Handbook of Local and Regional Development

The *Handbook of Local and Regional Development* provides a comprehensive statement and reference point for local and regional development. The scope of this Handbook's coverage and contributions engages with and reflects upon the politics and policy of how we think about and practise local and regional development, encouraging dialogue across the disciplinary barriers between notions of 'Local and Regional Development' in the Global North and 'Development Studies' in the Global South.

This Handbook is organized into seven inter-related sections, with an introductory chapter setting out the rationale, aims and structure of the Handbook. Section I situates local and regional development in its global context. Section II establishes the key issues in understanding the principles and values that help us define what is meant by local and regional development. Section III critically reviews the current diversity and variety of conceptual and theoretical approaches to local and regional development. Section IV addresses questions of government and governance. Section V connects critically with the array of contemporary approaches to local and regional development policy. Section VI is an explicitly global review of perspectives on local and regional development from Africa, Asia-Pacific, Europe, Latin and North America. Section VII provides reflection and discussion of the futures for local and regional development in an international and multidisciplinary context.

With over 40 contributions from leading international scholars in the field, this Handbook provides critical reviews and appraisals of current state-of-the-art conceptual and theoretical approaches and future developments in local and regional development.

Andy Pike is Professor of Local and Regional Development in the Centre for Urban and Regional Development Studies (CURDS), Newcastle University, UK.

Andrés Rodríguez-Pose is a Professor of Economic Geography at the London School of Economics, UK.

John Tomaney is Henry Daysh Professor of Regional Developmental Studies and Director of CURDS, Newcastle University, UK, and Professor of Regional Studies, Institute for Regional Studies, Monash University, Australia.

"This indispensible Handbook is one-stop shopping for any course on regional or urban development. Those seeking to understand how regions can develop or transform their economies in an increasingly competitive global environment must read the groundbreaking analyses assembled by Pike, Rodríguez, and Tomaney."

Joan Fitzgerald, *Professor of Urban Policy and Director, Law, Policy and Society Program, Northeastern University, Boston, USA.*

"A must read for all those wanting seriously to understand spatial patterns in development and to engage in the difficult art of modern local and regional development policy. Conceptual foundations, governance and the tools of policy delivery are revealed by cleverly bringing together theoretical advances in different fields."
Fabrizio Barca, *Director General, Ministry of Finance and Economy, Italy.*

"A comprehensive review of the theory and practice of local and regional development, emphasizing the capabilities, learning and governance, with a robustly comparative and international perspective, edited by major scholars in the field."
Michael Storper, *Professor of Economic Geography, London School of Economics; Professor of Economic Sociology, Sciences Po, Paris and Professor of Urban Planning, UCLA, USA.*

"This is a path-breaking collection of cutting-edge thinking on local and regional development written by a large number of influential scholars whose collective wisdom has clearly defined this important field of enquiry. The work sets a new benchmark for understanding, scholarship and practice."
Henry Yeung, *Professor of Economic Geography, National University of Singapore, Singapore.*

Handbook of Local and Regional Development

Edited by
Andy Pike, Andrés Rodríguez-Pose
and John Tomaney

LONDON AND NEW YORK

First published 2011
by Routledge
2 Park Square, Milton Park, Abingdon, Oxon OX14 4RN

Simultaneously published in the USA and Canada
by Routledge
52 Vanderbilt Avenue, New York, NY 10017

First issued in paperback 2020

Routledge is an imprint of the Taylor & Francis Group, an informa business

Typeset in Bembo by Glyph International Ltd

British Library Cataloguing in Publication Data
A catalogue record for this book is available from the British Library

Library of Congress Cataloguing in Publication Data
Handbook of local and regional development/edited by Andy Pike, Andrés Rodríguez-Pose and John Tomaney.
    p. cm.
1. Economic development–Handbooks, manuals, etc. 2. Regional planning–Handbooks, manuals, etc. I. Pike, Andy, 1968-
II. Rodríguez-Pose, Andrés. III. Tomaney, John, 1963-
HD82.H27525 2010
307.1′4–dc22   2010012512

ISBN 13: 978–0–367–66014–7 (hbk)
ISBN 13: 978–0–415–54831–1 (pbk)

For Michelle, Ella, Connell and my parents

To my friends, colleagues and students at the LSE, who have taught me more than I ever imagined

For my parents, Jim and Sylvia Tomaney

Contents

Section IV: Government and governance

Section V: Local and regional development policy

Section VII: Reflections and futures   549

Tables

Figures

Contributors

Editors

Andy Pike is Professor of Local and Regional Development in the Centre for Urban and Regional Development Studies (CURDS), Newcastle University, UK. His research interests are in the geographical political economy of local and regional development. He is widely published in international journals and co-author of *Local and Regional Development* (Routledge, 2006, with Andrés Rodríguez-Pose and John Tomaney). He has undertaken research projects for the OECD, European Commission and national, regional and local organizations. He is currently working on brands and branding geographies and decentralization, spatial economic policy and spatial inequalities. He is an editor of *Regional Studies* and leads the Postgraduate Local and Regional Development programmes in CURDS.

Andrés Rodríguez Pose is a Professor of Economic Geography at the London School of Economics, UK. He is the current holder of an IMDEA Social Sciences Professorial Research Fellowship and of a Leverhulme Trust Major Research Fellowship. He has a long track record of research in regional growth and on development policies and strategies and has acted as consultant on these fields to the European Commission, European Investment Bank, World Bank, OECD, and International Labour Organization, among others. He directed a major World Bank/Cities Alliance report entitled *Understanding Your Local Economy*. His books include *The Dynamics of Regional Growth in Europe* (Oxford, 1998), *The European Union: Economy, Society and Polity* (Oxford, 2002), and *Local and Regional Development* (Routledge, 2006, with Andy Pike and John Tomaney). He has published more than 70 papers in peer-reviewed journals, is the joint managing editor of *Environment and Planning C,* and sits on the editorial board of 16 scholarly journals.

John Tomaney is Henry Daysh Professor of Regional Developmental Studies and Director of the Centre for Urban and Regional Development Studies (CURDS), Newcastle University, UK, and Professor of Regional Studies, Institute for Regional Studies, Monash University, Australia. His research focuses upon the relationship between territory, democracy, identity and justice, especially at the local and regional scales. He is widely published in international journals and co-author of *Local and Regional Development* (Routledge, 2006, with Andy Pike and Andrés Rodríguez-Pose). He is also Associate Director of the UK Spatial Economics Research Centre (SERC) and is an Academician of the Academy of Social Science (UK).

Contributors

Peter Ache is Professor of European Metropolitan Planning at the Centre for Urban and Regional Studies (YTK), Helsinki University of Technology (TKK), Finland.

Harald Bathelt is Professor in the Department of Political Science and the Department of Geography and Planning at the University of Toronto, Canada.

John T. Bowen, Jr. is Assistant Professor in the Department of Geography, Central Washington University, Ellensburg, Washington, USA.

Gillian Bristow is Reader in Economic Geography, School of City and Regional Planning, Cardiff University, UK.

Tony Champion is Emeritus Professor of Population Geography in the Centre for Urban and Regional Development Studies (CURDS), Newcastle University, UK.

Shiuh-Shen Chien is Assistant Professor in Regional Development and Planning Geography, National Taiwan University, Taiwan.

Susan Christopherson is J. Thomas Clark Professor in the Department of City and Regional Planning, Cornell University, USA.

Jennifer Clark is Assistant Professor in the School of Public Policy, Georgia Institute of Technology, US.

Allan Cochrane is Professor of Urban Studies in Social Policy and Criminology at The Open University, UK.

Neil M. Coe is a Reader in Economic Geography in the School of Environment and Development, University of Manchester, UK.

Mike Coombes is Professor of Geographic Information in the Centre for Urban and Regional Development (CURDS), Newcastle University, UK.

Kevin R. Cox is Distinguished University Professor of Geography at The Ohio State University, USA.

Colin Crouch is Professor of Governance and Public Management at the Business School of Warwick University, UK.

Andrew Cumbers is a Senior Lecturer in Political and Economic Geography at the University of Glasgow, UK.

Kavita Datta is a Senior Lecturer in Human Geography at Queen Mary, University of London, UK.

Stuart Dawley is a Lecturer in Economic Geography at the Centre for Urban and Regional Development Studies (CURDS), Newcastle University, UK.

Bolesław Domański is Professor in the Institute of Geography and Spatial Management, Jagiellonian University, Poland.

Michael Dunford is Professor of Economic Geography at the University of Sussex, UK.

Aram Eisenschitz is Senior Lecturer in the Department of Social Science at Middlesex University, UK.

Yara Evans is a Visiting Research Fellow in the Department of Geography, Queen Mary, University of London, UK.

David C. Gibbs is Professor of Human Geography, University of Hull, UK.

J.K. Gibson-Graham is the pen-name of Katherine Gibson and the late Julie Graham, feminist political economists and economic geographers who work, respectively, at the University of Western Sydney, Australia, and the University of Massachusetts Amherst, USA. Julie Graham died in 2010 after a long illness.

John Goddard is Emeritus Professor of Regional Development Studies at the Centre for Urban and Regional Development Studies (CURDS), Newcastle University, UK.

Sara Gonzalez is Lecturer in Human Critical Geography at the School of Geography, University of Leeds, UK.

Ian Gordon is Professor of Human Geography at the London School of Economics, UK.

Jamie Gough is Senior Lecturer in the Department of Town and Regional Planning, Sheffield University, UK.

Nancey Green Leigh is Professor in the City and Regional Planning Program, Georgia Institute of Technology, USA.

Costis Hadjimichalis is Professor of Economic Geography and Regional Planning, Department of Geography, Harokopio University, Greece.

Robert Hassink is Professor of Economic Geography in the Department of Geography at the University of Kiel, Germany, and Adjunct Professor at the Department of Sociology and Human Geography at the University of Oslo, Norway.

Joanna Herbert is a Visiting Research Fellow in the Department of Geography at Queen Mary, University of London, UK.

Andrew Herod is Professor of Geography at the University of Georgia, USA.

Martin Hess is Lecturer in Human Geography in the School of Environment and Development, University of Manchester, UK.

Ray Hudson is Professor of Geography and Pro-Vice-Chancellor, Durham University, UK.

Bob Jessop is Distinguished Professor of Sociology and Co-Director of the Cultural Political Economy Research Centre, Lancaster University, UK.

Andrew E.G. Jonas is Professor of Human Geography, University of Hull, UK.

Martin Jones is Pro-Vice-Chancellor and Professor of Human Geography at Aberystwyth University, UK.

Claudia Klaerding is Research Assistant in the Department of Geography at the University of Kiel, Germany.

Roger Lee is Professor Emeritus of Geography at Queen Mary, University of London, UK.

Thomas R. Leinbach was Arts and Sciences Distinguished Professor Emeritus, University of Kentucky, USA. After a long illness, he died in late 2009.

John Lovering is Professor of Urban Development and Governance in the School of City and Regional Planning, Cardiff University, UK.

Danny MacKinnon is Senior Research Fellow in Urban Political Economy at the University of Glasgow, UK.

Gordon MacLeod is Reader in Urban and Regional Studies in the Department of Geography, Durham University, UK.

Neill Marshall is Professor of Economic Geography in the Centre for Urban and Regional Development Studies (CURDS), Newcastle University, UK.

Jon May is Professor of Geography at Queen Mary, University of London, UK.

Cathy McIlwaine is Reader in Human Geography at Queen Mary, University of London, UK.

Abid Mehmood is a postdoctoral researcher in the School of Architecture, Planning and Landscape, Newcastle University, UK.

Giles Mohan is Reader in the Politics of International Development at The Open University, UK.

Kevin Morgan is Professor of Governance and Development in the School of City and Regional Planning at Cardiff University, UK.

Frank Moulaert is Professor of Spatial Planning at the KU Leuven, Belgium. He is also a visiting professor at Newcastle University (APL), UK, and MESHS-CNRS, Lille, France.

Etienne Nel is Associate Professor in the Geography Department at the University of Otago, New Zealand.

Phillip O'Neill is Professor and Foundation Director of the Urban Research Centre, University of Western Sydney, Australia.

Seán Ó Riain is Professor of Sociology, National University of Ireland, Maynooth.

Diane Perrons is Professor of Economic Geography and Gender Studies at the London School of Economics, UK.

Jane Pollard is Senior Lecturer in Urban and Regional Development Studies in the Centre for Urban and Regional Development Studies (CURDS) and School of Geography, Politics and Sociology, Newcastle University, UK.

Dominic Power is Professor in Economic Geography in the Department of Social and Economic Geography, Uppsala University, Sweden.

Allen J. Scott is Distinguished Professor in the Department of Geography and the Department of Policy Studies, UCLA, USA.

Franz Tödtling is Professor and Head of the Institute for Regional Development and Environment at the Vienna University of Economics and Business, Austria.

Ivan Turok is Professor of Urban Economic Development in the Department of Urban Studies, University of Glasgow, UK, and Honorary Professor, University of Cape Town, South Africa.

Dina Vaiou is Professor in the Department of Urban and Regional Planning of the National Technical University of Athens, Greece.

Mário Vale is Associate Professor in the Institute of Geography and Spatial Planning, University of Lisbon, Portugal.

Paul Vallance is Research Associate in the Centre for Urban and Regional Development Studies (CURDS), Newcastle University, UK.

Dave Valler is Reader in Spatial Planning in the Department of Planning, Oxford Brookes University, UK.

Antonio Vázquez-Barquero is Professor of Economics at the Universidad Autónoma de Madrid, Spain.

Aidan H. While is Senior Lecturer in Town and Regional Planning, University of Sheffield, UK.

Jane Wills is Professor of Geography at Queen Mary, University of London, UK.

Andrew Wood is Associate Professor of Geography at the University of Kentucky, USA.

Felicity Wray is Post Doctoral Research Fellow in the Urban Research Centre, University of Western Sydney, Australia.

Acknowledgements

As part of our project of broadening local and regional development – substantively, disciplinarily and geographically, we have incurred many social debts in the process of assembling this collection. At the outset, we would like to thank Andrew Mould for encouraging us to develop the Handbook and supporting its production. In putting together the Handbook, very many thanks are due to all the contributors to this volume for their commitment and delivery of insightful, thoughtful and thought-provoking chapters. The Centre for Urban and Regional Development Studies (CURDS), Newcastle University, UK, continues to provide a distinctive and unique research culture and outlook that has inspired and inflected this collection. We have benefited directly from the advice, scepticism and dialogue with David Bradley, Tony Champion, Mike Coombes, Stuart Dawley, Andy Gillespie, John Goddard, Neill Marshall, Jane Pollard, Ranald Richardson, Alison Stenning, Gianpiero Torrisi, Vassilis Tselios and Paul Vallance. The insights and questions of the PhD and MA postgraduates in the Local and Regional Development programmes in CURDS and the Local Economic Development programme at LSE have further contributed to the development of the Handbook. Thanks to Pedro Marques and Emma Wilson in CURDS for helping to prepare the manuscript and Michelle Wood for the cover art. Andrés Rodríguez-Pose would like to acknowledge the generous financial support of a Leverhulme Trust Major Research Fellowship and of the PROCIUDAD-CM programme. All the editors acknowledge the support of the UK Spatial Economics Research Centre (SERC) funded by the ESRC, Department for Business, Enterprise and Regulatory Reform, Department for Communities and Local Government and Welsh Assembly Government.

Introduction

A handbook of local and regional development

Andy Pike, Andrés Rodríguez-Pose and John Tomaney

Introduction

The problematic of development regionally and locally sits at a difficult and uneasy conjuncture. Improvement of living conditions, decentralisation, prosperity, wellbeing and life chances for people and places internationally is ever more important in a world of heightened inequalities and inequities and intensifying environmental pressures. Yet powerful social forces are shifting the context and shaping formidable challenges to the understanding, role and purpose of local and regional development. Even before the tumultuous events triggered by the financial crisis at the end of the opening decade of the twenty-first century, numerous assessments already pointed toward the mounting discredit and ineffectiveness of development models nationally, questioned the role of states and other institutions in promoting development and even challenged the purpose and rationale for any form of spatial policy. Doubt was cast too upon the relative weaknesses and inabilities of local and regional agency to influence the profound and transnational challenges of – inter alia – energy and food insecurity, climate change and demographic shifts in the context of globalisation. Other views, however, countered that local and

regional development was broadening beyond a narrow focus on the economic to encompass the social and the ecological. They argued too that centralisation provided opportunities to give particular meanings to development and contest prevailing orthodoxies, better tailor policy and resources to local and regional conditions and mobilise latent economic and social potential. Indeed, it was contended that it was regional and local institutions that were especially well placed for constructing and nurturing the collective capacities to adapt to and mitigate constant, far-reaching and disruptive global change. Amidst such differing views in a changing and challenging context, this collection is timely in seeking to take stock and consider current thinking and practice in local and regional development.

Building upon our previous integrative work (Pike *et al.* 2006, 2007), the genesis of this Handbook lies in an effort to begin more systematically and rigorously to map out the terrain of local and regional development in an international and multi-disciplinary context. The powerful and contradictory currents buffeting, questioning and reinforcing development regionally and locally underline the need for a broadly based collection that attempts to bring together and reflect upon current thinking and provide a reference point for multi-disciplinary and international work in the field. More specifically, the Handbook aims:

i) To provide critical reviews and appraisals of the current state of the art and future development of conceptual and theoretical approaches as well as empirical knowledge and understanding of local and regional development.
ii) To connect and encourage dialogue between the (sub-)disciplinary domains between 'Local and Regional Development' in the Global North and 'Development Studies' in the Global South through the international outlook and reach of its coverage and contributors.
iii) To engage with and reflect upon the politics and policy of how we think about and practise local and regional development.

To fulfil such aims, contributions have been sought from leading voices concerned with issues of development across the disciplines internationally. We make no claim to any exhaustive comprehensiveness – no doubt other topics, authors, disciplines and/or geographies might have been included – but we have sought to identify and incorporate what we believe are the most important and resonant issues for local and regional development. To frame what follows, this introduction identifies and elaborates three central themes motivating and animating the Handbook: the meanings given to local and regional development in an international and multi-disciplinary context; addressing the tensions between context sensitivity and place in their articulation with universalising, 'placeless' concepts, theories and models of local and regional development; and, connecting considerations of development regionally and locally in the global North and South. The organisation of the Handbook is then outlined.

Defining development regionally and locally

The definitions and meanings of development regionally and locally become centrally important when considered in a more international and multi-disciplinary context. The geographical differentiation and change over time in what constitutes 'local and regional development' within and between countries are amplified internationally. Changing and contested definitions of development seek to encompass and reflect geographical variation and uneven economic, social, political, cultural and environmental conditions and legacies in different places across the world. The search for any singular, homogenous meaning is further undermined by the socially determined definitions of development that reflect the relationships and articulation of interests amongst social groups and their interpretations and understandings of their predicament. The question of 'what kind of local and regional development and for whom? (Pike *et al.* 2007) is deliberated, constructed and articulated in different ways in different places – albeit not necessarily in the conditions of their choosing and with varying degrees and kinds of autonomy for reflective and critical engagements with dominant and prevailing orthodoxies (Gough and Eisenschitz, Cochrane, Gibson-Graham, Lovering, this volume).

Such diversity about what local and regional development means does not, however, imply that we confront a relative, context-dependent concept. Far from it, perceptions of local and regional development across the world share numerous characteristics and a growing sense that "causes and solutions... are increasingly integrated across borders and disciplines, and revolve around common if differently-experienced patterns of change and the capacity to control it" (Edwards 2007: 3). A first such current connecting local and regional development internationally is the shifting and sometimes turbulent context that imparts complexity, inter-dependency, risk, uncertainty and rapidity of change upon any considerations of the development of localities and regions. Adaptation and adaptive capacities in regions and localities have come to the fore in order to cope with the kinds of volatile, far-reaching and profound changes unleashed by global economic challenges and successive regional and local crises – such as the Asian crisis of 1997 and the 2007–8 financial crisis. Such concerns have propelled the rapid emergence of 'resilience' as a developmental notion internationally, notwithstanding its conceptual and theoretical weaknesses arising from its heterogenous (sub-)disciplinary origins in Ecology, Economics, Engineering and Geography (Pike *et al*. 2010). A second and related international current is evident in the broadening of notions of development regionally and locally beyond its longstanding economic and quantitative focus to encompass sustainable social, cultural, political and environmental dimensions and more qualitative, even subjective, concerns about quality of life and wellbeing (see, for example, Cypher and Dietz 2004, Geddes and Newman 1999, Morgan 2004, Pike *et al*. 2007, Stimson and Stough 2008). In part, this change has been stimulated, first, by the widening of the notions and narrative of sustainability beyond a narrow concern with the state of the physical environment and resources to encompass the economic and the social (Christopherson, Hadjimichalis, Jonas *et al*., Morgan, this volume). Second, such change has been prompted by the – early stage and perhaps tentative – engagement between 'Local and Regional Development' in the global North and the historically broader conceptions and understandings of development within 'Development Studies' in the global South (Mohan, this volume). As the shifting context and broadening of local and regional development issues cross international, institutional and disciplinary boundaries at different spatial levels, it prompts some reflection upon our frameworks of understanding and their (sub-)disciplinary roots.

The shifting international context of disruptive and uncertain change, coupled with the widening and intersecting domains of economy, society, environment, polity and culture that impinge upon a broader, more rounded sense of what local and regional development is, means that any single discipline – regardless of its predicament or status – is ill-equipped and perhaps ultimately unable to capture the evolving whole. We see no need, then, to claim or establish disciplinary status for 'local and regional development' or its like or the dominance of any singular conceptual and theoretical framework (cf. Rowe 2008). Indeed, we argue that a more fruitful way forward is to recognise that "at the very least…there is no 'one best way' to achieve development. No one model should be privileged, nor should any one approach to economic theory" in order to stimulate an ambition to "reimagine growth and development as an inherently thick process, encompassing multiple social processes that can be illuminated differently by insights from different disciplinary fields" (De Paula and Dymski 2005: 14, 11). Local and regional development has such long established multi- and inter-disciplinary roots that reach up and out from especially economics, geography, planning and urban studies (Bingham and Mier 1993) and, we argue below, can extend and intertwine with 'Development Studies' in productive ways capable of invigorating our ability to engage with current and future challenges.

Rather than consensus and unifying, singular approaches, an aspiration for dialogue, establishing 'trading routes', negotiating 'bypasses' and 'risky intersections' (Grabher 2006), even contributing to 'post-disciplinarity' (Sayer 1999), underpins such multi- and inter-disciplinary approaches to local and regional development. Such endeavour may have potential if a meaningful 'spatial turn' in broader social science is underway and disciplinary boundaries are genuinely becoming more open and porous. Checks and balances in conceptual and theoretical dialogue emerge in an open context of accountability, analysis, exchange and argument; offering the potential for the diversity of an 'engaged pluralism' which is active, inclusive and emancipatory in its intent (Sheppard and Plummer 2007).

Such broad-based and all-encompassing approaches to what local and regional development are are not without problems. Critics may ask what unites local and regional development and gives it coherence in such a plural context? Does such a diverse and varied conceptual and theoretical backdrop allow academics and policymakers simply to pick the theories to suit their interests and justify their interventions? We argue that the stance outlined here need not descend into such a relativist free-for-all. Rather, we see value in approaching local and regional development with multi- and inter-disciplinary insight and in promoting a dialogue aimed at stimulating understanding and explanation of the problematic of development in different local and regional contexts. This stance promotes an appreciation of politics, power relations and practice in multi-level, multi-agent and devolving systems of government and governance. It raises the normative dimensions of value judgements about the kinds of local and regional development we should be pursuing and the adaptation of frameworks in the light of foundational concerns such as accountability, democracy, equity, internationalism and solidarity (Pike *et al.* 2007, Hadjimichalis and Hudson 2007). This Handbook is our contribution to this agenda and specifically includes new and sometimes contrary contributions from leading voices working internationally in an array of (sub-)disciplinary bases in Community Studies, Development Studies, Economics, Gender Studies, Geography, Planning, Political Science, Social Policy, Sociology and Urban Studies.

Context sensitivity and place

The longstanding and thorny question of how to reconcile the general and the particular remains central to frameworks of understanding and the practices of local and regional development in an international and multi-disciplinary frame. Localities and regions in South Korea, Surinam and Sweden face shared issues and concerns in securing and enhancing livelihoods, prosperity and wellbeing in the context of globalisation, urbanisation and decentralisation processes. But how they address those issues and concerns is mediated by their highly geographically differentiated contexts, which reflect specific and particular growth trajectories, developmental aspirations and strategies, institutional arrangements of government and governance and other broadening dimensions shaping their development paths and strategies. In these circiumstances, the challenge is how we reconcile more general concepts and theories to understand, explain and analyse global development challenges with the need meaningfully to incorporate context and place into the development equation.

An enduring view holds that local and regional development is especially dependent upon context as a consequence of its engagement with social processes in geographically differentiated and uneven spaces and places. In some ways, an inherent reading of context is ingrained in our understandings whereby the "the very nature of local or regional development – where context exerts a pivotal influence – impedes the translation of theory into practice" and shapes decisively policy intervention because of "the important influence context plays in determining the success or failure of economic development programs…not all local growth strategies work in all circumstances" (Beer 2008: 84, 85). There is even a sense that the complex, uncertain and rapid changes shaping local and regional development has heightened the importance of the specificity and particularity of geographical differentiation and uneven development in the Global North and South. Here, adjectives and conceptions of a 'spiky' and 'sticky' rather than 'flat' and 'slippery' world contest for our understanding and explanations (see, for example, Rodríguez-Pose and Crescenzi 2008, Markusen 1996). Reflecting and understanding the richness of experiences and distinctiveness of places is clearly important but in some ways serves to underline the contingent nature of development regionally and locally. Development in this reading is witnessed at specific and particular times and places when certain conditions and tendencies meet in localities and regions.

A strong emphasis upon context has, however, its downsides and critics. Taken too far, it risks portraying local and regional development as particular, unique and unrepeatable episodes from which other people and places can learn little. From the perspectives of regional economics and regional science (see, for example, Capello and Nijkamp 2009), overly privileging context obfuscates the isolation of cause-and-effect relationships, undermines 'observational equivalence' and frustrates the analyst's search for more widely applicable and generalisable knowledge and approaches as well as the "common element" upon which to base comparative and systematic international understandings, methods and analysis (Stimson and Stough 2008: 177; see also McCann 2007, Overman 2004). If, in caricature, 'it is all different everywhere' such critics argue that each situation ends up with a bespoke, idiosyncratic and contingent account of little explanatory use in any different context. Lessons cannot be learned and strategies and policies cannot be developed.

But such views of an overly narrow adherence to such deductive and positivist approaches to social science risk affording insufficient conceptual and theoretical weight to context and geographical differentiation. At worst, the particularities of place are treated as some kind of unexplained residual in mathematical models. This is important because if we conceive of "the economy of any country as a purely macro-economic phenomenon (e.g. national GDP, unemployment, inflation, export performance, and so on)…we often fail to grasp its full meaning because we tend to abstract away from its underlying geography" (Scott and Garofoli 2007: 7). Overly abstracted views are especially problematic where such general concepts and theories have developed into universalising, somehow 'placeless' logics whose general applicability is appealing to academics and policymakers and their needs for broadly based understanding, explanation and comparison. Economic geography, for example, is wrestling with exactly this tension in the wake of the emergence of 'new economic geography' or 'geographical economics' (see Clark, *et al.* 2000). In policy circles, current international debates mirror this issue in the opposition between a 'spatially blind' conception of local and regional development informed by 'new (economic) growth theory' and its emphasis upon the agglomeration and spill-over benefits arising from the geographical concentration of growth (World Bank 2009) and the 'place-based' view of tackling persistent economic inefficiencies and social exclusion in specific places to promote more balanced and distributed endogenous growth as the basis for EU cohesion policy (Barca 2009; see also Rigg *et al.* 2009, and Tödtling, this volume). In development debates too, place has morphed into an ecological determinism in accounts that seek to demonstrate how low-income countries of the Global South are trapped by their geography (Mohan and Power 2009).

At the heart of this question of how better to address the differences that context and place make to our general concepts and theories of local and regional development is the nature of our abstractions. De Paula and Dymski (2005) reject Krugman's (1995) argument that the notion of development could be salvaged by stronger links to neo-classical economics and its language of formal mathematical expression. They go on to critique the weak analytical and explanatory purchase of such 'thin' abstractions. Instead they claim that "theoretical models can best help us imagine new possibilities if they are institutionally specific, historically informed, and able to incorporate diverse social and psychological processes" (De Paula and Dymski 2005: 3). Such combinations of clear conceptualisation and the theoretical purchase of 'thick' abstractions offer some promise for local and regional development in affording heightened sensitivity to context dependence and an enhanced ability to situate and interpret the import of the particularity of place in appropriate conceptual, theoretical and analytical frameworks (Markusen 1999). Contributions to this Handbook and elsewhere offer some examples of how this approach might be furthered including adaptations of Sen's capabilities approach (Perrons, this volume), evolutionary approaches to path dependency, lock-in and related variety (Hassink and Klaerding, this volume), culture and creativity in an urban context (Power and Scott, this volume) and regulation theory-informed policy evaluation (Valler, this volume). Important too is Rodríguez-Pose and Storper's (2006) emphasis upon the role of community and institutions in providing the pre-conditions and key elements characteristic of appropriate and successful development capable of resolving informational and coordination problems regionally and locally. Given the "enormous challenges" of "finding exactly the right mix of arrangements to fit any concrete situation" because "All-purpose boilerplate approaches are certainly unlikely to be successful in any long-run perspective" (Scott and Garofoli 2007: 17) and the absence of any "universal model or framework guaranteeing success for regional economic development" (Stimson and Stough 2008: 188), our intention is that the contributions to this volume can help prompt critical reflection upon the appropriateness of our frameworks of understanding and policy and an aspiration of better matching and adapting general ideas and frameworks to particular regional and local circumstance in more context-sensitive ways.

Connecting local and regional development in the Global North and South

Strong and enduring traditions exist in the study and practice of local and regional development within and beyond the academy. 'Local and Regional Development' characteristically focuses upon localities and regions in the advanced, historically industrialised and urbanised countries of the 'Global North' (see, for example, Blakely and Bradshaw 2002, Fitzgerald and Green Leigh 2002, Pike et al. 2006, Stimson and Stough 2008). 'Development Studies' is founded upon a concern with the 'Global South' and has primarily – although not exclusively – been concerned with the national scale and, latterly, the regional, local and community levels (see, for example, Cypher and Dietz 2004, Mohan, this volume). Such traditions have run in parallel, with limited interaction and cross-fertilisation, and been marked and separated by the language, concepts, theories and terminology of the 'First', 'Second' and 'Third World', the 'Developed' and 'Less Developed Countries', 'Less Favoured Regions' and their recent change toward notions of 'emerging economies', 'transition economies', 'post-socialist economies' and 'High', 'Middle' and 'Low Income Countries' (Scott and Garofoli 2007, Domański, O'Neill, this volume). The legacy of such bounded fields of study lingers in recent contributions that circumscribe the geographical focus and reach of their studies such as Rowe's (2008: 3) recent collection and its focus upon "advanced western nations". Yet there is growing recognition that such compartmentalised and discrete approaches make little sense in an increasingly globalised world and create unhelpful gaps in our understanding (see, for example, Murphy 2008, Pike et al. 2006, Pollard et al. 2009, Rigg et al. 2009). In the context of an international and multi-disciplinary engagement with development at the regional and local level, much can be gained and learnt from connection and deeper interaction, building upon the insights of genuinely cross-national comparative work in a global context (see, inter alia, Beer *et al.* 2003, Markusen 1996, Niklasson 2007, Pike *et al.* 2006, Scott 2002, Poon and Yeung 2009).

The arguments for closer linkages and cross-disciplinary, international dialogue are several. First, the dissatisfaction and critique of the development project in the Global South in Development Studies, especially amongst post-colonial writers (Blunt and McEwan 2002, Hart 2002), echoes critical reflection upon the prevailing local and regional development models in the Global North (Geddes and Newman 1999, Morgan 2004, Gonzalez, Turok, this volume). From seemingly different starting points, both strands of work have questioned the underlying basis of the 'developmentalism' of linear, programmatic stages through which each and every country, region and locality must travel to effect development (Cypher and Dietz 2004, McMichael 1996). Moreover, such an approach offers only a "simplistic perspective of progress" and that "the discussion of development could not be restricted to the economic sphere per se, that is, it could not be oblivious to the urgent questions of poverty, neither to ethnic and gender inequalities" (De Paula and Dymski 2005: 4). A rethinking is shared, then, about the goals and processes of development and its underlying concepts and theories such that

> instead of relying on one or two organizing ideas, we recognize the need for many – for a thick theoretical approach – because of the diversity of circumstances and of the many divides that arise within the nations of the South. Indeed, these divides equally affect the nations of the North, and make development theory equally applicable to the 'advanced' nations as well.
>
> (De Paula and Dymski 2005: 23)

This view rejects any call for the dominance and adoption of any one conceptual and theoretical framework – particularly given our approach to reflecting diversity and variety in frameworks of understanding in this Handbook. In particular, this stance recognises that the differences that connecting local and regional development in the Global North and South make are conceptually and theoretically important. There is value in 'theorising back' (Yeung and Lin 2003) from empirical analysis in the Global South at dominant western, Global North perspectives (Nel, Chien, Vázquez-Barquero, Green Leigh and Clark, Dunford, this volume). With parallels for local and regional development, Murphy (2008: 857) frames the dilemma for Economic Geography: "Is the subdiscipline better served by sticking to research topics and locations that have driven many significant theoretical developments over the past 20 years or does a more intensive, extensive and coordinated engagement with the Global South offer an important opportunity to test, extend or retract these theories?" One key area centres on the impulse to question and broaden the meanings given to local and regional development beyond narrow concerns with economy and its quantitative dimensions. Development Studies work is vitally important here in its emphasis upon livelihoods, basic living standards, poverty reduction, capabilities and non-market forms of value, prosperity and wellbeing (Sen 1999). Problematising the meanings given to development allows us to question the assumption that places with higher levels of economic wealth – measured in an indicator like GDP per capita – have achieved more development and are higher up the development ladder than other countries with relatively lower levels of economic wealth. Ostensibly 'poorer' places on wealth measures may actually be pursuing more appropriate, fulfilling and sustainable forms of development regionally and locally (Morgan, Perrons, Turok, this volume).

Second, 'Local and Regional Development' and 'Development Studies' intersect through people and places across the world facing common issues and changing contexts. Albeit that they begin from markedly different starting points and along different pathways and trajectories of change with highly uneven social and spatial outcomes. Shared and common boundary crossing phenomena configure the development problematic in differentiated ways as part of intensified but highly uneven internationalisation and even globalisation (Bowen and Leinbach, Coe and Hess, Dawley, Hudson, Lee, O'Riain, this volume). Examples of such common issues explored in this Handbook include the spatially imbalanced geographical concentration of growth based upon agglomeration economies and spill-overs within nations (Ache, Dunford, this volume), sharpening inter-territorial competition (Bristow, Crouch, Gordon, this volume), shifting migration and commuting patterns (Coombes and Champion, Vaiou, Wills *et al.*, this volume) and decentralising, multi-level and multi-agent government and governance (Cox, Goddard and Vallance, Jessop, Jones and MacLeod, Mohan, Wood, this volume, Rodríguez-Pose and Ezcurra 2009). Interconnection, inter-dependency and integration in the context of globalisation frame shared concerns around the "increasingly desperate search of households throughout the world for safety, for security, and for freedom from want and freedom from the fear of want" (De Paula and Dymski 2005: 5). As Edwards (2007: 3) puts it:

> HIV infection rates…are as high among certain groups of African-American women in the United States as in sub-Saharan Africa, and for similar reasons. The erosion of local public spheres around the world is linked to decisions made by media barons in Italy, Australia and the US. The increasingly differentiated interests within the faster-growing 'developing'

countries (China, India, Brazil and South Africa) make it difficult to see why Chad or Myanmar would be included as comparators but Ukraine, Belarus, Appalachia and the Mississippi delta would not.

Such shared issues and common ground challenge existing categorisation and typologies. In response, emergent understandings interpret a "worldwide mosaic of regional economies at various levels of development and economic dynamism and with various forms of economic interaction linking them together. This notion allows us to describe global geographic space as something very much more than just a division between two (or three) broad developmental zones" (Scott and Garofoli 2007: 13). Developmental impulses and problematics – however geographically differentiated in their definition, articulation and expression – shape the selective incorporation and exclusion of a far wider range of different countries than hitherto, conditioning the potential and paths for territories "arrayed at different points along a vast spectrum of development characteristics" (Scott and Storper 2003: 33).

Recognising shared and common issues for development at regional and local levels is not to suggest homogeneity and sameness. Because, third, continued differentiation and the need to recognise context and place in understanding and policy – as discussed above – are central to the 'thick' abstractions needed to provide conceptual and analytical purchase upon heightened and evolving heterogeneity and geographically differentiated unevenness in the Global North and South. While finance is a shared issue for development policy internationally (Wray, Marshall and Pollard, this volume), for example, macro-economic instability remains a particular problem for regional and local development initiatives in many parts of the emerging world in ways that have generally been less familiar until recently to relatively more advanced western economies

(Sepulveda 2008; see also Vázquez-Barquero, this volume). Echoing our concern with context and place, "Centrally mandated development policies are… usually ill-equipped to respond to the detailed idiosyncrasies of individual regions and industrial communities" (Scott and Garofoli 2007: 8). Places across the world face problems in devising and delivering development strategies and adapting and translating concepts and models originated elsewhere. A sense of exhaustion is apparent with traditional 'top-down' approaches that appear too rigid and inflexible (Pike *et al.* 2006), where 'success' stories are increasingly harder to find. While the number of examples of botched national 'top-down' development strategies continues to grow, the cases of successful interaction between the state and the market in the development realm continue to be the exception – and constrained to East Asia (i.e. Wade 1990) – rather than the rule. This predicament has triggered the search for, and experimentation with, more sustainable, balanced and integrated alternatives and complements to longstanding top-down approaches jointly constructed through locally owned, participatory development processes and partnerships between state, capital, labour and civil society (Herod, Gough and Eisenschitz, Moulaert and Mehmood, this volume). But in contrast to the redistribution and equity enshrined in the spatial Keynesianism of the post-war period, the influence of new (endogenous) economic growth theory means "Development strategies today are less and less concerned with the establishment of an autarchic and balanced national economy, than they are with the search for a niche within the global division of labour" (Scott and Garofoli 2007: 5) (see World Book 2009, Rigg *et al.* 2009). In a context of increased bottom-up regional and local agency working in facilitating national frameworks, the unequal capacity and resource endowments of places may mean unequal development outcomes arising from such 'self-help'. In a more growth-oriented rather than redistributive spatial

policy framework internationally, what is to be done for the localities and regions with limited economic potential and chronically weak conditions for growth?

This characterisation of local and regional development in the Global North and South creates, establishes and enlarges the common ground and shared concerns with the well-being and livelihoods of people and places across the world. Given our emphasis upon the importance of context and place, this is not to suggest that different places can be treated the same through the rolling-out of unversalising, 'one-size-fits-all' models or assuming and promulgating the dominance of a specific set of ideas and practices from particular core parts of the world in the peripheries. Knowledge networks are distributed as well as concentrated and flows are diverse, varied and nuanced – cross-cutting, permeating and transcending boundaries as well as being channelled and controlled by various powerful interests (Bathelt, Cumbers and MacKinnon, Vale, this volume). Originating in development economics in India, the wider travels and import of Sen's capabilities approach provides one such example of Global South to North mobility. Our aspiration is not just about 'going South', doing more work to take and test Global North perspectives on local and regional development in more varied contexts or diffusing 'leading-edge' notions, techniques and practices from core to periphery (see Murphy 2008). Rather, it is that making such interconnections and encouraging dialogue might stimulate fresh thinking, new options and novel possibilities for often entrenched and intractable problems. We have identified only two areas of shared interest here – defining development at the local and regional level and tackling context specificity/particularity and place – with which to begin such an open, even democratized, discussion (De Paula and Dymski 2005). Our argument connects to Edwards' (2007: 3) calls: "for development professionals to recognise that problems and solutions are not bounded by artificial definitions of geography or economic condition, and to reposition themselves as equal-minded participants in a set of common endeavours. By doing that, we could instantly open up a much more interesting conversation." Ideally, such dialogue can extend and be of use not just to academics and researchers but to policymakers and practitioners in the Global North and South too. A central task to kick-start this dialogue has been to situate local and regional development in its international context. Contributors to the Handbook explicitly deliver on this in their international locations and outlooks contained within the Global North and South examples discussed in numerous of their contributions and cemented in the specific Section VI: Global perspectives (see p. 483). This part specifically explores the legacies and traditions of different approaches to local and regional development supra-nationally and nationally in Africa, Asia-Pacific, Latin America, North America and Europe. If the Handbook can act as a source and reference point for ideas, new thinking, inspiration even, then it will have served its purpose in beginning this broader conversation.

Organisation of the Handbook

In placing development locally and regionally in an international and multi-disciplinary frame, we have organised the contributions into seven connected parts. Section I: Local and regional development in a global context situates the development problematic against the backdrop of intensified internationalisation. It provides critical reviews and appraisals of the persistent importance of institutional and organisational issues shaping the kinds of development achievable at a regional and local level in the context of globalisation (O'Riain), the contextual influences upon collective action and policy choices in the face of inter-territorial competition (Gordon) and the imperial echoes of the historical evolution of development as capitalist incorporation at national, regional and local scales in the disciplinary domain of 'Development Studies' (Mohan).

Section II: Defining the principles and values of local and regional development addresses the fundamental bases and normative dimensions informing and giving meaning to particular definitions of development. Interventions here confront and reflect critically upon the potential of ameliorating socio-spatial inequalities through more inclusive models of growth and development (Perrons), the tensions and possibilities of 'inclusive growth' locally and regionally (Turok), the transformative potential of the sustainability narrative and the role of the 'Green State' and the public realm in delivering its regional and local outcomes (Morgan) and the prospects of approaches that reach upwards and outwards from the regional and local in constructing alternatives to currently dominant orthodoxies (Cochrane).

Section III: Concepts and theories of local and regional development demonstrates the diversity and variety of contemporary thinking through critical engagements with recent and emergent approaches. An initial set of contributions addresses the relationships and dynamics of spatial circuits and networks of value production, circulation, consumption and regulation shaping development prospects within and beyond localities and regions (Hudson, and Coe and Hess) and the particular role of labour individually and collectively in shaping the definition, meaning and practice of development regionally and locally in an international context (Herod). The next set reviews influential recent work concerning: path dependence, lock-ins, path creation, related variety and co-evolution emerging from evolutionary approaches (Hassink and Klaerding); the role, legacies and contingencies of socio-institutional relations and structures shaping spatial distribution and proximity in different kinds of innovation, knowledge and learning (Bathelt); the agglomerative and place-bound character of development based upon culture and creativity (Power and

Scott); the roles of path dependency and heterogeneity in moulding the diversity and variety of post-socialist transition experiences (Domański); and the complex and multi-faceted relationships of current migration and commuting patterns to local and regional development (Coombes and Champion). The remaining group of contributions in this section reflect recent, somewhat more disruptive interventions that question the possibility of regional and local development in cross-cutting territorial and relational space (Lee), the potential and spatialities of more social forms of innovation (Moulaert and Mehmood) and the possibilities of post-development and community economies (Gibson-Graham).

Questions of the state, institutions, power and politics are considered in Section IV: Government and governance. Interventions here engage with and prompt reflection upon the political and institutional questions of how we think about and practise local and regional development. The first batch of contributions address: the different dimensions of statehood, the state apparatus, and state power as well as governance and metagovernance (Jessop); the differentiated conceptions and forms of geographical political economies of power (Cumbers and MacKinnon); the compatibility of territorial and relational readings of space and place in devolved economic governance (Jones and MacLeod); and the burgeoning institutional fixes constructed within and beyond the state as part of attempts to contain the spatially uneven contradictions of capital accumulation (Cox). The second batch considers 'ecostate' restructuring in the local and regional development politics of carbon control (Jonas, While and Gibbs), the democratic deficits and politics of new institutional forms attempting to govern and regulate city and city-regional competition (Crouch), the changing nature of the state in capitalism and geographical specificity in the politics of local and regional development (Wood) and the relationships and tensions in spatial

planning for broader forms of territorial development policy (Ache).

Connecting current conceptual and theoretical developments to emergent approaches to intervention is the central concern in Section V: Local and regional development policy. This section captures and reflects contemporary approaches, policies and experiences of institutions in places seeking to promote and encourage local and regional development internationally. A first set of contributions critically appraises the potential and pitfalls of approaches focused upon: indigenous and endogenous development (Tödtling); the ubiquitous, dominant and malleable policy discourse of territorial competitiveness (Bristow); the complex and culturally nuanced emergence of regional and local gaps in venture finance provision (Wray, Marshall and Pollard); the possibilities, problems and politics of 'green' economic development (Christopherson); the wider and deeper potential of 'ordinary' SMEs and entrepreneurialism beyond the paradigmatic (Hadjimichalis); the potential and pitfalls of attracting and embedding exogenous forms of development regionally and locally through transnational corporations (Dawley); the new policy directions required in the context of multi-scalar and multi-local spaces of innovation networks (Vale); universities forging leading roles in science and technology-led development and attempting to broaden their civic engagement and roles (Goddard and Vallance); and globe-spanning logistics networks coordinating economic interactions between people and places (Bowen and Leinbach). The second set offers a more local and urban twist to development questions in considering the international (im)migration underpinning service economies in cities (Wills *et al.*), the character and consequences of neoliberal urbanism in Europe (Gonzalez) and the division and cohesion of gender and ethnicity in southern European cities undergoing socio-spatial transformations (Vaiou).

Section VI: Global perspectives demonstrates the international connections and inter-dependencies between local and regional development in the Global North and South. Distinctive supra-national and national histories and approaches to development regionally and locally are discussed comprising the experience of Africa (Nel), urban-focused industrialisation and development in Asia-Pacific (Chien), the local indigenous development connecting productivity, competitiveness, inclusion and sustainability in Latin America (Vázquez-Barquero), the traditions of metropolitan and territorial regionalism shaping local and regional development in North America (Green Leigh and Clark) and the definition and classification of areas and the mechanisms and distributional consequences of financial resource allocation in framing the evolution of cohesion and policy in Europe and its implications for China (Dunford).

Section VII: Reflections and futures closes the collection by addressing critical issues and normative political questions about the further direction and trajectories of development regionally and locally in an international frame. Contributions here consider the language and discursive constructions that shape how we think about local and regional development (O'Neill), the vital question of how we evaluate local and regional development policy and the shortfalls of current approaches and gaps in the coverage and rigour of our uneven analysis of evidence (Valler), the critique of the Neoliberal character of 'New Regionalism' held up as a key idea in promoting development regionally and locally (Lovering) and a return in the current context critically to reflect upon the future potential of what's left of the radical agenda that invigorated vibrant local and regional intervention and development during the 1980s (Gough and Eisenschitz). We then reflect upon some of the central messages and future directions of local and regional development in the final chapter. In sum, this Handbook represents only the start of what we envisage will be a challenging and difficult but fruitful and worthwhile dialogue and praxis about the problematic of development regionally and locally in a multi-disciplinary and international context.

Acknowledgements

We would like to thank the authors for their contributions and commitment to this collection. Thanks to Giles Mohan for insightful comments on a draft of this introduction. This chapter draws upon research undertaken as part of the UK Spatial Economics Research Centre (SERC) funded by the ESRC, Department for Business, Enterprise and Regulatory Reform, Department for Communities and Local Government and Welsh Assembly Government. The usual disclaimers apply.

References

Barca, F. (2009) *An Agenda for a Reformed Cohesion Policy: A Place-Based Approach to Meeting European Challenges and Expectations*, DG Regio: Brussels.

Beer, A. (2008) "The theory and practice of developing locally" in J. E. Rowe (Ed.) *Theories of Local Economic Development: Linking Theory to Practice*, Ashgate: Farnham, 63–89.

Beer, A., Haughton, G. and Maude, A. (2003) *Developing Locally: An International Comparison of Local and Regional Economic Development*, Policy Press: Bristol.

Bingham, R. D. and Mier, R. (Eds.) (1993) *Theories of Local Economic Development: Perspectives from Across the Disciplines*, Sage: Newbury Park, CA.

Blakely, E. and Bradshaw, T. (2002) *Planning Local Economic Development: Theory and Practice (3rd Edition)*, Sage: Thousand Oaks, CA.

Blunt, A. and McEwan, C. (2002) *Postcolonial Geographies*, Continuum: New York.

Capello, R. and Nijkamp, P. (Eds.) (2009) *Handbook of Regional Growth and Development Theories*, Edward Elgar: Cheltenham.

Clark, G. L., Feldman, M. P. and Gertler, M. S. (2000) *The Oxford Handbook of Economic Geography*, Oxford University Press: Oxford.

Cypher, J. M. and Dietz, J. L. (2004) *The Process of Economic Development (2nd Edition)*, Routledge: New York.

De Paula, S. and Dymski, G. (2005) "Introduction" in S. De Paula and G. Dymski (Eds.)

Reimagining Growth: Towards a Renewal of Development Theory, Zed: London, 3–26.

Edwards, M. (2007) "A world made new through love and reason: what future for 'development'?", openDemocracy, http://www.opendemocracy.net/globalization-institutions_government/world_reason_4566.jsp. Date accessed: 10 November 2009.

Fitzgerald, J. and Green Leigh, N. (2002) *Economic Revitalization: Cases and Strategies for City and Suburb*, Sage: Thousand Oaks, CA.

Geddes, M. and Newman, I. (1999) "Evolution and conflict in local economic development", *Local Economy*, 13, 5, 12–25.

Grabher, G. (2006) "Trading routes, bypasses, and risky intersections: Mapping the travels of 'networks' between Economic Sociology and Economic Geography", *Progress in Human Geography*, 30, 2, 1–27.

Hadjimichalis, C. and Hudson, R. (2007) "Rethinking local and regional development: Implications for radical political practice in Europe", *European Urban and Regional Studies*, 14, 2, 99–113.

Hart, G. (2002) "Geography and development: development/s beyond neoliberalism? Power, culture, political economy", *Progress in Human Geography*, 26, 6, 812–822.

Krugman, P. (1995) *Development, Geography and Economic Theory*, MIT Press: Cambridge, MA.

Markusen, A. (1996) "Sticky places in slippery space: A typology of industrial districts", *Economic Geography*, 72, 2, 294–314.

Markusen, A. (1999) "Fuzzy concepts, scanty evidence and policy distance: the case for rigour and policy relevance in critical regional studies", *Regional Studies*, 33, 869–884.

McCann, P. (2007) "Observational equivalence? Regional studies and regional science", *Regional Studies*, 41, 9, 1209–1221.

McMichael, P. (1996) *Development and Social Change: A Global Perspective*, Pine Forge Press: Thousand Oaks, CA.

Mohan, G. and Power, M. (2009) "Africa, China and the 'new' economic geography of development", *Singapore Journal of Tropical Geography*, 30, 1, 24–28.

Morgan, K. (2004) "Sustainable regions: Governance, innovation and scale", *European Planning Studies*, 12, 6, 871–889.

Murphy, J. T. (2008) "Economic geographies of the Global South: Missed opportunities and promising intersections with Development Studies", *Geography Compass*, 2, 3, 851–879.

Niklasson, L. (2007) *Joining-Up for Regional Development*, Statskontoret: Stockholm.

Overman, H. G. (2004) "Can we learn anything from economic geography proper?", *Journal of Economic Geography*, 4, 5, 501–516.

Pike, A., Dawley, S. and Tomaney, J. (2010) "Questioning 'resilience': An evolutionary political economy of geographies of adaptation and adaptability", *Cambridge Journal of Regions, Economy and Society*, 3, 1, 59–70.

Pike, A., Rodríguez-Pose, A. and Tomaney, J. (2006) *Local and Regional Development*, Routledge: London.

Pike, A., Rodríguez-Pose, A. and Tomaney, J. (2007) "What kind of local and regional development and for whom?", *Regional Studies*, 41, 9, 1253–1269.

Pollard, J., McEwan, C., Laurie, N. and Stenning, A. (2009) "Economic geography under postcolonial scrutiny", *Transactions of the Institute of British Geographers*, 34, 137–142.

Poon, J. P. H. and Yeung, H. W. C. (2009) "SJTG Special Forum: Continental drift? Development issues in Asia, Latin America and Africa", *Singapore Journal of Tropical Geography*, 30, 1, 3–34.

Rigg, J., Bebbington, A., Gough, K. V., Bryceson, D. F., Agergaard, J., Fold, N. and Tacoli, C. (2009) "The World Development Report 2009 'reshapes economic geography': Geographical reflections", *Transactions of the Institute of British Geographers*, 34, 128–136.

Rodríguez-Pose, A. and Crescenzi, R. (2008) "Mountains in a flat world: Why proximity still matters for the location of economic activity", *Cambridge Journal of Regions, Economy and Society*, 1, 3, 371–338.

Rodríguez-Pose, A. and Ezcurra, R. (2009) "Does decentralization matter for regional disparities? A cross-country analysis", *Journal of Economic Geography*, Advance access at: http://joegoxfordjournals.org/content/early/ by section.

Rodríguez-Pose, A. and Storper, M. (2006) "Better rules or stronger communities? On the social foundations of institutional change and its economic effects", *Economic Geography*, 82, 1, 1–25.

Rowe, J. E. (2008) "The importance of theory: Linking theory to practice" in J. E. Rowe (Ed.) *Theories of Local Economic Development: Linking Theory to Practice*, Ashgate: Farnham, 3–27.

Sayer, A. (1999) *Long Live Postdisciplinary Studies! Sociology and the Curse of Disciplinary Parochialism/Imperialism*, Department of Sociology, Lancaster University, Lancaster LA1 4YN, UK, http://www.comp.lancs.ac.uk/sociology/papers/Sayer-Long-Live-Postdisciplinary-Studies.pdf.

Scott, A. J. (2002) "Regional push: Towards a geography of development and growth in low- and middle-income countries", *Third World Quarterly*, 23, 1, 137–161.

Scott, A. J. and Garofoli, G. (2007) "The regional question in economic development" in *Development on the Ground: Clusters, Networks and Regions in Emerging Economies*, Routledge: London, 3–22.

Scott, A. J. and Storper, M. (2003) "Regions, globalization, development", *Regional Studies*, 37, 6–7, 579–593.

Sen, A. (1999) *Development as Freedom*, Oxford University Press: Oxford.

Sepulveda, L. (2008) "Spatializing industrial policies: A view from the South", *Regional Studies*, 42, 10, 1385–1397.

Sheppard, E. and Plummer, P. (2007) "Toward engaged pluralism in geographical debate", *Environment and Planning A*, 39, 11, 2545–2548.

Stimson, R. and Stough, R. R. (2008) "Regional economic development methods and analysis: Linking theory to practice" in J. E. Rowe (Ed.) *Theories of Local Economic Development: Linking Theory to Practice*, Ashgate: Farnham, 169–192.

Wade, R. (1990) *Governing the Market. Economic Theory and the Role of Government in East Asian Industrialization*, Princeton University Press: Princeton, NJ.

World Bank (2009) *World Development Report 2009: Reshaping Economic Geography*, World Bank: Washington DC.

Yeung, H. W. C. and Lin, G. C. S. (2003) "Theorizing economic geographies of Asia", *Economic Geography*, 79, 2, 107–128.

Further reading

Markusen, A. (1999) "Fuzzy concepts, scanty evidence and policy distance: the case for rigour and policy relevance in critical regional studies", *Regional Studies*, 33, 869–884. (On the conceptual, theoretical and methodological challenges for local and regional development.)

Pike, A., Rodríguez-Pose, A. and Tomaney, J. (2007) "What kind of local and regional development and for whom?", *Regional Studies*, 41, 9, 1253–1269. (On the definitions and meaning of local and regional development.)

Scott, A. J. and Garofoli, G. (2007) "The regional question in economic development" in *Development on the Ground: Clusters, Networks and Regions in Emerging Economies*, Routledge: London, 3–22. (On connecting Global North and South perspectives.)

Section I

Local and regional development in a global context

2

Globalization and regional development

Seán Ó Riain

Introduction

Globalization has prompted us to rediscover the region as a force in economic development. Apparently rendered powerless or, worse, irrelevant by economic globalization, the capacity of regions to generate economic and social development has paradoxically been rediscovered by policy makers and scholars alike. Localized inter-personal ties and networks are seen as important resources and sources of 'social capital'. The integration of such localized networks into 'micro-regions' – territorialized complexes of relationships and institutions – is increasingly seen as playing a critical role in production, industrial organization and social reproduction. Finally, 'macro-regions' such as the EU or the NAFTA area are important sources of diversity in the global economy – and of new scales of governance of globalizing processes. Through these local, micro-regional and macro-regional processes, 'regions' are now seen as playing a crucial role in constituting economic globalization.

Furthermore, where once scholars emphasized that regional resources for development were largely determined by historical and cultural legacies, recent research shows that regional economies can be constructed in a variety of ways by different constellations of socio-political actors. The discovery of the region as a space for generating development and shaping global processes opens up new spaces of social and political struggle and strategy within globalizing economic structures. The stakes of these struggles increase as regional inequalities grow within countries, new regions emerge globally and new patterns of socio-spatial inequality are constructed. But there are opportunities for social as well as economic renewal, as regions play an increasingly important role in social reproduction.

Exaggerated rumours? Rediscovering the region in an era of globalization

In the era after the Second World War a system of relatively stable national economies was institutionalized through an international order of 'embedded liberalism' (Ruggie, 1982). These economies were tied together through a negotiated regime of multilateral trade but buffered from the full effects of these international markets by institutions limiting trade and capital flows. The national economy and the bureaucratic firm acted

17

as 'time space containers' (Giddens, 1984), institutionalizing a 'spatial fix' for capitalism (Harvey, 1989).

Regions were embedded within the opportunity structures – and constraints – of international corporate hierarchies and national economic strategies. In advanced capitalist economies, large oligopolistic firms – in their most dominant form, 'national champions' – flourished and dominated within their markets and regional locations. Keynesian state strategies sought to narrow regional inequalities as part of the project of building 'national' economies (Brenner, 2004).

The globalization of the economy has consisted in large part of the weakening and even destruction of these institutional buffers between national economies and global markets. Despite attracting the most attention, the globalization of trade has been relatively modest – with world trade growing about twice as fast as world output in recent decades. More significant has been the continuing expansion of transnational production structures with about half of all trade internalized within multinational enterprises by the 1990s (Dunning, 2000; Held et al., 1999). As oligopolistic firms extended their global reach with the rise of transnational corporations (TNCs), relations among nations often tracked the international divisions of labour operating through these TNCs (Hymer, 1971). The majority of trade is in fact channeled through these corporate structures. The structures of the corporations have themselves been reconstituted, however, with hierarchical forms increasingly supplemented and even supplanted by networks and alliances and associated new forms of industrial governance (UNCTAD, 1998; Gereffi et al., 2005). Most significant of all has been the massive expansion of global finance, dwarfing all other forms of globalization and led by the financialization of the US economy (Held, 1999; Krippner, 2005).

Regions appeared at first glance to have been marginalized by these developments as global processes dominated and regional actors faced enormous difficulties in shaping local economic development. Latest, and arguably most famously, in a long line of analysts, Thomas Friedman (2006) proclaimed that 'the world is flat' as regional and national differences were eroded and rendered less important by the technological, economic and social processes of globalization.

Giddens (1991) argued that globalization occurs through a process of time-space distanciation where time and space are universalized and 'lifted out' or made independent of their immediate contexts. He argued that communication across distance depends upon the existence of expert systems, or systems of knowledge which actors understand and trust (such as the technical language of high-tech industry), and upon symbolic tokens, or media of communication that can serve as coordinating mechanisms for long-distance social relations where social cues and monitoring are absent or opaque (e.g. money). Reich (1991) argued that new information and communication technologies made it possible and even necessary to reorganize firms into 'global webs' and employees into global telecommuters. Regions were relegated to places where inputs for regional development could be created, but where little leverage could be gained over the process of development itself.

Other authors have portrayed a fundamentally different global economy where corporations have colonized local spaces and time has annihilated space in a process of time-space compression (Harvey, 1989). However, regions do not disappear but instead become more crucial to capitalist accumulation in providing a 'spatio-temporal fix' to problems of profitability and over-accumulation. Capital searches out new locations for activity in an effort to cut costs at the firm level and to develop new sources of demand and profitability at the systemic level. Even as neoliberal political discourse promotes market exchange as a universal ethics, power is in fact re-centralized and new forms of domination emerge (Harvey, 2005). While the kinds of forces that Friedman, Giddens and Reich observe are real and important, their impact is to generate uneven and unequal development, not a 'flat' world (Christopherson *et al.*, 2008).

In the process, new regional centres of capitalist production enter the dynamic sectors of capitalism, while other regions experience de-industrialization and decline. Brenner (2004) argues that these shifts in recent decades have produced a structural shift towards an increased centrality of urban agglomerations, rather than national economies, in the organization of capitalist accumulation, making strategies of 'locational competition' and urban entrepreneurialism more central (Brenner, 2004; Cerny, 1995). Even as regions become more central to capitalist accumulation the range of policy strategies available is narrowed to 'entrepreneurial' efforts to enhance 'competitiveness'. Questions of social reproduction and increasing inequality loom ever larger, even as policy is increasingly constrained in addressing these issues. Inequality between regions within countries has increased (Barnes and Ledebur, 1998; Heidenreich, 2009) and inequalities within metropolitan regions themselves have increased (Pastor *et al.*, 2009).

A third group of scholars are more sanguine about the prospects for regional development within contemporary capitalism. Piore and Sabel (1984) famously argued that the demands for increased flexibility and specialized learning make embedding the global workplace in local spaces even more critical, an argument that has received wide support from the new economic geography and economic sociology. Under what we might call time-space embedding, the social structure of regions becomes critical to economic development as efficient production and constant innovation require the construction of shared physical spaces where workers can interact and communicate on a face-to-face basis and where shared goals and meanings can be created and maintained (Piore and Sabel, 1984; Saxenian, 1994; Storper, 1997).

Distinctive local strategies of regional development can be expected to persist and, indeed, it is the distinctive social and cultural histories of places that are most likely to generate the kinds of social ties and 'social capital' that are to be the basis of effective regional development. The mobilization of regional 'relational assets' (Storper, 1997) has been crucial to the emergence of dynamic regions that have begun to close the gap with more established core regions (Heidenreich, 2009; Breznitz, 2007).

The global region

Recent research has spawned a wide variety of attempts to blend these insights from 'global' and 'local' perspectives on economic restructuring and regional development, creating something of a plague of 'glocalisms' in economic geography. A barrage of studies identified a large number of clusters and agglomerations within a globalizing economy. Empirically, we find that the global economy is increasingly organized through 'global regions', with an expanding number of concentrated specialized agglomerations of activity tied together through corporate networks of production and innovation, trade relations, flows of capital and labour mobility of various kinds.

While analysts saw either global or local processes as structurally or historically determined, there was little prospect of combining the two perspectives to understand the emergence of this network of regions. However, scholars increasingly understand local and global socio-spatial structures as mutually constitutive and have been increasingly interested to analyse both the social and the spatial dimensions of global regions as socio-political constructions (for a subtle analysis of scale, territory, place and networks as processual constructions see Brenner *et al.*, 2008).

Piore and Sabel (1984) located the flexibilities and trust that underpinned the success of the 'Third Italy' and other similar

19

industrial districts in informal social relations rooted in local face-to-face interactions and long-established regional industrial cultures. However, Herrigel (2008) notes that flexibility is increasingly founded, not on informal relations, but on the formalization of procedures, standards and measures of outcomes and performance. These formalized indicators – and crucially the discussions around them – render the tacit explicit and potentially open up the networks of the economy to new entrants. Sabel (1994) argues that such monitoring across organizational boundaries can serve as an occasion for conflict but also for learning through the dialogue around the interpretation of such measures. Similarly, Lester and Piore (2004) see such 'benchmarks' as technical instruments that can be the occasion for the stimulation of the formation of public spaces within industries that ultimately prove crucial to innovation. While the mechanisms are relatively poorly understood, the basic point is significantly different from the initial studies of industrial districts – the new analysis of regional industrial systems emphasizes the ability to construct dialogue and public spaces through the use of particular 'open' mechanisms of organizational networking and coordination.

Similarly, while researchers have found even more widespread evidence of the importance of agglomeration, their interpretation of these 'local' spaces has shifted. Piore and Sabel presented a picture of the Third Italy that emphasized its self-contained character as a local culture, a 'world in a bottle' (Sabel and Zeitlin, 2004). Similarly, the imagery of the new international division of labour with an orderly hierarchy of regions in the global production system has been complicated. For example,

a substantial and growing proportion of the trade today is in components – that is, that it is a spatial fragmentation of production and not simply a spatial dispersion (disagglomeration). Fragmentation means that external linkages now interpenetrate territorially embedded production systems at multiple levels and in multiple ways, which potentially challenges the established imagery of clusters and districts as sticky Marshallian knots of thick localized ties in a dispersed global network.

(Whitford and Potter, 2007: 509)

Similarly, the advantage of particular clusters was often linked to their constitutive role in global production and innovation networks – acting as centres of corporate control (Sassen, 1990), as centres of innovation (Saxenian, 1994), as logistics and operations hubs for macro-regions (Ó Riain, 2004), and so on.

The rethinking of the social and spatial foundations of agglomeration, flexibility and learning offers more room to move for policy and political actors. Social relations can be reconstructed to support new modes of organizing in a global economy. However, even as this offers hope to regional advocates, the threat of international competition is reopened as regions around the world seek to emulate the best known models of such industrial districts.

This is true in part because the building blocks of globally networked regional economies have themselves become more widely available, particularly as inter-firm networks, metrics and standards become more important and intra-corporate organizational integration is weakened (Storper, 2000). Storper argues that international convergence in production techniques and quality and other conventions is only partly driven by dynamics of competition, trade and international investment. There is also a more generalized diffusion of modes of organization of production and innovation (Giddens' globalizing 'expert systems' and 'symbolic tokens') often into regions that have little direct relation with the regions of origin of these new forms of economic organization. The generalized diffusion of Japanese manufacturing methods or of the Silicon Valley mode of work organization are important examples, where the influence of these 'models' of work organization has spread well beyond the specific networks of regions that are tied to the central nodes in Japan and California. The organizational 'building blocks' of networked production, although initially embedded in the regional cultures and institutions of Japan and Silicon Valley (Dore, 1973; Saxenian, 1994), have become more widely available to regions seeking to emulate or adapt features of these dynamic industrial centres.

From firms to regions?
Global regions and the social reproduction of capitalism

Regional development in an era of global networks has increasingly become a question of mobilizing and reassembling local and global elements in ways that sometimes seek directly to emulate models elsewhere and at times result in new and innovative modes of organization. In this sense, there is more scope here for innovative regional strategies than is captured by the imagery of urban entrepreneurialism and competitiveness (Le Galès, 2002). Regions are increasingly taking on the mantle worn in the Fordist era primarily by the dominant firms. These firms provided modes of 'organizational integration' (Lazonick, 1996) for the industrial system. We have already seen that regional complexes are increasingly important to the dynamics of competition, the organization of markets and the insertion of economies into international economic regimes. Furthermore, where large firms played a key role in organizing cooperation at the point of production and led the management of the capital–labour relation, regional industrial systems are increasingly important to the institutional coordination of the wage relation and class relations, in an era where inter-firm careers are increasingly common (Benner, 2002).

The social world of the large firm provided a complex organizational mechanism

for providing the social infrastructure for innovation, production, careers, the raising of finance, the reproduction of the labour force, and other critical elements of capitalist economic organization. Firms increasingly externalized many elements of their activities in the face of structural and policy shifts promoting financialization of the economy and the dominance of new conceptions of the firm as a bundle of financial assets (Fligstein, 2001). In the process, regions have become increasingly important to this work of the social reproduction of capitalism.

Regions have long been recognized as centres for the reproduction of labour, hardly surprising given the immobility of labour relative to capital. In effect, creation of pools of labour, ideally highly skilled, has always been a basic condition of regional development strategies – and particularly the ability of regions to attract mobile capital. However, the (in)famous 'creative class' theory (Florida, 2002) goes beyond this to argue that the attraction of mobile labour is a critical element of regional strategy and that the construction of a cosmopolitan urban environment is therefore critical to effective regional development.

But even Florida's latte-sipping 'creatives' find themselves involved in the mundane business of workplace conflicts and career negotiations. Here too the region plays a newly significant role. The ability to build a career across firms within a region is central to the reproduction of a skilled workforce in the most dynamic regions such as Silicon Valley (Saxenian, 1994). The workplace bargain between mobile workers such as software developers and their employers is based, not on the expectation of lifelong employment, but on the expectation of cash, learning and career benefits from particular projects benefits that can be realized in the global but also, more significantly, the regional labour market (Ó Riain, 2000, 2004). There are opportunities and attractions in more mobile labour markets but there are also risks and insecurities. Despite often glaring differences in wages and conditions, this 'precarity' extends increasingly to all workers especially those in the rapidly growing informational and service sectors and including even members of the 'creative class' (Ross, 2008; Kerr, 2010).

Surprisingly for an era of capital mobility, regions prove important to the organization of capital. Integration within the division of labour is increasingly provided across, rather than within, firms. New forms of modular contracting allow firms to recombine their networks (Sturgeon, 2002, 2003) and the network of inter-firm relations across global regions proves important in allowing this recombination to occur (Saxenian, 1994, 2006). Furthermore, industry and professional associations often play a role within regional economies that were played by the major disciplines (such as production management, marketing, personnel, and so on) within large firms (Jacoby, 1988). Flows of investment capital to the most successful regions have been organized through the embeddedness of venture capitalists within the regions themselves – most famously in Silicon Valley but also, increasingly, through networks of venture capitalists that link centres such as Silicon Valley with more peripheral regions (Saxenian, 1994; Saxenian and Sabel, 2008; Zook, 2005). The literature on regions and the decline of Fordism emphasized the effect of capital flows – and particularly outflows on regions (Bluestone and Harrison, 1982; Scott and Storper, 1986; Storper and Walker, 1991). However, regions can themselves become central to the constitution of particular flows of capital.

Finally, regions are increasingly placed at the centre of the innovation process that is at the heart of contemporary capitalist development. Regional studies have shifted in recent decades from asking where industry has gone, to investigating how new centres of innovation-based growth have emerged. A variety of frameworks have emerged that utilize concepts of economies of agglomeration, endogenous development, networks and governance to identify 'territorial systems of innovation' (Moulaert and Sekia, 2003). While Moulaert and Sekia point to the conceptual ambiguity in these frameworks, research programmes around industrial districts, innovative milieux, new industrial spaces, learning regions and more have pointed to the critical importance of territorialized processes in an innovation economy.

The decline of Detroit, and even the geography of IBM, has been displaced from the centre of regional studies by the study of Silicon Valley and its many imitators. Mowery (2009) shows that there has been a rapid increase in the numbers of scientists and engineers working in small firms as part of an 'open system of innovation' and Block and Keller (2008) document a significant shift in the sources of the most innovative scientific breakthroughs in the US, with Fortune 500 company labs dominating in the 1970s but federal labs, universities and collaborations among smaller firms taking the lead in the past decade.

Lester and Piore (2004) argue that the decline of corporate labs such as those in AT&T and IBM and the general externalization and rationalization by large firms has destroyed the public spaces that were essential to innovation within US firms. In the process, new public spaces outside the corporations have become crucial – even though weakly supported. Crucially, they argue that public policy – including regional development policy – will be sorely misguided if it follows exhortations to mimic the private sector. It is precisely the replacement of these public resources and spaces that have been neglected by the private sector that is the primary task of the public sector – and of the region.

Varieties of capitalist regions

The 'global region' is therefore constructed out of global elements even as it plays a critical role in constituting globalization.

However, it is not simply at the mercy of global flows and processes but is involved in providing the conditions for the mobilization of labour, capital and knowledge – and in shaping how they are organized and combined into particular pathways of development.

This in turn opens up the possibility that there may well be many types of regions within the global economy. We have seen that some of the differences between regions can be described in terms of their location within global networks (core vs peripheral, etc.) or their roles within those networks ('centres of corporate control', 'manufacturing platforms', etc.). However, in addition to these structural features of regional differences, there are also differences that can be traced to the constellations of organizations through which the region operates.

The influential literature on 'varieties of capitalism' poses two main types of capitalist economy – liberal market economies such as the US and UK, and coordinated market economies such as Germany and Japan. Furthermore, liberal market economies are seen as better suited, institutionally, to promote innovation-based industries through their flexible capital and labour markets and close university–industry ties (Hall and Soskice, 2001). But the degree of coordination within liberal economies is badly understated in this literature. It turns out that there are a wide variety of coordinating mechanisms at work within the liberal market economies (and indeed important elements

of markets in the coordinated economies) (see Peck and Theodore (2007) for a more detailed discussion of the difficulties with this approach).

Moreover, even within liberal market economies, there are also a variety of regional forms of coordination. Dunning (2000: 24–25) describes six types of spatial cluster, drawing on previous work by Markusen (1996) and others. In Table 2.1, organizes the six types along two different dimensions: (1) the extent to which private or public actors predominate in the region, and (2) the organizational structure of the region and mode of coordination by these dominant actors. While each of these spatial cluster types seeks to mobilize local resources in pursuit of a niche within the global economy, the effects of politics and institutional legacies and strategies on the form each 'global region' takes is clear.

Private firms take the lead in many global regions. In some a single 'flagship firm' acts as the hub around which many smaller, dependent firms form spokes – for example, around Boeing in Seattle or around Pohang Steel in Korea. This differs from the classically integrated firm which generated relatively few 'spokes' around itself. The opposite of this 'hub and spoke' structure is the classical 'industrial district' structure of networks of small firms with no single dominant firm, such as in Northern Italy's textile industry (Piore and Sabel, 1984). Industrial districts, however, are susceptible to transformation

Table 2.1 Varieties of global regions

		Lead sector	
		Firm-centred	Public or quasi-public institution-centred
Organisational structure	Dominant actor	Flagship firms/'Hub and spoke'	Government institutions at centre
	Network of actors	Industrial district	Public–private learning economies
	Attraction of external actors	Export-processing zones	Science and technology parks

Source: Based on Dunning (2000)

into 'hub-and-spoke' structures if lead firms become dominant and smaller firms become dependent upon them (Harrison, 1994). It appears that the Finnish high-tech cluster is going through a process like this as the once relatively decentralized industrial structure that spawned Nokia is incorporated within Nokia's umbrella and becomes dependent upon it. In the process, Nokia is rendered vulnerable by the lack of diversity and innovation in its products and organizational structure (Saxenian and Sabel, 2009). Private firms are also central to a third form of regional cluster – the export processing platform. In this case states seek to attract firms from beyond the region and are often able to build agglomerations through heavily subsidized infrastructure, low taxes and other incentives. There may be smaller 'hub-and-spoke' structures within the platform regions. However, the challenge for regions such as Ireland, Singapore and many others is to turn this agglomeration into more deeply embedded clusters – whether those be of the hub-and-spoke or industrial district variety. Regions rarely stay completely stable but are constantly shifting in their structure and development.

Other regions are based primarily around public sector organizations or clusters of public-private networks. Mirroring the hub-and-spoke structure of a single dominant organization, some regions are based around a major public facility – a federal lab such as Los Alamos in the US, a military research facility such as in Aldershot in the UK, or a university. Closely related is the more diversified region which consists of a network of larger public and private institutions – primarily R&D laboratories and universities. These clusters are based on the promotion of 'institution-building learning economies and the sharing of collective knowledge' (Dunning, 2000: 25), with the Research Triangle in North Carolina in the US perhaps the best-known example. Finally, science and technology parks form the third public sector-led region, with the institutional and material infrastructure for science and technology-based firms put in place in an effort to attract external firms – although with the significant possibility that what it produces in practice is a slightly more sophisticated export platform. The most successful examples, like Hsinchu Science Park in Taiwan, blend elements of this model with the public-private learning economy and the industrial district by fostering genuine networking and technical community within the park.

Contingency, politics and the global region

Regional development is not a pathway to escaping the challenges of globalization. However, it may provide the opportunity to shape the ways that regions participate in the global economy. Our brief review of the varieties of forms of organization of spatial clusters reveals the persistent importance of institutional and organizational factors, even in a world of regional development where global structural pressures are great, global networks are increasingly important and global models and metrics are widely diffused. There are significant variations in private sector-led regions while public organizations remain important, even within liberal economies.

Capital flows have certainly reshaped regions in significant ways, with the international integration of corporate operations changing the internal dynamics of regions. In addition, financialization of the economy particularly in the US and other liberal economies (Krippner, 2005) has threatened the basic organizational and social infrastructures of production and innovation. In the process, some regions are abandoned while others experience boom periods. In the face of the financial crisis, however, we are likely to see regions emerge as more vital than ever in the processes of global economic recovery as they provide one of the major reservoirs of productive and innovative capabilities.

The 'technical communities' of workers are also critical to the network of global regions. Ethnic diasporas, especially of technical professionals, provide important conduits of information and social ties between regions around the world. Crucially, these migration and mobility linkages enable peripheral regions to generate regional development and innovation through ties to core regions that go well beyond the typical transfers involved in attracting foreign investment or setting up export platforms (Saxenian, 2006). In the process, the innovation system of core regions has increasingly stretched beyond their own borders to incorporate more peripheral regions such as the extension of the Silicon Valley network to include innovation and production in places such as Israel and Taiwan, and perhaps to a lesser extent India and Ireland (Saxenian, 2006; Breznitz, 2007; Ó Riain, 2004).

The increasing internationalization of professional associations, scientific organizations and universities also forms a transnational technical community that is part of the infrastructure of regional development. Debates about integration into global networks now involve discussions about how best to attract and build, not only investment by firms, but also the institutional networks within which those firms and systems of innovation are embedded. Regional policy makers are increasingly involving themselves in building the social structures and institutions within which new forms of economic organization operate – in the process becoming 'lay' economic sociologists and geographers.

Public actors continue to matter therefore. New forms of developmental statism have emerged that place the mobilization of regional 'relational assets' (Storper, 1997) at the heart of their efforts. 'Developmental network states' have played an important role in the growth of high-tech regions in the US and its networks of global regions (Block, 2008; Breznitz, 2007; Ó Riain, 2004). These states have been instrumental in forming new professional labour forces, in supporting and shaping innovation and innovation-based firms, in underwriting emerging technical and industrial communities, and in promoting the intersection of local and global networks (Ó Riain, 2004). Regions that are tied to national states (e.g. Ireland and Singapore) are particularly well placed to mobilize the political and institutional resources that underpin regional development.

Cerny dismisses such strategies as subservient to the broader project of liberal marketization and simply incorporating regions into ever more dominant capitalist social relations:

> The outer limits of effective action by the state in this environment are usually seen to comprise its capacity to promote a relatively favorable investment climate for transnational capital – i.e., by providing an increasingly circumscribed range of goods that retain a national-scale (of subnational-scale) public character or of a particular type of still-specific assets described as immobile factors of capital. Such potentially manipulable factors include: human capital (the skills, experience, education, and training of the work force); infrastructure (from public transportation to high-technology information highways); support for a critical mass of research and development activities; basic public services necessary for a good quality of life for those working in middle- to high-level positions in otherwise footloose (transnationally mobile) firms and sectors; and maintenance of a public policy environment favorable to investment (and profit making) by such companies, whether domestic or foreign-owned.
>
> (Cerny, 1995)

However, our exploration of the broader role of the region in the social reproduction of labour, capital and knowledge points to more far-reaching possibilities for the political

25

shaping of regional social and economic outcomes. The substantial list of areas of interventions offered by Cerny leaves a significant range of action that goes well beyond ensuring competitiveness. Network state developmentalism integrating many of the elements of human capital, R&D, infrastructures and welfarism and incentives that Cerny describes has had profoundly different developmental consequences than alternative modes of regional or national development such as clientelism, simple corporate boosterism, growth machines or financialization. It is perhaps best to see 'competition state' strategies as one form of regional development, rather than as the structurally determined outcome that Cerny poses.

In addition, each of these areas can be structured in ways that make significant differences for patterns of inequality. Despite progressive emphasis on the decline of demand-side Keynesian strategies, much of the pattern of inequality in different societies is shaped by the supply-side, where more or less equal investments can be made in different groups of workers, and the organization of production, where significant differences in workplace organization persist despite the kinds of global convergences noted above (e.g. Cole, 1991; Lorenz and Valeyre, 2007; Heidenreich, 2004). It is telling that the social democracies that continue to combine innovation and equity have also emphasized many of the kinds of policies that Cerny describes. The trade-off between competitiveness and equality in regional development seems less pre-determined than the 'competition state' theory suggests.

In the face of the current global financial and economic crisis, most regions are already experiencing severe economic declines. However, the crisis has also seen increased attention being paid once again to Keynesian-inspired efforts at stimulating demand. While some of these efforts are being undertaken at the national level (such as in the US), increased attention has been focused on macro-regions such as the European Union

and their role in both stimulating and regulating credit and finance. This is particularly interesting because patterns of regional inequality in Europe show increasing inequalities between regions within nations, but decreasing inequalities between regions in different nations within the EU (Heidenreich, 2009). If the EU can rise to the challenge of an integrated fiscal and regulatory response to the crisis (which appears unlikely in mid-2009 but may become even more necessary as the crisis continues), the European economy in 2015 may be managed more heavily through macro-regional macro-economic coordination and micro-regional coordination of production and innovation. If this global and macro-regional capacity for macro-economic coordination can be built, then regional capabilities and regional development are likely to be critical building blocks of any emerging 'New Deal'.

There is reason to believe that such a 'New Deal' can go beyond economic production to enhance social well-being and participation, in an enriched model of 'integrated area development' (Moulaert and Sekia, 2003). While many analysts of global regions have emphasized their role in production and innovation, we have emphasized here that those contributions are intimately tied to the role of the region as a centre of social reproduction. This provides the opportunity to link sustainable economic development to social progress and egalitarian forms of development. While this is politically difficult, it is not impossible – research on varieties of capitalism and on regional variation in production systems shows that there remains significant scope for designing alternatives to neo-liberal economic organisation. Changes in global governance will no doubt be essential to protect such alternative pathways from the threats posed by financial liberalization and related processes. However, such political and institutional changes will not emerge from expert elites but will need to be backed by supportive and sustainable coalitions. We might expect that regions that provide more successful models of social and economic development will be central to those coalitions.

References

Barnes, W. R. and Larry Ledebur, C. (1998) *The New Regional Economies: The U.S. Common Market and the Global Economy Cities & Planning Series*. Thousand Oaks, Calif: Sage Publications.

Baron, J., Burton, M. D. and Hannan, M. (1996) 'The Road Taken: Origins and Early Evolution of Employment Systems in Emerging Companies', *Industrial and Corporate Change*, 5:2, 239–275.

Benner, C. (2002) *Work in the New Economy*. Oxford: Blackwell.

Block, F. (2008) 'Swimming Against the Current': The Rise of a Hidden Developmental State in the U.S.", *Politics & Society*, 36:2, 169–206.

Block, F. and M. R. Keller (2008) "Where do Innovations Come From? Transformations in the U.S. National Innovation System 1970-2006." Report published by The Information Technology and Innovation Foundation. Available at http://www.itif.org/index.php?id=158.

Bluestone, B. and Harrison, B. (1982) *The Deindustrialization of America*. New York: Basic Books.

Brenner, N. (2004) *New State Spaces*. Oxford: Oxford University Press.

Brenner, N., Jessop, B. and Jones, M. (2008) "Theorising Socio-Spatial Relations", *Environment and Planning D: Society and Space*, 26: 389–401.

Breznitz, D. (2007) *The Innovation State* New Haven: Yale University Press.

Cerny, P. (1995) "Globalization and the Changing Logic of Collective Action", *International Organization*, 49, 595–625.

Christopherson, S., Garretsen, H. and Martin, R. (2008) "The World is not Flat: Putting Globalisation in its Place". *Cambridge Journal of Regions, Economy and Society*, 1, 343–349.

Cole, R. (1991) *Strategies For Learning: Small-Group Activities in American, Japanese, and Swedish Industry*. Berkeley: University of California Press.

Dore, R. (1973) *British Factory-Japanese Factory: The Origins of National Diversity in Industrial Relations*. London: Allen and Unwin.

Dunning, J. (2000) "Regions, Globalization, and the Knowledge Economy: The Issues Stated", in J. Dunning (ed.) *Regions, Globalization and the Knowledge-Based Economy*. Oxford: Oxford University Press.

Fligstein, N. (2001) *The Architecture of Markets: An Economic Sociology of Twenty-First-Century Capitalist Societies*. Princeton, NJ: Princeton University Press.

Florida, R. (2002) *The Rise of the Creative Class*. New York: Basic Books.

Friedman, T. (2006) *The World is Flat*. London: Penguin Books.

Gereffi, G., Humphrey, J. and Sturgeon, T. (2005) 'The Governance of Global Value Chains', *Review of International Political Economy*, 12, 78–104.

Giddens, A. (1991) *The Consequences of Modernity*. Oxford: Blackwell.

Hall, P. and Soskice, D. (2001) *Varieties of Capitalism*. Oxford: Oxford University Press.

Harrison, B. (1994) *Lean and Mean*. New York: Basic Books.

Harvey, D. (1989) *The Condition of Postmodernity*. Oxford: Blackwell.

Harvey, D. (2005) *A Brief History of Neoliberalism*. Oxford: Oxford University Press.

Heidenreich, M. (2004) "Knowledge-Based Work: An International Comparison", *International Management: Thematic Issue on Cultures, Nations and Management*, 8: 3, 65–80.

Heidenreich, M. and Wunder, C. (2008) "Patterns of Regional Inequality in the Enlarged Europe", *European Sociological Review*, 24:1, 19–36.

Held, D., McGrew, A., Goldblatt, D. and Perraton, J. (1999) *Global Transformations: Politics, Economics and Culture*. Stanford: Stanford University Press.

Herrigel, G. (2007) 'Flexibility and Formalization: Rethinking Space and Governance in Corporations and Manufacturing Regions', in K. Bluhm and R. Schmidt (eds) *Changes in SMEs: Towards a New European Capitalism?* Basingstoke, Palgrave Macmillan.

Hymer, S. (1971) "The Multinational Corporation and the International Division of Labor", in R. B. Cohen, N. Felton, M. Nkosi and J. van Liere (eds) *The Multinational Corporation: A Radical Approach* (1979), Cambridge: Cambridge University Press.

Jacoby, S. (1988) *Employing Bureaucracy: Managers Unions and the Transformation of Work in American Industry 1900–1945*. New York: Columbia Press.

Kerr, A. (2010) "The Culture of Gamework", Chapter 17 in M. Deuze (ed.) *Managing Media Work*. Thousand Oaks, CA: Sage Publications.

Krippner, G. (2005) "The Financialisation of the American Economy", *Socio-Economic Review*, 3:2, 173–208.

Lazonick, W. (1991) *Business Organisation and the Myth of the Market Economy*. Cambridge: Cambridge University Press.

Le Gales, P. (2002) *European Cities*. Oxford: Oxford University Press.

Lester, R. K. and Piore, M. (2004) *Innovation – The Missing Dimension*. Cambridge: Harvard University Press.

Lorenz, E. and Valeyre, A. (2007) "Organizational Forms and Innovative Performance: A Comparison of the EU-15", in E. Lorenz and B. Lundvall (eds) *How Europe's Economies Learn*. Oxford: Oxford University Press.

Markusen, A. (1996) "Sticky Places in Slippery Space: A Typology of Industrial Districts", *Economic Geography*, 72, 29–313.

Moulaert, F. and Sekia, F. (2003) "Territorial Innovation Models: A Critical Survey", *Regional Studies*, 37:3, 289–302.

Mowery, D. (2009) "Plus ca change: Industrial R&D in the 'Third Industrial Revolution'", *Industrial and Corporate Change*, 18:1, 1–50.

Ó Riain, S. (2000) "Net-Working for a Living: Irish Software Developers in the Global Workplace", in M. Burawoy *et al.* (eds) *Global Ethnography*. Berkeley: University of California Press.

Ó Riain, S. (2004) *The Politics of High Tech Growth: Developmental Network States in the Global Economy (Structural Analysis in the Social Sciences 23)*. New York/Cambridge: Cambridge University Press.

Ó Riain, S. (2006) "Time–Space Intensification: Karl Polanyi, the Double Movement, and Global Informational Capitalism", *Theory and Society*, 35, 5–6, 507–528.

Pastor, M., Benner, C. and Matsuoka, M. (2009) *This Could be the Start of Something Big: How Social Movements for Regional Equity are Reshaping Metropolitan America*. Ithaca, NY: Cornell University Press.

Peck, J. and Theodore, N. (2007) "Variegated Capitalism", *Progress in Human Geography*, 31:6, 731–772

Piore, M. and Sabel, C. (1984) *The Second Industrial Divide*. New York: Basic Books.

Reich, R. (1991) *The Work of Nations*. New York: Vintage Books.

Ross, A. (2008) "The New Geography of Work: Power to the Precarious?", *Theory, Culture and Society*, 25: 7–8, 31–49.

Ruggie, J.G. (1982) "International Regimes, Transactions and Change: Embedded Liberalism in the Postwar Economic Order", *International Organization*, 36: 379–415.

Sabel, C. (1994) "Learning by Monitoring: The Institutions of Economic Development", in N. Smelser and R. Swedberg (eds) *The Handbook of Economic Sociology*. Princeton, NJ: Princeton University Press.

Sabel, C. and Zeitlin, J. (2004) "Neither Modularity nor Relational Contracting: Inter-firm Collaboration in the New Economy", *Enterprise and Society*, 5, 388–403.

Sassen, S. (1990) *The Global City*. Princeton, NJ: Princeton University Press.

Saxenian, A. (1994) *Regional Advantage: Culture and Competition in Silicon Valley and Route 128*. Cambridge, MA: Harvard University Press.

Saxenian, A. (2006) *The New Argonauts: Regional Advantage in a Global Economy*. Cambridge, MA: Harvard University Press.

Saxenian, A. and Sabel, C. (2008) "Venture Capital in the 'Periphery': The New Argonauts, Global Search, and Local Institution Building", *Economic Geography*, 84:4, 379–394.

Saxenian, A. and Sabel, C. (2009) *A Fugitive Success: Finland's Economic Future*. Helsinki: SITRA. Available at: http://www.sitra.fi/julkaisut/raportti80.pdf?download.

Scott, A. and Storper, M. (eds.) (1986) *Production, Work, Territory: the Geographical Anatomy of Industrial Capitalism*. Boston: Allen Unwin.

Storper, M. (1997) *The Regional World: Territorial Development in a Global Economy*. London: Guilford Press.

Storper, M. (2000) "Globalisation and Knowledge Flows: An Industrial Geographer's Perspective", in J. Dunning (ed.), *Regions, Globalization and the Knowledge-Based Economy*. Oxford: Oxford University Press.

Storper, M. and Walker, R. (1991) *The Capitalist Imperative: Territory, Technology and Industrial Growth*. Oxford: Basil Blackwell.

Sturgeon, T. (2002) "Modular Production Networks: A New American Model of Industrial Organization", *Industrial and Corporate Change*, 11, 451–496.

Sturgeon, T. J. (2003) "What Really Goes-on in Silicon Valley? Spatial Clustering and Dispersal in Modular Production Networks", *Journal of Economic Geography*, 3, 199–225.

Whitford, J. and Potter, C. (2007) "Regional Economies, Open Networks and the Spatial Fragmentation of Production", *Socio-Economic Review*, 5, 497–526.

Zook, M. A. (2005) *The Geography of the Internet Industry: Venture Capital, Dot-coms and Local Knowledge*. Oxford: Blackwell Publishers.

Further reading

Brenner, N. (2004) *New State Spaces*. Oxford: Oxford University Press. (A sophisticated theory of the interconnections between globalization, urban restructuring and new state forms and spaces.)

Gereffi, G., Humphrey, J. and Sturgeon, T. (2005) 'The Governance of Global Value Chains', *Review of International Political Economy*, 12, 78–104. (A review and development of the global value chains commodity chains perspective.)

Harvey, D. (2005) *A Brief History of Neoliberalism*. Oxford: Oxford University Press. (A wide-ranging account of the economic, political and spatial dimensions of neoliberalism.)

Heidenreich, M. and Wunder, C. (2008) "Patterns of Regional Inequality in the Enlarged Europe", *European Sociological Review*, 24:1, 19–36. (Evidence from the EU of growing inequalities between regions within countries and of convergence among regions across countries.)

Le Galès, P. (2002) *European Cities*. Oxford: Oxford University Press. (A wide-ranging investigation of how cities are changing in the face of globalization, in ways that go well beyond enhancing competitiveness.)

Lester, R. K. and Piore, M. (2004) *Innovation – The Missing Dimension*, Cambridge, MA: Harvard University Press. (A study of the role of public spaces in the innovation process and the role of industrial districts and universities in developing those spaces.)

Piore, M. and Sabel, C. (1984) *The Second Industrial Divide*. New York: Basic Books. (One of the classic accounts of the importance of regional economies in a world of flexible specialization.)

Saxenian, A. (2006) *The New Argonauts: Regional Advantage in a Global Economy*. Cambridge, MA: Harvard University Press. (A rich exploration of the ways in which the technical communities typically found in regions such as Silicon Valley are emerging on a transnational basis, promoting a network of global regions.)

Whitford, J. and Potter, C. (2007) "Regional Economies, Open Networks and the Spatial Fragmentation of Production", *Socio-Economic Review*, 5, 497–526. (Reviews the 'state of the art' in the analysis of regional production networks.)

3

Territorial competition

Ian Gordon

Introduction

The notion of territorial competition refers to a form of collective action, undertaken on behalf of economic interests within a particular territory, which serves to advance these in competition with those of interests located in (some or all) other territories (Cheshire and Gordon, 1995, 1996). From one perspective, this involves an extension to broader spatial scales of the types of location marketing traditionally practised by private developers. Alternatively, it may be seen as extending local governments' use of public goods provision to attract/retain desired residents into the productive economy. A more distinctive third dimension to the process involves specific investment in organisational assets to create a market in membership of the territory's economic community (Gordon and Jayet, 1994).

The concept was developed in the context of integrating European economies in the 1980s and 1990s, where such competition attained a new importance. In North America particularly, local competitive activity in the form of boosterism had been a well-known phenomenon for very much longer (see e.g. Cobb, 1982; Ward, 1998). The idea of 'territorial competition' is intentionally much

broader, however, encompassing not only attraction of inward investment, but all/any forms of collective action which served its purposes. The point is not to treat all these forms as equivalent, but rather to direct attention to the choices made among them in different contexts, instead of treating the practice of one or another in isolation.

Defining territorial competition in this broad way might seem to make it synonymous with local/regional economic development in general, and thus not worth discussing separately in this volume. But there are two distinguishing features which give analyses of territorial competition a particular flavour. The first is that they do not presume that such competition is necessarily functional – whether for a territory which is pursuing it, or for a wider set of areas – or indeed dysfunctional. Rather that is a key question to be investigated, both theoretically and empirically. Second, their dual emphasis on collective action and particular economic interests raises questions about the political processes underlying specific forms of territorially competitive activity (or their absence). From this perspective, there is nothing inevitable about a commitment to any serious form of local/regional economic development – even given a more solid understanding (than in the past) of how these can/should be pursued. Rather it is expected to depend on those structures, institutions and constraints which shape political action, and inaction, within the areas concerned. Nor does the idea of territorial competition presume that the interests to which it is directed will naturally or necessarily be those of the local economy/residents as a whole. Rather the expectation is that the mixture of interests which are effectively served will reflect the same political processes that determine whether and in what ways 'places' actually develop one form or another of competitive/developmental activity.

The perspective is thus essentially one of political economy – giving a central role to the interaction between 'political' and 'economic' processes – and might be seen as an extended/generalised version of the North American analyses of 'growth machines' (Molotch, 1976). However, the aspiration of those writing within a 'territorial competition' framework is not simply to provide a critical exposé of the gulf between idealised expectations of place-based economic development and the thrust of 'actual existing' competitive activity. The aim is rather to develop the kind of realistic understanding of the behavioural and political economy factors which is necessary if ways are to be found to correct the biases in how local/regional development functions or fails in particular kinds of context.

The significance of such factors is substantially affected by the territorial dimension, since the areas on behalf of which competitive actions are to be pursued will generally be far from closed in economic terms, or completely autonomous politically. This presents a pair of key issues about: the extent to which such activities could or should have effects outside the initiating areas ('spatial externalities' in the jargon); and how higher levels of government/governance – whether regional/national or international – may constrain these territorially competitive activities, whether just to conserve their own power

resources or to optimise outcomes across a wider territory.

Over the past quarter century, territorial competition seems to have become a global phenomenon, spreading beyond Europe/North America to play a strong role (for good and bad) in the development of newly industrialised and transition economies (Rodríguez-Pose and Arbix, 2001; Chien and Gordon, 2008; Hermann-Pilath, 2004, Jessop and Sum, 2000), and with sub-national agencies in many countries playing key roles in the competition for FDI (Oman, 2000). In each context, a characteristic interplay between political and economic factors shapes the form, intensity and outcomes of local economic development policies – sometimes with important consequences for national development too. But the expectation is that these will play out in different ways, depending on a set of economic, political and institutional characteristics which figure within a general model of territorial competition. In the remainder of this chapter, we shall look in turn at: the economics of place competitiveness; the politics of territorial competition; and a normative framework for assessing outcomes from the process and regulating it; before summarising key issues.

Place competition, place competitiveness and territorial competition

Spatial competition may be understood in several different ways in relation to local economic development policies. In particular, there are three that need to be distinguished, which for convenience we will refer to as place competition, place competitiveness and territorial competition (though these terms are not used consistently in the literature).

Place competition: At the most basic level, it is a simple matter of fact that individuals and businesses located in a particular area tend to compete not only with each other, but also with people/businesses located in other areas. The competitive position of each, in terms of price and quality, reflects a combination of factors – associated with: the assets they have available; the technologies they can deploy; costs/prices in the local market; extraneous influences on supply/demand in their specialisms; and 'pure chance'. Their combined effect across all local businesses/individuals produces some places which are 'winners' in terms of aggregate activity/earnings levels, while others are 'losers' in the place competition. Whether or not this division has evident local causes, it is likely to have local consequences – though not all of the place's businesses/residents will be affected in the same way (or at all).

What it means for a business to be 'located' in an area can vary greatly, depending on: who owns it; the status/role of local operations; and how far these are embedded in the local economy. Direct benefits from the competitive success of local business establishments (in product markets) and local residents (on labour markets) clearly accrue to those who own the crucial assets, notably: shareholders, who may or may not live within the area (in the first case); and those with increasingly valued kinds of human capital, who may or may not remain within it (in the second case). In addition, their success is likely to have some positive income spillovers within the local/regional economy, in terms of property values, money wages and (probably) employment rates.

Spatial economic theory suggests that the effects on property values will tend to be localised, because these assets are immobile, whereas the labour market effects may get rapidly and widely diffused. For the average resident, real (expected) earnings may not actually change, though there will generally be both winners and losers within any affected economy. If the supply of local residential/ commercial space is somewhat inelastic, the success of some local businesses will mean higher costs for all, thus lowering the demand

for others who sell price-sensitive products in external markets. Despite such uncertainties, the existence of spill-over effects means that members of the local community may reasonably believe that they have some stake in the competitive success of local businesses and residents – even when there is no collective involvement either in producing competitive assets or in sharing out their benefits.

Place competitiveness: Outcomes of such inter-place competition may be wholly or largely determined by exogenous factors. There are cases, however, where the competitive position of representative firms in an area is substantially influenced by the presence or absence of quasi-public goods, i.e. of competitive assets which are freely available, on a non-rivalrous basis, to all located within the area. Relevant examples could include: facilities traditionally provided (if at all) by local authorities (e.g. education, transportation, specialist research institutes); others dependent for their existence/sustainability on appropriate regulation of private activities by such an authority (e.g. via development planning); and a further set whose provision essentially depends on private activity, but where economic incentives cannot be counted on to secure (any or adequate) provision (e.g. pools of skill/tacit knowledge and support services, or networks of established cooperation). What these competitive assets have in common is that they are endogenous in character, in the sense that their availability is not fixed but rather reflects the shaping of an area through a combination of its economic history and its political economy (Massey, 1984).

The importance of place competitiveness in terms of such assets has been substantially enhanced over the past quarter century or so by two broad shifts in the form and intensity of economic competition. The first involves the market for mobile industrial or commercial investment projects, which grew substantially in importance as constraints on trade, communications and multi-plant co-ordination of productive activities were successively overcome (between the 1960s and 1980s). As far as inward investment was concerned, this enlarged the pool of potential projects which could be 'won', even by less established centres. As a result, however, the practice became much more competitive, since firms with plants to locate could now actively consider many more locations, and play these off against each other. And, at the same time, the existing activity base of economic 'territories' (both old and new) became more vulnerable both to the relocation of specific functions from established centres that could now be made to operate in some cheaper location, and to onward movement by footloose recent arrivals, tempted by better 'deals' offered elsewhere. The second involves a quite widespread (though still ongoing) shift in the basis of product market competition from simple price (or value-for-money) criteria to quality (or rather to the distinct qualities of differentiated products). This shift toward some version of 'flexible specialisation' (Piore and Sabel, 1984; Storper, 1989) seems partly to have reflected changes in the tastes of (more affluent) consumers, facilitated by new production technologies which made short production runs much more economic. But in the advanced economies it also represented a defensive response by home producers who could no longer attempt to match prices from plants in those low-wage economies that now offered feasible locations for relatively standardised products.

In Porter's (1990) terms, this shift allowed businesses, and the places that housed their core functions ('home bases'), to develop distinctive forms of 'competitive advantage' as an alternative to the 'race to the bottom' which pure price competition (and comparative advantage) promised in an increasingly globalised economy. The kinds of local public goods that appear to sustain competitive advantage of this kind are themselves qualitative – in relation to capabilities of local suppliers, complementary skill/knowledge pools,

knowledgeable consumers and vigorous competition – and combine in ways that allow fortunate places to offer distinctive kinds of environment relevant to firms occupying different types of market niche. As with Krugman's (1995) more aggregative emphasis on the strength of agglomeration economies, Porter's evidence for the beneficial effects of clustering implied that such places could enjoy continuing dynamic benefits (i.e. faster growth), rather than simply one-off (or temporary) boosts to the level of local activity.

Territorial competition: One further step beyond this, 'territories' – or some body acting on their behalf – may be seen as playing an active collective role in securing the conditions to promote competitive success for firms and individuals based in their area. This is the strong sense of purposive 'territorial competition', rather than of simply de facto 'place competition' or 'place competitiveness'.

For this concept to be applicable, it is necessary first of all for there to be substantial aspects of place competitiveness which can be manipulated in predictable/positive ways by some collective agency in the territory. That is partly a technical issue, as to whether such agencies possess both the relevant expertises and effective autonomy to apply them. But it is also a political one, because of the diversity of economic interests within any territory, which not only complicates the process of mobilising collective action but also increases the likelihood of it being captured by particular sectional interests.

There is a theoretical precedent for such purposive activity in Tiebout's (1956) treatment of inter-jurisdictional competition between (nearby) local authorities offering rival bundles of local public goods/tax rates to attract residents. Within the framework of his analysis, such competition serves – as authoritative decision-making on its own could not – to stimulate provision of an optimal mix of public goods – including those generated directly by an optimal pattern of residential segregation. This outcome depends crucially on three assumptions which are a good deal more problematic when translated to the context of competition for economic activity rather than residents: a large number of competing jurisdictions, each of efficient size and with free mobility between each; absence of any impacts spilling over territorial boundaries; and jurisdictions simply motivated to maximise growth (in Tiebout's version) or 'profits' (Bewley, 1981). Where these do not apply, competition alone will not necessarily secure desirable outcomes, independent of the processes through which policies are shaped and regulated.

Famously, Krugman (1996a) has argued against the pursuit of 'competitiveness' policies on behalf of territories (whether national or urban/regional), for reasons most commonly identified with the claim that unlike firms they 'cannot go bankrupt'). The relevance of that argument is not clear – since firms do not compete only to avoid extinction. But it can be understood as part of a broader concern about the lack of mechanisms to ensure that policies advocated in these terms are actually geared to advancing overall economic interests, rather than some (disguised) sectoral benefits involving larger costs for others in the economy, as he believes to be much more commonly the case (Krugman, 1996b). Just as at the national scale protection for the steel industry may be (falsely) claimed to advance overall US competitiveness (Krugman, 1996b), so at the urban scale boosterist arguments may be used to generate profits for developers while residents suffer in fiscal and environmental terms (Molotch, 1976).

The politics of territorial competition

Even where there is a strong functional argument for a public agency to take on some particular role – and widespread understanding

of it – we cannot assume that it will necessarily be pursued in practice in any serious/effective way. In general, governmental activities tend to be sustained through a high degree of inertia – with demands and supports flowing from established sources, organised client groups, vested staff interests, public expectations and programmed operations. Getting additional or novel responsibilities into the portfolio requires more pressure, to overcome initial hurdles and win a start-up budget, in situations where potential beneficiaries are liable to be less well organised than in cases where policy activity itself sustains organisation. This has two likely consequences. The first is that where new activities do make it on to the agenda and crowded budgets of public agencies they may not be very substantially resourced. The second is that, where they are, the form in which they are pursued may strongly reflect the particular political forces that managed to get them there.

The emergence since the 1980s of a new set of arguments for local economic development policies and/or more strategic forms of territorial competition is a case in point, for places lacking a longer history of such activity. For such arguments, and the real economic circumstances they invoke, to generate robust forms of competitive activity depends on a combination of:

at the micro-level: effective mobilisation by potential beneficiaries with the capacity to organise themselves into a successful promotional coalition within a suitably defined territory; and

at the macro-level: tolerance and/or active support by higher levels of government for local agencies to take on independent/competitive roles in pursuit of economic development for their territories.

The micro-level requirement has two aspects. The more basic is the presence within the territory concerned of a set of actors with significant 'spatially dependent' economic interests and the political/economic resources to pursue these (Cox and Mair, 1988). Such interests may include: ownership of land or immobile infrastructure; dependence on local markets, particularly where sales rely on persona; contact/reputation, or non-local expansion is otherwise constrained (as historically with state-based banks, utilities, etc. in the US; Wood, 1996); or other locally networked assets. For public authorities it may involve: dependence on a local tax-base (as in e.g. North America, though much less in Western Europe); for individual public officials it may involve: career prospects linked to measured local economic performance (as in China; Chien and Gordon, 2008). Their strength is institutionally variable therefore, but within nations is also likely to vary with different patterns of specialisation, and the balance between local and (multi-)national firms. Additionally, however, these interests need some basis for getting round the fundamental dilemma of collective action, as Olsen (1971) identified it: namely that it is rarely in the immediate interest of those with a recognisable stake in the success of some collective action, actually to expend significant resources of their own in pursuing it. Where no such basis exists, the likely outcome is some purely symbolic 'competitive' activity. This warrants a critical look at how substantively significant much advertised developmental action actually is. But where particular bases are found for escaping this dilemma, these will have consequences, first for the composition of the promotional coalitions that emerge, and then (consequentially) for the set of 'collective interests' and policies that come to be pursued – which also require careful examination (Cheshire and Gordon, 1996).

Some circumstances may just be generally supportive of cooperation, on the basis of solidaristic sentiments (as in the case of national minorities such as Catalans in Spain). But at best these provide a starting point, and other factors will generally produce biased outcomes. Three common forms can

be identified. The first starts from Olsen's observation that very small groups of actors with large individual stakes in a particular set of linked outcomes can more easily secure their mutual engagement than can any larger group. This leads to an expectation that major-landowning/development interests are the most likely core for a viable coalition (as in Molotch's 'growth machines' in the US). A second involves a bias toward historically dominant sectors, including staple industries in structural decline, on the basis that these are liable to have the strongest habits of cooperation, and most generally credible construction of what the territory's collective interests might be. The last embodies a bias toward (greater) localism on similar grounds. At a general level, the political economy perspective raises a suspicion that such coalition-building is more likely to serve elite interests than those of the average local resident, and to encourage an understanding of local development processes that conflates the two.

Beyond this, the specific kinds of bias that have been identified suggest potentially serious biases toward types of policy which are less likely than others to advance a territory's strategic economic prospects, by: focusing excessively on attracting inward investors to prestige new property developments; a form of 'lock-in' which concentrates on reinvigorating mature/obsolete sectoral complexes, rather than on renewing the local economic base; and/or defining the economically relevant territory too narrowly, ignoring complementarities with neighbouring areas, which are treated instead as the key competitors.

At the macro-scale, two key considerations are the degree of centralisation of, first, the state and, second, of national politics. On the one hand, state centralisation (as in say the UK or France as against effectively federal states) simply limits the scope of territorial agencies for genuinely independent action, as in the case of West European states before the 1980s, where both economic policies and fiscal control were jealously guarded monopolies of the central government. One factor in the eventual rise of territorial competition here seems to have been recognition that within a Single European Market where urban services became freely tradable urban competitiveness became a matter of national economic interest. In some developmental states elsewhere, notably China (Chien and Gordon, 2008), mobilisation of local competitive forces, within a framework of continuing central control, has been seen more directly as a servant of national economic objectives.

In relation to politics, the issue is rather different, relating to the role that territory plays in the processes through which national power is acquired. On the one hand are highly integrated systems in which political conflict/competition is fought out on a nation-wide basis in relation to generally recognised ideological differences and/or socio-economic groupings (as has tended to be the case in Western Europe, or in India through the 1950s/1960s). On the other are systems where national power is to a greater degree acquired through politicking in a series of semi-independent territorial polities, serving as arenas for political contests played out on different bases. This has always been the case in the US, but is also true in Brazil (Ames, 1995) and became so in India after the 1980s when the dominant Congress party lost its political cohesion (Schneider, 2004). In these situations, where power has to be built up sub-nationally, the territorial division of economic activity (as of the 'pork barrel') is an inescapable aspect of politics, and constrains any potential development of nation-wide ideological or class-based competition. Territorial competition is then (for better or worse) an expected and natural component of the political system. By contrast, in the former case, serious territorial competition presents a potential challenge to the maintenance of an integrated national politics (and party system) structured around such nation-wide issues. In the face of such

threats, national (or EU-wide) regional policies have been promoted to sustain political cohesion – rather than the 'economic and social cohesion' to which EU policies are nominally directed. And these may be adapted to assist, integrate (and domesticate) nascent forms of territorial completion, through conditional funding in relation to national goals and programmes (Gordon, 1990).

To summarise, while the pursuit of material interests of one kind or another is fundamental to the politics of territorial competition – and hence to the policy mix and outcomes to be expected from it – this does not mean that any reasonably free market economy should be expected to develop a common form of territorial competition, operating with similar intensity, and producing the same mix of outcomes. Rather the political economy perspective suggests that territorial competition – and thus local economic development as conventionally understood – should operate in ways that are highly contingent, but related in intelligible ways to a small set of factors. These include the character of national politics, the institutional/regulatory regimes under which territorial agencies operate, local economic structures, and the significance of territorial assets for interests within the local economy (Figure 3.1). In no case, however, can it be presumed that an effective capacity to engage in territorial competition can necessarily be mobilised, or that this would serve a set of community-wide economic interests.

Outcomes: good, bad and regulated

Like other kinds of policy, economic development policies launched under a territorially competitive initiative may yield unsatisfactory outcomes – whether through poor policy choice or failure to assure the necessary conditions for implementation (including actual provision of all required resources, including finance, skills and compliance). Other chapters

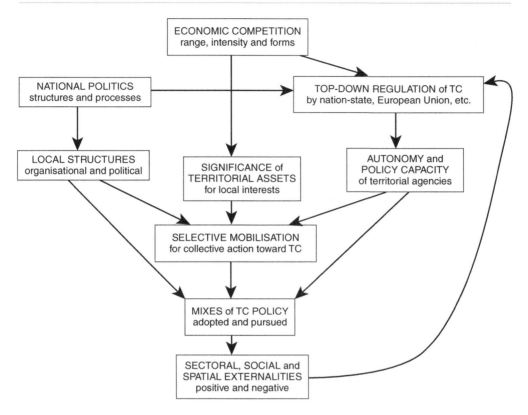

Figure 3.1 Processes shaping territorial competition (TC).
Source: Adapted from Chien and Gordon (2008: 7)

in this volume provide ample examples of this. But territorial competition presents some specific issues in relation to the desirability of outcomes which can be related to the conditions under which such activity comes into being in particular places and times.

One starting point for thinking about the problem is a simple normative distinction between policies which are (and may be expected to be):

Purely wasteful – with no net gains;

Zero–sum in their effects – i.e. purely redistributive, with gains for some being matched by losses for others; and

Economically productive/capacity-building – with overall net gains across the system (Cheshire and Gordon, 1998).

The distinctions here are not quite as simple as they look. In the first case, even the most 'wasteful' policy is likely to yield benefits to somebody, even if only to those who worked on it, the politician publicly launching it, or the mobile firms who succeed in extracting a high price for their locational favours. The basis on which we should judge whether some policies are 'purely wasteful', however, is whether they involve net losses overall to the territorial agency's legitimate stakeholders. In the second case, 'zero–sum' policies are ones that escape the 'pure waste' category, by yielding net benefits to stakeholders within the agency's own territory, but do so simply by capturing benefits from elsewhere (maybe in the form of mobile firms or product market share), or imposing comparable costs on other areas. Essentially then, they are spatially redistributive in their effects, possibly in ways that improve spatial equity, but as likely, or more, not to do so. In most cases we might expect there to be no equity issue, since competitive interactions of this kind most commonly involve areas in a similar economic position, and/or within the same functional economic region (for the latter see e.g. LeRoy, 2007).

To the extent that economically stronger areas have more assets to deploy in such competition, however, in the absence of external assistance to assist the competitive efforts of others, there is likely to be some bias toward outcomes that reduce rather than enhance spatial equity. Often, however, substantial effort may be required to achieve this outcome, including effort expended in contests where the territory ultimately loses out to other active competitors, as well as in those where it 'wins'. Taking these 'transaction costs' into account, the aggregate result of seeking to compete on this basis will generally involve negative-sum outcomes (i.e. net costs overall), rather than simply a zero balance.

For the active territorial 'players' (i.e. places pursuing such gains, through e.g. policies to attract mobile firms) the expected pay-off might still be expected to be positive – at least relative to the position they could expect to be in if they refrained from competing. This is often presented as a 'prisoner's dilemma' situation, in that active players may not actually achieve gains as compared with the status quo but be forced into competition by the knowledge that they will end up worse off if they refrain and allow others to take all the spoils (see e.g. Ellis and Rogers, 2000). That danger can seem particularly real, given a great excess demand for mobile investment projects, meaning that agencies cannot tell when the next desirable project might come along. For example, Thomas (2008) cites an estimate from Loveridge (1996) of just 200–300 large-scale projects annually in the US being pursued by some 15,000 investment attraction agencies.

However, if almost everyone participates in such competition, e.g. by offering cash incentives/tax breaks to firms who will locate a plant in their area, the expected net benefits may be very low, with only a modest penalty for abstinence. For any given project potentially available to, and desired by, all territories, models of the competitive process demonstrate how the 'winning' area will have to offer an incentive (of financial plus any natural advantages) at least equal to the perceived value of this project for the area which attaches the second highest value to it (King and Welling, 1992). From the perspective of an average territory, participation in such contests may then move toward the 'purely wasteful' category, with zero expected gains and significant entry costs. In the US, at least, these entry costs increasingly include the employment of site consultants, who offer territories the prospect of net gains through access to superior information, but serve primarily to boost competitive activity (Markusen and Nesse 2007; Thomas, 2007). Indeed it is striking that in a recent listing of nine ways to curtail the 'economic war' among the US states, at least two-thirds were clearly directed at issues involving waste for the states involved, while only one focused on issues of 'zero-sum' inter-state predation (LeRoy, 2007). OECD's international study similarly emphasises the advantages for states in pursuing transparent, rules-based approaches and avoiding rent-seeking (Oman, 2000). A careful econometric review of likely impacts of state and local economic development incentives in the US concludes that:

> for an average incentive project in a low unemployment local labor market, benefits and costs are of similar magnitude....whether the net benefits are positive or negative is unclear.
>
> (Bartik, 2005: 145)

The implication is that for a substantial proportion of such projects the balance will be clearly negative (even without taking account of the fixed costs of competing). Examples of such purely wasteful financial competition are numerous, including cases where regions within a developing economy end up competing with each other for FDI projects, as in the Brazilian 'car-wars' documented by Rodríguez-Pose and Arbix (2001).

The same logic applies where territories offer not actual cash payments (maybe because that is unlawful in their position) but rather a standard package of generalised concessions or locational attractors, fitted to the needs of a typical firm with mobile projects. In such cases, for projects with few locational constraints, all regions within a country (if not further afield) are effectively competing with each other, and monopoly power rests with the firm just as in the textbook case of tax/subsidy competition. This monopoly power derives ultimately from an excess demand from territories for mobile projects, which no individual agency can significantly modify. But it is substantially reinforced when areas pursue undifferentiated attraction and incentive policies, which allow firms to extract the maximum rent, by pitting all potential locations against each other.

By contrast, the economically productive/capacity-building category of policies includes not just the now familiar range of 'high road' initiatives aimed at boosting the long-run productivity of local business and public sector activity (Sengenberger and Pyke, 1992; Malecki, 2004); but also selective attraction of inward investors within specific target groups, using incentives that emphasise and reinforce distinctive actual/potential strengths of the particular territory. Pursuit of distinctiveness – with a locational offer that other territories could not match – could then serve as a means of countering the monopoly power of the mobile firm, both at the point of inward location and subsequently, when it might otherwise threaten an onward move. Where successful, this strategy would allow territories themselves to show net benefits from induced inward investment (Wins, 1995). From the perspective of the territorial com-

petition literature, we can thus identify three broad types of pathology in the way that subnational economic development activities are characteristically conducted – whether in advanced or developing economies, and whether in liberal democracies or more authoritarian regimes. These involve: a tendency for territorial agencies to pursue policies that are unlikely to yield net benefits for their constituents; an over-emphasis on competing against other areas (often within their own functional regions) for a limited pool of investment projects, whether directly or via generalised promotional strategies; and a failure to focus effectively on developing distinctive assets that could build a competitive advantage in particular economic niches, where territories could credibly establish some market power. As Turok (2009) indicates, this requires more than simply espousing the idea, or adopting some conventional notion of how distinctiveness can be achieved (whether through high-tech, creativity or iconic design).

These failings might be seen simply as components of a 'low road' development (or perhaps underdevelopment) strategy, for which other chapters offer a more detailed critique. Where the Territoral Competition (TC) perspective differs from other parts of the Local Economic Development (LED) literature is in suggesting that these pathologies are not simply reflections of ignorance, incompetence or lack of sophistication on the part of LED practitioners. Rather they are seen as predictable outcomes of the problematic politics of building collective territorial action, and of more or less rational behaviour on the part of those actively engaged in it. An obvious example is the neglect of spatial externalities by those territorial agencies which focus on the competitive aspect of their relations with other areas (including their neighbours), rather than the potential for collaboration. The seriousness of this problem clearly varies both with the extent to which agencies (including local governments) are free to pursue whatever competitive initiatives they choose, and with the particular pattern of incentives facing them.

In the first respect there has been a marked contrast, between a general lack of constraint on state/local competition in North America, and the situation in Western Europe, where national governments have traditionally restrained 'wasteful' domestic competition, and the EU has buttressed this with an effective cross-national regime limiting the use of state aid for competitive purposes (Sinnaeve, 2007). In relation to incentive structures there may be a similar pattern of difference among advanced economies, with those (notably the US) which make sub-national governments substantially autonomous in fiscal terms encouraging more cut-throat competition, than those where fiscal federalism dilutes the financial gains (or even eliminates them, in the UK case). Elsewhere, as in China, the central state may actually purposively design the incentive structure to encourage, not simply tolerate, vigorous local competitive action (Chien and Gordon, 2008). Translating some version of the European regulatory system to other national/regional contexts seems a rational response to the evident neglect of spatial externalities by which territories' competitive activities are unconstrained, though there is scepticism of its feasibility in the US case (Sinnaeve, 2007; Thomas, 2005).

From the TC perspective, however, neglect of such externalities is not the only issue involved in the pathology of predatory incentive competition. As important are: the excessive localism of the 'territories' on behalf of which agencies act (relative to the scale of functional economic units); and the seemingly irrational bias toward inward investment as the central priority in much competitive activity (Cheshire and Gordon, 1998). These are important in themselves, because a large proportion of incentive-based competition actually involves nearby areas which should logically be collaborating on a common development strategy, and because much of this appears wasteful even from the perspective of

the area which is supposed to benefit – if not from special interests in these areas.

Beyond this, however, the TC analysis wants to situate these issues in a root problem of the building of effective collective action to pursue competitive strategies on behalf of a representative set of interests across coherent economic units. Without some active, independent source of leadership, it is argued, the structures and forms of intervention that are developed will be subject to some combination of: weakness in resource terms, leading to the adoption of superficial, symbolic policies, including a substantial element of copying of conventional/fashionable initiatives (isomorphism, as Chien (2008) terms it), rather than development of tailored/differentiated strategies; and structural biases, reflecting the unrepresentative sub-sets of interests which are able spontaneously to build viable coalitions to promote competitive initiatives, including particularly those with stakes in development projects for which inward investment is an essential requirement.

Conclusion: competition, competitiveness and local economic development

Place competitiveness as well as place competition are clear realities in an economic environment, where market competition is pervasive and strong place characteristics play a crucial role in protecting communities from race-to-the bottom forms of pure price competition. There is a functional role thus to be filled by collective actors who can respond coherently, rationally and in a representative way to the challenge of building and sustaining the appropriate combination of territorial assets.

Vigorous market competition between places ought to provide both motive and the right set of incentives to steer public agencies toward more effective performance in support of this activity. However, the capacity to fill these roles is not naturally or necessarily available, and the collective action problem in evolving appropriate action coalitions is such that rhetoric about competition and competitiveness will often not be matched by organisations and activity which are both genuinely substantial/strategic and representative of the collective economic interests of functional relevant territories. To understand the limits of actual existing LED activity and the forms of 'competition' in which it engages – and progressing beyond these – it is necessary then to attend to the ways in which contextual influences on the political base of territorial competition shape (and bias) the choice of policies and the way they are implemented.

References

Ames, B. (1995) 'Electoral Rules, Constituency Pressures, and Pork Barrel: Bases of Voting in the Brazilian Congress', *Journal of Politics*, 57, 324–343.

Bartik, T.J. (2005) 'Solving the Problems of Economic Development Incentives', *Growth and Change*, 36, 139–166.

Bewley, T. (1981) 'A Critique of Tiebout's Theory of Local Public Expenditure', *Econometrica*, 49, 713–740.

Cheshire, P. and Gordon, I.R. (eds) (1995) *Territorial Competition in an Integrated Europe*. Aldershot: Avebury.

Cheshire, P.C. and Gordon, I.R. (1996) 'Territorial Competition and the Predictability of Collective (In)Action', *International Journal of Urban and Regional Research*, 23(3), 383–399.

Cheshire, P.C. and Gordon, I.R. (1998) 'Territorial Competition: Some Lessons for Policy', *Annals of Regional Science*, 33, 321–346.

Chien, S-S. (2008) 'The Isomorphism of Local Development Policy: A Case Study of the Formation and Transformation of National Development Zones in Post-Mao Jiangsu, China', *Urban Studies*, 45, 273–294.

Chien, S-S. and Gordon, I.R. (2008) 'Territorial competition in China and the West', *Regional Studies*, 42, 1–18.

Cobb, J.S. (1982) *The Selling of the South: The Southern Crusade for Industrial Development, 1936–90*. Baton Rouge: Louisiana State University Press.

Cox, K. and Mair, A. (1988) '*Locality* and *Community* in the Politics of Local Development', *Annals of the Association of American Geographers*, 78, 307–325.

Ellis, S. and Rogers, C. (2000) 'Local Economic Development as a Prisoners' Dilemma: The Role of Business Climate', *Review of Regional Studies*, 30, 315–330.

Gordon, I.R. (1990) 'Regional Policy and National Politics in Britain', *Environment and Planning C: Government and Policy*, 8, 427–438.

Gordon, I.R. and Jayet, H. (1994) 'Territorial Policies between Co-operation and Competition', CESURE working paper, 12E/94. University of Lille, Lille.

Hermann-Pillath, C. (2004) 'Competitive Governments, Fiscal Arrangements, and the Provision of Local Public Infrastructure in China: A Theory-Driven Study of Gujiao Municipality', *China Information*, 18, 373–428.

Jessop, B. and Sum, N-L. (2000) 'An Entrepreneurial City in Action: Hong Kong's Emerging Strategies in and for (Inter)Urban Competition', *Urban Studies*, 37, 2287–2313.

King, I. and Welling, L. (1992) 'Commitment, Efficiency and Footloose Firms', *Economica*, NS 59, 63–73.

Krugman, P.R. (1996a) 'Making Sense of the Competitiveness Debate', *Oxford Review of Economic Policy*, 12, 17–25.

Krugman, P. (1996b) *Pop Internationalism*. Cambridge, MA: MIT Press.

LeRoy, G. (2007) 'Nine Concrete Ways to Curtail the Economic War among the States', pp. 183–197, in A. Markusen (ed.) *Reining in the Competition for Capital*. Kalamazoo, MI: WE Upjohn Institute for Employment Research.

Loveridge, S. (1996) 'On the Continuing Popularity of Industrial Recruitment', *Economic Development Quarterly*, 10, 151–158.

Malecki, E.J. (2004) 'Jockeying for Position: What it Means and Why it Matters to Regional Development Policy When Places Compete', *Regional Studies*, 38, 1101–1120.

Markusen, A. and Nesse, K. (2007) 'Institutional and Political Determinants of Incentive Competition', pp. 1–41, in A. Markusen (ed.) *Reining in the Competition for Capital*. Kalamazoo, MI: WE Upjohn Institute for Employment Research.

Massey, D.B. (1984) *Spatial Divisions of Labour*. London: Routledge.

Molotch, H. (1976) 'The City as a Growth Machine', *American Journal of Sociology*, 82, 309–331.

Olsen, M. (1971) The *Logic of Collective Action*, Cambridge, MA: Harvard University Press.

Oman, C. (2000) *Policy Competition for Foreign Direct Investment: A Study of Competition among Governments to Attract FDI.* Paris: OECD.

Piore, M. and Sabel, C. (1984) *The Second Industrial Divide.* New York: Basic Books.

Porter, M.E. (1990) *The Competitive Advantage of Nations.* New York, The Free Press.

Rodríguez-Pose, A. and Arbix, G. (2001) 'Strategies of Waste: Bidding Wars in the Brazilian Automobile Sector', *International Journal of Urban and Regional Research*, 25(1), 134–154.

Schneider, A. (2004) 'Accountability and Capacity in Developing Country Federalism: Empowered States, Competitive Federalism', *Forum for Development Studies*, 33–59.

Sengenberger, W. and Pyke, F. (1992) 'Industrial Districts and Local Economic Regeneration: Research and Policy Issues', pp. 3–29, in F. Pyke and W. Sengenberger (eds) *Industrial Districts and Local Economic Regeneration.* Geneva: International Institute for Labour Studies.

Sinnaeve, A. (2007) 'How the EU Manages Subsidy Competition', pp. 87–101, in A. Markusen (ed.) *Reining in the Competition for Capital.* Kalamazoo, MI: WE Upjohn Institute for Employment Research.

Storper, M. (1989) 'The Transition to Flexible Specialisation in the U.S. Film Industry: External Economies, the Division of Labour, and the Crossing of Industrial Divides', *Cambridge Journal of Economics*, 13, 273–305.

Thomas, K.P. (200) 'The Sources and Processes of Tax and Subsidy Competition', pp. 43–55, in A. Markusen (ed.) *Reining in the Competition for Capital.* Kalamazoo, MI: WE Upjohn Institute for Employment Research.

Tiebout, C.M. (1956) 'A Pure Theory of Local Expenditures', *The Journal of Political Economy*, 64, 416–426.

Turok, I. (2009) 'The Distinctive City: Pitfalls in the Pursuit of Differential Advantage', *Environment and Planning A*, 41, 13–30.

Ward, S.V. (1998) *Selling Places: The Marketing and Promotion of Towns and Cities, 1850–2000.* London: Routledge.

Wins, P. (1995) 'The Location of Firms: An Analysis of Choice Processes', in P.C. Cheshire and I.R. Gordon (eds) *Territorial Competition in an Integrating Europe.* Aldershot: Avebury.

Wood, A. (1996) 'Analysing the Politics of Local Economic Development: Making Sense of Cross-National Convergence', *Urban Studies*, 33, 1281–1295.

4

Local and regional 'Development Studies'

Giles Mohan

Introduction: What is development?

Discussing local and regional development in the Global South necessitates engaging with empire, race and nation. The whole idea and practice of development is marked by imbalances of power about who decides what defines development, who its agents are, and what territories it constitutes. It is vital, therefore, to begin by asking how we understand development. My starting point is Hart's (2001: 650) distinction between 'D' and 'd' development whereby:

> 'big D' Development (is) defined as a post-second world war project of intervention in the 'third world' that emerged in the context of decolonisation and the cold war, and 'little d' development or the development of capitalism as a geographically uneven, profoundly contradictory set of historical processes.

Hart follows the Polanyian view that unleashing of markets generates a 'counter-movement'. Hence, "Far from the counter-movement representing some sort of external intervention in an inexorably unfolding teleology, these opposing tendencies are contained within capitalism" (Hart 2001: 650). This forces us to consider not only how Global capitalism must be actively "created and constantly reworked" (ibid.), but in a Gramscian sense how it can be resisted and made otherwise.

Within this counter-movement the relationship between power and knowledge is a form of governmentality (Watts 2003). In practice, this means analysing "the rationalities of rules, the forms of knowledge and expertise they construct, and the specific and contingent assemblages of practices, materials, agents and techniques through which these rationalities operate to produce governable subjects" (Hart 2004: 92). Governmentality has been used to examine international NGOs and multilateral agencies, and the intersection of different spaces of power (e.g. Ferguson and Gupta 2002). Hence, knowledge about development and its practical application in 'management' and 'planning' is very much about control and discipline.

From its inception in the Enlightenment, development has involved trusteeship, which saw science and state direction coming together to secure the basis of social harmony through a process of national development. Colonial trusteeship was all about the mission to civilize others and to give experience to the 'child-like' colonial peoples. While trusteeship was often rejected after 1945, because of its colonial connotations, the idea 'implicitly reappears' many times in post-war conceptions of international development (Cowen and Shenton 1996). During this period many former colonial administrators went on to take posts with NGOs like OXFAM or taught university courses on development administration and management (Kothari 2006). This is not to view colonial administration as a homogenous set of practices and ideas but rather to seek to understand the continuities to 'post-colonial' times, even as important changes have taken place in the ideology of development.

While the D/d development framework gives us a dialectic for understanding how development functions structurally that is not to say that historical changes do not occur. An important issue for studying development is the ways in which discourses and practices have evolved. McMichael's (2000) characterization of development having moved from 'developmentalism' to 'globalism' is instructive here, as is his observation that such moves have been a response to the crises of a previous regime. McMichael argues that developmentalism, essentially a social-democratic welfarism, was a response to the crisis of nineteenth-century monetary control via the gold standard and the destablizing effects of the two World Wars. As we will see, this Keynesian developmentalism came during the period of formal decolonization and underpinned state-led, protectionist and redistributive development policy. Globalism, by contrast, is a counter-mobilization to the constraints of social protectionism, which seeks to engender market rule through institutional coercion which has weakened the power of some states.

But how does the discipline of Development Studies function as part of the governmentality of development? In general there has been a tendency, generated by both those outside development studies and within it, to treat the developing world as so exceptional as to require a different set of analytical concepts or development studies imports concepts into inappropriate situations. This exceptionalism is manifested in a number of ways.

First is a 'provincialising' impetus arguing that globalization has missed out much of the developing world, so for all intents and purposes we can ignore them. They simply do not matter to the dominant forces that shape the contemporary world. But as the brief discussion of McMichael's work (ibid.) shows, globalization has affected the Global South in numerous ways and is significant for the lives of those living there, even if they are relatively powerless. Increasingly, the neoliberal consensus of McMichael's globalism informs all development policy, whether in the Global North or South, which has seen a convergence of concerns around entrepreneurialism, cost recovery and devolution, and with it an attempt to apply similar institutional economic theories to planning.

Second is an 'exoticizing' tendency, which runs that 'the other' in the Global South are so different culturally and politically that 'we' can never really comprehend them. This lack of comprehension is manifested in mono-causal explanations (Chabal 1996), with policy makers accepting crude takes on politics, which they would never accept in analysing their own situations. Or we see potentially patronizing 'participatory' approaches, which are discussed later, that encourage the 'beneficiaries' to reveal their needs through child-like, playful techniques that actually conceal the ignorance of the policy researcher.

Third is a spatial and intellectual separation which parcels together inappropriate territories and scales. On the one hand, we get a geographical separation with Development Studies focusing on the 'over there' regions, which generates a spatial, ethical and epistemological distance between the producers of the knowledge about development and the subjects of this knowledge. As Eyben (2006) argues, such distancing absolves elites in the Global North from much of the responsibility for poverty in both their own countries and the Global South. On the other hand, we get an intellectual separation with economics, politics, etc. doing their own things, but Development Studies does all these things, but at a more superficial level (Pieterse 2001). This lack of learning and dialogue undermines all knowledge about the world. However, one of the advantages of Development Studies is that it has, with varying degrees of success, tried to move beyond the economism that has afflicted local and regional development studies in the Global North (Pike *et al.* 2006). Through the work of theorists such as Sen (1999) and political moves of 'social development' researchers challenging the economism of institutions like the World Bank (Booth 1994), Development Studies' apparent eclecticism is better attuned to a world of concrete and complex problems as opposed to the sometimes debilitating disciplinary divisions of academia.

Colonialism, uneven development and post-colonialism

The origins of both D/d development lie in the colonial period. Industrialization in Europe was funded to a great extent from the profits of these overseas activities while the growth of wealth consequent upon the industrial revolution saw increased demand for tropical luxury goods as well as those used in industrial production. This heightened demand saw more formal colonization from the 1870s as systems were established for intensive production, which in turn led to the emergence of an international division of labour based around states and nationally centered MNCs (Hirst and Thompson 1996). Ideologically, the colonial mission was justified through a twin movement of protecting the competitiveness of the metropole *vis-à-vis* other imperial powers, but also as a necessary

process of enlightening the peoples of the Tropics. The colonies thus became national property to be nurtured and milked of their surplus yet tied to a discourse of modernity which promised to bring civilization and religion to the 'savages'.

In terms of the double-movement of D/d development the periphery fulfilled a number of functions. First and foremost it was a source of cheap raw materials as well as a market for manufactured goods. In terms of disciplining labour the prosperity generated by colonialism was a way of placating the working classes in the developed core while the colonies could be a sink for surplus labour, thereby ameliorating the tensions generated by unemployment. At a politico-cultural level nationalist and racist ideologies created 'others' which was a means of cementing working-class solidarity at home. Concomitantly this primary affinity to one's fellow countryman or woman undermined international labour solidarity. And despite overbearing economic motives there was undoubtedly a hegemonic role in the acquisition of colonies as a means of cementing Global dominion.

Crucially for understanding the origins of development and trusteeship, the colonial state was established in order to facilitate economic exploitation and maintain order. In this sense its role was more functionalist than any state form before or since. As Young (1994: 75) observes of colonialism in Africa, "African societies were to encounter a colonial master equipped with doctrines of domination and capacities for the exercise of rule that went far beyond those available in earlier times and other places". The initial conquest required strong coercion but force had diminishing returns so that other means of promoting hegemony were required.

In terms of territorial boundaries colonial dominions were often built up in piecemeal fashion and both the colonial and post-colonial states were faced with problems of political integrity (Davidson 1992). Not only were state forms imported but also languages and other cultural vestiges that 'colonized the mind' and reinforced the political and economic subordination. Not surprisingly given the economic imperative and lack of legitimacy these political structures were centralized, leading to what Mamdani (1996) labels the 'decentralized despotism' of the colonial state. For Mamdani (1996: 8, 18) this "crystallized a state-enforced separation, of the rural from the urban and of one ethnicity from another...two forms of power under a single hegemonic authority. Urban power spoke the language of civil society and civil rights, rural power of community and culture". This model was decentralized insofar as it empowered local elites with the colonial district commissioner exercising a high degree of local discretion, while preaching a discourse of local community.

The early phases of colonialism were concerned with repression and consolidation whereas the mature colonies saw high rates of urbanization as land was gradually given over to production. These changes were accompanied by a change in colonial ideology centered on development. Britain's 1929 Colonial Development and Welfare Act enshrined the idea of development as a way of placating and sanitizing (literally) the growing urban populations. The contradictions of colonialism threw up varied political responses. Therefore, the concern with development and other seemingly philanthropic acts was stimulated by an emerging political threat and recognition of the colonial project's weakness. Phillips asserts that the inability to overcome entrenched socio-economic structures and the rise of nationalist opposition was disadvantageous to capitalist accumulation. She notes that:

> widespread acceptance of development as a legitimate objective, and the subsequent acknowledgement of a responsibility on the part of the advanced countries for aiding this process, can be interpreted initially as no more than a response to the political crises of

the colonised countries. But this in no way undermines the argument that the development initiative was necessary as a means to overcoming obstacles to the further accumulation of capital.

(Phillips 1977: 17)

This contradiction saw numerous forms of resistance ranging from hidden acts of defiance, to guerrilla movements and formalized independence movements. Crucially anti-colonial nationalism concealed other social divisions, particularly the class nature of imperialism. With decolonization these social divisions became more apparent and once again development emerged as one key discourse attempting to mobilize the nation in order to contain these contradictions.

With the ending of formal colonization in the period from 1947 to the mid-1960s, control of the world system was achieved via new forms of imperialism which operated, in many respects, at arms-length. New forms of US-backed geo-economic governance were put in place through the Bretton Woods Institutions, ideological legitimation was actively stoked through the Cold War, and development policy was based around a seemingly benign theory of modernization and 'catch-up'.

Independence came to Latin America around a century before Asia and Africa, but the region remained tied into imperialist relations. As such it was no coincidence that many of the radical underdevelopment theories should emerge from this region and quickly find resonance among the newly independent countries of Africa and Asia. At independence there was a strong sense of optimism among Western-based theoreticians and many leaders of developing countries. This period of what McMichael (2000) terms 'developmentalism', from the early 1950s, came on the heels of the relative success of Soviet planning in the inter-war period, the post-war reconstruction of Europe under Marshall Aid and the Bretton Woods conference on international economic cooperation.

Learning from these, development economics was founded on the Keynesian rejection of mono-economics and the belief in 'mutual benefits' between rich and poor countries, which saw a positive role for aid (Hettne 1995).

In terms of interventions "development necessitated plans, written by economists, and strong, active governments to implement them" (Hettne 1995: 38). This 'positivist orthodoxy' hinged on a benevolent state, which acted in the common good and was peopled by impartial, technocratic elites. As Cooke (2003) notes this saw the change from colonial development to a focus on development management, with colonial service training centres in the North becoming the new Development Studies departments. Cooke argues that despite this change the essential architecture of intervention did not alter and was still based around notions of trusteeship and 'knowing best' what the Third World needed. Crucially the assumption was that proprietary rights would endure after independence so the colonialists were not unduly concerned.

Modernization theory built on a critique of Keynesianism and focused attention on why development failed to occur given these well-conceived theories and supposedly geared-up state structures. Modernization theory was very much an American body of work, richly funded by the US government, reflecting a belief in American superiority and inseparable from the Cold War concerns of the time. It retained teleological models of evolutionary change, but focused on the social and political barriers to self-sustained growth. Given its roots in the classical sociology of Western Europe, where such processes had largely occurred, modernization theory naturally appeared as a form of Westernization. The practical ramifications of modernization theory go to the heart of the Cold War since it justified concerted investigation of foreign countries and aid budgets targeted at socio-cultural (read ideological) change.

In a perverse way, the Cold War permitted ruling regimes in the South a degree of autonomy as they could play the superpowers off against one another. However, a country's ability "to exploit such a relationship, or to be damaged by it, depends on various conjunctural factors and agendas which are rarely under their control" (Corbridge 1993: 188). For example, India's import substitution industrialization programme of the 1950s and 1960s was made possible through American food aid subsidizing agricultural production, but tied India into a pro-American stance.

Many post-independence regimes espoused a brand of state socialism which had its roots in the centralized nationalist struggles which prevailed especially in English colonies (Davidson 1992). As 'non-alignment' became increasingly impossible as a result of the Cold War, anti-imperial political ideologies centered on Marxist-Leninism emerged (Corbridge 1993). With them came discourses of centrality and modernist rational planning which were distilled in import-substitution policies and/or Soviet-style five-year plans (Conyers and Hills 1984).

Another key discourse inherent in this kind of socialism was development. Following independence the social tensions in many countries became more apparent so national development became one means of attempting to contain them. As legitimacy becomes increasingly threatened:

> the government of a developmentalist state authorises its rule over the association of people who form the state, according to a principle of legitimacy which leads the government to claim that it represents the common interest of the people and is thus concerned with 'national development'.
>
> (Rakodi 1986: 435)

Hence, in the early days of independence "the national plan appears to have joined the national anthem and the national flag as a symbol of sovereignty and modernity"

(Conyers and Hill 1984: 42). The drawing of a national plan allowed the state to fall back on an authoritative document as a defence against clan-based pressures, it promised future prospects thereby securing compliance in the present, and presented a competent analysis for donors to work around.

However, all such interventions were at the expense of the rural areas and decentralized political administration. While many states were centralized, this centralization lay in tension with sub-national planning and decision-making. The legacy of Mamdani's 'decentralized despotism', discussed above, conditioned the structure and possibilities of post-colonial planning. For various reasons centralization has been exacerbated by the dependent nature of post-colonial states and the internal logic of their bureaucratic development. In this way spatial planning interventions may, as Samoff (1979) notes with respect to Tanzania, "be understood as the self-protective reaction of the bureaucratic bourgeoisie to challenges to its power and economic base" (p. 55). Hence, Slater (1989) shows how decentralization within post-colonial states functions as a form of rule. First, where territorial disaggregation threatens national integration the response very often was to "control local government by strict legislation and through the new politicized structure of the district administration" (Subramaniam 1980: 586), since it factionalizes and fragments political opposition. This usually involved placing political appointees in key positions in local government and ensuring elected members complied with party policy. Second, as Boone (2003) shows, regimes often promoted development programs that notionally built upon local energies because this absolves them of responsibility for welfare provision while earning political capital by apparently being sensitive to local issues. Longer standing ministerial hierarchies have also contested devolution of power and sought to maintain control of key resources, which as we will see has been a key feature of the attempts

under structural adjustment to bypass the central state.

But despite this centralized manipulation of decentralized planning, it failed as a development strategy for more local reasons. One is due to local patronage and elite structures. For example, in Uganda's decentralization program Francis and James (2003) identify the patronage outcomes of decentralization in which the limited fiscal resources passing through local government are contested by the locally powerful. Such 'elite capture' (Crook and Manor 1998) strengthens local governance in their favor. A further factor in the failure of decentralized planning, and one that the participatory approaches discussed below ostensibly address, is that the impoverished who are the intended targets of interventions have little time and energy for becoming involved in local politics and are skeptical anyway given the legacies of colonial divide and rule. Finally, there is the weak capacity of much sub-national government, although this speaks of the political misuse of decentralization which promises much, yet never really devolves resources to localities (Crook and Sverrisson 2001).

The Second World War marked the triumph of US hegemony and with it a set of institutions for managing Global relations. The Bretton Woods System was established at an international summit in 1944 and sought to build a system for managing the Global economy following the rivalries which had, in part, precipitated the Second World War. The International Monetary Fund (IMF) was set up as a central fund which member countries paid into and could then draw upon in times of balance of payment disequilibria. The International Bank for Reconstruction and Development (IBRD), more commonly known as the World Bank, was also established to assist in post-War reconstruction and financed sectoral programs or discrete infrastructure projects.

The Bretton Woods System worked reasonably well throughout 1950s and 1960s, but began to break down in the 1970s when the international regulation of exchange rates was abandoned for flexible, market rates which coincided with the deregulation of international banking and the oil boom of the 1970s (Hirst and Thompson 1996). This meant that creditworthy countries could borrow money privately to finance their deficits and fund development projects. During this period the Bretton Woods Institutions, especially the IMF, lost much of their raison d'être and were restructured and reoriented toward being 'development' institutions (Mohan *et al.* 2000).

The oil crises, debt and disciplinary neoliberalism

The neoliberal counter-revolution of the late 1970s and 1980s was based intellectually on a refutation of Keynesian theory and a hard-to-deny realpolitik about the venal nature of political regimes in the Global South. In analyzing the spread of neoliberalism Peck and Tickell (2002) make the case for a process-based analysis of "neoliberalization", arguing that the transformative and adaptive capacity of this political-economic project has been repeatedly underestimated. Amongst other things, this calls for a close reading of the historical and geographical (re)constitution of the process of neoliberalization and of the variable ways in which different "local neoliberalisms" are embedded within wider networks and structures of neoliberalism. Neoliberalism operates at multiple scales and more attention needs to be paid to the different variants of neoliberalism, to the hybrid nature of contemporary policies and programs and to the multiple and contradictory aspects of neoliberal spaces, techniques and subjects.

While the Cold War lasted until the late 1980s changes were already afoot which signaled its demise and the apparent 'triumph' of liberal capitalism. In the early 1970s, labour unrest in the core capitalist countries was rife and the power of the unions was seen as excessive. At the same time the oil-producing states in the Middle East formed OPEC, whose oil price rises precipitated a period of recession that fueled the labor unrest. The price rises and recession hit the developing world hard as the markets for their raw materials declined and their oil bills increased. What was an oil crisis for many was a windfall for the oil producers who had excess revenue. These so-called 'petrodollars' needed to be put to use and so at a time when the Bretton Woods System began to break down there was a great deal of cheap credit available to developing countries which needed to shore themselves up against their own recessions and to stave off legitimacy crises. Debate exists about the efficacy of this lending, but it turned even sourer when interest rates rose sharply in the late 1970s and ushered in the debt crisis for most developing countries.

Hence, from the late 1970s, a period of restructuring began which was premised upon the state strategies of Thatcherism in the UK and Reaganomics in the USA. With the collapse of the Soviet bloc a decade later, the way was open for a new form of political and economic hegemony, based around a logic of capitalism, a discourse of neoliberalism and a politics of thin multilateralism among a handful of powerful liberal states (Agnew and Corbridge 1995). This was known as the 'Washington Consensus'. For its architects, the key was not the oil crisis itself, but the erroneous way that most developing countries had responded. Rather than opening up to world market competition, they looked inward via various import-substituting mechanisms, heavy borrowing and a swathe of inflation-inducing measures. From this analysis, the conclusion ran that developing economies must become more externally oriented and, concomitantly, freed from malevolent dirigisme.

The Structural Adjustment programs which followed sought to correct these 'market-distorting' problems by seeking to remove the state from as many areas of economic life as possible. The pressing need to stem the balance of payments problem and begin debt repayment meant that revenue generation and cutting expenditure were paramount. The policies which flowed from this involved the privatization of State Owned Enterprises, the introduction of user charges for state services, and a variety of civil service reforms.

In the process of adjustment the state was restructured since deregulation of markets entails the reregulation of political space which leans towards authoritarianism. Contrary to the zero-sum 'state or market' model some parts of the state were strengthened while others were trimmed. In general during adjustment the presidential and executive branches of the state took over much of the decision-making which was bolstered by the repressive power of the military. In such cases conservative-technocratic politicians became leaders with the business class and the middle classes providing political support. For example, in Cote d'Ivoire President Houphouet Boigny clamped down so heavily on opposition parties that a situation arose of "multi-partyism without opposition" (Aribisala 1994: 140).

In addition, there was the problem of institutional capacity in terms of implementing development initiatives. Under neoliberal regimes we saw a small, technocratic clique generally placed in the finance ministries that 'formulated' policy in collaboration with World Bank and IMF officials. Hutchful's (1989: 122) analysis of Ghana concluded: "What has emerged in Accra is a parallel government controlled (if not created) by the lender agencies". This lack of accountability contradicted the calls for transparency and democracy in the liberalization process and persists today under the second-generation structural adjustment programs (Hickey and Mohan 2008).

The one-size-fits-all neoliberal approach tends to underestimate the variations within and between states and regimes in less developed countries. At a theoretical level this led the neoliberals to restate their argument, but added insights which complicated their position without radically altering it. For example, social capital theories brought questions of political culture to the fore, but only insofar as it contributes to capitalist democracy (Fine 2001). More problematically, the actual implementation of adjustment programs ran headlong into the political realities of diverse countries. The state institutions through which deregulation was taking place were also part of the political apparatus which stood to lose power to markets and therefore fought to protect their position. Some institutional 'weaknesses' were therefore more like filibusterism. It was these broad movements which drove the 'good governance' agenda of the 1990s.

The publication of *Sub-Saharan Africa: from crisis to sustainable growth* (World Bank 1989) marked a watershed in thinking about governance, both on the African continent and beyond. In the document, the (World Bank 1989: 60) argued that "political legitimacy and consensus are a precondition for sustainable development". The new governance agenda saw "democracy is a necessary prior or parallel condition of development, not an outcome of it" (Leftwich 1993: 605, original emphasis). This opens the way for a whole range of institutional and democratic reform programs aimed at getting the politics right in order to bring about economic development. This was a significant change from the early days of the adjustment era where politics and the state were seen as a hindrance.

Neoliberalism impacted upon subnational planning in a number of ways. The good governance agenda of the donors included a measure of decentralization. In the 1970s, decentralization was centered on the public and, to a lesser extent, the voluntary sector. Almost a decade later, and well into the 'adjustment era', Rondinelli et al. (1989) included privatization and deregulation as forms of decentralization. The World Bank's own policies reflect these trends in which decentralization "should be seen as part of a broader market-surrogate strategy"

(World Bank 1983: 23). Since the mid-1980s, then, decentralization became one of the mainstays of the localizing good governance agenda and promoted in a wide range of countries (Crook and Sverrisson 2001; Mohan 1996).

However, neoliberal policies have for many increased social hardships (Easterley 2006) which led to political tensions; the so-called 'IMF riots' of the 1980s and 1990s being the most visible examples (Walton and Seddon 1994), although the civil war in Sierra Leone in the 1990s has also been blamed in part on the austerity of the economic reforms. In such cases decentralization can be a means to placate sub-national political tensions by apparently devolving power downwards, but without really liberating resources that might help ameliorate the uneven development which neoliberalism tended to exacerbate. In Sierra Leone, following the cessation of hostilities, the donors supported a program to empower local chiefs in an attempt to re-establish political legitimacy, while totally missing the point that the civil war had been a complex response to a social system in which the privilege of the chiefs marginalized young people who went on to become the protagonists in the civil war. In this sense strengthening of local government and increasing fiscal accountability is used as a means of deflecting attention from the fact that these debilitating policy measures were devised and implemented centrally and undemocratically (Slater 1989).

The chieftaincy case in Sierra Leone demonstrates that one outcome of trying to reform the state or bypass it altogether as obstructing the market was to champion 'non-state' actors, most notably civil society organizations in the form of business associations and international NGOs. The motivations for donors and lenders using NGOs was twofold, both revolving around a cynical view of the state and a rather naïve, apolitical view of civil society. The first concerns delivery and efficiency in service provision, the so-called 'service delivery gap'. Major lenders and donors were wary of using inefficient states to deliver program funds so they channelled them through the supposedly less corrupt, more efficient and locally sensitive NGOs. In a parallel to their market philosophy, it is better to have inefficient NGOs than inefficient states. The second reason relates to the governance philosophy that strengthening civil society will automatically lead to deepened democracy. However, the idea that the 'local' can become a site for empowerment ignores the ways that the state is able to manipulate and control local politics as we have already seen.

Related to the rise of NGOs is that despite a de facto centralization the donors' vision of the state included a measure of decentralization and participation in the building up of civil society. Participation in development became orthodoxy from the mid-1990s onwards, when all the main development agencies had guidelines on how to make development more participatory (e.g. World Bank 1994). The move to Poverty Reduction Strategies (PRSs) at the start of the millennium, based on popular participation and country 'ownership' as the major vehicle for development aid and planning, signaled a scaling-up of participation from localized projects (Hickey and Mohan 2008).

One of the key messages of participation in development has been that power relations need to be reversed with the development practitioner 'handing over the stick' to the participating beneficiaries (Chambers 1997), whereby the former gives control to the latter over the representation of their lifeworlds. At the heart of this epistemological and political reversal is a belief that scientific approaches to finding out the needs of marginalized people are biased against them as they rely on Western forms of cognition and rationality. Practically, this means that rather than rely on formal literacy and/or quantitative understandings of the world, preference is given to visual techniques and alternative literacies.

Although the past three decades have seen a neoliberal attack on statist approaches, there has been an increasing tendency within contemporary Development Studies to focus on D-development rather than d-development processes of development, in ways that often obscure the underlying politics of development. Following Polanyi (1960), the development of capitalism always disembeds people from their social relations with policy seeking to prevent social breakdown by the state assuming trusteeship over subject populations in order to contain, maintain, and re-embed them around discourses of organic community (Cowen and Shenton 1996). It is here that participation is promoted as a way to reconnect citizens with the much more complex and fragmented political field created by neoliberal globalization. Thus participation becomes a populist response to neoliberalism, which functions ideologically in two ways. First is the agency versus structure argument in which the promise of agency-centered development diverts attention from the structural causes of inequality and marginalization. Second, discourses of localism, civil society and decentralization (Schuurman 1997) are part of a neoliberal move to delegitimize the state as a development actor and concomitantly to engender the freedom-seeking individual, ideally pursuing his/her freedoms through the market.

Conclusion: South-South development or neoliberalism without (obvious) imperialism

So far it is argued here that all Development Studies has been implicated in imperial relations and that much of what appears humanitarian intervention is driven by a need to contain the contradictions of capitalist incorporation for countries and peoples of the Global South. In this way much knowledge about development has functioned to legitimize the need for and scope of these D-development interventions while all the time obscuring the causes of these contradictions emanating from d-development. These were then periodized from the colonial to neoliberal regimes and finished by arguing that recent attempts to 'devolve' development are part and parcel of these longer moves to obfuscate the effects of Global capitalism.

In the transition from developmentalism to globalism we saw a step-change in the discourses and practices of development policy, even if the overarching dialectic between D/d development remained valid. In this the central state had been key, but now paradoxically bypassed through Civil Society Organizations and private firms while also being strengthened in some ways. This shows that rather than a zero-sum relationship between state and markets, as some neoliberals would argue, political power is central to the creation and maintenance of markets. In the Global South, the donors have been the major vehicle for this institutional process which has created what Harrison (2004) terms 'governance states' where donors are embedded at the heart of government through things like direct budget support while all the time espousing a discourse that they are passing the 'ownership' of development to the sovereign states they deal with. So, we see decentralization as part of a strategy seeking to weaken states and normalize the market.

But as Polanyi argued the creation of markets generates a counter-movement which needs to be contained, and here a discourse of localism, community and participation has arisen over the past two decades to help contain some of these negative consequences. Such discourses promise sensitive empowering local decision-making, responsive to revealed 'needs'. But given that many of the structural causes of poverty remain off the radar and certainly not addressed at a Global or national level, then such localism becomes functional to the marketization agenda as it further fragments and disempowers the poor, again all the time claiming to give them ownership and voice.

In this localizing agenda, Development Studies is not alone since we see a revived localism in policy discourses in the Global North (e.g. Stoker 2004, Pike *et al* 2006). However, if localism it is to avoid being defensive and ignorant of structural constraints then it needs to be politicized in different ways as argued elsewhere (Hickey and Mohan 2005). First, where participatory planning has had transformative outcomes, it has been promoted as part of a broader project that is at once political and radical, such as in Porto Alegre, Brazil. Second, such participatory approaches have sought to engage with underlying processes of development rather than remain constrained within the frame of specific interventions. For example, in the case of Kerala, India, participation is tied to a state-level program of social justice that privileges social development. Third, each approach is characterized by an explicit focus on participation as citizenship, aiming to transform politics in ways that progressively alter the processes of inclusion that operate within particular political communities, and which govern the opportunities for individuals and groups to claim their rights to participation and resources.

References

Agnew, J. and Corbridge, S. (1995) *Mastering Space: Hegemony, Territory and International Political Economy*, London: Routledge.

Aribisala, F. (1994) 'The Political Economy of Structural Adjustment in Cote d'Ivoire', in A. Olukoshi *et al. Structural Adjustment in West Africa*, Lagos: Pumark.

Boone, C. (2003) 'Decentralization and Political Strategy in West Africa', *Comparative Political Studies*, 36, 4, 355–380.

Booth, D. (1994) 'Rethinking Social Development: An Overview', in Booth (ed.) *Rethinking Social Development: Theory, Research and Practice*, Harlow: Longman, 3–41.

Chabal, P. (1996) 'The African Crisis: Context and Interpretation', in R. Werbner and Ranger, T. (eds) *Postcolonial Identities in Africa*, London: Zed Books, 29–54.

Chambers, R. (1997) *Whose Reality Counts? Putting the First Last*, London: Intermediate Technology Publications.

Conyers, D. and Hills, P. (1984) *An Introduction to Development Planning in the Third World*, Chichester: John Wiley.

Cooke, B. (2003), 'A New Continuity with Colonial Administration: Participation in Development Management', *Third World Quarterly*, 24, 1, 47–61.

Corbridge, S. (1993) 'Colonialism, Post-colonialism and the Political Geography of the Third World', in P. Taylor (ed.) *Political Geography of the Twentieth Century: A Global Analysis*, London: Belhaven Press, 171–206.

Cowen, M. and Shenton, R. (1996) *Doctrines of Development*, London: Routledge.

Crook, R. and Manor, J. (1998*) Democracy and Decentralisation in South Asia and West Africa: Participation, Accountability and Performance*, Cambridge: Cambridge University Press.

Crook, R. C. and Sverrisson, A. S. (2001) *Decentralisation and Poverty-Alleviation in Developing Countries: A Comparative Analysis or, is West Bengal Unique?* IDS Working Paper No. 130. Brighton: Institute of Development Studies.

Davidson, B. (1992) *The Black Man's Burden: Africa and the Curse of the Nation-State*, Oxford: James Currey.

Easterly, W. (2006) *The White Man's Burden: Why the West's Efforts to Aid the Rest Have Done So Much Ill and So Little Good*, New York: Penguin Press.

Eyben, R. (2006) 'The Road not Taken: International Aid's Choice of Copenhagen over Beijing', *Third World Quarterly*, 27, 4, 595–608.

Ferguson, J. and Gupta, A. (2002) 'Spatializing States: Towards an Ethnography of Neoliberal Governmentality', *American Ethnologist*, 29, 4, 981–1002.

Fine, B. (2001) *Social Capital versus Social Theory: Political Economy and Social Science at the Turn of the Millennium*, London: Routledge.

Francis, P. and James, R. (2003) 'Balancing Rural Poverty Reduction and Citizen Participation: The Contradictions of Uganda's Decentralization Program', *World Development*, 31, 2, 325–337.

Harrison, G. (2004) *The World Bank and Africa: The Construction of Governance States*, London: Routledge.

Hart, G. (2001) 'Development Critiques in the 1990s: Cul de Sac and Promising Paths', *Progress in Human Geography*, 25, 4, 649–658.

Hart, G. (2004) 'Geography and Development: Critical Ethnographies', *Progress in Human Geography*, 28, 1, 91–100.

Hettne, B. (1995) *Development Theory and the Three Worlds*, Harlow: Longman.

Hickey, S. and Mohan, G. (2005) 'Relocating Participation within a Radical Politics of Development', *Development and Change*, 36, 2, 237–262.

Hickey, S. and Mohan, G. (2008) 'Poverty Reduction Strategies, Participation and the Politics of Accountability', *Review of International Political Economy*, 15, 2, 234–258.

Hirst, P. and Thompson, G. (1996) *Globalisation in Question*, Cambridge: Polity Press.

Hutchful, E. (1989) 'From "Revolution" to Monetarism: The Economics and Politics of the Adjustment Programme in Ghana', in B. Campbell and J. Loxley (eds) *Structural Adjustment in Africa*, London: Macmillan.

Kothari, U. (2006) 'Spatial Imaginaries and Practices: Experiences of Colonial Officers and Development Professionals', *Singapore Journal of Tropical Geography*, 27, 235–253.

Leftwich, A. (1993) 'Governance, Democracy and Development in the Third World', *Third World Quarterly*, 14, 3, 605–624.

Mamdani, M. (1996) *Citizen and Subject: Contemporary Africa and the Legacy of Late Colonialism*, Oxford: James Currey.

McMichael, P. (2000) *Development and Social Change: A Global Perspective*, London: Sage.

Mohan, G. (1996) 'Adjustment and Decentralisation in Ghana: A Case of Diminished Sovereignty', *Political Geography*, 15, 1, 75–94.

Mohan, G., Brown, E., Milward, B. and Zack-Williams, A. (2000) *Structural Adjustment: Theory, Practice and Impacts*, London: Routledge.

Peck, J. and Tickell, A. (2002) 'Neoliberalizing Space', *Antipode*, 34, 3, 380–404.

Phillips, A. (1977) 'The Concept of "Development"', *Review of African Political Economy*, 8, 7–21.

Pieterse, J. (2001) *Development Theory: Deconstructions/Reconstructions*, London: Sage.

Pike, A., Rodríguez-Pose, A. and Tomaney, J. (2006) *Local and Regional Development*, London: Routledge.

Polanyi, K. (1960) *The Great Transformation: The Political and Economic Origins of our Time*, Boston: Beacon Press.

Rakodi, C. (1986) 'State and Class in Africa: A Case for Extending Analyses of the Form and Functions of the National State to the Urban Local State', *Environment and Planning D: Society and Space*, 4, 4, 419–446.

Rondinelli, D., McCullough, J. and Johnson, R. (1989) 'Analyzing Decentralization Policies in Developing Countries: A Political-Economy Framework', *Development and Change*, 20, 57–87.

Samoff, J. (1979) 'The Bureaucracy and the Bourgeoisie: Decentralization and Class Structure in Tanzania', *Studies in Society and History*, 21, 1, 30–62.

Schuurman, F. (1997) 'The Decentralisation Discourse: Post-Fordist Paradigm or Neo-liberal Cul-de-Sac?' *European Journal of Development Research*, 9, 1, 150–166.

Sen, A. (1999) *Development as Freedom*, Oxford: Oxford University Press.

Slater, D. (1989) 'Territorial Power and the Peripheral State: The Issue of Decentralization', *Development and Change*, 20, 501–531.

Stoker, G. (2004) 'New Localism, Progressive Politics and Democracy', *The Political Quarterly*, 75, 117–129.

Subramaniam, V. (1980) 'Developing Countries', in D. Rowat (ed.) *International Handbook on Local Government Reorganisation: Contemporary Developments*, London: Aldwych Press, 582–593.

Walton, J. and Seddon, D. (1994) *Free Markets and Food Riots: The Politics of Global Adjustment*, Oxford: Blackwell.

Watts, M. (2003) 'Development and Governmentality', *Singapore Journal of Tropical Geography*, 24, 1, 6–34.

World Bank (1983) *World Development Report*, Washington, DC: World Bank.

World Bank (1989) *Sub-Saharan Africa: From Crisis to Sustainable Growth*, Washington, DC: World Bank.

World Bank (1994) *The World Bank and Participation*, Washington, DC: World Bank.

Young, C. (1994) *The African Colonial State in Comparative Perspective*, New Haven: Yale University Press.

Key readings

On the changing ideology of development theory

Cowen, M. and Shenton, R. (1996) *Doctrines of Development*, London: Routledge.

Hart, G. (2001) 'Development Critiques in the 1990s: Cul de Sac and Promising Paths', *Progress in Human Geography*, 25, 4, 649–658.

McMichael, P. (2000) *Development and Social Change: A Global Perspective*, London: Sage.

On the state in developing countries

Davidson, B. (1992) *The Black Man's Burden: Africa and the Curse of the Nation-State*, Oxford: James Currey.

Watts, M. (2003) 'Development and Governmentality', *Singapore Journal of Tropical Geography*, 24, 1, 6–34.

Schuurman, F. (1997) 'The Decentralisation Discourse: Post-Fordist Paradigm or Neo-liberal Cul-de-Sac?' *European Journal of Development Research*, 9, 1, 150–166.

On the contested terrain of decentralization

Mamdani, M. (1996) *Citizen and Subject: Contemporary Africa and the Legacy of Late Colonialism*, Oxford: James Currey.

Section II

Defining the principles and values of local and regional development

5

Regional disparities and equalities

Towards a capabilities perspective?

Diane Perrons

Introduction

The contemporary world is characterized by difference rather than uniformity and inequality on a global scale is stark and largely undisputed despite unparalleled wealth, advances in human ingenuity, and a vast array of policies to promote development and redress regional and gender inequalities. Interestingly, some of the widest regional and gender gaps exist in affluent countries and regions and among those experiencing high rates of economic growth, especially in India and China (Milanovic 2005b; Quah 2007).

Uneven development is variously viewed as an intrinsic characteristic of capitalist economic development and/or a necessary stage through which countries pass in their pathway to a high-income society. Depending on welfare regime or variety of capitalism, high levels of inequality are also found in mature high-income regions and income inequality is associated with higher levels of disadvantage in other spheres including health, education and crime (Wilkinson and Pickett 2009). If the meaning of regional development is to incorporate some sense of wellbeing, it is important to take note of inequalities within regions when measuring regional performances.

In this chapter I explore the polarized character of contemporary growth processes and identify connections between growth and inequality as it is experienced by different social groups at the regional level. I consider the gulf between the highly developed institutional policies for promoting equality and diversity at all spatial scales and enduring inequality of outcomes. With some exceptions, a second gulf exists between policy aspirations for greater equality between social groups, reflected, for example, by the European Union's (EU) requirement of gender mainstreaming in the Structural Funds, or the equality and diversity strategies of regional bodies such as the Regional Development Agencies (RDAs) in the UK, and the attention paid to equality and diversity in the academic literature on regional development, whether in the regional studies or regional science variants (McCann 2007; Morgan 2004; Pike *et al.* 2007).

My argument is that current conceptions of regional development and regional growth are defined too narrowly and in ways that inhibit the analysis and discussion of connections between economic change and wellbeing. I locate my argument within recent appraisals of regional studies especially regarding 'what kind of regional development and for whom' (Pike *et al*. 2007) and the capability perspective with respect to inequality and development (Sen 1999; Nussbaum 2003; Robeyns 2003). I review tendencies towards rising inequality at different geographical scales and then identify links between regional development and equalities policies. Finally, I make a provisional attempt to widen orthodox measures of regional growth by drawing on the capabilities perspective to calculate a more comprehensive measure of regional development together with a gender-sensitive version in an attempt to bridge at least some aspects of these divisions. This approach is already used by the UNDP in the Human Development Index and is emerging within the UK's Equalities and Human Rights Commission (EHRC) in their equality measurement framework. The empirical illustration in the final section relates to the UK but, in principle, the ideas and methods could be extended to a variety of locations and used in comparative work.

Widening inequalities: regions and gender

In the last 25 years, world income has doubled and society has never been more opulent (Sen 1999). Nonetheless at a global scale, inequality between nations is wide and, depending on measures used, increasing (Milanovic 2005a). Using GDP per capita, Branco Milanovic (2005a) shows that inequality increased steadily from 1950 when each country is taken as a single unit, but when weighted by population, declined somewhat over the same period, largely as a consequence of dramatic growth in post-reform China. When China is excluded from the calculation, inequality has been fairly stable, if anything, increasing slightly in the last decade (see also Quah 2007). Both Milanovic (2005b) and Quah (2007) also find that fast-growing countries have experienced high levels of regional and interpersonal inequality. In China, regional inequalities have been

widening, with especially rapid growth in the urban regions in the East (Lu and Wei 2007; Ng 2007; Dunford, this volume). Gender inequalities are also wider in these Eastern regions having expanded with the economic reforms as enterprises and local authorities secured greater autonomy over wage setting (Ng 2007). Similarly, the UNU WIDER study (Kanbur and Venables 2007) found wide regional disparities in 58 developing and transition countries and in the 26 countries for which temporal data was available, spatial inequalities were rising. This study also found that on balance these increases were associated with increasing integration in the global economy through trade and exports, meaning that it is not exclusion from the global economy that is the source of inequality but rather the form of inclusion (see Perrons 2009). Kuznet (1955) identified an inverted-U relationship between economic growth and interpersonal income inequality, indicating how inequalities would be small within low-income countries, rise as development unfolded, but then narrow as the benefits of growth became more widespread. In recent times this relationship is no longer clear as inequalities have been rising in high-income countries especially those following a neo-liberal model, but also in Scandinavia. This new pattern leads Tony Atkinson to suggest that it makes sense to speak more of a U-shaped rather than inverted-U model and to 'episodes' rather than trends in inequality (Atkinson 2007; see also Monfort (2009) who develops these ideas in more detail).

Overall regional inequalities in GDP per head declined in the EU between 1985 and 2006 as measured by the coefficient of variation at the NUTS 2 level. For the EU 15 these declines were most notable up until the mid-1990s, whereas for the EU 27, the decline continued up until 2005. These contrasting figures indicate how the new poorer member states have caught up to some degree but that among richer regions convergence has been slower (Monfort 2009). However, this summary figure disguises some important variations in the patterns of growth and spatial cohesion. What has happened is that the strong decline in inequalities between countries has been moderated by increases in regional disparities within countries, i.e. some regions in poorer EU countries have experienced rapid growth and moved closer to EU averages but moved further away from other regions within their own territories, that continue to be marginalized, and across the EU as a whole the overall gap remains immense and shows little sign of narrowing or change (Monfort 2009). Thus as an index of the EU (EU = 100), GDP per capita measured in purchasing power standards (PPS) London scored 355.9 in 2006 while the value for the poorest region, Nord-Vest in Romania, was 24.7; when measured ten years earlier these figures were 289.9 for London and 25.5 for Nord-Vest, indicating that growth has been concentrated in an already rich region that has moved further ahead (Eurostat 2009). Of greater significance for this chapter is the way that interpersonal earnings inequalities are higher in the most affluent regions and although these inequalities can be moderated by tax policies these cannot be guaranteed and in regions closely following a neo-liberal regime, personal income disparities are very wide, with the negative consequences for other aspects of social well-being (Wilkinson and Pickett 2009). Phillipe Monfort (2009), using EU data, finds a positive relationship between regional disparities and interpersonal income disparities for most countries. More specifically, in countries where regional inequalities increased rapidly between 1995 and 2005, interpersonal disparities likewise increased significantly. What this means is that regional development analysts who focus only on convergence at the European level could conclude that progress was being made while inequalities were rising at the regional level within countries and within the regions.

With respect to OECD countries interpersonal income and earnings inequalities

have been increasing and while the gender pay gap has narrowed it remains wide and at the current rate of narrowing will endure for a long time. Further, the narrowing in the gender pay gap is largely due to widening class inequalities such that men in the lower deciles have experienced a decline in their earnings relative to other men, and while some women have moved into higher earnings categories the gender pay gap at the top of the distribution remains wide (OECD 2008; Perrons 2009).

At the national level, interpersonal income inequality is higher in neo-liberal regimes such as the UK and the USA in contrast to Scandinavian Europe or Japan, and given the association between income disparities and rising regional disparities, regional growth does not guarantee rising affluence for all. In London, for example, the most affluent region in the UK, and ranked first among the European regions in 2006, 41 per cent of children are being brought up in poverty (48 per cent in Inner London) and the gender wage gap in the upper deciles is roughly one-third higher than the UK average, while at the lowest decile it is similar to the poorest regions (Figure 5.1) (CPAG 2008). Taking women and men separately, the inter-decile range is especially high for men in London; they earn five times as much as the lowest decile and this gap has risen significantly over the last decade (Figure 5.2). Elsewhere, while the gender gap remains high as illustrated in Figure 5.1, the extent of inequality between women is less marked with inequality between women being marginally higher among women in Northern Ireland than among men. What this data shows is that the highest paid jobs are found in what are regarded as the most prosperous regions on the GDP measure. Where overall earnings inequalities are high at the national level these inequalities are magnified in the most prosperous regions where the high-paid jobs are disproportionately concentrated. These high-paid jobs are found alongside a wide range of other forms of employment,

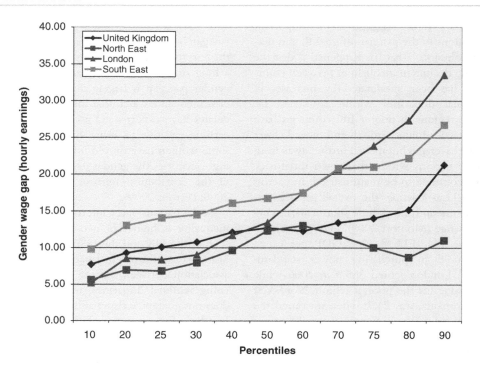

Figure 5.1 Gender wage gap in earnings, UK regions, 2008.
Source: Calculated from National Statistics (2009b) (ASHE data)

including personal services which tend to be among the lower paid, so the overall outcome is one of greater earnings polarization in London compared to other regions of the UK (Kaplanis 2007). As Leslie McCall (2001: 6) found with respect to the US, despite some narrowing of racial and gender inequalities at the national level, the best jobs are found in the more affluent regions and are still "heavily dominated by whites and men". If measures of regional development are supposed to reflect the character of the regions and if affluent regions are used as a model for other regions to emulate, then it would seem to be important to develop a measure that reflects regional well-being more broadly including internal inequality.

Marxian theories suggest that capitalist development is inherently uneven. More orthodox approaches suggested that widening internal inequality is a stage in the development process that ultimately tends towards equality (Kuznets 1955). Even this framework has been challenged by new growth theory and its application within spatial economics which shows how economies of agglomeration lead to clustering and uneven development. These findings have led to many empirical studies on clustering and are linked more generally to ideas of endogenous development associated with the Italian industrial district or regional innovation models and have formed important elements of consultancy and policy making in the field of regional development over the last three decades. This approach tends to be rather inward looking, focusing on connections within the region, yet despite the volume of literature and advice, the relationship between clusters of activity and the development and growth of regions remains rather unclear or fuzzy (Markusen 1999;

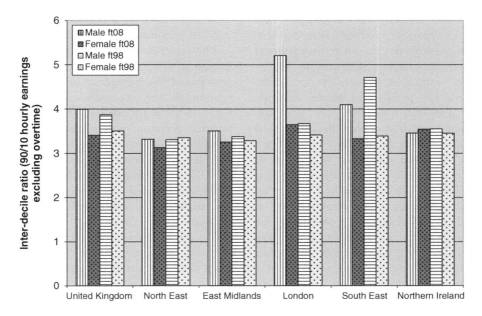

Figure 5.2 Inequality in wages among men and among women in the regions (full-time workers, hourly earnings excluding overtime) 1998 and 2008. The data plotted is the 90/10 inter-decile ratio for 1998 and 2008 using hourly earnings excluding overtime. What stands out is the high level of the gap between men in London and its steep rise over the last decade. Elsewhere the gender differences are less marked and in Northern Ireland the gap between women is higher than that between men. It is important to note that in absolute terms, as shown in Figure 5.1, there is a wide gender wage gap in earnings at this level.

Source: Calculated From National Statistics (2009b) (ASHE data)

Dunford and Greco 2006; McCann 2007). What are more certain are the theoretical predictions of unevenness and continuing patterns of regional inequality, measured by statistics on regional growth.

Positive and negative externalities are associated with concentration, agglomeration and clustering (EC 2008). As gains arise from economies of scale within production in both public and private firms and from external economies derived from proximity of related activities, unevenness itself is not necessarily problematic. Within both Marxist and new growth theories unevenness arises from productive efficiency: from economies of concentration and centralization within the Marxist perspective and economies of scale and proximity within new growth theory. In both cases, these economies, which mean that fewer inputs generate the same or

a larger quantity of output, potentially provide for gains to all. Many of the gains take the form of externalities arising from either clustering or from the division of labour within the firm. These gains, which can be cumulative, have to be recognized by individual agents in order to be realized, but in general terms arise from collective endeavour, that is, from cooperative aspects of activities rather than directly from the private activities of any single producer/supplier. A parallel case would be the classic illustration of extinguishing a fire through passing buckets along a chain rather than by individuals running back and forth. Given that even in a global economy there are some limits on the overall scale of desired output, if these collective gains are realized in one location they are less likely to be realized in another. As Ray Hudson (2007: 1156) succinctly points out, "some (regions) will 'fail' as part of the price of others succeeding". Further, these technical properties do not respect political or administrative boundaries so are just as present within as between regions. This being so the 'problem' of uneven development does not necessarily arise from the unevenness itself but from the differential appropriation or distribution of what are effectively social gains, that is from social choices made with respect to the distribution of collective efficiency gains. There is an argument therefore that the gains should be shared rather than privately appropriated, just as the negative externalities or losses in the form of congestion, higher rents or pollution are socialized.

The logic of this argument suggests there is no inherent reason why a geographically unbalanced distribution of economic activity should be associated with inequality in well-being. Further, given that inequality within the more affluent regions tends to be higher than in other regions and inequality itself is associated with lower scores on other aspects of social well-being, it is important to take a broader view of what constitutes overall regional development, especially given the existence of other state policies that advocate greater equality. This recognition opens the way for thinking about ways in which the regional growth and development might be measured to take account of inequalities and how the regional development and equalities agendas could be considered potentially complementary.

In this respect the EU's economic and social cohesion policy consists of two elements: an efficiency element which relates to the levels of productivity or the extent to which regional resources are efficiently utilized and an equity element which relates to reducing disparities in the standard of living but in practice there is no reason to assume that these different dimensions would move in synchrony. For example, regional disparities in GDP per capita may narrow but interpersonal inequalities within regions rise, so using

GDP per capita as a singular measure of regional performance is limited.

There is an extensive literature on the limitations of GDP per capita as a measure of growth and well-being from simple critiques relating to the compositional definition, e.g. to what is included and excluded and whether polluting 'goods' should count as contributing to economic growth, to the capabilities perspective as utilized within UNDP methodology and discussed further in this chapter, to demands for even broader understandings of well-being based on ideas of happiness (see Layard 2005). Elsewhere, I have disaggregated GDP into two constituent elements – an employment rate and a productivity rate – and mapped the distribution of EU regions (Perrons 2009; see also Dunford 1996), but in this chapter I develop a more comprehensive measure of regional development having first reviewed the links between equalities and cohesion policies which make such a broader measure more necessary.

Policies for equality and regional cohesion

Equality between women and men has been enshrined in the EU since its inception, the 50th anniversary being celebrated in 2007. Over time equalities policies have become more prominent; gender mainstreaming was adopted in 1997 and formally implemented in the Structural Funds from 1999, meaning that all policies, at all stages of design, implementation and evaluation have to be monitored for their gender implications. Subsequently equalities legislation has been extended to other areas of social disadvantage including ethnicity, sexual orientation, age and disability but these issues have not yet been mainstreamed. Specifically Article 2 of the EU Treaty sets out the fundamental value of gender equality; Article 3 relates to gender mainstreaming; Article 13 requires member states to combat discrimination by sex, race, ethnicity, religion/belief, disability, age and sexual orientation; and Articles 137 and 141 refer to securing gender equality in the labour market and to the principle of equal pay for work of equal value.

Gender mainstreaming was firmly embedded in the Structural Funds for the period 2000–2006 and moved gender from the margins of social policy to the mainstream of economic thinking and served to "shake traditional gender norms" especially in "gender conservative contexts" (Aufhauser 2007:1). In addition, gender mainstreaming has ensured that the gender implications of regional growth, planning and transport, which traditionally were considered purely technical or gender-neutral concerns, are articulated and taken into account in the design and monitoring of regional programmes. Thus projects put forward for Structural Funding have to pay attention to gender equality issues in both formulation and subsequent evaluation. Various tool kits have been designed to enable regional and local agencies to fulfil these requirements and a range of projects have been funded by the EU, under the European Social Fund and to a lesser extent as part of the general regional programmes under Objectives 1 and 2 and assessed from a gender perspective.

In the regulation of the Structural Funds and Community Strategic Guidelines on Cohesion for the period 2007–2013, although gender remains prominent it has become more of a cross-cutting theme. The policy stance towards regional equality has also shifted from a focus on redistribution towards lagging regions to one of enhancing growth and competitiveness within all regions. Within this more narrowly economic and competitive context equalities issues seem more ephemeral, even though women's employment has been of central importance to employment growth in the early years of the twenty-first century, with six of the eight million jobs created in the EU since the launch of the Lisbon Strategy being taken up by women and leading the EU (2007: 5) to remark that the "female labour force continues

to be the engine of employment growth in Europe".

Regional policy in the UK also reflects the shift from redistribution to promoting growth and competitiveness in all regions but at the same time the Regional Development Agencies, as public bodies, have a legal duty to promote gender equality. The UK's Equalities legislation covers six key characteristics of inequality: gender, ethnicity, disability, sexual orientation, age, religion/belief, but there is only explicit legislation to promote equality in the case of race and gender (see Ahmed (2007) for a parallel discussion of legislation with respect to race). The Regional Development Agencies have produced separate schemes and plans to promote gender and race equality within their own organizations and in the delivery of their services. With respect to gender, the legislation only came into effect in 2007 so that, while plans have been made to meet the legislative requirements, they have not yet been evaluated, but nonetheless contain ex-ante criteria for evaluation.

Some of the measures for success do not mean necessarily that progress has been made in securing greater gender balance but more simply that gender issues have been considered. The South West Regional Development Gender Equality Scheme, for example, indicates that with respect to economic inclusion, the measure of success would be to ensure that the level of and reasons for gender-related worklessness are clearly understood across geographical areas (SWRDA 2008). Nonetheless they carry out gender audits in relation to regeneration schemes and simply thinking through some of the gender implications at least raises awareness of the relations between regional planning and gender equality issues.

Plans for promoting gender equality are legal requirements and reflect high levels of aspiration towards securing equality but similarly to other policies, the relation between these objectives and others with which they may potentially conflict are rarely specified.

characteristics would expand the data requirements further. To simplify the process 'spotlight' indicators may be chosen to enable the EHRC to report on change on a few characteristics consistently over time while 'roving' indicators (Vizard and Burchardt 2008: 22) may be defined to highlight specific concerns as they change from year to year, but these have yet to be defined.

While such measures may more closely approximate lived experiences there is a danger that they simultaneously lose the power to provide an indication of equality, i.e. an indicator (rather than complete picture) of potential social concern or achievement. There is clearly a risk that its "very comprehensiveness... (could) drown out the sense of direction so important for purposeful policy-making" (Hirschman 1958: 205; also cited by Pike et al. 2007: 1263). While this framework might provide a useful way of mapping inequality and have resonance with people's experiences it is almost certainly too detailed to utilize in a practical way to estimate regional well-being. Moving away from the comprehensiveness, philosophical purity and individualist human rights stance of the EHRC's approach, below, I modify a subset of the capabilities defined by the EHRC to

provide a reflection of regional well-being to contrast with the narrowly economic focus of current measures.

Measuring gender and diversity in the regions: a capabilities approach

Using statistics to define regions creates a partial view of regional well-being. Regions with high levels of Gross Valued Added (GVA) per capita are generally portrayed as successful and creative; those with lower GVA used to be portrayed as lagging regions (reflecting the idea that they may catch up one day) but now are more likely to be portrayed as 'failing' or 'being challenged'. Table 5.1 portrays a GVA ranking of the regions and shows that the most prosperous regions are in the South of England with London ranking first followed by the South East and East. This pattern has been fairly stable over the last 15 years with some movements between closely ranked regions. For example, the East region displaced Scotland in 1993 as the third most prosperous region, Wales displaced Northern Ireland in the lowest position from 1992, and in the majority of years

Table 5.1 Regional rankings workplace-based gross value added per capita (current prices) 2006, household disposable income per capita 2005

Region	Index of UK	Rank GVA per capita	Index of UK	Rank disposable income per capita
London	155	1	120	1
South East	109	2	113	2
East	95	3	107	3
Scotland	95	4	95	5
South West	94	5	100	4
East Midlands	91	6	94	6
West Midlands	89	7	91	9
North West	87	8	92	7
Yorkshire and the Humber	86	9	92	8
North East	81	10	86	12
Northern Ireland	81	11	87	11
Wales	77	12	89	10

Source: Calculated from National Statistics (2009)

the North East falls just behind Northern Ireland (in 2006 their relative positions with respect to the UK are identical, their order in Table 5.1 being purely alphabetical). If disposable household income is used instead of work-place-based GVA per capita, the ranking is very similar and likewise is stable over time. In both cases the data show a divide between London and the South East, especially London and the other UK regions; the work-place-based measure highlighting the concentration of high-value economic activity; the residence-based measure reflecting a lower but still high average level of income in London but that affluence is spread more widely across the South and East, in part reflecting London's wide commuter belt.

Ranking the regions on GVA per capita disguises many characteristics of the region. I develop an index based on six of the capabilities identified by the EHRC; though I collapse these into five measures. This composite measure is completely contrary to the EHRC's methodology and ethos, but nonetheless still provides a more comprehensive measure and reflection of regional development that takes internal inequality within the regions into account and could counter or be juxtaposed alongside the narrowly economic perspective. The capabilities I draw on are to be: alive, healthy and knowledgeable; to have an adequate standard of living, and finally to engage in productive and valued activities.

With respect to life and health I use infant mortality as a single measure. Infant mortality has declined significantly across all regions of the UK since the 1980s but regional differences persist and reflect a number of aspects of well-being including the quality, provision and take-up of services, as well as parental health and well-being.

For knowledge, I calculate a composite measure based on the proportion of people securing five GCSE at grades A–C and the proportion securing three A levels; these qualifications are obtained at leaving secondary school at 16 and after two years, further

education 16–18 respectively. Northern Ireland performs best on both measures and the East is consistently in third place. For other regions there is much greater variation between these measures. London is a particularly interesting case; it ranks fifth on GCSE but eleven on three A levels. In addition, London comes first when regions are ranked on the proportion of the working population with degrees. This difference between the school population and the working population indicates commuting but also that London attracts learned people, through its educational institutions and work opportunities, rather than generating a high percentage of graduates from young people raised there. This difference also raises the question of whether measures of regional development should provide a sense of life in the regions or the characteristics of the region that might be attractive to inward investment. Probably both are required to reflect these different dimensions. In this chapter my focus is on the former so only includes GCSEs and A levels as the measure of knowledge.

For the standard of living and productive and valued activities, I use three criteria: employment, measured by the employment rate; earnings, based on a composite measure of median earnings to give a broad sense of well-being together with the index of earning inequalities, to reflect differences within the region; plus child poverty to reflect how well economies provide for the well-being of the most junior citizens (Poverty Site 2009).

I measure these elements using the UNDP's methodology for the HDI and combine them to form the Regional Development Index (RDI). Using some slightly different elements (gender-differentiated statistics for education and employment; the gender wage gap for earnings; but the same child-related measures) I then calculate a Gender-sensitive Regional Development Index (GRDI) (Figures 5.3 and 5.4).

In calculating these indices I have drawn on the EHRC's Equality Measurement Framework to reflect how equalities issues

GVA				RDI
1	London		South East	1
2	South East		East	2
3	East		South West	3
4	Scotland		Scotland	4
5	South West		East Midlands	5
6	East Midlands		Northern Ireland	6
7	West Midlands		Wales	7
8	North West		North East	8
9	Yorkshire and The Humber		North West	9
10	North East		Yorkshire and The Humber	10
11	Northern Ireland		West Midlands	11
12	Wales		London	12

Figure 5.3 Models of regional development gross value added and the Regional Development Index, 2006–2008. The years for the different elements of the index vary slightly between 2006 and 2008.
Source: Data for these indices National Statistics (2009a and 2009b)

are represented in a high-income country but draw directly on the simpler framework and methodology developed by the UNDP to calculate the RDI and GPDI (UNDP 2007: technical note 356–360). This is very much a preliminary, illustrative attempt to open discussion on ways of measuring regional development rather than a proposal for a definitive set of measures, which would require much deeper consideration of the items to be included and how they should be measured. In relation to gender, for example, ideally a

range of other items should be considered including violence, pension rights and so on. By moving away from conventional GDP measures and towards a wider understanding of development which has some resonance with the capabilities perspective this exercise may assist in thinking about 'what regional development means and for whom' (Pike *et al.* 2007).

Figure 5.3 contrasts the rankings of regions on the RDI model with the GVA per capita view. The most notable difference between

GVA				GRDI
1	London		Wales	1
2	South East		South East	2
3	East		South West	3
4	Scotland		Scotland	4
5	South West		East	5
6	East Midlands		North East	6
7	West Midlands		East Midlands	7
8	North West		North West	8
9	Yorkshire and The Humber		Northern Ireland	9
10	North East		Yorkshire and The Humber	10
11	Northern Ireland		West Midlands	11
12	Wales		London	12

Figure 5.4. Models of regional development gross value added and the Gender Regional Development Index, 2006–2008. The years for the different elements of the index vary slightly between 2006 and 2008. Source: Data for these indices National Statistics (2009a and 2009b)

these different ways of portraying regional development is the way that London moves from first to last position; the West Midlands ranking also declines. By contrast the positions of Northern Ireland and Wales improve considerably. The changes for other regions are less dramatic and Scotland retains fourth place on each of the indices.

Figure 5.4 contrasts the rankings of regions on the GRDI model with the GVA per capita and similarly shows how the relative position of London changes but also shows a dramatic reversal in the position of Wales. Both the RDI and the GRDI incorporate the judgement that inequality and distribution matter to well-being and may more closely approximate the experience of living in the region. Focusing on gender (see Figures 5.1, 5.2 and 5.4) likewise indicates the way in which the fruits of competitiveness have

benefited men to a greater extent than women, and supports criticisms of the finance focus of the last 20 years of development in the UK. Likewise in the case of Wales, the North East and Northern Ireland which rank in the lowest positions on the GVA method, all improve when broader aspects of well-being are considered, suggesting that their portrayal as failing overlooks the ways in which their development may have been more socially inclusive.

Clearly greater equality is not necessarily an advantage if that equality is based on a lower overall level of well-being, though there are data to suggest that inequality itself is socially damaging independently of the absolute level of well-being (Wilkinson and Pickett 2009) but to base success on narrowly inclusive models of development would also be limiting. In the case of London, for example, its extremely high position on the GVA per capita measure presents a view of a successful and competitive region that while correct in some ways overlooks how experience of life in London is highly differentiated. Visually, walking across Waterloo Bridge at night provides a stunning vista of city life but closer inspection of nearby streets presents a very different image. Likewise the presentation of the North East, Northern Ireland or Wales as failing regions with decaying industrial economies overlooks the existence of wealthy as well as desolate villages and the greater prominence of more egalitarian public sector employment. To address specific problems it is important to examine the relevant statistics separately and in this sense a composite measure disguises important differences. Nonetheless, given the way that the single GVA per capita measure is used as a summary measure to influence regional policies it is important to consider alternative more comprehensive measures. Developing different ways of measuring economic development at least provides a stimulus for thinking about what constitutes development, and for linking interpersonal inequalities with spatial inequalities, issues that have been linked and on the agenda for a long time at an international level and within EU and UK policies at the regional and local levels but less so within the regional studies academic literature.

As the data in Figures 5.3 and 5.4 shows, what appears to be the most successful region on measures of economic growth is problematic when questions of distribution and equity are taken into account. Given that government policies promote both competitiveness and cohesion, growth and equalities and especially since gender issues are mainstreamed in the European Structural Funds and within the Regional Development Agencies in the UK, it seems important that measures of regional development take account of inequality when measuring performance. The indices outlined in this chapter provide one possible way of so doing.

Conclusion

The processes generating current inequalities are so profound and embedded that it may be necessary to move beyond marginal adjustments to the current neo-liberal orthodoxy through redistribution and begin to specify more inclusive models of growth and development in order to realize policy aspirations for greater interpersonal and spatial equality. In this chapter I have addressed this issue and attempted to redress current policy fragmentation or disjuncture between equalities policies focused around individual deficits, and growth policies focused on abstract economic entities or regions with little attention given to the lived experiences of the inhabitants. To do so I proposed an index of regional development that incorporates aspects of interpersonal equality derived from a capabilities perspective and drew contrasts with more orthodox measures based on GVA. While the estimated indices are very provisional they may serve to open academic debate and policy discussion regarding the different ways in which regions can be portrayed.

Taking equalities aspirations seriously and looking at interpersonal dimensions of inequality provides a different view of the regions compared to one based on growth alone. With respect to the UK, while there are parallels between measures based on GVA per capita, this relationship is not consistent. In particular it does not relate to the most prosperous region, London, which moves from first place on the GVA per capita measure to last place on the regional development and gender-sensitive regional development indices owing to wide social divisions between residents. So London is not a prosperous region as such but a region where prosperous people and firms reside alongside high levels of interpersonal inequality and child poverty. Given that regions lower down the distribution rank more highly on measures linked with social welfare suggests that rather than being portrayed as failing regions, greater attention could be given to how they manage their economies and resources.

Linking measures of inequality with growth provides a way of overcoming the separation between the economic and the social and potentially returns the economy to its rightful position as a part of society (Polanyi 1957) that in principle could be oriented towards social and political ends of the majority rather than a minority. Such measures could also stimulate thinking about alternative, more inclusive models of regional development, appropriate at a time when the efficacy of neo-liberalism is in question. Rather than continually developing political and redistributive solutions to economic problems, more inclusive models of development would render such policies less necessary.

References

Ahmed, S. (2007) 'You End up Doing the Document Rather than Doing the Doing: Diversity. Race Equality and the Politics of Documentation', *Ethnic and Racial Studies*, 30 (4): 390–609.

Atkinson, A. (2007) 'The Distribution of Earnings in OECD Countries', *International Labour Review*, 146 (1–2): 41–60.

Aufhauser, E. (2007) *Strategies for Integrating Gender Equality into Regional Policy*, Paper prepared for the Seminar on 'Development of strategies for gender mainstreaming in national balance developmental model'. Seoul, South Korea, 28 May.

CPAG (2008) 'Child Poverty: The Statistics', *Analysis of the Latest Poverty Statistics*, London: Child Poverty Action Group http://www.cpag. org.uk/info/briefings_policy/CPAG_poverty_ the_stats_1008.pdf (accessed March 2009).

Dunford, M. (1996) 'Disparities in Employment, Productivity and Output in the European Union: The Roles of Labour, Market Governance and Welfare Regimes', *Regional Studies*, 30 (4): 339–357.

Dunford, M. and Greco, L. (2006) *After the Three Italies*, Oxford: Blackwell.

EC (2007) *Equality Between Women And Men Brussels Report From The Commission To The Council, The European Parliament, The European Economic and Social Committee and The Committee Of The Regions*. Brussels: COM(2007)49 final

http://eur-lex.europa.eu/LexUriServ/site/ en/com/2007/com2007_0049en01.pdf.

EC (2008) *Green Paper on Territorial Cohesion Turning Territorial Diversity into Strength*. Brussels: COM (2008) 616 final http://ec.europa.eu/ regional_policy/consultation/terco/paper_ terco_en.pdf (accessed March 2009).

EHRC (n.d.) *The Equality Measurement Framework*, London: Equalities and Human Rights Commission http://sticerd.lse.ac.uk/tex-tonly/case/research/equality/Briefing_ Equality_Measurement_Framework.pdf (accessed March 2009).

Eurostat (2009) Regional Statistics http://epp. eurostat.ec.europa.eu/portal/page/portal/ region_cities/regional_statistics/data/main_ tables.

Greed, C. (2005) 'Overcoming the Factors Inhibiting the Mainstreaming of Gender into Spatial Planning Policy in the United Kingdom', *Urban Studies*, 42 (4): 719–749.

Hirschman, A.O. (1958) *The Strategy of Economic Development*, New Haven, CT: Yale University Press.

Hudson, R. (2007) 'Regions and Regional Uneven Development Forever? Some Reflective Comments upon Theory and Practice', *Regional Studies*, 41 (9): 1149–1160.

IMF (2007) *World Economic Outlook Spillovers and Cycles in the Global Economy* http://www.imf. org/external/pubs/ft/weo/2007/01/pdf/ text.pdf.

Kanbur, R. and Venables, A. (2007) 'Spatial Disparities and Economic Development', in D. Held and A. Kaya (eds) *Global Inequality*, London: Polity.

Kaplanis, I. (2007) *The Geography of Employment Polarisation in Britain Publication*, IPPR, available on line http://www.ippr.org.uk/publication-sandreports/publications.asp?title=&author=Ka planis&pubdate=&policyarea=&search=search.

Kuznet, S. (1955) 'Economic Growth and Income Inequality', *The American Economic Review*, 45 (1): 1–28.

Layard, R. (2005) *Happiness: Lessons from a New Science*, London: Penguin.

Lu, L.C. and Wei, Y.D. (2007) 'Domesticating Globalisation, New Economic Spaces and Regional Polarisation in Guangdong Province', *China, Tijdschrift Voor Economische en Sociale Geografie*, 98 (2): 225–244.

McCall, L. (2001) *Complex Inequality: Gender, Class and Race in the New Economy*, New York: Routledge.

McCann, P. (2007) 'Observational Equivalence? Regional Studies and Regional Science', *Regional Studies*, 41 (9): 1209–1222.

Markusen, A. (1999) 'Fuzzy Concepts, Scanty Evidence, Policy Distance. The Case for Rigour and Policy Relevance in Critical Regional Studies', *Regional Studies*, 33 (9): 869–883.

Milanovic, B. (2005a) *World's Apart*, Princeton and Oxford: Princeton University Press.

Milanovic, B. (2005b) '*Half a World: Regional Inequality in Five Great Federations*', World Bank Policy Research Working Paper No. 3699, available at SSRN: http://ssrn.com/abstract=647765.

Monfort, P. (2009) *Regional Convergence, Growth and Interpersonal Inequalities across EU*, Report Working Paper of Directorate General Regional Policy European Commission http://ec.europa.eu/regional_policy/policy/future/pdf/9_monfort_final_formatted.pdf.

Morgan, K. (2004) 'Sustainable Regions: Governance, Innovation and Scale', *European Planning Studies*, 12 (6): 871–889.

National Statistics (2009a) *National Statistics Online Regional Trends* http://www.statistics.gov.uk/StatBase/Product.asp?vlnk=14356.

National Statistics (2009b) *National Statistics Online ASHE Annual Survey of Hours and Earnings* http://www.statistics.gov.uk/downloads/theme_labour/ASHE_2008/2008_gor_ind2.pdf.

Ng, Y.C. (2007) 'Gender Earnings Differentials and Regional Economic Development in Urban China, 1988–97', *Review of Income and Wealth*, 1: 148–166.

Nussbaum, M.C. (2003) 'Capabilities as Fundamental Entitlements: Sen and Global Justice', *Feminist Economics*, 9 (2–3): 33–59.

OECD (2008) *Growing Unequal. Income Distribution and Poverty in OECD Countries* http://ocde.p4.siteinternet.com/publications/doifiles/812008051P1G018.xls.

Perrons, D. (2009) 'Spatial and Gender Inequalities in the Global Economy: A Transformative Perspective', in O. Kramme and P. Diamond (eds) *Social Justice in the Global Age*, London: Polity.

Pike, A., Rodríguez-Pose, A. and Tomaney, J. (2007) 'What Kind of Local and Regional Development and for Whom?', *Regional Studies*, 41 (9): 1253–1269.

Polanyi, K. (1957) *The Great Transformation. The Political and Economic Origins of our Time*, Boston: Beacon Press.

Poverty Site (2009) *The Poverty Site, Joseph Rowntree Foundation* http://www.poverty.org.uk/16/index.shtml?2#num (accessed March 2009).

Quah, D. (2007) *Life in Unequal Growing Economies*, authors' web page http://econ.lse.ac.uk/staff/dquah/p/lug-1pr.pdf (accessed March 2009).

Rees, T. (2000) 'The Learning Region? Integrating Gender Equality in Regional Economic Development', *Policy and Politics*, 28 (2): 179–191.

Robeyns, I. (2003) 'Sen's Capability Approach and Gender Inequality: Selecting Relevant Capabilities', *Feminist Economics*, 9: (2–3): 61–92.

Sen, A. (1999) *Development as Freedom*, Oxford: Oxford University Press.

SWRDA (2008) *Gender Equality Scheme: Action Plan 2007–10*, Exeter: South West of England Regional Development Agency.

UNDP (2007) *Human Development Report 2007/2008. Fighting Climate Change: Human Solidarity in a Divided World*, New York: United Nations, available at http://hdr.undp.org/en/media/HDR_20072008_EN_Complete.pdf (accessed March 2009).

Vizard, P. and Burchardt, T. (2008) *Developing a Capability List for the Equality and Human Rights Commission*, Paper Prepared for the 30th General Conference of The International Association for Research in Income and Wealth Portoroz, Slovenia, 24–30 August http://www.iariw.org/papers/2008/vizard.pdf (accessed March 2007).

Wikinson, R. and Pickett, K. (2009) *The Spirit Level. Why More Equal Societies Almost Always Do Better*, London: Allen Lane.

Further reading

Monfort, P. (2009) *Regional Convergence, Growth and Interpersonal Inequalities across EU*, Report Working Paper of Directorate General Regional Policy European Commission http://ec.europa.eu/regional_policy/policy/future/pdf/9_monfort_final_formatted.pdf (Investigates the relationship between intra- and inter- regional inequalities).

Perrons, D. (2009) 'Spatial and Gender Inequalities in the Global Economy: A Transformative Perspective', in O. Kramme and P. Diamond (eds) *Social Justice in the Global Age*, London: Polity. (Attempts to integrate regional and gender inequalities and suggest a more inclusive form of development.)

Pike, A., Rodríguez-Pose, A. and Tomaney, J. (2007) 'What Kind of Local and Regional Development and for Whom?', *Regional Studies*, 41 (9): 1253–1269. (Raises questions about the character and purpose of regional development.)

6

Inclusive growth

Meaningful goal or mirage?

Ivan Turok

Introduction

The challenge at the heart of local and regional development is to build a more productive economy while cutting poverty and inequality. Governments around the world espouse the values of social justice and inclusion while trying to raise productivity, boost investment and create jobs. This tension has been expressed in different ways at different times – between efficiency and equity, wealth creation and distribution, self-interest and solidarity, prosperity and fairness, or competitiveness and cohesion. Meanings vary, but they allude to a common belief that spatial development policy should craft together different values and realities, and promote what is often summarised as inclusive growth. This stems partly from a moral sense that everyone should gain from a more affluent society, along with a pragmatic realisation that this should provide a more secure foundation for long-term economic progress and stability.

The commitment to shared prosperity and a broad economic development agenda has been called into question over the last two decades by the global trend of rising inequality. A range of studies have found that the gap between rich and poor has grown since the 1980s and that the number of people falling below the poverty line has also increased in most advanced economies (OECD, 2008; Dickens and McKnight, 2008; Heidenreich and Wunder, 2008; International Institute for Labour Studies, 2008). Inequality is higher still in most countries of the global South, with the locus of poverty shifting from rural areas towards cities (UN-Habitat, 2008). Global social and spatial divisions seem to have been growing despite expanding world output, prompting questions about why growth isn't being shared more fairly and the 'rising tide' isn't lifting all boats (Green, 2008). Social mobility also seems to have stagnated in many places, levels of trust and engagement in public institutions have diminished, and localised concentrations of poverty have persisted, risking entrenched exclusion and alienation from mainstream society (OECD, 2008; Irvin, 2008).

Meanwhile, highly educated groups have gained rich rewards from global technological change and financial deregulation, bolstered by cuts in top tax rates to attract talent (Toynbee and Walker, 2008; *Economist*, 2009). People have been encouraged to believe that the success of the few ultimately makes everyone better off. Traditional welfare policies have been replaced by more individualised systems, with people reliant on private savings for their pensions and loans to fund university education. Labour markets and public housing systems have been liberalised to attract investment and enable 'adjustment' to global forces through lower wages, flexible work patterns and migration. And redistributive social and spatial policies have been revised to support national growth objectives (Fothergill, 2005; Pike *et al.*, 2006; Hildreth, 2009). In the global South, structural adjustment programmes and enforced privatisation have curtailed the developmental capacity of many governments. The widespread assumption has been that the state is generally ineffectual, if not obsolescent, and that it has no alternative but to embrace market processes if it wants to improve long-run economic performance on the basis that markets are rational, efficient and can't be bucked.

The global downturn has raised serious doubts about this orthodoxy. The credit crunch, collapse in world trade and jobs crisis have provoked unprecedented state activism to stimulate national economies, rescue failing banks and bolster struggling firms and industries. Grave concerns have emerged about the dominant Anglo-Saxon model of financial capitalism, with its speculative tendencies, neglect of the real economy and extravagant rewards for the few. Unfettered market mechanisms and 'sound macroeconomic principles' have patently failed to deliver steady and sustained growth, let alone trickle down, prompting calls for concerted intervention to reform economic structures, tackle sectional interests and protect the most vulnerable from the burden of the slump. If the rising tide left some people and places behind, a prolonged falling tide could usher in a new age of austerity and cause extensive hardship, especially with state resources depleted by indebtedness from bailing out the financial system. Faced with the paradox of rising incomes alongside greater anxiety

and discontent over the last two decades, some observers have gone further to suggest replacing the goals of wealth creation and material consumption by the broader values of well-being, happiness and mutuality (Layard, 2006; Jackson, 2009).

The purpose of this chapter is to review some of the main arguments surrounding the challenges of poverty, inequality and economic development. I consider different perspectives on the relationship between growth and inequality and discuss the merits of two orthodox policy responses – social protection and welfare-to-work. Despite the different circumstances of the global North and South, I suggest there are some common guiding principles for a more effective and dynamic approach. I argue that inclusive growth is a meaningful goal rather than a mirage, although it requires clearer specification and cannot be achieved without active state involvement in market mechanisms, which tend towards unequal and uneven outcomes. Rewarding employment is the most important pragmatic route to shared prosperity, and requires governments to perform different functions at different levels. Local and regional development has a vital role to play, complemented by national policies that redistribute resources and regulate markets.

The chapter begins by considering the different dimensions of poverty and inequality, emphasising the need for a broad perspective covering both relative and absolute poverty. It then proceeds to examine the dynamics of change, distinguishing between temporary and persistent poverty, for individuals and across generations. The idea of equality of opportunity is more widely supported than equality of outcome, especially in seeking to improve economic performance. The underlying causes of poverty are then outlined, including individual, cultural and structural explanations. This provides the basis for exploring different policy responses in the remainder of the chapter.

The concepts of poverty and inequality

Absolute poverty is defined by the number of people below a given threshold or poverty line. This is the minimum income per head required to achieve an adequate standard of living in a given country. It depends on the precise definition of essential needs and is influenced by the cost of food, shelter, transport and other essential resources consumed by an average adult. The standard international poverty line used by the United Nations and World Bank is $2 a day, or $1.25 for extreme hardship. This concept has been broadened over time to include lack of access to services such as water, sanitation, health, education and information (United Nations, 1995). This breadth is reflected in the Millennium Development Goals launched in 2000, which devote particular attention to poor health and low life expectancy (UN-Habitat, 2006).

These dimensions have since been extended further to reflect people's own definitions of poverty through 'livelihoods' approaches. These stress personal capacities as well as needs, and include access to 'assets' such as skills and knowledge; savings and credit; land, housing and natural resources, and social and community networks. Ideas of resilience and stability are also important in recognising vulnerability to poverty if people's resources are insufficient to cope with unexpected shocks (such as natural disasters, conflict, family illness or death) or stresses (such as loss of seasonal employment or income, or steadily rising food or fuel prices) (Rakodi, 2002; Scoones, 2009). Livelihoods approaches also encourage locally embedded, place-based understandings of poverty and marginalisation, rather than highly generalised indicators introduced top-down.

An absolute poverty line can give the impression that the problem is soluble with limited economic and social change. It says nothing about the persistence of poverty and whether it is caused by deficiencies of individuals or wider labour market or demographic processes. It tends to imply that the appropriate response is to provide a basic income and public services to those without a means of living. The simplest way to finance this is by expanding overall tax revenues through economic growth. Most of the global South needs the additional resources because of the scale of hardship and modest national incomes. Wealthier countries may not need growth to fund poverty programmes, although the extra taxes avoid having to divert funds from other purposes. There is no need in either case to interfere with the basic structure of the economy or the distribution of income. Poverty can apparently be tackled through light touch government collecting taxes due on increased economic activity, i.e. via growth followed by targeted social spending.

Absolute poverty also neglects the social context, including the subjective feelings and attitudes of people on low incomes relative to wider norms and standards. Much research has shown that people are poor mainly in relation to the wider society, not independently of their social environment (Wilkinson and Pickett, 2007, 2009). The social and economic distance or stratification between groups is often more important than the absolute level of income in determining well-being, especially in countries where most people have attained basic living standards. This is because health and welfare are influenced by 'psychosocial' factors – whether people feel valued and respected by others, in control at work and in their domestic lives, and enjoy strong friendships. Large differences in social status, reinforced by gaps in material wealth and consumption, can damage self-esteem and contribute to a range of stress-related diseases, obesity, addictions and even violent crime. Many of these costly problems are not confined to the poor, but apply across society as a whole. It is well known that poverty harms those who suffer insecurity and poor diets, but Wilkinson and Pickett show that it means greater anxiety and depression, poorer social relationships, worse health and higher mortality for society overall. Hence, they argue that greater equality makes everyone better off. Their evidence in relation to social outcomes is strong, but the relationship between equality and economic outcomes may be more complex, as indicated below.

The concept of relative poverty reflects a concern about social disparities and is usually measured by some fraction of typical incomes in a country. This link allows the poverty line to change as a society becomes wealthier. The OECD and European Union use the threshold of 60 per cent of the median household income. This is the point at which people are thought to struggle to share the ordinary expectations of the majority. People below this level lack what most people take for granted. The median income is used rather than the mean in order to compare against households in the middle of the spectrum and ignore being influenced by the super-rich. There is still an empirical connection between relative poverty and income inequality – more unequal societies have higher levels of relative poverty (OECD, 2008), but they are not identical concepts. The implication for policy is that tackling relative poverty requires a shift in underlying social relationships, which may include intervening in the distribution of income and property, and challenging the systems that create and perpetuate unequal educational outcomes, segmented occupational hierarchies and other skewed opportunity structures.

A shortcoming of the relative poverty measure is that it can conceal rising real incomes for people in the bottom half of the spectrum if middle-income earners do even better. For example, a remarkable five hundred million people in China (some 40 per cent) were lifted out of a dollar a day absolute poverty by rapid industrialisation and economic growth between 1981 and 2004, although income disparities increased as well during this period (UN-Habitat, 2008). This sharp fall in material poverty meant undoubted

social progress – these people were genuinely better off – yet relative poverty may have grown because people above them did even better. The wider point is that both relative and absolute poverty are important concepts, along with some broader notions of livelihood and inequality. A partial, one-dimensional perspective may misrepresent particular local or national conditions.

Another important point is that poverty and its implications vary greatly in different contexts. Relative poverty is linked more directly to the distribution of income than to the economic growth rate, whereas it may be the other way round with absolute poverty. This may mean that a more pressing priority for countries of the South is to generate additional resources for pro-poor policies, whereas social inequality is a greater concern in wealthier countries, where redistribution is more viable. This simple distinction ignores the possibility that growth may be generated through poverty programmes, for example, by bringing unemployed labour into productive use. It also ignores differences within and between countries and the underlying causes of poverty and inequality. More light can be shed on this by considering the dynamics of poverty.

Poverty dynamics

Poverty is not static and people's experiences and risks vary widely. Analysis of poverty dynamics can reveal the trajectories of different households and their chances of falling into or escaping poverty. This helps to go beyond describing how many people are poor at any point in time to know how long they remain poor and whether they experience recurrent periods. People whose income falls below the poverty line for a temporary spell may not even consider themselves poor, for example, those moving between jobs, absent through childbirth and students. Many others experience prolonged or recurrent low income, causing hardship, mounting debt and demoralisation. Research shows a significant relationship between overall inequality and persistent poverty at the country level. Unequal societies are prone to developing a section of the population who are trapped in poverty for long periods, damaging their well-being and their children's prospects (OECD, 2008; Irvin, 2008). Such cumulative impacts are major social concerns, implying deep-seated problems requiring fundamental responses.

The full consequences of persistent poverty may be apparent in lack of change across generations, or social immobility. When children 'inherit' much of their economic status from their parents, this creates a perception of unfairness and lack of opportunity. Countries with a high transmission of disadvantage from one generation to the next may also be less productive than those where people have a more equal chance to succeed, as they waste the skills and talents of those from deprived backgrounds. Research suggests a relationship between equality of opportunity, social mobility and equality of outcome: "the more unequal a society is, the more difficult it is to move up the social ladder, simply because children have a greater gap to make up" (OECD, 2008: 204). This is salutary for those who assert that everyone has a fair chance of success and that individual effort is the key. It justifies the state trying to narrow the gap in life chances and reduce inherited inequality by creating a high-quality education system, taxing inheritance and investing in vulnerable communities.

Almost everyone agrees that equality of opportunity is important, both for economic and moral reasons. This corresponds well with most notions of equity and fairness, namely that people should have an equal chance to reach their potential in life. However, equality of opportunity is hard to measure and difficult to achieve – not least because of the powerful influence of parental resources, knowledge and ongoing support on their children's opportunities and capabilities. In the UK, the decline in social mobility over the last three decades has become an explicit policy concern because poorer groups are consistently held back by their social backgrounds and restricted opportunities, despite a core government objective over the last decade to shift the focus from inequality of income to opportunity, i.e. meritocracy rather than equality (Irvin, 2008). The latest policy response aims to widen access to education for individuals from the earliest years through to university and beyond, and to give poorer parents some additional support (HM Government, 2009). Policy-makers have been less inclined to address the underlying structural obstacles to social progress.

There is far less agreement about equality of outcomes than opportunities, especially for economic development (International Institute for Labour Studies, 2008). From a meritocratic perspective, inequality is actually fair and beneficial if it reflects individual skill and effort, but detrimental if it results from inherited wealth or unjustified discrimination based on factors such as race, gender, disability or place of residence, for reasons explained above. Market economists also see inequality as providing incentives to individual enterprise and risk-taking, which is deemed to underpin an efficient and prosperous economy, and improve society as a whole through higher incomes and opportunities for all. Critics counter that individual effort does not necessarily generate wider benefits, especially if it is associated with opportunistic behaviour, greed and excess (Irvin, 2008; Toynbee and Walker, 2008). Creativity and innovation in modern economies are delicate phenomena that depend less on individual initiative than on a combination of trust, cooperation, state support and private risk (Hutton and Schneider, 2008). Even the founder of free-market economics Adam Smith argued that economies do not work well if guided by self-interest alone – they need to be steered by a broader framework of social values, rules and conventions, or 'moral sentiments' that people internalise in judging how to behave (Smith, 2002).

The important point is that the dynamics of poverty vary in different contexts and the main policy challenge is persistent poverty and inequality, for individuals and across generations. A high level of inequality seems to have corrosive social consequences, although it is possible there are some economic advantages from limited inequality if it reflects rewards to individual talent and endeavour, rather than inheritance. Government policy should be concerned above all with helping people to escape from poverty in ways that can be sustained, and preventing others from falling into poverty. This includes support for young children to limit their life chances being curtailed at an early age. Policies of amelioration and mitigation are necessary to limit the worst effects of poverty, but they don't provide lasting solutions.

The analysis of poverty dynamics also requires a spatial dimension. 'Place' can be enabling or disabling for the poor, reinforcing or counteracting other forces in all kinds of ways. For example, the opportunity structures of neighbourhoods can work together to facilitate upward mobility or they can trap people in environments with poor access to jobs and amenities. Neighbourhoods that seem just as poor on the usual deprivation indicators can actually have contrasting trajectories because of their different locational assets. Some function as escalators assisting people to gain a foothold in the labour market or housing system because they are well located, have good schools or other facilities, or have strong outward-oriented social networks. These areas may appear to be poor because of the steady influx of low-income residents and the departure of people as they become better off. Other places function as poor enclaves – they are more isolated from opportunities and their services suffer under pressure from the concentration of poor households (Robson, 2009). Policies need to be more sensitive to the role different places perform within the urban system. Escalators have potential for reducing poverty that might be enhanced, while enclaves

require more comprehensive support on the grounds of need.

Causes of poverty and inequality

It is clear from the above that the causes of poverty can be wide-ranging and complex, depending partly on whether the reference point is the household, community, region or nation, and their particular circumstances. Interpretations are frequently contested because of the significant issues at stake and the difficulties involved in untangling the different factors at work. Separating the causes of poverty from the symptoms and consequences is not straightforward, especially when the processes are subtle and feedback effects occur. This gives considerable scope for ideological and political differences to emerge. Yet understanding what lies at the root of the problem is clearly important for formulating effective policy responses that go beyond palliatives to offer lasting solutions.

The simplest kind of explanation is where poverty is a temporary phenomenon affecting individuals or areas. People may experience poverty for a short period as a result of unforeseen events, such as redundancy, illness or an environmental hazard (fire or flooding) removing their livelihood. Localities may experience a temporary downturn because of difficulties afflicting a major employer or unseasonal conditions disrupting tourism, food supply or energy production. National economies may witness periodic recessions as a result of business cycles, volatile currency movements or stock market fluctuations. The consequences typically include higher unemployment and lower earnings, with the scale of the problem often accentuated by the spread of uncertainty and loss of confidence among investors and consumers.

The second type of explanation attributes poverty to the characteristics of individuals and households. People may be particularly vulnerable to poverty because they lack relevant skills and capabilities, or are unable to work through sickness, disability or old age. Governments are tempted to define poverty as being the result of personal deficiency, absolving them of responsibility. Unemployment is treated as if it is voluntary – there are plenty of vacancies available, but people lack a work ethic (e.g. HM Treasury, 2001). Some groups experience discrimination in the labour market because of gender, ethnic or religious backgrounds. People's risk of poverty varies at different stages of the life course, with children and older people being particularly vulnerable in countries with low levels of social protection. Adults with large numbers of dependants are also at risk, especially single parents. The biggest increase in poverty over the last two decades has occurred among working-age adults without jobs, along with their children (OECD, 2008). The implications of this important link between poverty and joblessness are discussed later.

Analyses focused on individual characteristics are generally better at describing the incidence of poverty (who is affected) than at explaining the origins or scale of the problem. There are essentially two kinds of more general explanation – cultural and economic. Cultural analyses typically attribute poverty to the attitudes, behaviour and agency of the individuals and groups at risk. For example, young men may be put off going to college or getting a job by peer pressure and socialisation in deprived areas, or the availability of easier sources of income. Marginalised communities may suffer from depressed expectations and a weak social fabric, with households prone to domestic disputes, family breakdown, teenage pregnancies and behavioural problems among children, thereby lowering educational attainment and repeating the cycle of poverty. In the UK policy discourse, the notion of an 'underclass' has been replaced by a supposed culture of low aspiration among deprived communities (HM Government, 2009).

Economic and structural analyses acknowledge cultural dimensions of poverty, but consider these more consequential than causal. For instance, long-term unemployment may damage people's confidence, undermine their motivation and reinforce their sense of exclusion, but attributing their economic status to poor attitudes would be misleading. Primacy must be afforded to the conditions shaping the opportunities for individuals and communities, including shifts in industries and occupations and the geography of jobs. Economic decline and restructuring are powerful drivers of unemployment and low income, varying in scale and composition across localities and regions. De-industrialisation in many advanced and middle-income economies has eroded the prospects for less-skilled male manual workers. Meanwhile, highly qualified professional, managerial and technical workers have enjoyed strong growth in earnings and investment income, thereby widening inequality (OECD, 2008). Natural population growth and in-migration have also enlarged the supply of labour in some places, harming the job prospects of local residents. Underlying these processes may be pervasive differences in the socio-economic position of different sections of the population, reinforced by selection mechanisms that restrict disadvantaged groups escaping from poverty in significant numbers. Other obstacles faced by the poor may relate to mundane matters such as low transport mobility or lack of vocational training facilities. A full analysis of poverty needs to be context specific and reflect the combined effects of different forces, individual and structural, cultural and economic.

Traditional responses: social protection

Governments have conventionally responded to poverty by extending social protection. Programmes are funded out of general taxation and distribute resources either through welfare benefits (cash transfers) or in-kind welfare services. Cash is paid to people who cannot support themselves because of unemployment, sickness, old age or caring responsibilities. Child support grants, disability allowances and basic pensions tend to be universal and given without testing individual incomes. Other benefits are means-tested to target the poor and limit the cost to the state, although this can stigmatise recipients and reduce take-up. They include subsidies towards the cost of food, clothing, housing, utilities or public transport. Some unemployment benefits and pensions are more generous than basic state provision, on condition that recipients contributed financially while they were working.

Benefit payments put money into people's hands and are therefore the most direct means of easing the burden of income poverty. Having control over the resources, people can meet their particular needs and preferences without outside influence. Raising benefit levels may be a good way of injecting spending power into the economy during a recession because the poor tend to spend more of their income on goods and services than the wealthy, and spend it fastest since they need it most (Elmendorf and Furman, 2008).

A drawback may be that welfare recipients are less inclined to seek work, depending on benefit levels, their duration and prevailing wage rates. Means-testing can worsen the disincentive effect because of the high marginal tax rates faced when moving into work. Targeted benefits can therefore create a poverty trap and reinforce exclusion, instead of a stepping stone towards inclusion and independence. More than a million people in the UK were transferred on to Incapacity Benefit during the 1980s and 1990s in response to rising unemployment (Brown *et al.*, 2008). They were written-off on the basis that their age, manual skills and location gave them little chance of regaining employment. Without support, their morale and skills deteriorated, their physical and mental health suffered, and a range of wider social problems became ingrained. These conditions proved difficult to reverse when the labour market subsequently recovered and whole communities were scarred by the experience (Audit Commission, 2008).

The poverty response of many cash-strapped governments in the global South has been to limit welfare payments to bare subsistence level and confine them to dependants such as children and pensioners. In practice, the income may still be spent across the whole family, thereby diluting the benefits for target groups. Restricting social grants to children can also encourage poor women to have more children, thereby complicating their ability to get a job and become self-reliant. Some states add conditions to benefit receipt in order to address the health and educational effects of poverty. In some South American countries parents only receive grants for their children if they attend school and get regular health checks.

This begins to address a concern that grants neglect the root causes of poverty and therefore provide no lasting solution. They alleviate the condition, but don't lift people out of poverty in a sustainable way by increasing their employability or entrepreneurial skills, for example. Nor do they prevent people from falling into poverty in future by counteracting the triggers, such as educational failure or loss of employment. This is not to underestimate the importance of an income safety net for people who are destitute because of the obvious benefits for their health and well-being. Scandinavian countries have addressed the tension between out-of-work poverty and welfare dependency by creating generous benefit systems that are time-limited, with a condition that recipients actively seek work and the state acting as employer of last resort.

The other main type of government response to poverty – welfare services – has a more direct bearing on the contributory factors. Quality provision in health, education and child-care can both treat some of the effects of poverty and improve individual capabilities. This can benefit society as a whole through better educated and healthier citizens. For example, social housing can give people stability and security, and enable them to focus on improving other aspects of their lives, including building a livelihood. Quality public services can also help to redistribute resources because they retain the support of middle-income groups, who would otherwise opt out to the private sector. Comprehensive education systems can offset the gap in life chances between people from different social backgrounds by helping to level the playing field. There may be a degree of paternalism involved in the state assuming it knows what forms of spending are best for children and families, rather than giving grants. In the global South, basic services such as water, sanitation, electricity, schools and clinics are vital to tackle extreme hardship in informal urban settlements and rural areas. As well as transforming child mortality and life expectancy, they can prevent the spread of disease and improve skills and resilience.

The 2009 World Development Report provided a novel formulation of these arguments in advocating an approach to 'uneven but inclusive growth' that placed universal basic services centre-stage (World Bank, 2009). The top priority in the global South was to provide essential services throughout the country to create the conditions for growth. A vital objective of this 'neutral' national policy was to unify each country by improving living conditions and reducing territorial disputes. The Report argued that growth is inevitably unbalanced and focused in the major cities as a result of agglomeration economies. Responsive social services in rural areas can equip people with the competences to access urban employment, while preventing others from being pushed into migrating for the wrong reasons, namely poor local facilities. Lagging regions would benefit from urban prosperity through remittances and circular migration. Improvements in transport connectivity would facilitate economic integration between cities and their hinterlands. The Report was critical of spatial development policies that seek to steer productive investment towards lagging areas, on the grounds that this will hold back national economic growth. It was strangely silent on direct measures that local and national governments can take to accelerate economic development, in cities and elsewhere, presumably because this goes beyond basic public goods. In line with the New Economic Geography, the assumption was that growth would emerge naturally through the concentration of population and lower barriers to trade between places, even if this takes generations.

Welfare-to-work

An alternative approach to inclusive growth has emerged in some countries, partly in recognition that welfare programmes may not provide sufficient basis for improved living standards, especially if people are trapped in unfavourable circumstances without opportunities to enhance their position. Paternalistic systems may also result in some welfare recipients developing lifestyle habits and expectations that cannot be accommodated indefinitely. A more active, resourceful and self-reliant citizenry is generally healthier, especially where state capacity is restricted and people ultimately have to support themselves. Governments need the practical ideas and hands-on involvement of local communities to develop relevant projects and programmes that can build skills and competences, improve livelihoods, provide work experience and address other barriers to economic and social progress.

A broader motivation is the traditional separation of social policy from economic considerations, in effect relegating it to a lower status and making it difficult to develop an integrated approach. Social programmes may be viewed as remedial, introduced after the event to compensate people and places left behind by economic change or palliatives chasing the symptoms of poverty around different public agencies without getting to the heart of the problem. They may be treated as pure costs or deductions from the resources generated by the productive economy, rather than as investments that can prevent the occurrence of poverty or contribute to long-term economic performance through, for example, ensuring the production and maintenance of a healthy, educated and motivated workforce.

Welfare-to-work is intended to give employment greater priority in tackling poverty and inequality. It is consistent with a large body of research showing that involuntary unemployment is the main determinant of social exclusion in advanced economies, where paid jobs are the principal source of income, daily routine, social status, personal identity and social interaction outside the family (Gordon and Turok, 2005). Consequently, employment offers the best route out of poverty because it provides a secure livelihood, meaning, dignity and structure to people's lives. Work enables people to realise their potential, is good for their health and well-being, and is where they meet most of their friends and partners. More people seeking employment also benefits the economy through increased labour supply. Some governments regard welfare-to-work as a more politically acceptable way of redistributing resources than unconditional grants, since the participants will be contributing to society.

One element of welfare-to-work is an active benefits regime, requiring recipients to take deliberate steps to improve their employability (through participation in work experience, vocational training or drug rehabilitation schemes) and actively look for work. Efforts to shift benefit claimants from passive recipients to active jobseekers can be harsh and punitive ('workfare'). Elsewhere, the ethos is more supportive, with an emphasis on positive encouragement to cooperate rather than negative sanctions for lack of compliance. A second part of the package is making 'work pay' and ensuring that low-income households have a real incentive to

choose paid work, using a minimum wage and tax credits. A third component is to align organisations responsible for providing welfare benefits with those delivering employment and training services to ensure an integrated approach, perhaps with a focus on supporting particular target groups, such as single parents or people with disabilities.

An additional element in some countries is to decentralise programmes to the local level in order to allow for more flexible tailoring to local labour market conditions and individual needs. Area-based initiatives can also enable more effective outreach into disadvantaged communities and stronger engagement with employers to persuade them to make vacancies available to target groups and to assist with subsequent job retention and progression. Decentralisation also offers the potential to connect public health, social care, training and anti-poverty programmes because of their common interest in getting more people engaged in meaningful activity that builds confidence, self-esteem and well-being.

An important limitation of welfare-to-work is the assumption that sufficient jobs exist to absorb people coming off welfare. It is partial in emphasising the supply-side of the labour market and neglecting the level and composition of labour demand. At worst it shifts the responsibility for unemployment on to the individual by implying that if they look harder and moderate their wage expectations they can find work. Evidence shows that the policy has been least effective in depressed local labour markets, where needs are greatest (Sunley et al., 2005). It was introduced as a standard national programme in the UK, in the interests of scale and consistency, but this has prevented adaptation in line with different local conditions.

A second weakness is the risk of creating a group of 'working poor'. This seems to have been an outcome in the USA during the 1990s when people in the lowest decile of the distribution saw their incomes stagnate or fall, despite sizeable employment growth

(Convery, 2009). Similar concerns have emerged in the UK over the last decade, where half of all poor children now live in households with someone in work (Lawton, 2009; Tripney *et al.*, 2009). Another striking UK finding is that around 70 per cent of people who get a job subsequently return to benefits within a year (Convery, 2009). Welfare-to-work programmes are insufficient to ensure that work is a genuine route out of poverty by improving job advancement to more rewarding positions, and freeing up entry-level jobs for the next cohort of job-seekers and school leavers. Additional measures are required to support progression, including stronger workplace regulation and a higher minimum wage to protect workers in this precarious section of the labour market. Such measures are likely to be more successful if integrated with the wider policies outlined in the conclusion.

Conclusion: Towards a broader approach

It has been argued that the pursuit of economic growth through market mechanisms can militate against social justice objectives. Furthermore, the prevailing social policy orthodoxy is an inadequate response to the challenges of uneven and unequal development. Rising unemployment, poverty and inequality require a broader and bolder approach. This is particularly apparent in current circumstances to prevent the economic difficulties from being translated into deep-seated social problems that are much more complex to resolve. The goal of inclusive growth is meaningful, but it needs a more precise definition since this policy arena is hotly contested and ambiguities abound. There are crucial differences between aiming to reduce absolute and relative poverty, and between equality of opportunity and outcome. Different definitions of the issue imply different kinds of anti-poverty strategy. The detailed composition of policy is also bound to vary between places and at different points in time, depending on economic and demographic conditions, industrial and occupational structures, and levels of education and skills.

There is a good case for putting full and rewarding employment at the heart of inclusive growth strategies because of the wide-ranging benefits for society and the economy. An employment focus can draw diverse interests together around a common agenda, including the business sector, trade unions, community groups, health professionals, social services and organisations responsible for education, training and economic development. A more rounded approach than welfare-to-work is required, with policies to strengthen labour demand as well as supply, creating more and better jobs paying wages that lift workers and their families out of poverty. Employment can be made a cross-cutting priority, using the full range of public sector powers as purchaser, investor, legislator and service provider. Public sector action is required to support people and places marginalised by market processes. Governments can encourage labour-intensive forms of growth through public works programmes, subsidise temporary work placements to give people relevant experience and become employers of last resort when other options are exhausted. National regulation of the labour market is important to protect vulnerable workers from insecure and unreasonable conditions. Health policies can support responsive work-related services to prevent accidents, stress and other ailments from causing people to lose contact with the labour market and falling into long-term sickness.

Countries such as the UK have not traditionally been very successful at ensuring an inclusive labour market with equal opportunities for people from different areas and social backgrounds, partly because of the centralised nature of economic and social policy. Local and regional development can help to overcome these weaknesses and promote more dynamic and effective interventions. Being rooted in place allows for greater sensitivity to local needs and circumstances, and a richer understanding of shifting conditions. Decisions taken locally are closer to many economic realities and better targeted to opportunities for productive investment, business development, enhanced skills, recycled land, improved infrastructure and other activities that add value and enhance long-term growth and development prospects. It is often easier to encourage different stakeholders to cooperate at this level because their common interests are more apparent. Harnessing the active participation and energy of communities has most potential at this scale. The integration of social, economic and environmental aspects of development can also be simpler because the need for coordination is more apparent and bureaucracies tend to be smaller.

References

Audit Commission (2008) *A Mine of Opportunities: Local Authorities and the Regeneration of the English Coalfields*, London: Audit Commission.

Brown, J., Hanlon, P., Turok, I. *et al.* (2008) 'Establishing the potential for using routine data on Incapacity Benefit to assess the local impact of policy initiatives', *Journal of Public Health*, 30(1), pp. 54–59.

Convery, P. (2009) 'Welfare to work – from special measures to 80% employment', *Local Economy*, 24(1), pp. 1–27.

Dickens, R. and McKnight, A. (2008) *The Changing Pattern of Earnings: Employees, Migrants and Low Paid Families*, York: Joseph Rowntree Foundation.

Economist (2009) 'Special report on the rich', 4 April, *Economist* Magazine.

Elmendorf, D. and Furman, J. (2008) *If, When, How: A Primer on Fiscal Stimulus*, Washington: Brookings Institution.

Fothergill, S. (2005) 'A new regional policy for Britain', *Regional Studies*, 39(5), pp. 659–667.

Gordon, I. and Turok, I. (2005) 'How urban labour markets matter', in Buck, I., Gordon, I. Harding, A. and Turok, I. (eds.) *Changing Cities*, London: Palgrave, pp. 242–264.

Green, D. (2008) *From Poverty to Power*, Oxford: Oxfam International.

Heidenreich, M. and Wunder, C. (2008) 'Patterns of regional inequality in the enlarged Europe', *European Sociological Review*, 24(1), pp. 19–36.

Hildreth, P. (2009) 'Understanding "new regional policy"', *Journal of Regeneration and Renewal*, 2(4), pp. 318–336.

HM Treasury (2001) *The Changing Welfare State: Employment Opportunity for All*, London: HM Treasury.

HM Government (2009) *New Opportunities: Fair Chances for the Future*. Cm 7533, London: HM Government.

Hutton, W. and Schneider, P. (2008) *The Failure of Market Failure: Towards a 21st Century Keynesianism*, London: National Endowment for Science, Technology and the Arts.

International Institute for Labour Studies (2008) *World of Work Report 2008: Income Inequalities in the Age of Financial Globalization*, Geneva: International Labour Office.

Irvin, G. (2008) *Super Rich: The Rise of Inequality in Britain and the United States*, London: Polity.

Jackson, T. (2009) *Prosperity Without Growth: The Transition to a Sustainable Economy*, London: Sustainable Development Commission.

Layard, R. (2006) *Happiness: Lessons from a New Science*, London: Penguin Books.

Lawton, K. (2009) *Nice Work if You Can Get It*, London: IPPR.

OECD (2008) *Growing Unequal: Income Distribution and Poverty in OECD Countries*, Paris: OECD.

Pike, A., Rodríguez-Pose, A. and Tomaney, J. (2006) *Local and Regional Development*, London: Routledge.

Rakodi, C. (2002) 'Building sustainable capacity for urban poverty reduction', in Romaya, S. and Rakodi, C. (eds) *Building Sustainable Urban Settlements*, London: ITDG Publishing, pp. 91–105.

Robson, B. (2009) *Understanding the Different Roles of Deprived Neighbourhoods*, London: Department of Communities and Local Government.

Scoones, I. (2009) 'Livelihoods perspectives and rural development', *Journal of Peasant Societies*, 36(1), pp. 171–196.

Smith, A. (2002) *The Theory of Moral Sentiments*, Cambridge: Cambridge University Press.

Sunley, P., Martin, R. and Nativel, C. (2005) *Putting Workfare in Place – Local Labour Markets and the New Deal*, Oxford: Blackwell.

Toynbee, P. and Walker, D. (2008) *Unjust Rewards: Exposing Greed and Inequality in Britain Today*, London: Granta.

Tripney, J. *et al.* (2009) 'In-Work Poverty: A Systematic Review', *Research Report 549*, London: Department of Work and Pensions.

United Nations (1995) *World Summit on Social Development*, New York: United Nations.

UN-Habitat (2006) *State of the World's Cities 2006/7*, Nairobi: UN-Habitat.

UN-Habitat (2008) *State of the World's Cities 2008/9*, Nairobi: UN-Habitat.

Wilkinson, R. G. and Pickett, K. E. (2007) 'The problems of relative deprivation: Why some societies do better than others', *Social Science and Medicine*, 65, pp. 1965–1978.

Wilkinson, R. G. and Pickett, K. E. (2009) *The Spirit Level: Why More Equal Societies Almost Always Do Better*, London: Allen Lane.

World Bank (2009) *Reshaping Economic Geography*, Washington: World Bank.

Further reading

Rising inequality globally

OECD (2008) *Growing Unequal? Income Distribution and Poverty in OECD Countries*, Paris: OECD.

Toynbee, P. and Walker, D. (2008) *Unjust Rewards: Exposing Greed and Inequality in Britain Today*, London: Granta.

The damaging social consequences of inequality

Wilkinson, R. G. and Pickett, K. E. (2009) *The Spirit Level: Why More Equal Societies Almost Always Do Better*, London: Allen Lane.

Employment as a route out of poverty

Gordon, I. and Turok, I. (2005) 'How Urban Labour Markets Matter', in Buck, I., Gordon, I. Harding, A. and Turok, I. (eds) *Changing Cities*, London: Palgrave. pp. 242–264.

Turok, I. and Edge, N. (1999) *The Jobs Gap in Britain's Cities: Employment Loss and Labour Market Consequences*, Bristol: The Policy Press.

7

The Green State

Sustainability and the power of purchase

Kevin Morgan

Introduction

Nothing has done more to spark new imaginaries of local and regional development in the past generation than the notion of "sustainability". Despite its fuzziness as a concept, or perhaps because of it, the principle of sustainable development has resonated around the globe, being equally applicable in the global North as it is in the global South. Indeed, if there is one grand narrative that has the scale and scope to compete with neo-liberalism, it is surely sustainable development, which is still a relatively new idea in terms of mainstream politics.

By comparison, the neo-liberal narrative has both a longer lineage and a narrower focus, concerned as it is to substitute the market for the state wherever it is profitable to do so. Whatever its shortcomings, the neo-liberal narrative has dominated the intellectual imagination of elites for many years, shaping the way they viewed and valued the world, be it economy, society or nature.

But with the credit crunch climacteric triggered by a fatal amalgam of financial greed and light touch regulation the political credentials of the neo-liberal narrative have been seriously damaged, at least for the moment, spawning new opportunities for alternative narratives that view and value things differently. Will the sustainable development narrative fill this vacuum or will the neo-liberal narrative reinvent itself after a period of contrition?

The answer will depend on a whole series of imponderables, not least the influence of the Green State – that is, a polity that strives to take sustainability seriously. To explore these issues in more depth the chapter is structured as follows: section two argues that, notwithstanding its fuzziness, sustainability can be regarded as a new developmental narrative because it brings with it a new set of values; section three explores the return of the state, and the prospects for a "green" state; and section four draws on the above arguments to explore the world of public food provisioning, a litmus test of sustainability.

From needs to capabilities: sustainability as a new developmental narrative

As a concept that embraces economy and society as well as the environment, it is worth remembering that sustainable development is a relative newcomer to mainstream political debate. Though it had some currency in the environmental movement, the concept was introduced to an international audience by the pioneering Brundtland Report in 1987. This is the source of the celebrated definition of sustainable development as "development that meets the needs of the present without compromising the ability of future generations to meet their own needs" (WCED 1987: 43).

In the Brundtland conception, this definition contained two key concepts: (1) the concept of 'needs', in particular the essential needs of the world's poor, to which overriding priority should be given; and (2) the idea of limitations imposed by the state of technology and social organization on the environment's ability to meet present and future needs. While the concepts of social needs, ecological limits and inter-generational equity commanded most attention, the Brundtland Report contained equally strong messages about democratic governance, calling for greater public participation and more devolved decision-making in resource management. But the strongest message of all concerned the "quality of growth" because:

> Sustainable development involves more than growth. It requires a change in the content of growth, to make it less material- and energy-intensive and more equitable in its impact. These changes are required in all countries as part of a package of measures to maintain the stock of ecological capital, to improve the distribution of income, and to reduce the degree of vulnerability to economic crises.
>
> (WCED 1987)

A perennial criticism of the Brundtland Report is that its definition of sustainable development is too vague to be of any practical benefit. But this is to miss the point because it is essentially "a normative standard that serves as a meta-objective for policy" (Meadowcroft 2007: 307). Like other normative concepts – democracy and justice, for

example – the concept of sustainable development will mean different things in different places because it is the concrete context that will determine the weight given to the social, economic and ecological dimensions of the concept. As a context-dependent concept, sustainable development needs to be understood as a spatial concept because it is grounded in the material circumstances of people and place, which is why local and regional context is so important to the politics of sustainability.

Since the concept was launched, some interpretations have given more weight to the environmental dimension, while others cleaved to the social dimension. Proponents of ecological modernization, for example, claim that capitalism can be rendered ever more sustainable through a progressive 'greening' process that helps to secure the twin goals of economic growth and environmental protection, a position that is totally at odds with "the radical green demand for a fundamental restructuring of the market economy and the liberal democratic state" (Carter 2007: 227). More radical schools of thought incline to a post-materialist interpretation of sustainable development, challenging the restless pursuit of consumption for its own sake and asking whether growth is actually necessary for prosperity (Jackson 2009).

However, the most important critique of the Brundtland conception albeit a sympathetic critique came from Amartya Sen, the architect of the capabilities approach to development. Although he welcomed the new prominence given to the idea of sustainable development, Sen asked whether the conception of human beings implicit in it is sufficiently capacious:

> Certainly, people have 'needs', but they also have values, and, in particular, they cherish their ability to reason, appraise, act and participate. Seeing people in terms only of their needs may give us a rather meagre view of humanity.
>
> (Sen 2004)

Sen's capabilities approach harbours radical implications for development studies, which have a tendency to conflate ends and means, reducing human development to economic growth (Morgan 2004). The capabilities approach enriches our understanding of development, particularly as regards the social dimension, because it defines the expansion of human freedom as both the primary end and the principal means of development. Sen identifies a number of substantive freedoms that are intrinsically significant ends in themselves, and not merely of instrumental significance for economic growth, though they are important in that respect as well. These substantive freedoms include "elementary capabilities like being able to avoid such deprivations as starvation, under-nourishment, escapable morbidity and premature mortality, as well as the freedoms that are associated with being literate and numerate, enjoying political participation and uncensored speech and so on" (Sen 1999: 36).

The capabilities perspective, with its stress on the social dimension of sustainability, is also a good antidote to partial definitions of sustainable development − as when human beings are considered to be no more than their living standards or when sustainability is reduced to mere environmentalism. When the partial view of Brundtland is supplemented with the broader perspective of Sen, we have the makings of a more capacious, more judicious conception of sustainable development − a conception that requires human beings to be actively involved in shaping their own destiny, a process that can be fostered by a state that takes sustainability seriously.

The return of the state?

The 'return of the state' was perhaps the only predictable aspect of the credit crunch crisis of 2008/09. Having been defined as part of the problem for so many years by the architects of neo-liberalism, the state was suddenly enrolled for crisis management duties, especially to bail out the banks and socialize their losses. But this is wholly consistent with the neo-liberal narrative, where the state is allotted a limited 'nightwatchman' role other than in times of crisis, when it is called upon to restore order. The neo-liberal state, in other words, tends to be much more active in practice than it is in theory (Harvey 2005).

The 'return of the state' has to be qualified in one important respect because, in many ways, it never really disappeared − at least not in practice. Even in the US, where anti-state ideology is most rife, the actual role of the state − federal, state and local − has always been greater than neo-liberal ideology is prepared to acknowledge.

If neo-liberalism failed to roll-back the state as much as it might have desired, it was spectacularly successful in devaluing the state and demeaning the public realm. As a result it created the impression that the national state has been rendered relatively powerless by globalization, which would penalize states that stepped outside the narrow parameters of the neo-liberal consensus. These (alleged) external pressures on the state were paralleled by very real internal pressures, particularly when the public sector was subjected to the narrow commercial logic of marketization, what one critic described as a Kulturkampf against the very notion of service and citizenship, the hallmarks of the public realm (Marquand 2004).

This is the political context in which the 'return of the state' is taking place, a process that began not with the credit crunch crisis but, rather, with the climate change crisis. As the greatest market failure of all time, the climate change crisis created a new ecological vocation for the state (Stern 2006). Where neo-liberals want to shrink the state, ecologists want to transform it into a Green State. Only the state, they argue, has the systemic capacity to induce more sustainable forms of production, consumption and regulation; and only states, especially when acting in concert, can counter the ecological damage wrought by globalization (Eckersley 2004). Like sustainable development, the Green State is a normative concept because it is essential, in this view, to have a conception of what the state ought to be doing: it is, in other words, "a green ideal or vision of what a 'good state' might look like" (Eckersley 2005: 160).

This normative turn in state theory chimes with the compelling philosophical argument of Martha Nussbaum, who argues that states should be held responsible for furnishing the social basis for key human capabilities, and she identifies ten universally applicable capabilities to which all men and women have a right "by virtue of being human" (Nussbaum 2000: 100). This normative-based capability approach rejects the utilitarian preference-based approach of neo-classical economic theory because of its desiccated conception of human beings. As Nussbaum says, "we have to grapple with the sad fact that contemporary economics has not yet put itself onto the map of conceptually respectable theories of human action" (Nussbaum 2000: 122).

As the state plays such a big role in these ecological and capability theories, it is surprising that so little attention is paid to its skills and powers. All the evidence suggests that the state's political capacity – to regulate the economy, deliver public services and procure goods and services, for example – needs to be substantially enhanced if it is to fashion more sustainable forms of development. The following section explores this theme of state capacity with respect to public food provisioning, a theme that is germane to the concerns of this chapter in two ways. First, the prosaic world of public food provisioning – in schools, hospitals, care homes, prisons and the like – is an intrinsically significant end in itself from a capability perspective. Second, the barriers to public food provisioning are a microcosm of a larger political paradox, which is that states often fail to deploy one of the greatest powers at their disposal – the power of purchase.

Public food provisioning: promoting sustainability through the power of purchase

States have a number of powers at their disposal to promote sustainable development, the most important of which are the powers of taxation, regulation and procurement. Of these, the power of purchase tends to be the most neglected, not least because it is often perceived as a lowly 'back office' function, which is truly paradoxical since public procurement is potentially one of the most powerful levers for effecting behavioural change among its private sector suppliers. The public sector constitutes an enormous market in virtually every country, accounting for up to 16 per cent of GDP in developed countries and as much as 20 per cent of GDP in developing countries. Although the power of purchase has been deployed for strategic ends usually for military purposes the story of public procurement is largely a tale of untapped potential (Morgan 2008a).

Politicians are belatedly waking up to this untapped potential because many states are turning to the power of purchase to promote their pet projects, including sustainable development. Although many sectors have a special significance in the sustainability debate – especially high CO_2-emitting sectors like energy and transport, for example – the agri-food sector has a unique status despite the neo-liberal belief that it is just like any other "industry". Quite apart from its umbilical link with nature, the exceptionalism of the agri-food sector stems from the fact that we ingest its products. Food is therefore vital to human health and well-being in a way that other sectors are not, and this is the reason why every state attaches such profound significance to it. Because of its unique role in human reproduction, food is the ultimate index of our capacity to care for ourselves, for others and for nature (Morgan 2008b).

The agri-food sector looms large in the sustainability debate because green campaigners believe it has the potential to offer multiple dividends:

> access to nutritious food is vitally important to human health and well-being – a health dividend;
> locally procured food can help to fashion new markets for small farmers, growers and producers – a local economic dividend;
> more sustainable food chains help to contain climate change by reducing the carbon footprint of the agri-food sector – an ecological dividend;
> more localized food chains allow consumers to reconnect with producers – a cultural dividend;
> less intensive and more welfare-conscious agri-food systems promote animal welfare – an ethical dividend;
> more fairly traded food chains enable consumers in the global north to express their solidarity with producers in the global south – a political dividend (Morgan 2008b).

Some or all of these dividends are being sought by local food campaigns in Europe and North America. Although some of these campaigns have attracted criticism for catering exclusively for an elite of high-income, quality-conscious consumers, and for privileging the local/green agenda over the global/fair agenda, these are not irredeemable features of the local food movement (Morgan 2008b). As we will see, public food reformers in Europe have consciously tried to overcome these problems by focusing on better food for all, particularly in school canteens, and by combining locally produced seasonal food with globally sourced, fairly traded food (Morgan and Sonnino 2008).

Local food movements are not confined to the rich countries of the global North, though the latter dominate the "alternative food" debates in the developed countries. To get a more textured understanding of local food movements, let us examine public food

reform in four countries which have been at the forefront of the debate.

Values for money: public food provisioning in Europe

School food reformers have been in the vanguard of public food reform in Europe largely because a moral panic about childhood obesity focused political attention on the diets of children. One of the key aims of school food reformers has been to persuade local authorities to serve healthier school meals by using fresh, locally produced ingredients. However, this seemingly simple and unpretentious ambition encountered a whole series of regulatory barriers, the most important of which was EU public procurement regulations that prohibited the explicit use of local food clauses in public sector catering contracts. Although these regulations applied equally throughout the EU, member states interpreted them very differently. Perhaps the biggest contrast of all was between Italy and the UK, arguably the opposite ends of the food culture spectrum in Europe. To understand these radically different interpretations of common EU regulations, we have to understand the political values that govern the procurement process as well as the cultural values that attach to food in Italy and the UK.

The quality of school food in the UK declined precipitously after the neo-liberal reforms of the Thatcher governments in the 1980s. These reforms transformed the school food service from a compulsory national subsidized service for all children to a discretionary local service. The most debilitating part of these reforms was the abolition of nutritional standards and the opening up of public contracts to private sector competition under a process called compulsory competitive tendering. While these provisions succeeded in creating a new low-cost catering culture, they also exacted a heavy toll on the quality of the food and the skills of the caterers.

Nothing less than a school food revolution is now underway in the UK, following a popular backlash against the neo-liberal reforms. While new and demanding nutritional standards were introduced by the Labour government in 2006, catering managers are struggling to overcome a public procurement culture in which low cost was allowed to masquerade as best value (Morgan and Sonnino 2008).

If public sector practices are slow to change, the political rhetoric around public procurement has been transformed because of its potential for promoting more sustainable forms of development. Launching a new public sector food procurement initiative, the sponsoring department said:

> If we are what we eat, then public sector food purchasers help shape the lives of millions of people. In hospitals, schools, prisons and canteens around the country, good food helps maintain good health, promoting healing rates and improve concentration and behaviour. But sustainable food procurement isn't just about better nutrition. It's about where the food comes from, how it's produced and transported, and where it ends up. It's about food quality, safety and choice. Most of all, it's about defining best value in its broadest sense.
>
> (Defra 2003)

As well as illustrating the multi-functional nature of sustainability, this statement also illustrates how far the vision of the state has changed from the neo-liberal heyday of Thatcherism, when lowest cost was the highest goal. The injunction to define 'best value in its broadest sense' was a clear indictment of the old procurement culture, where it was defined very narrowly.

Italian public authorities have always worked with a much broader understanding of 'best value' because food is imbued with deep cultural values and strong territorial associations given the fact that Italy, unlike the UK, had maintained the links between products and places. Far from being a symptom of primordial tradition, this food culture has been continuously fashioned by modern state interventions designed to help public bodies to purchase high-quality local food. While the UK was abolishing nutritional standards in the 1980s, Italy was promoting the Meditteranean diet into its public catering system. This was reinforced by Finance Law 488 (1999) which encouraged schools and hospitals to utilize 'organic, typical and traditional products as well as those from denominated areas'. The City of Rome, one of the leading school food services in Italy, now seeks 'guaranteed freshness' from its suppliers, rewarding them for abbreviating the time and space between harvesting and consumption (Morgan and Sonnino 2008).

The interplay between culture and politics has allowed public bodies in Italy to practise local food procurement without falling foul of EU procurement regulations. Although it is illegal to specify local products that can only be supplied by local producers (because this offends the EU principle of non-discrimination), it is possible to use certain quality marks – such as fresh, seasonal, organic, certified – that allow public bodies to purchase local food in all but name. These EU regulations worked to the advantage of Italy, with its strong links between produce and place, and against the UK, with its placeless foodscape.

The fact that Italy and the UK interpreted EU procurement regulations in such different ways clearly reflected their respective food cultures – local and seasonal in the former, placeless and processed in the latter. But contrasting food cultures are only part of the explanation. Equally important was the fact that state power was utilized in Italy to fashion markets, in this case for high-quality certified products; while in the UK it was used to mimic markets, by forcing public sector managers to compete with the private sector on the basis of price. Fashioning markets through national state action in the Italian case had the effect of creating sub-national economic development opportunities for local and regional producer associations.

Even so, the school food revolution in the UK proves that neither food culture nor public policy is set in aspic; on the contrary, both can be rendered more sustainable if the power of purchase reflects a range of values rather than a single, narrowly conceived economic metric.

Fome Zero: public food provisioning in Brazil

Brazil has attracted enormous international attention in recent years for its innovative state policies to reduce hunger and enhance food security. *Fome Zero* (Zero Hunger) is the umbrella strategy for more than 30 national programmes designed to combat the symptoms and causes of hunger in the largest economy in Latin America. Launched in 2003, Fome Zero was the social policy flagship of President Lula's Workers' Party government, which was elected in 2002. While some programmes were already established, the Lula government improved their quality, extended their reach and added some radically new ones. Three of the most significant programmes are the following (Rocha 2009).

Bolsa Familia: created in 2003, the Bolsa Familia (Family Grant) programme is a highly targeted, conditional cash-transfer scheme and it is the centre-piece of the government's social policy in terms of its coverage and its impact on poverty. By 2007 it was reaching all of its target of 11.1 million families, equivalent to 45 million people or a quarter of the total population. With 76 per cent of these transfers devoted to food, the programme helps poor families to improve their diets.

Programa Nacional de Alimentacao Escolar: the PNAE (National School Meals Programme) was launched in 1955, giving Brazil one of the first national school food systems in the developing world, and over 36 million

children are covered today. As federal funding only covers the cost of the food, this programme relies on partnerships with municipal governments, which have to meet the costs of personnel and infrastructure. Since 2001 a new emphasis has been placed upon basic foods (such as fresh fruits and vegetables) and the promotion of local food as opposed to processed food.

Programa de Aquisicao de Alimentos: the PAA (Food Procurement Programme) was launched as a new federal programme in 2003 to assist the poorest farmers by purchasing directly from them. The publicly purchased products help to build food stocks that are utilized in state food programmes, such as school meals or food banks. PAA is present in over 3,500 municipalities throughout the country and in 2006 it helped to maintain the income of more than 11,000 small farmers. The programme also helps to reduce local price fluctuations by building food stocks, providing stability for farmers to form cooperatives and associations, which is one of the requirements of PAA support.

To be effective, these federal programmes require a politically committed local government partner, which is especially important for a successful school meals programme because the council has to share the local delivery costs and animate the service.

There is no better example of a committed local partner than Belo Horizonte, the fourth largest city in Brazil and the capital of Minas Gerais state. With the election of Patrus Ananias as mayor in 1993, the city government declared food to be a right of citizenship, and Belo launched a whole series of food security programmes with citizen groups in civil society, making the city a beacon of urban food security in Brazil (Rocha 2001). In a food-insecure world, Belo is also extolled as a model for other countries, developed as well as developing, because it is seen as "the city that ended hunger" (Lappe 2009). Belo's pioneering role in promoting urban food security was officially recognized when its mayor, Patrus Ananias, was promoted to the federal government as Minister for Social Development and Fight Against Hunger.

These national and local food security strategies suggest one thing above all – that politics matters. Without the Workers' Party government, federally in Brazil and locally in Belo, the principle of food security would never have received such robust political support. The big question surrounding Fome Zero concerns its political sustainability because President Lula, with whom it is closely associated, has to retire after two terms despite his personal popularity. Food policy experts like Cecilia Rocha believe that the strategy will outlive the Lula government because food citizenship has taken root in civil society and because food security has been institutionalized, rendering it the responsibility of the state rather than of governments (Rocha 2009).

Home grown: public food provisioning in Ghana

Ghana is to Africa what Brazil is to Latin America, which is to say a pioneer of public food provisioning. Despite occasional bouts of political instability since 1957, when it won its independence, Ghana is now considered to be one of the most stable and best governed states in Africa. Political stability furnished the most important condition for the Home Grown School Feeding initiative, a radically new development strategy that aims to secure a double dividend of health and wealth by (1) providing children with nutritious school food, and (2) creating new markets for local producers by purchasing the food locally instead of importing it from developed countries like the US in the form of food aid. However laudable it might seem, imported food aid actually undermines the indigenous agri-food sector in developing countries, making it less likely that they can feed themselves (Morgan and Sonnino 2008).

Launched in 2006 with support from the UN and the Dutch government, the Ghana School Feeding Programme (GSFP) had three national objectives: (1) to reduce hunger and malnutrition; (2) to increase school enrolment, attendance and retention, especially of girls; and (3) to boost domestic food production. Although Ghana did extremely well to get such an ambitious programme off the ground – since other African states failed to do so – the GSFP has proved to be a very steep learning curve, especially as regards governance and procurement.

To implement the programme a wholly new multi-level governance system was created at national, regional, district and community levels, a serious mistake because the new bodies had no legal mandate and co-existed with the legally constituted state institutions which kept their distance. The public procurement process has also failed to live up to expectations because it was difficult to calibrate supply and demand at a local level, not least because agriculture is dominated by small subsistence farmers, some of whom have as little as 1.6 hectares of land each. Although the agricultural sector has been growing in Ghana, its development is stymied by a combination of inefficient farming practices and poor marketing outlets for farm produce. A combination of supply-side bottlenecks, weak procurement skills and poor governance has meant that the GSFP has been more challenging than anyone envisaged.

While the UN was correct to say that the home-grown model offers a new and more sustainable development strategy for developing countries, it was wholly wrong to suggest that it could provide "quick wins" in the battle against hunger. The fate of the GSFP ought to be of concern to every developing country because, despite its modest name, it is about so much more than just school food: on the contrary, it embodies the entire drama of development in microcosm. Learning to design a home-grown school feeding system involves a whole series of other learning curves – in governance, procurement and rural development, for example. The home-grown model therefore needs to be understood as a learning-by-doing exercise in which the end product, the provision of nutritious food, is just one part of a much larger process (Morgan and Sonnino 2008).

Conclusions

The central argument of this chapter is that food is one of the most important prisms through which to explore local and regional development because of its unique role in human health and well-being. It was also argued that the public provision of food is a litmus test of the state's commitment to sustainability because, insofar as it addresses human health, social justice and environmental integrity, it embodies the foundational values of sustainable development. Over and above this general point, three more specific conclusions emerge from the analysis.

First, sustainability can be regarded as a new developmental narrative to the extent that it incorporates social and economic as well as environmental values. The capability perspective helps to keep the social and economic dimensions in the frame because it identifies a set of capabilities that are essential for fully human functioning – an approach that focuses on what people are actually able to do and to be, a more compelling metric than the conventional metric of per capita income. However, sustainability will mean different things in different contexts, which is why it is important to understand it in spatial terms. The significance of spatial context – between North and South at the global level and between localities and regions at the national level – helps to explain why different people in different places produce such variable interpretations of what sustainability means for them.

Second, politics matters. State steering played a critical role in each of the country case studies – reinforcing the traditional food system in the case of Italy, reforming it in the others. The influence of the Green State will

depend on its organizational capacity, its political values and, above all, the balance of power in civil society – a combination of internal and external factors that will vary from country to country.

Finally, public food provisioning strategies serve different priorities in different countries. If cultural and ecological values are the priorities of provisioning strategies in Europe, food security is the overriding priority in Brazil and Ghana. But in all these cases, the power of purchase is now informed by values that are more capacious than the neo-liberal template, where low cost masquerades as best value.

References

Carter, N. (2007) *The Politics of the Environment*, Cambridge: Cambridge University Press.

Cities Alliance (2009) *2009 Annual Report: Building Cities and Citizenship*, Washington: Cities Alliance. Available at: http://www.citiesalliance.org/ca/sites/citiesalliance.org/files/Anual_Reports/AR09_FullText_0.pdf.

Defra (2003) *Unlocking Opportunities: Lifting the Lid on Public Sector Food Procurement*, London: Defra.

Eckersley, R. (2004) *The Green State: Rethinking Democracy and Sovereignty*, London: MIT Press.

Harvey, D. (2005) *A Brief History of Neoliberalism*, Oxford: Oxford University Press.

Jackson, T. (2009) *Prosperity Without Growth?*, London: Sustainable Development Commission.

Keil R. (2007) "Sustaining modernity, modernizing nature: the environmental crisis and the survival of capitalism," in R. Krueger and D.C. Gibbs (eds) *The Sustainable Development Paradox*, London: Guilford, 41–65.

Krueger, R. and Savage, L. (2007) "City-regions and social reproduction: a 'place' for sustainable development?", *International Journal of Urban and Regional Research*, 31, 215–23.

Lappe, F. M. (2009) "The City That Ended Hunger", www.yesmagazine.org/article.asp?ID=3330.

Marquand, D. (2004) *Decline of the Public*, Cambridge: Polity Press.

Meadowcroft, J. (2007) "Who is in charge here?: Governance for sustainable development in a complex world", *Journal of Environmental Policy and Planning*, 9 (4), 299–314.

Morgan, K. (2004) "Sustainable regions: Governance, innovation and scale", *European Planning Studies*, 12 (6), 871–889.

Morgan, K. (2008a) "Greening the realm: Sustainable food chains and the public plate", *Regional Studies*, 42 (9), 1237–1250.

Morgan, K. (2008b) *Local and Green v Global and Fair: The New Geopolitics of Care*, BRASS Working Paper 50, Cardiff University.

Morgan, K. and Sonnino, R. (2008) *The School Food Revolution: Public Food and Sustainable Development*, London: Earthscan.

Nussbaum, M. (2000) *Women and Human Development*, New York: Cambridge University Press.

Rocha, C. (2001) "Urban food security policy: The Case of Belo Horizonte, Brazil", *Journal for the Study of Food and Society*, 5 (1), 36–47.

Rocha, C. (2009) "Developments in national policies for food and nutrition security in Brazil", *Development Policy Review*, 27 (1), 51–66.

Sen, A. (1999) *Development as Freedom*, Oxford: Oxford University Press.

Sen, A. (2004) "Why we should preserve the spotted owl", *London Review of Books*, 26 (3), February.

Stern, N. (2006) *The Economics of Climate Change*, London: HM Treasury.

World Commission on Environment and Development (1987) *Our Common Future*, Oxford: Oxford University Press.

Further reading

Morgan, K. and Sonnino, R. (2008) *The School Food Revolution: Public Food and the Challenge of Sustainable Development*, London: Earthscan.

Nussbaum, M. (2000) *Women and Human Development: The Capabilities Approach*, Cambridge : Cambridge University Press.

Sen, A. (1999) *Development as Freedom*, Oxford: Oxford University Press.

8

Alternative approaches to local and regional development

Allan Cochrane

Introduction

Traditionally, and certainly until the 1980s, regional policy was understood in terms that started from the identification of 'distressed' or otherwise economically disadvantaged regions, and local economic development was similarly framed within a discourse of economic decline or decay. Policy tended to focus on the attempt to attract new industries, even to encourage relocation from more prosperous to less prosperous regions. Since the mid-1990s, however, emphasis has been placed on self-help, looking for ways in which regions might be able to generate growth and prosperity through the initiative of locally based actors, businesses and public agencies. Similarly, a more positive interpretation of the potential role of cities has become noticeable as a policy driver in recent years (Cochrane 2007).

In this context, over the last couple of decades, local and regional development has increasingly been framed in terms of 'competitiveness', in what has persuasively been described as the 'new conventional wisdom' (Buck *et al.* 2005). This 'new conventional wisdom' is globally fostered through organisations such as the OECD and the World Bank and is seen as suitable for application in

the countries of the global South as much as those of the global North (see e.g. Charbit *et al.* 2005, Hall and Pfeiffer 2000). From the perspective of the World Bank, it is regional uneven development that fosters growth – and they offer a policy approach in which what is described as 'unbalanced growth' is somehow coupled with 'inclusive development' (World Bank 2008).

Successful cities and regions are understood to be those which are competitive, in the sense that they are able to respond effectively to the opportunities generated by the workings of the global economy. Competitive places are generally said to have 'entrepreneurial' political leadership, as well as a flexible and educated or creative labour force, able to support the requirements of a (new) knowledge economy. This vision of development somehow manages to incorporate a belief in the ability of government and partnership agencies to shape development while at the same time leaving them with little policy option. They are required to find some way of fitting in with the inexorable requirements of global markets.

Within this understanding of the problem, instead of being victims of wider structural forces, regions and city-regions become more or less active participants in shaping their futures. Within what is seen to be an increasingly globalised world, they are given the responsibility of carving out their own economic and social spaces. And all this seems to have been reinforced by the shift of public policy emphasis to city-regions (see e.g. Charbit *et al.* 2005, Harrison 2007, Ward and Jonas 2004).

Moving beyond competitiveness

However, competitiveness is ultimately an unconvincing way of capturing the process by which different forms of local and regional development are generated. At best the labelling of places as 'competitive' is a retrospective one – in other words, instead of explaining what is happening, it starts from outcomes and labels 'successful' places 'competitive'. Because they are successful, the argument runs, they must have been competitive. In other words, the 'new conventional wisdom' identified by Buck *et al.* (2005) must, as they note, be seen as a political or ideological project, as much as a realistic assessment of development processes (see also Bristow 2005, this volume).

Even within a competitiveness paradigm there has been some significant variation, so that, for example, Florida (2002) called on rather a different vision identifying the context within which he argued creative industries might be expected to flourish. His celebration of a creative class even appeared to open up the possibility of progressive engagement by suggesting that bohemianism was an attractive feature in encouraging development. In practice, however, Florida's approach generated its own still sharper emphasis on competitiveness, ranking cities by the extent to which they exhibited the features supposedly needed for success. It became another template apparently capable of global application in a world of fast policy transfer, with Florida himself marketed as a guru whose ideas were eagerly consumed and propagated through city networks (see Peck (2005, 2010) for a critique).

The 'smart growth' movement is another US export that has found proponents in Europe and elsewhere, with its emphasis on compact development, green space and the use of market mechanisms as drivers of change. It promises a means of squaring the circle of sustainability and economic growth while in practice being fundamentally incorporated into the competitiveness agenda. It has become a selling point for those metropolitan regions taking it up as a planning model (see e.g. Krueger and Gibbs 2008). Keil powerfully describes the way in which sustainability has been mobilised as a political strategy, 'as one of the possible routes for neoliberal renewal of the capitalist accumulation process', enabling 'prosperous development with rather than against "nature"' (Keil 2007: 46). Sustainability is re-imagined as providing the necessary underpinning for successful 'market-based' capitalist development (see also Krueger and Savage 2007, While *et al.* 2004b).

Similar points could be made about a range of policy approaches that seem to offer ways of meeting the challenges of neoliberalism in different contexts. The shift in the political rhetoric of the World Bank and other global agencies, for example, that has seen the problem of the global 'slums' re-imagined, in terms that emphasise their entrepreneurial potential and refer to the possibility of 'empowering' their residents, is quite remarkable (see Cities Alliance 1999, Robinson 2010). However, here, too, it is impossible to miss the extent to which this remains a policy of adaptation or a repositioning within a competitive environment – the tools may be different, but the broad framework of assumptions remains that of the 'new conventional wisdom'.

In their review of the international experience, reviewing a set of case studies from North America and Western Europe, Savitch and Kantor (2002) suggest that even in terms of the global market-place, those localities where a more social-democratic and less neo-liberal agenda has been pursued tend to have better outcomes for local populations. So, there may be scope for some variation at the edges but there seems little seriously to challenge the main economic and political drivers. In the following sections, therefore, an attempt will be made to consider some of the strategies that seek more directly and explicitly to challenge the dominant model.

Developing alternative models I – the New Urban Left

The competitiveness logic has taken such a hold on contemporary policy discourse that it is sometimes hard to remember the relatively recent history of radical initiatives which quite explicitly sought to develop alternative approaches. It has almost become a forgotten history, and certainly one on which no public policy professional with an interest in promotion is likely to draw explicitly (although see Peck (2011) for a recent discussion). This section focuses on the specific experience of the UK, but it is worth noting that similar issues were being raised by urban social movements in other European countries and other cities across the world (see e.g. Castells 1978, Fisher and Kling 1993).

The first half of the 1980s was the time of the 'New Urban Left' or the 'New Municipal socialism' in the UK, with its promise of different approaches to economic development (see e.g. Boddy and Fudge 1984, Cochrane 1986, 1988, Gyford 1985, Lansley et al. 1989). Several councils set up enterprise boards (most notably London and the West Midlands), while others created larger employment or economic development departments (most notably in Sheffield).

The arguments underpinning these developments were clear: if local government continued to restrict itself to operating as provider of social services, picking up the pieces of economic decline and unemployment, then

it would never be able to meet the needs of local residents. Instead it was important to move actively into trying to manage or shape the local economy, generating welfare through such intervention and not just acting as a 'safety net'. The Enterprise Boards (and particularly the Greater London Enterprise Board) saw themselves as having the task of influencing economic change through the negotiation of planning agreements with enterprises (including a range of worker co-operatives) in which it invested or otherwise supported. The Greater London Council (GLC) developed a series of major plans and strategies for the London economy – most notably in the form of the London Industrial Strategy, but also in strategies for the labour market and the finance sector (GLC 1985, GLC 1986a, 1986b). In Sheffield similar initiatives were developed with the aim of working with businesses and trade unions to develop employment that would guarantee security for city residents and encourage investment in training. A plan was developed for the reclaiming and reuse of the Lower Don Valley, previously a major centre of large-scale steel production and heavy engineering (see e.g. Blunkett and Green (1983) and Lawless and Ramsden (1990) for discussions of Sheffield's approach to public policy).

The emphasis of all these initiatives was on the possibility of longer term investment that would enable older industrial communities to survive, through a process of repositioning, rather than a simple (and ultimately hopeless) defence of existing industry. It was argued that the 'New Right' (or neo-liberal) policies of Thatcherism led to closure of industry and the destruction of communities, without offering any prospect of revival. Aram Eisenschitz and Jamie Gough (1996) have forcibly argued that while these initiatives (which they label neo-Keynesian local economic development policies) might have mitigated the effects of neo-liberalism, they also made it easier for the ends of neo-liberalism to be achieved, because of the way in which they encouraged flexibility, sponsoring the creation of new 'competitive' enterprises and fostering training programmes that fitted workers for the new regime.

But this was not how it was understood at the time. The local authorities taking the lead in developing the new economic policies became the focus of government attention, which led to the abolition of the metropolitan counties (such as GLC and West Midlands). As a result the enterprise boards that survived became more narrowly focused and began to redefine themselves as regional investment banks working closely with other financial institutions (see e.g. Cochrane and Clarke 1990). As Robin Murray noted, what the supporters of the New Urban Left saw as 'liberated economic zones have had their frontiers pushed back, their conduct questioned, and their lack of popular support exposed' (Murray 1987: 47).

The economic initiatives of the New Urban Left were not only rooted in a particular political moment – the new dominance of Thatcherism, the failure of the Labour Party leadership in the face of economic crisis and political challenge, community and trade union resistance to cuts – but also in a strong municipal tradition: this was a movement that saw the capturing of the local state and its mobilisation to achieve radical ends as opening up new opportunities (see Boddy and Fudge 1986). With the partial exception of London under the mayoralty of Ken Livingstone in the early years of the twenty-first century, little remains of this vision, as the Labour Party has not only lost its hegemony in urban local government, but also any interest in pursuing a radical localist agenda.

Developing alternative models II – the politics of localisation

But this does not mean that there are no alternatives to the new conventional wisdom emerging in more informal – yet potentially

powerful – ways. If the New Urban Left still saw its role as challenging forms of capitalist development, some of these approaches seem to owe more to an understanding of the world which emphasise the possibility of building non-capitalist practices even within a broadly capitalist economy. Although they do not explicitly draw on the work of J.K. Gibson-Graham (1996), the underlying assumptions about the possibilities associated with the existence of multiple economic spaces are similar.

At their most generalised these approaches come together in the identification of the social economy as somehow distinct from the formal economy, or – at any rate – the commodified economy, the space of the market. In a sense the social economy is defined by what it is not (that is, not traded in the market or provided by the state) but it seems to carry a greater promise – of community action, collective working, self-help, charitable activity, conviviality. In some versions, it is identified as the 'third sector' to distinguish it from the private and public sectors. Jamie Gough and Aram Eisenschitz (2006) describe it as 'associationalism'.

Ash Amin, Angus Cameron and Ray Hudson (2002) identify two justifications for involvement in the social economy which are relevant in this context. The first suggests that it is in the social economy where community building and the development of social capital takes place and the second that it is within the social economy and through engagement with it, particularly at local level, that social justice from below might be delivered through forms of empowerment (Amin et al. 2002: 7). Amin et al. (2002) are generally sceptical of the grander claims made for the social economy in tackling social exclusion. In particular, they note that (with a few exceptions) little direct employment is created through such initiatives, although more indirect help is provided (e.g. through training programmes). Success, they note, is the exception rather than the expectation (Amin et al. 2002: 116).

Alongside this broad discovery of and engagement with the social economy, a series of movements have developed in recent years which have opened up new ways of thinking about local economies and their linkages, emphasising and celebrating localness and the features associated with it. They have drawn attention to the benefits of building trust and confidence at community level and have deliberately focused on the small scale and local as offering a way forward. Some have even called for a process of 'relocalisation' (Hopkins 2008). The important point here is that these are social movements, not government initiatives. They have tended to combine a commitment to self-help with a strong desire to identify alternatives to dominant economic practices.

Perhaps the best known of these in the UK are LETS (Local Exchange Trading Schemes), but similar or related initiatives are to be found in other countries, including Argentina, France, Germany, Italy, Holland, Belgium, Canada, Australia, the US, Hungary and New Zealand (see Aldridge and Patterson 2002, North 2005, 2006, 2008, Williams et al. 2003: 157–158). These schemes basically involve the creation of local associations whose members are prepared to exchange goods and services with each other in return for payment in a locally based currency. According to one survey conducted at the end of the 1990s, the average membership of LETS in the UK was just over 71 members and the average turnover was the equivalent of £4,664 (Williams et al. 2003: 158). This suggests that their economic impact is likely to be relatively small, but Williams et al. (2003) conclude that modest impact can be identified, particularly in giving some people a base on which to build in developing more secure employment but – more important – in providing additional work for some of those in more precarious forms of employment or self-employment. From this perspective, they can be seen as a form of collective self-help, not a potential alternative to what is provided through the formal economy but nevertheless good 'at providing alternative forms of livelihood' (Williams et al. 2003: 152).

The extent to which LETS can be maintained over time or generalised more widely remains questionable, however, precisely because of their localisation within quite specific networks of trust and reciprocity. They tend to rely on what Roger Lee (1996) has called moral geographies of localism. In some cases, too, as Williams et al. (2003) note, the very success of LETS in opening up opportunities for members may undermine their grander ambitions, because they may be able more fully to move into commercial exploitation of the goods and services they offer. LETS are particularly attractive for those who are self-employed in managing their working lives, but the balance between working in the social economy and the formal economy may change over time as (or if) their livelihoods become more secure.

However, the underlying principles of LETS also point to more radical (non- or anti-capitalist) possibilities. As Peter North argues, one of the justifications for the schemes is that:

Users of local currencies, irrespective of their values, will find they are structured into localized relations as the economic signals produced by a local currency steer rational economic agents towards more readily available locally or ethically produced goods and services, organic or environmentally benign food and the like, that has been produced under a local surveillance that ensures only sustainable practices are used. Structuration occurs as users find that while there will always be people willing to spend local currencies with them, to pass these local units on they will need to develop a local supply chain that meets their needs and which also accepts the local currency. They will have to pay close attention to the needs of and the quality of their relationships with these other local traders, as there are few pressures to compel anyone to accept relatively unlimited local currencies from someone who is not seen as a 'good community member' (perhaps as they are perceived to be polluting, exploiting others or unfriendly)... it is argued, local currencies actively create local-scale, humane economies by rewarding those who build these localized networks.

(North 2005: 225–226)

In this context, they can be seen as offering the possibility of genuine political action, and many of the members identify political commitment as a reason for involvement (Williams *et al.* 2003: 158). The core promise is that (localised) trust can be translated into action. The building of relatively discrete local economies is seen as a means of challenging the power of global economic processes, through practices of localisation. From this perspective, local currencies can be seen as working to localise social relations, containing markets by limiting their spatial extent.

Here, the overlap with the transition towns movement (which now involves communities in England, Scotland, Wales, Ireland New Zealand, US, Australia, Italy, Chile, Germany, Canada, Finland, Japan and Holland) highlights the extent to which a wider vision of local and regional development may be possible. The transition towns movement was born out of the belief that globally the moment of peak oil production was approaching or had already been reached. The implication of this is that the time has come for people collectively to plan for the lives that they would have to lead without cheap oil. Although intertwined with concerns about climate change, the main driver is rather a different one – not focused on the attempt to reduce carbon emissions to maintain existing economic and social relations, but rather looking for ways of changing those

relations to build an improved life in a low-oil, low-carbon economy. It is argued that what is needed is a vision focused on the local and the small scale as a means of enabling people to work together and live well together. Building resilience means rebuilding trust through local social relations and local economies. The politics of the movement is one that eschews any top-down campaigning or political structures, instead favouring a network approach, and celebrating the 'viral spread' of the idea community by community, 'town' by 'town' (Hopkins 2008).

A narrow focus on the local, however, even in the context of these wider ambitions, still raises questions about what is possible and what the constraints set by the wider political, social and economic context might be. In the context of their review of activity in the social economy, based on a series of local case studies, Amin *et al.* (2002) point out that the more successful initiatives are those that access resources beyond the local. In the Tower Hamlets (London) case they note that 'what is interesting is that while all the projects...are 'local' in that they serve the needs of specific areas within the borough, they rely on inputs from activists, networks, and other resources from outside the immediate area' (Amin *et al.* 2002: 113) They talk about the importance of 'non local localness', of initiatives that are 'place based but not place bound' (Amin *et al.* 2002: 115).

This suggests that scaling up is important not just so that lessons can be learned for wider implementation, but also to ensure that place-based initiatives may be able to flourish. Thad Williamson, David Imbroscio and Gar Alperowitz (2002) take a similarly strong line in the US context, actively seeking to build forms of local dependency writings (see Cox 1997). They outline and explore a whole series of specific initiatives, drawing on federal, state and local government, as well as community-based and third sector agencies, to develop what they describe as a new agenda aimed at delivering what they call a 'place respecting political-economy in the face of the triple threat of sprawl, internal capital mobility, and globalization' (Williamson *et al.* 2002: 310). Like Amin *et al.* (2002) they stress that it is only by calling on resources from a range of agencies, formally identified with a range of government levels and spatial scales, that it is possible to deliver 'community centred, place stabilizing policies' (Williamson *et al.* 2002: 310). In other words, for them, even the building of such places requires a set of policy interventions that are not simply local – community -based self-help may be necessary, but it is not sufficient.

Doreen Massey's consideration of a global politics of place takes the argument further. She points to the significance of the agreement negotiated while Ken Livingstone was mayor of London which brought Venezuelan oil to London, while transport planning expertise was made available to Caracas as a good example of how such a politics might develop in a reciprocal way (Massey 2007, 2010). In practise, of course, the scheme was brought to an end with Livingstone's defeat in the 2008 mayoral elections, but the principle that the politics of local and regional development are more than local is one that remains important.

Possibilities and constraints

It sometimes appears as if the possibilities faced by regions and localities are highly restricted – either they learn to play the competitiveness game within a globalised (neo-liberal) economy or they are doomed to decline. However, it is apparent that not all of those being positioned in this way are prepared to accept such a role. There continues to be substantial variation between places and 'success' may be defined in a range of different ways. Andy Pike, Andrés Rodríguez-Pose and John Tomaney explore what some of these different ways of understanding success might be – moving beyond narrow economic criteria to consider other forms of well-being – and suggest that policy makers should aspire to delivering 'holistic, progressive and sustainable local and regional development' (Pike *et al.* 2007: 1262).

There is also accumulating evidence that community-based initiatives can be successful, not only in resisting change being imposed by the drive of the property development industry and government policy commitments to 'urban renaissance', which generally imply gentrification and the reshaping of existing communities. Libby Porter and Kate Shaw (2009) bring together a series of case studies of community initiative and community action oriented towards economic development and regeneration (often in resistance to or engagement with state policies oriented towards renaissance and gentrification) from a range of cities across the world, which highlight both the scope within which action is possible and some of the limits placed on it. They question approaches which suggest that urban regeneration in practice is simply an expression of neo-liberal power, highlighting the scope for local action, while acknowledging the limits placed on it. It is only by focusing on the scope for action and initiative in particular places and in particular contexts that judgements about what is possible can be made.

The extent to which local initiative can more fundamentally challenge the direction of change remains open to question, however. As we have seen, some (such as those associated with transition towns) believe it is only local action linked through networks that can challenge the direction of change associated with global capitalism; others, however, emphasise the need to work across levels, to construct a politics that is global and local, regional and national, reaching out to draw in other economic and political actors, at the same time as also being drawn into their spheres of influence. And, of course, there remain those who are sceptical about the overall potential of local and regional action, if it is not set within some wider programme or agenda for change – part of a wider movement, which goes beyond viral connections and networks.

References

Aldridge, T. and Patterson, A. (2002) 'LETS get real: constraints on the development of Local Exchange Trading Schemes', *Area*, 34, 4: 370–381.

Amin, A., Cameron, A. and Hudson, R. (2002) *Placing the Social Economy*, London: Routledge.

Atkinson, R. and Moon, G. (1994) *Urban Policy in Britain. The City, the State and the Market*, Basingstoke and London: Macmillan.

Blunkett, D. and Green, G. (1983) 'Building from the bottom. The Sheffield experience', *Fabian Tract 491*, London: The Fabian Society.

Boddy, M. and Fudge, C. (eds) (1984) *Local Socialism? Labour Councils and New Left Alternatives*, Basingstoke: Macmillan.

Bristow, G. (2005) 'Everyone's a "winner": problematising the discourse of regional competitiveness', *Journal of Economic Geography*, 5, 3: 285–304.

Buck, N., Gordon, I., Harding, A. and Turok, I. (2005) *Changing Cities. Rethinking Urban Competiveness, Cohesion and Governance*, Basingstoke: Palgrave Macmillan.

Castells, M. (1978) *City, Class and Power*, London: Macmillan.

Charbit, C. and Davies, A. with Hervé, A. (2005) *Building Competitive Regions. Strategies and Governance*, Paris: OECD.

Cochrane, A. (1986) 'Local employment initiatives: towards a new municipal socialism?' in Lawless, P. and Raban, C. (eds) *The Contemporary British City*, London: Harper and Row.

Cochrane, A. (1988) 'In and against the market? The development of socialist local economic strategies, 1981–1986', *Policy and Politics*, 16, 3: 159–168.

Cochrane, A. (2007) *Understanding Urban Policy. A Critical Approach*, Oxford: Blackwell.

Cochrane, A. and Clarke, A. (1990) 'Local enterprise boards: the short history of a radical initiative', *Public Administration*, 68, 3: 315–336.

Cox, K. (ed.) (1997) *Spaces of Globalization. Reasserting the Power of the Local*, New York: Guilford.

Eisenschitz, A. and Gough, J. (1996) 'The contradictions of neo-Keynesian local economic strategy', *Review of International Political Economy*, 3, 3: 434–458.

Fisher, R. and Kling, J. (eds) (1993) *Mobilizing the Community. Local Politics in the Era of the Global City*, Newbury Park, CA: Sage.

Florida, R. (2002) *The Rise of the Creative Class: And How It's Transforming Work, Leisure, Community and Everyday Life*, New York: Basic Books.

GLC (1985) *The London Industrial Strategy*, London: Greater London Council.

GLC (1986a) *The London Financial Strategy*, London: Greater London Council.

GLC (1986b) *The London Labour Plan*, London: Greater London Council.

Gibson-Graham, J. K. (1996) *The End of Capitalism (As We Knew It): A Feminist Critique of Political Economy*, Oxford: Blackwell.

Gough, J. and Eisenschitz, A. with McCulloch, A. (2006) *Spaces of Social Exclusion*, London: Routledge.

Gyford, J. (1985) *The Politics of Local Socialism*, London: George Allen & Unwin.

Hall, P. and Pfeiffer, U. (2000) *Urban Future 21: A Global Agenda for Twenty-first Century Cities*, London: Spon.

Harrison, J. (2007) 'From competitive regions to competitive city-regions. A new orthodoxy but some old mistakes', *Journal of Economic Geography*, 7, 3: 311–332.

Hopkins, R. (2008) *The Transition Handbook. From Oil Dependency to Local Resilience*, Dartington: Green Books.

Krueger, R. and Gibbs, D. (2008) '"Third wave" sustainability? Smart growth and regional development', *Regional Studies*, 42, 9: 1263–1274.

Lansley, S., Goss, S. and Wolmar, C. (1989) *Councils in Conflict. The Rise and Fall of the Municiapal Left*, Basingstoke: Macmillan.

Lawless, P. and Ramsden, P. (1990) 'Sheffield in the 1980s. From radical intervention to partnership', *Cities*, 7, 3: 202–210.

Lee, R. (1996) 'Moral money? LETS and the social construction of local economic geographies in Southeast England', *Environment and Planning A*, 28, 8: 1377–1394.

Leyshon, A., Lee, R. and Williams, C. (eds) *Alternative Economic Spaces*, London: Sage.

McCann, E. and Ward, K. (eds) *Assembling Urbanism: Mobilizing Knowledge and Shaping Cities in a Global Context*, Minneapolis: University of Minnesota Press.

Massey, D. (2007) *World City*, Cambridge: Polity.

Massey, D. (forthcoming 2011) 'A counter hegemonic relationality of place', in McCann, E. and Ward, K. (eds) *Assembling Urbanism: Mobilizing Knowledge & Shaping Cities in a*

Global Context, Minnesota: University of Minnesota Press.

Murray, R. (1987) *Breaking with Bureaucracy. Ownership, Control and Nationalisation*, Manchester: Centre for Local Economic Strategies.

North, P. (2005) 'Scaling alternative economic practices? Some lessons from alternative currencies', *Transactions of the Institute of British Geographers*, 30: 221–233.

North, P. (2006) 'Constructing civil society? Green money in transition Hungary', *Review of International Political Economy*, 13, 1: 28–52.

North, P. (2008) *Money and Liberation. The Micropolitics of Alternative Currency Movements*, Minneapolis: University of Minnesota Press.

Peck, J. (2005) 'Struggling with the creative class', *International Journal of Urban and Regional Research*, 29, 4: 740–770.

Peck, J. (forthcoming 2011) 'Creative moments: working culture, through municipal socialism and neoliberal urbanism', in McCann, E. and Ward, K. (eds) *Assembling Urbanism: Mobilizing Knowledge & Shaping Cities in a Global Context*, Minnesota: University of Minnesota Press.

Pike, A., Rodríguez-Pose, A. and Tomaney, J. (2007) 'What kind of local and regional development and for whom?', *Regional Studies*, 41 (9): 1253–1269.

Porter, L. and Shaw, K. (eds) (2009) *Whose Urban Renaissance? An International Comparison of Urban Regeneration Strategies*, London: Routledge.

Robinson, J. (forthcoming 2011) 'The spaces of circulating knowledge: city strategies and global urban governmentality', in McCann, E. and Ward, K. (eds) *Assembling Urbanism: Mobilizing Knowledge & Shaping Cities in a Global Context*, Minnesota: University of Minnesota Press.

Savitch, H. and Kantor, P. (2002) *Cities in the International Marketplace. The Political Economy of Urban Development in North America and Western Europe*, Princeton: Princeton University Press.

Ward, K. and Jonas, A. (2004) 'Competitive city-regionalism as a politics of space: a critical reinterpretation of the new regionalism', *Environment and Planning A*, 36, 12: 2119–2139.

Williams, C., Aldridge, A. and Tooke, J. (2003) 'Alternative exchange spaces', in Leyshon, A., Lee, R. and Williams, C. (eds) *Alternative Economic Spaces*, London: Sage Publications.

Williamson, T., Imbroscio, D. and Alperovitz, G. (2002) *Making a Place for Community. Local Democracy in a Global Era*, New York: Routledge.

World Bank (2008) *World Development Report 2009. Reshaping Economic Geography*, Washington, DC: World Bank.

Further reading

Amin, A., Cameron, A. and Hudson, R. (2002) *Placing the Social Economy*, London: Routledge. (Critically reviews claims that the social economy offers new and more empowering ways of delivering development.)

Hopkins, R. (2008) *The Transition Handbook. From Oil Dependency to Local Resilience*, Dartington: Green Books. (Classic statement of the vision behind transition towns and transition culture.)

Leyshon, A., Lee, R. and Williams, C. (eds.) (2003) *Alternative Economic Spaces*, London: Sage. (Reviews a series of different ways of developing alternative forms of economic development at local level and beyond.)

North, P. (2008) *Money and Liberation. The Micropolitics of Alternative Currency Movements*, Minneapolis: University of Minnesota Press. (Widely framed discussion of experiments in the development of alternative currencies, the underlying tensions and possibilities.)

Williamson, T., Imbroscio, D. and Alperovitz, G. (2002) *Making a Place for Community. Local Democracy in a Global Era*, New York: Routledge. (A powerfully argued case for the centrality of community as a basis for successful, fair and sustained development.)

Section III

Concepts and theories of local and regional development

9

Spatial circuits of value

Ray Hudson

Introduction

Economic activity involves the production, circulation and consumption of value, typically embodied in material artefacts or in services. Such activity is inherently geographical, in two senses: first, it involves interactions between people and elements of the natural world to transform materials into socially useful objects; second, it involves flows of these objects, their constituent components and the value embodied in them between the various sites of production, exchange and consumption in which economic activities take place (Hudson, 2005). Value is a slippery concept, however, and it can be defined in different ways depending on the particular social relations in which economic activity is embedded and the places in which it occurs. In mainstream capitalist economic activities and discourses about them value is typically defined as the market price that a commodity can command. In other sorts of economies value is defined differently, for example, in terms of scarcity or the intrinsic worth of materials and things.

Definitions of value also depend upon theoretical perspective, however. While a mainstream economist would define the value of a commodity in a capitalist economy as given by market price, a Marxian political economist would argue that it is necessary to distinguish between the use value and exchange value aspects of a commodity and penetrate below the surface appearance of price relations to uncover the real basis of value and so define value in terms of the socially necessary labour time required to produce a commodity. However, the value of commodities produced by workers typically exceeds the value of their labour-power, their capacity to work that they sell on the labour market. The surplus labour that workers undertake forms the basis for the creation of surplus value which in turn becomes the source of profits, rents and wages and as such underlies the formation of market prices (Hudson, 2001). However, capitalist economies also encompass other definitions of value as activities are grounded in different value systems to those of the dominant mainstream – for example, in the 'Third Sector' value may be defined by the quantity of embodied labour time, by an allocated price or by what is seen as the intrinsic worth of activities and things while within the family it may be defined in terms of love and respect. Capitalist economies therefore are made up of a heterogeneous mixture of contested forms and flows of value, linked by complex relationships and transfers between them.

Value flows around circuits and networks of varying spatial reaches, and in the course of such flows values are transferred between firms and places (Hadjimichalis, 1987). In the mainstream capitalist economies the dominant flows of value are expressed in circuits of capital of varying complexity and extent. Moreover, capital seeks to penetrate the spaces of other value systems, so that it becomes dominant over increasingly extensive areas. It does so in two ways. First, through processes of primitive accumulation and accumulation by dispossession. This involves the appropriation of elements of nature by capital and of value produced under non-capitalist relations of production and their translation into capitalist forms of value. Second, it does so through the extension of the spaces of surplus value production and the intensification of capitalist relations of production within them. Flows and transfers of value are therefore intimately related to the production of spatially uneven development and the political recognition of regional and local development problems. While it has long been recognised that capital accumulation involves the growing reach of capitalist relations of production and the expansion of circuits of capital (for example, see Lenin, 1960, originally 1917), in recent years there has been a burgeoning literature of global commodity chains, value chains and production networks, signifying the emergence of new forms of combined and uneven development in an era of neo-liberal globalisation.

What I want to do in this chapter is summarise and reflect on these issues, on the relationships between these new and older geographies of value transfer, on the changing geographies of spatial transfers of value, and on the implications of these spatial circuits of value for local and regional development. The remainder of the chapter is organised as follows. First, I briefly discuss the way in which Marxian Political Economy

(MPE) conceptualises value and circuits of capital. The next section discusses the ways in which these circuits are shaped spatially, especially as a result of corporate structures for organising the production process. One consequence of this is the production of uneven development and regional problems. Next, therefore, I discuss the ways in which state policies seek to respond to regionally uneven development and their necessarily limited success in this endeavour. The following two sections discuss counter-tendencies and actions that seek to create a greater degree of regional closure, in part via developing activities grounded in different concepts of value and value systems and in part by seeking to confine value flows within the boundaries of the region. The final section seeks to draw some conclusions.

Producing value: Marxian Political Economy (MPE) and circuits of capital

Drawing on MPE, capitalist production can be usefully thought of in terms of continuous and repeated circuits, enabling the production of value and the creation of surplus value to be located within them. In fact the primary circuit of capital can be seen as encompassing three analytically distinct yet integrally linked circuits: commodity capital; money capital; productive industrial capital (see Hudson, 2005: 21–37). Although at this level of abstraction it is implicit, it is also clear that such circuits have definite geographies, with different locations forming sites of production and exchange, linked by flows of value and capital in the forms of money, commodities and labour-power. However, here I want to focus on the circuit of productive industrial capital (Figure 9.1) as it provides key insights to understanding the creation and realisation of surplus value, of profits, and transfers of value and the dynamism of geographies of production within the social relations of capital. This circuit requires that

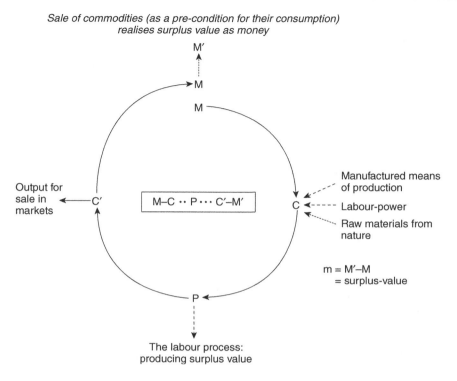

Figure 9.1 The circuit of industrial capital.
Source: Adapted from Hudson (2005)

capital be first laid out in money form to purchase the necessary means of production (elements of constant and fixed capital in the forms of factories and buildings, tools, machinery, manufactured inputs and raw materials) and labour-power. The reproduction of labour-power – and so the successful reproduction of circuits of capital – is critically dependent upon unwaged work in families and community organisations, work that is informed by different value systems to those of mainstream markets. This is also indicative of a more general point – that there are limits to commodification within a capitalist economy and that the reproduction of commodity relations depends upon the reproduction of other forms of social relations.

Labour-power and the means of production are then brought together in the production process, in the workplace, under the supervision of the owners of capital or their managers and representatives. Two things happen in the moment of production. First, existing use values, in the form of raw materials, machinery and manufactured components, suitably revalued according to their current cost of production, are transferred to new commodities. Second, surplus value is created. This augmentation of value is possible precisely because labour-power is the unique fictitious commodity. For capital purchases not a fixed quantity of labour but rather the workers' capacity to work for a given period of time. In this time, workers create commodities that embody more value than was contained in the money capital used as wages to purchase their labour time. This difference in value is the surplus value, the additional new value created in production, which, along with existing values transferred in the production process, is realised in money form as profits on successful sale of the commodity.

It is, however, critical to note that the exchange value of commodities is defined not by the absolute amount of labour time that they embody but by the socially necessary labour time required to produce them. Socially necessary labour time is defined as the amount of undifferentiated abstract labour needed to produce a commodity under average social and technical conditions of production. Since commodities sell in markets at a given price, the process of competition via markets has important implications for the transfer of value between companies. Companies deploying production technologies that require less labour time than the socially necessary average and so yield better-than-average productivity thus benefit from a transfer of value from those companies that use technologies that give a lower-than-average productivity. This continuous intercorporate transfer of value is a critical source of dynamism reshaping the corporate landscapes of capitalist production and an ever-present stimulus to individual companies to engage in R&D activity in search of more effective ways of organising production and creating new products (Hudson, 2001: 147–185).

To summarise so far, capitalist production can be thought of as simultaneously a labour process, producing material use values, and a valorisation process, reproducing value and producing surplus value, which is embodied in commodities and, having been realised, flows through the economy. It is also a process of materials transformation, although I do not have space to elaborate upon this here (but see Hudson, 2001, 2005, 2008). The smooth flow of capital around the circuit is thus necessarily interrupted as capital is fixed and materialised in specific commodified forms (aircraft, automobiles, power stations, shoes and so on). In some cases the value and surplus value that these commodities embody can be realised quite quickly and capital then

thrown back into circulation. In others, however, the process of amortisation following sale can take years, even decades, as capital is fixed in built and manufactured forms of great durability and duration. Moreover, realisation is by no means guaranteed for any commodity. Capitalist production is an inherently speculative and risky process, with a constant danger that the circuit might be broken or interrupted in non-renewable ways.

Assuming that sale is successful, however, the difference between the amount of money capital advanced at the start of the round of production and that realised at the end of it is equivalent to the difference in the value of commodities at the beginning and the end of the round. This is critical in understanding the rationale and dynamism of capitalist production. It also emphasises that the totality of production involves more than simply the transformation of materials to produce goods or services. It also involves a myriad other service activities associated with transportation, distribution and sale, since the determination of socially necessary labour time is contingent upon "socially necessary turnover time", the speed with which commodities can be distributed through and across space (Harvey, 1985). Furthermore, the meanings with which goods and services are endowed, the identities that they help create and form, are of central importance as consumers purchase commodities in the belief that they will be useful to them, materially and symbolically.

In summary, the circuit of productive industrial capital conceptualises commodity production and consumption in terms of the creation, realisation and flows of value. To the extent that realised surplus value is advanced as capital, then the scale of accumulation expands. Thinking in terms of the circuit of industrial capital also emphasises that commodity production is inherently geographical in a double sense. First, material transformations are predicated on relationships between people and nature: that is, upon a social-natural dialectic. Second, space is integral to the biography of commodities, which move between varied sites of production and consumption around the circuit: that is, a socio-spatial dialectic as value embodied in commodities flows between sites and nodes distributed over space. The circuit of productive capital thus involves complex relationships between people, companies, nature and space in processes of value creation and realisation and in flows of value through time/space. Conceptualising the production process in terms of successive journeys around the circuit of industrial capital aids understanding of developmental trajectories within capitalism. In particular, it helps reveal what happens to the money equivalent of the newly produced surplus value and the ways in which value flows through time as an integral part of the circuit of industrial capital. However, analysis at this high level of abstraction reveals nothing about the spatiality of flows of capital and surplus value, the locations from which and to which value flows. Seeking to understand these issues requires a different approach.

The spatiality of flows of value: geographies of capitalism, accumulation by dispossession and the spatial extension of circuits of capital

Flows of money, commodities and value are always flows over space as well as through time. Moreover, with the passage of time the spatial reach of circuits of capital has expanded, albeit unevenly, increasingly becoming global. In part, this spatial extension has been effected through processes of accumulation by dispossession (Harvey, 2003). This form of accumulation refers to an ongoing process of the appropriation of value created under non-capitalist relations of production and its translation into capitalist concepts of value and not simply to the initial early phase of global capitalist development, a

phase of primitive accumulation now consigned to the pages of history. Crucially it involves the replacement of non-capitalist modes of production with the capitalist mode of production as the dominant organisational force in the economy and in this way the penetration of capitalist social relations into spaces from which they were previously excluded. Often this has been a violent process, especially, although by no means only, historically secured by military means and physical force linked to processes of (neo)colonialism but it is now more often pursued by more subtle means, such as Intellectual Property Rights legislation and the force of the rule of law (for example, see Prudham, 2007; Sneddon, 2007). In either case, however, the role of the (national) state in underwriting the political construction of accumulation by dispossession has typically been central.

At the same time, and often as a direct result of the effects of accumulation by dispossession, capitalist social relations of production and processes of proletarianisation (that is, the transformation of people into workers dependent upon selling their labour-power in order to live) have increasingly penetrated spaces from which they were formerly excluded. This spatial extension has been a critical formative moment in the development of uneven development, with transfers of value between locations, both within and between companies. Increasingly, this has been a process cast at the international rather than simply intra-regional scale (most recently and spectacularly into much of China), with the circuits of commodity, money and productive capital successively becoming internationalised (Palloix, 1977).

The spatiality of these flows of value has been decisively shaped by the changing configurations of geographies and systems of production and of exchange and trade. Unequal exchange results from the exchange of commodities produced under capitalist relations of production with products produced under non-capitalist production relations

(Emmanuel, 1972). Increasingly, however, geographies of production and the spatial extension of capitalist relations of production rather than those of exchange became decisive in shaping the spatialities of flows of value. This spatial expansion has also formed an important strategy through which capital has sought to counter tendencies to over-production and for the rate of profit to fall (Harvey, 1982). Initially capital reorganised production on an intra-national scale (see, for example, Lipietz, 1977; Massey, 1984). Subsequently, the reach of flows of value was further extended as divisions of labour in production became organised on an international scale (see, for example, Frobel *et al*, 1980; Lipietz, 1987) and intra- and international divisions of labour became linked in complex ways. More recently, the growing significance of strategies of outsourcing and offshoring as supply chains became both more complicated and distanciated with the incorporation of a greater range of functions such as back-office activities and places into globalised production systems. This has been registered in the burgeoning literatures on global commodity chains, global value chains and global production networks and their relationship to regional development trajectories (see, for example, Gereffi and Korzeniewicz, 2004; Gereffi *et al*., 2005; Hudson, 2008; Smith *et al*., 2002; Wai-chung Yeung, 2009).

The growth of distanciated supply chains, spatially stretched over great distances, and the growing blurring of the boundaries between manufacturing and services as a result of outsourcing back-office activities is an expression of important changes in the organisation of capitalist production. The development of modern capitalism and the practices of major capitalist enterprises have increasingly emphasised the significance of advertising, brand management and symbolic register of commodities and their socially ascribed meanings (see, for example, Williams, 1980; Pike, 2009). Many major companies have in effect become

brand managers, out-sourcing the production of non-core services, components and final products to other companies – some of whom themselves are major brand owners – within hierarchically tiered supply chains. These chains are characterised by sharp inequalities in power among their constituent firms which shape the intra-chain magnitude and direction of flows of value. The organisation of global supply chains involves complex transfers of value between both companies and locations, with the dominant companies siphoning off monopoly rents as a consequence of brand ownership and with the dominant direction of net flows being to the lead companies and key centres of control and finance.

State policies, territorial development and global value flows: tensions between corporate and territorial development logics

Given that uneven development is inherent to capitalist economies as a result of capital's need to create surplus value and transfer value between locations according to the dictates of dominant corporate imperatives and priorities, there are clearly unavoidable tensions between the logics of territorial development and corporate profitability and growth, between the logics of place and space, since companies wish to move value to maximise corporate advantage while those with responsibility for the development of cities and regions wish to capture value and hold down value-creating activities in their place. This frequently leads to the apparently paradoxical outcome that factories and workplaces are closed in one place not because they are unprofitable but because they are less profitable than in another place.

In terms of mainstream state logic, those responsible for seeking to manage the contradictions of uneven development and for promoting local and regional development seek to position places more favourably within the spatial circuits of capital, accepting its concept of value. They employ a variety of tactics in pursuit of this objective – attracting inward investment, encouraging the growth of endogenous enterprise and local small firms and so on. In recent years there has been a growing emphasis on a neo-liberal conception of development, based on maximising global flows into and out of regions. This has further exacerbated the tensions between a corporate logic that seeks to maximise profits by globalising value flows and a territorial development logic that seeks to maximise intra-regional flows and connections and the volume of activity within a given region. Companies seek to minimise employment levels and wage costs per unit output and maximise surplus value production whereas those responsible for regional development seek to maximise the quantity and/or quality of jobs and the wage incomes that they bring. Nonetheless, those responsible for regional development strategies typically see themselves as having no alternative to seeking to work within the constraints arising from this clash of logics. Thus they seek to create, enhance and capture value "in ways that are not easily replicable elsewhere" (Rutherford and Holmes, 2007: 202). However, as the history of capitalist development makes abundantly clear, even if regions succeed in enticing companies to locate and create value within their boundaries, there is no guarantee that capital will be invested where surplus value is produced or indeed where it is collected.

There are also tensions within those parts of the administrative apparatus of the state concerned with local and regional development as to whether the priority is enhancing the strength and international competitiveness of the national economy through the use of local and regional development policies or developing localities and regions per se. While the administration of such policies was typically devolved to the regional level within the structures of central government ministries, decisions about their content and the criteria to be used in administering them remained firmly at central level within national states. Such policies often seem more concerned with reshaping the contours of profitable production spaces, or addressing national economic policy objectives, than meeting the developmental needs and concerns of particular places. Furthermore, implementation of such policies was often seen to create vulnerable urban and regional economies, ensembles of 'global outposts' at the extremities of corporate chains of command and control (Austrin and Beynon, 1979) and dependent upon decisions within distant national political capitals and the offices of transnational corporations (Firn, 1975). Despite attempts to encourage endogenous development and claims as to the emergence of new forms of qualitatively different embedded branch plants, such fears remain (Hudson, 1994, 1995). For example, in 1998 Fujitsu and Siemens closed brand-new state-of-the–art integrated circuit plants in North East England, facilities that had been heavily subsidised via state regional policy grants, as world market prices for these products collapsed.

Counter-tendencies, I: Seeking greater closure of local and regional economies within the mainstream

There are clearly limits to the degree to which any local or regional economy can and, arguably, ought to be closed off from the wider world economy and a key policy issue is to optimise the balance between intra-regional and extra-regional production, trade and value flows. In certain circumstances increasing intra-regional transactions is perfectly compatible with the mainstream logic of capital as it can cut both production and transport costs and enhance profits. Recognition of this underlay the creation of major integrated chemicals and steel complexes, for example, as by-products from one process became inputs to another process rather than valueless wastes. The same logic underpins the concept of eco-industrial development (EID), predicated on companies collaborating for mutual economic benefit, closing material loops via recycling, recovering or reusing wastes and enhancing eco-efficiency via exchanging different kinds of by-product, based on bilateral commercial agreements, driven by concerns to minimise risks and wastes and maximise profits, and retain flows of value within the local or regional economy (Scharb, 2001; Stone, 2002). It is, however, important to remember that there are limits to EID and similar attempts to increase regional closure as at least some raw materials and components are typically imported into the region and some finished products exported so that flows of value into and out of the region are unavoidable.

There are also limits as to what can be produced for sale regionally because of the size of regional markets and regional consumption preferences. Nonetheless there is considerable scope in many regions to enhance intra-regional transactions and the resilience of economies via public procurement policies. Consider, for example, the regionalisation of food supply chains over much of the European Union for schools, hospitals and other public sector activities (Hadjimichalis and Hudson, 2007). Such developments create markets to sustain regional agriculture and food-processing industries and increase the intra-regional retention of value.

Counter-tendencies, II: Creating alternative concepts and localised circuits of value

The chronic failure of state territorial development policies to manage the mainstream capitalist economy so as to deliver their claimed and intended effects has led to attempts to explore alternative conceptions of paths to local and regional development

(see, for example, Pike *et al.*, 2007). This involves moving beyond that which follows from the logic of capital and redefining what counts as 'the economy', admitting the validity of differing concepts of value and processes of valuation and the outputs of goods and services that arise from them. While goods and services produced within the social economy may be exchanged for money in markets, they do so at market prices that reflect an ethical and moral commitment and as such undercut prices in mainstream markets. Nonetheless there is competition within markets in the social economy and uneven development among and flows of value between social economy organisations as a result (Hudson, 2009). In addition, however, social economy activities may also be based upon different concepts and definitions of value that do not find monetary expression in the currencies of the mainstream (for example, Time Dollars defined in terms of the amount of time required to create a product or deliver a service). Such activities may also involve attempts to create localised flows of value (for example, via LETS – Local Exchange Trading Systems) detached from the dominant circuits of capital and the mainstream economy. More generally, these explorations of alternatives signal a more general concern with the developmental potential of the social economy and, more generally, of the 'Third Sector'.

Much of the recent impetus for this revival of interest in the social economy derives from the perception in policy circles that a localised social economy could offer a more effective way of dealing with localised problems of social exclusion, poverty, unemployment and worklessness. Much socially useful and environmentally enhancing activity that was formerly disregarded or consigned to the margins is now being accorded much greater recognition and significance as part of the social economy or 'Third Sector' in many parts of the world (Amin *et al.*, 2002; Amin, 2009; Leyshon *et al.*, 2003). Because such activity is often locally based, meeting local needs from locally produced products, based upon recycling and reuse of existing goods and materials, in a variety of ways it has a much lighter environmental footprint as well as creating socially useful work. Paradoxically, however, it is typically those places most ravaged by economic decline that lack the resources needed to develop a vibrant social economy and the developmental alternatives and alternative localised circuits of value that it could offer. Furthermore, as successful social economy organisations seek to extend their scale of operations and spatial reach, they typically move nearer to the logic of the mainstream economy and its definitions of value and criteria for exchange, blurring the line between the mainstream and alternatives to it as the bulwarks and shelters they provide are subject to strong convergence pressures from the mainstream (Hudson, 2009).

Conclusions

Capitalist development is driven by strong imperatives to maximise profits and this has led companies increasingly to organise their activities on an expanded spatial scale, seeking both to appropriate value from non-capitalist activities and extend capitalist relations of production into previously forbidden territory. Flows of value between companies and places are an integral part of the competitive imperatives that lie at the heart of capitalist social relations. A corollary of this is that companies are engaged in an ongoing process of reorganising their activities over space, transferring value between locations while investing in some places and disinvesting from others. Devalorisation is always place specific and, combined with the transfer of value from places because of their particular location in wider circuits of capital, is central to the creation of local and regional development problems. Equally, the search for new sources of surplus value and the intensification of capitalist social relations erodes the

space in which alternative concepts of value and more localised circuits of value could flourish. This poses a political challenge for national states and other social forces that seek to combat these problems of uneven development and as such the logics of corporate profitability and territorial development, of capitalist and non-capitalist social relations, come into sharp conflict. However, the production of uneven development is a necessary feature of the expansion of capitalist social relations and capital accumulation so that there are definite limits as to the extent to which value flows can be regionalised and local and regional economies insulated from the effects of wider and dominant circuits of capital.

Acknowledgement

Thanks to the editors for their helpful comments on an earlier draft of this chapter; the usual disclaimers apply.

References

Amin, A. (ed.) (2009) *The Social Economy: International Perspectives*, Zed Press, London.

Amin, A., Cameron, A. and Hudson, R. (2002) *Placing the Social Economy*, Routledge, London.

Austrin, T. and Beynon, H. (1979) *Global Outpost: the Working Class Experience of Big Business in North East England*, University of Durham, mimeo, Department of Sociology.

Coe, N. M., Hess, M., Yeung, HW.-C., Dicken, P. and Henderson, J. (2004) 'Globalizing regional development: a global production networks perspective', *Transactions of the Institute of British Geographers*, New Series, 29: 468–484.

Emmanuel, A. (1972) *Unequal Exchange*, Monthly Review Press, New York.

Firn, J. R. (1975) 'External control and regional development: the case of Scotland', *Environment and Planning A*, 7: 393–414.

Frobel, F., J. Heinrichs and Kreye, O. (1980) *The New International Division of Labour*, Cambridge University Press ,Cambridge.

Gereffi, G. and Korzeniewicz, M. (eds) (2004) *Commodity Chains and Global Development*, Praeger, Westport .

Gereffi, G., Humphrey, J. and Sturgeon, T. (2005) 'The governance of global value chains', *Review of International Political Economy*, 12: 78–104.

Hadjimichalis, C. (1987) *Uneven Development and Regionalism: State, Territory and Class in Southern Europe*, Croom Helm, London.

Hadjimichalis, C. and Hudson, R. (2007) 'Re-thinking local and regional development: implications for radical political practice in Europe', *European Urban and Regional Studies*, 14: 99–113.

Harvey, D. (1982) *The Limits to Capital*, Blackwell, Oxford.

Harvey, D. (1985) 'The geopolitics of capitalism', in D. Gregory, and J. Urry, (eds). *Social Relations and Spatial Structure*, Macmillan, Basingstoke, 128–163.

Harvey, D. (2003) *The New Imperialism*, Oxford University Press, Oxford.

Hudson, R. (1994) 'New production concepts, new production geographies? Reflections on changes in the automobile industry', *Transactions of the Institute of British Geographers*, 19: 331–345.

Hudson, R. (1995) 'The Japanese, the European market and the automobile industry in the United Kingdom. Towards a new map of automobile manufacturing', in R. Hudson and E. W. Schamp (eds) *Europe? New Production Concepts and Spatial Restructuring*, Springer, Berlin, 63–92.

Hudson, R. (2001) *Producing Places*, Guilford, New York.

Hudson, R. (2005) *Economic Geographies*, Sage, London.

Hudson, R. (2008) 'Cultural political economy meets global production networks: a productive meeting?', *Journal of Economic Geography*: 1–20.

Hudson, R. (2009) 'Life on the edge: navigating the competitive tensions between the "social" and the "economic" in the social economy and in its relations to the mainstream', *Journal of Economic Geography*: 1–18.

Lenin, V. I. (1960) *Imperialism: The Highest Stage of Capitalism*, Lawrence and Wishart, London (originally 1917).

Leyshon, A., Lee, R. and Williams, C. C. (eds) (2003) *Alternative Economic Spaces*, Sage, London.

Lipietz, A. (1977) *Le Capital et Son Espace*, Maspero, Paris.

Lipietz, A. (1987) *Mirages and Miracles*, Verso, London.

Massey, D. (1984) *Spatial Divisions of Labour*, Macmillan, London.

Palloix, C. (1977) 'The self-expansion of capital on a world scale', *Review of Radical Political Economics*, 9: 1–28.

Pike, A., Rodríguez-Pose, A. and Tomaney, J. (2007) 'What kind of regional development and for whom?', *Regional Studies*, 41: 1253–1269.

Pike, A. (2009) 'Geographies of brands and branding', *Progress in Human Geography*, 33: 619–645.

Prudham, S. (2007) 'The fiction of autonomous invention: accumulation by dispossession, commodification and life patents in Canada', *Antipode*, 39, 406–429.

Rutherford, T. D. and Holmes, J. (2007) '"We simply have to do that stuff for our survival": labour, firm innovation and cluster governance in the Canadian automotive parts industry', *Antipode*, 9: 194–221.

Scharb, M. (2001) 'Eco-industrial development: a strategy for building sustainable communities', *Review of Economic Development Interaction and Practice 8*, Cornell University and US Economic Development Administration, 43.

Smith, A., Rainnie, A., Dunford, M., Hardy, J., Hudson, R. and Sadler, D. (2002) 'Networks of value, commodities and regions: reworking divisions of labour in macro-regional economies', *Progress in Human Geography*, 26: 41–64.

Sneddon, C. (2007) 'Nature's materiality and the circuitous paths of accumulation: dispossession of freshwater fisheries in Cambodia', *Antipode*, 39: 167–193.

Stone, C. (2002) 'Environmental consequences of heavy-industry restructuring and economic regeneration through industrial ecology', *Transactions of the Institute of Mining and Metallurgy*, 111: A187–191.

Wai-chung Yeung, H. (2009) 'Regional development and the competitive dynamics of global production networks', *Regional Studies*, 43: 325–352.

Williams, R. (1980) *Problems in Materialism and Culture*, Verso, London.

Further reading

Harvey, D. (2003) *The New Imperialism*, Oxford University Press, Oxford.

Hudson, R. (2001) *Producing Places*, Guilford, New York.

Hudson, R. (2005) *Economic Geographies*, Sage, London.

Massey, D. (1984) *Spatial Divisions of Labour*, Macmillan, London.

10

Labor and local and regional development

Andrew Herod

Introduction

Workers have long organized themselves into various social, economic, cultural, and political groupings. Often, such entities have focused their attention most directly on what happens in the workplace and have sought to negotiate better wages and working conditions or to secure greater control over the production process. Workers' organizations, though, have also played important roles beyond the workplace, as they have tried to improve workers' lives as consumers and citizens and not just as producers. For instance, in 1895 members of the Christian socialist movement established the International Co-operative Alliance with the intent of setting up transnational cooperative trading associations (Gurney 1988), whilst labor unions and other worker organizations have also fought for things like public education and improved public health facilities. Importantly, both these types of activities – those focused specifically on the workplace and those beyond it – have had often dramatic impacts on patterns and processes of local and regional development. Thus, increases in wages can bring more money into an economy from outside. Equally, struggles to improve work's qualitative dimensions, such

as by reducing the number of working hours, can shape how local and regional economies function by giving workers more leisure time in which to spend their wages, thereby affecting how money circulates locally/regionally and what impact this will have on, say, the retail or entertainment sectors (see Pike *et al.* (2006) for an example from the UK). At the same time, workers' organizations can play direct and active roles in encouraging or discouraging local and regional economic development beyond the workplace, as when they may throw their weight behind the construction of housing for workers or attempt to limit the redevelopment of particular urban areas which might result in the factories in which they work being replaced by high-end residential units.

Given, then, that workers' organizations can shape local and regional development through their activities in both the workplace and beyond it, in this chapter I undertake two tasks. First, I provide a brief theoretical analysis of how the activities of workers' organizations can be linked to the unfolding patterns and processes of local and regional development, particularly with regard to their proactive efforts to mold the economic landscape in particular ways. Second, I detail a number of case studies in which such organizations have deliberately sought to shape the local and regional economic landscape through their activities. These examples are not meant to be an exhaustive account of all the ways in which workers and their organizations shape local and regional development but, rather, to be illustrative and to stimulate further thinking about labor's role in making the economic landscape of capitalism and other political-economic systems.

Theorizing labor's role in local and regional development

Workers are geographical creatures. They have a vested interest in ensuring that the economic landscape is made in some ways and not in others. As intimated above, much of this is done in an indirect way through their actions within the workplace. Hence, workers' efforts to increase their wages will indirectly impact upon how the economic landscape evolves around their places of work, ensuring that it remains, they no doubt hope, one of prosperity rather than poverty. However, it is important to recognize that workers also play a role in shaping the broader economic landscape beyond the workplace, both proactively and reactively. Three important bodies of theory have emerged within the critical geographic literature in the past two decades or so which seek to link workers' political and economic practices with the impacts of such actions on local and regional development patterns.

The first of these bodies revolves around the concept of what Harvey (1982) called "the spatial fix." Largely developed out of his effort to spatialize Marx, Harvey suggested that if capital is to engage in accumulation successfully, then it has to ensure that there is a certain geographical configuration of infrastructure placed in the landscape. It is essential, he argued, that labor and raw materials are brought together at particular locations so that work can be done and surplus labor

extracted from workers. This will generally require that factories or mines or other workplaces are situated in specific places, that workers are provided with housing sufficiently close to work (either directly by a firm, as with company housing, through the market, or by the state), that roads or other types of infrastructure are available to move goods and people around, and so forth. The realization of any surplus value generated, however, also requires investment in infrastructure. Often, this is the same infrastructure – roads can be used both for bringing raw materials to a site and for taking away finished products – but sometimes it requires different types of infrastructure, such as shops in which finished goods can be purchased. Thus, as Harvey (1982: 233) put it, collectively capital must invest in "factories, dams, offices, shops, warehouses, roads, railways, docks, power stations, water supply and sewage disposal systems, schools, hospitals, parks, cinemas, restaurants – the list is endless" so that the capitalist system is maintained.

There are several important issues which emerge from such a conceptualization. First, the form of the economic landscape is seen to be both a reflection of, but also constitutive of, the capitalist accumulation process – the demands of securing and realizing profit require a certain physical configuration of the landscape, whilst this configuration shapes how accumulation processes unfold, as goods, capital, information, and workers flow between particular places along the networks emplaced in the landscape. There is, in other words, a socio-spatial dialectic (Soja 1980) at play. Second, it is important to bear in mind that there may be significant divisions within collective capital – one group may wish for one particular type of spatial fix, whereas another may wish for a different type, such that the actual economic landscapes which eventually materialize are the result of struggle. Third, not only is there a synchronous socio-spatial dialectic at work but there is also a diachronic one, for landscapes have certain path dependences to them. Thus, the landscapes which facilitated accumulation at one historical moment increasingly come to limit its possibilities as the social relations of capitalist accumulation change, although this varies from place to place and over time, given that the rate at which capitalism's social relations develop will vary historically and geographically. Fourth, and perhaps most significant for our purposes here, although Harvey outlined an important way of thinking about how patterns of local and regional development are related to the internal machinations of capitalist accumulation, he did not have a particularly active conception of labor in this process – workers appeared more or less simply as factors of production. In response, a number of writers (e.g., Herod 2001) began to explore how workers – either individually or as part of a collective entity like a labor union – similarly seek to place in the landscape their own spatial fixes, fixes which they see as important for their own ability to reproduce themselves socially and biologically on a daily or generational basis. Specifically, such writers argued that workers struggle over the geographical location of work and over the location of those other things (businesses, schools, roads, recreation facilities, and so forth) which allow them to live their lives and which have tangible impacts upon local and regional development patterns. As with capital, though, different segments within the working class and its organizations of collective representation might prefer quite different spatial fixes to be implemented in the landscape. Equally, the landscapes which facilitated their self-reproduction at one historical moment may not at later moments, a fact which leads workers to seek to rework the economic landscape. Through their struggles over the economic landscape's form, then, workers and their organizations shape patterns of local/regional development.

If the spatial fix is one concept which helps link the political and economic activities of workers and their organizations to how patterns of local and regional development

are generated, a second – closely related – one is that of what Cox and Mair (1988) have called "local dependence." Specifically, Cox and Mair suggest that social actors are differentially tied to various places through capital investments and other economic bonds, kinship ties, political relationships, and the like. At the same time, they have disparate abilities to move elsewhere. Thus, whereas some capital is quite flighty, that with large amounts of investment fixed in particular places (like utility companies) or with significant ties to particular places (such as a reliance on highly trained labor that is only available in certain places) is less so. Likewise, whereas young workers with few responsibilities may readily pick up and move elsewhere, older workers who own houses they may not easily be able to sell or who may find it hard at their stage in life to find another job are more fixed in place. These considerations mean that certain firms and individuals are more dependent upon the continued economic vitality of the communities in which they live and/or are invested than are others. The result, Cox and Mair argue, is that they are much more likely to engage in boosterist local politics than are those firms and individuals who can more easily move on somewhere else should the local or regional economy begin to sag. Equally, they may be more likely to seek to reduce their own local dependence by externalizing it, through, for instance, drawing down their investments in their own fixed capital and using rented factories or office buildings (if they are firms) or seeking to sell their homes and move into rented accommodation in the same community (if they are workers). Consequently, those workers who are relatively spatially fixed in particular places often work hand-in-hand with local capitalists to ensure that investment is brought to their community, forming business coalitions to stimulate and/or continue local and regional development efforts. This means that whereas sometimes workers may mobilize around their class interests, at other times they may defend their territorial ones, with their choice dramatically shaping local/ regional development patterns.

The third way in which workers and their organizations have been theorized to play a significant role in shaping patterns of local and regional development is through the practice of seeking deliberately to mold the built environment for purposes of transforming social relations – that is to say, through engaging in spatial engineering for social engineering purposes. Thus, workers and their organizations have often attempted to establish various communities which reflect their social values, and in the nineteenth and twentieth centuries many unions went about building utopian communities of one sort or another. In the case of New York City's garment workers in the 1920s, for instance, the union built worker cooperative housing with the goal of creating a "workers' city" which would both give them greater security against being evicted by their landlords but also represented in bricks and mortar their vision of a more emancipatory built environment (Vural 1994). Likewise, in Berlin after the Second World War unions built some 10 per cent of all housing constructed in the city in some years, with goals similar to those of the New York garment workers (Homann and Scarpa 1983). Their objective in all of this has been to put "social thought in three dimensions" (Fishman 1977: 7), to create built environments which are, perhaps, more emancipatory than those within which they would otherwise find themselves.

Some diverse examples of labor shaping local and regional development

Having outlined some of the theoretical issues concerning labor's shaping of local and regional development, in this section I present several case studies intended to give a flavor of how workers and their organizations have actually made the economic landscape in particular ways. At a very local scale,

one example of a union having a significant impact on local development patterns is that of the International Ladies' Garment Workers' Union (ILGWU) in New York City. Faced with the loss of jobs in the industry in the 1970s and 1980s as a result of building owners transforming their manufacturing lofts into office space for the service-sector firms which were increasingly looking for cheap space in Manhattan's Garment District, the union sought to limit conversions as a way to preserve manufacturing space (Herod 1991). Through lobbying the city government, in the early 1980s the union was successful in having established a Special Garment Center District preservation zone in which building owners' abilities to rezone and convert their lofts would be restricted. The result was that space was saved for apparel manufacture that otherwise would have been converted into office space, such that garment manufacturers were able to weather some of the pressures they were facing. Through its ability to shape zoning patterns, then, the ILGWU was able to impact upon local development patterns not just in midtown Manhattan (location of the special district) but also elsewhere, as service-sector office users, denied locations in the garment district, were forced to look for space in other parts of the city.

If the ILGWU's activities in New York City represent a very local intervention into the dynamics of urban real estate, the American Federation of Labor-Congress of Industrial Organizations (AFL-CIO) has more broadly played important roles in shaping the urban fabric. One way in which this has been the case is through the housing policies pursued by various unions, which in the early post-war period encouraged both suburbanization and urban redevelopment as a solution to union workers' housing needs (Parson 1982, 1984; Botein 2007). Other examples are those of the AFL-CIO's Building Investment Trust, a real estate fund established in 1988 and worth some $2.1 billion as of 2009, and its Housing Investment Trust, first established as the Mortgage Investment Trust in 1965 and which by its own reckoning has financed close to 500 housing projects, creating or preserving more than 80,000 homes. During the first decade of the 2000s, the HIT committed some $2.6 billion to finance the development and/or preservation of over 33,000 housing units, with such investments generating over 22,000 union construction jobs and leveraging some $1 billion in additional investment capital for community development. Two notable projects have been the Chicago Community Investment Plan, a $500 million initiative announced in 2005 to help the city address housing and community development needs, and the HIT's Gulf Coast Revitalization Program to rebuild communities impacted by Hurricane Katrina (AFL-CIO 2009; see also Hebb and Beeferman 2009).

The US, though, is not the only place in which the AFL-CIO has been involved in building housing and local communities. Hence, beginning in the 1960s the Federation began using some of its constituent members' pension funds, together with US government monies, to construct housing and other types of infrastructure and make small loans to workers in Latin America and the Caribbean (Herod 2001). Such activities were part of a broader campaign designed to limit the appeal of communism to workers in the countries in which they were located, based upon the belief that improving workers' material conditions would make them less susceptible to communist ideology. In Brazil, for instance, a 448-unit housing complex was constructed in São Paulo and schools and community centers in a number of rural communities, whereas in Colombia low-cost worker housing projects were built in 15 cities throughout the country. Similar such projects were completed in many other countries in the hemisphere, with important impacts on local and regional economies. Likewise, other countries' labor movements played roles in shaping economic development in developing countries as a way to hinder communism's spread (Weiler 1988). Such examples

show not only how unions shape local and regional development but also how they may work simultaneously at different geographical scales to do so – hence, US unions building housing in Latin America worked both transnationally but also at the scale of the neighborhoods impacted by such projects.

Organized labor has also played a significant role in shaping patterns of local and regional development in Eastern Europe during both the communist and post-communist period. Hence, under communism the role of labor unions was to serve as "transmission belts" of the economy, which is to say that they were supposed to be the social entities who made sure that the production quotas determined by central economic planners were achieved. Although there was some variation in how this was done – unions in countries like East Germany and the Czech Republic, which had industrialized before 1945, were generally less authoritarian than were those in countries like Bulgaria and Romania, which largely industrialized after the Second World War (Herod 1998) – the unions generally served to mobilize/discipline the workforce to fulfill quotas and engage in "socialist emulation." Equally, unions served as conduits through which workers might acquire consumer goods (TVs, cars) or gain access to economic and social benefits (vacations at union-owned resorts, coupon books for rationed food, etc.). Consequently, unions – even as arms of the state – were central actors in processes of economic development. Significantly, though, they have also been key participants in the transformation of the region's economic landscape associated with what has come to be called "the transition." Hence, many unions assumed enthusiastic roles in processes of enterprise privatization and were active advocates of economic restructuring in the early 1990s, in the belief that privatization, the introduction of market reforms, encouragement of an entrepreneurial system and culture, and the restructuring of enterprises was required to kick-start local and regional

123

economies after almost half a century of central planning. Indeed, in Poland Solidarność (Solidarity) was a major advocate of neoliberal policies in the 1980s (Ost 1989) and many others across the region took similar stances – one adviser to the Czech national labor federation ČMKOS, for instance, suggested that unemployment in the early 1990s in the Czech Republic was too low and that "[a]n increase [in it] would be healthy," since this would likely bring higher productivity and thus, perhaps, higher wages for those workers who remained employed. At the same time, numerous Western labor organizations, from the AFL-CIO to entities like the International Metalworkers' Federation and the German metalworkers' union IG Metall, ran training seminars and otherwise worked with new and reformed unions in the region to help them reimagine themselves along Western lines (Herod 1998, 2001). The result of these activities has been that unions both within Eastern Europe and from beyond it have contributed in myriad ways to the processes of local and regional development which continue to unfold.

Unions have played similar roles in shaping patterns of local and regional development in other parts of the world, as in Mexico. In this case, they have done so as part of a corporatist arrangement with the *Partido Revolucionario Institucional* (PRI – Institutional Revolutionary Party), which ruled Mexico for much of the twentieth century. Thus, the *Confederación de Trabajadores de México* (CTM – Confederation of Mexican Workers) was for many years a central pillar in corporatist politics in Mexico and played important roles in designing industrial policy (including the creation of import substitution industrialization programs and, later, the Border Industrialization Program which encouraged establishment of the maquiladora plants that have industrialized Mexico's northern border). Likewise, in Germany and Scandinavia the idea of "co-determination," in which unions and workers participate in

decisions concerning how work should be organized and in long-term planning for companies and plants in particular communities, is central to how industrial relations work and has important impacts upon local/regional economies – in the 1970s, for instance, Scandinavian unions began initiating research projects aimed at developing alternative technologies for use in manufacturing (Bansler 1989; Lundin 2005) so as to help reduce negative impacts on the local environment and give workers more influence over how the work process is structured. Equally, in countries like China unions have not only been involved in shaping industrial policy but also in establishing and running businesses themselves. Hence, according to the All-China Federation of Trade Unions, by the late 1990s Chinese unions had set up 120,000 enterprises and operated more than 100 Sino – foreign joint ventures and overseas-based businesses, with such trade union-run enterprises employing 980,000 workers and generating approximately one-third of union incomes through the profits they earned (ACFTU 1999). More recently, entities like the Shanghai Federation of Trade Unions have established employment agencies for migrant workers and those workers laid off by the restructuring of state enterprises, whilst other unions have made small business loans to migrant workers looking to start businesses (*China Daily* 2009). Certainly, the fact that the official unions in China are presently arms of the state means that these practices raise significant questions concerning where labor organizations end and the state begins. At the same time, though, should such organizations gain greater autonomy as a result of growing worker pressure, then they will have considerable influence, as independent unions, on local and regional development patterns.

Finally, unions have impacted upon local and regional development directly through their collective bargaining activities. Although there are literally millions of examples of this, a particularly pertinent one involves the International Longshoremen's Association (ILA), which represents dockworkers in East Coast ports in the United States. Beginning in the 1950s, shipping companies began to deploy containers – essentially, large metal boxes – as a means to transport goods. The result was that much of the labor-intensive work of loading and unloading ships which, out of necessity, had historically been done at the waterfront could now be done at inland warehouses – whereas previously every piece of cargo had to be handled on the piers, now only the containers themselves did. In response to fears of job losses, however, the ILA successfully negotiated a series of work-preservation rules, one of the principal ones being an agreement that any container packing or unpacking work which would otherwise have been done at warehouses located within 50 miles of ports in which it represented dockers had to be done instead within these ports – this rule, in other words, forced work which might have migrated inland to remain at the waterfront whilst it also forced work that had already been shifted inland to be brought back to the piers, with all of the resultant impacts on local and regional work patterns (Herod 2001). At the same time, though, the union also successfully forced the employers to agree to a reworking of the scale at which collective bargaining took place in the industry. In particular, whereas traditionally bargaining had occurred on a port-by-port basis – New York employers negotiated with New York dockers, Philadelphia employers with Philadelphia dockers, etc. – the ILA's national leadership sought to develop a national, coastwide contract as a way of presenting a unified face to those employers who operated out of multiple ports along the coast. Perhaps the most significant impact of this new system on local and regional economies was that it augured the beginning of a national wage rate based upon conditions in New York (where dockers' wages were highest), which dramatically increased the amount of money cycling into

waterfront communities from Maine to Texas.

Concluding comments

Putting all of this together, it is obvious that workers can have dramatic impacts upon local and regional economic development in a number of ways. First, they can help bring capital into their locality or region from outside through successfully negotiating higher wages and/or securing employer agreement that more investment being expended on their workplaces. This can help buoy the local/regional economy, which can have various multiplier effects, and can also have significant impacts upon how work is structured – for instance, new investment may be in the form of improved workplace technologies which can perhaps enhance efficiency (hence bringing more factory orders to a region). Second, they can dramatically shape patterns of local and regional development by themselves moving into or out of particular localities or regions – if a region cannot produce a labor force in situ through natural increase, for instance, then insufficient labor migration may starve it of workers whereas too much may swamp it, with all of the consequences for patterns of local and regional development of either alternative. Third, workers can shape local and regional economies through the impact that their own actions have on the actions of other social actors. Hence, if workers become too powerful in particular places they may encourage capital to flee their regions. Likewise, the local and/or national state may seek to rein in workers' economic and political power in such situations, for fear that without so doing they may be unable to attract capital or that accumulation may be affected. Finally, workers can dramatically shape local/regional economies through directly intervening to shape the physical layout of the built environment as they seek to secure the particular spatial fixes they feel are necessary to ensure their own social and biological reproduction.

References

ACFTU (All-China Federation of Trade Unions) (1999) "Voluntary industry corporate industries of Chinese trade unions," January 20, posted at www.acftu.org.cn/template/10002/file.jsp?cid=100&aid=39; last accessed September 27, 2009.

AFL-CIO (American Federation of Labour-Congress of Industrial Organizations) (2009) Building Investment Trust (www.aflcio-bit.com) and Housing Investment Trust (www.aflcio-hit.com/wmspage.cfm?parm1=885).

Bansler, J. (1989) "Trade unions and alternative technology in Scandinavia," *New Technology, Work and Employment*, 4.2: 92–99.

Botein, H. (2007) "Labour unions and affordable housing: An uneasy relationship," *Urban Affairs Review*, 42.6: 799–822.

China Daily (2009) "Trade unions prepare migrant workers for job market," January 30, posted at www.chinadaily.com.cn/china/2009-01/30/content_7432306.htm; last accessed September 27, 2009.

Cox, K. R. and Mair, A. (1988) "Locality and community in the politics of local economic development," *Annals of the Association of American Geographers*, 78.2: 307–325.

Fishman, R. (1977) *Urban Utopias in the Twentieth Century: Ebenezer Howard, Frank Lloyd Wright, and Le Corbusier*, New York: Basic Books.

Gurney, P. (1988) " 'A higher state of civilisation and happiness': Internationalism in the British co-operative movement between c. 1869–1918," in F. van Holthoon and M. van der Linden (eds) *Internationalism in the Labour Movement 1830–1940*, Volume 2, London: E. J. Brill, 543–564.

Harvey, D. (1982) *The Limits to Capital*, Oxford: Blackwell.

Hebb, T. and Beeferman, L. (2009) "Can private pension funds be socially responsible?: The US experience," *Journal of Comparative Social Welfare*, 25.2: 109–117.

Herod, A. (1991) "From rag trade to real estate in New York's Garment Center: Remaking the labour landscape in a global city," *Urban Geography*, 12.4: 324–338.

—— (1998) "The geostrategics of labour in post-Cold War Eastern Europe: An examination of the activities of the International Metal-workers' Federation," In A. Herod (ed.) *Organizing the Landscape: Labour Unionism in Geographical Perspective*, Minneapolis: University of Minnesota Press, 45–74.

—— (2001) *Labour Geographies: Workers and the Landscapes of Capitalism*, New York: Guilford.

—— (forthcoming 2011) "Spatial engineering for social engineering in company towns," in A. Vergara and O. Dinius (eds) *Company Towns in the Americas: Landscape, Power, and Working-Class Communities*, Athens, GA: University of Georgia Press.

Homann, K. and Scarpa, L. (1983) "Martin Wagner, the trades union movement and housing construction in Berlin in the first half of the Nineteen Twenties," *Architectural Design*, 53.11/12: 58–61.

Lundin, P. (2005) "Designing democracy: The UTOPIA-project and the role of labour movement in technological change, 1981–1986." Paper no. 52, Centre of Excellence for Studies in Science and Innovation, The Royal Institute of Technology, Stockholm, Sweden.

Ost, D. (1989) "The transformation of Solidarity and the future of Central Europe," *Telos*, 79 (spring): 69–94.

Parson, D. (1982) "The development of redevelopment: Public housing and urban renewal in Los Angeles," *International Journal of Urban and Regional Research*, 6.2: 393–413.

Parson, D. (1984) "Organized labour and the housing question: Public housing, suburbanization, and urban renewal," *Environment and Planning D: Society and Space*, 2.1: 75–86.

Pike, A., O'Brien, P., and Tomaney, J. (2006) "Devolution and the Trades Union Congress in North East England and Wales," *Regional and Federal Studies*, 16.2: 157–178.

Rusnok, J. (1993) Statement by Jiří Rusnok, adviser to Czech Moravian Chamber of Trade Unions (ČMKOS), quoted in A. Hawker "Low unemployment perplexes officials," *Prague Post*, August 4–10: 5.

Soja, E. (1980) "The socio-spatial dialectic," *Annals of the Association of American Geographers*, 70.2: 207–225.

Vural, L. (1994) "Unionism as a Way of Life: The Community Orientation of the International Ladies' Garment Workers' Union and the Amalgamated Clothing Workers of America," unpublished Ph.D., Department of Geography, Rutgers University, New Brunswick, NJ.

Weiler, P. (1988) *British Labour and the Cold War*, Stanford, CA: Stanford University Press.

Further reading

Cravey, A. (1998) "Cowboys and dinosaurs: Mexican labor unions and the state," in A. Herod (ed.) *Organizing the Landscape: Labor Unionism in Geographical Perspective*, Minneapolis: University of Minnesota Press, 75–98. (Documents the role played by unions in shaping industrial policy in Mexico and how more recent neoliberal policies have transformed the geography of industrial development in the country.)

Herod, A. (1998) "Theorising unions in transition," in J. Pickles and A. Smith (eds) *Theorising Transition: The Political Economy of Change in Central and Eastern Europe*, London :Routledge, , 197–217. (This chapter details some of the ways in which unions helped structure the transition from Communism to post-Communism in Eastern Europe, and with what consequences for patterns of economic development.)

—— (2010) "Spatial engineering for social engineering in company towns," in A. Vergara and O. Dinius (eds) *Between Managerial Ideologies and Workers' Power: Twentieth-Century Company Towns in the Americas*, Athens, GA: University of Georgia Press, in press. (Examines how spatial engineering has been conducted for purposes of social engineering, from the scale of individual workplaces all the way up to entire landscapes.)

Hudson, R. and Sadler, D. (1986) "Contesting work closures in Western Europe's old industrial regions: Defending place or betraying class?," in A. Scott and M. Storper (eds) *Production, Work, Territory: The Geographical Anatomy of Industrial Capitalism*, Boston: Allen & Unwin, 172–194. (Investigates the politics around steel mill closures in Europe in the 1980s and how different groups of workers' responses to these shaped local economies.)

Humphrey, C. R., Erickson, R. A., and Ottensmeyer, E. J. (1989) "Industrial development organizations and the local dependence hypothesis," *Policy Studies Journal*, 17.3: 624–642. (Explores the politics surrounding the creation of local boosterist coalitions and the usually minimal formal influence in such coalitions of unions.)

Lee, C. K. (2003) "Pathways of labour insurgency," in E. J. Perry and M. Selden (eds) *Chinese Society: Change, Conflict and Resistance* (2nd edn), New York: Routledge, 71–92. (Focuses upon contemporary labor struggles in China and what this means for the activities of the official trade unions.)

Peck, J. (1996) *Work-Place: The Social Regulation of Labor Markets*, New York: Guilford. (Shows how labor markets are spatially regulated and how workers' organizations can shape how they operate, thereby influencing patterns of development.)

Waterman, P. and Wills, J. (eds) (2001) *Place, Space and the New Labour Internationalisms*, Oxford: Blackwell. (This edited collection contains several chapters which highlight how unions shape local and regional development.)

Wills, J. (2001) "Community unionism and trade union renewal in the UK: Moving beyond the fragments at last?," *Transactions of the Institute of British Geographers*, 26.4: 465–483. (Examines how community unionism can impact upon local economies.)

11

Local and regional development

A global production network approach

Neil M. Coe and Martin Hess

Introduction: regional development as neither 'inside-out', nor 'outside-in'...

Regions have been central to the agenda of economic geography and the wider social sciences for at least twenty years now. Processes of economic globalisation – as manifested, for example, in the expansion in the scale and scope of the activities of transnational corporations (TNCs) and neoliberally inspired inter-regional competition for investment – have focused attention on the need for regional-level interventions among a broad community of academics and policy makers. In this chapter, drawing upon the global production networks (GPN) perspective (Henderson *et al.*, 2002) we outline a conceptual framework that seeks to delimit regional development dynamics in a globalizing context. This approach focuses on the dynamic 'strategic coupling' of global production networks and regional assets, an interface mediated by institutional activities across different scales. Our contention is that regional development ultimately depends on the ability (or not) of this coupling to engender processes of value creation, enhancement and, most importantly, capture (Coe *et al.*, 2004).

In so doing, we seek to connect across two by now well-established bodies of work which have offered analytical perspectives on the links between globalisation dynamics and notions of 'regional development'. On the one hand, the so-called 'new regionalism' literature has placed significant emphasis on endogenous institutional structures and their capacity to 'hold down' global networks (for an overview, see MacLeod, 2001). For example, Amin and Thrift (1994) coined the term 'institutional thickness' to encapsulate the socio-cultural factors lying at the heart of economic success, a notion encompassing a strong and broad local institutional presence, a high degree of interaction among local institutions, the emergence of progressive local power structures and the development of a sense of common enterprise. In favourable circumstances, the outcome of institutional thickness is argued to be a regional economy characterised by dynamic, flexible institutions and high levels of trust and innovation.

Appealing though such concepts are, the functional connections between institutional thickness and regional development have been made far less clear. First, while institutional thickness may be a necessary condition for regional success, it is certainly not sufficient, as evidenced by many peripheral regions with dense institutional networks and yet relatively stagnant economies. Second, the necessity of purely local institutional building may be questionable in contexts where the re-scaling of national government/governance functions is giving greater powers to regional economic institutions. In reality, regional institutional configurations are often characterised by overlapping networks of locally initiated institutions, those with powers devolved or 'hollowed-out' from the national state, and regional 'branches' of national institutions. Third, and most important here, is the need to explore more fully the interactions between extra-regional firm networks and institutional thickness, and their influence upon economic development. The critical factor for economic success is often not necessarily intense local networks, but the ability to anticipate and respond to changing external circumstances: as Amin (1999: 375) has argued, "it is the management of the region's wider connectivity that is of prime importance, rather than its intrinsic supply-side qualities".

On the other hand, work on inter-firm networks – such as the global commodity chain (GCC) and global value chain (GVC) approaches – has been focused on the organisational structures of global production systems and how particular regions 'slot into' these networks with varying impacts on the potential for industrial upgrading (Gereffi and Korzeniewicz, 1994; Gereffi et al., 2005). While analysis of the governance structures, input-output systems, territorialities and institutional frameworks of global commodity chains has no doubt made important contributions to our understanding of development processes in a globalising world, such work has received sustained criticism for some of its perceived conceptual shortcomings (e.g. Dicken et al., 2001). Most important here is the extent to which questions of spatiality and geographical scale have been integrated into GCC/GVC analyses. Arguably, due to a seeming preoccupation with the

national scale, it has often had "surprisingly little to say about regional and subnational processes, because of the focus on the international dimensions of commodity chains and global divisions of labour" (Smith et al., 2002: 49). A related issue is the neglect of regional institutions in shaping processes of industrial upgrading. Whereas national and supra-national regulatory bodies have been given consideration as institutional frameworks for commodity chains, regional institutions have hardly been mentioned, although their activities may be integral to capturing the value created in particular localities.

In this chapter, we argue that neither the 'inside-out' nor the 'outside-in' perspectives offered respectively by these two strands of work is adequate in its own right: instead, regional development is best understood by working at the intersection of these two approaches. As such, it contributes to a discernible rapprochement between the two literatures over the last few years. The new regionalism literature now undoubtedly places more weight on the extra-local dynamics shaping economic growth within regions (both knowledge, capital and labour flows and also the wider institutional structures within which regions are embedded) (MacKinnon et al., 2002). Bathelt et al. (2004), for example, describe the importance of both 'local buzz' and 'global knowledge pipelines' in driving innovation and economic growth. (See also Bathelt, this volume.) Moreover, GCC/GVC studies have become increasingly concerned with how regional clusters and industrial districts are incorporated into global production systems, and the ensuing implications for local economic development and industrial upgrading (Humphrey, 2001). Local institutional formations are integral, for example, to Neilson and Pritchard's (2009) analysis of the position of the tea and coffee industries of South India in global value chains.

Our argument develops over three further sections. Next, we explain our conceptualisation of the 'strategic coupling' of global production networks and regional economies. Second, we evaluate the role of institutions of different kinds in mediating the intersection of regions and production networks. Third, we consider the limits to this conceptualisation, and explore the potential for extending notions of regional development beyond what tend to be economistic, firm-centric approaches. Three definitional issues merit brief consideration before proceeding, however. First, and most prosaically, we use the term 'region' as a 'taken-for-granted' sub-national scale of economic space. The wide range of cultural, political and historical forces behind the forging of regional spaces is not our primary consideration here. Second, our notion of regional development is a relative one, and is not something that can necessarily be measured by arbitrary quantifiable indicators of economic success. Regional development is seen as a process that can be characterised as a local improvement in economic conditions. Third, regional development is, by definition, an interdependent or relational process. The fortunes of regions are not only shaped by what is going on within them, but also through wider sets of relations of control and dependency, of competition and markets.

Global production networks, strategic coupling and regional development

The GPN framework offers a heuristic framework for understanding the developing geographies of the global economy. It emphasises the complex intra- , inter- and extra-firm networks that constitute all production systems, and explores how these are structured both organisationally and geographically. A GPN can be broadly defined as the globally organised nexus of interconnected functions and operations of firms and non-firm institutions through which goods and services are produced, distributed and consumed (Henderson et al., 2002). The operationalisation of the framework depends on the analysis of three interrelated variables. First, processes of value creation, enhancement and capture are scrutinised. Second, the distribution and operation of power of different forms within GPNs is considered. Third, the embeddedness of GPNs — or how they constitute and are reconstituted by the economic, social and political arrangements of the places they inhabit — is investigated.

The GPN approach can usefully be distinguished from GCC/GVC approaches in five key respects. First, through the explicit consideration of extra-firm networks, it necessarily brings into view the broad range of non-firm organisations — for example, supranational organisations, government agencies, trade unions, employer associations, NGOs, and consumer groups — that can shape firm activities in the particular locations absorbed into GPNs. Second, GPN analysis is innately multi-scalar, and considers the interactions and mutual constitution of all spatial scales from the local/regional to the global. Third, this is an avowedly network approach that seeks to move beyond the analytical limitations of the 'chain' notion. Production systems are seen as networked 'meshes' of intersecting vertical and horizontal connections in order to avoid deterministic linear interpretations of how production systems operate and generate value. Fourth, the governance characteristics of GPNs are taken to be much more complex, contingent, and variable over time than is suggested in GCC/GVC analyses. Fifth, and finally, a central concern of GPN analysis is not to consider the networks in an abstracted manner for their own sake, but to reveal the dynamic developmental impacts that result for both the firms and territories that they interconnect.

This broad approach can usefully be applied to understanding regional development in the contemporary era. Most importantly from this perspective, analytical attention must be paid to both endogenous growth factors within specific regions and also to the strategic needs of the translocal actors that coordinate GPNs, most notably large TNCs. Regional development can thus be conceptualised as the dynamic outcome of the complex interaction between region-specific networks and global production networks within the context of changing regional governance structures. It is the interactive effects between these two fields that contribute to regional development, not just either inherent regional advantages or the industrial structures of global industries. As a result, regional development is a highly contingent process that cannot necessarily be predicted by inventories of regional institutions or broad positions in global value chains.

In this view, endogenous factors are necessary, but not sufficient, to generate regional growth in an era in which competition is increasingly global. There is no doubt that, for development to take place, a region must benefit from economies of scale and scope derived from the local human, technological and institutional resource base; the term 'regional assets' can be used to describe this necessary precondition for regional development. These assets can produce two types of economies. First, economies of scale can be achieved through highly localised concentrations of specific knowledge, skills and expertise in certain industries. Second, economies of scope can exist if regions are able to reap the intangible benefits of learning and the cooperative atmosphere – sometimes known as spillover effects – that come from hosting a range of interconnected activities. However, the economies of scale and scope embedded within specific regions are only advantageous – and bring about regional development – insofar as they can complement the strategic needs of translocal actors situated within global production networks. As shown in Figure 11.1, when such complementarity exists, a strategic coupling process will take place through which the advantages of regions interact with the strategic needs of actors in GPNs. This strategic coupling process has three important characteristics: it is strategic in that it needs intentional and active intervention on the part of both institutions and inward investors to

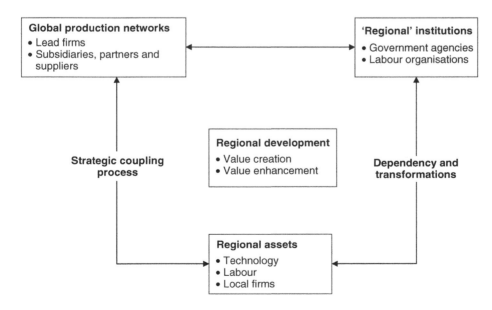

Figure 11.1 Global production networks and regional development.
Source: Authors' research

131

occur; it is time-space contingent as it is subject to change and is a temporary coalition; and it transcends territorial boundaries as actors from different spatial scales interact (Yeung, 2009).

The coupling process is seen to work through the processes of value creation, enhancement and capture. In GPN analysis, value is used to refer to the various forms of economic rent that can be realised through market as well as non-market transactions within production systems. Rent is created in a situation where a firm has access to scarce resources that can insulate them from competition by creating barriers to entry for competitors' firms. Firms may be able to generate rents within GPNs in a number of ways (Kaplinsky, 2005: 62–84): from asymmetric access to key product and process technologies (technological rents), from the particular talents of their labour force (human resource rents), from particular organisational skills such as 'just-in-time' production techniques (organisational rents), from various inter-firm relationships involving the management of production linkages with other firms (relational rents) or from establishing brand-name prominence in major markets (brand rents). In certain sectors and circumstances additional 'exogenous' rents may accrue to some firms as a consequence of preferential access to natural resources (resource rents), the impacts of government policies (policy rents), the uneven availability of infrastructure (infrastructure rents) and the nature of the financial system (financial rents).

This conception of value as economic rent has two significant implications for analysing regional development. First, different forms of rent can be created and captured by actors in GPNs meaning that regions may be best served by focusing on the particular form (or forms) of rent that suits their particular configuration of labour, capital and state institutions. A region with a highly competitive labour market, an active pool of venture capitalists and a pro-growth coalition of institutions is very differently placed to one

that is characterised by a weakly organised and abundant supply of labour, a virtual absence of finance capital and an unstable institutional structure. Endowed with different configurations of assets, such regions are likely to perform very different roles in terms of value creation within global production networks. Second, it should be noted that value takes on different forms across GPNs. At the time when value is created in one region, it may take a particular form, e.g. relational rent extracted from relationships with highly specialised suppliers. When this value is transferred to other regions, it may take on other forms, e.g. technological and/or brand-name rents. The potential multiplicity of rent forms indicates that the analysis of value creation and capture in regional development must go beyond simply tracking the market values of goods and services produced.

The multi-scalar institutional interface

The fact that a region is 'plugged into' a GPN does not automatically guarantee a positive developmental outcome because local actors may be creating forms of rent that do not maximise the region's economic potential. Hence, regional assets can become an advantage for regional development only if they fit the strategic needs of global production networks. The process of 'fitting' regional assets with strategic needs of GPNs requires the presence of appropriate institutional structures that simultaneously promote regional advantages and enhance the region's articulation into wider networks. It is crucial here that the notion of 'regional' institutions includes not only regionally specific institutions, but also local arms of national/supranational bodies (e.g. a trade union's 'local' chapters), and extra-local institutions that affect activities within the region without necessarily having a presence (e.g. a national tax authority). These multi-scalar regional institutions are important because they provide the 'glue' that ties down GPNs in particular localities.

Three dimensions of such institutional structures are crucial to regional development. The first dimension involves the creation of value through the efforts of regional institutions in attracting the location of economic activity, e.g. training and educating the local workforce, offering incentive packages, promoting start-up firms and supplier networks, facilitating venture capital formation, and encouraging entrepreneurial activities. Second, value enhancement essentially involves knowledge and technology transfer and processes of industrial upgrading. The influence of regional institutions – government agencies, trade unions, employer associations, etc. – can be especially significant here. On the one hand, regional institutions may develop specific regional assets (e.g. research capacity, supply networks, skills development) that underpin processes of upgrading for local firms. On the other hand, regional institutions may work directly with lead firms in GPNs to help them develop their value enhancement activities as part of a move towards higher quality inward investment. Over time, more value-enhancement activities may occur in these regions where lead firms are induced to bring in their core technologies and expertise. The development of sophisticated local supplier networks may also be important in enhancing the value activities of lead firms through the 'reverse' transfer of local knowledge and experience.

The third dimension of regional institutions in promoting regional development rests with their capacity to ensure value capture. It is one thing for value to be created and enhanced in some regions, but it may be quite another for it to be captured for the benefit of these regions. Issues of power and control are critical in the analysis of value capture. Understanding power in GPNs necessitates a move beyond 'centred' conceptions of power as an asset that can be accrued, towards networked or relational understandings of power (Allen, 2003). In this interpretation, power is generated through network relationships and hence varies according to the actors involved in the network, the structural and informational resources that they have at their disposal, and the effectiveness with which they are mobilised. Moreover, power structures at a given point in a network will influence and be influenced by power structures at other stages of the network. Power relations in supply networks are therefore transaction specific. A GPN can be seen as a series of exchange relationships, and variations in the power balance along the network will affect the ability of its members to capture value. Equally, any given relationship cannot be purely about power as there is always a measure of mutual interest and dependency involved. While the relationships among participants are rarely symmetrical, participants in GPNs to some degree depend on each other and work together for mutual benefit. It is not just firms that are enmeshed in these networked forms of power, but also a wide range of institutions – the state and various supra-state organisations, labour unions, trade associations, NGOs, etc. – that may also shape the structure and nature of GPNs. As a result, "GPNs resemble contested organizational fields in which actors struggle over the construction of economic relationships, governance structures, institutional rules and norms, and discursive frames" (Levy, 2008: 944). Where this is perhaps most visible is in the context of global North–South relations. While firms and industries in developing and emerging economies may experience various forms of upgrading, as numerous studies have shown (e.g. Humphrey and Schmitz, 2002; Scott, 2008), the challenge remains for regions – especially in the global South – to develop the institutional thickness necessary to 'fit' this upgrading with wider regional development goals (see Coe *et al.* (2004), for the example of BMW's GPN in Germany and Thailand).

Arguably, the more a region is articulated into GPNs, the more likely it is to be able to reap the benefits of economies of scale and scope in these networks, but the less likely it is able to control its own fate. A real risk in such relationships is the possibility of institutional capture, whereby the engagement between local institutions and external firms is asymmetrical, leading to the direct and indirect subsidisation of the activities of inward investors through economic development strategies that prioritise the needs of such firms at the expense of indigenous firms (Phelps, 2000). Christopherson and Clark (2007) similarly argue that the reality of power relations between GPNs and regional institutions is that TNCs are able to co-opt regional growth agendas in their favour, especially in terms of influencing regulatory policy (e.g. concerning the commercialisation of innovation), driving the research agendas of publicly supported research centres and dominating the regional labour market in terms of both skills, and pay and conditions. Importantly for these authors, such dominance does not just reflect the power of individual large firms, but also wider, systemic aspects of neoliberal market governance (e.g. engendering inter-place competition). Another risk is the possibility of institutional lock-in (Grabher, 1993) whereby regional institutions are unable to respond quickly enough to the rapidly changing demands of GPNs and as a result either become disconnected from the network or trapped in a form of strategic coupling that does not best utilise the region's assets. This is particularly a risk in advanced economies with established institutional infrastructures.

However, in certain circumstances, regional institutions may mobilise their region-specific assets to bargain with transnational firms such that their power relations are not necessarily one-way in favour of the latter. The bargaining position of such institutions is particularly high when their region-specific assets are highly complementary to the strategic needs of transnational firms (e.g. specialised knowledge pools in the biotechnology sector). The likelihood of value capture in specific regions is generally enhanced by a cooperative set of state, labour and business institutions that offer unique combinations of region-specific assets to lead firms in GPNs. Overall, the capacity of regions to capture value is a dynamic outcome of the complex bargaining process between regional institutions and lead firms in global production networks.

What kind of regional development? Exploring the dark sides of strategic coupling

In order to make the strategic coupling of global production networks and territories work for local and regional development, it is important to bear in mind the profound power asymmetries which characterise the bargaining process that determines the location of value capture. As numerous studies have shown (see, for example, Phelps and Raines, 2003), the embedding of GPNs into regional economies is of course no guarantee of positive developmental outcomes, even if it results in new or enhanced opportunities for value capture at the local level. Indeed, depending on their position of power within a network, some local firms may benefit from their insertion into GPNs, contributing to regional economic growth and innovation, while other actors within the region may only receive marginal benefits or become excluded in the process. In other words, although the articulation of regions in global production networks can produce significant economic gains on an aggregate level, in many cases it also causes intra-regional disarticulations, for instance, through uneven resource allocation and the breakup of existing cultural, social and economic networks and systems. This 'dark side' of strategic coupling not only affects firms and their growth potential, but also, and maybe more importantly, the opportunities and livelihoods of people and households, and hence raises serious questions about the nature and distribution of the value generated, enhanced and captured within the region.

Figure 11.2 provides a typology and examples of the negative consequences that can and frequently do result from the connections between regional economies/territorial assets and GPNs (or lack thereof). On the one hand, it is useful to think about both significant changes in the level or existence of region-GPN connections – ruptures – as well as ongoing areas of tension and contest between different local and non-local actors – frictions. On the other hand, by distinguishing between inter- and intra-regional effects, this typology also highlights Hudson's (2007: 1156) argument that regions need to be conceived of as both territorial and networked entities, "a product of a struggle between territorializing and de-territorializing processes". As the concept of strategic coupling affirms, that struggle transcends territorial boundaries and involves actors at different geographical scales. In this context, it is often implicitly assumed that harmonious interests exist between 'regional' actors with regard to mobilising regional assets to meet the strategic needs of GPNs and thus improve regional development. In reality, however, intra-regional conflicts of interest will arise about the positive and negative impacts of

globalised regional development and the appropriation of value (cf. Phelps and Waley, 2004). For development policy, this means moving beyond the primacy of what Christopherson and Clark call investment regionalism (focused on overall economic growth and value-added) to include the reduction of intra-regional inequality through distributive regionalism: "The search for ways to connect investment regionalism, centered on regional innovation systems, with distributive regionalism, centered on equity, access, and quality of life is a search for a model of sustainable economic development" (Christopherson and Clark, 2007: 148).

For the concept of strategic coupling to realise its potential (see also Coe *et al.*, 2008), it is important to reconsider the meaning of regional development and the underlying notions of value and innovation. By defining value as various forms of rent – in addition to more conventional readings of surplus value – a GPN perspective on regions emphasises the economic dimensions of development in a way which is similar to many territorial innovation models (TIMs). In their critique of technologist and market-competition-led development concepts, Moulaert and

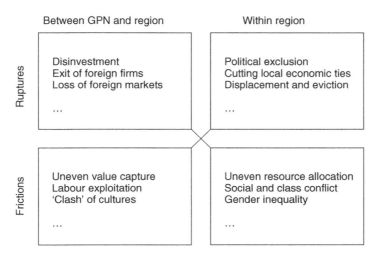

Figure 11.2 (Dis)embedding global production networks.
Source: Authors' research

Nussbaumer (2005: 46) pointed out the dangers of a reductionist development view which largely neglects the non-economic dimensions of territorial development:

> Most of the TIM models stress the instrumentality of institutions for economic restructuring and improved competitiveness of regions and localities. But none of these models makes reference to improving the non-economic dimensions and non-market-led sections of economy in localities […] According to the TIM, quality of life in local communities coincides with growing prosperity and will be produced as positive externalities of higher economic growth; no distinction is made between well-being and growth, between culture and business climate and so on.

To avoid such reductionism, strategic coupling therefore needs to adopt a more comprehensive view of what constitutes value beyond the firm and development beyond the economic (Hess, 2009).

Outside the firm and corporate networks, value is created by people and households when they try to produce their livelihoods through accessing and transforming available resources. As Bury (2008: 310; emphasis in original) argues, global players like TNCs can have significant impacts on this process:

> TNC activities often affect *what* resources households access in the pursuit of livelihoods as well as how these resources are accessed. Thus, TNCs can affect the rules and practices governing household access to resources as well as the different resource combinations utilized to produce livelihoods.

This is not only an issue for developing economies and extractive industries, from which he draws his example, but a fundamental problem that shows the dark side of strategic coupling. As illustrated in Figure 11.2, the political exclusion of some parts of civil society, the disarticulation of existing regional economies or growing gender inequalities are just a few possible outcomes that affect value creation, capture and the production of livelihoods. Regional development policy, therefore, in addition to pursuing a more distributive form of regionalism, must also be open to the potential of strategic decoupling from some GPNs if the contribution of such global ties to value creation and capture does not outweigh the detrimental effects for the economy and society affected. It is important in this context to bear in mind that no region or locality is completely detached from the global economy, and while development in some places may be strongly linked to one specific GPN, in most cases regions are inserted into a multitude of GPNs. Any development strategy aimed at enhancing economic well-being, social justice and participation/democracy must therefore reflect decisions about which networks should be engaged with and which should be decoupled from, thereby actively shaping the regions' positionality with respect to wider economic systems.

Conclusion

Local and regional development is a highly contested and political process. By forming different, temporal and multi-scalar coalitions, a multiplicity of actors struggle over the generation and distribution of value in its various forms and the ways to achieve social and economic development. GPNs and the regional contexts in which they 'touch down' create an open, dynamic relationship with contingent developmental outcomes, a political project based on multiple dimensions of power and agency on both sides. While some literature (cf. Levy, 2008) assumes that hegemonic power rests with global players and global structures, a GPN perspective on local and regional development emphasises that power relationships are reciprocal, but not necessarily symmetrical or exclusively in favour of non-local actors, with local institutions and local civil society rendered powerless. This chimes with Friedman's (2006: 428) assertion that analytical approaches should refuse "victimology and assume agency on all sides in the zones of encounter – not autonomy, or the freedom to act unimpeded by others, but rather agency, the drive to name one's collective and individual identity and to negotiate the conditions". What constitutes regional development and how to achieve it is at the centre of these negotiations. The concept of 'globalising' regional development (Coe *et al.*, 2004) as a process of strategic (de)coupling offers a lens through which value creation, enhancement, and capture by firms, institutions and households can be analysed. Translating that analysis into concrete politics will require social innovation to produce the necessary institutional, communication and governance structures which ultimately determine local and regional, economic and social development.

Acknowledgements

Many thanks to the editors of this volume for their perceptive comments on an earlier version of the chapter. We would also like to acknowledge that this chapter draws on ideas developed jointly with Peter Dicken and Henry Yeung.

References

Allen, J. (2003) *Lost geographies of power*, Oxford: Blackwell.

Amin, A. (1999) 'An institutionalist perspective on regional economic development', *International Journal of Urban and Regional Research*, 23, 365–378.

Amin, A. and Thrift, N. (1994) 'Living in the global', in A. Amin and N. Thrift (eds) *Globalisation, institutions and regional development in Europe*, Oxford: Oxford University Press, 1–22.

Bathelt, H., Malmberg, A. and Maskell, P. (2004) 'Clusters and knowledge: local buzz, global pipelines and the process of knowledge creation', *Progress in Human Geography*, 28, 31–56.

Bury, J. (2008) 'Transnational corporations and livelihood transformations in the Peruvian Andes: an actor-oriented political ecology', *Human Organization*, 67, 307–321.

Christopherson, S. and Clark, J. (2007) *Remaking regional economies: power, labor and firm strategies in the knowledge economy*, New York: Routledge.

Coe, N. M., Dicken, P. and Hess, M. (2008) 'Global production networks: realizing the potential', *Journal of Economic Geography*, 8, 271–295.

Coe, N. M., Hess, M., Yeung, H. W-C., Dicken, P. and Henderson, J. (2004) 'Globalizing regional development: a global production networks perspective', *Transactions of the Institute of British Geographers*, 29, 468–484.

Dicken, P., Kelly, P. F., Olds, K. and Yeung, H. W-C. (2001) 'Chains and networks, territories and scales: towards a relational framework for analysing the global economy', *Global Networks*, 1, 89–112.

Friedman, S. F. (2006) 'Periodizing modernism: postcolonial modernities and the space/time borders of modernist studies', *Modernism/Modernity*, 13, 425–443.

Gereffi, G. and Korzeniewicz, M. (eds) (1994) *Commodity chains and global capitalism*, Westport, CT: Praeger.

Gereffi, G., Humphrey, J. and Sturgeon, T. (2005) 'The governance of global value chains', *Review of International Political Economy*, 12, 78–104.

Grabher, G. (1993) 'The weakness of strong ties: the lock-in of regional development in the Ruhr area', in G. Grabher (ed.) *The embedded firm: on the socio-economics of inter-firm relations*, London: Routledge: 255–278.

Henderson, J., Dicken, P., Hess, M., Coe, N. M. and Yeung, H. W-C. (2002) 'Global production networks and the analysis of economic development', *Review of International Political Economy*, 9, 436–464.

Hess, M. (2009) 'Investigating the archipelago economy: chains, networks, and the study of uneven development', *Journal für Entwicklungspolitik*, 2, in press.

Hudson, R. (2007) 'Regions and regional uneven development forever? Some reflective comments upon theory and practice', *Regional Studies*, 41, 1149–1160.

Humphrey, J. (2001) *Opportunities for SMEs in developing countries to upgrade in a global economy* (http://www.inti.gov.ar/cadenasdevalor/, accessed 5 March 2009).

Humphrey, J. and Schmitz, H. (2002) 'How does insertion in global value chains affect upgrading in industrial clusters?', *Regional Studies*, 36, 1017–1027.

Kaplinsky, R. (2005) *Globalization, poverty and inequality*, Cambridge: Polity.

Levy, D. L. (2008) 'Political contestation in global production networks', *Academy of Management Review*, 33, 943–963.

MacKinnon, D., Cumbers, A. and Chapman, K. (2002) 'Learning, innovation and regional development: a critical appraisal of recent debates', *Progress in Human Geography*, 26, 293–311.

MacLeod, G. (2001) 'New regionalism reconsidered: globalization and the remaking of political economic space', *International Journal of Urban and Regional Research*, 25, 804–829.

Moulaert, F. and Nussbaumer, J. (2005) 'The social region: beyond the territorial dynamics of the learning economy', *European Urban and Regional Studies*, 12, 45–64.

Neilson, J. and Pritchard, B. (2009) *Value chain struggles: institutions and governance in the plantation districts of South India*, Chichester: Wiley-Blackwell.

Phelps, N. (2000) 'The locally embedded multinational and institutional capture', *Area*, 32, 169–178.

Phelps, N. and Raines, P. (eds) (2003) *The new competition for inward investment. Companies, institutions and territorial development*, Cheltenham: Edward Elgar.

Phelps, N. and Waley, P. (2004) 'Capital versus the districts: a tale of one multinational company's attempt to disembed itself', *Economic Geography*, 80, 191–215.

Scott, A. J. (2008) 'Patterns of development in the furniture industry of Thailand: organization, location and trade', *Regional Studies*, 42, 17–30.

Smith, A., Rainnie, A., Dunford, M., Hardy, J., Hudson, R. and Sadler, D. (2002) 'Networks of value, commodities and regions: reworking divisions of labour in macro-regional economies', *Progress in Human Geography*, 26, 41–63.

Yeung, H. W-C. (2009) 'Regional development and the competitive dynamics of global production networks: an East Asian perspective', *Regional Studies*, 43, 325–351.

Further reading

Bury, J. (2008) 'Transnational corporations and livelihood transformations in the Peruvian Andes: an actor-oriented political ecology', *Human Organization*, 67, 307–321. (Provides a discussion of the effects global actors, specifically TNC, have with regard to regional development and livelihood production.)

Coe, N. M., Dicken, P. and Hess, M. (2008) 'Global production networks: realizing the potential', *Journal of Economic Geography*, 8, 271–295. (Offers an overview of current state of research on global production networks and evaluates the potential for further developments.)

Coe, N. M., Hess, M., Yeung, H. W-C., Dicken, P. and Henderson, J. (2004) 'Globalizing regional development: a global production networks perspective', *Transactions of the Institute of British Geographers*, 29, 468–484. (Develops the concepts of 'globalising regional development' and 'strategic coupling', grounded in a global production networks perspective.)

Levy, D .L. (2008) 'Political contestation in global production networks', *Academy of Management Review*, 33, 943–963. (Critically investigates global production networks and related approaches as political systems, using a neo-Gramscian approach.)

Phelps, N. and Raines, P. (eds) (2003) *The new competition for inward investment. Companies, institutions and territorial development*, Cheltenham: Edward Elgar. (A collected volume containing many examples of regional development, investment regionalism and the role of institutions.)

12

Evolutionary approaches to local and regional development policy

Robert Hassink and Claudia Klaerding

Introduction

Local and regional development policies are affected by policy-related theoretical concepts and they, in turn, are influenced by meta-theoretical paradigms or turns in academic writing. In the economic geography and regional planning literature, for instance, there has been a cultural turn, a learning turn, a relational turn and most recently an evolutionary turn (Scott 2000), the latter being this chapter's main focus. It aims first at presenting some key evolutionary concepts (Boschma and Frenken 2007; Martin and Sunley 2006; Boschma and Martin 2009) and their relevance to local and regional development policy.

Innovation has become the key focus of local and regional development polices due to the increasing importance both of the knowledge economy in general and of the regional level with regard to diffusion-oriented innovation support policies (Amin 1999; Cooke and Morgan 1998; Asheim *et al.* 2003; Asheim *et al.* 2006b; Fritsch and Stephan 2005; Klaerding *et al.* 2009; Boschma 2008). The regional level is more and more seen as the level that offers the greatest prospect for devising governance structures to foster learning in the knowledge-based economy, due to four

mechanisms, namely knowledge spill-overs, spin-offs, intra-regional labour mobility and networks (Cooke and Morgan 1998; Boschma 2008). Partly supported by national and supranational support programmes and encouraged by strong institutional set-ups found in successful regional economies such as Silicon Valley in the USA, Baden-Württemberg in Germany and Emilia-Romagna in Italy, many regions in industrialised countries have been setting up science parks, technopoles, technological financial aid schemes, innovation support agencies, community colleges and initiatives to support clustering of industries since the second half of the 1980s. The central aim of these policies is to support regional endogenous potential by encouraging the diffusion of new technologies. Since the mid-1990s, these policies have been influenced by theoretical and conceptual ideas, such as regional innovation systems (Cooke *et al.* 2004), the learning region (Morgan 1997) and clusters (Enright 2003). These concepts originated in industrialised countries, but have also recently become important for developing and emerging economies, particularly concerning regional innovation systems (Lundvall *et al.* 2006; Cooke *et al.* 2004; Cooke and Memedovic 2003) and clusters (Schmitz and Nadvi 1999; Schmitz 2004).

However, recently it has been increasingly doubtful whether lessons can be learned from successful regional economies in order to create 'Silicon Somewheres' (Hospers 2006; Hassink and Lagendijk 2001). Furthermore, the scale issue, that is, the role of the regional level *vis-à-vis* the national and supranational level in supporting innovations, has been critically evaluated recently (Fromhold-Eisebith 2007; Uyarra 2009). Finally, complaints have become louder about regional innovation policies becoming too standardised (Tödtling and Trippl 2005; Visser and Atzema 2008).

In this chapter we will argue that the evolutionary perspective positively contributes to local and regional development policies by introducing some key explanatory notes, such as path dependence, lock-ins and co-evolution. Moreover, it has a positive and refining influence on existing concepts, that is, regional innovation systems and clusters, in particular. In the following some key evolutionary notes will first be presented in Section 2. In Section 3, three policy-related concepts, namely the learning region, regional innovation systems and clusters, will be discussed from an evolutionary perspective. Conclusions are drawn in Section 4.

Evolutionary thinking and local and regional development policy

Recently not only many economic geographers have introduced evolutionary thinking into their discipline (Boschma and Frenken 2007; Boschma and Martin 2009; Schamp 2000; Martin and Sunley 2006; Frenken 2007); also in other disciplines, such as economics, planning and sociology, this has been the case (Frenken 2007). In contrast to neoclassical theory, this school takes history and geography seriously by recognising the importance of place-specific elements and processes to explain broader spatial patterns of technology evolution. Evolutionary economic geography deals with "the processes by which the economic landscape – the spatial organization of economic production, distribution and consumption – is transformed over time" (Boschma and Martin 2007: 539). From evolutionary thinking the following notes are essential to local and regional development policy: path dependence, lock-ins, path creation, related variety and co-evolution. These concepts can potentially explain why it is that some regional economies lose dynamism and others do not.

"A path-dependent process or system is one whose outcome evolves as a consequence of the process's or system's own history" (Martin and Sunley 2006: 399). Closely related to the discussion around path dependence and regional evolution is the issue of lock-ins hindering necessary restructuring processes in regional economies (Martin and Sunley 2006; Grabher 1993; Hassink 2009). Grabher (1993) has defined these obstacles as three kinds of lock-ins, which together can be referred to as regional lock-ins. First, a functional lock-in refers to hierarchical, close inter-firm relationships, particularly between large enterprises and small- and medium-sized suppliers, which may eliminate the need for suppliers to develop critical boundary-spanning functions, such as research and development and marketing. Second, a cognitive lock-in is regarded as a common world-view or mindset that might confuse secular trends with cyclical downturns. Third, and closely related to cognitive lock-ins, is the notion of political lock-ins that might come up in a production cluster (Grabher 1993). Political lock-ins are thick institutional tissues aiming at preserving existing traditional industrial structures and therefore unnecessarily slowing down industrial restructuring and indirectly hampering the development of indigenous potential and creativity.

The evolutionary perspective also contributes to the understanding of the emergence of new industries in a spatial perspective. The theoretical concepts of windows of locational opportunity and new industrial spaces both stress the locational freedom of newly emerging industries, whereas path creation emphasises the inter-dependence between paths and hence less locational freedom. These concepts are highly relevant for local and regional development policies, as they can support policy-makers in predicting where new industries might emerge (Martin and Sunley 2006).

Moreover, the evolutionary perspective contributes to thinking about the relationship between specialisation vs. diversification and regional economic growth and stability (Frenken *et al.* 2007; Martin and Sunley 2006; Essletzbichler 2007). On the one hand, variety is seen as a source of regional knowledge spill-overs, measured by related variety within sectors. On the other hand, in the case of unrelated variety, variety is seen as a portfolio protecting a region from external shocks. According to Martin and Sunley (2006: 421) "there is a trade-off between specialization and a short-lived burst of fast regional growth on the one hand, and diversity and continual regional adaptability on the other".

Another key note derived from evolutionary thinking is that of co-evolution, which can be applied in theorising about local and regional development policy. In a co-evolutionary perspective, it is not only firms and industries, but also local and regional innovation policy, and in a broader sense the institutional environment of firms and industries, that affect the dynamism of regional economies (Nelson 1994; Murmann 2003).

Theoretical concepts seen from an evolutionary perspective

In addition to the relevance of some key notes from the evolutionary approach, evolutionary thinking has also influenced other, sometimes older theoretical concepts with a strong relevance for local and regional innovation policy. In the following we will deal with arguably the most relevant concepts (for an extensive overview of these so-called

territorial innovation models, see Moulaert and Sekia 2003).

Learning regions

Of the recently born offspring of the family of territorial innovation models, the learning region concept seems to be most focused on overcoming and avoiding regional lock-ins (Schamp 2000; OECD 2001; Boschma and Lambooy 1999b; Morgan 1997). Although there are several definitions and perspectives, most scholars consider learning regions as a regional innovation strategy in which a broad set of innovation-related regional actors (politicians, policy-makers, chambers of commerce, trade unions, higher education institutes, public research establishments and companies) are strongly, but flexibly connected with each other, and who stick to the following set of "policy principles" (OECD 2001):

i) carefully coordinating supply of and demand for skilled individuals

ii) developing a framework for improving organisational learning, which is not only focused on high-tech sectors, but on all sectors that have the potential to develop high levels of innovative capacity

iii) carefully identifying resources in the region that could impede economic development (lock-ins)

iv) positively responding to changes from outside, particularly where this involves unlearning

v) developing mechanisms for coordinating both across departmental and governance (regional, national, supranational) responsibilities

vi) developing strategies to foster appropriate forms of social capital and tacit knowledge that are positive to learning and innovation

vii) continuously evaluating relationships between participation in individual learning, innovation and labour market changes

viii) fostering redundancy and variety of industries and networks

ix) ensuring the participation of large groups of society in devising and implementing strategies.

These characteristics of a learning region, however, only describe the method of working and the attitude of regional economic policy-makers. The concrete contents of the innovation policy need to vary according to the economic profile and demand in individual regions (Tödtling and Trippl 2005).

Furthermore, partly based on the learning region concept, the EU has started a new generation of regional policies (Landabaso *et al.* 2001), which aim at improving the institutional capacity for innovation of less-favoured regions. These, in turn, should lead to higher absorption capacity for innovation funds from national and European governments.

Recently, however, critical voices on the learning region have become louder (Hassink 2007; Cooke 2005). Particularly, its fuzziness, its normative character, its strong overlapping with other similar concepts and its squeezed position between national innovation systems and global production networks have been criticised. Evolutionary thinking around path dependence and lock-ins has been an important impetus for the emergence of the learning region, but it has not contributed much to refining and improving this criticised concept.

Regional innovation systems

The basis of regional innovation systems (RIS) is regional networks and interdependencies between firms and organisations such as research institutes, financial service providers, technology transfer agencies or regional governments as well as institutions in terms of norms, rules, routines and conventions (Cooke *et al.* 1998). The systemic dimension of RIS results from the coupling of three subsystems (Cooke *et al.* 1997) leading to synergy effects of enhanced regional innovation capacities (Edquist 2001). The first subsystem of finance refers to the availability of regional budgets and capacities to control and manage regional infrastructures. The cultural setting of regions constitutes the second subsystem and defines the milieu within which the knowledge networks are embedded. Interactive learning is identified as the third subsystem and represents the core element of RIS as new knowledge is created and exploited. By defining more or less favourable conditions of these subsystems the RIS approach becomes particularly relevant for regional innovation policies. Several EU programmes already adapt to the idea of RIS (Landabaso *et al.* 2001).

Cooke *et al.* (1998) argue that regional policy interventions appear to be most effective when regions display characteristics such as high financial autonomy and control of infrastructures, high political competences and dense knowledge networks which have been observed for the case of Baden-Württemberg. At the same time, though, there is no best-practice or one-size-fits-all model of RIS. Instead tailor-made policy measures are required according to specific regional arrangements (Tödtling and Trippl 2005; Boschma 2008). For instance, 'globalised' and 'dirigiste' RIS such as Singapore seem less integrated into regional networks. In contrast, business relations at the national and global scale as well as multinational corporations play key roles for promoting innovation (Cooke 2004).

The RIS approach relates to the evolutionary thinking in two ways (see also Uyarra 2009; Iammarino 2005): first of all, it is a dynamic approach. By drawing on different case studies Cooke (2004) illustrates that RIS change over time: regions such as Catalonia can be classified in different RIS typologies during the years of 1995 to 2005. Second, we argue that it clearly refers to the identified key notes of path dependence, co-evolution and lock-ins.

The notion of path dependence can be identified in the definitions of the central elements of RIS, namely region and innovation. Both are considered to evolve over time, and thus follow specific trajectories. According to Cooke *et al.* (1997, 1998) regions are continuously formed by unique political, cultural and economic processes leading to inner cohesiveness, homogeneity and shared regional identity. They display institutions and organisations which are understood as results of search and selection mechanisms for specific economic problems (Cooke *et al.* 1998; Boschma 2008). However, different empirical definitions regarding spatial boundaries of regions and RIS, respectively, make it difficult to provide clear policy advice (Doloreux and Parto 2005). Also, some authors question the assumed independence of regional systems from national influences which seem to be predominant (Bathelt and Depner 2003).

Also, innovations are understood as inherently path dependent because they are conceptualised as social and evolutionary processes which are characterised by constant learning and accumulation of knowledge (Cooke *et al.* 1998). Innovations are generated through feedback loops and thereby refer to knowledge which has been gathered in the past. Hence, innovative outcomes and technological standards within a region crucially depend on previous knowledge trajectories.

Besides the idea of path dependence the RIS approach emphasises co-evolutionary processes. Cooke *et al.* (1998) argue for mutual interdependencies between institutions, organisations and firms. On the one hand, organisations and firms are claimed to be embedded in institutional settings which regulate economic interactions. On the other hand, organisations and firms impact upon institutions in two ways: they are able to both, reinforce institutions by reproducing established behaviour and to introduce new sets of practices which challenge the existing institutional context. Due to multiple systemic intra- and inter-regional linkages RIS are potentially flexible and capable of adjustments. However, institutions and organisations are seen as rather reluctant to make changes and transformations can turn out to be a slow and long-term process (Boschma 2008).

This represents a crucial turning point for regional development as lock-in situations are likely to appear. In this case, institutional and organisational set-ups of regions do not match the demands of new markets or technologies any longer (Boschma and Lambooy 1999a). Both, the co-evolution of institutions and organisations and their relative stabilities become problematic for regional growth because they reinforce an economic or technological path which is already outdated. The RIS approach, therefore, is well suited to analyse regional lock-ins because they result from strong systemic relations between the institutional, organisational and policy levels (Cooke *et al.* 1998). Because of these relations policy measures to combat lock-ins have simultaneously to consider changes within the economic and institutional environment. Tödtling and Trippl (2005) suggest, for instance, the creation of knowledge networks including new industries and technologies as well as renewing the educational and scientific infrastructures of the region. Boschma (2008) argues to diversify and broaden the regional economic base to allow for multiple development paths which are not selective towards particular regions or sectors. To achieve highly flexible institutions and organisations RIS should, similar to the learning region approach, also promote rather loose systemic relations and a culture that supports openness and willingness to change (Cooke *et al.* 1998).

Clusters

According to Porter (2000: 16) clusters can be defined as "a geographically proximate group of interconnected companies and associated institutions in a particular field, linked by commonalities and complementarities".

In recent years they have become the target for policy-makers and a key concept in supporting innovativeness and competitiveness initiated at several spatial levels (supranational, national, regional) (see, for instance, Porter 2000; Asheim *et al.* 2006a; Borrás and Tsagdis 2008; OECD 2007). Clusters, therefore, like learning regions and RIS, seem to be an empirical and theoretical basis for newly oriented regional development policies based on innovation.

Martin and Sunley (2003), however, are very critical about the ambiguities and identification problems surrounding the cluster concept. In fact, the concept bears many characteristics of what Markusen (1999) has coined a fuzzy concept, which is characterised by both lacking conceptual clarity, rigour in the presentation of evidence and clear methodology and difficulties to operationalise. An important criticism of clusters concerns the fact that the literature strongly focuses on how clusters function, whereas their evolutionary development is disregarded, i.e. how clusters actually become clusters, how and why they decline, and how they shift into new fields (see Brenner 2004; Lorenzen 2005; Staber 2009). Existing studies on the emergence of clusters (e.g. Klepper 2007; Fornahl *et al.* 2009) tend to suggest that the processes responsible for the functioning of a cluster cannot explain its emergence. In addition to this, examples of declining clusters (Hassink 2009; Hassink and Shin 2005) illustrate that the economic advantages that stem from cluster dynamics are not permanent. In fact, the decline of clusters seems to be caused by factors that were advantages in the past (Martin and Sunley 2006).

A reaction to this criticism is the recently emerging literature on cluster life cycles, with clear links to key evolutionary notes such as path dependence, lock-ins and path creation (Menzel and Fornahl 2007; Press 2006). It considers the stage of the cluster in its life cycle and recommends adapting policies to the position of the cluster in its life cycle. By doing this the cluster is put in an evolutionary perspective. The life cycle of clusters goes from emerging to mature and declining stages, albeit not in a deterministic way (Figure 12.1; see also Lorenzen 2005; Enright 2003). Menzel and Fornahl (2007: 3) highlight the difference between industrial and cluster life cycle and its consequences for local peculiarities and hence fine-tuned policies:

> Comparisons of clustered and non-clustered companies during the industry life cycle highlight additional differences: clustered companies outperform non-clustered companies at the beginning of the life cycle and have a worse performance at its end.... This shows that the cluster life cycle is more than just a local representation of the industry life cycle and is prone to local peculiarities.

In a next step Menzel and Fornahl (2007: 35–36) describe the different stages and the particular policy consequences of these stages in development:

> During the emergent phase, the companies are too heterogeneous to make use of synergies, while they are too close in the declining stage to endogenously maintain their diversity.... During the emergence of the cluster, the goal must be to focus the often thematically scattered companies on particular points. These focal points generate first synergies within the cluster and enable it to enter the growth stage. After the growing stage, the intention must be to steadily maintain a certain heterogeneity of the cluster to avoid a decline and to enable new growth paths. Measures to enforce these strategies are, for example, the selective promotion of start-ups that either lead to a widening of the thematic boundaries of the cluster or to

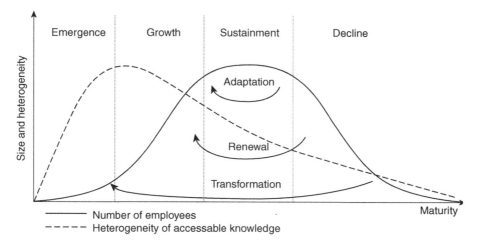

Figure 12.1 Interaction between size and heterogeneity of clusters over the life cycle.
Source: Adapted from Menzel and Fornahl (2007)

its focussing, depending on the stage of the cluster.

Clusters can display long-term growth if they retain their knowledge diversity (Saxenian 1994) and benefit from related variety to other industries. There are also examples of clusters renewing themselves and entering new growth phases (Trippl and Tödtling 2008). Clusters are therefore able to enter new life cycles in other industries and leave a maturing industry if they manage to go through processes of renewal and transformation (Figure 12.1).

Conclusions

This chapter has shown that the recent evolutionary perspective contributes to local and regional innovation policy in two ways. First, it introduces new notes that are highly relevant to local and regional economic development policies, such as path dependence, lock-ins, path creation, related variety and co-evolution. Second, it has had a positive and refining influence on existing concepts of local and regional economic policy, particularly on regional innovation systems, by considering the evolutionary development

of regional innovation systems through time, and on clusters, by extending this concept with the policy-relevant life cycle approach. Critical issues, however, can be seen in its limited empirical testing and the relegation of the political economy and agency of institutions within and beyond the firm in the evolutionary approach (MacKinnon *et al.* 2009). Furthermore, given the embryonic stage of evolutionary thinking in local and regional studies, there is still much room to "further incorporate aspects related to policy formation and evolution, as opposed to the present tendency to 'black box' policy processes" and "to develop a more sophisticated and nuanced understanding of the dynamics and limits of policy making and policy actors, and the increased complexity of policy making in a situation of multi-level, multi-actor governance" (Uyarra 2009).

One of the key influences of the evolutionary perspective on local and regional development policies is that they cannot be based on the principle of one-size-fits-all or best practice (Tödtling and Trippl 2005; Visser and Atzema 2008). These policies, instead, should reflect the different conditions and problems of the respective regional economies and innovation systems. A too strong focus on the existing regional industrial base,

145

however, might lead to negative path dependence and lock-ins. Therefore, "the paradox of regional policy holds that it can be very effective and successful in conserving economic activity by means of evolutionary policies, yet it has difficulty triggering, or even opposes new economic activity necessary for long-term development" (Boschma and Frenken 2007: 16). Evolutionary local and regional development policies should focus both on related variety in order "to broaden and diversify the regional economic base" and, at the same time, on "building on region-specific resources and extra-regional connections" (Boschma 2008: 328).

References

Amin, A. (1999) "An Institutional Perspective on Regional Economic Development", *International Journal of Urban and Regional Research* 23, 365–378.

Asheim, A., Cooke, P. and Martin, R. (eds) (2006a) *Clusters and Regional Development; Critical Reflections and Explorations*, London, New York: Routledge.

Asheim, B., Isaksen, A., Nauwelaers, C., Tödtling , F. (eds) (2003) *Regional Innovation policy for Small–Medium Enterprises*, Cheltenham: Edward Elgar.

Asheim, B.T., Boschma, R., Cooke, P., Laredo, P., Lindholm-Dahlstrand, Å. and Piccaluga, A. (2006b) "Constructing Regional Advantage. Principles, perspectives and policies", *Final Report European Commission*, DG Research, Brussels.

Bathelt, H. and Depner, H. (2003) "Innovation, Institution und Region: Zur Diskussion über nationale und regionale Innovationssysteme", *Erdkunde* 57, 126–143.

Borrás, S. and Tsagdis, D. (2008) *Cluster Policies in Europe; Firms, Institutions, and Governance*, Cheltenham: Edward Elgar.

Boschma, R. (2008) "Regional Innovation Policy", in B. Nooteboom and E. Stam (eds) *Microfoundations for Innovation Policy*, Amsterdam: Amsterdam University Press, 315–341.

Boschma, R.A. and Frenken, K. (2007) "Introduction: Applications of Evolutionary Economic Geography", in K. Frenken (ed.) *Applied Evolutionary Economics and Economic Geography*, Cheltenham: Edward Elgar, 1–24.

Boschma, R.A. and Lambooy, J.G. (1999a) "Evolutionary Economics and Economic Geography", *Journal of Evolutionary Economics* 9, 411–429.

—— (1999b) "The Prospects of an Adjustment Policy Based on Collective Learning in Old Industrial Regions", *GeoJournal* 49, 391–399.

Boschma, R. and Martin, R. (2007) "Editorial: Constructing An Evolutionary Economic Geography", *Journal of Economic Geography* 7, 537–548.

—— (eds) (2009) *Handbook of Evolutionary Economic Geography*, Cheltenham: Edward Elgar

Brenner, T. (2004) *Local Industrial Clusters: Existence, Emergence, and Evolution*, London: Routledge.

Cooke, P. (2004) "Introduction: Regional Innovation Systems – an Evolutionary Approach", in P. Cooke, M. Heidenreich and H-J. Braczyk (eds) *Regional Innovation Systems. The Role of Governance in a Globalized World*, London: Routledge, 1–18.

—— (2005) Learning Regions: A Critique. Paper presented at the 4th European Meeting on Applied Evolutionary Economics, Utrecht, 19–21 May.

Cooke, P. and Memedovic, O. (2003) *Strategies for Regional Innovation Systems: Learning Transfer and Applications*, Policy Papers, UNIDO, Vienna.

Cooke, P. and Morgan, K. (1998) *The Associational Economy: Firms, Regions, and Innovation*, Oxford: Oxford University Press.

Cooke, P., Heidenreich, M. and Braczyk, H-J. (eds) (2004) *Regional Innovation Systems: The Role of Governances in a Globalized World*, London: Routledge.

Cooke, P., Uranga, M. G. and Etxebarria, G. (1997) "Regional Innovation Systems: Institutional and Organisational Dimensions", *Research Policy* 26, 475–491.

—— (1998) "Regional Systems of Innovation: An Evolutionary Perspective", *Environment and Planning A* 30, 1563–1584.

Doloreux, D. and Parto, S. (2005) "Regional Innovation Systems: Current Discourse and Unresolved Issues", *Technology in Society* 27, 133–153.

Edquist, C. (2001) "Innovation Policy – A Systemic Approach", in D. Archibugi and B.-Å. Lundvall (eds) *The Globalizing Learning Economy: Major Socio-economic Trends and European Innovation Policy*, Oxford: Oxford University Press, 219–238.

Enright, M. J. (2003) "Regional Clusters: What we Know and What we Should Know", in J. Bröcker, D. Dohse and R. Soltwedel (eds)

Innovation Clusters and Interregional Competition, Berlin: Springer, 99–129.

Essletzbichler, J. (2007) "Diversity, Stability and Regional Growth in the United States, 1975–2002", in K. Frenken (ed.) *Applied Evolutionary Economics and Economic Geography*, Cheltenham: Edward Elgar, 203–229.

Fornahl, D., S. Henn and M.P. Menzel (eds) (2009) *The Emergence of Clusters. Theoretical, Empirical and Political Perspectives on the Initial Stage of Cluster Evolution*, Cheltenham: Edward Elgar.

Frenken, K. (ed.) (2007) *Applied Evolutionary Economics and Economic Geography*, Cheltenham: Edward Elgar.

Frenken, K., van Oort, F. G. and Verburg, T. (2007) "Related Variety, Unrelated Variety and Regional Economic Growth", *Regional Studies* 41, 685–697.

Fritsch, M. and Stephan, A. (2005) "Regionalization of Innovation Policy: Introduction to the Special Issue", *Research Policy* 34, 1123–1127.

Fromhold-Eisebith, M. (2007) "Bridging Scales in Innovation Policies: How to Link Regional, National and International Innovation Systems", *European Planning Studies* 15, 217–233.

Grabher, G. (1993) "The Weakness of Strong Ties; The Lock-in of Regional Development in the Ruhr Area", in G. Grabher (ed.) *The Embedded Firm; on the Socioeconomics of Industrial Networks*, London, New York: Routledge, 255–277.

Hassink, R. (2007) "The Learning Region: A Constructive Critique", in R. Rutten, and F.W.M. Boekema (eds) *The Learning Region: Foundations, State of the Art, Future*, Cheltenham: Edward Elgar, 252–271.

—— (2009) "Locked in Decline? On the Role of Regional Lock-ins in Old Industrial Areas", in R. Boschma and R. Martin (eds) *Handbook of Evolutionary Economic Geography*, Cheltenham: Edward Elgar.

Hassink, R. and Lagendijk, A. (2001) "The Dilemmas for Interregional Institutional Learning", *Environment and Planning* C 19, 65–84.

Hassink, R. and Shin, D-H. (2005) "Guest Editorial: The Restructuring of Old Industrial Areas in Europe and Asia", *Environment and Planning* A 37, 571–580.

Hospers, G-J. (2006) "Silicon Somewhere? Assessing the Usefulness of Best Practices in Regional Policy", *Policy Studies* 27, 1–15.

Iammarino, S. (2005) "An Evolutionary Integrated View of Regional Systems of Innovation: Concepts, Measures and Historical Perspectives", *European Planning Studies* 13(4), 497–519.

Klaerding, C., Hachmann, V. and Hassink, R. (2009) "Die Steuerung von Innovationspotenzialen – die Region als Handlungsebene", *Informationen zur Raumentwicklung* 5, 295–304.

Klepper, S. (2007) "The Evolution of Geographic Structures in New Industries", in K. Frenken (ed.) *Applied Evolutionary Economics and Economic Geography*, Cheltenham: Edward Elgar, 69–92.

Landabaso, M., Oughton, C. and Morgan, K. (2001) "Innovation Networks and Regional Policy in Europe", in K. Koschatzky, M. Kulicke and A. Zenker (eds) *Innovation Networks: Concepts and Challenges in the European Perspective*, Heidelberg/New York: Physica-Verlag, 243–273.

Lorenzen, M. (2005) "Why do Clusters Change?", *European Urban and Regional Studies* 12, 203–208.

Lundvall, B, Intarakumnerd, P. and Vang, J. (eds) (2006) *Asia's Innovation Systems in Transition*, Cheltenham: Edward Elgar.

MacKinnon, D., Cumbers, A., Pike, A., Birch, K. and McMaster, R. (2009) "Evolution in Economic Geography: Institutions, Political Economy, and Adaptation", *Economic Geography* 85, 129–150.

Markusen, A. (1999) "Fuzzy Concepts, Scanty Evidence and Policy Distance: The Case for Rigour and Policy Relevance in Critical Regional Studies", *Regional Studies* 33, 869–886.

Martin, R. and Sunley, P. (2003) "Deconstructing Clusters: Chaotic Concept or Policy Panacea?", *Journal of Economic Geography* 3, 5–35.

—— (2006) "Path Dependence and Regional Economic Evolution", *Journal of Economic Geography* 6, 395–437.

Menzel, M-P. and Fornahl, D. (2007) "Cluster Life Cycles – Dimensions and Rationales of Cluster Development", Jena: Jena Economic Research Papers 2007–076.

Morgan, K. (1997) "The Learning Region: Institutions, Innovation and Regional Renewal", *Regional Studies* 31, 491–503.

Moulaert, F. and Sekia, A. (2003) "Territorial Innovation Models: A Critical Survey", *Regional Studies* 37, 289–302.

Murmann, J. P. (2003) *Knowledge and Competitive Advantage. The Co-evolution of Firms, Technology, and National Institutions*, Cambridge: Cambridge University Press.

Nelson, R. R. (1994) "The Co-evolution of Technology, Industrial Structure, and

Supporting Institutions", *Industrial and Corporate Change* 1, 47–63.

OECD (2001) *Cities and Regions in the New Learning economy*, Paris: OECD.

—— (2007) *Competitive Regional Clusters*, Paris: OECD.

Porter, M. E. (2000) "Location, Competition, and Economic Development: Local Clusters in a Global Economy", *Economic Development Quarterly* 14, 15–34.

Press, K. (2006) *A Life Cycle for Clusters? The Dynamics of Agglomeration, Change, and Adaption*, Heidelberg, New York: Physica-Verlag.

Saxenian, A. (1994) *Regional Advantage: Culture and Competition in Silicon Valley and Route 128*, Cambridge, MA, and London: Harvard University Press.

Schamp, E. W. (2000) *Vernetzte Produktion: Industriegeographie aus institutioneller Perspektive*, Darmstadt: Wissenschaftliche Buchgesellschaft.

Schmitz, H. (ed.) (2004) *Local Enterprises in the Global Economy: Issues of Governance and Upgrading*, Cheltenham: Edward Elgar.

Schmitz, H. and K. Nadvi (1999) "Clustering and Industrialization: Introduction", *World Development* 27, 1503–1514.

Scott, A. J. (2000) "Economic Geography: The Great Half-century", *Cambridge Journal of Economics* 24, 483–504.

Staber, U. (2009) "Clusters from an Evolutionary Perspective", in R. Boschma and R. Martin (eds) *Handbook of Evolutionary Economic Geography*, Cheltenham: Edward Elgar.

Tödtling, F. and Trippl, M. (2005) "One Size Fits All? Towards a Differentiated Regional Innovation Policy Approach", *Research Policy* 34, 1203–1219.

Trippl, M. and Tödtling, F. (2008) "Cluster Renewal in Old Industrial Regions – Continuity or Radical Change?" in C. Karlsson (ed.) *Handbook of Research on Cluster Theory*, Cheltenham: Edward Elgar.

Uyarra, E. (2009) "What is Evolutionary About 'Regional Systems of Innovation'? Implications for regional policy", *Journal of Evolutionary Economics* 20 (1), 115–137.

Visser, E-J. and Atzema, O. (2008) "With or Without Clusters: Facilitating Innovation through a Differentiated and Combined Network Approach", *European Planning Studies* 16, 1169–1188.

Further reading

Boschma, R. (2008) "Regional Innovation Policy", in B. Nooteboom and E. Stam (eds) *Micro-foundations for Innovation Policy*, Amsterdam: Amsterdam University Press, 315–341.

Martin, R. and Sunley, P. (2006) "Path Dependence and Regional Economic Evolution", *Journal of Economic Geography* 6, 395–437.

Tödtling, F. and Trippl, M. (2005) "One Size Fits All? Towards a Differentiated Regional Innovation Policy Approach", *Research Policy* 34, 1203–1219.

13

Innovation, learning and knowledge creation in co-localised and distant contexts

Harald Bathelt

Introduction

Since the 1990s, reflexive processes of knowledge generation have become key factors in globalisation, and what Giddens (1990) calls the radicalisation of modernity. While knowledge has developed into a core resource shaping the so-called knowledge-based economy (Lundvall and Johnson 1994), learning is the key process driving knowledge generation and innovation (Lundvall 1988; Gertler 1995). A substantial part of the literature has focused on analysing interactive learning processes in localised contexts, even though radical innovations in information and communication technologies (ICTs) have generated new possibilities of transferring knowledge around the globe. Despite the potential of ICTs to open up new opportunities for economic interaction, as emphasised by a growing body of literature (e.g. Leamer and Storper 2001; Moriset and Malecki 2008), knowledge regarding the effects of these changes on the geographies of learning, production and innovation is still limited. I use this as a starting point for my analysis of the effects of new communication technologies and organisational forms on processes of learning and knowledge creation.

As highlighted by Pike (2007), there are at least two opposing strands in the literature suggesting that innovation and learning are either focused on local and regional contexts, or driven by global connectivities through relational ties (Allen *et al.* 1998; Amin 2004). This chapter contributes to a relational perspective of economic action (Bathelt 2006) by arguing that an analytical focus on any distinct geographical entity, or a binary discussion of the advantages of local versus global or regional versus extra-regional linkages, would result in an over-simplification of the multi-faceted and multi-tiered processes of learning and knowledge creation. Much of this discussion on the role of the region in the global knowledge economy also suffers from focusing on territorial units while neglecting the individual and collective agents at the heart of economic decision-making processes.

In this context, this research questions the assumed priority of local over non-local interaction that is still, at least implicitly, characteristic of some of the cluster literature. As Oinas (1999) recognised, there is relatively little empirical evidence to support broad claims on the predominance of proximate relations and localised learning in economic interaction. Others have argued that the "local" cannot be seen in isolation from other spatial levels in that local knowledge and competencies are continuously and system-atically enriched and challenged by global linkages (Amin 2004). Such work suggests that the "local" and the "global" are insepara-bly interwoven (Amin and Thrift 1992). The argument put forward in this chapter sug-gests that permanent co-location and face-to-face (F2F) interaction may be efficient in some economic contexts but not in others. Business leaders located in one region, for example, simply may not like one another or have opposing goals, thus hampering oppor-tunities for regional interaction. Conversely, interaction and learning in global production contexts have become quite widespread. Therefore, different settings can be structured in a way so as to enable efficient processes of economic interaction and knowledge gen-eration, even over a large distance. The goal of this chapter, thus, is to move beyond a simple dichotomy of local versus global spheres and, instead, inform a broader discus-sion concerning the potentialities for learn-ing and knowledge generation in settings not characterised by permanent co-location.

Rather than emphasising the advantages of proximity per se, I argue that it is impor-tant to analyse the preconditions, characteris-tics and outcomes incurred through F2F and other forms of interaction in different spatial settings. Temporary proximity through regu-lar business travel and intensive meetings during international trade fairs may, for instance, suffice to replace the need for per-manent co-location. Furthermore, new com-munication media combined with specific settings for interaction might mitigate, and even overcome, the need for permanent co-location. In order to more fully develop this argument, I integrate economic geography literature and studies in the field of social psychology (Bathelt and Turi 2008). Such studies shed light on how F2F interaction operates, and how computer-mediated com-munication (CMC) can make up for some of the problems arising during remote collabo-ration. Experiments conducted by social psy-chologists are well suited to enquire about

the potentialities of virtual interaction and their spatial consequences, as they are designed to overcome the role existing institutions have in stabilising prior communication patterns.

Structurally, this chapter next highlights important findings from the literature about the role of F2F interaction in section two. Section three emphasises the advantages of permanent co-location and regular F2F con-tacts in clusters creating what I refer to as "local buzz". Section four argues that perma-nent co-location should be viewed as an exception rather than a rule in complex pro-duction chains which have a global reach. Section five shows that temporary F2F inter-action and "global buzz" during international trade fairs provide opportunities to overcome possible problems in communication and knowledge exchange between agents located in different regional, cultural, or national contexts. Section six argues that computer-mediated interaction across locations can open new potentialities in innovation, not likely available to permanent F2F encounters within groups and corporations. Finally, sec-tion seven draws conclusions arguing that the combination of different forms of F2F-based and virtual interaction generates new opportunities for integrating production and innovation processes at the global scale.

Role of proximity and F2F interaction

While ICTs have provided new and unpre-cedented opportunities for knowledge trans-fers over distance, a large body of literature continues to stress the benefits stemming from geographic proximity between economic agents. Studies in economic geography have made a concerted effort to advance our understanding of the importance of "being there" (e.g. Gertler 1995), with respect to stimulating "local buzz" and transferring and implementing new technologies (Bathelt *et al.* 2004). Social psychologists have similarly examined remote and proximate collaboration, especially since the advent of modern ICTs. In examining the efficiency of CMC on group processes and outcomes, this research has lent special attention to the social and cognitive factors arising during F2F interaction. In explaining how integrational and informational aspects of F2F interaction afford the transfer of complex messages and the stimulation of trust under conditions of uncertainty, studies in social psychology provide a deeper understanding of the processes underlying "being there".

In their foundational analysis on the social psychology of telecommunications, Short *et al.* (1976) have identified a range of non-verbal cues such as facial expression, direction of gaze, posture and physical distance arising during F2F interaction. They distinguish two types of functions played by these non-verbal cues. First, the informational function is concerned with the passage of information from one individual to another through illustrative and emblemic gestures, and other non-verbal cues. Second, the integrative function refers to "all the behaviour that keeps the system in operation, regulates the interaction process, cross references particular messages to comprehensibility in a particular context, and relates the particular context to the larger contexts of which the interaction is but a special situation" (Birdwhistell 1970: 26).

While these aspects of F2F encounters enable the transfer of complex messages, collectively they serve to reduce uncertainties between communicators and, in turn, engender trust. The latter point is particularly important in economic contexts of learning and knowledge exchange (Leamer and Storper 2001). Studies have shown that cooperative work environments and successful business transactions require the development of trust (Nelson and Cooprider 1996; Dasgupta 2000). In such situations, geographical proximity acts as a factor of cohesion by supporting long-lasting cooperative behaviour thanks to the repetition of commitment. As discussed

next, this is prominent in successful clusters which are characterised by permanent co-presence and F2F interaction between agents. In contrast, distant agents have fewer opportunities for the kinds of interaction that maintain and develop personal or emotional trust (Ettlinger 2003).

Furthermore, F2F interaction creates opportunities for controlling the performance of other agents (Crang 1994), and can become a mechanism to exercise power over others (Allen 1997). The absence of a visual channel reduces possibilities for an accurate expression of the socio-emotional context and decreases the information available about the self-images, attitudes, moods and reactions of others. The benefits and shortcomings of mediums other than F2F interaction, thus, hinge upon their ability to allow for the actualisation and transfer of non-verbal cues. As argued below, different configurations of learning and knowledge creation exist that involve a different mixture of co-location, F2F meetings and virtual communication.

Permanent co-presence in clusters and local buzz

Much of the research in economic geography has been led by the assumption that spatial proximity is of key importance to understand economic interaction because it "is still a fundamental way to bring people and firms together, to share knowledge and to solve problems" (Storper and Walker 1989: 80). As pointed out by Hudson (2007), the new regionalism literature that has developed since the 1990s emphasises the role of within-in-region growth, institutional and learning dynamics. There is significant empirical evidence which supports this view. In the context of urban or regional agglomerations of industries, or clusters (Porter 1990; Gordon and McCann 2000; Malmberg and Maskell 2002), recent research has linked the importance of proximate relations to the thick web of information and knowledge connecting local agents and circulating between them. The resulting knowledge flows establish a rich information and communication ecology referred to as "noise" (Grabher 2002) or "buzz" (Storper and Venables 2004). This local buzz consists of specific information flows, knowledge transfers and continuous updates, as well as opportunities for learning in organised and spontaneous meetings (Bathelt *et al.* 2004). The importance and quality of a cluster's buzz is related to a number of features which are partly overlapping and make this setting especially valuable for processes of learning and knowledge creation.

First, the co-presence of many specialised firms of a particular value chain and regular F2F contacts between specialists from these firms generate a specific milieu for the exchange of experiences, information and knowledge within a cluster. In this milieu, F2F encounters and the associated non-verbal cues generate informational and integrational advantages in communication. This enables in-depth knowledge exchange as specific information about technologies, markets and strategies is circulated in a variety of ways in planned and unplanned meetings. This can lead to a strong local embeddedness of firms, supporting fine-grained information flows and interactive learning (Granovetter 1985).

Second, the agents in a cluster share similar technical traditions and views which have developed over time. They are based on similar day-to-day routines and problem-solving, and a joint history of regular F2F communication. Through this, new information and technologies are easily understood. When people of a similar technological background and realm of experience in a region converse with one another, they almost automatically know what others are talking about. Highly skilled experienced specialists, who have lived in a region for a longer time period, know one another and may have become acquainted with several firms as a result of switching jobs in the area. As positions change hands, knowledge that would be difficult to

acquire by other means is transferred between firms (Malmberg and Power 2005).

Third, the diversity of the relationships and contacts within a cluster strengthens and enriches tight networks of information flows, common problem solutions and the development of trust. Within these networks, agents are linked in multiple ways with each other as business partners, colleagues, peers, friends or community members. As a result, resources can be transferred from one type of relationship to another (Uzzi 1997). Multiplex ties help firms to quickly access new information and speed up its circulation within the cluster.

Fourth, through the shared history of relationships firms learn how to interpret local buzz and make good use of it. As a result, communities of practice become more rooted over time (Wenger 1998). This helps to transfer knowledge in a precise manner, interpret new information in the context of a cluster's technological competence and extract those knowledge parts that might be valuable in future applications. All of this is possible because co-presence and ongoing F2F encounters in a cluster enhance the likelihood that people develop compatible technology outlooks and interpretative schemes.

Interaction and learning are, of course, also related to ongoing transaction relations between regional firms, even if their extent is limited. They are, furthermore, enhanced through cross-corporate involvement in community activities, industry associations, clubs and the like. The advantages of permanent co-presence and frequent F2F interaction are supported by the fact that firms draw from a joint regional labour market characterised by job mobility and overlapping competencies (Malmberg and Maskell 1997; Malmberg and Power 2005). Through these processes, local buzz is circulated and reinforced in powerful ways. Permanent co-location can translate integrational and informational advantages of F2F interaction to become part of the wider institutional repertoire available to all local agents. In many ways, this serves to establish and deepen relational proximity and trust (Amin and Cohendet 2004; Bathelt 2006). It helps to establish reliable conditions for interactive learning and durable inter-firm relationships.

From research on path-dependent developments we know, however, that problems can develop if local communication patterns become too rigid and inward-looking, preventing trans-local knowledge flows and necessary adaptations to market and technology changes. From a spatial perspective, negative lock-in can result in a situation where localised industrial systems collectively run into problems due to rigid technological and organisational structures (Grabher 1993; Asheim *et al.* 2006). Too much local interaction may lead agents to rely too heavily on existing technologies and well-established problem solutions (Granovetter 1973). Through this, they may lose their openness for new solutions. Clusters might, in turn, become insular systems that are vulnerable to external shifts. As argued next, this may require that important inputs be acquired through systematic outside-cluster interaction.

Organisational co-presence in global networks

In a cluster, spatial proximity and shared institutional, social and cultural characteristics can create conditions for firms to engage in economic transactions and develop long-term producer–user relations (Rallet and Torre 1999). Yet, focusing on internal cluster interaction is not sufficient to generate long-term growth and competitiveness. Of course, much research has shown that the national level is still key in providing the institutional conditions for economic and social well-being (Gertler 1995; Pike and Tomaney 2004). To overcome limitations, firms may strive for strengthening interregional and international linkages, which is, however, not a routine process with guaranteed success. One way of trying to accomplish this is to establish

organisational proximity by merging with or acquiring complementary firms in other parts of the world to create reliable conditions for future interaction and wider market access (Boschma 2005; Torre and Rallet 2005). This requires that international mergers and acquisitions share a certain degree of cognitive proximity between the firms to enable the respective agents to interact with one another, and integrate their different cultures into a new overarching structure (Nooteboom 2000). At the same time, their respective capabilities must be sufficiently different to allow them to benefit from interactive learning. While international mergers and acquisitions can be viewed as processes of bridging multiple distances and establishing a framework for closer inter-firm linkages at an international scale, the same processes also create stress on existing network relations at the regional level. The argument put forward here is that a simple binary of local versus global relationships is simply not enough. Relational ties stretch across regional and national territories while, at the same time, being embedded into these entities (Bathelt 2006; Hudson 2007). As emphasised by Allen and colleagues (1998: 5), regions are "series of open, discontinuous spaces constituted by the social relationships which stretch across them in a variety of ways".

At a global scale, this argument of different types of proximities, which can be substituted for one another, may distract from the limitations to interaction that exist due to particular spatial structures. In the context of global production configurations or peripheral locations, for instance, firms may not easily find adequate partners for close-by transactions. They have no choice but to establish linkages over space providing access to distant markets and technologies developed elsewhere. F2F interactions in local context are often not an option for these firms. In global value chains, interaction does not build upon permanent F2F contact (Dicken *et al.* 2001; Gereffi *et al.* 2005). It often relies on a mixture of different types of more or less hierarchical network relations associated with existing personal ties, organisational bonds, and/or repeated visits at international trade fairs.

A single specific distance to be minimised in order to establish regular F2F interaction usually does not exist in complex production networks. Firms serve global markets and cooperate with partners located in different parts of the world. From the perspective of market access, it might be imperative for a firm to be reasonably close to its major markets to be able to customise products and learn from interaction with customers. From the view of research and development (R&D), it might be more important to have R&D facilities close to production to benefit from constant feedback and learning-by-doing. Depending on which aspect dominates, the locational structure of firms can be quite different. No matter how and where marketing, production or R&D are established, any setting is likely to be associated with proximities on one end and distances on the other. To have a single large plant within one cluster could under these circumstances cause problems in producer–user interaction because of large distances to international markets.

In sum, geographical proximity and "being there" are important issues of corporate organisation (Gertler 1995), but it has to be specified exactly which proximities are key: proximity to specific markets, production, or knowledge pools. In reality, spatial proximity and permanent F2F interaction might be possible with some relevant agents but not with all. As a consequence, there is no predefined territorial or non-territorial level which is best suited to support knowledge creation and innovation (Pike 2007). There is clearly no simple "either/or" between local and global learning dynamics as both are often intrinsically intertwined (Amin 2004). Many firms have learned how to organise economic action without permanent co-presence and have developed alternative

settings which work well without requiring co-location and F2F interaction on a daily basis. These settings have become expressions of new geographies of circulation through which knowledge can be created and exchanged at a distance (Thrift 2000; Amin and Cohendet 2004). An example for such interaction encompasses multinational firms within which managers go back and forth on a regular basis between different sites and countries. Through this, they generate a context similar to co-presence, but between distant places. Another example is given by learning processes and knowledge exchange during international trade fairs, as discussed in the next section.

Temporary F2F interaction and global buzz

A specific setting through which global knowledge flows are circulated and new linkages explored exists at leading international trade fairs (Borghini et al. 2004; Maskell et al. 2006). These events open up many possibilities for knowledge creation, network and market development at a global basis. F2F meetings with other participants at trade fairs enable firms to systematically acquire information and knowledge about competitors, suppliers, customers, and their technological and strategic choices (Bathelt and Schuldt 2008a). Temporary F2F contacts provide a sufficient basis to reassure ongoing interaction, even involving complex communication and learning.

Through different routes, global information concerning trends and ideas in an industry, as well as all sorts of news and gossip, flow back and forth between the participants who are temporarily clustered at trade fairs. Agents benefit from integrational and informational cues transported through repeated, intensive, often short F2F encounters which lead to a specific communication and information ecology referred to as "global buzz" (Bathelt and Schuldt 2008b). Similar to local buzz, global buzz is a multidimensional concept which enables unique processes of knowledge dissemination and creation through interactive learning and learning-by-observation. Its constitutive components are related to the dedicated co-presence of global supply and demand, intensive temporary F2F interaction, a variety of possibilities for observation, intersecting interpretative communities, and multiplex meetings and relationships. Central to these processes are verbal and non-verbal cues, visual stimuli, feelings and emotions, which are omnipresent during these events (Entwistle and Rocamora 2006).

International trade fairs bring together leading, as well as less well-known, agents from an entire industry or technology for the primary purpose of exchanging knowledge and learning about the present and future development of their industry, centred around displays of products, prototypes and innovations. This enables agents to get an overview of the developments and trends in the world market, and provides myriad opportunities to make contact, ask questions and engage in F2F communication with other agents from the same value chain (Rosson and Seringhaus 1995; Sharland and Balogh 1996; Prüser 2003). Exhibitors and visitors benefit enormously from the large variety of different types of informal and formal meetings held with a large variety of agents (Bathelt and Schuldt 2008a).

During these trade fairs, focused communities with similar technical traditions and educational backgrounds meet, which have developed over time based on similar day-to-day experiences. Participation within these communities helps reduce uncertainties and the degree of complexity in fast-changing product and technology markets. Within their contact networks, agents are linked in different ways and exchange facts, impressions, gossip, as well as small talk. This helps transmit experiences with existing products and interpretations of new developments in understandable ways (Borghini et al. 2006; Entwistle and Rocamora 2006).

Mixing different types of business-related and other information also helps to check out other agents and establish initial communication which can be continued later on. Through regular attendance at international trade fairs, firms are able to find suitable partners to complement their needs, learn about new developments, and undertake the first steps towards the establishment of durable inter-firm networks with distant partners. In the next section, the arguments about knowledge creation and learning are extended to contexts without F2F interaction.

CMC vs. F2F collaboration in economic interaction and learning

While the above arguments suggest that permanent, regular or temporary F2F contacts are of central importance to processes of economic interaction, learning and knowledge creation, such encounters are still limited in global production contexts. Instead, many firms rely to a great extent on virtual communication through ICTs to organise production, research and market interaction. Traditional studies in social psychology have emphasised the structural differences that exist between CMC and F2F interaction, pointing at different learning and networking potentials. Social presence theory, for instance, suggests that the absence of non-verbal, vocal and physical cues denies users important information about the characteristics, emotions and attitudes of other agents; thus resulting in communication that is less sociable, understandable and effective (Walther et al. 2005).

As argued below, however, potentialities of CMC might be much greater than suggested in social presence theory. Interaction patterns based on new ICTs have challenged established interpretations which emphasise the disadvantages of CMC compared to F2F settings. A growing body of research has, in fact, contested the presumed differentiation of verbal and non-verbal cue functionalities, at least with respect to their outcome. Social information-processing theory, for instance, rejects the position that CMC is inherently impersonal and that relational information is inaccessible to CMC users (Walther *et al.* 2005). Instead, it assumes that individuals deploy whatever communication cues they have at their disposal when motivated to develop relationships. This can provide the basis for the establishment of social relations, as is also the position of equilibrium theory (Olson and Olson 2003).

These conceptions raise questions regarding the general superiority of local F2F-based encounters over CMC in distant interaction and learning. In the context of corporate innovation projects and group collaboration, contextual differences between F2F interaction and CMC have been shown to affect the process and outcome of communication in sometimes unexpected ways. For example, Wainfan and Davis (2004) show that the group structure in CMC is often broader, yet more agile than in F2F teams. Accordingly, there is greater breadth in collaboration themes due to a wider involvement of experts. Although it might be harder to form social networks, it is also more difficult to distract or deflect the participants' attention by involving them in side conversations. In reducing non-verbal cues, other factors such as common ground, power and status become much less important in CMC. In the localised context of a firm, contextual cues such as seating position, office location, and even clothing have been found to influence communication patterns during employee meetings (Dubrovsky *et al.* 1991). As shown by Sproull and Kiesler (1991), individuals using CMC feel less constrained by conventional norms and rules of behaviour. The lack of "social baggage" attached to electronic messaging can help overcome some detrimental hierarchical and social structures impeding decision making within a group setting.

Studies have shown that CMC participants make more explicit proposals, defer less

to high-status members, and are less inhibited than F2F collaborators (Dubrovsky *et al.* 1991; Hollingshead and McGrath 1995). Rice (1984) has found that when faced with a dilemma, F2F groups begin by analysing the problem, whereas CMC collaborators tend to start a discussion by proposing a solution. Studies have suggested that anonymity decreases conformance pressure in CMC settings and allows group members to be less inhibited in their expression of ideas (Baltes *et al.* 2002). Furthermore, ideas expressed under anonymous conditions are more likely to be evaluated based on their merit, rather than the status of the person presenting them. This points at the potential of CMC settings to break with existing problem solutions and generate opportunities for innovation, analogous to the weak-tie argument of Granovetter (1973).

Although there are also clear limitations to interaction, these studies indicate that the systematic use of CMC enables complex interaction, and can stimulate learning and network formation even without frequent F2F contact. When including opportunities of using video-based CMC formats and the combination of these virtual encounters with occasional planned F2F meetings, the range of possibly efficient spatial configurations involving local and non-local F2F and computer-mediated exchanges drastically widens.

In the context of innovation projects in multinational firms, Song *et al.* (2007) have documented that knowledge dissemination between agents is greatest when both settings are combined. There appear to be parts of innovation processes where F2F meetings are key to the development of new ideas and concepts, while other parts benefit from work at dispersed workplaces with regular CMC adjustments. Permanent co-location may foster knowledge dissemination within R&D but impede knowledge dissemination between R&D and production. In global production contexts, co-localisation of R&D staff conversely may lead to the separation of R&D and production. At the corporate level, efficient learning requires that uncertainties and ambiguities are reduced, and that both explicit and tacit knowledge in both weak and strong relationships, planned and unplanned meetings, and both nearby and far away are transferred. This heterogeneity suggests that optimal innovation conditions require that co-location is complemented by CMC technologies (Nonaka and Takeuchi 1995). Similar conclusions can be drawn regarding inter-firm interaction.

Conclusion

This chapter aims to demonstrate that advancements in ICTs are drastically changing the ways in which firms conduct business and link practices of regional and cross-regional learning (Leamer and Storper 2001; Grabher *et al.* 2008). It puts forward a relational argument suggesting that the region and other geographical entities are not a priori bounded spaces of economic action (Amin 2004). Instead, as argued by Bathelt (2006), learning and knowledge creation in such a perspective are systematically influenced by structures of social and institutional relations (contextuality), the past legacies of such relationships (path dependence), as well as the principal open-endedness of potential decision making (contingency). In a spatial perspective, relational action is not limited to, and indeed cuts across, specific territories. Relational linkages might be grounded in local or regional development paths; however, they likely extend well beyond these boundaries through personal ties or organisational networks which have been established in the past or result from global production contexts. As such, this chapter suggests that there is no "either/or" dichotomy of local versus global learning dynamics (Hudson 2007) but that relational bonds are capable of benefiting from both: discrete territorial advantages as well as trans-territorial relationships and networked competencies. Therefore, there is no simple proximity to

be minimised in economic production and innovation. Proximities at one end of the production context will likely produce distances at another.

Studies examining F2F interaction and CMC demonstrate that the two mediums possess unique properties. Each medium has its relative strengths and weaknesses, which play themselves out differently during different tasks. On the one hand, when analysing corporate work processes and project groups, CMC is weaker under time constraints and tends to produce poorer decisions. That being said, it allows for knowledge dissemination between more people, and does so quicker. F2F interaction, on the other hand, is stronger in conveying tacit knowledge, which is critical in periods of uncertainty and ambiguity. However, the social baggage which accompanies F2F interaction can be a burden to successful innovation.

In response to inefficiencies of CMC and the importance of geographic proximity, corporate actors explore organisational structures combining both aspects, thus enabling knowledge generation over distance. For Torre and Rallet (2005), a solution lies in the temporary mobility of individuals. The need for F2F interaction in terms of learning and knowledge exchange does not necessitate that individuals permanently co-locate. What it requires is that individuals meet regularly in certain time intervals. In some circumstances, problems can be solved through the mobility of individuals, as in the case of business travel. In other circumstances, individuals collaborating in projects only need to meet F2F during particular phases of the innovation process, especially during times of high complexity and uncertainty. During these periods, F2F interaction as "organised proximity" is critical. In other stages of the innovation process, it may suffice or even be more efficient to rely on CMC settings for interaction. Organised proximity, of course, is not a purely geographical concept: it is relational and urges greater interaction among the members of a project, organisation or

157

value chain (Bathelt 2006). It refers to the establishment of a collective culture that generates shared interpretations of new information even if the agents are located in different places. Such commonality in thinking and solving problems is critical to learning and knowledge generation.

In scenarios where proximity is simply untenable, the value of virtual interaction using modern ICTs dramatically increases. In these cases, actors are quite willing to put up with and overcome the deficiencies of virtual interaction. Trade-offs are inevitable and staying competitive requires pinpointing a firm's own mixture of settings for interacting in production, distribution and innovation (Bathelt and Turi 2008). Under all circumstances, one has to keep in mind that one decisive disadvantage of CMC compared to F2F communication is related to difficulties in establishing initial trust. While this may require that complex innovation projects over distance have to involve agents already sharing trust from former cooperation in a co-localised setting, it does not rule out other projects based on CMC even in complex contexts. In fact, the combination of CMC with other interactive settings may overcome the dilemma of establishing trust.

Just as sound innovation strategies incorporate advantages of both local and global integration, so too do firms increasingly rely on CMC and F2F interaction in combination with each other. To argue that virtual interaction will eventually eliminate the benefits accrued from geographic proximity makes little sense when evaluating complex economic realities. It also appears misleading to assume a general superiority of local over non-local economic networks. Instead, modern ICTs have allowed distant and close collaboration to occur simultaneously. Both phenomena incur different costs, and generate different benefits. The firms and networks best able to make use of both options will likely develop sophisticated learning capabilities and an "integrative competitive advantage"

in the globalising knowledge economy in the future.

Acknowledgements

Earlier versions of this chapter were presented in 2008 at the Conference on "Industrial Cluster and Regional Development" in Kaifeng (China), the Symposium on "Knowledge and Economy" in Heidelberg and the Summer Institute in Economic Geography in Manchester. I would like to thank the participants of these meetings for valuable feedback and comments. In particular, I would like to thank Phil Turi for collaborating with me in this research, and for co-developing some of the arguments put forward regarding the role of CMC (for a detailed analysis, see Bathelt and Turi 2008). I am also indebted to the editors for stimulating suggestions on how to develop my arguments further. Financial support from the Social Sciences and Humanities Research Council of Canada is greatly appreciated.

References

Allen, J. (1997) 'Economies of power and space', in R. Lee and J. Wills (eds), *Geographies of Economies* (pp. 59–70), London: Arnold.

Allen, J., Massey, D. and Cochrane, A. (1998) *Rethinking the Region*, London, New York: Routledge.

Amin, A. (2004) 'Regions unbound: Towards a new politics of place', *Geografiska Annaler*, 86 B, 33–44.

Amin, A. and Cohendet, P. (2004) *Architectures of Knowledge: Firms, Capabilities, and Communities*, Oxford, New York: Oxford University Press.

Amin, A. and Thrift, N. (1992) 'Neo-Marshallian nodes in global networks', *International Journal of Urban and Regional Research*, 16, 571–587.

Asheim, B., Cooke, P. and Martin, R. (2006). 'The rise of the cluster concept in regional analysis and policy: A critical assessment', in B. Asheim, P. Cooke and R. Martin (eds), *Clusters and Regional Development: Critical Reflections and Explorations* (pp. 1–29), London, New York: Routledge.

Baltes, B. B., Dickson, M. W., Sherman, M. P., Bauer, C. C. and LaGanke, J. S. (2002) 'Computer-mediated communication and group decision making: A meta analysis'. *Organizational Behavior and Human Decision Process*, 87 (1), 156–179.

Bathelt, H. (2006) 'Geographies of production: Growth regimes in spatial perspective 3 – Toward a relational view of economic action and policy', *Progress in Human Geography*, 30, 223–236.

Bathelt, H. and Schuldt, N. (2008a) 'Between luminaires and meat grinders: International trade fairs as temporary clusters', *Regional Studies*, 42, 853–868.

Bathelt, H. and Schuldt, N. (2008b) *Temporary Face-to-Face Contact and the Ecologies of Global and Virtual Buzz*. SPACES online, 6 (2008-04). Toronto, Heidelberg (URL: http://www.spaces-online.com, date accessed 13 April 2009).

Bathelt, H. and Turi, P. (2008) 'Local, global and virtual buzz: The importance of face-to-face contact and possibilities to go beyond', in Research Center for Yellow River Civilization and Sustainable Development (eds), *Keynote Papers and Session-Papers' Abstracts of the 7th International Conference on "Industrial Cluster and Regional Development"* (pp. 37–53), Kaifeng, China: Henan University.

Bathelt, H., Malmberg, A. and Maskell, P. (2004) 'Clusters and knowledge: Local buzz, global pipelines and the process of knowledge creation', *Progress in Human Geography*, 28, 31–56.

Birdwhistell, R. L. (1970) *Kinetics and Context*, Philadelphia: University of Philadelphia.

Borghini, S., Golfetto, F. and Rinallo, D. (2004) *Using Anthropological Methods to Study Industrial Marketing and Purchasing: An Exploration of Professional Trade Shows*, Paper presented at the Industrial Marketing Purchasing Conference, Copenhagen (URL: http://www.europa.eu.int/comm/enterprise/enterprise_policy/spec/documents/fondazione_fiera_milano.pdf, date accessed 14 February 2006).

Borghini, S., Golfetto, F. and Rinallo, D. (2006) 'Ongoing search among industrial buyers', *Journal of Business Research*, 59, 1151–1159.

Boschma, R. A. (2005) 'Proximity and innovation: A critical assessment', *Regional Studies*, 39, 61–74.

Crang, P. (1994) Its showtime – On the workplace geographies of display in a restaurant in southeast England. *Environment and Planning D – Society and Space*, 12 (6), 675–704.

Dasgupta, P. (2000) 'Trust as a commodity', in D. Gambetta (ed.), *Trust: Making and Breaking Cooperative Relations* (pp. 49–72), Oxford: Department of Sociology, University of Oxford (URL: http://www.sociology.ox.ac.uk/papers/dasgupta49-72.pdf, date accessed 8 February 2008).

Dicken, P., Kelly, P. F., Olds, K. and Yeung, H. W.-c. (2001) 'Chains and networks, territories and scales: Towards a relational framework for analysing the global economy', *Global Networks*, 1, 89–112.

Dubrovsky, V. J., Kiesler, S. and Sethna, B. N. (1991) 'The equalization phenomenon: Status effects in computer-mediated and face-to-face decision making groups', *Human–Computer Interaction*, 6, 119–146.

Entwistle, J. and Rocamora, A. (2006) 'The field of fashion materialized: A study of London Fashion Week', *Sociology*, 40, 735–751.

Ettlinger, N. (2003) 'Cultural economic geography and a relational and microspace approach to trusts, rationalities, networks, and change in collaborative workplaces', *Journal of Economic Geography*, 3, 145–172.

Gereffi, G., Humphrey, J. and Sturgeon, T. (2005) 'The governance of global value chains', *Review of International Political Economy*, 12 (1), 78–104.

Gertler, M. S. (1995) '"Being there": Proximity, organization, and culture in the development and adoption of advanced manufacturing technologies', *Economic Geography*, 71, 1–26.

Giddens, A. (1990) *The Consequences of Modernity*, Stanford: Stanford University Press.

Gordon, I. R. and McCann, P. (2000) 'Industrial clusters: Complexes, agglomeration and/or social networks', *Urban Studies*, 37, 513–532.

Grabher, G. (1993) 'The weakness of strong ties: The lock-in of regional development in the Ruhr area', in G. Grabher (ed.), *The Embedded Firm: On the Socioeconomics of Industrial Networks* (pp. 255–277), London, New York: Routledge.

Grabher, G. (2002) 'Cool projects, boring institutions: Temporary collaboration in social context', *Regional Studies*, 36, 205–214.

Grabher, G., Ibert, O. and Flohr, S. (2008) 'The neglected king: The customer in the new knowledge ecology of innovation', *Economic Geography*, 84, 253–280.

Granovetter, M. (1973) 'The strength of weak ties', *American Journal of Sociology*, 78, 1360–1380.

Granovetter, M. (1985) 'Economic action and economic structure: The problem of embeddedness', *American Journal of Sociology*, 91, 481–510.

Hollingshead, A. B. and McGrath, J. E. (1995) 'Computer-assisted groups: A critical review of the empirical research', in R. A. Guzzo and

E. Salas (eds), *Team Effectiveness and Decision Making in Organizations* (pp. 46–78), San Francisco: Jossey-Bass/Pfeiffer.

Hudson, R. (2007) 'Regions and regional uneven development forever? Some reflective comments upon theory and practice', *Regional Studies*, 41, 1149–1160.

Leamer, E. E. and Storper, M. (2001) 'The economic geography of the Internet age', *Journal of International Business Studies*, 32 (4), 641–665.

Lundvall, B.-Å. (1988) 'Innovation as an interactive process: From producer–user interaction to the national system of innovation', in G. Dosi, C. Freeman, R. R. Nelson, G. Silverberg and L. L. G. Soete (eds), *Technical Change and Economic Theory* (pp. 349–369), London, New York: Pinter.

Lundvall, B.-Å. and Johnson, B. (1994) 'The learning economy', *Journal of Industry Studies*, 1, 23–42.

Malmberg, A. and Maskell, P. (1997) 'Towards an explanation of industry agglomeration and regional specialization', *European Planning Studies*, 5, 25–41.

Malmberg, A. and Power, D. (2005) ('How) do (firms in) clusters create knowledge?', *Industry and Innovation*, 12 (4), 409–431.

Maskell, P., Bathelt, H. and Malmberg, A. (2006) 'Building global knowledge pipelines: The role of temporary clusters', *European Planning Studies*, 14, 997–1013.

Moriset, B. and Malecki, E. J. (2008) *Organization vs. Space: The Paradoxical Geographies of the Digital Economy*, Paper presented at the Annual Meeting of the Association of American Geographers, Boston.

Nelson, K. M. and Cooprider, J. G. (1996) 'The contribution of shared knowledge to IS group performance', *MIS Quarterly*, 20 (4): 409–432.

Nonaka, I. and Takeuchi, H. (1995) *The Knowledge-Creating Company*, New York: Oxford University Press.

Nooteboom, B. (2000) *Learning and Innovation in Organizations and Economies*, Oxford: Oxford University Press.

Oinas, P. (1999) 'Activity-specificity in organizational learning: Implications for analysing the role of proximity', *GeoJournal*, 49, 363–372.

Olson, C. and Olson, J. (2003) 'Mitigating the effects of distance on collaborative intellectual work', *Economics of Innovation and New Technology*, 12 (1), 27–42.

Pike, A. (2007) 'Editorial: Whither regional studies?', *Regional Studies*, 41, 1143–1148.

Pike, A. and Tomaney, J. (2004) 'Guest editorial', *Environment and Planning A*, 36, 2091–2096.

Porter, M. E. (1990) *The Competitive Advantage of Nations*, New York: Free Press.

Prüser, S. M. (2003) 'Die Messe als Networking-Plattform [Trade fairs as a platform for networking]', in M. Kirchgeorg, W. M. Dornscheidt, W. Giese and N. Stoeck (eds), *Handbuch Messemanagement: Planung, Durchführung und Kontrolle von Messen, Kongressen und Events* [Handbook of Trade Fair Management: Planning, Execution and Control of Trade Fairs, Conventions and Events] (pp. 1181–1195), Wiesbaden: Gabler.

Rallet, A. and Torre, A. (1999) 'Is geographical proximity necessary in the innovation networks in the era of the global economy?', *GeoJournal*, 49, 373–380.

Rice, R. E. (1984) 'Mediated group communication', in R. E. Rice and Associates (eds), *The New Media: Communication, Research and Technology* (pp. 129–156), Beverly Hills: Sage.

Rosson, P. J. and Seringhaus, F. H. R. (1995) 'Visitor and exhibitor interaction at industrial trade fairs', *Journal of Business Research*, 32, 81–90.

Sharland, A. and Balogh, P. (1996) 'The value of nonselling activities at international trade shows', *Industrial Marketing Management*, 25, 59–66.

Short, J., Williams, E. and Christie, B. (1976) *The Social Psychology of Telecommunications*, New York: Wiley.

Song, M., Berends, H., van der Bij, H. and Weggeman, M. (2007) 'The effects of IT and co-location on knowledge dissemination', *The Journal of Product Innovation Management*, 24 (1), 52–68.

Sproull, L. and Kiesler, S. (1991) *Connections: New Ways of Working in the Networked Organization*, Cambridge, MA: MIT Press.

Storper, M. and Venables, A. J. (2004) 'Buzz: Face-to-face contact and the urban economy', *Journal of Economic Geography*, 4, 351–370.

Storper, M. and Walker, R. (1989) *The Capitalist Imperative: Territory, Technology, and Industrial Growth*, New York, Oxford: Basil Blackwell.

Thrift, N. (2000) 'Performing cultures in the new economy', *Annals of the Association of American Geographers*, 90, 674–692.

Torre, A. and Rallet, A. (2005) 'Proximity and localization', *Regional Studies*, 39, 47–59.

Uzzi, B. (1997) 'Social structure and competition in interfirm networks: The paradox of embeddedness', *Administrative Science Quarterly*, 42, 35–67.

Wainfan, L. and Davis, P. K. (2004) *Challenges in Virtual Collaboration: Videoconferencing, Audioconferencing, and Computer-Mediated Communications*, Santa Monica: RAND Corporation.

Walther, J. B., Loh, T. and Granka, L. (2005) 'Let me count the ways: The interchange of verbal and nonverbal cues in computer-mediated and face-to-face affinity', *Journal of Language and Social Psychology*, 24 (1), 36–65.

Wenger, E. (1998) *Communities of Practice: Learning, Meaning, and Identity*, Cambridge: Cambridge University Press.

Gertler, M. S. (2004) *Manufacturing Culture: The Institutional Geography of Industrial Practice*, Oxford, New York: Oxford University Press.

Malmberg, A. and Maskell, P. (2002) 'The elusive concept of localization economies: Towards a knowledge-based theory of spatial clustering', *Environment and Planning A*, 34, 429–449.

Rallet, A. and Torre, A. (2009) 'Temporary geographical proximity for business and work coordination: When, how and where?', *SPACES* online, Vol. 7, Issue 2009-02. Toronto and Heidelberg: www.spaces-online.com.

Further reading

Argyris, C. and Schön, D. (1978) *Organisational Learning: A Theory of Action Perspective*, Reading, MA: Addison Wesley.

14

Culture, creativity, and urban development

Dominic Power and Allen J. Scott

The cultural economy

The cultural economy has, in recent years, been the object of significant attention in studies of urban development. The rising importance of cultural activities in this regard is scarcely surprising given the increasing convergence between systems of cultural expression on the one hand and the economic order on the other (Lash and Urry 1994). Inspired by such intersections, cities and regions around the world have looked to 'creativity' and 'culture-led development', and the 'creative industries' to help address the development deficits attributed to deindustrialization and global outsourcing. Moreover, it is far from wishful thinking to base regional growth agendas on the cultural economy. For a variety of reasons, from the rise of popular culture to increasing disposable incomes, markets for cultural products have expanded rapidly in the last few decades. However, the cultural economy is not just about economic development, since the marketplaces, products and channels at its centre are now the dominant forums within which many social, cultural and political development processes find form and expression. As this has occurred, there has been a marked growth and spread of a group of

industries that can be loosely identified as suppliers of products with powerful aesthetic and semiotic content (Pratt 1997; Power 2002; Power and Scott 2004). These industries are based on an enormous and ever-increasing range of outputs (e.g. music, computer games, film and television, new media, fashion design, visual and performance arts, and so on).

The industries that make up the contemporary cultural economy are bound together as an object of study by three important common features. First, they are all concerned in one way or another with the creation of products whose value rests primarily on their symbolic content or the ways in which they stimulate the experiential reactions of consumers. Second, they are generally subject to the effects of (Ernst) Engels' Law, which suggests that as disposable income expands so consumption of non-essential or luxury products will rise at a disproportionately higher rate. Hence, the richer the region, the higher expenditure on cultural products will be as a fraction of individuals' budgets. Third, firms in cultural products industries are subject to competitive and organizational pressures such that they frequently agglomerate together in industrial districts or dense specialized clusters, while their outputs circulate with increasing ease on global markets.

It must be stressed at once that there can be no hard and fast line separating industries that specialize in purely cultural products from those whose outputs are purely utilitarian. On the contrary, there is a more or less unbroken continuum of sectors ranging from, say, detective novels or recorded music at the one extreme, through an intermediate series of sectors whose outputs are varying composites of the cultural and the utilitarian (such as shoes, sunglasses, or sports bicycles), to, say, cement or petroleum products at the other extreme. At the same time, one of the peculiarities of modern capitalism is that the cultural economy continues to expand at a rapid pace not only as a function of the growth of discretionary income, but also as an expression of the incursion of sign-value into ever-widening spheres of productive activity at large as firms seek to intensify the design content, styling, and quality of their outputs in the endless search for competitive advantage (Scott 2008).

It is such incursions alongside the growth in cultural industries that makes the cultural economy such an important topic for local and regional development; something we specifically address in the final section of this chapter. Our central contention is that the industries and agents involved in the cultural economy are central to a series of new opportunities and challenges to local and regional social well-being and economic development.

Production, organization and work in the cultural economy

Over much of the last century, the leading edges of economic development and growth were largely identifiable with sectors characterized by varying degrees of mass production, as expressed in large-scale machine systems and a persistent drive to product standardization and cost cutting. Throughout the mass-production era, the dominant sectors evolved through a succession of technological and organizational changes focused above all on process routinization and the search for internal economies of scale. These features are not especially conducive to the injection of high levels of aesthetic and semiotic content into final products. Indeed, in the 1930s and 1940s many commentators expressed grave misgivings about the incursion of industrial methods into the sphere of the cultural economy and the concomitant tendency for complex social and emotive content to be evacuated from forms of popular cultural production (e.g. Horkheimer 1947; Adorno 1991). These misgivings were by no means out of place in a context where much of commercial culture was focused on an extremely narrow approach to entertainment and distraction. The specific problems raised by the Frankfurt School in regard to popular commercial culture have in certain respects lost some of their urgency as the economic and political bases of mass-production have given way before the changes ushered in over the late 1970s and early 1980s, when the new economy started its ascent. This is not to say that the contemporary cultural economy is not associated with a number of serious social and political predicaments. But it is also the case that as commercial cultural production and consumption has evolved in the major capitalist societies, so our aesthetic and ideological judgements about their underlying meanings have tended to shift.

In contrast to mass machinofacture, sectors in the contemporary cultural economy tend to be composed of relatively disintegrated production processes, with processes of disintegration being greatly facilitated by various kinds of computerized and digitized technologies. Equally, and nowhere more than in segments of the cultural economy, production is often quite labor-intensive, for despite the widespread use of electronic technologies, cultural products industries also tend to make heavy demands on both the brainpower and handiwork of the labor force. These industries are typically composed of swarms of small producers (with low entry and exit costs), complemented by many smaller numbers of large establishments. Small-scale producers in the cultural economy are frequently marked by neo-artisanal forms of production, or, in a more or less equivalent phrase, by flexible specialization, meaning that they concentrate on making particular categories of products (clothing, advertisements, cultural performances, etc.) but where the design specifications of each batch of products change repeatedly. To be sure, large firms in the cultural economy occasionally tend toward mass-production (which would generally signify a diminution of symbolic function in final outputs), but are nowadays increasingly prone to organization along the lines of "systems houses" (Scott 2002). The latter term is used in the world of high-technology industry to signify an establishment whose products are relatively small in number over some fairly extended period of time, and where each unit of output represents huge inputs of capital and/or labor. Examples of systems houses are computer games producers, the major Hollywood movie studios, large magazine publishers (but not printers), television network operators, and, to a lesser degree, fashion houses.

These large-scale producers are of particular importance in the cultural economy because they so frequently act as the hubs of wider production networks incorporating many smaller firms. Equally, and above all in the entertainment industry, they play a critical part in the financing and distribution of much independent production. In addition, large producers right across the cultural economy are increasingly subject to incorporation into the organizational structures and spheres of influence of giant multinational conglomerates through which they tap into huge financial resources and marketing capacities. While these giant firms are absolutely central to the cultural economy, it is also important to note that their power is constantly under threat and subject to change

(Peterson and Berger 1996). Technological change is often central to these processes and the recent shifts brought about by new possibilities for disintermediation and distribution in the music, television and film industries are evidence of how quickly accepted industrial norms, structures and hierarchies can change. Indeed, one can imagine that at least some segments of the cultural economy – resting as it does on fluid and unpredictable trends and hard-to-protect intellectual property – may be entering into a new phase of development marked by yet more intense competition and reduced levels of oligopolistic power.

The actual work of production in the cultural economy is typically carried out within shifting networks of specialized but complementary firms. Such networks assume different forms, ranging from heterarchic webs of small establishments to more hierarchical structures in which the activities of groups of establishments are coordinated by a dominating central unit, with every possible variation between these two extreme cases. Much of the cultural economy can be described as conforming to a contractual and transactional model of production (Caves 2000). This model also extends to employment relations, with part-time, temporary, precarious, nonstandard, and freelance work being prevalent (Ross 2008). The instabilities associated with this state of affairs often lead to intensive social networking activities among skilled creative workers as a means of keeping abreast of current trends and opportunities and of finding collaborators, customers and employers (Scott 1998; Neff *et al.* 2005). Within the firm, these same workers are often incorporated into project-oriented teams, a form of work organization that is rapidly becoming the preferred means of managing internal divisions of labor in the more innovative segments of the modern cultural economy (Grabher 2001). By contrast, in sectors such as clothing or furniture, where low-wage manual operators usually account for a high proportion of total employment, piece-work and sweatshop conditions are

164

more apt to be the prevailing modes of incorporating workers into the production process, though these sectors are also characterized by high-wage, high-skill segments in activities such as design and commercialization.

These features of the modern cultural economy differentiate it quite markedly from the older model of mass-production. In contrast to what was often seen as the dispiriting and endless uniformity of the outputs that flowed from the mass-production system, the cultural economy is marked by extremely high levels of product variety in regard to both form and substance. As a corollary, the cultural economy is associated with a major transformation of market structures, with monopolistic competition à la Chamberlin (1933) becoming increasingly the norm. Chamberlinian competition, which resembles in some respects imperfect competition as formulated by Robinson (1933), is based on the notion that distinctive market distortions appear when producers have strongly developed firm-specific characteristics. Under a regime of monopolistic competition there may be many individual firms all making a particular class of products, but each firm's output also has unique attributes (design, place-specific associations, brand, etc.) that can at best be reproduced by other firms only in the form of inferior imitations. The increasing importance of cultural and symbolic content in contemporary patterns of consumption means that monopolistic competition has become an ever more feasible option for firms throughout the entire economy. The constant rebranding and repackaging characteristic of product markets today is helping to usher in an economic system where even small firms can sometimes vie with goliaths in the creation of virtual product monopolies.

Nodes and networks in the cultural economy

Cultural products industries almost always operate most effectively when the individual establishments that make them up exhibit at least some degree of locational agglomeration. A growing body of literature has shown that there is a persistent tendency of producers in the cultural economy to cluster together in geographic space (Christopherson and Storper 1986; Pratt 1997; Coe 2000; Scott 2000; Hesmondhalgh 2002; Power and Hallencreutz 2002; Rantisi 2002; Power and Scott 2004; Vinodrai 2006). This tendency follows at once from the economic efficiencies that can be obtained when many different interrelated firms and workers lie in close proximity to one another so that their complex interactions are tightly circumscribed in space and time. Agglomeration also occurs for reasons other than economic efficiency in the narrow sense. It is also partly a result of the learning processes and innovative energies that are unleashed from time to time in industrial clusters as information, opinions, cultural sensibilities, and so on, are transmitted through them, and these processes are usually especially strong in cases where transactional intensity is high. Moreover, outputs that are rich in information, sign value, and social meaning are particularly sensitive to the influence of geographic context and creative milieu. Molotch (1996, 2003) has argued that agglomerations of design-intensive industries acquire place-specific competitive advantages by reason of local cultural symbologies that become congealed in their products, and that imbue them with authentic character. This intensifies the play of Chamberlinian competition in the cultural economy because monopolistic assets now not only emerge from the productive strategies of individual firms, but also from their wider geographic milieu (Hauge et al. 2009).

The association between place and product in the cultural industries is often so strong that it constitutes a significant element of firms' successes on wider markets. Place-related markers, indeed, may become brands in themselves that agents can exploit to increase their competitive positions, as exemplified by the cases of Jamaican reggae, Scandinavian design, Hawaiian shirts, or Persian carpets. Successful cultural products agglomerations, as well, are irresistible to talented individuals who flock in from every distant corner in pursuit of professional fulfillment, in a process that Menger (1993) has referred to as "artistic gravitation." This gravitational force signifies that the labor pools of dynamic agglomerations are constantly being replenished by selective in-migration of workers who are already predisposed to high levels of job performance in the local area. Local supplies of relevant skills and worker sensibilities are further augmented by the specialized educational and training institutions that typically spring into being in productive agglomerations.

These remarks indicate that a tight interweaving of place and production system is one of the essential features of the new cultural economy of capitalism. This interweaving is obviously an important point of leverage for agents that are primarily interested in local and regional development (such as local authorities or tourist boards) but it is also a lever commonly used by agents interested in making a living from cultural products. In cultural products industries, as never before, the wider urban, leisure and social environment and the apparatus of production merge together in potent synergistic combinations. Some of the most advanced expressions of this propensity can be observed in world cities like New York, Paris, London, or Tokyo. Certain districts in these cities are typified by a more or less organic continuity between their place-specific settings (as expressed in streetscapes, shopping and entertainment facilities, and architectural background), their social and cultural infrastructures (museums, art galleries, theaters, and so on), and their industrial vocations (for example, advertising, graphic design, audiovisual services, publishing, or fashion clothing). The social networks and scenes that define production also leave an indelible stamp on the character of the city (Neff 2005;

Currid 2007). In a city like Las Vegas, the urban environment, the production system, and the world of the consumer are all so tightly interwoven as to form a virtually indivisible unity. The city of work and the city of leisure increasingly interpenetrate one another.

Global connections

In spite of the predisposition of firms in particular cultural products industries to locate in close mutual proximity to one another, inputs and outputs flow with relative ease across national borders and are a steadily rising component of international trade. The international flow of cultural goods and services is reinforced by the operations of transnational media conglomerates whose main competitive strategy appears increasingly to be focused on the creation of worldwide blockbuster products, as exemplified dramatically by the market offerings of major firms in the computer games and film industries. At the same time, with ever greater global interconnectedness many different cultural styles and genres become accessible to far-flung consumers so that highly specialized niche markets are also proliferating alongside the blockbuster markets in which major corporations largely participate. With the further development of computerized distribution technologies for cultural products, the process of globalization will assuredly accelerate, and this is especially true for cases where digitization of final outputs is feasible.

Observe that globalization in the sense indicated does not necessarily lead to the locational dispersal of production itself. On the contrary, globalization qua spatial fluidity of end products helps to accentuate agglomeration because it leads to rising exports combined with expansion of localized production activities. Concomitant widening and deepening of the social division of labor at the point of production then helps to intensify clustering because it generates increased positive externalities. Locational agglomeration and globalization, in short, are complementary processes under specifiable social and economic circumstances. That said, the falling external transactions costs associated with globalization will sometimes undermine agglomeration from the other end, as it were, by making it feasible for some kinds of production to move to alternative locations. It is now increasingly possible for activities that could not previously escape the centripetal forces of agglomeration to decentralize to alternative locations, such as sites with relatively low labor costs. This may result in a wide dispersal of certain types of production units, such as DVD processing plants and server farms for the gaming industry, or in the formation of alternative clusters or satellite production locations, as illustrated by the sound stages and associated facilities that have come into existence in Toronto and Sydney in order to serve US television and film production companies.

The overall outcome of these competing spatial tensions in the modern cultural economy is a widening global constellation of production centers. The logic of agglomeration and increasing-returns effects suggests that one premier global center will occasionally emerge in any given sector, but even in the case of the international motion-picture industry, which is overwhelmingly dominated by Hollywood, it can be plausibly argued (above all in a world of monopolistic competition) that multiple production centers will continue to exist if not to flourish. The scenario of thriving multiple production centers is all the more to be expected given that policymakers are investing more and more effort in local economic development projects based on the cultural economy, and where this effort also includes the fostering of associated distribution and marketing systems.

Large multinational corporations play a decisive role across this entire functional and spatial field of economic activity, both in coordinating local production networks and in ensuring that their products are projected onto wider markets. This remark, by the way, should not induce us to neglect the fact that small independent firms continue to occupy an important place in almost all cultural products agglomerations. In the past, multinationals based in the United States and Europe have led the race to command global markets for nearly all types of cultural products, but producers from other countries are now entering the fray in ever-greater numbers, even in the media sectors that have hitherto been considered as the privileged preserve of North American and European firms. In the same way, different cultural products industrial agglomerations around the world are increasingly caught up with one another in global webs of co-productions and creative partnerships (Lorenzen and Täube 2008; Lorenzen 2009). Indeed no localized group of firms can nowadays be completely self-sufficient in terms of state-of-the-art knowledge creation, and worldwide inter-agglomeration networks and circuits of interaction are an increasingly vital element of any individual agglomeration's performance. Concomitantly, global productive alliances and joint ventures are surging to the fore in the modern cultural economy, drawing on the specific competitive advantages of diverse clusters, but without necessarily compromising the underlying force of agglomeration itself.

In these industries where volatile and unpredictable changes in fashion are a given and where product differentiation is the dominant strategy pursued by firms, places which can "act as switching centres for the transmission of ideas harvested from a wide range of sources" (Weller 2007: 43) become privileged points on the landscape of production and consumption. The depth and intensity of global connections and flows makes switching centers, meeting places, and interactive spaces vitally important for all sorts of strategic knowledge and networks. Key to these sites is their role as foci of a highly globalized yet centralized culture and fashion media system (Breward and Gilbert

DOMINIC POWER AND ALLEN J. SCOTT

2006) that allows knowledge to be imported, created, and disseminated on a world-wide scale. It is not only the resident workers and entrepreneurs of these nodes who are important agents of local cultural development; short-term visitors to trade fairs, passing tourists, bloggers following fashion trends and gossip from far away are all examples of actors important to the emergence of the urban milieu. Moreover, the nodes themselves may be short-lived, periodic or episodic, as demonstrated by the important role played by trade fairs as switching points within global circuits of knowledge and value chains demonstrate (Power and Jansson 2008).

Once all of this has been said, the advent of a new cultural economy and the flow of its outputs through circuits of international commerce have not always been attended by benign results. This situation has led to numerous political collisions over issues of trade and culture. Notwithstanding such notes of dissonance, we seem to be moving steadily into a world that is becoming more cosmopolitan and eclectic in its modes of cultural consumption. Certainly for consumers in more economically advanced locales, traditional local staples are now but one element of an ever-widening palette of cultural offerings comprising African music, Japanese comic books, Indian films, Middle Eastern tourist resorts, Argentinean wines, Thai cuisine, Brazilian telenovelas and other exotic fare. This trend is an outcome of and a contributing factor to the recent, if still incipient, advent of a multifaceted and extensive global system of cultural products agglomerations. Thus globalization appears less to be leading to regional cultural uniformity than it is increasing the variety of options open to individual consumers.

Cultural industries and local and regional economic development policy

Cultural products industries are growing rapidly; they tend (though not always) to be environmentally friendly; and they frequently (though again not always) employ high-skill, high-wage, creative workers. Cultural products industries also generate positive externalities in so far as they contribute to the quality of life in the places where they congregate and enhance the image and prestige of the local area. Moreover, as noted above, they tend to be highly localized and often place-bound. This fact has made them increasingly attractive to policy-makers intent on finding new solutions to problems of urban redevelopment and local economic performance.

A sort of first-generation approach to the systematic deployment of cultural assets in the quest for local economic growth can be found in the aggressive place-marketing and local boosterism pursued by many municipal authorities since the early 1980s. This activity is often based on a local patrimony of historical or artistic resources, but it also assumes the guise of energetic property redevelopment programs. In many cases cultural grand projects have anchored initiatives to remake and market places: for instance, the success of the Guggenheim Museum in Bilbao as part of an initiative that has turned an old and stagnant industrial area into a world-renowned tourist center and a new focus of inward investment. An alternative (or, rather, a complementary) second generation of policy approaches has, since the mid- to late 1990s, come under the scrutiny of regional authorities. In this instance, the objective is less the attraction of tourists or migrants, than it is to stimulate the formation of localized complexes of cultural industries that will then export their outputs far and wide. In the advanced economies this approach has found expression in many different kinds of policy initiatives focused on diverse formulations such as 'creative industries', 'experience industries', 'content industries', 'cultural industries,' 'heritage', and so on. There is an extensive literature that draws critical attention to the difficulties associated with policy discourses on the creative and cultural industries

(O'Connor 2000, 2005; Hesmondhalgh 2002; O'Connor 2004; Power and Scott 2004; Pratt 2005; O'Connor and Xin 2006; Galloway and Dunlop 2007; Mato 2009; Miller 2009). Whether understood as terms denoting a distinctive economic grouping, a means of classifying 'cultural' or 'knowledge' production, a framework for conjoining certain types of intellectual or artistic labor, these discourses are inherently tied into two wider policy concerns, namely deindustrialization and knowledge economy more generally. Nonetheless there is an emerging agreement that some sort of productive industrial focus is necessary as a complement to cultural policy in the narrow sense. Sectors such as design, film/TV, popular music, games, and fashion in virtually all European countries are now the object of policies focusing on supportive of firm networking, labor training, cluster initiatives, localized institutional infrastructures, and so on.

This type of approach is critically dependent on a clear understanding of the logic and dynamics of the agglomeration processes that shape much of the geography of the modern cultural economy. For any given agglomeration, the essential first task that policymakers must face is to map out the collective order of the local economy along with the multiple sources of the increasing-returns effects that invariably emanate from its inner workings. This in itself is a difficult task due both to the problems of defining just where the cultural economy begins and ends, and to the intangible nature of many of the phenomena that lie at the core of localized competitive advantages. That said, it is this collective order more than anything else that presents possibilities for meaningful and effective policy intervention in any given agglomeration. Blunt top-down approaches focused on directive planning are unlikely in and of themselves to accomplish much at the local scale, except in special circumstances. In terms of costs and benefits and general workability, the most successful types of policies will as a general rule be those that concentrate

on the character of localized external economies of scale and scope as public or quasi-public goods. The point here is both to stimulate the formation of useful agglomeration effects that would otherwise be undersupplied or dissipated in the local economy, and to ensure that existing externalities are not subject to severe misallocation as a result of market failure. Finely tuned bottom-up measures are essential in situations like this.

Policymakers thus need to pay attention to three main ways of promoting collective competitive advantage, which, on the basis of the modern theory of industrial districts can be identified as (1) the building of collaborative inter-firm relations in order to mobilize latent synergies, (2) the organization of efficient, high-skill local labor markets, and (3) the potentiation of local industrial creativity and innovation (cf. Scott 2000; Malmberg and Power 2005). The specific means by which these broad objectives can be pursued are many and various depending on empirical circumstances, but basic institution-building in order to internalize latent and actual externalities within competent agencies and to coordinate disparate groups of actors is likely to be of major importance. Complementary lines of attack involve approaches such as the initiation of labor-training programs, creating centers for the encouragement of technological upgrading or design excellence, organizing exhibitions and export drives, and so on, as well as socio-juridical interventions like dealing with threats to the reputation of local product quality due to free-rider problems (especially in tourist resorts), or helping to protect communal intellectual property. In addition, appropriately structured private–public partnerships could conceivably function as a vehicle for generating early warning signals as and when the local economy appears to be in danger of locking into a low-level equilibrium due to adverse path-selection dynamics. The latter problem is especially apt to make its appearance in localized production systems because the complex, structured interdependencies within them often give rise to long-run developmental rigidities.

While economic development based on cultural products sectors will in all likelihood continue to occur in the world's richest countries, a number of low- and middle-income countries are finding that they too are able to participate in various ways in the new cultural economy, sometimes on the basis of traditional industries and cultures. Even old and economically depressed industrial areas, as we have seen, can occasionally turn their fortunes around by means of well-planned cultural initiatives. To be sure, the notion of the cultural economy as a source of regional development is still something of a novelty, and much further reflection is required if we are to understand and exploit its full potential while simultaneously maintaining a clear grasp of its practical limitations. In any case, an accelerating convergence between the economic and the cultural is currently occurring in modern life, and is bringing in its train new kinds of urban outcomes and opening up new opportunities for policymakers to raise local levels of income, employment, and social well-being.

References

Adorno, T. (1991) *The Culture Industry: selected essays on mass culture*, London, Routledge.

Breward, C. and D. Gilbert (eds) (2006) *Fashion's World Cities*, New York: Berg.

Caves, R. (2000) *Creative Industries: contracts between art and commerce*, Cambridge, Mass.: Harvard University Press.

Chamberlin, E. (1933) *The Theory of Monopoly Competition*, Cambridge, Mass: Harvard University Press.

Christopherson, S. and M. Storper (1986) "The city as studio – the world as back lot – the impact of vertical disintegration on the location of the motion-picture industry", *Environment and Planning D-Society & Space* 4(3): 305–320.

Coe, N. (2000) "The view from out West: embeddedness, inter-personal relations and the development of an indigenous film industry in Vancouver", *Geoforum* 31(4): 391–407.

Currid, E. (2007) *The Warhol Economy, How Fashion Art & Music Drive New York City*, Princeton, NJ: Princeton University Press.

Galloway, S. and S. Dunlop (2007) "A critique of definitions of the cultural and creative industries in public policy", *International Journal of Cultural Policy* 13(1): 17–31.

Grabher, G. (2001) "Locating economic action: projects, networks, localities, institutions", *Environment and Planning A* 33(8): 1329–1331.

Hauge, A., A. Malmberg and D. Power (2009) "The spaces and places of Swedish fashion", *European Planning Studies* 17(4): 529–547.

Hesmondhalgh, D. (2002) *The Cultural Industries*, London: Sage.

Horkheimer, M. (1947) *The Eclipse of Reason*, New York: Oxford University Press.

Lash, S. and J. Urry (1994) *Economies of Signs and Spaces*, London: Sage.

Lorenzen, M. (2009) "Creativity in context: content, cost, chance and collection in the organization of the film industry", in A. Pratt and P. Jeffcutt (eds) *Creativity, Innovation, and the Cultural Economy*, London: Routledge.

Lorenzen, M. and F. Täube (2008) "Breakout from Bollywood? The roles of social networks and regulation in the evolution of Indian film industry", *Journal of International Management* 14: 286–299.

Malmberg, A. and D. Power (2005) "(How) do (firms in) clusters create knowledge?", *Industry and Innovation* 12(4): 409–431.

Mato, D. (2009) "All industries are cultural", *Cultural Studies* 23(1): 70–87.

Menger, P. (1993) "L'hégémonie parisienne: économie et politique de la gravitation artistique", *Annales: Economies, Sociétés, Civilisations* 6: 1565–1600.

Miller, T. (2009) "From creative to cultural industries", *Cultural Studies* 23(1): 88–99.

Molotch, H. (1996) "LA as design product: how art works in a regional economy", in A. Scott and E. Soja (eds) *The City: Los Angeles and urban theory at the end of the twentieth century*, Berkeley: University of California Press.

Molotch, H. (2003) *Where Stuff Comes From: how toasters, toilets, cars, computers and many other things come to be as they are*, London: Routledge.

Neff, G. (2005) "The changing place of cultural production: the location of social networks in a digital media industry", *Annals of the American Academy of Political and Social Sciences* 597(1): 134–152.

Neff, G., E. Wissinger and S. Zukin (2005) "Entrepreneurial labor among cultural producers: 'cool' jobs in 'hot' industries", *Social Semiotics* 15(3): 307–334.

O'Connor, J. (2000) "The definition of 'cultural industries'" from http://www.pedrobendas-solli.com/pesquisa/icc1.pdf.

O'Connor, J. (2004) "Cities, culture and 'transitional economies'" in D. Power and A. Scott *Cultural Industries and the Production of Culture*, London: Routledge.

O'Connor, J. (2005) "Creative exports", *International Journal of Cultural Policy* 11: 45–60.

O'Connor, J. and G. Xin (2006) "A new modernity?: The arrival of 'creative industries' in China", *International Journal of Cultural Studies* 9(3): 271–283.

Peterson, R. and D. Berger (1996) "Measuring industry concentration, diversity and innovation in popular music", *American Sociological Review* 61: 175–178.

Power, D. (2002) "'Cultural industries' in Sweden: an assessment of their place in the Swedish economy", *Economic Geography* 78(2): 103–127.

Power, D. and D. Hallencreutz (2002) "Profiting from creativity? The music industry in Stockholm, Sweden and Kingston, Jamaica", *Environment and Planning A* 34(10): 1833–1854.

Power, D. and A. Hauge (2008) "No man's brand – brands, institutions, and fashion," *Growth and Change* 39(1): 123–143.

Power, D. and J. Jansson (2008) "Cyclical clusters in global circuits: overlapping spaces and furniture industry trade fairs", *Economic Geography* 84 (4): 423–448.

Power, D. and A. Scott (2004) *Cultural Industries and the Production of Culture*, London: Routledge.

Power, D. and A. Scott (2004) *A Prelude To Cultural Industries and the Production of Culture. Cultural Industries and the Production of Culture*, London: Routledge.

Pratt, A. (1997) "The cultural industries production system: a case study of employment change in Britain 1984–91", *Environment and Planning A* 29: 1953–1974.

Pratt, A. (2005) "Cultural industries and public policy: an oxymoron?", *International Journal of Cultural Policy* 11(1): 31–44.

Rantisi, N. (2002) "The competitive foundations of localized learning and innovation: The case of women's garment production in New York City", *Economic Geography* 78(4): 441–462.

Robinson, J. (1933) *The Economics of Imperfect Competition*, London: Macmillan.

Ross, A. (2008) "The new geography of work: power to the precarious?", *Theory Culture Society* 25(7–8): 31–49.

Scott, A. (1998) "Multimedia and digital visual effects: an emerging local labor market", *Monthly Labor Review* 121: 30–38.

Scott, A. (2000) *The Cultural Economy of Cities: essays on the geography of image-producing industries*, London: Sage.

Scott, A. (2008) *The Social Economy of the Metropolis: cognitive-cultural capitalism and the global resurgence of cities*, Oxford: Oxford University Press.

Scott, A. J. (2002) "A new map of Hollywood: the production and distribution of American motion pictures", *Regional Studies* 36(9): 957–975.

Vinodrai, T. (2006) "Reproducing Toronto's design ecology: career paths, intermediaries, and local labor markets", *Economic Geography* 82(3): 237–263.

Weller, S. (2007) "Fashion as viscous knowledge: fashion's role in shaping trans-national garment production", *Journal of Economic Geography* 7(1): 39–66.

Further reading

Anheier, H. K. and Y. R. Raj (eds) (2008) "The cultural economy", *Cultures and Globalization Series*, No. 2, London: Sage.

Power, D. and A. Hauge (2008) "No man's brand – brands, institutions, fashion and the economy", *Growth and Change* 39(1).

Power, D. and J. Jansson (2008) "Cyclical clusters in global circuits: overlapping spaces and furniture industry trade fairs", *Economic Geography* 84(4): 423–448.

Scott, A. J. (2008) *Social Economy of the Metropolis: cognitive-cultural capitalism and the global resurgence of cities*, Oxford: Oxford University Press.

15

Post-socialism and transition

Bolesław Domański

Introduction

The concepts of post-socialism and transition are commonly used as territorial and temporal descriptors referring to the countries which experienced state socialism and to the period after the fall of this system. The rationale behind studying local and regional development in post-socialist areas lies in the belief that the social system of socialism as it actually existed had distinct features which could make development processes to some extent different from their attributes in other areas. From the evolutionary perspective, we cannot understand current structures and processes, if we do not know their historical roots.

The objective of this chapter is to identify the structures and mechanisms which are reproduced, transformed and/or created in the post-socialist era. This involves the analysis of various economic, social, cultural, and political factors which operate at different geographical scales (local, regional, national, European, global) and which originated in the pre-socialist, socialist, and post-socialist milieu. The focus is primarily on European post-socialist countries.

At the outset a brief survey is necessary of the specific qualities of local and regional

development under socialism. This leads to a discussion on the current impact of the structural, institutional and cultural legacies of socialism, and the emergence of new mechanisms of development. In this context the chapter addresses the issues of the winners and losers in contemporary local and regional development, the spatial disparities which result and their explanations. The roles of the key actors are considered from the relational and institutional perspective, including global forces, local agency and public policies. The chapter is concluded by a debate on how far the transformation processes can be conceptualized as transition, modernization, and Europeanization or as a unique process.

What was specific about local and regional development under socialism?

The economic and political system

The socialist system was underlain by a belief in the necessity and possibility of creating new social reality. This mission was pursued by the centralized power, which attempted to control all economic, social and political activity, among other things, through state ownership of the means of production and means of consumption. Priority was given to economic growth and an accompanying ideology of industrialization as the means of progress. The socialist economic policy is described as an 'extensive development strategy' as high rates of growth in output were pursued by maintaining high rates of growth in inputs rather than by increasing efficiency. There were soft budget constraints and as a consequence an unlimited expansion drive, in which overinvestment resulted in shortages, which in turn justified further investment. As a result the economy was limited by supply rather than by demand and became an economy of structural shortage (Nove 1986; Kornai 1992).

The fundamental feature of the system was the existence of non-market relationships between enterprises and the administrative allocation of social goods in society which by and large replaced the 'anarchy' of market exchange. This gave rise to the power of gatekeepers – state agents controlling access to scarce resources. Large industrial producers from the priority sectors integrated the role of employers and gatekeepers and hence gained enormous influence in local and regional space. This merger of the spheres of distribution and production represented industrial paternalism underlain by labor shortages. Industrial gatekeepers sought control over the labor market and, as a result, the administrative allocation of scarce goods and services by key state producers became the major source of social and spatial inequalities (Domański 1997). This was a special type of segmentation of the labor market.

In sum, this social order was distinct from capitalism as major economic activities were not conducted by private firms, accumulated private wealth and unemployment were not the principal determinants of social inequalities, and market relationships were largely replaced by non-market mechanisms of distribution of goods in the economy and society. The socialist economies of Central and Eastern Europe were relatively isolated from the world economy, largely over-industrialized, dominated by big state-owned enterprises and a limited number of SMEs.

Regional development and spatial disparities

The emphasis on industrial expansion contributed to the fast growth of industrial areas. This generally enhanced disparities between more developed and less developed regions; new growth centers mainly emerged in areas of resource extraction. Numerous medium-sized and small towns dominated by a single industry and/or factory were created and/or expanded. Capital cities and regional administrative centers were in a privileged position due to the system of administrative allocation of social goods. There was a profound crisis for non-industrial small towns. They had lost their traditional central place functions due to the nationalization and concentration of the retail trade and services, together with the capturing of allocative functions by state-owned industrial and agricultural employers.

Another effect was the reproduction of, and even an increase in, the urban–rural contrast in terms of the standard of living. Vast rural regions were typical areas of multiple deprivation: poor housing conditions, limited educational opportunities, inadequate health services, etc. In addition, spatially concentrated industrial growth generated permanent demand for labor supply, which was satisfied by mass migration of young people from rural areas leaving behind a disproportionate share of the elderly.

Rural commuters constituted an underprivileged group produced by the creation of new jobs with limited housing opportunities in urban places. They were paid wages, but denied access to housing and social services available in towns. Underlying all this was inadequate public transport provision oriented to serving the needs of major industrial employers.

Urban issues

Large cities and medium-sized industrial towns experienced faster growth and enjoyed relatively better life chances than small towns and rural areas. However, they suffered at least to some degree from so-called 'crippled urbanization' (Domański 1997).The endemic feature of urban growth under socialism was the imbalance between industrial expansion and underdeveloped housing and social infrastructure provision. This can be accounted for by the absence of mechanisms linking local economic and population growth with the supply of infrastructure and services. There was no local taxation and there were no multiplier effects – mechanisms, whereby local authorities and independent agents could develop provisions in response to the demand created by the employees. Planning, which was meant to substitute for these mechanisms, failed since the socialist system lacked agents capable of enforcing local and regional plans. Local and regional authorities always had very limited bargaining power with the economic entities which controlled the basic assets and represented branch ministries – the pillars of the socialist system of power. Thus large industrial employers were able to disregard territorially organized administration and shift scarce resources to their advantage (Smith 1989; Domański 1997).

Vast groups of town dwellers experienced deprived access to many social goods due to industrial paternalism; women and the elderly were most affected. Industrial towns offered limited secondary and tertiary educational opportunities, being oriented at supplying the manual workers sought by industrial employers. There were company enclaves in towns and some urban places became company towns. The deteriorating conditions in old residential districts resulted from a preoccupation with the supply of new dwellings and the neglect of the existing housing stock, which reflected both the ideologically laden emphasis on the new at the expense of the old and the pressure of major employers demanding a new labor force. Last but not least, the serious environmental problems that arose in many places stemmed from the lack of environmental concern.

All in all, industrial towns were privileged vis-à-vis other urban places which might suffer from stagnation, but they often experienced pathological growth themselves. The activity of huge industrial enterprises did not contribute to the development of the socialist town but rather represented development in the town, bearing some resemblance to the effects of industrialization on early capitalist towns. This was underlain by suppressed local initiative, deficient social institutions and the absence of territorial self-government.

Post-socialism: the role of path-dependence vs. new mechanisms

The emphasis in many publications on post-socialist transition is on macro-economic and political institutional changes, namely privatization, liberalization, democratization, and internationalization. The major focus here is on the one hand on the impact of socialist and pre-socialist legacies and on the other on the emergence of new mechanisms and factors of local and regional development.

The restitution of private ownership of land and other assets was a complex, inevitably conflict-ridden process, which took different forms in individual countries. It produced fragmented ownership in certain domains and areas, and its concentration in others. One specific institutional legacy is an uncertain legal status of some areas and inconsistencies in the cadastre system which may frustrate tax collection and investment. A different division of power and relationships between the state and local/regional authorities was molded in various countries. There were powerful agents responsible for ownership transfer, e.g., Treuhand in eastern

Germany. Finally, new foreign-controlled players, including global transnational corporations (TNCs) and international bodies (e.g., IMF, EU), began to play an important role. All these institutional transformations entailed change in economic linkages and power relationships discussed later.

From the point of view of local and regional development, the critical change took place in the functioning of the labor markets (Rainnie et al. 2002). The shift from a situation where employers had to search for employees to an employer-dominated market and unemployment led to the erosion of the gatekeeping role of large employers as distributors of social goods in local communities. The re-emergence of demand-led multiplier effects eradicated the former imbalance between the production of capital goods and the supply of consumer products and services in urban areas. At the same time, new mechanisms of social and spatial inequalities appeared based on the segmentation of the capitalist labor market and the spatial reorganization of economic activities, worsening access to social goods for certain groups and places. Spatial variation in housing costs became a significant factor in migration. Suburban migration of the middle-class increased, whereas the mobility of the poorer segments of society was impeded (Pickles and Smith 1998; Bradshaw and Stenning 2004).

The fundamental material legacy of the pre-socialist and socialist past lies in the economic structures of towns and regions, their infrastructure and environmental situation which usually foster continuity and sometimes change in development trends. They are also affected by local educational levels and facilities and the demographic structures formed in the past.

Important as the changing formal institutions and material structures are, we cannot ignore the impact of the range of informal institutions and practices embedded in social networks and culture. There is enormous variation in social images, aspirations and activities at national, regional and local scales. This finds economic expression in entrepreneurship levels and attitudes to work and can be related to earlier migrations and contacts with relatives and friends in Western Europe and North America. One should not forget about the differences in the nature of the socialist regimes, some of which left more room for individual economic activity and contacts with abroad. The devastating impact of the erosion of trust in the relationships between citizens and public institutions characteristic of state socialism lasted longer in some regions than in others. A widespread belief in the irreparable crisis inherent in the socialist system, with its lack of hope, made the inhabitants of some Central European regions more open to radical change in the early days of the transformation. Where people widely believed that vast changes were necessary and/or inevitable, they were more prone to face up to new challenges, even though they could be disappointed with the consequences of the reforms. The significant differences in contemporary public attitudes, civil activity and institutions persist. Many authors point to the legacy of the old cultural divide between Western and Eastern Christendom and Western Christianity and Islam. A specific merger of political and economic power structures, patron–client relations, an aversion to transparency and high corruption levels may be rooted in the former Tsarist, Soviet and Ottoman monopolization of power (Turnock 2003; Van Zon 2008).

On the whole, there are clear indications of both continuity and new mechanisms of local and regional development related to the (re)introduction of a capitalist economy and the integration into global networks and dependencies. Path dependence can be identified especially in the case of some patterns of ownership, the layers of investment, the reproduction of demographic and educational structures as well as public attitudes and civic activity built upon pre-socialist foundations. The new labor market segmentation and migration patterns represent more recent mechanisms. We may now explore how this manifests itself in the development of regions and localities.

Regional disparities and their explanations in post-socialism

Metropolitan areas

The most obvious winners of the post-socialist transformation are metropolitan areas. They benefit from the development of advanced producer services, a broad range of consumer services and the location of new manufacturing plants, being the most attractive place for both foreign investment and the growth of small- and medium-sized indigenous firms. Partners for cooperation can more easily be found here, so large investors are more likely to become regionally embedded.

The success of metropolitan areas rests on the size of their market, a pool of skilled labor and good accessibility. Therefore they take advantage of their favorable position inherited from the past and profit from new locational factors which came to the fore with the advent of the market economy. The growing diversified economic base, international linkages and the increasing standard of living nurture agglomeration forces which may sustain their further growth. This is especially true of the metropolitan areas based on major cities, which host high-order service functions. The development of polycentric urban regions may be slowed by their industrial legacy.

Industrial regions and towns

The intensively industrialized regions and localities found themselves in a dubious situation with the fall of socialism, which prioritized industrial growth. They lost their privileged access to public resources at the same time as their major firms were made to face up to previously unknown foreign competition. Their performance is conditioned by the success of the sector and/or of individual enterprises.

The effects of deindustrialization are most dramatic in single-industry or, still worse, one-factory towns, which are the product of early capitalist or socialist industrialization. The places that relied on shrinking sectors, such as manufacturing of textiles, heavy engineering and military equipment, and resource extraction became especially vulnerable. Towns dominated by huge defense-related producers, expanded during the Cold War arms race, were often developed in peripheral regions for strategic reasons.

The seeds of the crisis in many industrial towns and regions can be found in their economic structure and its social and institutional consequences. The structurally unsustainable dependence upon individual sectors and on large plants, commonly with obsolete technology, was accompanied by weak SMEs and an underdeveloped tertiary sector with a distorted educational structure. The situation could be exacerbated by environmental problems. From the point of view of locational factors which have become important in the market economy, many industrial towns lack a large enough market, adequate services and attractive living conditions, a quality labor force, and sometimes good accessibility. The symptoms of a crisis have sometimes triggered a defensive reaction geared toward maintaining the old local/regional trajectory and opposing changes – a path-dependent mechanism of institutional lock-in (Grabher and Stark 1997). Thus deindustrializing towns can not only experience the disappearance of their former economic activities, but, to make matters worse, may not be able to mobilize local financial and cultural assets to launch themselves on a new development path. This is accompanied by the growing intra-urban social disparities typical of post-socialist towns.

Still, towns and regions dependent on growing industrial sectors and firms may do well. For example, one can observe the growth of several export-oriented resource-producing regions in Russia (Bradshaw 2006). Large old industrial regions with good accessibility may undergo successful restructuring, despite a decline of traditional sectors, attracting new manufacturing and service activities thanks to their large market, technical skills and other economies of agglomeration.

Peripheral non-metropolitan rural areas

The inferior position of non-metropolitan rural regions has been significantly aggravated in the post-socialist era. Poor accessibility associated with the inadequate road system has undermined their attractiveness to investment and has become a barrier to spill-over effects from the growth of metropolitan areas. Fragmented private agriculture with hidden unemployment, the collapse of state farming, the closures of socialist branch plants, and the shortage of young and educated people lie at the root of the generally low standard of living, limited market and poor human capital. All this hinders the multi-functional endogenous development of rural regions (Turnock 2003). A more favorable situation can be found in some border regions which may now profit from local transborder trade and service activity. This is especially the case with areas adjacent to the old EU countries. Other more successful poor areas may include the main transportation corridors.

Spatial dynamics and disparities: continuity or change?

There is a fundamental question concerning continuity or change in patterns of local and regional development in post-socialist countries. In general, diversified metropolitan regions perform better than industrial towns and regions and non-metropolitan rural areas. This indicates the reproduction of some earlier spatial structures, but also newly emerging patterns in the form of the fast growth of suburban and outer metropolitan zones along with the crisis of some industrial areas.

Thus, both elements of continuity and change are evident, though some sort of continuity seems to prevail. This is evident in the strengthening of many developed regions and the formidable barriers to development faced by peripheral ones. The continued privileged position of the former can be interpreted as the result of self-reinforcing processes fostered by forces of agglomeration built upon earlier structures and their conformity with the new needs of market, accessibility and quality of labor. They also offer the best innovation and learning potential. A stable settlement hierarchy with a dominant position for major cities is vital here. A small market, low standard of living, and demographic distortions in peripheral rural areas cause limited local entrepreneurship and slow development. Eastern regions can be particularly disadvantaged from the foreign investment and export linkage point of view when compared to areas in geographical proximity to Western Europe. On the other hand, the structural legacies may put certain towns and regions at a disadvantage due to their dependence on shrinking industrial sectors and the vulnerability of single-factory towns.

The salient mechanisms underlying current local and regional development trends are of an economic nature, but demographic, social and cultural determinants have a profound effect. The impact of local and regional structures has been strengthened rather than superseded by new international relationships. The importance of local trajectories of development manifests itself in the fact that prosperous towns and pockets of unemployment or stagnation are often found next to each other in both growing and declining regions, reflecting successful or unsuccessful local restructuring processes and adjustment to the circumstances of the global economy.

All things considered, there seems to be a general increase in regional disparities encouraged by both endogenous and exogenous factors, which facilitate the development of more advanced regions, metropolitan areas in the main, and marginalize the weak regions. This results in the reproduction of the prosperity and backwardness from the pre-socialist era, which was – through different mechanisms – maintained under socialism. Thus, the contemporary spatial patterns of local and regional development appear as a structure of long duration.

There are obviously differences in spatial disparities and processes between post-socialist countries depending on the size of countries, their historical divisions, and the dominant position of the capital in the urban hierarchy, e.g., Budapest in Hungary *vis-à-vis* Warsaw in Poland.

Global forces, local agency and public policies: key players in the relational perspective

Finally, we may take into consideration the changing role of various agents of local and regional development and relationships among them. The obvious effect of the opening of former socialist economies and societies was greater dependence of towns and regions on processes and phenomena in faraway places. The earlier dependence on Soviet decision-makers and central decision-making bodies, mainly industrial ministries, has been replaced by the influence of transnational corporations and international organizations. TNCs' investment is an evolutionary process involving learning and bargaining with various local stakeholders. The scope of their embeddedness in networks of local relationships is vital from the point of view of the multiplier effects they generate in the regional economy and the endurance of their activity in particular places. The role assigned to particular places by TNCs affects their upgrading or downgrading in global value chains and affects their development prospects. Foreign investors are responsible for strengthening more developed regions at the expense of weak ones since they are orientated to nationwide or international markets and search for a quality workforce.

The impact of the World Bank and the European Bank for Reconstruction and Development is often underscored as providers of blueprints for market reforms and the source of funds supporting macro-economic stability of post-socialist states. The aspirations to join the EU, and accordingly West European influence, became important to the new Member States. It is too early to judge the effects of EU funds on the development of problem regions.

The nation state has been instrumental in the transformation process due to its central role in the overhauling of the institutional system regulating various spheres of social and economic activity. This gave room for formal or informal bargaining between domestic and foreign firms and governmental bodies for favorable solutions concerning public support, domestic market protection, etc. Despite common external influences, the regulations and policies adopted in particular post-socialist states differ significantly, e.g., labor-market regulations and the division of competences between central, regional and local levels of public administration (e.g., Swain 2007). The lack of coherence and stability of national policies along with the low effectiveness of many government institutions undermines their strategies. Long-range innovation policy is especially missing.

There has been no consistent and comprehensive regional policy. There are public incentives offered to large investors in the form of tax exemptions or public subsidies. Despite some efforts to use them as instruments for attracting investors to problem areas (e.g., in the Polish Special Economic Zone program), they are usually standard forms of public support – the preference is for attracting foreign investors to the country rather than directing them to selected regions.

Government support for peripheral areas is mostly through infrastructure, especially road, investment. Several post-socialist countries have redrawn their regional administrative boundaries, e.g., preparing for EU accession. Older ethnic and religious divisions re-emerged as the basis for regionalist and some-times separatist tendencies. Political breakup and military conflicts hindered the economic development of some areas.

The salient change has been a revival of elected local government which may repre-sent the community, provide public services and have its own revenues. It has a significant impact as the activity of local leaders may mobilize the community, breaking out from dependency culture and creating the atmos-phere of local success. The role of regional authorities is usually less prominent, though they can be involved in the allocation of the EU structural funds now.

NGOs and trade unions are part of a broad institutional setting missing under state socialism. Trade unions lobby for govern-mental support for certain places, whereas NGOs may both strengthen local social and economic activity and oppose certain invest-ments, e.g., on environmental grounds.

All these main groups of actors are linked by a multitude of relationships of competition, conflict, cooperation, and control. Crucial relationships forged anew under post-socialism include those between foreign and domestic enterprises, between firms and public author-ities, and between state institutions and local government. In comparison with state social-ism, post-socialist regions are characterized by an increased role of both global actors and local agents.

The local and the regional should not be seen just as an arena, an obstacle or receiver responding to changes prescribed at the national or global scale. There is copious evi-dence that local and regional actors, the role of which was denied under state socialism, are vital. The activities of local governments and other institutions, together with the quality of human capital and public attitudes, constitute the basis for citizen mobilization and enterprise strategies. Local agency mat-ters a great deal, hence endogenous capacities for development are crucial. The enhancing of these capacities should be the main task of public policies at all levels, which cannot only be preoccupied with the improvement of technical infrastructure (Gorzelak et al. 2001). The strengthening of linkages between peripheral regions and fast-growing metro-politan areas is also important so that the former could benefit from the multiplier effects of the latter.

Conclusion: transition as modernization or a unique process?

The validity of the notion of transition is questioned as implying a short-term, teleolog-ical change from socialism to capitalism treated as a single ideal type. Critics point out that the idea of transition ignores the evolutionary nature of post-socialist changes and suggests that they end with the achievement of a cer-tain predefined state (Grabher and Stark 1997; Pickles and Smith 1998). In fact, transition constitutes a specific form of the concept of modernization. Thus we may ask about the nature of post-socialist transformation from the point of view of local and regional devel-opment processes. How far can it be concep-tualized as transition or modernization?

"Modernization" views development as progress. It appears as a teleological (aiming at a certain known end), uniform, linear, and normalizing process. The "underdeveloped" countries and regions have to follow the path of the "developed" ones, moving to higher stages of development, epitomized by the latter. This rests on the geographical dicho-tomy of core and periphery; the process of development means that peripheral regions become similar to the areas regarded as "advanced" (core). In the context of post-socialist Europe, this means adoption of the West European economic and political models.

"Europeanization" is another concept belonging to the modernization perspective. It substitutes for the socialist model of modernization, which formerly dominated Central and Eastern Europe.

The problem with the interpretations conveyed by the notions of transition, modernization and Europeanization is that they offer a partial, one-sided understanding of post-socialist transformation. There is undoubtedly an element of modernization and there is a process of becoming more similar to West European countries, but they cannot be treated as general models explaining post-socialist changes. The post-socialist transformation comprises multiple processes of change, including the (re)introduction of liberal democracy, marketization, technological modernization, globalization and, in some cases, European integration. Many processes are rooted in structures, social cognition, practices and sequences of events from the pre-socialist and socialist eras; hence they are in a broad sense path-dependent. This means that current patterns and changes cannot be understood without a broader historical perspective. There is no single pre-determined final stage and/or model to be achieved, the transformation is not a process of normalization which would simply lead to copying the attributes of advanced West European regions (Bradshaw and Stenning 2004; Domański 2005). Any deterministic interpretation can be challenged on the grounds that the processes of post-1989 development could have taken a different form in many post-socialist regions.

The belief in a single "jump" from socialism to capitalism presumes the ability to totally revamp social systems in a brief period of time, thus showing some resemblance to the faith of the socialist leaders from the past. Post-socialism constitutes a structural shift including elements of modernization mediated by the reproduction of former socialist and pre-socialist mechanisms and spatial patterns together with the creation of new ones. There were piecemeal changes and

meandering policies. It has been a unique process in some respects; certain factors and mechanisms may remain specific to post-socialist regions like to post-colonial ones.

The experience of local and regional development under socialism and post-socialism confirms that national, regional and local structures, mechanisms, and culture make a difference even at a time of major economic and political shocks. This also shows that many social, economic and spatial structures are structures of long duration. This is visible in economic structures, settlement and infrastructural networks as well as in human minds and behavior. Culture appears no less important than institutional structures in the path-dependent processes. In the evolutionary and relational perspective, post-socialist transformation can be seen as a critical juncture in which the development paths of regions and localities are molded by the interaction of older structures and the agency of various local, regional, national and global players.

References

Bradshaw, M. (2006) "Observations on the Geographical Dimensions of Russia's Resource Abundance", *Eurasian Geography and Economics* 47, 724–746.

Bradshaw, M. and Stenning, A. (eds) (2004) *East Central Europe and the Former Soviet Union: The Post-socialist States*, Harlow: Pearson.

Domański, B. (1997) *Industrial Control over the Socialist Town: Benevolence or Exploitation?*, Westport: Praeger.

Domański, B. (2005) "The Economic Performance and Standard of Living of Post-communist European Countries since 1989: Factors and Processes Behind", *Geographia Polonica* 78, 107–126.

Gorzelak, G., Ehrlich, E., Faltan, L. and Illner, M. (eds) (2001) *Central Europe in Transition: Towards EU Membership*, Warsaw: RSA Polish Section.

Grabher, G. and Stark, D. (eds) (1997) *Restructuring Networks in Post-socialism: Legacies, Linkages and Localities*, Oxford: Oxford University Press.

Kornai, J. (1992) *The Socialist System: The Political Economy of Communism*, Oxford: Clarendon.

Nove, A. (1986) *Socialism. Economics and Development*, London: Allen & Unwin.

Pickles J. and Smith, A. (eds) (1998) *Theorising Transition: The Political Economy of Post-communist Transformations*, London: Routledge.

Rainnie, A., Smith, A. and Swain, A. (2002) *Work, Employment and Transition: Restructuring Livelihoods in Post-communism*, London: Routledge.

Smith, D. (1989) *Urban Inequality under Socialism*, Cambridge: Cambridge University Press.

Swain, A. (ed.) (2007) *Re-constructing the Post-Soviet Industrial Region: The Donbas in Transition*, London: Routledge.

Turnock, D. (2003) *The Human Geography of East Central Europe*, London: Routledge.

Van Zon, H. (2008) *Russia's Development Problem: The Cult of Power*, Basingstoke: Palgrave Macmillan.

Further reading

Bradshaw, M. and Stenning, A. (eds) (2004) *East Central Europe and the Former Soviet Union: The Post-socialist States*, Harlow: Pearson. (Broad treatment of various post-socialist states.)

Domański, B. (1997) *Industrial Control over the Socialist Town: Benevolence or Exploitation?*, Westport: Praeger. (Industrial paternalism in socialist towns.)

Kornai, J. (1992) *The Socialist System: The Political Economy of Communism*, Oxford: Clarendon. (Economic mechanisms of socialism.)

Pavlínek, P. and Smith A. (2000) *Environmental Transitions: Transformation and Ecological Defence in Central and Eastern Europe*, London: Routledge. (Environmental issues.)

Pickles J. and Smith, A. (eds) (1998) *Theorising Transition: The Political Economy of Post-communist Transformations*, London: Routledge. (Transition debate and various aspects of trans-formation.)

Rainnie, A., Smith, A. and Swain, A. (2002) *Work, Employment and Transition: Restructuring Livelihoods in Post-communism*, London: Routledge. (Labour market issues.)

Turnock, D. (2003) *The Human Geography of East Central Europe*, London: Routledge. (Broad treatment of various post-socialist states.)

Van Zon, H. (2008) *Russia's Development Problem: The Cult of Power*, Basingstoke: Palgrave Macmillan. (Economy and power relations in Russia.)

16

Migration and commuting

Local and regional development links

Mike Coombes and Tony Champion

Introduction

At the outset it is not unreasonable to ask the rationale for exploring links between migration and commuting in the context of local and regional development. A simple answer is that they are both ways in which people are spatially mobile, with both these forms of mobility having potentially important implications for the places that act as origins and destinations and also – especially in the case of commuting – impacts on the places in between and on the environment more generally. Moreover the salience of this answer has grown steadily as mobility has become an ever more important feature of modern societies. In more recent years this growing mobility has attracted increasing academic interest, to a degree which has even led to some talk of a "mobility turn" across a range of the social sciences (Urry 2008). There is also a less obvious reason for examining links between commuting and migration, and this is that these links are far more complex and multi-faceted than they may seem at first sight. It is this reason which motivates much of the discussion here.

Although it is an oversimplification, it can be argued that in earlier work migration and commuting were often posed as corollaries.

In daily life, people were seen to decide their home location by choosing between migrating to be nearer their workplace or commuting from where they currently live. At the broader scale of cities and labour markets, much regional science and associated policy debates distinguished sharply between a labour supply available within daily commuting distance – which might adjust rapidly to changing labour demand – and that which might be gained or lost through the slower adjustment of migration. Commuting analyses have accordingly been largely restricted to a subregional scale, whereas migration research extends from the global to the very local. In keeping with the view of commuting as displacing migration – in fact commuting has been referred to as "daily migration" – a frequent distinction is made between local and non-local migration, with this spatial distinction depending on whether the move was further than most people are likely to be prepared to commute. In fact this same separation of local from non-local migration also appears in studies of migration by the many population groups outside the labour force, despite commuting patterns being irrelevant to them, as reflected in the demographer's distinction between "residential mobility" (address changing within a place that does not alter its overall population) and "migration" (between places).

A few stylized facts serve to illustrate ways in which diverse recent trends have eroded this apparently straightforward distinction between migration and commuting:

i) More households have more than one earner, and in many multi-earner households more than one member has a job whose location and pay supports longer distance commuting, so household migration decisions involve difficult trade-offs that may lead to one or more persons still commuting a long distance.

ii) More people have complex working patterns like "weekly commuting" which may be associated with temporary contract positions or with lifestyle and life-chance decisions which might involve preference for family upbringing in a more rural location or in a place with better access to high-ranking schools.

iii) More work is IT-enabled and this can foster "teleworking" which may appear to negate commuting but there is often still repeated travel, in some cases to the previous workplace: thus the stereotyped migration from metropolis to countryside enabled by teleworking with the same employer is linked to longer distance but more occasional journeys to the same workplace.

At the same time, migration patterns include the moves of distinct groups such as people who are approaching retirement and who may accept long commuting flows for a relatively short period between the place they are retiring to and the work they will retire from. This longitudinal perspective can find other possible links through time, such as people who initially accept long-distance commuting as part of a move to a more remote location they aspire to live in, but then weary of the commuting and change

their job – perhaps "downshifting" – so as to remain in the area they have chosen as home.

At this point it is necessary to acknowledge that the above examples of links between migration and commuting had to be presented as stylized facts, or anecdotal life histories, because the hard empirical evidence on these links between aspects of mobility is very patchy. The reasons are not hard to find as far as the more longitudinal links are concerned: longitudinal datasets are scarce and few cover both migration and commuting behavior. To make matters worse, in any one year relatively few people migrate, so migrants are a small minority of most survey samples, and in fact in some surveys any migrants disappear due to the survey method being based on repeat contact at the same address. Without going too far into the data minutiae – especially as the detail varies between datasets and indeed countries – both migration and commuting measures are strongly affected by the rising problems for surveys in representing modern life styles and behavior. In particular, measures of migration and commuting depend on identifying the "home" location for each person. That concept is based on traditional norms of a single settled address in a defined household, norms which cannot cope with the more transitory behavior of growing numbers of people especially young adults and international labour migrants.

The discussion so far has centered on individuals and households, but the decisions made at this micro scale have significant ramifications at neighbourhood and wider scales. This means there are key local, regional and even national policies that could benefit from a better understanding of the ways in which migration and commuting patterns are linked (Rees et al. 2004). The final part of this introductory section outlines the way in which commuting and migration are linked in different ways at different scales, and it then uses these differences to break down the remainder of this chapter into two broad sections.

Given the emphasis here on local and regional development policy issues, it is important to stress the need for clarity on the limits of – and the distinction between – the local and regional categories. The local category is clearly a scale above that of the individuals and households who make the migration and commuting decisions, and here it is distinguished from wider scales such as the labour market area. As such there is a substantial focus on the neighbourhood level of policy, but similar issues arise for whole small settlements such as the towns and villages that form part of the labour market areas of larger cities. The ways that migration behavior links with commuting to pose policy issues at this neighbourhood scale are dealt with in the last section of this chapter. In the current British policy lexicon, the issues at this scale mostly fall into the "places" agenda centered on areas' relative attractiveness to potential residents, and their appeal to employers too where relevant. More specifically, both commuting and migration patterns are influenced by the extent of locally available jobs appropriate to the types of residents attracted by the distinctive mix of housing and other conditions in that area. One example of the policy questions at this scale is the challenge of creating new residential areas that can help toward a lower carbon future by fostering local working and hence in-migration by people who will then not commute very far.

The regional scale is probably best termed the city region nowadays, for reasons that we set out below. Policy issues at this scale tend to privilege economic concerns and migration is increasingly central to such debates, particularly in seeking to attract and retain the people who will be most valuable to the city region economy. In fact, very similar issues are increasingly part of national policy debates, so that legislation over international immigration is often designed to maximize national economic gain. One way by which the national and city regional scales differ is, of course, that at this sub-national scale policy options are strictly limited. In most countries the city region scale is the focus of only limited policy leverage in general, with no leverage whatsoever over migration and commuting flows. Despite this, many city regions responsible for economic development have identified changing the balance of inflows and outflows across their boundaries as critical in growing their city region's economic strength. We look first at these city region issues before going on to examine the more local scale.

The city region scale

It is only recently that the city region has emerged internationally as a dominant spatial framework for sub-national economic analysis and development planning. Earlier policies used macro-economic regions distinguished by their industrial structure, such as the USA's agricultural "corn and hog belt" or the Ruhr coal-and-steel region. Policy to address industrial decline and restructuring initially took the form of special arrangements by central government, such as the 1930s examples of the Tennessee Valley Authority in the USA and the Special Areas in the UK. Later there was a widespread development of "regional planning" to combat widening core–periphery disparities – such as the polarization between the Paris region and the rest of France (le désert français), or between north and south Italy – but this was delivered through agencies for broad administrative regions or the provinces of federal countries. With the recent acceleration of globalization, rather smaller scale functionally defined entities have come to the fore. In the words of Scott (2001: 1–4):

> The new regionalism [is] rooted in a series of dense nodes of human labour and community life…. Such entities are becoming the focal points of … a new global-city capitalism…. City regions are coming to function as the basic motors of the global economy.

This worldwide development has major implications for regional economic development policy (see, for example, Neuman and Hull 2009).

The sustained growth of international migration flows is one aspect of the globalization that has led to this shift of spatial focus in development planning. Once again there are data limitations here related to the "loss" of migrants who leave, but the broad picture is one of increasing movement affecting most areas. The point made above about city regions having little or no leverage to influence arrivals or departures was starkly illustrated by the consequences for English sub-regions of the European Union (EU) decision to incorporate eight Central and Eastern Europe countries as member states ("the A8 countries") in 2004. Stenning *et al.* (2006) showed inflows across England which were unprecedented in their volume and

geographical spread and for which no policy response had been prepared. As shown in Figure 16.1, whereas immigration from traditional non-A8 sources was still heavily concentrated on the global city region of London, migration from the A8 countries was much less focused on this international "gateway city" and more strongly represented in smaller – and even rural – labour markets that had little experience of accommodating immigrants (see also Coombes *et al.* 2007). The subsequent global "credit crunch" economic downturn may have shrunk these inflows so much that the balance may have turned to net outflow (datasets on out-migration are too weak for this hypothesis to be tested). The link with commuting arises here too because these international labour migrants may use one area to live in even though their work (largely gained via agencies) is in a rather distant part of the country. In short, a

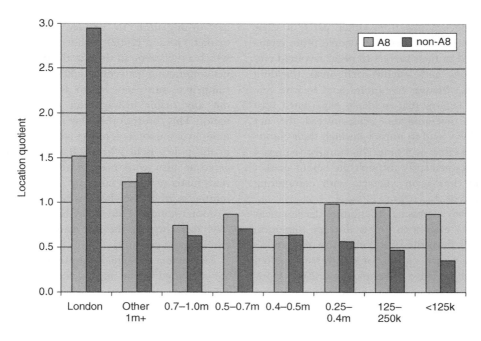

Figure 16.1 Distribution of England's immigration from A8 and non-A8 countries, 2005–2006, by travel to work area population size groups. Location quotient denotes the relationship to the share expected from the distribution of total population, e.g., a quotient of 3 means.

Source: Calculated from National Insurance Number data provided by the Department for Work and Pensions

city region policy-maker may aspire to alter the balance of the labour force through the cumulative effect of net international migration flows, but few city regions have the powers to influence either the number or the composition of these inflows and outflows.

For most city regions in most times, its migration exchanges with other parts of its own country are likely to be larger than its international migration flows. In fact most city regions have little more control over these intra-national flows, just as there are few countries that have policy leverage over the commuting flows across their city region borders. Even in the case of China where policy regimes exist to control intra-national migration and limit where people can work, people move but remain unrecorded. While these flows are largely beyond city region policy influence, they are by no means random in their patterns. In particular, across the world there is a well-established tendency for the key/capital city regions to gain younger adults from other parts of their countries but then lose people more established in their careers to other favoured city regions and amenity-rich areas (Fielding 2007). Mature economies tend to have few city regions that suddenly experience very large net migrant gains; instead the net inflows tend to impact through their cumulative effect over time. This cumulative impact works primarily through the labour market and thus again interacts with commuting patterns.

The increasing economic development policy interest in longer distance migration stems from the observation that migration's impact on a city region's skills base is often highly selective (Champion et al. 2007). Continuing loss of highly skilled and better paid people can progressively reduce the regeneration potential of a city region economy through its negative impacts on entrepreneurship and the availability of the skills mobile employers seek, as well as having indirect effects on the municipal tax base and private sector confidence. While the "knowledge economy" idea may have been overplayed recently, knowledge-rich sectors have tended to accelerate urban and regional growth (Pike et al. 2006), prompting city region policies to attract talented/skilled/creative migrants who are relatively scarce, as recommended by Richard Florida (2008) in his work on the rise of the creative class in the USA and in his advice to people choosing where to live (Florida 2008). Thus many policies centered on migration focus on those people in the labour force whose scarcity makes them among the best paid, a fact which makes them more likely to commute longer distances. In fact, even if the appropriate jobs are attracted to the city region, the people whose rare skills make them the most sought-after sometimes use their labour market power to avoid moving to the area, instead becoming "occasional commuters" (Green et al. 1999). At a more mundane level, commuting can act to more locally diffuse growth which otherwise might have required net in-migration to balance the labour market. Gordon (2002) outlined the way in which a succession of shifts in the balance of net commuting between neighbouring areas can help to satisfy new labour demand without any major in-migration to the city region. This absorption of new job opportunities by commuters is in fact all too familiar in the policy field where job creation targeted at areas with many workless people finds many new jobs taken by people commuting in from elsewhere, as recognized by Gordon's notion of the "leaky bucket" in his 1999 paper arguing the case against localized employment creation.

The extent to which commuting flows are contained within an area is measured by calculating the area's self-containment (Goodman 1970). Returning to the issue mentioned above of providing workers for local jobs, the key measure is demand-side self-containment, defined as the share of work trips ending in the area which start within the area and so do not cross its boundary. The other measure is the supply-side equivalent, which is the proportion of local working residents whose workplaces are within the boundary of the area. Coombes (forthcoming) details the ways in which these measures can be used when analyzing commuting data to identify labour market areas. This focus on commuting patterns as identifying the regions around cities which are closely tied to them dates back to at least the 1940s when the United States first defined its Standard Metropolitan Areas – a practice that is now widespread across countries with modern economies (Cattan 2001). One consequence is that updated commuting data prompts the updating of labour market area definitions: the pervasive trend across modern economies for more long-distance commuting means that more people will cross a previously defined labour market area boundary, so to meet a given level of self-containment the boundary will need to be drawn more widely. Despite the pervasiveness of the growth in longer distance commuting resulting in declining self-containment, there are relatively few direct empirical demonstrations of the trend. One exception is Pike et al. (2006) where 25 of Britain's medium-sized labour market areas (defined on the basis of fixed boundaries) were analyzed over two intercensal decades. Looking at both the demand- and supply-side containment levels, average values fell from around 80 per cent in the commuting data from the 1981 Census to under 75 per cent in 1991 and by 2001 they stood at 70 per cent (demand-side) and just over 65 per cent (supply-side). Put another way, the average area was able to provide local work for around four out of five of its working residents in 1981, but 20 years later over a third of local working residents were commuting to work outside that area boundary.

The trend toward more dispersed labour market areas is being exacerbated by commuting patterns becoming less heavily centralized on large city centers. Diverse commuting patterns are enabled by growing car use, while also being prompted by declining employment in traditional sectors where local working was common and by job decentralization to city edges. More people working further from their homes also means that – with the distance between settlements remaining constant of course – adjacent towns and cities which previously had been the foci of discrete labour market areas can become parts of the same polycentric labour market area. This process has been illustrated in detail within Denmark by Nielsen and Hovgesen (2005) and by Lambregts et al. (2006) for the Randstad area in the Netherlands.

One way that polycentric labour market areas have been conceptualized is that they encompass several sizable settlements between which at least some people can commute and so do not need to migrate. Yet this is to think of migration only as labour migration (i.e., residential moves which by definition are prompted by a change of workplace). In fact, far more people change where they live for other reasons, so most migration flows are dominated by people moving for these other reasons. Most of these non-labour migrants do not move far. It is worth recalling here the traditional contrast between commuting flows, which are not expected to cross city region boundaries, and the moves of labour migrants whose crossing of those boundaries is expected, precisely because the new workplace is too far away for commuting to be practicable. In the same way, non-labour migrants are mostly expected to stay within city region boundaries, so that their unchanged workplace can still be accessed (although non-work migrants who have retired can be among longer distance movers).

Indeed the coupling of housing and labour markets, along with other sub-regional geographies, features increasingly prominently in the contemporary economic development policy discourse on city regions (e.g., OECD 2007). Here defining functional economic areas is a necessary preliminary to avoid policy-related analyses misreading the geography over which the relevant market processes operate (e.g., Coombes 2009).

The local scale

The evolving polycentric areas mentioned above represent a situation where a blurring is occurring in the traditional distinction between the regional and the local. Turning now to the scale of the settlements and neighbourhoods found within city regions, the links between migration and commuting are more complex and so it should not be expected that areas which are relatively self-contained in terms of one of these types of mobility are also likely to be have few cross-boundary flows of the other type. For example, more deprived areas tend to have few local jobs so that those residents who are in work probably have to commute out, meaning the area has low self-containment of its commuting flows, but the fact that the area will not be very attractive to many residents of other areas is likely to mean that it has few migration connections with other parts of the city region and so is highly self-contained in migration terms.

At this scale, residential preference is a key driver of different areas' prospects, and this has a feedback through the characteristics of neighbourhoods. In particular, migration patterns can be highly selective so that, even if an area is close to balance between its overall inflows and outflows, this may disguise major net shifts in different groups' movements (e.g., the affluent moving out while poorer people move in). Whether the better-off are tending to move in or out will relate to local characteristics such as:

i) housing types and condition
ii) reputation of schools, secondary-level ones in particular
iii) levels of crime or antisocial behavior
iv) retail and leisure facilities
v) access to open space and the quality of the local environment including the public realm.

Unfortunately for less favoured areas, there tends to be a cumulative process in which the localities shunned by people with the economic power to choose from a wide set of options can see many of these characteristics get worse as the better-off leave. In the policy field this leaves a harsh dilemma: whether to accept that some areas must be the least favoured – the spatial equivalent of "the poor are always with us" – or to spend most regeneration funding on the areas least likely to become favoured places to live. The commuting aspect comes into play here through a key area characteristic not mentioned in the list above, job accessibility. Less favoured areas include old inner-city neighbourhoods, outlying public sector housing developments (like the outer metropolitan banlieues around Paris) and earlier settlements created to serve now-ceased single industries (as in former coalfield areas like the Ruhr). The basic urban economics of rent gradients focused on key employment nodes ensure that the likelihood of new investment is greater in those areas with easier opportunities for commuting. This can involve the gentrification of previously unfavoured areas and the transformation of CBD fringes with "loft living" as the iconic form of a completely new population migrating into a job-rich part of the city, as originally demonstrated by Zukin (1988) for New York and more recently by Nathan and Urwin (2005) for London and other UK cities.

Whereas a specific migration stream can rapidly change an area's character, as with gentrification, by contrast the major change in commuting patterns – the trend toward the greater spatial separation of home and workplace – tends to be gradual but also very generalized. Over a long time span, however, this too can have profound impacts on communities. For example, areas within a city region with middle-income residents will usually be located where there is good access to jobs but, as people become able and willing to commute longer distances, the competition for those jobs will grow because they can be reached by people living further away. If the city region has a lack of employment generally, then the residents of the middle-income areas gain little from the new option of commuting further, while losing some of their "local" jobs to commuters from further away (cf. Coombes and Raybould 2004). This process has been overshadowed by the more acute policy problems caused by major losses of particular types of jobs in distinct parts of city regions, especially due to decentralization from inner urban areas (Renkow and Hoover 2000). Here the link with migration and commuting has prompted debates about "spatial mismatch" (Preston and McLafferty 1999) because the remaining industrial jobs are in peripheral areas and pay wage rates which make it an economic impossibility for inner-city residents to either commute the longer distance to those areas or to migrate to the more expensive housing there.

The challenges of making appropriate job opportunities accessible to each area's residents are part of a broader policy remit, as in England's Sustainable Communities Plan (ODPM 2003). This framework includes a growing recognition of environmental aspects to sustainability. A key concern is that the growing mobility of people (Echenique 2007) – as highlighted by, but far from limited to, commuting patterns – directly links to growing carbon emissions, with the transport sector a key driver of this growth. The link to migration is less obvious and yet deeply pervasive: the drift of people is away from larger settlements to less densely populated areas where car use is most intense. Analysing UK National Travel Survey data, Banister (1997) shows a clear correlation between increasing settlement size and decreasing commuting distance. Even after allowing for personal characteristics and various aspects of geographical context, Coombes and Raybould (2001) confirm that short-distance commuting is most likely in larger settlements. Champion (2009) found that, even after allowing for the greater propensity for longer distance commuting among recent in-migrants, car owners and

certain other groups, people in more rural areas are still more likely to commute longer distances than urban residents.

These patterns reveal two limitations to policy advocating "smart growth" or more compact cities to reduce people's daily travel. Simply restricting the land available for development on the urban fringe may just lead to "leap-frogging" with migrants choosing more distant settlements from which they can still commute back. Equally those planning policies aiming for a closer spatial matching of housing and employment bring no guarantee that workers will take the jobs made available close to their homes. People make their decisions based on many other factors, such as rising fuel costs or road-use taxes (see Champion (2001) and Downs (2005) for further discussion of this conundrum in relation to the UK and USA respectively).

There are also social aspects of sustainability which may be undermined in communities where long-distance commuting is widespread. For example, do long-distance commuters actually gain the well-being they expected from a rural lifestyle if much of their time is in, or traveling to, a city? English city dwellers continue to state a strong preference for living in a more rural area (Champion and Fisher 2004), but not all who move to areas stereotyped as rural are counterurban migrants and people's moves may not match with their motivations (Halliday and Coombes 1995).

A concluding word on policy

Returning finally to local and regional policy considerations, a recurring feature of the preceding discussion has been an echo of Cheshire and Magrini (2009) in that key drivers of the trends which are creating uneven outcomes in modern economies are very largely beyond the remit or influence of sub-national governance structures. International-scale mega trends like oil prices affect the likelihood of continuing growth in personal mobility, while economic globalization helps to drive international migration. Then there are national (or EU) policies seeking to regulate cross-border migration, and the new recognition of the need for environmental sustainability (although the latter can seem like lip service when the primary political concern is sustained economic growth, without a "green new deal" to achieve both objectives). Whatever the policy outcomes are at these (supra-)national scales, local and regional policy may have the objective of creating sustainable communities but they have few policy levers that can bear down strongly on the decisions people make about their commuting and migration behavior. It should also be admitted that research has yet to provide very clear evidence on some key issues. For example, there is much European policy interest in a polycentric pattern of regional development with greater connectivity between places, aided by more investment in public transport infrastructure. Yet it is unknown whether this would really be a more sustainable scenario, rather than simply abetting the growth in personal mobility which may be inherently unsustainable. The best that local and regional policymakers and planners can do in these circumstances is to work toward an environment that maximizes the potential for people to reduce their mobility, such as mixing together jobs and housing within city regions and aiming for a better balance between city regions in both the quantity and the quality of employment and other life-chance opportunities.

References

Banister, D. (1997) "Reducing the need to travel", *Environment and Planning B* 24, 437–449.

Cattan, N. (2001) *Functional Regions: A Summary of Definitions and Usage in OECD Countries*, Paris: OECD (DT/TDPC/TI(2001)6).

Champion, T. (2001) *The Containment of Urban Britain: Retrospect and Prospect*, Milan: FrancoAngeli.

Champion, T. (2009) "Urban–rural differences in commuting in England: a challenge to the rural sustainability agenda?", *Planning Practice and Research* 24, 161–183.

Champion, T. and Fisher, T. (2004) "Migration, residential preferences and the changing environment of cities", in M. Boddy and M. Parkinson (eds) *City Matters*, Bristol: Policy Press, 111–128.

Champion, T., Coombes, M., Raybould, S. and Wymer, C. (2007) *Migration and Socio-economic Change: A 2001 Census Analysis of Britain's Larger Cities*, Bristol: Policy Press.

Cheshire, P. and Magrini, S. (2009) "Urban growth drivers in a Europe of sticky people and implicit boundaries", *Journal of Economic Geography* 9, 85–115.

Coombes, M. (2009) "English rural housing market policy: some inconvenient truths?", *Planning Practice and Research* 24, 211–231.

Coombes, M. (2010) "Defining labor market areas by analyzing commuting data: innovations in the 2007 review of Travel-to-Work Areas", in J. Stillwell, O. Duke-Williams and A. Dennett (eds) *Technologies for Migration and Population Analysis: Spatial Interaction Data Applications*, Hershey, PA: IGI Global.

Coombes, M. and Raybould, S. (2001) "Commuting in England and Wales: 'people' and 'place' factors", *European Research in Regional Science* 11, 111–133.

Coombes, M. and Raybould, S. (2004) "Finding work in 2001: urban-rural contrasts across England and Wales in employment rates and local job accessibility", *Area* 36, 202–232.

Coombes, M., Champion, T. and Raybould, S. (2007) "Did the early A8 in-migrants to England go to areas of labor shortage?", *Local Economy* 22, 335–348.

Downs, A. (2005) "Smart growth: why we discuss it more than we do it", *Journal of the American Planning Association* 71, 367–378.

Echenique, M. (2007) "Commentary: mobility and income", *Environment & Planning A* 39, 1783–1789.

Fielding, A.J. (2007) "Migration and social mobility in urban systems: national and international trends", in H.S. Geyer (ed.) *International Handbook of Urban Policy*, Volume 1, Cheltenham, UK: Edward Elgar, 107–137.

Florida, R. (2008) *Who's Your City?*, New York: Basic Books.

Goodman, J. (1970) "The definition and analysis of local labor markets: some empirical problems", *British Journal of Industrial Relations* 8, 179–196.

Gordon, I. (1999) "Targeting a leaky bucket: the case against localized employment creation", *New Economy* 6, 199–201.

Gordon, I. (2002) "Unemployment and spatial labor markets: strong adjustment and persistent concentrations", in R. Martin and P. Morrison (eds) *Geographies of Labor Market Inequality*, London: Routledge, 55–82.

Green, A., Hogarth, T. and Shackleton, R. (1999) "Long-distance commuting as a substitute for migration: a review of trends", *International Journal of Population Geography* 5, 49–67.

Halliday, J. and Coombes, M. (1995) "In search of counterurbanization: some evidence from Devon on the relationship between patterns of migration and motivation", *Journal of Rural Studies* 11, 433–446.

Lambregts, B., Kloosterman, R., Van Der Werff, M., Roling, R. and Kapeon, L. (2006) "Randstad Holland: multiple faces of a polycentric role model", in P. Hall and K. Pain (eds) *The Polycentric Metropolis: Learning from Mega-city Regions in Europe*, London: Earthscan, 137–145.

Nathan, M. and Urwin, C. (2005) *City People: City Centre Living in the UK*, London: Centre for Cities.

Neuman, M. and Hull, A. (2009) "The future of the city region", *Regional Studies* 43, 777–787.

Nielsen, T. and Hovgesen, H. (2005) "Urban fields in the making: new evidence from a Danish context", *Tijdschrift voor Economische en Sociale Geografie* 96, 515–528.

ODPM (2003) *Sustainable Communities Plan*, London: Office of the Deputy Prime Minister.

OECD (2007) *OECD Territorial Reviews: Madrid, Spain*, Paris: OECD.

Pike, A., Champion, T., Coombes, M., Humphrey, L. and Tomaney, J. (2006) *The Economic Viability and Self-containment of Geographical Economies*, London: Office of the Deputy Prime Minister.

Preston, V. and McLafferty, S. (1999) "Spatial mismatch research in the 1990s: progress and potential", *Papers in Regional Science* 78, 387–402.

Rees, P., Fotheringham, A. and Champion, T. (2004) "Modeling migration for policy analysis", in J. Stillwell and M. Clarke (eds) *Applied GIS and Spatial Analysis*, Chichester: Wiley, 259–296.

Renkow, M. and Hoover, D.M. (2000) "Commuting, migration and rural–urban population dynamics", *Journal of Regional Science* 40, 261–287.

Scott, A.J. (2001) *Global City-regions: Trends, Theory, Policy*, Oxford: Oxford University Press.

Stenning, A., Champion, T., Conway, C., Coombes, M., Dawley, S., Dixon, L., Raybould, S. and Richardson, R. (2006) *Assessing the Local and Regional Impacts of International Migration*, London: Communities and Local Government.

Urry, J. (2008) "Moving on the mobility turn", in W. Canzler, V. Kaufmann and S. Kesselring (eds) *Tracing Mobilities: Towards a Cosmopolitan Perspective*, Aldershot: Ashgate, 13–24.

Zukin, S. (1988) *Loft Living*, London: Radius.

Further reading

Champion, T., Coombes, M. and Brown, D. (2009) "Migration and longer distance commuting in Rural England", *Regional Studies* 43, forthcoming. (A direct analysis of the link between recent migration and current longer distance commuting in English rural areas.)

Champion, T., Coombes, M., Raybould, S. and Wymer, C. (2007) *Migration and Socio-economic Change: A 2001 Census Analysis of Britain's Larger Cities*, Bristol: Policy Press. (An analysis of whether Britain's largest cities attract the talented people that they need for securing their future prosperity.)

Coombes, M. (2010) "Defining labor market areas by analyzing commuting data: innovations in the 2007 review of Travel-to-Work Areas", in J. Stillwell, O. Duke-Williams and A. Dennett (eds) *Technologies for Migration and Population Analysis: Spatial Interaction Data Applications*, Hershey, PA: IGI Global. (A demonstration of innovative methods for the analysis of interaction data which shows variation in levels of commuting self-containment at different spatial scales.)

Coombes, M. and Raybould, S. (2001) "Commuting in England and Wales: 'people' and 'place' factors", *European Research in Regional Science* 11, 111–133. (A regression analysis identifying human or environmental factors associated with shorter distance commuting, which is environmentally preferable.)

Hall, P. and Pain, K. (eds) (2006) *The Polycentric Metropolis: Learning from Mega-city Regions in Europe*, London: Earthscan. (A detailed study of evolving urban forms in Europe from one particular viewpoint.)

Renkow, M. and Hoover, D.M. (2000) "Commuting, migration and rural–urban population dynamics", *Journal of Regional Science* 40, 261–287. (Econometric modeling suggests that in the US more of the trend to longer distance commuting is due to the preferences of people than to industrial restructuring.)

Stenning, A., Champion, T., Conway, C., Coombes, M., Dawley, S., Dixon, L., Raybould, S. and

Richardson, R. (2006) *Assessing the Local and Regional Impacts of International Migration*, London: Communities and Local Government. (A quantitative analysis of the large sudden inflow of East European migrants to England in 2004 to 2005 with short case studies of city regions.)

Urry, J. (2008) "Moving on the mobility turn", in W. Canzler, V. Kaufmann and S. Kesselring (eds) *Tracing Mobilities: Towards a Cosmopolitan Perspective*, Aldershot: Ashgate, 13–24. (Revised version of a key review of the new social science interest in mobility.)

17

Within and outwith/material and political? Local economic development and the spatialities of economic geographies

Roger Lee

Introduction

All development is local. It must necessarily take place. In this sense the notion of local development is tautologous. But local development is rarely, if ever, completely bounded by place. And this is not just a question of how 'local' or 'development' may be defined. Local development intrinsically involves mutually formative and politically significant intersections of territorial and relational spatialities – themselves inseparable and constituted together – across a multitude of organisational and geographical sites. Another way of putting this is that the 'local' shapes 'development' at the same time as 'development' shapes the 'local'. The one is always insinuated in, and formative of, the other. For example, the diversity of class, gender or ethnic divisions of labour within cities or regions reflects the day-to-day spatialities and social relations of the particular forms of economic activity and the environmental and social topographies through which they take place in those cities and regions. But they also reflect wider economic geographies and the place of particular cities or regions within them as well as the class/gender/ethnic relations associated with these wider geographies. It is the diverse nature of these

multiple geographies as much as the engagement or lack of engagement of cities and regions in them that shape and are shaped by the trajectories of urban and regional development or underdevelopment.

These complex geographies raise difficult issues – intensely political as well as material – in conceptualising, theorising and practising local development. Neither the material or the political nor the within and the outwith can be understood in isolation. Following Don Mitchell (2003), David Harvey (2006: 239) highlights the politics arising out of the intersection of territorial and relational geographies (see also Cumbers *et al.* 2008):

> It is only when relationality connects to the absolute spaces and times of social and material life that politics comes alive.

However, the use of the word 'only' here is problematic. It was used in an essay discussing different notions of space and does not mean, I think, that politics can arise in no way other than in the connection of absolute and relational spaces. Like economy, politics cannot but take place. Thus a very much alive politics is associated within both territorial and relational spaces. Both the politics of different territorial spaces (e.g. the differential access of particular groups to those spaces, or the priority given to, and achieved by, such spaces in the pursuance of polices to promote the provision for and sustenance of local development) and of different relational spaces (e.g. power relations along global commodity chains (Gereffi 2005), networks of value (Smith *et al*. 2002) or production (Dicken *et al*. 2001; Coe *et al*. 2008) generate significant political struggles.

Nevertheless, as the global spread and retreat of financially driven circuits of value reveal, it is doubtless the case that the intersection of relational and territorial spatialities clearly does raise profound geo-political questions including those associated with local and regional development. And to repeat, these intersections are mutually formative. Changes in one generate changes in the other. This is a continuous dynamic that must, somehow, be resolved to enable economies to function. Where resolution is impossible or inadequate (for example, in resolving the need for territorially based financial regulation with the hyper-spatial flexibility of flows of finance, or in coping with the territorial consequences for employment and local economic activity or the spatial restructuring of multi-site corporate organisations) uneven development is likely to result. In other words, the resolution of the differential dynamics of territorial and relational spatialities is a major driver of the politics and policies of local development.

These are the themes addressed by this chapter. Its focus is on thinking local and regional development from the standpoint of economy/economic geography. By this I mean not merely that the economic aspects of development are its focus but, rather, that the inherent socio-spatialities of economy/economic geography frame the concerns of the chapter. It attempts to think local development less from the perspective of the locality (however defined) than from the equally complex frame of the formative socio-spatialities of economy/economic geography (see the

consistent application of such ideas by Ray Hudson, e.g. 1989, 2001). The chapter begins by considering the material spatialities of economy (what I call circuits of value) before moving on to consider the political significance of the social relations that direct them. It then explores the significance of these spatialities and the questions that they raise for local political transformations and local development including the (im)possibilities of endogenous development. I then move on to examine the potentially transformed conditions for local economic development towards the end of the 2000s in the face of the financially induced fracturing of circuits of capital – not least financial circuits (Plender 2009). The concluding comments return to reflect on the insights on the possibilities of local economic development that may be offered by considerations of the ordinary economy. It thereby considers the paradox that, in "a period of inconclusive struggles between a weakened capitalism and dispersed agencies of opposition, within delegitimated and insolvent political orders" (Balakrishnan 2009: 26), radically new geographies of local development become imperative. While local economic development may be impossible, it may be the only possibility to be pursued.

Spatialities of circuits of value and local economic development

There is something irreducibly material and irreducibly geographical about economies/economic geographies. Economic geographies are constituted of circuits of value which necessarily involve the incessant movement and transformation of value – from consumption via exchange to production via exchange to consumption – for which territorial and relational geographies are not only the essential conditions of existence but also the objectives (the expansion, extraction and recirculation of value) of this movement and transformation. Upon the possibilities of such spatial and temporal repetition is all social life materially predicated.

Circuits of value are simultaneously both social and material. Figure 17.1 is, therefore (and notwithstanding the continued use of such a model of economy used, largely uncritically, by mainstream economics), a practical impossibility as it abstracts from the social relations which drive such circuits. It shows the flows of value which must take place across space and through time if the economic geographies constituted of such circuits are to be sustained and, schematically, identifies the elements and processes of reflexive evaluation and regulation to which such circuits are necessarily subject. Figure 17.2 represents a capitalist circuit of value in which the social relations of capital (labour:capital relations) and the imperative of the production of surplus value and its accumulation shape its trajectory. It points, again schematically, to

a range of possible social evaluations to which such circuits are necessarily subject and the regulatory relations and technologies involved.

Figures 17.1 and 17.2 emphasise the movement and transformation of value across space and through time inherent to circuits of value and their economic geographies. But circuits also require at least temporary spatial fixity to enable the consumption, exchange and production of value to take place. It is this complex of relationships between movement/relationality and fixity/territoriality circuits of value that lies at the problematic heart of 'local' economic development. And it is these inherently complex spatialities rather than any apparent failings in the field of local economic development which explains its lack of "a coherent theoretical framework" (Rowe 2009: xvi). It follows that, unless the developmental effects of these spatialities are fully

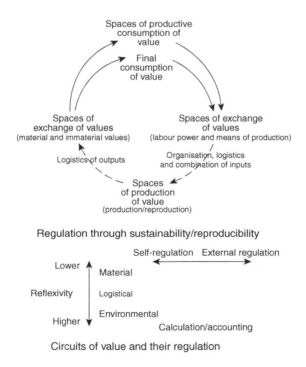

Figure 17.1 Circuit of value.
Source: Author's research

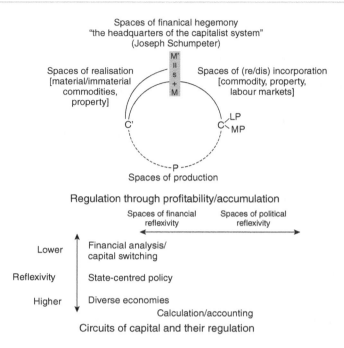

Figure 17.2 Circuit of capital.
Source: Author's research

incorporated, efforts to deal with this lacuna from within the field are doomed to failure.

Local development as problematic

Local development is problematic because – even leaving aside the question of what may be meant by the 'local' – there is a contradiction between territories of development and the relationalities of circuits of value. The geographies of circuits of value are constituted of the relational networks and circuits of the production exchange and consumption of value. These circuits cross, and locate – in whole or in part – within territories. Further, they are heavily dependent upon territories for their conditions of existence with respect, for example, to legal relations, economic policies and regulation, to say nothing of the built environment and the economic significance of social institutions,

civil society and locally embedded socio-political relations. Such necessary territorial conditions of existence of circuits of value point to the place-based nature of circuits of value. But they do not involve the place boundedness of circuits of value. Furthermore, just as places are, to an extent, substitutable in the dynamic geographies of circuits of value, so too can they be used to structure the geographies of the circuits. Particular parts of circuits may be placed in those locations that offer the greatest benefits to powerful participants in the circuit regardless of local developmental consequences.

Can economic development be local?

Given the necessary but fluid relationships between movement and stasis in circuits of value and the geographically substitutable relationships between places which are, nevertheless, necessary conditions of exist-ence of circuits of value, to what extent can economic development become, or remain local? It is possible to envisage at least five possible answers to this question:

i) Localisation of circuits of value. But then how much of a circuit of value within a locality would constitute local economic development: above or below 50 per cent? 75 per cent? 100 per cent?

ii) Localisation of any surplus created within circuits of value in a locality. The same questions of how much would constitute local economic development applies here too. Reten-tion of the surplus without local con-trol over it may constitute only a highly partial form of local economic development. But this raises further questions around the locus of control of this surplus – the spaces of hegem-ony in Figure 17.2. All economic geographies – even Robinson Crusoe single-person economic geographies – must have loci of control over their developmental trajectories. In capitalist economies these are the places of con-trol over capital including, for example, corporate headquarters. But, in recent years these loci of control have taken place and been created and practised in a hierarchy of financial centres which control the switching of finance capi-tal into and out of places and activities around circuits of value. Although they are, of course hegemonic only in certain spaces and times and are con-stantly vulnerable, they can and do exert hegemonic control thereby rais-ing profound questions about the nature of their regulation by appropri-ate authorities (see Lee 2011).

iii) Localisation of the spaces of hegem-ony. Depending on the extent of the localisation this would imply a form of local economic autarky in terms of

decisions governing the spatial and temporal switching of flows of value.

iv) Localisation of parts (as a whole or merely fragments) of circuits of value – production, exchange, consumption. Here the degree and form of local economic development would be shaped by which parts of circuits of value are present within a locality and how fragmentary their localisation may be.

v) Localisation of spaces of incorporation (e.g. labour markets, property markets) and/or of logistical relations (e.g. the movement of commodities). Local control over the relations of exchange does not, of course, imply any control over production or consumption.

Shaped and driven from both within and without, local economic development can be only partially local. 'Development' it may (or may not) be but 'local' it isn't in anything other than a partial sense. This is a central problem for local development policy and practice. It is perfectly possible to think of locally autarkic circuits of value, for example, but almost impossible to envisage that these could make anything more than a marginal contribution to local economic development (see, for example, Lee *et al.* 2004). From this perspective, then, 'local economic develop-ment' means little more than the grounding of bits of circuits of value in ways that might be considered to enhance local economic activity.

Social relations and the spatialities and politics of circuits of value

But this is not all. What has been discussed thus far has focused primarily on a concep-tion of economic activity considered in purely material terms – as circuits of value. This is an inadequate formulation.

Social relations and circuits of value

While circuits of value may have the superficial appearance of material flows of value through consumption, exchange and production, the nature, trajectory and purpose of these flows are shaped by social relations of value (compare Figures 17.1 and 17.2). Social relations of value are the shared, contested, or imposed understandings about the nature, norms and purposes of circuits of value. They make sense of, give direction to and, above all, define the parameters and the criteria of evaluation of circuits of value. Within circuits of capital (circuits of value shaped and driven by capitalist social relations of value) such criteria are primarily financial and concerned with accumulation and profitability. Any consideration of circuits of value not founded in these social relations is wholly incomplete. And this inherently social nature of the economic is inescapably political. It brings a whole new set of political and power relations into play.

Social relations and the evaluation and coherence of economic geographies

Economic geographies are, then, constructed not only out of material circuits of value but out of evaluations of these circuits. Social relations of value provide the templates for valuing value. They are, therefore, integral to economic geographies. And this is significant. Different social relations of value shape the construction of different economic geographies. But such evaluations must be capable of taking into account what is materially, environmentally and technologically possible. Further, the existence of an accepted, acceptable or imposed set of social relations of value (no matter how socially marginal or politically vulnerable that acceptance, acceptability or imposition may be) is also a necessary feature of all economic geographies.

Unless effective mechanisms of regulation and evaluation are in place to maintain specific criteria by which value is assessed – and thereby to impose a particular trajectory upon economic practices and the spaces through which they take place – value may be ever changing, not only in form and specification, but also in the mode and criteria of its evaluation. Under such circumstances, the sustenance of the practical coherence of economy across space and time may be severely hampered.

(Lee 2006: 416)

But such coherence is not merely a question of economic logistics; it is a deeply political process. Different sets of social relations of value involve not only different bases of power and different relations of power but different spatialities – fragmented feudalism versus expansionary capitalism, for example (Poulantzas 1974). What is more, different sets of social relations also powerfully constrain the politics of choice. They define the limits of the possible in terms of the norms, standards and objectives of circuits of value. They identify what is good or bad; better or worse.

Politics and the spatialities of circuits of value

In such circumstances the politics arising from the conjunction of territorial and relational spatialities is all too apparent. The policy and practice of local economic development are those of relations of power played out between the drivers of the spatialities of territories and the drivers of the spatialities of relational circuits of value. And these relations of power are asymmetric in that the spatialities of circuits of capital are driven primarily by assessments of the financial consequences (which are far from necessarily congruent with any local developmental consequences) – assessments that are potentially global in extent. Furthermore – and as indicated above – such assessments are normally made outwith the locality with little, if any, concern for local developmental consequences beyond those that might affect the financial performance of the relevant circuits of value. However, one of the consequences of the global financial crisis which began in 2007 is that the global reach of these financial assessments is likely both to be curtailed and substantially nationalised (temporarily at least), if not further localised.

And this politics is central to the question of local development. As a result of the decentred nature of the capital:labour relation, the significance and geographical indifference of finance capital and the Brennerian (Brenner 1977) centrality of competition within capitalist circuits of value, capitalist spatialities are inherently expansionary. Thus, if local development is both territorial and relational – its characteristics shaped by interactions between relational and territorial spatialities – then a critically significant framing of this interaction and the politics that arises from it is that of the uneven geographical and temporal dynamics of circuits of capital (Fagan and Le Heron 1994) and other circuits of value and their diverse engagement in material configurations of economic activity.

Circuits of value and the making of the world economic geography

It is important to stress the complexity of the geographical and temporal dynamics of circuits of value that constitute what is so misleadingly referred to simply as 'globalisation'. As Peter Dicken points out (2007: 29), globalisation is far from an "all-embracing, inexorable, irreversible, homogenising force". Quite the reverse. Globalisation is a process not a condition. It involves the multiple interactions of more (or less) geographically expansive circuits of value, especially circuits of capital, diverse networks of influence,

social relations, metrologies and semiotics with local circumstances and the resultant social and material contradictions and contested transformations of the local and the global. Capitalism is, then, highly diverse (see e.g. Peck and Theodore 2007). It demands a geographical critique of what can easily become essentialist notions of state, capital, labour civil society brought to bear upon it in analyses lacking the geographical imagination vital to its comprehension (see, for example, Lee 2002).

In the contemporary world, this politically charged set of interactions takes place between the geography of an expansive capitalism and a world already full of history and geography. The power geometries and politics to which these intersections give rise are captured in Eric Hobsbawm's description (1979: 310) of the making of the capitalist world economy:

> The capitalist world economy has grown up as an international, and increasingly worldwide, system evolving largely as a function of the development of its 'advanced' sector, and in the first instance largely for the benefit of that sector. With certain exceptions, it therefore transformed the remainder of the world, insofar as this was not temporarily left to its own devices as lacking, for the time being, economic interest, into a set of subsidiary and thus dependent economies.

Hobsbawm here describes dynamic circuits of capital pushing out selectively into the domains – both already capitalist and (today increasingly rare) non-capitalist – which surround them (see Wallerstein (e.g. 1979) for a different take on the making of the world economy).

The relations and contradictions between the dynamics of capitalist circuits of capital and those of the circuits of value into which they seek to expand are captured by Ernest Mandel (1975) in his suggestion that the growth and spread of the world economic geography consists of three interrelated moments:

i) ongoing capitalist development in the domain(s) of established capitalist circuits of value
ii) pre-capitalist and partial capitalist development [and, it might be added, non-capitalist development] outside these domain(s)
iii) struggles between the expansion of i) and the resistance of ii).

The process of the formation and transformation of the world economic geography may, then, be understood in terms of a set of intersections of circuits of capital and circuits of value (see Figure 17.3). Expansionary circuits of capital (IV) push out from the major centres of capital accumulation and intersect with non-capitalist circuits of value (III) (Gibson-Graham (2006, 2008) offers many examples) and/or with local, partial or declining circuits of capital (V). Given the geographically expansionary and increasingly global nature of circuits of capital, it would be rare to discover autonomous circuits of value (I) and inconceivable to find isolated circuits of capital (II).

In Figure 17.3 struggles to establish or to resist capitalist social relations of production take place primarily at the intersections where labour power and the means of production or commodities are transferred between circuits of value to circuits of capital. As a result of such intersections, the material and social bases of local development may be undermined – in whole or in part – while the restructuring of capitalist and non-capitalist social relations occurs as local circuits are linked to wider bases of valuation. But Figure 17.3 underplays the extent and significance of financial relations in seeking out capitalist and non-capitalist circuits of value for integration into wider capitalist circuits. It also implies that capitalist social relations may spread mainly through the establishment of capitalist systems of production, whereas exposure not only to financial flows but also to the possibilities and imperatives of consumption opened up by capitalism is a major factor dissolving existing systems of production-consumption relations.

Furthermore, global circuits of capital now not only involve the circulation of commodity capital (international trade), production capital (see, for example, Palloix 1977) and production sites, but massive global flows of finance capital (banking capital as well as

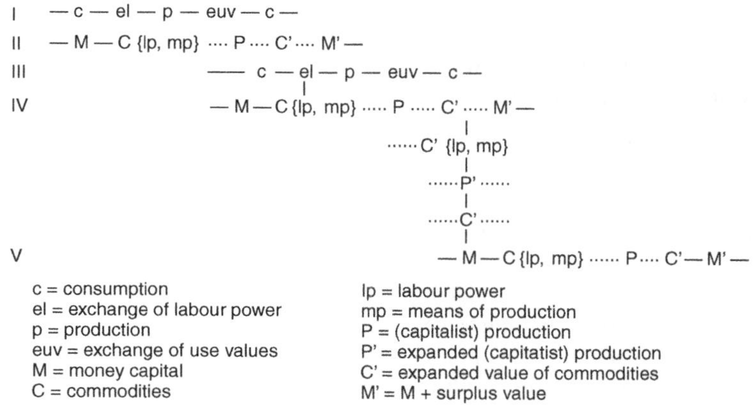

I	— c — el — p — euv — c —
II	— M — C {lp, mp} .... P .... C'.... M' —
III	—— c — el — p — euv — c —
IV	— M — C {lp, mp} ..... P ..... C' ..... M' —
	...... C' {lp, mp}
	...... P' ......
	...... C' ......
V	— M — C {lp, mp} ...... P.... C' — M' —

c = consumption
el = exchange of labour power
p = production
euv = exchange of use values
M = money capital
C = commodities

lp = labour power
mp = means of production
P = (capitalist) production
P' = expanded (capitalist) production
C' = expanded value of commodities
M' = M + surplus value

Figure 17.3 Intersecting and non-intersecting circuits of value.
Source Author's research

direct and portfolio investment). Flows of commodity capital subject the circuits of value with which they connect to potentially devastating forms of evaluation from outwith as a growing proportion (currently around 30 per cent) of global production enters into international trade. Prices of commodities are, thereby, brought ever more intensely into competitive relationships with each other and so become increasingly affected – and hence disciplined – not only by local production costs and patterns of consumption but by global evaluations shaped increasingly by financialisation (Lee *et al.* 2009), especially of commodities.

The often highly uneven – in both space and time – historical geography of financial capital flows reflects the hyper-mobility of many forms of such capital. They incorporate the economic geographies in which they are insinuated into wider circuits of capital. This not only increases the dependence of these geographies on the conditions of investment in the regions from which the flows of capital derive but imposes new forms of evaluation upon the recipient geographies. Even flows of directly invested productive capital engage in dizzying constructions and destructions of economic geographies – often under severe conditions of financial evaluation (see, for example, Lee 2003).

Orchestrating circuits in networks

What is more, these relations are orchestrated not merely through markets but, as indicated above, through global commodity chains, networks of value, or global production networks. Such networks are "extremely complex structures with intricate links – horizontal, vertical and diagonal – forming multidimensional, multilayered lattices of economic activity" (Dicken 2007: 15). It is through them that circuits of value (circuits of production, exchange and consumption extended across space and through time) are choreographed by networks of inter- and intra-firm relations.

But there is more to such networks than this. They are shaped by capitalist relations of value defined, implemented and enforced through calculations of value and profitability and the consequent switching of capital undertaken within spaces of hegemony. In the years leading up to the financial crisis of the late 2000s these spaces came to be dominated by financially shaped circuits of capital now shaped to an extent by state and near-state regulated finance. However, no matter how apparently 'free' markets may appear to be, production networks are always heavily embedded via relations of governance in the territories across which they create and perform their relational geographies.

The geographies of these networks thereby reflect, once again, intersections between territorial and relational geographies. But these geographies are also closely shaped by the power relations of participants – producers, consumers, market makers and suppliers of logistics – within the networks. Thus networks of production take place through distinctive spatialities which, until the late 2000s (at least and probably beyond) had become both more intensely interconnected and geographically extensive. The increasing spatial extent and growing interconnection within and between production networks or the fracturing of such links have clear implications for the possibilities of the capture of value through local development, notwithstanding the crucial significance of the embeddedness of the networks in the places within which many of their conditions of existence are to be found.

Spatialities of circuits of capital, local political transformations and the (im)possibility of endogenous development

However, the consequences of a geographically expansionary or a receding capitalism go well beyond those of disruptions to local circuits of value and the possibilities of the capture of value and local development. The creation of a capitalist world economic geography involves not only the expansion of a circuit of capital into, but the transformation of the social relations of production and consumption within, places. The geographical expansion of capital as a social relation necessitates the creation and/or transformation – ruthlessly if that is what it takes – of pre-existing social relations in places. Specifically, the reach of circuits of capital takes place through the:

i) purchase of labour power which presumes the existence of labour as a commodity (or the possibility of transforming labour into a commodity – labour power – capable of being bought and sold across a market), as well as of the means of production

ii) (geographical) restructuring of production

iii) sale both of means of production – which presumes the existence of a system of capitalist property relations – and of commodities which introduces capitalist forms of exchange

iv) subjection of local circuits of value to financial evaluation and financialisation from within the spaces of hegemony.

The struggles associated with the geographical expansion of capital identified by Mandel may have one of four possible outcomes:

i) transformation of non-capitalist social relations as a result of their replacement by capitalist social relations

ii) the mere interconnection of capitalist with the pre-capitalist social relations

iii) the partial adjustment of local social relations towards a capitalist form

iv) the rejection of and isolation from capitalist social relations and the development of alternative circuits of value.

These transformations demand, in turn, wider socio-political change. Within Europe, for example, labour came to be alienated from the ownership of the means of production more readily in the west than in the east. From the sixteenth century onwards, this pattern of uneven development gave rise to a momentous division (Okey 1982) with profound geo-economic and geo-political consequences which continue to reverberate well after the collapse of communism and the fall of the Berlin Wall in November 1989. And, with the geographically constrained adoption of capitalist social relations and criteria of evaluation of circuits of value in China (albeit within a communist/state socialist regulatory framework), capitalist economic geographies now dominate, even if they do not necessarily fully determine, the global economic geography.

Within Russia, the failure to recognise the significance of deep-seated pre-capitalist relations of circuits of value in Russia during the sudden attempt to introduce capitalism into the country during the 1990s contributed to the severe crisis of 1998. The liberalisation of trade, large-scale privatisations and macro-economic control – especially of inflation – were presumed to induce the spread and growth of capitalism. But, as John Thornhill (1998: 14) posing the revealing question 'Who lost Russia'? ('lost', that is, to capitalism), wrote at the time:

> while the reformers' model may have been valid for part of the economy, it did not capture the whole picture. The legacy of 74 years of Communist rule [and, it might be added, before that, the centralised feudality of the Czarist regimes] meant that large swathes of the economy were seemingly immune to market [i.e. capitalist] disciplines. 'Privatised' companies continued to be run like Soviet-era quasi ministries, subtracting rather than adding value to their inputs. They failed to pay either their taxes or their workers' wages.

Loss-making industries reverted to barter trade, plunging workers into a largely non-cash economy.

Unsurprisingly, the consequences of these kinds of disruption have not been confined to economic disruption. For example, the almost continuous decline of especially male life expectancy in the Soviet Union during the 1990s was one manifestation of the effects of the 'shock therapy' of mass privatisation administered to the post-socialist countries during the decade (Stuckler *et al.* 2009). Although countries with high levels of social capital suffered less, there could hardly be a clearer demonstration of the all too probable links between 'development' and social and environmental ill-being (e.g. Lee 2010a). The links between certain quantitative measures of 'development' and their manifestation as social and environmental underdevelopment are all too obvious (see Pike *et al.* 2007).

The case of Russia points once again to the limited and highly problematic possibilities of local development within spatially extensive and highly dynamic circuits of capital. The comforting but uncritical distinction between endogenous and exogenous development in accounts of local economic development (see, for example, Stimson and Stough 2009) is undermined not only by the mutually formative relations between territorial and relational spatialities but by the disruption of endogenous relations by external norms and metrics of value and by the perpetual geographical switching of circuits of capital in response to financial evaluations or state directives from the spaces of capitalist hegemony (Figure 17.1 and 17.2). Not only is this distinction unsupportable given the constant interactions between territorial and relational spatialities, it is politically naïve, reactionary or both.

Think, for example, of the widespread repetition of the then UK Chancellor of the Exchequer (later to be Prime Minister) Gordon Brown's careless remark "British jobs for ... British workers" made at a UK Labour Party conference in June 2007. Brown is an advocate of endogenous growth but misses the point that the endogenous notions of "British jobs" and "British workers" are meaningless in a globally connected economic geography. In such a context, there is a profound distinction to be made between the economic geography of Britain (or any other territory for that matter) and the British economic geography. The latter is, of course made up of circuits of value extending well beyond Britain and they in turn both shape, and are shaped by, the economic geographies taking place within the territory of Britain. Yet conventional economic notions of endogeneity refer not to the spatialities involved – these are ignored – but to the relative significance of supply- and demand-side influences on sustained changes in the so-called natural rate of growth (for a regional example, see Lanzafame 2009). This is a crucial issue for policy as it not only has the effect of extending and constricting what is economically possible but, as indicated above, has powerful reactionary political resonances too.

Fractured spatialities and transformed conditions of local economic development?

The economic and political uncertainties and vulnerabilities of globalisation have, perhaps, never been more apparent than they are at the end of the 2000s, and herein lies a set of possibilities for local development. In many ways – and notwithstanding the arguments pursued above on the constraints on local economic development in a spatially extensive world – there has rarely been a more pregnant time to consider these possibilities. Ways of doing things – of practising circuits of value, for example – need to change and this opens up spaces for the insertion of diverse economic practices less encumbered or constrained by circuits of capital into established and entrenched relations of power.

But there is a further and associated consideration highlighted by the financial turmoil of these years. The material spatialities of globalisation do not merely wax and wane but may be transformed along very different social relations of value and hence along very different political dimensions. Two examples of these qualitatively and politically different social relations of value shaping the vectors of globalisation would include global justice and responsibility (Massey 2004) not merely within but across territories and relational spaces. As J. K. Gibson-Graham (2008: 622), following Doreen Massey (2005, 2007; and see Cumbers *et al.* 2008) on the simultaneity and togetherness – conflict ridden or not – of social life puts it, this would involve a "move from a structural to an ethical vision of determination". In terms of local economic development it follows from this move that:

> [T]he academic task becomes not to *explain* why localities are incapable of looking beyond their boundaries but to *explore* how they might do so.
>
> (emphasis in original)

And what may bring such profound transformations to greater significance is the destabilisation, not merely of the spatialities of economic growth but of the social relations of value resulting from the profoundly geographical nature – in both cause and possible resolution – of the global financial crisis at the end of the first decade of the twenty-first century (McCarthy 2009). In the late 2000s, the further disturbance of hegemonic relations between global North and global South as a result of the financial crisis opens up the possibilities of new spatialities and, along with them, of new mutualities of development between South and South, as well as between North and South.

A central feature of the latter is the need to redress the massive global imbalances and levels of uneven development within and between North and South in terms of consumption in the former (to be reduced) and wage levels in the latter (to be increased) and, at the same time, to recognise the differentiated geographies and uneven development especially – but not only (see Cienski *et al.* 2009; Wagstyl 2009) – within the global South. This is not merely a question of market reform but of the restructuring of the provision of social security with particular attention being paid to the needs of the elderly and others marginal to circuits of value.

Further, the relations of development between North and South in the form, for example, of copyright, intellectual property, expertise (which, vitally, recognises the complex nature and developmental power of local expertise), infrastructure projects, aid and trade policy require fundamental reform. In terms of South–South relations, localities might be opened up to each other through supportive circuits of value and flows of policy and ideas shaped by social relations driven by collective and mutually supportive developmental agendas (see, for example, Manuel 2009). If able to recognise and to make such a critique, localities may look beyond their boundaries in sustaining a local economic development not based merely upon the local grounding of circuits of capital in locations deemed most effective by profit-driven criteria emanating from spaces of capitalist hegemony. Such transformations would enable the redrawing of power geometries and hence the source and nature of the evaluations which shape the spatialities of economic development.

So what might such transformed conditions of local economic development look like? Table 17.1 is little more than a list – merely indicative and illustrative and doubtless thoroughly incomplete – but, hopefully, it provides one way at least of framing some possibilities as a way of looking forward. The distinctions between the various conditions listed in Table 17.1 are not made merely on one dimension – for example, that of the quantitative and spatial extent of their effects. They also represent a range of different notions of what may be meant or imagined by 'local development'. And here the social relations of value and the politics associated with them are crucial. Table 17.1 is, therefore, arranged broadly in terms of the degree of fissure of the conditions of local economic development from the spatialities and social relations of capitalism. Thus as well as differentiating between different modes of local economic development, the table also provides a snapshot – however much out of focus – of the complex intersections between the spatialities of circuits of value and the politics deriving from them. However, the sections in the table should not be taken to imply that the distinctions highlighted by them are anything other than porous. The snapshot is both out of focus and in soft focus. The conditions of local economic development are more accurately envisaged as being arranged along a continuum. Certainly many could and should well appear in more than one row of the table.

A critical feature of such potential transformations in local economic development

Table 17.1 Conditions of and policies for local economic development

conditions of ...	*... and policies for ...*	*..... local economic development*
I capitalism **(regulated) financially** **driven circuits of capital**	market-based policies of spatial development	• driven by circuits of value emanating primarily from elsewhere • surplus appropriated largely by (financial) capital
locational development **and variegated localised** **economic geographies** • localising/clustering • internationalising • regionalising • globalising	policies of attraction and support for capital: e.g. • enhancing potential for localising processes – policy-driven clustering – institutionalised clustering – universities. etc. • recognising potential of regionalising processes (e.g. EU) for local development policy	• coping with internationalising and globalising processes • grounding and holding down high-speed fragments of circuits of value
locally regulated/reformist **capitalism**	• interventions to take '[C]apitalism beyond the crisis' (Sen 2009: 4) • regulatory and reformist policies to shape capitalism so generating 'variegated capitalism' (Peck and Theodore 2007) 'It is government's duty to promote growth while securing non-material values people hold dear' (Anon 2009) • 'The audacity of help' (Thornhill 2009: 17)	• local attempts to lock down capitalism (e.g. Coe *et al.* 2004; Yeung 2009) e.g. • Bologna and the 'third' Italy • China – localised capitalism; geographically graduated relations of value • credit unions (see, for example, Fuller and Jonas 2002; but also Pickard 2009) • green new deal 'designed to power a renewables revolution, create thousands of green-collar jobs and rein in the distorting power of the finance sector while making more low-cost capital available for pressing priorities' (New Economics Foundation n.d.) • Black 2009

(continued)

Table 17.1 *(Cont'd)*

II resistance to capitalism **militant particularism** (Harvey 2001) 'the place of socialist politics' (Harvey 1996: 32). A relational world necessitates 'the move from tangible solidarities … to a more abstract set of conceptions that would have universal purchase' but 'in that move, something [is] bound to be lost' (Harvey 1996: 33)	local (national state, city, region) interventions to displace capitalist social relations	radical social relations but constrained in terms of spatial extent and hence of transformation, e.g, Hayter and Harvey 1993 • living wage/housing, etc., i.e. distributional issues rather than economy-wide
the social economy 'non-profit activities designed to combat social exclusion through socially useful goods sold in the market and which are not provided by the state or the private sector. (Amin: *et al.* 2002: vii)	policies designed to enhance the 'meeting social needs and enhancing social citizenship (Amin *et al.* 2002: 125)	local initiatives operating in parallel with mainstream economic relations, e.g. • on-line person-to-person finance (e.g. Zopa.com) • a range of detailed examples illustrative of the inherent limitations of the social economy (but see Benjamin 2009; Clark 2009) is offered in Amin *et al.* (2002)
the ordinary economy (Lee 2006) 'Values matter and they are affected by our theories' (Layard 2009: 19)	policies to enhance the realisation of the multiple, simultaneously practised values in all circuits of value across multiple differentiated localities	widespread practice of often small-scale initiatives operating on the basis of alternative values, e.g. • gardens for food (RHS 2009; but see Pudup 2008) • community enterprises and companies (e.g. pubs, shops, post offices) (see, for example, Brignall 2009; Jenkins 2009)
III post-capitalism **diverse economies**	'performative practices for other worlds' (Gibson-Graham 2008) including designing and thinking policy otherwise	the practice of autonomous economic geographies with circuits of value driven by locally agreed and practised social relations, e,g. • LETS (see, for example, Lee *et al.* 2004; Leney 2009) • Fuller *et al.* (2010) offer a range of examples
democratised economic **geographies**	policies based on the democratic right to the economy (Gowan 2009) and city (Harvey 2009)	relations of economic engagement and practice driven by inclusive democratic relations

Source: Author's research

concerns the scale and institutional infrastructure involved. Micro-level initiatives may have great political and social significance – not least through the realisation of autonomy from the practices and relations of power within circuits of capital – but their material consequences are limited and localised. For Amin (2002: 125) the social economy, for example, "can never become a growth machine or an engine of job creation, or a substitute for the welfare state, but it can stand as a symbol of another kind of economy". By comparison the reform of banks through the credit union movement or the provision of retail banking through a (re-)nationalised post office, for example, or the financing of local authorities via National Savings, pension funds and other institutional investors to enable green infrastructural investment and schemes such as gardens for food, to take just two examples, are institutionally well-founded measures which address wider questions of carbon emissions as well as enhancing skills and local employment and so increasing the possibilities of the local capture of value.

Such initiatives involve political compromise in using existing mainstream institutions. Further, while such institutions have national, and even international, coverage and reach, they require reform and reorientation more fully to sustain the possibilities of local economic development offered by initiatives beyond capitalist circuits of value. A good example would be the reform of social security rules and the bases of personal taxation to encourage diverse economies. Similarly, the spatial constraints of many such initiatives require institutions which enable extra-local linkages to enable mutual support involving, for example, flows of resources such as knowledge to sustain innovation, and access to extra-local markets to sustain demand. In essence what is necessary here is the involvement of institutions capable of recognising and working with the relationality of circuits of value, so linking the extra-local with the local while, at the same time, the social relations of the territorial institutions from which local economic development derive many of its conditions of existence are reformed to enable local economic development.

Concluding comments

This chapter has argued that a recognition of the formative relations between territorial and relational spatialities is vital for any effective form of local development and, at the same time, that these intersections pose critical difficulties for any form of local development founded on localities. But this does not mean that localities are somehow powerless. A recognition of the possibilities for local development arising from the intersections of relational and territorial space, and for thinking local development otherwise than from the evaluative constraints and norms of the social relations of value of the mainstream economy presents a range of policy options.

Of course, these are neither easy to implement nor to sustain in any materially effective fashion. However, the notion of the ordinary economy accepts the material singularity of circuits of value as irreducible but also argues that:

> the economy is an integral part of everyday life, full of the contradictions, ethical dilemmas and multiple values that inform the quotidian business of making a living.
>
> (Lee 2006: 414)

Here, perhaps, within this multiplicity of values lie the possibilities of democratic geographies of economic development reaching well beyond the prevailing norms and values of the geographies of capitalism. But, like all economic geographies, such have to be constructed. The possibilities are great but not infinite. And they are not infinite not least – but not only – because of the inherent materialites of economic geographies (see Lee 2010a). To be capable of effective social sustenance, all economic geographies have to be capable not only of producing at least as much value as is needed merely to maintain a population, a city or a region at a minimally acceptable level of living but they must also be capable of being continuously reproduced across space and through time. So policy-making must be hard-headed. One round of a circuit of value – alternative or otherwise – is a waste of effort and a material contradiction in terms, notwithstanding the politically liberating effects that even such a limited alternative might engender.

However, the significance of such political liberation is not to be gainsaid. A critical imagination is also vital for effective policy-making (see Lee 2010b). There are only limited options facing policy-makers in trying to make the 'local' fit for prevailing mainstream norms of economic 'development'. What must also be designed into policy is the pursuance of alternatives. These must be materially and environmentally effective but will likely be driven by quite different social relations of value and, thereby, environmental norms. Whether policy-making within the state – at whatever level – is capable of thinking like this and so going beyond its role as "a committee for managing the common affairs of the whole bourgeoisie" (Marx and Engels 1968: 37) is, of course, a moot point.

Certainly, given prevailing social relations of value, conventional institutions of policy-making and implementation within the state are probably not only incapable of the imagination necessary to design and implement the kinds of policies necessary to breathe sustainable economic life back into localities abandoned by mainstream circuits of value, they also lack the political and institutional legitimacy to do so. And yet:

> [E]conomic geographies cannot … be reduced to a consideration of one static set of dominant social relations of value as such would be an impossibility. Rather they are constituted geographically, socially and politically – and hence practised – as co-present and dynamic hybridizations of alternative, complementary or competing social relations which may vary over the shortest stretches of time and space.
>
> (Lee 2006: 421)

The political problem of policy lies, first, in the recognition of the diverse developmental possibilities presented by this impossibility, second, in the critique of mainstream options required to create a real democracy of choice based on the realisation of the futility, constraints and limitations of mainstream options and, third, in the political mobilisation necessary to sustain the kind of profound economic, social and environmental change capable of offering some kind of hope for dealing with the current conjuncture (Gowan 2009; Lee 2010b). However the dynamics of territorial and relational spatialities imply that economic practice and policy must also be dynamic; solutions are inevitably temporary.

But these are issues not merely for policy-makers. Quite the contrary. The point of a democratic form of economic development is that it should be informed by social relations of value which reflect democratically agreed preferences. But first there has to be a meaningful democracy of choice. As Rajaram and Soguk (2006: 367) argue, "'[T]he political' begins with the imposition of permanence onto an unhinged and fluid spatiality". The point is to rupture and fragment such permanence. As Balakrishnan (2009: 26) has concluded, "[I]n the absence of organized political projects to build new forms of autonomous life, the ongoing crisis will be stalked by ecological fatalities that will not be evaded by autonomous growth."

Herein lies the real – i.e. ecological and political – significance of alternative forms of development and the alternative geographies through which they may take place. Such development does not represent only imaginative material responses to thinking development otherwise. The practice of such responses is able to release the imagination to design and implement ecologically sound alternatives around which policy choices might be freely and effectively made. But, of course, such policies are dependent upon the adoption set of social relations of value capable of sustaining them. Thus the problem of policy is less that of logistics than of politics. The politics remains central.

Acknowledgements

As ever, colleagues and friends have been immensely generous in offering guidance and advice. Particular thanks to Peter Dicken, Ray Hudson and to the editors of this book for offering such generous and incisive insights. Despite their generosity, I doubt that I am able to come anywhere near their degree of insight. Thank you once again to Ed Oliver, cartographer and web manager in the Department of Geography at QMUL, who drew the diagrams with his all too easily taken-for-granted elegance and patience.

References

Amin, A., Cameron, A. and Hudson, R. (2002) *Placing the social economy*, London: Routledge.

Anon (2009) 'Editorial: De-fetishising GDP', *Financial Times*, 30 January, p. 9.

Balakrishnan, G. (2009) 'On the stationary state', *New Left Review*, 59: 5–26.

Benjamin, A. (2009) 'Give the third sector a fighting chance', *Guardian* (Society), 13 May, p. 4.

Black, L. (2009) 'Posts of gold', *Guardian* (Society), 18 February, p. 1.

Brenner, R. (1977) 'The origins of capitalist development: a critique of neo-Smithian Marxism', *New Left Review*, 104: 25–92.

Brignall, M. (2009) 'Last orders? Locals fight back', *Guardian* (Money) 21 March, pp. 6–7.

Cienski, T., Escritt, T. and Wagstyl, S. (2009) 'Regulators warn against single view of east Europe', *Financial Times*, 5 March, p. 8.

Clark, M. (2009) 'How to build a better future', *Guardian* (Society – Social Business supplement), 18 February, p. 1.

Coe, N. M., Dicken, P. and Hess, M. (2008) 'Global production networks: realizing the potential', *Journal of Economic Geography*, 8: 271–295.

Coe, N. M., Hess, M., Wai-chung Yeung, H., Dicken, P. and Henderson, J. (2004) '"Globalizing" regional development: a global production networks perspective', *Transactions of the Institute of British Geographers*, 29: 468–484.

Cumbers, A., Routledge, P. and Nativel, C. (2008) 'The entangled geographies of global justice networks', *Progress in Human Geography*, 32: 183–201.

Dicken, P. (2007) *Global shift: Mapping the changing contours of the world economy*, London: Sage Publications, Thousand Oaks, 5th edition.

Dicken, P., Kelly, P., Olds, K. and Wai-chung Yeung, H. (2001) 'Chains and networks, territories and scales: towards a relational framework for analysing the global economy', *Global Networks*, 1: 89–112.

Fagan, R. and Le Heron, R. (1994) 'Reinterpreting the geography of accumulation: the global shift and local restructuring', *Environment and Planning D – Society and Space*, 12: 265–285.

Fuller, D. and Jonas, A. E. G. (2002) 'Institutionalising future geographies of financial inclusion: national legitimacy versus local autonomy in the British credit union movement', *Antipode*, 34: 85–110.

Fuller, D., Jonas, A. and Lee, R. (eds) (2010) *Interrogating alterity: Alternative economic and political spaces*, Farnbrough: Ashgate.

Gereffi, G. (2005) 'The global economy: organisation, governance and development', in Smelser, N. and Swedberg, R. (eds) *The handbook of economic sociology*, Princeton: University Press Princeton.

Gibson-Graham, J. K. (2006) *A postcapitalist politics*, Minnesota: Minnesota University Press.

Gibson-Graham, J. K. (2008) 'Diverse economies: performative practices for "other worlds"', *Progress in Human Geography*, 32: 613–632.

Gowan, P. (2009) 'Crisis in the heartland', *New Left Review*, 55: 5–29.

Harvey, D. (1996) *Justice, nature and the geography of difference*, Oxford: Blackwell.

Harvey, D. (2001) 'Militant particularism and global ambition: the conceptual politics of place, space, and environment in the work of Raymond Williams', in Harvey, D. (ed.) *Spaces of capital: Towards a critical geography*, Edinburgh: Edinburgh University Press.

Harvey, D. (2006) 'Space as a keyword', in Castree, N. and Gregory, D. (eds) *David Harvey: A critical reader*, Oxford: Blackwell.

Harvey, D. (2009) Opening speech at the Urban Reform Tent, 29 January, World Social Forum: Belem.

Hayter, T. and Harvey, D. (1993) *The factory and the city: The story of the Cowley automobile workers in Oxford*, London: Mansell.

Hobsbawm, E. J. (1979) 'The development of the world economy', *Cambridge Journal of Economics*, 3: 305–318.

Hudson, R. (1989) *Wrecking a region: State politics, party politics and regional change in north east England*, London: Pion.

Hudson, R. (2001) *Producing places*, London: The Guilford Press.

Jenkins, S. (2009) 'Postman Pat makes a better banker than Fred the Shred', *Guardian*, 18 March, p. 31.

Lanzafame, M. (2009) 'Is regional growth in Italy endogenous?', *Regional Studies*, 43: 1001–1013.

Layard, R. (2009) 'Now is the time for a less selfish capitalism', *Financial Times*, 12 March, p. 19.

Lee, R. (2002) 'The economic importance of geography', *Financial Times*, 30 October, p. 20.

Lee, R. (2003) 'The marginalisation of everywhere? Emerging geographies of emerging markets', in Peck, J. and Wai-chung Yeung, H. (eds) *Remaking the global economy: Economic-geographical perspectives*, London: Sage Publications.

Lee, R. (2006) The ordinary economy, *Transactions of the Institute of British Geographers*. 31: 313–432.

Lee, R. (2010a) 'Economic society/Social geography', in Smith, S. J., Pain, R., Marston, S. A. and Jones III (eds) *The Sage Handbook of Social Geographies*, London: Sage Publications.

Lee, R. (2010b) 'Spiders, bees or architects? Imagination and the radical immanence of alternatives/diversity for political-economic geographies', in Fuller, D., Jonas, A. and Lee, R. (eds) *Interrogating alterity*, Farnham: Ashgate.

Lee, R., (2011) 'Spaces of hegemony? Circuits of value, finance capital and places of financial knowledge', in Agnew, J. and Livingstone, D. (eds) *Handbook of geographical knowledge*, London: Sage.

Lee, R., Clark, G., Pollard, J. and Leyshon, A. (2009) 'The remit of financial geography – before and after the crisis', *Journal of Economic Geography*, 9 (5): 723–747.

Lee, R., Leyshon, A., Aldridge, T., Tooke, J., Williams, C. and Thrift, N. (2004) 'Making geographies and histories? Constructing local circuits of value'. *Environment and Planning D: Society and Space*, 22: 595–617.

Leney, F. (2009) 'Noted for trust'. *Financial Times* (Weekend), 28 February 2009: p. 1.

Mandel, E. (1975) *Late capitalism*, London: New Left Books.

Manuel, T. (2009) 'Let fairness triumph over corporate profit', *Financial Times*, 17 March, p. 13.

Marx, K. and Engels. F. (1968) *Manifesto of the Communist Party, 'Marx and Engels Selected Works'*, London: Lawrence and Wishart.

Massey, D. (2004) 'Geographies of responsibility.' *Geografiska Annaler*, 86 (B): 5–18.

Massey, D. (2005) *For space,* London: Sage Publications.

Massey, D. (2007) *World city*, Oxford: Polity Press.

McCarthy, C. (2009) 'Britain is not a regulatory island', *Financial Times*, 1 April, p. 13.

Mitchell, D. (2003) *The right to the city: Social justice and the fight for public space*, New York: Guilford.

New Economics Foundation http://www.new-economics.org/gen/z_sys_publicationdetail.aspx?pid=258 accessed 13 April 2009.

Okey, R. (1982) *Eastern Europe 1740–1980: Feudalism to communism*, London: Hutchinson.

Palloix, C. (1977) 'The self-expansion of capital on a world scale', *Review of Radical Political Economics*, 9: 1–28.

Peck, J. and Theodore, N. (2007) 'Variegated capitalism', *Progress in Human Geography*, 31: 731–772.

Pickard, J. (2009) 'Low-income borrowers pay high rates', *Financial Times*, 4 April, p. 4.

Pike, A., Rodriguez-Pose, A. and Tomaney, J. (2007) 'What kind of local and regional development and for whom?' *Regional Studies*, 41 (9): 1253–1269.

Plender, J. (2009) 'Homeward bound', *Financial Times*, 30 April, p. 9.

Poulantzas, N. (1974) 'Internationalisation of capitalist relations and the Nation-State', *Economy and Society*, 3 (2): 145–179.

Pudup, M. B. (2008) 'It takes a garden: cultivating citizen-subjects in organized garden projects', *Geoforum*, 39: 1228–1240.

Rajaram, K. and Soguk, N. (2006) 'Introduction: Geography and the reconceptualization of politics', *Alternatives: Global, Local, Political*, 31 (4): 367–376.

Rowe, J. E. (ed.) (2009) *Theories of local economic development: Linking theory to practice*, Farnham and Burlington: Ashgate.

RHS (2009) 'RHS members to help nation grow', *The Garden*, May, p. 297.

Sen, A. (2009) 'Capitalism beyond the crisis', *The New York Review of Books*, 14 March, p. 4.

Smith, A., Rainnie, A., Dunford, M., Hardy, J., Hudson, R. and Sadler, D. (2002) 'Networks of value, commodities and regions: re-working divisions of labour in macro-regional economies', *Progress in Human Geography*, 26: 41–64.

Stimson, R. and Stough, R. R. (2009) 'Regional economic development methods and analysis: linking theory to practice', in Rowe, J. E. (ed.) *Theories of local economic development*, Farnham and Burlington: Ashgate Publishing.

Stuckler, D., King, L. and McKee, M. (2009) 'Mass privatisation and the post-communist mortality crisis: a cross-national analysis', *The Lancet*, 373 (9661): 399–407.

Thornhill, J. (1998) 'Who lost Russia?', *Financial Times*, 28 August, p.14.

Thornill, J. (2009) 'The audacity of help', *Financial Times*, 12 March, 17.

Wagstyl, S. (2009) 'How to annoy someone from central or eastern Europe', *Financial Times*, 28 March, 11.

Wallerstein, I. (1979) *The capitalist world economy*. Cambridge: Cambridge University Press.

Yeung, H. W-c. (ed.) (2009) 'Special issue: Local and regional development in Asia', *Regional Studies*, 43 (3).

Zopa.com http://uk.zopa.com/ZopaWeb/ accessed 13 April 2009.

Further reading

Dicken, P. (2007) *Global shift: Mapping the changing contours of the world economy*, London, Thousand Oaks: Sage Publications, 5th edition. (On the complex geographies of globalisation.)

Gibson-Graham, J. K. (2006) *A postcapitalist politics*, Minnesota: Minnesota University Press (On the developmental possibilities arising from decentring economic thought.)

Fuller, D., Jonas, A. and Lee, R. (eds) (2010) *Interrogating alterity: Alternative economic and political spaces*, Farnham: Ashgate.

Harvey, D. (2006) 'Space as a keyword', in Castree, N. and Gregory, D. (eds) *David Harvey: a critical reader*, Oxford: Blackwell, pp. 270–293. (On notions of space and spatialities.)

Lee, R. (2010a) 'Economic society/Social geography', in Smith, S. J., Pain, R., Marston, S. A. and Jones, III (eds) *The Sage Handbook of Social Geographies*, Thousand Oaks, New Dehli, Singapore: Sage Publications London, 205–221. (On notions of the inherent sociality of circuits of value.)

Leyson A, Lee, R. and Williams, C. (eds) (2003) *Alternative economic spaces*, London: Sage Publications. (On examples of alternative economic practices.)

18

Spaces of social innovation

Frank Moulaert and Abid Mehmood

Introduction

The concept of 'social innovation' has gained prominence in scientific research, public debate, collective action and public policy (Moulaert and Nussbaumer, 2007). In the scientific world, the concept has been used for a long time, but it regained momentum over the last twenty years. Its contemporary applications range from the nature and functions of social innovation in countering mainstream perceptions of technological and organizational innovation, to the innovative behaviour of social, economic and political agents in socially innovative initiatives (Klein and Harrisson, 2007). Thus, it broadens the explanations of human progress and development from economic and technological only to social and socio-cultural ones (Moulaert and Nussbaumer, 2008).

This chapter provides an overview of different approaches to social innovation that have been developed in a diversity of disciplines in social science for the last twenty years approximately, with a particular focus on the quite recent discussions on the spatiality of social innovation. It dwells on the question if the introduction of social innovation principles in different sectors of economy and society leads to a wider acceptance of the

working modalities of the capitalist economy or, instead, opens new opportunities for human development. The next section looks at the dangers of social innovation becoming a fashion or decorum for local, regional and international development to conceal (un) social practice, thus stripping it from its core policy and scientific message. Section III then highlights various definitions and perspectives on social innovation especially in terms of social transformation, social economy and exclusion. Subsequently, the analytical dimensions of social innovation concepts and theories that are relevant for the study of the spatiality of social innovation initiatives and processes are presented. In the penultimate section, two types of 'spaces of social innovation' are presented and analysed: places that pursue local development through integrated area development (IAD) and spatial networks of social innovation initiatives. The conclusion points at possible directions for future research on spaces of social innovation.

Social innovation, fad or robust analytical concept?

Since the end of the revolutionary 1960s in the US and Europe, the term social innovation has received growing interest from academic and policy circles, with a proliferation of varying interpretations as a consequence. The very loose usage of the term generates a risk that it would begin to lead a life as a fashion and no longer reflect its scientific contents and its relationships with political reality and ideological debates. What happens when scientific themes become fashionable is that the various social and economic sectors use them in different meanings, thus spreading substantial ambiguity. One such example is its use in business administration through Corporate Social Responsibility (Moulaert, 2009: 11) which often turns up as an attempt at improving the image of capitalism instead of an ethically concerned initiative to humanize business activities. Similar examples can be observed in the cases of more environmentally concerned actions such as green economy, green banking and green New Deals as forms of green Keynesianism, as in the United Nation's Environmental Program's drive for a global green new deal (UNEP, 2009). Although this programme is in essence ethically honourable, without a clear understanding of its socially innovative content, a bias towards the logic of the global market economy remains tempting. In addition, there is a danger that social innovation is used as a cheap active welfare policy, fitting the World Bank's poverty relief agenda, which in some cases ends up in paying half a decent welfare income to those unemployed who have become active (Mestrum, 2005, ch. 2) instead of capacitating and empowering people to take their destiny in their own hands, as capability theorists (Sen, 1985; Nussbaum, 2001) and social innovation advocates (Kunnen, 2010; Gibson-Graham and Roelvink, 2009; Moulaert et al., 2000) argue. Similar directions of fashionable word use can be observed in the European Union's views of future territorial cohesion policy, for example (Faludi, 2007). As Servillo (2007) argues the diversity of views of territorial cohesion objectives across policy agendas and levels is so wide that the term itself is completely hollowed out to a near slogan status.

But at the same time there is relevant optimism that offers arguments in favour of scientific work built on the concept of social innovation, or socio-political movements pursuing social innovation initiatives. Social innovation has shown its power as a challenger to one-sided interpretations of the role of technological innovation in business and economics (Hamdouch and Moulaert, 2006). Social innovation as a socio-political mobilizing theme has become apparent from the studies carried out under the banner of the European Commission's Framework Programmes in the SINGOCOM and KATARSIS projects for various neighbourhoods and cities in Europe and North America (MacCallum et al., 2009). Elsewhere, the *Center for Social Innovation (CSI)* at Stanford University and *Centre de recherche sur l'innovation sociale (CRISES)* in Montreal are engaged in interesting work on social innovation research (Powell and Steinberg, 2006; Klein and Harrisson, 2007). The variety of perceptions and applications of the term in both of these research centres is striking but interesting. CSI remains more concerned with mainstream acceptance of the term connecting it with productivity and how workers within a corporation can be made to collaborate by promoting different types of social innovation in corporate business culture, social interaction and work organization. But at the same CSI also contributes to put sustainability on the corporate agenda, to improve the working of the social economy, in collaboration with social economy agents and providing instruments to improve the management of NGOs to work towards social efficiency, etc. In this way CSI has certainly contributed to a deeper ethical foundation to business practice and networking. CRISES in Montreal, then, provides a more socially innovative focus on the concept of economy, society and urban revitalization. It puts a particular stress on the networks of public-private agents as a regional system of social innovation (Klein and Harrisson, 2007; Lévesque and Mendell, 1999). CRISES' approach is genuinely concerned about the development of the local and regional communities which it analyses and works with especially in Canada and Latin-America. We could indeed argue that its researchers have given a more tangible content to the 'humane' dimension of spatial development by stressing the role of participation, governance and multi-partnerships in setting and implementing development agendas (MacCallum, 2008; Agger and Löfgren, 2008; Mandarano, 2009).

The fulfilment of the market dream which many neoliberal ideologists, but also market-economy practitioners pamper ultimately involves universal commodification, i.e. allocation of all use-values through the market's price mechanisms. But from the analyses we have looked at, we have learned that the further removed from the logic of the capitalist market, the better the nature of social innovation is analysed and implemented in authentic terms of human development in which original human values of solidarity and shared creativity form the base-source. This is, for example, the case in 'Spaces of Social Economy' (Amin et al., 1999) or the Alternative Economic Strategy Network (Cumbers and Whittam, 2007). Indeed the tendency towards 'a commodified world' puts a heavy burden on social relations geared towards solidarity, reciprocity and cooperation, and leads to an uncertain future for a plural economy (Williams, 2005). This does not mean however that more mainstream research or management learning centres (such as CSI) and networks are just there to cover up the evils of the corporate world by veiling them with an image of CSR. In fact CSI has significantly contributed to make sustainability and social innovation tangible in business development plans and tractable in actual corporate practice, thus contributing in their own way to economic plurality through ongoing research and regular publications.

Defining social innovation

With the growing research and literature on social innovation in various languages and within different perspectives it is increasingly complex to arrive at a fixed contemporary definition of the term. The SINGOCOM project (2001–2004) funded by European Commission FP-5 programme, developed an Alternative Model of Local Innovation (ALMOLIN) that embraced the following definition of social innovation:

> Social innovation is path dependent and contextual. It refers to those changes in agendas, agency and institutions that lead to a better inclusion of excluded groups and individuals into various spheres of society at various spatial scales. Social innovation is very strongly a matter of process innovation, i.e. changes in the dynamics of social relations, including power relations.

It further added that:

> as social innovation is about social inclusion, it is also about countering or overcoming conservative forces that are eager to strengthen or preserve social exclusion situations. […] social innovation therefore explicitly refers to an ethical position of social justice. The latter is of course susceptible to a variety of interpretations and will in practice often be the outcome of social construction.

According to this definition social innovation cannot be considered as an *ad hoc* and overnight problem-solution approach to community issues. For it requires connecting to ongoing social relations within the concerned communities and the carefully negotiated and co-produced socially creative strategies to overcome crisis situations. Social innovation to be effective to the development of a community should therefore be path-dependent, spatially embedded and socially re(produced). We will return to this in sections iv and v.

Looking at earlier works on social innovation we find that as far back as the eighteenth century, Benjamin Franklin evoked social innovation in proposing minor modifications within the social organization of communities in Philadelphia (as analysed by Mumford, 2002); and in 1893, Emile Durkheim highlighted the importance of social regulation in the development of the division of labour which accompanies technical change (Durkheim, 1893). Technical change itself can only be understood within the framework of an innovation or renovation of the social order to which it is relevant (Weber, 1968 [1921]). At the start of the twentieth century, Max Weber examined the relationship between social order and innovation, a theme which was revisited by French philosophers and social scientists in the 1960s (Chambon *et al.*, 1982). Among other things, Weber affirmed that changes in living conditions are not the only determinants of social change. Individuals who introduce a behaviour variant, often initially considered deviant, can exert a decisive influence; if the new behaviour spreads and develops, it can become established social usage (Weber, 1968 [1921]). In the 1930s, Joseph Schumpeter considered social innovation as structural change in the organization of society, or within the organizational forms of enterprise or business (1947). Schumpeter's theory of innovation went far beyond the usual economic logic, and appealed to an ensemble of sociologies (cultural, artistic, economic, political, and so on), which he sought to integrate into a comprehensive social theory that would allow the analysis of both development and innovation (Schumpeter, 1932; Becker and Knudsen, 2005).

Finally, in the 1970s, the French intellectuals of the '*Temps des Cerises*' organized a debate of wide social and political significance on the transformation of society, and on the role of the revolts by students, intellectuals and workers. A major part of the debate was echoed in the columns of the journal *Autrement*, with contributions from such prominent figures as Pierre Rosanvallon, Jacques Fournier and Jacques Attali. In their book on social innovation, Chambon, David and Devevey (1982) built on most of the issues highlighted in this debate. According to these authors:

> Socially innovative [...] practices are more or less directly aimed at allowing an individual – or a group of individuals – to deal with a social need – or a set of needs – that could not be satisfied from other means.
>
> (Chambon *et al.*, 1982: p 8, our translation from the original text)

This definition is very general and does not really stress on the process dynamics of the problem. However, this short book in the series *Que sais-je?* remains the most complete 'open' synthesis on the subject of social innovation to this day. In brief, the authors examine the relationship between social innovation and the pressures bound up within societal changes, and show how the mechanisms of crisis and recovery both provoke and accelerate social innovation. Another link established by Chambon *et al.* concerns social needs and the needs of the individual, individually or collectively revealed. In practice, social innovation signifies satisfaction of specific needs thanks to collective initiative, which is not synonymous with state intervention. According to Chambon *et al.*, in effect the state can act, at one and the same time, as a barrier to social innovation and as an arena of social interaction provoking social innovation from within the spheres of state or market. Finally, these authors stress that social innovation can occur in different communities and at various spatial scales, but is conditional on processes of consciousness raising, mobilization and learning. Many other definitions of social innovation are available in the literature. It is not our concern to provide an exhaustive overview, but to reveal those analytical dimensions that will allow us to understand the agency and structure-process dimensions of social innovation as well as their spatiality. This is what we will do in the next section.

Social innovation: intrinsically social

The key to understanding social innovation is its intrinsically social nature. In the same way as technological innovation cannot be understood outside the logic of techniques (e.g. technology can be defined in different ways, ranging from 'socially neutral' to socially embedded explanations), social innovation cannot be apprehended outside the dynamics of society and its different components. Broadly speaking we can address this societal character of social innovation from two perspectives: its politico–ideological significance as a driving force in society; and the way different social sciences have addressed this societal character. Later in this section we will draw some analytical lessons from these societal dynamics, on how to combine 'micro' and 'macro' perspectives and what they mean for the analysis of the spatiality of social innovation. We will do so while trying to avoid the maelstrom of debates on the spatiality of social reproduction (scalar geography, politics of scale, relational geography, political ecology) which are all relevant to the discussion on the spatial character of SI as agency and process but bypass the ambition of this short chapter.

Politico-ideological significance

We experience the politico–ideological significance of social innovation by being citizens, members of movements or just by being conscious and reflective. A clear mobilizing power that social innovation offers as a concept and as an issue for public debate is in its reaction to the economistic and technologist interpretations of innovation. Similarly, it offers an intellectual, ideological and political reaction to privatization discourse and practice. It also holds the potential to fill the gap between 'fall of public man' (Sennett, 1977) on the one hand, and the rise of the communities of interest on the other hand,

especially those under the nationalist and self-interest agendas. The latter view of public life has been severely criticized by several progressive authors (e.g. Raes, 1997). Filling this gap then means the building of communities from the social innovation point of view which can be instrumental to rebuild both the public sphere and the neutral state that entitles all members of the different communities to the same basic rights. The conception of community as the enabler of citizenship rights (Silverman, 2004) advocates a broadening of the notion of citizenship by the inclusion of further rights, while at the same time recognizing the responsibilities of citizens within their communities and society (Moulaert, 2010). In this vein, social innovation can also be considered as guaranteeing basic rights to avoid or overcome social and economic alienation, exclusion, deprivation, and poverty both in the material and ethical sense. MacCallum *et al.* (2009) provide a number of examples of how people can join hands in very extreme situations of deprivation to work their way out collectively. In today's policy arena, the global institutions do refer to many such experiences but they do not draw the conclusions that they would be expected to draw from such cases. They prefer to stick to the 'microcosmos' the 'good practice communities', in this way not recognizing the general demands for the basic rights that are voiced *in* and *across most communities*. They do not in fact recognize the hopes, fears and clashes of communities as working grounds for general citizenship rights building under the auspices of a neutral state.

Finally, there is the politico-ideological significance in terms of 'micro' ethics which very often have a community basis. The Slow-food movement is a good example. It grew from discontent about fast-food production and provision, as a threat to the high-quality food provided by local agriculture, food stores and restaurants, especially but not exclusively in smaller cities (Knox and Mayer, 2008). From a political point of view, 'micro ethics' which are in support of friendly communication and tangible expression of solidarity are at the heart of debates, practices, sharing experiences and feelings in the workplace, the community house, the public squares and bars; from the outside they may appear unimportant, but in fact they are vital for social interaction and know-how building. People in their very small microcosm react to 'fast society' in all its aspects such as the new management practices (bureaucratic taylorism, work organization codes), hypermobility, and commodification of political life (markets for votes). These reactions provide grounds for new social movements or reinvigorate existing ones.

Social innovation in contemporary social science

But social innovation has also been constructed through social science practice. Different social science disciplines have recently delivered new or revised concepts (sometimes just 'notions') and related theories of social innovation, corresponding to their problematics and problem-solving codes. Table 18.1 looks particularly at how the concept of social innovation has been used from the point of view of different disciplines. Five fields with specific contemporary approaches have been identified: management science and organization theory; approaches covering the links between economy, society and environment (e.g. social economy, environmental economics, economic sociology …); fine arts and creativity; spatial development analysis (urban sociology, social geography); public administration and governance. In the literature covering these fields five dimensions of social innovation have been striking: purpose or as the French say more explicitly *finalité* of a SI initiative; organizational changes linked to the initiative; the role of special agents: leaders, charismatic individuals and (artistic) creators; the role of path-dependency and structural constraints; and the tension between normative

viewpoints on social innovation and what 'path-dependency' allows (Moulaert and Nussbaumer, 2008, ch. 3). We will illustrate the relationship between these dimensions in section five, when we talk about 'place-linked' social innovation, by presenting the dynamics of integrated area development, but also by explaining the wider spatial dynamics of SI observed in social movements, city-networks, wide-area social learning and communities of SI practice.

We notice from Table 18.1, and the literature that backs it up, that compared to the 'older' ones, the recent scientific approaches to social innovation put more stress on the 'micro' perspective of social innovation initiatives and governance − except maybe in the fifth strand on 'Governance and public administration' (Moulaert and Nussbaumer, 2008: 52–66). The guidelines for SI analysis in contemporary social science indeed stress agency, micro initiatives, and bottom-linked governance. Table 18.2 then brings to the front and combines what we believe to be the main concepts and explanatory categories that should play a role in SI analysis, borrowing from both 'old' and 'new' literature. On the one hand, Weber and Durkheim stress the transformation of social relations within economy and society, or the social organization within economic and political communities. Schumpeter can be considered as a bridge figure between the 'macro' and 'micro' approaches. Not only does he address the relationships between development and innovation, he particularly highlights the role of the entrepreneur as a leader who, facing many contradictions, introduces innovations in the organizational modes of society. He stresses the multidimensional character of development and entrepreneurship, the role of different types of innovation in human agency and the relationship between organizational change and innovative behaviour. His approach thus links in with the 'micro' foci presented in Table 18.1, but places them within their societal dynamics (for the latter see especially Schumpeter, 1947).

Table 18.1 Dimensions of social innovation (SI) in five scientific disciplines

Dimensions of social innovation / Discipline	Purpose (or finalité) of the SI initiative	Transformation of social relations – organizational aspects	Role of special agencies (leadership, creative individuals)	Place and space – path-dependence and spatial embeddedness	How to bypass the tension between norms and reality?
Management sciences and organization theory	Improve coherence of the organization in achieving its objectives (work ethics, profitability, ecological impacts)	Create a climate for the exchange of information and ideas. 'Horizontalize' the decision and communication systems	The innovative individual 'Agents' are nurtured by the organization	Recognition of 'path-dependence' through the enterprise and organizational culture	Tangible objectives. Normalize relationships between the work and executive staff. Dynamic learning processes
Approaches covering links between economy, society and environment	Integrate social and ecological objectives to the corporate agenda	Human relations on the work place. Quality of work and social relations		Tension between mainstream and ethical entrepreneurship (represented by the tensions between professional associations)	'Societalization' of a firm's relationships with its environment
Fine and creative arts	Social innovation (in a broader sense) – processes of creative communication – sociocultural emancipation	Open cognitive processes. Communication between individuals. Role of interpersonal activities and relations	Special attention towards initiatives of individual creativity	Historical inspiration of the contemporary social innovation (prominent examples and experiences)	Role of information and its reception by the creative community. Discovery of solutions and constraints. Interactive revision and refinement of suggested solutions
Spatial development approaches (Integrated Area Development)	Satisfaction of human needs...	... in agreement with changes in the governance relationships	More focus on the role of the community and its social agents	Important influence of the historical reproduction of institutional capital	... through multi-level governance and creation of networks of cooperation between agents of the community
Governance and public administration	Effective, transparent (even democratic) administration	Dehierarchization – network communication	Civil society movements. Ombudspersons	Bypass bureaucratic rigidities	Simplification of the structures – regular evaluation of reorganizations

Source: Authors' research

Table 18.2 The intrinsically social character of social innovation – spatiality

Dimensions of social innovation ... (or: shedding light on) ... in relation to "Dimensions of social innovation"	"Finalité de l'initiative" – Purpose of the "initiative"	Transformation of social relations	Role of special agencies	Place and space	Path-dependency and spatial embeddedness
"Finalité de l'initiative" – Purpose of the "initiative"	The social economy pillar of social innovation: satisfy unmet or unsatisfactorily unmet needs (social economy, Franklin, Mumford, CSR, sustainable dev. agendas)	The potential innovation in social relations (governance, empowerment, networks of cooperation and their spatialities) has an impact on the content and reach of the initiative	... individuals as initiative leaders, creators, artists, network coordinators; lobbyist, gurus ... groups as ensembles of the previous (Schumpeter, Mumford, social entreprise, sociology as an art ...)	Initiatives can be place-bound, confined to local spaces, or related to a wider spatiality – or a combination of several of these	History of the initiative, the relationship between its *resource* and *place base* and its ambitions – includes the social reproduction of ethics in 'place' and 'space' (local development models and analysis, institutional sociology and economics, IAD)
Transformation of social relations	Role of 'scale' (size) of initiative determines aspects of social relations that matter (corporate organization, community governance, global network)	The sociology pillar of social innovation: transformation of social relations to make them more cooperative and communicative [referring to a purpose or 'finalité']	Individual and collective mobilizers, platform builders and manifesto designers (analysis of social movements, socio-political mobilization	Consolidation and transformation of social relations can be place-bound, confined to local spaces, or related to a wider spatiality – or a combination of several of these. Governance systems (state, civil society ...) and their spatially articulated interactions (relational geography)	Spatially articulated path-dependency of governance systems, community development networks, etc. (political history, devolution and regionalization analysis, geographical scale theory)
Role of special agencies	Identification of spontaneous and functional leaderships 'fitting' the initiative. Potential tensions between both (mobilizing versus collective management)	According to the relevant social relations and their dynamics, particular types of agencies can be catalysed	Special leaderships (individual, collective) have been empirically observed as key factors in social innovation initiatives and processes	Spatial dynamics, place reproduction foster or discourage particular leaderships (community development, networking dynamics in spatial relationships)	Leadership is socially reproduced versus leadership fits community needs (collaborative planning, stakeholder involvement ...)

(continued)

Table 18.2 (Cont'd)

Place and space	An SI initiative (or a set of initiatives) is often place-oriented, addressing challenges and needs of their population(s) and communities (community development and its wider spatial structure)	Both places and the spatial relations in which they are embedded are socially intrinsic. The potential of places to socially innovate depends significantly on the transformative power of social relations (regulation approach, scalar politics, relational geography, political ecology)	Agencies can have a significant impact on place-making, moving boundaries, building bridges between spatially fragmented social capitals (neighbourhood development, social capital analysis)	Place and space dynamics are key to SI processes, and as 'incubator sites' and 'incubator networks' of SI initiatives …	… However, their path dependency and spatial embeddedness does not necessarily catalyse SI in a desired or forecasted way
Path-dependency and spatial embeddedness	Strong and lasting SI initiatives can affect the direction of the development paths of places and their wider social relations. They lead to innovation in change culture, institutions … (institutional sociology)	Transformations in society (e.g. regime changes), socio-political movements for institutional change, 'open' governance with public arenas for discussing development change (social transformations)	Significant leadership can affect the course of history, if the 'historical and political conjuncture' allows for it (political science, regime theory)	Places with a strong path-dependency and spatial embeddedness will have a strong tendency to 'persist'; whereas socially and culturally more fragmented and less robust places may leave less opening for change dynamics	Path-dependency and spatial embeddedness are key to understanding the societal roots and the resources (or lack) of SI initiatives, processes and their sustainability as well as reception by society and its communities

Source: Authors' research

Spaces and places of social innovation

Many of the types of social innovation mentioned in the previous section as collective action (politico-ideological perspective) or analytical categories (scientific perspective) are about '(re)moving boundaries': overcoming social and political boundaries, reconfiguring identities, reconstructing social relationships, (re)building community identity, re-appropriating (public) space through social mobilization and social political action. But the removal of boundaries can also be taken literally, i.e. the elimination or displacement of spatial confines. Examples can be observed in business administration of cooperative firms that have gone international, and in corporate social responsibility that has become a worldwide cultural discourse and has affected the practice in local, regional and global business networks. The alter-economies such as co-operative, solidarity and sustainable economy take place at different spatial scales, for example, through networking, building local institutions, multi-scalar empowerment of governance, etc. The story of the pipelines in Nigeria, for instance, is about the struggle to overcome exclusion. The highly volatile and accident-prone infrastructure of oil and gas distribution cuts through hundreds of communities particularly in the Niger Delta, and has been causing social, economic and environmental degradation in the region. After a long period of suffering, the communities actively began to establish gender- and environment-based alliances and developed networks with local, national and international NGOs for the enforcement of proper environmental standards, improvement of regulatory frameworks, ensure public participation, and invoke social, economic and political will at all spatial scales (Ogwu, 2009). The Niger Delta experience provides a good illustration of how spatial scales are interconnected. Resistance from local populations feeds solidarity movements built up at higher spatial scales and is in turn empowered by them.

To analyse the relationship between space and SI we use the conceptual and theoretical anchor points set out in Table 18.2. The categories in the table are sufficiently suggestive as to spatial outcomes of SI: space (spatial forms, scales and scalar articulations such as boundaries, reconfigurations, networks …), place (local identity rebuilding, defragmentation of urban space …) and space–place interactions. But space–place strategies and dynamics often belong to the heart of the social innovation strategies and processes themselves. Let us look at two types of spatial social innovation or social innovation that are intrinsically (but not exclusively) space-based.

Integrated area development

Social innovation opens new perspectives for local and regional development (Moulaert and Nussbaumer, 2005), by stressing the use and organization of space as a new opportunity-set for change initiatives, by democratizing territorial governance dynamics and by linking local and regional bottom-up development agendas to the multi-scalar social relations that should enhance them. In terms of neighbourhood cooperation, inhabitants, organizations, movements, diverse public and private agents, etc. come together and create opportunities to communicate with each other to build up a neighbourhood development strategy. This often happens spontaneously through actions initiated to overcome severe problems of deprivation. Thus, neighbourhood development agencies with an area-based development agenda should learn interactively how they can build in the spatial dimensions, for example, by integrating housing functions with public space, reorganizing space in order to accommodate a diversity of social relations, establishing a park hosting different functions and actively involving people coming from inside and outside the neighbourhood in socio-political networking.

The spatial perspective of social innovation particularly allows explaining the relationships between the satisfaction of human needs on the one hand and social empowerment on the other hand through the reproduction of community social relations, in the form of 'Integrated Area Development' (IAD) (Moulaert et al., 2000; Moulaert et al., 2010). The IAD framework seeks to create opportunities to socially redress 'disintegrated areas' (Moulaert and Leontidou, 1995) by bringing together different types of actors and their aspirations, solutions for the threats to sustainable development (economic, ecological, socio-cultural and political), restoring links with other areas in the city and rebuilding a neighbourhood and community identity. To this purpose it helps to valorize the diversity of historical social, institutional, artistic cultures and traditions as resources for community-based development. And it is essential to transform governance relations from a local or bottom-up to a bottom-linked architecture, in which different governance scales (e.g. neighbourhood, city, region, national and international) empower each other.

Spatial networking as SI

Different types of *spatial social innovation* fall under this label: networking of social innovation agents operating in different places; establishing communication and governance modes allowing for democratic decision-making within multi-site and multi-place networks; up-scaling of governance of locally initiated initiatives with the purpose of empowering them and improving their politico-institutional leverage. The latter is, for example, what happened through the networking of Micro Finance Institutions (MFI) in the ProsperA network that was created "to promote the culture and practice of social performance by reinforcing the capacities of MFIs and local networks" (Antohi, 2009: 44). In Europe the European Microfinance Platform (e-MFP) formalized in 2006 comprises about a hundred organizations and individuals active in microfinance

and its main objective is to promote cooperation among European MF bodies active in developing countries, by enabling communication, exchange knowledge, advance good practice and enhance policy issues with European institutions and governments (http://www.e-mfp.eu/about-e-mfp). Part of the strategy of the federations such as ProsperA and e-MFP is to have social performance recognized in the microfinance mainstream. As for social innovation in general, there may be a price to be paid to the *Quantum Mammon* here, namely concerning the nature of the objective criteria by which social performance should be measured (op. cit: 44–45).

Alternative supply chains are another spatialized social innovation, e.g. the geography of the value-added chains as applied in regional and international fair trade. As to the regional, we refer to the direct delivery of agricultural products from farm to consumer (e.g. farmer markets and cooperatives), which reduces the share of the distribution sector (often big supermarket chains) in the value-added buildup between crop and consumption, with a fairer share going to local farmers and a better control on the health content of the produce (Knox and Mayer, 2008). Internationally speaking then, the recalibration of value-added chains to the benefit of the income of producers is probably even more crucial in countries of the global South. As in the Northern regional sustainability and fair-trade perspective, the agricultural sector is again the main focus both in the analysis of and recommendations for policy change in international trade. Here a confrontation with existing WTO regulations and ongoing liberalization of markets is unavoidable. These (de)regulatory dynamics continue to diffuse industrialization of the global South despite the fact that, in the last two decades the growth of manufacturing as percentage of GDP in developing countries has not helped in reducing their income gap with the developed world (Arrighi et al., 2003). Even within the agriculture sector, extreme trade protection strategies result in mutual dependency between the elements of the value-added chains (Stevens, 2001). An interesting case of how the financial instability can be countered by means of social economy is found in the example of business incubation initiatives in Brazil. After large-scale job losses in the wake of the 1980s' economic crisis, the solidarity economy practices were gradually articulated with public policy and supported by different types of institutions, including universities, by the establishment of incubators. Not only has this led to a new theory and practice strand but also to the formation of social technologies acquired through the sociology of knowledge of historical experiences (Dubeux, 2011).

Conclusion

Over the last twenty years research on the meaning of SI has advanced significantly. Several scientific disciplines have taken the concept on board, because it helps to understand the social dimensions of innovation, and to detail the content of human development in terms of needs satisfaction, coalition building, resources deployment, empowerment and bottom-up governance, community dynamics and path-dependency. Its multidimensional and practice-oriented nature has also given a major impetus to interdisciplinary and transdisciplinary research methodology (Social Polis:http://www.socialpolis. eu/; Novy *et al.*, 2012; Moulaert, 2010).

As to the spatiality of social innovation, more research is needed. Social innovation *as* and *through* community development has been studied in a quite detailed way since the Neighbourhood in Crisis and EU Urban I programmes (Moulaert *et al.*, 2010). More work on scalar dynamics, multi-level governance and place–scale relations in social innovation is needed however. Referring to the examples in the previous sections, for instance, the role of different places in the reproduction of fairer value-added chains should be

related to the modes by which the networks that connect and reproduce them are formed and governed. Are they bottom-up organizational initiatives? Have they grown from the convergence of initiatives in different places suffering comparable conditions of alienation and exploitation? What has been the role of critiques of international organizations – also from inside, in designing alternatives for international trade and bottom-linked transnational governance? Far from suggesting that social innovation analysis should overrule methodology in the fields already addressing these issues, the message is that SI, in its different complementary meanings and theoretical orientations, can help to analyse in a sociologically coherent way spatially embedded agencies of social change with multiscalar processes that either determine or steer them (Moulaert and Nussbaumer, 2008, ch. 6). In this way SI research, relational geography and scalar politics analysis could engage into a methodological enriching interaction.

References

Agger, A. and Löfgren, K. (2008) 'Democratic assessment of collaborative planning processes', *Planning Theory*, 7(2): 145–164.

Amin, A., Cameron, A. and Hudson, R. (1999) 'Welfare as work? The potential of the UK social economy', *Environment and Planning A*, 31(11): 2033–2051.

Antohi, M. (2009) 'Capital for innovation', in D. MacCallum, F. Moulaert, J. Hillier and S. Vicari (eds) *Social Innovation and Territorial Development*, Aldershot: Ashgate, pp. 39–62.

Arrighi, G., Silver, B. and Brewer, B. (2003) 'Industrial convergence, globalization and the persistence of the north–south divide', *Studies in Comparative International Development*, 3(81): 3–31.

Becker, M.C. and Knudsen, T. (2005) 'Translation of and introduction to "Entwicklung" (J. Schumpeter)', *Journal of Economic Literature*, 43(1): 108–120.

Chambon, J.-L., David, A. and Devevey, J-M. (1982) *Les innovations sociales*, Paris: Presses Universitaires de France.

Cumbers, A. and Whittam, G. (eds) (2007) 'Reclaiming the economy: alternatives to market fundamentalism in Scotland and beyond', *Scottish Left Review Press*, Edinburgh.

Durkheim, E. (1893) *De la division de travail social*, Paris: Presses Universitaires de France.

Dubeux, A. (2010) 'Business incubation of solidarity economy: a methodology for social innovation in Brazil', in F. Moulaert, D. MacCallum, A. Hamdouch and A. Mehmood (eds) *Social Innovation: Collective Action, Social Learning and Transdisciplinary Research*, Oxford : Blackwell forthcoming.

Faludi, A. (ed.) (2007) *Territorial Cohesion and European Model of Society*, Cambridge, Mass: The Lincoln Institute for Land Policy.

Gibson-Graham, J.K. and Roelvink, G. (2009) 'Social innovation for community economies', in D. MacCallum, F. Moulaert, J. Hillier and S. Vicari (eds) *Social Innovation and Territorial Development*, Aldershot: Ashgate

Hamdouch, A. and Moulaert, F. (2006) 'Knowledge infrastructure, innovation dynamics and knowledge creation/diffusion/accumulation processes: a comparative institutional perspective', *Innovation*, 19(1): 25–50.

Klein, J-L. and Harrisson, D. (eds) (2007) *L'innovation sociale: émergence et effets sur la transformation des sociétés*, Montréal: Presses de l'Université du Québec.

Knox, P. and Mayer, H. (2009) *Small Town Sustainability. Economic, Social, and Environmental*, Basel: Birkhäuser.

Kunnen, N. (2010) 'Research strategies for asset & strengths based community development', in F. Moulaert, D. MacCallum, A. Hamdouch, and A. Mehmood (eds) *Social Innovation: Collective Action, Social Learning and Transdisciplinary Research*, Oxford: Blackwell, forthcoming.

Lévesque, B. and Mendell, M. (1999) L'économie sociale au Québec: éléments théoriques et empiriques pour le débat et la recherché, *Cahiers du CRISES*, No. 9908, http://www.unites.uqam.ca/econos/Levesque-Mendell.pdf, accessed 25 October 2009.

MacCallum, D. (2008) 'Participatory planning and means–end rationality: a translation problem', *Planning Theory and Practice*, 9(3): 325–343.

MacCallum, D., Moulaert, F., Hillier, J. and Vicari, S. (eds) (2009) *Social Innovation and Territorial Development*, Aldershot: Ashgate.

Mandarano, L.A. (2009) 'Social network analysis of social capital in collaborative planning', *Society and Natural Resources*, 22(3): 245–260,

Mestrum, F. (2005) *De rattenvanger van Hamelen – De Wereldbank, armoede en ontwikkeling*, Antwerp: EPO.

Moulaert, F. (2009) 'Social innovation: institutionally embedded, territorially (re)produced', in D. MacCallum, F. Moulaert, J. Hillier and S. Vicari (eds) *Social Innovation and Territorial Development*, London: Ashgate.

Moulaert, F. (2010) 'Social innovation and community development: concepts, theories and challenges', in : F. Moulaert, F. Martinelli, E. Swyngedouw and S. Gonzalez (eds) *Can Neighbourhoods Save the City? Community Development and Social Innovation*, Oxon: Routledge (in press).

Moulaert, F. and Nussbaumer, J. (2005) 'The social region: beyond the territorial dynamics of the learning economy', *European Urban and Regional Studies*, 12(1): 45–64.

Moulaert, F. and Nussbaumer, J. (2008) *La logique spatiale du développement territorial*, Sainte-Foye: Presses Universitaires du Québec.

Moulaert, F. and Leontidou, L. (1995) 'Localités désintégrées et stratégies de lutte contre la pauvreté', *Espaces et Sociétés*, 78: 35–53.

Moulaert, F. and Sekia, F. (2003) 'Territorial innovation models: a critical survey', *Regional Studies*, 3: 289–302.

Moulaert, F., Martinelli, F., Swyngedouw, E. and Gonzalez, S. (eds) (2010) *Can Neighbourhoods Save the City? Community Development and Social Innovation*, Oxon: Routledge (in press).

Moulaert, F. et al. (2000) *Globalization and Integrated Area Development in European Cities*, Oxford: Oxford University Press.

Mumford, M.D. (2002) 'Social innovation: ten cases from Benjamin Franklin', *Creativity Research Journal*, 14(2): 253–266.

Novy, A., de Souza, D.C. and Moulaert, F. (2012) 'Social cohesion in the city – empowering inhabitants to shape their city', *Urban Studies*, forthcoming.

Nussbaum, M.C. (2000) *Women and Human Development: The Capabilities Approach*, Cambridge: Cambridge University Press.

Ogwu, F.A. (2009) 'Petroleum pipeline distribution system: the case of oil and gas pipeline network in Nigeria: an environmental justice approach', http://www.lancs.ac.uk/fass/events/changingcultures/seminars/seminar6.htm, accessed 25 October 2009.

Powell, W.W. and Steinberg, R. (eds) (2006) *The Non-profit Sector: A Research Handbook*, 2nd edn, New Haven, CT: Yale University Press.

Raes, K. (1997) *Het moeilijke ontmoeten. Verhalen van alledaagse zedelijkheid*, Brussels: VUB Press.

Schumpeter, J. (1947) *Capitalism, Socialism and Democracy*, London: Harper.

Schumpeter, J. (2005 [1934]) 'Entwicklung', translated by Becker and Knudsen 2005.

Sen, A. (1985) *Commodities and Capabilities*, Oxford: Oxford University Press.

Sennett, R. (1977) *The Fall of Public Man*, New York: W.W. Norton.

Servillo L. (2007) 'Coesione Territoriale e Politiche Urbane in Europa' (Italian), unpublished Ph.D. thesis, Turin Polytechnic.

Silverman, M. (ed.) (2004) *Community-based Organizations. The Intersection of Social Capital and Local Context in Contemporary Urban Society*, Detroit: Wayne State University Press.

SINGOCOM (n.d.) project website <http://users.skynet.be/bk368453/singocom/index2.html>.

Stevens, C. (2001) 'Value chains and trade policy: the case of agriculture', *IDS Bulletin*, 32(3): 46–59.

UNEP (2009) *'Global Green New Deal: policy brief'*, United Nations Environment Programme, Geneva: UNEP-DTIE.

Weber, M. (1968 [1921]) *Economy and Society*, vol. 1 (trans.), New York: Bedminster Press.

Williams, C.C. (2005) *A Commodified World: Mapping the Limits Of Capitalism*, London: Zed Books.

Further reading

MacCallum, D., Moulaert, F., Hillier, J. and Vicari, S. (eds) (2009) *Social Innovation and Territorial Development*, Aldershot: Ashgate. (For alternative perspectives to spatial, economic and social change.)

Moulaert, F., Martinelli, F., Gonzalez, S. and Swyngedouw, E. (eds) (2007) 'Social innovation and governance in European cities: between path dependency and radical innovation', Special issue of *European Urban and Regional Studies*, 14(3). (For issues on social polarisation and exclusion.)

www.socialpolis.eu <http://www.socialpolis.eu> (A number of papers and reports produced under different fields and themes for the Social Platform for Cities and Social Cohesion, funded by EC SSH programme.)

19

Forging post-development partnerships

Possibilities for local and regional development

J.K. Gibson-Graham

Post-development as ontological politics

A post-development approach to world-making has arisen from a critique of the idea that development, especially economic development, is yoked to capitalist growth. This approach extends the long tradition of critique that has accompanied the hegemonic rise of a mainstream development project focused on the 'problem' of less developed regions of the world (Escobar 1995; McGregor 2009). The deconstructive project of post-development thinking unhinges notions of development from the European experience of industrial growth and capitalist expansion, decentres conceptions of economy and de-essentializes economic logics as the motor of history, loosens the discursive grip of unilinear trajectories on narratives of change, and undermines the hierarchical valuation of cultures, practices and places. In essence, this project has proposed a complete unravelling of the unexamined certainties of modernist social science as applied to social and economic development.

The post-development agenda is not, however, anti-development. As we see it, the challenge of post-development is not to give up on development, but to imagine and practise development differently. Thus post-development thinking does not attempt to represent the world "as it is", but the world "as it could be". In this sense it breaks from the commitment to epistemological realism that underpins so much mainstream and radical social analysis. Accepting the inevitable performativity of language – its power to create the effects that it names (Butler 1993, 2; Law and Urry 2004) – post-development thinking attempts to perform new worlds by generating new and experimental discourses and practices of development.

Boaventura de Sousa Santos outlines what is at stake when we reject the intellectual landscape that has been colonized, as he sees it, by the hegemonic monocultures of modern science and high culture, linear time, hierarchical classification systems, scalar spatial framings and capitalist growth dynamics (2004: 238–239). Freed from these systems of thinking, the positivity of "development" and "developed" or "leading" regions is not set against the negativity of "under-development" and "less developed" or "lagging" regions. Instead we are able to appreciate how developmental thinking has produced a sociology of absences – "non-existent" places, regions and nations where any vestige of (self-defined) development has been "disqualified and rendered invisible, unintelligible, or irreversibly discardable" (2004: 238). As a counter to this evacuated landscape, post-development thinking works to reinstate and create multiple and different knowledges, temporalities, forms of recognition (as opposed to classification), trans-scale relationships and dynamics of productivity. By establishing ecologies of difference at the centre of world being, we can take an ontological and political leap and begin to imagine and enact a wide range of possibilities for local and regional development.

One way to illustrate the difference a post-development approach makes is to contrast it with the latest in high modernist thinking on regional development as represented in the World Development Report entitled *Reshaping Economic Geography* (World Bank 2009). In this document places are located on a developmental continuum determined by their distance (to markets), density (of market activity) and divisions (preventing freedom of trade and migration). Development is conceived as inherently uneven, unidirectional and capitalist (though not needing to be named as such, because economists have rendered non-capitalist economic activity non-credible or non-existent):

> Growing cities, ever more mobile people, and increasingly specialized products are integral to development. These changes have been most noticeable in North America, Western Europe, and Northeast Asia. But countries in East and South Asia and Eastern Europe are now experiencing changes that are similar in their scope and speed. World Development Report 2009: Reshaping Economic Geography concludes that such transformations will remain essential for economic success in other parts of the developing world and should be encouraged.
>
> (World Bank 2009: xix)

This report has a different message: economic growth will be unbalanced. To try to spread it out is to discourage it – to fight prosperity, not poverty. But development can still be inclusive, even for people who start their lives distant from dense economic activity. For growth to be rapid and shared, governments must promote economic integration, the pivotal concept, as this report argues, in the policy debates on urbanization, territorial development, and regional integration. Instead, all three debates overemphasize place-based interventions (World Bank 2009: http://go.worldbank.org/RBDWKOYC90 accessed 9 November 2009).

We are familiar with the sectoral transformations needed for economic growth – the changes in work and organization as agrarian economies become industrialized and service oriented. This report discusses the spatial transformations that must also happen for countries to develop. Higher densities, shorter distances, and lower divisions will remain essential for economic success in the foreseeable future. They should be encouraged. With them will come unbalanced growth. When accompanied by policies for integration calibrated to the economic geography of nations, these changes will also bring inclusive development – sooner, not much later (World Bank 2009: 32),

What is so remarkable about this report is its pragmatic "acceptance" that economic growth is uneven and its refusal to inquire into the causes and consequences of this unevenness for places on the "lagging" end of the development continuum (Rigg *et al.* 2009). Here we see the normative vision of Chicago School economics laid out with celebratory naiveté – complete with a unidirectional and singular trajectory of development that will enrol all places into one integrated system modelled on advanced capitalist economies. The report and its recommendations will, no doubt, reverberate through all the international institutions that the World Bank is connected to, influencing policy and practice on the ground (Mitchell 2005). Its performative effect will be to perpetuate a vision of the world in which localities and regions are presented with no alternative but to hitch themselves to the engine of capitalist growth or, where this is not feasible, for people to move to successful regions. From a post-development perspective the report's hopeful adherence to world trickle-down seems anachronistic, its blind belief in the market foolish and the failure to account for the environmental consequences of continued growth, as we have known it, immoral. So what might post-development offer instead?

Local and regional post-development in theory

A post-development approach to local and regional development starts from the premise that space has not already been colonized by capitalism. When the prevalence, density and efficiency of capitalist economic relations are not used as the gauge of development we are free to apprehend social space in many different ways. Places are not situated within a hierarchy of valuation in which cultures are modern or primitive and economies advanced or backward. The bald indices of human development (infant mortality,

calories consumed, longevity, etc.) will still display vast disparities across regions of the globe. But there is no projection of a singular pathway towards improved well-being. Development objectives can be opened up to local assessment and it becomes possible to imagine many different development pathways that build on local assets, experience and expectations.

While the discourse of capitalist hegemony is rampant in economic science, the murky reality is that most of the world is sustained by diverse economic relations, many of which cannot be framed as capitalist. Within development studies this heterogeneity of economic relations in the global south, or majority world, is a major focus of the sustainable livelihoods approach (Chambers and Conway 1992; Scoones 1998). In both the majority and minority world the economic identity of localities and regions can be appreciated using a weak theory of economy that inventories the variety of enterprise types and forms of labour, property, transactions and finance that coexist in any one site. Table 19.1 shows the diverse economy frame that we have used to 'map' economic space. Capitalist economic relations (including capitalist enterprise in

Table 19.1 The diverse economy

Enterprise	Labour	Property	Transactions	Finance
CAPITALIST	**WAGE**	**PRIVATE**	**MARKET**	**MAINSTREAM MARKET**
ALTERNATIVE CAPITALIST	**ALTERNATIVE PAID**	**ALTERNATIVE PRIVATE**	**ALTERNATIVE MARKET**	**ALTERNATIVE MARKET**
State owned	Self-employed	State-managed assets	Fair trade	Cooperative Banks
Environmentally responsible	Reciprocal labour	Customary (clan) land	Alternative currencies	Credit unions
Socially responsible	In-kind	Community land trusts	Underground market	Community-based financial institutions
Non-profit	Work for welfare	Indigenous knowledge (intellectual property)	Barter	Micro-finance
NON-CAPITALIST	**UNPAID**	**OPEN ACCESS**	**NON-MARKET**	**NON-MARKET**
Worker cooperatives	Housework	Atmosphere	Household sharing	Sweat equity
Sole proprietorships	Volunteer	International waters	Gift giving	Family lending
Community enterprise	Self-provisioning	Open source IP	Hunting, fishing, gathering	Donations
Feudal	Slave labour	Outer space	Theft, piracy, poaching	Interest-free loans
Slave				

Source: Author's research

which surplus value is produced, appropriated and distributed on the basis of waged labour, private property, production for the market and mainstream finance) are only the tip of the economy iceberg. People in places and regions are sustained by a vast array of non-capitalist and alternative capitalist enterprises, unpaid and alternatively paid labour, alternative private and open-access property, non-market and alternative market transactions and alternative and non-market finance. In many of the so-called "lagging regions" within nations there is a vibrant diverse economy that has sustained people and ecosystems for generations (Carnegie 2008; Gibson-Graham 2005; Pretes and Gibson 2008). Colonial and modern development interventions have often undermined or destroyed local networks and practices of social and environmental habitat maintenance, thereby contributing to the poverty that is taken as an indicator of lack of development (Gibson *et al.* 2010). A post-development approach does not ignore the need expressed by many in such locations for change that will increase well-being, but starts from a standpoint of "not knowing" with respect to how to move forward, allowing both practical and normative visions to emerge from the local or regional context.

The very idea of development implies a dynamic of change over time. But when development dynamics are not conceptualized in terms of the systemic logics of the capitalist growth machine (e.g. commoditization, proletarianization, mechanization, specialization, capital accumulation, concentration, capital and labour migration) we are able to imagine many other dynamics that operate and could be purposefully stimulated. A post-development theory of change appreciates the complexity of interdependent developments and co-developments but sees ethico-political decisions, rather than structural imperatives, as capable of activating development pathways that will unfold in unpredictable ways. By humbly acknowledging up front the

uncertain outcomes of our actions, we can monitor and attempt to minimize the damage to extant, functioning economic and ecological systems, as new interventions are introduced.

When ethical action is seen as contributing to developmental dynamics, we are able to imagine supporting and initiating processes that produce widespread well-being directly (rather than via the circuitous route of capitalist industrialization) (Healy and Graham 2008). We can begin to explore the contributors to system resilience and start to mimic natural ecological dynamics that sustain habitats and maintain diversity (Gibson *et al.* 2010). With this widened vision of economic ecologies of productivity we can think about ways that local and regional development might build sustaining economies that start with the assets at hand in any place. To summarize, the post-development approach to local and regional development recognizes and builds upon the diversity of economic practices that sustain livelihoods; recognizes market and other transactions as constitutive of community; recognizes and expands the diversity of development pathways; emphasizes relationships rather than logics of development; acknowledges and builds upon the economic interdependence of individuals and groups; starts with what is in place and builds from there (in other words, it is assets-based and path-dependent). How might such a post-development approach inform policy and planning on the ground?

Post-development pathways

Cultural analyst Raymond Williams reminds us that the modern term "region" originates from the Latin words regionem – direction, boundary, district – and regere – to direct or to rule (Gibson 2001: 643):

> In imperial and church government, and later in the development of centralized

nation-states, region thus became not only a part, but a subordinate part, of a larger political entity.

(Williams 1983: 264–265)

In a similar hierarchy of meaning the term "local" became positioned as only ever the product of dynamic political and economic forces that operate at a larger scale. Thus local and regional development has traditionally been seen as subordinate to the rule of capital which operates on a global scale. The place of planning and policy is to align regions and localities in such a way as to capture the dynamism that emanates from the logic of capitalist development.

A post-development local and regional development agenda involves taking back the economy as an ethical and political space of decision and the locality and region as sites of differentiation and possibility. The normative vision that might guide development interventions will be grounded in the specificities of place. In this section we review various cases where communities and regions have attempted to create different development pathways as they travel, guided by clearly stated ethical principles. Our commitment to the slogan of the World Social Forum, "Another world is possible", has drawn us to experiments with building local and regional community economies in which well-being is increased directly by a variety of mechanisms, surplus generation is used as a force for constituting and strengthening communities, a commons is created, shared and replenished, and new economic subjects are created.

Cooperative culture guiding regional development

In the economically depressed and war-ravaged Basque region of Spain, Father José Maria Arizmendiarietta, a Catholic priest versed in emancipatory social theory, set himself the goal of promoting unity in a society fractured by civil war and political division (Gibson-Graham 2003). Starting in the 1940s, he initiated over the subsequent decades some 2000 study circles on socialist, humanist and religious topics. Out of these groups emerged the future leadership of a complex system of worker-owned cooperatives that forms the basis of what is today one of the most successful and resilient regional economies in Europe. Beginning in 1956 with one cooperative business making paraffin cooking stoves for a largely unserved domestic market, the Mondragón Cooperative Corporation (MCC) now spans a diverse range of sectors supplying international markets. It produces consumer goods (e.g. domestic appliances, furniture and sports equipment), capital goods, especially machine tools for the automotive, aeronautic and domestic appliance sectors, and industrial components. It is also involved in construction, health care, education, housing, social security and pension management, business services and retail. In 2008 the MCC employed just under 93,000 workers, with 83 per cent of those working in the Industry Area being worker-owner cooperators (http://www.Mondragón-corporation. com/ENG/Economic-Data/Most-relevant-data.aspx accessed 12 November 2009).

There are a number of keys to the success of the experimental development pathway initiated in Mondragón. At the core of regional economic transformation are a set of cooperative ethical principles including open admission, democratic organization, the sovereignty of labour, the instrumental and subordinate nature of capital, participatory management, payment solidarity and inter-cooperation. These principles guide all economic decisions. They have shaped the economic development of the community ensuring that meeting the needs of the many is put before individual gain. Potential members are, for example, assisted to raise the initial capital needed to become worker-owners and the relatively flat pay scale minimizes income disparities in the region.

Another principle, that of social transformation, is consciously enacted via the consolidation and reinvestment of the surplus (net profits) generated by the cooperatives. Early on in the growth of the cooperatives, it became clear that there was a need for an overarching financial institution that could manage cooperator savings and marshal the surplus of the entire cooperative complex to foster new cooperatives and create more jobs. With the formation of the *Caja Laboral Popular* or Working People's Bank , the cooperatives as a group made the decision to require that the profit shares of individual cooperators be deposited in the bank until retirement. This created a pool of surplus available for investment in new cooperatives including, eventually, one charged with the development and nurturing of cooperative businesses. They offer rigorous business planning and provide on-site assistance with cooperative start-ups, guiding their development for several years until they are able to manage on their own.

On the basis of internally generated wealth and expertise, Mondragón has been able to create a multi-sector cooperative economy and engender region-wide prosperity. This post-development pathway has not been without pitfalls and problems. The early success of Mondragón was built on the emergence of new communal subjects able to navigate ethical decisions around individuality and collectivity, present gain and responsibility to future generations. But maintaining high levels of worker-ownership has become one of the major challenges in an organization that in recent years has thrived by expanding into Europe and Asia, absorbing capitalist companies and including a non-cooperator workforce. Driven by a primary commitment to Basque regional development, the MCC has become a hybrid organization in which the ethical issues of cooperativism, place loyalty and internationalism require continual debate and renegotiation. The adherence to cooperative principles is an ongoing struggle rather than a fait accompli. On the MCC

website the inspirational views of Father Arizmendiarietta are still to be heard:

> The present, however splendid it may be, bears the seeds of its own ruin if it becomes separated from the future.
> http://www.Mondragón-corporation.com/ENG/Co-operativism/Co-operative-Experience.aspx (accessed 12 November 2009)

In the Basque region of Spain we have an example of a longstanding, experimental, path-dependent form of post-development that continues to inspire people around the globe to be the future they want to see.

Social/solidarity economy movements guiding regional development

In the Canadian province of Quebec another successful experiment in economic development driven by social values has unfolded over the past few decades. This French-speaking "nation" of some 7.5 million citizens has a long history of strong labour unions, cooperatives and mutual benefit associations. Over the past two decades community activism and other social and environmental movements have gained organizational strength. While once coexisting in relative isolation, in the late 1990s these sectors, organizations and issue-based movements identified themselves together as members of a "social" or "solidarity" economy. The social economy refers to "a set of activities and organizations stemming from collective entrepreneurship" organized around certain principles and operating rules that put community benefit before private profit (Mendell 2009: 186). The language of the social/solidarity economy has been an important mobilizing tool, allowing this new movement to demonstrate that they are an essential part of the Quebec economy. Recognition has led to political clout (Neamtan 2008).

The post-development pathway followed in Quebec has involved the development and integration of institutions capable of orchestrating an alternative style of economic development. Initially, drawing on funds marshalled by unions (Fonds de solidarité) community initiatives emerging from community economic development corporations were supported in low-income neighbourhoods. Many new social enterprises committed to providing "*new services* that meet *new needs* or *previously unsatisfied needs*" were developed (Mendell 2009: 179; emphasis in original). By the early years of the twenty-first century, the Quebec social economy included 935 childcare centres, 103 homecare enterprises, 671 credit unions, 180 worker cooperatives and 72 worker-shareholder cooperatives that together provided 167,302 jobs (190). These enterprises are not substitutes for public provision. Given the magnitude and job-creating power of the social economy in Quebec the movement has established a working relationship with the provincial government, demanding "the same kind of support for our collective enterprises that the government has given to the private for-profit sector" (Neamtan 2008: 272). Most importantly they gained operating costs for their coordinating institution, the *Chantier de l'Economie Sociale,* that have increased from $250,000 per annum in 1996 to 1998 to $650,000 per annum in 2006 to 2008 (Mendell 2009: 187).

The Chantier is a democratically organized representative body that negotiates with government on behalf of its social economy membership. It functions as a support organization that networks social enterprises, unions, cooperatives and non-profits, creating internal markets, securing public sector markets, providing training directly and ensuring that colleges and universities meet the training needs of the social economy. It is also a social innovation hub for the sector that produces regular community maps and identifies new opportunities for enterprises. Innovative initiatives are sought out not primarily in order to solve problems in the community, but to build capacity.

The Chantier is committed to economic democratization which means, among other things, collective and community ownership. One of the main barriers to community ownership and wealth-building is the lack of appropriate legal frameworks and accounting norms for social enterprise. To address this lack, the Chantier is developing social accounting techniques for measuring collective value-added as well as formulating new legal instruments and entities for the social economy (Mendell 2009: 189). It has created its own investment tools so that it can support enterprises focused on maximizing social and environmental returns on investment, rather than financial return to financial institutions and shareholders. In 2007, as part of its co-construction policy, the Chantier obtained a government grant to establish the Fiducie du Chantier de l'Economie Sociale, a financial institution that offers long-term patient capital for enterprise development. In a province in which the manufacturing and resource sectors, especially pulp and paper, are struggling or facing closures, the challenges for employment generation are great. So far social economy developments have generated impressive job growth in a multitude of small establishments. Whether this sector can ever fully replace the employment levels associated with large-scale industry is unclear. Post-development possibilities in Quebec have been realized by a partnership between social economy actors and policy makers in government. Together they have provided an enabling environment in which needs in households and neighbourhoods have been directly met with childcare, homecare, artistic outlets, accessible finance and housing. Surplus has been deployed to strengthen the social economy, which has been able to meet the issue of economic development "head-on, without losing our value system" (Neamtan 2008: 270).

Theory and post-development possibility

Mondragón and Quebec present inspirational experiments with ethically driven regional development that have created economies focused on producing direct social benefit. In both cases great importance has been placed on a non-capitalocentric language of economy and support for emerging economic subjectivities. The role of intellectuals in helping to consolidate new developmental pathways is publicly acknowledged. In the case of Mondragón, Father Arizmendiarietta introduced theories of economic and social justice and the model of the Rochdale cooperators to unemployed youths and helped them conceptualize new forms of economic organization. In Quebec, university-based researchers are involved in collaborative partnerships with government and movement actors mapping, documenting, conceptualizing and measuring the social economy as part of a strategic mobilization to gain prominence in policy arenas (Mendell 2009: 202). To take another example, in Brazil where solidarity economy activism has grown dramatically in recent years, social enterprises are being set up in university incubators. The incubator at Universidade Regional do Noroete do Estado do Rio Grande do Sul, for example, is part of a university extension programme that:

> promotes citizenship, work and social inclusion, supported by principles and values of the solidarity economy (co-operation, self-management, solidarity, valorization of the worker and sustainable development).
> (Lechat 2009: 164)

Building on Paulo Freire's vision of empowerment through popular education and participation, these incubators not only advise about business development but cultivate newly knowledgeable subjects of a distinctively Brazilian solidarity economy.

In all these contexts we see intellectuals or academics working alongside others in research collectives. This observation offers a key to thinking about the role of concepts and theories in local and regional post-development. As thinkers we can choose to contribute to an enabling environment in which specific, place-based strategies for increasing well-being will emerge. If we start from the premise that there is no one theory or pathway of local and regional development, how might we bring our conceptual training to bear on the making of new worlds?

We have shown how rethinking the identity of the economy produces a proliferation of ways of meeting material needs in the social economy. While there is a lively debate about theorizing the social economy (e.g. Amin 2009), the conceptual representation of diverse economies is still very much a work in progress (Gibson-Graham 2006, 2008). In particular there is a dearth of thinking about developmental dynamics outside the confines of systemic capitalocentric logics of change. How might we represent the dynamic properties of solidarity economies as they are currently unfolding? How do we represent regional and local development in terms of interdependent developments and co-developments that are consciously initiated by strategic ethical decisions but that evolve in unpredictable ways? There is research to be done in collaboration with practitioners on the ground to recognize new dynamics and help to analyse their trajectories. Graham and Cornwell (2009) have worked with two community organizations in Massachusetts to help identify the ethical dynamics of development that they have activated. They have theorized the tensions and pay-offs in a large cooperative housing organization between, for example, "deciding to meet the needs of all tenants for affordable food or to maintain and restore the commons – the housing complex itself" (Graham and Cornwell 2009: 52, emphasis in original). They identify the practices that are "reclaiming the commons" by increasing

233

publicly accessible garden space in the city of Holyoke, and the tough decisions being made about how to share out common space to landless immigrants keen to farm (2009: 53). Added to these complex dynamics of interdependence they identify unique dynamics of organizational growth that (1) is membership-led and community driven, (2) emerges though a process of organic/logical evolution, and (3) is fuelled by transforming individuals (2009: 55–62). By producing this collaborative knowledge of change, the organizations and the social economy of which they are a part become more credible (and therefore powerful) and available as inspirations and models for development in other regions.

In another context researchers have begun to draw on ecological dynamics of development to understand the choices about development pathways facing poor rural communities in the Philippines. In collaboration with community-based researchers, Gibson and colleagues (2010) have identified many of the diverse economic practices and cultural traditions that sustain local social and environmental well-being at the municipal level. Guided by Jacobs' ecologically inspired discussion of economic diversity and the resilience of regions (2000), they have theorized strategies for strengthening local economies by maintaining and proliferating diverse economic relations – including both a wider range of sectors as well as different transactions, forms of labour and enterprise types. Here we see conceptual extension as a means of bringing theory to bear on post-development possibilities.

The aim of post-development theorizing about local and regional development does not preclude involvement of people and places with capitalist enterprise, wage labour, formal markets or mainstream financial institutions. This is perhaps where there is most need for new concepts and theories that allow for truly interdependent development. How might localities and regions foster the development of socially and environmentally responsible capitalist enterprises that distribute a share of privately appropriated surplus to community well-being and environmental health as well as providing well-paid and secure employment? Working with capitalist corporations to enhance the resilience of diverse local economies will involve very different strategies than those usually pursued by local economic development agencies (see, for example, Gibson-Graham 2006: 181–183).

Finally, and perhaps most importantly, academics and public intellectuals are in a position to foster and spread the post-development ethos, including its stance of "not knowing" (or not knowing too much) and its consequent openness to possibility and plurality:

> future society probably must be pluralist in all its organizations including the economic. There will be action and interaction of publicly owned firms and private firms, the market and planning, entities of paternalistic style, capitalist and social. Every juncture, the nature of every activity, the level of evolution and the development of every community, will require a special treatment...not limited to one form of organization if we believe in and love man, his liberty, and justice, and democracy.
>
> (Arizmendiarrieta, quoted in Whyte and Whyte 1988: 239)

References

Amin, A. (ed.) (2009) *The Social Economy: International Perspectives on Economic Solidarity*, London: Zed Books.

Butler, J. (1993) *Bodies that Matter: On the Discursive Limits of "Sex"*, New York and London: Routledge.

Carnegie, M. (2008) "Development prospects in Eastern Indonesia learning from Oelua's diverse economy", *Asia Pacific Viewpoint* 49, 3, 294–304.

Chambers, R. and Conway, G. (1992) "Sustainable rural livelihoods: practical concepts for the 21st century", *IDS Discussion Paper* 296 IDS: Brighton.

Escobar, A. (1995) *Encountering Development: The Making and Unmaking of the Third World*, Princeton, NJ: Princeton University Press.

Gibson, K. (2001) "Regional subjection and becoming", *Environment and Planning D: Society and Space* 19, 6, 639–667.

Gibson, K. Cahill, A. and McKay, D. (2010) "Rethinking the dynamics of rural transformation: performing different development pathways in a Philippine municipality", *Transactions of the Institute of British Geographers* (forthcoming).

Gibson-Graham, J.K. (2003) "Enabling ethical economies: cooperativism and class", *Critical Sociology* 29, 2, 123–161.

Gibson-Graham, J.K. (2005) "Surplus possibilities: postdevelopment and community economies," *Singapore Journal of Tropical Geography* 26, 4–26.

Gibson-Graham, J.K. (2006) *A Postcapitalist Politics*, Minneapolis: University of Minnesota Press.

Gibson-Graham, J.K. (2008) "Diverse economies: performative practices for 'other worlds'", *Progress in Human Geography* 32, 5, 613–632.

Graham, J. and Cornwell, J. (2009) "Building community economies in Massachusetts: an emerging model of economic development?", in A. Amin (ed.) *The Social Economy: International Perspectives on Economic Solidarity*, London and New York: Zed Books, 37–65.

Healy, S. and Graham, J. (2008) "Building community economies: a postcapitalist project of sustainable development", (D. Ruccio (ed.) *Economic Representations: Academic and Everyday*, New York: Routledge, 291–314.

Jacobs, J. (2000) *The Nature of Economies*, New York: Vintage Books.

Law, J. and Urry, J. (2004) "Enacting the social", *Economy and Society* 33, 390–410.

Lechat, N. (2009) "Organizing for the solidarity economy in south Brazil", in A. Amin (ed.) *The Social Economy: International Perspectives on Economic Solidarity,* London and New York: Zed Books, 159–175.

McGregor, A. (2009) "New possibilities? Shifts in post-development theory and practice", *Geography Compass* 10, 1–15.

Mendell, M. (2009) "The three pillars of the social economy: the Quebec experience", in A. Amin (ed.) *The Social Economy: International Perspectives on Economic Solidarity,* London and New York: Zed Books, 176–207.

Mitchell, T. (2005) "The work of economics: how a discipline makes its world", *European Journal of Sociology* XLVI, 297–320.

Neamtan, N. (2008) "Chantier de l'Economic Sociale: building the solidarity economy in Quebec", in J. Allard, C. Davidson and J. Matthaei (eds) *Solidarity Economy: Building Alternatives for People and Planet*, Chicago: Changemaker Publications, 268–276.

Pretes, M. and Gibson, K. (2008) "Openings in the body of 'capitalism': capital flows, trust funds and diverse economic possibilities in Kiribati", *Asia Pacific Viewpoint* 49, 3, 381–391.

Rigg, J., Bebbington, A., Gough, K., Bryceson, D., Agergaard, J., Fold, N. and Tacoli, C. (2009) "The World Development Report 2009 'reshapes economic geography': geographical reflections", *Transactions of the Institute of British Geographers* 34, 2, 128–136 .

Santos, B. de Sousa. (2004) "The WSF: toward a counter-hegemonic globalization", in J. Sen, A. Anand, A. Escobar and P. Waterman (eds) *World Social Forum: Challenging Empires*, New Delhi: The Viveka Foundation, 235–245.

Scoones, I. (1998) "Sustainable rural livelihoods: a framework for analysis", IDS Working Paper No. 72 IDS, Brighton.

Whyte, W.F. and Whyte, K.K. (1988) *Making Mondragón: The Growth and Dynamics of the Mondragón Cooperative Complex*, Ithaca, NY: ILR, Cornell University.

Williams, R. (1983) *Keywords: A Vocabulary of Culture and Society,* Second Edition Oxford: Oxford University Press.

World Bank (2009) *The World Development Report 2009: Reshaping Economic Geography*, Washington: The International Bank for Reconstruction and Development/The World Bank.

Further reading

Amin, A. (ed.) (2009) *The Social Economy: International Perspectives on Economic Solidarity*, London and New York: Zed Books. (An introduction to debates about defining the social economy and ethnographies of social economies around the world.)

Cameron, J. and Gibson, K. (2005) "Alternative pathways to community and economic development: The Latrobe Valley Community Partnering Project", *Geographical Research* 43, 3, 274–285. (Documents post-development action research in a post-industrial region of Australia.)

Escobar, A. (1995) *Encountering Development: The Making and Unmaking of the Third World*, Princeton, NJ: Princeton University Press. (A founding text of post-development theory.)

Escobar, A. (2008) *Territories of Difference: Place, Movements, Life, Redes*, Durham, NC, and London: Duke University Press. (An extended analysis of post-development practice in Colombia's Pacific region.)

Gibson-Graham, J.K. (2006) *A Postcapitalist Politics*, Minneapolis: University of Minnesota Press. (Outlines post-development thinking for economic geography.)

McGregor, A. (2009) "New possibilities? Shifts in post-development theory and practice", *Geography Compass* 10, 1–15. (A review of the evolution of post-development thinking.)

McKinnon, K., Gibson, K. and Malam, L. (eds) (2008) "Critical geographies of the Asia-Pacific Special Issue", *Asia Pacific Viewpoint* 49, 3. (An introduction to post-development thinking and its application in a variety of localities and regions.)

Ziai, A. (ed.) (2007) *Exploring Post-development: Theory and Practice, Problems and Perspectives*, London: Routledge. (Outlines key debates of the post-development approach.)

Section IV

Government and governance

20

The state

Government and governance

Bob Jessop

Introduction

The state is a complex institution that has been studied from diverse entrypoints and standpoints. No single theory could ever exhaust its intricacies. This chapter defines its core features and presents five approaches that provide some theoretical and empirical purchase on its roles in local and regional development. It also advocates studying the state in terms of its central role in meta governance, i.e. in articulating government and governance at different scales and across different social fields. Analyses should also draw on several disciplinary perspectives, consider different kinds of state and political regime, and explore how they are embedded in wider sets of social relations. These suggestions imply that, despite recurrent tendencies to reify the state and treat it as standing outside and above society, the state and its projects cannot be adequately understood apart from their relations to wider sets of social relations.

The state

The state is so taken for granted in everyday life that social forces often discover many of its complexities only when they seek to change it. While such complexities have led some analysts to undertake particular case studies and ignore general questions about statehood, states, or state power, such issues are valid research topics. Five approaches are especially productive: the Weberian account in terms of the territorialization of political power; the Marxist approach to the state as a social relation; critical discourse analysis on the political imaginaries that frame the nature and purposes of government; the Foucauldian approach to technologies of government (or governmentality); and work on governance, multi-level governance, network governance, and meta governance.

Recognizing the complex nature of the state, Max Weber, the German social scientist, addressed it in terms of means rather than ends. He famously defined the modern state as a 'human community that (successfully) claims the monopoly of the legitimate use of physical force within a given territory' (Weber 1948: 78). Similar definitions from other scholars highlight its formal sovereignty *vis-à-vis* its own population and other states. Thus viewed, the state's key features are state territory, a state apparatus, and a state population. This does not mean that modern states exercise power mainly through direct and immediate coercion – this would be a

239

sign of crisis or state failure – but rather that coercion is their last resort in enforcing binding decisions. If state power is deemed legitimate, compliance normally follows without such recourse and is often mediated through micro-techniques that seem to have little if anything to do with the state (cf. Bratsis 2006; Miller and Rose 2008).

More generally, building on Weber and like-minded scholars, some theorists regard the essence of the state (both pre-modern and modern) as the territorialization of political authority. This involves the intersection of politically organized coercive and symbolic power, a clearly demarcated core territory, and a resident population on which political decisions are collectively binding. This draws attention to the variable ensemble of technologies and practices that produce, naturalize, and manage territorial space as a bounded container within which political power is wielded to achieve various, more or less consistent, and changing policy objectives. Almost all territorial states have territorial subdivisions with more or less wide-ranging political and administrative powers and some autonomy from the central state apparatus. This provides the framework for cooperation and competition among local and regional authorities as well as their relations to the national territorial state and, directly or indirectly, to trans- and supranational authorities and institutions. The growing importance of the supranational from the 1970s onwards (putting aside previous patterns of historical empire, suzerainty, dependency, colonization, and imperial conquest) casts doubt on the common assumption that states are typically national states or, even more inadequately, nation-states. This assumption is still reflected in attempts to make sense of the European Union, for example, as a rescaled 'national' state. In contrast, others ask whether the EU is reviving medieval political patterns (neo-medievalism), is a new form of territorial state, or represents an emerging post-sovereign form of authority (with emphasis in this case falling on the open method of coordination

that has been adopted in some policy areas). One might also ask whether the rapid expansion of transnational regimes indicates the emergence of global governance or even a world state.

We can supplement the Weberian definition by noting the role of discursive and material practices in constituting the territorial boundaries of states and in redefining the division between the state qua institutional ensemble and other institutional orders and the everyday life in a given society. Noting how the state is related to other institutional orders in society, such as economy, family, religion, sport, art, or 'civil society' does not exclude (indeed, it assumes) specifically state-generated and state-mediated processes. The form and dynamic of political struggle is typically relatively autonomous from other sites and forms of struggle and may well create major disjunctions between politics and the organization of other fields of life. Well-known examples include the disjunction between the organization of the real and/or financial economies and the boundaries of different tiers and branches of government, creating potential problems of economic performance and political governance. The so-called relative autonomy of the political is what motivates many interests and forces to conduct struggles addressed to the state and/or to seek to transform the state, its capacities, and the forms of its intervention. From the viewpoint of local and regional (as well as supranational) government and governance, such struggles could turn on the extent and forms of areal differentiation, centre-periphery relations, the scalar division of political responsibilities and rights to raise revenue, and the chance to jump scale to secure political advantage over rivals and adversaries. There are significant cross-national differences in these regards that shape the capacities of local, urban, metropolitan, and regional authorities to enhance economic growth, competitiveness, and effective subnational government. Political practices at these levels are never confined to a given area or scale, of course, any more than is the case for the conditions for economic performance (cf. Arts *et al.* 2009; Cox 1998; Jessop 2002).

Organized coercion is just one state capacity among many forms of 'hard power' and co-exists with forms of 'soft power' rooted in socio-cultural relations. Thus another influential theorist, Antonio Gramsci, defined the state as 'political society + civil society'; and analysed state power in modern democratic societies as based on 'hegemony armoured by coercion'. He defined hegemony as the successful mobilization and reproduction of the 'active consent' of dominated groups by the ruling class through its political, intellectual, and moral leadership. In turn, for Gramsci, force refers to coercion that aims to bring the mass of the people into conformity and compliance with the requirements of a specific mode of growth. This approach reminds us that the state only exercises power by projecting and realizing state capacities beyond the narrow boundaries of state; and that domination and hegemony can be exercised on either side of any official public–private divide (for example, state support for paramilitary groups like the Italian fascisti or, conversely, state education in relation to intellectual and moral hegemony). It also suggests a continuum of bases of state power ranging from active hegemony through passive revolution (change without popular mobilization) and force-fraud-corruption to an open war on sections of the population. Gramsci was also sensitive to the spatial aspects of state power: he analysed the problems of building national unity due to local and regional economic, political, social, and linguistic differences as well as to uneven development, focusing especially on the 'Southern Question', i.e. the challenges created by the 'backwardness' of Southern Italy (Gramsci 1971, 1978; cf. Agnew 1995; Jessop 2007).

One way to move beyond the Weberian and Gramscian focus on coercion and hegemony, even allowing for socio-spatial differentiation, is to explore the state in terms of 'governance + government' or 'governance

in the shadow of hierarchy'. An influential approach to local and regional development in this regard is that promoted by scholars inspired by Foucault (e.g. Isin 2000). They emphasize the micro-foundations of state power in specific techniques of governmentality, i.e. the distinctive rationalities and disciplinary practices involved in shaping individual conduct and the overall properties of a given population (Miller and Rose 2008). These techniques often cross-cut the public–private divide and involve diverse institutions, professions, and practices. This poses the question of how multiple micro-powers can be combined to produce the semblance of macro-order by bringing individuals into conformity with the requirements of specific modalities of macro-power relations and/or be deployed to manage the effects of fragmentation and exclusion through targeted economic and social policies.

A fourth source of insight into state power comes from 'critical discourse analysts' who explore how discourse(s) shape the state and orient action towards it (e.g. Hansen and Stepputat 2001; Scott 1998). The development of broad economic and political visions as well as specific policy paradigms is relevant here. Given the multiplicity of competing visions (at most there is a dominant or hegemonic discourse) that orient the actions of political forces, this reinforces the view of the state as a polyvalent, polycontextual phenomenon. This becomes especially clear when we consider the many scales and sites on which the state is said to operate and highlights once again problems of institutional integration and the distribution of state functions and powers.

These arguments, insights, and questions have been synthesized within the strategic-relational approach to the state developed by Jessop (1990, 2002, 2007). Inspired by Marx, Gramsci, and Poulantzas, Jessop analyses the state as a social relation. This elliptical phrase implies that, whether regarded as a thing (or, better, an institutional ensemble) or as a rational subject (or, better, the repository of specific political capacities and resources), the state is far from a passive instrument or neutral actor. It is an ensemble of power centres and capacities that offer unequal chances to different forces within and outside the state. A given type of state, a given state form, a given form of regime will be more accessible to some forces than others according to the strategies they adopt to gain or influence state power; and it will be more tractable for some economic or political strategies than others because of its preferred modes of intervention and resources. In turn, the effectiveness of state capacities depends on links to forces and powers that exist and operate beyond the state's formal boundaries. Moreover, since it is not a subject, the state does not and, indeed, cannot, exercise power. Instead its powers (plural) are activated in specific conjunctures by changing sets of politicians and state officials located in specific parts of the state. This differential impact on political forces' capacity to pursue their interests depends in part on their goals, strategies and tactics. Political forces will usually consider the prevailing and, perhaps, future balance of forces within and beyond a given state. How far and in what ways state powers (and any associated liabilities or weak points) are actualized depends on the action, reaction, and interaction of specific social forces located in and beyond this complex ensemble. If an overall strategic line is discernible, it is due to strategic coordination enabled by the grid of the state system and the parallel power networks that cross-cut and integrate its formal structures. Such unity is improbable because the state is shot through with contradictions and struggles and its political agents must always take account of (potential) mobilization by a wide range of forces beyond the state, engaged in struggles to transform it, determine its policies, or simply resist it from afar. The strategic-relational approach covers all aspects of social domination, including class, gender, ethnicity, 'race', generation, religion, political affiliation, or regional location.

Applying this approach

There are many ways to study states on different scales with this approach. Three major foci are: (1) the distinctive material, social, and spatio-temporal features of the state and its relations to the wider political system and lifeworld; (2) the state's role in reproducing the economic and extra-economic conditions for capital accumulation; and (3) the relations between the state as a complex organ of government and broader patterns of governance in the wider society.

First, one could analyse six interrelated dimensions of the state's institutional materiality, discursive features, and spatio-temporal matrices. These are modes of political representation and their articulation; the vertical, horizontal, and transversal articulation of the state as an institutional ensemble and its demarcation from, and relation to, other states; mechanisms and modes of state intervention and their overall articulation; the political projects and demands advanced by different social forces within and beyond the state system; the state projects that seek to impose relative unity on state activities through a distinctive statecraft and to regulate the state's boundaries as a precondition for such efforts; and the hegemonic projects that seek to reconcile the particular and the universal by linking the state's purposes into a broader – but always selective – political, intellectual and moral vision of the public interest. One should not explore these dimensions solely at the national level because they also depend on broader areal and scalar grids of political practice.

Second, regarding capital accumulation and/or economic development, one can explore the roles of the state at various scales from the neighbourhood up to the world market or world society in facilitating profitable economic activities by private capital; in securing the overall economic and social reproduction of the labour force as workers and citizens (or subjects); the dominant, nodal, and other scales on which the most important economic and social policies are made and implemented; and the modes of governance adopted by states to compensate for market failures. We can compare states in all four respects. Thus the Keynesian welfare national state that characterized economic and social policy formation and implementation of Atlantic Fordism can be contrasted with the tendentially emerging Schumpeterian workfare post-national regime in the after-Fordist period. The third term in this contrast refers explicitly to the shift from the dominance of the national scale in economic and social policy-making to a more complex scalar division in this regard. This is reflected in the increased importance of local and regional government and governance arrangements as well as the expansion of trans- and supranational regimes (for further discussion, see Jessop 2002).

Third, governance refers to mechanisms and strategies of coordination in the face of complex reciprocal interdependence among operationally autonomous actors, organizations, and functional systems. Four main forms exist: markets, hierarchies, networks, and solidarity; states have a major role in modulating them and ordering them in time-space (see below).

Exploring these themes highlights the role of strategic concepts in analysing state apparatuses and state power. Given social contradictions and political struggles as well as internal conflicts and rivalries among its diverse tiers and branches, the state's capacity to act as a unified political force – insofar as it does – is related to political strategies. State managers (politicians and career officials) are key players here but cannot (or should not) ignore the wider balance of forces. Relevant strategic concepts for analysing states in capitalist societies include state-sponsored accumulation strategies oriented to economic development, state projects oriented to state-building and securing its institutional unity, and hegemonic visions of the nature and purposes of the state for the wider society. These should be related initially to specific economic, political, and social imaginaries and then to the deeper structure and logics of a given social formation and its insertion into the world market, inter-state system, and world society. Such strategies, projects, and visions are most likely to succeed where they address the major structural constraints associated with the dominant institutional orders and the prevailing balance of forces as well as the conjunctural opportunities that could be opened by new alliances, strategies, spatio-temporal horizons of action, and so on. A dialectics of path-dependency and path-shaping operates in these regards. This account can be applied to specific political periods, stages, or conjunctures by examining four topics.

First, what, if any, is the dominant *Vergesellschaftungsprinzip* (or principle of *societalization*) and how is it related to state formation and transformation? Among the competing principles are marketization, internal or external security, environmental stewardship, citizenship, the rule of law, nationalism, ethnicity, and theocracy. Any of these (or others) could (and have) become dominant, at least temporarily. Thus a state could operate mainly as a capitalist state, military power, theocratic regime, representative democratic regime answerable to civil society, apartheid state, ethico-political state, and so on (cf. Mann 1986). It follows that capital accumulation is not always the best entrypoint for studying the complexities of the social world even though one might later ask whether states that seem to prioritize, say, national security and nation-building actually pursue policies that favour capital (e.g. East Asian developmental states). Different crystallizations of state power will obviously affect capacities for local and regional as well as national development (e.g. South Africa during and after apartheid, Eastern and Central Europe before, during, and after Soviet domination). Other effects follow from modes of insertion into the world market (e.g. rentier oil states like the United Arab Emirates, small open economies based on a rich ecology of industrial and post-industrial regional clusters and strong local and regional authorities like Switzerland, or low-tech, low-wage exporting economies like Cambodia). Both types of effect illustrate the importance of the embedding (or not) of government and governance in wider sets of social relations.

Second, what are the distinctive patterns of 'structurally inscribed strategic selectivities' of a given state considered as a complex institutional ensemble? Casual observation as well as theoretical and empirical study shows that, despite the formal equivalence among the member states of the United Nations, not all states are equally capable of exercising power internally and/or internationally. This depends on their specific state capacities and powers (in the plural) and their differential vulnerabilities to the activation of counterpowers by other social forces within and beyond the state. States have different problems at home and abroad; different histories; and different capacities to address these problems and reorganize themselves in response. Moreover, in international as well as domestic matters, some are more powerful than others. Even the more powerful states still face external pressures from other states, power centres, and the logic of the world market as well as from the internal impact of their own policies and resulting resistance. Recent US history, financially, economically, militarily, and geo-politically, illustrates this truism and, in the present context, attempts by the federal Administration to displace some costs of decline onto local authorities and states are reflected in fiscal crisis and overburdened government and governance arrangements. A counter-example is the capacity for innovation shown by local and state governments in response to climate change.

Third, how can one describe and explain the historical and substantive organization and configuration of political forces in specific conjunctures and their strategies and tactics, including their capacity to respond to the strategic selectivities inscribed in the state apparatus as a whole? This raises interesting issues about the extent, pattern, and 'policing' of the formal, institutional separation between the state apparatus(es) and other institutional orders; and about the degree of interpersonal or organizational overlap among them. It also raises questions about the changing scales of the state and politics. While the national scale tended to dominate in post-war states in such varied regimes as Atlantic Fordism, import-substitution industrialization, export-led growth, or state socialism, globalization allegedly tends to weaken national states as well as national economies and societies (cf. Collinge (1996) on the 'relativization of scale'). This has enabled the resurgence of local and regional states beneath the national state and prompted the growth of trans- and supranational forms of power. The relative strengths and weaknesses of these scales of political organization and their implications for local and regional development can be studied in terms of the above-mentioned six dimensions, especially inter-scalar articulation and scale jumping. The weakening of national states need not entail that other scales of political organization gain power. This would depend on the adequacy of particular forms of representation, intervention, and internal and external articulation of state apparatuses and the tasks that are set by accumulation strategies, state projects, and hegemonic visions. This raises important questions about the relation between government and governance.

A fourth step leads to the interaction of the relevant political forces on the asymmetrical terrain of the state system and/or at a distance therefrom as they pursue immediate goals, seek to alter the balance of forces and/or the overall configuration of state powers and selectivities.

Bringing governance into the picture

The current fascination with the nature and dynamic of governance at all levels from the local to the global is linked to disillusion with the market and state as coordination mechanisms. Governance is an ambiguous term that can refer to various modes of coordinating social relations marked by complex reciprocal interdependence. Four modes are widely discussed: ex-post coordination based on agents' formally rational pursuit of self-interest (anarchic market exchange); ex-ante imperative coordination of the pursuit of collective goals set from above by relevant authorities (hierarchical command); continuing self-organization based on networks, negotiation, and deliberation to redefine objectives in the light of changing circumstances (heterarchic coordination); and reliance on unconditional commitment to communities of different kinds and scope (coordination via trust and solidarity). Self-organization based on networks is generally regarded as having expanded at the cost of markets and hierarchies. This is supposedly related to its suitability for guiding complex systems that are resistant to top-down internal and/or external command but cannot be left reliably to the market's invisible hand. Many examples exist at local and regional level insofar as problems of economic performance, political legitimacy, and social cohesion (or exclusion) are seen to have specific local and regional features and, by virtue of these complexities, to require 'joined up' (multi-stakeholder) thinking and policies. Less research has been undertaken on solidarity even though it is well suited to governing local problems and is significant in new forms of community participation at local and regional level. This may be because it is harder to roll out and entrench on a national or supranational basis across the full range of policy fields.

States are not confined to hierarchical command but directly employ all four forms of governance in different ways. While states differ in how they combine these mechanisms, their relative weight seems to have shifted in the last 30 years from top-down command towards networked governance in response

to market and state failure, especially where cooperation must cross territorial borders (e.g. in the European Union or in international regimes). Based on negotiation and networks, governance in this sense operates on different scales of organization ranging from localized networks of power and decision-making through national and regional public–private partnerships to the expansion of international and supranational regimes. While the expansion of governance is often assumed to imply a diminution in state capacities, it could enhance the state's power to secure its interests and, indeed, provide it with a new (or expanded) role in meta-governance, i.e. the rebalancing of different forms of governance. This is certainly how its role is conceived in local and regional development, with its turn to governance and governmentality in the shadow of national (or, for the EU, supranational) government supervision and oversight. Indeed, as economic competitiveness becomes a major and comprehensive goal, states (on whatever scale) get more involved in redefining relations between the economic and extra-economic, steering the (re-)commodification of social relations, and coping with the repercussions of the growing dominance of economic logic in the wider society. However, while the micro-social conditions for economic competitiveness may sometimes be better handled now at subnational or cross-border levels, large national states may be better equipped to deal with territorial integration, social cohesion, and social exclusion because of their greater fisco-financial powers and redistributive capacities.

Important differences remain between government and governance regarding modes of economic and social intervention. First, while the sovereign state is essentially a political unit that governs but is not itself governed, self-organization provides the essence of governance. Second, while the sovereign state mainly governs activities on its own territorial domain and defends its territorial integrity against other states and intrusive forces, governance seeks to manage functional interdependencies, whatever their (often variable) territorial scope. These differences explain the growing interest in multi-level governance insofar as it can operate across scales and coordinate state and non-state actors around particular functional problems with a variable territorial geometry. Some theorists emphasize the vertical dimension of coordination (multi-level governance); others focus on the horizontal dimension (network governance). In both cases the state is accorded a continuing role in the organization of reflexive self-organization among multiple stakeholders across several scales of state territorial organization and, indeed, in essentially extra-territorial contexts. But this role is that of primus inter pares in a complex, heterogeneous, and multi-level network rather than as the sovereign authority in a single hierarchical command structure. Thus formal sovereignty is better seen as a series of symbolic and material state capacities than as an overarching, dominant resource. Other stakeholders contribute other symbolic or material resources (e.g. private money, legitimacy, information, expertise, organizational capacities, or power of numbers) to be combined with states' sovereign and other capacities to advance collectively agreed aims and objectives. Thus states' involvement in multi-level governance becomes less hierarchical, less centralized, and less directive and, compared to the clear hierarchy of territorial powers theoretically associated with sovereign states, it typically involves tangled hierarchies and complex interdependence.

If markets and states fail, so does governance. One response to this is the increased attempts by states (especially but not exclusively at the national territorial level) to manage the mix and operation of the four main modes of governance in the light of emerging problems, the mutual interactions of their different forms and effects, and the overall balance of forces. This is expected to improve the performance of each mode of governance and, through judicious re-mixing and recalibration of markets, hierarchy, networks, and solidarity, to achieve the best possible outcomes from the viewpoint of those engaged in metagovernance. In this sense it also means the organization of the conditions of governance in terms of their structurally inscribed strategic selectivity, i.e. in terms of their asymmetrical privileging of some outcomes over others.

Governments play a major and growing role in all aspects of metagovernance: they get involved in redesigning markets, in constitutional change and the juridical re-regulation of organizational forms and objectives, in organizing the conditions for self-organization, and, most importantly, in collibration. They provide the ground rules for governance and the regulatory order in and through which governance partners can pursue their aims; ensure the compatibility or coherence of different governance mechanisms and regimes; act as the primary organizer of the dialogue among policy communities; deploy a relative monopoly of organizational intelligence and information in order to shape cognitive expectations; serve as a 'court of appeal' for disputes arising within and over governance; seek to rebalance power differentials by strengthening weaker forces or systems in the interests of system integration and/or social cohesion; try to modify the self-understanding of identities, strategic capacities, and interests of individual and collective actors in different strategic contexts and hence alter their implications for preferred strategies and tactics; facilitate collective learning about functional linkages and material interdependencies among different sites and spheres of action; and assume political responsibility in the event of governance failure. In this last respect, another motive for metagovernance is to guide the effects of governance arrangements on political stability and social cohesion (or overall coordination) of different governance regimes and mechanisms (Jessop (2002) on national states;

Zeitlin and Trubek (2003) on Europe; Torfing and Sørensen (2007) on democratic network governance; Slaughter (2004) on the world order). Meta-governance also serves to modify the strategic selectivity of the state and shift the balance of forces in favour of one set of forces or another. Jumping scale is one aspect of this. This emerging role means that networking, negotiation, noise reduction, and negative as well as positive coordination occur 'in the shadow of hierarchy' (Scharpf 1994: 40). Unfortunately, since every practice is prone to failure, metagovernance is also likely to fail. This implies that there is no Archimedean point from which governance or metagovernance can be guaranteed success.

Concluding remarks

This chapter has explored different dimensions of statehood, the state apparatus, and state power as well as broader issues of governance and metagovernance. It has used occasional references to the local and regional aspects of these complex phenomena but it has proved impossible to explore these aspects in detail because of the priority of setting out the broader theoretical framework. If readers have found the latter interesting, they must now face the challenge of applying it in these fields.

References

Arts, B., Langendijk, A. and van Houtum, H. (eds) (2009) *The Disoriented State: Shifts in Governmentality, Territoriality and Governance*, Heidelberg: Springer.

Bratsis, P. (2006) *Everyday Life and the State*, London: Anthem.

Collinge, C. (1999) 'Self-organization of society by scale: a spatial reworking of regulation theory', *Environment and Planning D: Society and Space*, 17 (5), 557–574.

Cox, K. (1998) 'Spaces of dependence, spaces of engagement and the politics of scale: looking for local politics', *Political Geography*, 17 (1), 1–23.

Gramsci, A. (1971) *Selections from the Prison Notebooks*, London: Lawrence & Wishart.

Gramsci, A. (1978) *Selections from Political Writings (1921–1926)*, London: Lawrence & Wishart.

Isin, E.F. (ed.) (2000) *Democracy, Citizenship and the Global City*, London: Routledge.

Jessop, B. (1990) *State Theory: Putting the Capitalist State in its Place*, Cambridge: Polity.

Jessop, B. (2002) *The Future of the Capitalist State*, Cambridge: Polity.

Jessop, B. (2007) *State Power: A Strategic-Relational Approach*, Cambridge: Polity.

Hansen, T.B. and Stepputat, F. (eds) (2001) *States of Imagination: Ethnographic Explorations of the Postcolonial State*, Durham, NC: Duke University Press.

Mann, M. (1986) *Social Sources of State Power, Volume 1*, Cambridge: Cambridge University Press.

Miller, P. and Rose, N. (2008) *Governing the Present. Administering Economic, Social and Personal Life*, Cambridge: Polity.

Scharpf, F.W. (1994) 'Games real actors could play: positive and negative co-ordination in embedded negotiations', *Journal of Theoretical Politics*, 6 (1), 27–53.

Scott, J.C. (1998) *Seeing Like a State, How Certain Scheme to Improve the Human Conditions Have Failed*, New Haven: Yale University Press.

Slaughter, A.M. (2004) *A New World Order*, Princeton: Princeton University Press.

Torfing, J. and Sørensen, E. (eds) (2007) *Theories of Democratic Network Governance*, Basingstoke: Palgrave.

Weber, M. (1948) 'Politics as a vocation', in *Essays from Max Weber*, London: Routledge & Kegan Paul.

Zeitlin, J.M. and Trubek, D. (eds) (2003) *Governing Work and Welfare in a New Economy. European and American Experiments*, Oxford: Oxford University Press.

Further reading

The state

Jessop, B. (1990) *State Theory: Putting the Capitalist State in its Place*, Cambridge: Polity.

Painter, J. and Jeffrey, A. (2009) *Political Geography: An Introduction to Space and Power*, London: Sage (second edition).

Applying the approach

Brenner, N. (2004) *New State Spaces: Urban Governance and the Rescaling of Statehood*, Oxford: Oxford University Press.

Jessop, B. (1990) *The Future of the Capitalist State*, Cambridge:Polity.

Bringing governance in

Bevir, M. (ed.) (2010) *The Sage Handbook of Governance*, London: Sage.

Miller, P. and Rose, N. (2008) *Governing the Present*, Cambridge: Polity.

21

Putting 'the political' back into the region

Power, agency and a reconstituted regional political economy

Andrew Cumbers and Danny MacKinnon

Introduction

The concept of power has been present within regional studies since at least the 1970s, when the introduction of Marxist perspectives led to regions being analysed in the context of wider processes of capital accumulation and uneven development (e.g. Massey 1979). Power was also implicated in parallel debates over underdevelopment and dependency theory in the related field of Development Studies concerned with how the Global South (developing countries) continued to be exploited by the North through relations of informal imperialism (Potter *et al.* 2008) Until recently, however, there was a surprising lack of conceptual discussion about the role of power in local and regional development. In particular, regional studies and economic geography have lagged behind other areas of social science in engaging with post-structuralist conceptions of power (see Deleuze and Guattari 1987, Foucault 1980, Latour 1993).

Conventionally, power has been viewed as a fixed capacity that is held or possessed by a particular individual, group or organisation (Allen 2003). This definition of power as a 'centred' capacity identifies two distinct forms of power relation (ibid.). First, there is the instrumentalist or 'negative' notion of power 'over' others, whereby particular actors subject others to their will. According to Dahl's influential definition, "A has power over B to the extent that he or she can get B to do something that B would not otherwise do" (Dahl 1957, quoted in Sharp *et al.* 2000: 5). This meaning of power underpinned the community power debates of the 1960s and 1970s in which pluralists argued that power was dispersed between different local groups whilst elitists contended that it was wielded by a particular set of actors (the elite) within the community (see Stoker 1995). The second meaning, by contrast, views power as an associational process where people come together to develop collective projects in the pursuit of shared goals. This is a more positive or 'softer' sense of the power to get things done with power playing a facilitating rather than a constraining role.

Post-structuralist conceptions of power have become increasingly influential across the social sciences and humanities in recent decades, viewing power as a fluid and dynamic medium that is constructed and exercised through specific discourses and forms of knowledge that permeate society (Allen 2003, Deleuze and Guattari 1987, Foucault 1980, Latour 1993, Sharp *et al.* 2000).

This approach has begun to filter into regional studies in recent years, particularly through the concept of the 'relational region' (Allen and Cochrane 2007, Allen *et al*. 1998, MacLeod and Jones 2007). From this perspective, regions are increasingly viewed as sites of ongoing social processes between competing forces and actors rather than as coherent and fixed entities. According to Allen and Cochrane (2007: 1163):

> The diverse ways in which the 'coherence' of a region is constructed and acted upon by different, and often new, political actors is the result of a complex set of political mobilisations at any one point in time [...] the invention and reinvention of regions is a constant.

By viewing regions as 'open, discontinuous spaces' (Allen *et al*. 1998: 5), the concept of the relational region challenges traditional views of regions as territorially bounded or enmeshed in a hierarchy of nested scales (i.e. regional, national, supra-national, global). Instead, relational thinking views 'the region' as part of a set of horizontal spatial networks connecting the local with the global, informed by the actor-network theory of Latour (1993).

In this chapter, we aim critically to assess the value of post-structuralist conceptions of power in relation to underlying processes of local and regional development. In so doing, we recognise that they provide important insights into the fluid and dynamic processes by which localities and regions are constructed. At the same time, however, we agree with Hudson (2007) that regions continue to be the site of historically rooted and territorially embedded social relations (MacKinnon *et al*. 2009). Accordingly, we argue for the development of a revived and reconstituted ('new') political economy approach (Goodwin 2004, Hudson 2006). This emphasises the institutionalised processes through which regions evolve as part of the spatially

uneven development of capitalist social relations (MacKinnon *et al*. 2009, Smith 1984), incorporating certain post-structuralist insights on power, networks and space. We begin by assessing recent regional development discourses of established conceptions of power. We then discuss some of the possibilities and limitations of relational accounts of power and space. This is followed by a discussion of how certain post-structuralist insights might be integrated into a 'new' political economy approach to local and regional development.

Power in local and regional development: orthodox approaches

Power has rarely been an explicit theme of the 'new regionalist' literature of the 1990s and early 2000s, underpinned by the belief that regions had become more prominent as units of economic organisation and political action (Amin 1999, Lovering 1999, Morgan 1997). Nonetheless, certain strands of 'new regionalist' research were informed by an implicit notion of power derived from studies of urban governance and urban regime theory in particular (Stoker 1995), involving a blending of interests as private 'rentier' groups and local government came together to promote cities and attract mobile investment (cf. Logan and Molotch 1987).

For instance, the concept of territorial innovation systems is based on leading firms, universities, research institutes and regional government agencies working together to promote innovation (Cooke 1997). According to Asheim (2000: 427), the governance of territorial innovation systems is based on close "university–industry cooperation, where large and smaller firms establish network relationships with other firms, universities, research institutes, and government agencies based on public–private partnerships". The concept of a territorial innovation system overlaps substantially with the interactive model of innovation developed by theorists of innovation (Freeman 1994). In place of the traditional linear conception of innovation focused on large corporations and formal research and development in scientific laboratories, the interactive approach views new and improved products and services as emerging out of collaboration between different organisations, particularly large corporations and their suppliers, but also involving universities, industry bodies, research institutes and government agencies (Cooke and Morgan 1998).

The influential work of the 1980s and early 1990s on industrial districts also incorporated a sense of power as a collective capacity. As a number of scholars stressed, the success of the Italian districts was deeply rooted in local institutions and culture (Amin 2000). Within the strongly communitarian political cultures of Central and North Eastern Italy (socialist in Tuscany and Emilia-Romagna, Catholic in Veneto), political parties, local authorities, labour unions, industry associations and chambers of commerce developed a sophisticated reservoir of knowledge, skills and resources for the use of firms and entrepreneurs. In particular, the sharing of knowledge and ideas between small firms facilitated incremental forms of continuous innovation, although critics such as Harrison (1997) argued that the emphasis on small firm innovation was overstated in the face of the continued dominance of large firms.

The emphasis on collaborative inter-firm and inter-organisational relations also reflects the influence of network approaches. For instance, Cooke and Morgan (1993) advocated the network paradigm as a new approach to regional development, emphasising the interactive and cooperative properties of 'flat' horizontal networks compared to vertical hierarchies and markets based on economic rationality. More recently, researchers have contrasted the 'softer' kinds of power evident in alternative food networks against the hierarchical relations by which larger multinational corporations control mainstream commodity chains (Morgan et al. 2006).

In general terms, as Allen (2003) argues, the conception of power as a 'centred' capacity conflates the possession of the resources upon which power resides and the actual exercise of that power. As a result of its reliance upon this approach, 'new regionalist' research has seriously under-estimated the difficulties encountered by dominant coalitions in the negotiation and implementation of particular agendas and projects, failing to allow sufficient scope for contestation and resistance (MacKinnon et al. 2002).

There has also been little interest in unequal power relationships between different interests and groups. Research on territorial innovation systems and 'learning regions' (Cooke 1997, Morgan 1997), for instance, views relations between firms in the supply chain as harmonious and collaborative, prompting some case study research into the unequal relations between transnational corporations (TNCs) and small and medium-sized enterprises (SMEs) (Christopherson and Clark 2007), which may involve the former exercising power 'over' the latter. Other research has assessed the potential for regional institutional capacity to be 'captured' by TNCs in the face of intense inter-regional competition for mobile investment (Phelps 2000). By contrast, in the research on alternative food networks cited above, 'soft' power is invoked without much recognition of the scope for conflict (Morgan et al. 2006). This reflects how the prevailing conception of power as an associational capacity privileges cooperation over competition (Markusen 1996), failing to attach sufficient weight to one of the key underlying imperatives of capitalism.

'Spatial vocabularies of power': relational approaches

In contrast to the rather narrow conception of power that characterises much of the existing work in regional development studies, a number of human geographers have developed more sophisticated and multi-faceted perspectives on the operation of power, drawing upon post-structural theories (Allen 2003, Massey 2005, Sharp *et al.* 2000). One key source of inspiration here is Michel Foucault's 'capillary' conception of power as a fluid and mobile medium which circulates throughout society (Foucault 1980, Sharp *et al.* 2000). Deleuze and Guattari's (1987) writings also evoke a similar sense of the fluid and 'unfolding' properties of power, reflecting the immanence of the social relations between people and things.

Informed by such post-structuralist conceptions, Allen (2003) defines power as a relational effect of social interaction. In place of the conventional geographical assumption that power is territorially bounded and organised across nested spatial scales (the local, the regional, the national, etc.), Allen favours a more open topological approach which sees power as a product of the networks and associations constructed across space. This offers the important insight that the possession of power must be distinguished from the actual exercise or activation of this power (Allen 2003). As such, it is the processes through which power is exercised in particular temporal and spatial contexts that generate discernible material effects rather than the mere possession of power itself. For example, regional development agencies in England have the capacity and resources to develop regional economic strategies as the result of a specific Act of Parliament (Jones 2001, Pike and Tomaney 2009a). Yet it is the activation of these powers, partly through the implementation of their respective strategies, that allows RDAs to have material effects on the performance of the regional economy. This is crucially dependent upon building relations with a host of other regional organisations and interests (e.g. firms, business networks, universities, local government and trade unions), requiring frequent liaison and support.

One of the major contributions of Allen's (2003) work is to distinguish between different

modes of power and the relations of proximity and reach through which they are exercised spatially. Other modes of power besides domination and expertise include: coercion, grounded in the threat of force or negative sanctions; manipulation, involving the concealment of intent; seduction, which engages subjects' own interests and desires; and negotiation and persuasion, which are associated with associational forms of power through the construction of shared agendas. Interestingly, Allen suggests that the 'softer' types of power relation such as seduction and manipulation often have a greater spatial reach than authority. The fact that the latter is dependent upon recognition by others means that direct presence is often important, while domination often triggers an opposing reaction (Sharp *et al.* 2000). From the perspective of 'getting things done' at the regional level, key organisations such as RDAs remain dependent on localised interactions and the generation of trust between social actors, in order to achieve particular ends. In this respect, despite the limitations highlighted above, the 'positive' conception of power as a collective capacity (Cooke and Morgan 1998) remains valuable for research on local and regional development.

Before turning to our 'new' political economy approach, we offer three critical comments on post-structuralist conceptions of power and space. First, such approaches tend to restrict power to questions of its exercise and effects (Allen 2003), arguing that power is performed through the construction of spatially extensive networks and associations rather than being possessed by 'centred' organisations and interests. While this approach raises exciting new research questions, power does not need to be viewed in such binary terms (MacLeod and Jones 2007). The rejection of conventional notions of power as a capacity seems overly narrow and limiting, undermining the vital distinction between capacity or potential and effects by conceptually privileging the latter over the former (Sayer 2004). In response, there is a need to recover a sense of power as capacity, alongside the concern with effects, focusing attention on the practical 'entanglements' of different forms of power (Sharp *et al.* 2000). A fruitful line of inquiry here may be to examine uneven flows of power within and between regions, raising the intriguing research question of the extent to which uneven flows of power become temporarily 'congealed' around particular regional organisations and interests.

Second, topological perspectives also seem to neglect the role of prior processes of historical sedimentation through which regions are constructed (MacLeod and Jones 2001, Paasi 1996). Fundamentally, relational perspectives underplay the weight of inherited forms of attachment and belonging, reflecting the theoretical and political agenda of developing a progressive sense of place which originally inspired them (Massey 1994). This point is also evident in relation to the territorial embeddedness of global justice networks in terms of how these are constructed out of temporally and spatially specific practices and resources (Cumbers *et al.* 2008). We can only understand why some regions become sites for resistance and alternative political projects at a particular moment in time (e.g. Red Clydeside, Red Bologna or the Zapatistas in Chiapas) if we understand how they are constituted through past struggles and conflicts in uneven and variegated ways, endowing them with certain properties and identities (MacLeod and Jones 2001, Paasi 1996). Regions are, of course, subject to subsequent processes of transformation and 'becoming', but inherited attachments condition how these processes are played out.

Third, the undoubted appeal of relational approaches in liberating research from traditional conceptions of space and power is cast into sharp focus by the entrenched contours of uneven development under capitalism. To return to the fundamentals of Harvey's original insights on the spatial fix (see Harvey 1982), spatial inequalities between cities and regions are the result of past and existing

struggles whose objective is the possession of power and its operationalisation and reproduction in particular places (under capitalism surplus value is the dominant though not the only measure of economic power). Fundamentally, a political economy perspective emphasises the social and political processes surrounding the formation of the human landscape over time and the stubborn territorial 'permanences' that are constructed out of these processes (Harvey 1996). This raises important questions of agency – arguably underplayed in the writings of Harvey and other political economic theorists – concerning the social groups and interests that construct such permanences. While this is largely an empirical question, it directs attention towards the role of regional elites in regulating conflictual social relations through the mobilisation of distinctive ideological and political apparatuses (Lipietz 1994). Such 'permanences' are, of course, always temporary, being subject to transformation through social processes that are open, contested and contradictory, reflecting the dialectical tensions between fixity and mobility (Harvey 1982, 1996).

Towards a 'new' regional political economy: evolution, power and institutions

In this section, we aim to develop a more integrated approach which remains rooted in a historical-geographical political economy perspective while acknowledging the fluidity and relationality of power (Harvey 2006, Swyngedouw 1997). We favour a dialectical ontology which emphasises the role of class relations and struggles over value capture in driving processes of capital accumulation over time and across space (Harvey 1996). For capital, fixity is as important as mobility for particular periods so as to secure surplus value. For some local and regional actors, concerned with the promotion of sustainable economic development, efforts to capture a share of value from increasingly globalised production networks in the face of competition from other regions (Coe *et al.* 2004, Smith *et al.* 2002) involve the exercising of particular forms of power.

Our 'new' political economy approach (see Goodwin 2004, Hudson 2006) is open to the intersections between the fluid and immanent properties of power and historically rooted and sedimented social relations. It is supported by a critical realist philosophy which contends that capitalist social relations and the creation of value have a real existence, although they are always known and represented through particular cultural and discursive formations (Bhaskar 1989). Such an approach emphasises the importance of regional diversity and variety within an uneven economic landscape, echoing the concerns of the neo-Marxist economic geography of the 1980s and early 1990s (see Massey 1995, Storper and Walker 1989).

In addition, our 'new' political economy approach adopts an evolutionary methodology, highlighting the role of history and more specifically, path dependency, in shaping contemporary patterns of regional development (MacKinnon *et al.* 2009, Pike *et al.* 2009). It conceptualises the evolution of the economic landscape in terms of the interaction between pre-existing regional variety and market-based selection mechanisms (MacKinnon *et al.* 2009). Institutions play a crucial role in mediating such interaction, resulting in path dependence and uneven development.

We view our evolutionary political economy perspective as offering an important corrective to the rather timeless purview of power and space apparent in relational thinking about regions which effectively erases prior processes of historical construction and sedimentation (Jones 2009). The importance of such processes is highlighted by the problems facing old industrial regions, where the legacy of past forms of specialisation and associated social and cultural practices can stymie attempts at economic modernisation and restructuring, developed in response to

the meta-narratives of globalisation and competitiveness (Grabher 1993, Birch *et al.* 2009). Institutional legacies can, in this sense, exhibit powers of conditioning and constraint. As we have argued elsewhere (see MacKinnon *et al.* 2009), however, research must avoid the dangers of over-socialisation whereby specific 'carriers of history' (institutions, habits, technologies, firms) impart strong, self-reinforcing continuities which structure processes of regional economic evolution (Hudson 2005). In this respect, post-structuralist conceptions of power are particularly persuasive because of their emphasis on fluidity, openness and power as a process (Sharp *et al.* 2000). This helps to restore agency to regional actors operating in the context of certain pre-existing regional trajectories and practices.

Understanding the operation of regional power relations therefore requires a sense of regional evolution in the context of a broader landscape of uneven development, an awareness of institutional practices and the operation of the different modalities of power in and across specific regional spaces. Here, we turn to recent research into the economic geography of the life sciences industry by way of illustration (Birch and Cumbers 2009). This reveals a significant instance of 'regional success' in the development of a Scottish 'life sciences' cluster. Against a backdrop of industrial decline, over-dependence upon footloose foreign investment and an older (but still relevant) image of a branch plant economy, the life sciences cluster is significant as one of the few sectors to create professional and skilled employment and one that largely comprises small local knowledge-intensive firms (ibid.)

Understanding the cluster's emergence requires an approach that is not only able to situate it within the historical trajectory of Scotland's political economy and broader processes of uneven development, but is also alert to the operation of the different modalities of power set out above. In the first instance, a long tradition of bio-medical research in

Scottish universities, allied to public sector support for medical research dating back to the 1940s, were critical factors in the cluster's initial emergence. While these regional and national institutional arrangements have been critical, the growth of the Scottish life sciences cluster has been facilitated by wider spatial networks from the outset. Of particular importance are the global knowledge communities within which Scottish scientists and academics operate, and a considerable Scottish scientific diaspora which is reproduced by flows of labour and knowledge of varying durations to and from 'the region'.

The growth of the cluster in recent decades reflects the ability of Scottish actors to leverage power and capture value (in the form of new firm formation and employment) from networks controlled by large TNCs. This suggests the operation of fluid and dynamic power relations that provide opportunities for small and newer actors to reposition themselves within global production networks. In this case, Scottish life science success is explained by the particular positionality (see Sheppard 2002) of Scottish scientists and firms as originators of new products and intellectual property (particularly in the field of healthcare, diagnostics, agriculture and environmental services) in a sector that is heavily knowledge-dependent (Birch and Cumbers 2009).

Despite its success, the long-run evolution of the life sciences cluster still has to confront the asymmetrical power relations in which it is embedded. The major players and final customers of the Scottish life sciences sector are European (predominantly Swiss) and US pharmaceutical multinationals which play a key role in coordinating and controlling production networks. A key constraint on the cluster is the limited availability of finance (particularly venture capital) for firm growth (compared to the South East of England), and its attendant inability to foster larger 'lead' firms capable of playing a more strategic role within the global life sciences network (ibid.)

A final piece of the political-institutional jigsaw is the compelling evidence that Scottish enterprise has 'learnt' from earlier mistakes in its approach to regional development policy over a period of three decades of policy experimentation, avoiding 'cognitive lock-in' (Grabher 1993). This is apparent in its support for local indigenous enterprise and its provision of longer term support for innovation within the life sciences cluster. The evolution of this policy at the Scottish level has been based on sustained collaboration between key actors in government, universities and the business sector, facilitated by a shared commitment to the prosperity of Scotland as a pre-defined regional space (MacLeod 1998), and drawing upon the institutional memory of past successes and failures in economic development policy. In this sense, the development of a life sciences cluster can be seen as an 'effect' of innovation and the construction of relationships between government agencies, researchers and entrepreneurs. At the same time, however, power is also 'centred', congealing around key organisations and individuals, granting them a limited capacity to shape the evolution of the cluster within global production networks controlled by TNCs based elsewhere.

Conclusions

As we argued in the introduction to this chapter, regional studies and economic geography have tended to lag behind other parts of the social sciences and humanities in their engagement with post-structuralist conceptions of power. The prevailing conception of power in local and regional development studies is the associational sense of power as a collective capacity generated in the pursuit of a shared agenda. By contrast, post-structuralist theories view power as a fluid and mobile medium, informed particularly by Foucault's 'capillary' approach. Drawing upon these ideas, Allen (2003) defines power as a relational effect of social interaction, distinguishing between the possession of power and the actual exercising or activation of this power in particular contexts. In response, we argued that power can be both a capacity and effect, raising questions about the practical entanglement of different forms of power (Sharp *et al.* 2000). Relational approaches to regional development also tend to neglect the prior processes of historical construction and sedimentation through which regions are constructed. Finally, there is a need to relate flows of power to processes of uneven development and the creation of spatial 'fixes' and 'permanences' (Harvey 1982, 1996).

Our interest in the development of a 'new' political economy approach is informed by these criticisms of relational accounts of space and power. This approach is concerned with capitalist social relations, value creation and uneven development while remaining open to post-structuralist insights regarding the fluid and immanent properties of power. We adopt an evolutionary methodology, viewing uneven development as the product of an institutionally mediated process of interaction between pre-existing regional variety and market-based selection mechanisms (MacKinnon *et al.* 2009). While institutional legacies exhibit powers of conditioning and constraint, accounts of local and regional 'path dependency' must avoid an over-socialised approach whereby past practices are seen to almost determine future choices. In this context, post-structuralist conceptions of power relations as open and fluid can make an important contribution by restoring agency to regional actors. Indeed, we would argue that research on the practical entanglements of power in processes of local and regional development should examine the processes of 'fixing' by which particular actors and interests seek to stabilise and freeze fluid power relations in order to generate and capture value within global production networks. As our example of the Scottish biotechnology industry indicates, the exercise of purposive agency for development is often a product of such 'fixing' processes

with economic development strategies emerging out of efforts by regional elites to fit wider narratives such as the knowledge economy to the perceived needs of regional economies. In principle, our 'new' political economy approach is applicable to regional economic development in both the Global North and South, emphasising the interaction between local and regional conditions and wider processes of uneven development.

References

Allen, J. (2003) *Lost Geographies of Power*, Blackwell, Oxford.

Allen, J. and Cochrane, A. (2007) 'Beyond the territorial fix: regional assemblages, politics and power', *Regional Studies* 41, 1161–1175.

Allen, J., Massey, D. and Cochrane, A. (1998) *Rethinking the Region*, Routledge, London.

Amin, A. (1999) 'An institutionalist perspective on regional economic development', *International Journal of Urban and Regional Research* 23, 365–378.

Amin, A. (2000) 'Industrial districts', in Sheppard, E. and Barnes, T.J. (eds) *A Companion to Economic Geography*, Blackwell, Oxford, pp. 149–168.

Asheim, B.T. (2000) 'Industrial districts: the contributions of Marshall and beyond', in Clark, G., Feldmann, M.L. and Gertler, M.S. *The Oxford Handbook of Economic Geography*, Oxford University Press, Oxford, pp. 413–431.

Bhaskar, R. (1989) *Reclaiming Reality: A Critical Introduction to Contemporary Philosophy*, Verso, London.

Birch, K. and Cumbers, A. (2009) *Strengthening the Life Sciences in Scotland Policy Report, Centre for Public Policy for Regions*, Universities of Glasgow and Strathclyde, Glasgow.

Birch, K., MacKinnon, D. and Cumbers, A. (2009) 'Old industrial regions in Europe: a comparative assessment of economic performance', *Regional Studies*, 44(1): 35–53.

Christopherson, S. and Clark, J. (2007) 'Power in firm networks: what it means for regional innovation systems', *Regional Studies* 41, 1223–1236.

Coe, N., Hess, M., Yeung, H.W.C., Dicken, P. and Henderson, J. (2004) '"Globalizing" regional development: a global production networks perspective', *Transactions of the Institute of British Geographers NS* 29, 468–484.

Cooke, P. (1997) 'Regions in a global market: the experiences of Wales and Baden-Württemberg',

Review of International Political Economy 4, 349–381.

Cooke, P. and Morgan, K. (1993) 'The network paradigm: new departures in corporate and regional development', *Environment and Planning D: Society and Space* 11, 543–564.

Cooke, P. and Morgan, K. (1998) *The Associational Economy: Firms, Regions, and Innovation,* Oxford University Press, Oxford.

Cumbers, A., MacKinnon, D. and McMaster, R. (2003) 'Institutions, power and space: assessing the limits to institutionalism in economic geography', *European Urban and Regional Studies* 10, 325–342.

Cumbers, A., Routledge, P. and Nativel, C. (2008) 'The entangled geographies of global justice networks', *Progress in Human Geography* 32, 183–201.

Deleuze, G. and Guttari, F. (1987) *A Thousand Plateaus: Capitalism and Schizophrenia,* trans. B. Massumi, University of Minnesota Press, Minneapolis.

Foucault, M. (1980*) Power/Knowledge Selected Interviews*, Harvester Wheatsheaf, Hemel Hempstead.

Freeman, C. (1994) 'The economics of technical change', *Cambridge Journal of Economics* 18, 463–514.

Goodwin, M. (2004) 'Recovering the future: a post-disciplinary perspective on geography and political economy', in Cloke, P., Crang, P. and Goodwin, M. (eds) *Envisioning Human Geographies,* Arnold, London, pp. 65–80.

Grabher, G. (1993) 'The weakness of strong ties: the lock-in of regional development in the Ruhr area', in Grabher G. (ed.) *The Embedded Firm: On the Socio-economics of Industrial Networks,* Routledge, London, pp. 255–277.

Harrison, B. (1997) *Lean and Mean. Why Large Corporations Will Continue to Dominate the Global Economy,* Guildford Press, New York.

Harvey, D. (1982) *The Limits to Capital,* Blackwell, Oxford.

Harvey, D. (1996) *Justice, Nature and the Geography of Difference,* Blackwell, Oxford.

Harvey, D. (2006) *Spaces of Global Captialism: Towards a Theory of Uneven Geographical Development,* Verso, London.

Hudson, R. (2005) 'Rethinking change in old industrial regions: reflecting on the experiences of North East England', *Environment and Planning A* 37, 581–596.

Hudson, R. (2006) 'On what's right and keeping left: or why geography still needs Marxian political economy', *Antipode* 38, 374–395.

Hudson, R. (2007) 'Regions and regional uneven development forever? Some reflective

comments upon theory and practice', *Regional Studies* 41, 1149–1160.

Jones, M. (2001) 'The rise of the regional state in economic governance: 'partnerships for prosperity' or new scales of state power?', *Environment and Planning A* 33, 1185–1211.

Jones, M. (2009) 'Phase space: geography, relational thinking, and beyond', *Progress in Human Geography* 1–20. Onlinefirst, doi: 10.1177/0309132508101599.

Latour, B. (1993) *We Have Never Been Modern,* Harvester Wheatsheaf, Hemel Hempstead.

Lipietz, A (1994) 'The national and the regional: their autonomy vis-à-vis the capitalist world crisis', in Palan, R. and Gills, B. *Transcending the State–Global Divide: a Neo-Structuralist Agenda in International Relations,* Lynne Reimer: London, pp. 23–43.

Logan, J. and Molotch, H. (1987) *Urban Fortunes: The Political Economy of Place,* University of California Press, Berkeley, CA.

Lovering, J. (1999) 'Theory led by policy: the inadequacies of the "new regionalism" (illustrated from the case of Wales)', *International Journal of Urban and Regional Research* 23, 379–395.

MacKinnon, D., Cumbers, A. and Chapman, K. (2002) 'Learning, innovation and regional renewal: a critical appraisal of current debates in regional development studies', *Progress in Human Geography* 26, 293–311.

MacKinnon, D., Cumbers, A., Birch, K., Pike, A. and McMaster, R. (2009) 'Evolution in economic geography: institutions, political economy and regional adaptation', *Economic Geography* 85, 129–150.

MacLeod, G. (1998) 'In what sense a region? Place hybridity, symbolic shape and institutional formation in (post) modern Scotland', *Political Geography* 17, 833–863.

MacLeod, G. and Jones, M. (2001) 'Renewing the geography of regions', *Environment and Planning D', Society and Space* 19, 669–695.

MacLeod, G. and Jones, M. (2007) 'Territorial, scalar, networked, connected: in what sense a "regional world"?', *Regional Studies* 241, 1177–1191.

Markusen, A. (1996) 'Sticky places in slippery space: a typology of industrial districts', *Economic Geography* 72, 293–313.

Massey, D. (1979) 'In what sense a regional problem?', *Regional Studies* 13, 233–243.

Massey, D. (1994) 'A global sense of place', in Massey, D. (ed.) *Place, Space and Gender,* Polity, Cambridge, pp. 146–156.

Massey, D. (1995) *Spatial Divisions of Labour,* Second Edition, Basingstoke: Macmillan.

Massey, D. (2005) *For Space*, Sage, London.

Morgan, K. (1997) 'The learning region: institutions, innovation and regional renewal', *Regional Studies* 31, 491–504.

Morgan, K., Marsden, T. and Murdoch, J. (2006) *Worlds of Food: Place, Provenance and Power in the Food Chain*, Oxford University Press, Oxford.

Paasi, A. (1996) *Borders, Territories and Consciousness: The Changing Geographies of the Finnish–Russian Border*, John Wiley, Chichester.

Phelps, N.A. (2000) 'The locally embedded multinational and institutional capture', *Area* 32, 179–188.

Pike, A. and Tomaney, J. (2009) 'The governance of economic development in England in post-devolution UK', *Cambridge Journal of Regions, Economy and Society* 2, 13–34.

Pike, A., Birch, K., Cumbers, A., MacKinnon, D. and McMaster, R. (2009) 'A geographical political economy of evolution in economic geography', *Economic Geography* 85, 175–182.

Potter, R.B., Binns, T., Elliott, J.A. and Smith, D. (2008) *Geographies of Development*, Third Edition, Pearson, Harlow.

Sayer, A. (2004) 'Seeking the geographies of power', *Economy and Society* 33, 255–270.

Sharp, J., Routledge, P., Philo, C. and Paddison, R. (2000) 'Entanglements of power: geographies of domination/resistance', in Sharp, J., Routledge, P., Philo, C. and Paddison, R. (eds) *Entanglements of Power: Geographies of Domination/Resistance*, Routledge, London, pp. 1–42.

Shepheard, E. (2002) 'The spaces and times of globalization: place, scale, networks, and positionality', *Economic Geography* 78(3): 307–330.

Smith, A., Rainnie, A., Dunford, M., Hardy, J., Hudson, R. and Sadler, D. (2002) 'Networks of value, commodities and regions: reworking divisions of labour in macro-regional economies', *Progress in Human Geography* 26, 41–63.

Smith, N. (1984) *Uneven Development: Nature, Capital and the Production of Space*, Blackwell, Oxford.

Stoker, G. (1995) 'Regime theory and urban politics', in Judge, D., Stoker, G. and Wolman, H. *Theories of Urban Politics*, Sage, London, pp. 54–71.

Storper, M. and Walker, R. (1989) *The Capitalist Imperative: Territory, Technology and Industrial Growth*, Blackwell: Oxford.

Swyngedouw, E. (1997) 'Neither global nor local: "glocalisation" and the politics of scale', in K. Cox (ed.) *Spaces of Globalization*, Guilford Press, New York, pp. 137–66.

Further reading

Traditional approaches to power in regional development

Asheim, B.T. (2000) 'Industrial districts: the contributions of Marshall and beyond', in Clark, G., Feldmann, M.L. and Gertler, M.S *The Oxford Handbook of Economic Geography*, Oxford University Press, Oxford, pp. 413–431.

Cumbers, A., MacKinnon D. and McMaster, R. (2003) 'Institutions, power and space: assessing the limits to institutionalism in economic geography', *European Urban and Regional Studies* 10, 325–342.

On 'Spatial vocabularies of power'

Allen, J. (2003) *Lost Geographies of Power*, Blackwell, Oxford.

Allen, J. and Cochrane, A. (2007) 'Beyond the territorial fix: regional assemblages, politics and power', *Regional Studies* 41, 1161–1175.

On a 'new regional political economy'

MacKinnon, D., Cumbers, A., Birch, K., Pike, A. and McMaster, R. (2009) 'Evolution in economic geography: institutions, political economy and regional adaptation', *Economic Geography* 85, 129–150.

22

Territorial/relational

Conceptualizing spatial economic governance

Martin Jones and Gordon MacLeod

Introduction

This chapter forms part the ongoing project to research the governance of local and regional economic development in the United Kingdom following the era of political devolution and constitutional change. Since 1997, the political geographical processes of the UK have been altered through the granting of an elected Parliament for Scotland, a National Assembly for Wales, an Assembly for Northern Ireland, an elected London Mayor and Greater London Assembly, alongside Regional Development Agencies for the eight English regions. Each of these institutions are, to varying degrees, charged with responsibilities for generating and orchestrating economic development, against which they are being judged within the contemporary uncertain political climate.

As we have argued elsewhere (Jones and MacLeod 2004; MacLeod and Jones 2007), when analysing such an asymmetrical political landscape of economic development, it behoves researchers to appreciate the particular economic, cultural and political discourses, practices and inflections around and through which its nations and regions are, in Anssi Paasi's terms, institutionalized. In other words we need to appreciate the socio-spatial

processes through which certain territorial units emerge as a part of the spatial structure of society and become "established and clearly identified in different spheres of social action and social consciousness" (1986: 121). Stretching this terminology further, the post-1997 institutional accomplishments enacted in the name of devolution have led the UK to undergo a substantial re-institutionalization of the policy landscape for governing economic development. This has proved to be a particularly interesting process for generating research over the past decade (Tewdwr-Jones and Allmedinger 2006).

Our chapter introduces two theoretical approaches that in recent years have been deployed to interpret UK devolution and related prospects for economic governance. First, we examine how UK devolution has come to be conceptualized as a re-configuration and rescaling of the territorial state. We then consider an alternative approach, which has in part arisen out of a backlash against such territorial and scalar perspectives, and which advocates a self-styled 'relational' approach to space and topological as opposed to topographical conceptualizations of spatiality. Following a synthetic overview of these two approaches, we aim to transcend this potential theoretical impasse by demonstrating how each can offer a fruitful analysis of different expressions of devolution and the governance of economic development across the UK landscape. This argument is then presented through a discussion of: (1) the struggle to institutionalize the South West of England as a geopolitical unit; and (2) endeavours to foster a definitively new region called The Northern Way. Through these case studies we underline how these alternative territorial and topological perspectives can offer compatible – as opposed to entirely antagonistic – approaches for interpreting the process of devolution, state structuring, and economic governance.

Territorial approaches to the geography of devolution

One of the most discernible endeavours to conceptualize UK devolution, particularly among political economic geographers and planners, interprets it as a rescaling of the state and a territorial reworking of the geographies of government and governance. This has been a key message in some analyses of England's Regional Development Agencies (Jones and MacLeod 1999; Deas and Ward 2000; Gibbs and Jonas 2001) and the creation of Regional Spatial Strategies (Haughton and Counsell 2004; Bianconi et al. 2006). Others inspired by the neo-Marxist state theory of Bob Jessop (2002) conceptualize this rescaling of economic governance as part and parcel of a 'hollowing out' of the national state and a corresponding 'filling in' at other scales such as England's regions, the Northern Ireland Assembly, and the Welsh Assembly and its Regional Divisions (MacLeod and Goodwin 1999; Goodwin et al. 2005; Jones et al. 2005; cf. Shaw et al. 2009).

To date, however, many of these scalar-informed analyses of UK devolution have deployed a relatively superficial reading of the concept of rescaling. We contend that a deeper engagement with the now highly enriched theoretical vocabulary on the

"politics of scalar structuration' (Brenner 2001, 2004, 2009) might prove instructive in examining the territorial character of UK devolution. This approach "connotes a developmental dynamic in which the basic structures of collective social action are continually reproduced, modified and transformed in and through collective social action" and in doing so, highlights how "[p]rocesses of scalar structuration are constituted and continually reworked through everyday social routines and struggles" (Brenner 2001: 603).

A fundamental premise of this approach, then, is that geographical scale is conceptualized to be socially constructed rather than ontologically pre-given, and that through this process geographic scales "are themselves implicated in the constitution of social, economic and political processes" (Delaney and Leitner 1997: 93). Perhaps, then, we could pre-empt the claims from 'relational space' thinkers (below) by underlining how this is very much a relational approach to scale (Swyngedouw 1997; Howitt 2003), whereby scale is conceived as unfolding "relationally within a community of producers and readers who give the practice of scale meaning" (K. Jones 1998: 27). It also infers that spatial scales – such as localities and regions and all those others associated with the territorial organization of the state – are not merely the settings of political conflicts but one of their principal 'stakes' in this struggle (Brenner 2004). Thus, as cogently argued by Neil Brenner:

> traditional Euclidian, Cartesian and Westphalian notions of geographical scale as a fixed, bounded, self-enclosed and pregiven container are currently being superseded by a highly productive emphasis on process, evolution, dynamism and sociopolitical contestation.
>
> (Brenner 2001: 603)

In accordance with this foundational principle, Swyngedouw had earlier made a compelling case for an ontologically process-based approach to scale that:

> does not in itself assign greater validity to a global or local [or we would add national or nation-state] perspective, but alerts us to a series of sociospatial processes that changes the importance and role of certain geographical scales, re-asserts the importance of others, and sometimes creates entirely new significant scales. Most importantly, however, these scale redefinitions alter and express changes in the geometry of social power by strengthening the power and the control of some while disempowering others.
>
> (Swyngedouw 1997: 141–142)

Furthermore, Jones (1998) informs us how this process is performed through a politics of representation whereby political agents discursively present their political struggles across scales; action that, in turn, implicates spatial imaginaries like regions, localities, cities and nation-states to be continuously implicated as 'active progenitors', offering an already partitioned geographical 'scaffolding' around and through which such practices and struggles take place (N. Smith 2003; Brenner 2001, 2009). In our view, this framework unlocks considerable potential for analysing the geohistory and contemporary spatiality of a process like devolution; what we might term state spatiality (Brenner 2004). For on one level, it offers scope to examine the crucial role of nationalist and devolutionary political campaigners – as in the Scottish Constitutional Convention and the Campaign for a Welsh Assembly – to discursively present their territorially oriented political struggles through a scalar narrative but also across scales, stretching to London and beyond. Instructive in this regard is Agnew's work on Italy, where political parties have been central players in "writing the scripts of geographical scale [...and where] ...The boundaries they draw [...] define the

geographical scales that channel and limit their political horizons" (Agnew 1997: 101).

A politics of scalar structuration approach might also enable us to understand how England's regional planning boundaries, which were established during wartime in the 1940s, came to represent active progenitors in shaping the post-1994 map of Regional Government Offices and the post-1999 Regional Development Agencies (RDAs). And, in turn, through the introduction of particular spatially selective policies and state strategies – state spatial strategies (Brenner 2004) – England's newly revived regional scales are given additional licence to become both the objects of state policy and active subjects in delivering policy (Jones and MacLeod 2004; Raco 2006). Not that any of this should imply some Russian Doll-like neatly layered structure of territorial spheres each containing a discrete package of political powers and responsibilities. For as lucidly outlined by Jamie Peck, political strategies and policy endeavours explicitly tangle and confound scales, with the result that:

> the scalar location of specific political-economic functions is historically and geographically contingent, not theoretically necessitated. Functions like labor regulation or the policing of financial markets do not naturally reside at any one scale, but are variously institutionalized, defended, attacked, upscaled, and down-scaled in the course of political-economic struggles. Correspondingly, the present scalar location of a given regulatory process is neither natural nor inevitable, but *instead* reflects an outcome of past political conflicts and compromises.
>
> (Peck 2002: 340; emphasis added)

Deployed in this way, it may be that the theoretical and methodological principles of this politics of scalar structuration perspective can uncover the ways in which contemporary devolution is characterized by a rescaling of policy and planning responsibilities alongside the formation of new, revived, or strengthened state spaces and the extent to which associated strategies to enact territorial development are intricately intertwined with the redefinition of state intervention (Brenner 2004).

A relational approach to the geography of devolution

In recent years, the merits of a territorial or scalar approach to the understanding of political economic transformations have been questioned, largely though not exclusively from a coterie of geographers based in England who advocate a more radically relational approach to space (see inter alia Allen *et al*. 1998; Allen and Cochrane 2007; Amin 2002; 2004; Massey 2004; 2005). The critique has two dimensions. The first is concerned with normative democratic politics and has been most explicitly articulated in a pamphlet entitled *Decentering the Nation: A Radical Approach to Regional Inequality*, where the authors (Amin *et al*. 2003) disavow the 'spatial grammar' that punctuates the debate and the practice of UK devolution. Indeed they proclaim that by following the well-trodden path of a territorially rooted political discourse and strategy, New Labour's devolution – particularly in relation to England – has done little to disturb the London-centrism that has characterized the business of politics and economics for over the last 100 years.

In order to confront this entrenched hegemony of London, they advocate replacing the territorial politics of devolution with a 'politics of dispersal'. This envisages different parts of England playing equal roles in conducting a more mobile politics, perhaps involving national institutions like Parliament travelling from London to the various 'provinces', although presumably this very process would lead such regions to no longer be peripheralized as such. Amin *et al*. deem that

these acts of dispersal would instil new spatial imaginaries of the nation – multi-nodal as opposed to deeply centralized – enabling regions to become effective national players while also stretching the cognitive maps of regional actants to embrace external connectivity in fostering economic prosperity and social and cultural capital. Amin (2004: 37) has since argued that, in contrast to conventional mappings where devolution politics is territorially "grounded in an imaginary of the region as a space of intimacy, shared history or shared identity, and community of interest or fate", this relational spatial grammar works with the variegated processes of spatial stretching and territorial perforation associated with globalization and a society characterized by transnational flows and networks.

This leads directly on to the second dimension of the critique of a scalar or territorial logic: the possibility of an alternative ontology and conceptual orientation towards relational processes and network forms of organization that defy a linear distinction between place and space (Amin 2002). Amin's reasoning for this relates to how:

In this emerging new order, spatial configurations and spatial boundaries are no longer necessarily or purposively territorial or scalar, since the social, economic, political and cultural inside and outside are constituted through the topologies of actor networks which are becoming increasingly dynamic and varied in spatial constitution. [...] The resulting excess of spatial composition is truly staggering. It includes radiations of telecommunications and transport networks around (and also under and above) the world, which in some places fail to even link up proximate neighbours. [...] It includes well-trodden but not always visible tracks of transnational escape, migration, tourism, business travel, asylum and organized terror which dissect through, and lock, established communities into new circuits of belonging and attachment, resentment and fear. […] It includes political registers that now far exceed the traditional sites of community, town hall, parliament, state and nation, spilling over into the machinery of virtual public spheres, international organizations, global social movements, diaspora politics, and planetary or cosmopolitan projects.

(Amin 2004: 33–34)

Viewed through this ontology of relational space, cities, regions and nation-states thereby come with no automatic promise of territorial integrity "since they are made through the spatiality of flow, juxtaposition, porosity, and relational connectivity" (ibid.: 34). In turn, Amin cautions against fetishizing places as 'communities' that "lend themselves to territorially defined or spatially constrained political arrangements and choices" (ibid.: 42; also Closs 2007). Moreover, and without wishing to denigrate any calls for building effective regional voice and representation, he is deeply suspicious of any assumption that there is a defined 'manageable' geographical territory to rule over.

This mode of reasoning certainly offers a fundamental challenge to perspectives on the politics of scalar structuration, whose language of 'nested scales and territorial boundaries' is deemed to omit "much of the topology of economic circulation and network folding" characteristic of contemporary capitalism (Amin 2002: 395). It also places on trial a range of territorially oriented concepts such as community, locality as well as those of urban, city and region. Moreover, as highlighted by Raco (2006), relational thinking provides some alternative avenues for conceptualizing the identity spaces and the emerging 'space–place tensions' of devolution (cf. Taylor 1999): not least in that if spatial identities are indeed fostered through a mixture of flows and connections across different

scales, "then any attempt to 'fix' them through policy initiatives will be characterised by over-simplification and an inability to capture their dynamism and ever-changing character" (Raco 2006: 324).

Governing spatial economies: relational, territorial, networked

So where do these contrasting approaches take us? Is it appropriate to view the process of devolution as a rescaling of state spatiality and territorial restructuring, or as a topology of spatially stretched, variegated flows and territorially perforating trans-regional networks? Or perhaps it might actually be quite unhelpful to be posing the question in such stark either/or terms? This would certainly seem to be the view of the distinguished political geographer John Agnew. In the process of introducing his theoretical 'mapping' of politics in modern Italy, Agnew talks of an 'intellectual standoff' between those who perhaps overstate the novelty and impact of networks and those who may remain too committed to the enduring significance of territorial spheres. For Agnew (2002: 2), "[P]art of the problem is the way the debate is posed, as if networks invariably stand in opposition to territories [and, further, as if…] networks are seen as a completely new phenomenon without geographical anchors".

In an explicit endeavour to transcend this seemingly polarized debate between territorial/scalar and non-scalar or topological perspectives, Harriet Bulkeley (2005) posits two crucial arguments. The first concerns the false assumption that approaches to the politics of scale – or politics of scalar structuration – somehow offer a naïve view of political scales as pre-given, homogeneous and intact. She then adds that such accounts conceptualize the very processes through which such scalar constructions emerge with an emphasis on the fact that they are not neatly bound in territorial terms but take place through various actor networks and spaces of engagement (Cox 1998; Jones and MacLeod 2004). Bulkeley's second objection to the positioning of scales and networks as polar opposites concerns the extent to which networks – at least in terms of the objects which are enrolled in networks and indeed their very scope – are themselves scaled. It then follows that:

> once the concept of scale is freed from notions of contained and contiguous territories, it is clear that networks have a scalar dimension, both in terms of the ways in which they operate and the ways in which they are framed and configured by other networks/coalitions of actors.
>
> (Bulkeley 2005: 882)

To this extent, then, any conceptualization of the politics of scalar structuration or of rhizomatic or network topologies should recognize that "scales evolve relationally within tangled hierarchies and dispersed interscalar networks" (Brenner 2001: 605); and, moreover, that "geographical scales and networks of spatial connectivity are mutually constitutive rather than mutually exclusive aspects of social spatiality" (ibid.).

These claims can be demonstrated in two brief examples. In the case of the South West of England, there is powerful evidence of a scalar politics and territorially oriented praxis, where official governmental organizations and oppositional political actors identify contrasting spatial scales – respectively, the South West regional boundary and Cornwall – around and through which to wage their quite explicitly territorial politics of engagement and representation. And yet we can also interpret that the everyday performance of these political geographies is being conducted through the trans-territorial and spatially variegated actor networks of people, objects such as trains and cars, alongside face-to-face and radiated modes of communicating information, ideas and technologies (cf. Mol and Law 1994). In the second case,

that of The Northern Way, we encounter a quite explicit endeavour to establish a pan-regional economic strategy for the North of England forged through a multi-nodal arc of connectivity: a truly networked space. But again, this is a networked topology which interacts around and through the territorial geometries of RDA and Government Office administrative boundaries alongside other scales and territories of government.

'Programmed spatiality': building and contesting the South West Region

The Greater South West (GSW) – later termed the South West Region – was created by central government during the 1930s following surveys conducted by the Board of Trade and Ministry of Labour on the UK population and economy. Prior to the era of RDAs, the South West had a number of economic development agencies operating at different spatial scales, thereby creating fragmented partnerships at the standard region level. Accordingly, the South West RDA (SWRDA) received relatively widespread support for its potential to help make the region more economically competitive and more cohesive. However, in some instances this territorializing institutional arrangement has spawned numerous tangled hierarchies and perplexing policy networks which, far from rationalizing the landscape of governance, have intensified its complexity. Indeed the South West Regional Assembly has identified "that the nature of the relationships between the key players within the region and the boundaries between them are at times, unclear" (SWRA 2002: 15). All of which has left some organizations anxiously groping to define a clear sense of orientation and territorial identity.

The most active resistance against this devolved territorial fix has been led by Mebyon Kernow. Formed in the 1950s, Mebyon Kernow is a grass-roots regional movement, modelled on Breton-Welsh-Celtic lines and combining claims for cultural rights with strategies for economic devolution. Its activists regularly fight general and local elections with low-level success, but throughout the 1990s Mebyon Kernow gained credibility by developing closer alliances with the Liberal Democrats, the hegemonic mainstream party in the South West of England. Mebyon Kernow's own approach to the RDA model of regionalization is encapsulated in Bernard Deacon's contention that:

> By refusing to debate regionalism the UK government is threatening Cornwall's institutional integrity. It has placed Cornwall in an artificial regional construct – the South West which is very large and culturally incoherent.
>
> (Deacon 1999: 3)

This insurgent venture to disturb the post-devolution governmentalized territory of South West Britain was given a major impetus in 2000 with the formation of a Cornish Constitutional Convention (Senedh Kernow) – a cross-party organization supported by Cornwall's four LibDem MPs, members of political parties, community and cultural activists – and its campaign for a Cornish Assembly (Deacon *et al.* 2003). By late 2001, over 50,000 people had signed the petition for a Cornish Assembly and this was taken to the House of Commons for the attention of the Minister for Regions. Building on this work, the landmark documents Devolution for One and All (CCC 2002) and The Case for Cornwall (CCC 2003) offer a multidimensional blueprint – drawing connections between territory, identity, politics and economics – for a fully devolved Assembly modelled on the experiences of Wales and the Isles of Scilly and legitimized by Cornwall's 'variable geometry' (ibid.: 10).

The political strategy of Senedh Kernow also combines a territorial politics of scale with a networked choreography of placemaking. For while it is the case that – as

briefly alluded to above – most contemporary political endeavours enrol a spatially variegated and trans-scalar topology of actor networks, the very practice of relational networking is brought to life in the CCC's claim that devolution is about "cutting Cornwall in" to a partnership of the regions of the British Isles, Europe and the world. And also that "strong relationships will need to be established and maintained with Cornwall's 'peer group' of UK regions and nations.... In addition, relationships will need to be renewed with regions and nations along the 'Atlantic Arc', and new relationships developed in Europe" (CCC 2002: 7). Nonetheless, in highlighting all this there is little denying that, as recognized by Bernard Deacon from the Institute of Cornish Studies at the University of Exeter, the primary objectives of Senedh Kernow were waged through a politics of scalar structuration:

> While being studiously ignored in the Government's 2002 White Paper on the English regions [...], this 'inconvenient periphery' provides one of the few explicit examples of a struggle over scale.
>
> (Deacon 2004: 215)

'The Northern Way': enacting a multi-nodal networked region

Since 1999, and in accordance with government priorities, each RDA has worked hard to develop effective regional and sub-regional partnerships and to foster a robust Regional Spatial Strategy (Roberts 2009). However, in recent years, and especially following the rejection following a public referendum in 2004 of a directly elected regional assembly in the North East of England, the government has been encouraging the creation of alternative types of region. This includes three new growth areas: the M11 corridor (Cambridge to Stansted), Thames Gateway (East London–North Kent), and Milton Keynes–South Midlands (Allen and

Cochrane 2007; Allmendinger and Haughton 2009). A fourth invented region is The Northern Way. Prepared by the three northern RDAs – One North East, Yorkshire Forward, and Northwest, The Northern Way was launched in September 2004 and saw:

> The three regions [...] unit[ing] in a common purpose – to develop the full potential of the North and narrow the £30 billion economic divide with the rest of England.
>
> (John Prescott, Foreword in NWSG 2005b: 3)

The geographical shape of The Northern Way is particularly interesting given the theme of this chapter. For a start, the RDA boundaries magically disappear. And this trans-territorial porosity is given deeper inflection with those lines that do actually feature: rail and automobile routes and other tributaries emphasizing mobility, linkage, networks. But perhaps the most notable geographical signifier concerns the prominence given to eight city regions: Liverpool/ Merseyside, Central Lancashire, Manchester, Sheffield, Leeds, Hull and Humber Ports, Tees Valley, and Tyne and Wear (Gonzalez et al. 2006). These are presented as relational assets and the 'principal spatial focus' promoting faster economic growth (NWSG 2004). In substantive terms, the city-regions actually seem to correspond to traditional travel to work areas, shopping catchment areas and housing markets. Nonetheless, again the geographical references of The Northern Way discourse appear to be intentionally fuzzy and the spatial ontology relational, as each node is acknowledged to:

> cover areas extending well beyond the city centres at their core [and...]. They contain a spectrum of towns, villages and urban fringe areas, and they have mutually inter-dependent relationships with the countryside around them.
>
> (NWSG 2005a)

The period between the fall of 2004 and late spring 2005 saw the stakeholders in each city-region prepare City Region Development Programmes, which provided:

> for the first time an overview of the economic development potential and requirements of the North's major urban economies. They look at the flow of markets across administrative boundaries and draw out the consequences for the development of policy and investment in a coherent way within *these new geographies*.
>
> (NWSG 2005b: 9; emphasis added)

The vision of The Northern Way Steering Group (NWSG) was as unambiguous as it was ambitious: "nothing less than the transformation of the North of England to become an area of exceptional opportunity, combining a world-class economy with a superb quality of life" (NWSG 2005b: 6). To achieve this, the NWSG proposed three broad types of action:

> Investments that are pan-Northern and add real value by operating across all three regions, such as joint marketing programmes;
>
> Activities which need to be embedded into mainstream programmes in each region, such as meeting employer skills needs;
>
> Potential investments for which further evidence must be developed to demonstrate the long-term benefits which will accrue to the North's economy, such as major transport infrastructure.

Indeed, of the ten investment priorities that have been identified thus far, three relate explicitly to transport, described as improving 'the North's connectivity'. This involves the preparation of a Northern Airports Priorities Plan designed to 'improve surface access' to key northern airports; improving access to the North's sea ports; and the creation of a premier transit system in each city-region and stronger linkages between city-regions. Other significant initiatives include: three Science Cities (Manchester, York and Newcastle); an integrated technology transfer network structure across the North; the creation of up to four world-class research centres and an enhanced programme of Knowledge Transfer Partnerships; the Northern Enterprise in Education Programme (NEEP); a pan-northern Women into Enterprise Programme; pan-northern projects in chemicals, food and drink and advanced engineering; environmental technologies, financial and professional services and logistics (NWSG 2005a). City-region plans also placed the emphasis on openness, porosity and permeability, with Leeds aiming to "improve city regional, pan-regional and international connectivity", and Hull and Humber Ports advertising as "a global gateway". All in all:

> The Northern Way represents perhaps the most significant economic development collaboration in Europe in the current decade. Therefore, it has required a new way of working of the three RDAs and their partners in the regions, local partners in City Regions and Government Departments.
>
> (NWSG 2005b: 6)

In some regard, though, these audacious claims demand some critical interrogation. First, this initiative involved a minute budget: one that is top-sliced from existing RDA funds. Second, the old assertions about trans-regional institutional capacity and networking need to be measured alongside the mundane reality of centrally policed and territorially defined targets for mainstream government programmes. In stating this, however, the proliferation of newer regionalisms such as The Northern Way may actually be indicative of how the UK state is seeking to respond to the complex diversity of political and policy-related demands: neighbourbood, local, regional, trans-regional, trans-national, terrestrial, electronic and so on. At the same time, we can begin to identify how relational processes and trans-regional networked forms of governing are being opened up to permit fresh approaches with which different policy actors can communicate and work together more effectively not simply within their sector but across sectors and across scales (Allmendinger and Haughton 2009). In turn, these emerging debates are helping us move towards a more relational understanding of how policy development proceeds.

Conclusions

In this chapter we have discussed two alternative approaches to researching the governance of local and regional economic development in the UK. The first concerns a territorial 'politics of scalar structuration'. In recent years this has assumed increasing popularity as an approach with which to capture the relationships between a purported rescaling of policy and planning responsibilities and the transformation of existing, or indeed the creation of new, state spaces, themselves deeply intertwined with the geographical specificities of state power and state intervention. In discussing this, we wish to reiterate how the territorialization of political life is never fully accomplished, but remains a precarious and deeply contentious outcome of historically specific state projects. Consequently, spatial, territorial, and scalar relations are neither pre-given nor naturally necessary 'bounded' features of statehood but are rather deeply processual and practical outcomes of strategic initiatives undertaken by a wide range of social forces. In the context of the South West of England, the Cornish – in the various guises of Mebyon Kernow and Senedh Kernow – are particularly keen to denaturalize the contemporary territorialization of UK political life, promoting their brand of nationalist regionalism as a processual and practical route through which to confront the perceived contradictions of statist technocratic regionalization.

The second approach to spatial politics has thus far been presented as a counterweight to that of scalar structuration. Deploying this topological approach would envision a radically relational interpretation on devolution and constitutional change emphasizing the networked practices and processes of devolution, and would make a case that an ontological focus on territorial boundaries and scales does violence to the actor-networked assembling of such a process. This approach is particularly powerful as a way of interpreting how, in the age of globalizing (post-)neoliberalism something like economic development can be conceived as a highly mobile and radiated process whose lines of flight stretch spatial forms and whose registers spill over fixed territorial boundaries and disturbing any rational sense of scalar hierarchies, tangled or otherwise. The value of this thinking is clearly evident from our brief discussion of The Northern Way. Nonetheless, we contend that many everyday *realpolitik* acts of spatial politics – as in the case of a central government classifying a region as a 'problem' or local activists campaigning for devolved government and cultural rights – often distinguish a pre-existing or aspirant spatial scale or territorially articulated space of dependence through which to conduct their actually-existing politics of engagement (Cox 1998). Thus, when the various objectives and strategic priorities defined in the name of The Northern Way are finally tabled, there is every likelihood that RDA and city-regional territorial boundaries and borders will re-emerge as 'active progenitors': with the whole process of 'who getting what' type of investment being waged on territorially demarcated and scalar-defined terms.

We thus remain to be unconvinced that these two approaches might be compatible in research strategies (see also Pike and Tomaney 2009). At one level, we consider it both politically naïve and theoretically negligent to ignore the fact that much of the political challenge to devolution prevailing across England and elsewhere is being practised through an avowedly territorial narrative and scalar ontology. However, it would equally be quite absurd to deny that these practices and performances are also often enacted through topologically heterogeneous trans-regional and cross-border networks of 'fluidity' and circulation (Mol and Law 1994). In short, then, our bottom line is that mobility and fluidity should not be seen as standing in opposition to territories. As Anssi Paasi has remarked:

> There is no doubt that networks do matter, but so do 'geography', boundaries and scales as expressions of social practice, discourse and power. Geography, boundaries and scales are not 'intuitive fictions' and their rejection/ acceptance can hardly be 'written away' or erased in our offices but have to be reconceptualized perpetually in order to understand their material/discursive meaning in the transforming world.
> (Paasi 2004: 541–542)

We, therefore, call for a retaining of territorially oriented readings of political economy and, when and where appropriate, their conjoining with non-territorial or topological approaches (Allen *et al.* 1998; Amin 2002). And as we have outlined above, the growing body of work on the politics of scalar structuration is explicitly relational in its approach to territorial form. The ongoing rounds of devolution and constitutional change certainly offer the context for stretching these analyses further.

For instance, the Wales Spatial Plan, which since 2004 is providing the basis for economic development and spatial planning, explicitly deploys a relational 'fuzzy boundary' narrative. Six regions, governed through 'area groups' have been created, some of which are coterminous with local authority administrative areas, while others cut across these geographies. Conventional cartographies based on administrative regions thus exist alongside fluid relational spaces based on flows of people, goods and services. The Wales Spatial Plan is claimed to enable "partners to work together on common issues in a flexible way" (The Wales Spatial Plan 2008: Foreword), thus breaking away from the "shackles of preexisting working patterns which might be variously held to be slow, bureaucratic, or not reflecting the real geographies of problems and opportunities" (Allmendinger and Haughton 2009: 619). The research challenge is to use techniques such as qualitative GIS, so that these 'soft spaces' (Allmendinger and Haughton 2009) of economic development can be mapped by a variety of quantitative (official/survey) and qualitative (unofficial/stakeholder) data records (Jones and MacLeod 2009). Further, while our chapter is limited to the experience of the UK, we contend that at a time when the governance of economic development continues to be renegotiated in many countries across the world, this conceptual dialogue has a wider resonance (Everingham et al. 2006; Brenner 2009).

References

Agnew, J. (1997) "The dramaturgy of horizons: geographical scale in the 'reconstruction of Italy' by the new Italian political parties, 1992–1995", Political Geography, 16 (2): 99–121.

Agnew, J. (2002) Place and Politics in Modern Italy, University of Chicago Press, Chicago.

Allen, J. and Cochrane, A. (2007) "Beyond the territorial fix: regional assemblages, politics and power", Regional Studies, 41: 1161–1175.

Allen, J., Massey, D. and Cochrane, A. (1998) Rethinking the Region, Routledge, London.

Allmendinger, P. and Haughton, P. (2009) "Soft spaces, fuzzy boundaries, and metagovernance: the new spatial planning", Thames Gateway Environment and Planning A, 41: 617–633.

Amin, A. (2002) "Spatialities of globalization", Environment and Planning A, 34: 385–399.

Amin, A. (2004) "Regions unbound: towards a new politics of place", Geografiska Annaler, 86B: 33–44.

Amin, A., Massey, D. and Thrift, N. (2003) Decentering the Nation: A Radical Approach to Regional Inequality, Catalyst, London.

Bianconi, M., Gallent, N. and Greatbatch. I. (2006) "The changing geography of subregional planning in England", Environment and Planning C: Government and Policy, 24: 317–330.

Brenner, N. (2001) "The limits to scale? Methodological reflections on scalar structuration", Progress in Human Geography, 15: 525–548.

Brenner, N. (2004) New State Spaces: Urban Governance and the Rescaling of Statehood, Oxford University Press, Oxford.

Brenner, N. (2009) "Open questions on state rescaling", Cambridge Journal of Regions, Economy and Society, 2: 123–139.

Bulkeley, H. (2005) "Reconfiguring environmental governance: towards a politics of scales and networks", Political Geography, 24: 875–902.

Closs, Stevens A. (2007) "'Seven million Londoners, one London': national and urban ideas of community in the aftermath of the 7 July 2005 bombings in London", Alternatives, 32: 155–176.

Cornish Constitutional Convention (2002) Devolution for One and All: Governance for Cornwall in the 21st Century, Senedh Kernow, Truro.

Cornish Constitutional Convention (2003) Your Region, Your Choice: The Case for Cornwall. Cornwall's Response to the Government's Devolution White Paper, Senedh Kernow, Truro.

Cox, K. (1998) "Spaces of dependence, spaces of engagement and the politics of scale, or: looking for local politics", Political Geography, 17: 1–23.

Deacon, B. (ed.) (1999) 'The Cornish and the Council of Europe framework for the protection of national minorities', Joseph Rowntree Reform Trust, York.

Deacon, B. (2004) "Under construction: culture and regional formation in south-west England", European Urban and Regional Studies, 11: 213–225.

Deacon, B., Cole, D. and Tregidga, G. (2003) Mebyon Kernow and Cornish Nationalism, Welsh Academic Press, Cardiff.

Deas, I. and Ward, K. (2000) "From the 'new localism' to the 'new regionalism'? The implications of regional development agencies for city–regional relations", Political Geography, 19: 273–292.

Delaney, D. and Leitner, H. (1997) "The political construction of scale", *Political Geography*, 16 (2): 93–97.

Everingham, J-A., Cheshire, L. and Lawrence, G. (2006) "Regional renaissance? New forms of governance in nonmetropolitan", *Australia Environment and Planning C: Government and Policy*, 24: 139–155.

Gibbs, D. and Jonas, A. (2001) "Rescaling and regional governance: the English Regional Development Agencies and the environment", *Environment and Planning C: Government and Policy*, 19 (2): 269–280.

Giddens, A. (1984) *The Constitution of Society*, Polity Press, Cambridge.

Gonzalez, S., Ward, N. and Tomaney, J. (2006) "Faith in the city-region", *Town and Country Planning*, November: 315–317.

Goodwin, M., Jones, M. and Jones, R. (2005) "Devolution, constitutional change and economic development: explaining and understanding the new institutional geographies of the British state", *Regional Studies*, 39: 421–436.

Haughton, G. and Counsell, D. (2004) *Regions, Spatial Strategies and Sustainable Development*, Routledge, London.

Howitt, R. (2003) "Scale", in J. Agnew, K. Mitchell and G. Toal (eds) *A Companion to Political Geography*, pp. 138-157, Blackwell, Oxford.

Jessop, B. (2002) *The Future of the Capitalist State*, Polity, London.

Jones, K. (1998) "Scale as epistemology", *Political Geography*, 17: 25–28.

Jones, M. and MacLeod, G. (1999) "Towards a regional renaissance? Reconfiguring and rescaling England's economic governance", *Transactions of the Institute of British Geographers*, 24: 295–313.

Jones, M. and MacLeod, G. (2004) "Regional spaces, spaces of regionalism: territory, insurgent politics, and the English question", *Transactions of the Institute of British Geographers*, 29.

Jones, M. and MacLeod, G. (2009) *Conceptualising the Geography of UK Devolution*, Presented Paper, Royal Geographical Society/Institute of British Geographers Annual Conference, Manchester, September.

Jones, M., Jones, R. and Goodwin, M. (2005) "State modernization, devolution, and economic governance: an introduction and guide to debate", *Regional Studies*, 39: 397–403.

MacLeod, G. and Goodwin, M. (1999) "Reconstructing an urban and regional political economy: on the state, politics, scale, and explanation", *Political Geography*, 18: 697–730.

MacLeod, G. and Jones, M. (2007) "Territorial, scalar, networked, connected: In what sense a 'regional world'?", *Regional Studies*, 41: 1177–1191.

Massey, D. (2004) 'Geographies of responsibility', *Geografiska Annaler, Series B, Human Geography*, 86 (1): 5–18.

Mebyon, K. (1999) "A fresh start for Cornwall: the Manifesto of Mebyon Kernow", in *The Party for Cornwall*, Mebyon Kernow, Cornwall.

Mol, A. and Law, J. (1994) "Regions, networks and fluids: anaemia and social topology", *Social Studies of Science*, 24: 641–671.

Nash, F. (2002) "Devolution dominoes", *The Times Higher*, 1 February, p. 30.

NWSG (2004) *Moving Forward: The Northern Way*, Northern Way Steering Group.

NWSG (2005a) *Moving Forward: The Northern Way: Action Plan – Progress Report Summary*, Northern Way Steering Group.

NWSG (2005b) *Moving Forward: The Northern Way: Business Plan 2005–2008*, Northern Way Steering Group.

Paasi, A. (1986) "The institutionalization of regions: a theoretical framework for understanding the emergence of regions and the constitution of regional identity", *Fennia*, 16: 105–146.

Paasi, A. (2004) "Place and region: looking through the prism of scale", *Progress in Human Geography*, 28: 536–546.

Peck, J. (2002) "Political economies of scale: fast policy, interscalar relations, and neoliberal workfare", *Economic Geography*, 78: 331–360.

Pike, A. and Tomaney, J. (2009) "The state and uneven development: the governance of economic development in England in the post-devolution UK", *Cambridge Journal of Regions, Economy and Society*, 2: 13–34.

Raco, M. (2006) "Building new subjectivities: devolution, regional identities and the re-scaling of politics', in M. Tewdwr-Jones and P. Allmedinger (eds) *Territory, Identity and Spatial Planning*, Routledge, London.

Regional Studies (2002) *Special Issue: Devolution and the English Question*, edited by C. Jeffery and J. Mawson, 36 (7).

Regional Studies (2005) *Special Issue: Devolution and Economic Governance*, edited by M. Jones, M. Goodwin and R. Jones, 39 (4).

Roberts, P. (2009) "Regional development and regional spatial strategies in England", in J. Bradbury (ed.) *Devolution, Regionalism and Regional Development: The UK Experience*, Routledge, London.

Sandford, M. (2002) "The Cornish question: devolution in the South-West Region", *Report for the South West Constitutional Convention and* the Cornish Constitutional Convention, Constitution Unit, London.

Shaw, J., MacKinnon, D. and Docherty, I. (2009) "Divergence or convergence? Devolution and transport policy in the United Kingdom", *Environment and Planning C: Government and Policy*, 27: 546–567.

Smith, N. (2003) "Remaking scale: competition and cooperation in prenational and postnational Europe", in B. Brenner, B. Jessop, M. Jones and G. MacLeod (eds) *State-Space: A Reader*, Blackwell, Oxford.

Smith, R. (2003) "World city actor-networks", *Progress in Human Geography*, 27: 25–44.

SWRA (2002) "Who owns the skills & learning agenda?", *South West Regional Assembly Select Committee on Skills & Learning*, South West Regional Assembly, Exeter.

Swyngedouw, E. (1997) "Neither global nor local: 'glocalization' and the politics of scale", in K. Cox (ed.) *Spaces of Globalization*, pp. 137–166, Guilford Press, New York.

Taylor, P. (1999) "Place, space and Macy's: place-space tensions in the political geography of modernities", *Progress in Human Geography*, 23: 7–26.

Tewdwr-Jones, M. and Allmendinger, P. (eds) 2006) *Territory, Identity and Spatial Planning: Spatial Governance in a Fragmented Nation*, Routledge, London.

The Wales Spatial Plan (2008) *People, Place, Futures: The Wales Spatial Plan Update 2008*, Welsh Assembly Government, Cardiff.

Further reading

Amin, A. (2004) "Regions unbound: towards a new politics of place", *Geografiska Annaler*, 86B: 33–44.

Brenner, N. (2004) *New State Spaces: Urban Governance and the Rescaling of Statehood*, Oxford University Press: Oxford.

Pike, A. and Tomaney, J. (2009) "The state and uneven development: the governance of economic development in England in the post-devolution UK", *Cambridge Journal of Regions, Economy and Society*, 2: 13–34.

Regional Studies 41 (9) "Whither Regional Studies" contains several papers engaging with the implications of territorial and relational perspectives for the study of local and regional development (especially those by Allen and Cochrane, MacLeod and Jones, Morgan).

23

Institutional geographies and local economic development

Policies and politics

Kevin R. Cox

Introduction

Discussion of institutions and their significance is nothing new in the literature on
local economic development. Governance,
particularly urban governance, has been a
central focus for some time now, and the earlier idea of urban regimes still resonates.
More recently still the way in which institutional change has affected the changing form
of local and regional development policy and
subsequent politics has been a central organizing theme. This has been particularly so
given the significance accorded to fordism
and its successors, including neo-liberalism.

Quite aside from these literatures and their
particular foci, to talk about institutions and
local economic development can cover a
huge range of relationships. I am assuming
for a start that in referring to institutions we
are following Douglass North (1992) who
defined them as 'rules that shape interaction'.
Emphatically this is not to omit reference to
the other dominant sense of the term. This is
institutions as organizations or modes of
cooperation: the state, the firm, the family,
the economy, and so on. On close inspection
the notion of organization complements that
of rules, so that both definitions of 'institution' grasp something of significance to our
purpose here. There is, I would suggest, an

internal relation between organizations and
rules: they are mutually entailing. Organization
entails rules since unless agents within organizations know what they are supposed to
do – in other words, what the rules are –
then there can be no organization and hence
no cooperation towards some shared end;
only incoherence. Likewise, rules only make
sense as ways of regulating social life. This in
turn has been characterized by institutional
differentiation, but 'institutions' here in the
sense of organization. Organization and rules,
however, if they are to be understood in
terms that make sense for our current purpose, require some situating with respect to
ideas of social process more generally. In this
particular treatment I give pride of place to
the capital accumulation process. This will be
followed by an examination of three particular areas of critical interest in the literature.
These include a still quite pervasive localism;
over-simplified binaries of long-term change;
and the central role of the state. I will say more
about these at the end of the next section.

The centrality of the accumulation process

In anything to do with local economic development, I assume the accumulation process

to be central. I conceive it not just in terms of its surface form of continual expansion of values through the investment rather than consumption of the surplus along with the values originally laid out, but as a class relation. This is its necessary condition and it then reproduces that class relation; the workers' share of the product consists of no more than what is necessary to reproduce them as workers while capital's possession of the means of production is both confirmed and deepened. This process of reproduction is itself mediated by struggle; workers press for a larger share of the product while capitalists repel their claims by repeated economies in the use of labour power and so a continual reproduction of the industrial reserve army, which in turn keeps wages at a level consistent with the appropriation of surplus value. Accumulation is a class relation, therefore, both in its origins and in its reproduction.

If accumulation is to take place, then certain institutional conditions have to be assured. Commodity exchange, whether that between the employer and the worker or between one firm and another is not unproblematic. The state becomes of major importance, regulating these relations in various ways. There is the problem of what has been antiseptically referred to as 'firm governance'. Likewise, like all organizations, those of the working class require rules. The class relation is regulated in various ways. And so on.

This relation is complicated, however, by the fact that accumulation necessarily occurs over space. This means in turn that organization has to coordinate and regulate agents in different places with all the additional difficulties of divergent interests, possibilities of concealment and dissimulation, for example, that separation entails, and at whatever geographic scale this organization takes place. The necessarily antagonistic nature of the accumulation process heightens these effects. As Harvey (1985a) has emphasized in his idea of 'the geopolitics of capitalism' this antagonism assumes the form of tensions between fixity and mobility, both of which

are entailed by the accumulation process. This particular antagonism has in turn been fundamental to the idea of local economic development: a process through which accumulation can be promoted in particular localities, and positions in wider geographic divisions of labour defended.

The result is what can be called an institutional geography. To some degree this can be captured by various organizational forms. Firms have spatial divisions of labour which require internal regulation. The possibilities here are myriad, as are the tensions and the possibilities of transformation. Particular positions in the spatial division of labour may be independently owned rather than characterized by vertical or horizontal integration. As a result branches may not be owned outright. This means in turn that coordination has to occur through subcontracting relations and relations of trust, though it is not unknown for a lead firm to insert its own teams of 'advisers' to ensure product quality. To the extent that difficulties remain, a takeover may be envisaged so as to subordinate suppliers to the rule of administrative fiat. To the degree that this alters the relation between production facilities and particular localities – heightening the chance of a plant closure, dedicating a plant's product for one particular customer, altering stakes in local conditions of production – this is not inconsequential for local economic development and its politics.

Agents also enter into what might be called scalar divisions of labour. An example is what Andrew Wood (1997; 1993) and I have called the local economic development network. It is through this particular form of organization that inward investment gets orchestrated and realized. In the US the network comprises the gas and electric utilities operating at regional scales alongside the Chambers of Commerce and local governments in the different localities of which the region is comprised. In virtue of their command of site information, the utilities perform a gatekeeping role. Firms prospecting for sites necessarily go through their offices and the utilities then orchestrate the subsequent site-search process within respective service areas. This requires the cooperation of both local Chambers of Commerce and local governments. The former provide information, particularly with respect to local labour conditions. The role of local government is the provision of the necessary permits and infrastructural extensions. Both are essential if a site decision is to be firmed up. The utilities delegate considerable power in this process and a good deal can go wrong. To a substantial degree it is mediated by relations of trust, but to the extent that trust breaks down, refusal to bring prospecting firms to particular localities typically brings the uncooperating to heel; underlining the fact that rules are always backed up by sanctions. A similar process occurs in the United Kingdom with the counties performing the same functions as the utilities (Cox and Townsend 2005). This also underlines both the way in which the state's own scalar division of labour is an essential ingredient in local economic development and the tensions that it generates.

This very brief survey of the organizational forms relevant to local economic development might seem to exclude some of the characteristic ways in which people have thought about this relationship. The attention given in the literature to both regulation theory and urban regime theory has been of major proportions. Both of these appear more global in form, and less spatially differentiated than the forms identified above. While this might in fact be the way in which they have been drawn on, it does not have to be so. Closer inspection suggests that both of these cases can be thought fruitfully in the terms I have identified above. Neil Brenner's (2004) account of the organizational relations underpinning what he has called 'spatial Keynesianism' and then their subsequent transformation is an excellent example. Although he does not express it in these terms, what he describes is a scalar division

of labour with respect to local economic development. The initial, spatial Keynesian phase in post-war Western Europe involved a dispersion of economic activity away from major metropolitan centres towards areas of relatively high unemployment. The creation of new towns facilitated these ends, as did public ownership of key industries. These processes were tightly coordinated from the centre with limited discretion accorded the localities. Subsequently this has shifted to a form in which significant power is decentralized to the localities and the regions.

Urban regime theory is also notable for its spatializing limitations. Again, though, this does not have to be the case. Urban regimes bring together local government and business in ways aimed at enhancing local economic development. Some of this is of genuinely global significance. Regardless of their commitments to particular parts of a city, all developers can support policies aimed at enhancing its growth as a whole. But as Molotch (1976) pointed out many years ago, they also have interests in particular neighbourhoods and hence in the overall pattern that that growth will assume. This can be a major source of tension within urban regimes, compromising their effectiveness and calling for careful attention to governance arrangements if those tensions are to be held at bay, as Hoxworth and Clayton-Thomas (1993) have indicated.

So in thinking about the geography of institutions, as they relate to local economic development, one might imagine it as a patchwork of institutional fixes, like the local economic development network or an urban regime, each of which is internally differentiated spatially, but which can be regarded more globally as well. As with the urban regime case, and given the regional character of the local economic development network, each of the localities making it up can have some secondary interest in seeing investment attracted elsewhere in the region. Allowing for these scalar considerations, local economic development is not a zero-sum game, though that sense of something more global as significant to particular localities is clearly subject to discursive arbitration. And each of these institutional fixes, of course, should be thought of in terms of mitigating the contradiction between fixity and mobility at the heart of the geopolitics of capitalism and therefore of the politics of local and regional development. It is also, and emphatically, an institutional historical-geography. In other words, institutional fixes, regardless of geographical scale, change over time and over space. Inevitably this process of change is conditioned by tensions in the accumulation process and the changes are invariably contested.

In talking in this way about 'local economic development' I am aware that it has become a very contested term. There were always differences and they remain. In the US it is much more about enhancing local tax bases and the flow of value through the social relations of a locality, particularly sales and rents, while in Western Europe employment has been a primary concern. But ultimately development, regardless of the 'local economic' that precedes it and which obfuscates, is about the development of people. It is this prospective view that encourages interest in ideas of sustainability, democracy as intrinsic aspects of the concept (Pike *et al.* 2007). The accumulation process, however, except in very favourable circumstances of the super-profits stemming from some quasi-monopoly, is unlikely to give much leeway to these alternative definitions. As Marx observed, under capital development necessarily has a very one-sided meaning.

With this as background, in the remainder of this chapter I want to explore certain issues arising from a reading of the literature on institutions and local economic development. Some of these issues have been widely recognized while in other instances that is less the case. The topical areas that I have chosen are threefold, though they necessarily overlap with one another. In the next section of the chapter I examine claims of an unwarranted localism in the literature; this is the claim that those working on questions of urban governance have tended to focus on the urban rather than those wider arenas with their own interplays of forces and institutional frames that are thoroughly relevant for what transpires in urban areas.

Second, there is the whole vexed question of how to understand institutional change as it relates to local economic development policy and politics. There has been a tendency in the literature to think of this in quite discontinuous ways. The historical geography of institutions is broken up into discrete, institutionally coherent periods: fordism, post-fordism, neo-liberalism, managerialism, etc. I want to urge greater circumspection: a greater sensitivity, therefore, to the elements of continuity as well as well as to sharper changes in the institutions that underpin local economic development. Again, I will return to the logics of the accumulation process in order to press this point.

Finally, there is the issue of the state. A take-off point here are the quite profound differences in the ways in which the practices of local economic development and the politics surrounding them have unfolded in the US as compared with Western Europe. One could argue that this has to do with differing patterns of local dependence (Cox and Mair 1988); that there is nothing in Western Europe that corresponds to the cluster of utilities, banks, developers, even private universities and hospitals and the local media empires that provide the core of American growth coalitions. I am going to suggest here though that much of the difference resides in institutional variation and in particular, in territorial organizations of the state that are very different indeed.

Localism

What some, including Ward (1996), Harding (1999) and Jessop *et al.* (1999) have called localism is a major feature of the literature on institutions and local economic development. This refers to the singular focus on institutions in particular local contexts, a focus that has worked to the detriment of an institutional geography at wider geographical scales. In part this focus is a response to the interest in globalization and how localities might cope with its challenges. The subsequent interest has been in how new institutions of urban or local governance might be devised so as to facilitate territorial competition in wider arenas. In brief, through improved institutions fostering the integration of divisions of labour within urban areas, and enhancing the coordination of one local government with another and with local business, the foundations for growth can be maintained or rebuilt. New investment and a new, or at least fortified, economic base will be the result.

Much of this work has drawn inspiration from urban regime theory (URT). However, it should be noted that URT was also part of a critique of earlier work in studies of the politics of local economic development. It positioned itself not so much with respect to the practical challenges of the period as with certain research tendencies. In contrast to the more global, structural and economic emphases of the growth coalition literature urban regime theory located these as terms in binaries and itself as focusing on the missing terms. So instead of privileging the economic, the structural and the more global, the URT emphasis would be on the political, agency and the more local.

There might seem to be two approaches to mitigating this. One would be to pay greater attention to the politics of scale and how, for example, local growth interests make use of wider institutional contexts and occasionally intervene in order to transform them: in other words, activities aimed at improving urban governance don't stop at the city or metropolitan boundary. The other approach would be more lateral in character, foregrounding the creation of what Allen and Cochrane (2007) have called assemblages, and regardless of the ideas of territorial hierarchy that so frequently accompany work that draws on the idea of the politics of scale.

It might seem an obvious point that rules defined at higher levels of the state are an essential datum point for local economic development practice. There is, nevertheless, a tendency to take them for granted, as in the work on urban governance. Sayer and Walker (1992) have made the same point in a critical discussion of firm governance and rules designed to reduce transaction costs: "these (transaction costs) are no more than a residual after the greatest dangers of exchange have been dampened by the heavy hand of the state, as embodied in various laws of contract, tort, liability and regulation, and by customary sanctions regulating tolerable behavior and mutual responsibility" (p.117). When consideration is given to institutions like zoning, subdivision regulations, state limits on the bonded debt of local governments, or the rules that were embodied in the federal urban renewal legislation of 1949, this caveat clearly applies not just to the case of firm governance but to urban governance as well.

In the US, those with strong interests in what they would define as local economic development have often been at the centre of attempts to create new institutions at broader geographic scales. Marc Weiss (1987) has described how community builders with strong stakes in particular metropolitan housing markets played a key role, through their national lobbying groups, in obtaining national legislation that would, in effect, strengthen local zoning provisions. This was through tacking onto the FHA mortgage insurance legislation of the 1930s a provision that made insurance dependent in part on more stringent zoning on the part of municipalities. Weiss (1980) has written in a similar 'politics of scale' vein about the origins of urban renewal legislation in the US.

The politics of scale, moreover, has worked in both directions: not just bottom-up in order to secure some institutional fix for local growth interests, but also top-down so as to further the accumulation interests of firms less tied to specific localities. As Jon Teaford (1984: 200) has described, fire insurance companies were hugely important in persuading local governments to adopt more stringent building codes and water pressure standards, and to professionalize local fire departments. The more contemporary role of property insurance companies in redlining also comes to mind here.

The second way in which one might mitigate the localistic bias of the literature on institutions and local economic development is through the idea of assemblages. In applying the idea to local economic development, Allen and Cochrane's (2007) focus was on how regions get constructed but their essential point from our perspective is their emphasis on the extra-regional in putting together some coalition of forces with stakes in a particular geographical area. The sorts of understandings central to Stone's (1989) idea of urban regimes, therefore, and which facilitate cooperation around some local economic development project or agenda can extend beyond the city to incorporate other agents operating elsewhere at scales that might be similar but might not be as well: regional agencies, certainly, but also bond rating agencies, consultants, and other local governments. Their work also underlines the value of more relational understandings of institutional fixes.

The question of historical geography

Institutions have a historical geography. They vary over both space and time. No work on the institutions–local economic development nexus can avoid some assumptions about these variations. In numerous instances, though, they should be in question. For example, central to understandings of change in policies of local economic development

and their politics have been periodizations of institutions. The influence of regulation theory has been quite extraordinary. Within the last fifteen years or so it has been hard to read the literature without it being situated in some way, and rarely critically, with respect to the categories of 'fordism', 'post-fordism', and more recently 'neo-liberalism'. There are other examples. Mollenkopf's (1983) industrial city/post-industrial city is one. Harvey's (1989) distinction between the managerial and entrepreneurial city has been remarkably influential. The same goes for the idea of globalization and how it is supposed to exist in contrast to something, typically undefined, that preceded it. Sometimes this has merged with other binaries. The idea of glocalization (Swyngedouw 1997) exists in self-conscious contrast to the more state-centric arrangements characteristic of fordism.

In contrast, and along with Brenner and Glick's incisive critique of regulation theory, I want to suggest that institutional change has been much, more continual and gradual than this seeming orthodoxy would suggest. Many of the crucial institutional changes are ones that, significantly, tend to get downplayed in the local economic development literature, perhaps because they do not slot neatly into these binary approaches. A history of zoning would be an informative example; likewise the institutional changes governing home-ownership. There are still other organizational changes that laid down the conditions for the politics of local economic development as we have come to know it but which again would be very hard to squeeze into some framework defined by periods. The competition for branch plants which has been such a defining feature of the contemporary politics (and policies) of local economic development is inconceivable outside of, in the first place, the gradual – emphasize 'gradual' – development of the multi-locational firm and the creation of branch plants to attract in in the first place; and second, the, again gradual, emergence of new branches of production less dependent on the sorts of considerations emphasized by Weberian location theory.

One can make similar critical remarks about the 'geography' in the historical geography of institutions. But here, instead of the punctuation of time into discrete, mutually exclusive categories, the tendency has been to engage in a smoothing-out process which has marginalized the differences between places, and particularly between one country and another. Part of this is the result of attempts to universalize the periodizations of regulation theory or of arguments about local economic development policy. As Sayer (1989) has pointed out, what passes for post-fordism can vary hugely between one country and another, to the point at which the very term should be in question. Likewise, I would argue that Harvey's managerial/entrepreneurial distinction is a hybrid based on the American and British cases that does justice to neither of them. Since the Second World War American cities have always been far more entrepreneurial than managerial – virtually no public housing but always with serious concerns for a local tax base; while in Britain the entrepreneurialism that has emerged has been weak tea compared to its American cousin. Jessop makes similar over-generalizations in his (2002) book *The Future of the Capitalist State*.

In short, institutional historical geographies might usefully be brought back onto the research agenda rather than be made the object of exercises that are ultimately reductionist in character. Massey's (2005) happenstance circumstances and the coming together of various conditions and influences at particular points in space-time might offer at least one ingredient of a necessary corrective. Different institutional innovations have meant different things in different places. There is evidence that just-in-time has been operationalized in ways in Western Europe that are different from those in Japan (Mair 1991). But, and contra Massey's somewhat voluntarist posture, the logics of the accumulation process also have to assume a fundamental role. As Brenner and Glick (1991) have argued:

> Despite the heterogeneous modes of regulation of its constituent parts the world economy as a whole has possessed a certain homogeneity, indeed unity, in terms of its succession of phases of development. The world economy, has, it seems, been able to impose its quite general logic, if not to precisely the same extent on all of its component elements, despite their very particular modes of regulation.
>
> (p. 112)

The territorial structure of the state

If we are to take these methodological injunctions seriously, then one place to start would be an examination of the territorial structure of the state. The politics of local and regional development varies dramatically between the US and Western Europe, and state form is heavily implicated in this contrast. On the one hand, there is a radically decentralized state, whose fragmentation is deepened still further by the fact that it is a presidential rather than a parliamentary democracy. On the other hand, there are the highly centralized states of Western Europe, and which continue to be so, despite the exaggerated claims of many academics about 'hollowing out' (Cox 2009) and the intense interest that the topic of devolution is currently attracting, particularly in Western Europe (see, for example, the recent issue of *The Cambridge Journal of Regions, Economy and Society* (Cox 2009), on 'Rescaling the State'). In the American case, representation, the organization of the state and its outputs are all much more territorialized, and to a remarkable degree.

This gives immense scope for a similarly territorialized politics of local and regional development. The use of the primary system as a vehicle for selecting candidates, the importance of legislative committees, and the weakness of the party system give local representatives both an intense interest in satisfying the sorts of local interests espoused by growth coalitions, and the ability to do so. This applies to elections to state assemblies in the same way as elections to Congress. Through the primary system competing candidates have to carve out programmes appealing to specifically local electorates. Once elected the committee system gives them the opportunity to push these legislative agenda and to block those of others. When a bill leaves the committee stage, the weakness of the political parties allows the construction of all manner of coalitions, many bipartisan in character, with a view to promoting the interests of particular regions or particular sorts of locality. Epstein (1986) is especially useful on the distinctive nature of the American state.

The federal nature of the US intensifies these effects. The US has not one but fifty welfare states. Without this variety, territorial competition around the idea of 'business climate' would make no sense. The states are responsible for local government, which means that the localism of the American state can be expressed at the state level in city-specific agenda. A good deal of legislation is city-specific, and log-rolling among representatives lowers the barriers to getting it passed; if St Louis wants something from the Missouri state legislature then the delegation from the Kansas City area will be willing to agree so long as there is an understanding that the favour will be returned in the future (Shefter 1978; Burns et al. 2009). This means that there can be a quite remarkable flexibility in developing new institutions of metropolitan governance for particular cities. If the local will is there, converting it into a new institutional form is typically not that difficult, as Jonas and I (Cox and Jonas 1993) have demonstrated.

The West European case is almost diametrically the opposite and the scope for interests in the future of local economies to express themselves, accordingly much weaker. The party–representative relation is quite different. Party central offices can override local choices. Once elected strict party discipline is expected. Legislative committees, likewise, give less scope for the expression of local interests; in fact they are used far less than in the American case with the cabinet assuming a greater role in preparing bills for consideration. Finally, these are for the most part unitary states, and where they are federal their federalism is far less radical than in the American instance. Local economic development policy has been much more top-down than in the US. The sorts of interventions that characterized Western Europe in the twenty to thirty years after the Second World War – aid to depressed areas, New Towns in particular – would have been unworkable on the other side of the Atlantic. There were programmes designed to channel aid to depressed areas but the criteria defining them foundered on the shoals of log-rolling. The result was that very few areas were excluded (Barnekov et al. 1989: 111; see also Ellwood and Patashnik 1993).

This is to dwell on the enabling nature of the state's territorial structure. I would suggest, though, that it is also significant in the way it conditions local and regional interests. It is not just, for example, that local governments dispose of powers of raising revenue for both operating and capital expenses and of land use regulation which might appeal to local business coalitions; it is also that they too have stakes in the growth of respective local economies. They are accordingly extremely active agents in the politics of local and regional development. Local planning departments have as a major mission attracting in new investment to a degree that would be regarded as unusual in Western Europe. As a result, local governments will usually be at the centre of local growth coalitions, orchestrating their activities and their agenda. Likewise, every state has a Department of Development aimed at stimulating the growth of the state economy through inward investment, arguing through state congressional delegations for regulatory relief for dominant industries and so forth.

This is very different from the Western European experience. In the US, private interests in local and regional economies are attracted to local and state government because of the formal powers they possess. And if they aren't attracted, they will be solicited and duly organized. Without this very particular field of possibilities, a field defined by a radically different territorial organization of the state, it seems unlikely that the American politics of local and regional development would be as so – equally radically – territorialized that it is. Rather, and as in Western Europe they would look elsewhere: usually to sector–specific organizations that lobby at the centre.

Conclusions

The existing literature on institutions and local economic development, therefore, discloses numerous lacunae. It is also a literature replete with received wisdoms that merit a much closer and more critical look. Regulation theory and regime theory have been especially prominent. So too are various, quite questionable, assumptions about the territorial structure of the state, including some odd ideas about shared institutions and tendencies on either side of the Atlantic. How, therefore, might one proceed? I assume first of all that anything to do with local economic development has to be approached from the standpoint of the capital accumulation process, and its necessary conditions. These include institutions and geography. Capital unfolds over space, creating various institutional fixes as it goes. These occur at more local scales but at others too, sometimes in a layered fashion where the rules of the central state, like zoning law, underpin local

development; sometimes as part of a broader, coherent institutional structure of which the local is one part as in the national planning legislation encountered in Western Europe and for which there is little or no counterpart in the USA; and sometimes as a response to local initiatives seeking a way out of specifically local dilemmas – which is very common in the US and much less so in Western Europe. What is then crucial is to identify the tensions, often with strong spatial reflections, that will be generated by the accumulation process, and how they contribute to the formation of new institutional fixes, or to such a confrontation of opposing forces that the result is to reproduce the status quo. What emerges is inevitably unpredictable but always conditioned by past and present institutional geographies and by what will work given the constraints of the local economic development process. And if history is anything to go by, more gradual and less punctuated, and more geographically differentiated, than some might assume.

References

Allen, J. and Cochrane, A. (2007) "Beyond the Territorial Fix: Regional Assemblages, Politics and Power", *Regional Studies* 41(9), 1161–1175.

Alonso, W. (1971) "The Economics of Urban Size", Papers and Proceedings, *Regional Science Association* 26, 67–84.

Barnekov, T., Boyle, R. and Rich, D. (1989) *Privatism and Urban Policy in Britain and the United States*, Oxford: Oxford University Press.

Brenner, N. (2004) *New State Spaces*, Oxford: Oxford University Press.

Brenner, R. and Glick, M. (1991) "The Regulation Approach: Theory and History", *New Left Review* 188, 45–120.

Burns, N., Evans, L., Gamm, G. and McConnaughy, C. (2009) "Urban Politics in the State Arena", *Studies in American Political Development* 23, 1–22.

Cox, K. R. (2009) "'Rescaling the State' in Question", *Cambridge Journal of Regions, Economy and Society* 1–15.

Cox, K. R. and Jonas, A. E. G. (1993) "Urban Development, Collective Consumption and the Politics of Metropolitan Fragmentation", *Political Geography* 12(1), 8–37.

Cox, K. R. and Mair, A. J. (1988) "Locality and Community in the Politics of Local Economic Development", *Annals, Association of American Geographers* 78, 307–325.

Cox, K. R. and Townsend, A. R. (2005) "Institutions and Mediating Investment in England and the United States", *Regional Studies* 39(4), 541–553.

Cox, K. R. and Wood, A. M. (1997) "Competition and Cooperation in Mediating the Global: The Case of Local Economic Development", *Competition and Change* 2, 65–94.

Ellwood, J. W. and Patashnik, E. M. (1993) "In Praise of Pork", *The Public Interest* 110, 19–33.

Epstein, L. (1986) *Political Parties in the American Mould*, Madison: University of Wisconsin Press.

Harding, A. (1999) "North American Urban Political Economy, Urban Theory and British Research", *British Journal of Political Science* 29(4), 673–698.

Harvey, D. (1985a) "The Geopolitics of Capitalism", Chapter 7 in D. Gregory and J. Urry (eds), *Social Relations and Spatial Structures*, London: Macmillan.

Harvey, D. (1985b) "The Place of Urban Politics in the Geography of Uneven Capitalist Development", Chapter 6 in Harvey, D. *The Urbanization of Capital*, Oxford: Basil Blackwell.

Harvey, D. (1989) "From Managerialism to Entrepreneurialism: The Transformation in Urban Governance in Late Capitalism", *Geografiska Annaler B* 71(1), 3–18.

Hoxworth, D. and Clayton-Thomas, J. (1993) "Economic Development Decision Making in a Fragmented Polity: Convention Center Expansion in Kansas City", *Journal of Urban Affairs* 15, 275–292.

Jessop, B., Peck, J. and Tickell, A. (1999) "Retooling the Machine: Economic Crisis, State Restructuring and Urban Politic", Chapter 9 in A. E. G. Jonas and D. Wilson (eds), *The Urban Growth Machine*, Albany: State University of New York Press.

Jessop, R. (2002) *The Future of the Capitalist State*, Cambridge: Polity Press.

Mair, A. M. (1991) "The Japanization of Volkswagen?" Local Government Centre, Warwick Business School, University of Warwick, Coventry, England.

Massey, D. (2005) *For Space*, London: Sage Publications.

Mollenkopf, J. H. (1983) *The Contested City*, Princeton: Princeton University Press.

Molotch, H. (1976) "The City as a Growth Machine: Toward a Political Economy of Place", *American Journal of Sociology* 82, 309–332.

North, D. C. (1992) *Institutions, Institutional Change and Economic Performance*, Cambridge: Cambridge University Press.

Pike, A., Rodríguez-Pose, A. S. and Tomaney, J. (2007) "What Kind of Local and Regional Development and for Whom?", *Regional Studies* 41(9), 1253–1269.

Sayer, A. and Walker, R. (1992) *The New Social Economy*, Oxford: Basil Blackwell.

Sayer, R. A. (1989) "Postfordism in Question", *International Journal of Urban and Regional Research* 13, 666–695.

Shefter, M. (1978) "Local Politics, State Legislatures, and the Urban Fiscal Crisis: New York City and Boston", Chapter 6 in S. Tarrow, P. J. Katzenstein and L. Graziano (eds), *Territorial Politics in Industrial Nations*, New York: Praeger.

Stone, C. (1989) *Regime Politics: Governing Atlanta, 1946–1988*. Lawrence, KS: University Press of Kansas.

Swyngedouw, E. (1997) "Neither Global nor Local: 'Glocalization' and the Politics of Scale", Chapter 6 in K. R. Cox (ed.), *Spaces of Globalization*, New York: Guilford.

Teaford, J. (1984) *The Unheralded Triumph: City Government in America, 1870-1900*, Baltimore: Johns Hopkins University Press.

Ward, K. (1996) "Rereading Urban Regime Theory: A Sympathetic Critique", *Geoforum* 27, 427–438.

Weiss, M. A. (1980) "The Origins and Legacy of Urban Renewal", Chapter 4 in P. Clavel, J. Forester and W. W. Goldsmith (eds), *Urban and Regional Planning in an Age of Austerity*, New York: Pergamon Press.

Weiss, M. A. (1987) *The Rise of the Community Builders*, New York: Columbia University Press.

Wood, A. M. (1993) "Local Economic Development Networks and Prospecting for Industry", *Environment and Planning A* 25, 1649–1662.

Further reading

Brenner, R. and Glick, M. (1991) "The Regulation Approach: Theory and History", *New Left Review* 188, 45–120.

Cox, K. R. (2004) "The Politics of Local and Regional Development, the Difference the

State Makes and the US/British Contrast", Chapter 10 in D. Valler and A. Wood (eds) *Governing Local and Regional Economies: Institutions, Politics and Economic Development*, London: Ashgate.

Cox, K. R. and Townsend, A. R. (2005) "Institutions and Mediating Investment in England and the United States", *Regional Studies* 39(4), 541–553.

Harvey, D. (1985a) "The Geopolitics of Capitalism", Chapter 7 in D. Gregory and J. Urry (eds), *Social Relations and Spatial Structures*, London: Macmillan.

Massey, D. (1999) "Spaces of Politics", Chapter 14 in D. Massey, J. Allen and P. Sarre (eds), *Human Geography Today*, Cambridge: Polity Press.

24

Carbon control regimes, eco-state restructuring and the politics of local and regional development

Andrew E.G. Jonas, Aidan H. While and David C. Gibbs

Introduction

Environmental regulation is having an increasingly important impact on the practice and politics of local and regional economic development. For more than a decade, localities and regions have strived to incorporate principles of environmental sustainability into spatial development plans and policies (Haughton and Counsell 2004). For some practitioners and policy makers, promoting sustainable forms of local and regional development (e.g. eco-industrial parks, green infrastructure, biofuels and other 'alternative' sources of energy, environmental industry clusters, etc.) is not much more than a place marketing tool (Deutz and Gibbs 2004). For others, it is seen as good economic development practice – see, for example, the Cornwall Sustainable Energy Partnership in the United Kingdom (UK) (Aubrey 2007) and the Global Green USA (2005) report on Los Angeles in the United States (US), both of which aim to use renewable energy projects as a catalyst for economic regeneration. However, in general we would argue that such attempts to 'green' local and regional economies have met with very mixed success as suggested by a continuing preference for promoting economic competitiveness over

and above meeting environmental and social targets.

Nevertheless, mounting international concerns about carbon emissions and their impact upon enhanced global warming, as well as the increasing cost of energy and fears over peak oil, have given urgency to develop a low carbon economy, both nationally and at the local and regional scale (see, for example, DTI 2003; City of Chicago 2008; Lerch 2008). Could it be that the development of low carbon economies is supplanting sustainable development as the mantra of good practice in local and regional development? If so where, in what form and with what consequences for local firms, workers, residents, policy makers and politicians? More generally, what does a new era of carbon control and climate change portend for state theoretical approaches to local and regional development?

In addressing such questions, this chapter also considers the ways in which state environmental regulation in the form of territorial carbon control regimes (CCRs) might inform and inspire new theoretical and empirical work on local and regional development. The first part of the chapter sets out a framework for understanding state–economy–environment relations as part of broader processes of what elsewhere we are calling 'eco-state restructuring' (ESR) (While *et al.* 2009). Given the policy trajectory of climate change governance, the concept of ESR draws attention to the ways in which states are struggling with growing pressures to reduce or manage global warming, cut carbon emissions and promote economic development in environmentally less harmful ways.

In the second part of the chapter we examine how these new territorial forms of environmental regulation might map out unevenly onto different local and regional economies, representing opportunities for some places and threats for others. Environmental regulation under a more stringent state-orchestrated CCR creates conditions for a politics scaled around local and regional development. This scalar politics takes many possible forms, including a new politics of locality, a competition between localities and regions to be seen as leaders in climate change policy, the re-incentivization of territorial growth coalitions, and new regional or city-regional forms of governance. The chapter draws upon our ongoing research into spaces of collective provision, sustainability, and new forms of local and regional development in the United States and Europe.

Environmental economic geography and new forms of state environmental regulation

The emergence of economic geography as a distinctive subdiscipline towards the end of the nineteenth century, and having its own set of organising concepts and assumptions, is closely associated with the acquisition of knowledge of the spatial distribution of natural resources (Barnes 2002). Nevertheless, the development of a critical environmental dimension to economic geography was hampered by the wider discipline's flirtation with environmental determinism and colonialist discourses. Even under the liberal-modernist

project of spatial science there was little interest in developing a perspective on processes of industrial location and resource use *vis-à-vis* mechanisms of state territorial redistribution. The revival of economic geography – qua geographical economics – as a mainstream social science at the end of the twentieth century has continued this separation of the sub discipline from the critical analysis of the state and the environment.

That environmental economic geography has undergone a revival is thanks mainly to radical scholarship and the 'institutional turn' in some branches of economic geography (Gibbs 2006; Bridge 2008). Among other developments, it has enabled Marx's insights on production, accumulation, labour and nature in capitalism to be brought into contemporary work on industrial restructuring (Hudson 2005). Enriched by Marx's concepts of accumulation, crisis and metabolism, neo-Marxist approaches recognise that production in capitalism relies on the transformation of nature and that this contains inherent 'ecological contradictions' (O'Connor 1998). For some neo-Marxists, moreover, the state is a non-neutral instrument in mediating the contradictions of social nature (Castree 2008). Since capitalists 'accumulate for accumulation's sake', the state plays an increasingly important, yet spatially contingent, role in mitigating the damaging environmental outcomes of global production (Drummond and Marsden 1995).

One potential obstacle to further work along these lines is the intellectual divide existing between the primarily economic oriented work on clusters, new economic spaces and global production networks, on the one hand, and the corresponding institutional work on the role of the state in local and regional governance, on the other. Likewise researchers have struggled to achieve theoretical commensurability between the concrete concerns of work on urban and regional governance and the abstractions of state and regulation theories (Lauria 1997). The latter approaches occasionally make reference to environmental policy and regulation, but usually only as part of the broader problematic of social regulation rather than as a response to pressing local or global ecological and environmental imperatives (Gibbs and Jonas 2000). We can only assume that attempts to downscale state theories of the environment to the realm of local and regional development are likely to encounter similar challenges, not least those posed by the different levels of abstraction involved in such approaches (Bridge and Jonas 2002).

For example, institutional approaches in economic geography recognise that the transformation of the 'environment' generates externalities and transaction costs, which firms, workers and local and regional authorities struggle to externalise via inter alia the development of local and regional economies and governance structures; but we do not necessarily learn about the possibility of corresponding opportunities and pressures on local and regional economies emanating from the national scale (or increasingly the supranational scale in the case of the European Union) as a result of stringent environmental regulation (Gibbs and Jonas 2000). Likewise the new environmental economic geography certainly considers the ways in which the production, accumulation and circulation of environmental resources shapes commodity flows and exchanges on a global scale (Bumpus and Liverman 2008). For the most part, however, the state remains an unexamined entity in this process. In none of these perspectives is there much evidence of thinking critically about the relationship – or tension – between new forms of environmental regulation, the role of the state, and local and regional development in a more integral – ecology and economy – sense.

Even regulation theorists, for whom capitalism has often shown signs of impending ecological crisis (Lipietz 1987), the environment is treated as little more than an 'extra-economic condition' for the establishment of the mode of social regulation (MSR) (Jessop 1997, 2002). The political–ecological content

of the MSR itself is rarely discussed; nor is the possibility that local and regional MSRs – if they exist as such (see Peck and Tickell 1992) – contain institutional forms capable of marrying local accumulation strategies to the social regulation of ecological conditions. It seems that there is an urgent need for conceptual frameworks for local and regional development that situate ecological processes and environmentalism more centrally within wider modalities of capitalist state regulation (Krueger and Gibbs 2007).

The eco-restructuring of the state and the emergence of territorial carbon control regimes

Although regulation of the environmental and ecological impacts of human activity has always been part of the work of the modern state, we believe that the period since the 1970s represents a concerted extension of the scope and scale of state environmental regulation. For instance, some scholars argue that we are in a period of 'ecological modernisation' (Mol 2002). This period is characterised by the search for national societal contracts that take into account public concerns about possible ecological and technological limits to capitalist development trajectories. In contrast to some accounts within ecological modernisation, which predict a linear progression towards a more ecologically benign state (cf. Meadowcroft 2005), we suggest that there are different, overlapping and contested phases of ESR. Our use of the concept of ESR refers to the ways in which state and parastatal actors mobilise strategic interests and actors around economic development projects and social activities, which the state – or more accurately certain actors within the state apparatus – regard as consistent with very specific and strategic environmental goals and outcomes set at international and national levels (While et al. 2010). Moreover, these strategic goals vary according to different political constructions of environmental and economic crises at respectively international, national, regional and local scales.

For example, the period from the early 1970s and 1980s might be categorised as the era of 'pollution control', a period when there were growing public concerns about the impact of industrialisation and urbanisation on natural resources and human health. This period was succeeded by the era of sustainable development. This era was predicated on a reorientation of, rather than a challenge to, growth-oriented accumulation strategies. Whether it has been beneficial for the environment remains in some considerable doubt given a lack of prescription in environmental target-setting (Owens and Cowell 2002). For some writers, elements of the sustainability agenda have resonated with competitiveness and the rise of the neo-liberal 'competition state' (Keil 2007), allowing discourses of sustainable development to be internalised within neo-liberalism even as environmental protection, health care and social services have been drastically cut back (Gibbs 2006).

If pollution control and sustainable development have been the dominant – sometimes overlapping – dimensions of ESR in the period 1970 to 2005, since around 2005 state environmental regulation has entered a new phase (for further details, see While et al. 2010). This phase is marked by an instrumental goal of reducing as quickly and efficiently as possible the major greenhouse gas emissions, and especially carbon dioxide. Ostensibly this era of carbon crisis is recognition of the need to maintain carbon concentrations in the atmosphere at levels sufficient to avoid dangerous and irreversible climate change. The point we want to make is that carbon control is partly about protecting society from the environmental damage associated with global climate change, but it also serves other political-economic agendas that are nation-state specific, not least increased anxiety about the rising costs and future supply problems of oil and gas in the United States and countries in Europe (Schlosberg and Rinfret 2008). If the current era has been captured under such headings as low-carbon capitalism, peak oil, decarbonisation, or climate change (Newman et al. 2009), we choose to refer to it in terms of the rise of carbon control regimes (CCRs). Crucially, CCRs operate not just nationally but also around localities and regions.

The conditions for the emergence of CCRs at the national scale can be traced back to the 1980s and 1990s. The Intergovernmental Panel on Climate Change (IPCC) reported in 1990 on the seriousness of the dangers of climate change. Global warming was also a leading consideration at the 1992 Rio Earth Summit leading to the United Nations Framework Convention on Climate Change (UNFCCC) (Henson 2006: 272). The Kyoto Protocol of 1997 subsequently recognised the need for mandatory reductions, requiring industrialised countries to reduce their collective emissions of six greenhouse gases by 5.2 per cent over the period 2008 to 2012 compared to the year 1990 (United Nations 1988). Since then states have sought various ways of meeting international targets for emissions reduction.

Given that some states did not ratify Kyoto, we might expect to see different national CCRs emerge as the eco-restructuring of the state meshes with distinct national modes of regulation. For example, in the United States, the Chicago Climate Exchange (CCX) was established in 2003 to provide a voluntary but legally binding trading system for North America, supplemented by the Chicago Climate Futures Exchange, the world's first environmental derivative exchange. By 2008, CCX had nearly 300 members drawn from the private and public sectors, all making a legally binding commitment to meet annual reduction targets set against their emissions baseline (see www.chicagoclimatex.com, accessed August 2008). There are plans to further roll out the CCX model with separate territorialised climate trading systems in California,

New York and New England. In contrast to the CCX, which was based on voluntary agreements, the EU adopted a mandatory Emissions Trading Scheme for large companies in 2005 (Bailey 2007). CCRs in Europe will nevertheless incorporate principles of subsidiarity and to that extent we recognise that the eco-restructuring of the state must have a territorial – or scaled down – dimension.

The eco-restructuring of the state and the down-scaling of CCRs

The question of the state's territorial structure looms large in any analysis of the politics of local and regional development (Cox and Jonas 1993). Pressures for the rescaling – or, more precisely, the downscaling – of environmental policy have been examined by the likes of Bulkeley (2005) and Bailey (2007). Anticipating a debate about the use of scalar concepts in human geography (Marston et al. 2005; Jonas 2006), Bulkeley critiques a prevailing fetish for hierarchical notions of scalar politics as represented in a 'cascade model' of climate change governance. While it is quite likely that CCRs will be rolled out by international and national governments across localities and regions, we too caution against any approach that treats CCRs as if they operate around a neatly ordered hierarchy of international-national-local state 'scales'.

Nevertheless, what is clear is that local and regional authorities have continued to assume greater responsibility for environmental policy implementation, and increasingly this has had to be factored into economic development strategy. In part this expanded remit of local and regional environmental policy is simply a reflection of the increased demands being placed on nation-states, but there are important questions about how responsibility for environmental policy – including responsibility for reconciling competing pressures and demands around environmental regulation – is being passed down to local and regional institutions in different national contexts.

Although our present interest is in CCRs as a new dimension of state territoriality, our past research indicates that state institutions at various scales have responded to pressures and demands for environmental regulation by engaging in a search for a 'sustainability fix' (While et al. 2004). By this we mean that state environmental policy is always mediated by place- and scalar-specific interests, including the presence (or absence) of territorial development coalitions pursuing strong competitiveness vis-à-vis environmental sustainability agendas. For the state, the possibility that environmental concerns – including more recent concerns around reducing carbon emissions – are mediated (and often driven) in the first instance by local and regional interests (interests in, for example, economic development and the collective provision of services) leaves some scope for mediating between these different interests in the following ways: by (1) passing responsibility for carbon emissions reduction on to localities and their constituent firms (workplaces) and residents (living places); (2) introducing market-based mechanisms in environmental policy as a mechanism for stimulating inter-territorial competition; (3) providing incentives to public–private partnerships that pursue low carbon investment strategies – or what we have elsewhere termed 'carbon offsetting the urban growth machine' (While et al. 2010); and (4) developing new regional or city-regional forms of governance. We explore each of these four possibilities in a bit more detail before addressing the limits to progressive low carbon alternatives.

CCRs as a new locality politics

Carbon control is likely to mean some form of territorially based target within

287

nation-states, and perhaps a more free-wheeling form of 'cap and trade' that enables cities or regions to buy or sell carbon credits. National carbon reductions can be achieved without the need to devise specific targets for sub-national territorial units, but there are various political and technical advantages to devolving responsibility (though not nec-essarily power) for some of the hard deci-sions around climate change politics to individual localities. Aside from the vexed question of where the carbon costs of things that move – notably cars, airplanes, traded goods and services, labour power, etc. – are to be located, it would be fairly straightforward to find a proxy measure for sub-national carbon emissions in terms of energy use. Territorial carbon budgets would therefore sit alongside the range of other regulatory obligations and incentives for carbon reduc-tion that are being passed downwards to firms, individuals and public agencies, and hence also to localities. A distinct possibility is that it would be left to individual localities to determine how to respond to national expectations and requirements; in other words CCRs could reflect locality-specific priorities. Sub-national emissions reduction targets would mean that difficult local choices would have to be made about local invest-ment decisions on the basis of carbon impacts. Crucially, the trade-offs around different economic development strategies would not be restricted simply to industrial or commer-cial development, but would extend into residential development and household energy use. Local authorities will need to secure their own CCRs within the targets they have been set, weighing up the costs and savings of actions in the social, economic and environmental spheres.

Carbon reduction and inter-territorial competition

A second possibility is that carbon control simply becomes an additional incentive (or,

by implication, a disincentive) in inter-local and inter-regional competition. Alongside the usual bundle of goods and services that municipal or regional authorities are expected to provide to residents and investors, effective carbon control pricing strategies would be marketed for the savings they represent for local businesses and residents. Here the abil-ity to 'vote with one's feet' (Tiebout 1955) might be taken literally to mean providing prices and incentives for residents and firms to move to a local jurisdiction that reduces dependence on fossil fuels or invests in alter-native modes of transport. Indeed, cities and regions are likely to want to engage in a 'race to the top' and be seen as leaders in meeting more stringent emissions reduction targets. This might already be happening.

In July 2009, the UK government announced its plans to introduce Low Carbon Economic Areas (LCEAs) as part of a national Low Carbon Industrial Strategy (see http://www.number10.gov.uk/Page20072, accessed July 2009). LCEAs are designed to foster cooperation between regional development agencies, companies, and local authorities involved in the development of alternative energy supplies and low carbon industries and supply chains. This announcement was accompanied by a decision by Nissan Corporation to invest over £200 million in a new rechargeable lithium-ion battery facility to be located near its European car manufac-turing operations in the North East of England. The North East region claims to be the UK's – and the world's – first LCEA. However, other UK regions such as the South West have likewise claimed to be the 'first' LCEA (see http://www.clickgreen.org.uk/news/national-news/12340-south-west-named-uks-first-low-carbon-economic-area.html, accessed July 2009).

In the US, the CCX recognises that strong carbon management will help posi-tion member cities and states (see Table 24.1) for economic opportunities including the possibility for additional federal funds from the Obama Administration for major

Table 24.1 State and local government
membership of the Chicago Climate Exchange

States
State of Illinois
State of New Mexico

Counties
King County, Washington
Miami-Dade County, Florida
Sacramento County, California

Municipalities
City of Aspen
City of Berkeley
City of Boulder
City of Chicago
City of Fargo
City of Melbourne, Australia
City of Oakland
City of Portland

Source: Adapted from http://www.chicagoclimatex.
com/content.jsf (accessed August 2008)

infrastructural projects. Some cities (e.g. Seattle) even claim to have introduced a target of becoming 'emissions neutral' by 2050. Within a 'cap and trade' model, those cities, counties or states without effective carbon reduction strategies in place may be forced to buy extra carbon credits, compromising their ability to fund other aspects of collective provision. Economically marginal communities, however, might find it more difficult to find matching local funds for infrastructure investments or to engage the electorate in necessary carbon reduction measures, thereby compromising their chance of federal funds. In all likelihood, then, this type of CCR will reinforce the neo-liberal tendency for successful places – especially the global cities – to reinforce their already privileged status by attracting additional state funding or local tax revenues (Hodson and Marvin 2007). For example, in his capacity as Mayor of London Ken Livingstone was active in positioning the city as a world leader in governance for climate change with the further aspiration to 'lead the world in becoming a low-carbon city' (Mayor of London 2005, 2007). Such overt low carbon boosterism encourages us to add the slogan

'Look! No more emissions!' to the typologies of urban representational regimes identified in Short (1999).

Carbon offsetting territorial growth coalitions

Third, there will certainly be opportunities for rethinking the cost-benefit calculations of mobilising growth coalitions around the pursuit of pro-growth economic development strategies. Assuming carbon targets are distributed equally to places on a per capita basis, carbon control might offer incentives for mobile capital to seek out local alternatives to overheating growth hot-spots; alternatively, target regimes would offer incentives for regions and localities to invest in 'smart growth' planning and fiscal zoning tools designed to reduce carbon output. Such smart growth regulations have developed furthest in the US, but similar provisions have been transferred into UK planning policies (Falk 2004; Krueger and Gibbs 2008; and see the UK's Planning Policy Statement 1: Planning and Climate Change (2007) www.communities.gov.uk/publications/planningand building/ppsclimatechange, accessed June 2009). National governments might further opt to incentivise private–public regeneration partnerships by introducing some form of contract and convergence mechanism, with an emphasis on carbon-efficient use of land and infrastructure rather than a 'winner takes all' form of urban competition. One can envision a variety of ways in which carbon control can be deployed alongside existing neo-liberal measures used by state agencies to incentivize and activate territorial growth coalitions (cf. Jessop et al. 1999).

New forms of city-regionalism

Finally, unlike the concept of 'splintered urbanism' – where different parts of the same city-region have become ever more jurisdictionally fragmented and disconnected from each other (Graham and Marvin 2001) – the logic of carbon control involves forging new city-regional connections – or perhaps even reconnections. It is possible that carbon budgets will lead to the development of formal regional governance in places where businesses and politicians have already developed a strong culture of regional cooperation despite the fragmentation of local jurisdictional arrangements. Denver in the US appears to be a good example where regional cooperation has been instrumental in the development of infrastructure, including a new light rail network linking the central city to surrounding suburbs and centres of high-tech industry. The development and extension of the network, known as FasTracks, appears to represent a break from the Denver region's economic dependence on high energy consumption and fossil-fuel infrastructure. Regionalism in this respect might entail new city-regional interdependencies based on alternative energy supplies and infrastructures. Such interdependencies would be expected to reflect not just contiguous boundaries but also revenue sharing, new alliances between workers, employers and public agencies, the development of new industry clusters, or a shared public sense of environmental and health security (see e.g. Krueger and Savage 2007). CCRs might also be developed around cross-territorial networks of localities and regions, which share in common existing energy supplies and infrastructures or engage in the development of new environmental industries and alternative energy sources.

Towards alternative low carbon forms of local and regional development

There is much about the new era of carbon control that might be welcomed in terms of social justice, distributional equity and the pursuit of alternative forms of economic development (Agyeman et al. 2003). For example, in the UK initiatives such as the Transition Towns Movement provide fora for communities and residents in smaller towns and deprived communities to rethink their dependence on fossil fuels and traditional energy sources (Transition Towns 2006). This is crucial as it is becoming increasingly apparent that the poor and powerless in localities and regions both in the global North and the South will suffer most from the consequences of climate change.

In contrast with the weak trade-offs of sustainable development, the logic of CCRs at different scales means that countries, firms and places will be required to account for ecologically unsustainable behaviours. In this respect, there are important links to be explored between carbon budgeting and work on alternative economic spaces (Leyshon et al. 2003; North 2009). Seyfang (2007) envisages potential for social redistribution via personal carbon trading, which would not only tax unsustainable behaviour but allow green citizens to trade their unused credits, with the assumption being that as they emit less greenhouse gases than the wealthy, the poor would gain most from personal carbon trading. Work by the New Economics Foundation on the Green New Deal is exemplary in this respect (Green New Deal Group 2008); albeit the fate of the Foundation's version of the Green New Deal demonstrates how such progressive agendas can quickly be co-opted by mainstream political parties to serve wider state interests. Much may depend here on how much CCRs (and those devising them) reflect the need for a paradigmatic shift in economic development trajectories or, as in 'weak' forms of ecological modernisation, are envisaged as new sources of markets and innovation to kick-start more conventional economic growth (Barry and Doran 2006; Milanez and Bührs 2007). For example, one might compare the kinds of economic future envisaged in the aforementioned UK government's low carbon economy industrial strategy (www. hmg.gov.uk/lowcarbon, accessed June 2009) with those of low-impact developments outlined in Pickerill and Maxey (2009).

Nonetheless, it is perhaps one of the ironies of this period of ESR that the holistic perspective of sustainable development and especially its ethical-moral concern with uneven development and social equity has dropped out of the equation in the push to meet the more instrumental goal of carbon reduction. Indeed, our concept of 'carbon control regimes' anticipates that a less socially progressive low carbon future is a more likely trajectory of the current round of ESR. Carbon control portends a new cultural hegemony of increasing environmental surveillance as local and regional economies struggle to adjust to global economic and environmental crises. This is because carbon reduction measures could have disciplining effects not so much on capital as on labour by contributing to surveillance strategies – both in the workplace and living place – and forcing some employers to (threaten to) relocate and avoid CCRs or go out of business altogether.

Conclusions

This chapter has explored the unfolding relationship between local and regional development and the eco-restructuring of the state, and has introduced the concept of carbon control regimes (CCRs). The re-regulation of society and space around the goal of ecological protection continues to gather pace and move out in new directions and arguably away from sustainable development and ecological modernisation (cf. Mol 2002). A decisive shift might already have occurred, from pollution control and sustainable development – which comprised initial waves of state-environmental regulation in the late twentieth century – to the new territorial politics of carbon control. In our view, CCRs could mark a distinct phase in the dominant

discourse, rationalities and practices of state environmental regulation, particularly in terms of the use of market-based environmental policy instruments to re-regulate economy–environment and state–citizen relations. This phase involves a hard-edged instrumental concern with reducing carbon dioxide emissions into the upper atmosphere as a first order policy concern. It reflects a new realism about anthropogenic climate change and the rising costs of oil dependence in Western nations.

In the process, new carbon reduction policy instruments devised nationally could be passed down to local and regional institutions and state structures in the form of territorial CCRs. So if localities, regions and, increasingly, city-regions are to be seen as strategic sites for innovation, creativity and economic development, they are also likely to be places where experiments in carbon reduction are likely to take place. As policy makers and practitioners seek to adjust to the new political and economic imperatives of carbon control, new strategic and calculative practices will be introduced into local and regional development. Given the amount of economic activities and uses currently dependent on fossil fuels, local and regional 'environmental' policy under CCRs is likely to have potential implications for all areas of local and regional development strategy and practice. It calls into question the prevailing ecological and economic rationalities of infrastructural investments and energy uses which underpin connections across space as well as in situ. Notably, CCRs shift policy attention to the wider systems of urban and regional circulation: to flows of fuel, transportation, carbon and so forth. Infrastructure is a particularly important arena of investment and economic development where carbon reduction and economic development trade-offs are likely to be made. Different interests dependent on working and living in urban places undergoing infrastructural developments will position themselves differently in relation to CCRs.

A further aim of the chapter has been to contribute to recent debates about the rescaling of the state, particularly in terms of thinking through the processes underpinning the scalar politics of climate change governance (Bulkeley 2005). Our argument is that environmental regulation must be examined as a problem of territorial governance for the state (via new alliances with capital and labour), the scaling of which is contingent upon strategic action and political struggle around the adoption of low carbon forms and trajectories of local and regional development. Our prognosis is that carbon control will be layered on to regimes of inter-place competition, with economically successful city-regions being best equipped to retrofit economic, social and physical infrastructures in order to prosper within CCRs. Nonetheless, it is also emphasised that the fortunes (or perhaps survival) of particular places and regions will also be shaped by the uneven costs of climate change adaptation. As the territorial politics of carbon control intersects more closely with the politics of local and regional development, questions of environmental justice are likely to come forcefully into play. While there is certainly progressive potential in climate change policy, one danger is that the political-economic project of carbon control will be narrowly oriented towards an instrumental agenda of carbon competitiveness rather than opening up possibilities for alternative economic development. Underpinned by a powerful mandate for state intervention, the result could be new forms of carbon-based uneven development and associated geographies of inequality and injustice.

Acknowledgements

The authors are grateful to the British Academy (SG-45293) for funding our research in King County (Seattle) and Denver. We thank Kevin Ramsey and Andy Goetz for helpful information and advice relating to the US examples. The chapter has also benefited from comments on an earlier draft by the editors. The usual disclaimers apply.

References

Agyeman, J., Bullard, R.D. and Evans, B. (eds) (2003) *Just Sustainabilities: Development in an Unequal World*, London: Earthscan.

Aubrey, C. (2007) "On a roll", *Guardian* (Society Section), 20 June, p.9. (http://www.guardian.co.uk/society/2007/jun/20/regeneration.energy, accessed June 2007).

Bailey, I. (2007) "Neoliberalism, climate governance and the scalar politics of EU emissions trading", *Area*, 39, 431–442.

Barnes, T.J. (2002) "Performing economic geography: two men, two books, and a cast of thousands", *Environment and Planning A*, 34, 487–512.

Barry, J. and Doran, P. (2006) "Refining green political economy: from ecological modernisation to economic security and sufficiency", *Analyse and Kritik*, 28, 250–275.

Bridge, G. (2008) "Environmental economic geography: a sympathetic critique", *Geoforum*, 39, 76–91.

Bridge, G. and Jonas, A.E.G. (2002) "Governing nature: the re-regulation of resources access, production and consumption", *Environment and Planning A*, 34, 759–766.

Bulkeley, H. (2005) "Reconfiguring environmental governance: towards a politics of scales and networks", *Political Geography*, 24, 875–902.

Bumpus, A. and Liverman, D. (2007) "Accumulation by decarbonisation and the governance of carbon offsets", *Economic Geography*, 84, 127–155.

Castree, N. (2008) "Neo-liberalising nature: the logics of de- and re-regulation", *Environment and Planning A*, 40, 131–152.

City of Chicago (2008) Chicago Climate Action Plan, Chicago IL (available at www.chicagoclimateaction.org, accessed August 2008).

Cox, K.R. and Jonas, A.E.G. (1993) "Urban development, collective consumption and the politics of metropolitan fragmentation", *Political Geography*, 12, 8–37.

Department of Trade and Industry (DTI) (2003) *Our Energy Future – Creating a Low Carbon Economy,* London: DTI (http://www.dti.gov.uk/energy/whitepaper/ourenergyfuture.pdf, accessed December 2005).

Deutz, P. and Gibbs, D. (2004) "Eco-industrial development and regional restructuring:

industrial ecology or marketing tool?", *Business Strategy and the Environment*, 13, 347–362.

Drummond, I. and Marsden, T.K. (1995) "Regulating sustainable development", *Global Environmental Change*, 5, 51–64.

Falk, N. (2004) "Funding sustainable communities: smart growth and intelligent local finance", *TCPA Tomorrow Series*, Paper 13, London: Town and Country Planning Association.

Gibbs, D. C. (2006) "Prospects for an environmental economic geography: linking ecological modernisation and regulationist approaches", *Economic Geography*, 82, 193–215.

Gibbs, D.C. and Jonas, A.E.G. (2000) "Governance and regulation in local environmental policy: the utility of a regime approach", *Geoforum*, 31, 299–313.

Global Green USA (2005) *Solar City Report: How Los Angeles Can Gain the Economic and Environmental Competitive Edge*, Santa Monica, CA: Global Green USA (www.globalgreen. org/publications/archive, accessed June 2009).

Graham, S. and Marvin, S. (2001) *Splintering Urbanism: Networked Infrastructures, Technological Mobilities and the Urban Condition*, London: Routledge.

Green New Deal Group (2008) *A Green New Deal*, London: New Economics Foundation.

Haughton, G. and Counsell, D. (2004) *Regions, Spatial Strategies and Sustainable Development*, London: Routledge.

Henson, R. (2006) *The Rough Guide to Climate Change*, London: Rough Guides.

Hodson, M. and Marvin, S. (2007) "Understanding the role of a national exemplar in 'strategic glurbanization'", *International Journal of Urban and Regional Research*, 31, 303–325.

Hudson, R. (2005) *Economic Geographies*, London: Sage.

Jessop, B. (1997) "A neo-Gramscian approach to the regulation of urban regimes: accumulation strategies, hegemonic projects, and governance", in M. Lauria (ed.) *Reconstructing Urban Regime Theory: Regulating Urban Politics in a Global Economy*, Thousand Oaks, CA: Sage Publications, 51–73.

Jessop, B. (2002) *The Future of the Capitalist State*, Cambridge: Polity.

Jessop, B., Peck, J.A. and Tickell, A. (1999) "Retooling the machine: economic crisis, state restructuring, and urban politics", in A.E.G. Jonas and D. Wilson (eds) *The Urban Growth Machine: Critical Perspectives Two Decades Later*, Albany, NY: State University Press of New York, 141–159.

Jonas, A.E.G. (2006) "Pro scale: further reflections on the 'scale debate' in human geography",

Transactions of the Institute of British Geographers, 31, 399–406.

Jonas, A.E.G., While, A. and Gibbs, D.C. (in press) "Managing infrastructure and service demands in new economic spaces: the new territorial politics of collective provision", *Regional Studies*.

Keil, R. (2007) "Sustaining modernity, modernizing nature: the environmental crisis and the survival of capitalism", in R. Krueger and D.C. Gibbs (eds) *The Sustainable Development Paradox*, London: Guilford Press, 41–65.

Krueger, R. and Gibbs, D.C. (2008) "'Third wave' sustainability? Smart growth and regional development in the USA", *Regional Studies*, 42(9), 1263–1274.

Krueger, R. and Savage, L. (2007) "City-regions and social reproduction: a 'place' for sustainable development?", *International Journal of Urban and Regional Research*, 31, 215–223.

Lauria, M. (ed.) (1997) *Reconstructing Urban Regime Theory: Regulating Urban Politics in a Global Economy*, Thousand Oaks, CA: Sage Publications.

Lerch, D. (2008) *Post Carbon Cities: Planning for Energy and Climate Uncertainty*, Sebastopol, CA: Post Carbon Press.

Leyshon, R., Lee, R. and Williams, C. (eds) (2003) *Alternative Economic Spaces*, London: Sage Publications.

Lipietz, A. (1987) *Mirages and Miracles: The Crises of Global Fordism*, London: Verso.

Marston, S.A., Jones III, J. P. and Woodward, K. (2005) "Human geography without scale", *Transactions of the Institute of British Geographers*, 30, 416–432.

Mayor of London (2005) *Low Carbon Leader: Cities*, Weybridge: The Climate Group.

Mayor of London (2007) *Action Today to Protect Tomorrow: The Mayor's Climate Change Action Plan London* (http://www.london.gov.uk/ mayor/environment/climate-change/ccap/ index.jsp, accessed April 2007).

Meadowcroft, J. (2005) "From welfare state to ecostate", in J. Barry and R. Eckersley (eds) *The State and the Global Ecological Crisis*, Boston, MA: MIT Press, 3–24.

Milanez, B. and Bührs, T. (2007) "Marrying strands of ecological modernisation: a proposed framework", *Environmental Politics*, 16(4), 565–583.

Mol, A. P. J. (2002) "Ecological modernisation and the global economy", *Global Environmental Politics*, 2: 92–115.

Newman, P., Beatley, T. and Boyer, H. (2009) *Resilient Cities: Responding to Peak Oil and Climate Change*, Washington, D C: Island Press.

North, P. J. (2009) "Eco-localisation as a progressive response to peak oil and climate change – a sympathetic critique", *Geoforum*, available online at: http://www.sciencedirect.com/science?_ob=ArticleListURL&_method=list&_ArticleListID=1364503976&view=c&_acct=C000014659&_version=1&_urlVersion=0&_userid=224739&md5=eefb2349e0dd4ca13ed93eb2116dc0a1.

O'Connor, J. (1998) *Natural Causes: Essays in Ecological Marxism*, New York: Guilford Press.

Owens, S. and Cowell, R. (2002) *Land and Limits: Interpreting Sustainability in the Planning Process*, London: Routledge.

Peck, J. and Tickell, A. (1992) "Local modes of social regulation? Regulation theory, Thatcherism and uneven development", *Geoforum*, 23, 347–363.

Pickerill, J. And Maxey, L. (2009) *Low Impact Development: The Future in Our Hands*, Wordpress.com (http://lowimpactdevelopment.wordpress.com, accessed June 2009).

Schlosberg, D. and Rinfret, S. (2008) "Ecological modernization, American style", *Environmental Politics*, 17, 254–275.

Seyfang, G. (2007) "Personal carbon trading: lessons from complementary currencies", CSERGE Working Paper ECM 07-01, available at: http://www.uea.ac.uk/env/cserge/pub/wp/ecm/ecm_2007_01.htm.

Short, J. (1999) "Urban imagineers: boosterism and the representation of cities", in A.E.G. Jonas and D. Wilson (eds) *The Urban Growth Machine: Critical Perspectives Two Decades Later*, Albany, NY: State University Press of New York, 37–54.

Tiebout, C.M. (1955) "A pure theory of local expenditures", *Journal of Political Economy*, 64, 416–424.

Transition Towns (2006) *Transition Towns* (www.transitiontowns.org, accessed August 2007).

United Nations (1988) *Kyoto Protocol to the United Nations Framework on Climate Change* (http://unfccc.int/resource/docs/convkp/kpeng.pdf, accessed June 2007).

While, A., Jonas, A.E.G. and Gibbs, D.C. (2004) "The environment and the entrepreneurial city: searching for the urban 'sustainability fix' in Manchester and Leeds", *International Journal of Urban and Regional Research*, 28, 549–569.

While, A., Jonas A.E.G. and Gibbs, D.C. (2010) "From sustainable development to carbon control: the eco-restructuring of the state and the politics of local and regional development", *Transactions of the Institute of British Geographers*, 35(1): 76–93.

Further reading

Bulkeley, H. (2005) "Reconfiguring environmental governance: towards a politics of scales and networks", *Political Geography*, 24, 875–902. (An imaginative application of the concept of scalar politics to environmental governance.)

Bulkeley, H. and Betsill, M.M. (2003) *Cities and Climate Change: Urban Sustainability and Global Environmental Governance*, New York: Routledge. (Excellent monograph on the contradictory implications of climate change for urban sustainability governance.)

Department of Trade and Industry (DTI) (2003) *Our Energy Future – Creating a Low Carbon Economy*, London: DTI. (http://www.dti.gov.uk/energy/whitepaper/ourenergyfuture.pdf, accessed December 2005). (An example of policy thinking around low carbon economy in the United Kingdom; not especially critical.)

Gibbs, D.C. (2006) "Prospects for an environmental economic geography: linking ecological modernisation and regulationist approaches", *Economic Geography*, 82, 193–215. (Useful critical review of the ecological modernisation literature written for a specialist audience of economic geographers.)

Graham, S. and Marvin, S. (2001) *Splintering Urbanism: Networked Infrastructures, Technological Mobilities and the Urban Condition*, London: Routledge. (Landmark intellectual treatment of urban infrastructure under neo-liberalism.)

Green New Deal Group (2008) *A Green New Deal*, London: New Economics Foundation. (An imaginative manifesto for an alternative and progressive green economy.)

Krueger, R. and Gibbs, D. C. (eds) (2007) *The Sustainable Development Paradox*, London: Guilford Press. (A collection of chapters by leading critical geographers on the incorporation of sustainable development into urban political economy.)

Newman, P., Beatley, T. and Boyer, H. (2009) *Resilient Cities: Responding to Peak Oil and Climate Change*, Washington, D. C: Island Press. (Examines the implications of carbon control for urban planning; up to date and accessible.)

25

Competitive cities and problems of democracy

Colin Crouch

Introduction

Cities and regions are under increasing pressure to strengthen their economic competitiveness. As investment funds have become thoroughly internationalized, even globalized, local public elites have both opportunities and needs to strengthen the prosperity of their areas by attracting external investment and providing environments in which economic activities can flourish. The implications of these developments for local democracy are ambiguous and complex, and have been the object of a number of studies.

This is not necessarily a story of the quality of public services and urban amenities being driven down in a race to the bottom as city authorities offer tax breaks to inward investors, depriving themselves of resources to invest in the quality of life of their cities. Such processes do take place, particularly in developing and some transition economies, where national and local authorities seek competitiveness through low cost. But many localities seek instead to attract high-value-added activities and to make themselves attractive places to live in for skilled professionals (Florida 2002). This can involve the opposite strategy of increasing expenditure

on high-quality public facilities and social infrastructure (OECD 2006a: 137–152). More generally, living in a competitive city is likely to satisfy local citizens better than living in an uncompetitive one. The problems raised for democracy through local competitiveness strategies, at least in wealthier societies, are more subtle, and mainly relate to the following issues:

i) The geographical areas around which competitiveness strategies can be developed are unlikely to correspond to the contours of elected political authorities.

ii) This fact, together with other attempts at fitting political institutions to a search for competitiveness, places a premium on mixed forms of governance, threatening to dilute the role of democratic institutions within governance.

iii) Stress on competitiveness and inward investment tends to make local (and national) political authorities heavily dependent on corporate interests, which may also be reflected within the mixed governance discussed under (ii).

The following discussion will address each of these issues in turn.

Democracy and flexible geography

It is possible to identify geographical areas that, more or less, constitute economic units, in the sense that most journeys to work take place within them, supplier networks are dense within their boundaries, and collective institutions (such as technical colleges) in the area's specialisms are likely to be grouped within them. In advanced economies these areas can usually be identified as metropolitan regions, bringing together either a dominant city and several smaller ones, or a group of more or less equal cities. The OECD has identified at least 78 of these among its member states, and economic activity and dynamism in the wealthy countries are concentrated within these spaces (OECD 2006a). In some cases (e.g. the Öresund region of Sweden and Denmark), or the region around Vienna (Austria) and Bratislava (Slovakia) an economic region crosses national frontiers. There are advantages for competitiveness strategies if public decision-making can be made at the level of a defined economic region. However, not only are the boundaries of economic regions flexible in relation to political boundaries; they also change. Furthermore, the fact that an economic region exists for some purposes (say, commuting patterns) does not mean that it has the same boundaries for others (e.g. supplier relations). This triple flexibility presents democracy with problems (OECD 2006a: 101–135). Political authorities have boundaries that need to remain stable, subject only to periodic boundary reviews, if citizens are to identify with them. There are also advantages if local administrations can provide different services and infrastructures across a similar geographical scale, as there are usually dense links among them. Also, an integrated economic region can contain several million people, raising problems of scale for local democracy.

Advocates of "localism" argue that, as decision-making levels become removed from easy access by citizens, democracy becomes more difficult to practise (Stoker 2004a, 2004b). From a different perspective, advocates of public choice through market mechanisms (e.g. Tiebout 1956) consider it important that citizens be able to "vote with their feet" and move out of local jurisdictions that they find politically unacceptable or administratively inefficient without much disruption to their lives by moving house over long distances. They therefore advocate geographically small local government units.

Voluntary cooperation can of course develop among neighbouring authorities, and there are increasing examples of this, such as the Local and Multi-Area Agreements in the UK. There are however difficulties when a diversity of authorities, often of different political colour, try to tackle issues jointly. Local taxation systems designed to give local authorities autonomous sources of revenue (itself an important attribute of local democracy) often give them perverse incentives – for example, by encouraging suburban authorities to establish decentralized business districts in order to reap returns from business taxes, creating urban sprawl, when it might be both more efficient and environmentally better to concentrate certain activities within a central city.

Further, a high level of institutional fragmentation can mean that some local jurisdictions, generally central cities, bear the costs of public services used by the residents of other areas without receiving income for them – for example, coping with the strains imposed by commuting traffic and disposing of litter dropped in the city during the working day. In other words, lack of cooperation on a territorial base can lead to a mismatch between decision-makers, taxpayers, and beneficiaries of public services (OECD 2006a: 156–158).

A number of approaches have been developed in different parts of the world to reconcile these conflicting demands on cities, and have been summarized by the OECD (ibid. 158–200) as follows. Each contains a different balance between democracy, appropriateness of scale and flexibility, and none is able to optimize that relationship:

i) Functional models whereby governance structures are reshaped to fit or approximate to the economic area (e.g. by the creation of a metropolitan government and the amalgamation of municipalities). This can be done only occasionally, as it involves complex political processes, and may eventually lead to the erection of large authorities remote from citizens. It is advocated by those who believe in the superior efficiencies of scale and prioritize this goal over both flexibility of organizational form and local accountability (Newton 1982). Compared with some of the other forms to be discussed below, such formal structural reforms do produce bodies with democratic accountability, but the strength of this will depend on local acceptance of the enlarged structure – the "culture of cooperation" or "actor behaviour" that they induce (Kübler and Heinelt 2005). For example, in Stuttgart and Lyon the creation of metropolis-wide governments derived from long traditions of cooperation, in the latter case dating back to the 1960s.

ii) Inter-municipal joint authorities for specific tasks, such as agencies for transport, urban planning or economic development. These provide a more flexible form and retain actual democratic accountability at a more local level, but at the expense of democracy becoming more indirect, as the joint authority is not itself accountable, only its constituent municipalities. This has been an issue, for example, in France, where Urban Communities and Agglomeration Communities have been given an increasing range of responsibilities and larger and larger budgets without being run by a directly elected assembly (Lefevre 2004; OECD 2006b).

iii) Informal coordination bodies such as platforms, associations or strategic planning partnerships, often relying on existing networks of relevant actors, without necessarily following territorial boundaries. A problem is caused for democratic government by the fact that the appropriate boundary will probably vary according to the function or goal in question. This is of course an issue even where local government takes a tiered form of such entities as regions, provinces, counties, cities, districts. It is magnified when attempts are made to form different task-specific agencies that cut across this existing structure.

Both (ii) and (iii) are advocated by the "New Regionalism" school (Savitch and Vogel 2000). This school does not accept that political regulation should only be organized by public bodies. Rather, metropolitan governance is seen as organized by more or less formal and stable systems of different actors, involving structures of network cooperation between public and private actors with a relatively weak institutionalization (Walter-Rogg 2006). However, where there is a mix of private and public bodies in such flexible governance forms, flexibility is purchased at the expense of clarity in the specific identity of democratic bodies, as these are mixed with the representatives of private firms in the governance structures. This will be discussed again below.

Finally:

iv) Purely fiscal arrangements such as equalization mechanisms and tax-base sharing to deal with fiscal disparities and territorial spill–over as well as public–private partnerships and contract services. These again raise issues of public–private relations that will be discussed in a later section of this chapter.

A further problem for democracy is created by trends towards geographical segregation on class and ethnic grounds that frequently occur in very large urban spaces (Le Galès 2004; OECD 2006a: 190–200). There are conflicts over the location of large, essential but unattractive elements of urban infrastructure, such as major roads or waste-disposal plants, which everyone needs but no one wants to live near. Formal government at remote levels is unlikely to cope with these problems, and may make some of them worse because of its remoteness from street level. Further, the conditions of modern city life generate various social movements and protests that cannot easily translate themselves into formal political and administrative terms. These movements, while not democratic in the formal sense of having participated in elections, are indicators of the health of a vibrant civil society that is part of the infrastructure of democracy. Problems appear when one tries to distinguish between a democracy-reinforcing civil society group, and a lobby using its power to undermine democratic processes.

Flexible governance

The above discussion has introduced a number of themes that are usually discussed within the framework of governance theory. This theory maintains that the regulation of social life cannot be studied through the concept of formal political government alone, but through a range of mechanisms, the word governance being used to distinguish this broader idea from that of government. The other mechanisms usually discussed include markets, corporate hierarchies (or the authority of the firm), business associations and trade unions, networks, and communities. This much is agreed among a wide range of observers. There is however a major division between those who use these ideas purely analytically, and who see government as one among a number of modes of governance (e.g. Hollingsworth and Boyer 1997; Hollingsworth et al. 2002; Crouch 2005) and those who see a historical trend away from government towards other forms of governance, in particular networks (e.g. Giddens 1998; Greenwood et al. 2002; Leach and Percy-Smith 2001; Rhodes 1997). The intricacies of this dispute do not concern us here.

The whole process of authorities being concerned for the economic competitiveness of their areas brings the market to bear as a source of decision-making and regulation. Engagement with private firms in such matters as regional development authorities or contracting out public services brings private corporate hierarchies into local governance. The mobilization of civil society groups can be seen as engaging networks and communities.

Some, mainly British, scholars would also argue that the overall structure of "new" governance thereby produced is itself a network, with different participants linked horizontally rather than in a hierarchy coming down from formal government (Giddens 1998; Greenwood et al. 2002; Leach and Percy-Smith 2001; Rhodes 1997). During the 1990s "lightness" (or "living on thin air" in the memorable phrase of Charles Leadbeater (1999) became seen as a desirable characteristic of institutions. This was a period when many large enterprises were ostensibly "downsizing" and "delayering", and government seemed clumsy alongside it. One says that firms were "ostensibly" downsizing, because they were simultaneously often becoming enormous global businesses. Elimination of some middle layers of an organization and the use of sub contracting rather than direct employment enabled shrinking to be compatible with centralization of decision-making and the growth of an organization.

It was also the period when stock markets were discovering the possibilities of secondary markets and derivatives, enabling the trading of stocks and making money to become divorced from productive economic activities. Lightness was seen, not just as a literal quality of high-tech and services sector activities in contrast with "heavy" industry, but as a desired organizational characteristic of all institutions suited to the post-Fordist economy (Giddens 1998). Rapid mobility and flexibility of structures were considered to enable government to resemble, not just firms, but the market itself in its flexible and rapid adjustment to changing needs. The search for flexible forms of governance of local and regional economies is a key instance. Networks were preferred to formal associations for the same reason. The former can adjust quickly and flexibly; the latter have rather rigid structures and definitions of their scope.

Our main focus here is on the democratic quality of these different governance modes, as this might enable us to answer whether shifts among them in local and regional affairs are likely to have implications for democratic responsiveness. Only actual government can possess the formal quality of democratic accountability, though whether individual governments have the substantive quality of public responsiveness that might be assumed to follow from this attribute varies. Only markets, provided they are true markets, are certain to be responsive in this way, but the market cannot be called democratic. Only governments, associations and corporations are formal legal identities; this attribute makes them more accountable at law, but also makes them less flexible. Flexibility is most certainly possessed by the market and networks. Changes in governance arrangements will therefore have implications for this bundle of qualities: democracy, responsiveness, accountability, flexibility. It is however not necessarily easy to work these out a priori, and without well-founded knowledge of particular cases.

Burroni et al. (2005) are sceptical of those who claim to see a major historical trend to "light" governance, but do see a wide diversity of different combinations of governance modes. They speak of "kaleidoscopic" governance.

For example, Svensson and Östhol (2003) discuss the "growth agreements" in Swedish regional partnerships, which include measures for dealing with such problems as the public/private balance and accountability. However, the problem of which groups should be included within the networks has remained unresolved, as there are no clear tests for entitlement to participate once one has moved outside formal democracy.

Paradoxically, when authorities deal with individual firms such problems are not raised. Firms do not claim to be representative; they lobby authorities in pursuit of contracts and privileges for themselves, on the grounds of what their activities can achieve for economic growth in the territory concerned. That is the only legitimation that they need, but their participation raises problems for both the proper functioning of markets and the delivery of collective competition goods. Moulaert and colleagues (2001), after examining large new urban projects in a number of European countries, argue that the rhetoric of the market is used by public authorities to conceal granting privileged access to favoured corporate insiders. This confusion between the market and corporate hierarchies is a very common error in public policy-making. Similarly, according to Novy et al. (2001), new coalitions of city council, business and academics in Vienna made urban policy a fragmented, privatized, opaque and ad hoc area. A study of another, particularly large, project, that of the recent reconstruction of Berlin, describes how corporate actors used city authorities in order to unload market risk on to the city, with (the authors argue) strong negative effects (Häussermann and Simons 2000).

The role of networks in the governance of strong territorial economies is well known, from the Italian industrial districts (Burroni and Trigilia 2001) to Silicon Valley (Kenney 2000). Patrucco (2003) describes how different kinds of institution worked together to produce a true complementarity of communication and networks in the technological district of Brianza in northern Italy. Sydow and Staber (2002), Baumann (2002), Baumann and Voelzkow (2004), and Elbing *et al.* (2009) have similarly described the role of multi-participant project networks in German and British television. Formal levels of government do however often play a role in such innovations. Izushi (1999) describes the role of the Welsh Development Agency in promoting inter-firm cooperation among suppliers. Several studies show that, even when production becomes internationalized, inter-firm relations and other networks around technological issues retain important local or regional focuses: Swedish machinery producers (Larsson and Malmberg 1999); high-tech small ICT firms around Cambridge in the UK (Keeble *et al.* 1999), certain Dutch towns (Atzema (2001) and industrial districts of Italy (Burroni 2001, 2007); the biopharmaceutical sector around Oxford (Proudfoot 2004). Kaufmann and Tödtling (2000) report a similar mix of local and global for older industrial districts in Styria in Austria. They put the emphasis the other way round – on the fact that firms are inserted in European as well as local networks; but the findings also support the hypothesis of the continuing importance of the local.

The concept of networks is embraced very easily by policy-makers, partly because the idea has been associated with these and other "success stories", but also because the apparent looseness and non-specificity of the idea fits very well with the new "light" governance concept. It may seem that if local actors from polity, economy and civil society come together, pooling their different and often complementary governance resources, they will produce networks with a rich diversity of possibilities. But it is not clear whether central government policies of fragmenting their own organizations in order to equip them to participate in such governance, or requiring local authorities to interact with private firms results in the generation of networks. It is by no means new for firms having

a private interest in certain development projects to seek to influence local policy concerning them; has the rhetoric of network governance simply provided legitimation for what, from stricter constitutional perspectives, is a dubious practice?

The successful networked economies tend to be rather special places, produced by chance combinations of factors that are difficult to reproduce at will: there have been many unsuccessful attempts at creating new Silicon Valleys. At times the loose, light arrangements of new governance experiments may be not so much an ideal new model of institutions as the best that can be achieved in poor circumstances. This has been proposed by a recent literature on the advantages and disadvantages of light, flexible "projects" as opposed to heavy, firmly established institutions (Grabher 2002).

Grabher's contrast between "cool projects and boring institutions" is ironic, as "boring" turns out to imply useful stability, but Dornisch (2002) takes him rather literally when discussing the state of economic regeneration in the Łódź region of Poland. Formerly the site of a major textile and clothing industry, the region was in severe economic and institutional decline after the fall of the Soviet system, and (like most textile districts in Europe) competition from low-cost producers in Asia. There had to be highly contingent, improvised experiments with chance sets of actors. Dornisch sees advantages here. Because of the diversity, people are "learning through switching" (ibid.: 310), a quality uniquely produced by the transition context, and particularly suited to projects. He argues that it was precisely the "volatile discontinuity" and "loose coupling" of the project approach that helped achieve success and rapid moves away from unsuccessful paths (ibid.: 315). On the other hand, more recent research on the same area (Burroni *et al.* 2008) suggested that small-scale clothing manufacturing activities in the area had been unable to get beyond very informal arrangements and limited products, because of an absence of strong supporting institutions.

This research contrasted the Łódź case with certain similar areas in southern Italy, which had been able to take advantage of formal public policy and links to established major firms. In the Italian cases it was formal local government which guided innovative experiments. The idea of "governance without government" and of the role of light institutions does not seem to be confirmed; on the contrary, both local governments and formal business and labour associations invest in the experience of local development pacts in order to reinforce their own legitimacy within local society, and thereby help embed the pact itself as a form of real co-operation (Magnatti et al. 2005; Burroni 2005). The experience of the pacts also confirms Grabher's stress on the usefulness of stability, as it favours: (1) the creation of mutual trust between public and private actors, (2) cumulative learning processes, and (3) the creation of collective goods with medium- and long-term perspectives (Cersosimo and Wolleb 2001; De Vivo 2004; Magnatti et al. 2005).

Major examples of "mixed governance" in the UK are the Regional Development Agencies (RDAs). These are creatures of central government, there being no formal and democratic tier of regional government in most of the UK. English RDAs comprise individuals appointed by central government from various central government agencies, representatives of local authorities, private business, trade unions and the voluntary sector. Fuller et al. (2002) suggest that the lack of discretionary power and resources has undermined the capacity of RDAs to pursue strategic aims; and that in response to this they have concentrated on particular activities and have developed relations with certain partners only. A study of new forms of governance of redevelopment in Govan, a long-term depressed area in the Glasgow region in Scotland (where an RDA format had been established before the institution of devolution), also comments on the weak

leverage over wider policies and resource flows (Raco et al. 2003). However, these authors do report positive achievements of the system in bringing together public- and private-sector actors in flexible local development companies.

Research on RDA activity in North East England makes a different point, demonstrating the ambiguities of any observed trends away from government and towards networks (Pike 2002). The author argues that central government rather than local actors took the leading role, by creating 28 separate and temporary "task forces", designed to forge new entities between state and market. These have been very flexible units of central government engaged with local government and other public agencies, as well as some firms. But Pike sees a problem of identifying responsibility and legitimacy among the range of public agencies involved. He also reports concern at the role of patronage available to central government in such a situation, and at the creation of "cosy circles" of private and public insiders produced by such an opaque process of identifying salient participants.

A study of "partnership governance" in rural Wales similarly suggests that the rhetoric of partnership is used to remove competence from local government, either upwards to a regional level or down to "communities" – hence in fact enhancing the role of the central state (Edwards et al. 2001). The authors report that partnerships are able to cross old hierarchical lines and link unfamiliar partners, mainly within the public sector, in precisely the way expected by "new governance" writers. However, the authors make two further points that are unexpected from this perspective. The central state itself appears as far from being "hollowed out" and weakened; rather it takes new powers, particularly away from local government. Second, and related to this, the state uses the new flexible forms to depart from the universalism of the historical modern state, selecting privileged interlocutors from among the institutions in the territory. The research was carried out before the establishment of a democratic tier of regional government for Wales. Since then, however, the shift from formal local government to "communities" has been followed in England, symbolized in the renaming of the local government ministry as the Department for Communities and Local Government.

Parallel with this change has been a complex shift in the role of local government in England. Under the Sustainable Communities Act 2007 (UK Government 2007) local authorities were given the power to raise issues and carry out inquiries in a wide range of issues going beyond their specified formal competences. At the same time, however, local authorities in this country as well as many others are under increasing pressure to privatize or subcontract provision of their services to private firms, thereby losing substantive powers to take action themselves to provide services. The role of formal local democracy therefore shifts to being one of advocacy on behalf of citizens rather than acting as a public authority on their behalf. In this way the distinction between formal local government and informal community groups is reduced.

Another group of researchers has also questioned whether there is a decentralization to local levels in these new flexible structures, or in fact a centralization (North et al. 2001; Valler et al. 2000). They go on to make a further point, related to the "cosy circles" and "privileged interlocutors", and to the previously observed shift in the participation of business interests away from associations to individual firms, selected without formal or open process by the political centre out of a large number of potential contenders. Again, this is not the market but the engagement of private corporate hierarchies in governance. A further study of North East England similarly reports problems in the formation of small firm networks because of doubts over the legitimacy of so-

called "networks" and "communities" of such firms (Laschewski et al. 2002).

Private firms and local democracy

This last point leads us to the role of private firms in flexible new governance arrangements. This raises certain problems: the protection of special interests, sometimes those of dominant but declining sectors; the exclusion of the concerns of SMEs to the advantage of large corporations better equipped to lobby; the neglect of other legitimate non-economic social interests (OECD 2006a: 212–215). For example, research on Reading, a former railway town in South East England, describes the pressure imposed by central government to persuade the city authorities to operate through partnership with private and voluntary sectors when seeking a new role (Raco 2003). Reading has as a result become a successful regional retail centre, but the core group sharing governance with the city council in determining the policy were certain national property-development firms, not local businesses, representative business associations or the local population. It is difficult to judge whether this was a case of external groups helping a city find a future that it could not have produced from its own past legacies, or a solution serving a particular set of interests. Neither democratic political processes nor the market drove the policy.

Counsell and Haughton (2003) compared efforts to provide employment sites for large-scale inward investment in the two highly contrasting English regions: the declining North East and the prosperous South East of England. They found that new modes of governance had enabled different groups to try to use the system to advance their own interests, in particular taking advantage of the confused meaning given to the idea of "sustainable development". Based on research that he conducted on local regeneration partnerships in four urban areas in Northern and Eastern England (Barnsley, Rotherham, Hull and North East Lincolnshire), Davies (2004) reached several similar conclusions. He describes a complexity of governance modes, which he attributes to the paradoxical pressures placed on the government to achieve certain public regeneration goals while also giving primary weight to market forces. One consequence of this complexity was fragmentation and institutional instability; another was an increasing flow of power to central government. Partnerships did not, he argues, produce the strong role for network governance that Rhodes (1997) and other advocates of the new governance approach criticized above had predicted (Davies 2004: 581).

Conclusions

The arrival of economic competitiveness on the agenda of local and regional politics has had important implications for democracy. First, policy-makers have new incentives to align levels of political decision-making to those of identifiable regional and local economies; but it is not always clear what constitutes a regional or local economy, and in any case it is likely to change more quickly than the organization of elected authorities. Formal democracy either ignores economic change, gradually becoming incapable of producing strategy in this vital policy field; or it runs after such change and loses its stability. Various halfway approaches have been developed to cope with this dilemma.

Second, authorities have tried to produce more flexible structures of local and regional government, "kaleidoscopic" governance. But this can bring a decline in the sovereignty of political government as such. There is also evidence of a decline in the role of business associations and trade unions in favour of individual corporations in policy influence.

Finally, this role of private firms has important implications for democracy. As with the other issues being discussed in this chapter, there is a wealth of research evidence from a variety of cities and countries. While these do reveal the trends that have been discussed, they also show considerable continuing diversity.

Acknowledgement

This chapter draws heavily on work that the author carried out for two projects: as academic adviser to the Organization for Economic Co-operation and Development (OECD) for its report *Competitive Cities in the Global Economy* (OECD 2006a); and on local economic development with Luigi Burroni and Maarten Keune (Burroni *et al.* 2005).

References

Atzema, O. (2001) "Location and Local Networks of ICT Firms in the Netherlands", *Tijdschrift voor Economische en Sociale Geografie*, 92, 3: 369–378.

Baumann, A. (2002) "Convergence versus Path-Dependency: Vocational Training in the Media Production Industries in Germany and the UK", Ph.D. thesis, Florence: European University Institute.

Baumann, A. and Voelzkow, H. (2004) "Recombining Governance Modes: The Media Sector in Cologne", in Crouch *et al.* (2004), q.v., 261–282.

Biagiotti, A. and Burroni, L. (2004) "Between Cities and Districts: Local Software Systems in Italy", in Crouch *et al.* (2004), q.v., 283–305.

Burroni, L. (2001) *Allontanarsi crescendo. Politica e sviluppo locale in Veneto e Toscana*, Torino: Rosenberg & Sellier.

Burroni, L. (2005) "Economic Governance and European Cities", Florence: European University Institute, unpublished paper.

Burroni, L. (2007) *Distretti veneti e sfide globali, in Fabrizio Cafaggi. e Paola Iamiceli Reti di imprese tra crescita e innovazione organizzativa*, Bologna: Il Mulino.

Burroni, L., Crouch, C. and Keune, M. (2005) "Governance caleidoscopica, debolezza istituzionale e sviluppo locale", *Stato e Mercato*, 3/2005: 423–454.

Burroni, L., Crouch, C., Kamińska, M. E. and Valzania, A. (2008) "Local Economic Governance in Hard Times: The Shadow Economy and the Textile and Clothing Industries around Łódź and Naples", *Socio-Economic Review*, 6, 3: 473–492.

Burroni, L., and Trigilia, C. (2001) "Italy: Economic Development through Local Economies", in Crouch *et al.* (2001), q.v., 46–78.

Cersosimo, D. and Wolleb, G. (2001) "Politiche pubbliche e contesti istituzionali. Una ricerca sui Patti territoriali", *Stato e Mercato*, 3: 369–412.

Counsell, D. and Haughton, G. (2003) "Regional Planning Tensions: Planning for Economic Growth and Sustainable Development in Two Contrasting English Regions", *Environment and Planning C: Government and Policy*, 21: 225–239.

Crouch, C. (2005) *Capitalist Diversity and Change: Recombinant Governance and Institutional Entrepreneurs*, Oxford: Oxford University Press.

Crouch, C., Le Galès, P., Trigilia, C. and Voelzkow, H. (2001) *Local Production Systems in Europe: Rise or Demise?*, Oxford: Oxford University Press.

Crouch, C., Le Galès, P., Trigilia, C. and Voelzkow, H. (2004) *Changing Governance of Local Economies: Responses of European Local Production Systems*, Oxford: Oxford University Press.

Davies, J. (2004) "Conjuncture or Disjuncture? An Institutionalist Analysis of Local Regeneration Partnerships in the UK", *International Journal of Urban and Regional Research*, 28, 3: 570–585.

De Vivo, A. (2004) *Pratiche di concertazione e sviluppo locale. L'esperienza dei patti territoriali in Campania*, Milan: Angeli.

Dornisch, D. (2002) "The Evolution of Post-socialist Projects: Trajectory Shift and Transitional Capacity in a Polish Region", *Regional Studies*, 36: 307–321.

Edwards, B., Goodwin, M., Pemberton, S. and Woods, M. (2001) "Partnerships, Power and Scale in Rural Governance", *Environment and Planning C: Government and Policy*, 19: 289–310.

Elbing, S., Glassmann, U. and Crouch, C. (2009) "Creative Local Development in Cologne and London Film and TV Production", in Crouch, C. and Voelzkow, H. *Innovation in Local Economies: Germany in Comparative Context*, Oxford: Oxford University Press.

Florida, R. (2002) *The Rise of the Creative Class, and How it's Transforming Work, Leisure, Community and Everyday Life*, New York: Basic Books.

Fuller, C., Bennett, R. J. and Ramsden, M. (2002) "The Economic Development Roles of English RDAs: The Need for Greater Discretionary Power", *Regional Studies*, 36: 421–428.

Giddens, A. (1998) *The Third Way*, Cambridge: Polity.

Giordano, B. and Roller, E. (2003) "A Comparison of City Region Dynamics in the UK, Spain and Italy: More Similarities than Differences?", *Regional Studies*, 37, 9: 911–927.

Glassmann, U. and Voelzkow, H. (2001) "The Governance of Local Economies in Germany", in Crouch *et al.* (2001). q.v., 79–116.

Grabher, G. (2002) "Cool Projects, Boring Institutions: Temporary Collaboration in Social Context", *Regional Studies*, 36, 3: 205–214.

Greenwood, J., Pyper, R. and Wilson, D. (2002) *New Public Administration in Britain*, London: Routledge.

Häussermann, H. and Simons, K. (2001) "Developing the New Berlin: Large Projects – Great Risks", *Geographische Zeitschrift*, 89, 2–3: 125–134.

Hollingsworth, J. R. and Boyer, R. (eds) (1997) *Contemporary Capitalism. The Embeddedness of Institutions*, Cambridge: Cambrdge University Press.

Hollingsworth, J. R., Müller, K. H. and Hollingsworth, E. J. (eds) (2002) *Advancing Socio-economics: An Institutionalist Perspective*, Lanham: Rowman & Littlefield.

Izushi, H. (1999) "Can a Development Agency Foster Co-operation among Local Firms? The Case of the Welsh Development Agency's Supplier Association Programme", *Regional Studies*, 33: 739–750.

Kaufmann, A. and Tödtling, F. (2000), "Systems of Innovation in Traditional Industrial Regions: The Case of Styria in a Comparative Perspective", *Regional Studies*, 34: 29–40.

Keeble, D., Lawson, C., Moore, B. and Wilkinson, F. (1999), "Collective Learning Processes, Networking and 'Institutional Thickness' in the Cambridge Region", *Regional Studies*, 33: 319–332.

Kenney, M. (ed.) (2000) *Understanding Silicon Valley: The Anatomy of an Entrepreneurial Region*, Stanford, CA: Stanford University Press.

Kübler, D. and Heinelt, H. (2005) *Metropolitan Governance: Capacity, Democracy and the Dynamics of Place*, London: Routledge.

Larsson, S. and Malmberg, A. (1999) "Innovations, Competitiveness and Local Embeddedness: A Study of Machinery Producers in Sweden", *Geografiska Annaler: Series B: Human Geography*, 81, 1: 1–18.

Laschewski, L., Phillipson, J. and Gorton, M. (2002) "The Facilitation and Formalization of

Small Business Networks: Evidence from the North East of England", *Environment and Planning C: Government and Policy*, 20: 375–391.

Leach, R. and Percy-Smith, J. (2001) *Local Governance in Britain*, London: Palgrave.

Leadbeater, C. (1999) *Living on Thin Air*, London: Viking.

Lefevre, C. (2004) "The Governability of Metropolitan Areas: International Experiences and Lessons for Latin America", Report for the Inter-American Bank for Development.

Le Galès, P. (2004) *European Cities*, Oxford: Oxford University Press.

Magnatti, P., Ramella, F., Trigilia C. and Viesti, G. (2005) *Patti territoriali. Lezioni per lo sviluppo*, Bologna: Il Mulino.

Moulaert, F., Swyngedouw, E. and Rodríguez, A. (2001) "Large Scale Urban Development Projects and Local Governance: From Democratic Urban Planning to Besieged Local Governance", *Geographische Zeitschrift*, 89, 2–3: 71–84.

Newton, K. (1982) "Is Small Really so Beautiful? Is Big Really So Ugly? Size, Effectiveness and Democracy in Local Government", *Political Studies*, 30: 190–206.

North, P., Valler, D. and Wood, A. (2001) "Talking Business: An Actor-centred Analysis of Business Agendas for Local Economic Development", *International Journal of Urban and Regional Research*, 25, 4: 830–846.

Novy, A., Redak, V., Jäger, J. and Hamedinger, A. (2001) "The End of Red Vienna: Recent Ruptures and Continuities in Urban Governance", *European Urban and Regional Studies*, 8, 2: 131–144.

OECD (2006a) *Competitive Cities in the Global Economy*, Paris: OECD.

OECD (2006b) *Territorial Review of France*, Paris: OECD.

Patrucco, P. P. (2003) "Institutional Variety, Networking and Knowledge Exchange: Communication and Innovation in the Case of the Brianza Technological District", *Regional Studies*, 37: 159–172.

Pike, A. (2002) "Task Forces and the Organization of Economic Development: The Case of the North East Region of England", *Environment and Planning C: Government and Policy*, 20: 717–739.

Proudfoot, N. (2004) "The Biopharmaceutical Cluster in Oxford", in Crouch *et al.* (2001), q.v., 237–260.

Raco, M. (2003) "Assessing the Discourses and Practices of Urban Regeneration in a Growing Region", *Geoforum*, 34: 37–55.

Raco, M., Turok, I. and Kintrea, K. (2003) "Local Development Companies and the Regeneration of Britain's Cities", *Environment and Planning C: Government and Policy*, 21: 277–303.

Rhodes, R. (1997) *Understanding Governance*, Buckingham: Open University Press.

Savitch, H. V. and Vogel, R. K. (2000) "Paths to New Regionalism", *State and Local Government Review*, 32: 158–168.

Stoker, G. (2004a) *Transforming Local Governance*, Basingstoke: Palgrave Macmillan.

Stoker, G. (2004b) "New Localism, Progressive Politics and Democracy", *The Political Quarterly*, 75, 1: 117–129.

Svensson, B. and Östhol, A. (2003) "From Government to Governance: Regional Partnerships in Sweden", *Regional and Federal Studies*, 11, 2: 25–42.

Sydow, J. and Staber, U. (2002) "The Institutional Embeddedness of Project Networks: The Case of Content Production in German Television", *Regional Studies*, 36: 215–227.

Tiebout, C. (1956) "A Pure Theory of Local Public Expenditures", *Journal of Political Economy*.

UK Government (2007) *Sustainable Communities Act 2007*, London: HMSO.

Valler, D., Wood, A. and North, P. (2000) "Local Governance and Local Business Interests: A Critical Review", *Progress in Human Geography*, 24, 3: 409–428.

Walter-Rogg, M. (2006) "Metropolitan Governance Reform in Germany", paper presented at conference", Governance and Spatial Discontinuities: Reterritorialization or a New Polarization of Metropolitan Spaces?", INRS-Urbanization, 24–25 April 2006, Montreal, www.vrm.ca/documents/Montreal2006_Working_Paper_Walter_Rogg_Sojer.pdf.

Further reading

Kübler, D. and Heinelt, H. (2005) *Metropolitan Governance: Capacity, Democracy and the Dynamics of Place*, London: Routledge.

Le Galès, P. (2004) *European Cities*, Oxford: Oxford University Press.

OECD (2006a) *Competitive Cities in the Global Economy*, Paris: OECD.

26

The politics of local and regional development

Andrew Wood

Introduction

This chapter concerns work on the politics of local and regional development. I start out by situating the emergence of the literature within the context of significant changes in the political economies of North America and Western Europe. A shift in how cities are governed coupled with the growing intensity of inter-locality competition stirred significant academic interest in the politics of local and regional development. The chapter then examines three different theoretical approaches that grapple with the politics of local and regional development. The first concerns the concept of urban entrepreneurialism and the related rise of a new urban politics (Harvey 1989). The second centres on the concept of the growth machine (Molotch 1976; Logan and Molotch 1987). The chapter turns, third, to examine the notion of the urban regime (Stone 1989, 1993). Collectively these concepts have served to revitalize the study of the politics of local and regional development. There are, however, important differences within this literature and the chapter sets out to describe the relative strengths of the different approaches. Over the past two decades the frameworks have spawned an expansive

literature that has now moved well beyond the North American context in which it first developed. The final section examines the portability of the different approaches. In this section I emphasize their limitations and the need for a careful and measured appraisal of how well they travel.

The origin of work on the politics of local and regional development

The initial impetus for work on the politics of local and regional development can be traced to a series of profound changes in the nature of the advanced capitalist economies of North America and Western Europe. Variously described as a period of economic restructuring or deindustrialization, the late 1970s and 1980s marked a transition from the relatively stable period of post-1945 economic growth based on classic Fordist industries to one in which local and regional economic fortunes were far less certain or secure. This was a time in which questions of local and regional development took on significant urgency. In short, local and regional development became a political matter.

This is not to suggest that Fordism had been marked by a universal pattern of local and regional prosperity. The health and vitality of local economies had always fluctuated with shifts in the capitalist space economy. Certain localities and regions such as the coal-mining communities based on resource extraction or areas focused on traditional manufacturing industries such as clothing and textiles had long witnessed significant changes in their economic fortunes and trajectories. However, the 1970s marked the beginning of an era in which uneven development and the prospects for future economic growth took on major political significance. At the same time the period saw a profound shift in the nature of the policy response. Earlier periods of economic difficulty had generally been met by national-level programmes and policies focused on 'disadvantaged' regions designated to receive state resources designed to mitigate economic decline. However, in the new era the institutional architecture took a different form. In Britain the period saw the growth of a new set of local economic development agencies and activities attached to local government, marking a significant shift in the spatial scale at which questions of local and regional development were addressed (Campbell 1990; Eisenschitz and Gough 1993). In the United States the picture was more complicated but the period of economic restructuring generated a pattern in which local and state governments adopted a more proactive role in seeking to protect and enhance the development of local and regional economies. The transformation is captured in David Harvey's argument, explored shortly, about a shift from urban managerialism to urban entrepreneurialism (Harvey 1989).

While a turbulent economic time heralded academic work designed to theorize the politics of local and regional development we should be careful not to overstate the novelty of the practices captured by the transition to entrepreneurialism. In the US South state and local government agencies had long been active in seeking to cultivate economic development largely on the basis of attracting industry and investment from established regions (Cobb 1982). The Frostbelt to Sunbelt shift of industry and employment within the US was accompanied by the vigorous promotion of Sunbelt locations, heralding a competition for inward investment that came to embrace an ever wider range of locations. The general spread of inter-locality competition also saw the development of various metrics designed to describe and account for the demise of the traditional manufacturing regions that constituted the Rustbelt and the corresponding growth of the US South. Perhaps the most widely cited was the Grant-Thornton business index, an annual measure first produced in 1979 that ranked states according to the health of their 'business climate'. The index and the ideas attached to it provided a model for policy makers that emphasized low corporate tax rates, relatively cheap labor and low levels of unionization. While the Grant-Thornton measure was criticized and subsequently abandoned the competition for inward investment took on a decidedly neoliberal hue, despite the heavy involvement of state agencies in orchestrating local economic development.

Urban entrepreneurialism

While recognizing a raft of earlier initiatives designed to promote local economic development, the 1980s marked a much more general shift in the significance attached to economic development and the extent of inter-locality competition. David Harvey has described the shift as a general transformation from urban managerialism to urban entrepreneurialism (Harvey 1989). For Harvey, urban politics had come to focus increasingly on local economic development:

> The new entrepreneurialism has as its centrepiece the notion of public–private partnership in which traditional

local boosterism is integrated with the use of local government powers to try and attract external sources of funding, new direct investments or new employment sources.

(Harvey 1989: 7)

Urban entrepreneurialism involved more than simply a shift in the policy agenda to prioritize economic development in place of the traditional emphasis on collective service provision. As Harvey indicates, urban entrepreneurialism was also bound up with changes in the institutional arrangements through which cities are run involving a shift from government to governance. Urban entrepreneurialism marked the adoption of a much more proactive role on the part of local interests seeking to capture and embed flows of investment and the economic activities attached to them. Accordingly, the city's economic health and prospects became central to understanding the politics of the city.

Harvey's argument concerning the shift to entrepreneurialism is influential and widely cited. The thesis captures a diverse set of concrete changes which Harvey links to an underlying shift in the extent and nature of territorial competition. This, in turn, is related to deep and persistent crisis tendencies in the capitalist space economy. The theoretical basis for Harvey's argument positions the shift as both widespread and lasting. Indeed, the argument has served as the context for a wide range of studies that have sought to examine how urban entrepreneurialism plays out in different national and local contexts (see, for example, Hall and Hubbard 1998).

Harvey's arguments have clear resonance in the work of others. For Kevin Cox the transition marked the development of a 'new urban politics' in which questions of local economic development were increasingly moved centre stage (Cox 1993, 1995). For Harvey and Cox territorial competition represents one particular expression of deep-seated and fundamental contradictions and

conflicts inherent to capitalism. For these authors local or place-dependent coalitions of interest signify a territorial form of politics that can serve to mask more traditional forms of class-based political struggle. For Cox and Mair the sense of a shared dependence on a particular territory "provides a basis for the suspension of conflict in favour of a solidarity within each locality... that can be turned against the locally dependent in other localities" (Cox and Mair 1988: 307).

The concept of urban entrepreneurialism is grounded firmly within the Marxist tradition, emphasizing the way in which local politics is embedded within a wider set of economic and political structures. However, the same period also saw the emergence of a set of novel ideas and frameworks that strive to capture the essence of the new urban politics by emphasizing the role of local agents and interests in shaping the politics of development. Two concepts in particular have assumed particular significance and I consider each in turn. The first is Harvey Molotch's concept of the 'growth machine', introduced in 1976 (Molotch 1976) and later elaborated with John Logan in Urban Fortunes (Logan and Molotch 1987). The second is Clarence Stone's concept of the urban regime (Stone 1989).

The growth machine

The growth machine is a compelling and yet relatively simple concept. Molotch argues that whatever the differences between powerful elite interests within US cities the mantra that holds them together is an overriding concern with the economic growth of the city. Furthermore, this is a near-universal phenomenon:

the political and economic essence of virtually any given locality, in the present American context, is *growth*. I further argue that the desire for growth provides the key operative motivation towards consensus for members of politically mobilized local elite.

(Molotch 1976: 309–310; emphasis in original)

Building on the claim that growth provides the basis on which elites come together Logan and Moloth detail the local interests that lie at the heart of the growth machine. The principal animators are what Logan and Molotch term 'rentiers' or 'place entrepreneurs' defined as, "the people directly involved in the exchange of places and collection of rents"(Logan and Molotch 1987: 29). The fortunes of place entrepreneurs rest upon the intensification of land use and the realization of exchange value tied to rising land and property rents that accompany economic growth. The tie to land and property and the drive to intensify land use provide the foundation for growth machine activity. While propertied interests sit at the core of the growth machine these local actors have to mobilize the powers and resources of local government in order to secure the infrastructural conditions and the general political climate conducive to growth. Beyond those with direct interests in land and property Logan and Molotch identify a further set of interests in growth that includes local politicians, the local media (see Ward 2009) and utilities along with a set of 'auxiliary players' such as universities, professional sports teams, cultural institutions, local retailers and even organized labour (Logan and Molotch 1987:75–85). These different actors and institutions are seen to share a collective interest in the conditions of the local economy and the realization of urban growth. Logan and Molotch argue that.

the pursuit of exchange values so permeates the life of localities that cities become organized as enterprises devoted to the increase of aggregate rent levels through the intensification of land use. The city becomes, in effect, a "growth machine."

(Logan and Molotch 1987: 13)

Given their power and privileged position Logan and Molotch argue that urban development effectively serves to transfer resources and wealth to the propertied interests that comprise the rentier class.

Urban regimes

The growth machine thesis rests, as Molotch explicitly acknowledges, on evidence drawn from the American city. Clarence Stone's work on urban regimes developed from research on the post-war politics of Atlanta, Georgia. Stone's (1989) book *Regime Politics: Governing Atlanta, 1946–1988* has become a landmark study in the politics of urban development. In looking at the changing contours of urban politics over the post-war period Stone identifies a basic continuity in the arrangements for governing Atlanta. While the individual protagonists came and went two groups dominated Atlanta's urban politics, forming a single urban regime committed to promoting the economic growth of the city. The governing coalition comprised Atlanta's downtown business elite and, reflecting the city's post-war black electoral majority, Atlanta's black middle class represented by the city's mayor. While these two groups comprised the governing coalition the concept of the regime rested on more than simply the identification of those with an interest in economic growth. The regime is defined as "an informal yet relatively stable group *with access to institutional resources* that enable it to have a sustained role in making governing decisions" (Stone 1989: 4; emphasis in original). While Stone's work on Atlanta focused largely on the material resources or incentives that sustained the regime he later defines resources as "not just material matters but also such things as skills, expertise, organizational connections, informal contacts, and level and scope of contributing effort by participants" (Stone 2005: 329). In addition to focusing on the composition of the regime and the resources mobilized by different regime members regime analysis directs attention to the nature of the relationship among the different coalition partners. As Stoker suggests, "the underlying issue is the extent to which a regime achieves a sustained capacity to act and influence developments in key policy areas" (Stoker 1995: 62). It is important to note that a commitment to growth is just one of a number of strategies that can define an urban regime. Indeed in reviewing cities across the US Stone identifies four different regime types (Stone 1993). The 'development' regime, characteristic of post-war Atlanta, is committed to promoting economic expansion. Such regimes bear close resemblance to the growth machine identified by Molotch.'Maintenance' regimes seek to promote the routine delivery of urban services, while 'middle-class progressive' regimes set out to address the environmental implications of development or harness the gains from economic growth. The fourth type – the 'lower class opportunity' regime – seeks to structure urban development in order to widen the distribution of economic and social benefits and opportunities. In relying on the mass mobilization of urban residents this regime is distinct from the other forms.While the mantra of 'growth' holds the growth coalition together, Stone's framework allows for a much wider range of urban agendas that help to define the nature and scope of the governing coalition. In this sense the regime framework proves capable of embracing a far wider range of scenarios than that associated with the growth machine model (Stoker and Mossberger 1994).

The concepts of the growth machine and the urban regime have been widely deployed. Most of the subsequent studies have, understandably, focused on the politics of local economic development, although its precise form varies from case to case. The two frameworks share significant strengths. The first, which they share with the concept of urban entrepreneurialism, is the move from a traditional concern with the formal structure and functions of local government to a broader focus on the question of governance and specifically on the ways in which local agencies develop what Stone terms 'the capacity to govern'. Regime and growth coalition accounts focus attention on a range of powerful interests deemed to be particularly influential in determining the nature of urban politics. In this sense the work furthers the long-standing interest in the US literature in the question of 'who governs?' (Dahl 1961; Harding 1995; Hunter 1953). Yet the move also marks a welcome departure from a traditional pluralist understanding of the state by drawing attention to the fact that different actors have quite different stakes in the nature, scope and outcomes of urban governance. Furthermore, such approaches are adept at highlighting the contested nature of the state and the ways in which conflicts over the state's multiple roles are commonly expressed via tensions between different departments and branches of the state (O'Neill 1997). Furthermore, while focusing squarely on the relationship between state agencies and interests within civil society these interests are by no means taken as a set of equivalent constituencies. Indeed work in the growth machine and regime traditions places particular emphasis on the relationship between the state and local business interests. Second, while the frameworks recognize the structural or systemic power of business interests in influencing the capacity to govern the frameworks also posit considerable scope for local agency. As Stone indicates, "urban regime analysis … concerns how local agency fits into the play of larger forces. Local actors are shaped by and respond to large structures, but the appropriate lens for viewing this wider field is local agency" (Stone 2005: 324). Third, both models direct attention to the informal ways in which local interests seek to shape and influence the pattern of urban governance. For Stone regime theory strives to examine "the informal arrangements by which public bodies and private interests function together in order to be able to make and carry out governing decisions" (Stone 1989: 8–9). Accordingly, a key strength of such work is in delving beyond the formal arrangements by which urban decisions are made in order to examine the negotiations and compromises that underpin urban decision-making.

In short, the frameworks highlight a concern with the practices and discourses that help to constitute urban strategy. A concern with the informal arrangements of governance also has important methodological implications for it brings with it a requirement for detailed qualitative work designed to examine how urban agendas are constructed and particular decisions are made. It is no coincidence that work that deploys such concepts tends to undertake case studies of particular cities or, at most, a small number of cases. Furthermore, the emphasis on the stability and endurance of governing coalitions favours detailed ethnographic work. After all, Clarence Stone's major contribution is based on the detailed study of a single city, Atlanta.

The politics of local and regional development beyond the US

While the concepts of the urban regime and the growth machine were developed to examine the US city, their use in a wide variety of different local and national contexts suggests considerable flexibility. In this section I examine the portability of these frameworks. The earliest applications beyond the United States are found in research looking at the politics of local economic development in Britain (Bassett 1996, 1999; Bassett and Harloe 1990; Cooke 1988; Harding 1991; Lloyd and Newlands 1988). I suggest that this work serves to highlight some of the limits as well as the strengths of the growth machine and urban regime frameworks. I then turn to the recent use of these concepts to study the politics of urban development in China.

The merit of exporting the US-based theories beyond their original context has generated a significant and ongoing debate. In one corner scholars argue that the frameworks reflect conditions particular to the US (Ward 1996; Wood 1996; Jessop et al. 1999; Davies 2003). For Peck and Tickell, "the growth machine hypothesis ... remains a framework with which to understand the particularity of US politics" (Peck and Tickell 1995: 59). While this is not to deny the capacity of the frameworks to shed light on the US case it does bring into question their wider application. However, others see any such problems as surmountable. Dowding and colleagues use the regime concept to explore local politics in London (Dowding et al. 1999), while Mossberger and Stoker argue that once suitably modified the use of the regime framework beyond North America has "facilitated the development of a valuable and plausible political economy perspective" (2001: 830).

The relationship between local state institutions and business interests provides a useful window on the question of the wider utility of regime and growth coalition models. This is, after all, the relationship that lies at the core of both frameworks. For Mossberger and Stoker (2001) the regime concept is particularly helpful in examining the extent and nature of business engagement in urban governance. And yet Harding suggests that in practice work on Britain has largely failed to examine the nature and scope of business mobilization (Harding 1999). In part this reflects basic differences in state form, not least the susceptibility of local state institutions in the US to the power and influence of business interests (Wood 2004). Despite these differences the 1980s saw a sustained effort to incorporate business interests into local policy-making in Britain and a number of studies examined the nature and extent of business mobilization, albeit often highlighting the difficulties involved in creating a shared and coherent local business vision (Peck 1995; Peck and Tickell 1995; Raco 2003;

Rogerson and Boyle 2000; Valler 1996; Wood et al. 1998; Valler and Wood 2004). Similar findings have been reported in other contexts in which business interests have come to play a more active role in urban politics. The much vaunted growth of "public–private partnerships' might be taken to mark convergence on the US model. However, despite a similar concrete form, work beyond the US commonly positions such coalitions as heavily orchestrated by the state rather than driven by the spontaneous engagement of local business interests. In the case of Sydney, McGuirk argues that, "beyond project-specific public–private partnerships, the formation of partnership-style relations with government has largely been state-orchestrated" (McGuirk 2003: 215). In continental Europe such partnerships can be seen to reflect the prominent and long-standing tradition of corporatism, while work on Britain suggests a similar dynamic in which engagement between local government and the private sector rests heavily on rules and norms established by central government (Jones and Ward 1998).

The tendency for US models to underplay the influence of the central state reflects its highly decentralized form. However, it also raises a wider conceptual issue concerning geographic scale and what many see as the limited ability of the growth coalition and urban regime models to conceptualize the place of local politics within processes and relationships that operate beyond the urban scale (Lauria 1997; Stoker 1995; Tretter 2008). Rather than treat the urban as both constituted by and constitutive of these broader scale processes they are merely seen to provide the context in which the dynamics of local/urban scale governance play out. As McGuirk suggests:

> the determinants of urban politics are predominantly understood … to be the local mediation of conflicting interests, the negotiated construction of coalition agendas, and the ongoing bargaining that characterizes the interdependence of state and markets in a locality.
>
> (McGuirk 2003: 203)

Yet urban politics is shaped by an interdependent set of political economic relations and processes that operate across a range of spatial scales that extends well beyond the urban. In place of a fixed, bounded and territorial notion of the urban recent work has begun to embrace a relational view of scale that reflects the open and dynamic interrelationship between activities, relations and processes stretched over different spatial extents (Macleod and Jones 2007). Rather than fall into the "localist trap" (Stoker 1995: 67), studies "require a multiscalar perspective" that serves to problematize "the scalar organization of governance" (McGuirk 2003: 204).

Related to the sanctity of the urban scale is the tendency for traditional frameworks to privilege the internal dynamics of urban regimes or coalitions or what Stone terms "the internal politics of coalition building" (1989: 178). What matters is how the state/market dynamic plays out within the urban arena and interest centres on how urban agendas are produced by a set of local agents trying to develop workable strategies that enable and encourage collective action. The emphasis on the role of the local newspaper in serving "to bolster and maintain the predisposition for general growth" (Logan and Molotch 1987: 72) is one sign of the emphasis on the internal machinations of urban coalitions. While such accounts highlight the vitality and agency of local actors and the complex ways in which urban agendas are negotiated and pursued they commonly serve to marginalize the role played by much wider discourses and practices that have national or international scope. Developments such as the rise of the 'creative city' or the 'global city' are examined as de facto changes in the context in which urban politics plays out rather than as ideas and practices that are partly constituted and reproduced by local agency at the urban scale. Once again, the urban scale and processes and relations beyond the urban are treated as analytically separate phenomena.

The privileging of the local scale and its internal politics is one reason why regime accounts commonly drift towards the detailed empirical description of urban governance rather than interpreting concrete cases through reference to more abstract theoretical frameworks. On this point the contrast with Harvey's account of urban entrepreneurialism is particularly telling. While work in the regime and growth coalition traditions explicitly recognizes the significance of social stratification there is little attempt to interpret regime types or growth coalition politics through a broader interpretive framework. For this reason regime accounts commonly struggle to explain regime change other than through reference to the internal dynamics of regime building. Furthermore, while regime analysis identifies a plethora of regime types it is often difficult to assess the significance of the differences between them given the absence of a broader theoretical framework in which to position them.

While the contextual limit of the regime and growth coalition concepts remains an open question the frameworks have been ever more widely adopted. The case of China proves particularly intriguing. As indicated above, a common starting point for work in the regime and growth coalition traditions is the manner in which two sources of power are combined and mobilized in order to bring about certain results. The first is the power of governmental authority which, in the US case, is seen to rest on the legitimacy of elected government. While elected officials are beholden to local constituencies the state has the resources and authority that enable the development and pursuit of an agenda designed to meet the goals of coalition interests. Yet these various interests clearly differ in terms of their own power and significance. Molotch and Stone recognize that in capitalist societies economic

power rests firmly with the ownership and control of economic assets or, in other words, the owners of private capital. On this basis private business interests are deemed to be essential to the coalitions that assemble together in order to devise and shape urban agendas (Mossberger and Stoker 2001). Given the systemic power of business interests it is little surprise that the strategies and policies pursued by governing coalitions tend to favour the owners of capital rather than other interests and groups within civil society.

On this basis China represents an interesting paradox. As Stoker indicates:

> Regime theory takes as given a set of government institutions subject to some degree of popular control and an economy guided mainly but not exclusively by privately controlled investment decisions.
>
> (Stoker 1995: 56)

Growth coalitions and urban regimes rest on stable, established patterns of accommodation between the state and a range of powerful business interests often represented through collective business organizations. Yet it is also clear that even when these conditions are present the existence of regimes is not guaranteed – it is a necessary but not sufficient condition. The popular control of government allied to the strength of local business interests would both seem to militate against the application of regime and growth coalition models to the Chinese case. However, a number of recent changes broadly captured in the notion of 'transition' are seen to have opened up the possibilities for such work (Zhang 2002). The decentralization of governmental decision-making and the growth of revenues outside of the central planning process provide a key incentive for more entrepreneurial forms of urban governance. With regard to local business interests the movement towards the commodification of land and property is seen to have the potential to generate the local 'landed interests' at the heart of the urban growth coalition (Zhu 1999). Furthermore, the speed and intensity of economic growth would also seem to highlight the prevalence of development as a political issue. As Zhu suggests, "pro-growth seems to be at the core of urban policies in the face of fierce economic competition" (Zhu 1999: 537). Given the nature of these changes both the growth coalition and urban regime models have recently been applied to examine urban development in China (Yang and Chan 2007; Zhang 2002; Zhu 1999; Wang and Scott 2008). While this work provides a very welcome addition to the literature on the comparative politics of local and regional development the analytical contribution of the growth coalition and urban regime concepts is much less clear. Harding's (1999) earlier argument concerning the tendency for research on Britain to use the terminology rather than the analytical purchase of the American models continues to resonate.

Conclusion

Traditional frameworks for understanding the politics of local and regional development have now generated a wealth of studies that have significantly enriched our understanding. Harvey's thesis on urban entrepreneurialism and the rise of the new urban politics has proved particularly influential, linking the politics of local and regional development to a powerful set of wider changes in the nature of the capitalist economy. The concepts of the growth machine and the urban regime have also provoked a welcome array of studies. Yet in closing I suggest that we continue to exercise some caution when applying these models beyond the US context. First, we should recognize the differences between contexts and the extent to which the US-based models reflect their particular place of origin. Regime and growth coalition models direct attention to

agendas and strategies that reflect the decentralized nature of the US state. Land use regulation provides just one example where powers of land use zoning and regulation rest very firmly with local tiers of government. Accordingly, the politics of land use intensification is very much a local matter.

Arguably, the parochialism of the models reflects a more general failure to theorize the state. Just as the nature and territorial configuration of the state can be brought into question attention should be given to the geographic specificity of the business interests that animate urban coalitions. Again the US context provides a particular set of circumstances that are not always widely replicated. Central to the urban regime and especially the growth coalition model are interests intimately connected to land and property. While this by no means exhausts the range of interests that engage in coalition activities it does serve to highlight the geographic specificity of the interests involved, or, what Cox and Mair term, their local dependence (Cox and Mair 1988; Cox 1998). What matters for the 'landed interests' is the realization of exchange values in a particular place. In short, the politics of local and regional development in the US remains driven by a set of interests with local stakes. Recent work on China, like much of the literature on the politics of local and regional development, pays relatively short shrift to the geographic specificity of the interests caught up in the politics of local and regional development. The centrality of land-based interests to the politics of local and regional development also has critical implications for what counts as 'development'. The traditional models presented in this chapter tend to privilege the way in which local and regional politics is animated by interests in a particular form of economic development, centred on local economic growth and, more narrowly still, on the intensification of land use. Again, the models reflect their time and place of origin and, as such, it is difficult to see how such approaches might handle the emergence of more holistic and sustainable understandings of development centred on strategies of low or no growth (Pike *et al.* 2006).

The coupling between strong business interests and local governmental power and authority in the pursuit of economic growth sits at the very centre of US-based work on the politics of local and regional development. This parochial emphasis is problematic, placing undue emphasis on local events and interests while failing to take into account sources of power and authority across the range of geographical scales. In part the emphasis on the local scale stems from the fact that much of the US-based work is rooted in urban studies. However, in turn, this reflects the particular conditions prevalent in the US, most notably the significant power and authority of sub-national government allied with strong and active local business interests.

References

Bassett, K. (1996) "Partnerships, business elites and urban politics: new forms of governance in an English city?", *Urban Studies* 33, 539–555.

Bassett, K. (1999) "Growth coalitions in Britain's waning Sunbelt: some reflections", in A. Jonas and D. Wilson (eds) *The Urban Growth Machine*, Albany New York: State University of New York Press, 177–193.

Bassett, K. and Harloe, M. (1990) "Swindon: the rise and decline of a growth coalition", in M. Harloe, C. Pickvance and J. Urry (eds) *Place, Policy and Politics*, London: Unwin Hyman, 42–61.

Campbell, M. (ed.) (1990) *Local Economic Policy*, London: Cassell Educational.

Cobb, J. (1982) *The Selling of the South: The Southern Crusade for Industrial Development, 1936–1980*, Baton Rouge, Louisiana: Louisiana State University Press.

Cooke, P. (1988) "Municipal enterprise, growth coalitions and social justice", *Local Economy* 3, 1319–1336.

Cox, K. (1993) "The local and the global in the new urban politics: a critical view", *Environment and Planning D* 11, 433–448.

Cox, K. (1995) "Globalisation, competition and the politics of local economic development", *Urban Studies* 32, 213–224.

Cox, K. (1998) "Spaces of dependence, spaces of engagement and the politics of scale, or: looking for local politics", *Political Geography* 17, 1–24.

Cox, K. and Mair, A. (1988) "Locality and community in the politics of local economic development", *Annals of the Association of American Geographers* 78, 307–325.

Dahl, R. (1961) *Who Governs?*, New Haven, CT: Yale University Press.

Davies, J. (2003) "Partnerships versus regimes: Why regime theory cannot explain urban coalitions in the UK", *Journal of Urban Affairs* 25, 253–269.

Dowding, K., Dunleavy, P., King, D., Margetts, H. and Rydin, Y. (1999) "Regime politics in London local governance", *Urban Affairs Review* 34, 515–545.

Eisenschitz, A. and Gough, J. (1993) *The Politics of Local Economic Policy*, Basingstoke, Hampshire: Macmillan.

Hall, T. and Hubbard, P. (eds) (1998) *The Entrepreneurial City: Geographies of Politics, Regime and Representation*, Chichester: John Wiley & Sons.

Harding, A. (1991) "The rise of urban growth coalitions, UK style?", *Environment and Planning C* 9, 295–317.

Harding, A. (1995) "Elite theory and growth machines", in D. Judge, G. Stoker and H. Wolman (eds) *Theories of Urban Politics*, London: Sage, 35–53.

Harding, A. (1999) "North American urban political economy, urban theory and British research", *British Journal of Political Science* 29, 673–698.

Harvey, D. (1989) "From managerialism to entrepreneurialism: the transformation of urban governance in late capitalism", *Geografiska Annaler* 71B, 3–17.

Hunter, F. (1953) *Community Power Structure: A Study of Decision Makers*, Chapel Hill, North Carolina: University of North Carolina Press.

Jessop, B., Peck, J. and Tickell, A. (1999) "Retooling the machine: economic crisis, state restructuring and urban politics", in A. Jonas and D. Wilson (eds) *The Urban Growth Machine*, Albany, NY: State University of New York Press, 141–159.

Jones, M. and Ward, K. (1998) "Grabbing grants? The role of coalitions in urban economic development", *Local Economy* 13, 28–38.

Lauria, M. (ed.) (1997) *Reconstructing Urban Regime Theory*, Thousand Oaks, CA: Sage.

Lloyd, G. and Newlands, D. (1988) "The 'growth coalition' and urban economic development", *Local Economy* 3, 31–39.

Logan, J. and Molotch, H. (1987) *Urban Fortunes: The Political Economy of Place*, Berkeley: University of California Press.

Macleod, G. and Jones, M. (2007) "Territorial, scalar, networked, connected: in what sense a 'regional world'?", *Regional Studies* 41, 177–191.

McGuirk, P. (2003) "Producing the capacity to govern in global Sydney", *Journal of Urban Affairs* 25, 201–223.

Molotch, H. (1976) "The city as a growth machine: toward a political economy of place", *American Journal of Sociology* 82, 309–332.

Mossberger, K. and Stoker, G. (2001) "The evolution of urban regime theory: the challenge of conceptualization", *Urban Affairs Review* 36, 810–835.

O'Neill, P. (1997) "Bringing the qualitative state into economic geography", in R. Lee and K.Willis (eds) *Geographies of Economies*, London: Arnold, 290–301.

Peck, J. (1995) "Moving and shaking: business elites, state localism and urban privatism", *Progress in Human Geography* 19, 16–46.

Peck, J. and Tickell, A. (1995) "Business goes local: dissecting the 'business agenda' in Manchester", *International Journal of Urban and Regional Research* 19, 55–78.

Pike, A., Rodríguez-Pose, A. and Tomaney, J. (2006) *Local and Regional Development*, London: Routledge.

Raco, M. (2003) "The social relations of business representation and devolved governance in the United Kingdom", *Environment and Planning A* 35, 1853–1876.

Rogerson, R. and Boyle, M. (2000) "Property, politics and the neo-liberal revolution in urban Scotland", *Progress in Planning* 54, 133–196.

Stoker, G. (1995) "Regime theory and urban politics", in D. Judge, G. Stoker and H. Wolman (eds) *Theories of Urban Politics*, London: Sage, 195–212.

Stoker, G. and Mossberger, K. (1994) "Urban regime theory in comparative perspective", *Environment and Planning C: Government and Policy* 12, 195–212.

Stone, C. (1989) *Regime Politics: Governing Atlanta, 1946–1988*, Lawrence, Kansas: University Press of Kansas.

Stone, C. (1993) "Urban regimes and the capacity to govern: a political economy approach", *Journal of Urban Affairs* 15, 1–28.

Stone, C. (2005) "Looking back to look forward – reflections on urban regime analysis", *Urban Affairs Review* 40, 309–341.

Tretter, E. (2008) "Scales, regimes and the urban governance of Glasgow", *Journal of Urban Affairs* 30, 87–102.

Valler, D. (1996) "Locality, local economic strategy and private sector involvement: case studies in Norwich and Cardiff", *Political Geography* 15, 383–403.

Valler, D. and Wood, A. (2004) "Devolution and the politics of business representation: a strategic relational approach", *Environment and Planning A* 36, 1835–1854.

Wang, Y. and Scott, S. (2008) "Illegal farmland conversion in China's urban periphery: local regime and national transitions", *Urban Geography* 29, 327–347.

Ward, K. (1996) "Re-reading urban regime theory", *Geoforum* 27, 427–438.

Ward, K. (2009) "Urban political economy, 'new urban politics' and the media: insights and limits", *International Journal of Urban and Regional Research* 33, 233–236.

Wood, A. (1996) "Analysing the politics of local economic development: making sense of cross-national convergence", *Urban Studies* 33, 1281–1295.

Wood, A. (2004) "Domesticating urban theory? US concepts, British cities and the limits of cross-national applications", *Urban Studies* 41, 2103–2118.

Wood, A., Valler, D. and North, P. (1998) "Local business representation and the private sector role in local economic policy in Britain", *Local Economy* 13, 10–27.

Yang, Y. and Chan, C. (2007) "An urban regeneration regime in China: a case study of urban redevelopment in Shaghai's Taipingqiao area", *Urban Studies* 44, 1809–1826.

Zhang, T. (2002) "Urban development and a socialist pro-growth coalition in Shanghai", *Urban Affairs Review* 37, 475–499.

Zhu, J. (1999) "Local growth coalition: the context and implications of China's gradualist urban land reforms", *International Journal of Urban and Regional Research* 23, 534–548.

Further reading

Cox, K. and Mair, A. (1988) "Locality and community in the politics of local economic development", *Annals of the Association of American Geographers* 78, 307–325. (A theoretical argument concerning the territorialized nature of the politics of economic development.)

Hall, T. and Hubbard, P. (eds) (1998) *The Entrepreneurial City: Geographies of Politics, Regime and Representation*, Chichester: John Wiley & Sons. (A collection of essays extending the concept of the entrepreneurial city.)

Harvey, D. (1989) "From managerialism to entre-preneurialism: the transformation of governance in late capitalism", *Geografiska Annaler* 71B, 3–17. (The classic statement of the nature of urban entrepreneurialism.)

Jonas, A. and Wilson, D. (eds) *The Urban Growth Machine*, Albany, NY: State University of New York Press. (A collection of critical commentaries on the concept of the growth machine.)

Molotch, H. (1976) "The city as a growth machine: toward a political economy of place", *American Journal of Sociology* 82, 309–332. (The classic statement introducing the concept of the growth machine.)

Stoker, G. (1995) "Regime theory and urban politics", in D. Judge, G. Stoker and H. Wolman (eds) *Theories of Urban Politics*, London: Sage, 195–212. (An introduction to the strengths and limits of urban regime theory.)

Stone, C. (1989) *Regime Politics: Governing Atlanta, 1946–1988*, Lawrence, Kansas: University Press of Kansas. (The classic study introducing the concept of the urban regime.)

27

Spatial planning and territorial development policy

Peter Ache

Introduction

In Europe, the systematic education of planners turned one hundred in 2009, taking the W.H. Lever Chair for Civic Design in University of Liverpool's Department of Civic Design as the commonly agreed starting point (Hall, 1996, Albers, 1997). The British founder of a company producing 'bare necessities of life' (with the slogan 'A bar of soap is a piece of hope') stands actually at the beginning of a systematic approach towards the education of people who plan and develop our living environment. In those days it was Victorian Utopian Humanist thinking which made Lever experiment with the 1887 Port Sunlight garden city – or for similar reasons Krupp with the 1909 Margarethen Höhe in Essen, at that time the German steel capital – giving people of the heavy days of industrialization a better life and living environment. A lively picture of these conditions was provided by Friedrich Engels (1892), observing the 'conditions of the working class' and its methods very 'dense' description of urban issues.

One hundred years later, spatial planning is still at the point of attempting to give people better places to live in and, at the same time, allowing them to produce their own little

harbours of delight, as well as the motorways to commute between spatially separated functions of work and living (due to the very influential Charter of Athens (CIAM) 1933, LeCorbusier 1942; see also the New Charter of Athens, http://www.ceu-ectp.org/e/athens/). The aspect of 'social deliberation' is possibly still there or might have been surpassed by questions of sustainability (Sachs and Santarius, 2007). What became a systematic activity at the level of individual quarters or model towns (the policing of buildings is a long-standing historic practice especially; see e.g. Benevolo, 2000) has evolved into a system of elaborate and highly integrated layers of government and non-government action. Those planning territorial development systems have faced change time and again and have, at least in the European context, also seen the rise of a new layer, that of the European Union (Faludi, 2007), no matter how elaborate this level is or is not at the start of the third millennium.

The following sections will elaborate on aspects of these dimensions – which are by no means an exhaustive account of what planning is or can be (an overview on existing practice can be found in Ryser and Franchini, 2008). In the first section, formal planning systems will be addressed and the increasing 'hybridization' of planning activities outlined. Whereas over its history the planning task might have been easily captured by one dimension only, in today's world planners face much more complex tasks and need to invent new approaches to cope with those challenges. The second section will elaborate on new spatial structures and problem situations, mainly from a European perspective. The main point here is the enlarged spatio-functional context surpassing traditional spatial patterns and city perimeters and establishing polycentric metropolitan spaces at a European level. The management and the achievement of territorial cohesion (if at all) are major issues of the future. The third section will widen the perspective and look across European borders into those development features which have already been labelled as 'urban millennium'. The dire outlooks of population 'metapolises' (UN Habitat, 2006) of the southern hemisphere call for new planning governance and sustainability but are also full of social innovations. The concluding remarks at the end remind us that there is still a utopian function for cities in society.

Territorial development systems

Planning and territorial development, defined as a coordinated approach towards specific aims or objectives, is usually based on a set of processes and institutional structures and at least in part defined as an act of sovereignty with mandatory results. This statement might surprise in the face of the many different forms which the core activities in the professional field have taken, as is indicated by the notion of a change 'from government to governance'. Yes, planning has changed its instruments and procedures and much has happened over recent years in terms of empowerment, participation and new managerial approaches in planning. But try imagining a multi-billion Euro investment being fixed without a solid legally binding basis

(e.g. a local plan, even if this is increasingly negotiated between public and private parties) (Ennis, 2003). For the exploding population mega metropolises one instrument which helps in getting those cities straight is to empower citizens via ownership of land, enabling the citizens to take responsibility without being expelled (e.g. property rights, land titles and registers, cadastres; see UN Habitat, 2006). A 'planner' usually has to be 'registered' to have the full rights in professional terms (i.e. the role of professional associations regulating markets; see Geppert and Verhage, 2008). This starts usually at the higher education level with the question whether a course in planning has been 'accredited' (in the UK e.g. by the Royal Town Planning Institute; see Ache, 2008b). In sum, there are many complex 'system dimensions' structuring the field, and some of the core aspects, in particular institutional structures and plans, will be addressed in the following sections.

Over past years research but also practice related-projects (like the Interreg IIIB Baltic Sea Region; see http://commin.org/en/commin/) tried to develop a full picture of such dimensions of planning and territorial development systems. One such project was the 'compendium of European planning systems' (European Commission, 1997). In 2006, with the enlarging European Union a fresh overview was needed and provided, using a more generic approach to understand the governance of territorial and urban policies from EU to local level, acknowledging the more elaborate structure and changes inside territorial development (University of Valencia et al., 2006). The analysis of territorial development systems is an altogether difficult venture, given that there are not only differences between state systems (due to varying constitutional settings or basic laws) but also because of cultural differences which are expressed in varying professional traditions. Despite variations in what constitutes such systems in the various countries, on the basis of the compendium we can identify some structural similarities. At the national level we can find spatial planning frameworks as point of reference for lower tiers with a coordination function. At the regional level again spatial planning policies have been defined as frame of references for intra-regional development. At the level of regions there is also the overlap with regional policy, i.e. the economically driven development of regions. And, last but not least, at the local level spatial frameworks can be found, but then again, instruments stipulating and controlling land use (especially land use plans) are even more important. So, the usual composition of planning systems works with a multi-level government of three to four layers. With the European Union and the discussions outlined earlier, we are likely to see one additional layer arising (Faludi, 2008). One decisive element of such an analysis is the locus of power (i.e. who has the right to define what kind of development is intended and allowed) and between how many levels the power (in planning) is distributed. In a plan-led system like the one established in Germany, the existing levels are linked together by what is called the 'counter current principle', i.e. frameworks at national level have to be respected by lower tiers, whereas existing strategies or projects inform the comprehensive planning documents of the upper tier.

When looking into the predominant professional orientation and dimensions, the various systems in Europe have been categorized as follows (European Commission, 1997).

Urbanism tradition is the managing of space through the smallest geographical unit available, the physical structure, through building regulations. Countries that can be classified under the urbanism tradition don't have spatial plans on a higher scale, or are not developed when they do exist, but only have building regulations (e.g. Mediterranean Countries).

Land use management is the planning of space through the development of a local plan for the future use of land in accordance with the land's capabilities through zoning laws based on the regulation and control of land controlling the changes of use. All land use plans distinguish at least three categories of land use, namely: infrastructure, urban and open land. In the case where a country has a land use planning style it has a land use plan in the form of a municipal or other plans at the local level, for instance, a land use designation plan. Furthermore, plans on a higher scale are absent (e.g. UK).

Regional economic approach is the managing of space through the development of regional plans that are made by either the regions or the national level. Regional planning deals with the efficient placement of infrastructure and zoning of economic activities and population for the sustainable growth of a region; it addresses region-wide issues such as environment, social and economic concerns. It pursues a balanced spatial development in all fields (spatial justice). When a country can be categorized under the regional economic approach style it has regional plans, national plans with a regional focus and local plans that are there to execute the regional plans (usually because hierarchic relations among levels and spatial justice presuppose presence of a main tutorial level) (e.g. France).

Comprehensive integrated approach is the managing of space through a hierarchical system of spatial plans on several geographical levels taking into account all relevant sectors that have an impact on the spatial development. It is related with land use and cross-sectoral coordination. Countries that fall under the comprehensive integrated approach planning always have a hierarchy of plans and institutions with a planning competency. Furthermore one can see vertical and horizontal coordination between the different sectors and levels taking place (e.g. Nordic Countries, Germany).

The second part of the aforementioned report (University of Valencia et al., 2006) approached the issue of territorial development from a governance perspective, i.e. trying to pay attention to the general changes in state action. The conceptualization followed a multi-level approach, reflecting among others the shifting of responsibilities (but not always also resources) towards lower levels, which are observable in various states. Parallel to that, also the more formal approach towards territorial development opened to softer horizontally integrated approaches. Furthermore, not only at the EU level a strong connection with regional economic policy exists. In general, a discussion of a more integrated approach and the reorientation of planning systems is observable. The first impulse comes from the territorial cohesion theme (CEC, 2008) which is so prominent at the European level, demanding a more integrated territorial approach in all its development activities (EC, 2006, EC and Ministers for Spatial Development, 2005). The second point is that the existing planning systems increasingly evolve towards the comprehensive integrative and the regional economic management models (University of Valencia *et al.*, 2006). Ultimately the message is that territorial organization matters with the implication that coordination and development using integrated schemes is of the essence. This does not mean a strict hierarchical approach in the sense of primacy of any level over the other, but of agreed and discussed sets of aims and objectives. An important further aspect is the need for a more cooperative approach between national territories. This idea of 'territorial cooperation' has been built into the current ERDF regulations as one of the major policy orientations and it has therefore become a part of EU regional development policy (EC, 2006).

In addition to these large-scale systems shifts, are there further visible changes inside the planning systems, giving them a new character? A synthesis (Fürst, 2005) of such changes from a German perspective (arguing against the background of a rather elaborate plan-led system) includes:

i) The replacing of a rather technocratic approach with one emphasizing communicative action (towards planning diplomacy).

ii) A superseding of what might be called 'basic spatial ordering' with a development function including the development of a new regional governance (ultimately very closely connecting the two fields of planning with regional development).

iii) The embracing of project-based planning, i.e. using projects as drivers and components for more comprehensive plans.

iv) The incorporation of 'stakeholders' to promote 'problem ownership'.

v) The opening up of expert-led planning as a political arena via integration of wider groups (actually going beyond 'stakeholders').

vi) The attempt to control projects via Environmental Impact and Territorial Impact Assessment (regarding the latter see various projects of the ESPON research programme, http://www.espon.eu/).

vii) The adoption of management concepts on the side of institutions but also for processes.

viii) The management by objectives in the frame of sustainable development.

ix) The introduction of economic control instruments (e.g. licensing).

Planning, in sum, shows therefore several tendencies, establishing hybrid systems between still important formal foundations, which need to be politically and democratically legitimized, and new 'governance' features, of an increasingly softer nature and bringing in more parties to 'chart the courses of action into the future' (Friedmann, 1987). The next section will look into the new territories for which planning and development need to draft those courses of actions.

Spatial development problems

Spatial planning and territorial development policy look onto a considerable set of spatial problem situations (EC and DG Regional Policy, 2007, European Commission, 2008a, European Commission, 2008b, World Bank, 2009). The complexity of societal development lends itself to a matching set of not least 'unintended spatial consequences' of policies and practices. Looking into this landscape there is clearly an indication that we need more 'planning' instead of less. For instance, it is quite obvious that market interactions alone do not produce the best result, where best might be defined in the sense of a 'common good' or 'public interest'. This is a constant struggle in planning and territorial development (Hillier and Healey, 2008), battles 'lost and won' on an almost daily basis. By way of demonstration, looking at the actual global economic crisis and responses by various governments to control the onward effects, in many cases public investments into infrastructures are considered a possible solution. However, building broadband networks, motorways, investing in built structures in general (no matter how beneficial this might be for a local populace in the individual case) for instance, put strategies to harness the consumption of unspoilt unbuilt land immediately at risk and therefore the aims of sustainability.

This said, the core process driving land use in our modern Western societies is clearly the economy and its varying features over different periods of time. The question here is, which spatial form the economy takes, e.g. what links global flows and local conditions (Swyngedouw, 1992)? Two scenarios will be looked at to demonstrate those concerns. One is the work by Pierre Veltz (2004) who speaks about 'archipelago economies'. The second resulted from the ESPON research programme, namely the projects on territorial futures (ESPON 3.2 Project, 2007, Robert and Lennertz, 2007). The core of the first hypothesis builds on metropolitan spaces (the OECD defines a metropolis of at least one million inhabitants; OECD, 2006) which become the adequate 'ecosystems' of advanced technology and economy.

A threefold reinforcement process of increased mobility factors, innovation and quality-based competition, and general metropolization forms the positive feedback triangle. Metropolitan regions are the principal suppliers of the relational resources that fuel open-ended coordination processes, which cannot be set up either by decision making of a centralized techno-structure or through sheer market forces (Veltz, 2004). In terms of spatial structures, the resulting picture is that of a system of highly dynamic and well-connected metropolitan islands on which the better off and economic dynamic parts of society settle, which are floating in deserts of abandoned spaces (see below on the situation in East Germany).

In terms of further territorial futures, the ESPON 3.2 Project (2007) describes the economic core territory of the European Union, what was once called 'Blue Banana' (Brunet, 1989) or the 'Pentagon' (EC, 1999), as an 'oscillating' space, depending on whether those scenarios continue a trend, look at the effects of increased competitiveness or attempt to compensate at a regional level. In particular the competition scenario (following basically the ideas of the Lisbon strategy; Lisbon European Council, 2000) is alarming, describing a further concentration of growth processes on the European core territory. In fact, looking at one of the key indicators Europe is interested in, which is R&D activities, already today most of it is concentrated in the centre (e.g. about 60 per cent of all patents in 2002 came from that region; ESPON Project 3.1 and BBR, 2006 (October)).

This large-scale picture re-emphasizes the need to think about 'territorial cohesion', which will be the prominent issue for Europe over the coming years:

"The concept of territorial cohesion extends beyond the notion of economic and social cohesion by both adding to this and reinforcing it. In policy terms, the objective is to help achieve a more balanced development by reducing existing disparities, avoiding territorial imbalances and by making both sectoral policies which have a spatial impact and regional policy more coherent. The concern is also to improve territorial integration and encourage co-operation between regions".

(EC, 2004)

Territorial development policies financed by the Structural Funds of the EU have since their inception in the mid-1970s attempted to initiate a catch-up process (Ache, 2004). The results of it can be expressed as a relative process of cohesion, i.e. least developed regions can be more dynamic but they start from a very low level (in the EU from index values of 40 where the EU average is 100; European Commission, 2008b) – but this means also that we speak about generations to come or need ultimately to bring the most disadvantaged regions closer to the currently leading regions (Bröcker et al., 2004, Cheshire and Carbonaro, 1997).

Territorial cohesion at the level of the EU is at the moment the theme which might lever proper planning activities in addition to regional development policies, using an integrated comprehensive approach (to remain in the terminology of the previous section). However, at the same time the immediate policy orientation seems to turn away from a compensation pattern towards a 'strengthening of the strong' and hoping for spread effects. The guidelines for the Structural Funds are read here as an indicator for such an approach or model (EC, 2006). The texts however also emphasize the potentials of 'territorial capital' (European Commission, 2005, OECD, 2001) which is diverse in Europe (and should continue being diverse) and which should be utilized by the less advantaged regions to the maximum possible effect. It will be interesting to observe how the practice will work and whether we will see a possibly accelerating process of cohesion.

In any case, looking at such problems in various countries (like the UK, Finland or Germany) it is obvious that from a planning perspective the professional world will still have to cope with disadvantaged regions. In the UK context, the dominating southern region around London almost strangulates the rest of the country (Buck et al., 2005). In the Finnish context, the demographic change and internal migration movements will empty the expansive countryside (Steinbock, 2007). The unification of East with West Germany did not result in blossoming landscapes but, on the contrary, nowadays planners are talking about 'perforated cities' (Lütke-Daldrup, 2001, Sander, 2006), where entire quarters were abandoned and housing or infrastructure systems have fallen derelict. It is especially this latter phenomenon, which provides at the moment the most striking 'evidence' for the scenarios mentioned at the outset, in particular with reference to the 'archipelagos'. Beyond such already serious anecdotes, what are other spatial development trends for which answers have to be found in Europe?

Clearly one major issue relates to demographic changes, migration and multicultural societies. Births and deaths, ageing and the balance of inward to outward migration are the main drivers of demographic change. Their individual combination is a response to external factors in fields like economy, life-styles, general cultural setting and – talking about an individual – aspirations (ESPON Project 3.1 and BBR, 2006). Migration becomes the prime driver of regional population changes. Europe is one of the major net immigration areas globally:

All migratory flows, whether external or internal in relation to the EU, as well as in inter-and intra-regional movements, are regionally targeted and age-specific. A redistribution from less favoured to more favoured areas occurs. ... Demographic structures and trends in Europe highlight the potential for a further increase in regional polarisation, with declining and growing areas existing side by side. Urban areas and metropolitan agglomerations are the main winners from current demographic trends. They are the regions in which positive migratory balances reinforce positive natural increases or compensate for natural population losses in this era when families have fewer children. The south of Germany, central England and southern and western France, as well as Ireland, are representatives of this kind of region.

(ESPON 3.1, 2006: 11)

European cities are increasingly turning into the multi cultural stages of our societies (Sandercock, 1998, 2003). This implies new forms of potentials but also conflict not least over contested spaces (Harvey, 1997). In 2008/2009 the city of Rotterdam, I guess as one of the very first, saw the election of a new mayor with a migratory background and of Muslim faith. Looking at him in this high political office, citizens with a migratory background have finally arrived in the centre of our societies. And hopefully, the cynical comment made by Max Frisch on the politics in the 1950s and 1960s can be buried: "Wir riefen Arbeitskräfte, und es kamen Menschen" (We called labour force, and 'Menschen' came; Frisch, 1965). Beyond or on side of ethnic issues many more social problems characterize in particular our cities (Ache and Andersen, 2008, 2009).

In summary, the direct and indirect spatial effects of what can be called 'globalization' (Held and McGrew, 2000, Taylor, 2004) or 'glocalization' (Swyngedouw, 1992) create new spatial structures which also have an increasingly growing interdependency and responsibility (Massey, 2005). Urban development processes show a 'transitional' character in that they are no longer confined to tightly bounded cities but spread out into urban regions of unprecedented scale with the possible climax of a 70 million inhabitant

'Europolis' (Hall and Pain, 2006). The look across European boundaries proves that such a situation is already there, as the next section will demonstrate.

Urban millennium

The final point of this chapter tries to open the perspective which until now was mainly the perspective of the 'northern hemisphere' and Europe. The UN Habitat programme has labelled the new millennium as 'urban', i.e. alluding to the continuous streams of people into the population mega-metropolises, basically of the 'southern hemisphere' posing different planning problems to respond, like the principal organization of 'cities', urban social divides, or risk through environmental disasters, to name the important ones.

UN Habitat (2006) in view of the World Development Goal 7: 'Ensure Environmental Sustainability, Improving the Lives of at Least 100 Million Slum Dwellers' produced an extensive report on the state of the world's cities with alarming results regarding the negative side of things: "Africa is the least urbanised continent but by 2030 its urban population will exceed the total population of Europe." Also the World Development Report 2009 (World Bank, 2009) foresees a continued process of concentration of populations in mega-cities in the 'southern hemisphere', i.e. in situations of serious development problems. The United Nations (UN Habitat, 2006) speak about 'metapolises' with more than 20 million inhabitants which grow in particular in the developing countries. One out of every three city dwellers – nearly one billion people –already lives in a slum. The forecast for 2020 is 1.4 billion altogether. The problems are revealed through the criteria which are applied to measure 'slum conditions': durable housing, sufficient living area, access to improved water, access to sanitation, secure tenure (referring back to the formal instruments still needed in planning). The future of such a radically unequal and explosively unstable urban world has been captured by Mike Davis (2006), speaking about a 'planet of slums' and portraying a vast humanity 'warehoused in shantytowns and exiled from the formal world economy'.

Already in the year 2000 for the Global Conference on the Urban Future held in Berlin, Hall and Pfeiffer prepared a report based on the results provided by a 'World Commission URBAN 21' and a related expert group which worked for more than two years on millennial challenges of the urban world in 2025. One of the main sections formulates so-called 'urban essentials', i.e. dimensions of a sustainable city. These can be listed as follows: a sustainable urban economy – work and wealth; a sustainable urban society – social coherence and solidarity; sustainable urban shelter – decent affordable housing for all; a sustainable urban environment – stable ecosystems; sustainable urban access – resource-conserving mobility; sustainable urban life – building the liveable city; and sustainable urban democracy – empowering the citizenry.

All of these very broad issues are bound together with what Hall and Pfeiffer (2000) call 'good governance in practice'. The basic principles are laid down in strong urban government at a local level with adequate distribution of responsibilities and resources. The normative aim is set to sustainable development, i.e. the major concern lies with health and pollution, recycling and renewable energy, in general high sanitation standards. But also economic growth and social inclusion are obvious aims. The liveable city in the end is a city which provides proper housing and infrastructures, allowing citizens successfully to seize opportunities and develop their individual potentials accordingly. Here the question is also raised: what kind of planning can 'poor' cities afford? The answer meanders between a yes ascertaining universally applicable principles and solutions and a no, as the hyper-growth city will always be a fragmented city of planned and unplanned sections.

The report did not find unanimous acclaim and has been criticized by John Friedmann (2002) as a typical view from the developed world. As to the issues, they can also be critically reviewed, not least with a view towards the imprints and resulting responsibilities which colonial periods of the past left behind. For instance, most of the planning ideas and features of planning systems, including the education of planners, go back to those periods and might be considered culturally inadequate. In terms of the normative orientations for 'development', again most ideas were generated from a support philosophy, focusing on model orientations of 'exogenous' vs. 'endogenous' development (see Vázquez-Barquero, 2002) or following from 'growth pole' ideas (referring to the work by F. Perroux in the 1950s; see Parr, 1999a, 1999b).

One of the most conspicuous trends of the last decade has been the transformation of the state, creating new arenas for pluralistic debates and helping a more diversified range of actors to emerge. One-party or military governments have been replaced by multi-party systems and civil society organizations have gained voice. The decentralization of government functions and their devolvement to regional and local political and administrative levels is progressing, albeit slowly. The last decade has, however, also seen increased political destabilization in some parts of the world, internal conflicts, civil wars or 'failed states'.

Given the extended global economic relations nowadays, much of the 'development issues' therefore are subject to conflicting interests if not power games. Rather typical than a-typical continues to be the issue of resource exploitation. By way of an example, much of the communication technology for the Western information and communication society depends on 'tantal oxides' (coltan), for which the main global supplier nowadays is the Democratic Republic of the Congo (so at least the official title). As observers report, "Mineral firms 'fuel Congo unrest'" (BBC News, 2009), pointing out the power games not only between local groups (in part militia) but also between global economic interests and nation states, leaving much of the population in unrest or a state of flight. Urban areas and cities are in such a context often the locus of conflict.

In sum, does this constitute a perspective that inescapably results in a dystopia? And has the 'utopian' power of the city, as essentially the important place of individual freedom, escape, opportunity, innovation and creation of new solutions vanished? The European view might be largely covered by a 'veil of ignorance' in this respect, but looking into cities of the 'southern hemisphere' and their approaches towards social and environmental issues, there is a lot to be learnt. The 2006 Nobel Peace Prize went to Muhammad Yunus and the Grameen Bank, pioneers of microfinance, supporting social entrepreneurship which not least has a strong gender impact and aims at a self-sustained economy. Meanwhile, micro-credits re-enter the 'northern' cities as a tool to remedy unemployment under conditions of economic crisis.

Conclusions

In their edited publication on the 'Endless Metropolis', Burdett and Sudjic (2007) bring together the dimensions of a London School of Economics-based Urban Age Project:

> (It) is ... an exploration of the connec-tions between urban form and urban society, translating a conventionally constrained two-dimensional discourse into a three-dimensional dialogue. In (...) the insights of Jane Jacobs (...) that 'the look of things and the way they work are inextricably bound together'.

The project reflects on key investigation areas, like the changing nature of work and its impact on the physical form of the city; the effects of mobility and transport systems on social cohesion and economic viability; how the design of housing and neighbour-hoods affects local communities and urban integration; and how the public life and urban spaces of the city foster or impede tol-erance and conflict among the different con-stituencies (Burdett and Sudjic, 2007: 10). But there is also the intention to generate new ideas and impulses for the betterment of local living situations, understanding cities "as places where 'urban life becomes a source of mutual strength rather than a source of mutual estrangement and civic bitterness'" (Burdett and Sudjic, 2007).

Cities and metropolitan regions are not just concentrations of problems – which they are, too – but they are also the places where we create the solutions to problems in an ongoing set of experiments and failures. Planning professionals do what they can to create and shape those 'spaces of hope', some-times futile but many more times surpris-ingly effectively and efficiently.

And what could be the utopian dimen-sions? John Friedman (2002), one of the most out- and long-standing 'urbanists', keeps to a vision of a 'good city', consisting of both a manual of indispensable processes and normative indications for achievements. The 'good city' is a political act in the sense of Arendt's 'vita activa' (Arendt 1958). John Friedmann postulates as a common aim of the 'good city' human flourishing, a minimal agenda of appropriate homes, health, waged labour, and social networks and infrastruc-tures. A central instrument for this is 'good governance', in the end also good govern-ment, which consists of inspired and inspir-ing political actors with visions, publicly accountable, working transparently, satisfying the public information duty. All citizens have equal rights to the city, harnessing and forc-ing politics to be responsive. Suffice it to say that this society is free of aggression but not free from conflict, and solutions are found in peaceful ways. 'A Bias for Hope' (John Friedmann quoting Albert Hirschmann) is the overall guidance for that vision:

"The position I hold is for inclusive, democratic practices, for local citizen rights, for peaceful, multicultural diversity in the cities of this world, for cooperative rather than competitive solutions, and for meaningful intervention by states in the market economy to protect and further citizen rights"
(Friedmann, 2002).

References

Ache, P. (2004) Auf dem Weg zu, territorialer Kohäsion – Strukturprogramme und Raumentwicklung Raumplanung, 182–186.

Ache, P. (2008a) 'AESOP perspective: Strengthening our member schools in the changing landscape of planning', in Geppert, A. and Verhave, R. (eds) Towards a European Recongition for the Planning Profession, AESOP.

Ache, P. (2008b) 'Raumplanerausbildung in Europa – Situation und Perspektiven', Raumforschung und Raumordnung, 496–506.

Ache, P. and Andersen, H. (2008) 'Cities between competitiveness and cohesion: discourses, realities and implementation – introduction', in Ache, P., Andersen, H., Maloutas, T., Raco, M. and Tasan-Kok, T. (eds) Cities Between Competitiveness and Cohesion: Discourses, Realities and Implementation, NN: Springer.

Ache, P. and Andersen, H. (2009) 'Reconciling competitiveness with cohesion – ambivalent realities in metropolitan settings', DISP, 45 (1), 31–38.

Albers, G. (1997) Zur Entwicklung der Stadtplanung in Europa: Begegnungen, Einflüsse, Verflechtungen, Braunschweig, Vieweg.

Arendt, H. (1958) The Human Condition, Chicago: University of Chicago Press.

Baraquero, A. V. (2002) Endogenous Development: Networking, Innovation, Institutions and Cities, London and New York: Routledge Chapman & Hall.

BBC News (2009) Mineral firms 'fuel Congo unrest', BBC News. 21 July London: BBC.

Benevolo, L. (2000 21 July) Die Geschichte der Stadt, Frankfurt New York: Campus.

Bröcker, J., Roberta Capello, L. L., Roland Meyer, Jan Rouwendal, Nils, Schneekloth, A. S., Martin Spangenberg, Klaus Spiekermann, Daniel Van Vuuren R. V., Michael Wegener (2004) ESPON 2.1.1 Territorial Impact of EU Transport and TEN Policies.

Brunet, R. (1989) Les villes europeennes. La Documentation Francaise, Paris: RECLUS, DATAR.

Buck, N., Gordon, I., Harding, A. and Turok, I. (eds) (2005) Changing Cities. Rethinking Urban Competitiveness, Cohesion and Governance, Basingstoke and New York: Palgrave Macmillan.

Burdett, R. and Sudjic, D. (eds) (2007) The Endless City. The Urban Age Project by the London School of Economics and Deutsche Bank's Alfred Herrhausen Society, London: Phaidon.

Cheshire, P. and Carbonaro, G. (1997) 'Testing models, describing reality or neither convergence and divergence of regional growth rates in Europe during the 1980s', in Peschel, K. (ed.) Regional Growth and Public Policy Within the Framework of European Integration, Heidelberg: Physica Verlag.

CIAM (1933) The Charter of Athens, The Functional City Athens: CIAM.

Davis, M. (2006) Planet of Slums, London: Verso.

Dürrenmatt, F. (1980) Die Physiker, Neufassung: Diogenes Verlag.

Engels, F. (1892) Friedrich Engels, The Condition of the Working-class in England in 1844, London: Swan Sonnenschein & Co.

Ennis, F. (ed.) (2003) Infrastructure Provision and the Negotiating process, Aldershot: Ashgate.

ESPON 3.2 Project (2007) Spatial Scenarios, Bonn.

ESPON Project 3.1 and BBR (EDIT) (2006) (October)) ESPON ATLAS. Mapping the Structure of the European Territory, Bonn.

European Commission (1997) The EU Compendium of Spatial Planning Systems and Policies, Luxembourg: Office for Official Publications of the EC.

European Commission (1999) ESDP – European Spatial Development Perspective. Towards Balanced and Sustainable Development of the Territory of the European Union. Agreed at the Informal Council of Ministers responsible for Spatial Planning in Potsdam, May 1999.

European Commission (2004) A New Partnership for Cohesion – Convergence, Competitiveness, Cooperation. Third report on economic and social cohesion. Luxembourg: Office for Official Publications of the European Communities.

European Commission (2005) Territorial State and Perspectives of the European Union. Towards a

Stronger European Territorial Cohesion in the Light of the Lisbon and Gothenburg Ambitions. Scoping document and summary of political messages, Luxembourg: Ministers for Spatial Development, European Commission.

European Commission (2006) *Proposal for a Council Decision on Community strategic guidelines on cohesion* {SEC(2006) 929} (presented by the Commission) COM(2006) 386 final.

European Commission and DG Regional Policy (2007) *State of European Cities Report: Adding Value to the European Urban Audit*, Brussels: CEC

European Commission, (2008a) *Growing Regions, Growing Europe. Fifth Progress Report on Economic and Social Cohesion*, COM(2008) 371 final. Luxembourg.

European Commission (2008b) Regions 2020. *An Assessment of Future Challenges for EU Regions*, Commission Staff Working Document. Brussels: DG Region.

European Commission (2008c) *Green Paper on Territorial Cohesion. Turning territorial diversity into strength. Coomunication from the Commission to the Council, the European Parliament, the Committee of the Regions and the European Economic and Social Committee*, COM(2008)616 final, Brussels: CEC.

Faludi, A. (2007) 'Making sense of the "territorial agenda of the European Union", *European Journal of Spatial Development*. URL: http://www.nordregio.se/EJSD/refereed25.pdf.

Faludi, A. (ed.) (2008) *European Spatial Research and Planning*, Cambridge, MA: Lincoln Institute of Land Policy.

Friedmann, J. (1987) *Planning in the Public Domain: From Knowledge to Action*, Princeton, NJ: Princeton University Press.

Friedmann, J. (2002) *The Prospect of Cities*, Minneapolis: University of Minnesota Press.

Frisch, M. (1965) 'Zürich-Transit. Skizze eines Films. Überfremdung': Vorwort zum Buch "Siamo italiani. Gespräche mit italienischen Gastarbeitern", in Seiler, A. J. (ed.) *Siamo Italiani. Gespräche mit italienischen Gastarbeitern*, Zürich: EVZ.

Fürst, D. (2005) 'Entwicklung und Stand des Steuerungsverständnisses in der Raumplanung', *DISP*, 16–27.

Geppert, A. and Verhage, R. (2008) *Towards a European Recognition for the Planning Profession.* Leuven Heverlee: AESOP.

Hall, P. (1996) *Cities of Tomorrow. An Intellectual History of Urban Planning and Design in the Twentieth Century* (2nd edition), Oxford: Blackwell.

Hall, P. and Pain, K. (2006) *The Polycentric Metropolis: Learning from Mega-city Regions in Europe*, London: Earthscan.

Hall, P. and Pfeiffer, U. (2000) *Urban Future 21*, London: Spon Press.

Harvey, D. (1997) 'Contested cities: social process and spatial form', in Jewson, N. and MacGregor, S. (eds) *Transforming Cities: Contested Governance and New Spatial Divisons*, London and New York: Routledge.

Held, D. and McGrew, A. (2000) 'The great globalization debate: an introduction,' in Held, D. and McGrew, A. (eds) *The Global Transformations Reader. An Introduction to the Globalization Debate*, Oxford: Polity Press.

Hillier, J. and Healey, P. (eds) (2008) *Foundations of the Planning Enterprise. Critical Essays in Planning Theory*, (Volume 1), Aldershot: Ashgate.

Le Corbusier (1942). *Charte d'Athènes* (Athens Charter). Harper Collins: London.

Lisbon European Council (2000) Presidency Conclusions. Lisbon European Council, 23 and 24 March.

Lütke-Daldrup, E. (2001) 'Die perforierte Stadt. Eine Versuchsanordnung' *StadtBauwelt*, 40–45.

Massey, D. (2005) *For Space*, Oxford: Blackwell.

OECD (2001) *OECD Territorial Outlook*, 2001 Edition Paris: OECD.

OECD (2006) 'Competitive cities in the global economy", *OECD Territorial Reviews*, Paris: OECD.

Parr, J. B. (1999a) 'Growth-pole strategies in regional economic planning: a retrospective view', Part 1. Origins and Advocacy *Urban Studies*, 36, 1195–1215.

Parr, J. B. (1999b) 'Growth-pole strategies in regional economic planning: a retrospective view,' Part 2. Implementation and Outcome *Urban Studies*, 36, 1247–1268.

Robert, J. and Lennertz, M. (2007) *Territorial Futures. Spatial Scenarios*, ESPON Programme, ESPON 3.2 Project.

Ryser, J. and Franchini, T. (eds) (2008) *IMPP – International Manual of Planning Practice*, The Hague: ISoCaRP.

Sachs, W. and Santauris, T. (eds) (2007) *Fair Future, Resource Conflicts, Security and Global Justice*, London: Zed Books.

Sander, R. (2006) *Urban Development and Planning in the Built City: Cities under Pressure for Change – An Introduction*, Deutsche Zeitschrift für Kommunalwissenschaften.

Sandercock, L. (1998) *Towards Cosmopolis. Planning for Multicultural Cities*, Chichester: John Wiley & Sons.

Sandercock, L. (2003) *Cosmopolis II: Mongrel Cities in the 21st Century*, London: Continuum.

Steinbock, D. (2007) *The Competitiveness of Finland's Large Urban Regions*, Helsinki, Ministry of the Interior Finland.

Swyngedouw, E. A. (1992) 'The mammon quest. "Glocalisation", interspatial competition and the monetary order: the construction of new spatial scales', in Dunford, M. and Kafkalas, G. (eds) *Cities and Regions in the New Europe: The Global–Local Interplay and Spatial Development Strategies*, London: Belhaven.

Taylor, P. (2004) *World City Network. A Global Urban Analysis*, London: Routledge.

UN Habitat (2006) *The State of the World's Cities Report 2006/2007. The Millennium Development Goals and Urban Sustainability: 30 Years of Shaping the Habitat Agenda*, London: Earthscan.

University of Valencia *et al.* (2006) *ESPON Project 2.3.2 – Governance of Territorial and Urban Policies from EU to Local Level*, Draft Final Report, Valencia.

Veltz, P. (2004) *The Rationale for a Resurgence in the Major Cities of Advanced Economies. The Resurgent City*, Leverhulme International Symposium, LSE.

Whitelegg, J. and Haq, G. (eds.) (2003) *The Earthscan Reader on World Transport Policy Practice*, London: Earthscan.

World Bank (2009) *World Development Report, Reshaping Economic Geography*. Oxford: Oxford University Press.

Further reading

Ache, P., Andersen, H. *et al.* (eds) (2008) *Cities between Competitiveness and Cohesion: Discourses, Realities and Implementation*, The GeoJournal Library V93, Dordrecht: Springer. (A good introduction.)

European Commission (2008) *Growing Regions, Growing Europe. Fifth Progress Report on Economic and Social Cohesion*. COM(2008) 371 final. Luxembourg. (On 'spatial development problems'.)

Massey, D. (2005) *For Space*, Oxford: Blackwell. (Connecting to the conclusions.)

UN Habitat (2006) *The State of the World's Cities Report 2006/2007. The Millennium Development Goals and Urban Sustainability: 30 Years of Shaping the Habitat Agenda*, London: Earthscan. (On the 'urban millennium'.)

UN Habitat (2009) *Global Report on Human Settlements 2009: Planning Sustainable Cities* London, UN Human Settlements Programme. (On 'territorial development systems'.)

UN ECE (2008) *Spatial Planning. Key Instrument for Development and Effective Governance. With special reference to countries in transition*. New York and Geneva: United Nations. (On the 'urban millennium'.)

World Bank (2009) *World Development Report. Reshaping Economic Geography*, Oxford: Oxford University Press (On 'spatial development problems'.)

Section V

Local and regional development policy

28

Endogenous approaches to local and regional development policy

Franz Tödtling

Definition and genesis of the concept

Indigenous and endogenous approaches to local and regional development policy were introduced in the late 1970s and have become prominent since then both in advanced economies and in developing countries (see e.g. Stöhr 1990, Garofoli 1992, OECD 2003, Pike *et al.* 2006, Vázquez-Barquero 2006). They are based on the idea that local and regional development should be driven in a bottom-up manner by indigenous and endogenous forces and factors. There is a certain difference, however no clear borderline, between indigenous and endogenous development concepts. Pike *et al.* (2006: 155) refer to indigenous development as being based upon naturally occurring and/ or socially produced sources of economic potential growing from within localities and regions. They regard indigenous approaches as a means of nurturing such 'home-grown' assets and resources that may be more locally and regionally embedded, more committed and more capable of making enduring contributions to local and regional development. Such resources and factors include land, natural resources, the resident local labour force, historically rooted skills, and local entrepreneurship. Endogenous approaches are more broadly defined in comparison, referring to those that focus more on internal factors and processes of local and regional development instead of external ones (Stöhr 1990). Included here are also factors which are intentionally created or upgraded by policy makers and related institutions, such as infrastructure investments, schools, training organisations, universities and research organisations. Created endogenous factors, thus, refer to a highly educated workforce, and to knowledge and technologies developed in the region, which might lead to new products, processes or other new solutions. Endogenous forces include also social and political factors such as the engagement of social agents and civil society which trigger processes of self-help, local initiatives, and social movements aiming at the improvement of living conditions in a particular region. Due to the strong role of local forces and factors, such a development strategy has often also been called the "bottom-up approach". This refers to the idea that regional development is initiated and carried by local and regional actors and agents instead of central government or external agencies, and that it is oriented to the needs and objectives of the regional population.

In endogenous development various spatial levels and respective institutions play a role. The focus is on the local and regional levels where specific processes, institutions and agents are the key driving forces. At the local level we often find entrepreneurial processes, economic and social initiatives and movements, whereas at the regional level activities of regional government and associations, official programmes for (endogenous) economic development, cluster initiatives and innovation support including university–industry relationships may be identified. Endogenous local and regional development also depends, however, to a considerable extent also on national political and institutional structures (e.g. policy competences of regions, national economic policies), macro-regional conditions and institutions (e.g. EU regional policies and structural funds), and also on global regimes and institutions (e.g. trade regimes and related institutions).

Endogenous approaches to local and regional development have evolved as a counter-thesis to previous regional development approaches for less developed areas which have strongly emphasised external factors such as interregional trade (exports, imports) or the mobility of capital (firms), labour and technology between regions and countries. More specifically, endogenous regional development strategies were formulated as a response to often unsuccessful policies of the 1960s and 1970s which were strongly based on factors such as external demand (export base theory, trade theory), the attraction of leading international firms and technology to growth centres (growth pole theory), and the mobility of capital and labour between economically strong and weak regions (neo-classical growth theory). This previous external development paradigm has also been called "top-down regional development approach" (Stöhr and Taylor 1981) because it was often designed and implemented by central government or external agencies. A number of critical reviews and studies have pointed out that those external strategies had

not been very effective for improving the economic situation of less developed and peripheral regions and countries (Stöhr and Tödtling 1977, Stöhr and Taylor 1981). In particular, the gap to the economically leading regions, i.e. the core areas, could often not be reduced. A number of critical points had been raised regarding the external regional development paradigm. The first was that due to the strong orientation on external demand and on specific comparative advantages of respective regions only a small share of regional factors had been mobilised and used in previous development policies. In particular specific natural resources, tourist sites and low-cost labour had been exploited in less developed regions and countries, whereas other factors and potentials such as qualified labour, specific skills and competences had been rather neglected. Then, a key strategy had been the attraction of external firms and of branch plants. This, however, had benefited often central locations or growth centres in those regions, and there were few economic spill-overs to less developed areas. If these existed, they took the form mainly of labour commuting to the centres and the dispersal of branch plants to the hinterland, less through input–output linkages and technology diffusion to peripheral regions. Furthermore, the branch plants have lacked usually higher level functions such as office and managerial activities, R&D and innovation offering only low-quality jobs with few prospects of upward mobility for workers and employees. Then, the potential of mobile plants to locate in less developed regions had been reduced due to an increasing globalisation of the economy. New locations for multinational companies had been coming up in emerging economies such as South East Asia and Latin America as well as in Eastern Europe, offering abundant cheap labour as well as prospects for a high market growth. As a consequence, firms have been setting up new subsidiaries or branch plants in those new locations, and less so in backward regions of advanced countries.

A related problem was that the focus on branch plants in such external strategies did not raise the entrepreneurial potential and the innovation capability of less developed regions to a notable extent. As a consequence, there were few start-ups and a lack of innovations, in particular as regards new products. Last but not least, the external strategies often have deteriorated the environmental situation in the respective regions because ecological and sustainability aspects had not been taken into account.

As a reaction to these problems, scholars and policy observers since the 1980s were looking for new approaches for local and regional development. Policies in many advanced and developing countries were shifting subsequently more towards endogenous concepts. These were not based on a consistent new theory, but were defined rather as a counter-thesis to the external approach. The following elements and characteristics have been pointed out for such a new orientation (Stöhr and Tödtling 1977, Stöhr 1990, Garofoli 1992, Vazquez-Barquero 2006, Pike *et al.* 2006):

i) It was argued that regional economic development should take a long-term perspective and harmonise economic, social and environmental goals (Stöhr and Tödtling 1977, Morgan 2004). Economic growth, thus, should not only enhance regional production and average per capita income, but also improve the broader socio-economic situation, including the living conditions for the poor. Furthermore, it should not deteriorate the environmental and ecological situation of the region, an idea which more recently has been introduced as "sustainable regional development".

ii) Strategies were based to a higher degree on the mobilisation of endogenous regional factors and potentials, instead of external and mobile ones. Endogenous potentials were seen to

exist in particular in natural resources, landscapes and tourist sites, qualified labour and specific skills or competences of the respective regions. Porter (1990, 1998) more recently has pointed out in this context that such factors and potentials are not just "given" but can be created or upgraded through a long-term goal-oriented public policy as well as through corporate initiatives and actions.

iii) It was also argued that other sectors than manufacturing, such as agriculture, craft-based industries, tourism and other services, should be included in development strategies. The intention was to formulate integrated concepts trying to inter relate different but complementary sectors. This has included, the strengthening of input-output linkages and other relationships between those various sectors. Examples are complementarities and interrelations between agriculture, tourism and craft-based activities in rural and peripheral regions.

iv) Then, more attention has been given to the development problems and growth potentials of incumbent small firms as well as a stronger focus on entrepreneurship and new firm formation. This was due to the fact that less developed regions often had high shares of small and medium-sized firms in traditional sectors which did not benefit from the top-down strategies. The formation of new firms, on the other hand, was seen as key for generating growth and renewal in those regions.

v) Innovation has received a more prominent role than in the top-down approaches. Innovation was broadly defined, including technological, business and social innovations. The intention was to escape cost competition from low-wage countries through a

335

high quality of products and processes. Innovation, however, was also aimed at the solution of broader social and other problems and not confined to technology aspects of companies only.

vi) Regional specificities in culture, local demand and economic structure were regarded as relevant contexts and factors to be taken into account. Such peculiar local and regional characteristics cannot easily be copied by competitors, and are therefore seen as a source of unique competitive advantages for regional firms. In this context a certain level of "regional identity" was seen as a favouring factor for regional development. In business this took the form of branding of regional products, and of using new ways of marketing such as direct selling (e.g. of agricultural or handicraft products).

vii) Beyond narrow economic factors, social and political forces were pointed out to be relevant for local and regional development. This includes activities of social agents and the engagement of civil society triggering and supporting processes of self-help, local initiatives, and social movements aiming at the improvement of living conditions in particular regions. Decentralised decision making and policy competences at the local and regional levels were seen as favourable for economic development since it was assumed that there was a better understanding of problems, barriers and potentials for regional development at those lower levels and since it allowed a fine tuning of development strategies to the needs and goals of the regional population.

Endogenous approaches to local and regional development are based on bottom-up processes, initiated and carried out by local and regional actors, influenced and shaped by local and regional institutions and policy (Cooke and Morgan 1998). Space in this context is conceived as "territory", representing the clustering of social and economic relations, and having specific cultural and other features (Garofoli 1992). These relations and institutions lead to specific patterns of local and regional development or to different "worlds of production" (Storper 1997) instead of a uniform development model. Endogenous approaches to local and regional development, thus, take account of and build upon economic, social and institutional particularities in geographical space.

Key mechanisms for generating such a bottom-up process are development initiatives started and implemented by local and regional actors, using mainly regional resources and aiming at regional benefits (OECD 2003). They respond to the needs of the regional population and are created and controlled by individuals and groups of the respective community. Central objectives are often the creation of viable and worthwhile employment or the improvement of regional living conditions. An underlying hypothesis of this approach is that the basic prerequisites of development – initiatives and entrepreneurship – are available or latent in most regions. Actions initiated at the local and regional levels are seen to have several advantages compared to central or top-down approaches such as a direct problem perception, a high intensity of interaction, regional synergies, regional strategy formulation, and collective learning within regional networks.

It should become clear, however, that regional development is never the result of endogenous forces only. It is always the outcome of both endogenous and exogenous factors and processes, and their interaction. This leads to a plurality of development paths and of development models, partly also due to the effects of different economic policies. Furthermore, individual regions have a different capacity for endogenous development and therefore a differentiated need for central or external development inputs and efforts. It is a kind of paradox that peripheral and dis-advantaged regions, which were often the target of endogenous regional development strategies, have a rather low potential for such strategies and require more external resources and support for triggering a dynamic regional development (Hadjimichalis and Papamichos 1991).

Specific routes of endogenous local and regional development

Endogenous approaches to local and regional development were inspired by and further developed since the 1980s in related con-cepts such as industrial districts, local entre-preneurship, regional learning and regional innovation systems. First, studies on industrial districts such as "Third Italy" (e.g. Emilia Romana, Toscana, Veneto), Baden-Württemberg and other regions of Europe (Garofoli 1991, Cooke and Morgan 1998, Asheim 2000, Amin 2003) have advanced the concept of endogenous local and regional development. These districts were often spe-cialised in traditional sectors such as textiles and clothing, leather and shoes, furniture, and machinery, and they were characterised by competitive small firms, entrepreneurship and flexible specialisation. Although these firms have often been competing fiercely, they have also maintained cooperative links and subcontracting relations at the local and regional levels. It has been demonstrated that firms in such districts were strongly embed-ded into the respective local and regional economies through input–output links, knowledge exchange and collective learning, and various kinds of social relationships such as family ties, relations to local unions and other interest groups. There were also ele-ments of collective action, institutions and of policy support, such as the provision of serv-ices in the fields of R&D, product develop-ment, technology upgrading, sales and distribution, and marketing. Due to an ongoing

process of globalisation, however, local and regional relationships have been substituted by global market links and by production relocations to low-wage countries.

Industrial districts were often regarded as a role model for endogenous local and regional development, since they combined several relevant elements: local entrepreneurship, indigenous small firms in traditional sectors, competing successfully on the world market through a high quality of products, incre-mental product innovation and continuous upgrading of technology, cooperation with customers and suppliers (vertical) and com-petitors (horizontal), as well as collective action and policy support at the local level. As a consequence, they were copied by policy-makers in many regions across the world, even if the respective qualities such as a cer-tain entrepreneurial potential, social capital and trust as preconditions for cooperation, and supporting institutions did not exist in many localities and regions (Storper *et al.* 1998). Furthermore, industrial districts have been strongly challenged by the emerging economies in Asia, Latin America and in Eastern Europe, which have been catching up rapidly in some of these sectors. Industrial districts and their firms have reacted in vari-ous ways to this challenge: some have been relocating production activities abroad to low-cost countries, whereas others have undergone a process of mergers and take-overs by incoming foreign firms hollowing out the original model. Another strategy was the upgrading towards high-end product segments or towards activities such as design, R&D and marketing. The literature on industrial districts, thus, has demonstrated some key problems and issues of endogenous regional development. First, only a few regions have really good preconditions for an endogenous development route and strategy. Second, even regions showing good condi-tions are continuously challenged by globali-sation and changing external conditions such as new competitors, and the change of markets and technologies. Third, due to these challenges, external factors and strategies of development are increasingly used and combined with endogenous elements. In this process, endogenous and external factors become more and more interrelated and inserted into complex and multi-scalar webs of social and economic interdependencies (Amin 2004, McLeod and Jones 2007, Pike 2007).

Endogenous approaches to local and regional development policy have since the 1990s also been stimulated by research and policies of local entrepreneurship (Malecki 1994, Reynolds et al. 1994, Acs and Storey 2004, De Groot et al. 2004). Entrepreneurship is a key element in endogenous policy approaches because new firms usually originate from the region, they use local talent and labour, and have more local and regional input–output and knowledge links than external firms. Furthermore, they have their management and other key functions within the region. They, thus, are often strongly embedded in local social and economic networks. There have been a number of studies on local conditions and regional differences of entrepreneurship and new firm formation, effects on local and regional development in terms of employment and economic growth, barriers for the setting up of new firms, and related policies and their results. This research also shows the limits of the entrepreneurship approach to local and regional development. In particular less favoured regions have usually a limited entrepreneurial potential and there are many other barriers (Fritsch 1992, Reynolds et al. 1994, Armington and Acs 2002, Tödtling and Wanzenböck 2003). Furthermore, effects on local and regional development in terms of employment generation and economic growth remain often small, due to the small size and slow growth of many such companies. More recently local entrepreneurship has received strong attention in approaches to the regional knowledge economy (Keeble et al. 2000, Cooke et al. 2007, Julien 2007). In these studies and

respective policies local spin-offs from universities and research organisations, venture capital and the mobility of highly qualified people within the local labour market are put into the centre. Policy experiences regarding local entrepreneurship are summarised in OECD (2003) and OECD (2007). It has been pointed out that enterprise promotion as a local development strategy can be a critical component of a development strategy, but it does not constitute a development panacea. It favours those individuals who possess human capital, financial and other assets, and it cannot address all problems of disadvantaged regions. It also needs an extended time horizon of such policies to be successful.

Regional learning has been another route of endogenous local and regional development (Morgan 1997, Lundvall and Borràs 1998, Rutten and Boekema 2007). The central argument here is that globalisation increasingly challenges local and regional economies through rapid shifts of markets, production and technologies requiring fast adjustments. Furthermore, in a world of modern information and communication technologies and global flows of codified knowledge, the sources of competitive advantages become increasingly rooted in unique local competences, skills and tacit knowledge (Malmberg and Maskell 1999). Informal relationships and "untraded interdependencies" (Storper 1995) are key for the exchange of such local competences and skills. There are some preconditions for local learning, however, such as a common understanding of problems and issues, or the existence of trust for engaging in networks and knowledge exchange. As in the case of entrepreneurship such conditions cannot be found in every region (see Storper et al. (1998) for learning problems in the case of "late comers in the global economy"). Regional learning is strongly related to endogenous regional development since it builds on local competencies and skills, and the sharing of knowledge and of best practices. Regional learning approaches aim at a collective enhancement of know-how, and an upgrading of practices and technologies as has been demonstrated for selected industrial districts, clusters and in innovative milieux. Key mechanisms of regional learning are the mobility of qualified labour, knowledge exchange through cooperation and informal networks, and the setting up of spin-off companies. A certain limitation of local learning as a regional development strategy is that it often leads to incremental innovation only, less often to more radical innovations (Cooke et al. 2007). This tends to keep firms on their existing technology paths and runs the risk of leading to "lock-in" (Grabher 1993, Hassink and Shin 2005).

Finally, ideas of endogenous local and regional development show up in innovation approaches such as regional innovation systems and policies (Cooke et al. 2000, Doloreux 2003, Tödtling and Trippl 2005, Nauwelaers and Wintjes 2008). Here, innovations such as new products, processes or organisational practices are regarded as key drivers of local and regional development. These are often based on local knowledge or competencies. Key endogenous actors in regional innovation systems are R&D performing and innovating firms, universities, research organisations, and education institutions. Also, organisations for knowledge transfer, innovation finance and support organisations have an important role to play. Like in industrial districts and in regional learning an intensive interaction between firms (knowledge exploitation) and research organisations (knowledge generation) is seen to be required for a good performance. However, it should be pointed out that regional innovation systems are not only relying on endogenous actors and institutions. They are highly open and often multi-level systems, strongly related to the respective national innovation system as well as to international firms and institutions. Regional

innovation policies cannot be of a "one-size-fits-all" type for every region (Tödtling and Trippl 2005). In particular core regions and large cities often have better conditions for innovation, whereas less favoured regions frequently have severe constraints and regional innovation system deficits. Peripheral regions are often lacking industry clusters and organisations of knowledge generation and education (universities and research organisations). Their economies are based on SMEs facing many innovation barriers (Asheim et al. 2003). Old industrial areas on the other hand have industrial clusters as well as universities, schools and R&D organisations. However, these organisations and institutions are oriented on old clusters and technologies, and often re-enforce problems of lock-in. This implies that "endogenous" innovation strategies take different routes in distinctive regions since they have to be tailored to the specific innovation problems and barriers of such regions.

Endogenous local and regional development concepts have been applied in a number of policy programmes and development initiatives, supported by international organisations such as OECD, ILO and the European Commission. Examples are the LEADER and RIS/RITTS programmes for regions of the EU or the LEED programme by the OECD. Key ideas of this approach have also been integrated into the recent report regarding a reform agenda of the EU cohesion policy (Barca 2009). The concept has been promoted also by ECLA (Economic Commission for Latin America) in South America and has been applied in countries such as Guatemala, Costa Rica, Venezuela and Brazil. In Asia it was taken up by countries such as India and Pakistan. In most of these more recent approaches there is more emphasis on entrepreneurship, innovation and regional learning compared to earlier versions of endogenous development. Furthermore these more recent policy models take more account of global–local and multi-scalar interactions and linkages, and depart from ideas of self-reliance or regional autonomy.

Conclusions

Endogenous approaches to local and regional development have come up since the late 1970s as a counter-thesis to the external regional development paradigm. Core ideas and elements are the understanding of development as a bottom-up process, a key role of local and regional actors and initiatives, including social agents and civil society, a high importance of decision-making functions, as well as of policy competences and institutions at local and regional levels. It is conceived as an integrated approach taking account of sector- and other socio-economic interdependencies, and it has an emphasis on ecological aspects and on a sustainable use of natural and other resources.

Endogenous local and regional development policy was inspired by related concepts such as industrial districts, regional learning and innovation systems. These have partly distinct features and elements as was pointed out. However, they also share common elements characterising them as endogenous development. Such common elements are the search for local and regional specificities, uniqueness and identity also as a source of competitive advantages for firms, a key role of local and regional institutions, social capital and networks, a high importance of entrepreneurship and innovation, and the view that learning and innovation are, despite globalisation and modern information and communication technologies, to a high degree local processes, based on localised tacit knowledge and its exchange.

Endogenous local and regional development, thus, can be regarded as a stimulating and influential concept evolving since the 1980s. It has responded to the problems and limits of a one-sided top-down or external development approach. It has brought attention to indigenous and endogenous forces

and factors, including social and political processes, and it has emphasised the key role of local initiatives, entrepreneurship and innovation. It has prepared, thus, the ground for more recent concepts such as the fostering of entrepreneurship, regional learning and innovation. However, we should not overlook the weaknesses and limits of the endogenous development concept. It has been formulated too much as a "counter-concept" against the then prevailing top-down model and was lacking coherence as a theory of its own. It has focused initially too strongly on endogenous factors and actors, neglecting the fact that successful regional development is usually the result of both endogenous forces and external factors such as mobile capital, technologies, talent and knowledge. Basically, the concept of endogenous regional development has more or less tried to promote "islands of development" in a world of increasing social and economic interdependencies at all spatial levels. As a consequence it stands in stark contrast with and is challenged by recent, more unbound and relational approaches of economic geography.

Due to ongoing processes of European integration and globalisation, regions and countries are nowadays highly open systems with ever-increasing external flows of goods, services, finance and capital, people and knowledge. Furthermore, institutions and policies for economic development and innovation are increasingly characterised by multi-level governance, where regional actors and institutions are inserted in and strongly related to national and international (e.g. EU) levels and institutions. This was shown, for example, for Europe in recent studies on the role of Structural Funds and on regional innovation systems. Under such conditions endogenous regional development had to take new routes such as regional entrepreneurship and learning, and regional innovation policy. We have to be aware, however, that these newer variants are not applicable to all kinds of situations. Like the original model of endogenous regional development they tend to work better in already successful locations and regions, thus further increasing the gap to those at the bottom of the league.

References

Acs, Z. and Storey, D. (2004) 'Introduction: Entrepreneurship and Economic Development', *Regional Studies* 38(8), 871–877.

Amin, A. (2003) 'Industrial Districts', in Sheppard, E. and Barnes, T.J. (eds) *A Companion to Economic Geography*, 149–167, Oxford: Blackwell.

Amin, A. (2004) 'Regions Unbound: Towards New Politics of Place', *Geografiska Annaler* 86 B, 33–44.

Armington, C. and Acs, Z. (2002) 'The Determinants of Regional Variation in New Firm Formation', *Regional Studies* 36(1), 33–45.

Asheim, B. T. (2000) 'Industrial Districts: The Contribution of Marshall and Beyond', in Clark, G.L., Feldman, M.P. and Gertler, M. (eds) *The Oxford Handbook of Economic Geography*, 413–431, Oxford: Oxford University Press.

Asheim, B. and Gertler, M. (2005) 'Regional Innovation Systems and the Geographical Foundations of Innovation', in Fagerberg, J., Mowery, D. and Nelson, R. (eds) *The Oxford Handbook of Innovation*, 291–317, Oxford: Oxford University Press.

Asheim, B., Isaksen, A., Nauwelaers, C. and Tödtling, F. (eds) (2003) *Regional Innovation Policy for Small-Medium Enterprises*, Cheltenham: Edward Elgar.

Aydalot, Ph. and Keeble, D. (eds) (1988) *High Technology Industry and Innovative Environments: The European Experience*, London: Routledge.

Barca, F. (2009) *An Agenda for a Reformed Cohesion Policy – A Place-Based Approach to Meeting European Union Challenges and Expectations*, Independent Report to the Commissioner for Regional Policy, Brussels: EC.

Cooke, P. and Morgan, K. (1998) *The Associational Economy: Firms, Regions, and Innovation*, Oxford/ New York: Oxford University Press.

Cooke, P., Boekholt, P. and Tödtling, F. (2000) *The Governance of Innovation in Europe*, London: Pinter.

Cooke, P., DeLaurentis, C., Tödtling, F. and Trippl, M. (2007) *Regional Knowledge Economies*, Cheltenham: Edward Elgar.

De Groot, H., Nijkamp, P. and Stough, R. (2004) *Entrepreneurship and Regional Economic Development: A Spatial Perspective*, Cheltenham: Edward Elgar.

Doloreux, D. (2002) 'What we Should Know About *Regional Systems of Innovation Technology in Society*', 24, 243–263.

Fritsch, M. (1992) 'Regional Differences in New Firm Formation: Evidence from West Germany', *Regional Studies* 26 (3), 233–241.

Garofoli, G. (1991) 'Local Networks, Innovation and Policy in Italian Industrial Districts', in Berman, E., Maier, G. and Tödtling, F. (eds) *Regions Reconsidered – Economic Networks, Innovation and Local Development in Industrialised Countries*, London/New York: Mansell.

Garofoli, G. (ed.) (1992) *Endogenous Development in Southern Europe*, Aldershot: Avebury.

Grabher, G. (1993) 'The Weakness of Strong Ties: The Lock-in of Regional Development in the Ruhr-area' in Grabher, G. (ed.) *The Embedded Firm: On the Socioeconomics of Industrial Networks*, 255–278. London: T.J. Press.

Hadjimichalis, C. and Papamichos, N. (1991) '"Local" Development in Southern Europe: Myths and Realities', in Bergman, E., Maier, G. and Tödtling, F. (eds) *Regions Reconsidered – Economic Networks, Innovation, and Local Development in Industrialised Countries*, London/New York: Mansell.

Hassink, R. and Shin, D.-O. (2005) 'Guest Editorial: The Restructuring of Old Industrial Areas in Europe and Asia', *Environment and Planning A*, 37, 571–580.

Julien, P.-A. (2007) *A Theory of Local Entrepreneurship in the Knowledge Economy*, Cheltenham: Edward Elgar.

Keeble, D. and Wilkinson, F. (eds) (2000) *High-technology Clusters, Networking and Collective Learning in Europe*, Aldershot: Ashgate.

Lundvall, B.-A. and Borrás, S. (1999) *The Globalising Learning Economy: Implications for Innovation Policy*, Luxembourg: Office for Official Publications of the European Communities.

MacLeod, G. and Jones, M. (2007) 'Territorial, Scalar, Networked, Connected: In What Sense a "Regional World"?', *Regional Studies* 41(9), 1177–1191.

Malmberg, A. and Maskell, P. (1999) 'The Competitiveness of Firms and Regions: Ubifiquation' and the Importance of Localized Learning', *European Urban and Regional Studies*, 6(1) 9–26.

Malecki, E. (1994) 'Entrepreneurship in Regional and Local Development', *International Regional Science Review* 16 (1&2), 119–153.

341

Morgan, K. (1997) 'The Learning Region: Institutions, Innovation and Regional Renewal', *Regional Studies* 31, 491–503.

Morgan, K. (2004) 'Sustainable Regions: Governance, Innovation and Scale', *European Planning Studies* 12(6), 871–889.

Nauwelaers, C. and Wintjes, R. (eds) (2008) *Innovation Policy in Europe*, Cheltenham: Edward Elgar.

OECD (2003) *Entrepreneurship and Local Economic Development – Programme and Policy Recommendations*, Paris: OECD Publications.

OECD (2007) *OECD Framework for the Evaluation of SME and Entrepreneurship Policies and Programmes*, Paris: OECD Publications.

Pike, A. (2007) 'Editorial: Whither Regional Studies?', *Regional Studies*, 41(9), 1143–1148.

Pike, A, Rodriguez-Pose, A. and Tomaney, J. (2006) *Local and Regional Development*, London and New York, Routledge.

Pike, A., Rodriguez-Pose, A. and Tomaney, J. (2007) 'What Kind of Local and Regional Development and for Whom?', *Regional Studies* 41(9), 1253–1269.

Porter, M. (1990) *The Competitive Advantage of Nations*, New York: Free Press.

Porter, M. (1998) *On Competition*, Boston: Harvard Business School Press.

Reynolds, P.D., Storey, D.J. and Westhead, P. (1994) 'Cross-national Comparison for the Variation in New Firm Formation Rates', *Regional Studies* 28, 443–456.

Rutten, R. and Boekema, F. (eds) (2007) *The Learning Region: Foundations, State of the Art, Future*, Cheltenmham: Edward Elgar.

Stöhr, W.B. (ed.) (1990) *Global Challenge and Local Response – Initiatives for Economic Regeneration in Contemporary Europe*, London: Mansell.

Stöhr, W.B. and Tödtling, F. (1977) 'Spatial Equity: Some Antitheses to Current Regional Development Doctrine', *Papers of the Regional Science Association*, 38, 33–54.

Stöhr, W. and Taylor, D.R.F. (eds) (1981) *Development from Above or Below? The Dialectics of Regional Planning in Developing Countries*, Chichester: Wiley.

Storper, M. (1995) 'The Resurgence of Regional Economies, Ten Years Later: The Region as a Nexus of Untraded Interdependencies', *European Urban and Regional Studies* 2, 191–221.

Storper, M. (1997) *The Regional World: Territorial Development in a Global Economy*, New York: Guilford Press.

Storper, M., Thomadakis, S.B. and Tsipouri, L.J. (eds) (1998) *Latecomers in the Global Economy*, London: Routledge.

Tödtling, F. and Wanzenböck, H. (2003) 'Regional Differences in Structural Characteristics of Start-ups', *Entrepreneurship & Regional Development* 15, 351–370.

Tödtling, F. and Trippl, M. (2005) 'One Size Fits All? Towards a Differentiated Regional Innovation Policy Approach', *Research Policy* 34, 1023–1209.

Vazquez-Barquero, A. (2006) *Endogenous Development—Networking, Innovation, Institutions and Cities*, London: Routledge.

Further reading

On the concept and applications of endogenous development

Stöhr, W.B. (ed.) (1990) *Global Challenge and Local Response – Initiatives for Economic Regeneration in Contemporary Europe*, London: Mansell.

Vazquez-Barquero, A. (2006) *Endogenous Development—Networking, Innovation, Institutions and Cities*, London: Routledge.

On industrial districts as a model of local and regional development

Amin, A. (2003) 'Industrial Districts', in Sheppard, E. and Barnes, T.J. (eds) *A Companion to Economic Geography*, 149–167, Oxford: Blackwell.

Asheim, B. T. (2000) 'Industrial Districts: The Contribution of Marshall and Beyond', in Clark, G.L., Feldman, M.P. and Gertler, M. (eds) *The Oxford Handbook of Economic Geography*, 413–431, Oxford: Oxford University Press.

On the role of formal and informal institutions for local and regional development

Cooke, P. and Morgan, K. (1998) *The Associational Economy: Firms, Regions, and Innovation*, Oxford/New York: Oxford University Press.

For a review on entrepreneurship and regional development

Acs, Z. and Storey, D. (2004) 'Introduction: Entrepreneurship and Economic Development', *Regional Studies* 38(8), 871–877.

On the role and preconditions of learning in local and regional economies

Rutten, R. and Boekema, F. (eds) (2007) *The Learning Region: Foundations, State of the Art, Future*, Cheltenmham: Edward Elgar.

On innovation policies and regional development

Nauwelaers, C. and Wintjes, R. (eds) (2008) *Innovation Policy in Europe*: Cheltenham: Edward Elgar.

Tödtling, F. and Trippl, M. (2005) 'One Size Fits All? Towards a Differentiated Regional Innovation Policy Approach', *Research Policy* 34, 1023–1209.

29

Territorial competitiveness and local and regional economic development

A classic tale of 'theory led by policy'

Gillian Bristow

Introduction

Quite simply, competitiveness is everywhere. Regions and cities the world over are pre-occupied with the notion that they are rivals facing intense global competition for economic prowess. Local and regional economic development strategies are littered with the language of winning, of gaining competitive advantage over other places, of moving up the competitiveness league table, and of competing for key resources in the form of global capital investment, government funding, events, visitors, or skilled, 'creative' residents. They are not unique in this. The competitiveness imperative facing cities and regions mirrors the dominant thinking around national and supranational economic performance. Competitiveness is, for example, deeply embedded in the European Union (EU)'s Lisbon Agenda which explicitly states that its aim is 'to make the EU the most competitive and dynamic knowledge-based economy in the world' (Commission of the European Communities, 2000: 2). Competitiveness-thinking is also pervasive in the global South which has witnessed the rapid absorption of the North's mantras on competitiveness and the policy approaches deemed to enhance it (Wignaraja, 2003; UNCTAD, 2004). Indeed,

the 'new conventional wisdom' is that nations, regions and cities have to be more competitive to survive in the new marketplace being forged by globalisation and the rise of new information technologies (Buck *et al.*, 2005). Yet the notion that competitiveness is a concept that can be applied to places has been denounced as at best 'misleading' (Kitson *et al.*, 2004) and at worst a 'dangerous obsession' (Krugman, 1994), the use of which not only betrays a serious failure to understand how local and regional economies actually work, but results in, among other things, invidious and damaging place-based competition.

The purpose of this chapter is to provide a detailed review of the current thinking around the notion of territorial or place competitiveness. While competitiveness is increasingly applied to all places, the chapter focuses specifically on the use and relevance of the term in the context of local and regional economic development. It begins by trying to establish what place competitiveness actually means. This reveals it is an inherently confused concept with weak theoretical underpinnings. As such, it is argued that the rise to prominence of place competitiveness is a classic example of 'theory led by policy' (Lovering, 1999) whereby commentators are now seeking to justify use of the term long after it has become firmly embedded in policy discourse. This, in turn, is prompting increasing criticism of the sorts of policy agendas being prioritised under the rubric of competitiveness. The chapter then moves on to examine the growing interest in political economy approaches to understanding the dominance of competitiveness thinking. These approaches are valuable as a means of generating insights into why competitiveness has such appeal in local and regional development policy, and who is shaping and spreading its dominant ideas. It concludes by establishing what and where capacities might exist for the dominance of place competitiveness to be contradicted or challenged.

Place competitiveness: a chaotic concept

In spite of the growing volume of literature on the subject which typically cuts across a range of disciplines, there is precious little agreement about what place competitiveness actually means. Broadly speaking, there are two ways in which it can be understood – first, in the relatively narrow, economistic sense of competing over market share and resources, and second, in much broader developmental terms relating to the determinants and dynamics of a place's long-run prosperity. One of the major difficulties in understanding place competitiveness is that these different conceptions typically tend to get muddled together and confused.

For some authors, places are competitive in the same way as businesses compete for market share. This notion derives from the business economics literature with key authors such as Michael Porter, Robert Reich and Lester Thurow being hugely influential in spreading the notion that places vie with one another for economic advantage in a manner directly commensurable with that of firms. This idea of place competitiveness is thus a direct antecedent of the globalisation discourse in that it asserts that

in the wake of the post-war settlement and the rise of the neoliberal political economy, the structural properties of the global economy have drastically changed (Krugman, 1996).

Yet this assumes that places are actors with discrete control over their jurisdictions and that they are actively in competition with other, similarly constituted places in clearly defined and spatially connected factor markets – assumptions which are highly questionable. Whereas firms face a distinct bottom line and may go out of business if they are uncompetitive, places do not. While firms enter and exit markets, places do not. Furthermore, unlike firms, places may have more than one objective and are not driven simply by the pursuit of economic success or profit (Turok, 2004). As such, the competitive success of one place is not necessarily at the expense of another. Indeed, regions and cities are often locked in complex interdependencies and networks of relations, some of which are co-operative rather than necessarily conflictual or competitive. They create markets for one another, people commute between cities and places, and supply chains typically cross city boundaries. As Unwin (2006: 5) observes, 'nobody would claim that if Manchester's economy performs poorly, this is good news for Liverpool. The demand for Liverpool's goods and services will shrink and Manchester will no longer be able to supply it with goods and services as cheaply or of the same quality.' Thus the analogy of regions and cities acting as business entities and clearly cast as either winners or losers in a dog-eat-dog competitiveness game is fraught with difficulties (Bristow, 2005).

This is not to deny the existence of territorial competition. Rivalry manifestly does exist between places and indeed, the local economic development literature is littered with examples of spatial contests over the attraction and retention of mobile capital resources, skilled labour, tourists and events (Buck et al., 2005). This has spawned growing interest in the nature and type of assets required to make local and regional economies attractive or 'sticky places' (Markusen, 1996). However, the critical point is that this competitive behaviour does not necessarily lead to clearly defined performance outcomes for places as it does for firms. It may in fact have negative consequences not least in the opportunity costs that typically accompany incentive competition and bidding wars (Markusen, 2007).

In short, it is important to distinguish between competition and competitiveness (Kitson *et al.*, 2004). While places may compete with one another in certain ways, this is not to say they are competitive in the same way as firms are. Places are not competitive. Rather they develop and perform. However, inasmuch as the competition between places occurs for factors which help shape the development and sustenance of a business environment conducive to competitive firms, there are clear connections with the second, much broader conceptualisation of place competitiveness which sees it as pertaining to relative economic prosperity.

One of the principal proponents of this broader approach is Michael Storper who has played an important role in propagating the concept of regional competitiveness which he defines as:

> the capability of a region to attract and keep firms with stable or increasing market shares in an activity, while maintaining stable or increasing standards of living for those who participate in it.
>
> (Storper, 1997: 264)

This definition, which has since been widely applied to cities too, presents competitiveness as a wide-ranging, overall measure of economic performance. It is in fact derived from a widely used definition of national competitiveness. The implicit assumption made is thus that regions and localities are in effect scaled-down versions of a national, macroeconomy. Thus, a place is 'competitive' according to this view when it has the ability

to raise its standard of living and sustain 'winning' outcomes. Competitiveness thus resides principally in the competitiveness of the firms operating within a place, with a competitive place being one that has the conditions to enable it to generate high profits and wages through having a stock of high value-added growth firms.

The difficulty lies in understanding precisely what these 'conditions' are for competitive success and when a situation of 'competitiveness' has thus been achieved. Theoretical efforts to comprehend place competitiveness are strong in their assertion that the key ingredients shaping it are predominantly endogenous and reside within the environment within which businesses operate. A wide variety of 'soft' locational factors have been suggested as helping to create a favourable environment for the development of productive firms, including social capital or the norms and trust developed between businesses in a place, the local entrepreneurial culture, the quality of the local living or social environment, cultural resources, and place identity and international image (see Cambridge Econometrics *et al.* (2002) for a more detailed review). Since these 'soft' location factors are also those which might help attract in new investment and labour, the blurring of boundaries between place competitiveness and place competition is plain to see.

Other authors dispute the notion that competitiveness can be directly equated to local and regional prosperity and instead argue that competitiveness is 'revealed' through the performance of a place's firms. Michael Porter's work is again of seminal importance here. Porter has asserted that competitiveness is simply a proxy for productivity such that the productivity of a place is ultimately reducible to the productivity of its firms, whether domestic or foreign-owned subsidiaries (Porter, 1990, 1998, 2003). Furthermore, the local and regional environment plays a critical role in shaping firm productivity since, he argues, 'comparative advantage is created and sustained through a highly localised process' (Porter, 1990: 19).

There may be some justification for defining competitiveness in terms of productivity and for expecting a link between productivity and place prosperity. Camagni (2002) asserts that places compete in terms of absolute advantage or efficiency, not comparative advantage. A place may be thought of as having an absolute competitive advantage when it possesses superior technological, social, infrastructural or institutional assets that are external to, but which benefit individual firms and give them higher productivity. Similarly, and in a recent apparent change in his thinking, Krugman (2003) has argued that a region that is more productive will be able to attract (and retain) labour and capital from other regions. Furthermore, he suggests that these factor inflows will subsequently reinforce the region's absolute productivity advantage even further in a virtuous circle.

However, the conceptualisation of subnational (particularly regional) productivity remains somewhat vague. Labour productivity coupled with the employment rate represent what might be termed measures of 'revealed competitiveness' in that they are both central components of a place's economic performance and its prosperity, but of themselves say little about the underlying attributes and complex processes upon which they depend. Indeed, there is considerable confusion as to what actually causes some places to have higher productivity than others, whether it is differential factor endowments, differences in the available knowledge base, or the increasing returns that give local firms higher productivity (Gardiner et al., 2004).

For regions, there is growing interest in the evolutionary perspective which appears to offer some promise in respect of its ability to explain why some regions may develop firms with a competitive advantage (Boschma, 2004). The evolutionary approach emphasises dynamic competitive advantage or how economic transformation proceeds differently in different places, and highlights the ability of a regional economy to adapt to changing market conditions and the emergence of new technologies and competitors. It asserts that a region's competitive advantage is a product of its historical, path-dependent development and its capacity to create new development trajectories, such that place matters. This perspective is still, however, in its infancy and requires further interrogation and critical, empirical analysis.

The concept of place competitiveness is thus an inherently chaotic one which lacks a clear, unequivocal and agreed meaning within the academic literature. Fundamentally, this chaos reflects the absence of a clear theoretical or conceptual framework for understanding the competitive performance of places, particularly at the local and regional level. As Kitson et al. (2004: 997) observe in relation to regions, 'we are far from any agreed framework for defining, theorising and empirically analysing regional competitive advantage', although they themselves along with other authors such as Budd and Hirmis (2004), make some progress towards synthesising the different factors that need to be included. Instead, there are a range of disparate bodies of work, each of which tends to adopt a different perspective and to emphasise a different set of variables. What place competitiveness actually means and how it is to be achieved thus remains clouded in a considerable degree of mystery.

Theory led by policy

It is perhaps not surprising then that the policy discourse on place competitiveness is equally, if not more, muddled and confused. The concept of place competitiveness is typically defined in very broad terms in the policy discourse. In general, policy-makers have tended to favour the macroeconomic definition of place competitiveness which directly equates it with prosperity and performance.

Thus, for example, the UK government states that regional competitiveness 'describes the ability of regions to generate high income and employment levels while remaining exposed to domestic and international competition' (DTI, 2003: 3), a definition also utilised by the European Commission. However, to confuse matters the UK government also publishes a range of separate regional competitiveness indices where it deliberately shies away from making explicit claims about the causal relationships between firm innovation, productivity and overall regional economic performance.

Similar confusion is evident in relation to the competitiveness of cities and city-regions. For example, in a research report for the UK government's State of the Cities Report (ODPM, 2006), urban competitiveness is defined as

> the ability of cities to continually upgrade their business environment, skills base, and physical and cultural infrastructure, so as to attract and retain high-growth, innovative and profitable firms, and an advanced creative and entrepreneurial workforce, to thereby enable it to achieve a high rate of productivity, high employment, high wages, high GDP per capita, and low levels of income inequality and social inclusion.

This captures various, potentially contradictory elements of urban economic performance and refers to both absolute economic performance outcomes, as well as broader social and distributional goals. It is however insightful in that it reveals much about what place competitiveness has come to mean in practice. The policy discourse around competitiveness clearly tends to conflate the strategic pursuit of 'competitiveness' as meaning the search for improved economic performance, with engagement in competition for resources and the development of boosterist strategies for attracting high-quality, 'knowledge-based'

firms and skilled labour. Competitiveness is a catch-all for the pursuit of business-led growth and entrepreneurial place-selling.

In this regard, the discourse of place competitiveness constitutes a classic tale of 'theory led by policy' (Lovering, 1999), whereby commentators have found themselves engaged in ex-post rationalisation of a term that has already become embedded in common policy parlance. Thus, for example, in the ODPM (2006) report, efforts are made to develop a model of urban competitiveness which identifies GDP per capita as the principal measure of competitive advantage, with this being underpinned by various measures of revealed competitiveness including productivity, the employment rate, wage levels and profit rates. These are, in turn, deemed to be the outcomes of the key drivers of urban competitive performance, namely innovation, investment, human capital, economic structure, connectivity, the quality of life and the structure of decision-making – thereby capturing all the facets of competitiveness raised in the discourse around it, with no real or clear sense of how they are supposed to interact.

The implications of the theory led by policy approach are also becoming clear. The result is striking similarity in the competitiveness strategies being followed across different cities and regions around the world which are routinely characterised by a familiar 'hotch-potch' of property, retail and events-led interventions targeted at improving the quality of the business, cultural and social environment. In this regard, they ostensibly promote and encourage competition between places around their attractiveness and image, and carry the clear risk of exacerbating spatial inequalities (see Cheshire and Gordon, 1995). As well as being criticised for their ubiquitous 'one-size-fits-all' approach which ignores place specificities (Bristow, 2005), such strategies are also under increasing attack for the narrowness of the policy approach they propagate – an overt focus on the promotion of a place's assets rather than their development (Unwin, 2006), the reduction of a wide diversity of urban and regional problems to a simple, imported policy agenda (Bristow and Lovering, 2006) when in fact there may be multiple routes to growth (Turok, 2008), and the overwhelming emphasis upon a narrow, private sector-based route to place prosperity which rarely takes account of the non-economic variables essential to the social reproduction of everyday life (Jarvis, 2007). In particular, competitiveness strategies do not demonstrate any concern with who benefits from these productive firms and supposedly competitive places, nor indeed of the sustainability of these outcomes or their fit with the broader social needs, development objectives and environmental limits of a place. Competitiveness, it seems, is at one and the same time commonsensical, common place and 'care-less'.

Understanding the enduring policy appeal of competitiveness

The limitations of place competitiveness inevitably lead to a range of questions around how and why such a poorly understood concept has assumed such significance in local and regional economic development policy circles. This focuses attention on the policy process and the relative importance of ideas and interests in the formulation of strategic policy agendas and approaches. It also focuses attention on the ways and means by which these ideas are then spread through relevant networks of policy actors and across spatial scales. These are ostensibly questions concerning the political economy of competitiveness which until relatively recently have received only limited attention (Bristow, 2005). These questions are, however, rising to the fore in line with the emergence of discursive approaches to understanding the policy process.

Indeed, a number of authors have applied political economy approaches to demonstrate the hegemonic or dominant status of the competitiveness discourse across nations. For example, Fougner (2006) has argued that the spread of the global competitiveness discourse is a deliberate tactic on the part of developed countries and the OECD to maintain the neoliberal capitalist hegemony and rationality of governance within advanced capitalist countries and spread it to the global South. This in turn privileges the particular 'attractiveness'-oriented conception of competitiveness which has become dominant – in short, it makes sense to constitute states and their populations as competitive and entrepreneurial 'place-sellers' in a global marketplace for investment. Similarly, Rosamund (2002) demonstrates that the rise to prominence of competitiveness as a strategic imperative in the EU reflects its utility as a strategic device for asserting the sense of a functional European space economy. This, in turn, helps legitimise its broader agendas as regards both the Europeanisation of governance capacity and the deepening of integration processes.

More recently, the development of the Cultural Political Economy (CPE) approach has provided a potentially useful framework for understanding how and why particular ideas, such as competitiveness, arise, spread and become materially implicated in everyday life (see Jessop, 2005). The CPE approach first emerged from research into the 'entrepreneurial city' which was instrumental in the development of two key notions. The first of these was the assertion that cities or regions are actors or 'spaces for themselves' endowed with 'capacities to realise particular discursive-material accumulation strategies and hegemonic projects' (Jessop and Sum, 2000: 2310). This was significant in its direct implication that cities and regions are capable of pursuing innovative strategies to maintain or enhance their economic competitiveness *vis-à-vis* other economic spaces. As such, they are increasingly like nations. The second notion developed was that of 'economic imaginaries'. These are subsets of economic activity (such as competitiveness, innovation and workfare) which are discursive constructs transformed into sites and objects of observation, calculation and governance and thus used by the state to secure hegemony (Sum and Jessop, 2001).

The CPE approach asserts that the construction of an economic imaginary involves a number of distinct evolutionary stages. First, there is a process of 'selection' whereby particular discourses are prioritised in terms of their ability to interpret and explain particular events. Second is the process of 'retention' whereby these discourses are repeatedly incorporated into a wide range of institutional sites, roles, routines and strategies. Third is the process of 'reinforcement' whereby these discourses are restated and embedded in procedural mechanisms, governance structures, rules and regulations such that they become a naturalised discourse (Jessop, 2005). According to Jessop (2005) there are a range of institutions and actors such as government departments, business organisations, the OECD, the EU and the World Bank that are likely to seek to establish and institutionalise such imaginaries. They use a range of discursive vehicles or 'genre chains' (Sum, 2004) such as policy documents and strategy reports to reinforce these imaginaries to suit their particular purposes.

The value of the CPE approach lies in its ability to help avoid naïve acceptance of competitiveness, and instead to provoke interrogation of the political dynamics of its evolution and utility for advancing particular policy goals and discouraging others. It remains developmental and in need of refinement and testing, not least to consider how the spread of key economic imaginaries is linked with processes of state rescaling, as well as with material developments and change (Jones, 2008). Nonetheless, it provides a useful framework for understanding the policy appeal of place competitiveness and its durability (see Bristow, forthcoming).

What becomes clear when examining the political economy of competitiveness is its resonance with key interest groups and policy-makers. The intuitive appeal of competitiveness to business is relatively easy to understand. Businesses are familiar with Darwinian notions of cut-throat competition and survival of the fittest. So it is not surprising that business interests within places are keen to promote and support policies which prioritise and assist competitive firms and oil the wheels of the wider business environment. It is also easy to see how key proponents of the idea of competitiveness have effectively worked to spread its logic from nations, to regions and to cities. Powerful organisations such as the OECD and EU have developed prominent tools and techniques for benchmarking the competitive performance of places including competitiveness indices and league tables and a plethora of best-practice reports and policy transfer studies. In turn, a highly profitable, influential and networked regional and urban development industry has emerged, which is characterised by a range of high-profile consultants, development agencies and think-tanks. These work collectively to spread the key ideas around competitiveness between places and across the world, to share what is supposed to be best practice, and promote the imitation of successful, if ultimately rather stylised, forms of policy intervention.

The appeal of place competitiveness to policy-makers at all spatial scales is also easily understood when considering competitiveness ostensibly as an idea, promoted by particular and powerful interests. The vague and nebulous nature of the competitiveness concept acts perhaps as one of its principal strengths for policy-makers. It becomes a veritable garbage-can into which all relevant strategic actions for the support of particular goals can be thrown. For cities and regions, the most striking characteristic of competitiveness strategies is indeed their extreme vagueness and flexibility over time. In the event, the commitment to competitiveness can thus be interpreted as authorising key players in urban and regional governance to adapt to circumstances and opportunities as and when they arise, and especially as they have been proposed by potential investors, notably in the property development sector (Bristow and Lovering, 2006; see also Chien and Gordon, 2008). At times, competitiveness can also be used strategically to justify the support of particular ailing local businesses perhaps for political purposes or electoral gain. At other times, the cloak of competitiveness usefully absolves local policy-makers from responsibility inasmuch as the winds of global competition and change can be conveniently presented as variables which are essentially outwith local responsibility and control. Perhaps more disturbingly, competitiveness-speak may create a trap for local and regional policy-makers from which, once ensnared, they struggle to break free. To fail to pursue competitiveness or to opt out of the competitiveness game completely might be regarded as either a sign of weakness or a submission of defeat to erstwhile rivals.

Moving beyond competitiveness

It would thus appear as if there is no alternative for places but to adopt competitiveness-orientated policies. The story of inescapable globalisation, competitiveness and economic neoliberalism is indeed a very pervasive one such that even policies which appear not to be about competitiveness become subsumed to its clutches. As Massey (2000: 282) observes, 'every attempt at radical otherness [becomes] quickly commercialised and sold or used to sell....With all of this, one might as well ask what are, and where are, the possibilities for doing things differently?' To put it another way, the growing awareness of the limitations of competitiveness-oriented policies raises a number of critical questions around, first, the scope for a fundamental transformative shift in the extralocal rules of the game set by neoliberalism and its privileging of economic rationality; second, whether and how an enhanced sense of place and context can be

reinserted into the local and regional development policy lexicon; and finally, whether and how local strategic interventions can prioritise broader, more socially just and ecologically attuned development goals over narrow, entrepreneurial place-selling mantras.

In emphasising that competitiveness and indeed neoliberalism are social and political constructs, the CPE approach usefully highlights that they are not immune from challenge. While economic imaginaries such as competitiveness can be discursively constructed and materially reproduced at different sites and scales, they are only ever likely to be partially constituted and will remain contingent. As Jessop (2005: 146) observes, the process of material reproduction 'always occurs in and through struggles conducted by specific agents, typically involves the asymmetrical manipulation of power and knowledge, and is liable to contestation and resistance'. This means that there will always remain space for competing imaginaries to challenge the dominant ones.

While the probability that neoliberalism itself will be toppled may be unlikely, the potential for certain catalytic forces such as climate change, the onset of peak oil and the current economic crisis to destabilise it and provoke change should not be entirely ruled out and may indeed be gathering momentum. Certainly, these forces may be of such magnitude in the years ahead to impel a new, global concern with frugality, egalitarianism and localism in response to changing public and political opinion. As Leitner et al. (2007: 325) observe: 'what was made can be unmade', and indeed the first step in visualising a politics beyond neoliberalism may be to acknowledge that hegemonic does not necessarily mean everlasting.

A second step is to acknowledge that the dominant indicators of competitiveness and place prosperity provide an inordinately narrow, economic metric of development which focuses attention on instrumental inputs or means to development, rather than intrinsically significant longer term policy ends or outcomes (such as health, well-being and a sustainable natural environment) (Morgan, 2004). The search for a metric which treats progress and well-being as one of its premier indicators of development is gathering momentum at the international scale. For example, the Stiglitz-Sen Commission of high-profile international economists is currently reviewing a range of alternative metrics of development with a view to establishing how to improve the calculation of GDP; how to incorporate new measures of economic, social and environmental sustainability into national accounting; and how to devise fresh indicators for assessing quality of life. Given the prominent role played by such indicators in spreading key imaginaries, dismantling and reforming them will, in turn, go a long way towards changing political priorities and creating new ideals around the collective social improvement of the opportunities or 'capabilities' of all individuals, the pursuit of happiness, sustainability and overall well-being – the moral norms that unite us and provide constraints on the utility-enhancing choices nations may make (see Nussbaum, 2000).

Clearly, local and regional action to assist the development of a more progressive policy is also important. The growing critique of place competitiveness clearly shines a light on the capacities within localities to effect change. Regions and cities are not univocal subjects of the policy decisions and mantras developed elsewhere. They are instead characterised by agonistic politics between diverse and multiple interests and groups with varying aspirations and goals. They also have increasing capacities to make their own political choices in response to these demands, albeit within certain parameters (Hudson, 2007), not least in the proactive support for new metrics of development.

Indeed, there is evidently scope for new, alternative economic imaginaries to emerge out of the local contests and battles around competitiveness, which ultimately may themselves then be selected, retained and reinforced – a sort of transformation from below (Leitner et al., 2007). There is growing evidence that substantive matters of struggle around redistribution and the material conditions of economic growth and uneven development provide for substantive resistance to the global hegemony of competitiveness (Krueger and Savage, 2007; Leitner et al., 2007). Within a fragile and susceptible capitalism there are thus a wide variety of 'alternative' economic spaces and practices which are centred much less around capital accumulation and much more around the creation of 'smart growth' to shape more socially just, ecologically sustainable and ethical urban and regional environments, such as transition towns, local exchange and trading systems, not to mention a wide range of social and ethical business enterprises. The enduring question appears to remain what capacity exists for scaling up these often diverse localised struggles into some sort of broader political project capable of challenging the dominant thinking (Leyshon et al., 2003; Leitner et al., 2007).

While these practical experiments are inherently diverse, there are some commonalities in the discourses and visions for a more progressive local and regional development agenda which appear to be emerging in practice. They are linked by a desire to effect a more socially and environmentally oriented, smaller scale, place-based approach to local and regional development – ostensibly one which creates resilience in the face of the destabilising winds of economic and environmental change. Focusing on what unites rather than what divides these discourses is potentially very important inasmuch as it may open up new opportunities to examine the specific ordering and spatiality of projects required effectively to challenge conventional approaches (Holloway et al., 2007) – perhaps, for instance, through the development of new networks to achieve social change and address the challenges which increasingly straddle global and local boundaries.

Fortunately, these commonalities also usefully resonate with recent theoretical developments in the study of city and regions which emphasise the broader and more qualitative character of 'development' as opposed to simply economic performance or growth. As well as being inherently diverse, local and regional development trajectories and processes are also increasingly understood to be evolutionary, context-specific and path-dependent. As Pike *et al.* (2007: 1258) observe, 'from Hackney to Honolulu to Hong Kong, each place has evolving histories, legacies, institutions and other distinctive characteristics that impart place dependencies and shape – inter alia – its economic assets and trajectories, social outlooks, environmental concerns, politics and culture'. These developments have spawned some important questions for critical research including the extent to which these alternative practices are locally or regionally constructed and embedded, or to put it another way, whether in this case scale and also place matters (North, 2005). The formative links between these alternatives, their emergent economic geographies and the practices and values of mainstream capitalist activities also remain under-researched, with a clear imperative emerging to rethink the links between social and economic relations in regions. The management of collective consumption and social reproduction and the centrality of ecological resources to the evolutionary process that is local and regional development are also clearly missing links in dominant spatial development literatures. In short, there is a need for a wider utilitarian debate and analysis in local and regional studies – one that is characterised by a broader concern with progress or well-being, and the potentially diverse approaches to achieving it.

Conclusions

In conclusion, place competitiveness has become a ubiquitous and dominant mantra in local and regional development policy precisely because it lacks precision and is inherently chaotic. The emergent political economy approaches explored here provide valuable insights into understanding the subsequent malleability of the discourse and thus its utility to both policy-makers and the key groups keen to promote the interests it serves. However, it is also demonstrably a limiting, growth-first discourse with the potential to effect and enhance uneven development between places, while simultaneously failing to address more fundamental social and ecological matters concerning a place's development.

In this light, there is a developing literature which asserts that local and regional development and well-being should be conceived and implemented on the basis of a broader ontology in which the economic imperative – the global competitiveness of firms – is only one rationale. As has been demonstrated, however, the scope for the selection and retention of an alternative, more context-specific discourse around city and regional resilience will critically depend upon the relative importance of both the catalytic forces for extra-local change, as well as the more permissive factors within places. These surround the role of political choice within the constraints of capitalist social relations, and the opportunities for scaling up localised struggles around the competitiveness imperative. As such, there are likely to be multiple, complex and contingent pathways to alternative development strategies. What is also likely is that action at the local level will only go so far in fostering relevant changes. Nation states remain dominant actors in pertinent global discussions around the development of new metrics and regulatory regimes, as well as playing a critical role through devolution processes in shaping the powers, resources and capacities available at subnational scales to enable and empower strong local action. Practical action and policy change must also be informed by improved understanding of precisely how regions and cities actually work. The story of place competitiveness is illustrative of the very real and significant dangers of theory led by policy. It is a challenge to which theorists now need to respond.

References

Boschma, R. (2004) 'Competitiveness of regions from an evolutionary perspective', *Regional Studies*, 38, 1001–1014.

Bristow, G. (2005) 'Everyone's a "winner": problematising the discourse of regional competitiveness', *Journal of Economic Geography*, vol. 5. no. 3, 285–304.

Bristow, G. (forthcoming) *Critical Reflections on Regional Competitiveness*, Routledge, London.

Bristow, G. and Lovering, J. (2006) 'Shaping events, or celebrating the way the wind blows? The role of competitiveness strategy in Cardiff's "ordinary transformation"', in A. Hooper and J. Punter (eds) *Capital Cardiff 1965–2020: Regeneration, Competitiveness and the Urban Environment*, University of Wales Press, Cardiff (311–329).

Buck, N., Gordon, I., Harding, A. and Turok, I. (eds) (2005) *Changing Cities: Rethinking Urban Competitiveness, Cohesion and Governance*, Palgrave MacMillan, Basingstoke.

Budd, L. and Hirmis, A. K. (2004) 'Conceptual framework for regional competitiveness', *Regional Studies*, vol. 38, no. 9, 1015–1028.

Camagni, R. (2002) 'On the concept of territorial competitiveness: sound or misleading?', *Urban Studies*, vol. 39, 2395–2411.

Cambridge Econometrics, Ecorys-NEI and Martin, R. (2002) 'A study on the factors of regional competitiveness', *Report for the European Commission*, Director-General Regional Policy.

Cheshire, P. C. and Gordon, I. R. (Eds) (1995) *Territorial Competition in an Integrating Europe*, Avebury, Aldershot.

Chien, S-S. and Gordon, I. (2008) 'Territorial competition in China and the West', *Regional Studies*, vol. 42 no. 1, 31–49.

Commission of the European Communities (2000) *Lisbon European Council – Presidency Conclusions*, 23 and 24 March, Lisbon.

DTI (Department of Trade and Industry) (2003) *Regional Competitiveness and State of the Regions*, HMSO, London.

Fougner, T. (2006) 'The state, international competitiveness and neoliberal globalisation: is there a future beyond "the competition state:?', *Review of International Studies*, vol. 32, 165–185.

Gardiner, B., Martin, R. and Tyler, P. (2004) 'Competitiveness, productivity and economic growth across the European regions', *Regional Studies*, vol. 38, no. 9, 1045–1068.

Holloway, L., Kneafsey, M., Venn, L., Cox, R., Dowler, E. and Tuomainen, H. (2007) 'Possible food economies: a methodological framework for exploring food production–consumption relationships', *Sociologia Ruralis*, vol. 47, no. 1, 1–19.

Hudson, R. (2007) 'Regions and regional uneven development forever? Some reflective comments upon theory and practice', *Regional Studies*, vol. 41, no. 9, 1149–1160.

Jarvis, H. (2007) 'Home truths about care-less competitiveness', *International Journal of Urban and Regional Research*, vol. 31, no. 1, 207–214.

Jessop, B. (2005) 'Cultural political economy, the knowledge-based economy and the state', in A. Barry and D. Slater (eds) *The Technological Economy*, Routledge, London (144–166).

Jessop, B. and Sum, N-L. (2000) 'An entrepreneurial city in action: Hong Kong's emerging strategies in and for (inter)urban competition', *Urban Studies*, vol. 37, no. 12, 2287–2313.

Jones, M. (2008) 'Recovering a sense of political economy', *Political Geography*, vol. 27, no. 4, 377–399.

Kitson, M., Martin, R. and Tyler, P. (2004) 'Regional competitiveness: an elusive yet key concept?', *Regional Studies*, Vol. 38, no. 9, 991–999.

Krueger, R. and Savage, L. (2007) 'City-regions and social reproduction: a "place" for sustainable development', *International Journal of Urban and Regional Research*, vol. 31, no. 1, 215–223.

Krugman, P. (1994) 'Competitiveness: a dangerous obsession', *Foreign Affairs*, vol. 73, no. 2, 28–44.

Krugman, P. (1996) *Pop Internationalism*, MIT Press, Cambridge, MA.

Krugman, P. (2003) *Growth on the Periphery: Second Wind for Industrial Regions?*, The Allander Series, Fraser Allander Institute, Scotland.

Leitner, H., Peck, J. and Sheppard, E. S. (2007) 'Squaring up to neoliberalism', in H., Leitner, J. Peck and E. S. Sheppard (eds) *Contesting Neoliberalism*, The Guilford Press, New York (311–327).

Leyshon, A., Lee, R. and Williams, C. (2003) (eds) *Alternative Economic Spaces*, Sage, London.

Lovering, J. (1999) 'Theory led by policy: the inadequacies of the 'New Regionalism' (illustrated from the case of Wales)', *International Journal of Urban and Regional Research*, vol. 23, 379–396.

Markusen, A. (1996) 'Sticky places in slippery space: a typology of industrial districts', *Economic Geography*, vol. 72, 293–313.

Markusen, A. (ed.) (2007) *Reigning in the Competition for Capital*, W E Upjohn Institute, Michigan.

Massey, D. (2000) 'Entanglements of power reflections', in J. Sharp, P. Routledge and R. Paddison (eds) *Entanglements of Power: Geographies of Domination/Resistance*, Routledge, London, (279–286).

Morgan, K. (2004) 'Sustainable regions: governance, innovation and scale', *European Planning Studies*, vol. 12 6, 871–889.

North, P. (2005) 'Scaling alternative economic practices? Some lessons from alternative currencies', *Transactions of the Institute of British Geographers*, vol. 30, no. 2, 233–235.

Nussbaum, M. C. (2000) *Women and Human Development: The Capabilities Approach*, Cambridge University Press, Cambridge.

Office of the Deputy Prime Minister (ODPM) (2006) *State of the English Cities: A Research Report*, Volume 1 (available at: http://www.communities.gov.uk/publications/citiesandregions/state4), accessed 1 April 2009.

Pike, A., Rodriguez-Pose, A. and Tomaney, J. (2007) 'What kind of local and regional development, for whom?', *Regional Studies*, vol. 41, no. 9, 1253–1269.

Porter, M. (1990) *The Competitive Advantage of Nations*, Macmillan, Basingstoke.

Porter, M. (1998) *On Competition*, Harvard Business School Press, Cambridge, MA.

Porter, M. (2003) 'Building the microeconomic foundations of prosperity: findings from the microeconomic competitiveness index', in World Economic Forum (ed.) *The Global Competitiveness Report 2002–2003*, World Economic Forum, Oxford University Press, Oxford.

Rosamund, B. (2002) 'Imagining the European economy: "competitiveness" and the social construction of "Europe" as an economic space', *New Political Economy*, vol. 7, no. 2, 157–177.

Storper, M. (1997) *The Regional World*, Guilford Press, New York.

Sum, N-L. and Jessop, B. (2001) 'The pre- and post-disciplinary perspectives of political economy', *New Political Economy*, vol. 6 no. 1, 89–101.

Sum, N-L. (2004) 'From "integral state" to "integral world economic order": towards a neo-Gramscian cultural international political economy', *Cultural Political Economy Working Paper Series No. 7*, Institute for Advanced Studies in Social and Management Sciences, University of Lancaster, Lancaster.

Turok, I. (2004) 'Cities, regions and competitiveness', *Regional Studies*, vol. 38, 1069–1083.

Turok, I. (2008) 'A new policy for Britain's cities: choices, challenges, contradictions', *Local Economy*, vol. 23, no. 2, 149–161.

UNCTAD (2004) *Competition, Competitiveness and Development: Lessons from Developing Countries*, Report by the UNCTAD Secretariat, UNCTAD/DITC/DITC/CLP/2004/1.

Unwin, C. (2006) Urban myth: why cities don't compete', *Centre for Cities*, Institute of Public Policy Research (IPPR), Discussion Paper, no. 5, February 2006.

Wignaraja, G. (ed.) (2003) *Competitiveness Strategies in Developing Countries: A Manual for Policy Analysis*, Routledge, London.

Further reading

Blake, M. and Hanson, S. (2004) 'Rethinking Innovation: Context and Gender', *Environment and Planning A* vol. 37, 681–701.

Boland, P. (2007) 'Unpacking the theory–policy interface of local economic development: an analysis of Cardiff and Liverpool', *Urban Studies*, vol. 44, no. 5–6, 1019–1039.

Bristow, G. and Wells, P. (2005) 'Innovative discourse for sustainable local development: a critical analysis of eco-industrialism', *International Journal of Innovation and Sustainable Development*, vol. 1, no. 1/2, 168–179.

Gibbs, D., Deutz, P. and Proctor, A. (2005) 'Industrial ecology and eco-industrial development: a potential paradigm for local and regional development?', *Regional Studies*, vol. 29, no. 2, 171–183.

Gibson-Graham, J. K. (1996) *The End of Capitalism (as we knew it): A Feminist Critique of Political Economy*, Blackwell, Oxford.

Lagendijk, A. and Cornford, J. (2000) 'Regional institutions and knowledge – tracking new forms of regional development policy', *Geoforum*, vol. 31, 209–218.

Lagendijk, A. (2007) 'The accident of the region: a strategic relational perspective on the construction of the region's significance', *Regional Studies*, vol. 41, no. 2, 1193–1208.

30

Finance and local and regional economic development

Felicity Wray, Neill Marshall and Jane Pollard

Introduction

One often overlooked area in economic geography is a suite of questions concerning the role of finance in local and regional economic development. This is testimony to the relatively marginal location of finance in economic geography (Courlet and Soulage 1995, Martin 1999, Pollard 2003, Clark 2006, Pike and Pollard 2010) and a tendency to examine 'flows' of money, rather than the "processes and practices that shape and generate the flows" (Pryke 2006: 7). More particularly, it reflects a long-standing tendency in economic geography to treat firm finance as something of a 'black box' and a largely taken-for-granted aspect of production (Pollard 2003).

'Venture capital' is an umbrella term referring to specialist forms of finance – found most especially in the global North – that can be used to prove a business concept, help start up a business or allow businesses to expand. So-called 'classic venture capital' investments refer to equity used to help business start-ups. A second form of venture capital, 'merchant venture capital', refers to using equity to fund management buy-outs and buy-ins. The skill sets of merchant venture capitalists usually lie in financial engineering rather than fostering early stage entrepreneurs.

Venture capital has an important role in promoting local and regional development for several reasons. First, classic venture capitalists are often successful entrepreneurs and can contribute to local firm formation and growth and generally support entrepreneurship (Mason and Harrison 1995, 1996, 1997, 1999, Martin *et al.* 2005, Zook 2002). Second, by funding new ideas and helping to prove concepts, venture capitalists help underpin innovative knowledge economies and may play an integral part in the development of local technological infrastructure (Florida and Smith 1995, Saxenian 1994). Third, venture capitalists can add to a locality's institutional thickness, and act as both capitalists and catalysts for local and regional development (Keeble and Wilkinson 2000).

This chapter develops two interrelated arguments. First, we argue that analyses of venture capital remain relatively underdeveloped in economic geography; while many areas of economic geography have long been sensitised to cultural political economy approaches that stress the sociality of markets and different types and flows of knowledge, these debates have yet to touch analyses of venture capital in any significant way. Second, we argue that many analyses of the venture capital industry have – as is true of other parts of financial geography – focused on empirical cases in 'successful' regions and cities. Thus there is a corpus of work focused on venture capital in Cambridge (UK) (Klagge and Martin 2005, Keeble and Wilkinson 2000), Boston (Babcock-Lumish 2004) and Silicon Valley (Saxenian 1994, Zook 2004). In what follows, we outline the workings of the venture capital industry in two less affluent and less 'successful' English regions – the North East and the East Midlands. Our analysis suggests that variations in venture capitalists' financial knowledges play a significant role in explaining regional variations in venture capital activity and generate some more complex narratives about the relationship between finance and local economic development.

Research on the venture capital industry

To date, research on venture capital and regional development has tended to take one of three forms. First, important contributions have mapped the spatial distribution and take-up of venture capital investment (see, for example, Mason and Harrison 2002, Klagge and Martin 2005). Highlighting such spatial variations has allowed comparisons to be made between venture capital 'rich' and 'poor' regions (Figure 30.1). Such work has also distinguished between 'classic' and 'merchant' venture capital investments.

A second trend characterising work on venture capital in the UK context has been to highlight the spatial concentration of financial industries in the City of London and the rest of South East England (Mason 1987). This concentration shapes flows of venture capital and the reproduction of long-standing patterns of uneven regional development. Martin and Minns (1995), for example, highlighted the dominance of London and the

South East as a source and destination of flows of money and finance. Such concentration may pose significant challenges for the economic development trajectories of regions beyond London and the South East; many commentators stress the importance of physical proximity between venture capitalists and entrepreneurs to facilitate investments (Klagge and Martin 2005, Mason and Harrison 2002, 2003, Zook 2004).

A third trend in work on venture capital, and particularly that circulating in policy circles, is the way in which the availability and take-up of venture capital has tended to be conceived in the language of supply and demand. Thus, a lack of venture capital investments in a particular region is typically attributed either to a lack of entrepreneurial demand for finance or, alternatively, blamed on a lack of supply of funds from financial institutions who are risk averse (a phenomenon that has resurfaced in the current 'credit crunch'). A corollary of this supply and demand discourse is the idea that some places or regions endure 'finance gaps', reflecting a spatial mismatch between the demand and/or supply of finance.

The concept of a 'finance gap' has been very influential in UK policy circles. In 2002 the UK government injected a regional dimension into venture capital policy by introducing Regional Venture Capital Funds (RVCFs) to counteract the spatial concentration of venture capital funds/investments in London and the considerably lower rates of firm start-ups in regions outside London and the South East. This policy reflected a supply-side conception of 'the venture capital problem'; relatively low rates of new business formation in the UK were to be addressed by increasing the supply of equity in all the English regions and having those funds managed by managers assumed to have local knowledge and expertise. Mason and Harrison (2003) critiqued the policy on four counts: the lack of early stage venture capital skills available to manage the funds, the small size of the funds, the maximum investment

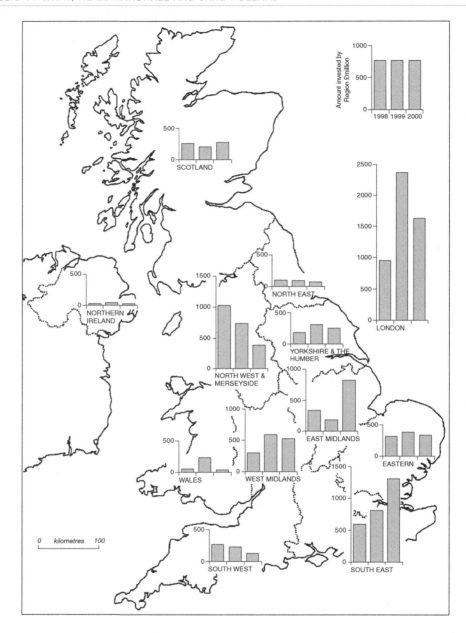

Figure 30.1 Regional distribution of venture capital investments by value, government office regions, 1998–2000.
Source: Adapted from Mason and Harrison (2002: 440)

limits on the funds which left them unable to address the main 'finance gap' in the English regions (investments in the £250,000 to £1 million range) and the neglect of the demand-side constraints that contribute to

equity gaps. They concluded a more comprehensive approach was required to address regional equity capital gaps in the UK.

What might this more comprehensive approach look like? In what follows, we draw on recent relational economic geography perspectives on cultures of money to argue that in addition to conceiving regional finance gaps as quantitative problems – of supply of and demand for venture capital – it is important to recognise and understand spatial variations in the qualitative dynamics – financial knowledges embodied by different agents involved in the venture capital industry – that produce and reproduce these perceived 'finance gaps'.

A relational perspective on venture capital

Previous political economic and institutional research has highlighted the uneven geographies of UK financial flows, institutions and financial infrastructure (Leyshon and Thrift 1995, Martin and Minns 1995, Martin *et al.* 2005). In the context of research on the venture capital industry, an interesting paradox has been revealed; the North East of England is venture capital 'rich', yet persistently endures the lowest volume of venture capital activity of all the English regions. This chapter argues that to understand this paradox, we need to complement political economic and institutional approaches – that devote relatively little attention to exploring the dynamics of money at the local level (Martin 1999, Pollard 2003) – with a finer grained analysis of the ways in which venture capitalists and entrepreneurs come together and do business.

More recent literatures on cultural political economies of money provide a starting point from which to complement current understandings of the processes and practices of the venture capital industry. Broadly, these literatures stress the socially constructed nature of the economy (Lee and Wills 1997, Crang 1997, Gertler 1997) and the assemblage of people, objects and activities that make up markets (see Du Gay and Pryke 2002). In the context of geographies of money, these literatures advocate getting beneath flows of money and unveiling the different forms of financial knowledge or 'calculative practices' (Callon 1998) that stabilise financial markets. These authors have encouraged a growing emphasis on examining the microdynamics of money.

A second hallmark of these literatures is greater sensitivity to the different systems of meanings that are established by individuals and groups in relation to the circulation of money. Here the networks through which money is circulated are critically important and are the means whereby money is mediated, appropriated and made sense of by particular communities. Drawing on Simmel (1978), Allen and Pryke (1999: 65) suggest it is possible to talk about "money cultures… made up of people who position themselves in relation to the circulation of money and are also positioned by it". Such a perspective makes it possible to talk about multiple money cultures that vary over place but which intersect with and are shaped by gender, ethnicity, age, class and so forth.

In similar vein, Communities of Practice (CoP) literatures (Wenger 1999, Lave and Wenger 1991) emphasise how people in a shared enterprise generate new knowledge and practices and draw attention to the communities that underpin and produce money cultures as well as fostering a greater awareness of how different networks of agents acquire, embody and mobilise financial knowledges. Conceptualising venture capitalists and entrepreneurs as communities of practice helps account for the different meanings and financial knowledges that agents attach to equity and their different ways of approaching the lending process. A further facet of the CoP literature is its important critique of accounts of regional learning that stressed the importance of physical proximity for knowledge exchange. Instead, CoP literatures argue that knowledge, in all its forms, can be exchanged through physically distant agents and that communities can access as well as circulate the same sets of knowledge at a distance (Vallance 2007, Faulconbridge

2006, Hall 2006, Amin and Cohendet 2004, Allen 2004). From this perspective, spatially dispersed venture capitalists may be connected to the same monetary networks, accessing and circulating similar financial knowledges, and ultimately be part of the same CoP, while physically proximate venture capitalists may belong to separate CoPs.

Finally, the preoccupation with mapping and quantifying the venture capital industry and the reliance on data collected by administrative region has tended to reinforce a spatially bounded treatment of the industry wherein regions are conceived as spatial containers for investment activity rather than as networks of social relations. As such, the spatiality of venture capitalists networks, which often transcend regional boundaries, has been relatively neglected. The 'relational turn' in economic geography (Amin 2004, Amin and Cohendet 1999, 2004, Allen 2000, Massey *et al.* 2003, Massey 2004, Marston 2000) refers to a set of more topological ways of seeing space that no longer correspond to neat scalar or territorial packages. Within this heuristic, places become defined as the sum of connections and networks of varying lengths, speed and duration that intersect and combine with human, technological and biological elements (Amin 2007: 102) and at all times "these combinations are always rubbing against historically shaped territorial formations" (ibid.). From this perspective neither networks nor territories are given preference. Rather places are sites of intersection between network topologies and territorial legacies (Amin 2007). The emphasis on connectivity and networks, plus the alternative spatial ontology advocated in relational approaches to economic geography is a useful framework to escape the territorially bounded readings of the venture capital industry and provides an alternative way of theorising the industry that recasts it as a stretched out and networked construction.

Relational approaches provide a different 'take' on the impact of actors and their patterns of behaviour on spatial economic

development (Bathelt and Glucker 2003, Ettlinger 2003). Their recognition of the networks of connections between venture capitalists, investors and entrepreneurs makes it possible to explore the relational advantage (Yeung 2005) of different financial networks and provide a more satisfactory way of understanding how financial knowledge is circulated across and within monetary networks with different spatial reaches. This allows us to explore how, if at all, the connectivity of professional finance agents in a locality makes a difference to the chances of local entrepreneurs securing finance and becoming investment ready.

In sum, these theoretical insights suggest an analytical treatment of the venture capital industry that problematises agency, creates a more socialised account of the industry and engages with the dynamics and intersections of money and finance in a variety of spaces. In the next section, we demonstrate the merit of such an approach to understand the emergence, production and dynamics of finance gaps at the local level. Specifically, we interrogate agents' embodied financial knowledges, behaviours and spaces of interaction and connectivity in a comparative study of two case study regions, the East Midlands and the North East of England.

Venture capital networks in the North East and the East Midlands

The North East and the East Midlands regions of England have interesting similarities, but also differences. The North East of England is usually described as an 'old industrial region' which occupies a peripheral position – economically and geographically – in relation to London and the South East (Pike 2006, Hudson 2005). The East Midlands is characterised by average performance when compared to other regions on a range of economic performance indicators (Crewe 1995) and considered to be a 'middling region' (Hardill *et al.* 2006). Both regions have had to reposition themselves and adapt to a decline in their traditional industries: coal-mining, steel-making, shipbuilding and chemicals in the North East, and textiles, steel and some limited coal-mining in the East Midlands.

Both regions have relatively small populations and the lowest rates (in England) of VAT registrations with an average of 45,330 and 123,818 registrations in the North East and East Midlands respectively between 2003 and 2005 (ONS 2006). Table 30.1 demonstrates that in terms of private equity-backed companies per '000 population, the number of start-ups per thousand population, and the location quotient of venture capital-backed companies (measured by the number of companies that receive equity per 1000 of total VAT registered businesses) neither region can be considered to be particularly dynamic in terms of venture capital activity compared with London and the South East. Table 30.2 provides further detail regarding the levels of venture capital investment, both classic and merchant. Between 2005 and 2007, the North East secures between 1 and 4 per cent of all merchant investments, while the East Midlands fluctuates between 4 and 6 per cent; London and the South East secured 41 per cent of these kinds of deals.

Figure 30.2 describes the indigenous equity funds of each region, including the fund managers, the size of fund and the maximum amount that can be invested. When compared with the East Midlands, the North East appears relatively 'rich' in terms of providers of equity, although the East Midlands Regional Venture Capital Fund (RVCF) is double the size of that in the North East. There are three noteworthy features of venture capital provision in the North East. First, the region is reliant on public sector managed equity. Second, it has a relatively even concentration of equity funds across four main institutions. Third, although the North East has considerably more venture capital finance than the East Midlands, it records fewer transactions than is the case in the East Midlands.

In what follows, we draw on observational research and semi-structured interviews with professional finance agents and entrepreneurs in the two regions (see Tables 30.3 and 30.4); all the entrepreneurs were seeking equity and the professional finance agents either supplied venture capital or coached entrepreneurs to become investment ready. Table 30.4 highlights how East Midland entrepreneurs tended to be slightly more concentrated in more innovative, higher value-added and high-technology sectors than their North Eastern counterparts who where slightly more concentrated in more traditional manufacturing. These sectoral differences partly reflect the industrial structures of each region.

Table 30.1 Business start-up rates, private equity backed companies and location quotients of equity backed companies, 2003–2005

	Start-ups per 1000 popn in 2003	LQ	No. of PEBC* per '000 popn in 2003	Start-ups per 1000 in 2004	LQ	No. of PEBC per 'ooo popn in 2004	Start-ups per 1000 in 2005	LQ	No. of PEBC per '000 popn in 2005
North East	17	0.83	1.46	17	1.21	2.16	17	0.68	1.64
East Midlands	28	0.52	1.50	28	0.58	1.68	29	0.52	1.39
London	38	0.93	3.59	38	0.91	3.53	38	0.93	3.88
South East	35	0.97	3.42	35	0.91	3.19	35	0.95	2.90

*PEBC = Number of private equity-backed companies.
Source: Wray (2007)

Table 30.2 Number and percentages of merchant and classic investments by region, 2005–2007

| | Pop–share 2003–2005 | Early stage/classic investments | | | | | | MBO/MBI merchant investments | | | | | |
| | | 2005 | | 2006 | | 2007 | | 2005 | | 2006 | | 2007 | |
		Number	%	Number	%	Number	%	Number	%	Number	%	Number	%
South East	16.2	104	21.18	90	18.00	88	17.53	47	15.26	55	15.07	44	12.61
London	14.8	75	15.27	104	20.80	110	21.91	70	22.73	107	29.32	100	28.65
South West	10	42	8.55	35	7.00	29	5.78	21	6.82	29	7.95	15	4.30
East of England	11	61	12.42	50	10.00	50	9.96	21	6.82	22	6.03	22	6.30
West Midlands	10.6	24	4.89	35	7.00	32	6.37	27	8.77	25	6.85	21	6.02
East Midlands	8.5	22	4.48	20	4.00	18	3.59	19	6.17	15	4.11	22	6.30
Yorkshire & Humber	10	20	4.07	10	2.00	19	3.78	20	6.49	29	7.95	35	10.03
North West	13.6	65	13.24	70	14.00	77	15.34	51	16.56	51	13.97	48	13.75
North East	5.1	16	3.26	10	2.00	19	3.78	3	0.97	11	3.01	15	4.30
Scotland	–	36	7.33	40	8.00	34	6.77	18	5.84	10	2.74	12	3.44
Wales	–	13	2.65	20	4.00	17	3.39	8	2.60	11	3.01	13	3.72
N. Ireland	–	13	2.65	16	3.20	9	1.79	3	0.97	–	0.00	2	0.57
TOTAL		491	100	500	100	502	100	308	100	365	100	349	100

Source: BVCA (2008: 29)

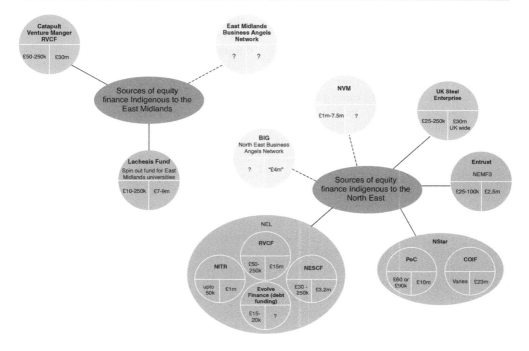

Figure 30.2 Regional financial architectures: indigenous supplies of equity.
Source: Wray (2007)

Table 30.3 Research summary

	North East	East Midlands
Entrepreneurs interviewed	20	20
Professional finance agents interviewed	21	17
Number of times non-participant observation was undertaken	13	6

Source: Wray (2007)

Table 30.4 Number of entrepreneurs interviewed by sector (informed by SIC codes)

	East Midlands	North East
Software consultancy and design	8	11
Manufacturing	1	5
Product design	5	0
Leisure/lifestyle	1	2
Research and experimental development in natural sciences and engineering	4	1
Railway maintenance	0	1
Biochemical analysis and testing	1	0

Source: Wray (2007)

The professional finance agents

There were important differences in the biographies and work histories of the venture capitalists interviewed in the two regions. North East finance agents came predominantly from backgrounds in commercial banking or public service. By contrast, 52 per cent of finance agents in the East Midlands had either been venture capitalists in well-known equity firms, worked in large private consultancy firms specialising in biotech or pharmaceuticals and/or were also successful entrepreneurs and active business angels. A further finding was that 15 of the 17 East Midland finance agents had arrived in the region from elsewhere; in the North East, by contrast, all but two finance agents were either from the region or had remained in the region from their days at university.

Each regional finance community of professional finance agents was governed by different norms and values which produced different kinds of behaviour. Very few interdependencies, linkages, reciprocal arrangements or instances of collaboration existed between North East finance agents; instead, a culture of hostility, suspicion and mistrust prevailed. Local finance agents felt their counterparts were more concerned with "having their own agendas to prolong their own existence" (Business Angel, February 2005), rather than fostering entrepreneurship, and were suspicious of the capabilities and conduct of local institutions claiming that they were "slow and cumbersome" (Finance Intermediary, February 2005), "ineffective and fragmented" (Corporate Financier, February 2005), produced "appalling business plans" (Business Angel, March 2005) or that "retired bank managers are not going to encourage and foster the ambitions of entrepreneurs" (Former Venture Capitalist, March 2005). Finance agents in the North East tended to operate in isolation from each other; they demonstrated that physical proximity does not necessarily breed familiarity and linkage.

In the East Midlands, by contrast, professional finance agents were bound together through a variety of linkages and interdependencies ranging from formal contracts to verbal commitments; they described working in a community predicated on trust, reciprocity and sharing financial knowledge and expertise. The collaborative behaviour and sentiments served to produce a high-quality 'buzz' in the financial milieu and a stock of localised capabilities and expertise that finance agents drew on regularly to react to gaps in provision or demand. East Midlands finance agents felt they accrued benefits from being in close proximity to other agents. Overall the East Midlands finance agents were a community of practice that operated in similar money cultures. To what extent these different ways of behaving/doing venture capital had an impact on local entrepreneurs and ultimately local development trajectories will be discussed in Section V.

The differences in the linkages and interconnections of the various financial communities were also reflected in their spatial reach. Over three-quarters of North East finance agents interviewed operated mostly at the scale of the region and were disconnected from wider investor networks. Three-quarters of North East finance agents did not consider engaging beyond the region important for them and their business, and they perceived there to be limited, if any, need for links between the North East's financial milieu and investors located elsewhere. Some explained the lack of links in terms of their perception that non-local investors did not see the North East as a profitable place to do business, while others admitted that they deliberately excluded themselves from non-local networks to reduce the threat of competition. Others suggested it was too expensive to engage non-locally, and believed there were positive benefits accruing from isolation: "being insular is a good thing; it helps us to make money" (Corporate Financier). The decision by North East finance agents to operate solely at the scale of the region meant they probably relied on more limited financial knowledges and had fewer opportunities to develop organisational proximity with investors from more successful and buoyant investment contexts.

In contrast, the East Midland finance agents argued it was important to be part of networks beyond the region. Reasons given included the opportunity to access funds for local entrepreneurs, to share and learn from best practice, to access other investment opportunities and to promote the East Midlands as an attractive place in which to invest. To maintain and forge these contacts agents employed a variety of strategies such as (1) membership of specialist networks, (2) attending non-local investment events and, (3) organising special events within the region where non-local investors were invited. From the perspective of local finance agents, the 'reward' for maintaining and undertaking this behaviour was the numerous organisational proximities and relational complementarities developed with finance agents beyond the region. Examples of outcomes included recruiting high-calibre non-executive finance directors for East Midlands entrepreneurs and well-attended local investment events. Additionally, with the concentration (82 per cent) of contacts located in Cambridge or Oxford, East Midlands finance agents were able to stay current with financial narratives produced by investors in centres of discursive authority. The myriad connections served to produce an extremely porous finance community, demonstrating relational advantage, and made it difficult to define where the East Midlands finance community started and finished.

Institutional and financial architectures

The dissimilar institutional terrain, financial architectures (Figure 30.2) and industrial histories of the two regions are an important influence on these different ways of behaving

and practising venture capital. The institutional terrain of the East Midlands was richer than the North East in terms of support agencies mentioned by entrepreneurs seeking finance and this helped filter how entrepreneurs accessed funds and financial advice.

The multiple ties that existed between the agencies may indicate an institutional capacity to coordinate a response to obstacles and problems in the East Midlands. The thinner institutional structure of the North East, the longevity of the two main institutions dedicated to supporting entrepreneurship (Entrust and RTC) and the lack of collaboration that finance agents mentioned suggest some institutional inflexibility in supporting regional entrepreneurship. An alternative perspective is that finance agents in the North East could be viewed as embedded in a set of 'trained incapacities' (Schoenberger 1997) and are unable or unwilling to react to change.

The ready supply of public sector equity in the North East (Figure 30.2), which the UK government requires to be invested solely within the standard region, arguably mitigates the need for finance agents to collaborate to secure finance. This financial architecture means that North East finance agents are operating in a limited market and are possibly in competition with each other to invest these funds, thus fuelling the observed culture of mistrust. Also the way in which the funds were spatially bounded helps to explain why North East finance agents attached little importance to engaging beyond the North East region. Similarly, the relative paucity of funds in the East Midlands arguably encouraged local finance agents to collaborate and forge non-local connections to secure funds for local entrepreneurs. A by-product of the financial architecture, however, was that it added to the relational advantage of the finance community due to the plethora of organisational proximities and relational complementarities formed with non-local investors. A further by-product was that local finance agents accessed and relied on financial knowledge from some of the

Table 30.5 Support agencies used by entrepreneurs in the North East and East Midlands

	East Midlands					North East		
	EMIN	Loughborough Innovation Centre	BioCity	The Hive	Connect Midlands	Entrust	Codeworks Connect	RTC (Regional Technology Centre)
Year Formed	2001	2002	2001	2001	2004	1981	2004	1987
Mission	A network of business incubators – to increase the volume, value and survival rates of new start businesses	Purpose-designed business incubator for new and growing companies that are technology or knowledge based	The UK's largest purpose-built bioscience and healthcare innovation centre	Purpose-built enterprise development centre to facilitate the university to create and support new ventures	A not-for-profit network linking high-potential technology businesses with training and finance	Enterprise agency supporting individuals, start-ups and established businesses to reach their objectives and goals	To create jobs and wealth in North East England by fostering the growth of the regions digital industries	A technology transfer company to help clients exploit new opportunities and improve competitiveness through the application of technology, knowledge and forward thinking

Source: Wray (2007)

most economically dynamic parts of the country. How do differences in institutional and financial architectures and in the behaviours of professional finance agents affect local entrepreneurs seeking to secure finance? By engaging with entrepreneurs it is not only possible to answer this question but demonstrates how different socio-institutional configurations affect local and regional economic development trajectories.

Entrepreneurs seeking finance

The contrasting institutional and financial configurations of the two regions influenced how local entrepreneurs navigated the financial landscape. Entrepreneurs interviewed in the East Midlands recognised and benefited from the 'focus on entrepreneurship' and 'numerous support frameworks' in the region. Consequently local entrepreneurs perceived the East Midlands as a 'pretty positive place' in which to set up and do business by virtue of its enabling and supportive environment. The myriad ties between the organisations meant East Midlands entrepreneurs were referred to appropriate contacts/institutions and found the financial landscape relatively easy to navigate. By contrast, most North East entrepreneurs found the fractured financial landscape difficult to navigate, likening it to a 'maze' and haphazard. A quarter of entrepreneurs called for 'greater clarity and consolidation' to make the support networks more focused. Entrepreneurs reported being unaware or unsure of which organisation to approach "there is just nothing that you can latch onto for (financial) assistance" (ibid.) in the region and generally entrepreneurs felt less well supported by the institutionally thin terrain. As one entrepreneur put it, "there needs to be more people who can pick up a small business and push them through the various milestones to get funding ... it's all very daunting".

The two sets of regional entrepreneurs also experienced different preparation processes to become investment ready. Within the East Midlands, entrepreneurs were coached by Connect Midlands whose remit was to ensure that entrepreneurs became investment ready and could pitch for business at investment events. Among the professional finance agents and the entrepreneurs, Connect Midlands was perceived to be a high-quality and well-respected intermediary. Of the nine entrepreneurs that used Connect Midlands' investment training, all were positive about their experiences and recognised the high-quality advice they received from the various finance agents recruited by Connect to deliver specialist sessions. The North East appeared to lack any official or structured investor readiness programme. Although Entrust claimed to offer such a programme in reality it provided limited, ad-hoc training from in-house employees. Of the eight entrepreneurs who received training, seven expressed their dissatisfaction, claiming it was poor quality, generic and had little added value. One entrepreneur, who paid £200, 'received very little advice and support... and were given standard guidelines of what is in a business plan which I could get from anywhere'. Another entrepreneur recognised there was a mismatch between his and the investors' financial knowledge so when presenting his idea at an Investors Forum it 'felt like an exam without any opportunity to revise for it'. This may reflect the work experience of those training entrepreneurs (in commercial banking or the public sector) unlike those tutors in Connect Midlands, who had relevant experience in the sector.

The high-calibre training offered by Connect Midlands meant East Midlands entrepreneurs tended to embody and perform similar financial knowledge to their professional counterparts, while North East entrepreneurs remained largely unaware of investor expectations and, in essence, operated in a separate money culture from that of potential investors. Evidence of the impact of these differences in the preparation process can be seen in the fact that 55 per cent of

East Midlands entrepreneurs understood correctly the required sections for a business plan, compared to only 15 per cent of North East (see Wray 2007).

Finally both sets of local entrepreneurs enacted and mirrored the behaviour of the local professional finance agents. Like their professional counterparts 65 per cent of East Midlands entrepreneurs attached value and importance to engaging beyond the region to increase their chances of securing finance. Of the 40 per cent of North East entrepreneurs that engaged beyond the North East, it was in a considerably more ad-hoc or sporadic way. So, while the behaviour of East Midland entrepreneurs added to the porosity and relational advantage of the local financial milieu, contributing to the dense ecology of interaction and knowledge sharing, North East entrepreneurs contributed to the relatively poor relational advantage of the local milieu.

The behaviour of East Midland entrepreneurs provides evidence to suggest that they are less dependent on regional intermediaries to secure finance on their behalf. Rather the training and support provided equips local entrepreneurs to take control of their own agendas in securing finance, whereas North East entrepreneurs remained (unknowingly) reliant on relatively ineffective training and isolated intermediaries. Different regional financial architectures underpin and sustain the dissimilar behaviour of each set of entrepreneurs.

Conclusion

Using the venture capital industry as a lens, this chapter has engaged with the dynamics of money and finance at the local level to make two key arguments. First, it has argued that the emergence and production of 'finance gaps' at the local level is far more complex and culturally nuanced than current research suggests. In so doing, it has highlighted the different types and flows of

knowledge held by venture capitalists and entrepreneurs which, in some regional contexts, make it difficult for agents to intersect and do business together. Second, the chapter has explored two regions not considered to have 'successful' venture capital scenes and has demonstrated considerable heterogeneity, in both venture finance agents and entrepreneurs, in the two regions. In addition to problematising the concept of 'the problem region', the chapter has highlighted how the management of equity at the local level shapes, and is shaped by, local economic, institutional and financial architectures. Drawing on literatures from communities of practice, cultural political economy and relational economic geography, this chapter has illustrated the importance of agency and variations in financial knowledges by way of complementing more structural and institutional analyses of the concentration of venture capital activity.

If, as is regularly stressed, promoting regional entrepreneurship is a vital ingredient of vibrant and diverse local economies, then there are a number of lessons that can be drawn from this analysis. First, a supply of money is not enough. Merely increasing the supply of equity in some places does not necessarily increase the number of deals conducted. Although the supply-side initiatives are not to be condemned, the existence and rules underpinning these funds may have helped to perpetuate the North East's relative isolation from other investment networks and had a negative impact on local entrepreneurs. This research has shown the need for more multi-dimensional and nuanced regional venture capital policies that embrace different socio-economic and institutional configurations rather than national polices rolled out across regions with little regard to local differences. Second, the research suggests the need for high-quality intermediaries and investment training programmes if entrepreneurs are to be able to embody the right kinds of financial knowledge and to do business more easily with venture capitalists.

The positive impacts of the investors training course in the East Midlands provides support for this recommendation. Finally, this research illustrates the significance of examining the sociality and spatiality of the venture capital industry in order to understand perceived 'finance gaps'. This analysis escapes the (usually) territorially bounded treatment of the industry, while paying greater attention to agency, and highlighting the connectivity and spatial reach of venture capitalists. The research has also added to a growing corpus of work grappling with the tension between territorial and relational approaches by empirically demonstrating the complex way in which networks, territories and socio-institutional structures intersect to produce distinct spatial configurations and challenges for local and regional development outcomes.

References

Allen, J. (2004) 'The whereabouts of power: politics, government and space', *Geografiska Annaler*, 86, 1, 19–32.

Allen, J. and Pryke, M. (1999) 'Money cultures after Simmel: mobility, movement and identity', *Environment and Planning D: Society and Space*, 17, 51–68.

Amin, A. (2007) 'Rethinking the urban social', *City*, 11, 1, 100–114.

Amin, A. and Cohendet, P. (2000) 'Organisational learning and governance through embedded practices', *Journal of Management and Governance*, 4, 93–116.

Amin, A. and Cohendet, P. (2004) *Architectures of Knowledge: Firms, Capabilities and Communities*, Oxford, New York: Oxford University Press.

Babcock-Lumish, T.L. (2004) 'The dynamics of innovation investment communities: the spatial structure of networks and relationships', University of Oxford School of Geography, *Economic Geography Working Paper Series* WPG 04–17.

Bathelt, H. and Glückler, J. (2003) 'Towards a relational economic geography', *Journal of Economic Geography*, 3, 117–144.

BVCA (2008) *BVCA Private Equity and Venture Capital Report on Investment Activity 2007*, London, BVCA.

Callon, M. (ed.) (1998) *The Laws of the Markets*, London: Verso.

Clark, G.L. (2006) 'Setting the agenda: the geography of global finance', in S. Bagchi-Sen and H. Lawton-Smith (eds) *Economic Geography: Past, Present and Future*, Routledge: London, 83–93.

Courlet, C. and Soulage, B. (1995) 'Industrial systems and territorial space', *Entrepreneurship and Regional Development*, 7, 287–308.

Crang, P. (1997) 'Cultural turns and the (re)constitution of economic geography' in R. Lee and J. Wills (eds) *Geographies of Economies*, London, New York, Sydney, Auckland: Arnold.

Crewe, L. (1995) 'The East Midlands', *Geography*, 80, 2, 166–171.

Du Gay, P. and Pryke, M. (2002) *Cultural Economy*, London: Sage.

Ettlinger, N. (2003) 'Cultural economic geography and a relational and micro space approach to trusts, rationalities, networks, and change in collaborative workplaces', *Journal of Economic Geography*, 3, 145–171.

Faulconbridge, J. (2006) 'Stretching tacit knowledge beyond a local fix? Global spaces of learning in advertising professional service firms', *Journal of Economic Geography*, 517–540.

Florida, R. L. and Smith, D. F. (1995) 'Venture capital formation, investment and regional industrialisation', *Annals of the Association of American Geographers*, 83, 434–451.

Gertler, M. (1997) 'In search of the new social economy: collaborative relations between users and producers of advanced manufacturing technologies', *Environment and Planning A*, 29, 1585–1602.

Hall, S. (2006) 'What counts? Exploring the production of quantitative financial narratives in London's corporate finance industry', *Journal of Economic Geography*, 6, 5, 661–678.

Hardill, I., Bentley, C. and Cuthbert, M. (2006) 'The East Midlands The Missing Middle?' in I. Hardill, P. Benneworth, M. Baker, and L. Budd, (eds) *In The Rise of the English Regions?*, Oxford, New York: Routledge.

Hudson, R. (2005) 'Rethinking change in old industrial regions: reflecting on the experiences of North East England', *Environment and Planning A*, 37, 581–596.

Keeble, D. and Wilkinson, F. (2000) *High-technology Clusters, Networking and Collective Earning in Europe*, London; Ashgate.

Klagge, B. and Martin, R. (2005) 'Decentralised versus centralised financial systems: is there a case for local capital markets?', *Journal of Economic Geography*, 5, 387–421.

Lave, J. and Wenger, E. (1991) *Situated Learning: Legitimate Peripheral Participation*, Cambridge: Cambridge University Press.

Lee, R. and Wills, J. (1997) (eds) *Geographies of Economies*, London: Arnold.

Leyshon, A. and Thrift, N. (1995) 'Geographies of financial exclusion: financial abandonment in Britain and the United States', *Transactions of the Institute of British Geographers*, 20, 312–341.

Marston, S. A. (2000) 'The social construction of scale', *Progress in Human Geography*, 24, 2, 219–242.

Martin, R. (1999) *Money and the Space_Economy*. Chichester: John Wiley.

Martin, R. and Minns, R. (1995) 'Undermining the financial basis of regions: the spatial structure and implications of the UK pension fund system', *Regional Studies*, 29, 125–145.

Martin, R., Berndt, C., Klagge, B. and Sunley, P. (2005) 'Spatial proximity effects and regional equity gaps in the venture capital market. Evidence from Germany and the UK', *Environment and Planning A*, 37, 7, 1207–1231.

Mason, C. and Harrison, R. (1995) 'Closing the regional equity capital gap: the role of informal venture capital', *Small Business Economics*, 7, 153–172.

Mason, C. and Harrison, R. (1996) 'Why business angels say no: a case study of opportunities rejected by an informal investor syndicate', *International Small Business Journal*, 14, 2, 35–51.

Mason, C. and Harrison, R. (1997) 'Business angel networks and the development of the informal venture capital market in the UK: is there still a role for the public sector?', *Small Business Economics*, 9, 111–123.

Mason, C. and Harrison, R. (1999) 'Financing entrepreneurship: venture capital and regional development', in R.L. Martin, (ed.) *Money and the Space Economy*, Chichester, Wiley 157–183.

Mason, C. and, Harrison, R. T. (2002) 'The geography of venture capital investments in the UK', *Transactions of the Institute of British Geographers*, 27, 4, 427–451.

Mason, C. and Harrison, R. T. (2003) 'Closing the regional equity gap? A critique of the Department of Trade and Industry's regional venture capital funds initiative', *Regional Studies*, 37, 8, 855–868.

Massey, D. (2004) 'Geographies of responsibility'. *Geografiska Annaler*, 86,1, 5–18.

ONS (2006) *Regional Trends* No. 36, London: The Stationery Office.

Pike, A. (2006) '"Shareholder value" versus the regions: the closure of the Vaux Brewery in Sunderland', *Journal of Economic Geography*, 6, 201–222.

Pike, A. and Pollard, J. S. (2010) 'Economic geographies of financialisation', *Economic Geography*, 86, 1.

Pryke, M. (2006) 'Speculating on geographies of finance', CRESC Working Paper Series, Working Paper No. 24, CRESC: Manchester

Pollard, J. S. (2003) 'Small firm finance and economic geography', *Journal of Economic Geography*, 3, 4, 429–452.

Saxenian, A. (1994) *Regional Advantage: Culture and Competition in Silicon Valley and Route 128*, Cambridge, MA: Harvard University Press.

Schoenberger, E. (1997) *The Cultural Crisis of the Firm,* and Massachusetts, USA, Oxford, UK: Blackwell.

Simmel, G. (1978) *The Philosophy of Money*, translated by T. Bottomore and D. Frisby London, Henley, Boston: Routledge & Kegan Paul.

Wenger, E. (1999) *Communities of Practice: Learning, Meaning and Identity*, Cambridge: Cambridge University Press.

Vallance, P. (2007) 'Rethinking economic geographies of knowledge', *Geography Compass,* 1, 4, 797–813.

Wray, F. (2007) *Money, Space and Relationality: Rethinking the Venture Capital Industry in the East Midlands and the North of England*, unpublished Ph.D. Dissertation, Centre for Urban and Regional Development Studies, Newcastle University, UK.

Yeung, H. W-C. (2005) 'Rethinking relational economic geography', *Transactions of the Institute of British Geographers*, 30, 37–51.

Zook, M. (2002) 'Grounded capital: venture financing and the geography of the Internet industry', *Journal of Economic Geography*, 2, 151–177.

Further reading

Klagge, B. and Martin, R. (2005) 'Decentralised versus centralised financial systems: is there a case for local capital markets?', *Journal of Economic Geography*, 5, 387–421. (A piece considering some of the policy dimensions of venture capital provision.)

Yeung, H. W-C. (2005) 'Rethinking relational economic geography', *Transactions of the Institute of British Geographers*, 30, 37–51. (A treatment of the main tenets of relational thinking in economic geography.)

Zook, M. (2002) 'Grounded capital: venture financing and the geography of the Internet industry', *Journal of Economic Geography*, 2, 151–177. (A case study of the significance of venture capital.)

31

Green dreams in a cold light

Susan Christopherson

Introduction

For many policy-makers in advanced economies, "green" economic development is the next new thing. It has been touted as a vehicle for economic regeneration along the lines of previous technological transformations, such as the computer and electricity. It is portrayed as a strong economic engine that will create millions of new jobs as well as a healthier planet (Gordon and Hays, 2008). The relationship between economic development and efforts to reduce greenhouse gases is a contentious one however. Some advocates of a "green" economy believe that a climate change-driven technological and economic transformation must incorporate a social justice agenda. They argue that our ability to achieve a healthier global environment will be limited if not impossible if "green" economic development does not improve the quality of life for people who have not benefited from globalization processes, such as trade liberalization. Other advocates of a "green economy" take for granted that technological change and government incentives will produce economic growth and jobs, and are less concerned with how those jobs are distributed or with where and how economic development will occur. They

believe that when the fate of the global climate is at stake, the end justifies the means.

For the most part, projections regarding climate-change-related economic development and the demand for "green" jobs have come from analyses of industries that have some association with a green economy (Apollo Alliance, 2008, 2009; Bezdek, 2007b; Pollin *et al.*, 2008; Pollin and Wicks-Lim, 2008; Renner *et al.*, 2008). These estimates are very optimistic. Bezdek (2007), for example, estimates that 40 million Americans could be employed in green industry jobs by 2030 and Pollin and co-authors (2008) project that two million Americans could be employed in green jobs by 2011. The authors of these optimistic reports generally agree that, in advanced economies, the greatest potential for creating employment is in building retrofitting and in enhancing energy efficiency. In developing economies, the potential scope for job creation is much broader, both because of out-sourced production for alternative energy equipment (such as wind turbines) and because basic energy needs have not been met for a substantial portion of the world's population. This unmet need could create, for example, new industries and jobs in small-scale energy production, as in photovoltaic equipment.

Overall, the existing studies estimate how much public and private investment will be required to create the job growth the authors project (Pollin and Wicks-Lim, 2008). However, there has been almost no analysis of where public and private investments are likely to occur, of how investment location decisions will affect the spatial distribution and density of green job creation or of how differently positioned communities will be affected by these investments.

A clear-eyed assessment of where and how economic development is likely to be structured in the "real" economy requires an assessment that "follows the money" and also looks at how political decisions affect the ability to adopt energy-saving technologies (Kelley, 2008). Three perspectives are critical to this assessment. The first is a recognition that green technologies and their applications will occur within a political economic framework that has emerged in conjunction with trade liberalization, devolution, and deregulation – what we loosely refer to as globalization – and the international division of labor constructed by these processes. The second perspective recognizes the ways in which economic development policy-making and at the national, sub-national and local scales will influence public and private investment in the green agenda. Because the structure and practice of economic development differ among national contexts, what is meant by "green economic development" is likely to differ, too. Finally, while local initiatives and social movements are central to effective responses to climate change, they will be affected dramatically by economic policy initiatives promulgated and adopted at geographic scales above those of the locality. These include government incentives to favor some technologies over others and decisions to invest in new forms of energy production or efforts to foster conservation (Gibbs, 2002).

In this chapter, I lay out a framework for understanding how the green economy will take shape and what that will mean for dif-ferent segments of the workforce and differently positioned places – disadvantaged inner city neighborhoods, suburban and rural communities – in advanced economies. The United States is used as the primary example because of its central role in world energy consumption and adoption of market-based strategies to respond to climate change. My goal, however, is to foster discussion of a conceptual framework that recognizes how green economic development is embedded in broader political economic institutions and reflects the priorities and power relations that drive those institutions.

The green economy – what is it?

Any attempt to understand the forces shaping so-called "green" economic development necessarily starts from a point of confusion because the concept of the green economy has been adopted and adapted by interest groups and corporations with vastly different interpretations and agendas. While the greening of the economy was once promoted by a small group of environmental activists, it is now integral to the agendas of multi national fossil fuel companies, such as BP, as well as of advocates for nuclear power, and agribusiness interests supporting subsidies for corn production. What this means is that we have to sort through myriad depictions of effective responses to climate change and to understand who will benefit from one actual agenda rather than another (Swyngedouw, 2006).

Despite extreme elasticity in the concept, the green economy is typically defined around: (1) renewable energy, including manufacturing of equipment to serve alternative energy producers in wind power, solar and geothermal as well as biomass, and (2) energy efficiency and conservation through new technologies, products, building retrofitting, and recycling. The broad and more philosophical than operational goal of these efforts is "sustainability", most frequently defined as approaches to the economy and environment that "meet the needs of the present without compromising the ability of future generations to meet their own needs" (United Nations General Assembly, 1987).

The ideas and initiatives swirling around the green economy exhibit all the contradictions and conflicts inherent in battles over economic globalization. They pit transnational corporations who thrive on inter-regional competition and production out-sourcing against localists who question the social utility of engagement with notions of global and inter-regional competition. The local version of sustainable development is very different from that proposed by transnational firms. This is particularly apparent in poor countries where applications are likely to be small scale and local because there are few profits to be made from providing poor people with energy of any kind (Barbier, 2009). The political debate about the global and local variants of the green economy has been increasingly "fuzzed over", however, as the green economy has gained iconic status. And, as with globalization, "There are no internal social tensions or internal generative conflicts. Instead the enemy is always externalised and objectified" (Swyngedouw, 2006: 25).

When one looks at whose version of green development dominates U.S. economic development policy, however, it is clearly that of those who project a green, sustainable economy built around economies of scale – big firms, big unions, and big utilities. For reasons described below, the big players have the most potential for shaping critical public policies around their interests and capturing the lion's share of public investment that will be needed to reconfigure the economy to respond to climate change.

In the broad debate over what is meant by a green sustainable economy and what public policy actions should take place to realize it, the question of scale is central. In the arena of electric energy production and distribution, for example, two options are presented. The first is the development of renewable energy in a way that makes it easily integrated with existing highly centralized and privatized energy production and distribution systems. In this scenario, sources of renewable energy, such as wind, would be developed at a scale that allows existing energy distributors to access the energy in a form that is consonant with an enormous centralized corporately owned "grid". To make this version of the green economy viable, the grid will have to be reconstructed to accommodate the variability of large-scale renewable energy sources, such as the ten-square-mile photovoltaic farms projected for the Western deserts of the U.S. In this "big-big" approach to the green economy, economic development policy supports the kinds of major investments that reconstruct the grid and encourage large-scale renewable energy sources such as wind and photovoltaic panel "farms" that are projected for construction in frontier and rural land.

At the other end of the spectrum are "distributed" energy solutions, such as municipal and regional power companies which rely on heterogeneous, regionally differentiated sources of renewable energy including wind, geothermal energy, and hydropower. Distributed energy approaches may be micro, operating at the level of the individual residence or business, or regional, as in the Austin Texas Water and Power District Austin Energy, but they are predicated on the idea that energy efficiency is more effectively achieved by relying on and tapping sources of energy that are available locally or regionally. In this view of the green economy, long- distance transmission and large-scale development should only be undertaken where regional and local energy options are not available and energy conservation efforts are not sufficient. The grid is a back-up system. While a "smart grid" would have to be constructed to handle the variability associated with renewable energy, economic development policy would also focus on building municipal and regional systems that rely on local sources of renewable power and are accountable to the citizens of a region.

A second arena in which the issue of scale is central to the green economy is that which constructs a choice between a green economy rooted in large-scale industrial development of replacements for existing sources of energy production and use (such as bio-fuels but including a range of new technologies, such as electric cars) and efforts to reduce our carbon footprint through energy efficiency measures. For the most part, energy efficiency measures (such as building retrofitting, green roof development or adaptation of photo-voltaic cells in building) are inherently local in their applications. These two directions, one focused on energy product replacement and the other focused on energy conservation, efficiency, and reduction are supported by different economic development coalitions but all under the banner of sustainability.

In the next section I use the example of the United States to further examine the policies and incentives that underpin "green" economic development as it is taking shape in advanced economies. In the U.S. case, the incentives largely favor market-based, large-scale solutions and de-emphasize the role of local capacity, energy conservation, and distributed technologies.

What kind of green economy?

As has already been suggested, possibly the most important thing to know about the green economy is that, despite the hype, it is not wholly new. It will emerge out of the business organizations that grow, mine, manufacture, and distribute products and services. It will also be significantly shaped by the strategies of firms that dominate those industries, firms such as Siemens, Mitsubishi, and General Electric Corporation. This is important to remember when assessing how the green economy is likely to take shape. While there are many interesting experiments and possibilities, it is critical to look at the dominant players, their interests and agendas.

The green economy is embedded in broader and deeper economic institutions. Policies to promote a green economy take shape within national governance regimes that measure economic development in different ways (more or less including measures of social welfare and long-term investment) and a global governance regime that, though partial, has been built around trade liberalization and intra-national deregulation of key industries. When powerful organizations and individuals step forward to recommend steps to curb climate change, they do so in such a way that their power and influence is maintained. Thus, there is strong pressure for continuity in the governance regime and institutional power as policies to transform environmental policy take shape (Sayer, 2008; Swyngedouw, 2006).

Green economic development and the jobs that are associated with it are developing in ways that parallel wealth, knowledge and technological resources among countries (Adger et al., 2006; Barbier, 2009). They also mirror the broader patterns associated with the division of labor in a global economy that has been restructured by trade liberalization. In 2006, 82 percent of investment in renewable energy was in the Organization for Economic Cooperation and Development countries, with Europe and the United States taking three-quarters of the investment. China had 7 percent, India 4 percent, Latin America and the rest of the developing world each had 3 percent – 3 percent for Latin America and 3 percent for all of the rest of the countries (Renner et al., 2008). Since 80 percent of the world's workforce lies outside the advanced economies, most workers are untouched by the green economy.

Five countries control 72 percent of global wind capacity, with Germany, Denmark, and Spain as most important (International Energy Agency, 2008). Japan and Germany account for 87 percent of grid, connected PV solar installations. One out of three of all solar panels and all wind turbines are made in Germany (ibid.).

At an international scale, the direction and content of responses to climate change have been affected by trade liberalization and the way in which national economies have responded to its challenges and opportunities. The emergence of national champions in green energy production, such as Vestas, Siemens, and Gamesa reflects long-term national investments in the research and development capacity and market development that are translating into now expanded market demand in advanced economies. These now transnational energy firms wield significant bargaining power when making decisions to locate in new markets, such as the U.S. and in out-sourcing to international supply networks (Christopherson and Clark, 2007). According to one report on the energy industries:

> Growth through acquisition is enabling the 'big' players to get even bigger while becoming more vertically integrated and thus able to raise entry barriers to keep out new entrants while limiting the growth of small companies. Even as recently as the late 1990s, it was possible for a company to grow through the ability to serve domestic demand, as demonstrated by India-based Suzlon. That window of opportunity, however, seems to be closing as large global players further extend their global reach.
>
> (Glasmeier *et al.*, 2007: 14)

As the U.S. and U.S. firms attempt to play "catch–up" with Europe in grasping the economic opportunities of the new green technologies and regulatory environments, the specificities of the U.S. market governance regime and economic development policy provide a context within which initiatives draw political support and public investment.

The context for green sustainable economy in the U.S.

In the United States, the green economy agenda is being built around four key features.

These features are consonant with the U.S. economy's orientation toward short-term gain, high-risk, high-return ventures, emphasis on market creation, financial products (rather than on manufacture) and strong inter-jurisdictional competition. Central to the U.S. approach is the development of new markets for alternative fuels, which can spur investment in land, equipment, and facilities related to wind, solar and hydro power. Market creation in the form of tradable quotas or "cap and trade" programs is at the core of the U.S. approach to climate change. This approach has been adopted despite European experience indicating that market creation approaches replicate the lack of transparency and complexity that has made utility privatization so problematic, while producing minimal improvements in eliminating pollution (Adam, 2008; Lohmann, 2006; Milner, 2008). Second, the conception of adaptation to a new energy regime emphasizes replacement of high carbon products with low carbon products, such as electric cars, light bulbs, paper products, furniture, and appliances. This is consonant with the perception of the green economy as a market stimulus. Policies that encourage reuse and recycling are accepted at the margins because they offer some conventional economic growth potential. Policies that might remove products from the market or lower demand for them are actively discouraged as antagonistic to economic growth.

The third feature of the U.S. green economy is the assumption that it is built on individual choices, rather than, for example, regulatory measures. The taken-for-granted conception of what should take place is a change in the behavior of individuals to replace old light bulbs with new ones and old autos with new ones. Community choices to build municipal energy systems or alter incentives across households are depicted as eccentric and "socialistic". A strong private property rights regime limits social responses to environmental damage. Pollution is an externalized cost, and there is little incentive for individual firms to reduce it. As a consequence, fossil fuel industries and highly polluting industries remain very profitable.

The fourth characteristic of U.S. governance affecting which policy initiatives attract support and how they are implemented is the policy-making environment, and particularly the extent to which choices regarding public investment are shaped by inter-jurisdictional competition. The economic development policy environment is important to how the green economy will take shape because it is through policy decisions that public investments will be made in firms, industries, and energy-saving initiatives. In the U.S., economic development policy has been built historically around inter-jurisdictional competition and carried out through firm-specific subsidies as opposed to approaches that emphasize building industries (through workforce development, for example). Economic development investments have declined at the local scale and become more significant at the state level as the scale of financing required to attract transnational firms has increased. These public investments focus almost exclusively on large, visible, international players for both political and economic reasons. As one economic development official aptly noted: "There is as much work in negotiating with a firm employing 20 people as one employing 400 people so we only work with the larger firms" (Personal interview, February 15, 2009).

Although it reflects these enduring features of the U.S. market regime, the direction and content of U.S. green economy agenda has also been profoundly affected by trade policy and deregulation since the 1980s. Trade liberalization and deregulation encouraged the "financialization" of the U.S. economy and hampered investment in the kinds of long-term research projects that produced global leaders in new green technologies in Germany and the Netherlands.

Deregulation also exacerbated propensities to externalize environmental costs in key transport industries. Deregulation of trucking, for example, greatly expanded the use of truck transport, which is more energy-dependent than other forms of freight transport, and subcontracting to owner-drivers. The vertical disintegration of the industry and intensified labor cost competition makes it very difficult to incorporate the social and environmental costs of truck transport in the total cost of freight transport (Christopherson and Belzer, 2009). Deregulation also encouraged speculation and market "gaming" in deregulated energy markets, particularly in electricity markets, raising the rates that consumers pay and mitigating against long-term investments that would provide for a stable market that could incorporate renewable energy at a reasonable cost (McCullough, 2009). It has, through privatization initiatives, encouraged market concentration and internationalization of ownership of energy distribution companies.

Within the policy sphere itself, the key decisions about where investments are to occur and what initiatives will be funded will be made at the sub-national state scale rather than by local officials. While some funds for local initiatives and energy-efficiency initiatives will come from the federal government, the implementation programs will be designed and priorities set by sub-national states. Although there are some exceptions, sub-national states generally favor large-scale expenditures, such as subsidies to transnational advanced manufacturing firms. They have little experience with or inclination to develop the labor-intensive programs and projects that increase energy efficiency in the local built environment.

Arrayed against the political and economic dynamics that favor large-scale investments and inter-jurisdictional competition are local, state, and regional sustainability organizations in the U.S., which have historical connections to consumer protection movements. These efforts, organized by thousands of not-for-profit organizations, have complex and fragmented agendas, including everything from protecting endangered species to addressing the regulatory barriers impeding the local installation of wind and solar power. Non-profit environmental and sustainability organizations have organized historically around single issues (consistent with consumer style political action in the U.S.) and their ability to address the broader structural and more abstract questions raised by green economic development policy is still open to question. Because of these political and economic dynamics, both long term and short term, the U.S. green economy is likely to assume a particular form, one which will affect both the number of jobs that will be created and where they will be located.

The emerging shape of the U.S. green economy

Although it is difficult to make definitive predictions about how policy decisions will affect the direction and content of the green economy in the U.S., there are some broad indicators of how and where investments in green economic activities will occur. While lobbyists and sector-based green activists use methods such as input/output analysis to project a potential number of jobs by industry (construction, electronic product manufacturing, etc.) the actual location of job-generating economic activity will depend on:

i) the scale of public and private investment to energy efficiency or renewable energy (energy efficiency being ubiquitous and local, and renewable energy in specific locations);

ii) what form investment takes (tax incentives or grants versus direct expenditures);

iii) at what scale it is generated (local, state, or national), and

iv) whether it is long term or short term.

The greater job-generating potential of energy-efficiency programs at the local level

is widely recognized and there are numerous efforts by non-profit organizations which lay out guidelines about how retrofitting might occur (Center on Wisconsin Strategies, 2008). The actual programs are, however, highly dependent on federal funding, which is inherently short term. For example, the U.S. federal government has allocated $3.2 billion to the 50 states through the U.S. Department of Energy in the form of flexible block grants to be used in a wide variety of projects, including transportation and new green building construction as well as building retrofits. In addition, The American Recovery and Reinvestment Act of 2009 (ARRA) has made available $45 million in funding in the form of a set-aside for green infrastructure, and water and energy efficiency projects. How this money is expended will determine how many jobs are created and for whom. Because of the range of possible projects included in the federal allocation, including transportation, relatively little will likely be spent on building retrofitting in cities. Much more likely to benefit are projects employing large construction companies in efforts to build new "green" schools and municipal buildings. States are vying with each other to produce model signature projects (in the guise of demonstrating "best practice") that can attract media attention and avoid political opposition. Regulatory change and small-scale programs, which can be easily generalized across towns and cities, are likely to receive less attention because, although they would create more jobs, they are less visible to the media.

At the state level, there is very little investment on the energy-efficiency side of green economic development. Instead, state legislators and public officials are investing massively to compete for firms manufacturing equipment for renewable energy facilities. These jobs are in transnational firms in highly concentrated industries. In wind energy, the top ten manufacturers supply over 95 percent of global capacity. The solar industry is moving toward highly integrated distributors who have already developed markets. These include BP and Shell Solar.

For state economic development policy-makers, the most prized green economy jobs are in manufacturing plants such as that built by Gamesa in Pennsylvania or Vestas in Colorado. These plants, many of them branch plants, will employ, however, only a fraction of the workforce. A study by Good Jobs First (Mattera, 2009) analyzing the subsidies and job creation projections for 28 green advanced manufacturing plants projected to be built in 14 U.S. states, indicates that the total investment across states is just under $5 billion. Total jobs projected for all these 28 plants is about 11,000 (ibid.: 13). Thus, state investments in a very small number of advanced manufacturing jobs are significantly greater than all federal investment in energy-efficiency programs that could create many more jobs. These selective investments in advanced manufacturing firms are consistent with contemporary U.S. economic development policy but raise questions about how overall investment allocations will translate into the millions of jobs that are projected as possible by green economy advocates.

Much of the enthusiasm for the advanced manufacturing green jobs is based on the idea that they will replace old manufacturing jobs that have been lost to trade liberalization. The locational choices of large transnational manufacturing firms producing for equipment for the emerging green economy suggests, however, that while traditional manufacturing states may be attracting investment, these firms are not locating in cities or in old industrial centers where job losses have been significant. Instead, they are locating in the same types of ex-urban locations that are attractive to all advanced manufacturing firms. This tendency is demonstrated by an examination of the recent location choices of transnational wind turbine plants in U.S. states. The primary Gamesa plant in Pennsylvania, for example, is located in Bucks County, with a median family income of

$75,000 as compared with a little over $50,000 in Pennsylvania as a whole. The county is 91 percent white. Lee County, Iowa, where Siemans has located its plant, has a median household income of $43,000, slightly lower than that for Iowa as a whole ($47,000) and is 9 percent white. One percent of its citizens are foreign born. Weld County Colorado, the location for Vestas, has an average household income of $53,000, higher than the U.S. average of $51,000 but lower than that estimated for Colorado as a whole ($59,000). The county is 97 percent of European extraction or Latino.

In general, green economy manufacturers choose green field sites and locations where they can pay relatively low wages while still providing for high-quality homes and amenities for their management. The concentrated structure and location patterns of these green industries replicates that in other advanced manufacturing industries. In knowledge-based economies, these activities are ex-urban and free-standing rather than part of an urban agglomeration economy. These, typically transnational, firms rely heavily on internationally out-sourced inputs, limiting the opportunity for the development of supply chains. Because of their location pattern, green advanced manufacturing plants are likely to contribute to regional inequality rather than reduce it.

In addition, while we know that the green economy offers many job opportunities at the local level and in small firms that is not where public and private investment is likely to occur. Research by Pinderhughes (2008) in the San Francisco Bay area, for example, finds that firms offering "green jobs" are overwhelmingly small privately owned firms. Their average employment is 28 and many of the firms have four to five employees. Without effective supportive from economic development policy, this small-scale, local approach to job creation in the green economy is likely to occur only in high-income places where citizens can afford to support it as a dimension of local amenities.

The green future is more about politics than technology

Those analysts close to the ground and attempting to construct actual change in the relationship between humans and the built as well as natural environment recognize that change is more about politics than about new technologies (Kelley, 2008). The kind of politics that green environmental experts recognize, however, is a micro-politics of land use and environmental regulation. What has been missing is a politics that addresses who will benefit and who will lose from policy decisions that determine how the green economy takes shape, a politics that addresses the socio-economic dimensions of going green or "sustainable".

In the United States, discussions about various courses of action are difficult because of a consensus-driven political culture. So, for example, it is considered impolite or worse to open the question of winners and losers as a consequence of taking one course of environmental action rather than another. Since losers are likely to be concentrated among the already disenfranchised, this makes for a strange environmental politics, one that speaks of apocalypse but emphasizes the need for consensus across classes of people who will experience change in very different ways. The voices of the potentially disenfranchised (poor urbanites pushed to the periphery by green cosmopolites, coal workers, rural residents) are hushed, and made to seem unimportant in the face of impending catastrophe. The absence of an open and encompassing political debate over what green environmental policy means for equity, however, comes with a cost. It enables the illusion that there is consensus over what to do and how to go forward. And it fosters the kinds of solutions that will only modestly affect the status quo, either environmentally or socio-economically.

References

Adam, D. (2008) "Britain's worst polluters set for windfall of millions", *Guardian*, September 12.

Adger, W., Paavola, J., Mace, M. and Huq, S. (eds) (2006) *Fairness in Adaptation to Climate Change*, Cambridge MA: MIT Press.

Apollo Alliance (2008) *Green-collar Jobs in America's Cities: Building Pathways out of Poverty and Careers in the Clean Energy Economy*. Retrieved May 2, 2008: http://www.apolloalliance.org/downloads/greencollarjobs.pdf.

Apollo Alliance (2009) *The Apollo Program: Clean Energy, Good Jobs*. Retrieved April 3, 2009: http://apolloalliance.org/wp-content/uploads/2009/03/ fullreportfinal.pdf.

Austin Energy http://www.austinenergy.com/About%20Us/Environmental%20Initiatives/index.htm.

Barbier, E. (2009) *A Global Green New Deal*. Report prepared for the Economics and Trade Branch, Division of Technology, Industry and Economics, United Nations Environment Programme. Available at http://www.unep.org/greeneconomy/docs/GGND_Executive_Summary.pdf.

Bezdek, R. (2007a) *Economic and Jobs Impacts of the Renewable Energy and Energy Efficiency Industries: U.S. and Ohio*, presented at American Solar Energy Society.

Bezdek, R. (2007b) *Renewable Energy and Energy Efficiency: Economic Drivers for the 21st Century*, American Solar Energy Society.

Center on Wisconsin Strategy (2007) *Milwaukee Retrofit: Capturing Home Energy Savings in Milwaukee*. Retrieved May 2, 2008: http://www.cows.org/pdf/bp-milwaukeeretrofit_050807.pdf.

Christopherson, S. and M. Belzer (2009) "The next move: metro-regions and the transformation of the freight transport and distribution system", in Nancy Pindus, Howard Wial and Harold Wolman (eds) *Urban and Regional Policy and Its Effects*, Washington, D.C.: The Brookings Institution.

Christopherson, S. and J. Clark (2007) *Re-making the Region: Power, Labor, and Firm Strategies*, London: Routledge.

Gibbs, D. (2002) *Local Economic Development and the Environment*, London: Routledge.

Glasmeier, A., R. Feingold, A. Guers, G. Hay, T. Lawler, A. Meyer, R. Sangpenchan, M. Stern, W. Stroh, P. Tam, R. Torres, R. Truly and A. Welch (2007) *Energizing Appalachia: Global Challenges and the Prospect of a Renewable Future*, Washington, D.C.: Appalachian Regional Commission.

Gordon, K. and J. Hays (2008) *Green-collar Jobs in America's Cities: Building Pathways out of Poverty and Careers in the Clean Energy Economy*, Apollo Alliance and Green for All.

International Energy Agency. World Energy OutLook. Paris: IEA/OECD.

Kelley, I. (2008) *Energy in America, A Tour of our Fossil Fuel Culture and Beyond*, Burlington: University of Vermont Press.

Larsen, B. and A. Shah (2002) *World Fossil Fuel Subsidies and Carbon Emissions*, Working Paper 1002, Washington, D.C.: The World Bank.

Lohmann, L. (2006) *Carbon-trading: A Critical Conversation on Climate Change, Privatisation and Power*, Development Dialogue, No. 48 – available at: http://www.thecornerhouse.org.uk/pdf/document/carbonDDlow.pdf.

Mason, C. (1987) "Venture capital in the United Kingdom – a geographical perspective", *National Westminster Bank Quarterly Review*. 47–59.

Mattera, P. (2009) *Highroad or Low Road? Job Quality in the New Green Economy. Washington: Good Jobs First*. Available at: www.goodjobs-first.org.

McCullough, R. (2009) *The New York Independent System Operator's Market – Clearing Price Auction Is Too Expensive for New York*, Portland, Oregon: McCullough Research.

Milner, M. (2008) 'Carbon prices rise amid tighter rules', *Guardian*, March 4.

Personal Interview, February 15, 2009.

Pinderhughes, R. (2007) *Green Collar Jobs: An Analysis of the Capacity of Green Businesses to Provide High Quality Jobs for Men and Women with Barriers to Employment*, Berkeley, CA: City of Berkeley Office of Energy and Sustainable Development.

Pollin, R. and J. Wicks-Lim (2008) *Job Opportunities for the Green Economy: A State by State Picture of Occupations That Gain From Green Investment*, Amherst: Political Economy Research Institute, University of Massachusetts, Amherst.

Pollin, R., H. Garrett-Peltier, J. Heintz and H. Sharber (2008) *Green Recovery, A Program to Create Good Jobs and Start Building a Low Carbon Economy*, Washington, D.C.: Center for American Progress.

Renner, M., S. Sweeney and J. Kubit (2008) *Green Jobs: Towards Decent Work in a Sustainable, Low Carbon World*, New York: United Nations Environment.Programme. Available at: www.unep.org/civil_society/Publications/index.asp.

www.unep.org/labour_environment/features/greenjobs.asp.

Sayer, S. (2008) *Geography and Global Warming: Can Capitalism be Greened?*, unpublished manuscript, Department of Sociology, Lancaster University, UK.

Swyngedouw, E. (2006) *"Impossible Sustainability and the Post-Political Condition"*, unpublished MS. Available from author at: Department of Geography, School of Environment and Development, Manchester University, Oxford Road, Manchester M13 9PL, UK.

United Nations General Assembly (1987) *Report of the World Commission on Environment and Development: Our Common Future*. Transmitted to the General Assembly as an Annex to document A/42/427, Development and International Co-operation: Environment.

Further reading

Barbier, E. (2009) *A Global Green New Deal*, Report prepared for the Economics and Trade Branch, Division of Technology, Industry and Economics, United Nations Environment Programme Available at http://www.unep.org/greeneconomy/docs/GGND_Executive_Summary.pdf.

Christopherson, S. and M. Belzer (2009) "The next move: metro-regions and the transformation of the freight transport and distribution system," in Nancy Pindus, Howard Wial and Harold Wolman (eds) *Urban and Regional Policy and Its Effects*, Washington, D.C.: The Brookings Institution.

Gibbs. D. (2002) *Local Economic Development and the Environment*, London: Routledge.

Renner, M., S. Sweeney and J. Kubit (2008) *Green Jobs: Towards Decent Work in a Sustainable, Low Carbon World*, New York: United Nations Environment Programme. Available at: www.unep.org/civil_society/Publications/index.asp www.unep.org/labour_environment/features/greenjobs.asp.

See also: www.greenchoices.cornell.edu.

32

SMEs, entrepreneurialism and local/regional development

Costis Hadjimichalis

Introduction

In the 1970s and early 1980s, during the Fordist crisis, researchers identified that some regions in developed capitalist economies grew faster, compared to established industrial cores. Regions such as Third Italy, the M4 axis in the UK, Southern Paris and Rhône-Alpes in France, Silicon Valley and Boston in USA, Murcia and Valencia in Spain and Baden-Württenburg in Germany were among those identified as successfully overcoming the crisis, with Third Italy attracting most attention (Sabel, 1989; Benko and Lipietz, 1992). A common characteristic of these new dynamic spaces was the predominance of industrial micro, small and medium enterprises (SMEs) in industrial districts (IDs) and a locally diffused entrepreneurial spirit, contradicting both dominant development theories and policies of the time based on large infrastructure projects and large industrial investment with strong guidance/assistance from the state. Soon these regions, their small firms and local social structure became symbols of success of small-scale flexible capitalism, "from below", with its highly individualistic, entrepreneurial and competitive character. The new paradigm became *l'enfant gâté* for neo-liberals and for some institutionalists and it turned to widespread local development policies in the 1990s. It became also the cornerstone of the "New Regionalism" literature which has dominated Anglophone economic geography and planning studies in the last 25 years. New Regionalism includes a whole series of analytical and policy-oriented concepts inspired from SMEs such as the highly influential "second industrial divide", "networked, learning and innovative firms and regions", "the embedded firm" and "endogenous local/regional development", to mention but a few (Piore and Sabel, 1984; Scott, 1988; Morgan, 1977; Cooke, 1988).

Individual states and supranational entities such as the EU, IMF and the World Bank introduced programmes assisting flexible, innovative and networked SMEs and through these promoting local/regional development. There is an open discussion, however, whether regional policies based on SMEs followed relevant concepts and theories, or vice versa (Hudson, 1999). In the EU, several policies and programs along those lines have been introduced, among which LEADER for rural areas and LEDA for urban centers. After the Lisbon Pact, in which development in the EU has being associated with competitiveness, innovation and entrepreneurship, in 2008 a "Small Business Act" for Europe was launched by the European Commission (EC), in which we read:

> Our capacity to build on the growth and innovation potential of small and medium-sized enterprises will therefore be decisive for the future prosperity of the EU. In a globally changing landscape characterized by continuous structural changes and enhanced competitive pressures, the role of SMEs in our society has become even more important as providers of employment opportunities and key players for the wellbeing of local and regional communities.
>
> (Small Business Act for Europe, 2008: 2)

The above quote was written before the current, major economic crisis of neo-liberalism. In the middle of disarray for corporate giants this communication by the EC was a prelude to the urgent assistance given today to SMEs by all governments and financial institutions acknowledging their basic function: to save employment and to safeguard local and regional well-being. Although still within the frame of the Lisbon Pact, this is a pragmatic and low-profile approach which keeps a distance from the grandiose claims made two decades earlier about SMEs by proponents of New Regionalism.

In this chapter I discuss these and other questions by focusing first on how SMEs have been associated with local/regional development to become part of a major paradigm. Second, I will shift the emphasis from paradigmatic to what we may call "ordinary" SMEs, arguing for the need to take them on board for a more nuanced and inclusive approach to local/regional development. And third, I will try an alternative categorization of SMEs as a continuum ranging from "ordinary" in all sectors to the celebrated, advanced ones in IDs.

The "discovery" of small industrial firms as engines for regional growth: the rise and crisis of a paradigm

Since the 1950s and until the crisis of Fordism, dominant models of regional development were based on industrialization via capital incentives or large state projects in growth poles, provision of public infrastructures and employment creation via inward investments from other regions. It was the period of what we can call "welfare regionalism" largely based on social democratic political principles, predominant in Europe and beyond at that time (Pike *et al.*, 2006). The state in the capitalist West with its top-down policies took an active role for development in "lagging" regions, as part of welfare policies in Europe, and at a different scale, in North America fostered also by the Cold War competition between West and East. The economic crisis of the 1970s was followed by a neo-liberal turn. Regional, top-down, welfare planning was being hit from all sides. From the left it was seen as maintaining uneven regional development and from the neo-liberal right as a wasteful luxury, pouring public money down the plughole without efficient results. It was in the early 1980s when the policy option "fostering dynamic regional growth" came to replace the old "reducing regional inequality". From integrated, comprehensive and nationally organized regional welfare planning, a transformation took place towards intensely competitive and geographically fragmented processes, what we may call "entrepreneurial regionalism". The search for alternatives in successful regions on both sides of the Atlantic led to the "great discovery" of small dynamic, competitive and highly entrepreneurial industrial firms.

As with other geographical discoveries, small firms and their embeddedness were always there, unknown maybe to those who "discover" them, but well known to local communities and to local scientists. A century earlier, the anarchist geographer Peter Kropotkin in his *Fields, Factories and Workshops* with the interesting subtitle: *Industry Combined with Agriculture and Brain Work with Manual Work* (1898/1968), opened the debate on small firms, indirectly criticizing Marx and the German social-democrats for the "iron law" of capital centralization. In this book, Kropotkin focuses on craft industries, their social division of labour and their relation with agriculture in different parts of Europe, including Central Italy, Lyon, Bavaria, the Jura and Sheffield, as well as India and Brazil. He noticed the division of work among small firms in small towns and villages and he pointed out that sectors like cotton mills "does not suffer at all from the division of production of one given sort of goods at its different stages between several separate factories" (1898/1968: 179) and for the German small firms a crucial factor for their success has been "the degree of association amongst the producers" (1898/1968: 249).

The work of Kropotkin and that of Alfred Marshal on small industry's agglomeration characteristics as well as the work of David Birch (1979, 1980) on how important small firms were in the job generation process – not to speak for research published in languages other than English – was of secondary interest, compared to Piore and Sabel's book *The Second Industrial Divide* (1984) which marked the recent "discovery" of small firms with a powerful critique of the "best is big" paradigm. Their book draws strongly on Italian small firms in IDs to oppose the model of flexible specialization to the Fordist model, by stressing the role of historical alternative to mass production. Despite the many inadequacies of this book, it became a major vehicle for the promotion and acceptance by the wider economic and planning community of the role of SMEs in local/regional development.

Along similar lines but using also variants of the French regulation theory, Scott and Storper paid particular attention to the "geography of flexible accumulation" via small high-tech firms in Silicon Valley, Orange County and Los Angeles, as well as in Third Italy and other "new industrial spaces" (Scott, 1988; Scott and Storper, 1988; Storper, 1997). Their approach to the relations between economy and territory was based on a novel emphasis on transaction costs, vertical disintegration and agglomeration.

In Italy itself and during the late 1970s, there was a vibrant debate on the role of SMEs from three different standpoints. First, there was the famous book by Bagnasco, *Tre Italie* (1977, never translated into English), making Third Italy famous, although Muscara, a geographer, and Paci, a sociologist, were first in identifying the patterns described by Bagnasco. Other, similar research on the social, cultural, economic and political foundations of small firms (not only industrial) followed (Paci, 1972; Mingione, 1988; Ardigò and Donati, 1976), but remaining unknown outside Italy. Second, there was the reintroduction of Marshall's concept of local external economies of scale by the Emilian school (Becattini, 1990; dei Ottati, 1994) and from a more critical perspective by Garofoli (1983). These scholars used such concepts to explain the efficiency of small firms in some "neo-Marshallian" IDs focusing on the advantages of territorial concentration and sectoral specialization. And third there was the "*fabrica difussa*" approach (Frey, 1974; Magnaghi and Perelli, 1978), which was highly critical of the use of small firms as subcontractors ("putting-out" and "splitting-in") and as a means to undermine working conditions, unionization and radical local political networks.

By the mid-1980s, the new paradigm of flex-spec small industrial firms as major engines of local/regional development was successfully established and has opened important windows for new research and policies. We can identify several positive aspects of it. First, it has shifted the focus to firms and production processes, not previously accepted as viable and profitable options for development. By the same token new regions and development paths became known, away from the old repertoire of industrial heartlands of North-Western capitalism. Second, it has shown cases of "spontaneous" growth, without direct welfare assistance from the central state, where small firms with strong entrepreneurial spirit initiated a "bottom-up" growth. Third, it has successfully combined analyses on market opportunities, on mobilization of existing resources (particularly knowledge and learning) and on new forms of production organization, i.e. flexibility and networking. And fourth, it has highlighted the role of competition and cooperation at the local level with the assistance of strong local cultural traditions, institutions and associations.

Soon, however, the new paradigm became a new orthodoxy, collapsing "very diverse processes and areas into one category and then to treat this as a symbol of the new era of accumulation", as Amin and Robins (1990) argue. In the euphoria that followed the "discovery" of dynamic SMEs, several misreadings, omissions and problems occurred. First, there was a simplistic binary opposition between mass production and flex-spec (Sayer, 1989), while Fordism was never hegemonic in the regions in which growth was directed by flexible small industrial production ensembles. Second, in the relevant literature, a very selective appropriation of the complexity and richness of SMEs has taken place, in which only certain general economic, organizational and institutional issues have been taken on board, while others such as power and inequalities among small firms and within industrial districts, the limitations of networking and learning, what cooperation, reciprocity and "social capital" really means for firms and labour, conditions of work, the informal economy, gender and ethnicity – to mention but a few – remain in the dark (Hadjimichalis, 2006b; Mingione, 1998; Smith, 1999). Third, there is a lack of

attention to the role of the state and to various protectionist and assistance measures it has introduced. From devaluation of national currency and labour legislation to particular incentives for SMEs and international agreements (such as the Multi-Fibre agreement), there was never such a thing as "without assistance from the central state" (Dunford, 2006; Hadjimichalis, 2006a). Fourth, by looking only at success in the context of neo-liberalism, there was interest in a few paradigmatic industrial sectors and on few advanced service providers only in a limited number of European and North American regions. Fifth, and as result of the above, there has been a remarkable neglect of other sectors such as tourism, trade and agriculture, to areas beyond North America and Europe and to those millions of "ordinary" small firms that form the majority of SMEs everywhere, being the real supporters of local employment and well-being (Navdi and Schmitz, 1994).

While such omissions would be expected from a neo-liberal perspective, it is rather puzzling for me that some radical theorists and researchers succumb to the charms of grand narratives, even when they strongly argue for the need to pay attention to differences, to the ordinary, to both global North and global South and to local processes. In the 1980s and 1990s, critical voices concerning the above issues from Anglophone scholars and from Southern Europe and Latin America remained largely peripheral. After 2000, however, on both sides of the Atlantic a major crisis-driven restructuring has taken place. Many SMEs in several IDs in California, Third Italy, Valencia and Murcia, Baden-Württenburg, Northern Portugal and Northern Greece, due to major changes at the global and national scales, are engaged in three interrelated restructuring processes:

i) Mergers and acquisitions and formation of large, vertically integrated firms and groups of firms, like Benetton,

Gucci, Prada, Zara and corporate "district business groups", which challenge from within the celebrated superiority of small-scale production (Bianchi and Bellini, 1991; Dunford, 2006; Harrison, 1994).

ii) De-localization of part of production or of all firms to low labour cost regions and countries. From Southern Europe they moved to Slovenia, the Balkans, Tunisia, Morocco, India and Vietnam. From Central Europe they went to Eastern Europe, Latin America and Asia and from California to Mexico, China and India (Hadjimichalis, 2006b; Labrianidis and Kalogeressis, 2007; Rabelloti et al., 2009).

iii) Extensive replacement of local labour by medium and highly skilled immigrants, to compensate increasing labour cost and/or the lack of skilled native labour. There are thousands of Chinese, Romanian, Filipinos and Moroccans in Italian IDs. Latinos and Asians work in California's SMEs and Moroccans, Pakistanis, Kurds, Albanians and those from Africa are present in all Southern European countries (Bialasiewicz, 2006; Ybarra et al., 2004; Mingione and Pugliese, 2002; Verducci, 2003).

These developments directly challenge grandiose claims about flex-spec small firms, in IDs as models for the future and about the social and cultural continuity of the paradigm based on trust, reciprocity and social capital. The power of Fordism has not disappeared, it has shifted to other regions; local networks and local embeddedness was not enough to control de-localization, and immigrants replacing native employees challenged the locally specific continuation of craft tradition. However, this is not a crisis of SMEs per se as possible motors for local/regional development, but a crisis of this particular paradigm of SMEs promoted by entrepreneurial regionalism.

From paradigmatic to ordinary SMEs and everyday entrepreneurialism

Although in the literature of small firms and local/regional development there are references only to the paradigmatic SMEs discussed above, the world of regions includes millions of other SMEs, less glossy and famous but nevertheless important for the local well-being. Small firms are in fact the predominant form of entrepreneurship worldwide. On average, 93 per cent of all enterprises in the EU have fewer than ten employees, in USA 50 per cent and in OECD countries 95 per cent. As large firms downsize and outsource several functions previously done inside, small firms' role in the economy is increasing. SMEs are defined as independent firms with fewer than 250 employees, as in EU and other countries, while in USA and Mexico they include firms with fewer than 500 employees (see Table 32.1). Small firms are generally those below 50 employees and in the EU must have an annual turnover of 40 million euro or less and/or a balance-sheet valuation not exceeding 27 million euro (OECD, 2006). Table 32.1 presents some data for selected countries, used later in the chapter as examples, in which micro and small enterprises form the majority of firms in all sectors. Employment in SMEs plays a crucial role as percentage of total, with Romania, Mexico and USA being less dependent on small firms. Italy and Greece have the largest figure of SMEs per 1000 people, while USA has the relative lowest figure.

From the literature of New Regionalism we learn mainly about innovative industrial firms and advanced service providers. The majority of small firms, however, belong to all kinds of services, trade and tourism, which account for two-thirds of economic activity and employment in OECD countries. SMEs also account in communications, constructions and business services. Despite this, the neglect of agricultural, tourist, services and

Table 32.1 Micro, small and medium-sized enterprises: a collection of published data for selected countries

	Income group	Year data	Definition of SME: number of employees			% SMEs in all sectors of the economy			SMEs per 1000 People	Employment in SMEs as % of total
			Micro	Small	Medium	Micro	Small	Medium		
Brazil	Lower middle	2001	0–9	10–49	50–249	92.9	6.2	0.9	27.1	56.5
Germany	High	2003	0–9	10–49	50–249	88.3	10.2	1.5	36.4	70.4
Greece	High	2003	0–9	10–49	50–249	97.5	2.1	0.3	72.2	74.0
Italy	High	2003	0–9	10–49	50–249	95.6	4.0	0.4	77.8	73
Romania	Lower middle	2001	0–9	10–49	50–249	91.5	1.5	18.0	18.0	40.2
UK	High	2003	0–9	10–49	50–249	89.7	9.0	1.4	37.6	56.4
USA	High	2002	0–9	10–99	100–499	79.3	19.9	0.8	19.6	50.2
Mexico	Middle	2002	0–30	31–100	101–500	96.0	3.1	0.9	29.3	48.5

Source: Data from International Finance Corporation (2005)

trade sectors continues up until today. This is because in these sectors economists and planners assume that SMEs are less dynamic than industry, entrepreneurship is weakly developed and it is perceived as a business with low entry barriers, low-tech and labour intensive (particularly feminized) and in some cases requires little capital. Above all, economists and some economic geographers do not take into account these sectors because of the high importance of the informal sector, a situation which was incomprehensible for many non-Southern scholars having experience from the development history of the Fordist factory, the mass worker and the welfare state. The "informal", as it has been used since the 1980s in Southern Europe (and in our research; see Vaiou and Hadjimichalis, 1997; Hadjimichalis and Vaiou, 1990, 2004), is not identical with the "household economy", "alternative market" or "non-market transactions". Nor is its use to be confused with developing world formulations about two separate economic sectors and with approaches in Development Studies which often see small firms as welfare or safety-net measures for poor people. What I am talking about, and what has been at the core of

Southern European debates, has to do with culturally embedded "ways of doing or performing" the economic, with processes and practices which permeate the ensemble of social relations and could contribute not only to the simple survival of local areas but to their dynamic entrance into global competition (Ardigò and Donati, 1976; Mingione, 1983).

Many of the micro and small firms in the informal sector are indeed backward, with a short-term planning horizon and a limited knowledge of the business environment. At the same time, however, there are thousands more that are performing the economic in innovative and novel ways as in the case of tourism in the Mediterranean, particularly in disadvantaged regions which usually have a strong representation of micro tourism firms (Melissourgos, 2008). Shaw and Williams (1994) argue that small tourist firms hold the key to strengthening and spreading the benefits from tourism locally and regionally because of the very nature of their family structure, of their dependence on local markets and hence the development of stronger backward and forward linkages, unlike larger ones who often operate like enclaves. SMEs in tourism have the ability to respond to dynamic changes in global markets (e.g. the current economic decline), where the markets are seasonal and notoriously fickle, and even to create jobs at a time when major operators are downsizing. They succeed through multiple employment: part-time agriculture, part-time industry, and part-time tourism.

For SMEs in the agricultural sector new opportunities have opened since the 1990s. In Europe, North America and Japan, the ecological/sustainable touristic trend across lagging regions, often mountainous, has the effect of revitalizing rural areas as cultural landscapes. This shift in meta-preferences has given a second chance to marginal areas, now as places for consumption and not for production (Calafati, 2006). A second and more important opportunity is organic farming. According to a report for Latin America by IFAD (2003), thousands of small family farmers in Mexico producing organic products like coffee in Chiapas and honey in Yucatan, cacao and bananas in Talamanca, Costa Rica, coffee in Guatemala, sugar cane in Argentina and fresh vegetables in El Salvador, were able to create new jobs and opened new competitive advantages beyond their local region. Since 1992, when the EU-Regulation 2092/91 about organic farming was implemented, many SMEs in rural regions started to produce organic products, with Italy being at the forefront in Europe, followed by France, Austria and Germany. Because consumers pay premium prices for organic products, small firms in this sector may obtain higher prices and thus create new growth potentials for lagging regions.

On the other hand, it is true that a high percentage of SMEs in many OECD countries are in the industrial sector and provide half of OECD industrial employment. Small firms are increasingly present in technology-intensive industries and in creative industries, particularly in large urban areas. They predominate in strategic sectors, such as business services, where human resources and

knowledge-based competitiveness play a major role. Not all of them, however, are innovative and networked as the ideal type depicted by New Regionalism, the so-called "high road". Side by side with the modern, flex-spec firm, where labour cost is combined with better wages, there are thousands of small traditional firms and sweatshops at the edge of survival along the so-called "low road", small dependent sub-suppliers and subcontractors and thousands of women homeworkers, operating in the informal sector. These firms attract no attention to OECD official policy recommendations which continue to focus on typical growth-oriented strategies, via competitiveness (see OECD, 2005, 2006, 2007).

The majority of dispersed and/or clusters of SMEs in developing countries operate under informal conditions such as in the shoe industry in the Sinos Valley, South Brazil and Guadalajara, Mexico and in India's textile industry in Tiruppur, Delhi and Mumbai (Navdi and Schmitz, 1998) and in the Bangalore technology district. Furthermore, many paradigmatic industrial SMEs in Third Italy's IDs operate also under informal conditions, either avoiding taxes and local payments under the local "tacit agreement", "give nothing, but ask for nothing" (in Veneto), or polluting the environment (the leather districts of Arzignano and Chiampo), or violating labour legislation and using economic migrants illegally (in Prato, Tuscany; Carpi, Emilia Romagna and Macerata; the Marche) (Bialasiewicz, 2006; Rabelloti et al., 2009).

To these small industrial firm variants we have to add labour variants such as paid and unpaid family labour, limited and unlimited time contracts, stable and precarious work, formal and informal labour, women's and children's labour, immigrant labour, etc. These forms of labour are present in the majority of IDs, and they constituted a coherent and indispensable ensemble of economic and social relations which made possible, until the post-2000 crisis, high profits for the few modern, paradigmatic small firms. And apart from micro and small firms in the same sector, there are also medium and large vertically integrated firms with brand names which compete with small ones. Many of those, particularly in fashion and design sectors, are using similar flex-spec and just-in-time production methods and outsource part of their production to dependent firms regionally and globally.

To illustrate the above, I will use two examples from my own work. The first concerns SMEs in the fur industrial district of Kastoria, Northern Greece, one of the few Greek IDs which demonstrate analogous social, cultural and economic characteristics with Italian IDs. Kastoria is a Byzantine town (2001: 36,000 people), known as the capital of fur production and trade in Greece, able to establish "Made in Kastoria" as an international brand name. In the entire prefecture there are more than 2500 micro, small and medium firms and only five with more than 80 employees, providing employment for about 18,000 people. From this remote place, 12 per cent of global fur trade and 90 per cent of global fur-coat production out of small pieces (a historical local specialization) is controlled. The key role is played by dynamic SMEs producing for exports (today mainly to the *nouveaux riches* of Russia) which are organized along the flex-spec, networked and learning paradigm, with strong social, cultural and institutional support from the local community and local government. There are, however, many other types of firms within the IDs, from "ordinary" homeworkers and sweatshops in the informal sector to advanced small independent design studios and medium vertically integrated firms. We cannot understand how Kastoria's local productive system operates, how it is so successful even in periods of crisis and how it promotes local/regional development, until we take on board all firm types and all forms of work. In Figure 32.1, three types of firms are shown (vertically integrated, dependent

subcontractors with homeworkers, horizontal advanced network which also use homeworkers) together with the nine basic stages of production for a mink fur-coat. Each type has positive and negative characteristics, with firm A controlling in-house the entire production apart from design; firm B controlling quality-packing and commercialization-distribution; and firm C controlling in-house as in A plus matching small pieces.

The second example is from an ordinary urban municipality, Ilion, part of the Athenian metropolitan area. Ilion is a working- to low- middle- class area, in Western Athens (2001: 82,000 people). The structure of local employment is divided between trade and services, industry and construction, with 56 per cent of employment provided within the boundaries of the municipality (see Figure 32.2). In a 2003 survey – after the 1999 major earthquake which hit Western Athens badly – 624 SMEs have been located within the urban tissue (in the ground floors of apartment buildings and in few separate premises), in sectors such as industry, producer services, local trade and construction (see Figure 32.2). Other SMEs belonging to non-local trade, personal services, food, restaurants and drinks, education and health (total 2100) are also depicted but not shown in this map (for further information see Hadjimichalis *et al.*, 2003). With three exceptions (one export fashion leather shoe firm and two high-tech producer service firms), all others could be classified as "ordinary firms": one to fifteen employees with a substantial presence of self-employment and immigrant labour, mainly family owned, using low–medium technology, not particularly innovative and the majority using some sort of informality. They are nevertheless embedded in local social and cultural relations, adequately networked among themselves and enjoying institutional support from a municipal agency, financed by the EU. No brand names, no export figures, nothing special,

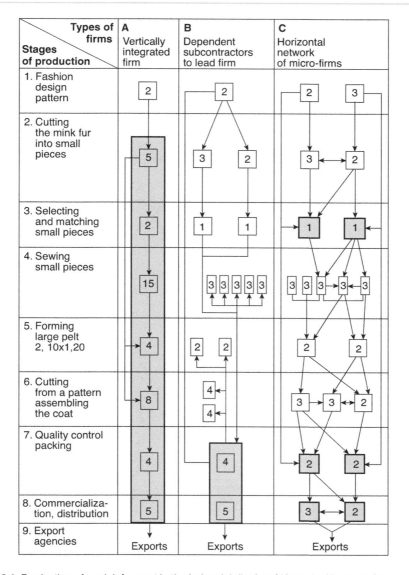

Figure 32.1 Production of a mink fur-coat in the industrial district of Kastoria, Northern Greece.

Source: Hadjimichalis and Vaiou 1997

Note: Numbers in squares show workers at each stage and/or at each micro firm.
       Grey areas show leading firms.

an ordinary socio–spatial structure similar to many others in urban areas like Ilion. The local economy and society, however, cannot do without them: they are diffused within the urban tissue keeping it alive, they have local backward and forward linkages, they provide local employment, they serve the needs of local people and local market within walking distance (particularly food and personal services), and, finally, they are rooted in the local tradition of petty trade and self-employment.

Figure 32.2 "Ordinary" SMEs in Ilion, Western Athens, 2003.
Source: Hadjimichalis *et al.* (2003)

Towards an alternative categorization: some concluding comments

The focus on SMEs as dynamic agents for local/regional development was (and remains) a welcome contribution and this applies also to the various concepts and formulations associated with them. But in practice, it often seems to be trapped in grandiose claims, ill-founded theorizations and an overemphasis on a few paradigmatic sectors and regions, ignoring the vast majority of ordinary SMEs which play a much more important role in the development of ordinary places, often "lagging" behind successful ones. Looking at ordinary SMEs in ordinary places we open a window to conceive development more broadly than just economic growth to incorporate sustainability, everyday life and well-being at the local level (see Pike *et al.*, 2007).

From a local/regional development perspective, small producers and service providers fall into many categories and many sectors and several types of firms and forms of labour could be distinguished, as the previous analysis has shown. The boundaries are unclear and I prefer to see them as a continuum between three main categories:

i) Geographically and sectorally dispersed small producers and service providers. Most of rural and urban small industry, service provision, agricultural production and tourism fall into this category. From the village carpenter and small family hotel to urban small firms such as grocery shops, cafés, design studios, web designers and small manufacturing diffused in the urban tissue – to mention but a few examples – their growth depends on demand mainly from local and national markets. The scope for division of labour and hence for economies of scale is small. The impact, however, to local/regional economy could be notable, if (a) there is an important amount of small firms and (b) their forward and backward linkages are highly localized/regionalized.

ii) Geographical clusters of small firms belonging to different or to similar sectors. In contrast to the previous case, there is wide scope for division of labour between firms and hence for specialization and innovation, essential for competing beyond local markets. There is, however, an unknown threshold, after which that clustering opens up efficiency gains beyond simply agglomeration economies. Also this clustering is not necessarily incompatible with the presence of large firms. In fact, large producers and service

providers by their very operation give birth to many small ones, e.g. large hotels and surrounding small restaurants, cafés and souvenir shops, or large manufacturers subcontracting part of their production to smaller producers, etc. In this type, we have both vertical and horizontal relations among firms and contribution to development is also a function of their forward/backward linkages. These clusters could be unplanned, derived from agglomeration economies, or planned as an intervention from local or central state for more efficient operation.

iii) Geographical clusters of small firms in the same sector of the type of Italian industrial district. The main characteristics in this case are: unplanned clustering within historical towns and/or planned relocation in designated district zones, historical sectoral specialization, predominance of small and medium-sized firms, close inter-firm collaboration and networking with mainly horizontal relations, a common socio-cultural identity which facilitates trust, a particular local social division of labour which reproduces skills and entrepreneurship, active local/regional institutions providing wide-ranging assistance and supportive local government and nation state. In this case there is a capture of agglomeration economies by all firms in the district, resulting in a collective efficiency and local/regional development. In many IDs large firms and corporate business networks could operate alongside small firms.

The above categorization is highly context and path dependent: in an economically and technologically advanced region, the ability to contribute to regional growth by a dispersed or networked small firm in an ID should be analysed with a different analytical framework from, say, a peripheral region in the same country, or in a small village in Asia or Latin America. We should also remember that SMEs belong to particular sectors and are regulated by local, national and international institutions and this is true for the few paradigmatic SMEs in IDs. And we should not forget that these are historical forms of capitalist organization competing under conditions not of their choice in the uneven global landscape. Like all other forms of capitalist production, they survive as long as two conditions are secured: (1) their social and spatial division of labour remains globally competitive *vis-à-vis* other similar SMEs, larger firms, sectors and regions, and (2) their internal system of economic and social reproduction remains unchallenged. The analysis based on the new orthodoxy of SMEs in IDs is unable to answer these questions and, after the realization of the limits and dead-ends of entrepreneurial regionalism, a radical change is needed to formulate more nuanced and inclusive policies for local/regional development taking into account all types of SMEs and forms of labour, in all sectors and regions.

References

Amin, A. and Robins, K. (1990) "The re-emergence of regional economies? The mythical geography of flexible accumulation", *Society and Space*, 8, 7–34.

Ardigò, A. and Donati, P. (1976) *Famiglia e Industrializzazione: continuità e discontinuità negli orientamenti di valore in una comunità a forte sviluppo endogeno*, F, Angeli, Milano.

Bagnasco, A. (1977) *Tre Italie: La problematica territoriale dello sviluppo italiano*, il Mulino: Bologna.

Becattini, G. (1990) "The Marchallian industrial district as a socio-economic notion", in F. Pyke, G. Becattini and W. Sengerberger (eds) *Industrial Districts and the Interfirm Co-operation in Italy*, ILO, Geneva, pp. 134–142.

Benko, G. and Lipietz, A. (1992) (eds) *Les Régions qui gagnent*, PUF, Paris.

Bialasiewicz, L. (2006) "Geographies of production and the contexts of politics: dislocation and new ecologies of fear in the Veneto *città diffusa*", *Society and Space*, 24, 1 41–68.

Bianchi, P. and Bellini, N. (1991) "Public policies for local networks of innovators", *Research Policy*, 20, 487–497.

Birch, D.L. (1979) *The Job Generation Process*, MIT Program on Neighborhood and Regional Change, Cambridge, MA.

Birch, D. L. (1980) *Job Creation in Cities*, MIT Program on Neighborhood and Regional Change, Cambridge, MA.

Calafati, A. (2006) "'Traditional knowledge' and local development trajectories", *European Planning Studies*, 14, 5, 621–632.

Cooke, P. (1988) "Flexible integration, scope economies and strategic alliances: social and spatial mediation", *Society and Space*, 6, 281–300.

Dei Ottati, G. (1994) "Cooperation and competition in the Industrial District as an organization model", *European Planning Studies*, 2, 4, 463–483.

Dunford, M. (2006) "Industrial districts, magic cycles and the restructuring of the Italian textiles and clothing chain", *Economic Geography*, 82, 1, 27–59.

Frey, L. (1974) "Le picole e medie imprese industriali di fonde al mercato del lavoro", *Inchiesta*, 14, 85–96.

Garofoli, G. (1983) *Industrializzazione disfuza in Lombardia*, IPER/F. Angeli, Milan.

Hadjimichalis, C. (2006a) "The end of Third Italy as we knew it?", *Antipode*, 32, 1, 82–106.

Hadjimichalis, C. (2006b) "Non-economic factors in economic geography and in 'New Regionalism': a sympathetic critique", *International Journal of Urban and Regional Research*, 30, 4, 858–872.

Hadjimichalis, C. and Vaiou, D. (1990) "Whose flexibility? The politics of informalisation in Southern Europe", *Capital and Class*, 42, winter, 79–106.

Hadjimichalis, C. and Vaiou, D. (2004) 'Local' illustrations for 'International' geographical theory, in J.O. Baerenhold and K. Simonsen (eds) *Space Odysseys*, Ashgate, Aldershot, pp. 171–182.

Hadjimichalis, C., Vaiou, D. Sapountzaki, K. Skordili, S. and Chalikias, Chr. (2003) *Social and Economic Impacts to SMEs and Employment in Western Athens from the 7.9.1999 Earthquake*, Final Research Report to OASP, Dept. of Geography, Harokopio University, Athens (in Greek).

Harrison, B. (1994) "The Italian Industrial Districts and the crisis of the cooperative form: part I", *EPS*, 2, 1, 3–22 and part II, *European Planning Studies*, 2, 2, 159–174.

Hudson, R. (1999) "The learning economy, the learning firm and the learning region: a sympathetic critique of the limits to learning", *European Urban and Regional Studies*, 6, 1, 59–72.

Kropotkin, P. (1898/1986) *Fields, Factories and Workshops: Industry Combined with Agriculture and Brain Work with Manual Work*, Greenwood Press, New York.

Labrianidis, L. and Kalogeressis, A. (2007) "Geographies of de-localization in Europe: conceptual issues and empirical findings", *6th Framework Programme*, http://afroditi.uom.gr/move/.

Magnaghi, A. and Perelli, B. (1978) "Ristrutturazione e diffuzione territoriale del ciclo produttivo:la fabrica diffusa in Italia", Proceedings ATTI-1, Seminario Internationale, Milano, pp. 213–225.

Melissourgos, G. (2008) *Local/Regional Development and the Geography of Locational Conflicts: Tourist Development in Greece and Spain*, unpublished doctoral dissertation, Department of Geography, Harokopio University, Athens (in Greek).

Mingione, E. (1983) *Urbanizzazione, classi sociali, lavoro informale*, F. Angeli, Milan.

Mingione, E. (1998) *Sociologia della vita economica*, Carocci, Rome.

Mingione, E. and Pugliese, E. (2002) *Il Lavoro*, Carocci, Rome.

Morgan, K. (1977) "The learning region: institutions, innovation and regional renewal", *Regional Studies*, 31, 5, 491–503.

Nadvi, K. and Schmitz, H. (1994) "Industrial clusters in less developed countries: review of experiences and research agenda", *IDS*, Sussex, mimeo.

OECD (2005) *Building Competitive Regions*, OECD, Paris.

OECD (2006) *The OECD Small and Medium Enterprise Outlook*, OECD, Paris.

OECD (2007) *Competitive Regional Clusters: National Policy Approaches*, OECD, Paris.

Paci, M. (1972) *Mercato del lavoro e classi sociali in Italia*, Il Mulino, Bologna.

Pike, A., Rodríguez-Pose, A. and Tomaney, J. (2006) *Local and Regional Development*, Routledge, London.

Pike, A., Rodríguez-Pose, A. and Tomaney, J. (2007) "What kind of local and regional development and for whom?", *Regional Studies*, 41(9): 1253–1269.

Piore, M. and Sabel, C. (1984) *The Second Industrial Divide: Possibilities for Prosperity*, Basic Books, New York.

Rabelloti, R., Carabelli, A. and Hirsch, G. (2009) "Italian Industrial Districts on the move: where are they going?", *European Planning Studies*, 17, 1, 19–41.

Recio, A. (1998) "Capitalismo, precarización y economía sumergida:notas para un debate", *Proceedings Economía sumergida: el estado della cuestión en España*, CGT, Murcia, pp. 225–271.

Sabel, C. F. (1989) "Flexible specialization and the re-emergence of regional economies", in P. Hirst and J. Zeitlein (eds) *Reversing Industrial Decline? Industrial Structure and Policy in Britain and Her Competitors*, Berg, Oxford, pp. 101–156.

Sayer, A. (1989) "Post-fordism in question" *International Journal of Urban and Regional Research*, 13, 4, 666–698.

Scott, A. (1988) *New Industrialised Spaces*, Pion, London.

Scott, A. and Storper, M. (1988) "The geographical foundations and social regulation of flexible production complexes", in J. Wolch, and M. Dear (eds) *The Power of Geography*, Allen and Unwin, London, pp. 21–40.

Shaw, G. and Williams, A. (1994) *Critical Issues in Tourism: A Geographical Perspective*. Blackwell Publishers, Oxford.

Smith, G. (1999) *Confronting the Present: Towards a Politically Engaged Anthropology*, Berg, Oxford.

Storper, M. (1997) *The Regional World: Territorial development in a global economy*, Guilford Press, New York.

Vaiou, D. and Hadjimichalis, C. (1997) *With the Sewing Machine in the Kitchen and the Poles in the Fields: Cities, Regions and Informal Work*, Exandas: Athens

Vaiou, D. and Hadjimichalis, C. (2003) *With the Sewing Machine in the Kitchen and the Poles in the Fields: Cities, Regions and Informal Work*, (Second edition)Exandas: Athens (in Greek).

Verducci, F. (2003) "Immigrazione e mutamento sociale. Lavoro ed integrazione sociale nel distretto industriale della calzatura", *Universita deglli Studi di Macerata*, Dip. Di Sociologia (mimeo).

Vinay, P. (1985) "Family life cycle and the informal economy in Central Italy", *International Journal of Urban and Regional Research*, 9, 1, 82–97.

Ybarra, A. San Miguel, B. and Hurdato, J. (2004) *El Calzado en el Vinalopò, entre la continuidad y la ruptura*, Universitat de Alicande/Ayutamiento de Elche, Elche.

Ybarra, J.A. (1986) "La informalización industrial en la economía valenciana: un modelo para el subdesarrolo", *Revista de trabajo*, 2, 28–39.

Further reading

Becattini, G., Bellandi, M., de Ottati G., and Sforzi, F. (2003) *From Industrial Districts to Local Development*, Edward Elgar, Cheltenham.

Bengo, G. and Lipietz, A. (eds) (1992) *Les Régions qui Gagnent*, PUF, Paris.

Hudson, R. (2000) *Production, Places and Environment*, Prentice Hall, Essex.

393

33

Transnational corporations and local and regional development

Stuart Dawley

Introduction

The activities of Transnational Corporations (TNCs), through Foreign Direct Investment (FDI) and processes of control and coordination, continue to orchestrate the process of global economic integration. Put simply, TNCs are one of the primary movers and shapers of the contemporary global economy (Dicken 2007). Since the 1970s the impacts of the contemporary TNC have been scrutinised across a variety of academic disciplines – *inter alia* economic geography, strategic management, economics and the international business literature – analysing economic growth, technological change, trade, market structures, finance and employment (Yeung and Peck 2003; Dunning and Lundan 2008). Perspectives developed within economic geography continue to make important and distinctive contributions to this inter-disciplinary endeavour.

On the one hand, economic geographers have led the move away from 'placeless' notions of global corporations to a more advanced appreciation of the geographical embeddedness of TNC activity (see, for example, Yeung and Peck (2003) on Dicken's work in this field). The character and behaviour of TNCs both shape, and are shaped by, a geographical

contradiction central to global economic integration – between the promotion of a space of flows and the continued significance of place (Phelps and Raines 2003; Jessop 1999). Examining the impact and possibilities for economic growth as part of the "variegated landscape of relations between TNCs and territories" is of greatest interest to economic geographers (Phelps and Waley 2004: 192). On the other hand, contributions from economic geography, industrial geography and regional studies have more specifically focused upon "unpacking the relationships between TNC activity and urban and regional development" (Yeung 2009: 198). Indeed, Yeung (2009: 199) goes on to suggest that a "geographical perspective argues strongly that TNCs and their activity are undisputedly one of the keys to understanding urban and regional development in today's globalizing world economy".

The current Global Production Network (GPN) approach (see Coe *et al.* 2008) offers a valuable framework in bringing together these interrelated concerns – TNCs, territories and local and regional development. At one level, the approach situates the roles and impacts of TNCs and territories as part of a broader "globally organised nexus of interconnected functions and operations by firms and non-firm institutions through which goods and services are produced and distributed" (Coe *et al.* 2004: 471). At another level, the notions of 'strategic couplings' and 'regional assets' connect investment strategies of 'focal firms' with a 'globalised' understanding of regional development. In so doing, the GPN approach has created a productive and expansive dialogue between economic geography and local and regional development studies, moving beyond the traditional focus on FDI and regional development in Europe and the USA to encompass contributions from the global North and South (*inter alia*).

This chapter aims to contribute to the recent reinvigoration of academic and policy interest in the dynamic interrelations between TNCs and regional development. The GPN approach offers much utility as a heuristic framework to explore and question the interplay of global networks of firms, non-firm institutions and territories. However, in developing such a holistic and inclusive network approach the GPN framework tends to underplay the tensions created by the differential powers of key agents shaping and moulding the fortunes of regions and their ability to attract and embed exogenous resources. As a result, this chapter seeks to refocus attention on the particular and enduring roles of the TNC and the nation state in shaping host region development. First, while according an active role to the socio-institutional and cultural regulation of investment behaviour, this chapter restates the centrality, power and causal role of the firm. The 'black box' of the TNC is explored, focusing on emerging dynamics of time-based competition and intensified intra-corporate competition and the role of TNC merger and acquisitions in shaping (dis) investment decisions within host regions. The discussion reveals how the prospects for local affiliates, host regions and communities are asymmetrically pitched within a diverse array of fluctuating, competitive and geographically selective processes of corporate restructuring and change. Second, the discussion

then focuses upon the enduring importance of national level institutions in shaping the interrelations between TNC investment behaviour and host region economies. Withstanding the widespread acceptance of state ceding power to capital within the contemporary neo-liberal context, the interrelations between TNCs and contexts of *home* and *host* nations continue to impact upon corporate strategies, and ultimately their relative power over institutions in host localities and regions. Building on the preceding discussion, the final section concludes by highlighting the changing roles, prospects and challenges for regional-level institutions in their ongoing relationships with TNCs – offering a series of insights into the GPN's notion of establishing 'strategic couplings'. The chapter begins, however, by briefly revisiting the traditional literature on TNCs, FDI and local and regional development prominent in the 1980s and 1990s within economic geography, industrial geography and regional studies.

In its contribution to local and regional development studies, the discussions developed within this chapter illustrate the complex and fluctuating ways in which "TNCs organise their economic activities across space in a variety of different ways, with important implications for the places that 'plug-in' in to these corporate networks" (Coe *et al.* 2007: 225). For local and regional development scholars and policy practitioners alike, the analytical challenge remains one in which "we generalize about the impact of TNCs at our peril…what is true in one set of circumstance may not be true in others…we need to avoid 'kneejerk' reactions, whether positive or negative" (Dicken 2007: 454).

From branch plants to embedded plants and back again?

Research into inward investment and peripheral region development represents a long tradition of inquiry (Firn 1975; Watts 1981; Pike 1997; Hudson 2000; Phelps *et al.* 2003). According to Yeung (2009) a clear distinction can be made between this strand of literature with its preoccupation with the impacts of FDI activity and that of the more contemporary concerns of the GPN literature which affords more attention to unravelling the 'black box' of the TNC, its organisation, production networks, multi-scalar institutional relations and influence on regional development. However, I would argue that while the GPN notions of *strategic couplings*, *regional assets* and *value* are useful heuristic devices, the traditional literature continues to offer a detailed series of insights into how such 'coupling' processes are constrained, enabled and expressed in host regions. In particular, the analytical frameworks developed in the traditional literature around 'studying regions by studying firms' still offer considerable utility in grounding the impacts and interrelations between TNCs and regional development (Markusen 1995).

The truncated experiences of inward investment industrialisation in peripheral regions during the 1960s and 1970s coalesced with the development of the branch plant economy tradition of conceptual and empirical inquiry. This work emphasised the structures of external ownership and the control and creation of functional roles for regions within broader corporate and geographical divisions of labour (Firn 1975; Dicken 1976; Hudson 2000). In short, peripheral regions became sites for the more routine capital-intensive and low-skilled elements of the production chain, while higher level command and conception activities were located in more advanced regions. As such the original policy expectations that inward investment would stimulate a 'growth pole' for peripheral regions received heavy criticism as the very nature of branch plant investments offered host economies little in the way of "skill formation, technology transfer, linkages opportunities, transmission of new managerial and entrepreneurial

know-how or reinvestment of profits" (Amin and Tomaney 1995: 202; Phelps 2009). Moreover, through the insertion into the extremities of corporate hierarchies peripheral host economies, such as the North East of England, were described as 'global outposts' (Hudson 1995) susceptible to the vagaries of external control, corporate rationalisation and capital flight as the cost/price nature of locational behaviour fuelled capital mobility (Bluestone and Harrison 1982; Hudson 2000).

With the failure of alternative forms of endogenous growth strategies to adequately cater for the huge employment demands within old industrial areas, the attraction of inward investment remained a key element of peripheral region development within states within Western Europe during the 1980s and early 1990s (Amin and Tomaney 1995). Indeed, the strategic direction of FDI-led growth was given new impetus in the early 1990s with the prospect that new processes of corporate reorganisation, operating with flatter and looser organisational structures, offered a qualitatively enhanced type of inward investment project for host region economies (see Table 33.1; Pike 1998; Young *et al.* 1994).

Situated within a loosely defined context of 'flexible' or 'post-Fordist' corporate reorganisation, new 'performance plant' inward investment projects carried heightened levels of autonomy, more complex functionality, specialised markets, heightened product and processes technologies and more qualified workforces (Amin *et al.* 1994; Phelps *et al.* 2003). Transnational corporate strategies were understood as increasingly responsive to geographical variations in markets and regulation, most notably at macro-regional levels. As a result production strategies became 'regionalised' or 'glocalised' (Hudson 2000) as companies sought to gain competitiveness through geographical proximity to markets and also localised production networks (for example, just-in-time supply chains). For host economies, the local economic development

Table 33.1 Dimensions of type of plant and local and regional development implications

	'Branch plant'	'Performance/networked branch plant'
Role and autonomy	External ownership and control; structured position and constrained autonomy; truncated and narrow functional structure involved in part-process production and/or assembly; cloned capacity and vertically integrated with limited nodes capable of external local linkage (e.g. suppliers, technology); state policy subsidised establishment via automatic grants to broadly designated areas	External ownership and control but possible enhanced strategic and operating autonomy as well as responsibility for performance increased within a 'flattened' hierarchical structure; wider functional structure involved in full process production tilted towards manufacturing rather than solely assembly; sole capacity with product (range), division or market mandate at the expense of rationalisation elsewhere; increased nodes capable of linkage (e.g. R&D with technology support, human resources with training); state policy support for establishment on selective and regulated basis (e.g. job creation, local content)
Labour process	Labour-intensive, semi- and unskilled work; 'routinised' and specific tasks within refined technical division of labour; high-volume production of low- to medium-technology products; standardised process technology; short-term, task-specific, 'on-the-job' training integrated with production	Capital and technology intensive, semi- and skilled work with increased need for diagnostic and cognitive skills; recombined job tasks and individual/team responsibility for performance; low- to high-technology and low- to high-volume production flexibility; flexible and reprogrammable process technology; longer term, coordinated with investment, 'on-' and 'off-the-job' training
Labour–management relations	Organised and unionised labour; job classifications, task assignments and work/supervision rules linked to seniority-based pay scales; formalised and collective negotiation and bargaining tied to employment contract; personnel management with administrative focus	Business unionism; reduction and streamlining of grading, job titles and meritocratic salary structure; shift to company-based non-(traditional) union arenas, individualised negotiation and bargaining tied to 'enabling' agreements; human resource management techniques
Labour market strategies	Employees considered interchangeable, replaceable and in need of constant supervision; limited screening and high labour turnover and absenteeism; reliance on external labour market	Rigorous scrutiny and increased selectivity in recruitment; employees as human resources needing investment; teamworking to reduce labour turnover and identify employee with the goals of the company; development of core internal labour market and peripheral (part-time, temporary) segments
Supplier linkages	Limited since integration with broader corporate structures of production and supply chains; intra-firm linkages substituted for local ties; limited local supply chain knowledge and greater awareness of potential suppliers in headquarters region	Outsourcing increase with JIT and synchronous suppliers; increased potential for local procurement and supplier agglomeration; first- and second-tier supply chain management; increased global sourcing and partnership relations; growth in dependence in the local supply network; geographically distributed production networks and JIT operated over (inter-)national distances

(continued)

Table 33.1 (*Cont'd*)

| Local economic development implications | Externally owned and controlled plants with limited decision-making powers locally ('dependent development', 'branch plant economy') vulnerable to closure or relocation ('footloose', 'runaway industries', 'hyper-mobile capital'); limited growth rates in employment and output; low technology and skills ('screwdriver plants'); few local linkages ('enclave development', 'dual economy', 'industrialisation without growth', 'cathedrals in the desert'); diversified industries not building upon or modernising existing regional industrial strengths; limited innovation potential and technology transfer from dedicated production processes and suppliers | New concepts of externally owned and controlled plant with increased decision-making autonomy for strategic and operational issues, more rooted and anchored in the local economy ('embedded firm'), higher levels of technology and skills, higher innovative potential, more local linkages and increased technology transfer through research and technological development functions; supplier links upgrading process technology improvement and partnership development with suppliers; potential for the plant to be a 'propulsive local growth pole', 'vehicle/catalyst for local economic development' and capable of setting in train 'sustainable development' |

Source: Adapted from Pike (1998: 886–887)

implications of this purported shift focused upon the enhanced potential to increase the local 'embeddedness' of plants and investment projects. The localisation of production was seen to offer new forms of 'development' of local economies through the deeper sets of backward and forward localised supplier linkages (Turok 1993; see Table 33.2) while, the workforce requirements, a swathe of Japanese and South Korean FDI projects within Wales, Scotland and the North East of England, were understood to be generating more highly skilled and intensively trained workforces within peripheral regions, triggering both skills and occupational uplift effects (Phelps and Fuller 2000; Raines 2003). Together, the qualitative shift in supplier linkages and the increased requirement for skilled and professional labour were perceived to offer a 'demonstration effect' of new industrial practices which would trigger the modernisation of peripheral region economies (Cooke and Morgan 1998; Peck and Stone 1993).

In terms of workforce requirements, a swathe of Japanese and South Korean FDI projects within Wales, Scotland and the North East of England were understood to be generating more highly skilled and intensively

trained workforces within peripheral regions, triggering both skills and occupational uplift effects (Phelps and Fuller 2000; Raines 2003).

Similarly in the United States in the 1980s and 1990s, examples of 'performance plant' FDI emerged through a series of Japanese automotive 'transplants' – *inter alia* Honda, Nissan and Toyota – creating a distinct break with the geographies and production systems of the then traditional US automakers. In geographical terms, "this 'new' automobile industry had a very different geography from that of the traditional one. With few exceptions, the old established automobile industry centres were not favoured" (Dicken 2007: 309). In particular, having first secured the key priority of establishing production in the increasingly protected US national market, the incoming Japanese investments targeted greenfield rural locations, initially clustered in a 'Transplant Corridor' in the American Mid-West before being decentralised across the Southern States (e.g. Mississippi – Nissan, Toyota; Texas - Toyota; Kentucky – Toyota). Key factors of location included local workforce characteristics, low levels of unionised labour, transport infrastructures suitable for 'just-in-time' supplier agglomerations,

Table 33.2 Alternative linkage scenarios: a summary of the main tendencies

	Developmental	Dependent
Nature of local linkages	Collaborative, mutual learning based on technology and trust; emphasis on added value	Unequal trading relationships; conventional subcontracting; emphasis on cost saving;
Duration of linkages	Long-term partnerships;	short-term contracts;
Meaning of 'flexibility'	high-level interaction to accelerate product development and increase responsiveness to volatile markets	price-cutting and short-term convenience for multinationals
Inward investors' ties to the locality	Deeply embedded; high investment in decentralised, multi-functional operations	Weakly embedded; branch plants restricted to final assembly operations
Benefits for local firms	Markets for local firms to develop and produce their own products; transfer of technology and expertise strengthens local firms	Markets for local firms to make standard, low-tech components; subcontracting means restricted independent growth capacity;
Quality of jobs	Diverse including high skilled, high income	many low-skilled, low-paid, temporary and casual;
Prospects for the local economy	Self-sustaining growth through cumulative expansion of the industrial cluster	Vulnerable to external forces and corporate decisions

Source: Adapted from Turok (1993: 402)

state-level grants and assistance and sites away from the competitive pressures of rival automotive assemblers (Kenney and Florida 1992). Subsequently, new local and regional flexible production enclaves emerged within non-traditional heartlands such as Kentucky, where Toyota's largest US plant (Georgetown) provides the focal point of a state-wide motor vehicle industry involving 52,859 jobs and to become ranked as the third largest car-producing state, behind only the traditional centres of Michigan and Ohio (Kentucky Cabinet for Economic Development 2007). Beyond the local and regional impact, the purported *demonstration effect* of Japanese transplants triggered a restructuring of production systems among US producers such as Ford and GM, Toyota's continued superiority supported the growth of a 42,000-strong US workforce across over ten vehicle and parts plants. For Toyota, its success was attributed to a company culture which "thinks globally, but act(s) locally…we have a hybrid system where we take the best of

every culture and distil that into a system that really works effectively in every country where we do business – and the ability to transplant that system throughout other countries is the key to growing globally" (Toyota's North American President cited in Schifferes 2007). Similar examples of Japanese automotive transplants in the UK – Toyota, Honda and Nissan – led to suggestions that FDI was stimulating a series of new growth trajectories around 'flexible production enclaves' in old industrial regions – analogous to a variant of a post-Fordist 'new industrial space' (Bryson and Henry 2005).

Since the early 1990s empirical inquiry has attempted to investigate and evaluate the notion of the locally embedded/performance plant within the UK, with a considerable weight of evidence continuing to illustrate the limited contribution of exogenous investment in stimulating regional transformation. One of the most comprehensive analyses of any purported shift from branch plants to embedded plants was provided by Phelps and

Raines (2003: 28), which concluded that in the inward investment heartlands of Wales and North East England there appeared "little support for the idea of the locally embedded plant". Although many of the overseas operations had developed enhanced roles and were more advanced than traditional branch plant stereotypes, there remained low levels of local sourcing, collaborative R&D linkages remain limited in scope and there were few regional attractions (e.g. suppliers, education and training) that were deemed important in attracting further rounds of investment. In essence, the experiences of FDI in the UK regions were subsequently described as 'extended enclaves' (Phelps et al. 2003) whereby the integration of an FDI project is extended beyond simply direct employment to involve partial connections with local bases of R&D, suppliers and education and training. In terms of contributing to the development of synergies or agglomerations within host regions, then, FDI spill-overs appear mostly associated with *existing* clusters of indigenous industry with only reduced or even negative agglomeration effects in FDI-led clusters (De Propis and Driffield 2006; Phelps 2009).

At one level, this brief review of the traditional literature indicates the many lines of analysis through which the precise local and regional development impacts of TNC investment or 'strategic couplings' can be scrutinised. At another level, the limited evidence of embeddedness and truncated contributions to local and regional development serve to restate the political economy of FDI and the regions during the 1980s and 1990s (Hudson 2000). The extent to which the same structures shaping the degree of linkages, embeddedness, performance plants continue to shape the prospects of more contemporary concerns of FDI-led clusters remains a matter for further conceptual and empirical research. However, the following sections indicate the importance of connecting and retaining a geographical political economy perspective within studies of TNCs

and regional development (Pike et al. 2006, 2008).

Restating the significance of the firm

With reductions in the growth of FDI flows in recent years, Phelps and Raines (2003) have identified a new terrain of intensified competition between territories for the attraction and retention of FDI and the mobile investment of TNCs. Central to these competitive dynamics are new forms of time-based competition, intensified processes of intra-corporate competition and increased merger and acquisition activity – all of which are impacting upon host regions in selective and geographically uneven ways. To better understand the corporate processes in which host regions are competitively pitched, research must look into the 'black box' of intra-corporate activity and redress fears that recent economic geography research has "sidestepped the issues of researching how business firms perform as the movers and shapers of the capitalist economy" (Yeung 2006: 2; O'Neill 2003; Dawley 2007a). It is important, therefore, that economic and political imperatives of TNCs – or focal firms – are not diluted within frameworks such as the GPN approach. As a purely economic agent, relative to other agents such as governments, the firm continues to possess structural power (Phelps and Waley 2004). Moreover, constitutive of the institutional contexts that they connect, firms increasingly exhibit political power, for example, using mobility to promote convergence across national regulatory environments (Phelps and Waley 2004). Here, Phelps and Wood (2006: 497) draw on the work of Crotty et al. (2003) to make the distinction between the bargaining power that TNCs can generate through the "gross mobility of capital (i.e. realized and non-realized threats of re-location of production) rather than just the net mobility of capital that highlights the true extent of regulatory arbitrage". As such, the structural power of the TNC continues to play a central role in determining the execution of their strategies across and between local affiliates, host region institutions and communities. The following discussion focuses upon three competitive dynamics currently shaping the uneven geography of their corporate investment and restructuring processes: *time-based competition; intensified intra-corporate competition;* and *TNC merger, acquisitions and restructuring.*

Time-based competition

Emerging from broader questions of the heightened mobility and turnover of multinational capital in time and space (Jessop 1999), the development prospects for host region economies are increasingly moulded by the shortening life span of individual FDI projects (Phelps and Raines 2003). Driven by the enhanced dynamism of 'time-based' competition (Schoenberger 1997; Van Egeraat and Jacobson 2005), disruptive technological change and market preferences, competitive pressures are forcing TNCs to reduce the *time-to-market* of products and shorten *product life cycles* (Stalk and Hoult 1990; Yeung 2006). According to Phelps and Raines (2003: 3), these competitive pressures expose host regions to the "heightened mobility of productive investments as the 'lives' of individual production facilities dwindle, their future existence repeatedly and frequently become subject to parent company review". Compounding the existing vulnerabilities of host peripheral regions within TNC spatial divisions of labour and accentuated by the recent shift towards deregulated trade and investment policy regimes (Peck and Yeung 2003), the emerging salience of time-based competition and product life–cycle perspectives provide important insights into the economic geographies of transnational investment activity. The recent interest surrounding time-based competition and product

life cycles necessitates a brief consideration of former approaches to the temporal and spatial dynamics of TNC investment activity and peripheral region development (Phelps and Raines 2003; Schoenberger 1997). The late 1970s and early 1980s reflected the heydays of cyclical models of TNC industrial location behaviour, built around the profit-cycle approach (Markusen 1994) and its influential antecedent the product-cycle model (Vernon 1966; Taylor 1986). Both approaches connected the cyclical evolution of products and sectors to the geographical dispersion and life course of TNC investments, with peripheral regions hosting the most labour-intensive, cost-sensitive and consequently ephemeral operations. However, with the rise of structuralist realism within economic geography in the mid-1980s, cyclical models of industrial change became discredited as essentialist, technologically deterministic and ultimately disembodied from the concrete phenomena of industrial behaviour (*inter alia* Sayer 1985; Walker 1985). Nevertheless, elements of both approaches connected with an emerging concern into investment volatility within the classic 'branch plant' critique of FDI that conceptualised a geographical division between core and peripheral localities within corporate spatial divisions of labour (Pike *et al.* 2006). Here, cyclical notions of investment vulnerability were replaced with a non-temporally determined exposure to corporate abandonment through spatial structures of production within broader social relations of production (Massey 1995; Yeung 2005). Continued scepticism surrounding the nature and scale of any qualitative transformation surrounding durability brought about by the 'performance plant' perspective were more recently reinforced by a series of 'performance plant' closures, rationalisations and postponed investments across the "periphery of the neoliberal economic heartland" (Phelps and Raines 2003; Dawley 2007b; Van Egeraat and Jacobson 2004). This was most vividly demonstrated with the decimation of the

UK's high-technology semiconductor fabrication industry almost entirely dependent upon FDI projects. Between 1998 and 2002 over 4,000 jobs were lost and a further 2,400 new jobs postponed due to a flurry of plant closures and aborted investments, geographically concentrated in the North East of England, Wales and Scotland's much-hyped 'Silicon Glen' electronic corridor. Encompassing some of the largest FDI projects within Europe, these flagship investments were emblematic of a 'new dawn' for the peripheral regions. The most acute example being that of Siemens Semiconductors in the North East of England, the German TNC closed its £1.1 billion investment after just over one year of commercial production with the loss of 1,200 high-skilled jobs (Dawley 2007a). While the collapse of the memory chip market was felt across the whole Siemens Semiconductors Corporation, the selective nature of rationalisation and closure exposes the weak position of the Siemens plant in the North East of England within the broader corporate division of labour. From its inception, the North East plant became locked into extracting the diminishing returns from an outgoing segment of the market – and therefore unable to compete with other Siemens plants, notably in Germany, in attracting and upgrading its product and process technologies. The fragility of the plant's path dependency was subsequently exposed as the 'weakest link in the chain' in the face of market collapse. In sum, the dynamics of intensified time-based competition create new challenges for host regional economies as the volatility of TNC investment increases and the life span of projects dwindles, accentuating further the vulnerabilities of peripheral host regions within TNCs spatial divisions of labour.

Intensified intra-corporate competition

Much academic and policy attention has focused upon the 'locational tournaments' (Mytelka 2000) pitched between nations and regions for the attraction of new greenfield inward investment projects. However, following an overall reduction in the growth of FDI flows and greenfield investment in recent years, Phelps and Fuller (2000) suggest competition for investment is now more focused upon capturing intra-corporate *repeat* or *reinvestment*. More acutely, such intra-corporate competition can also be pitched in a regressive battle to avoid disinvestment or closure (Pike 2005). But how can we better understand these new competitive contexts within which local affiliates and regions compete against each other to attract or preserve investment?

While much of the GPN work has thus far been preoccupied with inter- and extra-firm institutional relations, more emphasis needs to be placed on (focal) firm-level processes to open up the *black box* of intra-corporate activity during the geographical uneven and selective (dis) investment episodes. Even so, the GPN approach does offer a framework within which the agency of the corporation can be analysed as part of a more "pluralistic industrial geography", according an active role to the socio-institutional and cultural regulation of investment behaviour (Yeung 2001: 293). In this sense, while the capitalist 'firm' continues to respond to economic imperatives, the precise strategies and actions of capitals evolve in response to specific social, cultural, political contexts – both *internal* and *external* to the corporation (Schoenberger 2000; Yeung 2000). By conceptualising the firm as a complex socio-spatial and territorial construction, the behaviour of corporate actors and strategists need not be confined to a singular logic of profit maximisation, but instead reflect the influence of competing discourses, cultures and politics within the firm (Dicken and Malmberg 2001; Yeung 2001; Schoenberger 1997). In particular, three important dimensions offer critical insights into the investment strategies which shape the geographically uneven nature of investment decisions within and across TNC affiliates and regions. First, in seeking to reconnect historical contexts with economic-geographical analysis, investment decisions and corporate strategies are shaped by the evolution and path dependency of the institutional architecture of capital (Clark 1994). Path dependency can reflect the strategic disposition of corporate activities together with territorial embeddedness of firms and corporate cultures (Dicken and Malmberg 2001). Second, the embeddedness of a TNCs within its home nation has been proven to play an important role in influencing and enmeshing corporate strategies and behaviours within territorially distinctive assemblages of institutions and practices (Dicken 2000). Insights are derived from studies which reveal the distinctiveness of national business systems and varieties of capitalism that suggest "although firms do respond and react to (or anticipate) changing competitive conditions...the strategy they choose is most strongly shaped by the national legacy of their home county" (Bathelt and Gertler 2005; Gertler 2001: 14). Through the processes of TNC-driven international economic integration, the roles of home and host political, cultural and regulatory institutional environments serve to embed the firm-territory nexus and contextualise intra-corporate socio-spatial relations during (dis) investment episodes (Phelps and Fuller 2000).

Third, evidence of time-based competition and the shortening life span of individual FDI projects suggests elements of the product life-cycle approach still provide some practical bearing on the functional and spatial organisation of affiliates within the TNC networks (Phelps and Fuller 2000). In this way, the status and roles of TNC affiliates are connected to the life cycle of each plant's product and process technologies. Intra-corporate spatial divisions of labour emerge and are contested as TNC operations compete for parent company investment to obtain first-mover advantages and avoid being locked into declining product markets (Birkinshaw 1999; Phelps and Fuller 2000). Connecting

to Massey's (1995) work, and while not situating plants within rigid spatial structures, managerial hierarchies (including economic ownership) and technical divisions of labour continue to contribute to our understanding of socio-spatial power relations within corporate and global production networks (Phelps and Fuller 2000; Birkinshaw 1999). For example, the work of Schoenberger (1997) illustrates the variations in corporate subcultures and knowledge transmission across TNC networks, while Birkinshaw and Hood (1998) have focused upon the agency of entrepreneurial affiliates to alter their position within corporate socio-spatial hierarchies. For local and regional development, the discussions surrounding enhanced intra-corporate decision-making expose the complexities of the corporate decision-making process and the degree to which the prospects of regions are based, but also how they are very rarely purely financial decisions and instead are melded together under particular economic, political, institutional and cultural contexts (Phelps and Waley 2004).

TNC merger, acquisition and restructuring

To date the majority of literature focusing upon TNCs and local and regional development has been preoccupied with the arrival and departure of greenfield investment projects (cf. Ashcroft and Love 1991, 1993). However, less attention has focused upon the local and regional development impacts of in-situ corporate restructuring driven by TNC acquisition and merger activity. While not exclusively so, this is especially the case in traditional industries when firms with long regional histories become acquired and absorbed within broader TNC ownership structures. Put simply, we tend to look beyond 'the new in the old' despite these corporate dynamics representing some of the main FDI flows into host regions. This has been most starkly demonstrated through the pent-up and belated globalisation of the steel industry. Driven by a complex combination of new market conditions, technological change and above all pressures to consolidate in the face of persistent global overcapacity, the corporate anatomy of European steel production has been rapidly restructured from a fragmented sector dominated by a large number of predominantly national, sometimes nationalised, companies towards an increasingly smaller number of integrated TNC producers (Fairbrother *et al.* 2004). Within the UK the vestiges of the formerly nationalised British Steel Corporation merged with the Dutch steel company Hoogervens in 1999 to form Corus. The merger was driven by the need to achieve scale, market access and a more diversified product base, but the burden of post-merger rationalisation was to be most harshly felt in the UK's steel regions with the loss of 13,000 jobs (Dawley *et al.* 2008). Moreover, indicative of different national traditions of corporate governance rumours of "open warfare between the UK and Dutch parts of Corus" (*Financial Times* 2003) hampered corporate decision-making, especially in terms of the location of further disinvestment and job loss. Less than five years after the Corus merger, a corporate decision was made to write the steel plant on Teesside, North East England, out of the company's strategy reflecting its vulnerable position in producing cost-price commodity steel within an increasingly competitive global market. Moreover, Teesside's fate appeared pinned directly to the new corporate pressures to deliver investment returns generated by a 'financialised' capitalism and search for 'shareholder value' within restructuring plans (Pike 2006). Following merger, Corus' strategy sought "to selectively seek growth and shareholder value creation ... achieved through the development of those businesses where we can achieve market-leading positions" (Corus 2002). Although a spike in global steel demand sustained the plant through a series of international supply agreements, the fate of Teesside was further compounded in 2007 when Corus was acquired by Tata Steel, part of the Indian Tata industrial conglomerate. While Corus viewed the acquisition as essential in that it was "no longer sufficient to be European...this is a global industry" (Jim Leng, Deputy Chairman of Tata Steel cited in BBC News 2007), it marked further uncertainty for the future of Teesside. In December 2009, Tata announced that the Teesside steel operation was the source of its greatest losses within Europe and will be 'mothballed' with the loss of 1,500 jobs. While there is no counterfactual as to the direction the Teesside steel plant may have taken without being integrated within evermore transnational corporate structures, it nevertheless mirrors similar processes that have occurred within the Teesside petrochemicals industry (Sadler 1992; Chapman 2005). Together these processes raise important challenges in broadening and deepening our analysis of TNCs and local and regional development. In particular, this story indicates how analytical and policy attention must redress the tendency to overlook the significant ways in which TNCs and FDI can serve to reinvigorate or indeed 'hollow-out' (Williams *et al.* 1990) long-serving and established regional industries.

The state is dead...long live the state

Dicken's (2007) commentary on the often uneasy nexus between states and TNCs suggests that while historical variations have existed between states' FDI policies, in the last two decades policies have tended to converge in the direction of liberalisation. At the broadest level, historical variations existed between the more liberal approaches of developed countries than developing countries. But even within the developed countries there were wide variations between, for example, the UK's 'open door' approach from the 1970s onwards compared to that of France's more restrictive − even protectionist − stance.

Similarly, within the developing states, Singapore's longer term 'developmental' open door policy to FDI contrasted sharply for many years with the latecomer liberalisation of South Korea. However, moves towards greater harmonisation in neo-liberal policy approaches suggest that competition for investment is now more extensive and that the bargaining power is ever-more loaded in the favour of business (Stopford and Strange 1991).

However, this does not necessarily reduce the significance of the state, nor variations between states, in understanding the dynamic relations and frequently "murky firm–state nexus" in regulating, shaping and moulding patterns of investment or disinvestment (Phelps and Fuller 2000; Mackinnon and Phelps 2001a). While much attention has focused upon decentralisation of certain economic development roles to local and regional scales, these continue to be mediated by national modes of regulations ranging from policies on corporate governance and trade to labour market regulation (Macleod 2001). Recent case studies of attempts to stimulate FDI-led clusters and agglomerations in China (Yeung et al. 2006), South East Asia (Phelps 2008) and the UK (Phelps 2009) continue to reveal the integral role of state-level institutions and strategies in orchestrating their successes and failures.

Economic geography research has continued to explore the altered roles and capacities of nation-states in developing political and policy structures to promote and regulate the spatial strategies of TNCs' investment activities (Phelps and Waley 2004; Yeung 1998). After all, it remains the "complex, dynamic interactions between states and firms" that creates the context for 'regulatory arbitrage' within which TNCs play one state (and communities within them) off against another (Dicken 1998: 10). However, while states engage in regulatory arbitrage in the attraction of inward investment, they are at the same time relatively powerless to prevent companies attracted by national regulatory

environments emphasising deregulation and labour market flexibility from taking advantage of low exit costs to close or rationalise operations within host regions (Mackinnon and Phelps 2001a; Dawley 2007a). Thus, Dicken (2000: 284) suggests that the inter-firm, intra-firm, firm–place and place–place connections developed through processes of international economic integration are:

> fundamentally embedded within asymmetrical, multi-scalar power structures....Each of these sets of relationships is embedded within and across national/state political and regulatory systems which helps to determine the parameters within which firms and place interact.

Stark variations exist between national regulatory structures and FDI models. On the one hand, the US has developed a highly deregulated approach to competition for, and incentives given to, overseas TNCs (Phelps and Raines 2003). Similarly, until recently the UK's approach was typified as a "low cost to enter – low cost to exit" pro-business environment, which lacked a clear connection to an industrial, or even regional, policy (Mackinnon and Phelps 2001). Therefore, Loewendahl (2001: 219 cited in Phelps 2008) suggested that:

> UK industrial policy is based upon the ad hoc attraction of large-scale, job-creating inward investment to create short-term jobs in declining regions. There is no coherent strategy integrating sector targeting and economic development, at least at the central level, and government policy, has artificially dispersed foreign companies, missing out on any clustering benefits.

For many decades UK regional policy used the dispersal of FDI as a vehicle to diversify the industrial profile of peripheral regions, leading to few positive economic impacts beyond direct employment (Phelps 2009). Where FDI-based clustering – or sectoral grouping – did occur within the UK, for example, the 'Silicon Glenn' electronics corridor in Scotland, linkages remained truncated, few knowledge spill-overs were generated and labour poaching reflected a lack of a coordinated approach (Turok 1997). Indeed, ultimately the fragility of the Silicon Glenn cluster, based almost entirely dependent on the FDI, was brutally exposed in the early 2000s with a rapid and extensive spate of closures.

On the other hand, elements of the developmental state model prosecuted in certain East Asian nations, particularly Singapore, provide a significant counterpoint. In the immediate aftermath of independence, Singapore followed a necessarily indiscriminate approach to attracting FDI, driven by the need to stimulate large-scale employment. However, by the 1970s and 1980s the city-state's Economic Development Board pioneered the sectoral and functional targeting of FDI projects as part of an integrated industrial and cluster policy (Phelps 2009). Singapore's strength as a high-level business service centre continued to attract head office and R&D functions while low value-added functions were increasingly offshored, both organically and as part of a state-managed process to relocate TNC activities from the overheating economy. Initially, the Singaporean and Indonesian government coordinated the industrial development of the nearby Batam and Bintan islands to provide a low-cost hinterland. Subsequently, the Singaporean government deployed its power extraterritorially (i.e. beyond its sovereign territory) to establish and manage business parks in China, Vietnam and India – an expansion equivalent to 20 per cent of the industrial land in Singapore. Despite the gains from this programme being relatively modest – anchoring corporate functions in Singapore and internationalising domestic firms – larger benefits have accrued from attempts to embed FDI projects within

industrial clusters (see Phelps (2008) for a review of South East Asian clusters).

Within Europe, the liberalisation of the Central and Eastern European (CEE) economies as part of the transition process (Bradshaw and Swain 2004) led to striking rates of growth in the receipt of FDI in the 1990s. By 1998, CEE economies received one-tenth of all European inward investment flows, growing at a rate which outstripped FDI to the developing world (Raines 2003; Helinska-Hughes and Hughes 2003). Much of the growth in FDI was concentrated in Poland, Czech Republic and Hungary and focused primarily on manufacturing investments, especially from the US and other EU states. Following an initial impetus by TNCs to 'cherry pick' as part of the privatisation process, inward investment and FDI promotion has developed through a more sophisticated set of national institutional structures. Each of the first wave transition states developing – with EU PHARE support – inward investment promotion agencies (e.g. CzechInvest; PAIZ – Poland Inward Investment Agency) and sophisticated portfolios of inward investment incentives. While many of the state-level incentives structures have been phased out as part of the harmonisation of accession into the EU, within Poland, legacies of the incentivised structures continue to be used across 15 Special Economic Zones (*inter alia* tax exemptions, land and property assistance, etc.). While Poland has attracted considerable cost-sensitive manufacturing FDI, often relocated from former inward investment heartlands in the UK and Ireland, it has also become a location for product development and shared services centres, with FDI concentrating in regions with high levels of human capital and technological infrastructures (Raines 2003; OECD 2008). Within Krakow, for example, the Special Economic Zone programme developed a series of Technology Parks which have attracted TNC R&D investment from companies such as Motorola, IBM, Google and Delphi. In the case of Motorola, its decision to locate a software development centre in Krakow in 1998 followed the instigation of a 'locational tournament' across Central and Eastern Europe. Indicative of a qualitative shift in the nature of FDI attracted to Poland, a key driver for Motorola's investment was the ready availability of human capital. Krakow offers the second largest concentration of university students within Poland and a long history of university-based R&D within computer sciences. In addition, the relative wage levels within Poland coupled with the site and infrastructure support available within the Special Economic Zone programme also made Poland a low-cost, high-quality location relative to other European states (Motorola Plant Director, author's interview 2009). Yet the recent success of Krakow in attracting additional FDI in allied software development (e.g. Google, IBM, etc.) has raised a number of issues as to the sustainability of its low-cost profile as competition for the recruitment and retention of skills heightens. However, while the embeddedness of Motorola's investment remains limited to local training and education linkages and market access, the US TNC has instigated several rounds of reinvestment and has expanded to employ over 600 staff across two sites.

Local and regional institutions and TNCs

The themes developed within this chapter have served to restate the relative and differential powers of TNCs and nation-states in analysing the prospects for regions in attracting and embedding exogenous resources. The chapter has examined the power and causal role of the firm and explored a number of current corporate dynamics which shape the uneven geographical expression of (dis)investment. The chapter then examined the ways in which the investment strategies of corporation continue to be moulded and embedded by the enduring interrelations

between TNCs and national institutional contexts. Together, these perspectives illustrate the importance of adopting a geographical political economy approach to TNCs and regional development and as a result illustrate the importance of not losing sight of theoretical, empirical and policy lessons developed within the traditional literature on TNCs, FDI and local and regional development – reviewed at the outset of this chapter. Drawing on the preceding discussions, this final section of the chapter concludes with an examination of the changing roles, prospects and challenges facing regional-level institutions in their ongoing relations with TNCs.

In an attempt to 'globalise' regional development, Coe et al. (2004) restate the importance of local and regional institutional agency and capacity in promoting and negotiating issues of power and control with focal firms in global production networks. Within a global context of geo-economic deregulation and mobile capital, 'regional institutions' (including non-local institutions with regional influence) have an important role to play in promoting and coupling 'regional assets' with the strategic needs of focal firms within global production networks (ibid. Amin and Thrift 1994). Again, considerable attention has focused upon the roles and efficacy of local and regional institutions in both seducing 'flagship' FDI projects and embedding TNC investment within host economies within the existing research focused upon FDI and regional development (Mackinnon and Phelps 2001a; Phelps and Fuller 2000; Amin et al. 1994). Important insights for the GPN approach can be derived from this literature, especially in terms of developing proposals suitable for adoption within the policy community.

Within the UK, the neoliberal orthodoxy implemented during the 1980s and early 1990s created a highly competitive and ultimately wasteful environment within which regional agencies effectively competed against each other as 'hostile brothers' to seduce mobile investment. Even so, regions and nations such as the North East and Wales developed successful repertoires of rapid 'one-stop shop' multi-agency and multi-scalar institutional responses, referred to as Taskforces or coalitions, to delivering packages of assistance on sites, infrastructures, supply chain and labour market support for large-scale FDI projects. Crucially, the regional initiatives were necessarily mobilised under the guidance and funding support of the national agencies and government bodies. Over time regions began to move away from an indiscriminate attraction of FDI to an approach which increasingly targeted key sectors and corporate functions and a more explicit attempt to embed projects through 'aftercare' provision (Amin and Tomaney 1995). In part, this was driven by the pragmatism of a need to stimulate reinvestment in the face of flows of greenfield inward investment projects from the mid-1990s onwards. It also reflected attempts to mimic emerging best practice from institutions such as IDA Ireland with high-skilled FDI electronics investments driving the 'Celtic Tiger' (Amin *et al.* 1994). In addition to increasingly supporting the embedding of FDI projects, Raines (2003) indentifies two further shifts in inward investment promotion strategies around *differentiation* and *discrimination*. In terms of differentiation, agencies have increasingly focused upon promoting the distinctive 'regional assets' (in GPN parlance) such as sector, R&D or labour market strengths rather than more generic advantages. Discrimination builds upon the principles of differentiation, but emphasises the ways in which regions proactively 'target' specific projects or functions within sectors or sub-sectors to either upgrade or enhance existing strengths (see, for example, preferential rates in the UK former Regional Selective Assistance grants). Examples of differentiation and discrimination are clearly more readily applicable when part of a national sectoral and industrial programme, for example, the development

state models, especially Singapore. However, similar trends are occurring within regions of the UK. The North East of England has recently attempted to capture 'first mover' advantage in the offshore wind turbine power generation sector. Partially in the wake of the collapse of the former FDI-driven model of regional development pursued in the North East, the Regional Development Agency adopted a more balanced approach which sought to foster R&D strengths in areas including renewable energy – creating the UK's largest R&D and testing facility for offshore wind turbines. FDI is now being targeted to supplement the R&D activity but also to build outwards in the value chain into the mass production of the wind turbines – ironically reutilising the shipbuilding infrastructure that provides the regions industrial heritage. Built around a series of 'regional assets' (R&D; infrastructure; skills; market access) the North East's new targeted approach to FDI marks a stark contrast to its formerly indiscriminative approach built around low costs and institutional flexibility.

However, drawing on the geographical political economy approach adopted within this chapter, regions continue to be pitched into significant power asymmetries with TNCs across episodes of investment and disinvestment. This can be reflected in what Phelps (2008) terms the 'corporate capture' of land and infrastructure developments, skills and training support and more generally monopolise the efforts of regional institutions (Christopherson and Clark 2007; Lovering 2003). The most acute example of capture occurs when FDI projects are short-lived. In the case of the volatile Siemens Semiconductor investment in the North East of England examples existed of both labour and infrastructure capture. In terms of labour, the rapid 'ramp up' into production led to the recruitment of an 'off-the-shelf' skilled workforce, causing 'backfill' issues for employers within and beyond the region – with one in three high-skilled recruits drawn from outside the North East. In the aftermath of the shock closure of the plant, the limited absorptive capacity of the local labour market contributed to the majority of management and engineers leaving the region for new employment (Dawley 2007b). The labour market churn and limited 'regional capture' of the skills involved in this investment episode highlighted the ways in which TNCs internalise value from the host region (Phelps 2009). The challenge facing the region was further compounded by the limited power of regional – and national – institutions to capitalise on the relatively unique 'regional assets' of plant and infrastructural legacies. Siemens' ongoing ownership and overseas control of the mothballed plant meant numerous options to sell the plant to new investors were turned down, fuelling speculation that the company would not cede capacity to its rivals. Despite the efforts of national and regional institutions in securing a replacement investor, it took over two years before Siemens sold the plant, by which time much of the 'regional asset' of skills and experience of the previous round had dissolved. Therefore, if peripheral regions – already weakly positioned within intra-corporate spatial divisions of labour – are to respond to the shortening of FDI project life cycles then host economies require responsive policies to identify and integrate 'strategic couplings' between regional assets created by one round of investment and the strategic needs of future rounds of investment (Massey 1995; Coe *et al.* 2004). Few studies have examined the relative power of host regions to retain, reinvigorate or recycle the hard and soft infrastructural legacies of disinvesting TNCs. These questions raise further conceptual and policy-related challenges for research that explores the potential agency of localised points of resistance (local affiliates, institutions and communities) in moderating the powers and investment decisions of MNEs within host region economies (Phelps and Waley 2004; Coe *et al.* 2004).

References

Amin, A. and Thrift, N. (1994) 'Living in the global', in Amin, A. and Thrift, N. (eds) *Globalizaion, Institutions and Regional Development,* Oxford University Press, Oxford.

Amin, A. and Tomaney, J. (1995) 'The regional development potential of inward investment in the less favoured regions of the European Community', in Amin, A. and Tomaney, J. (eds) *Behind the Myth of European Union. Prospects for Cohesion,* Routledge, New York.

Amin, A., Bradley, D., Gentle, C., Howells, J., and Tomaney, J. (1994) 'Regional incentives and the quality of mobile investment in the less favoured regions of the EC', *Progress in Planning,* 41: 1–112.

Ashcroft, B. and Love, J. (1989) 'Evaluating the effects of external takeover on the performance of regional companies: the case of Scotland, 1965 to 1980', *Environment and Planning* A, 21 (2): 197–220.

Bathelt, H. and Gertler, M.S. (2005) 'The German variety of capitalism: forces and dynamics of evolutionary change', *Economic Geography,* 81: 1–9.

BBC News (2007) 'Q+A: Tata takeover of Corus', 31 January, http://news.bbc.co.uk.

Birkinshaw, J. (1999) 'Multinational corporate strategy and organisation: an internal market perspective', in Hood, N. and Young, S. *The Globalisation of Multinational Enterprise Activity and Economic Development,* (eds), Oxford University Press: Oxford.

Birkinshaw, J. and Hood, N. (1998) 'Multinational subsidiary evolution: capability and charter change in foreign-owned subsidiary companies', *Academy of Management Review,* 23: 773–795.

Bluestone, B. and Harrison, B. (1982) *The Deindustrialisation of America: Plant Closings, Community Abandonment and the Dismantling of Basic Industry,* Basic Books, New York.

Bradshaw, M. and Swain, A. (2004) 'Foreign investment and regional development', *in* Bradshaw, M. and Stenning, A, (eds) *East Central Europe and the Former Soviet Union: The Post-socialist States.* Pearson Education, Harlow.

Bryson, J. and Henry, N. (2005) 'The global production system: from Fordism to post-Fordism', in Daniels, P. *et al.* (eds) *Human Geography: Issues for the 21st Century,* Prentice Hall, Harlow. Second Edition.

Chapman, K. (2005) 'From "growth centre" to "cluster": restructuring, regional development, and the Teeside chemical industry.' *Environment and Planning A,* 37: 597–615.

Christopherson, S. and Clark, J. (2007) *Remaking Regional Economies: Power, Labor, and Firm Strategies in the Knowledge Economy*, Routledge, New York.

Clark, G. L. (1994) 'Strategy and structure: corporate restructuring and the scope and characteristics of sunk costs', *Environment and Planning A*, 26: 9–32.

Coe, N. M., Kelly, P. F. and Yeung, H-W. (eds) (2007) *Economic Geography: A Contemporary Introduction*, Blackwell, Oxford.

Coe, N. M., Hess. M., Yeung, H. W-C., Dicken, P. and Henderson, J. (2004) '"Globalising" regional development: a global production networks perspective', *Transactions of Institute of British Geographers*, NS, 29: 468–484.

Cooke, P. and Morgan, K. (1998) *The Associational Economy: Firms, Regions and Innovation*, Oxford University Press, Oxford.

Corus, (2002) *Frequently Asked Questions: Aluminium Businesses Disposal*,18 March, www.corusgroup.com

Crotty, J.(2003) 'Core industries, coercive competition and the structural contradictions of global neoliberalism', in Phelps, N.A. and Raines, P. *The New Competition for Inward Investment: Companies, Institutions and Territorial Development*, eds. Edward Elgar, Cheltenham.

Dawley, S. (2007a) 'Fluctuating rounds of inward investment in peripheral regions: semiconductors in the North East of England', *Economic Geography*, 83(1): 51–73.

Dawley, S. (2007b) 'Making labour market geographies: volatile "flagship" inward investment and peripheral regions', *Environment and Planning A*, 39 (6): 1403–1419.

Dawley, S., Stenning, A. and Pike, A. (2008) 'Recasting steel geographies: mapping corporations, connecting communities', *European Urban and Regional Studies*, 15 (3): 281–303.

De Propris, L. and Driffield, N. (2006) 'The importance of cluster for spillover from FDI and technology sourcing', *Cambridge Journal of Economics*, 30 (2).

Dicken, P. (1976) 'The multi-plant enterprise and geographic space', *Regional Studies*, 10 (4): 401–412.

Dicken, P. (1998) *Global Shift*, Paul Chapman: London, Third Edition.

Dicken, P. (2000) 'Places and flows: situating international investment' , in Clark, G. L. Feldman, M. P. and Gertler, M.S. *The Oxford Handbook of Economic Geography*. (eds) Oxford University Press, Oxford.

Dicken, P. (2003) '"Placing" firms: grounding the debate on the "global" corporation', in Peck, J. and Yeung, H. W-C. (eds) *Remaking the Global Economy: Economic-Geographical Perspective*. Sage Publications: London.

Dicken, P. (2007) *Global Shift*. Paul Chapman, London. Fourth Edition.

Dicken, P. and Malmberg, A. (2001) 'Firms in territories: a relational perspective', *Economic Geography*, 77: 345–363.

Dicken, P. and Thrift, N. (1992) 'The organisation of production and the production of organisation: why business enterprises matter in the study of geographical industrialisation', *Transactions of the Institute of British Geographers*, 17: 279–291.

Dunning, J. H. and Lundan, S. M, (2008) *Multinational Enterprises and the Global Economy*, Edward Elgar, Cheltenham, Second Edition

Egeraat, C. van and Jacobson, D. (2005) 'Geography of production linkages in the Irish and Scottish microcomputer industry: the role of logistics', *Economic Geography*, 81: 283–304.

Fairbrother, P., Stroud, D. and Coffey, A. (2004) *The Internationalisation of the World Steel Industry*, Working Paper 53, Cardiff University, School of Social Sciences, Cardiff.

Financial Times (2003) 'Observer: paper talk for varin', *Financial Times* (29 April).Accessed on 4 March 2008 at: http://search.ft.com/ftArticle?queryText=papertalkforvarin&aje=true&id=030429000577&ct=0.

Firn, J. (1975) 'External control and regional development the case of Scotland', *Environment and Planning A*, 7 (4): 393–414.

Florida, R. and Kenney. M. (1992) 'Restructuring in place: Japanese investment, production organization and the restructuring of steel,' *Economic Geography* (April): 146–173.

Gertler, M. (2001) 'Best practice? Geography, learning and the institutional limits to strong convergence', *Journal of Economic Geography*, 1: 5–26.

Helsinka-Hughes, E. and Hughes, M. (2003) 'Joining the competition: Central and European challenge to established FDI destinations' in Phelps, N. A. and Raines, P. (eds). *The New Competition for Inward Investment: Companies, Institutions and Territorial Development*, Edward Elgar, Cheltenham.

Hess, M. and Yeung, H.W-C. (2006) 'Whither global production networks in economic geography? Past, present and future', *Environment and Planning A*, 38: 1193–1204.

Hudson R. (1995) 'The role of inward investment', in Evans, R. *et al.* (eds) *The Northern Region Economy*, Routledge, London.

Hudson, R. (2000) *Production, Places and Environment: Changing Perspectives in Economic Geography*, Harlow, Prentice Hall.

Jessop, B. (1999) 'Reflections on globalisation and its (il)logics', in Olds, K. Dicken, P. Kelly, P. Kong, L. and Yeung, H. (eds) *Globalisation and the Asia- Pacific: Contested territories*, Routledge: London.

Kentucky Cabinet for Economic Development (October 2009) Available at: www.thinkkentucky.com/kyedc/pdfs/ky_auto_industry.pdf (accessed 16 June 2010).

Loewendahl, H. B. (2000) *Bargaining with Multinationals: The Investment of Siemens and Nissan in North-East England,* Ph.D. Thesis, University of Birmingham.

Lovering, J. (2003) 'MNCs and wannabes – inward investment, discourses of regional development, and the regional service class', in (eds) Phelps, N.A. and Raines, P. *The New Competition for Inward Investment: Companies, Institutions and Territorial Development*, Edward Elgar, Cheltenham.

MacKinnon, D. and Phelps, N.A. (2001a) 'Devolution and the territorial politics of foreign direct investment', *Political Geography*, 20: 353–379.

MacKinnon, D. and Phelps, N. A. (2001b) 'Regional governance and foreign direct investment: the dynamics of institutional change in Wales and North East England', *Geoforum*, 32: 255–269.

Macleod, G. (2001) 'Beyond soft institutionalism: accumulation, regulation and their geographical fixes', *Environment and Planning A*, 33: 1145–1167.

Markusen, A. (1994) 'Studying regions by studying firms', *Professional Geographer*, 46: 477–490.

Massey, D. (1995) *Spatial Divisions of Labour: Social Structures and the Geography of Production*, Macmillan. Basingstoke, Second Edition.

Mytelka, L. K. (2000) 'Locational tournaments for FDI: inward investment into Europe in a Global World', in Hood, N. and Young, S. (eds) *The Globalisation of Multinational Enterprise Activity and Economic Development*, Macmillan Press: Basingstoke.

OECD (2004) OECD *Territorial Reviews: Poland 2008,* OECD Publishing, Paris.

O'Neill, P. (2003) 'Where is the corporation in the geographical world?', *Progress in Human Geography*, 27: 677–680.

Pauly, L. W. and Reich, S. (1997) 'National structures and multinational corporate behaviour: enduring differences in the age of globalisation', *International Organisation*, 51: 1–30.

Peck, F. and Stone I. (1993) 'Japanese inward investment in the Northeast of England: reassessing "Japanisation"', *Environment and Planning C*, 11, 55–67.

Peck, J., and Yeung, H.W-C. (eds) (2003) *Remaking the Global Economy: Economic-Geographical Perspectives*, Sage: London.

Phelps N. A. (2008) 'Cluster or capture? Manufacturing FDI, external economies and agglomeration', *Regional Studies*, 42 (4): 457–473.

Phelps, N. A. (2009) 'From branch plant economies to knowledge economies? Manufacturing industry, government policy, and economic development in Britain's old industrial region', *Environment and Planning C: Government and Policy*, 27: 574–592.

Phelps, N.A. and Fuller, C. (2000) 'Multinationals, intracorporate competition and regional development', *Economic Geography*, 76: 224–243.

Phelps, N.A. and Raines, P. (2003) Introduction, in Phelps, N.A. and Raines, P. (eds) *The New Competition for Inward Investment: Companies, Institutions and Territorial Development*, Edward Elgar, Cheltenham.

Phelps, N.A. and Waley, P. (2004) 'Capital versus the districts: a tale of one multinational company's attempt to disembed itself', *Economic Geography*, 80: 191–215.

Phelps, N.A. and Wood, A. (2006) 'Lost in translation? Local interests, global actors and the multi-scalar dynamics of inward investment', *Journal of Economic Geography*, 6 (4): 493–515.

Phelps, N.A., MacKinnon, D., Stone, I. and Braidford, P. (2003) 'Embedding the multinationals? Institutions and the development of overseas manufacturing affiliates in Wales and North East England', *Regional Studies*, 37: 27–40.

Pike, A. (1998) 'Making performance plants from branch plants? In-situ restructuring in the automobile industry in the UK region', *Environment and Planning A*, 30: 881–900.

Pike, A. (1999) 'The politics of factory closures and task forces in the North East region of England', *Regional Studies*, 33 (6): 567–575.

Pike, A. (2001a) 'Reflections on the task force model in economic development', *Local Economy*, 16 (2): 87–102.

Pike, A. (2002) 'Task forces and the organisation of economic development: the case of the North East region of England', *Environment and Planning C*, 20: 717–739.

Pike, A. (2005) 'Building a political economy of closure: the case of R&DCo in North East England', *Antipode*, 37: 93–115.

Pike, A. (2006) "Shareholder value" versus the regions: the closure of the Vaux Brewery in Sunderland, *Journal of Economic Geography*, 6: 201–222.

Pike, A. Rodriguez-Pose. A. and Tomaney, J. (2006) *Local and Regional Development*, Routledge, London.

Raines, P. (2003) 'Flows and territories: the new geography of competition for mobile investment in Europe', in Phelps, N.A. and Raines, P. (eds) *The New Competition for Inward Investment: Companies, Institutions and Territorial Development*, 119–137, Edward Elgar, Cheltenham.

Sadler, D. (1992) *The Global Region: Production, State Policies and Uneven Development*, Pergamon Press, Oxford.

Sayer, A. (1985) 'Industry and space: a sympathetic critique of radical research,' *Society and Space*, 3: 3–30.

Sayer, A. (2000) *Realism and Social Science*, Sage, London.

Schiffere, S. (2007) 'The triumph of lean production', BBC News Website, http://news.bbc.co.uk/1/hi/business/6346315.stm (accessed: 16 June 2010).

Schoenberger, E. (1997) *The Cultural Crisis of the Firm*, Blackwell, Oxford.

Schoenberger, E. (2000) 'The management of time and space', in Clark. G.L. Feldman, M.P. and Gertler, (eds) *The Oxford Handbook of Economic Geography*, Oxford University Press, Oxford.

Stalk, G.R. and Hout, T. (1990) *Competing Against Time: How Time-based Competition is Reshaping Global Markets*, The Free Press, New York.

Stopford, J.M. and Strange, S. (1991) *Rival States, Rival Firms: Competition for World Market Shares*, Cambridge University Press, Cambridge.

Sunley, P. (1991) 'Game theories? Spatial divisions of labour and rational choice Marxism', *Antipode*, 23: 229–239.

Taylor, M. (1986) 'The product-cycle model: a critique', *Environment and Planning A*, 18: 751–761.

Turok, I. (1993) 'Inward investment and local linkages: how deeply embedded is Silicon Glen?', *Regional Studies*, 27: 401–417.

Turok, I. (1997) 'Linkages in the Scottish electronics industry: further evidence', *Regional Studies*, 31 (7): 705–711.

Vernon, R. (1966) 'International investment and international trade in the product cycle', *Quarterly Journal of Economics*, 80: 190–207.

Vernon, R. (1979) 'The product cycle in a new international environment', *Oxford Bulletin of Economics and Statistics*, 41: 255–267.

Watts, H.D. (1981) *The Branch Plant Economy*, Longman, London.

Walker, R. (1985) 'Technological determination and determinism: industrial growth and location', in Castells, M. (ed). *High Technology, Space, and Society*. Sage: Beverley Hills.

Williams, J. and Haslam, C. (1990) 'The hollowing out of British manufacturing and its implications for policy', *Economy and Society*, 19: 456–490.

Yeung, H.W-C. (1998) 'Capital, state and space: contesting the borderless world', *Transactions of the Institute of British Geographers*, 23: 291–309.

Yeung, H.W-C. (2000) 'Organising "the firm" in industrial geography I: networks, institutions and regional development', *Progress in Human Geography*, 24: 301–315.

Yeung, H.W-C. (2001) 'Regulating "the firm" and sociocultural practices in industrial geography II', *Progress in Human Geography*, 25: 293–302.

Yeung, H.W-C. (2003) 'Practising new economic geographies: a methodological examination', *Annals of Association of American Geographers*, 93: 442–462.

Yeung, H.W-C. (2005) 'Rethinking relational economic geography', *Transactions of Institute of British Geographers*, NS, 30: 37–51.

Yeung, H.W-C. (2006) *From Followers to Market Leaders: Asian Electronics Firms in the Global Economy*, Asia Pacific Viewpoint Lecture, the International Geographical Union Regional Congress, Brisbane, Australia, 3–7 July.

Yeung, H.W-C. (2009) 'Perspective review: transnational corporations, global production networks, and urban and regional development: a geographer's perspective on multinational enterprsie and the global economy', *Growth and Change*, 40 (2): 197–226.

Yeung, H.W-C., Liu, W. and Dicken, P. (2006) 'Transnational corporations and network effects of a local manufacturing cluster in moblile telecommunications equipment in China', *World Development*, 34 (3): 520–540.

Yeung, H. and Peck, J. (2003) 'Making global connections: a geographer's perspective', in Peck, J. and Yeung, H.W-C. (eds) *Remaking the Global Economy: Economic Geographical Perspectives*, Sage, London.

Young, S. Hood, N. and Peters, E. (1994) 'Multinational enterprises and regional economic development', *Regional Studies*, 28(7): 657–677.

34

Innovation networks and local and regional development policy

Mário Vale

Introduction

Localized innovation networks are related to the advantages of geographical agglomeration, in which spatial proximity facilitates the generation of externalities and localized learning processes critical to local and regional development. The role of agglomeration in the innovation networks is epitomized by notions of industrial district, cluster and milieu innovateur. These territorial innovation models highlight the particular territorial conditions that promote localized knowledge generation and diffusion through networks of innovative firms, universities and other institutions.

However, there are arguments concerning the effectiveness of distant networks in the creation and diffusion of knowledge (Oinas, 2000; Boschma, 2005; Torre and Rallet, 2005) as a result of the increasing use of ICT and lower transport costs that enable the effective operation of powerful communities of practice (e.g. engineers, entrepreneurs, computer experts, etc.) across space. Distant networking has been crucial for producing new knowledge and innovation. Production networks are often multi-scalar, ranging from local to global and the other way around (Dicken and Malmberg, 2001). Therefore, we

may ask if non-geographically bounded innovation networks imply different local and regional policies.

On the other hand, the absence of a clear understanding of different types of knowledge enrolled in the innovation process has been a constraint to design adequate innovation regional policies. According to Asheim and Gertler (2005), certain types of knowledge travel more easily across space than others. In fact, analytical knowledge type (know why) is essential codified knowledge, highly abstract and universal and to a certain extent less sensitive to spatial context when compared with synthetic (know how) and symbolic (know who) types that travel less easily because tacit knowledge is more relevant (especially on the symbolic type) and as a result both show certain levels of discrepancy between places. Considering that sectoral differences are related with distinct knowledge types it is quite clear that policy response needs to address these differences and respond effectively to firms and institution needs.

Current perspectives on regional innovation systems (Cooke, 1992; Cooke and Morgan, 1998) became the benchmark for innovation policy at regional level in a way complementary to the cluster approach. Both perspectives identify geographical proximity as a key element on the innovation process at regional level. The regional innovation system (RIS) perspective has been very influential in the policy design of important organizations such as the OECD and the European Commission.

The EU innovation policy is based on the RIS and therefore addresses the knowledge transfer university-firm, IPR, training, local and regional partnerships and alliances, as well as traditional mechanisms centred on incentives systems, venture capital, etc. Nevertheless, we argue that local and regional policy has to focus on local-distant networking and encompass different actions on knowledge 'pipelines' (Bathelt *et al.*, 2004), knowledge mobility and anchoring, and institutional development, which have to be coherent with the dominant knowledge types of each innovation network.

This chapter discusses precisely the adequacy of local and regional development policies to support innovation networks at regional level considering the globalizing economic world and the easier access to certain knowledge types, questioning the cluster-type policy orientation and the limitations of Regional Innovation Systems policy instruments. First, we review theoretical debate about the role of space in knowledge creation and why and how firms combine local and distant knowledge sources considering the implications of the global economy and the knowledge creation processes to localized innovation networks. Second, we examine the local and regional policy-relevant literature concerning knowledge and innovation in the region emphasizing the cluster and RIS policy orientations. Finally, we point out new directions to regional knowledge dynamics and innovation in multi-scalar spaces of innovation networks.

Space, knowledge and innovation networks

Innovation is a key element on the regional economic development. It is also a social process in the sense that it relates to capital, labour and the state, whose actors' interactions are precisely the basis of geographical inequality (MacKinnon *et al.*, 2009). Therefore, innovation isn't immune to capital accumulation dynamics, labour relations and institutions. Knowledge is a fundamental input to innovation and regional economic growth. Knowledge and innovation have a determinant role on the introduction of new products to the market, new production processes and organizational practices that are critical to the competitive advantage of firms and regions (Feldman and Stewart, 2006). However, the innovation network is perhaps the most relevant element to understand the innovation dynamics in a region:

> innovation is an emergent process based on gradually introduction interactions that link agents, knowledge, and goods that were previously unconnected, and that are slowly put in a relationship of interdependence: the network, in its formal dimension, is a powerful tool for making these connections.
> (Amin and Cohendet, 2004: 153)

Hence, the localized innovation systems have captured the attention of economists, geographers and regional scientists where proximity and relatedness of agents have been considered essential to understand their success. The industrial district (Bagnasco, 1977; Becattini, 1987), clusters (Porter, 1990, 1998) and milieu innovateur (Aydalot, 1986; Camagni, 1991) approaches illustrate the role of the industrial agglomeration and the innovation networks in localized systems. These theoretical underpinnings highlight the particular territorial conditions that promote localized knowledge generation and diffusion through networks of innovative firms, universities and other institutions (Antonelli, 1999; Cooke, 1996; Peck, 2003; Moulaert and Sekia, 2003; Amin and Cohendet, 2004). Although there are relevant differences among these theories of localized innovation, one can identify a common claim of prominence of tacit knowledge and localized learning. This particular type of knowledge and the intense local learning process cannot exist beyond the agglomeration of economic activities and institutions even in a globalized era:

> What is not eroded, however, is the non-tradable/non-codified result of knowledge creation – the embedded tacit knowledge – that at a given time can only be produced and reproduced in practice. The fundamental exchange inability of tacit knowledge increases its importance as the globalization of business markets proceeds. [...] the more easily codified (tradable) knowledge is accessed by everyone, the more crucial does tacit knowledge become in sustaining or enhancing the competitive position of the firm.
>
> (Maskell and Malmberg, 1999: 16)

Precisely, the cluster approach illustrates the relevance of spatial proximity to firms' competitiveness, as well as the organizational and productive structures that are essential to the cluster performance (Porter, 1998). Although social relations do not appear to be relevant in the theory, the innovation processes show intense local networking at least in the cases of high technology clusters, like Route 128 and Silicon Valley (Saxenian, 1991), involving suppliers and customers, all playing a crucial role in new ideas and technology development. Furthermore, highly specialized workers pool and local institutions favour knowledge generation and innovation dynamics in the cluster (Glasmeier, 1988).

The Marshallian industrial district generates localized knowledge that relies on the social relations, local labour market mobility and the local and regional institutions and, in this sense, the innovative agglomeration is a socio-territorial entity which is composed by a community of individuals and a set of firms both interrelated (Becattini, 1987).

Social capital, trust and local actors' networks are the foundations of the industrial district, where untraded knowledge flows stimulate collective learning processes. The benefits for the local producers arise from the localized externalities which constitute a common good to entrepreneurs, like the existence of local labour market skills and competences that evolved largely based on localized learning processes. The collaboration and cooperation among local actors is another specific element of the industrial district organization, as well as the relative high number of spin-offs that consolidate the local innovative agglomeration capabilities.

More important than innovative isolated firms is the local network of actors and institutions to support knowledge creation and use and localized learning processes that are critical to the agglomeration as a whole. This is quite evident on the GREMI's innovative milieu perspective where firms benefit from strong institutions' interaction to provide the right infrastructure and especially the adequate environment to sustain collective learning processes and the reduction of firms' risk and uncertainty (always inherent to an innovation process) (Camagni, 1991). The geographical outcome is a mosaic of competing and differentiated innovative regions with poor inter-regional mobility of knowledge since its generation and use is context specific and developed through localized social interactions (Crevoisier and Jeannerat, 2009).

Recently, the spatial proximity role on the knowledge and dynamics innovation has been contested by several authors that claim substantial changes occurred on the process of how firms and regions develop their knowledge and innovation strategies. Hence, arguments concerning the effectiveness of distant networks in the creation and diffusion of knowledge have been put forward (Amin and Cohendet, 2004; Boschma, 2005; Torre and Rallet, 2005). There are three reasons commonly stated to sustain the claim. The first one refers to the increasing use of ICT and lower transport costs that allow for the increasing mobility of capital and people and the effective operation of powerful communities of practice (e.g. engineers, entrepreneurs, computer experts, etc.) across space. Second, the growing importance of knowledge in the creation of economic value compels firms and institutions to seek outside their limits relevant knowledge to generate innovation and strengthen competitive advantage in the international and national markets, especially because innovation processes are increasingly more complex (Feldman and Stewart, 2006). Third, socio-cultural dynamics become more central in innovation and therefore interactions between firms and customers are more important (Grabher *et al.*, 2008) and consequently symbolic knowledge is required to produce and sell new products and services in several industries (and not only consumer-end industries).

These changes are not a clear sign of the dismissal of proximity learning processes, however. According to Morgan (2004), three reasons can be put forward against the dichotomy proximity vs. distant learning. First, the organizational and social learning has always been related with geographical proximity, since the latter operates through the former type of proximity. Second, distant networking hardly replaces trust, stability and richness of close relations – like face-to-face contacts. Third, the benefits of local buzz cannot be fully replaced by the professional communities of practice; otherwise the geography of innovation would be less spatially concentrated.

Although spatial proximity is extremely important to innovation networks, distant networking aiming at the production of new knowledge and innovation is emerging and allegedly "successful clusters are the ones that are able to build and maintain a variety of channels for low cost exchange of knowledge within relevant hot-spots around the globe" (Bathelt *et al.*, 2004: 33). The cluster external communication channels are called 'pipelines' and can take the form of different sorts of organizational arrangements, such

as strategic partnerships, communities of practice, projects, temporary clusters, etc. Examples of multi-local innovation systems range from more traditional industries – see Uzzi (1996) about the New York garment industry or Vale and Caldeira (2007 and 2008) on the footwear-fashion innovation networks – to creative industries (Scott, 2002; Grabher, 2002) and high technologies (Owen-Smith and Powell, 2004; Fontes, 2005). These local-distant networks are not confined only to Europe or North-America. In fact, North-South evidences on automobile industry related with flex-fuel technologies indicate knowledge networks irradiate from São Paulo (Brazil) and involve large system producers like Robert Bosch, Magneti Marelli and Delphi which develop further networks with OEMs, bio fuel producers, suppliers and research institutes (Van Winden *et al.*, forthcoming). On a different angle, Coe *et al.* (2003) refer to the transnational elite professionals from South-East Asia moving repeatedly around the globe through the East Asia–Vancouver/San Francisco corridor, thus articulating "South" and "North".

To a certain extent, distant networking does not go up against local relations; on the contrary it complements firms' local networks with distant relations, particularly in the initial stages of cluster formation, although distant networking may avoid lock-in effects on later stages (Bathelt *et al.*, 2004). As Mackinnon and Cumbers (2007) suggest, local buzz and global pipelines reflect the complementary rather than contradictory nature of localization and globalization processes. Therefore the argument illustrates a rather peculiar combination of local and non-local learning processes underlying both geographical and organizational proximities in the learning processes of cluster-based firms and institutions (Amin and Cohendet, 2004).

Thus the question is to know if distant networking may replace co-location, local buzz and tacitness of certain types of knowledge in the clusters (Storper and Venables, 2004). In other words, are the agglomeration advantages to local firms less relevant in a globalized and highly integrated economic world? Do vibrant local agglomeration with a proliferation of activities and events relevant to learning processes of actors in the cluster get replaced by more efficient distant networking to access new knowledge and increase firms competitiveness? Asheim and Gertler (2005) shed some light on these complex and rather arguable claims. According to the authors, the answer may be found on the type of knowledge that firms are generating and using to develop new products and services or to achieve innovative organizational processes. Therefore the adequate questioning is under what circumstances distant networking is likely to be more effective on firms' learning processes or on the contrary what may prevent these forms of distant learning?

According to Asheim and Gertler (2005), the three primary types of knowledge are analytical knowledge (know why), synthetic knowledge (know how) and symbolic knowledge (know who). The first one travels across space more easily than other types of knowledge since it is highly codified through IPR, published papers, etc. and it is relatively universal and available across regions and cities. Synthetic knowledge is about solving problems and is interactive learning oriented. Both codified and tacit knowledge are relevant to the firms and therefore it is more sensitive to space. The symbolic knowledge type is clearly an outcome of creative processes and for that reason it is very much place specific due to cultural and social-specific context that affects this type of knowledge creation. Hence, the types of knowledge may be related with sectoral knowledge bases, for instance, pharmaceuticals industry and analytical knowledge, mechanical engineering and synthetic knowledge and design and cultural production and symbolic knowledge. Precisely, Gertler (2008) shows that synthetic and symbolic forms of knowledge are less amenable to distant learning. Currently, the platform nature of new technologies – like

clean technology (Cooke, 2008) – illustrates the increasing significance of combinatorial knowledge which tends to merge analytical, synthetic and symbolic knowledge and thus goes beyond the classical sectoral cumulative knowledge nature.

To a certain extent it seems evident that proximity and distant networking are not opposing categories, as it is evident that the type of knowledge being mobilized affects the geographical spread of the firms and institutions networks. As innovation is a social process, learning is based on interaction of myriad actors, often in the same geographical bounded space (the cluster, the industrial district, the innovative milieu). However, production networks – and we may add knowledge networks – are often multi-scalar, ranging from local to global and the other way around (Dicken and Malmberg, 2001; Coe et al., 2004; Yeung, 2009), especially if different types of knowledge are being used to produce a new product or deliver a new service, allegedly giving rise to a multi-local production system through the articulation of different local production systems (Figure 34.1) (Crevoisier and Jeanneret, 2009).

Innovation and territorial development policies

In 2000, the Lisbon agenda aimed at a growth improvement through innovation, employment and social integration in the EU. Innovation policies were initially influenced by the linear innovation model principles but moved slowly to a more integrated approach. Accordingly, in the early 1990s the innovation policy stressed the RTD investment and expenditure, while currently it embraces start-up support, venture capital, technology transfer, etc.

At the same time, the territorial dimension of innovation policy has emerged in association with the regionalization process in Europe (Seravalli, 2009). The regional innovation system approach highlights the

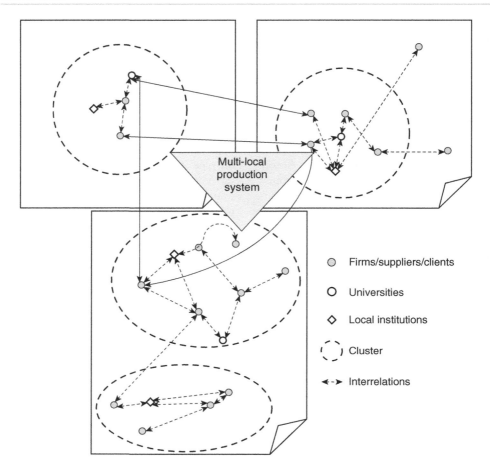

Figure 34.1 Emerging multi-local production systems.
Source: Based on Bathelt *et al.* (2004) and Crevoisier and Jeanneret (2009)

territorial innovation networks, in which firms' innovations depend on the "quality of 'home-base' institutions that act as a collective resource for both technological and non-technological innovation and learning" (Amin and Cohendet, 2004: 87). Accordingly institutional capacity of regions plays a central role in the innovation process, of which science and technology institutions, education and training organizations, entrepreneurial associations, and financial organizations (like venture capital) have been considered extremely relevant to regional innovation performance. The RIS approach

argues that collective learning is critical to stimulate innovation in the region, since it is an interactive and cumulative process in which firms play a central role in the system, though they depend on other regional institutions to exchange and exploit different kinds of knowledge (basic/applied, generic/specific, tacit/codified) (Tödtling and Kaufmann, 1999). Furthermore, knowledge dynamics and collective learning are path dependent, reflecting the past options and technological trajectories of regional agents to the present and future innovation outcomes (Krugman, 1991).

Among several RIS in Europe (Braczyk et al., 1998), the Welsh pioneer case stands as a good example in the EU. The restructuring process of Welsh economy was supported by the EU through the RITTS (Regional Innovation and Technology Transfer Strategy for the South Wales) and RTP (Regional Technology Plan) (Morgan, 1997). However, some criticisms of RIS can be found in the literature of regional development. In general, authors point out the limits of localized learning to the regional development process (Hudson, 1999), the tendency to give ex-post rationality to the regional innovation system policies (Lovering, 1999) and the bounded region concept which does not encapsulate the multi-local nature of knowledge dynamics.

Besides the RIS approach, cluster theory is another dominant policy framework on innovation and regional development. Actually, it has become a central component of regional development strategy in several EU countries, reflecting endogenous development aims in combination with innovative activities, often centred on high and medium-high technology firms and support institutions (Burfitt and Macneill, 2008). Cluster policy has been a major policy framework to promote innovation in the regions (Martin and Sunley, 2003) and eventually became a dominant paradigm to which regional authorities cannot escape since Porter's (1990) seminal work. Although it is not a straightforward concept, the cluster stresses the role of firms networking to generate and disseminate innovation in the regions and therefore "cluster policy emerged as a prominent economic development approach in numerous regions in Europe and beyond" (Burfitt and Macneill, 2008: 493).

Clusters include clients, suppliers, support industries, associated institutions and also competitors in a particular economic activity. These spatial agglomerations of related industries have been considered central to improve competitiveness of firms, regions and even nations due to transaction cost advantages and specialized inputs and their potential to generate dynamic learning effects through knowledge spill-overs, spin-offs, and higher rates of firm formation which have obvious benefits for the regional economies (Tödtling, 1999; Burfitt and Macneill, 2008). However, cluster policies have been in many ways vague and did not generate real positive effects in the regional economy. One of the reasons for this outcome results from a certain conceptual misunderstanding related to types, processes and spatial scale (Martin and Sunley, 2003). Moreover, the conceptual issues obstruct clear and realistic cluster policies and strategies formulation. In fact, this imprecision "generates arbitrary outcomes as policymakers struggle with imprecision and ambiguity at various stages of cluster policy development" (Burfitt and Macneill, 2008: 495).

Difficulties start early on with cluster selection and delimitation. As a matter of fact there is no metrics or rigorous NACE code-based analysis to identify a cluster (Martin and Sunley, 2003). Complications continue with the actors and organizations identification and/or new institutions formation that operate as active changing agents in the cluster and may design and implement new policies at cluster level (Cumbers and Mackinnon, 2004). Often an existing cluster's actors tend to be supported leaving behind emergent actors in the cluster.

Although cluster policies may be positive in specific cases, there is a risk of considering the approach as a solution for regional economic development. The lack of firm cooperation, the dominance of certain actors or firms, the limited institutional autonomy are constraints to cluster policy implementation which are not always considered by unwary policymakers (Burfitt and Macneill, 2008). Moreover, cluster policy strengthens local relations among the cluster actors which have been considered fundamental to promote innovation in the regional economy and quite often doesn't address properly the distant relations and global economic integration.

Hence, we discuss in the next section some critical policy orientations to promote innovation networks and regional development.

Local and distant innovation networks and regional development policies

In this section we point out some new directions to regional development policies in multi-scalar and multi-local spaces of innovation networks. Innovation systems approach has encapsulated a large part of the concepts discussed above. However, we claim that changing economic environment, producer–consumer relations and local and distant interrelations demand new policy orientations. The types of knowledge and its generation and use are much differentiated among regions and sectors. Knowledge dynamics have become more and more dependent on actors' interactions, whether they are firms, enabling organizations, clients or suppliers, and consequently knowledge networks have evolved at an extraordinary rate, changing the regional innovation models and entailing new policy orientations.

Recently, in the context of the Barca Report (2009), Farole et al. (2009) distinguish region competences at European level and point out some directions to different region types. According to the authors, innovation policies via the Lisbon agenda are better suited to core regions and regions adjacent to the European core that are on or near the technology frontier and where agglomeration forces make a difference. However, the 'picking winners' policy risks forgetting other regions and hampering their participation in the knowledge economy (Asheim et al., 2007). These regions also have available resources that may be useful to economic development through adequate policy action. The different regional capabilities ask for specific innovation policies although this doesn't imply necessarily 'uniqueness' policies,

especially in the cases of least developed regions where innovation and learning may benefit from the adoption of technologies from elsewhere (Lagendijk, 1999). Nevertheless, economic growth increasingly depends on the region innovation networks and its ability to reach distant innovative places and establish durable relations with other actors. The distant relations may support knowledge inflow in the region but in order to generate collective benefits it is necessary to anchor new knowledge in the region (Tödtling, 1999). Anchoring entails the local contextualization of new knowledge and learning through the local interdependencies of firms and institutions (Crevoisier and Jeannerat, 2009). Put simply, knowledge base, firms' networks and institutions are the starting point to design an adequate and consistent regional innovation strategy and policy.

Copying 'best practices' and successful models from elsewhere has often limited outcomes and too often drains important public resources, as can be illustrated by many science and technology parks or elusive cluster-building strategies, particularly in peripheral regions. Moreover, most successful examples are based on localized non-transferable regional assets that simply cannot be dislocated, as it is the example of localized untraded interdependencies (Storper, 1995). On the contrary, regional policy based on related variety may be more effective in developing innovative activities related to existing sectors, encouraging knowledge spill-overs (Asheim et al., 2007). Hence, innovation networks may well combine local and non-local knowledge to reinforce innovation dynamics via increasing variety (even if some less competitive firms are destroyed throughout the process) (Boschma and Frenken, 2006).

The authors infer that spin-offs may be more enduring than other new entrants in the regional economy since this type of innovative firm will build upon existing regional knowledge and therefore may well foster the regional innovation networks. Labour mobility across sectors and firms in the regions is another crucial area of regional policy, because knowledge circulation and collective learning depend heavily on skills transfer between sectors and firms (Antonelli, 1999). Although regional assets are a basis to design an adequate regional development policy, a solely regionally bounded perspective has limitations (Pike, 2007). As mentioned above, knowledge circulation through distant innovation networks has strong benefits for the regional economy when there is a regional anchoring capacity to absorb and use collectively new knowledge acquired elsewhere. The related variety policy approach has necessarily to encompass this type of concern and avoid innovation policies based exclusively on the region itself.

Cooke (2008) has suggested that a policy platform approach might overcome traditional limitations of sectoral and cluster innovation policies and include the related variety and long distant innovation networks concerns. According to Asheim *et al.* (2007: 24–25), the platform approach "represents a strategy based on related variety, which is defined on the basis of shared and complementary knowledge bases and competences". Policy response should promote those activities that may benefit from the local and regional skills and competences where cognitive proximity between existing and emerging activities may benefit the region's economic development. External knowledge sources connections, particularly specific knowledge sources, may be positive for local firms and the region may even benefit from knowledge spill-overs and thus reinforce innovation networks in the region. As Asheim *et al.* (2007) mentioned in a recent paper, "constructing regional advantage" requires a new perspective on regional policy in which regional actors should build external networks to access new critical knowledge to foster a region's related variety and increase

the combinatorial and complementary knowledge (keeping in mind the differentiated spatial friction upon the mobility of different knowledge types).

Typically, the platform policy approach is not immune to risks and even failure. The regional knowledge anchoring capacity is essential to avoid the hollowing out of localized knowledge systems. Obviously we refer to the process of local and regional competences and skills draining by the "pipeline" due to the usually strong attraction of external innovative agglomerations or as the result of uneven relations between local and external actors, although we cannot ignore power relations in inter-firm interdependencies even at regional level (Christopherson and Clark, 2007). Innovation's goal is to promote local and regional economic development; consequently knowledge connections require an integrated public policy because innovation networks are about both flows and agglomerations, meaning that both accessing and anchoring knowledge processes are critical to the regions' innovation dynamics. Regional success is closely related to local institutions' ability to articulate capital, labour and state interrelations within a local–distant interplay, but also with their capacity to disseminate knowledge in the region and ensure that benefits from knowledge inflow disseminate among actors to achieve collective gains at regional level.

Acknowledgements

The author wishes to acknowledge the support of the Integrated Project EURODITE – Regional Trajectories to the Knowledge Economy: A Dynamic Model, FP6 Contract No. 006187 (CIT3), sponsored by the European Union, as well as project members for their valuable contributions. The author is grateful to the editors of this book for the helpful comments on the original draft. Nonetheless, the usual disclaimers apply.

References

Amin, A. and Cohendet, P. (2004) *Architectures of Knowledge. Companies, Capabilities, and Communities*, Oxford: Oxford University Press.

Antonelli, C. (1999) "The evolution of the industrial organisation of the production of knowledge", *Cambridge Journal of Economics*, 23: 243–260.

Asheim, B. and Gertler, M. (2005) "The geography of innovation: regional innovation systems", in Fagerberg, J., Mowery, D. and Nelson, R. (eds) *The Oxford Handbook of Innovation*, Oxford: Oxford University Press.

Asheim, B., Boschma, R. and Cooke, P. (2007) "Constructing regional advantage: platform policies based on related variety and differentiated knowledge bases", *Papers in Evolutionary Economic Geography*, 0709, University of Utrecht.

Aydalot, P. (1986) *Milieux Innovateurs en Europe*, Paris: GREMI.

Bagnasco, A. (1977) *Tre Italie. La Problematica Territoriale dello Sviluppo Italiano*, Bologna: Il Mulino.

Barca, F. (2009) *An Agenda for a Reformed Cohesion Policy. A Place-based Approach to Meeting European Union Challenges and Expectations*, Brussels: European Commission.

Bathelt, H., Malmberg, A. and Maskell, P. (2004) "Clusters and knowledge: local buzz, global pipelines and the process of knowledge creation", *Progress in Human Geography*, 28 (1): 31–56.

Becattini, G. (1987) *Mercato e Forze Locali: il Distretto Industriale*, Bologna: Il Mulino.

Boschma, R. (2005) "Proximity and innovation: a critical assessment", *Regional Studies*, 39 (1): 61–74.

Boschma, R. and Frenken, K. (2006) "Why is economic geography not an evolutionary science? Towards an evolutionary economic geography", *Journal of Economic Geography*, 6 (3): 273–302.

Braczyk, H.-J., Cooke, P. and Heidenreich, M. (1998) *Regional Innovation Systems. The Role of Governances in a Globalized World*, London: UCL Press.

Burfitt, A. and Macneill, S. (2008) "The challenges of pursuing cluster policy in the congested state", *International Journal of Urban and Regional Research*, 32 (2): 492–505.

Camagni, R. (ed.) (1991) *Innovation Networks. Spatial Perspectives*, London: GREMI-Belhaven Press.

Christopherson, S. and Clark, J. (2007) *Remaking Regional Economies. Power, Labor, and Firm Strategies in the Knowledge Economy*, London: Routledge.

Coe, N., Kelly, P. and Olds, K. (2003) "Globalization, transationalism and the Asia-Pacific", in Peck, J. and Yeung, H. (eds) *Remaking the Global Economy*, London: Sage Publications.

Coe, N., Hess, M., Yeung, H., Dicken, P. and Henderson, J. (2004) "'Globalizing' regional development: a global production networks perspective", *Transactions of the Institute of British Geographers*, 29 (4): 468–484.

Cooke, P. (1992) "Regional innovation systems – competitive regulation in the new Europe", *Geoforum*, 23 (3): 365–382.

—— (1996) "Reinventing the region: companies, clusters and networks in economic development", in Daniels, P. and Lever, W. (eds) *The Global Economy in Transition*, Harlow: Longman.

—— (1998) "Clusters and the new economics of competition", *Harvard Business Review*, Nov.–Dec.: 77–90.

—— (2008) "Cleantech and an analysis of the platform nature of life sciences: further reflections upon platform policies", *European Planning Studies*, 16 (3): 375–393.

Cooke, P. and Morgan, K. (1998) *The Associational Economy. Companies, Regions, and Innovation*, Oxford: Oxford University Press.

Crevoisier, O. and Jeannerat, H. (2009) "Territorial knowledge dynamics: from the proximity paradigm to multi-location milieus", *European Planning Studies*, 17 (8): 1223–1241.

Cumbers, A. and Mackinnon, D. (2004) "Clusters in urban and regional development", *Urban Studies*, 41 (5): 959–969.

Dicken, P. and Malmberg, A. (2001) "Firms in territories: a relational perspective", *Economic Geography*, 77 (4): 345–363.

Farole, G., Rodríguez-Pose, A. and Storper, M. (2009) "Cohesion policy in the European Union: growth, geography and institutions", Working Paper written in the context of the report *An Agenda for a Reformed Cohesion Policy*, European Commission.

Feldman, M. and Stewart, I. (2006) "Knowledge transfer and innovation: a review of the policy relevant literature", Toronto: Ontario Ministry of Research and Innovation.

Fontes, M. (2005) "Distant networking: the knowledge acquisition strategies of 'out-cluster' biotechnology firms", *European Planning Studies*, 13 (6): 899–920.

Gertler, M. (2008) "Buzz without being there? Communities of practice in context", in Amin, A. and Roberts, J. (eds) *Community, Economic Creativity and Organization*, Oxford: Oxford University Press.

Glasmeier, A. (1988) "Factors governing the development of high-tech industries agglomerations: a tale of three cities", *Regional Studies*, 22 (4): 287–301.

Grabher, G. (2002) "Cool projects, boring institutions: temporary collaboration in social context", *Regional Studies*, 36 (3): 205–214.

Grabher, G., Ibert, O. and Flohr, S. (2008) "The neglected king: the customer in the new knowledge ecology of innovation", *Economic Geography*, 84 (3): 253–280.

Hudson, R. (1999) "'The learning economy, the learning firm and the learning region': a sympathetic critique of the limits to learning", *European Urban and Regional Studies*, 6 (1): 59–72.

Krugman, P. (1991) "History and industry location: the case of the manufacturing belt", *The American Economic Review*, 81 (2): 80–83.

Lagendijk, A. (1999) "Regional anchoring and modernization strategies in non-core regions: evidence from the UK and Germany", *European Planning Studies*, 7 (6): 775–792.

Lovering, J. (1999) "Theory led by policy: the inadequacies of the 'New Regionalism' (illustrated from the case of Wales)", *International Journal of Urban and Regional Research*, 23 (2): 379–395.

Mackinnon, D. and Cumbers, A. (2007) *An Introduction to Economic Geography. Globalization, Uneven Development and Place*, Harlow: Pearson Education.

Mackinnon, D., Cumbers, A., Pike, A., Birch, K. and McMaster, R. (2009) "Evolution in economic geography: institutions, political economy, and adaptation", *Economic Geography*, 85 (2): 129–150.

Martin, R. and Sunley, P. (2003) "Deconstructing clusters: chaotic concept or policy panacea?", *Journal of Economic Geography*, 3 (1): 5–35.

Maskell, P. and Malmberg, A. (1999) "The competitiveness of firms and regions: the 'ubiquitification' and the importance of localised knowledge", *European Urban and Regional Studies*, 6 (1): 9–25.

Morgan, K. (1997) "The learning region: institutions, innovation and regional renewal", *Regional Studies*, 31 (5): 491–503.

—— (2004) "The exaggerated death of geography: learning, proximity and territorial innovation systems", *Journal of Economic Geography*, 4: 3–21.

Moulaert, F. and Sekia, F. (2003) "Territorial innovation models: a critical survey", *Regional Studies*, 37 (3): 289–302.

Oinas, P. (2000) "Distance and learning: does proximity matter?", in Boekema, F., Morgan, K., Bakkers, S. and Ruten, R. (eds) *Knowledge, Innovation and Economic Growth*, Aldershot: Edward Elgar.

Owen-Smith, J. and Powell, W. W. (2004) "Knowledge networks as channels and conduits: the effects of spillovers in the Boston biotechnology community", *Organization Science*, 15 (1): 5–21.

Peck, J. (2003) "Places of work", in Sheppard, E. and Barnes, T. (eds) *A Companion to Economic Geography*, Oxford: Blackwell.

Pike, A. (2007) "Editorial: Whither regional studies?", *Regional Studies*, 41 (9): 1143–1148.

Porter, M. (1990) *The Competitive Advantage of Nations*, London: Macmillan.

Porter, M. (1998) "Clusters and the new economics of competition", *Harvard Business Review*, Nov. – Dec.: 77–90.

Saxenian, A. (1991) "The origins and dynamics of production networks in Silicon Valley", *Research Policy*, 20: 423–437.

Scott, A. J. (2002) "A new map of Hollywood: the production and distribution of American motion pictures", *Regional Studies*, 36 (9): 957–975.

Seravalli, G. (2009) "Competitive European regions through research and innovation. Different theoretical approaches to innovation policies", Working Paper written in the context of the report *An Agenda for a Reformed Cohesion Policy*, European Commission, Brussels.

Storper, M. (1995) "The resurgence of regional economies, ten years later: the region as a nexus of untraded interdependencies", *European Urban and Regional Studies*, 2 (3): 191–221.

Storper, M. and Venables, A. J. (2004) "Buzz: face-to-face contact and the urban economy", *Journal of Economic Geography*, 4 (4): 351–370.

Tödtling, F. (1999) "Innovation networks, collective learning, and industrial policy in regions of Europe", *European Planning Studies*, 7 (6): 693–697.

Tödtling, F. and Kaufmann, A. (1999) "Innovation systems in regions of Europe – a comparative perspective", *European Planning Studies*, 7 (6): 699–717.

Torre, A. and Rallet, A. (2005) "Proximity and localization", *Regional Studies*, 39 (1): 47–59.

Uzzi, B. (1996) "The sources and consequences of embeddedness for the economic performance of organizations: the network effect", *American Sociological Review*, 61 (4): 674–698.

Vale, M. and Caldeira, J. (2007) "Proximity and knowledge governance in localized production systems: the footwear industry in the North region of Portugal", *European Planning Studies*, 15 (4): 531–548.

423

—— (2008) "Fashion and the governance of knowledge in a traditional industry: the case of the footwear sectoral innovation system in the northern region of Portugal", *Economics of Innovation and New Technology*, 17 (1): 61–78.

Van Winden, W., van den Berg, L., Carvalho, L. and van Tuijl, E. (forthcoming) *Manufacturing in the New Urban Economy*, Abingdon: Routledge.

Yeung, H. (2009) "Situating regional development in the competitive dynamics of global production networks: an East Asian perspective", *Regional Studies*, 43 (3): 325–351.

Further reading

Asheim, B., Boschma, R. and Cooke, P. (2007) "Constructing regional advantage: platform policies based on related variety and differentiated knowledge bases", *Papers in Evolutionary Economic Geography*, 0709, University of Utrecht. (Explores new avenues on regional development policies in the construction of regional advantage supported by the idea of platform policies based on related variety and knowledge bases.)

Bathelt, H., Malmberg, A. and Maskell, P. (2004) "Clusters and knowledge: local buzz, global pipelines and the process of knowledge creation", *Progress in Human Geography*, 28 (1): 31–56. (Concerns the issue of localized and distant learning processes and questions the divide between codified (mobile) and tacit (localized) knowledge.)

Crevoisier, O. and Jeannerat, H. (2009) "Territorial knowledge dynamics: from the proximity paradigm to multi-location milieus", *European Planning Studies*, 17 (8): 1223–1241. (Moves away from the clusters and regional innovation system approaches to propose an interesting new concept of territorial knowledge dynamics.)

Gertler, M. (2008) "Buzz without being there? Communities of practice in context", in Amin, A. and Roberts, J. (eds) *Community, Economic Creativity and Organization*, Oxford: Oxford University Press. (Concerns the role of communities of practice and the innovation processes as well as the role of geographical proximity and relational proximity.)

Morgan, K. (2004) "The exaggerated death of geography: learning, proximity and territorial innovation systems", *Journal of Economic Geography*, 4: 3–21. (On the limits of distant learning and why geographical proximity still matters to innovation systems.)

35

Universities and regional development

John Goddard and Paul Vallance

Introduction

An interest in the potential contribution of universities to regional development has corresponded with a wider shift in economic geography towards modes of discourse and analysis in which knowledge and innovation are core concepts. The new knowledge produced through advanced scientific research in universities is a potentially vital input to innovation in technology-based industries that are seen by many academics and policy-makers alike as key to regional competitiveness in the post-industrial economy. Numerous studies have emphasised that local knowledge spill-overs from strong research universities were central to the formation of world-leading industrial clusters in sectors such as information technology and biotechnology. Conceptually, the recent prominence of institutional frameworks in economic geography, such as learning regions and national or regional innovation systems, has created a space for universities to be included in analyses, as part of the non-firm institutional structure of a territory that supports economic development. This chapter will reflect on this dominant viewpoint of the role universities play in regional development across three further sections. First, a

brief background identifies the major contextual factors that enable and constrain the relationship between universities and their regions. Second, the main body of the review focuses on the contribution of universities to innovation and technology-based development in their regional economies. Third, we argue that a broader interpretation of universities in regional development should be taken, beyond simply their role within the "knowledge economy".

Background: higher education and regional development drivers

Previous international studies comparing the involvement of universities in the development of different regions have demonstrated that this varies significantly depending on a number of national and regional features. A large-scale OECD (2007) review, encompassing 14 countries in five continents, found that the conjoint development trajectories of universities and regions are shaped by a combination of factors, including the historically formed industrial characteristics of the region, the extent to which higher education is incorporated into regional development policies, and the institutional make-up of the national higher education system. From the findings of another study, of 14 regions in seven European countries, Boucher *et al.* (2003) emphasise that the level of competition between higher education institutions within a region is another crucial factor, with the highest overall levels of engagement from individual institutions tending to be exhibited when there is a single large university in a 'peripheral' economic region. In past work we have analysed the interplay of these factors in an analytical framework bringing together drivers and constraints on regional engagement from both economic development and higher education policy and governance spheres (see Goddard and Puukka, 2008). The articulation of these two sides can be seen in a series of recent transformations that have taken place, to greater or lesser degrees, in the external environments of universities across a range of countries (OECD, 2007).

On the regional development side, universities are being attributed a changing role in public policy, where they are increasingly positioned as central to the building of 'knowledge economies' at regional or urban as well as national scales (Harloe and Perry, 2004; May and Perry, 2006). This can be seen as part of a more general shift in regional policy thinking towards measures that concentrate on building and mobilising the varied institutional capacity of a region to support bottom-up, endogenous development (Amin, 1999). In Europe, despite public expenditure on research as a whole falling significantly during the 1990s, this decrease was concentrated mainly in the funding of large-scale defence programmes and not higher education, meaning that the relative importance of universities within national and sub-national innovation systems has, in fact, generally risen (Larédo and Mustar, 2004). The recognition that academic and other publicly funded research may has significant economic returns has led to national science policy increasingly overlapping with

technology and innovation policies (see Lundvall and Borrás, 2005), and greater interdependencies between universities, industry and government in what Etzkowitz and Leydesdorff (2000) call "triple helix" relations. This has moved science policy into a realm where it also becomes the concern of sub-national economic governance actors, with the effect of introducing a regional dimension to this in many countries where it has hitherto been controlled overwhelmingly at the national level (Perry and May, 2007). Individual universities are responding to this rescaling in their environments by incorporating an explicit commitment to local and regional engagement into their mission statements alongside core teaching and research activities, entering into strategic partnership relations with key local public and private organisations, and establishing dedicated regional development offices (Charles, 2003).

Changes in the governance of higher education, mainly at the national level, are of equal importance in explaining why universities now interact more extensively with external partners, although in general less attention has been paid to these in the regional development literature. Here, even with trends towards globalisation, such as greater international movements of students and global connectivity of research links between universities (see e.g. Robins and Webster, 2002), national systems of higher education retain their importance and distinctiveness. In comparing higher education policy trajectories in the US, UK, Australia and Canada, Slaughter and Leslie (1997) found that despite some convergence towards more market-orientated systems in the face of reduced public funding bases, the precise content of these policies and the political conditions from which they arose still showed considerable differences between these countries. Marginson (2002) argues that the traditional 'nation-building' role of higher education has not become redundant, but that globalisation has forced governments to adapt their national systems to maintain success in a more internationally competitive environment. The provision of research funds by government has also been pushed in a more market-orientated direction, becoming diverted away from basic research in traditional academic disciplines and weighted towards supporting interdisciplinary fields (i.e. 'technoscience') that align with national economic priorities (Slaughter and Leslie, 1997). These more applied forms of research decentre the locus of knowledge production from its traditional home within universities, and direct academics to work in collaboration with a range of other types of private and public institutions within society (Gibbons *et al.*, 1994). These developments have coincided with the expansion of higher education sectors in many developed countries to accommodate mass student access, and correspondingly falling levels of public expenditure per student on higher education. This has forced universities to become more 'entrepreneurial' in seeking to maximise potential revenue from external sources through, for example, commercialising research or procuring funding from a broader base of government and industry bodies (Clark, 1998; Etzkowitz, 2004).

Universities, knowledge and regional development

This main review section will consider the contribution of the regional development literature to understanding the role of universities in local knowledge-based economic development. Reflecting the dominant recent understanding in economic geography more widely, links with industry and government arising from the drivers covered in the previous section have normally been considered strongest in supporting innovation at local scales. In particular, the input that strong research universities can make to the science base of a region has been identified as a key factor in the formation of clusters in certain technology-based industries,

of which the paradigmatic modern example is probably biotechnology (Cooke, 2002).

Empirical support for this has been provided by an economics literature on 'knowledge spill-overs'. Studies have generally shown, for certain knowledge-dependent industries, the existence of local (e.g. US state level) academic spill-overs in the form of a positive correlation between university research intensity and corporate innovation level, even after allowing for the effect of internal company R&D (e.g. Jaffe, 1989; Anselin *et al.*, 1997). This statistical analysis is used to explain the geographical concentration of production in these industries on the assumption that firms will locate close to strong research universities to access their knowledge externalities (Audretsch *et al.*, 2005). However, work using this methodology is normally more concerned with finding empirical evidence for the presence of local spill-overs than with explaining how or why they occur: knowledge is treated largely as a 'public good', without interrogating the challenges involved in translating it from an academic research to applied industrial context, and often without discriminating between the various formal and informal mechanisms through which 'spill-overs' may occur (Davies, 2008).

Work in economic geography, by contrast, has tended to explore the role of universities in local technology-based growth through case study accounts of certain regions. Of these the leading examples are probably the high technology districts in Silicon Valley and Cambridge (UK). In Silicon Valley, companies that were formed by alumni of Stanford University's electrical engineering programme, notably Hewlett Packard, are seen as critical to the emergence of the region as a technology centre in the post-war period (Castells and Hall, 1994; Saxenian, 1994; Cohen and Fields, 2000; Leslie, 2000). In Saxenian's (1994) study comparing Silicon Valley with its main US competitor region, New England's Route 128, relations between universities and firms reflect the wider industrial culture of the regions, hence acting as one of the institutional factors that explains the divergent development trajectories of these regions. In Silicon Valley, higher education institutions were well integrated into the regional industrial system: Stanford and latterly Berkeley universities adopted open attitudes to collaboration with firms, giving them access to the leading research being carried out there, as well as encouraging their members to be entrepreneurial themselves by establishing firms to commercialise their knowledge. Saxenian (1994: 42) also cites the role of state and community colleges, that like Stanford and Berkeley developed close links with local industry to ensure that there was a plentiful supply of graduates with relevant skills to underpin the growth of the region. In Route 128 by contrast, which in MIT and Harvard had comparable local academic assets, the more conservative and large-firm-dominated industrial culture meant that relations between these institutions and smaller technology enterprises were more remote. Consequently, practices such as promoting technology transfer and academic spin-offs which contributed to the dynamic milieu of Silicon Valley were generally taken up much later.

The socio-cultural elements of university–firm relations have also been emphasised in studies of the Cambridge high technology cluster in the South of England. Here, in a process similar to that reported in Silicon Valley, many of the firms that comprise the cluster are either direct spin-offs from Cambridge University, or subsequent generations of spin-offs from these original firms (Garnsey and Heffernan, 2005). For Keeble et al. (1999) the function of the university is not simply one of producing knowledge for dissemination in the cluster. They argue that processes such as spin-offs, the movement of graduate scientists into the labour market, and the establishment of close links with local firms and research consultancies have also helped to spread conventions for the "positive valuation of research interaction, dissemination, debate and collaborative endeavour" (ibid.: 323) within the region. This culture of cooperation between firms, based on norms and values that are more usually associated with academic rather than industrial practices, is seen by Keeble et al. to underpin high levels of local collective learning.

In both of these cases, however, the universities were probably only a driving force behind the growth of the industrial milieux in their early stages. Castells and Hall (1994: 20–21) emphasise that subsequent to the crucial contribution of university-based research and development in Silicon Valley, the industrial base of the region developed its own self-sustaining innovative capability and growth dynamics, in which the higher education sector has only a supporting, albeit vital, role in helping to meet local demand for professional labour. More recent research by Saxenian (2006) has highlighted the value of California's world-class universities in attracting talented international students, who subsequently stay in the region to enter Silicon Valley's labour market, and often go on to establish profitable business links with their home countries. Similarly, Garnsey and Heffernan (2005) link patterns of repeated spin-offs from Cambridge University and related firms with the longer term building of regional industrial competences, primarily contained in specialised labour markets. In the Cambridge biotechnology cluster, Casper and Karamanos's (2003) research shows that firms do have well-established links with Cambridge University (in the form of spin-offs, collaborations, graduates entering the local labour market, and employees sitting on advisory boards), but that these are not the exclusive or even dominant source of their scientific relations: these also exist with other universities and firms both inside and outside the region. Other case studies of biotechnology clusters from around the world have indicated that, while embedded universities and the basic research function they perform are central to the science base of most regions, the presence of other factors, such as the availability of venture capital directly to support enterprise, are at least as important to the success of regional systems (e.g. Feldman and Francis, 2003; Kaiser, 2003; Lawton Smith, 2004). In particular, recent studies that have highlighted the importance of global organisational networks in biotechnology have tended to focus on transnational corporations as the key actors within the industry, capable of establishing operations in multiple regions to access sources of specialist local knowledge (Coenen *et al.*, 2004; Zeller, 2004; Gertler and Levitte, 2005).

The work discussed above suggests that the emergence of successful high technology districts is contingent upon the convergence of a set of wider regional and extra-regional processes, some of which will be relatively independent of any direct effect universities have in the local economy. Garnsey and Lawton Smith (1998) make reference to complexity studies in explaining why Oxford emerged as a high technology centre later than Cambridge (UK), despite these areas having many comparable features. Some of the various factors they cite relate to differences between the respective universities and their commercialisation strategies, but others relate to the industrial and geographic structure of the Oxfordshire economy, which was less conducive to the formation of tightly knit clusters of small firms.

This line of argument is supported by the successful examples discussed above being widely regarded as unplanned developments, largely free of direct government intervention. While this seems to be basically accepted of Cambridge (Castells and Hall, 1994; Garnsey and Heffernan, 2005; Kitson *et al.*, 2009), many contend that the state played a vital part in the growth of Silicon Valley and Route 128 in the form of sustained and concentrated public spending on defence and aerospace during the Cold War period, from which universities like Stanford benefited and strengthened their links with large firms in the local economy (Saxenian, 1994;

Markusen, 1996; Leslie, 2000). Policy-led efforts to replicate these growth dynamics in less developed regions have commonly focused on reproducing one visible element of the institutional mix found in Cambridge and Silicon Valley – the presence of university-based science parks. These property-led developments (typically involving partnership with local government, development agencies or private finance) provide a space where technology firms can locate together proximate to the university (Quintas *et al.*, 1992). Research on science parks has, however, found little evidence for their general effectiveness in terms of granting firms within them any clear advantages, suggesting that physical co-location alone is not a sufficient factor for the formation of profitable relationships between academia and industry (Vedovello, 1997; Löfsten and Lindelöf, 2002; Siegel *et al.*, 2003). For instance, a survey of the first wave of such developments throughout the UK by Quintas *et al.* (1992), covering 38 parks with a direct connection to an academic institution built between 1972 and 1988, found that the host universities were just as likely to have research links with firms outside the park as those inside. It also did not find that these initiatives had led to large-scale incidence of academics forming successful companies on the park, leading the authors to conclude that the developmental potential of university spin-off firms had been overstated. In a wider ranging international study of the "technopole phenomenon", Castells and Hall (1994) show that state-led attempts to establish new centres of technological-based economic growth, whether by means of concentrating national scientific resources, or inducing investment from the private sector, have historically failed to produce the synergies between research institutes and technology firms required for extensive innovation. This is particularly the case when the centre is physically and functionally separated from existing industrial production. By contrast, an example of successful science-based cluster building around universities, the Finnish strategy reported by Cooke (2002), is attributed to the existence of close relations with both large and small firms: "The key reason for this [strategy seeming to work] is a policy of linkage between university research, R&D laboratories of large companies such as Nokia or AAB, some of their suppliers, and start-up firms spinning out largely from university research", all of which are "[t]ypically … co-located on or near the technology park" (Cooke, 2002: 68).

Over roughly the past ten years, many studies of universities in regional development have used a regional innovation systems (RISs) framework. Adapting the earlier national innovation systems approach to current understanding of the working of regional economies, this approach analyses the interrelationships between various organisational components (including firms and supporting governance, financial and knowledge infrastructure like universities) and the cultural or institutional environments that determine the innovative capability of a region (Cooke et al., 1998; Cooke, 2001; Iammarino, 2005). While much of the work on the localisation of university–firm links reviewed above is based, even if implicitly, on the assumption that a direct linear transference of knowledge from academia to industry is possible (Quintas et al., 1992), innovation system approaches by contrast are closely associated with a more complex evolutionary and non-linear conception of innovation, involving interactions and feedbacks between different networked agencies (Cooke et al., 1998; Etzkowitz and Leydesdorff, 2000). This position is more aligned with Gibbons et al.'s (1994) vision of "mode 2 knowledge", which prioritises "knowledge produced in the context of application", and displaces universities from their privileged location as the primary site of knowledge production in society by granting equal footing to, for instance, other public research laboratories, the R&D divisions of large corporations, networks of

smaller firms, government departments, think-tanks and consultancies.

Nevertheless it is clear that, because of their multifaceted character as educational as well as economic and cultural institutions in society, universities will have a distinct place within RISs compared to these other types of organisation. Charles (2006) identifies three forms of value that universities can add to a RIS: knowledge that is directly commodified through spin-offs or licensing of IP; human capital that upgrades skills and knowledge in the regional labour market; and social capital that builds trust and cooperative norms in local economic governance networks. Moreover, he sees that universities that are well integrated into their RIS, and have developed suitable intermediary mechanisms, can play a further key role by helping to join up these different circuits of knowledge within wider regional innovation processes. These varying functions are reflected in a distinction Gunasekara (2006) makes between approaches in the literature that emphasise universities having either "generative" or "developmental" roles in a RIS. A generative role, which he cites the "triple helix" framework as exemplifying (Etzkowitz and Leydesdorff, 2000), holds that entrepreneurial universities can, in their relations with industry and government, be a driving force of regional innovation and development through "knowledge capitalisation and other capital formation projects" (ibid.: 103). A developmental role, which is identified with literature employing the softer terms of regional engagement (e.g. Chatterton and Goddard, 2000), positions the contribution of universities in the less direct role of helping to build institutional capacity through their organisational partnerships with other regional governance actors, and the diverse external engagement activities of their employees within the region.

To which of these alternatives the higher education component of a RIS most closely conforms will clearly vary across different regional contexts and should be left as a predominately empirical question. For instance, Coenen (2007) compares the North East of England and Scania in Sweden. In the old industrial region of the North East, the relatively strong higher education sector is positioned as having a major part in affecting a path-breaking change in the economy:

> Being one of the few actors in the region with innovative potential, universities play a leading role in policy measures to induce a structural transformation of the regional industrial structure by offering a springboard for new business start-ups in knowledge-intensive and science-based (analytical) sectors such as biotechnology and nanotechnology. As such, a considerable part of the involvement of universities in strengthening the RIS is built on the model of the entrepreneurial university.
> (Coenen, 2007: 816–817)

For Scania, where by contrast strong indigenous knowledge-based sectors have developed in biotechnology and ICT, Coenen frames the primary challenge facing the RIS as a disconnection between the region's knowledge infrastructure and one of its key traditional industries – food production. Here, the university is seen to have a key part in integrating local food firms into the RIS: "the university plays the role of an extended R&D laboratory for an ailing industry where innovation support is provided to existing companies and where policy measures are emphasized to reduce the fragmentation and to increase networking" (ibid.: 817).

Other work has, like Coenen for the North East of England, focused on the position of universities at the forefront of innovation strategies in less favoured regions (e.g. Benneworth and Charles, 2005; Benneworth and Hospers, 2007). This represents a more general feature of the RIS approach. Rather than concentrating on explaining the success of "exemplary" cases like Cambridge or Silicon Valley, it compares the innovative

capabilities and deficiencies of a range of more "ordinary" regions (Charles, 2006; Coenen, 2007). Despite the higher than normal levels of local engagement often demonstrated by higher education institutions in these regions (Boucher et al., 2003), the absence of other conducive conditions means that their actual transformative potential within the economy is likely to be constrained. According to Cooke (2001) over-dependence on public sector institutions, which he sees as characteristic of most regions within Europe, may represent a weakness within RISs, indicating "market-failure" compared to the more enterprising, private sector-centred systems found in the USA where levels of innovation are generally higher.

A further issue concerning RISs is how they relate to other governance scales: clearly RISs are not self-contained, geographically bounded systems, but are instead partly produced through macro-level processes at the national or transnational level (Iammarino, 2005). This question is particularly salient when considering how universities are inserted into an RIS, since in most countries higher education remains a national system, rather than being governed at the regional level (Charles, 2006). The knowledge assets that universities add to local economies are also, as some authors have emphasised, constituted through international research networks and communities of academics (Maskell and Törnqvist, 2003; Coenen, 2007).

These scale issues have started to be addressed in a growing comparative literature on the multi-level governance of science policy in different national contexts. In contrast to innovation policy, which in most countries has a regional and, in the case of the EU (see Potts, 2002; Héraud, 2003; Larédo and Mustar, 2004), a transnational dimension, science policy is mainly national (Crespy et al., 2007; Perry and May, 2007). In the case of England, science and technology policy remains, by and large, a highly centralised system that is orientated towards supporting global "excellence" at the national level, and has little in the way of mechanisms through which science resources can be directed to help meet regional economic development needs (Charles and Benneworth, 2001). This means that, despite the system in theory being spatially neutral, in practice it reinforces a geographical imbalance in the state funding of research for universities and other public facilities towards a core Greater South East region that encompasses London, Cambridge and Oxford. The period after the return of a Labour government in 1997 however, in addition to the devolution of relevant powers to new parliaments or assemblies in Scotland, Wales and Northern Ireland, saw the emergence of some form of regional tier of science policy in England. Perry (2007) traces this development of what she calls a "minimalist system of multi-level governance" – in which local actors with only limited capacity concentrate on supporting or delivering priorities defined at the national level. The main catalyst for this change has been a parallel institutional growth in economic development governance organisations at the regional and trans-regional level, which facilitate the development of relationships between universities and local bodies with an interest in promoting science-based innovation and economic growth. For instance, all nine of the English regions have now established public–private partnership science and industry councils (Perry, 2007: 1058). The key actors within this process of constructing a new scale of science policy in England, particularly in less developed regions, were (centrally funded) regional development agencies (RDAs), which since their inception in 1999 led the way in incorporating universities into regional economic strategies aimed at boosting endogenous levels of innovation (also see Goddard and Chatterton, 1999; Kitagawa, 2004).

Broadly similar patterns of limited devolution to "minimalist" systems of multi-level science governance have been described in other traditionally centralised countries such as France and Japan (Crespy et al., 2007; Kitagawa, 2007). However, the relationship between national and sub-national levels is different in countries with a federal government structure, with individual states or provinces more likely to have the institutional scope and resources to pursue their own autonomous science as well as innovation policies (Perry and May, 2007). In the USA, for instance, various commentators have written about the widespread tendency for state-level university research policy to move in the more instrumental direction of supporting economic development through technology transfer programmes, although these are often at the expense of other higher education funding and may be vulnerable to budgetary cut-backs (Feller, 2004; Geiger and Sá, 2005). Salazar and Holbrook (2007) characterise the Canadian situation as one in which the federal structure blurs the distinctions between levels of governance, so that STI policy cannot be clearly attributed to either the federal or provincial governments, but instead operates predominately through a series of nationwide network programmes that link these levels.

Conclusion: A broader role for universities

A recurrent theme in our review has been that empirical research from different places shows the actual success of universities in stimulating regional growth often does not match the role prescribed it in theory. A critical evaluation of the literature indicates that those celebrated cases in which universities have reportedly played foundational roles in technology-led regional economic growth, such as Silicon Valley or Cambridge (UK), are the evolutionary product of a favourable or "serendipitous" (Kitson et al., 2009) set of geographically and historically contingent circumstances, that cannot be reproduced in any region solely through policies which focus on engendering links between academia and local industry. This may be particularly true of less developed economic regions where limited demand from private enterprise, and 'absorptive capacity' of local industry in general (Christopherson and Clark, 2007), constrains the overall economic impact that universities can have through business support or technology transfer programmes, despite the prominent position they may be assigned in regional innovation strategies.

Other recent reviews have come to similar conclusions. Some have raised primarily empirical and methodological concerns about the often inconclusive evidence or conflicting findings of studies in this field (Lawton Smith, 2007). A related issue is the problem of obtaining adequate data to measure or otherwise properly evaluate the regional economic impacts of university research and technology transfer activity (Thanki, 1999; Drucker and Goldstein, 2007). Others have focused on problematising underlying conceptual beliefs about the potential for knowledge produced through global academic research networks to be widely and effectively commercialised outside universities as the basis for specifically local economic development (Huggins et al., 2008; Power and Malmberg, 2008).

What these various commentaries point to is not so much that universities cannot play a significant role in regional development, but that the relatively narrow function assumed of them – as a source of knowledge generation and dissemination within a local economic innovation system – is overstated. A theme of this volume is that more holistic concepts of regional development are needed that do not just focus on economic growth and competitiveness (also Pike et al., 2007). In parallel with this, we suggest that a broader view of higher education institutions and their place in society would also be beneficial in more fully understanding the multidimensional contributions that they make to their localities at a sub-national level. This is sometimes revealed by case studies of how

individual universities interact with their region across a broad front (Goddard and Vallance, 2009). Several authors have noted the wider cultural and civic roles that universities have and their relevance to supporting local governance, business or community development (e.g. Chatterton, 2000; Charles, 2003; Gunasekara, 2006; Huggins et al., 2008), but in general these processes have not been examined to the same degree as those relating to the production and dissemination of economically valuable knowledge.

To advance the field beyond this may require a wider engagement with current thinking on the role of universities in civil society. For instance, in light of the increasingly social distributed nature of knowledge production described by Gibbons et al. (1994), Delanty (2001: 6–7) conceives a new role for the university as "the most important site of interconnectivity in what is now a knowledge society", "a key institution for the formation of cultural and technological citizenship" and "a site of public debate, thus reversing the decline of the public sphere". While this is a global agenda, facilitated by the diffusion of knowledge made possible by today's communications technology, public discourse is also local. It is rooted in the place-based life experience of individual citizens, including the academy and learners. Moreover, to focus on citizens raises the important urban dimension to higher education and the concept of the 'civic university' which mobilises its teaching and research to help meet the economic, social, cultural and environmental challenges confronting 'its' city (Goddard, 2009).

In a wide-ranging review of "universities and the public good", Calhoun (2006) has suggested that while knowledge may be generated in the public interest, it is not necessarily widely circulated: indeed excellence in the academy is often equated with exclusivity. While real knowledge may eventually be for the good of humanity as a whole, benefits "unequally trickle down". The rewards for research are tied up with the production of academic hierarchy and the relative standing of institutions. On the other hand, Calhoun (2006: 19) argues that:

> public support for universities is based largely on the effort to educate citizens in general, to share knowledge, to distribute it as widely as possible, and to produce it in accord with publically articulated purposes ... [including] economic development, especially insofar as this requires technical expertise and general education of participants.

One effect of bringing these kinds of debate into the study of universities and regional development is that it may help the local engagement missions of a more varied set of higher education institutions than just leading-edge research universities to be considered. For Power and Malmberg (2008) a weakness of existing work is that it conflates an institution's global 'excellence' in academic research with its 'excellence' in being able to support regional competitiveness. While regions do need access to global knowledge that comes with a strong research base, it is often non-research-intensive universities that have the deepest local or regional links. For instance, Glasson (2003) shows that two newer, teaching-orientated universities in England (Sunderland in the North East and Oxford Brookes in the South East) are highly regionally engaged, reflecting their histories as local polytechnic colleges, and bringing a range of direct and indirect benefits to their cities. On an international level, there are many countries where higher education does not necessarily resemble the Anglo-American research model that dominates global university ranking tables (Marginson, 2002). Ramachandran and Scott (2009) provide a rare example addressing these issues in a Global South context in their study of how university centres in the mainly rural North Central Coast Region of Vietnam fill important institutional gaps in local civil society by assuming a role similar

to development NGOs, with the notable difference that these centres are more likely to be permanent fixtures in the region.

Recognition of the diversity of higher education institutions that co-exist within a region or territory raises the further question of whether future research should remain focused predominately on case studies of single regions and universities, or whether tensions between the academic research and public service missions of universities should also be examined more often in the context of national funding systems and the uneven economic development of the territory. While many countries recognise the importance of supporting a diverse set of higher education institutions to meet national needs, matching this diversity to the developmental needs of different and especially lagging regions has not been a priority for the public funding of higher education in most countries. In England, for instance, the current system is one in which the sole criterion for research funding is to support academic excellence wherever it is located, and the funding of teaching is linked to graduate output to meet national needs, while funding for regional engagement is largely marginalised in so-called 'third stream' funding. Policy-concerned work in this field could make the case for public funding including a core dimension that recognises the contribution of a university to civil society in the place where it is located, and to support the evolution of networks of universities matched to the needs and opportunities of each part of a country (Goddard, 2009).

References

Amin, A. (1999) "An institutionalist perspective on regional economic development", *International Journal of Urban and Regional Research* 23, 365–378.

Anselin, L., Varga, A. and Acs, Z. (1997) "Local geographic spillovers between university research and high technology innovations", *Journal of Urban Economics* 42, 422–448.

Audretsch, D. B., Lehmann, E. E. and Warning, S. (2005) "University spillovers and new firm location", *Research Policy* 34, 1113–1122.

Benneworth, P. and Charles, D. (2005) "University spin-off policies and economic development in less successful regions: learning from two decades of policy practice", *European Planning Studies* 13, 537–557.

Benneworth, P. and Hospers, G. (2007) "The new economic geography of old industrial regions: universities as global-local pipelines", *Environment and Planning C: Government and Policy* 25, 779–802.

Boucher, G., Conway, C. and Van Der Meer, E. (2003) "Tiers of engagement by universities in their region's development", *Regional Studies* 37, 887–897.

Calhoun, C. (2006) "The university and the public good", *Thesis Eleven* 84, 7–43.

Casper, S. and Karamanos, A. (2003) "Commercializing knowledge in Europe: the Cambridge biotechnology cluster", *European Planning Studies* 11, 805–822.

Castells, M. and Hall, P. (1994) *Technopoles of the World: The Making of 21st Century Industrial Complexes*, London: Routledge.

Charles, D. (2003) "Universities and territorial development: reshaping the regional role of UK universities", *Local Economy* 18, 7–20.

Charles, D. (2006) "Universities as key knowledge infrastructures in regional innovation systems", *Innovation* 19, 117–130.

Charles, D. and Benneworth, P. (2001) "Are we realizing our potential? Joining up science and technology policy in the English regions", *Regional Studies* 35, 73–79.

Chatterton, P. (2000) "The cultural role of universities in the community: revisiting the university-community debate", *Environment and Planning A* 32, 165–181.

Chatterton, P. and Goddard, J. (2000) "The response of higher education institutions to regional needs", *European Journal of Education* 35, 475–496.

Christopherson, S. and Clark, J. (2007) *Remaking Regional Economies: Power, Labour, and Firm Strategies in the Knowledge Economy*, Abingdon: Routledge.

Clark, B. R. (1998) *Creating Entrepreneurial Universities: Organizational Pathways of Transformation*, Oxford: Pergamon.

Coenen, L. (2007) "The role of universities in the regional innovation systems of the North East of England and Scania, Sweden: providing missing links?", *Environment and Planning C: Government and Policy* 25, 803–823.

Coenen, L., Moodysson, J. and Asheim, B. T. (2004) "Nodes, networks and proximities: on the knowledge dynamics of the Medicon Valley biotech cluster", *European Planning Studies* 12, 1003–1018.

Cohen, S. S. and Fields, G. (2000) "Social capital and capital gains: an examination of social capital in Silicon Valley", in Kenney, M. (ed.) *Understanding Silicon Valley: The Anatomy of an Entrepreneurial Region*, Stanford, CA: Stanford University Press.

Cooke, P. (2001) "Regional innovation systems, clusters, and the knowledge economy", *Industrial and Corporate Change* 10, 945–974.

Cooke, P. (2002) *Knowledge Economies: Clusters, Learning and Cooperative Advantage*, London: Routledge.

Cooke, P., Uranga, M. G. and Etxebarria, G. (1998) "Regional systems of innovation: an evolutionary perspective", *Environment and Planning A* 30, 1563–1584.

Crespy, C., Heraud, J. and Perry, B. (2007) "Multi-level governance, regions and science in France: between competition and equality", *Regional Studies* 41, 1069–1084.

Davies, T. (2008) "University–industry links and regional development: thinking beyond knowledge spillovers", *Geography Compass* 2, 1058–1074.

Delanty, G. (2001) *Challenging Knowledge: The University in the Knowledge Society*, Buckingham: Open University Press.

Drucker, J. and Goldstein, H. (2007) "Assessing the regional economic development impacts of universities: a review of current approaches", *International Regional Science Review* 30, 20–46.

Etzkowitz, H. (2004) "The evolution of the entrepreneurial university", *International Journal of Technology and Globalisation* 1, 64–77.

Etzkowitz, H. and Leydesdorff, L. (2000) "The dynamics of innovation: from national systems and mode 2 to a triple helix of university–industry–government relations", *Research Policy* 29, 109–123.

Feldman, M. P. and Francis, J. L. (2003) " 'Fortune favours the prepared region': the case of entrepreneurship and the Capitol Region biotechnology cluster", *European Planning Studies* 11, 765–788.

Feller, I. (2004) "Virtuous and vicious cycles in the contributions of public research universities to state economic development objectives", *Economic Development Quarterly* 18, 138–150.

Garnsey, E. and Heffernan, P. (2005) "High-technology clustering through spin-out and attraction: the Cambridge case", *Regional Studies* 39, 1127–1144.

Garnsey, E and Lawton-Smith, H. (1998) "Proximity and complexity in the emergence of high-technology industry: the Oxbridge comparison", *Geoforum* 29, 433–450.

Geiger, R. L. and Sá, C. (2005) "Beyond technology transfer: US state policies to harness university research for economic development", *Minerva* 43, 1–21.

Gertler, M. S. and Levitte, Y. M. (2005) "Local nodes in global networks: the geography of knowledge flows in biotechnology innovation", *Industry and Innovation* 12, 487–507.

Gibbons, M., Limoges, C., Nowotny, H., Schwartzman, S., Scott, P. and Trow, M. (1994) *The New Production of Knowledge: The Dynamics of Science and Research in Contemporary Societies*, London: Sage.

Glasson, J. (2003) "The widening local and regional development impacts of the modern universities – a tale of two cities (and north–south perspectives)", *Local Economy* 18, 21–37.

Goddard, J. (2009) *Reinventing the Civic University*, London: NESTA.

Goddard, J. and Chatterton, P. (1999) "Regional Development Agencies and the knowledge economy: harnessing the potential of universities", *Environment and Planning C: Government and Policy* 17, 685–699.

Goddard, J. and Puukka, J. (2008) "The engagement of higher education institutions in regional development: an overview of the opportunities and challenges", *Higher Education Management and Policy* 20, 11–41.

Goddard, J. and Vallance, P. (2009) "Newcastle University: higher education with a purpose", in Mohrman, K., Shi, J., Feinblatt, S. and Chow, K. (eds) *Public Universities and Regional Development*, Sichuan: Sichuan University Press.

Gunasekara, C. (2006) "Reframing the role of universities in the development of regional innovation systems", *Journal of Technology Transfer* 31, 101–113.

Harloe, M. and Perry, B. (2004) "Universities, localities and regional development: the emergence of the 'mode 2' university?", *International Journal of Urban and Regional Research* 28, 212–223.

Héraud, J. (2003) "Regional innovation systems and European research policy: convergence or misunderstanding?", *European Planning Studies* 11, 41–56.

Huggins, R., Johnston, A. and Steffenson, R. (2008) "Universities, knowledge networks and regional policy", *Cambridge Journal of Regions, Economy and Society* 1, 321–340.

Iammarino, S. (2005) "An evolutionary integrated view of regional innovation systems: concepts, measures and historical perspectives", *European Planning Studies* 13, 497–519.

Jaffe, A. B. (1989) "Real effects of academic research", *The American Economic Review* 79, 957–970.

Kaiser, R. (2003) "Multi-level science policy and regional innovation: the case of the Munich cluster for pharmaceutical biotechnology", *European Planning Studies* 11, 841–857.

Keeble, D., Lawson, C., Moore, B. and Wilkinson, F. (1999) "Collective learning processes, networking and 'institutional thickness' in the Cambridge region", *Regional Studies* 33, 319–332.

Kitagawa, F. (2004) "Universities and regional advantage: higher education and innovation policies in English regions", *European Planning Studies* 12, 835–852.

Kitagawa, F. (2007) "The regionalization of science and innovation governance in Japan?", *Regional Studies* 41, 1099–1114.

Kitson, M., Howells, J., Braham, R. and Westlake, S. (2009) *The Connected University: Driving Recovery and Growth in the UK Economy*, London: NESTA.

Larédo, P. and Mustar, P. (2004) "Public sector research: a growing role in innovation systems", *Minerva* 42, 11–27.

Lawton Smith, H. (2004) "The biotechnology industry in Oxfordshire: enterprise and innovation", *European Planning Studies* 12, 985–1001.

Lawton Smith, H. (2007) "Universities, innovation, and territorial development: a review of the evidence", *Environment and Planning C: Government and Policy* 25, 98–114.

Leslie, S. W. (2000) "The biggest 'Angel' of them all: the military and the making of Silicon Valley", in Kenney, M. (ed.) *Understanding Silicon Valley: The Anatomy of an Entrepreneurial Region*, Stanford, CA: Stanford University Press.

Löfsten, H. and Lindelöf, P. (2002) "Science parks and the growth of new technology-based firms – academic–industry links, innovation and markets", *Research Policy* 31, 859–876.

Lundvall, B. and Borrás, S. (2005) "Science, technology, and innovation policy", in Fagerberg, J., Mowery, D. C. and Nelson, R. R. (eds) *The Oxford Handbook of Innovation*, Oxford: Oxford University Press.

Marginson, S. (2002) "Nation-building universities in a global environment: the case of Australia", *Higher Education* 43, 409–428.

Marginson, S. (2006) "Dynamics of national and global competition in higher education", *Higher Education* 52, 1–39.

Markusen, A. (1996) "Sticky places in slippery space: a typology of industrial districts", *Economic Geography* 72, 293–313.

Maskell, P. and Törnqvist, G. (2003) "The role of universities in the learning region", in Rutten, R., Boekema, F. and Kuijpers, E. (eds) *Economic Geography of Higher Education: Knowledge Infrastructure and Learning Regions*, London: Routledge.

May, T. and Perry, B. (2006) "Cities, knowledge and universities: transformations in the image of the intangible", *Social Epistemology* 20, 259–282.

OECD (2007) *Higher Education and Regions: Globally Competitive, Locally Engaged*, Paris: OECD.

Perry, B. (2007) "The multi-level governance of science policy in England", *Regional Studies* 41, 1051–1067.

Perry, B. and May, T. (2007) "Governance, science policy and regions: an introduction", *Regional Studies* 41, 1039–1050.

Pike, A., Rodríguez-Pose, A. and Tomaney, J. (2007) "What kind of local and regional development and for whom?", *Regional Studies* 41, 1253–1269.

Potts, G. (2002) "Regional policy and the 'regionalization' of university–industry links: a view from the English regions", *European Planning Studies* 10, 987–1012.

Power, D. and Malmberg, A. (2008) "The contribution of universities to innovation and economic development: in what sense a regional problem?", *Cambridge Journal of Regions, Economy and Society* 1, 233–245.

Ramachandran, L. and Scott, S. (2009) "Single-player universities in the south: the role of university actors in development in Vietnam's North Central Coast region", *Regional Studies* 43, 693–706.

Robins, K. and Webster, F. (eds) (2002) *The Virtual University? Knowledge, Markets and Management*, Oxford: Oxford University Press.

Quintas, P., Wield, D. and Massey, D. (1992) "Academic–industry links and innovation: questioning the science park model", *Technovation* 12, 161–175.

Salazar, M. and Holbrook, A. (2007) "Canadian science, technology and innovation policy: the product of regional networking?', *Regional Studies* 41, 1129–1141.

Saxenian, A. (1994) *Regional Advantage: Culture and Competition in Silicon Valley and Route 128*, Cambridge, MA: Harvard University Press.

Saxenian, A. (2006) *The New Argonauts: Regional Advantage in a Global Economy*, Cambridge, MA: Harvard University Press.

Siegel, D. S., Westhead, P. and Wright, M. (2003) "Science parks and the performance of new technology-based firms: a review of recent U.K. evidence and an agenda for future research", *Small Business Economics* 20, 177–184.

Slaughter, S. and Leslie, L. L. (1997) *Academic Capitalism: Politics, Policies, and the Entrepreneurial University*, Baltimore: The Johns Hopkins University Press.

Thanki, R. (1999) "How do we know the value of higher education to regional development", *Regional Studies* 33, 84–89.

Vedovello, C. (1997) "Science parks and university–industry interaction: geographical proximity between agents as a driving force", *Technovation* 17, 491–502.

Zeller, C. (2004) "North Atlantic innovative relations of Swiss pharmaceuticals and the proximities with regional biotech arenas", *Economic Geography* 80, 83–111.

Further reading

Higher education and regional development drivers

Goddard, J. and Puukka, J. (2008) "The engagement of higher education institutions in regional development: an overview of the opportunities and challenges", *Higher Education Management and Policy* 20, 11–41.

Harloe, M. and Perry, B. (2004) "Universities, localities and regional development: the emergence of the 'mode 2' university?", *International Journal of Urban and Regional Research* 28, 212–223.

Universities, knowledge and regional development

Coenen, L. (2007) "The role of universities in the regional innovation systems of the North East of England and Scania, Sweden: providing missing links?", *Environment and Planning C: Government and Policy* 25, 803–823.

Cooke, P. (2002) *Knowledge Economies: Clusters, Learning and Cooperative Advantage*, London: Routledge.

A broader role for universities

Huggins, R., Johnston, A. and Steffenson, R. (2008) "Universities, knowledge networks and regional policy", *Cambridge Journal of Regions, Economy and Society* 1, 321–340.

36

Transportation networks, the logistics revolution and regional development

John T. Bowen, Jr. and Thomas R. Leinbach

The logistics revolution and development

Over the past two decades, there have been profound changes in the way that goods move through the economy. Raw materials, intermediate goods, and final products move with greater speed, precision, and real-time "visibility" and do so via new or at least altered transportation networks. One result of these changes has been a newly "spiky world" (Florida 2005) whose peaks are places favored with superior accessibility. This chapter is about such places, the changes in transportation and logistics that have fueled their rise, and the development that their advantages have engendered.

One peak in this new topography, for instance, is Columbus, Ohio. Indeed, distribution – for Ambercrombie & Fitch, Borders Books, Petsmart, and scores of other companies – has become one of the engines of the Columbus economy. Overall, the Columbus transportation and warehousing sector directly employed 44,000 people (5 percent of the metro workforce) in 2007 and was growing much faster than the overall regional economy (City of Columbus 2009). Already in the mid-1990s it was estimated that the Columbus area was home to 150 distribution centers (Hesse and Rodrigue 2004). Ten are shown in Figure 36.1 to indicate the breadth of the companies involved. The appeal of Columbus to such businesses is obvious: a circle centered on Columbus with a radius of one-day's trucking distance encompasses much of the North American market, the city lies at the intersection of important east–west and north–south interstate highways and railroads, and its metro area contains two large airports. Yet what has happened in Columbus is hardly unique. A corridor of small towns along Interstate 81 in Pennsylvania and Maryland (Fuellhart and Marr 2007; Marr and Fuellhart 2008), California's Inland Empire (Bonacich and Wilson 2008), the Randstad in the Netherlands (de Ligt and Wever 1998), and the Pearl River Delta (Li and Cao 2005) are – at varying scales of analysis – just a handful of the other regions around the world whose development trajectories have likewise been affected by the new importance of logistics.

The rise of logistics, or the "logistics revolution" (Bonacich and Wilson 2008), comprises several intertwined changes:

i) the stronger integration of modes (intermodality) particularly via the containerization of cargo;

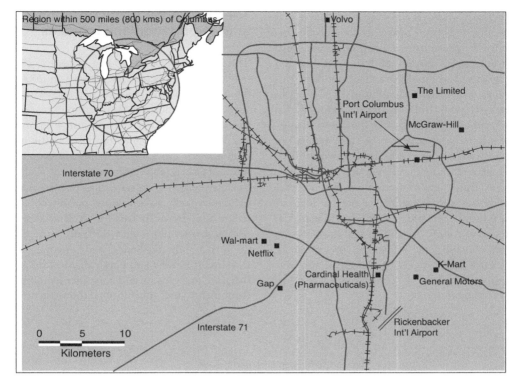

Figure 36.1 Distribution centers in the Columbus, Ohio area.
Source: Authors' research

ii) the shift from push to pull supply chains in which purchasing is driven by point-of-sale (POS) information;

iii) the overall reduction in levels of inventory, achieved partly by moving goods faster and just-in-time (JIT) from origin to destination;

iv) the application of electronic data interchange (EDI) and other information technologies to monitor and more precisely manage cargo flows in real time;

v) the development of more complex, often highly internationalized networks linking firms engaged in the production of some good;

vi) the outsourcing of logistics to specialized third party logistics (3PL) providers.

In lowering the cost of transportation – particularly the costs of inventory and transportation costs measured in terms of time – the logistics revolution has facilitated further internationalization of production, stronger levels of regional specialization, and enhanced economies of scale in many industries. These trends have consequences throughout the economy. Yet it is in places like Columbus that the transformation of transportation and logistics has been most pronounced.

In the sections that follow, we first map the geography of opportunities for regional development in transportation and logistics. While many traditional transportation hubs and gateways (e.g. seaports) have been rejuvenated by the logistics revolution, others have languished. At the same, new opportunities have been created for inland gateways

439

such as Columbus and even some places that are decidedly not "peaks" in the global economy. We then turn to examine the regional development impact of transportation and logistics. The rapid growth of goods movement has generated millions of new jobs directly and millions more indirectly in related industries (e.g., truck manufacturing). Further, new patterns of accessibility in transportation and logistics networks have had far-reaching development consequences. The third major section of the chapter addresses the implications of the logistics revolution for sustainability, particularly in terms of energy use and air pollution. Finally, we conclude by evaluating the potential rewards and dangers of making transportation and logistics a cornerstone of regional development policy.

The geography of opportunity in transportation and logistics

The movement of goods is a pervasive, yet spatially uneven economic activity. In 2008, for example, more than 40 percent of the world's containerized sea cargo traveled to, from, or through one of just 10 ports (Table 36.1). The concentration of traffic in such gateway cities fosters significant economies of scale (and diseconomies of scale, too – see below). Over time, the cost efficiency of a port such as Singapore permits it to secure a progressively larger hinterland, stimulating further traffic growth. Traffic growth, in turn, both facilitates and encourages investment in new and better physical infrastructure (e.g., automated container handling equipment) and institutional infrastructure

Table 36.1 The world's top containerports, 2008

Rank	Port	Thousands of twenty-foot equivalent units (TEUs)	Average annual growth since 2000 (%)
1	Singapore	29,918	7.3
2	Shanghai	27,980	22.2
3	Hong Kong	24,248	3.7
4	Shenzhen	21,414	23.4
5	Busan, South Korea	13,425	7.5
6	Dubai	11,828	18.4
7	Ningbo, China	11,226	37.0
8	Guangzhou	11,001	29.1
9	Rotterdam	10,800	7.0
10	Qingdao, China	10,320	21.9
11	Hamburg	9,700	10.9
12	Kaohsiung, Taiwan	9,677	3.4
13	Antwerp	8,664	9.9
14	Tianjin	8,500	22.2
15	Port Klang, Malaysia	7,970	12.1
16	Los Angeles	7,850	6.1
17	Long Beach	6,488	4.4
18	Tanjung Pelepas, Malaysia	5,600	38.3
19	Bremen/Bremerhaven	5,501	9.2
20	New York/New Jersey	5,265	7.1

Source: Bureau of Transportation Statistics (2009)

(e.g., expedited customs clearance procedures), and these developments in turn facilitate and encourage still further traffic growth. Such a virtuous cycle lies at the heart of Janelle's (1969) model of time-space convergence; transportation improvements permitting the convergence of places in time-space are more likely on routes linking important places, enhancing the accessibility advantages of already favored places. Janelle discussed this tendency in the context of road transportation within the American Midwest, but the same pattern is evident – albeit unevenly – on a global scale (Knowles 2006).

For instance, in 2006, the Maersk Line introduced the Emma Maersk, the first of a family of extremely large containerships, on a vast intercontinental itinerary with just 13 stops (Joseph 2006). Specifically, the 11,000 twenty-foot equivalent unit (TEU) containership was deployed on Maersk's Asia-Europe one route linking Aarhus, Gothenburg, Bremerhaven, Rotterdam, Algeciras, Suez Canal, Singapore, Kobe, Nagoya, Yokohama, Shenzhen, Hong Kong, Tanjung Pelepas (Malaysia) and back to Europe. The ship's huge size translated into lower unit costs, favoring this handful of ports. Further, the flow of traffic through Singapore and other large ports has been complemented by the development of "distriparks" adjacent to the port where consolidation, sampling, inventory management, product customization, merge-in-transit, storage, and other increasingly sophisticated logistics services are performed, further augmenting the port's pull on the traffic within its hinterland (Zhu et al. 2002). Giant vessels such as the Emma Maersk – like other transportation innovations – both draw upon and reinforce the resulting concentration of traffic.

And yet, the stature of hubs and gateways is by no means fixed. Yokohoma, for instance, ranked eighth among containerports in 1995 but had fallen to thirtieth by 2008. Shenzhen surged in the opposite direction as its two terminals (Yantian and Shekou) zoomed from their opening in the early 1990s to

become, combined, the fourth most heavily trafficked containerport in the world by 2008 (Table 36.1). The divergent fortunes of these two hubs reflect the fact that cargo flows are ultimately dependent upon patterns of economic activity. This basic fact has an important implication for regional development: regions with weak or declining economies are ill-positioned to harness the logistics revolution.

Shenzhen illustrates two of the prerequisites for new players in this sector of the economy. First, it has a strategically valuable location; specifically, Shenzhen is located near the center of the thriving Pearl River Delta (Figure 36.2). The Pearl River Delta is home to three of the ten busiest container ports in the world and the second busiest cargo airport. The airports in Guangzhou and Shenzhen meanwhile have been selected by FedEx and UPS, respectively, for their intra-Asian hubs. Second, the political commitment and financial capital to bring the new gateway to fruition were in abundance when Shenzhen's terminals were planned and then built. A strategic location and plenty of money and political will to build new infrastructure also help to explain the surge in the stature of Dubai, another fast-rising star among the ranks of the world's container ports.

A similar conjunction of factors explains the uneven growth of the world's top air cargo hubs (Table 36.2). Again, Dubai and Chinese gateways have enjoyed the fastest recent growth. One key difference between air and sea cargo, however, is the degree to which an air cargo hub can be affected, for better or for ill, by the decisions of a single carrier, such as FedEx in Memphis International. We return to this point in the last section of the chapter.

Memphis is an example of inland hub and, in that regard, it illustrates a broader trend for the handling and distribution of cargo to move farther toward the interior of continents and away from coastal gateways. This trend, which is evident in Europe but especially prominent in North America, is played

441

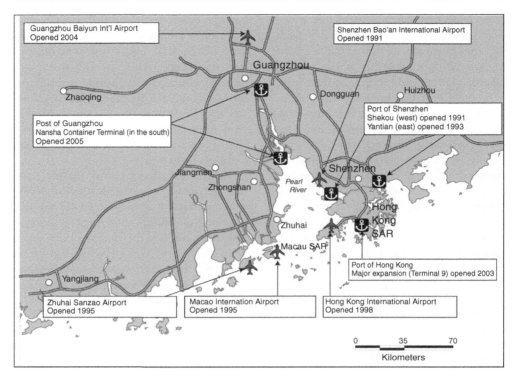

Figure 36.2 Transportation infrastructure expansion in the Pearl River Delta.
Source: Authors' research

out a two scales. First, mid-continent hubs such as Columbus and Memphis have become more prominent with the modal shift of goods traffic toward air cargo and trucks (Hesse and Rodrigue 2004). Second, land-hungry warehouses and distribution centers (DCs) have grown rapidly in areas located just inland from major seaports. For instance, Ikea's DC for the western US and Canada is located in Tejon Ranch, a privately owned logistics development 170 kilometers north of the ports of Los Angeles and Long Beach (Rodrigue and Hesse 2007). Conversely in Asia there has been less inward movement of logistics, with much of the handling of inbound, outbound, and trans-shipped cargo still done in the immediate vicinity of key ports, for instance. As a result the development impact of a hub like the Port of Singapore is concentrated in the

metropolitan area of which it is a part (Lee *et al.* 2008).

Finally, despite the concentration of traffic in favored hubs, it is not just in and near the "peaks" of the spiky world that the logistics revolution has affected regional development. In small, but strategically located towns such as Wilmington, Ohio and in gateways to peripheral regions such as Mombasa, Kenya in East Africa, transportation and logistics powerfully shape development trajectories, too. We return to this point in the final section of the chapter.

Transportation, logistics and regional development

Two broad kinds of impacts are considered here: the creation of jobs in the transportation

Table 36.2 World's top cargo hubs, 2008

Rank	Airport	Cargo (thousands of tonnes)	Average annual growth since 2000 (%)
1	Memphis Int'l	3,695	5.1
2	Hong Kong Int'l	3,661	6.2
3	Pudong Int'l (Shanghai)	2,603	15.9
4	Incheon Int'l (Seoul)	2,424	3.3
5	Ted Stevens Anchorage Int'l	2,340	3.3
6	Paris Charles de Gaulle Int'l	2,280	4.4
7	Frankfurt	2,111	2.7
8	Narita Int'l (Tokyo)	2,100	1.0
9	Louisville Int'l-Standiford Field	1,974	3.3
10	Changi (Singapore)	1,884	1.3
11	Dubai Int'l	1,825	15.3
12	Miami Int'l	1,807	1.2
13	Los Angeles Int'l	1,630	(2.8)
14	Amsterdam Airport Schiphol	1,603	3.0
15	Taipei Taoyuan Int'l	1,493	2.7
16	Heathrow (London)	1,486	0.7
17	John F. Kennedy Int'l (New York)	1,451	(2.8)
18	Beijing Capital Int'l	1,366	7.4
19	Chicago O'Hare Int'l	1,332	(1.2)
20	Suvarnabhumi (Bangkok)	1,173	3.8

Source: Airport Council International (2009)

sector (broadly defined to include warehousing and other logistics enterprises) and then the broader, catalytic effects of transportation accessibility and logistics capability upon the structure and performance of regional economies.

Jobs in transportation and logistics

The movement, storage, and handling of goods sustain millions of jobs directly across the world. In the United States, for instance, cargo transportation and warehousing employed at least 2.3 million people in 2006 or a little less than 3 percent of the workforce (US Census 2009). Between 1998 and 2006, employment in this sector grew five times faster than employment in the US economy generally, due in part to the outsourcing of logistics by manufacturing firms. Whether the growth of transportation and

logistics jobs is beneficial for regional economies depends upon the kinds of jobs created, including their associated wage and skill levels. Here the story is mixed. Some dockworkers in major US ports, for instance, have achieved substantial earnings increases due to the pivotal position they occupy in global supply chains, the strength of their union, and the high labor productivity achieved through the panoply of technologies related to containerization (Hall 2009). Yet the highest wages go only to those who occupy the most critical positions, such as the operators of giant cranes at portside; there are many more drayage truckers whose earnings are meager and under heavy pressure from newly arrived migrant workers (Bensman 2008). And the employment impact of some of the fastest growing segments of the transportation sector, especially warehousing, is muted by their heavy reliance on temporary employees (Bonacich and Wilson 2008).

Furthermore, globalization has enlarged the geographic scope of cargo flows so that there are more choices of hubs and corridors via which to move goods and concomitantly greater competition among workers in different places. Thus, port workers in Singapore, the world's busiest container port and one famous for its extraordinary speed and efficiency, were compelled by the government-linked Port of Singapore Authority to accept pay cuts in 2003 to fend off the challenge posed by lower cost ports elsewhere in Asia (Fang 2003).

Ultimately, what one may say of labor in the transport and logistics sector is that employment has grown rapidly in tandem with world trade and that there is a wide variety of jobs involved in the movement of goods; some are associated with very high skill and/or education levels and pay accordingly, but most are not. Of course, the overall employment impact of the sector extends to other parts of the economy, too, via the purchase of inputs (e.g., trucks, fuel, warehouse stacking systems, accounting services, etc.) and the spending of workers themselves. For instance, an input-output analysis of Cumberland and Franklin Counties in Pennsylvania (part of the I-81 corridor mentioned above) found a relatively low employment multiplier for warehousing and trucking combined (Fuellhart and Marr 2007). Specifically, these two industries employed 15,800 directly but supported 27,500 jobs overall – implying a multiplier of about 1.7405. This modest multiplier reflects low wages in the industry and the fact that the industry is near the end of the typical supply chain.

Cargo network accessibility and regional economic development

A limitation of input-output modeling – the methodology employed in the Pennsylvania study – is that it is based on a static picture of a regional economy; such studies therefore often fail to account for the way in which an improved transportation system alters a region's economic structure. The importance of that failing is evident in a mid-1990s analysis of several air cargo hubs (Oster *et al.* 1997). Two techniques were used to measure the broader effects of expanded hub employment in Memphis, Louisville, and Cincinnati in order to assess the likely impact of FedEx plans for a bigger hub at Indianapolis. The first approach, input-output modeling, found that the employment multiplier for the air transportation sector in these cities was a little more than 2. The second approach, econometric modeling, found much higher multipliers (e.g., 3.75 for Memphis). The difference between the two sets of multipliers has to do with how accessibility changes an economy. Input-output analysis assumes a steady relationship between airports and other elements of the economy, but as the carriers based at these hubs spawn more and denser linkages to places around the globe, their attraction as sites for certain other economic functions increases (SRI International 2001), apparently in a nonlinear fashion.

Certainly, the catalytic effects of accessibility figure prominently in the work of John Kasarda concerning air transport-centered development (e.g. Kasarda 2005; Kasarda and Sullivan 2005). Kasarda has argued that the contemporary economy places a premium on speed and agility, favoring locations near air transport hubs. The result is a new form of airport-centric development he terms the "aerotropolis," among whose hallmarks are airport-adjacent logistics parks, fulfillment centers, and distribution centers. Singapore is an example of an aerotropolis (Lindsay 2006), and there is little doubt that its centrality in the air cargo industry has fostered superior services in the air and on the ground, facilitating the city-state's movement up the value chain, especially in the electronics industry (Leinbach and Bowen 2005).

And yet Kasarda's work can be criticized for overemphasizing air accessibility. In an era of unprecedented intermodality, accessibility in multiple networks is becoming more important, particularly as manufacturers develop more sophisticated logistic strategies premised on multimodal hybrid networks and flexibility (Henstra *et al.* 2007). Geographically, such strategies favor, of course, places that have multimodal access. For instance, Sony replaced 14 European warehouses in 2001 with a single European Distribution Center at Tilburg, the Netherlands – a location that has excellent sea, air, and ground network accessibility as Schiphol Airport, the Port of Rotterdam, and major highways are all nearby (Lovell *et al.* 2005).

Externalities, sustainability and the logistics revolution

The increased volume of goods traffic has brought with it significant externalities including land take, road congestion, air pollution, noise pollution, and the "ugly blight" (Hunt 2006) of big box DCs. Some communities have decided there is a limit to their appetite for more business. For instance, Frankfurt, Europe's second largest air cargo hub, has imposed increasingly stringent restrictions on night-time operations. Because freighter aircraft operations are concentrated at night (to facilitate late-day pickups and early-morning deliveries), the Frankfurt restrictions are a significant impediment to growth for hometown carrier Lufthansa. Partly as a result of those concerns, in 2008 Lufthansa and DHL – which had been pushed from its hub at Brussels by similar night-time restrictions – formed a new cargo airline called AeroLogic to operate from a hub in Leipzig where there are no night-time restrictions (Lloyd's List 2008).

More generally, sustainable logistics are likely to become a major concern for the industry, policymakers, and academics in the future (Black 2007). Sustainable logistics means paying attention not only to local externalities such as those described above

but also the broader consequences of freight transportation including its contribution to global climate change and the exhaustion of easily accessed oil reserves. The logistics revolution, insofar as it has fostered faster, more frequent, small, often globally dispersed shipments militates against sustainability by favoring more energy-intensive modes (e.g., air); and yet the cost-effective management of supply chains, which is also a part of the logistics revolution, has meant in some cases a shift away from high cost (both financially and environmentally) modes. For example, Intel, which once moved 98 percent of its goods by air, has reduced that share to 88 percent (Lloyd's List 2008).

Of course, the airline industry is itself becoming more environmentally friendly with the development of more fuel-efficient aircraft like the Airbus A380 and new air traffic control procedures such as continuous descent. Other modes, too, are changing in a similar direction. Political pressure and increased fuel costs are likely to accelerate the pace of technological change within modes, encourage competition among modes on efficiency grounds, and perhaps spark a reversal of some of the trends (e.g., globalized production) that have defined the logistics revolution. The ramifications for patterns of economic development, including regional economic development, are likely to be far-reaching and should be a theme of further research in this area.

Conclusion

Drawn by the capacity of transportation and logistics to create thousands of jobs, many places have worked hard to gain, to keep, or to build upon an advantage in the world's supply and distribution networks. The rewards – and the dangers – in pursuing such a strategy are many. Consider the case of Wilmington, Ohio. In 2004, Germany's DHL chose Wilmington as its primary US air hub as part of a broader effort to challenge FedEx and UPS on their home turf. Like Columbus 100 kilometers to the north, Wilmington is well positioned to serve as a national distribution center, but a further factor in Wilmington's favor was the package of state and local government incentives, worth an estimated $400 million (Driehaus 2008). Wilmington's selection brought many new jobs; indeed, by 2008, DHL and its subsidiaries employed 7,000 people in a city of 13,000 people. But the good times did not last for long. In November 2008, DHL announced its decision to withdraw from the domestic overnight express market in the US, and to abandon its hub in Wilmington. In a matter of months, DHL employment in Wilmington fell by half with the strong likelihood of further steep job cuts (Nolan 2009; Dreihaus 2008). Other businesses that had been drawn to the Wilmington area by the accessibility afforded through DHL's hub also left. For example, DealerTrack, an overnight processor of car loans decided to move from Wilmington to Memphis, primarily to be close to the FedEx hub there (Risher 2009).

Ultimately, the story of Wilmington is about the dangers of basing regional economic development upon an industry as spatially dynamic as transport and logistics. The dangers are enlarged in places such as Wilmington that are not the "peaks" in the spiky world and that as a result have little locally or regionally generated traffic and just one or a few key players. Both characteristics help to explain the world of difference between the enduring significance of deeply rooted gateways such as Singapore and the scramble for position among smaller hubs competing on narrow, even fleeting advantages. Yet, as noted above, even Singapore is not invulnerable to the industry's dynamism. Indeed, the new Malaysian port at Tanjung Pelepas (see Table 36.1) has eaten into some of Singapore's business; Maersk and Evergreen, two of the world's largest shipping lines, moved their Southeast Asian transshipment business from Singapore to PTP,

partly due to the latter's lower handling costs (Richardson 2002).

Ultimately, in an industry whose purpose is movement, few spatial patterns are constant. Changes in the geography of freight flows and shifts in the strategies of major players such as DHL have reshaped the topography of advantage in the past and will undoubtedly do so again in the future. The state – through its infrastructure investments and policies toward aircraft noise, for instance – is likely to play an increasingly influential role in that topography, too. These myriad forces will bring new places to the fore in freight transportation flows: places like Hahn, Germany that are in the shadow of increasingly congested hubs – Frankfurt in Hahn's case – in developed countries (Behnen 2004) and new winners like Dar es Salaam and Mombasa in the trend toward increased traffic concentration in developing economies (Hoyle and Charlier 1995). The growth of traffic to, from, and through such communities can be expected to bring a familiar mixture of positive development impacts and negative externalities. Managing the balance of these outcomes, both in new hubs and in old ones, will remain an important challenge.

References

Behnen, T. (2004) "Germany's Changing Airport Infrastructure: The Prospects for Newcomer Airports Attempting Market Entry," *Journal of Transport Geography* 12 (4), 277–286.

Bensman, D. (2008) "Globalization and the Labor Markets of the Logistics Industry." A presentation at the Sloan Industries Studies Conference, Boston, May 2. Available online at www.web.mit.edu.

Black, W. R. (2007) "Sustainable Solutions for Freight Transport," in Leinbach, T. R. and Capineri, C. (eds) *Globalized Freight Transport: Intermodality, E-Commerce, Logistics, and Sustainablity*, Cheltenham: Edward Elgar, 189–216.

Bonacich, E. and Wilson, J. B. (2008) *Getting the Goods; Ports, Labor, and the Logistics Revolution*, Ithaca, NY: Cornell University Press.

Bureau of Transportation Statistics (2009) *America's Container Ports: Freight Hubs That Connect Our Nation to Global Markets*, June. Available online at www.bts.gov.

City of Columbus (2009) "Economic Advisory Committee Report and Recommendations," March 5. Available online at www.cityof columbus.org.

De Ligt, T. and Weger, E. (1998) "European Distribution Centres: Location Patterns," *Tijdschift voor Economische en Sociale Geografie* 89 (2), 217–223.

Dreihaus, B. (2008) "DHL cuts 9,500 Jobs in US, and an Ohio Town Takes the Brunt," *The New York Times*, November 11: B3.

Fang, N. (2003) "PSA Slashes Wages by Up to 14%," *The Straits Times* (Singapore), July 25.

Florida, R. (2005) "The World Is Spiky," *Atlantic Monthly* October, 48–51.

Fuellhart, K. and Marr, P. (2007) "Economic Impacts of Trucking and Warehousing in South-Central Pennsylvania," *Pennsylvania Geographer* 45 (2), 85–103.

Hall, P.V. (2009) "Container Ports, Local Benefits, and Transportation Worker Earnings," *Geojournal* 74 (1), 67–83.

Henstra, D., Ruijgrok, C. and Tavasszy, L. (2007) "Globalized Trade, Logistics, and Intermodality: European Perspectives," in Leinbach, T. R. and Capineri, C. (eds) *Globalized Freight Transport: Intermodality, E-Commerce, Logistics, and Sustainablity*, Cheltenham: Edward Elgar, 135–163.

Hesse, M. and Rodrigue, J.-P. (2004) "The Transport Geography of Logistics and Freight Distribution," *Journal of Transport Geography* 12 (3), 171–184.

Hoyle, B. and Charlier, J. (1995) "Inter-Port Competition in Developing Countries: An East African Case Study," *Journal of Transport Geography* 3 (2): 87–103.

Hunt, T. (2006) "Warehouse of the World: Out-of-Town Depots Are an Ugly Blight on the Landscape and Will Destroy our Civic Life," *Guardian*, July 12, 32.

Janelle, D. G. (1969) "Spatial Reorganization: A Model and Concept," *Annals of the Association of American Geographers* 72 (1), 8–15.

Joseph, G. (2006) "Emma Helps PSA, Maersk Make Peace," *The Business Times* (Singapore), October 3.

Kasarda, J. D. (2000/2001) "Logistics and the Rise of the Aerotropolis," *Real Estate Issues* 25 (4), winter, 43–48.

Kasarda, J. D. (2005) "Gateway Airports, Speed, and the Rise of the Aerotropolis," in Gibson, D.V., Heitor, M.V. and Ibarra-Yunez, A.

(eds) *Learning and Knowledge for the Network Society*, West Lafayette, Indiana: Purdue University Press, 99–108.

Kasarda, J. and Sullivan, D.L. (2005) "Air Cargo. Liberalization, and Economic Development," *Annals of Air and Space Law* 31.

Knowles, R. (2006) "Transport Shaping Space: Differential Collapse in Time-Space," *Journal of Transport Geography* 14 (6), 407–425.

Lee, S.W., Song, D.-W. and Ducruet, C. (2008) "A Tale of the World's Ports: The Spatial Evolution in the Global Hub Port Cities," *Geoforum* 39 (1), 372–385.

Leinbach, T. R. and Bowen, J. T. (2005) "Air Cargo Services, Global Production Networks and Competitive Advantage in Asian City-Regions," in Daniels, P.W. Ho, K.C. and Hutton, T.A. (eds) *Service Industries and Asia-Pacific Cities*, New York: Routledge, 216–240.

Li, P. and Cao, X.-S. (2005) "Evolution and Development of the Guangzhou-Hong Kong Corridor," *Chinese Geographical Science* 15 (3), 206–211.

Lindsay, G. (2006) "Rise of the Aerotropolis," *Fast Company* July/August, 76–85.

Lloyd's List (2008) "AeroLogic Lifts Off with EUR550m Joint Cargo Venture in Tow," February 4, 6.

Lovell, A., Law, R. and Stimson, J. (2005) "Product Value Density: Managing Diversity through Supply Chain Segmentation," *International Journal of Logistics Management* 16 (1), 142–158.

Marr, P. and Fuellhart, K. (2008) "A Transportation Assessment of the Warehousing and Trucking Industries in Franklin and Cumberland Counties, Pennsylvania," *Pennsylvania Geographer* 46 (1), 3–34.

Nolan, J. (2009) "No End in Sight for DHL-UPS Talks," *Dayton Daily News*, January 27: A6.

Oster, C.V., Rubin, B. M. and Strong, J. S. (1997) "Economic Effects of Transportation Investments: The Case of Federal Express," *Transportation Journal* 37 (2), 34–44.

Richardson, M. (2002) "Malaysia Aims to Become a Key Southeast Asian Shipping Hub: Singapore Faces a Rival Next Door," *New York Times*, February 1.

Risher, W. (2009) "DealerTrack moving to Memphis," *The Commercial Appeal* (Memphis), February 10.

Rodrigue, J.-P. and Hesse, M. (2007) "Globalized Trade and Logistics: North American Perspectives," in Leinbach, T. R. and Capineri, C. (eds) *Globalized Freight Transport: Intermodality, E-Commerce, Logistics, and Sustainablity*, Cheltenham: Edward Elgar, 103–134.

SRI International (2001) *Global Impacts of Fedex in the New Economy*. Available online at www.sri.com/policy/csted/reports/economics/fedex/.

US Census (2009) *County Business Patterns*. Available online at www.census.gov.

Zhu, J., Lean, H. S. and Ying, S. K. (2002) "The Third-Party Logistics Services and Globalization of Manufacturing," *International Planning Studies* 7 (1), 89–104.

Further reading

Bonacich, E. and Wilson, J. B. (2008) *Getting the Goods Ports, Labor, and the Logistics Revolution*, Ithaca, NY: Cornell University Press. (Contains a highly accessible, empirically grounded account of changes in the logistics and the implications of those changes for major stakeholders, especially labor unions.)

Kasarda, J. D. (2005) "Gateway Airports, Speed, and the Rise of the Aerotropolis," in Gibson, D. V. Heitor, M. V. and Ibarra-Yunez, A. (eds) *Learning and Knowledge for the Network Society*, West Lafayette, Indiana: Purdue University Press, 99–108. (Concisely describes Kasarda's ideas concerning the aerotropolis.)

Lasserre, F. (2004) "Logistics and the Internet: Transportation and Location Issues Are Crucial in the Logistics Chain," *Journal of Transport Geography* 12 (1), 73–84. (An insightful analysis of the implication of e-commerce for freight and logistics patterns.)

Leinbach, T. R. and Capineri, C. (eds) (2007) *Globalized Freight Transport: Intermodality, E-Commerce, Logistics, and Sustainablity*, Cheltenham: Edward Elgar. (Draws together experts from geography, political science, public policy and other fields on both sides of the Atlantic to present a rich overview of changes in freight transportation.)

37

(Im)migration, local, regional and uneven development

Jane Wills, Kavita Datta, Jon May, Cathy McIlwaine,
Yara Evans and Joanna Herbert

Introduction

Migration has a long and intimate relationship with local and regional development. On the one hand, policy-makers may use (im)migration as a means to develop a geographical area, seeking to attract desirable migrants as a means to fill labour shortages, foster economic growth and promote competitiveness. On the other hand, policy-makers may seek to promote emigration as a way of tackling under- and unemployment and raising additional capital in the form of remittances sent home by overseas workers. In the first case, migration provides a new source of labour and in the latter, the capital required for economic development. This chapter starts by exploring these twin development strategies focusing first on emerging policy frameworks that are designed to attract international migrants and then those that seek to promote the export of labour for economic development. In both cases, labour is positioned as the key agent in local and regional development even if that labour is not always physically present. Once these foundations are laid, the chapter then goes on to explore the consequences of labour migration in relation to uneven development. It is argued that there is a tendency for

migration to both reflect and perpetuate uneven development at a number of scales. As such, this chapter seeks to explore the difficult issues that lie at the heart of the intersection between labour migration and local and/or regional development. To do so, the chapter draws on current research in London and the UK, as well as secondary evidence about development in the rest of the world.

Changing immigration regimes

Structural shifts in global political economy have served to increase rates of population movement in recent years. The IOM (2008: 2) estimate that in 2005 some 191 million people were living outside their country of birth, a figure two and a half times the number in 1965, with these trends looking set to continue. International migration is now recognised as being one of the most critical challenges facing the world as well as one of its most crucial resources. Yet while international migration continues to increase as workers move to avoid conflict and/or take up employment, politicians remain accountable to national electorates. Internal divisions over the issue of immigration inevitably pull politicians two ways both in favour of, and against, immigration controls (Hollifield 1992; Freeman 1995). Politicians rarely adopt the pure political liberalism that would abandon any immigration controls and in the present period, most are adopting some form of hierarchical and stratified types of control.

As an example, the British government has recently sought to adapt its immigration regime. Recognising the economic advantages posed by certain forms of immigration – particularly in relation to skilled workers and those able to fill labour market shortages – new legislation has sought to create a hierarchical immigration regime that attracts the desirable and excludes the unwanted. In her speech to the Institute for Public Policy Research (IPPR) in September 2000, the Immigration Minister Barbara Roche signalled what has been a dramatic shift in policy by declaring: "We are in competition for the brightest and best talents. The market for skilled labour is a global market and not necessarily a buyers' market." Drawing parallels with the effective use of immigration as a strategy for economic development in countries like the USA, Canada and Australia, Roche anticipated a torrent of future legislation enacted by New Labour in the following years. In a scaled-up version of Richard Florida's (2002) arguments about the role of the 'creative class' in the dynamism of conurbations, the UK government has sought to open its borders to those who are seen as sufficiently highly skilled and entrepreneurial that they can contribute to the wealth of the nation. Rather than limiting immigration per se, the government has sought to manage it for economic advantage (Favell and Hansen 2002; see also Flynn 2005). As a result, and in contrast to the previous century, the UK has become a country of net immigration.

Thus, in tandem with developments elsewhere in the world, British immigration policy is being developed in the interests of the economy with: "borders that are open to those who bring skills, talent, business and creativity that boost our economy, yet closed to those who might cause us harm or seek to enter illegally" (Home Office and Commonwealth Office 2007: 2). The new points-based immigration regime is the centre-piece of this new approach to migration (Home Office 2006). Highly skilled migrants are positioned at the top of the hierarchy (in Tier 1) with full rights to the labour market and the benefit system. Those who are granted access to work for a particular employer in an identified shortage sector (that depends on research and analysis conducted by the Migration Advisory Committee) have to have a requisite level of English language skills to fulfil the terms of Tier 2. While this tier does not grant access to the benefit system it does afford migrants some possibility of applying for citizenship when they have been in the UK for as long as five years. In contrast, Tier 3 – covering so-called unskilled migration – has no such route to belonging. Ministers now expect all unskilled vacancies to be filled by migrants from the wider EU – and while full labour market access was granted to would-be immigrants from the first wave of EU succession states (Cyprus, Malta, Estonia, Croatia, Czech Republic, Hungary, Lithuania, Poland, Slovakia and Slovenia) from May 2004, any further vacancies are to be filled through time-limited quotas of Bulgarians and Romanians (the countries of the so-called A2). As in the past, those classified as unskilled from outside the EU can only gain access to the UK's labour market through family reunification, as international students or as refugees. But while student visas were once a relatively easy route for would-be migrants from the global South to enter the UK and stay despite immigration controls, educational providers (who are to be registered under Tier 4) are now expected to sponsor and monitor the activities of their students for violations of immigration control. Indeed, the UK government has renewed its efforts to control and monitor all international immigrants. Those who don't meet the terms of the points-based immigration regime are now subject to identification, detention and deportation back home.

The implementation of this new immigration regime has significant implications for local and regional development within the UK. Recent experience suggests that the policy-makers responsible for economic development in different parts of the country have had to develop a twin-track approach towards immigration reform. In the short term, policy-makers have had to try and attract – or repel – the migrants they need – or don't need – to underpin local and regional development strategies. In the longer term, they also have an obvious interest in influencing the trajectory of national policy developments as they unfold. This is often difficult, however, as local policy-makers tend to find themselves in a relatively weak position with regards to national immigration reform (Ellis 2006). Although sub-national localities are profoundly affected by changes in the rules governing the recruitment of international students and/or access to the labour market, for example, such rules are created and enforced by bodies operating beyond the regional and/or local scale. Policy-makers are thus entangled in the spatial politics of immigration policy whereby the interests of the nation may undermine local and regional interests. In addition, policy-makers often have to work through the intermediaries of the immigration regime, such as employers or educational establishments, if they are to influence rates of local migration.

Thus, in relation to the UK's new points-based regime, migrants granted access under Tiers 2, 3 and 4, as well as those being processed by the asylum system are spatially constrained once they arrive within the UK. Their terms of entry are tied to having a particular job, studying in a particular place or securing state support by living in a particular location (Phillimore and Goodson 2006). Attracting or repelling migrants depends upon the actions of those given authority by the national regime. Even in cases where

migrants have free movement – such as those under Tier 1 and those from the wider EU (including the so-called A8 migrants) – policy-makers are left to deal with the impact of the market itself. Thus the post-2004 arrivals from Eastern Europe have taken up low-waged employment across the UK in response to local labour market demand. Local and regional policy-makers have been left to deal with the impact of local in-flows, but they have little if any control over the nature of labour supply. Indeed, the A8 migrants have caused something of a policy crisis by settling in areas where local authorities and related agencies have little experience of responding to the needs of new populations or the challenges posed to community cohesion (McKay and Winkelman-Gleed 2005; Stenning and Dawley 2009). While migrant workers have generally been very beneficial for these economies they have also brought challenges in terms of service delivery. Local policy-makers have had to react to the impact of national-level policy and market forces (IPPR-CRE 2007).

In this context, different regions will tend to develop differentiated responses to the national immigration regime, seeking to secure local interests in relation to policy and its implications for regional and local development. In the UK, Scotland and London provide the most obvious examples of this locally-specific and differentiated response. The Scottish Parliament and associated policy-makers have been unusual in trail-blazing a very positive public policy agenda in relation to immigration. These bodies have seen immigration as a way to increase the size and skills of the local population, and to promote economic activity. Until it was superseded by the national points-based system, the Scottish Parliament sought to attract international graduates to Scotland after their studies. In what was called the Fresh Talent Scotland initiative, the Parliament provided funding for advisory staff and resources to attract skilled workers to the region. In this case, migrant workers were characterised as an asset to local and regional economic development and they have been encouraged to make Scotland their home (Houston *et al.* 2008).

In many ways, London has been similarly positioned in relation to the national immigration regime. Here, policy-makers have also recognised the extent to which the regional economy and its prosperity have come to depend upon supplies of foreign-born workers. In contrast to Scotland, however, London has had little difficulty in attracting new migrants such that recent statistics indicate that as many as 35 per cent of the working age population were foreign-born by the mid-2000s, with much greater concentrations among the low paid (see May *et al.* 2007; Wills *et al.* 2009a). In this regard, policy-makers have been more concerned about the implications of national legislation for local patterns of growth. In their response to the government's consultation about the case for managed migration outlined in the White Paper *Secure Borders, Safe Haven*, for example, the Greater London Authority (GLA 2002) opposed the proposed limits on numbers, reduced access to the asylum system and new barriers to citizenship. Indeed, it is significant that such concerns have persisted beyond the dramatic change in the leadership at the Authority following elections in 2008, with the Conservative Mayor, Boris Johnson, also championing London's particular interests in regards to the national immigration regime. Having agreed to explore the need to turn 'Strangers into Citizens' in a public dialogue with the broad-based community organisation London Citizens in the run-up to the election, Mayor Johnson has since commissioned research into the issue of irregular migration and has recently made the case for reform (LSE 2009). As he put it in a press release advocating a one-off regularisation of migrants issued in March 2009:

> [Irregular migration is a] huge issue for the capital … London is disproportionately affected with more irregular migrants … than anywhere else in the

UK. I believe it is perverse, particularly given the current economic climate that illegal immigrants can use public services such as the NHS and schools but are actually prevented from paying the taxes that fund these services … I believe we should carefully consider the merits of an earned amnesty for long-term migrants to maximise the economic potential of these people so they can pay their way. I do not want to be the Mayor of two categories of people in our great city, one group who live normally and another who live in the shadows unable to contribute fully to [the] rest of society.

> (GLA 2009)

Thus the national management of migration poses a range of challenges to actors positioned at local and regional scales. While some parts of a nation may have a policy commitment to increase in-migration (both domestic and international) as a means to support economic development, other regions may not. Moreover, different groups within any local community will also be differentially positioned in regard to the debate about immigration reform. Although (im)migration may be viewed as a route to increased competitiveness and economic growth by some, others are likely to see migrants as potential competitors for work, housing and resources. Indeed, those communities already facing the challenge of surviving in a subcontracted deflationary economy with poor employment prospects and diminishing public service provision have understandably been the most likely to view immigration with the greatest concern. In this regard, research exploring the reception and integration of new migrant communities in different localities across the UK has found a clear link between attitudes towards immigration and economic status (IPPR-CRE 2007). Those living in relatively affluent areas, with tight labour markets and above-average levels of skills (in this case, Edinburgh, Perth and Kinross in Scotland) tended not to see migrants as a threat to their lives. In contrast, those living in relatively poor areas, with high rates of unemployment, high levels of homelessness and/or overcrowding and below-average levels of skills (in this case Birmingham, and Barking and Dagenham in London) were likely to be much more concerned about increased rates of migration.

The prevailing political-economic geography of a nation – its uneven development – will thus underlie differential approaches to immigration in relation to strategies for local and regional development. Moreover, locally based policy-makers will inevitably have a different view to those determining the laws of the state. Such challenges are further magnified at the transnational scale, as we outline further below.

Remittance-sending for development?

Governments in the global South have increasingly come to view their workers as a resource to be exploited either in situ (via local economic development strategies and state-sponsored Export Processing Zones) or by moving abroad. The government of the Philippines has been something of a pioneer in this respect, promoting the export of labour. Developed over several generations, the country now has a strong culture of international labour migration in which official policies facilitate the out-migration of workers at all skill levels in the expectation that these 'bagong bayani' or 'new heroes' will send money back home. Such remittances now amount to greater sums than those sent in overseas development assistance from the global North to many parts of the global South (Datta *et al.* 2007). Recent figures available from the World Bank suggest that worldwide remittances exceeded US$ 305 billion in 2008, up from just US$ 2 billion in 1970 (Ratha 2007; World Bank 2006). This money is now critical to local and

regional development in large parts of the world. Our recent research to explore the labour market experiences and prospects of migrant workers in low-paid employment in London revealed very high levels of remitting, and given the diversity of the population, this practice impacted on many parts of the world. As illustrated in Figure 37.1, our interview survey of more than 400 migrants identified people from 63 different countries of origin and as many as 73 per cent were sending money back home (see also Datta *et al.* 2007; Wills *et al.* 2009a).

As might be expected, this, and other research, has illuminated the extent to which remittances appear to function as crucial safety nets for households in situations where cash-strapped national governments are unable or unwilling to provide any ongoing relief (de Haas 2005; Van Hear and Sørensen 2003). In a country like Zimbabwe, for example, extreme economic deprivation has meant that nearly half of all households are heavily dependent upon migrant remittances for their everyday needs (Styan 2007). Migration can thus underpin life itself, being essential to survival (and thereby sometimes referred to as 'subsistence remittances') as well as bringing more lasting development. Indeed, a certain level of development is usually necessary before remittances are able to generate more general growth and activity beyond the household scale. In this regard, researchers have documented a potential continuum between so-called 'unproductive' and 'productive' investments. In the case of the former, remittances are used for essential household expenditure. In the latter, remittances have proved important in the purchase of land and housing, and in the development of local businesses which can then impact on local development rates (de Haas 2006).

This nexus between remittances and development is being increasingly recognised by governments, banks and public officials. As an example, Peru has recently pioneered the Quinto Suyo programme to tap the ambitions of Peruvian migrants resident in the

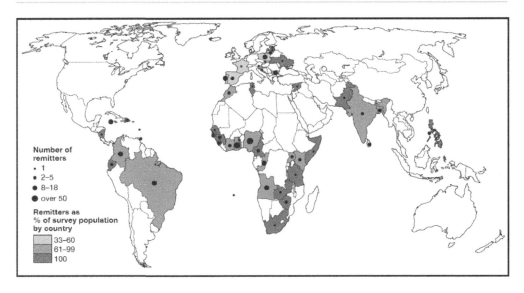

Figure 37.1 Remittance flows from London to the rest of the world.
Source: Authors' survey

US, Spain, Italy and Japan, allowing them directly to purchase housing in Peru through collaboration between Peruvian banks and foreign intermediaries (Conthe and García 2007). Governments have similarly started to support the collective development efforts of migrants themselves. In circumstances in which migrants are already working together to foster development – via informal connections, charitable work and hometown associations (Mohan 2008) – some governments are reinforcing this work. In the Mexican tres-por-uno (three for one) programme, for example, each 'migradollar' sent from abroad is complemented by three dollars from various governmental levels to be spent on local development work (Faist 2008).

Such examples illustrate the ways in which policy-makers in migrant-sending countries are beginning to recognise the potential development gains to be made from the money migrants are earning abroad. Indeed, by providing additional financial and physical infrastructure, local policy-makers can facilitate the developmental impact of the money

being remitted back home (see also Taylor *et al.* 1996). Yet remittances also have dangers for development in the poorest parts of the globe. Most obviously, there is evidence that remittances can intensify inequalities between migrant and non-migrant households with attendant implications for community relations (Osella and Osella 2000). In addition, there is a tendency to become increasingly reliant on foreign-earned cash. While domestic industries such as construction may flourish due to migrant investment in housing, for example, such activities simultaneously become highly dependent upon migrant remittances (Portes 2001). Such so-called 'productive' investments can also result in land and housing booms and consequent inflation in sending areas, which further marginalises non-migrant households without remittance income supporting their household (Ballard 2003). A dependency on remittances may thus 'infect' entire communities with particularly detrimental consequences for local economic development, engendering dependency, a withdrawal from broader livelihood opportunities and the neglect of any indigenous potential for growth. There is no certainty that remittances will facilitate sustainable development or that they will fuel greater equality at local, regional, national or international scales. Moreover, in providing a potential source of development funding, remittances can provide fodder for neoliberal ideologues who are eager to shift responsibility for development from the state to the poor, with migrants in host countries making huge sacrifices in order to bolster ailing economies back home (Datta *et al.* 2007).

(Im)migration and uneven development

Thus far, this chapter has argued that there are potential synergies between migration and local and/or regional development, but also that these synergies are by no means easy to sustain on the ground. While it is clear that migrants can provide the labour power and skills needed to underpin growth, and can generate the capital to support economic activities in the global South, it is also very difficult to ensure such positive feedback in practice. As we have seen, policy developed at one spatial scale may not suit development plans and needs at another; one group of people may be well served by migration while others are not; one place may benefit from migration while another is plunged into further decline. Any positive nexus between migration and development is thus fraught with potential pitfalls and problems.

In this section we argue that there is a tendency for migration to both reflect and perpetuate uneven development at a number of scales. Moreover, we suggest that despite recent arguments about the role of 'brain circulation' (Saxenian 2006) in local and regional development, much migration still involves the deskilling of migrants that then further undermines the potential benefits of labour migration for the economic development of both home and host locations. It is

also clear that migration can erode the space for 'high road' strategies of local and regional development in destination locations, again reinforcing uneven development at the sub-national scale.

Most obviously, migration is a product of uneven development. People are more likely to move when they are unable to support themselves in sustainable ways in their place of origin, and migrant flows often (although by no means always) reflect the uneven landscape of economic activity. If some poor localities and regions lose their labour power through (domestic or international) migration, it can then further reinforce their decline. In their explication of the so-called 'brain drain', for example, scholars and activists have highlighted the way in which skilled workers in one place are enticed elsewhere, further eroding the skills base of their home-nation. Given the low skills base in many African countries, it is not surprising that they have taken the lead in voicing these concerns, especially with regard to health workers. While the largest global suppliers of health personnel are from middle-income countries like India, the loss of doctors and nurses from poorer countries like Zimbabwe, Guinea-Bisssau and Uganda is deleterious to wider development goals (Skeldon 2008). As many as three-quarters of all native-born doctors emigrate from Zimbabwe within a few years of qualifying (Farrant *et al.* 2006) and more generally, about one-third of all African graduates now reside outside their country of birth – rising to as many as 42 per cent of skilled Ghanaians, and 36 per cent of skilled Nigerians (Grillo and Mazzucato 2008). Migration tends to suck the wealthiest and best-educated citizens from their homes in the South only to see them work in often inferior conditions in low or unskilled jobs in the lands of the North – thus contributing not only to a 'brain drain' but also to 'brain wastage'. Rather than being a positive cycle, and despite the impact of remittances, migration can thus be deleterious to local and economic development in the poorest parts

455

of the world. There is a danger that migration reinforces the uneven development it could otherwise do so much to reduce.

There is also a danger that the potential development impact of migration in host countries can also be undermined by the terms of migration itself, which often leads to 'brain wastage'. A combination of immigration control, labour market conditions, language skills and the non-transferability of professional qualifications means that many skilled workers are progressively deskilled and de-professionalised when they cross international borders for work.

Research in London, for example, has found many graduates working in low-waged employment in cleaning, catering and hospitality, facing significant barriers to progression in the labour market (Wills *et al.* 2009a). The low wages on offer mean that workers are often struggling to survive and are unable to remit large sums of money back home. It also implies that their skills are not fully exploited in relation to economic growth and success. Unless they are properly recognised, the resources proffered by migrant labour tend to be degraded as cheap labour, and deskilling means that valuable skills are lost.

On the other hand, recent evidence from Silicon Valley in the USA suggests that there is nothing inevitable about the 'brain drain' or 'brain wastage' of skilled migrants as they move across borders. Instead, the nature of the immigration regime, the actions of employers and the state can all help to foster what Saxenian (2006) refers to as 'brain circulation'. Her research among highly skilled information and communication technological (ICT) workers exposes the way in which such migrants can act as conduits to development in both host and home-nations; taking skills from one place to another, and augmenting the scope for innovation and valorisation in both (Saxenian, 2006). Indeed, such logic has underpinned the recent changes in the UK's immigration regime, outlined above, with priority access for highly skilled

workers now advocated on the basis of the economic needs of the nation.

Yet in practice, the UK government has provided very little access for the highly skilled from the poorest parts of the world who are often unable to meet the points threshold in relation to their qualifications, previous salary and English language proficiency, forcing them to take up less qualified work. In addition, Saxenian herself highlights the importance of the local regional context into which migrants return. While she documents the traditions of entrepreneurialism and efforts to foster a business culture in countries like Taiwan, such local conditions are often absent in poorer parts of the world. Moreover, as Gertler (2008: 107) suggests, the wider geo-political context in which economic activity takes place is also critical to the transplantation of business energy and ideas. Thus, while brain circulation is certainly possible, thus far at least, it has been characterised by the flows of workers between relatively developed economies (such as India and Taiwan) and the global North only in very particular conditions and contexts.

There are also dangers that immigration can distort development trajectories in host country states. In recent years, 'high road' strategies have been advocated as a means to foster sustainable local and regional economic development through skills, training and increased productivity that generate increased profits for employers and better wages for workers in a locally 'Fordist' platform for growth. It is argued that state-led investment in human capital can raise productivity and sustain the wage increases that can generate increased wealth to be shared (Malecki 2004; see also Pike *et al.* 2006). Yet given a supply of cheap workers, there is less incentive for policy-makers to pursue the high road rather than the low road to growth. Indeed, in conditions of the oversupply of cheap labour, there is no labour market pressure for employers to raise wages, improve training and raise productivity as a means to survive. The free hand of the market tends to reinforce a 'race to the bottom' in labour standards. Thus, despite its great wealth, a city like London has witnessed a sharp deterioration in the wages and conditions on offer to the low paid during the past twenty years. At a time when the city has had both high rates of local unemployment and high rates of labour in-migration, low-skilled labour has been in oversupply. In conditions in which there are as many as three low-skilled workers for each low-skilled job, wages have stagnated and even fallen for those doing the lowest paid jobs (see Wills *et al.* 2009a, 2009b).

Moreover, given the low wages and poor conditions of work for those at the bottom of the labour market, those who are able to claim benefits have often proved unwilling to engage in the labour market at all. In reviewing the evidence of the economic impact of immigration on the UK, the House of Lords' Select Committee on Economic Affairs (2008) has been particularly exercised by these long-term effects of migration. As they put it:

> Immigration, encouraged as a 'quick fix' in response to perceived labour and skills shortages reduces employers' incentives to consider and invest in alternatives. It will also reduce domestic workers' incentives to acquire the training and skills necessary to do certain jobs. Consequently, immigration designed to address short term shortages may have the unintended consequences of creating the conditions that encourage shortages of local workers in the longer term.
>
> (House of Lords 2008: 39)

There is thus a danger that (im)migration can undermine the labour market position of the most marginalised and their communities in destination locations, again reinforcing uneven development rather than contributing to its demise.

Conclusions

This short overview has explored the relationships between (im)migration and local and regional development at a number of different spatial scales. While there is scope for a positive relationship between immigration and development, there are also many reasons that negative change can occur. In this context it is important to highlight the growth of 'bottom-up' community efforts to challenge this negative cycle. In London, for example, migrant workers have sought to work with a wide alliance of local people to tackle this situation through efforts to generate 'high-end' roads to development through living wages, and associated increases in training, productivity and labour market reform (see Wills *et al.* 2009c; Pattison 2008). Irregular migrants are also organising to demand regularisation, giving them the chance to improve their conditions of work (Wills *et al.* 2009a). Such organisation is replicated in migrant-sending locations where workers and their community bodies are trying to create sustainable employment opportunities, to win living wages from international corporations and to influence the migration process itself (Hale and Wills 2005). There is also a role for government and other agencies in the global South to realise the potential development gains from remittances – and returning migrants – with efforts to provide the physical and financial infrastructure needed to stimulate new economic activity and reduce the uneven impact of migration itself. As such, community-led strategies have the potential to ensure a more positive relationship between migration and local and regional development, North and South.

References

Ballard, R. (2003) *Remittances and Economic Development*, London: House of Commons Select Committee for Migration and Development.

Conthe, P. and García, A. (2007) 'New mechanisms for developing primary and secondary housing finance markets: the case of Peru', *Housing Finance International*, 46–56.

Datta, K., McIlwaine, C., Wills, J., Evans, Y., Herbert, J. and May, J. (2007) 'The new development finance or exploiting migrant labour? Remittance sending among low-paid migrant workers in London', *International Development Planning Review*, 29, 1: 43–67.

De Haas, H. (2005) 'International migration, remittances and development: myths and facts', *Third World Quarterly*, 26: 1269–1284.

Ellis, M. (2006) 'Unsettling immigrant geographies: US immigration and the politics of scale', *Tijds*, 97, 1: 49–58.

Faist, T. (2008) 'Migrants as transnational development agents: an inquiry into the newest round of the migration-development nexus', *Population Space and Place*, 14: 21–42.

Farrant, M., MacDonald, A. and Sriskandarajah, D. (2006) 'Migration and development: opportunities and challenges for policymakers', IOM Migration Research series No. 22, Geneva: IOM.

Favell, A. and Hansen, R. (2002) 'Markets against politics: migration, EU enlargement and the idea of Europe', *Journal of Ethnic and Migration Studies*, 28: 581–601.

Florida, R. (2002) *The Rise of the Creative Class and How it's Transforming Work, Leisure and Everyday Life*, New York: Basic Books.

Flynn, D. (2005) 'New borders, new management: the dilemmas of modern immigration policies', *Ethnic and Racial Studies*, 28, 3: 463–490.

Freeman, G. (1995) 'Modes of immigration politics in liberal democratic states', *International Migration Review*, 29, 4: 881–902.

Gertler, M. (2008) 'The new Argonauts: regional advantage in a global economy', *Economic Geography*, 84, 1: 105–108.

Greater London Authority (GLA) (2002) *Response to Secure Borders, Safe Haven*, London: GLA.

Greater London Authority (GLA) (2009) *Mayor Condemns Government Immigration Failure*. Press Release, 9-3-2009, 126. Available from http://www.london.gov.uk/view_press_release.jsp?releaseid=21277 (last accessed 13 May 2009).

Grillo, R. and Mazzucato, V. (2008) 'Africa < > Europe: a double engagement', *Journal of Ethnic and Migration Studies*, 34, 2: 175–198.

Hale, A. and Wills, J. (2005) (Eds) *Threads of Labour: Garment Industry Supply Chains from the Workers' Perspective*, Oxford: Blackwell.

Hollifield, J. (1992) *Immigrants, Markets and States: The Political Economy of Post-war Europe*, Cambridge, MA: Harvard University Press.

Home Office (2006) *A Points-based System: Making Migration Work for Britain*, Paper 6741, London: Home Office.

Home Office and Commonwealth Office (2007) *Managing Global Migration: A Strategy to Build Stronger International Alliances to Manage Migration*, London: Home Office.

House of Lords (Select Committee of Economic Affairs) (2008) *The Economic Impact of Immigration*, Volume 1, London: HMSO.

Houston, D., Findlay, A., Harrison, R. and Mason, C. (2008) 'Will attracting the "creative class" boost economic growth in old industrial regions? A case study of Scotland', *Geografiska Annaler: Series B, Human Geography*, 90, 2: 133–149.

International Organisation for Migration (IOM) (2008) *World Migration 2008: Managing Labour Mobility in the Evolving Global Economy*, Geneva: IOM.

IPPR-CRE (2007) *The Reception and Integration of New Migrant Communities*, London: IPPR.

London School of Economics (LSE) (2009) *Economic Impact on London and the UK or an Earned Regularisation of Irregular Migrants in the UK*, London: LSE.

Malecki, E. (2004) 'Jockeying for position: what it means and why it matters to regional development policy when places complete', *Regional Studies*, 38, 9: 1101–1120.

May, J., Wills, J., Datta, K., Evans, Y., Herbert, J. and McIlwaine, C. (2007) 'Keeping London working: global cities, the British state, and London's new migrant division of labour', *Transactions of the Institute of British Geographers*, 32: 151–167.

McKay, S. and Winkleman-Gleed, A. (2005) *Migrant Workers in the East of England*, London: Working Lives Research Centre, London Metropolitan University.

Mohan, G. (2008) 'Cosmopolitan states of development: homelands, citizenships, and diasporic Ghanaian politics', *Environment and Planning D*, 26: 464–479.

Osella, F. and Osella, C. (2000) 'Migration, money and masculinity in Kerala', *The Journal of the Royal Anthropological Institute*, 6: 117–133.

Pattison, V. (2008) "Neoliberalization and its discontents: the experience of working poverty in Manchester", in A. Smith, A. Stenning and K. Willis (eds) *Social Justice and Neoliberalism: Global Perspectives*, London: Zed Press, 90–113.

Phillimore, J. and Goodson, L. (2006) 'Problem or opportunity? Asylum seekers, refugees, employment and social exclusion in deprived urban areas', *Urban Studies*, 43, 10: 1715–1736.

Pike, A., Rodriguez-Pose, A. and Tomaney, J. (2006) *Local and Regional Development*, London: Routledge.

Portes, A. (2001) 'Introduction: the debates and significance of immigrant transnationalism', *Global Networks*, 1, 3: 181–193.

Ratha, D. (2007) *Leveraging Remittances for Development, Policy Brief*, Washington D.C.: Migration Policy Institute.

Saxenian, A. (2006) *The New Argonauts: Regional Advantage in a Global Economy*, Cambridge, MA: Harvard University Press.

Skeldon, R. (2008) 'Of skilled migration, brain drain and policy responses', *International Migration*, published online (document identifier: 10.1111/j.1468-2435-2008.00484x).

Stenning, A. and Dawley, S. (2009) 'Poles to Newcastle: grounding new migrant flows in peripheral regions', *European Urban and Regional Studies* (16: 273–294).

Styan, D. (2007) 'The security of Africans beyond borders: migration, remittances and London's transnational entrepreneurs', *International Affairs*, 83, 6: 1171–1191.

Taylor, J. E., Arango, J., Hugo, G., Kouaouci, A., Massey, D. S. and Pellegrino, A. (1996) 'International migration and community development', *Population Index*, 62, 3: 397–418.

Van Hear, N. and Sørensen, N. (eds) (2003) *The Migration–Development Nexus*, Geneva: the United Nations and International Organisation for Migration.

Wills, J., Datta, K., Evans, Y., Herbert, J., May, J. and McIlwaine, C. (2009a) *Global Cities at Work: New Migrant Divisions of Labour*, London: Pluto Press.

Wills, J., Datta, K., Evans, Y., Herbert, J., May, J. and McIlwaine, C. (2009b) 'Religion at work: the role of faith-based organisations in the London living wage campaign', *Cambridge Journal of Regions, Economy and Society* (2, 443–461).

Wills, J. with Kakpo, N. and Begum, R. (2009c) *The Business Case for the Living Wage: The Story of the Cleaning Service at Queen Mary*, London: Queen Mary, University of London, available from: http://www.geog.qmul.ac.uk/staff/willsj.html.

World Bank (2006) *Global Economic Prospects: Economic Implications of Remittances and Migration 2006*, Washington, D.C.: World Bank.

Further reading

Datta, K. (2009) 'Transforming South–North relations? International migration and development', *Geography Compass*, 3, 1: 108–134.

Datta, K., McIlwaine, C., Wills, J., Evans, Y., Herbert, J. and May, J. (2007) 'The new development finance or exploiting migrant labour? Remittance sending among low-paid migrant workers in London', *International Development Planning Review*, 29, 1: 43–67.

Somerville, W. (2007) *Immigration under New Labour*, Bristol: Policy Press.

Wills, J., Datta, K., Evans, Y., Herbert, J., May, J. and McIlwaine, C. (2009) *Global Cities at Work: New Migrant Divisions of Labour*, London: Pluto Press.

38

Neoliberal urbanism in Europe

Sara Gonzalez

Introduction

Neoliberal urbanism is a concept increasingly used to describe the progressive privatization of public space and public realm (housing, civic facilities, etc.) and the commodification of our cities as profit-making machines. Some authors however believe that the particular history and institutional characteristics of European cities make them at least more resilient to these transformations. Through case studies of three European cities located in three different national contexts, Newcastle (UK), Milan (Italy) and Bilbao (Spain), this chapter will look at these debates uncovering the chameleonic nature of neoliberal urbanism, stressing how it adapts and changes in different local governance modes. The case studies draw on fieldwork carried out in three different projects making this a post-hoc comparative analysis. The methodology was qualitative and based on discourse analysis of main policy documents and interviews with key informants such as politicians, policy makers and academics.

European cities as strategic neoliberal sites

Neoliberalism is a political–economic philosophy that seeks the application of competitive forces and free market principles to all areas of social and economic life. It advocates the free flow of goods, capital and services across the world economy, reduced public spending and minimal state regulation, particularly in the labour market. Beyond these common points however, neoliberalism is a slippery idea. As it has implanted itself in different geographical and historical contexts it has adapted and changed. Although it initially emerged in the 1980s as a set of policies to "roll back" (Peck and Tickell, 2002) the state and enclose public services by the early 1990s it had morphed into "more socially interventionist and ameliorative forms epitomized by the Third Way" (ibid.: 41) seeking to "roll out" new regulatory policies designed to ensure that markets work effectively (Brenner and Theodore, 2002).

Logically, the urban realm does not escape the neoliberal tide. As Harvey (2008) reminds us capitalism's 'creative destructive' tendency is always related to urban restructuring. The overarching goal of neoliberal urban development policies is to "mobilize city space as an arena both for market oriented economic growth and for elite consumption" (Brenner and Theodore, 2002: 21). Far from a retreat of the state, neoliberal policies are actually either carried out or enabled by the public sector (Moulaert *et al.*, 2003) in a wide range of ways: private–public partnerships, deregulation of planning, privatization of housing and liberalization of rent controls, mega-urban projects, gentrification, urban surveillance, city marketing and branding to mention some.

In the face of this 'pessimistic' diagnosis, a group of European academics has sought to question this, according to them, totalizing analysis, arguing that in the case of European cities these neoliberal trends are mitigated. This so-called European city perspective seeks to reinvigorate a Weberian theoretical approach that brings out the specific role of political and institutional aspects of European cities, toning down the effects of macro-economic structures. The accent is on the collective actor aspect of European cities as active communities where actors such as Mayors, Chambers of Commerce or neighbourhood associations have path-shaping influence (Le Galès, 2002). The European city approach is also held as a normative project to "disclose the good qualities of European Cities and to emphasize the political role of cities" (Häussermann and Haila, 2005: 61). The European city approach can provide a useful counterpoint to the neoliberal urbanism thesis by emphasizing the role of local and regional politics as well as identity politics. The different levels and quality of welfare systems, housing subsidy schemes, pension systems, political-cultural, landownership patterns, morphological legacies, all play specific roles in shaping European cities (Häussermann and Haila, 2005; Musterd and Ostendorf, 2005). In my analysis of three European cities I want to find the methodological middle ground that is able to grasp the particular local configuration of actors, resources and powers that make neoliberalism take root in different ways.

The remaking of the political economic space of three European cities

Milan, Bilbao and Newcastle are three medium-sized European cities embedded in complex scalar choreographies from the European Union to the neighbourhood level. Significantly, they belong to different nation-states with diverse models of social regulation and regimes of accumulation. Table 38.1 summarizes key indicators to compare these cities showing the differences in terms of demographic trajectories, location in the 'imaginary' urban and global hierarchies and main economic characteristics. In the face of current hegemonic discourses of urban competitiveness, the three cities suffer from what I term aspirational complex as they are neither national capitals nor international global centres but medium-sized cities located in secondary exchange networks.

Table 38.1 Comparative indicators of Bilbao, Milan and Newcastle

	Demographic data			Economic data	Global rankings	
	City population	City-region population	Demographic trajectory	"Regional" GDP per capita, PPS (EU27=100)	Urban audit	Global connectivity
Bilbao	351,179	867,777	Growth set-back	31,600 (133.7)	No data	In the top 35 European cities
Milan	1,299,633	3,906,726	Recent resurgence	31,900 (135.1)	Knowledge hub	In the top 10 Global cities
Newcastle	271,600	1,089,300	Continuous decline	24,500 (103.7)	Transformation pole	No data

Source: Compiled by author from Demographic data: Eustat (2006) for Bilbao, Istat (2008) for Office of National Statistics (2007) for Newcastle and Turok, and Mykhnenko (2007) for demographic trajectory. Economic data: Eurostat (2009), Global rankings: EC (2007), Taylor (2003), Taylor *et al.* (2002)

461

Bilbao as a global city

A major oil-based manufacturing industrial city in the Basque Country, Bilbao was hit particularly hard by the international industrial crisis of the 1970s and by 1986 some towns in the Bilbao city-region reached unemployment rates of 30 per cent (Torres Enjuto, 1995; Rodriguez and Martinez, 2003). Following the establishment of democracy after 40 years of Francoist dictatorship, a socialist government introduced a corporate liberal-internationalist (Holman, 1996) modernization programme consistent with the destructive moment of neoliberalism in the form of roll-back. Nationalized industrial companies were privatized and rationalized, a process that was reinforced by Spain's accession to the European Common Market in 1986. This crisis had a particular spatial dimension as heavy industry was located along the riverfront and in working-class communities of Bilbao. The main steel factory in the metropolitan area of Bilbao went from almost 8,000 permanent contract workers to 300 in 2002. From the end of the 1980s a series of regeneration plans concentrated on cleaning up these areas and moving the industrial port from the river out to the sea, opening up prime development land.

From the late 1980s a more creative moment of what we can call regionalist neoliberalism emerged to "position [the Region] with advantage in the competitive international context of the most innovative city-regions" according to one regional leader (Intxaurraga, 2002: 11). Bilbao, as the largest and economically most important city, was re-invented as a 'global city' (BM30, 2001). Moderate Basque nationalism (the ruling force in the region up to recent elections in 2009) has adapted its traditionally entrepreneurial regionalist claims (del Cerro Santamaria, 2007) to a neoliberal context, investing in innovation, technology and an industrial policy inspired by Porter's cluster theory (Ahedo, 2006). Its urban strategy has been to use spectacular architecture and design to place Bilbao in the international circuits of tourism, conferences and private investment. Most of the big regeneration projects in the Bilbao city-region have been funded by the financially autonomous regional and provincial governments, such as the Guggenheim Museum, costing about $100 million (Zulaika, 1997). Local authorities have consciously sought to attract international star architects such as Calatrava, Foster, Isozaki, Zaha Hadid or Pelli responding to the demands of a 'brand society' according to Bilbao's Deputy Mayor (Author's interview, 2008). Former working-class spaces (factories or residential areas) have been transformed in the flagship projects for the new Bilbao, 'rolling out' the gentrification frontier from the more traditional bourgeois neighbourhoods of the city by pushing up rent and property prices (Vicario and Martinez Monje, 2003).

Most significant is the city's adoption of a series of "network forms of local governance based upon public–private partnership, 'quangos' and the 'new public management'" (Brenner and Theodore, 2002: 369). The most important is Bilbao Ría 2000 (BR 2000), established in 1992 as a multi-level public–public partnership between regional/local and central government bodies owning land and planning powers in and around Bilbao. It functions as a company and aims to generate profits from assembling and selling land to private developers to then reinvest in other urban projects. Although a 100 per cent public institution, BR 2000 is a good example of neoliberal urbanist practices (increasingly copied abroad: Gonzalez, 2009a). This model is based on land revenues (Rodríguez et al., 2001) and therefore dependant on a changing market which can put revitalization plans in jeopardy even as they are carried out (Reviriego, 2008); it has relegated local authorities' planning departments to a secondary role by assuming more planning powers in key regeneration areas (Rodriguez et al., 2001); and regeneration has become a predominantly technical affair as BR 2000 practitioners are mainly engineers working to a mandate of "maximum efficiency" (ibid.) rather than civic consensus or social engagement. Public participation is not encouraged. It thus represents an example of the erosion of "traditional relays of local democratic accountability" (Brenner and Theodore, 2002: 369) as decision making is 'elitized', making it easier for business elites to influence development decisions.

In Bilbao, the local governance coalition is mainly made up of public actors, such as the regional and provincial governments, state-owned railway companies and port authority, and bears the heavy imprint of Basque Nationalist Party control due to their dominance of both regional government and the Bilbao local authority for 30 years. Links with the private sector are not formalized but take place through traditional networks. The particularities of urban neoliberalism in Bilbao combine an economic 'global' strategy to place central areas of Bilbao in the international marketplace while at the same time mobilizing a political 'new regionalist' project to bypass the Spanish nation-state.

Milan, node of a global network

Milan was at the core of Italy's industrialization during the country's economic miracle in the 1950s and 1960s hosting large factories like Pirelli and Alfa Romeo or important infrastructures like the Exhibition Fair, all of which employed a large part of the population providing a social and cultural ferment to the city. During the 1980s many of these industrial referents began to relocate out of the centre of Milan, triggering a fast process of deindustrialization and deproletarianization; between 1971 and 1989, industrial jobs in the Province of Milan fell by 280,000 (Foot, 2001). Like in Bilbao, this change had a particular spatial footprint, hitting jobs in neighbourhoods and municipalities in the North of Milan, but unlike Bilbao, there was not so much severe unemployment as a

change in its employment structure towards smaller firms and the service sector (increasingly technology and knowledge) (OECD, 2006). Workers' rights and conditions worsened under the liberalizing labour market, following EU policy guidelines and the rescaling of labour bargaining processes from the national to the local scale (such as the 'Milan Pact').

Local planning has also shown recent elements of neoliberal urbanism. From the 1960s up to the 1980s there was an attempt to plan comprehensively for the city-region with a strong public intervention sometimes going against real estate interests. This attitude was replaced in the 1980s by a more fragmented project-based approach (Balducci, 2005) characterized by deregulation of planning (PIM, 2004), entrepreneurialism and an emphasis on growth (Healey, 2007), leading to a process of urban sprawl and suburbanization which has seen the city implode to its outer region into an infinite city (Bonomi and Abruzzese, 2004) with consequent traffic and pollution problems (OECD, 2006).

The lack of planning and governance capacity in the 1980s was not so much related to an international neoliberal trend as to the incapability of weak local governing coalitions to put forward strong public visions, following instead "single economic interests" (Dente, 2005: 320). Besides, a clientelistic corruption network led by the governing Socialist Party was discovered in Milan (Foot, 2001), the scandal bringing down the entire national political system. Subsequently local governance in Milan has been dominated by right-wing and regionalist parties more interested in efficient urban management including privatization and outsourcing of local services than integrative urban planning (Dente, 2005). With these political scandals and the city's recent decline as a centre for international innovation, Milan "seems to have lost part of its historical drive" (OECD, 2006: 12).

In response, a new spirit has emerged among sections of the local elite who are now presenting Milan as a 'node in a global network' of knowledge and communication, encouraged by Peter Taylor's (2004) ranking of Milan as the eighth city in the world in terms of global connectivity (Gonzalez, 2009). This has given impetus and coherence to a series of otherwise disconnected big urban projects. One of these projects is the International Expo 2015 under the slogan "Milan, world city-metropolis" which, according to the Head of Planning of Milan, has started a new "magical moment" for "ascending Milan" according to Masseroli (Carbonaro, 2008: 5). Other projects include the Fashion City, the New Exhibition Fair and the regeneration of various ex-industrial or exhibition spaces within the city (Balducci, 2005; Healey, 2007; Gonzalez, 2009). We find the traditional mix of famous architects and landmark architectures with little respect for the surrounding communities, limited consultation and piecemeal approach (Balducci, 2005), risking turning Milan into a "free for all city" (Rete Comitati milanesi, 2007). Environmental campaigners fear the Expo is already giving more momentum to the construction of mega-developments, such as a new regional super-motorway (Legambiente, 2009).

The governing local coalition in Milan is made up of a loose public–private partnership embedded in clientelistic and sometimes corruption-ridden networks (Piana, 2005) where the impetus comes mainly from the local business class and national corporations. But the coalition has also stretched out geographically to encompass national and international developers, further weakening the voice of local actors and those outside the property market arena (Pasqui, 2006). Like in Bilbao, local elites see in these schemes a glocal project to bypass the nation-state and position Milan as a global city in the international sphere. This is linked to a localist/regionalist form of entrepreneurial politics favoured by the right-wing conservatives and regionalist parties who seamlessly combine neoliberal policies with a strong attachment to the local territory (Gonzalez, 2009).

Newcastle, a European cultural and knowledge city

Newcastle and its region has the lowest GVA (gross value-added) output per head in England as well as some of the highest rates of child poverty, welfare dependency, unemployment and long-term sickness. Like much of Northern England, the city has suffered from a long period of economic decline (Robinson, 2002) since the 1930s, transforming from a "booming core in the 19th century to a marginalized and near-bust periphery by the end of the 20th century" (Hudson, 2005: 581). The city and the region have been constant public policy targets, from interventionist and top-down regional policies after the Second World War to a more entrepreneurial urban policy (Martin, 1993). This was exemplified most strongly in the work of the Urban Development Corporations (UDCs), one of which is located in Newcastle, central government appointed agencies to take control of large former industrial areas and docklands (Imrie and Thomas, 1993) and prioritizing private sector needs, growth over redistribution, physical over social development and effectively supplanting democratically elected local authority planning powers (Deas et al., 2000). In the Newcastle region, they also had a strong role in the deindustrialization of the region, turning many industrial sites into residential or commercial spaces (Byrne, 1999).

UDCs and other similar regeneration strategies have also contributed to the aim of breaking up "the bastions of Labour-union support" (Healey, 1994: 187) and traditional industrial working-class culture in Newcastle. With the arrival of New Labour, nationally driven regeneration programmes have developed a more social approach, specifically targeting deprived working-class communities in Newcastle through welfare to work-types of policies and bringing in middle-class population through tenure mix and gentrification. The West End of Newcastle, for example, has been subject to 17 different government programmes amounting to over £500m from 1979 to 2000 (Coaffee, 2004). Some of this funding has attempted to engage poor communities in urban governance, a strategy that Gough (2002) considers a neoliberal "top-down community socialization", by integrating the poor into low-wage labour relationships, disciplining the youth and de-politicizing class struggle. Other programmes, this time initiated by the local authority, such as Going for Growth, have directly advocated for demolition of working-class housing and gentrification (Cameron, 2003).

Most of the symbolic regeneration efforts to place Newcastle in the international sphere and change its industrial image have been focused in the waterfront along the River Tyne. From a so-called 'no-go area', it has been turned into the centre of Newcastle's corporatized nightlife, with bars, nightclubs and restaurants (Byrne and Wharton, 2004; Chatterton and Hollands, 2003), expensive flats and cultural attractions (a music centre designed by the ubiquitous global architect Norman Foster, a contemporary art gallery and an iconic bridge). Here public investment has led the way in redefining the internal and external identity of a former industrial site in the hope of attracting private development, tourists and residents (Miles, 2005), an example of which was Newcastle's bid to host European Capital for Culture in 2008. Another parallel strategy in recent years is the 'Science City' project, which aims to turn Newcastle into "one of the world's premier locations for the integration of science, business and economic development" (Strategy for Success, 2007). Partly funded by central government and regional agencies, it aims to create areas of scientific interest for the private sector drawing on neoliberal-inspired regional innovation policy ideas such as the 'triple helix' (Moulaert and Sekia, 2003) but the OECD (2006a) has already deemed it ambitious. The project has also created a real estate development opportunity freeing up the site of the former Tyne Brewery.

The local governance coalition in Newcastle is formed by the local authority, central government and myriad partnerships and quangos that run regeneration budgets and deliver social services. As a highly centralized country, central government still controls most of the budget and Newcastle City Council has relatively little financial autonomy, often dependent on private developers to shape and take the lead in urban development (Gonzalez and Vigar, 2008) with real estate development typically dominated by large landowners and construction (Healey, 1994). Despite the regional devolution process from 1997, regional institutions are still relatively weak, largely unaccountable and generally business-led. In sum, the local governance coalition in Newcastle is more public sector dependent than in other English cities and constrained by financial restrictions and the power of national and big landowners and construction industries.

Conclusions: Neoliberal 'Eurbanism'?

Returning to the discussion at the beginning of the chapter, it is clear that the three cities demonstrate an array of 'mechanisms of neoliberal localization' as identified by Brenner and Theodore (2002). But can we say that there is a homogenizing trend of neoliberal urbanization in Europe? And is it distinctively European?

All three cities have opted for urban mega-projects to attract private investors and have relied on mega-urban events (European Capital of Culture bid and EXPO) or symbolic icons (the Guggenheim) to initiate and sustain urban regeneration. In effect, a rather similar new urban landscape is being built by the same global star architects, resulting in what Muñoz (2008) calls urbanalization, the repetition of similar branded, financially efficient and disconnected landscapes for consumption. At the same time, their respective existing urban fabrics are rich enough to preserve local distinctiveness, and all have experienced political contestation with civil society winning some important victories.

Regeneration in all three cities has been based to an extent on rolling forward the gentrification frontier to working-class areas, more decisively and state-led in Newcastle, and less clearly in Milan and Bilbao, where public housing stock is anyway marginal and therefore gentrification has happened more as a by-product.

New forms of urban governance have emerged in all three cities involving more actors, particularly from the private and community sector. This is particularly the case in Newcastle while in Milan and Bilbao this is again not a top-down trend but takes place through ad-hoc institutional arrangements. In the three cities, but mostly so in Milan followed by Bilbao, there has been an internationalization of governance practices with international developers, architects, policy gurus, academics and private companies having a bigger say about the trajectories of the cities.

One of the most striking similarities among the three cities is the use of international competitiveness discourses and their aim to scale up the international hierarchy of cities. Bilbao has been re-imagined as a global city and Milan as a hub in an international network while Newcastle aspires to be a world-class science and innovation centre. But the reasons and mechanisms for this are different. In Milan and Bilbao, local and regional elites combine an entrepreneurial approach with a strong attachment to the local territory. It is therefore local forces who push for neoliberal policies in order to jump scales not necessarily 'protecting' European cities from neoliberal policies (as suggested by the European City approach) but, on the contrary, I would argue in the cases of Bilbao and Milan, reappropriating them.

It is difficult to assess whether these identified trends are particularly European. Recent reports on European cities have been unable to find common trends across cities,

constructing instead various typologies that correspond more with the economic hierarchy of the cities or the particular national situations (EC, 2007; Turok and Mykhnenko, 2007). Our analysis here confirms that the nation-state and wider and more traditional geo-categories like 'southern Europe' are still at play. So, in conclusion we seem to find a process of homogenization and neoliberal convergence in terms of urban governance practices, new landscapes, discourses of competitiveness and the emergence of cities as strategic economic centres. The European City approach's critique of this convergence holds if one sees neoliberalism as a relatively monolithic phenomenon but, as argued by Peck and Theodore (2007: 757): "a process-based conception – sensitive to conjuncture, contingency, and contradiction – are less vulnerable to such blunt critiques, since they are explicitly concerned with the manner in which (partially realized) causal processes generate uneven and divergent outcomes." There are, therefore, differences in the institutional settings where neoliberalization is taking root giving way to different localized 'neoliberal eurbanisms': a process of central state-led neoliberalization in Newcastle; a market-led neoliberal regionalism in Milan and a (local) state-led neoliberal regionalism in Bilbao.

In the face of the global economic downturn, however, neoliberal urbanist policies are failing: the construction industry in Spain is in crisis, flagship regeneration projects across the UK have been mothballed and the Milan Expo 2015 is being questioned by environmentalists and architects. The recession can indeed open up space for alternatives. The opportunities, however, arise in different contexts and different forms as the myriad protests, movements, factory occupations, etc. today express (Mayer, 2009). The challenge is therefore – as ever – to find alliances and linkages between localized demands and global claims. Recently Harvey (2008: 40) has promoted Lefebvre's slogan of the "The Right to the City" as "both working slogan and political ideal", demanding "greater democratic control over the production and utilization of the surplus" (ibid.: 37). This goes radically beyond the normative (and conservative) ambitions of the 'European city' approach. Similarly, Uitermark (2009) argues that a 'just city' (different to the 'good city' or the 'sustainable city') is one in which there is an equitable allocation of scarce resources and where residents have control over their living environment. The decommodification of the housing market must be the central idea in an alternative urban and regional kind of development (Hodkinson, 2010). But there are plenty of other ideas currently being experimented (Leitner *et al.*, 2007): transition towns, participatory budgeting, slow cities, urban farming, self-managed social centres and factories, etc. It is difficult to see, however, how local initiatives could amount to a radical change within the current capitalist system. As Marcuse (2009: 187) argues it is a bit pointless to imagine a less greedy capitalism as "greed is not an aberration of the system; it is what makes the system go". A just urban and regional development must therefore be imagined beyond the current system which makes predicting exactly how it would exactly be very difficult beyond several rather general ideas:

Cities that would not be for profit but would seek a decent and supportive living environment" [...] "eliminating profit as means and motivation in the political sector, eliminating the role of wealth and the power linked to it from public decisions.

(Marcuse, 2009: 195)

References

Ahedo Santiesteban, M. (2006) "Business systems and cluster policies in the Basque Country and Catalonia (1990–2004)," *European Urban and Regional Studies*, 13, 25–39.

Balducci, A. (2005) "Una visione per la regione milanese," in M. Magatti *et al.* (eds) *Milano, nodo della rete globale*, Milan: Bruno Mondadori, 231–264.

BM30 (2001) *Bilbao as a Global City. Making Dreams Come True*, Bilbao: BM30.

Bonomi, A. and Abruzzese, A. (2004) *La città infinita*, Milan: Bruno Mondadori.

Brenner, N. and Theodore, N. (2002) *Spaces of Neoliberalism: Urban Restructuring in North America and Western Europe*, Oxford: Blackwell.

Byrne, D. (1999) "Tyne and Wear UDC – turning the uses inside out: active deindustrialisation and its consequences," in R. Imrie and T. Huw (eds) *British Urban Policy: An Evaluation of the Urban Development Corporations*, London: Sage, 128–143.

Byrne, D. and Wharton, C. (2004) "Loft living – Bombay calling: culture, work and everyday life on post-industrial Tyneside. A joint polemic," *Capital and Class*, 84, 191–198.

Cameron, S. (2003) "Gentrification, housing redifferentiation and urban regeneration: 'going for growth' in Newcastle upon Tyne," *Urban Studies*, 20, 2367–2382.

Carbonaro, M. (2008) "l'effeto-Expo sulla 'Milano che sale,'" *Il Sole 24 Ore* 21–26 April, 5.

Chatterton, P. and Hollands, R. (2003) *Urban Nightscapes. Youth Cultures, Pleasure Spaces and Corporate Power*, London: Routledge.

Coaffee, J. (2004) "Re-scaling regeneration: experiences of merging area-based and city-wide partnerships in urban policy," *The International Journal of Public Sector Management*, 17, 443–461.

Deas, I., Robson, B. and Bradford, M. (2000) "Re-thinking the Urban Development Corporation 'experiment': the case of Central Manchester, Leeds and Bristol," *Progress in Planning*, 54, 1–72.

Del Cerro Santamaria, G. (2007) *Bilbao. Basque Pathways to Globalization*, London: Elsevier.

Dente, B. (2005) "Governare l'innovazione," in M. Magatti *et al.* (eds) *Milano, nodo della rete globale*, Milan: Bruno Mondadori, 313–335.

European Commission (2007) *The State of the European Cities Report*, Brussels: European Union, *Regional Policy*. Online. Available HTTP: http://ec.europa.eu/regional_policy/sources/docgener/studies/pdf/urban/stateofcities_-2007.pdf (accessed 5 August 2009).

Eurostat (2009) "Regional GDP per inhabitant in the EU27," *Eurostat newsrelease*, 23/2009, 19 February.

Foot, J. (2001) *Milan Since the Miracle. City, Culture and Identity*, London: Berg.

González, S. (2009) "(Dis)connecting Milan(ese): deterritorialised urbanism and disempowering politics in globalising cities," *Environment and Planning A*, 41, 31–47.

González, S. (2009a) "Urban policy tourism: the Bilbao effect and the Barcelona model 'in motion,'" mimeograph. Available from the author.

González, S. and Vigar, G. (2008) "Community influence and the contemporary local state: potentials and contradictions in the neo-liberal city," *City*, 12, 64–78.

Gough, J. (2002) "Neoliberalism and socialization in the contemporary city: opposites, complements and instabilities," in N. Brenner and N.Theodore (eds) *Spaces of Neoliberalism. Urban Restructuring in North America and Western Europe*, London: Blackwell, 58–79.

Harvey, D. (2008) "The right to the city," *New Left Review*, 53, 23–40.

Häusserman, H. and Haila, A. (2005) "The European city: a conceptual framework and normative project," in Y. Kazepov (ed.) *The Cities Of Europe*, London: Blackwell, 43–63.

Healey, P. (1994) "Urban policy and property development: the institutional relations of real-estate development in an old industrial region," *Environment and Planning A*, 26, 177–198.

Healey P. (2007) *Urban Complexity and Spatial Strategies: Towards a Relational Planning for our Times*, London: Routledge.

Hodkinson, S. (2010) "Housing in common: in search of a strategy for housing alterity in England in the 21st century," in D. Fuller, A. Jonas and R. Lee (eds) *Alternative Economic and Political Spaces: Interrogating Alterity*, Farnham: Ashgate.

Holman, O. (1996) *Integrating Southern Europe: EC Expansion and the Transnationalization of Spain*, London: Routledge.

Hudson, R. (2005) "Rethinking change in old industrial regions: reflecting on the experiences of North East England," *Environment and Planning A*, 37, 581–596.

Imrie, R. and Thomas, H. (1993) *British Urban Policy: An Evaluation of the Urban Development Corporations*, London: Sage.

Intxaurraga, S. (2002) "Presentación," in Departamento de Ordenacion del Territorio y Medioambiente (ed.) Euskal Hiria, Vitoria Gasteiz: Gobierno Vasco.

Le Galès, P. (2002) *European Cities: Social Conflicts and Governance*, Oxford: Oxford University Press.

Legambiente (2009) "Expo 2015, a un anno dalla vittoria di Milano non c'è ancora l'ombra di un progetto," Comunicato Stampa. Online. Available HTTP http://www.legambiente.

org/section.php?p=single&type=comunicato&id=462 (accessed 5 August 2009).

Leitner, H., Peck, J. and Sheppard, E.S. (eds) (2007) *Contesting Neoliberalism*, New York: Guilford Press.

Marcuse, P. (2009) "From critical urban theory to the right to the city," *City*, 13, 185–197.

Martin, R. (1993) "Reviving economic case for regional policy," in M. Hart and R. Harrison (eds) *Spatial Policy in a Divided Nation*, London: Jessica Kingsley, 270–290.

Mayer, M. (2009) "The 'right to the city' in the context of shifting mottos of urban social movements," *City*, 13, 362–371.

Miles, S. (2005) " 'Our Tyne': iconic regeneration and the revitalisation of identity in NewcastleGateshead," *Urban Studies*, 42, 913–926.

Moulaert, F. and Sekia, F. (2003) "Territorial innovation models: a critical survey," *Regional Studies*, 37, 289–302.

Moulaert, F., Swyngedouw, E. and Rodriguez, A. (2003) *The Globalized City. Economic Restructuring and Social Polarization in European Cities*, Oxford: Oxford University Press.

Muñoz, F. (2008) *Urbanalización. Paisajes comunes, lugares globales*, Barcelona: Gusto Gili.

Musterd, S. and Ostendorf, W. (2005) "Social exclusion, segregation and neighbourhood effects," in Y. Kazepov (ed.) *Cities of Europe*, Oxford: Blackwell, 170–189.

OECD (2006a) *OECD Territorial Reviews*, Milan, Italy, Paris: OECD.

OECD (2006b) *OECD Territorial Reviews: Newcastle in the North East*, The United Kingdon, Paris: OECD.

Pasqui, G. (2006) "Chi decide la città. Gli effetti dei grandi interventi sull'arena decisionale," in Consorzio Metis-Politecnico di Milano (eds) *Milano oltre Milano. Racconti della città che cambia 1990–2005*, Milan: Skira, 10–11.

Peck, J. And Theodore, N. (2007) "Variegated capitalism," *Progress in Human Geography*, 31, 731–772.

Peck, J. and Tickell, A. (2002) "Neoliberalizing space," in N. Brenner and N. Theodore (eds) *Spaces of Neoliberalism. Urban Restructuring in North America and Western Europe*, London: Blackwell, 33–57.

Piana, L. (2005) "New Ligresti City," *L'Espresso*, 26 May.

PIM (2004) *Dal mondo nuovo alla citta' infinita: cento anni di trasformazioni e progetti nell'area milanese*, Milan: Centro Studi PIM.

Rete Comitati milanesi (2007) "Comunicato," Milan: C/O Cooperativa Barona E. Satta. Online. Available HTTP http://eddyburg.it/

index.php/article/articleview/8996/0/38/ (accessed 10 August 2009).

Reviriego, J.M. (2008) "La crisis inmobiliaria amenaza grandes obras en Bilbao," El correo, 18th January 2008. Online. http://www. elcorreodigital.com/vizcaya/20080118/vizcaya/ crisis-inmobiliaria-amenaza-grandes-20080118.html (accessed 10 August 2009).

Robinson, F. (2002) "The North East. A journey through time," City, 6, 317–334.

Rodriguez, A. and Martinez, E. (2003) "Restructuring cities. Miracles and mirages in urban revitalization in Bilbao," in F. Moulaert, A. Rodriguez and E. Swyngedouw (eds) The Globalized City. Economic Restructuring and Social Polarization in European Cities, Oxford: Oxford University Press, 181–207.

Rodriguez, A., Martinez, E. and Guenaga, E. (2001) "Uneven redevelopment: new urban policies and socio-spatial fragmentation in metropolitan Bilbao," European Urban and Regional Studies, 8, 161–178.

Strategy for Success (2007) "Milestone for Newcastle Science City," News article. Online. http://www.strategyforsuccess.info/page/news/article.cfm?articleId=2155 (accessed 10 August 2009),

Taylor, P. (2003) "European cities in the world city network," Proceedings of a Conference at The Centre of Comparative European History Berlin 2002, European Science Foundation. Online. http://repub.eur.nl/publications/index/914872951/ (accessed 10 August 2009).

Taylor, P., Walker, D.R.F. and Beaverstock, J.V. (2002) "Firms and their global service networks," in S. Sassen (ed.) Global Networks Linked Cities New York, London: Routledge, 93–115.

Taylor, T. (2004) World City Network: A Global Urban Analysis, London: Routledge.

Torres Enjuto, M. C. (1995) Industria y Territorio en Bizkaia, Bilbao: Instituto Vasco de Administracion Publica.

Turok, I. and Mykhnenko, V. (2006) "Resurgent European Cities?," Glasgow: Centre for Public Policy for Region. Working paper No. 2. September.

Turok, I. and Mykhnenko, V. (2007) "The trajectories of European cities, 1960–2005," Cities, 24: 3, 165–182.

Uitermark, J. (2009) "An in memorian for the just city of Amsterdam," City, 13, 348–361,

Vicario, L. and Martinez Monje, P.M. (2003) "Another "Guggenheim effect"? The generation of a potentially gentrifiable neighbourhood in Bilbao," Urban Studies, 40, 2383–2400.

Zulaika, J. (1997) Cronica de una seduccion, Madrid: Nerea.

Further reading

Bagnasco, A. and Le Galès, P. (eds) (2000) Cities in Contemporary Europe, Cambridge: Cambridge University Press. (Analysis of recent urban processes in Europe.)

Brenner, N. (2004) New State Spaces, Oxford: Oxford University Press. (Macro-analysis of changes in European cities since the 1970s.)

Brenner, N., Marcuse, P. and Mayer, M. (2009) "Special issue: Cities for people, not for profit," City, 13, nos. 2-3. (Critiques and proposals in the face of urban neoliberalism.)

England, K. and Ward, K. (2007) Neoliberalization. States, Networks, Peoples, Oxford: Blackwell. (Spatial manifestations of neoliberalism.)

Harvey, D. (2005) A Brief History of Neoliberalism, Oxford: Oxford University Press. (A concise introduction to the concept of neoliberalism.)

Kazepov, Y. (ed.) Cities of Europe, Oxford: Blackwell. (Presentation of framework and case study work from the 'European city' school.)

39

Gender, migration and socio-spatial transformations in Southern European cities

Dina Vaiou

Introduction

In the context of processes implied in the term "globalization", Southern European countries, formerly "sending" economic migrants to the European and global North, have become "receiving" of ever more diverse flows: temporary and transnational migrants, "*sans papiers*", refugees, human trafficking circuits, as well as movements of elite groups. Women's migration forms an important part in these flows, leading to modified approaches of migrant movement/settlement as well as representations of "the migrant". These processes deeply affect the ways in which local development may be examined and evaluated in Southern European cities, where migrants are primarily directed.

Local development as it is approached in this chapter does not refer to industrial districts, innovative success stories and dynamic enterprise clusters, as is the case in the vast literature accumulated since the 1970s (for a review see Hadjimichalis 2006a; also Becattini *et al.* 2003). The term is rather used as a reference to the ways in which migrant women and men, as active agents, develop practices of survival and integration within and beyond the economy, combining in different ways global/local constraints

and opportunities. The vital contribution of migrants to the productive structures of Southern European cities and regions is not discussed here but it is taken as an indispensable backdrop (for an elaboration see Hadjimichalis 2006b).

I first discuss some features of an emerging "Mediterranean model" of migration which accounts for much of the economic success in Southern Europe since the 1990s; then these features are further elaborated in relation to local development through examples drawn from research in Athens (Vaiou *et al.* 2007) and references to Barcelona and Naples; in a third step, the gendering of migrant settlement experiences is examined in relation to socio-spatial transformations. Athens is used as "canvas" to discuss patterns of migrant settlement and dynamics of local development. This tactic does not lead to a comparative study nor does it intend to underestimate differences among cities and homogenize diverse experiences of migration. It is rather an attempt to go beyond widespread arguments about "deviance" from mainstream patterns and "idiosyncratic" characteristics and critically examine the ways in which alternative understandings may be developed about recent development patterns in Southern European cities.

A Mediterranean model?

The changing nature of global migrant movements after 1989 alongside specific local development patterns in Southern European countries has led many researchers to talk of a "Southern European" or "Mediterranean" model of migration (among many see King 2000, Macioti and Pugliese 1991, Bettio *et al.* 2006, Tastsoglou and Hadjiconstanti 2003). Differences among countries and particular localities are significant, while the complex geographies of movement/settlement cannot be understood in a simple North–South scheme, especially in view of the recent transit flows. However, common features can be identified, three of which are discussed here: the informal, cities as migrants' destinations and the growing demand for female labor.

The attractions of the informal

Informal activities and practices are an important historical feature of Southern European economies and societies and form part of dynamic and innovative processes of local development (for a detailed discussion of the multiple meanings and uses of the term "informal", see Vaiou and Hadjimichalis 1997/2003). Through such practices large social groups have found ways of integration not only in the labor market, but also in broad areas of social and economic life, including access to housing and property, ways of avoiding taxation and circumventing bureaucratic procedures, and securing caring services for children, the sick, the old and the disabled. In short, the informal has been central in the development of a know-how of survival which legitimated, among other things, the limited and sometimes controversial involvement of the state, the latter going hand in hand with limited expectations from, or in some cases mistrust towards, the state. Therefore, informal practices enjoy widespread social acceptance and they have to be

seen as a "cause" or a parameter of attraction, rather than as an effect of the new migratory flows (see among many Reyneri 1998).

Migrants are attracted to Southern European countries, on the assumption that it is easy to make a living, or even make money, even without a residence/work permit. Finding an informal job comes out prominently in many migrants' own accounts about the reasons for choosing particular countries and places. Opportunities and earnings vary among countries and localities but there are widespread expectations that, sooner or later, they can somehow regularize their status (see, for example, Pugliese (2002) for Italy, Martinez Veiga (1998) for Spain, Bagavos and Papadopoulou (2006) for Greece) – an expectation which has so far been verified, at least in part, through a series of "legalization processes" which aim to regulate migrants' status and, mainly, to restrict new entries.

The main requisite in order to acquire a residence/work permit is a legal employment contract and proof of having paid social security contributions for a specified period of time (Solé *et al.* 1998, Pavlou and Christopoulos 2004), a result of which is the fragilization of the legal status of migrants who often oscillate between legality and illegality. They seem to be caught in a vicious cycle between a growing demand for (informal) low-paid, flexible labor and the reproduction of that demand also through the migrants' acceptance of informal jobs – for lack of alternatives outside the informal. Despite differences among migrant groups, to do with particular migration strategies and individual or family projects, women migrants seem to be more vulnerable than men in this vicious cycle.

Migrant settlement in Southern European cities

An important aspect of recent migrations to Southern Europe – and one that remains less discussed – is the settlement of migrants in central areas of cities. In the 1990s, metropolitan areas, like Milan, Rome, Naples, Barcelona, Madrid, Lisbon, Athens, and many smaller cities have begun to host a multi-ethnic/multi-cultural urban population of various origins, with profound effects on urban dynamics. The literature on these effects emphasizes mainly segregation and/or spatial marginalization of migrants, especially when it refers to the beginning of the 1990s (see, for example, Malheiros 2000, Iosifidis and King 1998). In many cases arguments are drawn from Northern European cities, for which there is much more evidence, both for earlier and for more recent migrations. Southern patterns, however, do not seem to verify a simple geography of urban center–periphery division, based as they are on different histories of urban development and modes of urban governance particular to specific cities and their respective countries.

After the Second World War, many Southern European cities have followed processes of "additive growth", with a considerably reduced influence of central plans and provisions (Leontidou 1990). Such processes have contributed to the growth of neighborhoods with poor social and technical infrastructures; at the same time they account for a certain homogeneity of urban space with limited divisions and tensions. It is in such areas that post-1989 migrants seek to settle. Formerly unused spaces in apartment blocks and other buildings become re-integrated in urban life and new activities diversify urban realities. Migrants do not settle in some remote periphery, but rather in centrally located socially mixed neighborhoods, with diverse typologies of housing stock and many opportunities to find a job in an extensive and varied formal and informal labor market, as well as better possibilities to escape controls. A relatively fast improvement in housing conditions becomes a prime parameter for social integration, supporting ideas that integration in the city takes place before integration in the host society (Germain 2000);

hence a renewed interest in the much contested notion of "neighborhood", which is also reflected in EU policies of the early 1990s (examples here include projects like the Quartiers en crise or Développement social urbain).

A growing demand for "female labor"

Feminization of migration has been singled out as one of the major general trends in recent migrations (Castles and Miller (1993) among the first), referring to women moving independently from men and/or families, albeit in widely different proportions among different ethnic groups. Since the early 1980s, in Southern Europe this presence is related to demographic and economic changes which have led to a growing demand for female labor, particularly in cities, for a restricted range of "women's jobs", most prominently domestic helpers, carers and "entertainers". Low birth rates and high life expectancy gradually led to an aging population in need of caring, at a time when local women have been entering paid work at an ever increasing pace (Bettio and Plantenga 2004), thus contributing to a general rise of the standards of living. In this context, caring and domestic labor cannot be accommodated in the context of families, in line with the familistic model of welfare, prominent in Greece, Spain and Italy, and to a lesser degree Portugal. The state is a "carer of the last resort", as Bettio et al. (2006: 272) call it, in a system based mainly on monetary transfers (pensions, subsidies, etc.).

The caring gap which develops in the last decades is partially covered by migrant women from Eastern Europe and the Balkans in Greece, from Latin America in Spain, from Africa in Italy, from former colonies in Portugal. It is to these areas of work that a lot of recent research has been devoted (among many, Andall 2000, Campani 2000, Papataxiarchis et al. 2008, Parella Rubio

2003, Ribas 1999), combining a variety of sources and methods and highlighting a variety of aspects and perspectives. Migrant women's labor covers caring needs, at prices which make it accessible even to lower income households, securing at the same time a rather stable income for themselves and their own families. By the same token it contributes to a new gendered model of caring, which remains in the context of families and among women and leaves men mostly uninvolved.

The features of the "Mediterranean model" briefly sketched above account for migrants' practices which form part of local development in the places where they settle for longer or shorter periods of time, i.e., in multi-functional and socially mixed central neighborhoods of Southern European cities. Informal practices and employment patterns, small family businesses, modes of access to housing, networks of mutual support and exchange of caring services all point to patterns which are historically embedded in these places and highly gendered. However, they acquire new dynamics and modalities as they mix with migrants' different habits, cultures, ways of doing and being in the city – which are further examined in the next section.

Athens and other Southern European cities

As already mentioned, cities in Southern Europe receive the bulk of recent migrants, thus becoming a prime site of major transformations. In 2001 and according to the population census, migrants were 7.5 percent of the population resident in Greece (or 797,000 people) and 11 percent of the population of Greater Athens (or 321,000 people), although many researchers consider these figures an underestimate. Almost half of the migrants residing in Greater Athens live in the central municipality of Athens and not in some remote periphery (Figure 39.1).

A closer look at migrant settlement within the municipality of Athens reveals interesting patterns to do with the forms of concentration (Figure 39.2). An extensive nucleus is immediately identifiable in an area which includes the "heart of the city" and a range of neighborhoods at its immediate vicinity. The latter are part of the intensive urban growth of the 1960s and 1970s and retain a strong presence of local households. Some 215 ethnicities have been identified in the resident migrant population, with Albanians being the vast majority (51.1 percent), followed at a distance by Poles and Bulgarians (5.0 percent and 3.8 percent respectively), with quite different migration patterns and gender composition.

A similar pattern has been identified in Barcelona where most of the recent migrants have settled in the city itself and in the poorer parts of the Old City (Ciutat Vella) from where locals and internal migrants of the previous decades had partially left (Fullaondo and Elordui 2003; for mappings at various scales see Martori *et al.* 2005, Elordui and Cladera 2006). In Naples, migrants who are in "transit" and intend to move soon to the Centre or North of Italy tend to settle in housing complexes in the periphery, already abandoned by locals and run down. When their plan is to stay more permanently, however, they seek low-cost housing in very central neighborhoods (Schmoll 2008).

In these central, densely populated and socially mixed areas support networks and integration mechanisms from below are in operation, along with (and sometimes against) policies from above. Migrants' activities and everyday practices contribute to new dynamics and to the constitution of places-within-places, in the cities of destination where women's involvement is determinant. This last remark aims to underline the particular ways in which women and men interpret, live and attribute meanings to the spaces of the everyday, the neighborhoods of their new settlement. Three interrelated aspects of their contribution to local development are

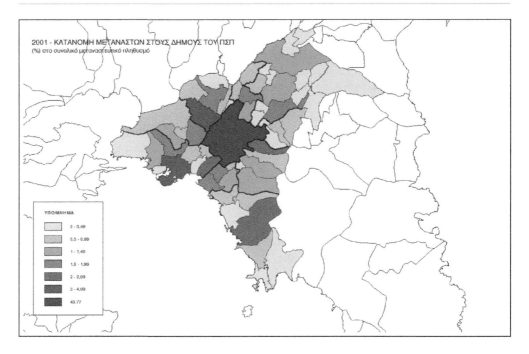

Figure 39.1 Migrant distribution in the municipalities of Greater Athens (% of total migrant population). Source: Vaiou *et al.* (2007). Adapted from Population Census data (2001)

discussed here: revitalization of the housing market, intensification of local commercial activity and the intensive (re)use of public spaces.

Revitalization of the housing market

The influx of migrants to the city center creates a considerable demand for housing, particularly after a first period of temporary arrangements, in the case of Athens in cheap hotels, overcrowded and rundown flats and even public squares. The municipality of Athens, like most historic centers of Greek cities, includes a rich typology of urban neighborhoods, resulting from a complex set of micro-local histories. After 1980, young households with better incomes started moving towards suburban areas, in search of better living environments. This movement,

however, never reached the dimensions of an "exodus" (Emmanuel 2002). It rather led to successive reorderings of the built stock in many central neighborhoods, such as manufacturing micro-firms in basements and lower floors of apartment buildings or, later, empty flats. Such restructurings kept prices low and attracted students, lower income households and, after 1990, migrants.

Migrants live in basements and lower floors of the same apartment buildings in which students and professional premises (lawyers, doctors, engineers, etc.) occupy the middle ones, while higher income, mainly elderly households remain in the upper floors – a pattern which contradicts theoretical arguments of gentrification based on rent gaps (e.g. Smith 1996). Migrants have upgraded through personal labor many old flats and paid higher rents than were proper for what they rented, usually in older apartment blocks. Initially, newcomers usually

Figure 39.2 Migrant concentration in the municipality of Athens (LQs)
Source: Vaiou *et al.* (2007). Adapted from Population Census data (2001)

cohabited with friends or relatives and/or sought smaller and cheaper flats and, most importantly, owners who would accept them. As their job situation and incomes became more stable, they looked for better housing conditions, usually in the same neighborhood, where networks and ties were already being established (Vaiou *et al.* 2007).

The case of Neapolitan "bassi" is indicative of how migrants have contributed to put back into the property market stock which was unused or poorly used and partially devalued. The difficult living conditions in these flats are compensated by the centrality of their location and the opportunities to earn a living that the city center offers (Peraldi 2001). They are also compensated by

the possibilities for contacts and networking in the context of everyday activities (Coppola 1999). In a similar vein, in the neighborhood of Raval in the Old City of Barcelona property prices had gone down due to the rundown condition of old stock – which attracted incoming migrants, mainly single men. The latter formed a first link in migrant networks, attracting more migrants who looked for housing near their compatriots. This process led to rent increases and to the re-insertion in the market of premises that were in poor condition (Garcia Armand 2005).

After more than two decades since the end of the 1980s, there is an observable tendency for migrants to buy flats in older apartment buildings, where prices per square meter are

475

lower. Albanian households in Athens are the main protagonists in this process, since they tend to pursue longer term migration projects, and women among them are key actors. In a situation of limited household resources, women's work, predominantly as domestic helpers and carers, yields a much more stable income (and possibilities to save) than men's seasonal or occasional work mainly in construction; on the other hand, and in this context, women have a decisive say in matters of housing (location, size, internal arrangement, etc.), not only "here" (in the place of destination), but also "there" (in the place of origin), where they also invest in housing purchase and/or improvement. In interviews with Albanian and Bulgarian women this continuous concern with securing better housing conditions "back home" comes out vividly; it clearly determines practices of income spending in both places and affects housing markets in several cities and towns of the Balkans and former USSR where most migrant women in Athens come from. Remittances not only cover immediate survival needs "there", but also trigger developments in the housing market and the growth of construction activity, with significant multiplier effects.

Intensification of commercial activity

As migrants settle more permanently, they begin to contribute to local economies through their activities and their incomes mostly spent locally, with immediate effects on local shops and services. It has been estimated that migrants accounted for 1.1 percent out of the 4.5 percent GDP growth in the 1990s (Labrianidis and Lyberaki 2001). Extensive fieldwork in neighborhoods of Athens, including detailed land use mapping, revealed a considerable number of shops addressed to migrants, as well as shops owned or run by them (Vaiou et al. 2007). In one such neighborhood, Kypseli, with more than

25 percent migrant population, 53 such shops were identified in an area of about 700 by 700 meters. These shops not only serve the different ethnic groups living in the area, but also a broader community of customers from the immediate vicinity and sometimes from other parts of the city.

Mini-markets, bakeries, money transfer offices, call centers, hairdressing salons, barbers, video clubs, internet cafes, fast-food stands, (ethnic) restaurants – all seem to fill a gap in the market, exceeding the local areas and the specific ethnic communities. These shops attract customers through specialized offers, long opening hours, higher quality service and affordable prices. They also play a stabilizing role in the neighborhood: they make the migrants' presence more visible, promote different selling/buying habits and usually function as points of reference for various groups of migrants and as contact places between migrants and locals. At the same time they are important employment and income generators. In this process migrant women are again key actors, both as consumers and as workers, in "family businesses" or in shops of their own.

The majority of migrant women living in Kypseli are employed: more than 70 percent of women from the Balkans (but 49 percent of women from Albania who usually come with their families), 50–70 percent of women from Africa and Poland (but less than 30 percent of women from Arab countries). Their paid work may take them to any part of the metropolitan area, but their daily activities as "homemakers" evolve mostly in the neighborhood: in local shops, in the weekly open markets, in municipal health consultancies, schools and other services. They not only buy for day-to-day needs "here", but also invest in consumer goods and appliances for homes "back home"; for the latter case neighborhood shops are preferred, even though they may be somewhat more expensive, because items can be paid off through monthly installments, which are made possible through personal contacts with local shop-owners. And it is women rather than men who determine such decisions to spend family or personal income, based on short- and longer term projects.

Similar processes of migrant women's involvement as consumers and as workers in local commercial activities and services are identified for the Old City of Barcelona (Aramburu 2002). Women may be earning their income all around the city, as domestic helpers, carers of elderly people, employees in shops and services, but they spend locally, in the immediate vicinity of their home (Garcia Armand 2005). In their role as "homemakers" they not only contribute to an intense local commercial activity, but also to a slow but visible change of attitudes. Examples like these help explore the "hidden" aspects of place-making which relate to household processes and extend over space at various scales.

Intensive use of public spaces

The numerous presence of migrants in public spaces of Southern European cities has been an important part of urban transformations since the early 1980s (for Italy) and 1990s (for Greece and Spain). At times, public squares and parks are used as temporary sleeping places for newcomers, usually men; but most intensely they are used as meeting and recreation spaces for various ethnic groups who thus make their presence visible to other migrants as well as to locals. Piazza Municipio or Galleria Umberto in Naples are associated with the presence of Somalis and Eritreans respectively, while the area of the Central Station, characterized by a continuous presence of migrants from Senegal and the Maghreb, is thought by many to be an "arabized" locality (Cattedra and Laino 1994). Plaza dels Ángels or Plaza dels Caramelles in the Raval are intensely frequented by women migrants from Pakistan, Bangladesh, the Philippines or Latin America who oversee their children playing in a public

space full of tourists (who visit the adjacent Museum of Modern Art or the Centro de Cultura Contemporana de Barcelona) and students from the nearby Department of Geography and History of the University of Barcelona ("Un barrio con futuro", special issue of the local newspaper *El Raval*, November 7, 2007).

In Athens particular micro-spaces are appropriated, regularly or occasionally, by different ethnic groups in all the central public squares, parks and gardens. In the neighborhood of Kypseli two different public spaces illustrate emerging development patterns: the main square and the municipal market (the agora). The agora, a covered market which for many years was a landmark for the area, was occupied in December 2006 by local left-wing activists to prevent its demolition by the Municipality and to stop a plan to build an office block and a large underground garage. The act initiated a broader mobilization in the neighborhood (and beyond) demanding public spaces and defending a site of collective memory. It now works as a self-managed social center and hosts various cultural, political and artistic projects and events of local and city-wide reach (Figure 39.3). Migrants from the area are active in the center, which has become a meeting point with locals, while the evening school offering free courses of Greek language by volunteer teachers contributes to build contacts among people of various ethnic backgrounds.

The main square of Kypseli, one of the very few public open spaces in the neighborhood, is bustling again with activity since the early 1990s. Migrant children from a variety of countries and places communicate in a whole host of languages and body movements, while their mothers learn to accept different playing habits, "other" attitudes towards children, "strange" ways of sitting and socializing. Repopulation of the square by migrant women and children has brought back also local, mainly elderly women, hesitant in the beginning but later eager to reuse

Figure 39.3 Kypseli, Athens: public event in the Agora
Source: Author's image

an emblematic place in their neighborhood (Figure 39.4). In their narratives, the square of their memories comes out as a different place where a complex mix of languages, music rhythms, smells and bodily appearances are encountered, gradually tolerated and often positively appreciated. Bodily presence and common daily practices contribute to contact and familiarization with "others" – which in turn mobilizes (informal) processes of networking, mutual support and, perhaps eventually, integration. Here the practices of women and men are distinctively different and imply a multiplicity of relations initiated and organized around shared experiences and practices of caring.

Gendering migrant settlement

The numerous presence of women in recent migration flows is by now well documented, both in terms of general numbers and in terms of autonomous presence within these flows, thereby challenging representations of "the migrant" as a man, young, economically active, moving alone. Approaches which integrate women's experiences and gender perspectives question the ways in which migration as a global set of processes can be understood. Such approaches also question in different ways established understandings of local development and point to some "hidden" aspects of local/global links which require a multi-scalar perspective. Decisions to migrate are part of complex migration projects which involve people and households/families in different countries and important negotiations of gender power, which are linked to the changing spatialities of migrant households.

Between global restructurings, countries and individuals, families are constituted as dispersed in different places, support networks are formed in neighborhoods, integration mechanisms are devised, linked to (micro)

Figure 39.4 Kypseli, Athens: the main square (2007).
Source: Author's image

spatial scales and collective action. In these processes, migrant women's involvement emerges as quite distinct from that of men. The absences and presences of migrant men point to lives more focused around paid work and disconnected from the caring aspects of everyday life. Women's invisible and under-valued everyday activities on the other hand contribute to constitute "familiar places" within Southern European cities and play an important role in transformations and devel-opments both "here" and "there". Their eve-ryday and longer term practices related to paid work, housing, household provisioning, populating public spaces and services and networking account to a large extent for the revitalization of urban neighborhoods which were on the verge of being devalued.

The organization of care, characteristic of the Mediterranean model, reveals important sites where masculinities and feminities are negotiated personally and socially, among migrants, between migrants and locals, and among locals. The minutiae of everyday life, and the different involvement of women and men, permit a clearer view of the gendered aspects of migrant settlement, in which power is enacted but also resisted. Attention to these gendered aspects reveals different dynamics of local development and of the changing spatialities of everyday life across places and borders, which constitute slow but deep challenges for local development. To what extent such patterns may survive the deepening economic crisis is an open question for Southern European cities and societies.

References

Andall, J. (2000) *Gender, Migration and Domestic Service. The Politics of Black Women in Italy*, Aldershot: Ashgate.

Aramburu, M. (2002) *Los otros y nosotros: Imágenes del inmigrante en Ciutat Vella de Barcelona*, Madrid: Ministeio de Educación, Cultura y Deporte.

Bagavos, Ch. and Papadopoulou, D. (eds) (2006) *Migration and Integration of Migrants in Greek Society*, Athens: Gutenberg (in Greek).

Becattini, G., Bellandi, M., dei Ottati, G. and Sforzi, F. (2003) *From Industrial Districts to Local Development. An Itinerary of Research*, Cheltenham: Edward Elgar.

Bettio, F. and Plantenga, J. (2004) "Comparing care regimes in Europe", *Feminist Economics*, 10:1, 85–113.

Bettio, F., Simonazzi, A. and Villa, P. (2006) "Change in care regimes and female migration: the 'care drain' in the Mediterranean", *Journal of European Social Policy*,16:3, 271–285.

Campani, G. (2000) *Genere, etnia e classe*, Pisa: ETS.

Castles, S. and Miller, M. (1993) *The Age of Migration. International Population Movements in the Modern World*, London: Macmillan.

Cattedra, R. and Laino, G. (1994) "Espaces d' immigration et formes urbaines: considéra-tions sur le cas de Naples", *Revue Européenne des Migrations Internationales*, 10:2, 175–185.

Coppola, P. (1999) "Nuovi abitanti, nuove mixité. Napoli: tracce di una città meticcia", in Brusca (a cura di*) Immigrazione e multiculturalità nell' Italia di oggi*, Milano: F. Angeli, 414–422.

Elordui, Z. and Cladera, J. (2006) "Residential mobility and foreign immigration settlement in the Metropolitan area of Barcelona", paper presented at the 6th Urban and Regional Studies Conference, Roskilde, Denmark.

Emmanuel, D. (2002) "Housing conditions in Greater Athens", *Geographies*, 3, 46–70 (in Greek).

Fullaondo, A. and Elordui, Z. (2003) *Análisis de la distribución territorial de inmigración extranjera en Barcelona*, Barcelona: Centre de Política de Sól i Valoracions (CPSV).

Garcia Armand, A. (2005) "El rol de las mujeres en el devenir de un barrio intercultural: el Raval de Barcelona", in M. Nash, R. Tello and N. Benach (eds) *Inmigración, género y espacios urbanos. Los retos de la diversidad*, Barcelona: edicions Bellaterra.

Germain, A. (2000) *Immigrants and Cities: Does Neighbourhood Matter?*, Montréal: Institut National de la Recherche – Urbanisation, Culture et Société.

Hadjimichalis, C. (2006a) "Non-economic factors in economic geography and in 'new regionalism': a sympathetic critique", *International Journal of Urban and Regional Research*, 30:3, 690–704.

Hadjimichalis, C. (2006b) "The end of Third Italy as we knew it?", *Antipode*, 38:1, 82–106.

Iosifidis, T. and King, R. (1998) "Socio-spatial dynamics and exclusion of three immigrant groups in the Athens conurbation", *South European Society and Politics*, 3:3, 205–229.

King, R., Lazaridis, G. and Tsardanidis, C. (eds) (2000) *Eldorado or Fortress? Migration in Southern Europe*, London: Macmillan.

Labrianidis, L. and Lyberaki, A. (2001) *Albanian Migrants in Thessaloniki. Trajectories of Prosperity and Oversights of the Public Image*, Thessaloniki: Paratiritis (in Greek).

Leontidou, L. (1990) *The Mediterranean City in Transition*, Cambridge: Cambridge University Press.

Macioti, M.I. and Pugliese, E. (1991) *Gli immigrati in Italia*, Bari: Laterza.

Malheiros, J. (2000) "Urban restructuring, immi-gration and the generation of marginalized spaces in the Lisbon region", in R. King, G. Lazaridis and C. Tsardanidis (eds) *Eldorado or Fortress? Migration in Southern Europe*, London: Macmillan, 207–232.

Martinez Veiga, U. (1998) "Immigrants in the Spanish labour market", *South European Society and Politics*, 3:3, 105–128.

Martori, J., Hoberg, K. and Suriñach, J. (2005) "Segregation measures and spatial autocorre-lation. Location patterns of immigrant minor-ities in the Barcelona region", paper presented at the 4th Congress of the European Regional Science Association, Vrije Universiteit Amsterdam.

Morini, C. (a cura di) (2001) *La serva serve. Le nuove forzate del lavoro domestico*, Rome: Derive-Approdi.

Papataxiarchis, E., Topali, P. and Athanasopoulou, A. (2008) *Worlds of Domestic Labor. Gender, Migration and Cultural Transformations in Early 21st Century Athens*, Athens: University of the Aegean (in Greek).

Parella Rubio, S. (2003) *Mujer, inmigrante y traba-jadora, La triple discriminación*, Barcelona: Anthropos.

Pavlou, M. and Christopoulos, D. (eds) (2004) *Greece of Migrants. Social Participation, Rights and Citizenship*, Athens: Kritiki and KEMO (in Greek).

Peraldi, M. (2001) *Cabas et containers. Activités marchandes informelles et réseaux migrants trans-frontaliers*, Paris: Maisonoeuvre at Larose.

Pugliese, E. (2002) *L'Italia tra migrazioni internazi-onali e migrazioni interne*, Bologna: il Mulino.

Reyneri, E. (1998) "The role of the underground economy in irregular migration to Italy: cause or effect?", *Journal of Ethnic and Migration Studies*, 24:2, 313–331.

Ribas, N. (1999) *Las presencias de la inmigración femenina. Un recorrido por Filipinas, Gambia y Marruecos en Cataluña*, Barcelona: Icaria-Antrazyt.

Schmoll, C. (2001) "Immigration et nouvelles marges productives dans l' aire métropolitaine de Naples", *Bulletin de l' Association des Géographes Français*, 76:4, 403–413.

Schmoll, C. (2008) "Naples dans les mouvements migratoires: une interface Nord-Sud?", *Bulletin de l' Association des Géographes Français*, 83:3, 313–324.

Smith, N. (1996) *The New Urban Frontier. Gentrification and the Revanchist City*, London: Routledge.

Solé, C., Ribas, N., Bergalli, V. and Parella, S. (1998) "Irregular employment amongst migrants in Spanish cities", *Journal of Ethnic and Migration Studies*, 24:2, 333–346.

Tastsoglou, E. and Hadjicostandi, J. (2003) "Never outside the labour market, but always outsiders: Female migrant workers in Greece", Special Issue: *Gender and International Migration: Focus on Greece* (E. Tastsoglou and L. Maratou-Alipranti, eds), *The Greek Review of Social Research*, 110A, 189–220.

Vaiou, D. (2002) "In the interstices of the city: Albanian women in Athens", *Espace, Populations, Societes*, 3, 373–385.

Vaiou, D. (2006), *Analysis of Demand for Female Migrants' Labour. The Greek Case* [online], FeMiPol Working Paper GR-WP 4.1, at: www.femipol.uni-frankfurt.de.

Vaiou, D., Bacharopoulou, A., Fotiou, Th., Hatzivasileiou, S., Kalandides, A., Karali, M., Kefalea, R., Lafazani, O., Lykogianni, R., Marnelakis, G., Monemvasitou, A., Papasimaki, K. and Tounta, F. (2007) *Intersecting Patterns of Everyday Life and Socio-spatial Transformations in the City. Migrant and Local Women in the Neighbourhoods of Athens*, Athens: L-Press (in Greek).

Vaiou, D. and Hadjimichalis, C. (1997/2003) *With the Sewing Machine in the Kitchen and the Poles in the Fields. Cities, Regions and Informal Work*, Athens: Exandas (in Greek).

Further reading

Anthias, F. and Lazaridis, G. (eds) (2000) *Gender and Migration in Southern Europe*, Oxford: Berg. (One of the first collections of essays on gender and migration with a Southern European focus.)

Dyck, I. and McLaren, A. (2004) "Telling it like it is… Gender, place and multiculturalism in migrant women's settlement narratives", *Gender, Place and Culture*, 11:4, 513–534. (A reflection on methodological issues and knowledge production related to gender and migration.)

Green, N. (2002) *Repenser les migrations*, Paris: Presses Universitaires de France. (Analysis of migrations, with interesting comparisons between France and the USA and a chapter about the passage from "the migrant (man)" to "the migrant (woman)".)

Häussermann, H., Siebel, W. (2001) "Integration and segregation. Thoughts on an old debate", *Deutsche Zeitschrift für Kommunalwissenschaften*, 40:1, 125–138. (A discussion on the role of integration policies and their effects on urban neighborhoods.)

Kearns, A. and Parkinson, M. (2001) "The significance of neighbourhood", *Urban Studies*, 38:12, 2103–2110. (An analysis of the significance of the much debated concept of "neighborhood".)

Quassoli, F. (1999) "Migrants in the Italian underground economy", *International Journal of Urban and Regional Research*, 23:2, 212–231. (A discussion of the role of informal activities on migrant settlement in Italy.)

Silvey, R. (2006) "Geographies of gender and migration. Spatializing social difference", *International Migration Review*, 40:1, 64–81. (A review of the contribution of geography to gender and migration research.)

Section VI

Global perspectives

40

The experience of local and regional development in Africa

Etienne Nel

Introduction

The recent history of local and regional development in Africa has been one marked with experiences ranging from disappointments and desperate attempts to cope with the effects of marginalization to ambitious supranational programmes and efforts to achieve unique forms of 'African development'. From the outset it is important to point out the complexity and diversity which characterizes Africa, which was, as of November 2009, home to over one billion people living in 54 different countries (BBC, 2009). These countries range from some of the world's poorest such as Chad and Malawi through to relatively affluent middle-income countries such as South Africa and Mauritius which are experiencing sustained economic growth and integration into the global economy (Ayeni, 1997). Significant language, religious and cultural differences and the existence of governments which range from at least one case of an absolute monarchy, to military states and true democracies complicate the picture and prevent the drawing of uniform conclusions.

Africa's recent past has clearly been one of the most traumatic on the planet. Economic collapse, debt, corruption and disease have proven to be significant obstacles to development and major inducements to policy-makers to implement appropriate responses (Konadu-Agyemang and Panford, 2006). Colonialism divided Africa into a series of artificial dependencies which cut across pre-existing tribal borders and imposed a system of resource extraction within the broader context of an International Division of Labour (Griffith, 1995; Niang, 2006). The initial optimism of the post-Second World War independence era and the pursuit of both pan-Africanism and various 'grand development' schemes was sadly curtailed by the 1980s debt crisis, maladministration, corruption and the marginal role Africa now plays in the global economy, which has since been compounded by the negative effects of trade liberalization, low growth rates in commodity prices and currency devaluation (Griffith, 1995). The fact that Africa has the fastest growing population rates in the world has not aided matters in countries which are experiencing minimal levels of economic growth, while the devastating effects of AIDS is severely straining fragile economies and government resources. In the view of Griffith (1995: 191) 'Africa is the most disadvantaged continent in terms of poverty, political unrest, quality of life and human suffering'. As a result the potential value of well-formulated local and regional development it is apparent.

At a continental level, Africa in the twenty-first century faces both enormous challenges and opportunities. It has some of the richest mineral resources in the world and there is a very strong sense of regional identity which has led to the formation of several key regional political and economic unions. Within countries, the Washington Census (the World Bank and IMF's concepts of state economic management) has curtailed previous forms of state intervention while larger 'regional' initiatives within countries are very much on the back-burner. Themes of decentralization and community empowerment have become a hallmark of the survival endeavours of marginal towns and communities, often with direct reliance on the NGO sector for support. Its is apparent that significant policy and strategic changes are taking place in Africa; however, it seems that 'the current regional trend in Africa has received little scholarly attention especially in a systematic and comprehensive way. This is due partly to the fact that the processes are currently unfolding and there is still uncertainty in the outcomes' (Adejombi and Olukoshi, in Cambria Press, 2008).

This chapter overviews Africa's experiences in regional and local development over the last 60 or so years. It starts with a brief review of the pre-Independence scenario before focusing on national development schemes and pan-Africanism as pursued in the 1950s through to the 1970s. Following what has been referred to as the 'lost decade' of the 1980s in Africa, as a result of the debt crisis and structural adjustment, focus shifts to look at recent pan-regional initiatives, national policies and various local coping strategies. Given the shear size and complexities of the continent and its 54 countries it is impossible to capture the micro-detail of what is happening in each country; rather emphasis is placed on generic themes and the examination of specific illustrative cases as appropriate.

The pre-independence and early independence eras in Africa, 1950–1980s

European colonialism imposed an artificial division of space on the pre-existing tribal kingdoms of Africa. Empires such as the Ashanti and Monomotapa, which were regional in extent, and which had developed regional trading routes within African and with the Middle East were subsumed in a European order which divided the continent into European 'spheres of influence' (Best and de Blij, 1977; Griffith, 1995). That 'development' did take place is undeniable; however, this often took the form of linking the colony to the mother country through defined systems of transport and resource abstraction, which made once economically independent areas dependent on external economies for inputs, jobs, products and even food, as economies were restructured, often becoming mono-economies to supply products such as cotton (from the Sudan) and copper (from Zambia) to Europe (Ayeni, 1997; Makinda and Okumu, 2008). Regional development in the sense of the creation of industrial-mineral and commercial-agricultural complexes was a hallmark of this period with the granting of lands to European settlers and companies and significant state and private investment in key industrial-mineral complexes. Examples include tea production in the Kenyan Highlands, cotton production in the Sudan, tobacco in what is now Zimbabwe and cocoa in West Africa. Key mineral-industrial nodes include the Witwatersrand in South Africa, once the wealthiest gold-producing area in the world, the Copperbelt complexes in what are now Zambia and the Congo and the industrial cities of present-day Zimbabwe (Best and de Blij, 1977). These complexes were all linked to large, purpose-designed ports with dedicated high-volume rail linkages (Davidson, 1994; Griffith, 1995). An examination of historical railway maps of Africa provides insight into the nature of this historical, extractive economy and its selective influence on the continent. The dense rail network in industrialized South Africa stands in contrast to the effective absence of any rail connectivity in poorly developed Chad, while in countries such as Mozambique and Angola, short unconnected railway lines link ports to single resource supply zones in the interior (Davidson, 1994).

At the international scale, the concept of 'spheres of influence' in the British, French, Portuguese, Spanish and German parts of the continent led to the formation of close cross-border trade and administrative links which was most noticeable in French West Africa where two Federations were formed under French rule. Later in the British sphere the Central African and East African Federations were formed (Best and de Blij, 1997; Griffith, 1995; Konadu-Agyemang and Panford, 2006). At the time of Independence Africa was left with highly skewed and dependent economies, characterized by what were often mono-economies, dependent on European trade and economic linkages, and weak and poorly diversified skills bases and economies. While attempts were made to throw off what were perceived to be the 'shackles' of colonial oppression through efforts to promote unique forms of African development such as 'Afro-Socialism' and the active courting of links with the then USSR, China and the Eastern bloc, true economic independence from the West proved difficult to attain (Ayeni, 1997).

The early Independence era in countries such as Ghana, Zambia, Ethiopia and Tanzania was characterized by bold attempts to implement nationally appropriate strategies which often had a strong rural focus and an appeal to 'self-reliance' principles. The most extreme case was Tanzania which actively sought to cut off links with the external world and pursued an ambitious policy of rural development through a 'villagization' development scheme known as Ujaama. These strategies had their roots in pan-Africanism as espoused by key African leaders such as Nkrumah from Ghana and the belief in African self-reliance as advocated by leaders such as

Kaunda in Zambia and Nyerere in Tanzania. In parallel, other countries and regimes, such as Kenyatta's Kenya chose to pursue more Western market-based development strategies often with equally limited success (Davidson, 1994; Ayeni, 1997).

In this era the local state tended to have few powers of direct decision-making. Key powers rested with the central state which, in most cases, actively strove to develop national assets, often through targeted spatial development schemes. Some of the most apparent include significant investment in capital cities and in certain cases the creation of brand-new administrative capitals with Dodoma in Tanzania, Lilongwe in Malawi and Abuja in Nigeria being the most obvious. Investment in airports, sports stadia and administrative complexes has created artificial pseudo-western cities in what are often some of the poorest countries on the planet. The redevelopment of Abidjan in Ivory Coast is a case in point under the rule of Houphouet-Boigny (Bell, 1986; Griffith, 1995).

Another distinctive feature of this period which overlapped with attempts at self-reliance, was the desire for and pursuit of prestige projects to drive development. With the support of the global financial bodies there was, for example, significant investment in major river basin/large dam/HEP schemes. One of the most significant was the development of Lake Volta in Ghana which created a vast dam to supply electricity to the newly built aluminium smelter at Tema and which was also meant to facilitate irrigated farming and fishing. Parallel initiatives included Cabora Basa in Mozambique, Kariba between Zambia and Zimbabwe, the Aswan High Dam and multiple dam projects in Morocco. In almost all cases the schemes have not delivered the full range of anticipated benefits (Best and de Blij, 1977).

Within countries Western-style interventions such as a focus on the development of growth centres and support for industrial development nodes was supported to some degree within most African countries (Ayeni, 1997).

One of the most comprehensive assessments of this process was provided in the study by Alan Whiteside in 1981 who overviewed the pursuit of these strategies in various parts of Africa. Despite significant investment in infrastructure and industry, capital city dominance of the economies was not significantly altered and in countries such as Zimbabwe, which pursued growth centre planning through to the 1990s, the vast majority of the growth centres failed to 'take off'. Problems include insufficient resources, inadequate incentives and a lack of market-based reasons for firms establishing in such centres. That said, in political terms, Zimbabwe was a forerunner in establishing relatively high degrees of political decentralization (Gooneratne and Mbilinyi, 1992).

The most comprehensive form of regional development pursued in Africa in this era was undoubtedly South Africa's Regional Industrial Development Programme which meshed regional and growth centre planning with its then racist ideology of developing 'racial reserves' for the different tribal groupings in the country. Over 50 growth points were established and a package of incentives once described 'as the most generous in the world' were made available to prospective industrialists. Significant state investment, estimated at some 10 per cent of government expenditure in the late 1980s was needed to prop up a highly inefficient system which aided some 10 per cent of national industries and supported over 100,000 jobs (Rogerson, 1988; Nel, 1999). The cessation of the policy in the early 1990s witnessed the collapse of many of the former growth points and the closure of most of the firms, to the detriment of former employees in particular. Exceptions occurred in places which were better resourced and able to continue growing in the absence of incentives, such as the towns of George, Saldanha Bay and Isithebe. Studies have shown that firms generally failed to develop economic links with the host area and often remained on site only for the duration of the incentives, ceasing operations when the

funding ceased. Extensive abuse of the system was also noted and, if anything, the South African case is something of an anti-model with respective to the concept of regional development anchored in these outlying industrial growth centres (Rogerson, 1988; Nel, 1999).

The contemporary context

Regional development (internal)

In parallel with international experience traditional regional development interventions fell into abeyance in the 1980s and 1990s, often resulting from limited success and budget constraints. Where regional development persisted in the period from the 1980s through to the 1990s it tended to have quite a distinctive project-based focus. This is shown in a comprehensive overview of Regional Development practice in the 1990s in Africa by the United Nations Commission for Human Settlement (UNHCS, 1997) which indicates the following broad themes:

i) River basin development – primarily in West Africa along the Niger River and Lake Chad
ii) Lake basin development, e.g. around Lake Victoria
iii) National development planning, e.g. in Zambia with associated efforts to address regional inequalities
iv) Growth centre planning, e.g. in Ghana, Nigeria and Kenya
v) New capital city development, e.g. Malawi, Nigeria and Tanzania
vi) Integrated rural development, e.g. in Tanzania.

In his critique of these approaches and the apparently limited success of the initiatives implemented, Ayeni (1997) indicates that these schemes suffered from both the application of inappropriate planning and theory and they were bedevilled with implementation problems. Difficulties included spatial bias in implementation, poor policy analysis, the overwhelming focus of growth and migration on the big primate cities, and broader economic changes including structural adjustment which severely curtailed the role the state could play in the space-economies of African states.

One of the more successful and long-standing collaborative regional development arrangements exists in the Sengal River basin. Following the signing of the Bamako Convention in 1963 between Guinea, Mali, Mauritania and Senegal a series of enduring programmes have been enacted, revolving around the provision of water management, communications and power-generating infrastructure. High levels of engagement between partners have reduced conflict and facilitated economic development in areas such as fish farming and rice cultivation (Alam and Dione, 2006).

The recent revival and focus on more sophisticated and diverse forms of regional development in the developed world has few parallels in Africa. With certain South African exceptions, there are few examples of contemporary regional strategies such as global city development, science parks or high-tech industrial zones. Another exception has been South Africa's reinvigoration of regional development in the late 1990s when a 'Spatial Development Initiative' programme focusing on defined transport and economic growth corridors was initiated, in parallel with the establishment of high-tech or export-orientated 'Industrial Development Zones' (Simon, 2003). While the former has only achieved limited success, in the case of the latter, significant investment in purpose-designed facilities with an export-orientated focus and having special tax concessions have seen the establishment of key port and industrial zones at Coega (near Port Elizabeth), East London and Richards Bay which are yielding initial success. Another noteworthy trend has been the recognition given to the emergence of various 'industrial clusters' and 'innovation systems' in Africa in recent years

which generally have emerged with little, if any state support. Examples range from sophisticated manufacturing for the global car market, as exemplified by the Durban auto-cluster in South Africa, to more informal activities such as fish processing in Uganda and furniture manufacturing in Egypt (Oyelaran-Oyeyinka and McCormick, 2007).

In parallel, there has been widespread experimentation with the concept of export processing in countries ranging from Liberia to Botswana and Zimbabwe. Earlier research by the ILO (in Nel, 1994) however found results to be disappointing. In addition to concerns about the limited success of interventions such as these, there remain the pressing challenges posed by rural areas which are subject to environmental degradation and economic decline, which also merit some form of regional support (Gooneratne and Obudho, 1997).

Regional development (supranational)

A distinctive feature of regional development practice and policy in Africa is widespread subscription to the principles of cross-border linkages within the continent for purposes of facilitating trade, social, cultural and economic exchange, peace-keeping and the overall promotion of pan-Africanism. International connectivity has a relative long history in the continent. The world's oldest customs union is in fact the Southern African Customs Union formed in 1910, which now includes South Africa, Botswana, Namibia, Lesotho and Swaziland (Kyambalesa and Hougnikpo, 2006). In addition, political Federations established in the 1950s in East and Central Africa laid the basis for later regional arrangements.

Makinda and Okumu (2008) argue that the proliferation of regional groupings in Africa came about because of the perceived need for both collective security and development in the post-Cold War era and in response to regional conflicts within the continent.

According to Adejombi and Olukoshi (in Cambria Press, 2008), slow economic progress and increasing marginalization of the continent at the global level have given significant impetus to new regional development strategies. The small size of national economies and the logic of establishing a collective voice through supranational arrangements (Griffith, 1995) has created what Bell (1986: 108) argues is a 'powerful case' for regional cooperation. The net result has been the veritable blossoming of a range of key initiatives discussed below.

The post-independence era in Africa was characterized by clear commitment in many parts of Africa to the principle of pan-Africanism and the determination of a unique and collaborative vision for the continent (Makinda and Okumu, 2008). This was initially advocated by first-generation independence leaders such as Lumumba, Kenyatta, Nyrere and Nkrumah. The latter argued for the idea that 'Africa Must Unite' (Griffith, 1995). Despite this, early attempts at a union between Guinea and Ghana and calls for greater degrees of regional integration met with little success in the 1960s and 1970s (Davidson, 1994). These concepts have since developed significantly, crystallizing in 1980 with the Lagos Plan of Action which laid the basis for seeking greater degrees of self-reliance through supranational arrangements. In 1963 the Organization of African Unity was formed as a loose political union amongst most of Africa's states. This has since evolved into the African Union, established in 2001, which has now set up a Pan-African Parliament and which has as one of its goals the formation of an African Economic Community (Janneh, 2006).

In addition to continent-wide initiatives, a not insignificant range of customs and nascent economic unions exist in Africa which has variously assisted with issues such as the provision of unified telecommunications networks in Southern Africa and the formation of regional peace-keeping forces in West Africa. As Ayeni (1997: 53) notes, if these organizations can succeed they 'would have serious repercussions for processes of regional development all over the continent'. The key unions are as follows:

i) The Southern African Customs Union (SACU), established in 1910 as a customs union with joint revenue-sharing arrangements on tariffs derived from external trade (Kyambalesa and Hougnikpo, 2006).

ii) The East African Community (EAC), first established in 1967 and revived in 2000, leading to the establishment of a customs union in 2005. A common market and political union are planned and a joint Legislative Assembly has been set up (Kyambalesa and Hougnikpo, 2006).

iii) The Economic Community of Central African States (ECCAS), which was established in 1985 to promote regional economic cooperation, free trade and a customs union and eventually a Common Market in central Africa (Kyambalesa and Hougnikpo, 2006).

iv) The Economic Community of West African States (ECOWAS) was established in 1975 by the Treaty of Lagos. It seeks collective 'self-sufficiency' through the development of an economic and monetary union and a trading bloc. Key organizations which it has established include a Community Court of Justice and a common peace-keeping arrangement (Kyambalesa and Hougnikpo, 2006; Konadu-Agyemang and Panford, 2006).

v) The Common Market for Eastern and Southern Africa (COMESA), which was formed in 1994, replacing the earlier Preferential Trade Area, establishing a free trade area between nine of the member countries. There is an agreement to expand free trade arrangements with the EAC and SADC, which if finalized will create free trade zones encompassing nearly

50 per cent of the countries in Africa (Kyambalesa and Hougnikpo, 2006; BBC, 2008).

vi) The Southern African Development Community (SADC) was formed in 1992 to replace an earlier political union in the region. The organization strives to promote socio-economic, political and security cooperation. Currently 12 countries have formed a free trade area and progress has been made with a range of joint projects in areas such as infrastructure, trade and health care (Kyambalesa and Hougnikpo, 2006).

The Africa Free Trade Zone (AFTZ) formed by links between SADC, COMESA and EAC agreed on in 2008, and mentioned above, will link 26 countries with a GDP of some US$624 bn (BBC, 2008). At a grander level are the current and proposed activities of the African Economic Community (AEC) which seeks to utilize the above-mentioned regional groupings as 'pillars' for their proposed activities. The AEC was founded in 1991 through the Abuja Treaty and has helped promote the development of the regional trading blocs (Niang, 2006; Kyambalesa and Hougnikpo, 2006). The AEC is supported by all of Africa with the exception of the Arab Maghreb Union. Future goals are a proposed continent-wide customs union by 2019 and an African Common Market by 2023. The establishment of the AFTZ is clearly a key step in the attainment of these eventual goals (Janneh, 2006).

At a political level the establishment of the Organization of African Unity (1963) and its replacement with the African Union (AU) in 2001 have been the primary continent-wide forms of regional political collaboration and cooperation. Head quartered in Addis Abba, the AU seeks to promote socio-economic and political integration, to seek consensus and present common positions and to promote peace and security (Konadu-Agyemang and Panford, 2006; Makinda and Okumu, 2008). A Pan-African Parliament has been created which incorporates the entire continent with the exception of Morocco. Mechanisms to promote peace-keeping, democracy and development have been put in place (Mohamoud, 2007). In 2007 a Union Government for Africa was mooted.

A parallel but linked international initiative which has been formally adopted by the AU is the New Partnership for Africa's Development (NEPAD) established in 2001 through the merger of South Africa, Algeria and Nigeria's Millennium Partnership plan and Senegal's OMEGA plan (Konadu-Agyemang and Panford, 2006). NEPAD seeks to put in place mechanisms across the continent to eradicate poverty, promote sustainable growth and development, integrate Africa into the world economy and accelerate the empowerment of women (Niang, 2005; Mohamoud, 2007). Partnerships have since been developed with many of the world's key financial bodies and programmes focusing on agriculture, science, e-schools, infrastructure and building continental institutions are being developed. In practice, slow progress, the lack of civil society participation and perceptions that NEPAD is working too closely with the 'Washington Consensus' organizations, and the dominance of South Africa in the organization are clearly concerns for several member states (Makinda and Okumu, 2008).

Challenges experienced by the various regional blocs discussed above include: under-resourcing, member countries participating in overlapping organizations, the pursuit of self-interest, limited supranational policing mechanisms, friction between members, limited mandates and long-standing conflicts, particularly in the Great Lakes region (Kyambalesa and Hougnikpo, 2006). Other concerns include the limited nature of cross-border infrastructure development and a continued dependence not on intra-African but inter-continental trade (Konadu-Agyemang and Panford, 2006). The UNCTAD (2009) argues that while substantial progress has been made to establish regional institutions, intra-African trade, investment and people's mobility have not increased significantly, leaving Africa with some of the most fragmented markets in the world. As a result a key UN report released in 2009 (UNCTAD, 2009) argues the case for enhancing 'regional integration to build stronger and more resilient economies … Regional infrastructure, policy harmonization and increasing cross-border investment and labour mobility will help Africa benefit fully from economic opportunities provided by regional integration'.

One recent variant on the concept of regional development has been the promotion of a series of trans-frontier parks or game reserves, primarily between South Africa and its neighbours which has seen the removal of border fences and the creation of extensive, jointly managed international game parks (Simon, 2003).

Local development

Two broad themes characterize local development in Africa. The first is the formal empowerment of local governments through processes of decentralization to engage more directly with local development challenges. The second relates to processes which have always been in existence, namely the actions of local community groups desirous of improving living and economic conditions in their locality. This accords with the argument of Taylor (2005: 148) that in 'contrast to formal approaches to regionalism, the New Regionalism Approach … has been more sensitive to "bottom-up" processes that are not considered by the more orthodox approaches'. In the view of Gooneratne and Obudho (1997) given the scale of the African economic crisis communities have to pursue local development options. They also recognize the key role NGOs can play in supporting local initiatives, often in the absence of state support. A particular concern for a range of authors is the need for governments to allow and to facilitate 'local self-reliance'

by communities (Gooneratne and Mbilinyi, 1992; Taylor and Mackenzie, 1992).

In terms of the theme of local government decentralization, partially driven by structural adjustment requirements and partially by the widespread pursuit of democratic engagement, there has a been a dramatic shift in the locus of local government control from what in most countries was direct central government control of local governments to one which acknowledges and facilitates local control and decisions. The passage of decentralization policies in countries as diverse as Ghana and Zambia are hallmarks of this new era and the World Bank has noted how widespread the take-up of these policies has been (Gooneratne and Obudho, 1997; Hope, 2008). However, on-the-ground evidence in countries with well-established track records of decentralization practice over more than a decade indicates that deep-rooted operational challenges impede progress (Egziabher and Hlemsing, 2005) – these include lack of skilled staff in localities, limited funds and what Stockmayer (1999) has termed the consequential 'decentralization of poverty' from being the responsibility from the central state to the local. The net result is often the inability to effect change on the ground, to provide needed infrastructure and the common challenge of only servicing the areas and communities which can pay, to the detriment of the marginalized majority. For example, in a city such as Lusaka only 10 per cent of areas have regular refuse removal.

A variant of local development is the more focused approach of Local Economic Development (LED) which has attracted some degree of attention across Africa. Whilst many countries such as Swaziland and Zambia have expressed interest in the LED approach and have put in place limited policy support, applied practice across Africa is however limited (Gooneratne and Obudho, 1997; Egziabher and Helmsing, 2005). The one exception is South Africa which is regarded as something of a front-runner in the policy and practice of LED (Rodríguez-Pose and

Tijmsitra, 2005). LED is now a legal requirement of local governments in that country and, interestingly, local governments have been challenged to implement policies of 'developmental local government' which implies being conscious of encouraging development-related outcomes from all their actions (Nel, 1999; Nel and Rogerson, 2005). Experience varies widely in the country from that of small, impoverished rural municipalities, which are only able to support limited community projects in activities such as community tourism and farming to the large metropoles which are pursuing globally competitive marketing and investment strategies (Rogerson, 1997). Cities such as Johannesburg and Cape Town have positioned themselves on the world stage as 'global cities' replete with modern airports, sports stadia, convention centres, business and tourism support programmes and various forms of informal sector support (Nel and Rogerson, 2005). Evidence however suggests that outcomes, though often impressive, seldom devolve down to communities most in need in the big cities. In smaller urban centres the lack of progress is more evident where municipalities are unable to effect change, often through a lack of resources and staff. A net result of the limitations experienced by 'developmental local government' in both large and small centres have been widespread civil sector protests against local governments' restricted delivery in recent years (Nel *et al.*, 2009). At a broader level in Africa there is growing recognition of the role local governments can play in development processes as indicated by the recent establishment of the 'Municipal Development Partnership for Eastern and Southern Africa'. Based in Harare in Zimbabwe, this organization is promoting research and collaborative exchanges between local governments. It also works with the 'Africa Local Government Action Forum' which has a primary focus, amongst others, on the promotion of LED (MDP, 2009).

At the community level, the recognition in the 1970s that development along the lines proposed by the Diffusionist and Modernization approaches was not succeeding in addressing mass poverty in Africa galvanized a reinterpretation of development interventions and approaches. This included at one level the acknowledgement that 'basic needs'-type interventions were probably a more appropriate line to follow, and second, there was the recognition of the informal or 'second economy' as often being the largest part of the economy in many areas (Pacione, 2001; Hope, 2008). This led to the work of the ILO and Hart and the application of Reformist approaches throughout much of the continent in a targeted effort to support the newly recognized micro-entrepreneurial sector (Hope, 2008). In the 1980s the scale of the debt crisis and negative economic growth in the poorest communities forced many rural communities back into subsistence and the frequent reliance on barter and parallel economic systems. It is at this level that despite numerous constraints, NGOs have been the most active and governments have attempted various low-level support measures such as the provision of market facilities and extension support to farmers and entrepreneurs. In parallel, a significant volume of literature on this dimension of local development has emerged. Prominent in this regard were the research and policy proposals of Gooneratne and Mbilinyi (1992) based at the United Nations Centres for Regional Development regional office in Nairobi, Kenya. In addition, the work of Baker (1990) and Baker and Pederson (1992) and researchers based at the Africa Studies Centre in Uppsala in Sweden exposed the realities of rural and urban livelihoods, and local economic adaptation in order to survive. While the overall economic situation has improved in many parts of Africa since the 1980s and 1990s, for the majority of the poor, self-reliance initiatives at the local/community and family levels remain critical survival. As outlined by Taylor and Mackenzie (1992) and Egziabher and Helmsing (2005), initiatives such as the production of charcoal, basic metal and craft products are often critical in assuring economic survival. In parallel, more recent writings on rural and urban livelihood strategies intimate just how important it is for communities to have multiple livelihood strategies and sources of income in order to ensure survival. While often poorly understood and difficult to directly support, it is apparent that for a significant number of Africa's residents this form of 'local development' is critical to their survival. Future research and policy support in these areas will be critical for the long-term well-being of Africa's residents (Egziabher and Helmsing, 2005).

Conclusion

As the world's poorest continent, and as the one least likely to attain the Millennium Development Goals, Africa's development challenges are clearly significant and profound. Africa suffers from the inherited legacy of regional development interventions set up to link the continent's key resource nodes, at a subsidiary level into the global economy. Post-Independence regional development interventions have tended to support either the capital cities or have been high-profile developments which have seldom achieved the envisaged success and they have seldom benefited those most in need. In the present era, of note at the international level are strenuous efforts to lay the basis for various regional economic unions which might well culminate one day in an African economic union. In parallel with state-driven regional development interventions, local development, either through emerging local government interventions or more long-established community-based endeavours, though often achieving only marginal success, remain critical for the economic well-being of the majority of Africa's population.

In terms of the way forward, future regional and local development in Africa

needs to take cognizance of several trends and realities. These include persistent poverty and marginalization, the rapid urbanization which is taking place, and the existence of major urban development and management challenges. In addition, as Ayeni (1997) argues, future strategies will need to be more participatory in focus, and adhere more to principles of decentralization. Major resource, funding and staffing constraints compromise the ability to effect change and clearly require urgent attention. That said, endeavours to promote trade between countries in Africa through lowering customs barriers, widespread embracing of the principles of decentralization, the uptake of the concept of LED and support for community-based interventions are cause for optimism about the future.

References

Alam, A. and Dione, O. (2006) "Fueling Cooperation: A regional approach to reducing poverty in the Senegal River Basin", in Fox, L. and Liebenthal, R. (eds) *Attacking Africa's Poverty: Experience From the Ground*, Washington: The World Bank, 95–116.

Ayeni, B. (1997) "Regional Development Planning and Management in Africa", in *United Nations Centre for Human Settlements (Habitat) Regional Development Planning and Management of Urbanization*, Nairobi: Habitat, 7–62.

Baker, J. (ed.) (1990) *Small Town Africa*, Uppsala: The Scandinavian Institute of African Studies.

Baker, J. and Pedersen, P.O. (eds) (1992) *The Rural Urban Interface in Africa,* Uppsala: The Scandinavian Institute of African Studies.

Best, A.C.C. and de Blij, H.J. (1977) *African Survey*, New York: John Wiley.

BBC (2008) "Africa Free Trade Zone is Agreed", http://news.bbc.co.uk/2/hi/7684903.stm, accessed 27 November 2009.

BBC (2009) "Africa's Population Tops One Billion", news.bbc.co.uk/2/hi/africa/8366591.stm, accessed 27 November 2009.

Cambria Press (2008) "The African Union and New Strategies for Development in Africa", www.canbvriapress.com/cambriapress.cfm?/template=4&bid=271, accessed 12 November 2009.

Davidson, B. (1994) *Modern Africa: A Social and Political History*, London: Longman.

Egziabher, T.G. and Helmsing, A.H.J. (2005) *Local Economic Development in Africa*, Maastricht: Shaker.

Gooneratne, W. And Obudho, R.A. (1997) *Contemporary Issues in Regional Development Policy*, Aldershot: Avebury.

Gooneratne, W. and Mbilinyi, M. (eds) (1992) *Reviving Local Self-Reliance in Africa*, Nagoya: United Nations Centre for Regional Development.

Griffith, I. (1995) *The African Inheritance*, London: Routledge.

Hope, K.R. (2008) *Poverty, Livelihoods and Governance in Africa*, New York: Palgrave.

Janneh, A. (2006) "Development in Africa and ECA", Statement by the UN Under-Secretary-General, UN, New York.

Konadu-Agyemang, K. And Panford, K. (2006) *Africa's Development in the Twenty-First Century*, Aldershot: Ashgate.

Kyambalesa, H. and Hougnikpo, M.C. (2006) *Economic Integration and Development in Africa*, Aldershot: Ashgate.

Makinda, S.M. and Okumu, F.W. (2008) *The African Union: Challenges of Globalization, Security and Governance*, London: Routledge.

Mohamoud, A.A. (2007) *Shaping a New Africa*, Amsterdam: KIT Publishers.

Nel, E.L. (1994) "Export Processing Zones", *Development Southern Africa*, 11, 1, 99–111.

Nel, E.L. (1999) *Regional and Local Economic Development in South Africa*, Aldershot: Ashgate.

Nel, E. and Rogerson, C.M. (2005) *Local Economic Development in the Developing World*, New Brunswick: Transaction Publishers.

Nel, E., Binns, T. and Bek, D. (2009) "Misplaced Expectations? The experience of applied local economic development in post-apartheid South Africa", *Local Economy*, 24, 3, 224–237.

Niang, A. (2006) *Towards a Viable and Credible Development in Africa*, Raleigh: Ivy House.

Oyelaran-Oyeyinka, B. and McCormick, D. (2007) *Industrial Clusters and Innovation Systems in Africa*, Tokyo: United Nations University Press.

Pacione, M. (2001) *Urban Geography*, London: Routledge.

Rodríguez-Pose, A. and Tijmstra, S. (2005) *Local Economic Development as an Alternative Approach to Economic Development in Sub-Saharan Africa*, Municipal Development Programme/World Bank: Washington DC.

Rogerson, C.M. (1988) "Regional Development Policies in South Africa", *Regional Development Dialogue*, Special Issue, 228–262.

Rogerson, C.M. (1997) "Local Economic Development and Post-Apartheid Reconstruction in South Africa", *Singapore Journal of Tropical Geography*, 18, 1, 175–195.

Simon, D. (2003) "Regional Development–Environment Discourses, Policies and Practices in Post-Apartheid Southern Africa", in Grant, J.A. and Soderbaum, F. *The New Regionalism in Africa*, Aldershot: Ashgate, 67–89.

Stockmayer, A. (1999) "Decentralization: Global fad or recipe for sustainable local development?", *Agriculture and Rural Development*, 6, 1, 3–6.

Taylor, D.R.F. and Mackenzie, F. (eds) (1992) *Development from Within: Survival in Rural Africa*, London: Routledge.

Taylor, I. (2005) "The Logic of Disorder: 'Malignant regionalization' in Central Africa", in Boas, M., Marchand, M.H. and Shaw, T.M. (eds) *The Political Economy of Regions and Regionalisms*, Basingstoke: Palgrave, 147–166.

United Nations Centre for Human Settlements (Habitat) (1997) *Regional Development Planning and Managment of Urbanization*, Nairobi: Habitat.

United Nations Conference on Trade and Development (UNCTAD) (2009) "Press Release – Economic Development in Africa 2009", PR/2009/022 25/06/09, UNCTAD, Geneva.

Whiteside, A. (1981) *Regional Development in Southern Africa*, Pietermaritzburg: University of Natal Press.

Further reading

Egziabher, T.G. and Helmsing, A.H.J. (2005) *Local Economic Development in Africa*, Maastricht: Shaker. (Comprehensive overview of local economic development in Africa.)

Gooneratne, W. and Obudho, R.A. (1997) *Contemporary Issues in Regional Development Policy*, Aldershot: Avebury. (Key overview of the state of regional development in Africa.)

Konadu-Agyemang, K. and Panford, K. (2006) *Africa's Development in the Twenty-First Century*, Aldershot: Ashgate. (Key overview of development to opportunities and challenges in Africa.)

Nel, E. and Rogerson, C.M. (2005) *Local Economic Development in the Developing World*, New Brunswick: Transaction Publishers. (Review of the state of local economic development in South and Southern Africa.)

Taylor, D.R.F. and Mackenzie, F. (eds) (1992) *Development from Within: Survival in Rural Africa*, London: Routledge. (Comprehensive overview of community economic development and self-reliance strategies.)

41

Globalization, urbanization and decentralization

The experience of Asian Pacific cities

Shiuh-Shen Chien

Asian Pacific cities in the global map

Despite the disruption by the financial crisis in the 1990s and doubts over the peaceful rise of China and India, the Asian Pacific region has become a global focus again, in which cities have played a role to facilitate the transformation. In terms of population, 11 of the top 19 world cities with population over 10 million are located in the region, with Tokyo at 35 million ranked at the top and Mumbai at 19 million as Asia's second most crowded city (as well as the fourth most crowded in the world) (United Nations Economic and Social Affairs 2008) (Table 41.1). In addition, many cities in the region are the size of nations not only in terms of population but also in terms of economic products. The size of Tokyo in terms of population is even bigger than the combined total population of the five Nordic countries of Norway, Demark, Sweden, Finland, and Iceland. Shanghai's economic performance in terms of GDP is almost 300 per cent of Cambodia. Besides, nine of the top ten world's highest skyscrapers are built in Asian cities – in height order: one in Dubai, one in Taipei, two in Kuala Lumpur, two in Shanghai, one each in Guangzhou, Nanjing, and Hong Kong. Twenty of the world's 30 most

polluted cities are in Asia, all of which are in China (World Bank China Quick Facts 2007); while the world's largest slum is observed in Dharavi of Mumbai, India. To sum up, local and regional development in Asia Pacific can be understood as an urban phenomenon.

During colonial times, cities in Asia Pacific simply functioned as primary commodity production and resource extraction centers for Western imperialism (Murphey 1969). Nowadays, these cities serve new roles in the globalization of Asian Pacific economy. Tokyo, Hong Kong and Singapore are the most recognized Asian global cities in terms of connectivity of banking and finance industry and command centers of headquarters. New Delhi positions itself as a global call center to clients dialing toll-free numbers in North America. Such call center services offer the opportunity for Indian workers to situate their own jobs within the global labor markets. In the context that the Philippines is the largest exporter of government-sponsored labor in the region, diverse types of private recruitment agencies have shaped many cities in the Philippines to involve global 'reproduction' networks (Kelly 2009). In addition, ciy-regions in Taiwan (like the Taipei-Hsinchu city-region and the Great Taichung Region) have transformed themselves into an important

Table 41.1 Cities with over 10 million population, 2007

Rank	City/urban area	Country	Population (millions)
1	Tokyo	Japan	35.7
2	New York–Newark	USA	19.0
3	Ciudad de México (Mexico City)	Mexico	19.0
4	Mumbai (Bombay)	India	19.0
5	São Paulo	Brazil	18.8
6	Delhi	India	15.9
7	Shanghai	China	15.0
8	Kolkata (Calcutta)	India	14.8
9	Dhaka	Bangladesh	13.5
10	Buenos Aires	Argentina	12.8
11	Los Angeles–Long Beach–Santa Ana	USA	12.5
12	Karachi	Pakistan	12.1
13	Al-Qahirah (Cairo)	Egypt	11.9
14	Rio de Janeiro	Brazil	11.7
15	Osaka–Kobe	Japan	11.3
16	Beijing	China	11.1
17	Manila	Philippines	11.1
18	Moskva (Moscow)	Russian Federation	10.5
19	Istanbul	Turkey	10.1

Source: United Nations (2007), World Urbanization Prospects

node for high-technology knowledge to connect with high-technology hubs elsewhere like Silicon Valley, Japan and China (Yang, Hsu *et al.* 2009).

This chapter reviews the dynamic development of Asian Pacific cities. Three driving forces that led to their formation and transformation are identified: globalization and cross-border investment, urbanization in relation to rural migrations, as well as decentralization empowering local self-interested agents to initialize territorial competition. The social polarization and conflicts within cities, urban rapid growth without livability, and risks of natural hazards and infectious diseases show the transformation of the region comes with complicated challenges for sustainability.

Globalization

Inward and outward investment

In terms of cross-border investment, economic globalization in relation to Asian Pacific urban development can be understood as a dual process. On the one hand, the inflow of foreign direct investment (FDI) helps developing cities increase productivity, transfer technology, and promote trade. In the case of the Pearl River Delta (PRD) in China, small and medium-scale, labor-intensive, processing-types of manufacturing and trade-creative FDI coming from Hong Kong have emerged as key not only for industrialization but also urbanization. With the so-called FDI-induced exogenous urbanization, Shenzhen has been transformed from a tiny fishery village to an important metropolis populated by more than seven million citizens and hundreds of thousands of illegal migrants (Sit and Yang 1997). Kunshan also has witnessed substantial inflow of manufacturing capital from Taiwan, transforming itself from a rural county in the late 1970s to one of the world's high-tech areas famous for the notebook industry and integrated circuit industry (Chien 2007). In 2006, about 2.5 billion laptop computers (one-fourth of the world production) were produced in Kunshan. But globalization is a two-edged sword, as these developing cities are more vulnerable to global economic shock. The 1997 Asia financial crisis rapidly increased unemployment and poverty incidence in Jakarta, causing Jakarta's public revenue to drop dramatically and be unable to support policies needed during the financial crisis (Firman 1999). On the other hand, some of Asia's industrialized cities skillfully utilize globalization as an opportunity to expand their economic powers and political influences by stimulating industrialization in the least developed Asian countries. Osaka, Japan's second largest city, recognized that a transfer of capital and technology overseas should be in relation to a strategy of industrial upgrading at home. With an internationally oriented local development strategy, Osaka supported local firms to make enclaves of investment in other overseas cities in order to upgrade its position in the changing international spatial division of labor (Hill and Fujita 1998). In addition, Singapore promoted cross-border operations not only in business firms but also in industrial zones management. In order to exert its regional influences in Asia, Singapore transferred their industrial management knowledge by co-building China Singapore Suzhou Industrial Park with the China authority (Yeung 2003).

External agents playing a role

From a perspective of a gap between Asian experience and so-called 'Western' theories on local and regional development, three kinds of external agents need to be particularly addressed: Chinese business diasporas (Yeung and Lin 2003), skilled expatriates and unskilled transnational workers, and international organizations and consultant agencies. First, among all foreign investors, Chinese diasporas have been the most special and essential in rapidly developing Asia Pacific cities (Olds and Yeung 1999). Many established ethnic Chinese business firms in the region were compelled to engage in

transnational operations to sustain their business growth and expansion. The transnational ethnic social networks were able to facilitate economic growth in a cross-border context because they could 'glue' multiple economic actors in different countries as well as 'lubricate' economic transactions among them (Chen 2000). Without their networks and embeddedness as brokers, it would have been questionable whether rural China cadres who were still deeply embedded in the communist legacy after Mao's death would know how to embrace globalization (Hsing 1996).

Second, globalization of Asian Pacific cities is also facilitated by professional expatriates and unskilled transnational laborers. The former are able to accumulate and transfer high-level financial and technological knowledge as well as social practices and discourse from the western to the Asia Pacific region. For example, transnational expatriates transplanted certain know-how, know-who and networks in developing complicated international financial and banking systems to Hong Kong and Singapore (Beaverstock 2002). However, in contrast, the hundreds of thousands of unskilled labor migrants moving around within the Asian Pacific region served as necessary city low-end human labor sources, like construction employers and domestic workers, while being kept socially excluded in the host society.

Third, international organizations and transnational development-related consultants also play roles in the transformation process of Asian Pacific cities. Besides the individual governmental budgets for urban infrastructure financing, three other public funding sources include the World Bank, Asian Development Bank (ADB) and Japan Bank for International Cooperation. Over past decades ADB funded 276 loan projects totaling US$16 billion and 595 technical assistant projects worth US$335 million (www.adb.org/Documents/Urban-Development/, accessed 28 February 2009). China, Indonesia and India were the top three recipients of these urban projects for new town development, flood protection, health care, waste management, air quality improvement, river governance, tourism, waterway rehabilitation and so on. Moreover, international development-related consultant firms also helped globalize cities in terms of diffusing development knowledge. In the case of Calcutta, certain Western planning technology was transplanted to become part of Calcutta's planning experience, mainly through the United States' Ford Foundation (Banerjee and Chakravorty 1994). In one proposal competition for Shanghai's new financial district, non-Chinese design professionals – the 'Global Intelligence Corps' – promoted several planning ideas, many of which are adeptly incorporated by Shanghai cadres into the official Shanghai development plan (Olds 1997).

Urbanization

Urban growth and rural migration

'Crowded' is possibly the most intuitive description for those paying a visit to any Asian city. In 2007, Asia's urban population was about 1,645 million, which is nearly half of the world's total urban population. Cities are growing at an unprecedented pace. While London took 130 years to grow from 1 million people to 8 million, Bangkok took 45 years and Seoul only 25 years (Asian Development Bank 2008; United Nations Economic and Social Affairs 2008). The rapid urban population growth is supplemented as well by the high yearly population growth rate: Karachi and Mumbai having over 5 percent and Pyongyang and Kuala Lumpur over 4 percent (Figure 41.1).

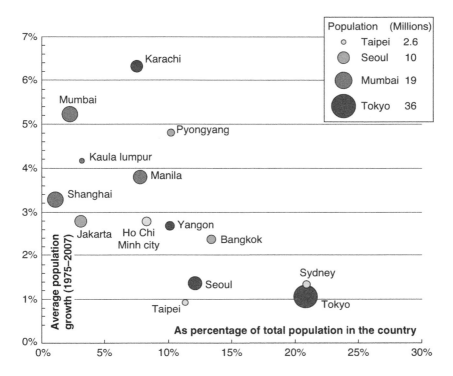

Figure 41.1 Population growth rates and its primacy by selected cities.
Source: Author's research

Along with that is an urban primacy phenomenon in Asia. Tokyo and Sydney occupy 20 percent of total population in Japan and Australia respectively (Figure 41.1), and capital regions in Southeast Asian countries, like Bangkok, Manila and Kuala Lumpur, are much bigger than their second city counterparts. Dhaka alone contributed 60 percent of Bangladesh's total GDP, and Seoul 50 percent of Korea's national account of GDP (Ruck and Munich Re Group 2004). In addition, megacities or megacity-regions have emerged, some of which are within a country, like Tokyo–Osaka–Kyoto in Japan, Hong Kong-Shenzhen-Guangdong in China; and some of which form a cross-border integration, like the Growth Triangle of Singapore Johor-Riau, and the Northern Triangle of Northern Malaysia, Southern Thailand, Northern Sumatra.

The growth of urban population is contributed to not only by the natural growth from a high birth rate, but by the social growth from rapid rural migration as well. It is because industrialization in many developing countries has come about together with limited rural development. As a consequence, peasants are made more vulnerable in rural areas and must rely on migrant work for survival. Rural areas were designated to supply labor for rapid industrialization in cities. Tokyo experienced a high rate of net domestic migration until 1970 with the peak early in the 1960s. During the post-Mao period, many of China's coastal cities also attracted migrants from other provinces and from different cities within the provinces. Unfortunately, those rural migrants were not granted urban citizenship and in many cases they were even treated badly as 'outsiders' to the urban society.

Economically intertwined urbanization

Urbanization in the Asia Pacific is economically intertwined between formal and informal sectors. In general, the level of urbanization is strongly correlated to per capita income; and spatial agglomeration is highly related to greater economic productivity. Related to that there is a changing economic structure in cities – increasing manufacturing (or so-called industrialization) and service industries along with the declining agriculture industry (Asian Development Bank 2008).

However, the city economy is not constituted of formal sectors alone, and informal sectors actually contribute greatly to functions and operations of cities. A research publication by ADB shows that by 2000 the relative size of the informal economy to the whole national output of products in Thailand and Sri Lanka and the Philippines is over 40 percent; in Korea and Malaysia and Bangladesh above 20 percent (Asian Development Bank 2008). Informal trade and enterprises in Manila and Chennai cover large fractions of solid waste management, and in Beijing and Delhi for electronic waste-recycling activities. In addition, dramatic urbanization also creates a shelter crisis in the sense that a large amount of people cannot afford legal housing and therefore a number of informal settlements have increased in both absolute and percentage terms.

Socially polarized urbanization

Urban landscapes in these cities are very socially polarized. On the one hand, a phenomenon that cities compete among one another to build skyscrapers is commonly seen. Table 41.2 shows that only four out of the top 20 highest buildings in the world are located outside Asia. And the skyscraper phenomenon is also predominated by Chinese cities – more than half of these 20 high-rise buildings are in cities in Taiwan, Hong Kong and China. These skyscrapers collectively symbolize an imagination of international development. Promoting skyscrapers is a shortcut for Asian cities to gain more world-class identity and prestige (Bunnell 1999). Similarly, Asian urbanization is also shaping a rise of scattered gated communities. These gated communities are financially constructed by larger private developers, physically located in the urban outskirts linked by freeways and flyovers, as well as materially serviced by high-quality security and daily services (gyms, laundries, and even groceries). Such kinds of new housing consumption serving an emerging mobile (trans-local and trans-national) high-class society can be found in Manila, Jakarta and Beijing.

On the other hand, however, many low-income and peasant groups are marginalized and even excluded during the process of urbanization. The consequence of a rapid increase in population has resulted in a shortage of housing and related infrastructure especially for the low-income household, forcing nearly half of the city population to live in conditions of miserable poverty and overcrowded slums. Dharavi in Mumbai has the approximately 6 million other inhabitants who have also lived in informal settlements or areas characterized as "slums". By 2000, more than 37 percent of the urban population in Bangladesh was living below the poverty line. In the context of post-Mao China, the new urban housing allocation system does not favor the socially and economically disadvantaged but favors people with political position and connections, those of higher social-economic backgrounds and those whose work units (*dan wei*) have greater organization authority. In addition, the expansion of the central business districts also contributed to the displacement of low-income groups toward peripheral areas of the cities. Under the guise of beautification or improvement of the city, urban renewal projects often involved serious human right violations and forced evictions. In Sydney, development also has had a negative impact upon the reduced supply of affordable rental housing, particularly in the case of public housing in western Sydney (Mee 2002).

Table 41.2 Top 20 world's highest buildings, 2007

Rank	Building	City	Height	Floors	Year
1	Burj Dubai	Dubai	818 m	162	2009
2	Taipei 101	Taipei	509 m	101	2004
3	Shanghai World Financial	Shanghai	492 m	101	2008
4	Petronas Tower 1	Kuala Lumpur	452 m	88	1998
5	Petronas Tower 2	Kuala Lumpur	452 m	88	1998
6	Nanjing Greenland Financi	Nanjing	450 m	66	2009
7	Sears Tower	Chicago	442 m	108	1974
8	Guangzhou West Tower	Guangzhou	438 m	103	2009
9	Jin Mao Tower	Shanghai	421 m	88	1999
10	Two International Finance	Hong Kong	415 m	88	2003
11	Trump International Hotel	Chicago	415 m	96	2009
12	CITIC Plaza	Guangzhou	391 m	80	1997
13	Shun Hing Square	Shenzhen	384 m	69	1996
14	Empire State Building	New York City	381 m	102	1931
15	Central Plaza	Hong Kong	374 m	78	1992
16	Bank of China Tower	Hong Kong	367 m	70	1990
17	Bank of America Tower	New York City	366 m	54	2009
18	Almas Tower	Dubai	363 m	68	2009
19	Emirates Office Tower	Dubai	355 m	54	2000
20	Tuntex Sky Tower	Kaohsiung	348 m	85	1997

Source: Data compiled from http://www.emporis.com/en/bu/sk/st/tp/wo, accessed 28 February 2009

Decentralization

Local entrepreneurial governance

Asian cities are very 'entrepreneurial' as local governments make efforts innovatively and proactively to promote development by creating new spaces of production (like China's special economic zones), promoting new spaces of consumption (like Singapore's casinos), and striving for new financial sources for growth (Jessop and Sum 2000). Kunshan made a bold decision to develop a locally initiated industrial zone without official permission from any upper level governments. However, due to its successful development, the zone was finally endorsed by Beijing and granted national approval (Chien 2007). Hosting hallmark events is also a popular local entrepreneurial strategy. Seoul, Sydney and Beijing are cases in point to show that the urban infrastructure can be upgraded and city marketing can succeed through a process of organizing for the Olympics Games. Another example of social development is an innovation of water 'marketization' for the poor. In order to deal with persistent problems of access to good water by the poor, Jakarta deregulated water markets in 1990 by permitting private homes with water connections to resell municipal water to the poor, with relative costless expansion in the standpipe system as a consequence (Crane 1994).

The rise of local entrepreneurial states in Asia is mainly triggered by a mechanism of decentralization with two dimensions – economic decentralization and political decentralization. The former refers to local governances empowered with more material resources and administrative competences for local development. Most Asian Pacific countries have experienced much economic decentralization. Fiscally speaking, local revenue relative to the national revenue is much higher on average, and local governments are able to promote better business environments with less institutional constraints.

In terms of the latter, with some exceptions like China and Vietnam, local elections have been widely implemented in Asia around the 1980s and 1990s. Bangkok held the first mayoral election in 1984, Taipei in 1994, Seoul in 1995, and Jakarta in 2007. Implementation of local democratization is highly connected to popular movements against authoritarianism and centralized decision-making systems.

Localities in competition

The emergence of entrepreneurial local states is related to territorial competition, referring to the intense competition among cities and regions for foreign investment. Outcomes of intercity competition are actually a mixed picture. On the positive side, a phenomenon of race to the top can be generated as a consequence. A story that there is a strong correlation between intensive competition for FDI and improvement of business environment in China is a case in point. Coastal China, which has accumulated more than 80 percent of the FDI since 1978, only required taxation and administrative fees of 4.1 percent of the sales revenues of companies in that region. The figure in other parts of China where there was relatively less competition for FDI is 5–6 percent. Representatives of business in the coastal southeast region only need to spend about 52 days per year with the local bureaucracy to process business licenses, while the requirement is from 62 to 72 days per year in other areas of China (Chien 2008).

However, territorial competition also provides negative consequences in a sense that in order to attract certain types of investment, local governments have to be willing to contrive all manner of incentives to major corporations and make a variety of concessions, such as tax abatements, reduced charges for providing physical infrastructure, or downgraded environmental and regulatory standards. When Disneyland announced plans to invest in a new project in China, there was fierce competition between Hong Kong and Shanghai. The cost for the Hong Kong government to win the bid was reportedly US$30 billion (ten times the investment paid by its Disney counterpart) to co-build the park but it obtained only 43 percent park ownership. What's more, all profits from Disney trademarked goods sold in the Hong Kong Disneyland are not shared with the Hong Kong government but go entirely to the Disney corporation (Douglass 2002).

Self-interested agents in action

Local entrepreneurial states in relation to embedded territorial competition actually need to be ignited by proactive agents whose interests are highly involved in the political economy of local development. In the context of a young Asian urban democracy like Bangkok, businessmen are more likely to have an advantage to win elections, and exchange political influence to back personal business interests. Therefore those business-cum-politicians are more materially motivated to exert their dominance in the process of industrialization and urbanization between national governments and people in the localities (Shatkin 2004). Despite no elections in China, local cadres are still able to be politically motivated by the performance-based personal management system. As career path is related to economic growth during their tenures, careerist local leaders strive and compete in order to achieve economic targets imposed from above (Chien 2008).

One note to be addressed is that decentralization has certainly opened an avenue for civil society, such as community-based organizations and non-governmental organizations that help the poor. New programs like the 'Community Mortgage Program' represent a promising paradigm shift to allow squatter associations in Manila to acquire lands by means of state-guaranteed credit to be repaid over a period of 25 years (Berner 2000).

But the changing state–society relations in Asian cities cannot produce much optimism because decentralization is more in favor of political families and international and domestic business interest groups. In Manila, industrial interests have created such developmental pressure on urban lands that civil societies representing the urban poor groups continue to face significant obstacles in their effort to influence the government (Shatkin 2000). In addition, the dominance of one political party and its hierarchical structure has thwarted the scope for effective bottom-up planning in Kolkata.

Challenges ahead

There are three major challenges ahead for Asian cities, calling for a new holistic, progressive and sustainable solution for further development (Pike et al. 2007). First of all, cities are struggling with problems of over-population and inadequate housing, unemployment, congested transportation and deteriorating environmental quality, all questioning whether urban transformation in Asia Pacific is livable or not. Urban transportation congestion is partly because of rapid urban sprawl and partly because of the huge numbers of private motor vehicles, which is a key cause of bad air quality in cities. In China, the inhabitants of every third metropolis are forced to breathe in polluted air every day, accounting for the estimated 400 thousand deaths every year. As many cities in Asia Pacific accumulate considerable economic wealth, building up their ability to address sustainability concerns for livability must be a next top priority.

The second challenge is the social contestation within cities, for two reasons: one is historical legacy and the other is because of ethnic migration. Singapore used to be a trade point in Southeast Asia connecting China, India, Malay and the West. This legacy makes Singapore nowadays host four completely different religions: Buddhism, Hinduism, Islam, and Christianity. All of them are very active in the society but with very limited interactions, creating a worry that a lack of mutual understanding may result in potential conflicts in the future. In addition, the concentration of Indo-Chinese-Australians in and around Sydney is negatively depicted by most media and policy-makers, while Sydney Muslims have been portrayed as non-existent in the context of anti-mosque local politics (Dunn 2004). Those unfriendly attitudes toward ethnic migrations, if not changed, may become hidden time bombs for social inclusion and harmony.

And the final challenge is environmental-related risks. Flooding has becomes much more frequent in Asian Pacific cities, partly because of rising sea levels due to climate changes and partly because of subsidence due to excessive groundwater extraction. In addition, natural catastrophes in high-density megacities cause widespread devastation. For example, the earthquake in Kobe in 1995 resulted in thousands of fatalities, US$100 billion in damages, making it the most costly natural disaster of all time (Ruck and Munich Re Group 2004). The Severe Acute Respiratory Syndrome (SARS) case in 2004 also shows that infectious diseases are easily spread within and between megacities. Diarrheal diseases, which are endemic in Delhi, infecting a great number of the urban poor, are caused mainly by impoverished quality of water supplies. More actions toward appropriate precautions and preventions are needed to reduce negative externality of megacities in terms of environmental and health risks (Yang, Hsu et al. 2009).

References

Asian Development Bank (2008) *Managing Asian Cities – Sustainable and Inclusive Urban Solutions*, Manila, Asian Development Bank.

Banerjee, T. and S. Chakravorty (1994) "Transfer of Planning Technology and Local Political Economy – A Retrospective Analysis of Calcutta's Planning", *Journal of the American Planning Association* 60(1): 71–82.

Beaverstock, J. V. (2002) "Transnational Elites in Global Cities: British Expatriates in Singapore's Financial District", *Geoforum* 33(4): 525–538.

Berner, E. (2000) "Poverty Alleviation and the Eviction of the Poorest: Towards Urban Land Reform in the Philippines", *International Journal of Urban and Regional Research* 24(3): 554–566.

Bunnell, T. (1999) "Views from Above and Below: The Petronas Twin Towers and in Contesting Visions of Development in Contemporary Malaysia", *Singapore Journal of Tropical Geography* 20(1): 1-23.

Chen, X.M. (2000) "Both Glue and Lubricant: Transnational Ethnic Social Capital as a Source of Asia-Pacific Subregionalism", *Policy Sciences* 33(3–4): 269–287.

Chien, S.-S. (2007) "Institutional Innovations, Asymmetric Decentralization and Local Economic Development – Case Study of Kunshan, in Post-Mao China", *Environment and Planning C: Government and Policy* 25(2): 269–290.

Chien, S.-S. (2008) "Local Responses to Globalization in China – a Territorial Restructuring Process Perspective", *Pacific Economic Review* 13(4): 492–517.

Crane, R. (1994) "Water Markets, Market Reform and the Urban-Poor: Results from Jakarta, Indonesia", *World Development* 22(1): 71–83.

Douglass, M. (2002) "From Global Intercity Competition to Cooperation for Livable Cities and Economic Resilience in Pacific Asia", *Environment and Urbanization* 14(1): 53–68.

Dunn, K. (2004) "Islam in Sydney: Contesting the Discourse of Absence", *Australian Geographer* 35(3): 333–353.

Firman, T. (1999) "From 'Global City' to 'City of Crisis': Jakarta Metropolitan Region Under Economic Turmoil", *Habitat International* 23(4): 447–466.

Hill, R.C. and K. Fujita (1998) "Osaka's Asia Linkages Strategy – Regional Integration in East Asia, Local Development in Japan", *Urban Affairs Review* 33(4): 492–521.

Hsing, Y. (1996) "Blood, Thicker than Water: Interpersonal Relations and Taiwanese Investment in Southern China", *Environment and Planning A* 28(12): 2241–2262.

Jessop, B. and N.-L. Sum (2000) "An Entrepreneurial City in Action: Hong Kong's Emerging Strategies in and for (Inter-) Urban Competition", *Urban Studies* 37(12): 2287–2313.

Kelly, P.F. (2009) "From Global Production Networks to Global Reproduction Networks: Households, Migration and Regional Development in Cavite, the Philippines", *Regional Studies* 43(3): 449–461.

Mee, K. (2002) "Prosperity and the Suburban Dream: Quality of Life and Affordability in Western Sydney", *Australian Geographer* 33(3): 337–351.

Murphey, R. (1969) "Traditionalism and Colonialism: Changing Urban Roles in Asia", *The Journal of Asian Studies* 29(1): 67–84.

Olds, K. (1997) "Globalizing Shanghai: The Global Intelligence Corps and the Building of Pudong", *Cities* 14(2): 109–123.

Olds, K. and H.W.-c.Yeung (1999) "(Re)shaping 'Chinese' Business Networks in a Globalising Era", *Environment and Planning D: Society and Space* 17(5): 535–555.

Olson, M. (1965) *The Logic of Collective Action: Public Goods and the Theory of Groups*, Cambridge, MA, Harvard University Press.

Pike, A., A. Rodríguez-Pose, *et al.* (2007) "What Kind of Local and Regional Development and for Whom?", *Regional Studies* 41(9): 1253–1269.

Ruck, M. and Munich Re Group (2004) *Megacities- Megarisks- Trends and Challenges for Insurance and Risk Management*, Munich, Germany, Munchener Ruckversicherungs-Gesellschaft.

Shatkin, G. (2000) "Obstacles to Empowerment: Local Politics and Civil Society in Metropolitan Manila, the Philippines", *Urban Studies* 37(12): 2357–2375.

Shatkin, G. (2004) "Globalization and Local Leadership: Growth, Power and Politics in Thailand's Eastern Seaboard", *International Journal of Urban and Regional Research* 28(1): 11–26.

Sit, V. and C. Yang (1997) "Foreign-Investment-Induced Exo-Urbanisation in the Pearl River Delta, China", *Urban Studies* 34(4): 647–677.

United Nations Economic and Social Affairs (2008) *World Urbanization Prospects the 2007 Revision*, New York, United Nations.

Yang, D.Y.-R., J.-Y. Hsu, *et al.* (2009) "Revisiting the Silicon Island? The Geographically Varied 'Strategic Coupling' in the Development of High-technology Parks in Taiwan", *Regional Studies* 44(3): 369–384.

Yeung, H.W.-c. (2003) *Strategic Governance and Economic Diplomacy in China: The Political Economy of Government-linked Companies from Singapore*. Regional Governance: Greater China in the 21st Century, The Centre of Contemporary Chinese Studies, University of Durham, UK; 24–25 October.

Yeung, H.W.-c. and G.C.S. Lin (2003) "Theorizing Economic Geographies of Asia", *Economic Geography* 79(2): 107–128.

World Bank (2009) China quick facts. Available at: http://web.worldbank.org/wbsite/external/countries/eastasiapacificext/chinaextn/0,,contentMDK:20680895~pagePK:1497618~piPK:217854~theSitePK;318950,00.html. Accessed 31 May 2009.

Further reading

Croissant, A. (2004) "Changing Welfare Regimes in East and Southeast Asia: Crisis, Change and Challenge", *Social Policy and Administration* 38(5): 504–524.

Douglass, M., T. Q. Le, *et al.* (2004) *The Livability of Mega-Urban Regions in Southeast Asia: Bangkok, Ho Chi Minh City, Jakarta and Manila Compared.* International Conference on the Growth Dynamics of Mega-Urban Regions in East and Southeast Asia. Singapore.

HO, K. C. and H.-H. M. Hsiao (eds) (2006) *Capital Cities in Asia-Pacific: Primacy and Diversity*, Taipei, Center for Asia-Pacific Area Studies, Academia Sinica.

Jones, G. and M. Douglass (eds) (2008) *Mega-Urban Regions in Pacific Asia: Urban Dynamics in a Global Era*, Singapore, Singapore University Press.

Lin, G.C.S. (1994) "Changing Theoretical Perspectives on Urbanization in Asian Developing Countries", *Third World Planning Review* 16(1): 1–23.

Marcottullio, P.J. (2001) "Asian Urban Sustainability in the Era of Globalization", *Habitat International* 25(4): 577–598.

Ng, M.K. and P. Hills (2003) "World Cities or Great Cities? A Comparative Study of Five Asian Metropolises", *Cities* 20(3): 151–165.

Schmidt, J. D. (1998) "Globalization and Inquality in Urban Southeast Asia," *Third World Planning Review* 20(2): 127–145.

42

Local development

A response to the economic crisis. Lessons from Latin America

Antonio Vázquez-Barquero

Introduction

For over 30 years, parallel to the intensification of the process of economic integration and globalization, multiple local development experiences emerged and unfolded in Latin American countries (Aghon et al., 2001; Altenburg and Meyer-Stamer, 1999; Vázquez-Barquero, 2002, 2007). Local initiatives change from one place to another because they are designed and implemented for a specific locality or territory. For the old industrialized regions, such as the Greater ABC in Sao Paulo, Brazil that is experiencing a strong industrial restructuring process; for rural areas with development potential, such as the region of the Sierra de los Cuchumatanes in Guatemala, that is in the early stages of the process of development; for places that are trying to eradicate poverty, as in the case of the UNDP project in Cartagena de Indias, Colombia, or to overcome the effects of a natural disaster such the earthquake in the case of Villa El Salvador, Peru.

But the economic, political and institutional environment in which local initiatives emerged has changed since the middle of 2007. Developed and emerging economies have found themselves affected by the financial crisis, which spills over into the real economy. The developed economies have begun a process of economic recession and the emerging economies have seen their growth rates substantially reduced, industrial activity has shrunk, internal and foreign demand is falling, unemployment rates grow, and poverty is increasing once again. Faced with this scenario, the response to the crisis should combine measures that aim both at re-establishing trust in the financial markets and expanding bank credit, and at increasing productivity and competitiveness. This chapter argues that local development policies are useful for approaching the problems that characterize the crisis of the real economy. As in the past, the objectives are to make the productive system more competitive, to create jobs and improve social well-being, and local development policy acts as a catalyst of the development mechanisms through local initiatives. They facilitate entrepreneurial development and the creation of firm networks; they encourage the diffusion of innovation and knowledge; improve urban diversity; and stimulate the development of the institutional fabric. The local development tools act on the determining forces of capital accumulation and contribute to economic and social progress.

This chapter is organized as follows. After describing the current crisis and its financial and economic effects, some policy measures adopted to counter the growing financial crisis by advanced and emerging economies are presented. Following this, the chapter argues that local development tools foster increased productivity and make economies more competitive, and, therefore, local initiatives can help overcome the crisis. The chapter ends with some final comments on the strengths and weaknesses of local development.

Economic and financial crisis: some facts

The current crisis is a global financial crisis that is spilling over into the real economy. It started in the United States in August 2007 with the lack of liquidity and the decline in solvency in the financial markets when the banking system incurred important risks because of the default on an important part of the subprime mortgages. After the collapse of the investment bank Lehman Brothers and the nationalization of the insurance company AIG, in September 2008, the crisis spread to international markets through the stock exchange, the international banking system, and the monetary standard (Bordo, 2008).

The financial crisis is contaminating the functioning of the economy and this generated a decline in the GDP during the last quarter of 2008, and this contraction is expected to worsen throughout 2009 (IMF, 2009a). According to the update of the IMF World Development Outlook of July 8, the global activity will contract by 1.4 per cent in 2009. GDP, in real terms, will decline by 2.6 per cent in the United States; and by 4.8 per cent in the Eurozone; it will fall by 6.2 per cent in Germany; and by 4.2 per cent in Spain. The forecasts for Latin America show a GDP growth rate decline of 2.2 per cent; of 1.5 per cent for Argentina; of 1.3 per cent for

Brazil; and of 7.3 per cent for Mexico. Growth projections in the most dynamic emerging economies have been revised for 2009 (GDP growth rate of 7.5 per cent in China; and of 5.4 per cent in India); while for Russia a significant fall of 6.5 per cent in 2009 is foreseen.

The advanced economies are experiencing a strong restructuring process in their service sectors. Financial activities are redimensioned, following the shutdown of investment banks and their absorption by commercial banks. In any case, as a consequence of the reduction of financial activities, job loss increased and branch networks are being restructured. It is estimated that up to January 2009, 325,000 jobs were lost in the global banking system, and 20 banks have declared themselves bankrupt in Europe.

At the heart of the crisis is the restructuring of industrial activities in developed and emerging countries. In the Eurozone, a rapid decline in industrial production took place during the second semester of 2008, and continued in 2009. Eurostat reported that in April 2009 compared to the same period a year ago, the European Industrial Production fell 21.6 per cent in the Eurozone; 24.2 per cent in Italy; 23.2 per cent in Germany; 21.2 per cent in Sweden; and 19.7 per cent in Spain. Activities in sectors such as automobiles, consumer electronics, suppliers for the construction sector, textiles and garments and the food processing industries, have sharply reduced their production.

In emerging economies industrial restructuring is also taking place, because of the sharp contraction of international demand, foreign trade and direct investment. In China a noticeable slowdown in the growth of industrial production can be seen, dropping from 11.4 per cent in September to 5.4 per cent in December 2008. Furthermore, thousands of companies have closed down, especially in the provinces of Guangdong and Zhenjiang, during this period, and the steel, car, petrochemical, and textile sectors are, as the Chinese authorities recognize the need for profound restructuring. In Korea, industrial production has fallen since October 2008 and it is foreseen that it will continue to fall during 2009, as indicated by the reduction in car sales and exports.

According to the International Labor Organization, unemployment is increasing as a consequence of the recession of the international economic system. The OECD (2009) report states that the unemployment rate in the United States was 5.8 per cent in 2008 and is foreseen to worsen and surpass 9.3 per cent in the course of 2009 (10.1 per cent in 2010). Unemployment rose in the Eurozone during the second semester of 2008, and it is foreseen that this trend will continue throughout 2009, reaching 10.0 per cent at the end of the year (12.0 per cent in 2010). In Spain, which has the highest unemployment rate in the Eurozone, the foreseen unemployment rate will be over 18 per cent in 2009 (20 per cent in 2010). In the emerging economies, unemployment is on the rise because of plant shutdowns. In China, the unemployment rate was 9.2 per cent in 2007 and the situation may worsen during the coming months if the growth rate of the economy falls below 8 per cent in 2009, and this is because the capacity of the economy will be reduced for the absorption of the new workers in the labor market.

The economy's incapacity to absorb new workers and the increased unemployment rate are having a negative effect on the living conditions of the people, especially in the territories with a low per capita income. During the last 30 years poverty was reduced spectacularly throughout the world; according to the estimates of Chen and Ravallion (2008) the share of the poor has fallen from representing 51.8 per cent of the developing world population in 1981 to 25.2 per cent in 2005 (in Latin America it fell from 11.5 per cent to 8.4 per cent). Nevertheless, the tide may turn during the near future, if international demand is reduced, the slowdown of global economic growth continues, and the labor absorption capacity worsens.

Inequalities increase in the emerging economies, which is why the reduction in the growth rate may increase social unrest, especially when it combines with an increase in poverty and a worsening in the functional and regional income distribution. In Latin America, where the number of poor fell by more than 12 million between 2002 and 2005, the poverty rate continues to be high: 21.0 per cent of the total population for Argentina in 2006; 33.0 per cent for Brazil; and 31.7 per cent for México. Income distribution continues to be very unequal in Latin American countries as shown by the Gini coefficient: in Brazil it was 0.590 in 2007; in México it was 0.506 in 2006. In China, where the number of poor fell from 835 million in 1981 to 208 million in 2005, income distribution worsened in a singular manner since the beginning of the reforms in 1978, as the Gini coefficient increase from 0.33 in 1980 to 0.49 in 2005 shows.

Structural policy measures for the economic crisis

The current economic crisis is like no other, as it affects, in a singular manner, the financial system, and is destroying the productive fabric of most of the dynamic regions and countries, which is why it cannot be resolved, as on other occasions, by monetary policy measures alone. What is needed are policies that stimulate the quantitative expansion of the money in circulation, but the reality in the economies also asks for a treatment that combines a number of measures that aim, on the one hand, at re-establishing the trust in the financial system and extending bank credit, and, on the other hand, at improving the productivity of firms and making economies more competitive.

A necessary condition for overcoming the economic crisis is to make the financial system of the advanced and emerging economies work again. The combined action of several countries has as its main objective to satisfy the needs for liquidity, if and when the banking system requires it, and to act decisively in cases of bankruptcy of financial firms and banks. Therefore, actions aimed at rescuing banks in difficulties vary from country to country: the nationalization in the case of insolvent banks and firms, as announced in the United Kingdom and the United States; the injection of funds into solvent banks that are short of liquidity; the encouragement of mergers between financial entities; and the support of the banks' recapitalization through public and private funds, as the Federal Deposit Insurance Corporation in the United States is doing (Tamames, 2009).

The banks' task of recovering their role as financial intermediaries, as well as to activate the functioning of the markets through the credit system is not easy. The adjustment of the assets nominal value to their real value is a win-lose game and countries are seeking a negotiated solution to the problem. In any case, changing the rules and norms of the financial system's functioning seems urgent, and this requires an agreement between the economic operators and the institutional agents. The purpose is to recover trust in the financial system so that the market regains its role within the economic activity.

Nevertheless, economic recovery requires a number of stimuli to foster increased productivity and competitiveness. The International Monetary Fund (2009b) describes some measures that the G20 countries have adopted, or plan to adopt. Among these the following should be emphasized:

i) A fiscal stimulus to demand. On the one hand, some of the G20 countries have announced reductions in personal income tax, indirect taxes, and corporate income taxes. But they also plan to stimulate consumption through a line of credit to citizens with low income levels.

ii) Increased spending on transport and communications infrastructure, either through the central or local administrations, is an initiative that the majority of the G20 countries take into consideration.

iii) Policies for entrepreneurial development play a key role among the measures that the countries have announced they will try in their attempt to neutralize the effects of the economic crisis. Among these are support to small and middle-sized companies, the fostering of strategic activities, such as high technology or defense, and the development of renewable energies.

iv) Social policy measures can also be found among the initiatives that have been proposed during the last months. Some actions aim at improved health care (such as those that affect the endowment of hospitals and doctors) and education (improving the quality of human resources); but also measures that aim at supporting vulnerable groups such as the unemployed, poor, and pensioners.

Local development and the economic recovery

Local development policy emerged and developed in poor and late developing countries, as an answer on behalf of localities and territories to the challenges of poverty, productive restructuring and increased competition. Is local development a strategy for fostering entrepreneurial development in places that are affected by the current crisis? Why are local development tools useful in times of crisis?

The search for a territorial response to the crisis

Local development and structural policies share the same objectives: increased productivity, improvement in social cohesion, and conservation of natural and cultural resources.

But their approach to the crisis problem is different. Whilst structural policies choose a functional approach, local development policies define their actions under a territorial viewpoint that seems more effective in the process of structural change. The reason for this is that actions carried out in territories must interact with the social, institutional, and cultural dimensions of the places. Therefore, measures are more efficient when they make use of local resources and are articulated toward the investment decisions of the local actors.

Two aspects condition the results of policy actions: the development potential that exists within the territory, and the organizational capacity of the local actors. From this perspective, all localities and territories have their development potential. This is true for rural areas, such as the Cuchumatanes in Guatemala, as well as for dynamic cities, such as Rosario in Argentina. At the local, regional or national level one can find a determined production structure, labor market, technical knowledge, entrepreneurial capacity, natural resources, social and political structure, or tradition and culture, on which local initiatives are based.

On the other hand, the development of a locality or territory requires public and private actors to carry out the investment programs in a coordinated manner. In Latin America, the local development projects are coordinated and managed through new forms of governance where public and private actors, international organizations, and non-governmental organizations participate. In Villa el Salvador, Peru, the 'Autoridad Autónoma del Parque Industrial del Cono Sur' was created, and unites public and private actors with the goal of building up the industrial park. In Jalisco, Mexico, local entrepreneurs, including the managers of multinational corporations, participate jointly with public actors in the creation of local supplier networks.

Finally, the local development strategy differs from one case to another, because the demands of each territory are different, the capacities of the inhabitants, companies, and local community change, and, also, the priorities to be incorporated in their development policies differ from one local community to another. Territorial strategic planning has turned, therefore, into a valuable instrument for the rationalization of decision-making and management in cities and rural areas. There are multiple examples of this, such as Rosario and Córdoba in Argentina, or cities and regions in El Salvador, Guatemala, Honduras, Republica Dominicana, Ecuador, and Colombia where UNDP and ILO encourage the creation of Local Economic Development Agencies, on the basis of strategic plans.

Innovation, a strategic factor in production adjustment

Understanding the crisis as an opportunity for transforming the production system, and making the economy stronger and more competitive at the international level, should be at the core of the strategy for overcoming the crisis. The key element is the introduction and diffusion of innovations throughout the productive fabric. Local development policies face the question of the adjustment and restructuring of production systems in order to make firms more competitive in product and factor markets. Income growth and the changes in demand have led to the diversification of production in cities as well as in rural areas. The development of the tourist activity in the cities of Cartagena de Indias and Havana, as well as the strength of cultural tourism in Chiapas and in the Yucatan Peninsula show how changes in international demand stimulate a diversification of production and therefore create the conditions for the continuous introduction of innovations that upgrade local resources and make them competitive.

When economic integration increases, firms try to develop their competitive advantages in local and international markets. In this way, production systems are always evolving and, frequently, the activation of change is carried out on the basis of a renovation of traditional know-how by introducing new knowledge during the structural change process. In the case of Cuchumatanes, for instance, reproduction and feeding techniques have improved in ovine production, and the technological package that led to the restructuring of natural coffee production into organic coffee was perfected and brought about increased coffee output and quality (Cifuentes, 2000). The adaptation and transfer of technology allowed the differentiation of production that has made local products more competitive in national and international markets.

In other localities and territories the question is not so much the differentiation of production or the reduction of cost but the finding of new products for markets in which local companies may maintain their competitive advantage. This is the case in Tapachula, in Mexico, for instance, where the coffee producers had to react in the face of strong competition from Vietnam in their markets, with whom they could not compete over prices. The answer was to change their production activities and start cultivating tropical flowers for markets such as the United States, for which the farmers had to adopt new production technologies from abroad, to enter into new markets, and to adapt their knowledge to the new productive and commercial reality.

Firms and territories can also opt for the production of new goods and services for which the demand in markets is increasing, such as for products that incorporate high-tech components and for which a strong internal and international demand exists, as occurs in the electronics cluster in Jalisco, Mexico (Rasiah, 2007).

Local initiatives and increasing productivity

It is through development actions that local initiatives can make an important contribution in the search for overcoming the economic crisis. Its strength rests on the fact that the local policy tools used stimulate capital accumulation, and therefore contribute to increasing productivity and competitiveness (Vázquez-Barquero, 2002).

One of the objectives of local initiatives is fostering entrepreneurship and the formation and development of firm networks. The start-up and development of firms is a necessary condition in the development process, as firms transform savings into investment through entrepreneurial projects; furthermore, when the development of networks and clusters of firms is encouraged, it favors the appearance of external economies of scale and the reduction of transaction costs.

Fostering firms' development is used often by local initiatives in Latin America, as seen in the case of the Cuchumatanes mountain area (Cifuentes, 2000). The project was launched by Guatemala's Ministry of Agriculture, Cattle and Food in 1994, and affected 9,000 poor rural families, with a net income per family of less than $1,200 per year. In order to favor sustainable development, the improvement of local entrepreneurial and managerial capabilities was encouraged. The experience and knowledge of self-management that existed within the local population before the civil war was recovered, and cooperatives and associations of peasants began to acquire full legal capacity. Moreover, more informally structured organizations, or Interest Groups were encouraged, and this brought people with common productive and commercial interests together.

On the other hand, fostering cluster development has become more frequent during the last decade, as shown by the case of Jalisco, in Mexico. The Jalisco state government created the Jalisco Development Corporation (JDC), whose main objective was the formation and development of an electronic cluster (Rasiah, 2007). The JDC helps strong systemic coordination locally and fosters clustering and human resource synergies, and motivates new firm creation. In this way, the cluster makes an important contribution toward differentiation of production and division of labor, and the diversification of the local productive fabric, job creation and economic development.

Another main axis of local development policy is the diffusion of innovation and knowledge throughout the local productive fabric, which allows for the introduction of new products and the differentiation of existing ones, changes in production processes, and the opening of new markets. All of this contributes toward the increase of productivity and competitiveness of the companies.

A particularly interesting case is that of the Technological Centre do Couro, Calçado e Afins (CTCCA) of Novo Hamburgo, Rio Grande do Sul in Brazil. This is a private, non-profit institution established in 1972 and founded for the purpose of helping the footwear firms during the early stages of their export activity, by providing services that would allow them to maintain the quality standards required by international markets. After more than 30 years, it has become an institution capable of stimulating research activity and product and process development in the shoe industry of Brazil.

Actions for training of human resources are strategic instruments for local development policy, for it is through this that knowledge is incorporated into the production of goods and services and in the management of their own development strategy. When training activities are included in the development strategy, the improvement in the quality of human resources can help increase productivity, stimulate competitiveness, and even affect the cultural model in which the development process must seek support.

In Rafaela, an industrial district in Argentina, training is a recurring objective issue in all the institutions created throughout the 1990s. Initially, the town promoted the improvement of personnel skills in order to strengthen municipal management. The Center for Entrepreneurial Development and the Regional Center in Rafaela consider training skills strategic in obtaining entrepreneurial and technological development for Rafaela, as does the Institute for Qualification and Study for Local Development, a municipal entity founded in 1997 to foster changes and transformations in the local community.

Finally, initiatives targeting the building up and improvement of overhead social capital and of infrastructures are instruments frequently used in local and regional development policies. Firms prefer locations in accessible places that are well endowed with services which allow them to make good use of economies of agglomeration and to have good accessibility to product and factor markets. Furthermore, the improvement of infrastructures attracts industrial and service activities to rural and peripheral localities and regions, generating economies of diversity and favoring an increase in productivity.

Sometimes, the question is to build up infrastructures, as in the Cuchumatanes Project, where in order to reach Guatemala City and international markets a link from the mountain area to the Panamericana highway was built. Other times, the question is the creation of a town, as in the case of Villa El Salvador, located 20 km south of Lima and close to the Panamericana highway (Aghon *et al.*, 2001). This is an initiative that allowed the transformation of a deserted area into a city that at present has a population of over 400,000 inhabitants. A Self-managed Urban Community was created, and one of the main projects was the buildup of an industrial park in order to provide industrial land, equipment and the services required by micro-firms and small and medium-sized firms.

At times, the purpose is for transport infrastructures to become a tool for sustainable development like that of Curitiba, Brazil (Cambell, 2001). During the late 1990s, a project was launched that tries to integrate urban infrastructure actions (construction of a road that connects 14 neighborhoods in the periphery of the city) with business initiatives which use the premises (community huts) in which micro-firms and small enterprises can be located with the support of the services available through professional and entrepreneurial training. The urban transport system was transformed into a surface metro system and it became the strategic element for local development.

Final comments

Advanced and emerging countries experience a process of important productive and social change due to the financial crisis and the bank credit crunch, which start to have profound effects on the real economy. Therefore, for solving these problems it would be helpful to combine measures that lead to the recuperation of trust in the financial institutions and to expand bank credit; with actions directed toward increasing productivity and competiveness.

This chapter sustains that local development is an instrument for helping to overcome the economic crisis. Its strength is inherent to its strategy which focuses on the question of productive adjustments under a territorial perspective. This allows finding out concrete solutions to the problems of specific territories, using precisely the development potential that is not utilized because of the crisis. Its merits lie in that local development is a strategy that stimulates increasing returns to investments and, therefore, helps increase productivity and competitiveness.

Yet, local development also seeks social progress and sustainable development. Development is a process in which economic growth and income distribution are two aspects of the same phenomenon, given that the public and private actors, when they choose and carry out their investments, do so for the purpose of increasing productivity and improving social well-being. Local development is, likewise, a strategy that is based on the continuous improvement of available resources, and particularly the natural and historic and cultural resources, and in this way contributes to increasing the sustainability of the territory.

Finally, local development is not a strategy whose results are guaranteed. Local development policy seeks economic and social progress and job creation by stimulating entrepreneurial development; but, an excess of external aid would reduce the creative capacity of entrepreneurs and local actors and therefore would limit the results of local initiatives. Furthermore, it is a policy whose results depend on an efficient coordination of the measures and the actors in the territory; but it would lose effectiveness when actions are carried out in an isolated manner because the positive feedback effects from the interaction between the development instruments would be neutralized. Finally, local development is a participatory policy in which the local actors are the ones who design and control its implementation; therefore, its results would be affected when actions and/or objectives are imposed in a unilateral way, by local and external actors.

References

Aghon, G., Alburquerque, F. and Cortés, P. (2001) *Desarrollo Económico Local y Descentralización en América Latina: Un Análisis Comparativo*, Santiago de Chile: CEPAL/GTZ.

Altenburg, T. and Meyer-Stamer, J. (1999) "How to Promote Clusters: Policy Experiences from Latin America," *World Development*, 27: 1693–1713.

Bordo, D. M. (2008) "An Historical Perspective on the Crisis of 2007–2009," Working paper, 14569, Cambridge, MA: National Bureau of Economic Research.

Cambell, T. (2001) "Innovation and Risk-taking: Urban Governance in Latin America," in Scott, A.J. (ed.) *Global City-Regions. Trends, Theory, Policy*, Oxford: Oxford University Press, pp. 214–235.

Chen, S. and Ravaillon, M. (2008) "The Developing World is Poorer than we Thought, but no Less Successful in the Fight Against Poverty," Policy Research Working Paper, 4703, Washington: The World Bank.

Cifuentes, I. (2000) *Proyecto Cuchumatanes. Transferencia de servicios técnicos a las organizaciones de productores*, Huehuetenango, Guatemala: Ministerio de Agricultura, Ganadería y Alimentación.

IMF (2009a) World Economic Outlook. April 2009. *Crisis and Recovery*. International Monetary Fund, Washington.

—— (2009b) "World Economic Crisis. Stimulus Measures Bolstering Demand Amid Crisis," *IMF Survey Magazine: Policy*, February 6. Washington: International Monetary Fund.

OECD (2009) *Economic Outlook*, 85, June, Paris: OECD.

Rasiah, R. (2007) "Cluster and Regional Industrial Synergies: The Electronics Industry in Penang and Jalisco," in A. Scott and G. Garofoli (eds) *Development on the Ground*, London: Routledge, pp. 223–250.

Tamames, R. (2009) *Para salir de la crisis global. Análisis y soluciones*, Madrid: Editorial EDAF.

Vázquez-Barquero, A. (2002) *Endogenous Development: Networking, Innovation, Institution and Cities*, London: Routledge.

—— (2007) "Endogenous development: analytical and policy issues," in A. Scott and G. Garofoli (eds.) *Development on the ground*, London: Routledge, pp. 23–43.

Further reading

Alburquerque, F., Costamagna, P. and Ferraro, C. (2008) *Desarrollo económico local, descentralización y democracia*, Buenos Aires: UNSAM.

Courlet, C. (2008) *L'Économie territoriales*, Grenoble: Presses Universitaires de Grenoble.

Friedman, J. and Weaver, C. (1979) *Territory and Function*, London: Edward Arnold.

Garofoli, G. (1992) *Endogenous Development and Southern Europe*, Aldershot: Avebury.

Massey, D. (1984) *Spatial Divisions of Labour. Social Structures and Geography of Production*, London: Macmillan.

Sen, A. (2001) *Development as Freedom*, 2nd edition, New Delhi, Oxford: Oxford University Press (Chapter 48).

43

North American perspectives on local and regional development

Nancey Green Leigh and Jennifer Clark

Introduction

This chapter explores distinctions in US and Canada local and regional development patterns that are framed by two approaches. The first approach is functional regional development – metropolitan regionalism – which is focused on the scale of the city-region. The second is territorial regionalism which defines the region not by the boundaries set by urban and industrial growth, but through natural resource or social-cultural spatial definitions. A further factor generating regional and local development distinctions between the two North American nations is their degree of governmental decentralization.

In Canada, coordination at the federal level has produced regional development characterized by priority-setting and targeted investment in city-regions and in industries and technologies. In the US, limited territorial-regional development programs are coordinated at the federal level while city-regional development is an ad hoc collaboration among states, local jurisdictions (towns, cities, and counties), and private interests. The resultant US regional development projects are generally aimed at discrete rather than comprehensive goals (e.g. transportation coordination; water resource management; targeted poverty alleviation and other specific economic development strategies).

Looking beyond the national level, this chapter explores international influences that are shaping the two nations' local and regional development patterns. These include trade and immigration policies, divergent approaches to regional innovation systems and the coordination of national, provincial, and regional technology-led economic development. We conclude this chapter with a discussion of early evidence as to how the two nations' local and regional development practices are being affected by the Global Recession as well as to the pre-existing challenges of climate change, inequality, and globalization.

Country overview

Canada and the United States are, respectively, the world's second and third largest countries by physical size, but Canada has only one-ninth of the US population (Table 43.1). In fact, Canada has approximately 3.5 million fewer people than the State of California (36.8 million in 2008). In both countries, however, the population is overwhelmingly urban (80 percent), though Canada's largest cities are significantly smaller than those in

515

Table 43.1 Key indicator comparison – United States and Canada

Indicator	Canada	United States
Land area	9,093,507 sq km	9,826,630 sq km
Administrative divisions	10 provinces/3 territories	50 States/1 District
Population (2008 est.)	33.2 million	303.8 million
Net migration rate	5.62 migrants/1,000 population	2.92 migrants/1,000 population
GDP (2008 est.)	$1.567 trillion	$14.33 trillion
Agriculture	2%	1.2%
Industry	28.4%	19.2%
Services	69.6%	79.2%
GDP per capita (2008 est.)	$40,200	$48,000
Distribution of family income/GINI Index	32.1 (2005)	45 (2007)
Trade	United States	Canada
Exports (2007)/imports(2008 est.)	78.9/54.1	21.4/15.7
Year became independent nation	1867*	1776

* Became fully self-governing in 1931.
Source: Compiled from CIA The World Factbook; www.cia.gov/library/publications/the-world-factbook/; Annual Estimates of the Resident Population for the United States, Regions, States, and Puerto Rico: April 1 2000 to July 1 2008 (NST-EST2008-01) from Population Division, U.S. Census Bureau, release date: December 22 2008

the US (Figure 43.1). Ninety percent of all Canadians live within 160 km (100 miles) of the common border that Canada and the US share. Immigration is a larger driver of population growth for Canada than for the US, but Canada does not experience the same level of illegal immigration, largely because it does not share a border with a relatively poorer developing nation (Mexico).

Administratively divided into ten provinces and three arctic territories, Canada is both an independent sovereign democracy and a federal state. The US democracy is a constitution-based federal republic, and includes 50 states, the District of Columbia, and several territories. Among the many differences between the US and Canada, one of the most significant is Canada's official bilingualism that formally recognizes its cultural diversity and inherent regional distinctions. Although the US is broadly diverse, it holds onto a single national identity and recognizes cultural distinctions and regional difference at the sub-national scale.

Both Canada and the US are considered affluent, industrialized nations with significant levels of advanced technology. Their gross domestic products are over the trillion-dollar level, though US GDP is 11 times

greater than that of Canada's. Further, nearly 30 percent of Canada's GDP is still generated by industry, as opposed to services (70 percent), while industry only generates 20 pecent of US GDP. US GDP per capita is 20 percent greater than that of Canada's, but this is accompanied by a 40 percent greater level of family income inequality. Greater income inequality is a documented trend accompanying the shift to higher levels of service-based economies, and over the last three decades most of the gains in US household income have gone to the top household quintile (Blakely and Leigh 2010).

Significant increases in trade and economic integration between Canada and the United States have come about since the enactment of the 1989 US-Canada Free Trade Agreement (FTA) and its 1994 successor, the North American Free Trade Agreement (NAFTA) that incorporated Mexico. The US absorbs nearly 80 percent of Canadian exports annually, resulting in a large trade surplus for Canada. Further, most US energy imports (oil, gas, uranium, and electric power) come from Canada.

Largely attributable to its abundant natural resources, Canada's economic growth from 1997 to 2007 was accompanied by balanced

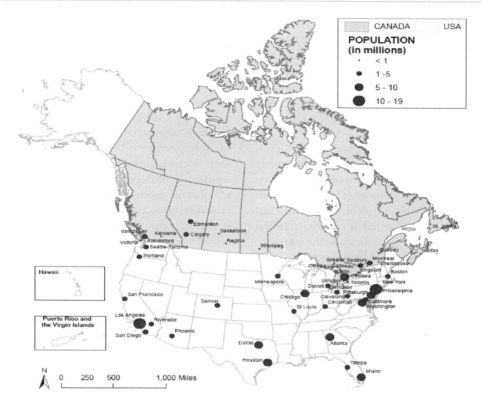

Figure 43.1 Top 25 metropolitan areas in the US and Canada, 2006.
Source: (1) Natural Resources Canada; (b) Statistics Canada; (c) US Census
Note: Maps of Hawaii, Puerto Rico, and the Virgin Islands are not to scale

federal budgets, unlike the US which has experienced trade and budget deficits over the same period. The US set off a Global Recession in 2008 due to its sub-prime mortgage crisis, falling home prices, slowdown in construction, failures in the banking and investment industries, and tightening of all types of credit. Canada's economy was significantly affected.

Two analytical frameworks for local and regional development

North American regionalism has evolved along two major trajectories: functional and territorial. Functional regional development, or metropolitan regionalism, is focused on the scale of the city-region and parallels much of the regional development practices emerging in other developing countries (Pike 2009). Territorial regionalism defines the region not by the boundaries set by urban and industrial growth, but through natural resource or social-cultural spatial definitions. The tension between these regionalisms has been consistent in the US and less pronounced in Canada. Canadian coordination at the federal level has produced regional development projects characterized by priority-setting with provinces and targeted investment in city-regions, in industries, and in technologies (Wolfe and Holbrook 2000). While the challenge for Canadian federal regional policy has long been smoothing out the uneven development patterns between affluent and lagging provinces and rural and urban areas, these policies at the federal scale of governance have been consistent and coordinated (if not wholly effective) (Wellar 1981; Savoie 1986; Wolfe and Holbrook 2002; Doloreux and Dionne 2008).

The historical experience in the US is described in Friedman and Weaver's *Territory and Function* (1979) and Markusen's *Regions* (1987). The US experience with territorial regionalism is intermittent, with occasional federal policies targeted at specific technical challenges (rural electrification, the interstate system) or disadvantaged regions (Appalachian Regional Commission). The US experience with metropolitan regionalism is rooted in the continuing interest and concern of planners with metropolitan and urban governance and the challenges of urbanization, exemplified by the work of Clarence Stein, Lewis Mumford, Robert Moses and other metropolitan planners and regionalists (Caro 1974; Sussman 1976; Friedmann and Weaver 1979; Weir 2000). However, this strategy has been erratic in implementation with moments of dramatic policy shift (e.g. metropolitan governance in the Twin Cities and Portland; progressive cities initiatives, the Smart Growth Movement), and long periods of significant federal and state disinvestment (Clavel 1986; Orfield 1997; Dreier, Mollenkopf *et al.* 2001).

Influence of decentralization on regional and local development

A further factor generating regional and local development distinctions between the two North American nations is their degree of governmental decentralization. It has long been acknowledged in local and regional development that the delineation of administrative boundaries (i.e. a city or county's legal boundaries) for a territory can create problems for planning and policy-making

when they do not coincide with natural environmental boundaries (i.e. watersheds) or functional economic boundaries (i.e. a metropolitan economy that encompasses multiple county units of government or even states).

Because Canada is divided into only ten regional administrative units or provinces and three territories below the national level, there is much greater capacity to implement regional approaches than there is in the US that is divided into 50 states. Further inhibiting regional approaches in the US is the fact that states are subdivided into counties, each with their own local government. The total number of counties is over 3,000, compared to 288 Census Divisions in Canada – the most analogous geographic unit. Furthermore, the number as well as land area of counties varies widely amongst US states (for example, the State of California with a land mass of nearly 156,000 square miles has 58 counties while Georgia's nearly 58,000 square miles are divided into 156 counties (Blakely and Leigh (2010)). Finally, in addition to its county units, the US has approximately 35,000 municipalities and towns.

In the US, local economic development has historically been defined as job or wealth creation (Fitzgerald and Leigh 2002). With few exceptions, the approach has been market-based and modeled explicitly on export base theory. Consequently, policy has taken two interrelated forms: (1) tax-based subsidies to individual firms (usually basic) intended to influence their location decisions, and (2) redevelopment incentives to increase property values (Malizia and Feser 1999). In the first case, that of firm-specific subsidies, results are measured in terms of jobs created. In the second, the measure of success is an increase in the local tax base. Redevelopment has been particularly favored in cities because of its potential to increase property values (Sagalyn 1997; Fainstein 2001).

The efficacy of these strategies has been critiqued for 60 years but those responsible for implementation have shied away from accounting for their results. When they have done so, stated objectives were rarely achieved (Bartik 1991; Bingham and Mier 1997). More recently, ideas counter to this economic development practice have gained popularity. They include concepts such as regional innovation systems, the creative class, industry clusters and sustainable economic development (Porter 1998; Cooke 2002; Florida 2002; Newby 1999; Leigh and Fitzgerald 2002). These strategies tend to emphasize regional solutions to shared problems and a reorientation of investment to innovative institutions, human capital, and emerging (green) technologies rather than direct firm subsidies (Clark and Christopherson 2009).

In Canada, the practice of local economic development, particularly the focus on firm attraction, retention, and expansion strategies has been generally consistent with US practice. However, while the Canadian model is business-oriented, it has included a broader commitment to distributional equity. In other words, the distributional concerns surface in assessing both the allocation of costs and benefits of development. While this practice is uneven across Canada (as it is in the US), the growth of neoliberalism within Canada in the past 15 years has eroded the commitment to social services and distributional equity (Reese and Fasenfest 1996; Reese and Rosenfeld 2004).

The US has limited territorial-regional development programs coordinated at the federal level while city-regional development is an ad hoc collaboration among states, local jurisdictions (towns, cities, and counties), and private interests. Much of the country's local and regional development patterns are shaped by political fragmentation and competition between jurisdictions. The federal government does not have a pro-active policy of encouraging cooperation between states, and instances where states encourage cooperation between counties or municipalities are rare.

There are, however, instances where states have banded together to protect their common regional interests and obtain federal resources. For example, the Northeast-Midwest Institute was formed during the 1970s when states in those two regions (which came to be called the Rustbelt) were beginning to experience severe de-industrialization effects. The Institute, focused on creating economic vitality, environmental quality, and regional equity for Northeast and Midwest states, has close ties to Congress through the Northeast-Midwest Congressional and Senate Coalitions. These bipartisan coalitions advance federal policies that can enhance the region's economy and environment (see www.nemw.org). State governors from the South also formed an organization to promote their regional economy and quality of life in the 1970s. The Southern Growth Policies Board represents the 13 southern states as well as Puerto Rico and partners with legislative groups as well as others to promote its development agenda (see www.southern.org).

The United States' limited territorial-regional development projects are generally aimed at discrete rather than comprehensive goals (e.g. transportation coordination; water resource management; targeted poverty alleviation and other specific economic development strategies). However, the most significant transportation project for regional development was not specifically targeted to regions. It was the National Interstate and Defense Highways Act of 1956 which led directly to the auto-dominated pattern of local and regional development that is now creating significant problems for the goals of sustainability. Other federally funded "Development" highways were later piggy-backed onto the 1956 Act and targeted some of the country's poorest regions.

The Tennessee Valley Authority Act of 1933 is an early example of the federal government's targeted regional development program. In a letter to Congress, President Franklin D. Roosevelt described the new entity's responsibilities as: "planning for the proper use, conservation, and development of natural resources of the Tennessee River drainage basin and its adjoining territory for the general social and economic welfare of the Nation" (Owen 1973: 14, requoted in Forrest 2002). Subsequent major federal targeted regional development programs include the Appalachian Regional Commission (1965), Delta Regional Authority (Mississippi 1965), Denali Commission (Alaska 1998), Interagency Task Force on the Economic Development of the Southwest Border (1999), and the Northern Great Plains Authority (2002).

The largest impetus for US local and regional development planning, however, is found at the metropolitan level. While the quote below is from 2008 (Mitchell-Weaver *et al.* 2000), observe that the roots of US metropolitan regionalism began in the early nineteenth century. Moving into the twentieth century, they write that US metropolitan planning was a reaction to the second industrial revolution and focused on four themes: housing reform, park and boulevard planning (a component of the City Beautiful Movement), using social statistics and land use data to plan for metropolitan expansion, and government reform targeting professionalization and annexation. This planning was initiated by civic associations, the most famous of which continues to be the Committee on Plan of New York which published its first plan for the metropolitan area in the 1920s. The committee is now known as the Regional Plan Association and encompasses 31 counties in the tri-state area of New York, New Jersey and Connecticut. It has made two major revisions to the metropolitan plan and is now focused on implementing the third plan in the areas of community design, open space, transportation, workforce and the economy (see www.rpa.org).

The federal government did not become involved with metropolitan problems until the Great Depression. There has never been a major movement to create actual metropolitan government at the federal level; there have been efforts to create greater intergovernmental cooperation such as the Advisory Commission on Intergovernmental Relations

established by federal legislation in 1959, and the creation of coordinating agencies in the form of Councils of Governments and Metropolitan Planning Agencies. Support for these efforts began to wane under the Reagan Presidency (Mitchell-Weaver *et al.* 2000). By the 1990s, however, sprawling metropolitan areas became a key focus of federal, state, and local government. In 1996, the US Environmental Protection Agency partnered with non-profit and government organizations to create the Smart Growth Network which advocates for compact growth (see Smart Growth Network, www.smartgrowth.org). Growing attention has been focused on intra-metropolitan changes such as declining inner-ring suburbs, new residential growth in some downtowns while others are hollowing out, new suburban and exurban immigrant populations, and widening inequality (Lee and Leigh 2007).

The importance of metropolitan areas to national and state economies argued in the quote below is reinforced and extended by two additional concepts. First, clusters of metro areas are growing into "megaregions" that cross state boundaries and represent a new form of functional regionalism (Goldfeld 2007). Second, the largest metro areas have become global cities that are characterized by Sassen (2006: 54–55) as "partly denationalized territorializations with considerable regulatory autonomy through the ascendance of private governance regimes" (2007: 54–55). Katz *et al.* (2009: 23) argue that:

> America doesn't really possess a national economy, or even a collection of 50 state economies. Instead, America's long-term prosperity stands or falls on the more local prosperity of its 363 distinct, varied, clustered, and interlinked metropolitan economies, dominated by the 100 largest metros—many of which cross county and state jurisdictions and incorporate multiple city centers, suburbs, exurbs, and downtowns in a way that the old hub-and-spoke model

of urban geography never did. In that sense, America is quite literally a "MetroNation," utterly dependent on the success of its metropolitan hubs.

Targeted local and regional development policies

Emerging technologies and industries have had a significant influence on North American local and regional development policies. Industry cluster strategies dominated the local and regional economic development policy discourse and practice in the 1990s, stimulated by the success of Silicon Valley and Michael Porter's "diamond" model for national and regional competitiveness (Porter 1990). In recent years, cluster strategies have merged with local and regional technology-led development strategies, including sustainable or green technologies and industries (Martin and Mayer 2008). Concurrently there has been a renewal of local and regional development policies focused on human capital, regional capacities, and innovation systems.

The merger of regional economic development strategies and technology-led or innovation-based policy has led to multi-scalar innovation systems in many industrialized countries including in North America (Pike *et al.* 2006). The intentional placement of the region as the central scale of economic development investment characterizes these systems and policy approaches (Perry and May 2007). This model of technology-led economic development integrating innovation and commercialization strategies with regional development objectives arrived in the US and Canada in the 1980s (Roessner 1985; Feller 1997). The impetus to reorient economic development policy was precipitated by a popular perception of a wide gap between innovation and commercialization in both Canada and the United States.

The emerging economic development models in North America integrated technology investment with traditional economic development practices using a targeted industry or technology approach, often based on a clusters framework (Doutriaux 2008). The celebrated success of Silicon Valley, particularly during a period when other regions were experiencing precipitous declines, shaped much of US regional development since the 1980s (Saxenian 1994). These strategies developed as cluster-based approaches, often linked to research centers and frequently based in universities. While primarily articulated at the regional scale in the US, the cluster-based approach was adapted in other countries as national industrial policy or as science and technology policy in an effort to initiate, through policy and planning the connection between technology and the growth seen as the root of the Silicon Valley success story (Bluestone and Harrison 1982; Atkinson-Grosjean 2002; Hospers *et al.* 2008).

In the United States and Canada, the technology-led economic development strategies neither began with the major policy transformations of the 1980s nor followed the same path. In both countries, the "Centers of Excellence" or "Innovation Centers" model represented a simultaneous expansion and deviation from the network of national government labs implemented over the post-Second World War era and sponsored by a variety of national-level agencies. The emphasis of the traditional research centers was a sector of the economy (e.g. energy or defense) rather than a specific industrial sector (e.g. automobiles or semiconductors) or a targeted technology (e.g. biotechnology, nanotechnology, or optics and photonics). This new economic development involved several key elements: inclusion of technology transfer, emphasis on the collaboration between academic and industry researchers with the goal of commercialization, reorientation toward an emerging technology rather than an established industry sector, and recognition of the role of regions as engines and containers of agglomeration economies (Rood 2000).

In the mid-1990s, the US and Canada undertook two different national strategies aimed at institutionalizing technology-led economic development at the sub-national scale. These two paths, the decentralized US approach and the coordinated Canadian approach, in many ways mirrored the previous policy path dependencies in each country and their divergent approaches to the role of government in the distributional consequences of economic development planning.

In Canada, the National Centers of Excellence (NCE) program began as a partnership of Industry Canada and three other federal agencies: It was based in universities and emphasized a "distributed network approach." This approach took two directions. It paired a national network of scientific excellence with a local network of firms and industry actors. Thus, the Centers of Excellence were embedded in existing regional industrial clusters and connected across Canada to a national research network (Globerman 2006). In general, funding of scientific priorities has been set by the federal government and implemented through the university networks and regional institutions (Salazar and Holbrook 2007).

In the US, the technology-led development model took several paths following parallel but less coordinated tracks at the state and national levels. At the national level, a Centers of Excellence model was implemented incrementally through the existing framework of the National Science Foundation. These centers never emerged as linked, in design or in practice, to regional innovation systems or as active and consistent coordinators of regional economic development strategies. A version of that center model, closer in character to the Canadian NCE project, emerged instead at the state level in the US. Beginning in the late 1990s, several states in the US recognized the potential of university-based technology-led development strategies as a mechanism for broader regional economic development

spillovers through investment in research and development infrastructure and an emphasis on technology transfer (Feller 1997). In particular, the Centers of Excellence in Ontario impressed state-level policy-makers in the US. In New York, Georgia, and Texas the model emerged as explicit components of state-driven regional innovation systems intended for economic development and based, in part, on an industry clusters analysis (Christopherson and Clark 2007).

In New York, the implementation of these centers was accompanied by promises of impressive job growth, a traditional economic development metric from industry investment. Like the Canadian NCE program, the state-level Centers of Excellence programs oriented toward existing industry clusters, regional technology specializations, or specified national or state priorities (e.g. genomics or stem cells). Unlike the Canadian programs, the proliferation of state-level technology-led regional economic development strategies developed without explicit multi-scalar coordination, thus magnifying existing issues of interjurisdictional competition for public and private investment (Malecki 2004; Christopherson and Clark 2007).

At the center of the collaborative, Canadian approach has been the "distributed network model" in which technology-led economic development strategies interact with and complement existing concentrations of capital (human, social, and venture) in dominant urban areas. The distributed network model explicitly takes the tension between the goal of providing national access to education and research resources with the imperatives of the highly concentrated and localized geographies produced by both agglomeration economies and the policies intended to support them (e.g. technology transfer). Although it remains unclear whether lagging regions are advantaged through the distributed network model, the Canadian approach attempts to avoid working against the economic success of peripheral regions (Doloreux 2004; Trippl and

Tödtling 2007; Doloreux and Dionne 2008). In the US, the absence of a coordinated strategy results in a devolution of equity and distributional concerns to the state and local scale.

Evolving perspectives

Prior to the Global Recession which began in 2008, there were key distinctions in how the two nations' local and regional development practices responded to the challenges of climate change, inequality, and globalization. For example, Canada was one of the original signatories of the Kyoto Protocol in 1998, but the two-term Bush Administration refused to sign. However, a local level movement begun by the Mayor of Seattle led to more than 900 towns and cities signing the treaty by early 2009. Further, five years after Canada signed onto the Kyoto Protocol, rising oil prices made Alberta's oil sand production commercially profitable for the first time in decades. Oil sand production is estimated to emit three to five times more greenhouse gases than conventional production. In the US, green economy initiatives at all government levels are one of the key features inserted by the new Obama Presidential Administration into the multi-billion stimulus package initiated by the outgoing Bush Administration and left for passage and implementation by its successor. Beyond the stimulus package, the new Administration quickly began to move to control US greenhouse gas emissions. As the major consumer of Canadian oil, this move may cause US firms to meet their oil needs elsewhere, thereby creating conflict between the two nations and challenging the possibility of a North American Climate Change Agreement to complement the existing Free Trade Agreement.

The Global Recession has the potential significantly to alter the path of world development, although the full extent and nature of the alteration will not be known for some years. Canada's banking sector, known for conservative lending practices and strong capitalization, cannot be implicated in the economic downfall. However, a key fallout of the mismanaged US banking sector is the decline in US housing and commercial construction and sales, new car sales, and world commodity prices. This, in turn, particularly affects the regional economies of Canada that supply these different segments of the US market. Moreover, it is possible that the heated incentives competition for global capital (Markusen 2007) that has been pursued by economic developers in both countries in recent decades will be halted.

Prior to the Global Recession's onset, efforts in both Canada and the US to promote local resilience and sustainability were gaining momentum (see, for example, the MacArthur Foundation-funded Building Resilient Regions network: brr.berkeley.edu). In Canada, struggling rural economies were part of the impetus while a key driver of the US movement has been the urban tragedies of the attack on New York's World Trade Towers and financial industry on September 11, 2001, and Hurricane Katrina hitting New Orleans in 2005. In particular, Katrina showed just how devastating the impacts could be on a concentrated urban poverty population of a region that mismanaged its flood plains and disaster responses.

For evolving North American perspectives, we can consider whether local and regional sustainability and resiliency initiatives, as well as the megaregion movement, suggest the emergence of a new regionalism that seeks to incorporate the perceived conflicting goals of competitiveness and sustainability. In the US, prior even to President Obama signaling support for green economy initiatives, this does appear to be the case. However, while it is too soon to know whether these will generate fundamental changes in the theory and practice of functional and territorial regional development, they clearly warrant close watching.

References

Atkinson-Grosjean, J. (2002) "Canadian Science at the Public/Private Divide: The NCE Experiment", *Journal of Canadian Studies*, 37(3): 71.

Bartik, T. (1991) *Who Benefits from State and Local Economic Development Policies?*, Kalamazoo, Michigan: The Upjohn Institute for Employment Research.

Bingham, R.D. and R. Mier (eds) (1997) *Dilemmas of Urban Economic Development*, Thousand Oaks: Sage Publications.

Blakely, E.J. and N. Green Leigh (forthcoming 2010) *Planning Local Economic Development*, 4th edition, Thousand Oaks: Sage Publications.

Bluestone, B. and B. Harrison (1982) *The Deindustrialization of America: Plant Closings, Community Abandonment, and the Dismantling of Basic Industry*, New York: Basic Books.

Bozeman, B. and C. Boardman (2004) "The NSF Engineering Research Centers and the University-Industry Research Revolution: A Brief History Featuring an Interview with Erich Bloch", *Journal of Technology Transfer*, 29(3–4): 365.

Caro, R. A. (1974) *The Power Broker*, New York: Random House, Inc.

Christaller, W. (1933) *Central Places in Southern Germany*, Jena: Fischer.

Christopherson, S. and J. Clark (2007). *Remaking Regional Economies: Power, Labor, and Firm Strategies in the Knowledge Economy*, New York: Routledge.

CIA – The World Fact Book https://www.cia.gov/library/publications/the-world-factbook/geos/ca.html.

Clark, J. and S. Christopherson (2009) "Integrating Investment and Equity: A Critical Regionalist Agenda for a Progressive Regionalism", *Journal of Planning Education and Research*, 28 (Spring): 341–354.

Clavel, P. (1986) *The Progressive City: Planning and Participation, 1969–1984,* New Brunswick, NJ: Rutgers University Press.

Cooke, P. (2002) "Regional Innovation Systems and Regional Competitiveness", in M. Gertler and D. Wolfe (eds) *Innovation and Social Learning*, New York: Palgrave Macmillan.

Doloreux, D. (2004) "Regional Innovation Systems in Canada: A Comparative Study", *Regional Studies*, 38(5): 481.

Doloreux, D. and S. Dionne (2008) "Is Regional Innovation System Development Possible in Peripheral Regions? Some Evidence from the Case of La Pocatière, Canada", *Entrepreneurship and Regional Development*, 20(3): 259.

Doutriaux, J. (2008) "Knowledge Clusters and University–Industry Cooperation", in C. Karlsson (ed.) *Handbook of Research on Innovation and Clusters*, Northampton, MA: Edward Elgar.

Dreier, P., J. Mollenkopf, *et al.* (2001) *Place Matters: Metropolitics for the 21st Century*, Lawrence, Kansas: University Press of Kansas.

Fainstein, S. S. (2001) "Competitiveness, Cohesion, and Governance: Their Implications for Social Justice", *International Journal of Urban and Regional Research*, 25(4): 884.

Feller, I. (1997) "Manufacturing Technology Centers as Components of Regional Technology Infrastructures", *Regional Science and Urban Economics*, 27(2): 181.

Fitzgerald, J. and N. Leigh (2002) *Economic Revitalization: Cases and Strategies for City and Suburb*, London: Sage Publications.

Florida, R. (2002) *The Rise of the Creative Class: And How It's Transforming Work, Leisure, Community, and Everyday Life*, New York: Basic Books.

Forrest, T.J. (2004) "Regional Theory, Regional Policy and Southern Poverty", unpublished manuscript, City and Regional Planning Program, Georgia Institute of Technology, April.

Friedmann, J. and C. Weaver (1979) *Territory and Function: The Evolution of Regional Planning*, London: E. Arnold.

Globerman, S. (2006) "Canada's Regional Innovation Systems: The Science-based Industries", *Canadian Journal of Political Science*, 39(2): 432.

Goldfeld, K.S. (ed.) (2007) *The Economic Geography of Megaregions*, The Trustees of Princeton University.

Hospers, G.-J., F. Sautet and P. Desrouchers (2008) "Is There a Need for Cluster Policy?", in C. Karlsson (ed.) *Silicon Somewhere: Handbook of Research on Innovation and Clusters*, Northampton, MA: Edward Elgar.

Katz, B., M. Munro and J. Bradley (2009) "Miracle Mets: How U.S. Metros Propel America's Economy and Might Drive Its Recovery", *Democracy: A Journal of Ideas*, Spring 2009, pp 22–35. http://www.brookings.edu/articles/2009/0311_metro_katz.aspx, accessed 18 March, 2009.

Lee, S. and N.G. Leigh (2007) "Intrametropolitan Spatial Differentiation and Decline of Inner-ring Suburbs: A Comparison of Four U.S. Metropolitan Areas", *Journal of Planning Education and Research*, 27 (2): 146–164.

Malecki, E. J. (2004) "Jockeying for Position: What It Means and Why It Matters to Regional

Development Policy When Places Compete", *Regional Studies*, 38(9): 1101.

Malizia, E. E. and E. J. Feser (1999) *Understanding Local Economic Development*, New Brunswick, NJ: Center for Urban Policy Research.

Markusen, A.R. (1987) *Regions: The Economics and Politics of Territory*, Totowa, NJ: Rowman and Allenheld.

Markusen, A. (ed.) (2007) *Reigning in the Competition for Capital*, Kalamazoo, Michigan: W.E. Upjohn Institute for Employment Research.

Martin, S. and H. Mayer (2008) "Sustainability, Clusters, and Competitiveness: Introduction to Focus Section", *Economics Development Quarterly*, 22(4): 272–277.

Mitchell-Weaver, C., D. Miller and R. Deal Jr. (2000) "Multilevel Governance and Metropolitan Regionalism in the USA", *Urban Studies*, 37 (5–6): 851–876.

Newby, L. (1999) "Sustainable Local Economic Development: A New Agenda for Action?", *Local Environment*, 4(1): 67–72.

Orfield, M. (1997) *Metropolitics: A Regional Agenda for Community and Stability*, Washington DC: The Brookings Institution Press.

Perry, B. and T. May (2007) "Governance, Science Policy and Regions: An Introduction", *Regional Studies* 41(8): 1039–1050.

Pike, A. (ed.) (2009) *Whither Regional Studies?*, London: Routledge.

Pike, A., Rodríguez-Pose, A. and Tomaney J. (2006) *Local and Regional Development*, New York: Routledge.

Porter, M. E. (1990) "The Competitive Advantage of Nations", *Harvard Business Review*, 68(2): 73.

Porter, M. E. (1998) "Clusters and the New Economics of Competition", *Harvard Business Review*, 76(6): 77.

Reese, L. A. and D. Fasenfest (1996) "Local Economic Development Policy in Canada and the US: Similarities and Differences", *Canadian Journal of Urban Research*, 5(1): 97.

Reese, L. A. and R. A. Rosenfeld (2004) "Local Economic Development in the United States and Canada: Institutionalizing Policy Approaches", *American Review of Public Administration*, 34(3): 277.

Roessner, J. D. (1985) "Prospects for a National Innovation Policy in the USA", *Futures*, 17(3): 224.

Rood, S.A. (2000) *Government Laboratory Technology Transfer: Process and Impact*, Aldershot [England], Burlington, USA: Ashgate.

Sagalyn, L.B. (1997) "Negotiating for Public Benefits: The Bargaining Calculus of Public-private development", *Urban Studies*, 34(12): 1955.

Salazar, M. and A. Holbrook (2007) "Canadian Science, Technology and Innovation Policy: The Product of Regional Networking?", *Regional Studies*, 41(8): 1129.

Sassen, S. (2006) *Territory, Authority, Rights: From Medieval to Global Assemblages*, Princeton, NJ: Princeton University Press.

Savoie, D. J. (1986) *Regional Economic Development: Canada's Search for Solutions*, Toronto: Buffalo, University of Toronto Press.

Saxenian, A. (1994) *Regional Advantage: Culture and Competition in Silicon Valley and Route 128*, Cambridge, MA: Harvard University Press.

Sussman, C. (1976) *Planning the Fourth Migration: The Neglected Vision of the Regional Planning Association of America*, Cambridge, MA: MIT Press.

Trippl, M. and F. Tödtling (2007) "Developing Biotechnology Clusters in Non-high Technology Regions – The Case of Austria", *Industry and Innovation*, 14(1): 47.

Weir, M. (2000) "Coalition Building for Regionalism", B. Katz (ed.) *Reflections on Regionalism*, Washington DC: The Brookings Institution.

Wellar, B. S. (1981) *National and Regional Economic Development Strategies: Perspectives on Canada's Problems and Prospects: Colloquium Proceedings*, Ottawa, Canada: University of Ottawa Press.

Wolfe, D. and J. A. Holbrook (2000) *Innovation, Institutions and Territory: Regional Innovation Systems in Canada*, published for the School of Policy Studies, Queen's University by McGill-Queen's University Press, Montreal.

Wolfe, D. and J. A. Holbrook (2002) *Knowledge, Clusters and Regional Innovation: Economic Development in Canada*, published for the School of Policy Studies, Queen's University by McGill-Queen's University Press, Montreal.

Zysman, J. and L. D. A. Tyson (1983) *American Industry in International Competition: Government Policies and Corporate Strategies*, Ithaca, NY: Cornell University Press.

Further reading

Blakely, E.J. and N. Green Leigh (forthcoming 2010) *Planning Local Economic Development*, 4th edition, Thousand Oaks: Sage Publications.

Clark, J. and S. Christopherson (2009) "Integrating Investment and Equity: A Critical Regionalist Agenda for a Progressive Regionalism",

Journal of Planning Education and Research, 28 (Spring): 341–354.

Cooke, P. (2002) "Regional Innovation Systems and Regional Competitiveness", in M. Gertler and D. Wolfe, *Innovation and Social Learning*, New York: Palgrave Macmillan.

Friedmann, J. and C. Weaver (1979) *Territory and Function: The Evolution of Regional Planning*, London: E. Arnold.

Goldfeld, K.S. (ed.) (2007) *The Economic Geography of Megaregions*, The Trustees of Princeton University.

Lee, S. and N.G. Leigh (2007) "Intrametropolitan Spatial Differentiation and Decline of Inner-ring Suburbs: A Comparison of Four U.S. Metropolitan Areas", *Journal of Planning Education and Research*, 27 (2): 146–164.

Markusen, A.R. (1987) *Regions: The Economics and Politics of Territory*, Totowa, NJ: Rowman and Allenheld.

Markusen, A. (ed.) (2007) *Reigning in the Competition for Capital*, Kalamazoo, Michigan: W.E. Upjohn Institute for Employment Research.

Mitchell-Weaver, C., D. Miller and R. Deal Jr. (2000) "Multilevel Governance and Metropolitan Regionalism in the USA", *Urban Studies*, 37 (5–6): 851–876.

Reese, L. A. and D. Fasenfest (1996) "Local Economic Development Policy in Canada and the US: Similarities and Differences", *Canadian Journal of Urban Research*, 5(1): 97.

Sassen, S. (2006) *Territory, Authority, Rights: From Medieval to Global Assemblages*, Princeton, NJ: Princeton University Press.

44

Area definition and classification and regional development finance

The European Union and China

Michael Dunford

Introduction

Area development policies are widely implemented. In each case such measures involve the definition and classification of geographical areas, the establishment of information systems to support policy initiatives, the determination of strategic policy goals, the establishment of policy instruments and the allocation of financial and other resources to plan, implement, monitor and evaluate the measures adopted. The aim of this chapter is to deal with two of these dimensions of area development policies: the definition and classification of areas and the allocation of financial resources. These issues will be considered in relation to the experience mainly of the European Union but also of contemporary China.

Defining regions

A region is essentially a part of the land surface of the earth. In the geographical literature regions are defined in three ways as, respectively, uniform, functional and administrative areas. Most useful for economic development purposes are functional areas which combine places characterized by strong

degrees of interdependence and strong complementarities. Examples include market areas that combine market centres where the function is performed and the places in which the people who use those market centres reside. A classic case is afforded by Christaller's (1933) theoretical account of the size, number and spacing of market centres and market areas in Southern Germany. Another example is a travel-to-work area which combines places of employment and the places where the people who work in those places of employment live. As this definition implies, functional areas are essentially city regions.

The degree of emphasis placed on functional definitions of regions varies. In part this variation reflects the shifting relative importance attached in geography to the study of regions as self-contained entities (as in the regional tradition and more recent 'territorial' approaches to regional development studies) and as places that can only be understood in terms of their relationships with other places (as in the locational tradition and in recent relational approaches to economic geography) (Wrigley, 1965; Pike, 2007).

Although functional definitions are from a scientific point of view the most useful, most used are regions defined for administrative purposes. Once a regional division is put in

527

place it can acquire a historical justification especially if its development is associated with the creation of relatively strong regional identities and with the development of social movements that press for the preservation of the resulting regional entities. Also possible however is the opposite: the creation of new political and administrative arrangements and new regional divisions designed specifically to make a break with the past. A step of this type can occur as part of projects of economic and political transformation (Dulong, 1975, 1978). An example is the initial creation of a regional tier of the administration in Gaullist France in the 1960s where the creation of Commissions de développement économique régionale (CODER) was part of a programme of state-directed economic and social modernization in which regional planning was a vital instrument and where an important aim was to recompose regional elites in established regions with powerful traditional elites considered as obstacles to economic and political modernization. A case in point was Brittany where a new region was defined so as not to coincide with earlier definitions (Dulong, 1975). A longer view of European development would include many striking instances of these two types of change as the processes of political integration saw the creation of a European nation state system out of an earlier patchwork quilt of political entities, and as the state system was itself successively modified through the interaction of further projects of integration, attempts to preserve the territorial integrity of existing states and attempts to preserve historical identities. Administrative regions can coincide with uniform regions, functional regions or neither. There are reasons related to the criteria that an administrative system should satisfy that suggest that an administrative region should make functional sense. A situation in which administrative and functional regionalizations coincide is however in practice difficult to achieve (Parr, 2007; Dunford, 2010), although non-achievement has important consequences for

the rationality of administrative systems. In addition, it leads to the existence of functionally over- and under-bounded administrative areas with significant repercussions for the meaningfulness of widely used statistical indicators.

The NUTS classification

A European regional policy was first put in place at the start of the 1970s. At that point in time a geographical division of the territory of the community was required for the analysis of regional problems, for the design and implementation of this new policy including decision-making about eligibility for regional aid and for the compilation of harmonized regional statistics to inform analysis and policy decisions. The result was the establishment of the Nomenclature des Unités Territoriales pour la Statistique (NUTS). In the 1960s what came to be called NUTS LEVEL II areas were identified as the framework used for Member State regional policies, whereas NUTS LEVEL I were identified as the principal entities for the analysis of community regional issues such as the subnational impact of customs union and economic integration, and NUTS LEVEL III areas were considered as useful in the diagnosis of regional problems and in identifying where regional policy measures were required. Today the periodic report on the social and economic situation and development of the regions of the Community, which the Commission is required to prepare every three years draws mainly on NUTS LEVEL II data.

The NUTS is intended to provide a single uniform breakdown of the territory of the European Union into a hierarchical set of statistical regions. The main building blocks of the NUTS system are general-purpose administrative divisions of each Member state. The current NUTS system is a three-level hierarchical classification of regions in which each Member State is subdivided into a whole number of NUTS LEVEL I regions, each of which is in turn subdivided into a whole number of NUTS LEVEL II regions and each NUTS LEVEL II region is subdivided into a whole number of NUTS LEVEL III regions. As EU concern with areas not derivable from the these three NUTS levels and especially with smaller territories (mountainous areas, disadvantaged agricultural areas, coastal zones, deprived urban areas) increased, smaller NUTS LEVEL IV and NUTS LEVEL V areas were also identified. At present however former NUTS LEVEL IV and 5 areas are classed as Local Administrative Units 1 and 2.

As the administrative systems in the different Member States differ quite significantly combining national territorial communities into an EU-wide system was far from straightforward. It was however the path that in the past was chosen most often: issues of data availability and regional policy implementation required that the NUTS nomenclature be based primarily on the institutional divisions currently in force in the Member States. One consequence of these differences is that in many Member States construction of the first three intra-Member State tiers permitted the use of only two levels of the administrative system and therefore required construction of a non-administrative NUTS Level.

The exceptions to the adaptation of NUTS classifications to existing administrative arrangements are mainly found in the new Member States in central and eastern Europe where the establishment of NUTS classifications was often accompanied by the top-down imposition of new sub-national administrative arrangements.

Until relatively recently the NUTS classification was changed as a result of the initiative of the statistical offices of the individual Member States, although subsequent steps in the procedure were largely determined by the way in which the classification was compiled. Any change in a national administrative tier used to establish a particular NUTS level saw an almost automatic change in the NUTS classification (Council of the European

Communities, 2003). Other changes such as the creation of new NUTS LEVEL II areas in the UK had to be examined in detail. In some of these cases negotiations with Member States were protracted and difficult (Council of the European Communities, 2003). The reasons why lay in the impreciseness of the statistical criteria and the room they left for manoeuvre in a situation where the change in classification might have an impact on eligibility for Structural Fund support.

In 2003 a reliance on 'gentlemen's agreements' between Member States and Eurostat to establish NUTS classifications came to an end with the approval of a NUTS Regulation. The Regulation calls for the use of objective criteria to define regions, the stability of the nomenclature (laying down clear rules for the management of change with a view to preventing changes in the classification during negotiations over the allocation of regional assistance) and comparability in the sizes of the populations of areas at each level of the hierarchy (see Table 44.1).

Assessing the NUTS classification

As indicated in the last section the administrative systems in the different Member States differ sharply. These differences reflect different decisions about the division of responsibilities, estimates of the population sizes required to meet responsibilities efficiently and effectively and distinct histories of sub-national governance. Creating a harmonized EU system of sub-national territorial communities was consequently an extremely problematic task.

Table 44.1 Threshold population sizes for NUTS LEVEL I, II and III areas

Level	Minimum	Maximum
NUTS LEVEL I	3 million	7 million
NUTS LEVEL II	800,000	3 million
NUTS LEVEL III	150,000	800,000

Source: EU (2003)

The reasons for the choice of national administrative arrangements as the foundation for the NUTS classification are absolutely clear: on the one hand data is produced for these entities at a Member State level; on the other hand sub-national administrations play a role in the design and implementation of EU-funded regional development programmes.

One consequence is the heterogeneity of NUTS regions. To some extent this problem derives from the fact that population is the only criterion for the allocation of national administrative and non-administrative areas to different levels of the NUTS hierarchy. Even in narrowly demographic terms however the areas vary very widely. The reason why is that mean size is used to match administrative tiers and non-administrative areas to particular NUTS levels, although in the case of non-administrative areas changes under the Regulation are only accepted if they reduce the degree of dispersion measured

by the standard deviation of the populations of areas at that level in the EU as a whole. Although this provision improves the situation, it is clear from Figure 44.1 that while the mean size of NUTS LEVEL II areas standing at 1,831,000 lies between the threshold values of 800,000 and 3 million, a substantial number of NUTS LEVEL II areas lie outside these limits. The smallest had a population of just 26,400 while the largest (Ile de France) had a population in excess of nearly 11.4 million.

A more fundamental problem arises from the fact that the features of important geographical distributions do not necessarily coincide with administrative boundaries: areas chosen in deciding on territorial breakdowns should ideally reflect the geographical distribution of the phenomena under investigation. In relation to many of the issues dealt with in Cohesion policy functional areas and in particular travel to work areas would make more scientific and policy sense. What is more the harmonized application of rules for

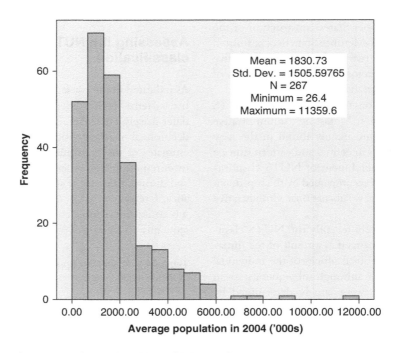

Figure 44.1 Average population of NUTS LEVEL II areas in 2004.
Source: Author's elaboration from Eurostat data

defining functional regions would ensure the international comparability of the regions in the individual Member States. Insofar as cohesion policy deals mainly with issues to do with the geography of economic activities and employment travel-to-work areas make sense. The difficulty is that if a number of other distinct subjects require analysis (access to schools, for example) the number of potential functional regionalizations increases.

As far as regional economic development is concerned travel-to-work areas have a strong rationale. One of the major disputes in the regional economic policy area concerns the extent to which differences in employment rates reflect 'demand-side' (differences in employment opportunities) or 'supply-side' (unemployed do not get jobs that exist) factors. In this context there is a significant difference between two types of area: areas with low levels of employment that are not within easy travelling distance of anywhere with a tight labour market; and areas with low employment rates that are within commuting distance of areas with tight labour markets. In areas of the first type that are a part of concentrations of travel-to-work areas (TTWAs) with low employment rates, demand for labour needs to be stimulated as if jobs are not created within the travel-to-work area concerned only with temporary or permanent migration affords an answer to low employments rates. In this case searching for TTWAs and in particular for concentrations of TTWAs with low employment rates plays a particularly important role in the diagnosis and design of regional policies. To this important consideration must be added another: areas defined as assisted areas should not be defined so narrowly as to cut off support from nearby functionally interdependent areas that are zones of potential growth. The use of administrative areas that are not also functional areas raises a number of particularly important difficulties in relation to one of the most important indicators used for EU regional policy purposes: Gross Domestic Product (GDP) per head.

The difficulty arises as GDP is usually measured by place of employment, whereas population is measured by place of residence. Measuring GDP by place of employment makes sense as regional policy is designed to augment the wealth-creating capacities of economically disadvantaged areas. If however GDP per head is calculated for administrative areas that are not at the same time travel-to-work areas the GDP per capita indicator will be seriously misleading either because the administrative areas exclude the places of employment of the people who live there or the places of residence of the people who work there. At present, for example, Inner London has by far the highest GDP per head of NUTS LEVEL II areas in the EU. This figure is artificially high. The reason why is that Inner London includes a very large number of places of employment for people who do not reside in Inner London, while relatively fewer residents work outside of Inner London. Inner London in other words excludes many of the suburbs of London and a vitally important commuter zone that lies beyond the limits of Greater London.

The importance of the use of a set of reasonably objective criteria in the definition of areas is also highlighted by the fact that measured indicators of disparities and therefore, for example, maps of aid eligibility designed to target disadvantaged areas depend upon the ways in which regions are created. Figure 44.2 (A) and (B) explores a simple hypothetical example (Dunford, 1993). Suppose a country is divided into 16 areas (A1, A2, ..., D4) with identical populations but different levels of GDP per head, and that these areas are grouped first into four and then into two regions (see Figure 44.2 (A)). The standard deviation expressed as a percentage of the mean decreases from 38.5 per cent (16 areas) to 10.6 (four areas: A1..B2, A3..B4, C1..D2 and C3..D4) and 3.22 (two areas: A1..B4 and C1..D4). It is important to note however that the choice of regional boundaries can affect the result. If in Figure 44.2 (A) the 16 areas are divided horizontally rather than vertically

	A	B	C	D
1	5	10	10	5
2	10	10	10	10
3	10	15	20	10
4	5	10	10	5

(A)

	A	B	C	D
10	5	10	10	5
11	10	10	10	10
12	10	15	20	10
13	5	10	10	5

(B)

Figure 44.2 Measured inequality and regional division.
Source: Author's own elaboration

into two groups (A1..D2 and A3..D4) the indicator falls to 9.67 instead of 3.22. Alternatively if four areas are identified in the manner indicated in Figure 44.2B the coefficient of variation will equal 24.7. Measured regional disparities depend, therefore, not just on the degree of spatial concentration of economic activities, but also on the regional division of the country: the number of areas and the choice of boundaries affect the measure of disparity, just as the delimitation of electoral districts shapes the outcome of elections. Clearly the ideal solution is to use functional economic areas which combine places of work with corresponding places of residence, although disparities between politically identified areas are significant as determinants of the resources over which different communities can exercise political leverage.

The pertinence of this simple example is demonstrated in practice by the ways in which changes in regional boundaries have in practice affected eligibility for EU regional aid. In the case of the Republic of Ireland, for example, there was just one NUTS LEVEL II area up to the point in time when the higher levels of GDP per capita in the more developed south and east were so high as to raise the Republic as a whole over the threshold for Objective 1 status (GDP per head less than 75 per cent of the EU average). At that point in time the Irish government negotiated a division of Ireland into two NUTS LEVEL II areas in the context of the Agenda 2000 agreement. The Agenda 2000 agreement was an agreement relating to the EU budget for the period 2000–06 that was finally reached at the Berlin summit in 1999. This agreement was profoundly shaped by the implications for in particular EU agricultural and structural policies of the soon-to-start eastern enlargement. Also in 1999 in Ireland two regional assemblies comprising nominated members of indirectly elected regional authorities were established. As a result of this division the Border, Midland and Western region retained Objective 1 status for the purpose of the Structural Funds for the period 2000–06. The Southern and Eastern region qualified for Structural Funds assistance under the phasing-out regime for Objective 1 until December 2005.

A more recent example relates to the German Land of Sachsen-Anhalt which was divided into three NUTS LEVEL II areas (Table 44.2). For the period 2007–13 Magdeburg and Dessau were identified as Convergence regions as their average GDP per capita at PPS in 2000–02 was less than 75 per cent of the EU15 average. Halle however was identified as a phasing-out area as its average per capita GDP at PPS exceeded 75 per cent. As Table 44.2 shows however Sachsen-Anhalt as a whole is small enough to qualify as a NUTS LEVEL II area. Had it in fact not been subdivided the whole of the area would have qualified for funding under the Convergence objective.

Table 44.2 Statistical indicators for Sachsen-Anhalt, 2000–04

	NUTS 2 regions			Sachsen-Anhalt
	Magdeburg	Halle	Dessau	
Population	1178061	835933	521421	2535415
Demographic change, 2000-03 (%)	−3.00	−3.90	−4.90	−3.70
Employees	476971	339396	195632	1011999
Employee change 2000-03 (%)	−2.80	−6.40	−4.30	−4.30
GDP change 2000-03 (%)	9.20	3.80	8.40	7.20
GDP per employee in 2004 (€)	44455	44459	44171	44402
GDP per capita at PPS in 2003 (EU25=100)	75.50	77.60	70.90	75.20
GDP per capita at PPS in 2000-02 (EU25=100)	72.27	75.07	65.99	74.54
Unemployment rate in 2003 (%)	17.6	21.3	21.3	19.6

Source: Statlisches Landesamt Sachsen-Anhalt, Eurostat, calculations of the Staatskanzlei Sachsen-Anhalt, Author's calculations

It is finally important to recognize that the generation of statistics for territorial entities involves a significant degree of information loss. These information losses are particularly problematic in situations such as the one depicted in Figure 44.3 (A, B, C, D and E) of non-correspondence of the administrative boundaries especially of relatively large territorial entities with one of the geographical distributions central to many policy areas. Figure 44.3(A) plots population density by LAU LEVEL II administrative units (Cubitt, 2007). Figure 44.3(B), 44.3(C) and 44.3(D) plot the same data by NUTS LEVEL III areas,

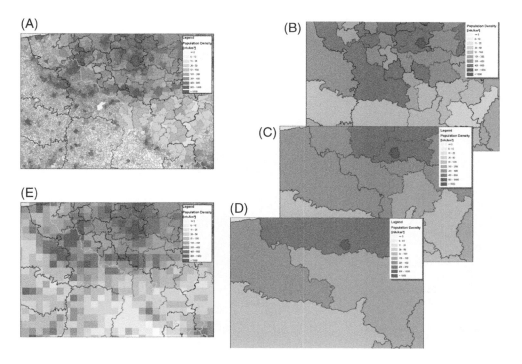

Figure 44.3 Geographies of population density.
Source: Adapted from Cubitt (2007)

NUTS LEVEL II areas and NUTS LEVEL I areas respectively. As this figure makes clear, movement up the NUTS hierarchy results in quite extraordinary losses of detail, while the average values for NUTS LEVEL I areas in particular can potentially be quite misleading. Figure 44.3(E) finally plots the same data using grid squares. The use of geo-referenced data of this kind provides a significantly superior representation of the underlying distribution than the NUTS administrative divisions.

To these considerations should finally be added the fact that development is at present defined in a relatively restricted manner. Wider definitions of the meaning of development require consideration of the distribution of wealth and income, the ways in which wealth and income are used and economic sustainability. In regional development studies some writers are calling for a more explicit consideration of foundational principles of development such as equity and justice (Pike *et al.*, 2007).

A wider concept of development implies a wider set of indicators and, since the scale and the extent of interdependence of different phenomena vary, greater complexity in the definition of appropriate areas.

Areas for regional development assistance in China

China differs from the European Union in that it is a sovereign state with, as the top decision-making institution, the system of the National People's Congress and, as the top executive institution, the State Council. The State Council exercises uniform leadership over a series of sub-national tiers of administration and determines the specific division of powers and responsibilities. China is divided into 22 provinces, five autonomous regions and four municipalities directly under the Central Government (Figure 44.4). The provinces and

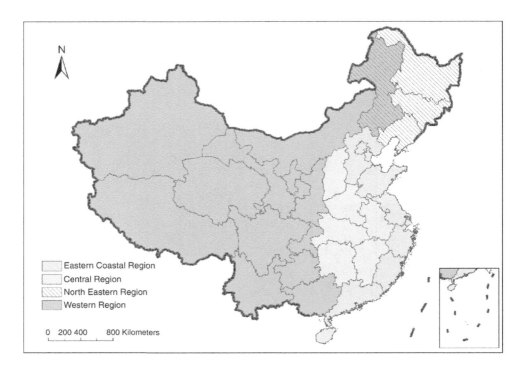

Figure 44.4 Administrative divisions in China and the four economic belts.
Source: Author's research

autonomous regions are divided into autonomous prefectures. Autonomous prefectures are divided into counties, autonomous counties and cities. The counties and autonomous counties are divided into townships, ethnic townships and towns. The municipalities directly under the Central Government and large cities in the provinces and autonomous regions are divided into districts and counties. The result is a four-level system, a three-level system if the prefectural level is absent and a two-level system where municipalities under the Central Government are divided only into districts (see http://www.china.org.cn/english/Political/28842.htm).

Chinese national regional development strategies have for the most part operated at a very large geographical scale. In the 1960s, China was divided into an Eastern, Central and Western region. After 1964 the priority was the development of a Third Front (or third line of defence) of strategic industries dispersed in mountainous areas in Sichuan, Guizhou and Yunnan in south-west China. Essentially the aim was to develop rail and other infrastructures and to develop strategic industries (such as chemical, metallurgical, energy, machine-making, electronics and aviation) away from the north-east of China and from the coast in the face of fears of conflict with the Soviet Union and with the United States which at that time was conducting a war in Vietnam. In the 1980s the orientation of development changed radically, yet these industries laid foundations for a more recent drive to develop western China.

The early 1970s saw the normalization of relations with the United States and a major change of course in China with the adoption of a strategy of modernization (the four modernizations) and in 1978 of reform and opening up. This change of course saw a remarkable acceleration in Chinese economic growth at the expense of a marked increase in geographical and social inequalities in part as externally oriented growth was concentrated in Special Economic Zones and open cities on the east coast of China.

Although the aim was to accelerate growth (or in Marxist terms develop the productive forces) permitting some areas and some people to get rich first, the 1980s nonetheless saw the first of a set of initiatives to address China's growing regional disparities and to support the restructuring and development of economically disadvantaged areas. Accordingly, the 'Sixth Five-year Plan' (1981–85) divided the whole country into coastal areas and hinterland. The 'Seventh Five-year Plan' put forward the concepts of 'eastern, central and western' regions. The 'Eighth Five-year Plan' envisaged strategic development trends for seven cross-provincial economic zones. The 'Ninth Five-year Plan' strengthened the financial, investment and policy supports to central and western regions. The 'Tenth Five-year Plan' put forward proposals for an overall plan for regional development, involving a 'great western development drive' (xibu da kaifa), the restructuring of old industries and industrial areas in north-eastern China and the rise of central China with coastal areas continuing to take the lead in development. (The Great Western Development Strategy was started in 2000. It covered the provinces of Gansu, Guizhou, Qinghai, Shaanxi, Sichuan, and Yunnan, five autonomous regions (Guangxi, Inner Mongolia, Ningxia, Tibet, and Xinjiang), and one municipality (Chongqing). This region contains 71.4 per cent of mainland China's area, but, as of the end of 2002, only 28.8 per cent of its population and, as of 2003, just 16.8 per cent of its total economic output. The programme involved investment in: infrastructure (transport, hydropower plants, energy and telecommunications), the enticement of foreign investment, increased ecological protection (such as reforestation), the promotion of education, and retention of talent flowing to richer provinces. As of 2006, a total of 1 trillion yuan had been spent building infrastructure in western China.

A largely similar regional division of China underpinned the balanced regional development strategy in the Eleventh Five-year Plan which called for development that reflects the carrying capacity of the environment and the development regional resource endowments, that addresses the weaknesses of disadvantaged areas, and that involves a clear zoning of economic activities, stronger interregional interaction, an equitable allocation of public services and reduced disparities in living standards. To these ends it called for: advancing the development of the Western Region, revitalizing north-east China and other old industrial bases, promoting the rise of the Central Region, Encouraging the Eastern Region to take a lead in development, and supporting the development of old revolutionary bases (the areas from where the Chinese Communist Party and the Red Army drew its strength in the period from the start of the Long March in 1934 to the Communist victory in 1948), ethnic minority areas and border areas.

Chinese regional development policies involve several types of action:

1 an investment policy under which, for example, the Central Government provides 29 per cent of resources for drinking water projects in the east and 63 per cent in the west;
2 a tax policy under which corporate income tax stands at 15 per cent in the west and 30 per cent in the east with until recently 15 per cent for multinational and other companies in Special Economic Zones) and where there are special value-added tax arrangements for north-east China and selected cities in central China;
3 a credit/loan policy under which disadvantaged areas get more long-term credit; and a tax transfer policy under which some formula-driven elements operate to the advantage of disadvantaged areas. The tax policy and investment policy area classifications differ.

Alongside successive regional development strategies spatial poverty reduction programmes were put in place. In 1994, 592 poverty counties were identified. A 2001 revision also identified 592 poverty counties (plus all 73 counties in Tibet) removing poverty counties in eight eastern provinces. These areas receive earmarked funds for enterprise support, construction and preferential loans and are given preferential treatment in the allocation of investment subsidies. In addition, a partnership system pairs each western province (except Tibet which is paired with all provinces) with an eastern province which is required to support poverty reduction programmes. To this spatial strategy the Eleventh Plan added a strategy for promoting the formation of priority development zones in part to move in the direction of a model of development that is more sustainable from an environmental point of view. Four classes of area were to be identified:

i) Optimized development zones: regions with high-density land development and a declining resource and environmental carrying capacity.
ii) Prioritized development zones: regions with relatively strong resource endowment and environmental carrying capacity as well as favourable conditions for the agglomeration of economic activities and people.
iii) Restricted development zones: regions with weak resource endowment and environmental carrying capacity, poor conditions for agglomeration of economic activities and people, and which are crucial to wider regional or national ecological security.
iv) Finally, prohibited development zones: legally established nature reserves.

These zones were to be identified through area classification exercises conducted first at a national level and subsequently at a provincial level. This classification raises many important issues. It raises demographic issues to do with the relocation of people, and the livelihoods that support them; issues to do with the household registration (*hukou*) system; industrial issues to do with the development of non-polluting industries in optimized, restricted and forbidden development areas; investment issues; environmental issues to do with different environmental regulations in different areas; and not least fiscal issues. On this last front, measures to restrict development were to prove extremely controversial due to the negative impact that they would have on sub-national government revenues in a period in which central government was asking sub-national administrations to invest more in health and education.

Most striking finally are the ways in which the evolution of regional policy thinking reflects the evolution of development models in China. Just as in the European Union regional policy where regional policy was redesigned to reflect more closely the economic growth-oriented goals of the Lisbon Agenda and the Sapir Report (Dunford, 2005), in China regional policy is changing in important ways to reflect the goal of harmonious development understood as social harmony and harmony with nature and will change further to reduce the degree of dependence of China on export-oriented growth.

Solidarity, cohesion and the allocation of financial resources in the EU

In order to achieve their strategic goals and to meet their responsibilities governments require financial resources. The aim of this section is to identify the ways in which in the European Union (EU) and in its constituent Member States financial resources are acquired and allocated in particular to activities relating to regional economic development. The EU is a union of sovereign nation states. The powers of the EU are those powers that the Member States agree to confer on it in order for the EU to achieve its objectives as set out in successive Treaties.

Competences that relate to territorial development are for the most part competences that are shared with its Member States and a set of sub-national, regional and local authorities.

The EU budget

In absolute terms the European Union (EU) budget is large. At present it stands at over €100 billion per year: in 2007 appropriations stood at €115.5 billion. As a share of EU income and public expenditure it is however small, standing at less than 1 per cent of Gross National Income (GNI) and at less than 2.5 per cent of public expenditure. As a share of GNI however it has recently decreased in size.

As in the past the most recent 2007–13 New Financial Framework was largely determined by national interests (Mrak and Rant, 2004). The reason why was that national interests expressed in terms of the global and partial (related to particular issues) net cash flows/net budgetary balances (NBB) gave rise to coalitions that corresponded very closely with the actual coalitions that shaped the negotiation of the budget. The underlying data are plotted in Figure 44.5. On the vertical axis is plotted each Member State's NBB defined as total expenditure allocated to a country less its total contributions comprising traditional own resources, the VAT source and the GNI source plus net receipts from the UK rebate. Net contributors have negative NBBs and net recipients positive NBBs. Each column also identifies partial NBBs defined as the net cash flows attributable to individual issues: Member State receipts from the issue minus Member State contributions to financing of that issue. In Figure 44.5 NBBs and partial NBBS are all expressed as shares of GNI.

These data suggest that new Member States and net recipient old Member States wanted high spending especially on the Common Agricultural and Cohesion policies,

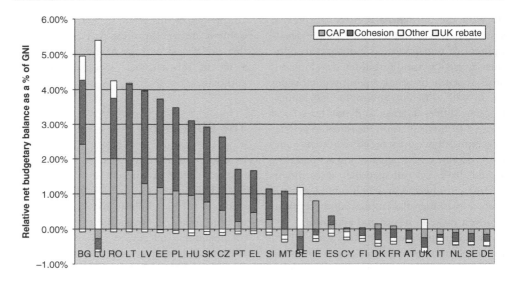

Figure 44.5 The 2007–13 new financial framework: net budgetary balances, partial budgetary balances and GNI.
Source: Author's elaboration from data in Mrak and Rant (2004)

old Member States wanted low spending especially on Cohesion policy, and Belgium and Luxembourg as well perhaps as the European Commission probably wanted high administrative spending. Mrak and Rant (2004) showed that the main drivers of the New Financial Framework stemmed from (1) the existence of strong and opposing coalitions that prevented major reductions in cohesion spending, (2) the ability of the Gang of Six to secure low overall spending and in the face of the retention of the October 2002 Franco-Germen agreement to extend the Common Agricultural Policy via a limited financial commitment to the Lisbon objectives.

The financial resources for Cohesion policy

As indicated in the last section Cohesion Policy was allocated €308,041 million in 2004 prices (€347,410 in current prices) for the period 2007–13. This sum was divided into a financial profile of annual allocations.

The new Cohesion Policy architecture identified three objectives and three financial instruments: a convergence objective; a regional competitiveness and employment objective; and, a European territorial cooperation objective; 81.4 per cent overall financial resources were allocated to the convergence objective 15.8 per cent to the regional competitiveness and convergence objective and 2.5 per cent to the European territorial cooperation objective.

In spite of the strong concentration of resources on convergence areas, aid intensity does not increase as relative national prosperity decreases. In Figure 44.6 Member States are ranked according to their GNI at PPS per head in 2003–5, while aggregate aid per capita is recorded on the vertical axis, using as a denominator national population figures. EU12 countries with the exception of the two newest Member States (Bulgaria and Romania) and Cyprus receive between €373 (Czech Republic) and €252 per head (Poland). As Figure 44.6 shows there is a clear tendency for aid per capita to increase at first as GNI per capita increases and only to

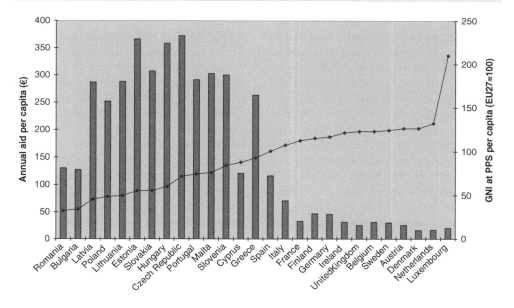

Figure 44.6 Aid per capita in 2007–13 (current prices) and GNI at PPS per head (EU27 = 100).

decline once GNI per capita reaches around 84 per cent (in the case of Slovenia) of the EU27 average.

If the population figures used in computing aid intensities relate to the populations resident in eligible areas (and not national population figures as in Figure 44.6) and the convergence, phasing-out, phasing-in and competitiveness and employment objectives are considered separately some striking additional results emerge. Average annual aid intensities indicate that annual aid per capita to convergence regions which stands at €184 in assisted areas is not far ahead of that for the phasing-out areas which receive €141. The phasing-in areas receive €82 per head per year, and the regional competitiveness and employment (RCE) areas receive €21. Also striking is the fact that amongst the convergence regions the highest aid intensities are for Portugal (€344) and Greece (€333). Of the new Member States the Czech Republic (€269) and Estonia (€239) do well. Romania and Bulgaria receive €84 and €81 respectively even though their per capita GNI at PPS stood at just 32.7 and 34.4 per cent of

the EU27 average compared with 71.8 per cent in the case of the Czech Republic. Estonia's GNI at PPS was lower at 55.6 per cent but was not as low as that of the two newest Member States. The aid intensity for Poland (€166) is close to that for the UK (€163) and Germany (€155).

Criteria for the allocation of financial resources

The financial allocations are the result of published and unpublished criteria that differ from one strand of policy to another. The outcomes however were not simply a result of the application of these criteria but reflected also a set of overarching constraints (Bachtler *et al.*, 2007: 24) and a series of compromises made in particular during European Council negotiations. Of these overarching constraints the most important was an absorption cap designed to restrict financial resources to a share of national Gross Domestic Product that the recipients could spend effectively. This cap is important mainly as it overrides mechanisms which allocate resources according to need and in accordance with the original principle of concentration of resources. Another factor driving down per capita Structural Fund flows to the lowest income Member States was the setting of the share of the Cohesion Fund for Member States that joined the Union on or after 1 May 2004 at one-third of their total financial allocation (Structural Funds plus Cohesion Fund). The effect of this constraint is to increase the relative importance of Cohesion Fund resources which in contrast to Structural Fund resources are confined to investments in transport and environmental infrastructures.

As already mentioned the underlying criteria vary from one strand of policy to another. Consider the case of the convergence objective. As is well known, areas eligible for the convergence objective are NUTS 2 areas whose per capita GDP at PPS is less than 75 per cent of the Union average. The allocation of resources for each Member State is the sum of the allocations for its individual eligible regions. The way in which regional allocations are initially derived centres on the so-called Berlin mechanism implemented in 2000–06. Three steps are involved. First, each region's population is multiplied by the difference between its GDP per capita measured at PPS and the EU25 average to derive a sum expressed in €. Second, the sum derived from the first step is multiplied by a relative prosperity coefficient reflecting the relative GNI at PPS of the Member State in which the eligible region is situated. As a result the sum is larger the lower regional GDP per capita and the lower is the relative prosperity of the Member State concerned. The third step involves the computation of an additional sum that reflects the existence of relatively high unemployment compared with other eligible areas. This sum is derived by multiplying the number of people out of work in that region as a result of the fact that the unemployment rate is in excess of the average unemployment rate in all EU

convergence regions by a premium of €700. If, for example, 1,000 people are out of work, the unemployment rate is 10 per cent and the average rate is 5 per cent, excess unemployment stands at 500 and the region would receive an additional €350,000.

The main driver of the allocation of resources is relative GDP per capita and relative GNI per capita. The unemployment driver however generates a quite different geographical distribution allocating resources in particular to a number of EU15 Member States (Italy, Germany, Spain and France). More strikingly the published indicative allocation of resources differs markedly from the outcome derivable from the application of this variant of the Berlin mechanism. The main reason why is that the resulting allocation of resources is inconsistent with the spending caps, and that the resources in excess of the caps that were initially allocated to low-income Member States are re-allocated.

Government finance in EU Member States

In 2007 the EU budget appropriations stood at €115.5 billion, and that as a share of EU income and public expenditure they stood at less than 1 per cent of GNI and at less than 2.5 per cent of public expenditure. It means that it is the Member States and sub-national tiers of national government that account for most European public expenditure. The aim of the first part of this section is to put some figures to these roles before attention is paid to some of the mechanisms for fiscal redistribution inside EU Member States.

In 2007 EU27 general government expenditure (excluding the expenditure of public corporations) stood at 45.8 per cent of GDP (EUROSTAT, 2008). Government revenues were equal to 44.9 per cent of GDP. For the EU15 expenditure stood at 46.1 per cent (0.8 per cent more than government revenue). This figure was a long way beneath the 1995 figure of 52.5 per cent.

Within the EU27 there are very wide variations in government expenditure per capita. In 2007 general government expenditure expressed in Euros and adjusted for Purchasing Power Parities (PPP) was highest (setting aside Luxembourg) in Sweden (16,465), Denmark (15,418), Austria (15,320), the Netherlands (14,907) and France (14,451). At the other end of the spectrum lie formerly Communist new Member States in eastern and central Europe. The lowest scores for Bulgaria (3,580) and Romania (3,723) are approximately 22 per cent of the figure for Sweden. Expressed in Euros (without the PPP adjustment) the range extended from 28,787 in Luxembourg and 21,104 in Denmark to 1,421 in Bulgaria and 2,083 in Romania. By far the most important contribution was made by central government which accounted for 25.1 per cent of EU27 GDP. States present in only four countries accounted for 4.2 per cent and local government for 11.2 per cent, although these figures differed substantially from one country to another.

National governance and fiscal equalization in the EU

As emphasized in the last section the Member States account for a large share of public expenditure, and are mainly responsible for a wide range of activities. One indication of the scale and scope of Member State activities is provided by the functional (as opposed to government departmental) analysis of UK public expenditure: in 2006–07 UK public expenditure amounted to 41.3 per cent of GDP. Social protection (13.4 per cent of GDP), health (7.1 per cent), education (5.5 per cent), general public services (3.6 per cent), economic affairs (2.9 per cent) and defence (2.4 per cent) were the most important areas of activity. Considered in its widest sense a number of these areas of expenditure play an important role in local and regional development.

In each Member State similar sets of responsibilities are divided up between national and sub-national tiers of government. Generally speaking sub-national government has sole or shared responsibilities for a wide but varying range of activities: land use planning, economic development, infrastructure provision, and the provision of a range of local services that may include education, health and employment.

The division of responsibilities across different tiers of government requires a corresponding allocation of financial resources such that all sub-national authorities can meet these responsibilities and in particular can provide citizens with largely comparable services at similar levels of overall taxation. If all tax revenues are collected centrally, resources can be allocated so as to secure equal service provision making allowance for differences in needs and costs through formula-driven methods of resource allocation that allocate more resources to areas with relatively high costs or greater needs.

If conversely some taxes are raised at a sub-national scale situations will arise in which there are mismatches between the revenue-raising capabilities of sub-national governments and the costs of providing similar services: some areas will have high tax revenues and low costs and others will have low tax revenues and high costs. In this situation ensuring that citizens receive comparable services at similar levels of taxation requires movement in the direction of fiscal equalization either through fiscal redistribution (horizontally across tiers of government or vertically from higher to lower tiers of government) or tax-sharing arrangements (where different tiers of government are entitled to fixed shares of specified taxes).

In EU Member States equalization measures of this kind serve at least to reduce these disparities. Some years ago Wishlade *et al.* (1996) estimated the size and impact of fiscal transfers in seven Member States (France, Germany, Italy, Portugal, Spain, Sweden and the UK). As this study showed, irrespective of whether a flow (in which regions is public money spent) or benefit concept (in which regions do the benefits of public expenditure accrue) of the distribution of expenditure is used, the richer regions in the eight countries studied transfer significant sums to the poorer regions. At an EU scale, however, whether a region is a part of an economically strong or an economically weak Member State makes a great difference: areas with similar levels of GDP per head are net recipients of public expenditure flows in rich countries such as Germany but net contributors in poorer countries such as Spain.

Finance for regional development in China

In China fiscal revenue is far smaller as a share of GDP than it is in EU Member States. As Figure 44.7 shows fiscal revenue declined from 30.1 per cent of GDP in 1978 to 10.3 per cent in 1995. After 1995 it rose to reach 18.4 per cent in 2006. Of course this figure underplays the role of the state in economic life as many assets and many enterprises are state-owned.

In China there are significant disparities in the resources available to sub-national authorities. An unequal distribution of revenue conflicts with principles of equal access to public services: sub-national governments are not able to finance basic public services such as education, medical care and social security. As Figure 44.8 shows in 2005 per capita fiscal revenue varied from RMB9957 in Shanghai to 1,202 in Anhui. These variations were a reflection of large variations in fiscal revenue (RMB7,980 in Shanghai to 435 in Tibet) that were not invariably rectified by transfers (RMB6,921 in Tibet to 521 in Fujian). Although there are very large per capita transfers to some provinces with little fiscal revenue there are also large positive transfers to relatively rich provincial level cities such as Shanghai and Beijing. This situation is a consequence of a number of features of the Chinese fiscal system.

As Figure 44.9 shows from 1979 onwards central government expenditure declined as a share of the total standing at around 30 per cent

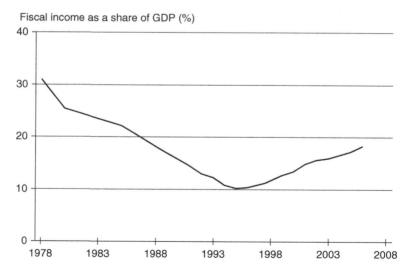

Figure 44.7 Fiscal revenue as a share of GDP, 1978–2006.
Source: Author's elaboration from People's Republic of China, National Bureau of Statistics. Note that figures for some years up to 1990 were interpolated

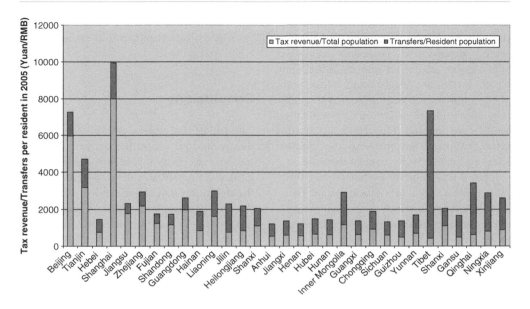

Figure 44.8 Fiscal revenue and fiscal transfers per inhabitant, 2005.
Source: Author's elaboration from People's Republic of China, National Bureau of Statistics

until 2003. The share of local government increased to reach in the order of 70 per cent. As a result of the introduction of a tax-sharing system in 1994 central government's share of total fiscal revenue rose from 22 per cent in 1993 to 52.8 per cent in 2006. As the division of responsibilities was not changed central government came to receive twice as much revenue as it spent, whereas local government received about two-thirds of what it spent.

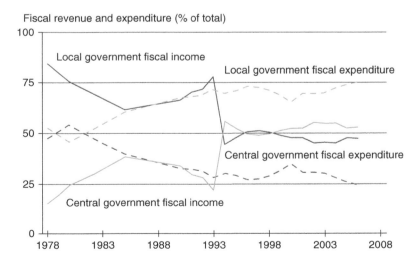

Figure 44.9 Fiscal income and expenditure in China.
Source: Author's elaboration from People's Republic of China, National Bureau of Statistics. Note that figures for some years up to 1990 were interpolated

In China there are five levels of government and five levels of public finance with the central government providing near-pure public goods and other responsibilities split across levels of government: nine years of compulsory education is provided mainly at a county level, while rural cooperative health care involves four levels up to the county. Central government expenditure accounts for 30–35 per cent of the total.

Central government revenues derive from 21 tax items. At a sub-national level there are 31 tax items of which the most important is a resource tax. Extra-budget income from, for example, land development accounts for one-third to one-half of local revenue. Alongside these two sets of tax items there are a number of tax-sharing items. An example is value-added tax of which 75 per cent goes to central government and 25 per cent to sub-national government.

The gap between sub-national government revenue and expenditure is covered by central government fiscal transfers although their contribution to fiscal equalization is limited. These transfers fall into three groups:

1. General transfers (33 per cent of the total) are mainly compensation for losses caused by the 1994 reform. Only 10 per cent of this transfer is in reality formula-based. In this case relative underdevelopment is considered with a national average of 60 per cent and, for example, 90 per cent for Tibet.
2. Specific transfers (33 per cent of the total) are divided into a first set of funds earmarked for service provision, and a second part which does not require match-funding comprising 210 vertically managed items whose allocation is based on precedent/quotas and not science; and
3. a tax rebate (33 per cent of the total) which is a legacy of 1994 reform and was designed to ensure that the revenue of sub-national governments did not fall. In addition, there are sub-national

inter-provincial transfers but these transfers are not unified into an integrated system.

Conclusions

The aim of this chapter was to consider two interconnected issues that generally receive too little attention in academic discussions of local and regional area development policies: the definition and classification of areas and the mechanisms and distributional consequences of financial resource allocation. Area development policies by definition involve the identification of geographical areas to which spatial policies will apply and the establishment of criteria determining the eligibility of different areas for different types of support. In this chapter I have shown how in the EU and in China administrative definitions of regions are the foundation for most area development policies. In the EU a set of rules have been established in an attempt to harmonize different national administrative systems. This NUTS system plays three important roles. First, it provided the framework for the development of harmonized regional statistics. Second, it served as the foundation for the socio-economic analyses of the EU regions. Third, it provides a framework for EU regional policy and in particular it is used in deciding on eligibility for regional aid: with the establishment of the Structural Funds the classification of areas eligible for support under Objective 1 or the Convergence objective was carried out for NUTS LEVEL II regions, while the classification of areas eligible under other priority objectives has involved the use of NUTS LEVEL II areas. In the Chinese case area development policies also rest on administrative divisions of the country. Although China has not developed a set of formal rules similar to those embodied in the NUTS system the different levels of the Chinese administrative system are roughly comparable with tiers of the NUTS system, although some levels of the Chinese system are subject to more rapid and frequent changes.

The reasons for the choice of national administrative arrangements as the foundation for area development policies are absolutely clear: on the one hand data are produced for administrative entities; on the other hand sub-national administrations play a role in the design and implementation of regional development programmes. Administrative areas are however especially in the EU heterogeneous. A more fundamental problem arises from the fact that the features of important geographical distributions do not necessarily coincide with administrative boundaries. In relation to many of the issues dealt with within development policy functional areas and in particular travel-to-work areas would make more scientific and policy sense. The importance of the use of a set of reasonably objective criteria in the definition of areas is also highlighted by the fact that measured indicators of disparities and therefore, for example, maps of aid eligibility designed to target disadvantages areas depend upon the ways in which regions are created.

As far as financial issues are concerned emphasis was placed on the importance of examining the geographical distribution of public finance considered as a whole. Generally speaking the per capita financial resources available to sub-national government should enable the uniform provision of public services. As such these resources should be roughly proportional to the population served with some allowance for variations in the costs of equal service provision due to variations in need and cost structures. Area development resources exist alongside and complement normal public service provision providing additional resources to deal with economic adjustment and economic development but are by comparison relatively small. In the EU case attention was paid mainly to EU area development policies. Equal service provision is a responsibility at present of Member States and involves the use of a variety of schemes for fiscal equalization. Equalization

occurs however only at a Member State level. At an EU level there are very wide disparities. In relation to resources for area development it was pointed out that aid for 2007–13 is not proportional to relative GNI. Although the underlying Berlin mechanism allocates most resources to the most disadvantaged areas capping mechanisms in particular result in a situation in which aid at first increases with GNI and only subsequently falls.

In the Chinese case large disparities in the availability of fiscal resources per capital were noted. Although the Chinese government compensates for the lack of financial resources in some provinces with very large transfers to areas in the west of China, it also supports politically powerful and economically advanced areas. An unequal distribution of resources is an impediment to the Chinese government's ambitions to improve health, education and social security provision. The importance of fiscal reform is accentuated by several other factors. One is the need to release savings and to expand the domestic market to underpin China's future economic growth. Another is the fact that the prevention or the restriction of development in ecologically sensitive areas will under the current fiscal system place limits on revenue generation in these areas. Additional transfers will be required therefore not just to enable sub-national authorities to meet their health, education and social security responsibilities but also to compensate these areas for ecological protection schemes that will improve environmental conditions not only in the areas affected but in other parts of China. As these considerations also indicate, finally, questions of the definition and financing of area development intersect in important ways with definitions of the meaning of development and the choices made with respect to development models.

References

Bachtler, J, Wishlade, F and Méndez, C. (2007) *New Budget, New Regulations, New Strategies:*

The 2006 Reform of EU Cohesion Policy, European Policy Research Paper, 63. Glasgow: European Policies Research Centre.

Commission of the European Communities (2007) Commission Regulation (EC) No. 105/2007 of 1 February 2007 amending the annexes to Regulation (EC) No. 1059/2003 of the European Parliament and of the Council on the establishment of a common classification of territorial units for statistics (NUTS).

Commission of the European Communities (2008) Commission Regulation (EC) No. 11/2008 of 8 January 2008 implementing Regulation (EC) No. 1059/2003 of the European Parliament and of the Council on the establishment of a common classification of territorial units for statistics (NUTS) on the transmission of the time series for the new regional breakdown.

Council of the European Communities (1993) Council Regulation (EEC) No. 2082/93 of 20 July 1993 amending Regulation (EEC) No. 4253/88 laying down provisions for implementing Regulation (EEC) No. 2052/88 as regards coordination of the activities of the different Structural Funds between themselves and with the operations of the European Investment Bank and other existing financial instruments. Official Journal L 193, 31/07/1993 P. 0020–0033.

Council of the European Communities (2003) Regulation (EC) No. 1059/2003 of the European Parliament and of the Council of 26 May 2003 on the establishment of a common classification of territorial units for statistics (NUTS). Official Journal of the European Union L154/1. 21/6/2003.

Cubitt, R. (2007) *European Regional Classification, Statistics and Geography*, Second High-level EU China Seminar, European Union Open Days, Brussels, 8–9 October.

Dulong, R. (1975) *La question bretonne*, Paris: Armand Colin.

Dulong, R. (1976) 'La crise du rapport Etat/société locale vue au travers de la politique régionale', in Nicos Poulantzas (ed.) *Le crise de l'Etat*, Paris: Presses Universitaires de France, 209–232.

Dulong, R. (1978) *Les régions, l'état et la société locale*, Paris: Presses Universitaires de France.

Dunford, M. (1993) 'Regional disparities in the European Community: evidence from the REGIO databank', *Regional Studies*, 27(8): 727–43.

Dunford, M. (2005) 'Growth, inequality and cohesion: a comment on the Sapir Report', *Regional Studies*, 39(7): 972–978.

Dunford, M. (2010a) 'Area definition and classification: the case of the European Union', in Graham Meadows and Wang Yiming, *Chinese and European Cohesion and Regional Development Policies*, Brussels: European Commission.

Dunford, Michael (2010b) 'Financing solidarity: matching resources and responsibilities through the budget for European Cohesion Policy and Member State financial arrangement', in Graham Meadows and Wang Yiming, *Chinese and European Cohesion and Regional Development Policies*, Brussels: European Commission.

European Parliament and Council of the European Communities (2005) Regulation (EC) No. 1888/2005 of the European Parliament and of the Council of 26 October 2005 amending Regulation (EC) No. 1059/2003 on the establishment of a common classification of territorial units for statistics (NUTS) by reason of the accession of the Czech Republic, Estonia, Cyprus, Latvia, Lithuania, Hungary, Malta, Poland, Slovenia and Slovakia to the European Union.

European Parliament and Council of the European Communities (2008) Regulation (EC) No. 176/2008 of the European Parliament and of the Council of 20 February 2008 amending Regulation (EC) No. 1059/2003 on the establishment of a common classification of territorial units for statistics (NUTS) by reason of the accession of Bulgaria and Romania to the European Union.

EUROSTAT (2008) *Government Finance Statistics*, Luxembourg: Office for Official Publications of the European Communities.

Mrak, M and Rant, V (2004) Financial perspective 2007–2013: domination of national interest. http://ec.europa.eu/dgs/policy_advisers/conference_docs/mrak_m_rant_dom_national_interests.pdf.

Parr, J. (2007) 'On the spatial structure of administration', *Environment and Planning A*, 39(5): 1255–1268.

Pike, A. (2007) 'Editorial: whither Regional Studies?', *Regional Studies*, 41(9): 1143–1148.

Pike, A., Rodríguez-Pose, A. and Tomaney, J. (2007) 'What kind of local and regional development and for whom?', *Regional Studies*, 41(9): 1253–1269.

Wishlade, F., Yuill, D., Taylor, S., Davezies, L., Nicot, B.H. and Prud'homme, R. (1996) *Economic and Social Cohesion in the European Union: the Impact of Member States' Own Policies*, Rapport définitive à la Commission Européenne (DG XVI), Glasgow: European Policies Research Centre.

Wrigley, E.A. (1965) 'Changes in the philosophy of geography', in Peter Haggett and Richard J.

Chorley (eds) *Frontiers in Geographical Teaching*, London: Methuen, 3–20.

Fan, C.C. (2001) 'The political economy uneven development: the case of China', *Progress in Human Geography*, 25(3): 517–519.

Further reading

Fan, C.C. (1995) "Of belts and ladders: state policy and uneven regional development in post-Mao China", *Annals of the Association of American Geographers*, 85(3): 421–449.

Section VII

Reflections and futures

45

The language of local and regional development

Phillip O'Neill

Introduction

Novel theoretical vocabularies infuse people's very beliefs and social practices. Along with theoretical redescriptions go practical effects such as changed views about the object of inquiry, altered practices of study, and the establishment of new social groupings and institutions.

(Cutler 1997: 4; cited by
Barnes 2001b: 548)

It should be obvious that there is nothing like an economy out there, unless and until men [*sic*] construct such an object.

(Louis Dumont 1997: 24;
cited by Barnes 1998: 99)

I like the fact that both language and the region are indeterminate devices. Language is a choice among an endless list of words and combinations of words and symbols. Similarly, a region is a choice of the way we represent the world we live in. When we write from a regional perspective we create a way of viewing the world for a particular purpose, and there is a tradition in this. Wishart (2004)

shows how we have used natural regions to present the world as organised into tracts of land based on physical characteristics such as climate; how we have used nodal regions to show the role of central places in providing commercial services to their hinterlands; administrative regions to show how institutions can divide the world politically or bureaucratically; and vernacular or cultural regions for showing how romantic imaginations of people can coincide with distinct bio-physical landscapes.

Regionalising our world, though, is not a dispassionate act of convenience or special interest. When we write regions onto our world we are effectively assigning to it our spatial imaginaries, which are the calculations and desires that we have of, and for, our world. Jon Murdoch (2006) explains how our spatial imaginaries are enacted by our spatial deliberations and performances such as through our planning activities, our fiscal spending patterns and through infrastructure provision. In this way, spatial imaginaries are our way of choosing order and sequence from the spatial menu available to us. Murdoch calls this a process of building governmentalities into that complex set of interacting entities that we summarise with the word 'space'. Thus Murdoch sees two things happening when we create spatial imaginaries: first, we "*select* the spatial attributes thought to be of most significance" in our interaction with the world; and, second, we intervene "*in* space on the basis of this selection" (2006: 156, emphasis in original). Murdoch's point is important to this chapter. It advises us that regionalising our world is more than a convenient tidying-up of a world that is a bit messy. Rather it is an imposition of a range of ordering desires to create spatial formations that determine human activity. As such, regionalising our world is a powerful act that warrants raised awareness.

The purpose of this chapter, then, is to explore the intriguing relationship between language and region by focusing on the way language and its devices drive the ways we mobilise the idea of regional development. The chapter commences with some basic views of the role of language in framing our view of the region as a economic entity. This is followed by three case studies of how language has been used to represent the regional economy in the last half century: first, as a space where neo-classical economic logics drive human activity; second, as a site where income and expenditure flows can be aggregated into discrete Keynesian entities; and, third, drawing on the Marxist language of historical materialism, as class-based building blocks, or localities. The chapter concludes with observations of emerging languages of regional development and an argument for language consciousness as a prerequisite for desirable regional development outcomes.

The role of language

The approach taken in this chapter is post-structuralist, meaning the adoption of a view that we live unavoidably in a language-encased and therefore a language-enabled world. The approach is guided in general by Jon Murdoch (2006) and by the long list of works by Norman Fairclough and Bob Jessop who have systematically joined the study of

language with the study of society and its politics to show how deeper understandings of our world are possible. The approach to language in this chapter follows closely an approach that Fairclough has termed the critical discourse analysis approach, or CDA. As well, in relation to regional development questions, the chapter draws heavily on the work of Trevor Barnes, one of human geography's leading analysts of the role of language in the development of geographical thought.

What does language enable?

A first understanding of the role of language is that it sets up the tasks at hand. Different language selections enable different types of regional analysis. Hence to describe a region we draw on unique words and language structures to produce a compendium of facts and knowledge. For example, we compose language in a particular way when we analyse the dynamism of a region to show changes in industrial sectors through time. We choose a different portfolio of language to build abstract understandings and models of regional development processes. And we choose differently again for policy language that can justify, for example, certain taxation, expenditure or regulatory interventions on behalf of a region.

More than words are used in each of these types of regional analysis. There are also maps, diagrams, tables of numbers and calculations, mathematical equations and statistical indicators. These are also language devices, dependent on unique symbols in carrying meaning to an audience. Throughout this chapter all these devices are understood to be part of what we call language.

Language enables five things for understanding regional development. *First*, it makes informed observation possible. Language – words, numbers, symbols, images – brings an otherwise disconnected list of unnamed landscape items into common understanding (see Fairclough 2003). Language is a social agreement on how to name the things we are talking about: a mountain, a motorway, an abandoned factory site. Language also helps us group items into useful categories: men and women, employed and unemployed, revenue and expenditure. These are simple functions of language, naming and classifying; yet they draw attention to our inability to say anything at all about our world when a word to capture the presence of a thing or category of things is unavailable or in dispute (see Gottdiener 1995).

Second, language drives analysis. Language sets up the idea of the region as having worth or value, gives a way of expressing this worth such as through measurement or comparison, and guides the monitoring of changes through time such as by providing a way of talking about time and of standardising regional conditions from one moment or period of time to another. Language also guides us in depicting a region's strength, its vulnerability and its stability. And language provides a way of showing a region's connections and the ways these might produce strength and autonomy, or dependence. Often these notions of strength and connection depend on the use of language metaphors, a language tactic we explore in the next section.

Third, language guides the way we use abstractions, though we mostly do this subconsciously since language itself is a process of abstraction, a thought event where we convert an observation, thought or feeling into a symbol (a written word, an equation or an image) or an utterance (a spoken word). The arrangement of letters that make up the words 'thermal power station', for instance, converts a massive industrial installation with coal stockpiles covering many hectares into a small set of letters on a page capable of conveying the same meaning to the reader that would be conveyed by a direct viewing of the power station in reality.

But language also enables the assembly of more complex abstractions. The world can be depicted as a human or natural system,

for example, only through the device of language. The Chicago School's powerful and enduring representation of the city by a concentric zone model, for instance, converted observations of a growing and decaying mid-western US city in the 1920s into a template for understanding the dynamism of cities worldwide. Language enables abstract generalisations. For example, language enables us to invent the idea of inequality to describe compounded differences in income, education and employment across groups of households, and to make judgements about the desirability of these differences.

Fourth, language enables us to express our feelings about a region, to imagine something else, a different state of affairs under different imagined conditions; to chose alternative spatial imaginaries. In other words, language provides the opportunity for normative thinking and judgments. Such thinking capacity opens regional analysis to political debate about the desirability of what is going on in a region and what possibilities there are for change (see Barnes 2001b).

Fifth, language enables us to provide relative fixity to relationships between time and space. Fairclough (2003, esp. p. 151), citing Harvey (1996), shows that while space and time are central concepts in society and societal analysis, they are also social constructs. Through language constructions, space and time become core categories in locating conditions and events, showing how they are changing, positioning people's reactions to them, and creating the parameters for contest, conflict and resolution. Obviously, then, space and time are key language-based concepts for the study of regions and pivotal to how we understand regional change and development.

In summary, then, language-consciousness is vital to effective regional analysis. As Nigel Thrift (1990) demonstrates, language establishes and drives everything that can said about the region, what the region is, what the region is composed of, why the region is an important scale of areal analysis and the nature of our analytical and policy aspirations.

Features of language that deserve attention

Barnes (for example, in Barnes and Duncan 1992) and Fairclough (especially 1992, 1995, 2003) have shown the importance of a language self-consciousness in regional analysis writing and, therefore, of the need for an understanding of basic linguistics and of the need for scholars to acquire the basic skills of language analysis. We now turn to a brief discussion of the features of language helpful in developing a language self-consciousness.

We start with the basic unit of language, the word. A word is an utterance recordable as a simple collection of letters which represent a word as a symbol or sign. A word thus refers to an object or an idea, the thing that is being signified by the sign. The signifier–signified link drives linguistic study, while the evaluation of the permanence of signifier–signified relationships is at the heart of the post-structuralist debate (see Gottdiener 1995).

Of course, words are usually delivered in sentences so that their meaning can be enhanced by being surrounded by other words. The words that are chosen and the way they are grouped and presented vary according to different contexts. Context means that both the selection of words and the meaning of these words vary according to who is the composer (the speaker or writer) and who is the audience (the readers or listeners), as you would know.

What I seek to emphasise here is that words are delivered through language structures that either systematically reproduce ways of thinking and understanding, or else challenge ways of thinking and understanding. This stabilisation or unsettling of meaning is fundamental to the processes of scholarship about regions. As we see in the case studies of regional development below, any approach to regional development has a set of language expressions and devices that are stabilised by their being agreed on by a user community; meaning that research practice lives within a stable set of pre-existing practices.

Barnes depicts the language within such set or stable practices as 'dead' language. Not that Barnes is deriding the use of dead language. Rather he notes that when a new approach to, say, regional analysis is being developed, there is conflict between the ideas encased in the language forms of the pre-existing or dead language of analysis and the ideas being developed by the new or alternative analysis. For the new ideas to become ascendant, by definition they must be propelled by a language that is more or less new. Prosaically, Trevor Barnes argues that the development of new ideas about the world involves a "redescription of the world in terms of novel vocabularies" (2001a: 164, citing Culler 1997). In other words, the language which postures as a replacement language of analysis is a living language, alive to new ideas and therefore to new ways of expressing these ideas.

There are many ways that language stabilises in sets of words that carry agreed meanings. Small groups of words in a pattern, so-called 'figures of speech' or 'common expressions', are known technically as 'tropes'. A trope is an important device in regional analysis. Most regional development concepts are expressed as tropes: the rate of economic growth, labour force participation rate, environmental sustainability, regulatory environment, industrial cluster, and so on.

More powerful and more complex than tropes are metaphors. Metaphors carry meaning across otherwise stable language worlds. They perform descriptive, comparative, explanatory and judgement roles. Technically, a metaphor is a figure of speech that carries an idea into a new domain through juxtaposing separate things with similar characteristics. A common metaphor in economic development is the biological metaphor of the human body and its development. A region might be described as being in a youthful, adult or mature stage of development, its progress monitored by growth rates, its component relations describable as its internal metabolism, its money flows seen as having circulatory properties, while periods of depression are seen to need external injections, and so on.

Barnes' work on metaphor and economic geography over many years shows the impossibility of conceiving the region as an economic entity without resorting to the adoption and stylisation of language metaphors in building our representations and, therefore, our understanding of the real world we seek to understand and change. In other words, metaphors are our pathway to shift from observation to theorisation (see Barnes 1991, esp. p. 112). The adoption of new ways to do regional analysis, then, involves the adoption of new metaphors as part of taking on new words and language structures. Emphatically, Barnes and Duncan (1992: 11) see that new metaphors "are the jolt, the *frisson*, that makes us see the world in a different way ... [M]etaphors create new angles on the world ... [and then] they gradually acquire a habitual use."

Barnes' analysis of metaphor, and his attention to language consciousness more generally, show how language drives our understanding of regions, leads the development of political concerns about regional performance, guides (or limits) the exploration of alternative regional economic pathways, and fosters new planning strategies. The way we talk about regions, from day-to-day conversations through to sophisticated academic analysis, is simultaneously language-limited and language-enabled. In the case of the metaphors deployed in all this talk we can see how metaphors that have become common and used uncritically – and therefore naturalised or dead – can produce unintended, uniform and uncritical decisions and actions. Without language consciousness, we become the slave of the defunct metaphor-maker, warn Barnes and Duncan (1992: 62).

Of course, beyond an understanding of trope and metaphor, there is a vast range of linguistic understandings and analytical skills for building a language-informed approach to regional analysis. Fairclough (esp. 1992 and 2003) provides a comprehensive guide to the field. Beyond words, expressions and metaphors, Fairclough (1992) identifies three other areas for language consciousness. One is the understanding of the power of language's structure and form; that the meaning language carries is tied into a writer's or speaker's language format and approach. Thus, when a language-user chooses between narrative, analytical, inferential or deductive approaches to talk about a region, this requires the selection of a matching vocabulary, metaphorical base, logical sequence and engagement strategy. A second language understanding advanced by Fairclough is the role of context, being the situation where language is authored and targeted, and the place for discursive practices to be enacted. Hence a political speech to a constituent audience about regional disadvantage will contain markedly different language to the language chosen for an academic journal, and to that written by a consultant in a report to a local government authority. A third area of understanding of the social practices of language, especially the reflexivity of language, is the idea that language development is inseparable from the triangulated relationship between author, audience and society. As much as an author might try to ignore these relationships, authorship is always overdetermined by the immanence of audience and society. The idea that authorship is actually negotiated with its audience is developed in the body of work emanating from the Russian Bakhtin writers' group, an early twentieth-century group of linguists and writers which explored the relationship between the act of authorship and the act of communication, the anticipated conversation to come (see Brandist 2002). This awareness is captured by the concept of *dialogism*, being the idea that all language is reducible to utterances that are part of a wider audience dialogue.

Clearly there is much to be conscious of in authoring for a regional development purpose. However, individual authors rarely develop their own sets of vocabularies, expressions, metaphors and language structures. Authors tend to belong to schools of thought, akin to what Kuhn (1962) called 'paradigms', or groups of work that share common research motivations (often including both research questions and political ideologies), analytical assumptions, investigative strategies (or epistemologies) and anticipated audiences. Three of these schools – neo-classical, Keynesian and localities – are now examined as case studies to demonstrate how language underpinned their development and mobilisation.

Case studies of language and regional development

Case study of neo-classical models of regional development

The neo-classical view of the region remains a major influence on the study of local and regional development. Perhaps as a consequence, the analysis and critique of the neo-classical approach has been a major theme of Barnes' prolific writings; and once again we draw heavily on Barnes' work in this section. The lineage of the neo-classical tradition in regional development studies is rather clear and simple (see Barnes 2001a). The neo-classical approach to the region coalesced in the 1950s with a concentration on applied economic theory and modelling. The timing here is significant because the development of the neo-classical approach cannot be isolated from the post-Second World War surge in the grand project of modernity underpinned by widespread acceptance of the idea that the application of rational, scientific-based knowledge to the management of human affairs could produce unproblematic and universally shared advances in the human condition. The neo-classical approach was thus, dialogically, propelled by scientifically derived understandings and received by a scientifically enthused audience.

Central to the rise of the neo-classical treatment of the region in the 1950s was the development of the discipline of regional science by economist Walter Isard. Central to Isard's work was the resuscitation of nineteenth-century German spatial imaginaries, specifically of a spatial economy underpinned by hierarchies of towns and cities, with patterns of rural land use and industrial investments explainable by simple, reproducible logics. Barnes (2003b, 2004) shows the links between Isard's seminal volume *Location and Space Economy* (1956) and the work of his fellow economists at MIT, especially Paul Samuelson. Barnes then traces Isard's work, and thus the new language of regional analysis, through the creation of the University of Pennsylvania's Department of Regional Science, its first PhD graduate William Alonso, the rise worldwide of the regional science discipline, and the incorporation of its work into regional policy and practitioner practices. While regional science as an identifiable discipline has declined markedly over the last three decades, regional science technologies endure in the toolboxes of regional development practitioners, for example, as the basis for calculating location efficiencies in GIS distance minimisation models, and in the spatial imaginaries of new economic geographers such as Paul Krugman and Masahisa Fujita within the economics discipline, albeit on its margins.

Features of the neo-classical approach

Barnes (1987) shows how early regional economic theories accepted naturally, as much as uncritically, neo-classical approaches to economy. The inclusion of a spatial dimension was designed to display how ordered, utility-maximising human behaviours played out on a relatively unproblematic a-social spatial surface. Subsequently, social theorists dubbed the rational spatial player 'economic man' or, humorously, *homo economicus*. Citing Olsson and Gale (1968: 229), Barnes (1987: 301) identifies the analytical ease of playing with a predictable human population, noting that "the players in the spatial economic game are blessed with the attributes of economic man", and so behave rationally and predictably.

The starting point for neo-classical spatial analysis is the construction of a spatialised economic surface. There are four famous historical spatial constructions of the domain of *homo economicus* (Figure 45.1). The first is Johann Heinrich von Thünen's concentric model of land use contained in his 1826 manuscript *The Isolated State*. This was the first published demonstration of neo-economics in a formal spatial setting. Von Thünen used rent theory to show how the occupancy of rural land nearer a town or city depends on the user's capacity to extract high rates of returns per square metre of land compared to the land productivity of competing users. Barnes (2003a) shows how von Thünen used geometry, relational algebra and calculus to construct a surface of possibilities for maximising economic returns, somewhat anticipating neo-classical marginal economics by half a century. The methodology pioneered what later became standard neo-classical model-making: commence with abstract assumptions that remove spatial contingency, and then progressively relax them to show the effect of movements in individual variables.

The second iconic neo-classical spatial model is Alfred Weber's location triangle, published in his *Theory of the Location of Industries* in 1909. The triangle shows the choices available to industrial investors if they are motivated solely by transportation cost minimisation. Weber (1929, see Barnes 2003a) extended von Thünen's analysis of rural land use into models of industrial location. Again, though, it was "a projection of pure economics into the spatial domain" (2003a: 78). Yet, intriguingly, its purpose was something more than a distillation of real life into a "a disembodied set of logico-mathematical procedures and diagrams" (Barnes 2003: 78). Barnes reveals how Weber sought to expose the "cultural aspects of modern capitalism" and therefore to expose it as something more

than "purely economic". Weber's strategy involved deploying the extant language and analytical techniques of neo-classicism. Ironically, Weber's heritage is seen as his contribution to a neo-classical spatial imaginary rather than to its repudiation.

Apparently the work of August Lösch is similarly misinterpreted. Barnes (1987) shows how Lösch extended Weber's analysis through his 1954 book *The Economics of Location*. The book showed how "spatial economic phenomena could be expressed in an explicitly abstract, formal, and rationalist vocabulary and directly connected to the empirical world" (1954: 546). Lösch's work continued the evolution of regional science as a law-seeking enterprise, the discovery of abstractions and generalisation that played across space irrespective of any local bumpy bits. Funnily, though, Lösch's construction of an idealised spatial surface was his way of demonstrating and explaining the idiosyncrasies of the real world rather then asserting the presence of the ideal in actuality. Perhaps this intention derived from Lösch being a student of heterodox economist Joseph Schumpeter, always one for elevating the contingency of real human behaviour as a prime economic force. Barnes (2003a: 81) quotes Derek Gregory (1994: 58):

> Lösch wanted to disclose, to make visible, the systematic order or a rational economic landscape – what he [Lösch] called "the rational and therefore natural order" – because he was convinced that such a demonstration held out the prospect of domesticating the "illogical, irregular, lawless" forces that ravage [a] chaotic reality.

In other words, Lösch sought to construct a spatial order in order to determine how the chaos of the observed world could be bettered; showing in Barnes' (2003a: 81) terms, a preference for a "logically constructed landscape" over "messy real places". As with Weber, this purpose was largely lost in the subsequent use of Lösch's work.

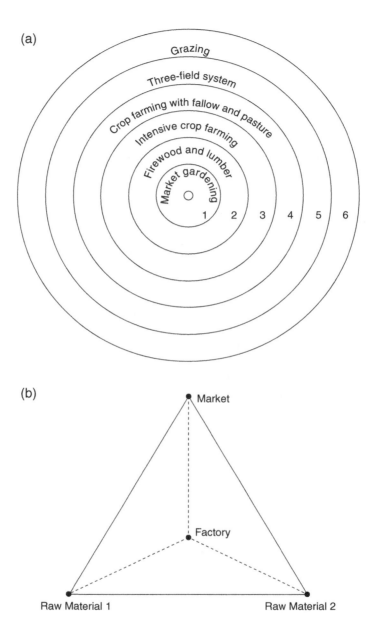

(a)

Grazing

Three-field system

Crop farming with fallow and pasture

Intensive crop farming

Firewood and lumber

Market gardening

1 2 3 4 5 6

(b)

Market

Factory

Raw Material 1   Raw Material 2

Figure 45.1 Neo-classical spatial analysis models
a) Von Thünen's concentric land use model
b) Weber's location triangle

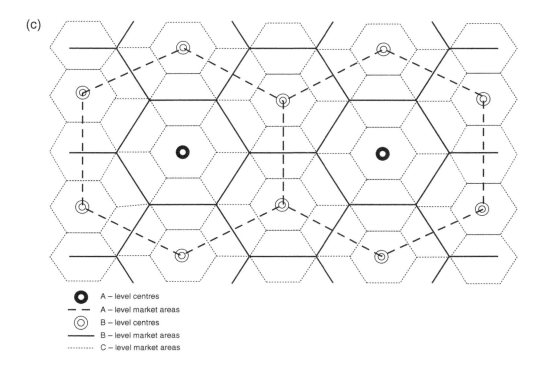

(c)

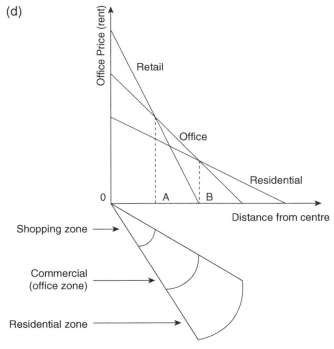

(d)

Shopping zone →

Commercial
(office zone) →

Residential zone →

Figure 45.1 Continued

c) Christaller's Central Place theory

d) Alonoso's bid-rent model of urban land use

Source: Adapted from Alonso (1964) Christaller (1993) Lösch (1954) Von Thünen (1996)

559

In any event, Barnes stresses that what was made of Lösch's work (say, by Berry and others) wasn't determined only by its language but by the beliefs and social practices that framed its reading. The two – language, and beliefs and social practices – proceed hand in glove, dialogically. In this sense, Lösch's work was very much part of what we now call a modernist view of the world, a "theoretical redescription" (Barnes 2001b: 548), taking a complex, unevenly composed world and recomposing it as a stylised space of rational predictable behaviour with, crucially, a process of "expressing the subject matter at hand in terms of a new vocabulary and syntax" (2001b: 548).

The third iconic spatial model is from Walter Christaller's 1933 dissertation *The Central Place in Southern Germany*. In this enduring work Christaller represented the settlement pattern of his home region as a geometric distribution of differently sized towns and cities based on the relative capacity of their retailers to attract consumption spending from households spread across a featureless plain. Christaller's neatly arranged set of nested hexagons has adorned geography and planning textbooks and lecture rooms ever since, the elegance of the representation at least as enticing as the power of any explanation on offer.

Similar figurative elegance can be found in William Alonso's bid-rent model of land use in a city. Alonso's (1964) urban land use theory sees the geographical location pattern of a city as derived from the opportunities householders have for maximising utility across "one-dimensional Euclidean space" (Barnes 1989: 305). In other words, the models of Christaller, Lösch and von Thünen imagined the geographical landscape as a set of "spatial opportunities" (1989: 306) to be surveyed by rational actors in pursuit of commercial activity. Says Barnes,

> In summary, neo-classical economic geographers assume that beneath the heterogeneous economic landscape lies a more fundamental variable, economic rationality…[such that] the extreme, geographical relationship among places, and the internal arrangement within them, all get reduced to the single logic of rational choice. Geographical diversity and complexity are thus explained away.
>
> (Barnes 1987: 32)

It is important to understand that this elimination of diversity and complexity is bound up in the language approaches of the neo-classical scholars – which we call their semiosis (see Fairclough 2003) – especially in the way they used the languages of mathematics and geometry and in the way they approached the task of theory-building. We now turn to an analysis of these language approaches.

The neo-classical approaches described above have four common features. *First*, as explained by Barnes (1989), they employ Cartesian perspectives. In other words, the neo-classical economic geographers reduced the earth's surface to a measurable grid of x and y coordinates where the location of human activity was determined by the solution of linear equations relating, for example, land use intensity to distance from a city centre; and commercial pull to population size and distance from competing centres. Non-linear perspectives and behaviours other than economic rationalist behaviours were ignored. As Barnes observes (2001b: 560), it was an approach that reflected a belief "that the economic landscape was fundamentally ordered and could be grasped all on a … sheet of paper" leading, according to Barnes (1989: 299), to an "emaciated view of place".

Second, the neo-classical approaches used the universalising languages of mathematics, especially relational algebra, and of statistics. On one hand this gave the neo-classical models the appearance of certainty; while, on the other, made the world's economic geography seem as if it were determined by a small number of knowable, measurable variables. Thus, as Barnes (1989) points out, an embrace of mathematics steered attention towards the enunciation of general principles without the need for attention to spatial or temporal subtleties. Likewise, any exploration of regional data was for the verification of abstract spatial principles rather than for their discovery.

Importantly, the language strategies of these neo-classical approaches shielded their proponents from unsettling observations and counter-logics. Two periods of history are important here. One is the broadening of the application of mathematics and geometry to fields of scientific inquiry in the nineteenth and early twentieth century. Regional economics was obviously caught up in this. The other is the quantitative revolution in the social sciences during the 1960s when rapidly expanding computing capacities magnified the power of researchers to manipulate large datasets. Regional economics and its regional science brother thus became infused with equations, graphs and numbers.

And then paralleling the quantitative revolution was the appropriation, often uncritically, of models and metaphors from the natural and related sciences. Barnes observes that:

> From physics emerged gravity and later entropy-maximising models; from sociology and land economics came models of land use, social physics, including the rank-size rule, and urban factorial ecology; and from geometry came network and graph theory and the analysis of topological forms that were incorporated into transportation studies:
>
> (Barnes 2003a: 84, citing Pooler 1977)

And Barnes adds that, "Marking all these different theoretical ventures was the emphasis on conceptual precision, deductive logic and analytical rigour, that is, rationalism"

(Barnes 2003a: 84), emphasising (2003a: 91) that mathematics in particular offered "an ineluctable principle that would guarantee the truth" (2003a: 91).

Third, the neo-classical spatial modellers used utility-maximising, *homo economicus* assumptions, taking these uncritically from their neo-classical economist colleagues. As noted above, space was seen only as a conceptual dimension onto which the predictable economic behaviours of humans could be mapped. Moreover the humans involved were impossibly rational, possessing complete information and making decisions solely to maximise their personal circumstances, which everyone did identically. The field of choice was all-knowable remotely and in advance rather than by empirical observation. Real space had no *a priori* existence or relevance; and humans were automatons.

Fourth, while the prime purpose of the neo-classical scholars was to determine the underlying reasons for human spatial behaviours, these reasons would be common from one spatial setting to the next, such that "behind the chaos and complexity of the world there is an order" (Barnes 1987: 473); and where "diversity, difference and disjuncture are excluded by definition" (1987: 473). In other words, the hermeneutic approach of the neo-classical spatial modellers involved the belief that human behaviour was commonly determined and therefore predictable once key exogenous variables were identified – in the same way that scientists sought to uncover an underlying order in the physical world (see Barnes 1988). Thus the modelling approach was nomothetic, or law-seeking (see Barnes 2003a: 82). On one hand this was a major departure from the predominantly descriptive approach of early regional geographers. On the other, it removed any possibility that geographic space and place were capable of generating forces of primary importance to the way people lived, conducted business and built productive landscapes. Paradoxically, economist's interest in the spatial landscape, then, showed little

561

interest in real geography and the condition of society at all.

In contrast, the application of Keynesian principles to the regional economy question was motivated principally by a determination to be able to change business and living conditions. We now turn to an examination of the Keynesian region and the language approach that characterised it.

Case study of Keynesian regions

Like most branches of post-Second World War economics, post-war regional economics was dominated by the application of the principles of economics developed by British economist John Maynard Keynes. There is a vast literature explaining the power of Keynesianism in constructing post-Second World War national economies as a set of Keynesian economic categories interacting in defined ways with reasonably predictable outcomes (see Bryan 2001). Importantly, Mitchell (2002) argues that Keynes and Keynesianism were instrumental in creating 'the economy' as a discrete object of human management. Thus Keynesian economics can be seen as building the idea of a *national* economy and then disaggregating it into spending categories each of which become a potential site for Keynesian-style government intervention.

These developments were necessary preconditions for the idea of the regional economy which enabled new ways of depicting and analysing the operation of spatial economies at the sub-national level. Common texts recording the canons of regional Keynesian economics are Nourse (1968) and Richardson (1972). Four features of the formulation – each steeped in language – are important. *First*, because Keynesian analysis privileged demand conditions as the driver of economic growth, the categories that constitute aggregate demand – rather than supply- or production-side drivers – became key attributes to be measured and promoted in regional economic management. These attributes

flowed directly from the basic Keynesian income identity,

$$Y = C + I + G + (X - M)$$

where Y is aggregate income
C is consumption spending
I is investment spending
G is net government spending, and
$(X - M)$ is export earnings minus import spending, a territory's net trade position.

Keynes proved mathematically that variations in income come from net changes in investment, government spending or export earnings; and the multiplier effects of these income changes are maximised when they are generated externally. For the region, not having its own capacity for fiscal deficits, the prime source of economic growth was seen to come from net growth in regional exports. This led to the development of 'export base theory' in regional economics, the simple Keynesian-inspired maxim that a region's economic performance was ultimately dependent on the performance of its tradable goods and services sector.

Second, even though Keynesian economics had little to say about spatial economic relationships, the overall Keynesian approach was dependent on there being a defined territory where the basic Keynesian entities are both observable and contained in their contribution to the thing known as 'the economy'. As noted, the Keynesian economy in its original formulation is a national economy. In the regional variation of Keynesian economics, though, the region – and not the nation – is seen as the scale where the basic Keynesian income identity plays out. That this scale jump was unexplained in the regional economics literature is surprising since the key characteristics and policy levers that ensured export earnings held a privileged growth position in a national economy – the existence of a separate national currency, controls over cross-border capital movements, the capacity to redistribute incomes across sectors, the ability to regulate the credit-creation capacity of the banking sector, and the capacity to generate fiscal deficits through taxation and government spending powers – were absent from the regional scale. Nevertheless, the mathematics of Keynesianism were applied enthusiastically to regional data, famously in regional input-output models and in the calculation of regional multipliers, still the information cash-cows of boosterist regional development agencies and consultancy firms worldwide.

Third, their national focus notwithstanding, Keynesian economics gave regional economics a territorially based set of economic relations, something neo-classical economics struggled to do. Hence, not only were there definable Keynesian relations between the non-household demand categories: investment, government spending and exports; these were held in tense spatial relations with their ameliorating opposites: saving, taxation and imports. Like the Keynesian national economy, then, the regional economy became a spatial imaginary replete with measurable economic categories and a mathematical schema that defined their inter relationships. Accordingly, Keynesianism gave regions an important political argument for the establishment of regional development agencies with budgetary and regulatory capacities, adopting the same Keynesian logics that were driving national economic management practices; even though the power of these capacities was often exaggerated.

Fourth, the application of Keynesian economic theory to the regions legitimised government intervention as desirable economic practice, irrespective of how effective regional Keynesianism proved to be. The elegant demonstration by Keynes that government action is capable of smoothing economic growth cycles provided also an argument by representatives of labour and capital and by community groups in support of ongoing regional development programmes. A regional Keynesianism was thus instilled simultaneously in both post-Second World War economic growth and social equity programmes.

In summary, regional Keynesianism, like national Keynesianism, provided Western political systems with an economic development language that maintained the centrality of private sector capitalism – during a period when a third of the world's population lived under various forms of socialism – by showing how state intervention and regulation could ameliorate capitalism's cyclical and social excesses and inequities. A different, radical language of regional economy based on class formation processes, however, emerged with the failure of Keynesian economics to maintain national economic growth in Western economies during the 1970s. This language, that of the localities school, is the subject of our next case study.

Case study of localities

The localities project, as it might be called, was an idea that was consciously formed and developed for the purpose of examining the spatialised roll-out of an exploitative capitalism across a landscape of economic regions each with its own unique social and cultural histories and contemporary circumstances. The localities project started with two concerns. One was the concern of human geographers that a search for abstract and generalised processes across all societies by both orthodox regional scientists and radical political economists was denying the possibility of regionally scaled social processes as determinants of social outcomes, and not just incidental contexts.

Mary Beth Pudup (1988) articulates this concern in detail. The demands of modern social science, says Pudup, displaced a traditional interest in regional identity and difference. In contrast, she says, the localities approach sought to attach contingency to general social processes by making their existence entirely dependent on an engagement with actually existing regional geographies. In addition, Pudup identifies a determination to marry an enlivened regional geography with a newly invigorated political economy of class, gender and conflict. The historical context here was the rise of anti-establishment politics in Britain in the late 1970s to counter the emergence of a Margaret Thatcher-led neoliberalist restructuring. The localities project sought a genuine engagement with class and gender questions. The predominately British project coincided with an American political economy which was focused on a differently scaled politics such as the city, in the case of David Harvey (e.g. 1985; see also Barnes 1989: 302–303), and the corporation in the case of scholars such as Barnett and Muller (e.g. 1975) and Bluestone and Harrison (e.g. 1982), and activists like Ralph Nader.

Barnes (1987) observes that the localities project retrieved an aspiration for the region as the scale where human behaviour displays "richness and diversity" (1987: 305), such that in exploring this richness and diversity one could uncover "the norms, institutions, symbols and social relationships" (1987: 306) that underpin the geographical world as well as "the role of the state at all scales, the role of local culture and society, the influence of past and present events, the importance of both macro- and micro-economic process, and so on" (Barnes 1988: 487).

Importantly, Barnes (1988) nominates Doreen Massey's work on south Wales as "a good example of an attempt to understand the broader geographical context in which acts [sic] are to be understood" (1988: 488), for Doreen Massey's article 'In what sense a regional problem?' (1979) is commonly seen as having led off the localities project. In this article Massey proposed the agenda for localities study. And while the article sought a generalist (historical materialist) explanation of spatial economic difference, it proposed the localities project as an attempt to talk about regional and uneven development by melding the language of class and the geographical language of the region.

Massey (1979) argued, then, that regional equality was the result of general processes:

"the imperatives of the overall process of [capitalist] accumulation" (1979: 234) to produce a differentiated regional landscape, which was in fact a "spatial division of labour" (1979: 234), exploited in various ways to maximise profits according to a "series of 'rounds' of new investment" (1979: 234). Massey observes:

'The economy' of any given local area will thus be a complex result of the combination of its succession of roles within the series of wider, national and international, spatial divisions of labour.
(Massey 1979: 235)

The key forces of the UK economy were thus identified as being strongly regional in character. For example, different economic sectors were identified as concentrated "in the areas most propitious in terms of their requirements for production" (Massey 1979: 235); while dominant, chiefly exporting industries became "the structuring elements in the new emerging pattern of regional differentiation" (1979: 235). Thereafter, the "regional problem" – Massey's spatial imaginary – was produced by the effects on the spatial division of labour within these industries of the unwinding of the UK's "imperial relationships" as a "dominant world capitalist economy" (1979: 235–236), and the rise of a corporations-based economy reinforced by "hierarchies of control" (1979: 236) involving the externalisation of ownership and control and the separation of research and development functions from direct production functions. This then produced an economic landscape overlain by both a hierarchy of production regions and a hierarchy of cities and regions with the tensions between them generating major and entrenched forms of social inequality. In summary, regional problems were seen as "the outcome of the changing relationships between the requirements of private production for profit and the spatial surface" (Massey 1979: 241) with the regional problem seen not as "a problem produced by regions, but by the organisation of production itself" (1979: 243).

Pudup (1988) claims that Massey's (and the localities project's) view of the region was a reaction to having learned the social process theories of other progressive disciplines and sought ways of inscribing these onto a spatialised surface. The features of locality studies, then, were:

i) the core place of regions in Britain's roll-out of industrial capitalism;
ii) the assertion that local economies could not be understood on their own terms;
iii) requiring reference to processes operating more broadly, and therefore more generally;
iv) the primary place of labour and local labour markets in industrial transformations; and,
v) through labour, the inseparability of local cultures and local political economies.

The driving interest for locality studies (and its inherent Marxism) was that these interplays explained the UK's highly spatialised "class structure, historical work culture and gender relations" (Pudup 1988: 382).

Despite the claim to regional and local contingencies, however, and a class-rootedness discernible at these scales, Thrift (1991) showed how locality studies were implicitly structuralist. According to Thrift, locality studies stemmed from "a specific need to understand the economic, social, cultural and political changes taking place in the UK in the 1980s" (1991: 459) using the framework of "Marxism through the substitution of space for time" (1991: 460). As such, says Thrift, they elevated place to be an essence that underpins human activity, a mixer that gives flavour and meaning to life, very much in a Vidalian tradition, though without primary causative status. Elsewhere, however, and emphasising its language encasement, Thrift cedes the spatial integrity of the

localities project. The localities work, he said, was important as an attempt to "find a vocabulary" that moved "away from ideas constituted with metaphors like landscapes, topographies and maps" (Thrift 1993: 93), quoting Morris 1987) seeing regions as "frames for varying practices of space, time and speed" (Thrift 1993: 94).

Thrift thus exposes the localities project as an attempt to produce new understanding of the spatial economy through the construction of an alternate method of analysis and a set of language tools for its operationalisation. We now turn to the final part of this chapter and consider the importance of language in driving the politics of regional development projects.

Conclusion: the politics of regional development language

Of course there are other regional development and economic languages that have steered the way we create and manage local economies. More recently, there are languages associated with post-Fordist approaches to the region which have evolved through a range of approaches tagged by labels such as institutional economics, new economic geography, competitive regions, and relational approaches. Like the case studies above, these approaches are also language dependent in the ways they construct particular views, or spatial imaginations, of regional economies.

In this part of the chapter, we reflect on language's role in the production of theory and politics, using Norman Fairclough as a guide, and we make some concluding comments on how language can be mobilised to secure better regional economic outcomes.

Norman Fairclough argues that the "relatively durable social structuring of language" intersects with the "relatively durable structuring and networking of social practices" (2003: 3) such that language singularly produces a "certain commonality and stability in the way the world is represented" (2003: 126). This view has important implications for the way we understand the process of regional development analysis and policy development and, therefore, how we tackle the regional analysis task from a language-conscious, or post-structuralist, perspective. Echoing Barnes, Fairclough asserts:

> When different discourses come into conflict and particular discourses are contested, what is centrally contested is the power of ... preconstructed semantic systems to generate particular versions of the world which may have the performative power to sustain or remake the world in their image, so to speak.
>
> (Fairclough 2003: 130)

Hence, as we have observed, language is critical to the processes of social change, especially in how we represent them and then bring forward new forms of, say, capitalism following crisis and envelop these in persuasive ideologies and fill them with everyday social practices.

For me, the enduring power of Fairclough's work is in its illustration of how language brings about changes in our knowledge, beliefs and values. Language shapes our identities; for example, as men and women, as consumers and workers. Language, too, shapes our mental world, our thoughts, feelings and beliefs. Language also brings into being changes in the material world through changes in architecture and design, for instance; and by changing the ways we respond to these changes. Finally, language enables us to respond to change as well as to project and imagine possible worlds different from the world we currently experience (see Fairclough 2003: 8, 124).

Beyond its theoretical worth, Fairclough's work is a guide to analysing the presence of language in social practices and social change. This chapter has shown the power of understanding the role of words, trope, metaphor and discursive practices in regional analysis and representation. Powerful skills of language analysis are available from study of Fairclough's texts (e.g. 1992, 1995, 2003). Beyond supplying the social scientist with such skills, however, Fairclough (in 2003) delivers a manifesto for critical discourse analysis, which can be read as a guide to a politically charged language consciousness in regional development studies. For Fairclough, semiosis – the broader act of signification and communication, including communication through visual images as well as language – is (at the risk of harping) an "irreducible element of all material social processes" (2003: 204).

In conclusion, consider four final claims. The *first* is that there is great political leverage to be gained from allowing both language and the region to be indeterminate devices. The strategic purpose of creating such uncertainty is to take advantage of what Fairclough calls an "oscillation" of social practices between a determination by fairly obstinate social processes and the opportunities afforded by the presence of social action and agency. Key to understanding this oscillation, says Fairclough, is the way practices develop as a stabilised configuration of diverse social elements which *always* include discourse (Fairclough 2003: 205). As discussed, discourse is part of all social activity; it drives all representations; and it figures centrally in the shaping of identity, practice and of ways of being (Fairclough 2003: 206). Hence by choosing a language of representation and analysis which exposes the region as a framework for observation, understanding and action, we cannot avoid watching the way our depictions of the region – our spatial imaginaries – shape identity, economic practices and ways of being. An infinite selection of language opportunities for an infinite number of regional analyses, then, doesn't paralyse our regional work. Rather, it forces us to consciously select the language and the regional framework that best match our purposes. And then it beefs up the power of social action and agency in the face of obstinate social processes.

The *second* claim is that language consciousness is a necessary precursor to achieving desirable regional economic outcomes. There is little doubt that the set of motivations underlying Norman Fairclough's persistence in his project to raise language consciousness among social scientists includes his frustration at deteriorating social and regional conditions in his home nation, the UK, under neoliberalist economic management regimes, his recognition of the role that language has played in maintaining a hegemony of neoliberalist practices, and his observation of a paucity of political responses from academic social scientists. Fairclough sees that it is necessary to expose the language strategies of neoliberalism. But, he stresses, this requires an enhanced set of language analysis skills among social scientists.

The *third* claim, then, is that regional analysis should always be moving from a language-limited approach to a language-enabling approach; or, in Barnes' words, to be moving from dead languages of analysis to new, living languages. Quite simply, Barnes instructs us, when our words, tropes, metaphors, models, equations and images are static, then we are lagging in matching our analytical words with an actually existing world which has moved on in time and space. As clumsy as the process often is, we should always experiment with new ways of saying things in order to build better understandings and more desirable outcomes.

The *fourth* claim is that the most enlivened regional politics comes from a serious acknowledgement of dialogism and intertexuality. Such an acknowledgement turns the idea of communicating academic findings on its head. An engaged language, as we have seen, is always a triangulation between author, audience and wider society. When this engagement is resisted, a failure to communicate is one result. Another is that the author forgoes access to the knowledge and experiences that come from the presence of an audience in the writing process. In the

quotation which opens this chapter, Dumont observes that the economy is very much a constructed thing. As regional analysts — through our spatial imaginaries — we are complicit in this construction. A language consciousness in our approach can only help us do our bit of the job better.

References

Alonso, W. (1964) *Location and Land Use: Toward a General Theory of Land Rent*, Cambridge: Harvard University Press.

Barnes, T. (1987) 'Homo economicus, physical metaphors, and universal models in economic geography', *The Canadian Geographer* 31, 299–308.

Barnes, T. (1988) 'Rationality and relativism in economic geography: an interpretive review of the homo economicus assumption', *Progress in Human Geography* 12, 473–496.

Barnes, T. (1989) 'Place, space and theories of economic value: contextualism and essentialism in economic geography', *Transactions of the Institute of British Geographers* 14, 299–316.

Barnes, T. (1991) 'Metaphors and conversations in economic geography: Richard Rorty and the Gravity Model', *Geografiska Annaler* 73, 111–120.

Barnes, T. (1998) 'Political economy III: confessions of a political economist', *Progress in Human Geography* 22, 94–103.

Barnes, T. (2001a) 'On theory, history, and anoraks', *Antipode* 162–167.

Barnes, T. (2001b) 'Retheorizing economic geography: From the quantitative revolution to the "cultural turn"', *Annals of the Association of American Geographers* 91, 546–565.

Barnes, T. (2003a) 'The place of locational analysis: a selective and interpretive history', *Progress in Human Geography* 27, 69–95.

Barnes, T. (2003b) 'What's wrong with American regional science? A view from science studies', *Canadian Journal of Regional Science* 26, 3–18.

Barnes, T. (2004) 'The rise (and decline) of American regional science: lessons for the new economic geography?, *Journal of Economic Geography* 4, 107–129.

Barnes, T. J. and Duncan, J. S. (eds) (1992) *Writing Worlds: Discourse, Text and Metaphor in the Representation of Landscape*, London: Routledge.

Barnett, R. J. and Muller, R. E. (1975) *Global Reach: The Power of the Multinational Corporations*, London: Jonathan Cape.

Bluestone, B. and Harrison, B. (1982) *The Deindustrialization of America: Plant Closings, Community Abandonment, and the Dismantling of Basic Industry*, New York: Basic Books.

Brandist, C. (2002) *The Bakhtin Circle: Philosophy, Culture and Politics*, London: Pluto Press.

Bryan, D. (2001) 'Global accumulation and accounting for national economic identity', *Review of Radical Political Economics* 33, 57–77.

Christaller, W. (1993) *Central Places in Southern Germany*, Jena: Fischer.

Cohen, T. (2001) *Jacques Derrida and the Humanities: A Critical Reader*, Cambridge: Cambridge University Press.

Fairclough, N. (1992) *Discourse and Social Change*, Cambridge: Polity Press.

Fairclough, N. (1995) *Critical Discourse Analysis*, London: Longman.

Fairclough, N. (2003) *Analysing Discourse: Textual Analysis for Social Research*, London: Routledge.

Fairclough, N., Jessop, B. and Sayer, A. (2003) 'Critical realism and semiosis', in J.M. Roberts and J. Joseph (eds) *Realism, Discourse and Deconstruction*, London: Routledge, 23–42.

Gottdiener, M. (1995) *Postmodern Semiotics: Material Culture and the Forms of Postmodern Life*, Oxford and Cambridge: Blackwell.

Harvey, D. (1985) *The Urbanization of Capital*, Baltimore: John Hopkins University Press.

Harvey, D. (1996) *Justice, Nature and the Geography of Difference*, Oxford: Blackwell.

Isard, W. (1956) *Location and Space-economy; A General Theory Relating to Industrial Location, Market Areas, Land Use, Trade, and Urban Structure*, Cambridge: Technology Press of Massachusetts Institute of Technology, and Wiley.

Kuhn, T.S. (1962) *The Structure of Scientific Revolutions*, Chicago: University of Chicago Press.

Losch, A. (1954) *The Economics of Location* (2nd edition; translated from the German by W.H. Woglom with the assistance of W.F. Stolper), New Haven, CT: Yale University Press (originally published 1940).

Massey, D. (1979) 'In what sense a regional problem?', *Regional Studies* 13, 233–243.

Mitchell, T. (2002) *Rule of Experts: Egypt, Techno-Politics, Modernity*, Berkeley: University of California Press.

Murdoch, J. (2006) *Post-structuralist Geography: A Guide to Relational Space,* Sage: London.

Nourse, H.O. (1968) *Regional Economics: A Study in the Economic Structure, Stability and Growth of Regions*, New York: McGraw Hill:

Olsson, G. and Gale, S. (1968) 'Spatial theory and human behaviour, *Papers in Regional Science*,' 21(1), 229–242.

Pudup, M.B. (1988) 'Arguments within regional geography', *Progress in Human Geography* 12, 369–390.

Richardson, H.W. (1972) *Regional Economics: Location Theory, Urban Structure and Regional Change*, London: Weidenfeld Nicolson.

Thrift, N. (1990) 'For a new regional geography 1', *Progress in Human Geography* 14, 272–279.

Thrift, N. (1991) 'For a new regional geography 2', *Progress in Human Geography* 15, 456–466.

Thrift, N. (1993) 'For a new regional geography 3', *Progress in Human Geography* 17, 92–100.

von Thünen, J.H. (1996) *Von Thünen's Isolated State*, an English translation of *Der Isolierte Staat* (translated by C.M. Wartenberg; edited with an introduction by P. Hall), Oxford: Pergamon Press (originally published 1826).

Wishart, D. (2004) 'Period and region', *Progress in Human Geography* 28, 305–319.

Further reading

Aylett, A. and Barnes, T. (2009) 'Language and research', in R. Kitchen and N. Thrift, (eds) *International Encyclopaedia of Human Geography*, Volume 6, 153–158. (On the ways language has shaped human geography and regional studies.)

Fairclough, N. (2003) *Analysing Discourse: Textual Analysis for Social Research*, London: Routledge. (A highly useful explanation and guide for social scientists concerning the techniques of language analysis.)

Murdoch, J. (2006) *Post-structuralist Geography: A Guide to Relational Space*, London: Sage. (An accessible text which explores post-structuralist approaches to the study of space and place.)

46

The evaluation of local and regional development policy

Dave Valler

Introduction

The past 20 years or so have witnessed the development of a substantial critique of evaluative work in local and regional economic development (LRED), most notably in the United States. As Clarke and Gaile argued in 1992, efforts to evaluate local economic development policy had become "a quagmire of good intentions and bad measures" (1992: 193), and a variety of contributions have since sought to change the bases for evaluative work. In general these have problematized traditional evaluative measures and methods, such as the focus on basic job creation/retention measures, and argued for a shift from narrow 'process' or 'formative' evaluation to a broader concern with the overall 'outcomes' and 'impacts' of policies (see, for example, Bartik, 2002; Bartik and Bingham, 1995; Reese and Fasenfest, 1997). This has also been associated with calls for a much wider range of criteria in evaluating LRED (Reese and Fasenfest, 1997; Molotch, 1991), albeit accepting the added complexity which would inevitably arise. Additionally, a number of contributions have exposed the essentially value-laden nature of evaluative processes and judgements and the often implicit theoretical positions adopted in evaluative work.

Yet despite this sustained period of attention there is little substantive basis upon which to frame judgements on some of the most basic questions regarding LRED. What counts as the 'success' or 'failure' of LRED in a locality or region, and why? Is the form of LRED in a place appropriate given the economic, social, political and cultural challenges being faced? Is the programme of LRED sustainable? My contention is that the lack of clear guidance on some of these most basic questions derives from a theoretical tendency to underplay both the broader context of economic and state restructuring and the locally specific conditions within which economic development activities are situated, and within which their distinctive contributions are defined. Responding to this requires the elaboration of an alternative theoretical standpoint sensitive to the particularity of place, and to the multiple roles that LRED activity comes to play across production, reproduction, consumption, ideological, political and cultural spheres. In this sense evaluation would become a more complex, comprehensive and contextualised exercise than it has been to date.

In this chapter I briefly outline some aspects of the critical commentary around LRED evaluation, together with some of the more important avenues which have emerged in response. In spite of the value of these subsequent contributions, little headway has been made in terms of situating local and regional economic development in context, or in establishing an explicit theoretical basis upon which 'success' or 'failure' might be judged. Indeed, it can certainly be argued that the theoretical foundations for LRED evaluation remain comparatively underdeveloped in a field dominated by more pragmatic and immediate concerns. As a result, evaluative exercises have been significantly limited in terms of interpreting the real 'meaning' of LRED policy and in appraising the overall impact of LRED as a strategic response rather than as a series of isolated projects. In light of this I argue for an approach based in regulation theory, a conceptual framework introduced in France in the 1970s which has subsequently come to exert considerable influence in studies of the state and social and economic policy more generally across a wide variety of contexts, both in Europe and in the US. This theoretical stance can assist significantly in locating LRED activity in a broader political-economic context, in explaining the evolution of LRED and its distinctive institutional and policy forms with reference to the evolution of the political economy and the state, and in establishing a framework within which to evaluate the scale, nature and overall contribution of LRED activity.

Evaluation: critical themes

While a broad concern for the measurement of policy performance has been apparent throughout the history of LRED policy, it is since the mid-1980s that a detailed and thoroughgoing critique of evaluation per se has emerged. This has incorporated, on the one hand, a direct examination of the conceptual and methodological challenges posed by LRED evaluation in particular, a point considered further below. However, it also acknowledged a changed political and governance

context within which demonstrating policy efficacy and value for money became much more significant. Here neoliberal ideology and the hegemony of public choice theory and new managerialism underscored an 'evidential turn' (Taylor, 2005: 601; see also OECD, 2008) in local policy-making, based on the instrumental use of systematic research and scientific knowledge, and emphasising as the ideal form of relevant knowledge "quantitative methodologies, empirically-tested and validated" (Sanderson, 2002: 6). In the UK this was associated with the Blairite mantra 'what matters is what works' and a new era of policy-making informed by evidence of what was 'proven' to be effective in achieving particular outcomes (Nutley, 2003: 3), while the US paralleled 'new managerialism' with total quality management. These more rigorous contexts would, of course, be far less sympathetic to the scattergun "shoot anything that flies, claim anything that falls" approach portrayed by some economic development practitioners in the mid-1980s (see Rubin, 1988). Third, particularly in the US, a serious questioning of the basic rationale for, and performance of, LRED policy effectively elevated the importance of evaluation processes and the pressure on individual programmes to justify their existence (see, for example, Peters and Fisher, 2004).

With regard to underlying conceptual issues, authors have argued that 'economic development' has cultivated very specific 'growth' objectives focused on job creation, business attraction and an enhanced local tax base. This is in contrast to any broader notion of 'development' and the associated construction of new innovative capacities, increased adaptability, and engagement with questions of social justice and quality of life (Reese and Fasenfest, 1997: 196–198; Wolman and Spitzley, 1996; see also Beauregard, 1999; Foley, 1992). Such a narrow focus is not, of course, entirely surprising, and as Beauregard (1999) demonstrates there are strong reasons for an employment focus in evaluations of local economic performance. Yet it betrays an underlying value system which effectively privileges formal, commercial and business-oriented economic activity at the expense of the informal sector and broader notions of democracy, equity, and social and environmental justice (Reese and Fasenfest, 1997; Pike *et al.*, 2007). In addition, it references a somewhat under developed theoretical basis for economic development activity whereby "state and local economic development strategies evolve incrementally without (any) underlying economic theory except that more jobs are good and less jobs are bad" (Beaumont and Hovey, 1985: 328; see also Valler and Wood, 2009, forthcoming). In this sense the task of evaluation is immediately coloured by a partial and in some senses limited understanding of the basic constitution of local economies (Beauregard, 1993).

Beyond these foundational concerns the evaluation of LRED activity faces numerous methodological challenges, not least because evaluation of a policy action requires an assessment of what would have happened in the absence of such activity. Coulson (1990) outlines the problems of 'displacement' (where job creation in one place is at the expense of jobs in another), 'deadweight' (where the outcome would have been the same in the absence of policy action), 'indirect impacts' (including multipliers), and 'leverage' (which can lead to accounting difficulties), all of which add to the complexity of evaluation. Further problems include, but are certainly not limited to: determining which outcomes can in fact be measured, and which 'proximate' outcomes might be appropriate where ultimate outcomes are difficult to measure; imprecise or inadequate information from respondents; potential biases in sampling; significant resource constraints; and the thorny issue of demonstrating clear causal relationships (see, for example, Bartik, 1992, 2002; Foley, 1992). Despite these obvious difficulties, however, an enormous literature has emerged around the evaluation of local economic development programmes, deploying a range of techniques designed to

overcome or allow for these and other methodological problems. Limitations of space preclude a detailed rehearsal of all the twists and turns of this debate, and readers are directed to relevant literature in Further reading below. However, some of the more important directions can be identified.

As a first step, there has been a general acceptance, at least in principle, of the need for a more sophisticated approach to evaluation, along with a clearer focus on outcomes (see, for example, OECD, 2004). This has a number of implications including, for example: a concern for unexpected results as well as delivery against predetermined criteria; a focus on the interaction of programmes and policies across a wide range of sectors; the need for longitudinal data; the use of comparative research and control groups; and questions over the specification of appropriate evaluation criteria. In practice, of course, this raises significant challenges including those alluded to above, and these may in turn constrain the evaluative exercise undertaken. Yet in many different national contexts, and across both academic and policy circles, it is apparent that the focus on outcomes evaluation has sharpened. In the UK, for example, HM Treasury issued a 'Framework for the Evaluation of Regeneration Projects and Programmes' in 1995, setting out a general framework for the ex-post evaluation of expenditure projects and programmes with regeneration objectives, covering social, environmental and economic objectives and distinguishing between 'monitoring' (the collection of performance data) and 'evaluation' (the examination of a policy to distinguish how effectively and efficiently it delivered predetermined objectives). In this sense there has been something of a turn towards outcomes evaluation in local and regional economic development and cognate fields even if, as the OECD admitted in 2004, the core task of determining programme effectiveness has tended to be 'somewhat obscured' by a focus on formative evaluation and the improvement of programme operations.

A second key dimension of the evaluation debate has been the call for more sophisticated and rigorous statistical approaches, particularly in response to the counter-factual problem. How might we identify the precise impact of firm- or area-based policies on levels of economic activity such as business creation/expansion, employment generation, and productivity growth? Bartik (1992, 2002), for example, has argued for experimental comparisons between 'control' and 'treatment' firms or areas where such policy differentiation is practicable, or statistical comparisons of economic impacts across recipient and non-recipient firms or areas where it is not. These methods would adopt randomized criteria to avoid selection biases and a variety of statistical techniques to allow for differences in other variables which affect outcomes, thereby "generating objective quantitative evidence on the bottom line for the program" (Bartik, 2002: 29). Evaluations should, however, examine not only the impacts of policies on local business growth, but also important public benefits, namely:

> fiscal benefits for government, and increased earnings for the unemployed or underemployed. Fiscal and employment benefits can be estimated using regional econometric models which are combined with special modules that consider the structure of local taxes and government budgets, and the local labor market.
>
> (Bartik, 2002: iii)

While a closer examination of these techniques is beyond the scope of this chapter, it is certainly worth noting challenges associated with the production of local and regional economic data which in the UK case has been characterized as limited, historically skewed towards manufacturing rather than services, and unresponsive in the face of economic restructuring (see 'The Allsop Review', HM Treasury, 2004). Similar concerns are frequently voiced in the US (for example,

Feser and Sweeney, 2006) and especially in developing and transition economies where data problems are often severe. Accepting this, though, it is apparent that detailed statistical investigation and appropriate modelling can offer important insights into the evaluation of individual economic development programmes. Already a vast literature exists around the economic impacts of enterprise zones (e.g. Boarnet, 2001), job-training schemes (e.g. Giloth, 2000), tax increment financing schemes (e.g. Dye and Merriman, 2000), and the effects of state and local taxes on business location and growth (see Bartik, 1991, 1992; Buss, 2001), amongst many other programmes. These studies have gone some way to produce relatively clear and defensible claims of programme impact in a field characterized by significant uncertainty and complexity. There are, however, obvious difficulties in this area which effectively limit the development of this type of evaluative work in practice. It is expensive, resource-intensive and complex; there are practical difficulties in identifying appropriate comparator groups; and there may be multiple sources of potential bias. It is telling, for example, that Bartik (2002: 12) is aware of only a single case of economic development evaluation in the US utilizing data from an experiment using random assignment.

A third – rather British-flavoured – strand in the debate highlights the concern with explanation, and the task of opening up the 'black box' of policy mechanics to identify more precisely how and why a policy works or fails (Ho, 1999: 424; Turok, 1989; see also Jones, 1999). In place of basic output measures or value-for-money indicators evaluation should seek a detailed understanding of the causal processes and mechanisms which generate specific outcomes in particular times and places. As Turok (1989) argues, this requires some form of theoretical apparatus in order to identify key processes and relations, to situate policy in context, and provide a convincing explanatory basis for the diversity of outcomes. The link between policy and outcome in LRED, for example, is often indirect and complex, requiring careful theoretical analysis and detailed empirical investigation. Additionally, local economic policy operates in a much broader context of economic, social, and political forces as well as distinct local conditions all of which are integral to the production of outcomes and cannot be detached from evaluative analysis. In this sense evaluation necessarily requires a convincing theoretical and empirical account of specific outcomes, which would in turn enable policy learning and the build up of cumulative knowledge in contrast to the shifting fashions and occasional leaps of faith which have tended to characterize LRED policy.

Developments along these lines have yielded fruitful theoretical insights, not least around the formulation of a 'realist' approach to evaluation (Ho, 1999, 2003). Here the focus is thrown on the causal properties and liabilities inherent in policy forms, properties which may or may not be realized depending on the diverse contexts in which they are situated. This then requires an explicit theorization of the proposed policy response, setting out the mechanisms through which specific programme elements would counter perceived problems and a consideration of context in relation to the measures adopted, in order to explain diverse policy outcomes. However, despite the obvious importance of such understanding, in practice these insights have been limited in terms of application and unfortunately somewhat marginalized in the face of more instrumental concerns. In part this probably signifies the need for further middle-range theoretical development in order to ground these more general philosophical insights, and to demonstrate the value of such explanation in comparison to more basic measures. It also suggests the potential value of analyses of cross-national policy transfer and learning, given the contingent and uneven outcomes created by 'policies in motion' (Peck, 2003: 229). Such processes of international experimentation

and differentiation can often throw causal dynamics into sharp relief (see also Hudson *et al.*, 1997; McCann, 2008).

Finally here, a number of authors have argued for evaluation to incorporate broader social, welfare and equity impacts which go well beyond traditional economic measures, a point which chimes with contemporary calls for a broader and more holistic definition of 'development' per se (see Pike *et al.*, 2007) and is consistent with the theoretical standpoint we elaborate below. Such impacts might include, for example, quality-of-life indicators such as life expectancy, educational attainment, health and income disparity, housing quality and the like, alongside further qualitative information regarding the nature of employment and economic activity generated (Reese and Fasenfest, 1997). These measures potentially offer a more rounded picture of LRED outcomes, though there are clearly serious difficulties involved in selecting appropriate indictors and attributing causality. An increasingly important concern is the question of political empowerment and the need to engage recipient communities in the design and conduct of LRED policies, giving rise to 'participatory' and 'empowerment' evaluation focused on stakeholder participation, capacity-building, and active learning rather than judgement or accountability (Brooks, 2008: 28; see Fetterman, 2001). This has, in some instances, supported a range of innovative participatory procedures and a significant re-examination of the respective roles of stakeholders, evaluators, and communities in evaluation processes. It has thereby underscored a more reflexive examination of the evaluative task, and generated an enhanced sensitivity to the complex and contested nature of LRED policy. It has also found particular resonance in developing economies where urban expansion and population growth, infrastructure shortfalls and burgeoning urban poverty may be accompanied by 'back-to-front' development taking place in advance of formal planning and regulatory procedures. In these contexts participatory approaches may go some way to recognize and validate the role of the urban poor in developing towns and cities (Majale, 2008: 273; see also Atav, 2007; Hordijk and Baud, 2006). However, the scale of participatory activity overall has been marginal in comparison to the emphasis on formal performance measures, targets and outputs which dominate contemporary governance arrangements. As the OECD (2004: 4) states, the conventional approach has been to:

> evaluate individual policy instruments and programmes against their explicitly stated objectives. In this way, programme evaluations tend to produce isolated and often disappointing findings, without due regard to the interaction and cumulative impact of policies that, by design or not, work in a 'target-oriented' way.
>
> (OECD, 2004: 4)

It is in this context that we seek a more convincing and comprehensive theoretical account which might facilitate broader and more satisfying judgement. This requires linkages to be drawn between the nature and conduct of LRED activity and the broader context of political-economic dynamics and state restructuring. For this we turn to the broad insights of regulation theory as the basis for an overarching conceptual frame for the evaluation of LRED activity (see also Valler and Wood, 2010, forthcoming).

A regulationist contribution?

The regulation approach

By now the contours of the original regulationist account are well known. Beginning from an assertion of the contradictory and crisis-prone nature of capitalist society, regulation theory emphasizes the social norms, mechanisms and institutions which may come

together to derive a contingent and necessarily temporary stability in capitalist accumulation processes (Aglietta, 1979, 1998; Boyer, 1990; Jessop, 1990, 1997; Lipietz, 1987; Peck and Tickell, 1992, 1995). This establishes a distinctive theoretical starting point in which the economy tends neither to an automatic equilibrium as in conventional economics, nor to an inevitable breakdown as in Marxist theory (Friedman, 2000: 61). Rather, an 'accumulation system', or characteristic set of relationships between production and consumption, emerges to a position of dominance within an economic arena and may come to be sustained in the medium term by a 'mode of regulation' or collection of social and institutional supports which together provide a degree of coherence and stability to an overall 'regime of accumulation'. Such stability is necessarily temporary, acting only to mute or disguise both the inherent contradictions of capitalist production and the tensions which necessarily exist within institutional forms. Each regime of accumulation thus contains the seeds of its own destruction, beyond which capitalist production and regulation must be thoroughly transformed to secure its future survival. Capitalism therefore proceeds historically through periods of stability and growth, when accumulation and reproduction are relatively steady, and periods of crisis, when the conditions for capitalist social reproduction are found wanting.

Within this overarching framework regulationists have offered specific accounts of political-economic restructuring, most notably around the emergence and consolidation of Fordism (Aglietta, 1979) and the putative transition to post-Fordism (Lipietz, 1987). Much of this early literature is well known and there is no need to rehearse it here. Additionally, a wide range of authors have deployed regulationist insights to position and inform their analyses across a variety of spheres, including, for example, UK urban politics (Goodwin et al., 1993), UK urban and regional development (Peck and Tickell, 1992; 1995), US urban policy (Florida and

Jonas, 1991), and US housing (Florida and Feldman, 1988). Such accounts have achieved notable advances in these various spheres by contextualizing particular policy fields in a broader political-economic and institutional arena, and making critical connections between economic, social, political, cultural and institutional practices. Regulationists have also elaborated on a number of apparent weaknesses in initial formulations of the regulationist approach, most notably in responding to accusations of structuralism and economic determinism. Yet the central theoretical and methodological contribution of regulation theory has proved notably robust, and it might be argued that as "a perspective and form of analysis" (Goodwin and Painter, 1996) regulation theory has come to exert significant influence. Though concern for the underlying "generative structures and mechanisms that shape the actual movement of social forces" (James, 2009: 184) was largely superseded after the late 1990s by a more concretized focus on 'governance' forms, the basic importance of sensitivity to macroeconomic change and political strategy and struggle continues to resonate (see especially James, 2009). Indeed, despite the relative absence of explicitly regulationist accounts of policy and institutional change since the late 1990s such insights offer a distinctively holistic and wide-ranging analytical frame within which to account for such change, albeit in combination with appropriate meso-level theorizations. Additionally, as we set out below, the approach also provides a foundation for an alternative, theoretically nuanced approach to evaluation, though this point has been little recognized to date.

Regulation theory and LRED

From a regulationist standpoint contemporary LRED activity is best viewed within the context of overall patterns of institutional change and policy experimentation directed towards the establishment of some form of 'post-Fordist' mode of regulation (Goodwin, 2001: 74). On the one hand the structures and practices of economic development activity at sub-national scales will be critically influenced by broader processes of restructuring in state–market relations, innovation and competition systems, formal regulatory frameworks, governance structures, patterns of social organization, political and ideological commitments, and economic, social and cultural policy. Clearly national policy shifts will impact directly on institutional forms and policy development and implementation in localities and regions. Yet this cannot in any sense be seen as a simplistic or undifferentiated projection of national changes onto localities. Rather, regulatory practices operating at a variety of scales necessarily find expression locally, both reflecting the pre-existing character of uneven development, and being actively constituted locally (Goodwin et al., 1993: 69).

Additionally, of course, localities and regions come to play different roles, with different degrees of success or failure, within overall national regimes of accumulation. For it is apparent that regions and localities are characterized by distinctive accumulation-regulation couplings and will be inserted differentially into both wider spatial divisions of labour and regulatory structures. As Peck and Tickell point out (1992: 352), "some regional economies … will be favoured by national accumulation strategies while others will not". But it is also clear that different regulatory functions operate at different spatial scales (Goodwin, 2001: 78; Peck and Tickell, 1992: 352), and that a whole variety of social, cultural and institutional forms contribute to distinctively local or regional regulatory effects. Peck and Tickell, for example, highlight the potential role of local growth coalitions, inter-firm networks, labour market structures and institutions, housing markets, venture capital arrangements, forms of local governance, local economic policies and relations in civil society (1992: 353). As a result economic development activity will also reflect the search for a 'regulatory fix' at the local or regional scale, as localities with distinctive economic, social, political, cultural and institutional histories seek to position themselves within the context of a broader accumulation strategy (Goodwin, 2001: 78).

Overall, then, regulation theory promises significant advances both in contextualizing LRED activities broadly within the search for a resolution to the crisis Fordism and the experimentation over new post-Fordist regulatory forms, and in approaching the diverse mechanisms and forms of regulation operating in particular (sub-national) spatial contexts. This has important theoretical implications for evaluative work. In particular we can derive two very broad basic criteria upon which to construct evaluations of changing policy forms and institutional frameworks. These relate to the specific contributions of economic development activities in (i) managing ongoing crisis tendencies, and (ii) facilitating the reproduction of capitalist social relations. Clearly, this is not to suggest that individual economic development initiatives could in any way be evaluated in these abstract terms per se. Rather, LRED activity, operating in conjunction with an array of socio-political, institutional and cultural forces and processes, may come to play distinctive roles in the production of 'regulatory effects', which are themselves necessarily "greater than, or qualitatively different from, the sum of individual effects" (Painter and Goodwin, 1995: 335). Such effects are emergent properties of a social system and are inherently relational. They may incorporate specific political compromises, institutional forms, social expectations or fiscal and organizational arrangements, but it is important to note that regulatory effects do not emerge directly from these individual elements, but through critical interrelations amongst these and other forms, and may therefore be specified only in terms of the broader system.

In this context the starting point for understanding the 'meaning' of LRED activity is in defining the ways in which localities

and regions come to find a degree of "local economic integrity" (Eisenschitz and Gough, 1993) or "structured coherence" (Harvey, 1985) which temporarily stabilizes capitalist reproduction in particular times and places. This emerges from the combination of a wide variety of processes and practices operating at multiple scales, each with their own geographies and spatial structures, and will therefore vary spatially (Painter and Goodwin, 1995: 335). For Harvey:

> At the heart of that coherence lies a particular technological mix – understood not simply as hardware but also as organizational forms – and a dominant set of social relations. Together these define models of consumption as well as of the labour process. The coherence embraces the standard of living, the qualities and style of life, work satisfactions (or lack thereof), social hierarchies (authority structures in the workplace, status systems of consumption), and a whole set of sociological and psychological attitudes towards living, enjoying, entertaining and the like.
>
> (Harvey, 1985: 140)

This, in turn, suggests a distinctive approach to evaluation focusing on the extent to which, and the ways in which, LRED activity reinforces, reshapes or even undermines such coherence in particular places. Clearly, LRED activity may be implicated in many aspects of such coherence, ranging across production and consumption relations, social and political forms, and cultures and attitudes. Indeed LRED policy may come to play a variety of roles – simultaneously economic, political, institutional and cultural – in the construction of successful regulatory processes.

Further, as we have outlined earlier, localities and regions are inserted differently in wider spatial divisions of labour and regulatory structures, and are characterized by distinctive social, cultural and institutional forms. Patterns of structured coherence therefore vary widely between places, and the contribution of LRED activities to such coherence will be similarly diverse. Evaluation must in turn be a more complex and comprehensive exercise than it has been to date. For if regulatory processes and effects are different in different places, evaluating the contribution of any one particular type of institution or activity across these places may involve measuring different things (see Valler et al., 2000). For example, in considering the potential contributions of workfare programmes to distinct forms of structured coherence in different places we might reflect on how the key emphases of workfare-based policy, namely "flexibility for enterprise; geographic rescaling of economic and social intervention; replacement of entitlements with obligations on the part of citizens; and coalitional power-holding spanning governmental, civil society, and profit motivated actors" (Krinsky, 2006: 158) might perform differentiated roles in, for example, responding to fiscal crisis, channeling and containing political opposition, enhancing labour market flexibility, overcoming important institutional scleroses and managing social polarization (see Valler and Wood, (2009) for further related discussion). The key point is that the contribution of these diverse roles in establishing or reinforcing effective regulation in particular places will be distinctive. From this viewpoint it is only once we have defined the form of structured coherence in a place that we may distil the contribution of LRED activities in these particular arrangements. In turn the broadest evaluative questions around LRED activities – of their 'success' or 'failure', 'appropriateness' or 'sustainability' – can only be determined in context, that is with regard to their specific contributions to particular accumulation–regulation couplings in localities and regions. Evaluative work should therefore reflect the particularity of place and the distinctive character of regulation in any given case.

Conclusion

A call for further attention to the theoretical foundations for evaluation must, of course, be tempered with some degree of caution. Plainly it would shift the focus away from the basic quantifiable output measures which dominate contemporary policy discourse, and require both policy-makers and academic commentators to look beyond immediate policy structures and prerogatives. It would generate additional complexity for evaluators in thinking through the emergent and differentiated regulatory affects which characterize specific places, and which are far less amenable to communication through basic, mechanistic data. In this sense there would be no simple off-the-shelf method for evaluation in the broadest sense. There are also critical conceptual challenges, not least the question of how to operationalize a focus on structured coherence, given that the notion is based on "loose and heterogenous" foundations (Jessop, 2006: 147). Yet if we wish to move away from "isolated and often disappointing findings" we must recognize that different types of question require different types of evaluation, and that 'success' or 'failure' can only be evaluated in context.

Taking this forward requires significant theoretical and methodological development to refine high-level abstractions into more specific middle-range concepts and concrete claims. As a starting point, approaching the tendency to structured coherence in particular territories would require, first, a detailed and frank assessment of the position of specific places within the wider global, national and regional division of labor; second, a clear understanding of the regulatory challenges and tensions posed by the location of a particular place – with its distinctive political-economic history and socio-cultural and institutional forms – within this broader environment; and third, a focus on the key interrelationships between economic, social, political, cultural and institutional relations which act to mitigate such crisis tendencies.

It is this focus on the emergent properties of a social system where the value of the approach lies, and against which the distinctive contribution of LRED policy in particular can be judged. Clearly, though, these are very first steps along these lines and there is much progress to be made in developing these insights. But despite the novelty of the approach such theoretical and methodological development also offers the tantalizing prospect of informing policy which seriously addresses the distinctive problems of localities and regions, rather than serially reproducing inappropriate LRED policies irrespective of local context.

Acknowledgement

This chapter draws directly on material from Valler, D. and Wood, A. (2010) 'Conceptualizing Local and Regional Economic Development in the USA', forthcoming in *Regional Studies*. Copyright permission provided by Taylor & Francis Books (UK).

References

Aglietta, M. (1979) *A Theory of Capitalist Regulation*, London: New Left Books.

Aglietta, M. (1998) 'Capitalism at the turn of the century: regulation theory and the challenge of social change', *New Left Review* 41–90.

Atav, A. (2007) 'Democracy to become reality: participatory planning through action research', *Habitat International* 31, 333–344.

Bartik, T.J. (1990) 'The market failure approach to regional economic development policy', *Economic Development Quarterly* 4, 4, 361–370.

Bartik, T.J. (1991) *Who Benefits from State and Local Economic Development Policies?*, Kalamazoo, Michigan: W. E. Upjohn Institute for Employment Research.

Bartik, T.J. (1992) 'The effects of state and local taxes on economic development: a review of recent research', *Economic Development Quarterly* 26, 1, 102–110.

Bartik, T.J. (2002) 'Evaluating the impacts of local economic development policies on local economic outcomes: what has been done and what is doable?', Upjohn Institute Staff Working Paper No. 03–89. W.E. Upjohn Institute for Employment Research: Kalamazoo, MI.

Bartik, T.J. and Bingham, R.D. (1995) 'Can economic development programs be evaluated?', Upjohn Institute Staff Working Paper No. 95–29. W.E. Upjohn Institute for Employment Research.

Beaumont, E.F. and Hovey, H.A. (1985) 'State, local and federal economic development policies: new federal patterns, chaos or what?', *Public Administration Review* 45, 327–332.

Beauregard, R. A. (1993) 'Constituting economic development', in R. D. Bingham and R. Mier (eds) *Theories of Local Economic Development* Newbury Park, CA: Sage, 267–283.

Beauregard, R.A. (1999) 'The Employment Fulcrum: Evaluating Local Economic Performance', *Economic Development Quarterly* 13, 1, 8–14.

Boarnet, M.G. (2001) 'Enterprise Zones and Job Creation: Linking Evaluation and Practice', *Economic Development Quarterly* 15, 3, 242–254.

Boyer, R. (1990) *The Regulation School: A Critical Introduction*, New York: Columbia University Press.

Brooks, Z. (2008) 'Participatory and empowerment evaluation tools for regeneration', *Journal of Urban Regeneration and Renewal* 2, 1, 27–38.

Buss, T.F. (2001) 'The Effect of State Tax Incentives on Economic Growth and Firm Location Decisions: An Overview of the Literature', *Economic Development Quarterly* 15, 90–105.

Clarke, S.E. and Gaile, G.L. (1992) 'The next wave: postfederal local economic development strategies', *Economic Development Quarterly* 6, 2, 187–198.

Coulson, A. (1990) 'Evaluating local economic policy', in M. Campbell (ed.) *Local Economic Policy*, London: Cassell, 174–194.

Dye, R.F. and Merriman, D.F. (2000) 'The effects of tax increment financing on economic Development', *Journal of Urban Economics* 47, 2, 306–328.

Eisenschitz, A. and Gough, J. (1993) *The Politics of Local Economic Policy*, Basingstoke: Macmillan.

Feser, E. and Sweeney, S. (2006) 'On the state of the geography in the U.S. Bureau of Labor Statistics covered wages and employment (ES-202)', *Series International Regional Science Review* 29, 247–263.

Fetterman, D.M. (2001) *Foundations of Empowerment Evaluation*, Thousand Oaks, CA: Sage.

Florida, R. and Feldman, M. (1988) 'Housing in US Fordism', *International Journal of Urban and Regional Research* 12, 187–210.

Florida, R. and Jonas, A. (1991) 'US urban policy: The post-war state and capitalist regulation', *Antipode* 23, 349–384.

Foley, P. (1992) 'Local economic policy and job creation: A review of evaluation studies', *Urban Studies* 29, 557–598.

Friedman, A.L. (2000) 'Microregulation and post-Fordism: Critique and development of regulation theory', *New Political Economy* 5, 1, 59–76.

Giloth, R.P. (2000) 'Learning from the field: economic growth and workforce development in the 1990s', *Economic Development Quarterly* 14, 340–359.

Goodwin, M. (2001) 'Regulation as process: Regulation theory and comparative urban and regional research', *Journal of Housing and the Built Environment* 16: 71–87.

Goodwin, M. and Painter, J. (1996) 'Local governance, the crisis of Fordism and the changing geographies of regulation', *Transactions of the Institute of British Geographers* 21, 635–648.

Goodwin, M., Duncan, S. and Halford, S. (1993) 'Regulation theory, the local state and the transition of urban politics', *Environment and Planning D: Society and Space* 11, 67–88.

Harvey, D. (1985) *The Urbanisation of Capital*, Oxford: Blackwell.

HM Treasury (1995) *A Framework for the Evaluation of Regeneration Projects and Programmes*, London: HM Treasury.

HM Treasury (2004) *Review of Statistics for Economic Policymaking – Final Report*, Norwich: HMSO.

Ho, S.Y. (1999) 'Evaluating urban regeneration programmes in Britain: Exploring the potential of the realist approach', *Evaluation* 5, 422–438.

Ho, S.Y. (2003) *Evaluating British Urban Policy: Ideology, Conflict and Compromise*, Aldershot, Hants: Ashgate.

Hordijk, M. and Baud, I. (2006) 'The role of research and knowledge generation in collective action and urban governance: How can researchers acts as catalysts?', *Habitat International* 30, 668–689.

Hudson, R., Dunford, M., Hamilton, D. and Kotter, R. (1997) 'Developing regional strategies for economic success: Lessons from Europe's economically successful regions?', *European Urban and Regional Studies* 4, 4, 365–373.

James, T.S. (2009) 'Whatever happened to regulation theory? The regulation approach and local government revisited', *Policy Studies* 30, 2, 181–201.

Jessop, B. (1990) 'Regulation theories in retrospect and prospect', *Economy and Society* 19, 153–216.

Jessop, B. (1997) 'A neo-Gramscian approach to the regulation of urban regimes', in M. Lauria, (ed.) *Reconstructing Urban Regime Theory*, London: Sage, 51–73.

Jessop, B. (2006) 'Spatial fixes, temporal fixes and spatio-temporal fixes', in N. Castree, and D. Gregory (eds) *David Harvey: A Critical Reader*, Oxford: Blackwell Publishing.

Jones, M. (1999) *New Institutional Spaces*, London: Jessica Kingsley.

Krinsky, J. (2006) 'The dialectics of privatization and advocacy in New York City's workfare state', *Social Justice* 33, 3, 158–174.

Lipietz, A. (1987) *Mirages and Miracles: The Crises of Global Fordism*, London: New Left Books.

Majale, M. (2008) 'Employment creation through participatory urban planning and slum upgrading: The case of Kitale', *Kenya Habitat International* 32, 270–282.

McCann, E. (2008) 'Expertise, truth, and urban policy mobilities: Global circuits of knowledge in the development of Vancouver, Canada's "four pillar" drug strategy', *Environment and Planning A* 40, 885–904.

Molotch, H. (1991) 'The political economy of urban growth machines', *Journal of Urban Affairs* 15, 29–53.

Nutley, S. (2003) 'Bridging the policy/research divide: Reflections and lessons from the UK', Paper presented at 'Facing the Future: Engaging stakeholders and citizens in developing public policy'. National Institute of Governance Conference, Canberra, Australia, 23/24 April. Available at: http://www.treasury.govt.nz/publications/media-speeches/guestlectures/pdfs/tgls-nutley.pdf.

OECD (2004) *Evaluating Local Economic and Employment Development: How to Assess What Works among Programmes and Policies*, Paris: OECD.

OECD (2008) *Making Local Strategies Work: Building the Evidence Base*, Paris: OECD.

Painter, J. and Goodwin, M. (1995) 'Local governance and concrete research: Investigating the uneven development of regulation', *Economy and Society* 24, 334–356.

Peck, J. (2003) 'Geography and public policy: Mapping the penal state', *Progress in Human Geography* 27, 2, 222–232.

Peck, J. and Tickell, A. (1992) 'Local modes of social regulation? Regulation theory, Thatcherism and uneven development', *Geoforum* 23, 3, 347–363.

Peck, J. and Tickell, A. (1995) 'The social regulation of uneven development: "Regulatory deficit", England's South East and the collapse of Thatcherism', *Environment and Planning A* 27, 15–40.

Peters, A. and Fisher, P. (2004) 'The failures of economic development incentives', *Journal of the American Planning Association* 70, 1, 27–37.

Pike, A., Rodríguez-Pose, A. and Tomaney, J. (2007) 'What kind of local and regional development and for whom?', *Regional Studies* 41, 9, 1253–1269.

Reese, L.A. and Fasenfest, D. (1997) 'What works best? Values and the evaluation of local economic development policy', *Economic Development Quarterly* 11, 3, 195–207.

Rubin, H.J. (1988) 'Shoot anything that flies, claim anything that falls: Conversations with economic development practitioners', *Economic Development Quarterly* 2, 3, 236–251.

Sanderson, I. (2002) 'Evaluation, policy learning and evidence-based policy making', *Public Administration* 80, 1, 1–22.

Taylor, D. (2005) 'Governing through evidence: Participation and power in policy evaluation', *Journal of Social Policy* 34, 4, 601–618.

Turok, I. (1989) 'Evaluation and understanding in local economic policy', *Urban Studies* 26, 2, 587–606.

Valler, D. and Wood, A. (2010) 'Conceptualising local and regional economic development in the United States', *Regional Studies* 44 (2): 139–151.

Valler, D., Wood, A. and North, P. (2000) 'Local governance and local business interests: A critical review', *Progress in Human Geography* 24, 3, 409–428.

Wolman, H. and Spitzley, D. (1996) 'The politics of local economic development', *Economic Development Quarterly* 10, 2, 115–150.

Further reading

Ho, S.Y. (2003) *Evaluating British Urban Policy: Ideology, Conflict and Compromise*, Aldershot: Ashgate (An excellent flavour of the reality of evaluative procedures in the context of a new era of public management in the UK.)

OECD (2004) *Evaluating Local Economic and Employment Development: How to Assess What Works among Programmes and Policies*, Paris: OECD. (An invaluable starting point, introducing evaluation issues across a wide range of policy forms together with important critical reflection.)

47

The new regional governance and the hegemony of neoliberalism

John Lovering

All change – no change?

The surge of academic interest in the region from the 1980s (which morphed into a focus on the 'city' and then the 'city-region' in the 2000s), paralleled by the explosion of employment in various agencies dedicated to 'regional development', has transformed the intellectual and policy landscape, and teaching orthodoxies (Pike *et al.* 2006). But the proliferation of journals, books, edited collections, conferences, consultancies, TV and radio programmes and websites that have followed contrasts oddly with the lack of any really significant change in hierarchies of regional economic development. Elvis Presley would not be impressed: there has been a lot more conversation than action. This chapter explores this apparent paradox. It argues that the emergence of an intellectual and policy 'New Regionalism' since the 1980s has been primarily an ideological and political development, in which theory, research and policy analysis has been, in effect, subordinate to the top-down reconstruction of spatial governance and the spatial imaginary by national governments. The latter has been intimately bound up with the globalisation of neoliberalism. I suggest here that the reconstruction of arguments for, and

institutions of, regional governance has done more than merely reflect the impact of neoliberal ideas and neoliberalising intentions. Rather, they have played a major role in constituting neoliberalism as a ubiquitous ideological and material force (this does not mean that anyone mentioned here actually intended this outcome).

Neoliberalism was exported with increasing vigour and success from its American heartland to much of the rest of the world from the late 1970s to the mid-2000s. It consisted essentially of the use of state power, paradoxically to 'undo' the legacies of earlier uses of state power (Hayek 1944). But being essentially an ethical and cognitive dogma, it has been remarkably weak on economics, both at the level of pure high theory and at the level of dirtier everyday practice. The wave of neoliberalisation that has swept around the planet over the past two to three decades was accordingly accompanied not by the boom that neoliberal advocates anticipated, but by overall economic growth rates that were relatively feeble by historical standards in all but a few geographically and socially exceptional cases. The neoliberal turn neither raised capitalism to new levels of dynamism, nor did it diminish capitalism's inherent tendency to uneven development (even before the outbreak of the new great Recession). Instead, it gave rise to the expansion and legitimisation of the 'political class' (Oborne 2007). Neoliberalising capitalisms are not freer, more open ones; on the contrary, they proliferate new forms of intervention in the 'life-world'. The expansion of the political class has, however, had some economic effects. It has created a major market for new policy 'discourses', which has been met – thanks to the contemporaneous neoliberalisation of the University and the emergence of a new cohort of academic commodity salespeople – by the creation of new degree and professional courses and other tools of credentialisation geared to the creation of new spatial development professions. All this scurrying about has created a significant number of jobs for those involved one way or another in the (global) reconstruction of spatial governance. And the regional scale, I suggest, is a case in point. The New Regionalism in ideas and in practices has been accompanied by a proliferation of private and public networks and bureaucracies, but cannot be attributed with a lot of innovatory economic change. It has been good for an in-group minority. But whether it has been as good for anyone else, and indeed for 'regions' in general, is much less certain.

Neoliberalism and regional analysis

The global economic recession which erupted in 2008–9 belatedly drew public attention to the pervasive, and dysfunctional, role of neoliberalism in the restructuring of national and global policy thinking, economic institutions, and patterns of economic and socio-cultural development which followed the crisis of the 'Keynesian' approach to policy in the 1970s (Davidson 2009). The recession has widened the debate on the inherent problems in the neoliberal *weltanschauung* to a wider audience, and has opened up new

questions concerning the principles which might inform a 'post-neoliberal' reconstruction (not that these have yet had much influence on practice – Turner 2009). The intellectual inadequacies of neoliberalism have been well known and widely available from long before the recent neoliberal adventure began (Davidson 2009, Krugman 2008). But in the regional (and latterly city-regional) policy fields a critical awareness of the significance of neoliberalism has been conspicuously absent, both before and after the outbreak of recession.

'Theorising' in the regional and latterly urban policy fields has all too often taken the postmodern form of a mutually agreeable sharing of acceptable discourses and assumptions. The work of a relatively small number of regional geographers and economists since the mid-1980s led to the construction of a well-defined new orthodoxy (a neat summary of which, presented in a celebratory light, is given in the biographical introduction to Richard Florida's 2005 *Cities and the Creative Class*; for a less flattering view see Lovering 1999, 2006). This has paralleled the emergence of a new cohort of 'ideas entrepreneurs' in the public policy field as the boundaries between official academic and policy work have become increasingly porous. With the advance of neoliberalism public policy-makers have increasingly sought legitimacy in fashionable academic theories. And entrepreneurial academics have been keen to package their insights as fashionable commodities. This has perhaps been particularly the case in the regional, and now urban, policy arenas where it has sometimes lapsed into 'theory led by policy'.

This tendency has been particularly evident where policy-makers and their intellectuals have found common ground in fixating on this or that supposedly magic policy bullet. In the early 1990s the leading global example was perhaps Michael Porter, whose work on clusters became an international hit in industrial and spatial policy circles. The most prominent example today is probably

Richard Florida, whose optimistic vision of the role of the so-called 'creative classes' in urban development has been packaged as a commodity and eagerly consumed by a global policy-maker audience, spending public dollars. Both of these cases exemplify the lack of interest on the part of fashionable policy voices in neoliberalism, and their preference for supposed technologically driven transformations such as the advent of Flexible Specialisation, the arrival of the 'New Economy' or the age of 'Smart' Business as explaining recent history. The weakness which has characterised the intellectual dimension of the rise of the New Regionalism (and New City-Regionalism) is best understood, I suggest, as a consequence of the peculiar political sociology of the restructuring of spatial governance in capitalist societies, and this is the central theme in the following discussion. To put it bluntly, the main consumers of these ideas are not too worried about how well grounded they are, for they like the conclusions to which they apparently lead.

The region as a policy object

Spatial policy is inevitably a matter both of ideas and of (formal and informal) institutions, all of which have taken different forms at different times. Countries at early stages in the nation-building phase generally devoted more attention to the development of an overarching sense of – and institutions for – national unity than to 'internal' geographical questions. Only later, when a national economic space was taken for granted, did internal geographical economic disparities come to be seen as important, especially where they connected to perceived political and cultural differences. Sometimes large states failed to address those problems adequately, and this became one reason why the number of states has quadrupled since 1950 to over 200 today. The recession of the 1930s gave rise to the first systematic spatial-economic strategies in Europe as a result of the decline

of former industrial regions into chronic unemployment and underutilisation of capacity. The resulting 'regional' policies gave rise to the spatial units which would be used by central governments for accounting, administration and implementation purposes for the following half century (Keating 1999: 55). In the Keynesian 'Golden Age' of rapid and relatively inclusive growth, regional and urban geography become not only analytical points of view but also sources of governmentality and of policy experiments.

The resulting rise of a regional development aspect of governance generated the notion of expert regional 'knowledges', and the construction of a new intellectual service sector with its own criteria of professional expertise. In pre-neoliberal times this knowledge was conceived in broadly 'Keynesian' and 'Myrdalian' terms. In this vision, tax-generated funds and planning constraints were mobilised to meet national spatial goals by encouraging the spatial redistribution of industry and to a lesser extent, manpower, to iron out regional economic imbalances; cooling 'hot spots' and warming up colder zones bypassed by market forces. As everyone knows, from the 1970s this approach withered under the joint impact of the proto-neoliberal taxpayer revolt which constrained the growth of public funding, and changing national economic policy goals and processes. The latter was not merely a 'technical' adaptation to changing real-world circumstances. More important was a profound shift of analytical perspective in elite (and increasingly global) policy-making circles, then the media, then 'public opinion' (and votes) concerning the role the state should play in economic management. This shift has been given many names according to the writer's perspective and the historical scale imagined, ranging from post-Fordism', the emergence of 'post-political' society, the advent of 'post-modernity', or even the 'New Enlightenment'. The perspective I argue for here sees the crucial dimension for our purposes as the ascendancy of neoliberalism as a new and relatively coherent ideological and organisational package (described from a sympathetic insider's point of view in Cockett (1995), and from outsider critics in Harvey (2002).

The resulting shift in modes of thinking, and policy, concerning the goals and methods of regional 'development' was followed from the 1990s by a similar reorientation concerning first cities and then 'city-regions'. Two themes have been particularly prominent at all three scales. The first was a cognitive shift towards seeing places as bounded 'entities' to be studied in their own right (although exactly how has always been controversial). The second was a normative bias towards the idea that places could and should improve their 'competitiveness' and thereby pull themselves up by their own metaphorical bootstraps. The proliferation of these ideas characterised what I called a decade ago the New Regionalism (Lovering 1999) in which the region is a privileged scale for capital (a 'crucible of innovation'), for civil society (the nursery of spatial 'identity') and for governance (and thence 'leadership'). Appropriate policies dedicated to these goals would, so the New Regionalist fable had it, reproducing neoliberal assumptions, improve regional 'bootstrapping capacity'.

Depoliticisation

An important but under-investigated aspect of this was that it implied the 'depoliticisation' of regional economic policy; what regions (or cities) needed was less politics, more business experts, and (for Florida specially) more pluralism and tolerance. This doctrine reproduced at the sub-national scale the depoliticisation of economic analysis and the determination of policy goals and methods which has been a key objective of neoliberalism at the national and international levels (Hui 2006). The extraction of politics and the delegitimising of fundamental debate over values, goals and methods differentiated this 'New Regionalism' from the 'Old Regionalism' at the level of

principle (if not always practice), because in the latter the central theoretical and practical question was distributional (and so inescapably 'political'); how should the state redistribute resources between places, and thence people? The 'depoliticised' approach that is now dominant regards regions/cities not as components of a mutually dependent moral and political community (parts of an implicit Aristotelian polity) but as quasi-individuals, obliged to find their own ways to economic vitality. Competing with equivalent others, they have both the opportunity and, crucially, the moral responsibility to boost their own capacities and skills in order to increase their market shares. By embedding this 'must try harder' bias in institutions and in discourses to which the new leaderships of reconstructed regional/urban governance were obliged to subscribe, New Regionalist ideas played a major role in validating and spreading neoliberal ideas and practice. But since the latter never stood much chance of achieving significant effects in terms of creating jobs and incomes, this meant that the New Regionalism was bound to become primarily an ideological and governance project.

The elephant in the new regional room – neoliberalism

This was never, of course, explicit. For many of those involved it was not even intended. The reconstruction of spatial governed focused on the region and then the city was presented as a requirement of simple good economic sense. Some added a 'sentimental' justification too, for such a restructuring of governance could also give new life to regional or urban 'identities'. But the influence of the parallel national and international shift towards neoliberalism was downplayed, denied, or more commonly simply overlooked (Cooke and Morgan 1996, Florida 2005).

Yet it would appear bizarre to a historically minded observer to suggest that such a radical cognitive and normative reorientation could be unaffected by the wider context in which neoliberalism has provided the overarching official *weltanschauung*, the most widely endorsed way of thinking, both cognitively and normatively, in state and business circles, and in academic and other communities, and in much of popular culture or 'civil society' for the past three decades (Harvey 2002, Gamble 2009, Hui 2006). To suggest that it has deeply influenced the goals of public policy, and the methodological principles adopted by economists and geographers amongst others would be relatively uncontroversial in economics and political philosophy. But in academic regional geography and urban policy studies both sides of the Atlantic this would often raise a dissenting eyebrow. In these academic corridors the term neoliberalism has more often been avoided as 'too political', or as quaintly economistic – out of date in an era supposedly defined by postmodernity and the cultural turn. Some commentators, especially those close to government policy-making circles, have diminished the significance of neoliberalism by detaching the term from its historical and social-scientific meaning and identifying it instead with (a journalistic reading of) the particular set of policy paradigms and packages associated with Reagan in the USA in the 1980s and Thatcher in the UK. As such, it is long since dead and gone, and not worth wasting too much time on today. In this mode Alan Harding in urban policy, for example, and Pike *et al.* in the regional field (2006: 28) admit the 'N' word only in their background historical sketches.

Reading neoliberalism in this way is reasonable enough if one's aim is less to relate policy approaches to their historical context than to fit them into neat boxes with party-political labels in a tidy chronological list. But this risks missing the wood for the trees, reducing policy to a series of pragmatic adjustments, or intrusions of a set of intellectual fashions that are essentially arbitrary. Above all, it forgets the vast literature on historical patterns in the rise and fall of policy paradigms since the origins of capitalism and the advent of the 'reformist state' from the late eighteenth century (Polanyi 1944). The relationship between the state and the economy has been reconceived and redesigned at intervals – triggered by recessions and crises – ever since, oscillating between a fairly well-defined set of oppositions, alternatively advocating and deprecating an active interventionist role on the part of the state. As Gamble (2009) puts it, the policy-intellectual preference has in effect wobbled between an 'efficient state' hypothesis (the most recent case being Keynesianism), and an 'efficient market' hypothesis (neoliberalism).

What is neoliberalism anyway?

So we need to spend a few moments pinning down just what this thing called neoliberalism is. Classical Liberalism crystallised out of a highly diverse set of eighteenth-century doctrines which shared the aim of reducing authoritarian government by Church or State. In the nineteenth and twentieth centuries Liberal theorists narrowed their social and ethical vision and focused in particular on the supposed virtues of private property rights, stressing the need to reorient the use of state power to avoid 'interfering' with what, after John Locke, they wished to see as Natural Rights. The degree to which the state should also address social inequalities and long-term visions of the Social Good became increasingly problematic for Liberal thought as the twentieth century approached the twenty-first. Early Liberals accepted the need for a major role here to create a healthy population and a decent social order (Liberals designed the British welfare state, implemented by Labour and then by Conservative governments between the 1940s and 1960s). Late twentieth-century neoliberals took a much less generous and more myopically economic approach, explicitly or implicitly relying on the Burkean claim that inequalities are acceptable so far as they are the result, and the cause, of general economic improvement. This reduction of classical Liberal thought to the harsher doctrine of 'neoliberalism' (the term was first used by Milton Friedman in 1953) was however motivated by concerns that were only in part economic. Its advocates saw themselves as the latest carriers of the moral message of the Enlightenment (Ebenstein 1997). By prioritising natural property rights and market forces governments could bring about immediate economic gains, and these would eventually bring about the only kind of ethical and social transformation that 'human nature', as Liberalism conceives of it, would allow to become sustainable. So in the 1990s (while many geographers were obsessing over the arrival of Postmodernity and the demise of Grand Theory) one of the most ambitious examples of Modernist grand theory was rising to global ascendancy in the world outside in the form of neoliberalism.

Neoliberalism is an ambitious programme which brings with it a set of epistemological, normative and methodological principles. As such it supplies not only 'off-the-shelf' policy guidelines. It also offers a vision of what 'development' means, and the ethical assumptions this entails. Liberalism rests on a radically naturalistic conception of the individual and thence society (Hayek 1944). It sees the attempt to deny this naturalism through irrational constraints on 'freedom', especially where these arise from collectivist institutions, as the ultimate cause of economic (and political) failures, including spatial ones. Where neoliberalism is the theory neoliberalisation became the practice – the extension of commodity production in place of non-market exchanges, the commodification of more and more areas of social life, and of space. As analysts like Frederic Jameson have insisted, neoliberalisation over the past three decades has radically extended the provenance of market forces and the capitalist dimension of social relations and culture.

Neoliberalism did not become ascendant from the 1980s through the 1990s because it was intellectually more sophisticated than its predecessors. 'neoclassical', 'new classical' or 'rational expectations' theories in economics were no better at explaining macroeconomic reality (Davidson 2007). The strength of the neoliberals has been organisational and ideological: they knew where to push and what to say to win over audiences (as traced by Cockett 1995). Because they imagined themselves to be heroic 'outsiders' to the academic and political Establishment, neoliberals have perhaps been more aware than their opponents that their agenda entails a ruthless but subtle realpolitik. In the circles that mattered neoliberalism became hegemonic largely because policy-makers and their target audiences were persuaded by the neoliberal assertion of the impossibility of business as usual. The contemporaneous transformation of the world political stage, as Soviet communism collapsed and the USA became the world's only superpower, helped validate this shift away from the 'efficient state' to the 'efficient market' assumption. This has had profound implications for analysis and policy thinking at all geographical scales. The 'neoliberal turn' largely explains, I suggest, why regional development in recent years has achieved so little in economic terms, and has paradoxically increased bureaucracy and 'ideological' interventions.

The globalisation of neoliberalism and the New Regionalism

Between the mid-1980s and mid-1990s governments, academics, and consultants, plus private 'ideas entrepreneurs' working for groups such as industrialist lobbies in the US and EU, developed a series of suggestions as to how spatial policies might be better geared to economic priorities. A common theme was the emphasis on 'clustering', inferred from observation of some successful industrial compels, such as aerospace and IT, as reported by the influential Michael Porter in the US. This resuscitated an old economic geographical theme in the new form of a policy package. Porterism insisted that 'clustering' was essential, and that it required supportive institutional adjustments. The idea that historically new technological and global-economic imperatives implied the need for a 'modernisation' of strategic imperatives and forms of governance became an orthodoxy. Subsequently, between the mid-1990s and mid 2000s, these orthodoxies were institutionalised in the form of policy recommendations, loan conditions, and political pressure from some of the world's most powerful organisations, not least the World Bank and European Commission (which after the demise of Delors in 1995 shifted from a broadly Keynesian to a broadly neoliberal orientation in many dimensions). In the European case, for example, the European Roundtable of Industrialists, arguably the 'peak' organisation representing corporate capital, played a major role in legitimating a reorientation of spatial policy from the early 1990s. Within a couple of years this had become the central plank of the European Regional Directorate, and numerous academic publications began to emerge reflecting this.

The top-down nature of the new regional policy agenda meant that in many regions it arrived as if dropped from a helicopter. In others they emerged more organically as the latest in a long series of regional experiments. In poorer countries, for example, the neoliberalisation of economic and regional strategy was more likely to come as part of a package of 'structural adjustment'. In the European Union, on the other hand, it has often come through the pressure on aspiring new members to demonstrate their acceptance of the 'European Acquis'. So today in Turkey, for example, part of the ritualistic dance which it has to perform to be accepted as a legitimate candidate for EU Membership (enthusiasm for which is sinking rapidly) is the establishment of formal regional structures. But Turkey has been highly centralised (at intervals a military quasi-dictatorship) since the republic was founded in 1923 and regions

do not have much pre-existing economic meaning. New Regionalist bodies such as Development Agencies therefore lack a plausible local economic rationale and popular political support, and are particularly prone to capture by maverick politicians or business special interests. At the opposite end of the EU the influence of neoliberal conceptions of economic imperatives and the New Regionalist turn has played the dominant role in the post-devolution economics of Wales. The emphasis on boosting competitiveness, and on supply-side polices such as 'skills training', offers a case study in importing and implementing New Regionalist orthodoxy, packaged in local-friendly talk of local special needs and autonomy. In both Wales and Turkey these developments are most significant not for what they are likely to do for regional economic development (little) but for what they reveal about how globalisation of policy discourses has impacted on the restructuring of spatial governance.

In Wales, devolution to the new National Assembly after 1999 allocated formal responsibility for 'regional' (now 'national') development to a newly elected body. But it lacked intellectual or political resources to do other than act out the global orthodoxy, especially since it was underwritten by Labour Party policy in London. The spatial pattern, and content, of economic development in Wales since devolution has been shaped more by the development of Cardiff – stereotypically neoliberal in its reliance on property markets and consumption – than by the well-meaning economic policy statements of the Welsh Assembly (Lovering and Bristow 2006). As in the Turkish case, there is a striking gap between the claims made for New Regional institutions and discourses, and the actual development of the space economy.

In general it would seem that the most interesting result of the creation of New Regional discourses and institutions, in terms of economic development, is that not much really happened as a result. At the level of detail different regional stories could of

587

course be told, and these details are not unimportant (such as the relative role of housing market boons, export industries versus service sectors, etc.). But there can be no denying that for all the organisational restructuring, consensus-building, network-ing at all scales, production of mountains of grey literature, lavish expenditure on market-ing and public relations material, and the employment of tens of thousands in region-ally badged institutions, the impact on the ranking of regions in terms of most indica-tors has been so modest as to be generally undetectable. The European Commission and the numerous European regional lobbies have been the noisiest advocates of new regional policy fashions since the 1990s, but there is little evidence of any significant change in the economic rankings of the component regions (Petrakos *et al.* 2005). The striking regional economic develop-ments in other parts of the world – for exam-ple, in India and South East China – have to be attributed to national developments within which New Regionalist 'bootstrap-ping' has had very limited significance. As analysis and as strategy, the New Regionalism hasn't worked. Yet like every good ideology, a chronic mismatch between theory and real-ity hasn't stopped it being influential.

The problematic agenda of New Regionalist policy

For most people in their target constituen-cies the proliferation of new regional institu-tions must seem like little more than another example of the expansion of the tax-funded 'quangocracy'. The construction of this new layer of governance has further expanded the political class (Oborne 2007). Since this has not been accompanied by noticeable regional economic gains it has sometimes prompted criticisms of an *ad hominem* nature. These focus on the supposed failings of leadership, or of key individuals, or the presence of too many sluggish bureaucrats as opposed to

dynamic businesspeople in policy-making circles. But what is really at stake here is not merely local failures of recruitment or of effort. The New Regionalism was never going to work; the creation of new policy principles and new institutions was never the application of practical wisdom to contin-gent problems. The new regional leaderships were never going to be able to deliver what was asked of them.

The focus on the supply side and lack of research into regional dynamics

The new regional strategic vision was justi-fied by appeal to a collection of generalised historical claims concerning the arrival of new ('post-Fordist') technologies, or the demise of state protectionism, the rise of the 'radical individual', or the world-historical transfor-mation of everything in sight implied by 'globalisation'; stories that converged on the idea that a restoration of competition and market forces should underlie the recon-struction of all economic governance. Those End of History assertions turned out, as they always do, to be premature. One example was the misinterpretation of the arrival of Flexible Specialisation to imply the end of mass pro-duction (of which there is now more than ever). Together with assertions about chang-ing industrial relations and consumer tastes these vague but intriguing notions congealed into claims for the arrival of the New Economy, which looked absurd within only a few years. Above all, the pressure to focus on 'supply-side' questions that was character-istic of neoliberal thinking led to chronic neglect of the demand side and of the real dynamics of spatial flows in economic devel-opment. Where Keynesian spatial policy had triggered efforts to understand the empirical macroeconomics of each region (or city, or city-region) the neoliberal influence directed attention elsewhere. In neoliberal eyes the real spatial agenda for each area (however exactly that is defined) is to learn how to 'bootstrap' itself into a more competitive state. Demand conditions are less important than the potential to change supply conditions; macroeconomic questions are someone else's responsibility.

In this spirit the construction of the new regional apparatus was accompanied by the production of mountain-high piles of reports, assessments, scoping studies, SWAT analyses and opinion surveys examining this or that spatial development or perceived local economic weakness. But few of these asked the most crucial questions about how regional economies actually function. In particular the relationship between external demand and internal variables – seen as vital to regional analysis in the Keynesian era since it constituted the 'export base' and its multipliers – has received very little attention since the 1970s. We now have libraries full of lists of regional and urban statistics and interview quotes, but hardly any exploring questions of economic significance. Economics has been displaced by Business Studies. The most fashionable writings manage to arrive at regional (or urban) development proposals without needing to descend to the level of local empirical detail at all; it is enough to invoke Global Truths and 'apply' them to local circumstances (for numerous examples relating to regions see the Michael Porter website; for cities see Richard Florida's, or in a more evasive vein Amin and Thrift 2002).

The political sociology of the New Regionalism – the Regional Service Class

The weaknesses of much of the information gathering inspired by new regional structures reflects the weaknesses of those structures themselves. And here we encounter perhaps the most problematic aspect of the new regional and urban apparatuses: their political sociology. New Regional 'theory' from the 1980s to the mid-1990s assumed in effect a fairly simple economistic basis for the

political character of the 'region', and of the institutions that should be built to articulate it. Regions are economic spaces that thrive by doing distinctive things (specialising), with (therefore) distinctive institutions and even social relations. But the spatiality conjured up by the recent restructuring of spatial governance has rarely coincided with that of the materiality of the capitalist economy and the geographies of empirical identities. Regions do not generally map onto fractions of capital, and have done less and less ever since the industrial revolution. Nor do they generally correspond to a unitary sense of identity and purpose. As a result the governance niches represented by the creation of new regional (city-regional) institutions, programmes, networks, and associations, have been occupied by individuals who have been generally unrepresentative of their regions, if only because their regions cannot be 'represented' by any single interest or discourse.

The occupants of these positions constitute what I suggest it is helpful to think of as the 'Regional Service Class' (or Urban, or City-Regional Service Class according to case). The concept of class is of course terribly unfashionable, especially in former Soviet countries where it was loaded with discredited associations. But the term captures the way in which occupations and shared discourses constitute distinct social groups, and in Weberian or Marxist versions it still has some value (as Florida rightly recognised in his conception of the Creative Classes). The concept of the Regional Service Class borrows from Karl Renner's attempt a century ago to characterise a growing social stratum at the nation-state (German) level (Lovering 2003). This 'service class' was neither capitalist nor worker. It performed functions for those more powerful (capital and the state), from whom it derived its slightly elevated economic and social status. For Renner the 'service class' raised new questions of origins (where does it come from?), composition (who is in it?), function (what does it do and how do it do it?) and also ethical and cognitive questions (what does it conceive to be the public Good?). These are useful hints as to how we might approach the new Regional Service Class (RSC), whose emergence has been perhaps the most significant empirical result of recent changes in spatial governance.

In the era of Keynesian regional policy the equivalent of the RSC would consist of central government functionaries, dedicated to the regional application or servicing of central policies. With the neoliberal turn and the related rise of the New Regionalism from the 1980s a new kind of RSC had to be constructed, with a new mission. In UK cases the new RSC often began in the 1980s as an embryonic group focused on inward investment. Over the following decade and a half this was expanded and encouraged to engage in a more ambitious, indeed holistic, sociocultural agenda for restructuring. The nature of the occupants of these roles, and the position they find themselves in, might best be illuminated by recalling the concept of territorial 'cadres' developed by van der Pijl in his important studies of the evolution of national and international economic development in the mid-twentieth century (1998). These describe how throughout recent history a small and identifiable set of policy cadres have played a key role of identifying from within the flux of events the emergence of a crisis, and securing support for a comprehensive policy shift to resolve it. The key 'cadres' of Keynesian capitalism operated in the apparatus of central government, the higher echelons of the business world, and the institutions most directly implicated in the development and exploration of ideological discourses – Universities, 'think-tanks' and consultancies, plus the media.

In this spirit we could define the RSC as those cadres working in the region who are officially engaged in the project of visualising the region and its relations to the wider world. Its business is cognitive and normative – producing and transmitting

ideas about what regional development consists of, and how to achieve it. But in one important respect this can never be a 'true' regional equivalent to Renner's service class. For regional service class can only have a somewhat tenuous relationship to industry and a complex or compromised relationship to central government. Since regions do not map onto economic circuits, production chains, or interest groups in any clear or consistent manner, the RSC is likely to suffer both an excess of 'autonomy' and a deficit of 'representativeness'. A glance at the rise of urban boosterism in the US is instructive here.

In his 1989 analysis of urban entrepreneurialism David Harvey highlighted the key roles played by urban coalitions formed by economic interests, in particular property developers, and urban political elites:

> The new urban entrepreneurialism typically rests, then on a public–private partnership focusing on investment and economic development with the specific construction of place rather than amelioration of the conditions within a particular territory as its immediate (though by no means exclusive) political and economic goal.
>
> (Harvey 1989: 8)

In the present context this can be regarded as an outline of the political economy of the 'Urban Service Class'. It suggests it will tend to be committed to focusing on policies that are likely to enhance property values and the urban tax base. To these ends it works with others to encourage what comes to be bracketed as 'regeneration' in various consumer- and investor-friendly forms. Harvey suggests that the natural focus of urban entrepreneurialism is property development and urban regeneration, for the housing and property markets are generally 'urban'.

What could be the equivalent at the regional level? Housing and property markets, not to mention manufacturing, do not fall into neat regional boundaries. Commodity chains and corporate industrial grouping very rarely follow a regional pattern. The region, even more than the city, sits awkwardly across functional economic boundaries. We may conclude that the character of a Regional Service Class is likely to be even more 'semi-detached' from its ostensible socioeconomic base than its urban parallel. If regions were the way some 1980s regional theories claimed then they might be expected to generate a coherent Regional Service Class. But they are generally not like that, and the construction of a Regional Service Class has accordingly had to be most 'unnatural', that is to say, driven, by the national state, from above and afar. As a result the de facto Regional Service Classes which have been constructed as part of the creation of new regional institutions of governance have usually been no more than what Allen and Cochrane nicely describe as an 'assemblage' (2007). This is a recipe for bureaucratic compromise, not a political expression of convergent economic interests (in Marxist language: a spatially identifiable fraction of capital). But this does not mean it cannot act as a Pijlian cadre. Rather, the fact that there is no preexisting self-evident economic interest which it can represent and strategise for suggests that it will enjoy a high degree of autonomy, able to make the running because no one else can.

Why new regional institutions incline towards symbols and performative governance

This helps explain why in so many regions the focus of the main players in economic governance is on what at first seem to be relatively trivial matters such as the construction of new imaginaries around regional identity, and regionally badged 'spectacle'. The reimagining of the city, in particular, has been a hot topic in recent research, and

has exercised many urban geographers, cultural theorists, planners and urban designers (Amin and Thrift 2002). What's missing in most of this literature is any recognition that the impulse to this reimagining and conscious 'reimaging' has been powerfully influenced by the political economy of economic governance, rather than some kind of autonomous general global economic and cultural shift. Under pressure to demonstrate that they are doing something worthwhile, especially when their funding is only partly provided by central government, they are likely to seize on 'symbolic' activities where performance is at once highly visible, and inoffensive to any major vested interest.

The reapolitik of institutional survival, in circumstances where the institution concerned cannot hope to satisfy any but a few local economic interests, encourages a tendency to excessive displays of the performance of governance. If you can't deliver much in material terms, you can at least put on a good show to demonstrate that your existence is worthwhile. It is no surprise that the 'performative turn' in regional and urban governance should recently have become so ostentatious and pervasive. There are few regions and cities in which the presence of the local regional development agency or similar actor is not noisily demonstrated to the public in light shows, firework displays, sponsorship of all sorts, festivals and goodwill events and lots of new signage. Here the New Regional (and urban) pattern echoes the broader tendency of neoliberalism; what ordinary people, and even most businesspeople, know about their local economy is shaped by the up beat story local agencies of governance tell about it. And the positive image that invariably results is consolidated by the everyday observation of the extraordinary new Cities of Spectacle that have transformed the visual horizon on most cities on the planet.

There may be unemployment and inequality, and you may not be able even to live here, but the well-manicured urban spectacle on display surely means that things are looking up! Walter Benjamin saw the arcade as a monument to the production of commodities. The urban experience is shaped by representations. And what better to represent the revitalisation of the region/city/city-region than a glorious new shopping mall, glamorous architecture, and lots of sexy new bars and restaurants? Those whose jobs depend on keeping the new spatial apparatus in business are likely to regard a focus on image management targeted at elite groups as a perfectly rational approach to 'economic development', for understandable reasons (for which they can find plenty of succour in the publications of a Porter or a Florida or a Landy). And the absence of a public discourse questioning the dominant conception of economic development, and a more democratic structure of spatial governance through which it could find expression, means there are few voices to disagree. A bias towards rhetoric, image management, and celebration is inherent in the neoliberalisation of spatial governance (Lovering 2007).

The New Recession and the future of Regionalism

The era of global neoliberalism was one of faltering and uneven growth, even before the recession broke out in 2008. It is inevitable that the attempt to create lots of little regional players competing in this semi-stagnant wider context should have little to show for itself. With the arrival of Recession the regional apparatus that has so laboriously been constructed over the past couple of decades now faces new challenges. How will these already feeble apparatuses of governance maintain their credibility (and funding) when they are unable to claim even modest economic success? Will the pressure to demonstrate governance through symbolic activities become even more intense? Or will it seem even more absurd to

subsidise floral displays on airport highways while doing nothing to address chronic unemployment?

These are of course political questions. As noted earlier, one of the most worrying aspects of the emergence of the new apparatus of spatial governance, thanks largely to the dominance within it of what I have called New Regionalist thinking, is that they have not been accompanied by a general local political engagement in the development of economic goals and strategies. Just the opposite; the depoliticising current inherent in the regional governance agenda in practice (if not in the more Utopian new regionalist theoretical speculations) has worked against this. The New Regional turn proved to be not an agenda for social inclusiveness and political regeneration, but for the consolidation of a professionalised political class, and a focus on policies intended to persuade the local public, rather than represent it.

Given this, the prospects for the Recession are particularly gloomy. Regional structures are far better placed to become specialists in spatialist ideology ('our region/city is the most famous/competitive/beautiful/important') than to become political spaces for new constituencies and new demands. And indeed the Recession has so far drawn forth a mainly conservative response which stresses the need to do what was already ostensibly being done, but even more energetically. If the recovery continues to take the form of renewed financial profitability alongside entrenched slow growth and chronic underemployment, the pressure will surely be towards more of the same. In this gloomy scenario the new regional governance continues to act out the logical corollaries of the absence of a macroeconomic strategy aimed at sustainable and high-quality employment. Having already developed, through lack of alternatives, skills in symbolic gestures and performative governance, the Regional Service Class may find it has acquired just the capacities that fit the new bill; a recipe for authoritarianism and further image management.

The reconstruction of spatial governance in reality has taken a very different form, with less attractive effects, from that anticipated in New Regionalist theorising. I have argued that this is largely because the latter failed to take into account the factor of neoliberalism (and the global hegemony of the US). Now that both of these are in question, we have the opportunity to subject the inherited wisdom to fresh challenges. And this will mean paying much more attention to the processes whereby the de facto Regional Service Class is constructed, and to what it does and why. There is an older and simpler language for this; it revolves around the word democracy. The challenges to dominant economic thinking and policy implicit in the notion of a Green New Deal, or of local empowerment, or of a remoralisation of the economy, all point at sub-national level to the need for a greater awareness and understanding of the content and behaviour of the Regional Service Class, and for measures that may help transform it into something very different from its neoliberal incarnation.

References and further reading

Regional development and governance trends

Bristow, G. and Lovering, J. (2006) 'Shaping events, or celebrating the way the wind blows? The role of competitiveness strategy in Cardiff's "ordinary transformation"', in A. Hooper and J. Punter (eds) *Capital Cardiff 1975–2020: Regeneration, Competitiveness and the Urban Environment*, Cardiff: University of Wales Press.

Pike, A. (2004) 'Heterodoxy and the Governance of economic development', *Environment and Planning A*, 36, 2141–2161.

Pike, A., Rodriguez-Pose, Andres and Tomaney, John. (2006) *Local and Regional Development*, London: Routledge.

Porter, M.E. (1990) *The Competitive Advantage of Nations*, New York: Free Press.

Petrakos, G. Rodrígues-Pose, A. and Rovolis. A. (2005) 'Growth, integration and regional disparities in the European Union', *Environment and Planning A*, 37, 10, 1837–1855.

Depoliticisation and the construction of a New Regionalist (and urban) orthodoxy

Amin, A. and Thrift, N. (2002) *Reimagining the Urban*, Cambridge: Polity Press.

Cooke, P. and Morgan, K.(2000) *The Associational Economy*, Oxford: Oxford University Press.

Florida, R. (2005) *Cities and the Creative Class*, London: Routledge.

Harvey, D. (1989) "From managerialism to entrepreneurialism: The transformation in urban governance in late capitalism", *Geografiska Annaler. Series B* 71 (1), 3–17.

Lovering, J. (1999) 'Theory led by policy: The New Regionalism', *International Journal of Urban and Regional Research* 23, 379–395.

Lovering, J. (2006) 'The new imperial geography', in Helen Lawton Smith and Sharmi Bakhti-Sen (eds) *Economic Geography, Past Present and Future* London: Routledge.

Lovering, J. (2007) 'The relationship between Neoliberalism and Urban Regeneration', *International Planning Studies* 12, 4, 343–366.

Oborne, P. (2007) *The Triumph of the Political Class*, London: Pocket Books.

Polanyi, K. (1994) *The Great Transformation: The Political and Economic Origins of our Time*, New York: Farrar & Rinehart.

Wang Hui (2006) 'Depoliticised politics from East to West', *New Left Review* 41, 29–45.

Weakness of Neoliberalism as economic theory, and origins of the recession

Davidson, P. (2009) *John Maynard Keynes*, Abingdon: Routledge.

Gamble, A. (2009) *The Spectre at the Feast: Capitalist Crisis and the Politics of Recession*, London: Palgrave.

Krugman, P. (2008) *The Return of Depression Economics*, London: Penguin Books.

The political economy of neoliberalism as a hegemonic policy discourse

Cockett, R.(1995) *Thinking the Unthinkable: Think-tanks and the Economic Counter-revolution 1931–1982*, London: HarperCollins.

Ebenstein, A. (2007) *Milton Friedman*, New York: Palgrave.

Hayek, F. (1944) *The Road to Serfdom*, Chicago: University of Chicago Press.

The politics of place and context

Allen, J. and Cochrane, A. (2007) 'Beyond the territorial fix: Regional assemblages', *Politics and Power Regional Studies* 41, 9, 1161–1175.

Lovering, J. (2003) 'The Regional Service Class', in Nicholas A. Phelps and Philip Raines, (eds) *The New Competition for Inward Investment: Companies, Institutions and Territorial Development* London: Edward Elgar.

van der Pijl, K. (1998) *Transnational Classes and International Relations*, London: Routledge.

Turner, B. (2009) 'Citizens, communities and conflict: Surviving globalization', *Citizenship Studies*, 13, 40, 431–437.

48

Local Left strategy now

Jamie Gough and Aram Eisenschitz

Introduction

Leftwing local initiatives often develop out of capitalist crises such as that which has developed globally since 2007 – Germany in the 1920s, Italy in the 1970s, Britain in the 1980s, the US in the 1990s, Latin America in the current decade. When living standards fall, when the proportion of those is unemployed or when poverty rises, when nation states either choose not to or are powerless to intervene, then a radical local politics may emerge. This politics may go beyond quantitative amelioration of economic conditions to develop qualitatively new social relations and genuinely liberatory politics. Crises do not always, however, lead to such local politics: the strategies adopted by the Left can be crucial, and these are the subject of this chapter. We put forward our own views on Left strategy, but include others' through critique. We consider more developed countries (MDCs) and urban areas in newly industrialised countries (NICs), where the majority of the population depend directly or indirectly on waged labour; we shall use the Marxist term 'the working class' to refer to this majority; we do not consider local struggles in the rural Third World.

Since the industrial revolution, the Left, with the partial exceptions of anarchism, syndicalism and utopian socialism, has tended to see the national and international scales as strategically the most important. Key flows of capital and commodities are at these scales, and nation states have greater powers and resources than local and regional government; accordingly, the focus of the Left has been to influence these economic flows and the nation state. But we shall argue in this chapter that the 'local' scale, stretching from home and workplace to region, is an essential scale for Left politics, and indeed has specific strengths for the Left. It is true that the place of the local within wider economic flows and higher scale state structures makes Left local strategy problematic and replete with tensions and pitfalls: localism has often been a trap for the Left. The purpose of this chapter is to shed light on some of these difficulties and dilemmas, in the present context of neoliberalism and its crisis. Such a discussion is particularly important in the present period due to the burgeoning of local economic initiatives and urban programmes, most of which do not advance Left politics and many of which militate against it. We therefore seek here to develop ideas for a distinctively Left approach to local development which prioritises the interests of the working class.

We first consider the dependence of Left local politics on its national and international political setting by using the example of Left initiatives in Britain since the late 1960s. We then consider the present difficult – but not hopeless – situation internationally for the Left after 30 years of neoliberalism. Section IV considers some strategic issues for a Left local politics that can begin to overcome working class fragmentation and depoliticisation. Section V considers how these principles might be carried through in particular kinds of local initiative.

The rise and fall of the local Left in Britain

In Britain from the late 1960s until the defeat of the miners' strike in 1985 there was an open political crisis, generated by unprecedentedly low profit rates of British capital, moves to austerity by capital and the state, and militant resistance to the latter by trade unions, social movements and residents' organisations (Glyn and Harrison 1980). While some of this resistance was nationally organised, much of it arose from local organisations. Regarding employment, previously non-militant groups of workers such as British Asians and women in Ford, Imperial Typewriters and Grunwick, as well as previously well-organised workers such as dockers, printers and car workers, undertook long disputes; workers occupied closed factories; even the two crucial national miners' strikes of 1973 and 1984–5 were strongly rooted in the mining communities. A well-organised national network of shop stewards was sometimes able to link strong workplace organisation to solidarity within and beyond the industry. Resistance around council house rents and squatting was also highly localised and differentiated, as were many of the actions of the women's and black movements. Responding to grassroots resistance, the 1970s and early 1980s also saw

radical initiatives issuing from some Left Labour councils – sometimes rather grandly dubbed 'municipal socialism'. Their main foci were the maintenance of their services and the tax revenue to fund them, and initiatives to sustain and improve local jobs and further equal opportunities (Boddy and Fudge 1984; Eisenschitz and Gough 1993: 75–86; GLC 1985, 1986; Gyford 1985). The latter local economic initiatives were inspired by the dominant strategy adopted by the trade union and Labour Left nationally, the Alternative Economic Strategy (Coventry *et al.* Trades Councils 1980; London CSE 1980) – a major statement of which was edited by the former British prime minister (Brown 1975). This strategy envisaged public investment in the private economy, with the state exerting increasing control, to improve innovativeness and productivity, widen and deepen skills, give workers greater say in their industries, and overcome social disadvantages within work; conversion to socially useful and eco products was also proposed. These ideas made a brief appearance in the manifesto and first year of the 1974 Labour government; but otherwise local authorities had to carve out their Left policies within tight legal and financial constraints, in opposition to national governments; after the decisive defeat of the miners and the government's 1986 abolition of the Metropolitan Counties, these efforts collapsed.

The subsequent 20 years in Britain have seen very few localised struggles, notable exceptions being the local-national revolt against the poll tax in 1990 and some site-based ecological protests; the few workplace-based strikes have generally remained isolated and been defeated. Neoliberal discipline was imposed in Britain more heavily and successfully than in other developed countries excepting the US, through maintaining a high value of sterling (deflating manufacturing in particular), imposing anti-trade union laws, and privatising much of the previously well-unionised public sector. The strongly credit-based expansions of 1992–9 and

2001–7 gave the appearance that neoliberalism had regenerated the British economy, even though economic inequality increased. Local public services increasingly excluded both clients and workers from influence. Local politics became dominated by a consensual, apparently apolitical 'partnership' between councils, business and community organisations which implemented 'pro-business' policies (Cochrane 2007). Trade unionists, especially at the workplace level, were largely shut out of local politics, including from Labour Party decision making. Where residential communities were formally drawn into urban programmes, as they increasingly were from the 1990s, they found that the key decisions were made elsewhere and that the militant community politics of the 1970s was ruled out (Atkinson 1999; Gough and Eisenschitz 2006: 148–156, 200–202). Deregulation and privatisation of housing and public transport effectively separated them from working-class political influence. Coming into the present crisis, then, popular organisations in Britain, including those at a local level, are numerically weakened and politically demoralised.

Because they promised a boost to production, some of the policies developed by Left councils in the 1980s have come into the mainstream, but in forms compatible with, and even reinforcing, neoliberalism. Supporting old and new industrial districts was pioneered by the 1980s Enterprise Boards, and now, as 'clusters', is the central strategy of the English Regional Development Agencies, shorn of considerations of job quality, equalities or workers' influence (Balls and Healey 2000; Gough 2003). Promotion of the social economy, seen in the 1980s as opening to workers' self-management, is now a central part of national and local anti-poverty policy, in the form of semi-private self-help and quasi-privatisation of public services (Amin *et al.* 2002). Training for oppressed groups has shifted from skilled waged work to self-employment and entrepreneurship. Lack of pressure from popular organisations has allowed the productive and disciplinary potential of these policies to be used while suppressing their radical potential.

This history suggests some general points. First, Left advance at any spatial scale is critically dependent on militant struggles by popular collective organisations; Left policies of government are a response to pressure from them. Second, the Left may be able to take initiatives in particular localities against the flow of national politics; but these initiatives are limited and fragile unless there is a revival of the Left at a national level. Third, a given policy may be used in politically very varied ways (Eisenschitz and Gough 1993: ch.2; Gough and Eisenschitz 2006: ch.8). In particular, for policies of the state and of the voluntary and community sector (VCS) to be implemented with empowering dynamics requires particular strategies and continuous pressure from popular organisations. We expand on these points below.

The legacy of neoliberalism

Since the 1980s neoliberalism has defeated, or inhibited the emergence of, Left local initiatives not only in Britain but worldwide. Offensives by firms to raise their profitability have increased job insecurity and weakened union organisation, exacerbated by cuts and privatisation in state employment. Increased mobilities of productive and money capital and commodities have undermined the old centres of union strength and the working-class community organisation that often went with that (Silver and Arrigi 2000). At the same time, an enormous reserve of labour has been opened up in the Third World through industrialisation of agriculture and explosive growth of cities, resulting in an urban working class of one billion people (Davis 2004), of which half are either un- or under-employed and a large proportion work in the informal economy (Petras and Veltmeyer 2001). An increasing part of the urban working class globally makes its living through crime, particularly the illegal drugs industry which has been created by criminalisation, and crime organisation disorganises and sometimes directly attacks progressive collectivities (Ramonet 2002).

Capital's demands and its mobility have weakened taxation, public spending and state regulation of business. Austerity has encouraged competition for welfare services and jobs within the working class, resulting in a steep rise in ethnic or religious identification and xenophobia throughout the world (Panitch and Leys 2002). Insecurity of personal and household income, widening of individual and household incomes, erosion of welfare services, and weakening of established community ties by enforced migration, have weakened cultures of collectivity and mutuality and encouraged anomie and possessive individualism (Vail *et al.* 1999; Sennett 1998; Beck 2001). In the developed countries, particularly, workers, even the poor, come to blame themselves for their problems (Galbraith 1992). The disavowal of responsibility for economic and social well-being by neoliberal states has further inhibited working-class political involvement. Socio-economic weakening of open, formal popular organisation, and states' and capital's repression, have meant that much collective organisation is (semi-) illegal, hidden within sub-cultures (Scott 2005). Thus neoliberalism has had major success in its central objectives – to atomise and individualise the world working class, weaken collective organisations in both production and social spheres, and depoliticise the population by imposing 'the rule of markets'.

Since the 1990s, however, there has been a certain revival of both militant unionism and urban struggles (Moody 1997; R. Cox 1999; Merrifield 2002; Leitner *et al.* 2007). This process has been highly uneven between countries due in part to differences in the severity of the attacks on living standards, in the effective fragmentation of the working class, and in direct repression. Resistance has also varied with territorially specific

political-economic traditions which can be durable over many decades and to some extent survive changes in global regulation such as neoliberalism; even among the MDCs there are enormous variations in 'national regimes' (Coates 2000). Thus in the US, Britain, Canada, Australia and Japan since the 1980s, and the former Eastern Block countries since 1989, collective resistance has been weak. By contrast, in many EU countries since the 1990s there have been militant struggles around jobs, pensions, unemployment and racism. In these countries local and regional governments have in some cases been able to maintain or innovate some top-down, mildly social democratic policies, partially shielding their populations from neoliberalism; in the US, the weakness of social democracy has meant that this role has in some places been played by innovative community development initiatives (Williamson *et al.* 2002). The newly industrialising countries, despite strong long-term growth, have seen accumulation and/or financial crises which have elicited much militant, even explosive, collective action – even in the face of brutal repression, as in China; this has tended to remain localised because of repression of national popular networks (Sanyal 2008). In those parts of the Third World with low or negative growth, the economic weakness of the working class has mostly enabled dictatorial regimes to prevent collective action for economic and social aims, or to channel it into inter-ethnic conflict; this is true of most of the Middle East and Africa, and to some extent India. It is in Latin America that popular resistance to neoliberalism has been strongest, including movements of the rural poor, struggles by unionised and unemployed workers and by indigenes, often organised at the neighbourhood level, mostly against the state; these have led to the formation of Left or social democratic governments (Panizza 2005). Overlaid on these national differences are, in many nations, large differences in the strength of the Left between regions and localities (Jonas 1996; Agnew 1997;

K. Cox 1998; Castree *et al.* 2004: ch.6). In the late 2000s, then, the possibilities for building Left initiatives at a local level start from very different positions in different continents, countries and localities. As we write the picture changes weekly, as protests against the effects of the global recession erupt across the Third World, former Eastern Bloc and the MDCs.

Strategic ideas for Left local politics

Class, collectivity and the local

In these circumstances, how can Left initiatives be built against neoliberal disempowerment using the local scale? Basic principles should be to combat neo liberal individualism and anomie by building wide, varied and comprehensive collective organisations of ordinary people, developing collective control over the economy, enhancing collective social reproduction, and thus extending democracy through all aspects of society. Empowerment must be collective to combat the market-fatalism that social atomisation has created, to provide force of numbers against capital and (often) the state, and to begin to plan production and reproduction according to genuinely social criteria. This implies that a social democratic strategy limited to progressive policies carried out top-down by the local state (for example, Allmendinger 2003) is inadequate. But equally, a libertarian/anarchist strategy limited to building islands of progressive practice such as individual social enterprises (Gorz 1982; Gibson-Graham 1996) or Foucauldian heterotopias (Genocchio 1995; MacCannell 2008) is inadequate in that it organises only a small elite, does not confront markets, and does not offer solutions for the majority of the population; it therefore cannot develop inclusive, strong organisations and action.

A strategy of collective organisation needs to be rooted in, though not limited to, the

local scale. This scale facilitates the involvement of increasing numbers of people through the immediacy and visibility of local problems of economic, social and cultural life. Collective organisation can draw on existing bonds of friendship, acquaintance and trust. The sharp constraints of money and time that most people have for participation in politics are easiest to overcome with local organisation. In some cases, though not all, longstanding local traditions of solidarity can be drawn on (Wills 1998). Thus Sklair (1998) argues that, even to confront the major global institutions and practices of power, local action is the essential starting point – even though this needs to be multiplied and linked at higher spatial scales. The local scale is thus essential to a strategy of collective organisation and action. It is then possible to build 'a sense of local community', not in its currently dominant form as reinforcement of local hierarchy and competition with other localities, but in a progressive way which can contest power (Cowley *et al.* 1977; Massey 1993; Craig and Mayo 1995).

Collective working-class organisations are, in the first place, oppositional to capital and the state rather than 'constructive', since by definition they do not have control over the major social resources. Trade unions form and develop through defence against employers. Residents' organisations make demands on the local state and on property, infrastructural and service capital. This organisation around immediate, daily needs can involve large numbers of people in organisation and activity. This practical-oppositional nature of working-class organisation is neglected by some purportedly 'Gramscian' strategists who see the central task of a progressive movement as being the construction of an alternative hegemonic ideology (Laclau and Mouffe 1985; Hall and Jacques 1989); this privileges the activity of Left intellectuals and marginalises all others', and dodges addressing the immediate material needs of the majority. It is also glossed over by theorists who deny or downplay the existence of 'power over' (Allen 2003) and who propose alternatives based on Deleuzian networks (Amin and Thrift 2002; Swyngedouw 2008); it is at best unclear how such networks can confront the major forms of power in contemporary society (Sklair 1998). Similarly, the oppositional nature of working-class organisation is neglected by those, including all the major global institutions, who propose the building of generic 'social capital' in working-class, especially poor, communities (World Bank 2000; Social Exclusion Unit 2001). This approach occludes how social capital and civil society are profoundly shaped by capital and the state (R. Cox 1999), and that local relations between people are specific to particular social projects and thus particular political strategies (Fine 2001; Das 2004).

The crucial organisations here are not only those of the poor – the target group for so many mainstream local economic initiatives – but those of the whole working class, including 'the middle class'. Throughout industrial capitalism the non-poor have had better formal organisation than the poor because of their stronger position in production and greater resources for organising; and in recent decades the poor have tended further to lose organisational capacity through economic and social atomisation and the drugs industry. A symptom of this problem is that in recent years the poor and deracinated have found expression for their anger in fruitless rioting, inter-ethnic fights, and battles with the police which lead nowhere, as instanced in South Los Angeles in 1992, British cities in 1981 and 1991, the Paris banlieux in 2004, and Greece in winter 2008–9. Besides, in the last 30 years the non-poor have acquired increasing reasons for self-organisation and militancy. Job loss, insecurity, deskilling, loss of autonomy within work, and erosion of pensions and welfare services started with unskilled workers but have moved 'upwards' through middle layers to professionals, and this tendency 'to share the misery' is obvious in the present crisis.

Thus during the crisis of 2001–3 in Argentina, the middle class played a substantial role in local mobilisations (Ozarow 2007). The struggle specifically against extreme poverty therefore needs to link collective action of the poor to mainstream working-class organisations; the latter have an interest in this since poverty is essentially a distillation and concentration of oppressions experienced by all the working class (Gough and Eisenschitz 2006). If this link is made, then the poor will have more effective means of organisation than the riot (cf. Zizek 2008). Left local strategy, then, can and should encompass organisation of the great majority of the population, from the poor to the middle class.

The local state, capital and social enterprises

While workers' organisations are in the first place oppositional, a Left strategy cannot be simply in opposition to the local state. Especially in the developed countries and the NICs, the local state has substantial powers and resources which the Left needs to use and develop. Basic services such as education, health, social housing and environmental services cannot be adequately provided for without the taxation and borrowing powers of the state, and the socialisation of the economy cannot proceed without the powers and funds of the state. The Left therefore needs to resist cuts in spending on useful services and restriction of local governments' abilities to tax and borrow, and defend direct state delivery of services against fragmentation into cost centres, contracting out, quangoisation and outright privatisation (Whitfield 2006). It needs to defend, or push for, egalitarian delivery of services which empower users and build their sociability, as, for example, in the revolutionary education practices of Reggio Emilia in Italy (Dahlberg and Moss 2006).

The Left also needs to defend the existing powers of the local state to regulate investment, for example, in the built environment, and to run trading enterprises. More ambitiously, it needs to push the local state to intervene in the local economy on the side of workers (Gough 1986; Totterdill 1989; Cumbers and Whittam 2007). The local economy is centrally important not just because most people's incomes depend on it, but also because it determines workers' autonomy, quality of labour and ability to organise within the working day. Local production politics has, however, to recognise that it may not be possible, in the medium term, to gain the necessary powers or funding.

'Support for state action' does not, though, mean allowing elected representatives and state officers a free hand. On the contrary, collective organisations in civil society need to impose continuous pressure on the local state, open up its processes of decision making to inspection, and become an integral part of that decision making — in short, a real and popular democracy. For example, any state policies involving employment and production need to be made in association with the relevant trade unions, and pupils, parents and teachers' organisations need to direct schools. Such possibility of real influence also encourages wider and more active participation in those collective organisations, which is the best insurance against their bureaucratisation, capture by 'leaders', or corruption (which are chronic problems everywhere). The Argentinian piqueteros negotiated for the neighbourhood in the street in order to put pressure on the state representatives and to prevent clientalist corruption (Starr 2005). Since the local state is formally controlled by political parties, Left trajectories for the local state are also furthered by the development of Left parties genuinely responsive to their membership and committed to working-class interests. Politicians from such parties who control local government can both 'take the local state outwards' through supporting popular organisations and actions, and take these organisations 'into the local state' by making it more

open and responsive to them (Wainwright 1994: ch.7).

A corollary is that the oldest and still most popular aim of the Left, extending democracy, is not achieved simply or mainly by extending formal methods of participation in local government: 'participation' needs to be of a form which achieves radical results. Collective organisations need to achieve real control and design of state services, investments and regulation of private interests (Eisenschitz 2008). If this does not happen, participation simply results in demoralisation of people and bureaucratisation of their organisations. In particular, decentralisation of state powers and spending from nation to region to locality to neighbourhood in the name of increasing participation — a current consensus from Right to Left — is meaningless unless the smaller scale facilitates greater popular control over resources and powers. Moreover, for the Left 'extending democracy' should not concern merely the state but private capital and indeed social enterprises: for socialists, the disempowerment of working people within production is central to their social, political and cultural disempowerment. If production is, then, to be subjected to greater democratic control, this must be partly through the direct actions of local collective organisations. Given these caveats, extensions of democracy into the state and economy can form virtuous circles, whereby ordinary people come to understand social mechanisms better, feel greater ability to change them, and thus propose more radical solutions.

These considerations raise important dilemmas concerning the contracting out of local state services to not-for-profit enterprises and the Voluntary and Community Sector (VCS). This type of contracting out has been a major aspect of reform of local government in, for example, Britain; the Labour government has argued that the VCS is more plural, democratic, responsive and innovative compared with the 'bureaucratic' and 'inflexible' state (Paxton and Pearce 2005). Some Centre-Left commentators of a postmodern or associationalist bent have supported this process on the grounds that it empowers civil society, democratises the services, and weakens the overbearing state (Amin and Thrift 2002). It is true that non-state organisations have sometimes delivered essential services in ways which are more visionary and innovative than departments of the local state. For brief periods of crisis, community enterprises may form something of an alternative that may be a means of reshaping the state. In the city of Mosconi in Argentina, for instance, there were 300 projects built by well-organised grassroots organisations that effectively developed a parallel local state (Starr 2005). But the Left needs to be cautious before calling for wholesale hand-over to the VCS. In the first place, these services remain dependent on state funding; the projects in Mosconi, for instance, relied on local and national state funding, World Bank-backed workfare schemes, and the goodwill of local oil firms (Schaumberg 2008: 378). Existing contracting out to the VCS is taking place for the same, neoliberal reasons as contracting out to private firms: to lower wages and conditions, and to depoliticise services by passing the buck for ensuring their quality. This has fragmented service delivery, created greater unevenness across localities, and made it more difficult for the local state to pursue pro-working-class policies (Mayer 2007). A strong, continuing role for the local state in delivery of services is in our view essential in order to ensure their universality, equity and quality, and in order that they can be democratically planned across the locality. But, as we have just argued, these very roles of the local state need to be opened up to much greater control by residents, clients and service workers. The Left needs to ensure that social enterprises funded to provide essential services do not undercut public sector employment conditions, are genuinely democratically accountable, are efficient, and are not corrupt. Under these conditions, their innovativeness can help to make the services directly run by the state more innovative. With this kind of approach, many different concrete articulations of the local state, community organisations, and collective social groups are possible in delivering essential services.

A related debate concerns the role of social enterprises and worker cooperatives in producing marketed commodities. Some associationalist (Cooke and Morgan 1998; Gibson-Graham 1996) and market-socialist (Nove 1983; Sayer 1995) authors argue that a comprehensive system of such enterprises, relating through markets, is a potential, feasible alternative to capitalist production. They argue that it is a desirable one since it allows workers much greater autonomy and control within their enterprises, increases innovativeness and productivity, and spatially decentralises decision making. If this were so, then the Left has a simple, comprehensive alternative to both state and market (Catterall *et al.* 1996); Mance (2009) speaks of social enterprises as 'the material base of post capitalist societies'. In the last decades there have indeed been many local Left initiatives to support such enterprises (Pearce 2003). However, once again, we think that the Left should not pursue producer cooperatives operating in free markets as the only strategy for production of commodities (Gough and Eisenschitz 2006: 216–21). Cooperatives tend to be undercapitalised and thus find it hard to out-compete the private sector. They often rely for survival on self-exploitation of the workforce. They typically need the state for both funding and coordination, so that they cannot so easily escape the state's 'dead hand'. We therefore believe that we need strategies for local state production and Left strategies within-and-against the existing private sector (see further section V). And since Left strategy for social enterprise, in both state-funded services and commmodity production, is far from straightforward, we also discuss this further in section V.

Connecting different aspects of local life

Left local strategies need to address all aspects of the locality holistically, in particular combating the characteristic splits in capitalist society between production and reproduction, the public sphere and the home, economy, social life and culture, and society and nature (Meszaros 1995: 464ff.). Left strategy should refuse the division between 'economic', 'social', 'environmental' and 'cultural' policy making. For example, democratisation of privately controlled production means not only pushing for more skilled and autonomous work (Hales 1980; Cooley 1987) but also changing its goods and services towards basic human needs (Mackintosh and Wainwright 1987: ch.7; Elson 1988). While reproduction of people under capitalism is centred on private domestic work and private use of commodities purchased, these are in fact strongly socially constructed, particularly by capital; Left strategy should aim to make this socialisation conscious and democratic, whether it be food and nutrition, the geography of retailing, the design of housing, or public transport versus the car. In each of these areas there can be collaboration between workers in the service and residents consuming it, redesigning the service for the benefit of both groups (Lavelette and Mooney 2000; on housing see Arkitektkontor 1974; on public transport see GLC 1985: ch.20). Moreover, safeguarding of ecosystems through local action nearly always involves decisions which span the spheres of production and social life respectively. Such actions across the two spheres are the best way of developing a culture of care for both humans and nature, by posing the question of the aims of production (use values versus private profit) and the nature of human and ecosystem needs. Such actions can expose the alienated nature of both production and consumption under capitalism (Pepper 1993).

Moreover, they imply collaboration between popular organisations in the respective spheres – trade unions, residents' groups and social movements – and hence their mutual support. These alliances can be very powerful: for example, in Glasgow during the First World War and in Turin in 1969–70,

strong and militant union organisation inspired revolts in the social sphere – rent strikes for rent controls in the former case, mass squatting of housing and free public transport in the second. These collaborations are not always easy, however; there are likely to be tensions between local groups due to their different preoccupations and foci: for example, workers in polluting industries may clash with local residents' groups; male workers may not see the point of expanding nursery provision; users of cars may be unwilling to see their use restricted. But the local level is the ideal scale at which to thrash out these disagreements and negotiate practical ways forward, since the different groups can meet face-to-face and also directly inspect the concrete local facts relevant to the dispute.

The problem of spatial scale

While the locality is a necessary and potentially powerful scale for Left action, the latter always needs to be linked into higher spatial scales. The world is constructed through the relations between territories, but by the same token each locality is constructed by its relations to others (Howitt 1993). The key task considered in this chapter, of constructing solidarity and collectivity within localities, is thus inseparable from constructing them at wider spatial scales (Swyngedouw 2000; Gough 2002). In modern society, social actors within any locality have powerful impacts on society and nature outside it. Conversely, progressive actions within localities can easily be undermined by markets in land, production, commodities and money operating at larger scales, by firms based outside the locality, and by spatially higher levels of the state (Obi 2005). The latter problem is worse the smaller the 'locality' (another reason why spatial decentralisation of state decision making can be counter-productive). The limitations of the local are less the more broad and inclusive are the local collective organisations (so that higher scale pressures do not so easily create divisions), and the more holistic are the initiatives being taken (so that the democratic forms of social and economic life in the locality have greater resilience). But the scale problem cannot be avoided. In consequence, local collective organisation always needs to seek the greatest solidarity and cooperation with similar organisations elsewhere. This solidarity is especially necessary when localities are linked by capital's investments: gains by workers in one workplace or locality can be easily undermined by capital (and workers) elsewhere in the same industry unless workers cooperate across space (Hudson and Sadler 1986). To the extent that a local civil society begins to direct local government in progressive ways, it needs to prevent undermining by both other local governments and the nation state. Thus Left organisation, strategy and transformation at higher spatial scales are essential to any Left local advance that is to last more than a year or two. To change the hallowed slogan, 'think and act locally and globally'.

Such cooperation across localities and nations cannot rely on the state nor even on national and international bureaucracies of popular organisations such as trade unions: it has to be built from the bottom up. Thus on employment, in recent years a new National Shop Stewards Network has been constructed in Britain, and many international campaigning organisations have been built from the grass roots (Moody 1997) – an early pioneer was the Transnational Information Exchange (Chapkis and Enloe 1983). In the last 15 years or so a loosely organised movement against neoliberal globalisation (or 'alter-globalisation movement') has emerged linking national, and to a lesser extent local, unions, community organisations and progressive NGOs, meeting through the Social Forums which were, significantly, initiated by the city government of Porto Alegre, Brasil. So far, this movement has not organised any large-scale actions, but has yielded many useful bilateral cooperations (Amoore 2005; Routledge and Cumbers 2009).

Through this kind of overall strategy, the depoliticisation wrought by neoliberalism can start to be reversed, as the social nature of daily life becomes increasingly evident and it begins to be more strongly subject to collective political debate and action. These processes are path dependent; in particular, existing consciousness and socio-economic practices may mean that apparently modest reforms can have radical dynamics. We have noted the very different degrees of collective organisation and militancy between countries and localities at present, and these will affect how bold initiatives can be. Moreover, Left tactics need to vary over time: in Britain, for example, rather than simply widening the VCS as in the 1980s, we need to radicalise and democratise it; and rather than simply resisting privatisation, we need to bring services back into public ownership. Tactical acumen is essential for the local Left.

Fields of action

Struggles around jobs

The workplace is the most essential scale for trade union organisation and contestation: larger scale workers' organisation has no base and no purchase without it. The daily interactions between workers within the workplace, and the recognition of their common situation there, are the basis for collective organisation. At the workplace scale workers can act rapidly, and in ways that provide a spectacle of resistance in walk-outs, pickets and occupations, helping to win support from other workers and residents in the locality (Hudson and Sadler 1986; Jonas 1998).

If the workplace is profitable, then it can be possible for workers to gain concessions from management through action restricted to that workplace (Castree et al. 2004: xvii–xviii, 18–23); this was often done, for example, in large manufacturing plants in

Britain in the 1960s, and this developed a strongly decentralised union movement. But when profitability is low or there is over-capacity in the industry, purely local action is insufficient: management can threaten to close the workplace if workers resist restructuring or wage cuts; and if workers are successful in keeping their plant open, this will tend to cause job loss elsewhere in the industry or multi-plant firm (Herod 1997; Harvey 1996: ch.1). The spatial divisions and competition between workers orchestrated by management can be combated only by cooperation between workers in different workplaces within the industry. The logic of such cooperation is then for unions to begin to monitor patterns of investment and disinvestment across the industry, at scales from the locality to the globe depending on the sector, and then begin to make demands on that investment: the germs of socialist planning (Gough 2002; Gough 2004: 269–283).

Where there is a locally centred industrial district or dense local subcontracting linkages between workplaces, unions can gain strength from organising within the industry across workplaces, sometimes using blockage of contracting linkages for bargaining (GLC 1985: ch.15; Castree *et al.* 2004: 162–165); powerful local solidarity can thus be developed. This approach can sometimes be used in industrial districts where workers and employers belong to the same minority ethnicity. The employers often use ethnicity to subordinate their workforce (Kakios and van der Velden 1984); but workers may use community bonds to organise their solidarity, as have the Turkish and Kurdish workers in the London clothing industry.

The local scale is also an essential one for organising the worst-organised workers. The extreme exploitation of most homeworkers can be addressed through community-based campaigns (Allen and Wolkowitz 1987). A large proportion of the workforce in MDCs now works in small, non-unionised workplaces of diverse sectors within each locality.

These have been addressed by 'community unionism' targeted on industrial neighbourhoods and using those spaces to develop solidarity (Wills 2001). 'Living wage' campaigns based in particular cities or neighbourhoods have successfully organised to improve wages of low-paid, often casualised, sometimes illegal-immigrant, service workers, including those that work in small work units such as caretakers and cleaners (Savage 1998; Figart 2004). Thus in recent years London Citizens, based in residential-community, minority-ethnic and church organisations, has worked with unions to secure a living wage well above the national minimum wage for groups of low-paid workers, something the unions alone had not achieved (Holgate and Wills 2007). In globally traded goods, such local campaigns can be further strengthened through international networks of solidarity (Ross 1997). Finally, the local scale is an essential one for organising the unemployed since – given the widespread failure of unions to organise them – they are outside (larger scale) production-related networks. In recent years local organisation has been the basis for regional and national marches and actions of the unemployed in some European countries, reconnecting them with employed workers and residents (Mathers 2007).

In times of acute crisis, workers' collective actions of different types can catalyse each other across a locality. Thus in the crisis of the early 2000s in Argentina militant neighbourhood assemblies and local organisations of the unemployed posed an alternative power to capital and state. With this support, workers in many localities tried to seize the means of production, despite more than half of workers being in the informal sector (Schaumberg 2008); some 170 cooperatives were formed as workers took control of (mostly small) closed factories (Dinerstein 2007).

Altogether, then, localities remain essential, though not sufficient, sites for workers' collective resistance to capital.

The organisation of production and investment

Despite the very limited resources and powers of local and regional government around production (albeit with big variation between countries), there are progressive policies which they may be able to implement or at least push for. First, the local state may be able to invest in and run trading enterprises. The local authority in Glasgow, USA, for instance, provided a local telecommunications network giving a cheaper and better internet connection for residents and attracting strong inward investment (Williamson *et al.* 2002: 152). Such investments or plans for them can be used to put in question the efficiency and social impacts of private production (on building work see Direct Labour Collective 1978; on telecoms see GLC 1985: ch. 16).

Second, there is powerful legitimacy for the local state to bring into use underused resources, be they unemployed workers or unused land and buildings. The political point is further reinforced if these resources are used for innovative forms of production, for example, worker cooperatives, skilled and autonomous forms of work, or socially useful products.

Third, investment money may be channelled into the locality by using political pressure on the major holders of savings, the pension funds and insurance companies; the latter are vulnerable to this pressure because they hold working people's savings. In social democratic countries such as Sweden trade unions have long had a say in how their industry's pension fund is invested; in other countries, unions and local governments can apply pressure for the same ends (Minns 1980; Blackburn 2003). Again, the point should be to democratise and politicise the process of investment and the choices it involves, for example, to prioritise high unemployment areas or green production.

Fourth, it is possible to take local initiatives in money circulation which put into question its capitalist forms. Local money (Monbiot 2009) can increase circulation and, if it stimulates corresponding production, is non-inflationary. Thus the city government of Curitiba in Brazil paid its own workforce partly in local money which it had organised for local municipal and private services to accept, leading to rapid local economic growth. In Argentina there was a massive growth in local voucher schemes from 1995 in response to economic collapse; the number of these *Trueques* peaked at 4,700 in the 2002 crisis; the vouchers were exchangeable between schemes, creating an effective second national currency. The schemes enabled the unemployed, particularly women, to market their labour power, micro-enterprises and a few larger worker cooperatives to be set up, abandoned buildings and land to be used, unsold production from local factories to be exchanged, and local services to gain adequate custom. Half of surveyed local households made over half their income through the schemes, and many subsistence goods could be purchased with vouchers (Gomez and Helmsing 2008). Local Exchange and Trading Schemes (LETS) organise direct exchange of individuals' labour time, enabling production and consumption of useful services, albeit limited to those without substantial fixed capital or economies of scale (Walker and Goldsmith 2001). Cooperatively owned credit unions or local government-owned people's banks can provide much better terms for savings and borrowing than the private sector (Fuller and Jonas 2003). All these forms of money make the link between production and consumption more direct and transparent, and thus encourage a social view of the local economy.

The Third Sector

The 'Third Sector', not-for-profit enterprises or the 'social economy' can play an important role in Left strategy, by demonstrating the possibilities for workers' or residents' control of the enterprise, social innovation, production directly to meet social needs, and efficient production without capitalist direction. South Central Farm in Los Angeles, for example, improved food quality and security, preserved traditions of a peasant community recently uprooted to the city, and enabled members to develop as individuals and as a collective; the potentially militant dynamic of such initiatives is shown by the strong fight waged to take the land into community ownership (Irazabal and Punja 2009: 11). However, social enterprises can equally well serve rightwing politics: they may survive through self-exploitation, with wages, hours and conditions inferior to the industry average; they may be used to habituate people to poor employment; they may be under-resourced self-help, an inferior substitute for formal welfare services; and the state may contract out to them in order to cut wages and conditions; in short, they may teach 'standing on your own two feet' rather than working-class cooperation (Eick 2007). In Britain at present, for example, the social economy inclines more to the rightwing than the leftwing model (Amin *et al.* 2002; Fuller and Jonas 2003).

To lead the social economy in a leftwards direction strategy is therefore vital (Medoff and Sklar 1994; Eisenschitz and Gough 2009). Social enterprises need to form the strongest possible ties to unionised workers in mainstream production, by being unionised and by tapping into the technical expertise of mainstream workers; they can then, reciprocally, show the latter the advantages of having immediate control over one's production process. Adequate capital should be secured from the local state (including as land and buildings), from socialised finance, or from recycling of profits from other social enterprises. Economic and political economies of scale should be sought through networking of community enterprises locally, nationally and internationally. There are global networks that attempt to build cooperation between the millions of people involved in

the social economy worldwide. These explicitly liberatory campaigns seek to generate synergies of alternative finance, local currencies, fair trade, ethical consumption and low-impact technologies, using a variety of ownership forms. The accumulation of political strength is important since the social economy has to constantly fight against being legally marginalised by lobbying from private business. With this kind of strategy, the social economy can complement and radicalise, rather than undermine, increases in workers' influence within mainstream production and the extension of democratic state-owned production.

In the medium term, however, a liberatory social economy is dependent on Left advance in the whole society, without which community-based organisations tend merely to manage their place within capitalist markets. Petras (1997) argues that Latin American NGOs from the 1980s moved from progressive politics to becoming neoliberalism's community face. In Argentina, the radical community-based initiatives in welfare and production of the early 2000s withered when the Kirchner government used the national scale to seize the political initiative from the Left. Only 10 per cent of the Trueques present in 2002 survived until 2007, and this was partly due to lack of support from and integration with local governments (Gomez and Helmsing 2008). In the US employee ownership of firms has not made any fundamental challenge to capitalism (Williamson *et al.* 2002). Particularly in times of economic decline, wider Left advance is needed for worker- and community-controlled enterprises to maintain their radical dynamics.

Fighting social oppressions

Various social oppressions are substantially – though never wholly – constructed within localities, and many radical struggles against them have had this scale (Gough and Eisenschitz 2006: 131–135, 224–228; Craig

607

and Mayo 1995). The oppression of women is rooted in local relations between home, neighbourhood and waged work. Campaigns for more social care for children and the infirm, better housing, housing suitable for varied households, closer proximity of home, waged work, welfare and services, more convenient and free public transport, and for women's equality within waged work, can lead to practical gains, and can show that apparently individual problems are social and have collective solutions (Rowbotham 1989; Greed 1994; Darke *et al.* 2000). Racism's deepest roots are in relations between the national and international scales. But racism is strongly expressed and developed within localities, and is fought there in campaigns for equality in housing, education and health care and against super-exploitation in waged work (Sivanandan 1990). Mainly locally based campaigns for safety in both homes and public spaces have been waged by black people, women, and lesbians and gay men (Rowbotham 1989; Bhavnani and Coulson 2005). Neighbourhood and local scales are vital cultural supports to all these struggles, since antagonistic groups there confront each other not as abstractions but face-to-face and thus, potentially, as full persons. For example, campaigns to stop deportation of refugees in Britain have had their greatest success in stubborn defence of refugees by their British neighbours who have befriended them (Hayter 2000); conversely, some of the worst racism in Britain is found in regions such as Cumbria and Lincolnshire with very few black or immigrant residents. Local settings can thus be powerful in overcoming prejudice and developing practical solidarity.

Housing and land

The last 25 years have seen rapid inflation in house prices throughout the MDCs and NICs, resulting for the majority of the working class in drain on income, poor accommodation, overcrowding, insecurity, and blocking of inter-local migration. This crisis has been caused by insufficient new building to meet monetarily effective demand, let alone need, plus a massive channelling of capital into property via direct investment and credit, much of it directed at speculative gain (Harvey 1989: ch.2; Turner 2008). The Left internationally has been extraordinarily unsuccessful in pushing for expanded supply of affordable housing. This is in part due to the legal, institutional and financial structures of housing provision being almost entirely in the hands of nation states, over which the Left has had virtually no influence.

The most substantial local struggles around housing under neoliberalism have been to defend poor people's occupation of, or tenure in, existing stock. In the 1970s and 1980s, there was mass squatting by the poor in the fast-growing northern Italian cities, and widespread squatting, mainly by young people, in high-value empty housing in central cities. However, state violence against squatters increased, and further rises in value have meant declining space available for squatting in major cities. There have also been struggles to oppose eviction of (largely long-standing) poor residents from CBD-fringe neighbourhoods to make way for commercial buildings and expensive apartments; in recent years the latter has been a central part of the vaunted 'urban renaissance' (Swyngedouw *et al.* 2002). In the 1970s and 1980s these defensive campaigns had some successes (Wates 1976; Tuckett 1988); but more recently there have been few successes and many defeats; most of the successes have been in defending or setting up work and living spaces for low-income creative self-employed people (Porter and Shaw 2008). This deterioration reflects, in part, the ever-increasing profits from CBD-fringe development, and the consequent increasing ruthlessness of developers and state in pushing it through; creative spaces can, however, sometimes be welcomed as adding 'vibrancy'. Another form of resistance, in Britain and Germany, for example, has been of social housing tenants to (semi-) privatisation of their homes; well-organised neighbourhood campaigns have had some successes here, though without reversing the national policies.

These campaigns, however, have been essentially defensive, and have not achieved new programmes to increase the supply of affordable housing. Yet given the manifest disaster of neoliberal housing provision, now exacerbated by the recession, Left campaigns for affordable housing could be very popular, as they were in the nineteenth- and early twentieth-century MDCs. Left strategy should focus on the partial de-commodification of housing, through state and cooperative ownership (Bowie 2008) funded by control of the major national and international investment funds, zero-carbon construction by state-owned or cooperative building firms backed by the builders' unions, and state appropriation of empty housing. While this is essentially a national task, local actions can dramatise the housing shortage, for example, through small-scale state and community building as well as resistance to city-fringe evictions, boycott by building workers of demolition of low-income housing (as in the Sydney 'green bans' in the 1970s: Mundey 1981), or coordinated mass squatting of empty property. The vast experience of self-build on squatted land in Third World cities over the last 50 years suggests another possible avenue; but this constructs slums unless tied to collective organisation of building, as in contemporary Venezuela, to legalisation of occupation, to provision of physical infrastructures by the state.

Such campaigns point towards social ownership of all land. Private ownership of land, extended by neoliberalism, is a deep, chronic generator of privatised culture (Low and Smith 2003), whereas its public ownership is a palpable assertion of the primacy of the social. Capital gains to private owners from change of land use are a gross example of unearned income, and so lack legitimacy: the Left should push for their full appropriation by the state (Massey and Catalano 1978: 188–190; Sandercock 1979: ch.6).

Again, national legislation is key. But local actions around major office and luxury-housing developments and the state's facilitation of them can make propaganda for the socialisation of land (Oudenampsen 2008; Holgersen 2008). More positively, with legislative backing social ownership of land may be developed as local community ownership, where gains from land development can be used for locally determined social good, whether in further fixed investment or in welfare services. This was indeed the strategy of the early twentieth-century Garden City movement in Britain; today the community trust in Letchworth has a property income of £6m, used for social purposes. Such landownership can breed radical political dynamics. Thus Boston's Dudley Street Neighbourhood Initiative managed to appropriate the private landlords, and used this political momentum to develop strong policies on jobs, health, education, transport and local services (Medoff and Sklar 1994). However, the Left needs to guard against governments using development values as an excuse to cut direct state funding, and in ways which exacerbate spatial uneven development. Thus in recent years in Britain, with little central state funding for social housing, local governments have been forced to negotiate social housing as 'planning gain' from private development, hence subordinating it to the market. The Development Trusts which have multiplied in poor neighbourhoods of Britain in recent years often own fixed assets; but this has been used to make anti-poverty measures a local responsibility dependent on low-value local resources (Development Trusts Association 2008). Community asset management can be used in depoliticising ways (Aiken et al. 2008). Community land ownership needs to be an additional gain, not compensation for cuts in other fields.

Participatory budgeting

Participatory budgeting, in which neighbourhood assemblies have control over the local state's spending in their neighbourhood, was pioneered in 1989 by the far Left government of Porto Alegre. It has since been taken up in many localities in Latin America and beyond (Sintomer *et al.* 2008), sometimes under strong pressure from the working class (Rogers 2005: 5). In Porto Alegre decisions on annual priorities for capital investment were discussed in open neighbourhood assemblies; these decisions were then centralised through delegates to boroughs and from them to the city, which then decided on distribution between boroughs. This method politicised local government and elicited extraordinary participation from the population, especially from previously marginalised women, black people, those without secondary education and unskilled workers; in the first five years, 8 per cent of the adult population was involved at some stage (Abers 1998). The process stimulated the formation of neighbourhood associations and self-organisation of blacks, disabled people and the elderly (Bairerle 2002). Over the years there was a shift from parochial defence of one's patch to support for the most needy neighbourhoods. Investment switched sharply from prestigious projects mainly used by the better-off to basic infrastructures such as street paving, sewers and schools. Spending became more efficient and less corrupt (Abers 1998).

But, even in Porto Alegre, participatory budgeting has had limitations (Baierle 2002). The delegation structure was not powerful enough to prevent the council bureaucracy from continuing its control over city-wide infrastructures. The city was hemmed in by the authority of State and Federal governments which were less democratic and radical. Most importantly, democracy in the city was strongly affected by the overall political atmosphere in the locality and beyond: the Brazilian trade unions were on the offensive in the 1980s but from the 1990s have been in retreat in the face of a neoliberal offensive which has greatly increased unemployment. Once again we see that formal democracy

of the local state cannot be effective if the working class is disempowered and unable to act in the economic and social spheres. Indeed, under these conditions formal democratic methods of government may function to contain discontent by dividing and co-opting community groups (Cockburn 1977); according to Sintomer *et al.* (2008) this has indeed been the most common experience of participatory budgeting in recent years.

Alternative accounting systems

Economic actors in capitalist society normally make decisions through a calculus of prices and incomes, assumed to arise from exchange in markets. This calculus tends to lock people's strategies into the order of capitalist society, and thus subordinate them to its forms of power (Mohun 1979). Conversely, alternative calculi can potentially challenge capitalist logics. In the field of local and regional politics in particular, in recent years capitalist accounting and criteria have been (increasingly) dominant; the Left needs to challenge precisely these notions of 'development' (Pike *et al.* 2007).

One alternative approach to accounting has been welfare economics, which uses price calculations but shifts from individual actors in markets to aggregate outcomes for social groups and the public good. Thus cost-benefit analysis puts a price on the impacts of, for example, a major infrastructure investment, including both social actors and phenomena such as noise excluded in the relevant market exchanges. Social impact assessments of (dis)investment decisions can demonstrate their wider benefits and costs, for example, how closure of a large workplace imposes costs on the state in lost taxes, income support and health spending and on suppliers in lost income (Glyn 1985). Calculation of a money value of domestic work has sometimes been used to argue for feminist policies (Peterson and Runyan 2005).

Such calculations can be useful in showing that capitalist society is not 'economically rational' even in its own terms, and in getting people to think socially. But they have limitations. Many calculations assume key prices and incomes as given, as when cost-benefit analysis values people's free time as a fixed fraction of their money income (Ball 1979). More profoundly, the calculations do not in themselves reveal the social relations which give rise to the initial miscalculation of costs and benefits. For example, the fact that a workplace closure imposes costs on the local state which may exceed the saving by the firm does not prevent the closure, since the state and the firm are separate social actors subject to quite different social relations. A genuinely radical dynamic here would need to question and violate these social relations, for example, by the state taking over the firm without compensation.

Another approach to social valuation is that of LETS. LETS does indeed change social relations of production by setting up direct exchange of work without money. Though creating another money (labour time units), it enables revaluation of people's labour, skills, caring work, and even humanity through increased (self-) esteem (Walker and Goldsmith 2001).

Other alternative calculi seek to value 'the non-economic', that is, neither labour nor products of labour. One such is accounting of aspects of the ecosystem, such as greenhouse gases, water and agricultural land. Again, this accounting is ideologically important for the Left in highlighting eco-societal impacts and long-term consequences of present actions, and in pointing the finger at both capitalist production dynamics and mindless consumption. But again, the accounting can be the basis for quite different political directions. Are carbon emissions to be fixed in advance, or made to respond to profits and incomes through trading of quotas? A Left strategy adopts the former approach, thus violating capitalist logic. Moreover, ecological production relations should be made more transparent by linking local people to the workers 'producing' the greenhouse gases, water and food they 'consume', partially bypassing the commodity form.

Finally, a recently developed strategy has been 'the economics of happiness' (Layard 2006; Michaelson et al. 2009). Like welfare economics, this starts from a critique of neo-classical economics, arguing that aspects of human well-being such as health, education, creativity and general happiness are mis-priced 'by markets' but nevertheless need to be accounted for in economic policy. This work can justify allocating economic resources to support these aspects of well-being. But the limitation of this work is that aspects of well-being are pictured as quasi-commodities which can be 'delivered' to individuals; again, the approach fails to focus on social relations. Thus Layard does not cri-tique capitalist social relations of production and the low self-esteem and unhappiness that are intrinsic to exploitation (Marx 1980; Sennett 1998), nor how capitalism generates indifference to others (Geras 1998). Well-being is not simply something which individuals have more or less of but is within relations to others. Thus Wilkinson and Pickett (2009) show that the well-being of a country's inhabitants is strongly correlated with low income inequality, that is, with its relations of distribution. At a smaller scale, Baker et al. (2004: ch.2) argue that a funda-mental aspect of well-being is being within relationships of care. Alternative calculi, then, can form powerful critiques of capitalist out-comes and point to social solutions. But the Left needs to act on these by challenging the relations of the economy.

Conclusion

Socialist tradition has emphasised solidarity and economic planning at national and inter-national scales. The local scale has been seen as problematic because of the subordina-tion of enterprises and local economies to competition at higher spatial scales, and because of the weaker powers of the local state compared with the national. Neoliberal globalisation is said to have exacerbated these problems. But we have argued that localities are a crucial site for Left strategy, because important social and economic relations are enacted and reproduced there, because of dense local relations between economy and social life, and because daily interactions and proximity facilitate building relations of solidarity and collectivity. Transforming social relations at higher spatial scales is certainly necessary, but local struggles are a dialectical moment in this.

The Left local strategy discussed here is above all a class policy, against the individualisation and division of the working class which is the foundation of all capitalist power and which has been deepened by neoliberalism. Accordingly, we have given primacy to collective self-organisation and practical collective economics rather than autonomous progressive action by capital and the state. The heart of a radical local politics is a journey from individual to collective modes of thinking and acting. This implies a development of place-based community, not as the commonly encountered self-subordination of the weak to the strong, but as the solidarity of the weak against the powerful. We hope we have shown that there are many promising tactics for carrying forward this strategy during the present crisis.

References

Abers, R. (1998) 'Learning democratic practice: distributing government resources through popular participation in Porto Alegre, Brazil', in M. Douglas and J. Friedmann (eds) *Cities for Citizens*, New York: Wiley.

Agnew, J. (1997) 'The dramaturgy of horizons: geographical scale in the "reconstruction of Italy" by the new Italian political parties, 1992–1995', *Political Geography*, 16 (2): 99–121.

Aiken, M., Cairns, B. and Thake, S. (2008) *Community Ownership and Management of Assets*, York: Joseph Rowntree Foundation.

Allen, J. (2003) *Lost Geographies of Power*, Oxford: Blackwell.

Allen, S. and Wolkowitz, C. (1987) *Homeworking: Myths and Realities*, Basingstoke: Macmillan.

Allmendinger, P. (2003) 'From New Right to New Left in UK planning', *Urban Policy and Research*, 21 (1): 57–79.

Amin, A. and Thrift, N. (2002) *Cities: Reimagining the Urban*, Cambridge: Polity Press.

Amin, A., Cameron, A. and Hudson, R. (2002) *Placing the Social Economy*, London: Routledge.

Amoore, L. (ed.) (2005) *The Global Resistance Reader*, London: Routledge.

Arkitektkontor, A.B. (1974) 'Urban redevelopment: the Byker experience', *Housing Review*, 23 (6): 149–156.

Atkinson, R. (1999) 'Discourses of partnership and empowerment in contemporary British urban regeneration', *Urban Studies*, 36 (1): 59–72.

Baierle, S. (2002) 'The Porto Alegre Thermidor? Brazil's "participatory budget at the crossroads", in L. Panitch and C. Leys (eds) *Socialist Register 2003*, London: Merlin.

Baker, J., Lynch, K., Cantillon, S. and Walsh, J. (2004) *Equality*, London: Palgrave.

Ball, M. (1979) 'Cost-benefit analysis: a critique', in F. Green and P. Nore (eds) *Issues in Political Economy*, London: Macmillan.

Balls, E. and Healey, J. (eds) (2000) *Towards a New Regional Policy*, London: The Smith Institute.

Beck, U. (2001) 'Living your own life in a runaway world: individualisation, globalisation and politics', in W. Hutton and A. Giddens (eds) *On the Edge, Living with Global Capitalism*, London: Vintage.

Bhavnani, K. and Coulson, M. (2005) 'Transforming socialist feminism: the challenge of racism', *Feminist Review*, 80: 87–97.

Blackburn, R. (2003) *Banking on Death, or Investing in Life?*, London: Verso.

Boddy, M. and Fudge, C. (eds) (1984) *Local Socialism*, Basingstoke: Macmillan.

Bowie, D. (2008) *Housing and the Credit Crunch*, London: Compass.

Brown, G. (ed.) (1975) *The Red Paper on Scotland*, Edinburgh: E.U.S.P.B.

Castree, N., Coe, N., Ward, K. and Samers, M. (2004) *Spaces of Work*, London: Sage.

Caterall, B., Lipietz, A., Hutton, W. and Girardet, H. (1996) 'The Third Sector, urban regeneration and the stakeholder', *City*, 5–6: 86–97.

Chapkis, W. and Enloe, C. (1983) *Of Common Cloth: Women in the Global Textile Industry*, Amsterdam: Transnational Institute.

Coates, D. (2000) *Models of Capitalism*, London: Polity Press.

Cochrane, A. (2007) *Understanding Urban Policy*, Oxford: Blackwell.

Cockburn, C. (1977) *The Local State: Management of Cities and People*, London: Pluto.

Cooke, P. and Morgan, K. (1998) *The Associational Economy*, Oxford: Oxford University Press.

Cooley, M. (1987) *Architect or Bee? the Human Price of Technology*, 2nd edn, London: Hogarth.

Coventry, Liverpool, Newcastle and North Tyneside Trades Councils (1980) *State Intervention in Industry: A Workers' Inquiry*, Nottingham: Spokesman.

Cowley, J., Kaye, A., Mayo, M. and Thompson, M. (1977) *Community or Class Struggle?*, London: Stage 1.

Cox, K. (1998) 'Spaces of dependence, spaces of engagement and the politics of scale; or, looking for local politics', *Political Geography*, 17: 1–24.

Cox, R. (1999) 'Civil society at the turn of the millennium: prospects for an alternative world order', *Review of International Studies*, 25 (1): 3–28.

Craig, G. and Mayo, M. (1995) *Community Empowerment*, London: Zed Books.

Cumbers, A. and Whittam, G. (2007) *Reclaiming the Economy: Alternatives to Market Fundamentalism in Scotland and Beyond*, Biggar: Scottish Left Review Press.

Dahlberg, G. and Moss, P. (2006) 'Introduction: our Reggio Emilia', in C. Rinaldi (ed.) *In Dialogue with Reggio Emilia*, London: Routledge.

Darke, J., Lewith, S. and Woods, R. (2000) *Women and the City*, Basingstoke: Palgrave.

Das, R. (2004) 'Social capital and the poverty of wage labourers: problems with social capital theory', *Transactions of the Institute of British Geographers*, 29 (1): 27–45.

Davis, M. (2004) 'Planet of slums', *New Left Review*, 26: 5–34.

Development Trusts Association (2008) *Poverty in the UK: The Role of Development Trusts*, London: Development Trusts Association.

Dinerstein, A. (2007) 'Workers' factory takeovers and new state policies in Argentina: towards an "institutionalisation" of non-governmental public action?', *Policy and Politics*, 35 (3): 529–50.

Direct Labour Collective (c.1978) *Building with Direct Labour*, London: Conference of Socialist Economists.

Eick, V. (2007) 'Space patrols – the new peacekeeping functions of nonprofits: contesting neoliberalism or the urban poor?', in H. Leitner, J. Peck and E. Sheppard (eds) *Contesting Neoliberalism: Urban Frontiers*, New York: Guilford Press.

Eisenschitz, A. (2008) 'Town planning, planning theory and social reform', *International Planning Studies*, 13 (2): 133–149.

Eisenschitz, A. and Gough, J. (1993) *The Politics of Local Economic Policy*, Basingstoke: Macmillan.

Eisenschitz, A. and Gough, J. (2009) 'Socialism and the "social economy"', Sheffield University Department of Town and Regional Planning Working Paper.

Elson, D. (1988) 'Market socialism or socialisation of the market?', *New Left Review*, 172: 3–44.

Figart, D. (ed.) (2004) *Living Wage Movements*, London: Routledge.

Fine, B. (2001) *Social Capital versus Social Theory*, London: Routledge.

Fuller, D. and Jonas, A. (2003) 'Alternative financial spaces', in A. Leyshon, R. Lee and C. Williams (eds) *Alternative Economic Spaces*, London: Sage.

Galbraith, J.K. (1992) *The Culture of Contentment*, Boston: Houghton Mifflin.

Genocchio, B. (1995) 'Discourse, discontinuity and difference: the question of "other" spaces', in S. Watson and K. Gibson (eds) *Postmodern Cities and Spaces*, Oxford: Blackwell.

Geras, N. (1998) *The Contract of Mutual Indifference*, London: Verso.

Gibson-Graham, J.K. (1996) *The End of Capitalism (As We Know It): A Feminist Critique of Political Economy*, Cambridge, Mass.: Blackwell.

Glyn, A. (1985) *The Economic Case against Pit Closures*, Sheffield: National Union of Mine Workers.

Glyn, A. and Harrison, J. (1980) *The British Economic Disaster*, London: Pluto Press.

Gomez, G. and Helmsing, A. (2008) 'Selective spatial closure and local economic development: what do we learn from the Argentine Local Currency System?', *World Development*, 36 (11): 2489–2511.

Gorz, A. (1982) *Farewell to the Working Class*, London: Pluto.

Gough, J. (1986) 'Industrial policy and socialist strategy: restructuring and the unity of the working class', *Capital and Class*, 29: 58–82.

Gough, J. (2002) 'Workers' strategies to secure jobs, their uses of scale, and competing notions of justice', Institute of British Geographers Economic Research Group Working Paper 02.02.

Gough, J. (2003) 'The genesis and tensions of the English Regional Development Agencies: class relations and scale', *European Urban and Regional Studies*, 10 (1): 23–38.

Gough, J. (2004) *Work, Locality and the Rhythms of Capital*, London: Routledge.

Gough, J. and Eisenschitz, A. (1997) 'The division of labour, capitalism and socialism: an alternative to Sayer', *International Journal of Urban and Regional Research*, 21 (1): 23–37.

Gough, J. and Eisenschitz, A. with McCulloch, A. (2006) *Spaces of Social Exclusion*, London: Routledge.

Greater London Council (1985) *London Industrial Strategy*, London: GLC.

Greater London Council (1986) *London Labour Plan*, London: GLC.

Greed, C. (1994) *Women and Planning*, London: Routledge.

Gyford, J. (1985) *The Politics of Local Socialism*, Boston: George Allen & Unwin.

Hales, M. (1980) *Living Thinkwork*, London: CSE Books.

Hall, S. and Jacques, M. (eds) (1989) *New Times*, London: Lawrence Wishart.

Harvey, D. (1989) *The Urban Experience*, Oxford: Blackwell.

Harvey, D. (1996) *Justice, Nature and the Geography of Difference*, Oxford: Blackwell.

Hayter, T. (2000) *Open Borders*, London: Pluto.

Herod, A. (1997) 'From a geography of labor to a labor of geography: labor's spatial fix and the geography of capitalism', *Antipode*, 29: 1–31.

Herod, A. (ed.) (1998) *Organizing the Landscape: Geographical Perspectives of Labor Unionism*, Minneapolis: University of Minnesota Press.

Holgate, J. and Wills, J. (2007) 'Organising labour in London: lessons from the living wage campaign', in L. Turner and D. Cornfield (eds) *Labour in the New Urban Battlefields: Local Solidarity in a Global Economy*, Cornell: Cornell University Press.

Holgersen, S. (2008) *Class Conflicts and Planning*, Saarbrücken: VDM Verlag.

Howitt, R. (1993) '"A world in a grain of sand": towards a reconceptualisation of geographical scale', *Australian Geographer*, 24: 33–44.

Hudson, R. and Sadler, D. (1986) 'Contesting works closures in Western Europe's old industrial regions: defending place or betraying class?', in A.Scott and M.Storper (eds) *Production, Work, Territory*, London: Allen & Unwin.

Irazabal, C. and Punja, C. (2009) 'Cultivating just planning and legal institutions: a critical assessment of the South Central farm struggle in Los Angeles', *Journal of Urban Affairs*, 31 (1): 1–23.

Jonas, A. (1996) 'Local labour control regimes: uneven development and the social regulation of production', *Regional Studies*, 30: 323–338.

Jonas, A. (1998) 'Investigating the local-global paradox', in A. Herod, (ed.) *Organizing the Landscape*, Minneapolis: University of Minnesota Press.

Kakios, M. and van der Velden, J. (1984) 'Migrant communities and class politics: the Greek community in Australia', in G. Bottomley and M.de Lepervanche (eds) *Ethnicity, Class and Gender in Australia*, Sydney: George Allen & Unwin.

Laclau, E. and Mouffe, C. (1985) *Hegemony and Socialist Strategy*, London: Verso.

Lavelette, M. and Mooney, G. (eds) (2000) *Class Struggle and Social Welfare*, London: Routledge.

Layard, R. (2006) *Happiness: Lessons from a New Science*, London: Penguin.

Leitner, H., Peck, J. and Sheppard, E. (eds) (2007) *Contesting Neoliberalism: Urban Frontiers*, New York: Guilford Press.

London Conference of Socialist Economists (1980) *The Alternative Economic Strategy*, London: CSE.

Low, S. and Smith, N. (2003) 'Introduction: the imperative of public space', in S. Low and N. Smith, (eds) *The Politics of Public Space* New York: Routledge.

MacCannell, J. (2008) 'The city at the "end of history"', in BAVO (ed.) *Urban Politics Now*, Rotterdam: NAi Publishers.

Mackintosh, M. and Wainwright, H. (eds) (1987) *A Taste of Power*, London: Verso.

Mance, A. (2009), *Solidarity Economics*. Online. Available: http://turbulence.org.uk/turbulence-1/solidarity-economics/ (accessed 15 March 2009).

Marx, K. (1980) 'Alienated labour and capital', in D. McLellan (ed.) *Marx's Gundrisse*, London: Macmillan.

Massey, D. (1993) 'Power-geometry and a progressive sense of place,' in J. Bird, B. Curtis, T. Putnam, G. Robertson, and L.Tickner, (eds) *Mapping the Futures: Local Cultures, Global Change*, London: Routledge.

Massey, D. and Catalano, A. (1978) *Capital and Land*, London: Arnold.

Mathers, A. (2007) *Struggling for a Social Europe*, Aldershot: Ashgate.

Mayer, M. (2007) 'Contesting the neoliberalization of urban governance', in H. Leitner, J. Peck and E. Sheppard (eds) *Contesting Neoliberalism: Urban Frontiers*, New York: Guilford Press.

Medoff, P. and Sklar, H. (1994) *Streets of Hope*, Boston: South End Press.

Merrifield, A. (2002) *Dialectical Urbanism: Social Struggles in the Capitalist City*, New York City: Monthly Review Press.

Meszaros, I. (1995) *Beyond Capital: Towards a Theory of Transition*, London: Merlin Press.

Michaelson, J., Abdallah, S., Steuer, N. Thompson, S. and Marks, N. (2009) *National Accounts of Well-being*, London: New Economics Foundation.

Minns, R. (1980) *Pension Funds and British Capitalism*, London: Heinemann.

Mohun, S. (1979) 'Ideology, knowledge and neo-classical economics: some elements of a Marxist account', in F. Green, and P. Nore (eds) *Issues in Political Economy*, London: Macmillan.

Monbiot, G. (2009) 'A better way to make money', *Guardian*, 20 January.

Moody, K. (1997) *Workers in a Lean World*, London: Verso.

Mundey, J. (1981) *Green Bans and Beyond*, Sydney: Angus and Robertson.

Nove, A. (1983) *The Economics of Feasible Socialism*, London: Allen & Unwin.

Obi, C. (2005) 'Globalization and local resistance: the case of Shell versus the Ogoni', in L. Amoore (ed.) *The Global Resistance Reader*, London: Routledge.

Oudenampsen, M. (2008) 'AmsterdamTM, the city as a business', in BAVO (ed.) *Urban Politics Now*, Rotterdam: NAi Publishers.

Ozarow, D. (2007) 'Argentina's Nuevos Pobres since the Corralito: from despair to adapting to downward mobility', unpublished thesis, London University – Institute for the Study of the Americas.

Panitch, L. and Leys, C. (eds) (2002) *Socialist Register 2003: Fighting Identities*, London: Merlin Press.

Panizza, F. (2005) 'Unarmed utopia revisited: the resurgence of left-of-centre politics in Latin America', *Political Studies*, 53: 716–734.

Paxton, W. and Pearce, N. (2005) *The Voluntary Sector and the State*, York: Joseph. Rowntree Foundation. Online. Available HTTP: http://www.jrf.org.uk/sites/files/jrf/1859353681.pdf (accessed 2 March 2009).

Pearce, J. (2003) *Social Enterprise in Anytown*, London: Gulbenkian Foundation.

Pepper, D. (1993) *Eco-socialism*, London: Routledge.

Peterson, V. and Runyan, A. (2005) 'The politics of resistance: women as nonstate, antistate, and transstate actors', in L. Amoore (ed.) *The Global Resistance Reader*, London: Routledge.

Petras, J. (1997) 'Imperialism and NGOs in Latin America', *Monthly Review*, Online. Available HTTP: http://www.monthlyreview.org/1297petr.htm (accessed 3 March 2009).

Petras, J. and Veltmeyer, H. (2001) *Globalization Unmasked*, New York: Zed Books.

Pike, A., Rodríguez-Pose, A. and Tomaney, J. (2007) 'What kind of local and regional development and for whom?', *Regional Studies*, 41 (9): 1253–1269.

Porter, L. and Shaw, K. (2008) *Whose Urban Renaissance?*, London: Routledge.

Ramonet, I. (2002) 'The Social Wars', Le Monde Diplomatique. Online. Available HTTP: http://mondediplo.com/2002/11/01socialwars (accessed 12 November 2008).

Ross, A. (ed.) (1997) *No Sweat*, New York City: Verso.

Routledge, P. and Cumbers, A. (2009) *Global Justice Networks: Geographies of Transnational Solidarity*, Manchester: Manchester University Press.

Rowbotham, S. (1989) *The Past is Before Us*, London: Pandora.

Sandercock, L. (1979) *The Land Racket*, Melbourne: Silverfish Books.

Sanyal, B. (2008) 'What is new in planning?', *International Planning Studies*, 13 (2): 151–160.

Savage, L. (1998) 'Geographies of organizing: Justice for Janitors in Los Angeles', in A. Herod (ed.) *Organizing the Landscape*, Minneapolis: University of Minnesota Press.

Sayer, A. (1995) 'Liberalism, Marxism and urban and regional studies', *International Journal of Urban and Regional Research*, 19 (1): 79–95.

Schaumberg, H. (2008) 'In search of alternatives: the making of grassroots politics and power in Argentina', *Bulletin of Latin American Research*, 27 (3): 368–387.

Scott, J. (2005) 'The infrapolitics of subordinate groups', in L. Amoore (ed.) *The Global Resistance Reader*, London: Routledge.

Sennett, R. (1998) *The Corrosion of Character: The Personal Consequences of Work in the New Capitalism*, New York: Norton.

Silver, B. and Arrighi, G. (2000) 'Workers, North and South', *Socialist Register 2001*, London: Merlin.

Sintomer, Y., Herzberg, C. and Rocke, A. (2008) 'Participatory budgeting in Europe: potentials and challenges', *International Journal of Urban and Regional Research*, 32 (1): 164–178.

Sivanandan, A. (1990) 'Britain's Gulags', in A. Sivanandan (ed.) *Communities of Resistance*, London: Verso.

Sklair, L. (1998) 'Social movements and global politics', in F. Jameson, and M. Miyoshi, (eds) *The Cultures of Globalization*, Durham: Duke University Press.

Social Exclusion Unit (2001) *Preventing Social Exclusion*, London: SEU.

Starr, A. (2005) *Global Revolt*, London: Zed Books.

Swyngedouw, E. (2000) 'Authoritarian governance, power, and the politics of rescaling', *Environment and Planning D: Society and Space*, 18: 63–76.

Swyngedouw, E. (2008) 'The post-political city', in BAVO (ed.) *Urban Politics Now: Re-imagining*

Democracy in the Neoliberal City, Rotterdam: NAi Publishers.

Swyngedouw, E., Moulaert, F. and Rodriguez, A. (2002) 'Neoliberal urbanisation in Europe: large scale urban development projects and the new urban policy', in N. Brenner and N. Theodore (eds) *Spaces of Neoliberalism*, Oxford: Blackwell.

Totterdill, P. (1989) 'Local economic-strategies as industrial-policy: a critical-review of British developments in the 1980s', *Economy and Society*, 18 (4): 478–526.

Tuckett, I. (1988) 'Coin Street: there is another way', *Community Development Journal*, 23 (4): 249–257.

Turner, G. (2008) *The Credit Crunch*, London: Pluto Press.

Vail, J., Wheelock, J. and Hill, M. (eds) (1999) *Insecure Times*, London: Routledge.

Wainwright, H. (1994) *Arguments for a New Left*, Oxford: Blackwell.

Walker, P. and Goldsmith, E. (2001) 'Local money: a currency for every community', in E. Goldsmith and J. Mander, (eds) *The Case against the Global Economy and for a Turn towards Localization*, London: Earthscan.

Wates, N. (1976) *The Battle for Tolmers Square*, London: RKP.

Whitfield, D. (2006) *New Labour's Attack on Public Services*, Nottingham: Spokesman Books.

Wilkinson, R. and Pickett, K. (2009) *The Spirit Level: Why More Equal Societies Almost Always do Better*, London: Allen Lane.

Wills, J. (2001) 'Community unionism and trade union renewal in the UK: moving beyond the fragments at last?', *Transactions*, Institute of British Geography, 26 (4): 465–483.

Williamson T., Imbroscio, D. and Alperovitz, G. (2002) *Making a Place for Community*, New York: Routledge.

Wills, J. (1998) 'Space, place, and tradition in working-class organisation', in A. Herod, (ed.) *Organizing the Landscape*, Minneapolis: University of Minnesota Press.

World Bank (2000) *World Development Report*, Washington DC: World Bank.

Zizek, S. (2008) 'Some politically incorrect reflections on urban violence in Paris and New Orleans and related matters', in BAVO (ed.) *Urban Politics Now*, Rotterdam: NAi Publishers.

Further reading

Long-term Left strategy

Meszaros, I. (1995) *Beyond Capital: Towards a Theory of Transition*, London: Merlin Press.

Pepper, D. (1993) *Eco-socialism*, London: Routledge.

Strategic possibilities of local action for the Left

Craig, G. and Mayo, M. (1995) *Community Empowerment*, London: Zed Books.

Eisenschitz, A. (2008) 'Town planning, planning theory and social reform', *International Planning Studies*, 13 (2): 133–149.

Harvey, D. (1996) *Justice, Nature and the Geography of Difference*, Oxford: Blackwell, 416–438.

Harvey, D. (2000) *Spaces of Hope*, Edinburgh: Edinburgh University Press, ch. 12.

Massey, D. (1993) 'Power-geometry and a progressive sense of place,' in J. Bird, B. Curtis, T. Putnam, G. Robertson and L. Tickner (eds) *Mapping the Futures: Local Cultures, Global Change*, London: Routledge.

Left local action in the current global context

Cox, R. (1999) 'Civil society at the turn of the millennium: prospects for an alternative world order', *Review of International Studies*, 25 (1): 3–28.

Gough, J. and Eisenschitz, A. with McCulloch, A. (2006) *Spaces of Social Exclusion*, London: Routledge, ch. 12.

Sklair, L. (1998) 'Social movements and global politics', in F. Jameson and M. Miyoshi (eds) *The Cultures of Globalization*, Durham: Duke University Press.

Examples of Left local action

Leitner, H., Peck, J. and Sheppard, E. (eds) (2007) *Contesting Neoliberalism: Urban Frontiers*, New York: Guilford Press.

Medoff, P. and Sklar, H. (1994) *Streets of Hope*, Boston: South End Press.

Merrifield, A. (2002) *Dialectical Urbanism: Social Struggles in the Capitalist City*, New York City: Monthly Review Press.

Routledge, P. and Cumbers, A. (2009) *Global Justice Networks: Geographies of Transnational Solidarity*, Manchester: Manchester University Press.

Local labour and economy

Castree, N., Coe, N., Ward, K. and Samers, M. (2004) *Spaces of Work*, London: Sage, ch. 6, 8 and 9.

Gough, J. (1986) 'Industrial policy and socialist strategy: restructuring and the unity of the working class', *Capital and Class*, 29: 58–82.

Gough, J. and Eisenschitz, A. (1997) 'The division of labour, capitalism and socialism: an alternative to Sayer', *International Journal of Urban and Regional Research*, 21 (1): 23–37.

Herod, A. (ed.) (1998) *Organizing the Landscape: Geographical Perspectives of Labor Unionism*, Minneapolis: University of Minnesota Press.

Mackintosh, M. and Wainwright, H. (eds) (1987) *A Taste of Power*, London: Verso.

Other local issues

Baierle, S. (2002) 'The Porto Alegre Thermidor? Brazil's "participatory budget" at the cross-roads', in L. Panitch and C. Leys (eds) *Socialist Register 2003*, London: Merlin.

Bowie, D. (2008) *Housing and the Credit Crunch*, London: Compass.

Greed, C. (1994) *Women and Planning*, London: Routledge.

Lavelette, M. and Mooney, G. (eds) (2000) *Class Struggle and Social Welfare*, London: Routledge.

49

Local and regional development

Reflections and futures

John Tomaney, Andy Pike and Andrés Rodríguez-Pose

Legacies

The terms and prospects for local and regional development are being transformed. The context for local and regional development in the thirty years after the end of the 1970s was the rise of neo-liberal globalisation. Neo-liberalism, with its origins in the pro-market reforms and deregulation of finance of, first, the Thatcher governments in the UK and, then, the Reagan administrations in the US shaped the international ideology of economic development to a greater or lesser degree across large parts of the world. Neo-liberalism recast the relationship of state and market, so that the chief role of the former was to facilitate the operation of the latter. Part of the political success of neo-liberal reforms was that they were accompanied by a period of relatively rapid economic growth, although ultimately they established the conditions which produced the severe financial crisis and recession after 2007 with its highly uneven local and regional character exacerbating existing inequalities and creating new ones.

Globalisation was the partner of neo-liberalism in the transformation of the world economy during this period. Globalisation – a term which passed from academic research to popular and political discourse – points to the growing integration of international markets. Frequently presented as an inexorable process, globalisation is, in fact, a politically constructed settlement, which favoured some social groups and places more than others (Hirst and Thompson, 1999). Globalisation facilitated the expansion and restructuring of international trade which was accompanied by rising living standards, but also by rising interpersonal inequalities (Milanovic, 2005) as well as intra-national – although, curiously, not international – disparities (Rodríguez-Pose and Crescenzi, 2008). Integrated financial, capital and trade markets, though, also became the mechanism for the rapid transmission of the global financial crisis whose initial trigger was the collapse of the American sub-prime housing market, but which had much deeper roots in the debt-fuelled forms of economic growth which were visible from Europe to the Middle East to North America and, in turn, were themselves related to new patterns of production, consumption and trade imbalances that were the outcomes of neo-liberal globalisation during this period (see Harvey (2005) for an overview of the history of global neo-liberalism).

Neo-liberal globalisation had a profoundly geographically uneven impact and prompted diverse responses by national and local governments and firms and non-governmental organisations in the developed and developing worlds. Indeed, while capturing something of the economic hegemony during this period, the idea of neo-liberalisation contains the danger of obscuring its variegated nature and the complex interplay of factors which have shaped – and will continue to shape – the prospects for local and regional development (see, for example, Peck and Theodore, 2007). Rather than attempting to distil conventional conclusions from the contributions to this Handbook, this chapter begins by reflecting on the main trends shaping the present and future of local and regional development. It then explores the principles and values that underpin local and regional development, before examining the potential conditions for successful local and regional development strategies. The chapter concludes by reflecting explicitly on the politics of local and regional development.

Contexts

As we noted in the introduction to this Handbook, an important current connecting localities and regions in the global North and South are the shared contexts to their development predicament. The scale of socio-economic inequality between and within countries and between and within regions and cities is a striking feature of the period from the end of the 1970s, despite the growth in world income. The measurement of socio-inequality is complex and by no means uncontroversial. At a global scale, the UNDP's Human Development Index (e.g. UNDP, 2007) reveals the extent of the gaps. Collier identifies (2007) a "bottom billion" of the world's population which resides in countries – notably in sub-Saharan Africa – characterised by "development traps", which have left them marginalised in relation to the world economy. Countries which experienced rapid growth during this period typically also saw marked increases in socio-economic and territorial inequality; China presents a notable example. In some accounts spatially imbalanced growth is assumed to be positive in the early stages of rapid industrialisation which will be mitigated at a later date (World Bank, 2009). Others, however, stress the political dangers of growing inequality associated with globalisation which arise when the proceeds of growth are not equally distributed, markets are imperfect and richer countries and regions are able to assert market power (Birdsall, 2001, 2006; Stiglitz, 2006; Perrons, Turok, Cochrane, this volume). Even in poor and middle-income countries the relationship between growth and human development is far from straightforward as the debate about the Millennium Development Goals reveals (ODI, 2008).

The growth of inequality is not restricted to poor or middle-income countries. Inequality also grew in OECD countries in the twenty years to 2008 (OECD, 2009). The European Union is characterised by doggedly persistent inequalities: the most recent official analysis detected some convergence of regional performance across Europe, which it attributed to strong regional policies (or Cohesion Policy in EU parlance), although inequalities remain large (European Union, 2007). Moreover, regional inequalities widened within countries with growth tending to be concentrated in capital city regions everywhere, and most markedly in post-socialist transition countries such as Warsaw, Prague, Bratislava and Budapest, which experienced rapid growth before 2007 (Domański, this volume). Such cities grew at the expense of the rest of the country, reflecting the shift of employment from agriculture and industry to services (with rural and old industrial regions undergoing the greatest relative decline) (European Commission, 2007). In short, regional inequalities remain entrenched across the world and, in many cases, are growing, although patterns of change are highly heterogeneous, affected by distinctive socio-economic structures, diverse patterns of change and variegated the policy responses to these.

On a global scale, the growth of spatial inequalities is closely linked to accelerating urbanisation. Rapid urbanisation (and rural depopulation) is a marked feature of developing and newly industrialising countries. It is, however, a feature of even the most urbanised societies such as Europe and Australasia. For instance, in Australia – in some accounts the most highly urbanised society on the planet – state capital cities continue to increase their share of the national population (Birrell and O'Connor, 2000). Social and economic inequalities between cities and their hinterlands continue to grow, but so do inequalities within cities, especially "global cities" in the developed and developing world. The management of these relationships is a pressing problem of public policy across the globe and likely to intensify in light of economic crisis and climate change (UN HABITAT, 2008; Chien, Gonzalez, Nel, Turok, this volume).

The prospects for local and regional development are being and will continue to be profoundly affected by the impacts of the global financial crisis (GFC) which unfolded after 2007 and marked the end of a long period of uninterrupted growth for many economies around the world. Although one of the proximate causes of the crisis lies in the exposure of the international banking system to defaults in the sub-prime elements of the US housing market, the larger causes are found in the imbalances which developed in the global economy between deficit economies (notably the US, the UK or Spain) and creditor countries (notably China and Germany), which in turn are linked to evolving patterns of international trade and investment. The rapid expansion of financial services on the back of debt-fuelled household consumption in many industrial countries, as well as other parts of the world such as the Middle East, underpinned economic growth, but contributed further to trade imbalances. The scale of the crisis and its translation into a "credit crunch" produced its impact on the "real economy", which

proved highly uneven between and within countries. For instance, New Zealand, the Baltic states, Ireland, Iceland, Greece and Spain which experienced rapid, debt-fuelled growth and widening regional inequality found themselves highly exposed to the consequences of the GFC and entered periods of draconian fiscal austerity in 2008. This reversal of fortune was especially dramatic in Ireland, for example, when it is recalled it was considered a model for other small, open economies during the 2000s (Bradley, 2006; Krugman, 1997).

Making long-term prognostications about the impact of the GFC on the prospects for local and regional development is fraught with danger. Some consequences of the GFC, however, seem evident and are likely to be long-lasting. Evidence from the UK (Martin, 2009) and Australia (Australia Parliament House of Representatives, 2009) highlights the uneven regional impact of the GFC and suggests its severest impacts are on already disadvantaged regions. An immediate consequence in many countries, including some which experienced rapid recent growth, is severe fiscal pressure as governments deal simultaneously with the unprecedented and massive costs of bank bailouts, stimulus measures, and rising unemployment in the context of collapsing revenues. These developments will undoubtedly undermine the medium- and long-term capacity for governments to intervene in the economy. Steeply rising debt levels, already leading to what may be a long-lasting claw-back in public expenditure, are likely to affect the sustainability of economic growth for some time. In particular, many lagging regions across the world, already dependent on heavy government or international organisation transfers are likely to suffer most from this process. Hence, how and where governments choose to retrench will shape the prospects for cities and regions across the world. In the medium term, local and regional authorities are likely to have fewer resources available to invest in development projects, especially in those regions which need them most.

A potentially far-reaching effect of the GFC arises from the debate about the future role of the financial services sector in the economy, emerging from criticism of the excesses which developed in the sector, notably in countries such as the US and UK, but also in countries such as Dubai and Iceland. The head of the UK's Financial Services Authority, Lord Turner, even suggested that the sector had grown "beyond a socially reasonable size", while much of its activities were "socially useless" (quoted in Inman, 2009; NEF, 2009). Reflecting on the growth of the financial instruments which were complicit in the emergence of housing bubbles and excessive consumer debt, and which lay behind much of the urban renewal programmes of the 1990s and 2000s, Paul Volcker, the former chairman of the US Federal Reserve Bank and later chairman of President Obama's Economic Recovery Advisory Board, said, "I wish someone would give me one shred of neutral evidence that financial innovation has led to economic growth – one shred of evidence" (quoted in Hosking and Jagger, 2009: no page). The extent to which pressure develops to reform the financial services so that it focuses on "socially useful" productive activities will shape the conditions for local and regional development and the amount and nature of resources available for investment in economic development, albeit in conditions of austerity.

Paradoxically, given the fiscal stresses described above, the GFC has seen the return of the state to centre stage in economic development. Although the actions of the state were central to the operation of neo-liberalism, its role was carefully limited in many states to the support of the development of markets and the financialisation of the economy. Even some of the ideologues of neo-liberalism now recognise that this model has died (Wolf, 2009). The shape of things to come in this respect is hard to divine but new forms of regulation at national and international scales have potential to reshape patterns of trade, investment and financial flows, which will affect the prospects for local and regional development through shaping the activities of transnational firms and the ways in which regions are inserted in global production networks (UNCTAD, 2009; Coe and Hess, Dawley, this volume).

The search for an effective governmental response to the GFC drew attention to the emergence of a new pattern of geopolitics, symbolised by the growing importance of the G20. Within this grouping the rising political and economic prominence of Brazil, Russia, India, and China (the so-called BRICs) is especially noteworthy. The relative insulation of these economies from the GFC, alongside their growing importance in the world trade system will have impacts for the distribution of economic activity globally and at the local and regional scales, although the models of economic development they embody (for instance, in relation to democratic structures and progress on reducing inequality) are notably different from each other and from the models which underpinned neo-liberal forms of globalisation. The Brazilian government of President Lula, for instance, has made tackling inequality a priority, notably through its food policies (Morgan, this volume). The future of globalisation will be shaped by China especially (Dunford, Chien, this volume) and it is possible that globalisation may start to adopt a very different form, where within developing country (i.e. intra-China, intra-Brazil or intra-India) and South–South trade flow become much more important at the expense of the currently dominating North–North flows. Changing patterns of trade, new forms of international regulation, the rise of sovereign wealth funds and new patterns of foreign direct investment (for instance, growing Chinese influence in the Middle East, Africa and Latin America especially in pursuit of natural resources) will shape the prospects for local and regional development in developed and developing countries and in rich and poor regions. These developments though suggest the need for new global understandings, albeit carefully contextualised. Storper and Scott (2003) in the context of globalisation and international economic integration, abjure older conceptions of the structure of world economic geography as comprising separate blocs (First, Second and Third Worlds), each with its own developmental dynamic. Instead, they suggest the need to build a common theoretical language about the development of regions and countries in all parts of the world, as well as about the broad architecture of the emerging world system of production and exchange. However, such a common theoretical framework requires an acceptance of the "provincial" character of much orthodoxy and the need for theories to be developed in – as well as developed for – the global South and to acknowledge the legacies of colonialism (Mohan, this volume).

Local and regional development policy in the 1990s and 2000s was heavily influenced by the notion of the knowledge economy. Developments in knowledge and the application of knowledge to knowledge (Carnoy and Castells, 2001) were deemed to be central to the growth of productivity, especially with the growth of information and communications technology. The idea that technological change and improvements in human capital are the sources of growth, the idea of the knowledge economy had a powerful appeal across the globe and led to influential attempts to identify "learning regions" as a focus for policy (Florida, 1995; Morgan, 1997; Hudson, 1999; Ó Riain, this volume). Such approaches emphasised, at various times and in various places, for example, the role of science parks and/or the role of university–industry relationships in regional development (e.g. OECD, 2007). These models were widely adopted in Australasia (Yigitcanlar *et al.*, 2008); Europe (Knight, 1995) and North America (Industry Canada, 1999), but were also adopted in developing countries, notably China (Wang, 2009). While the growth of the knowledge

economy will continue to provide threats and opportunities for local economies, the GFC provides a reminder that traditional concerns such as macro-economic structures, the fiscal and redistributive capacities of the state, the operation of land and property markets and the availability of credit for infrastructure investment — i.e. tangible as well as intangible assets — provide the context for the knowledge cities and regions and should not be neglected in discussion of local and regional development.

In 2007, the Intergovernmental Panel on Climate Change (IPCC, 2007) concluded that the warming of the climate system is unequivocal, with most of the observed increase in globally averaged temperatures since the mid-twentieth century being very likely due to the observed increase in anthropogenic (human) greenhouse gas concentrations. It predicted that anthropogenic warming and sea level rise would continue for centuries due to the timescales associated with climate processes and feedbacks, even if greenhouse gas concentrations were to be stabilised, although the likely amount of temperature and sea level rise varies greatly depending on the fossil fuel use intensity of human activity during the next century. The IPCC states that the probability that this is caused by natural climatic processes alone is less than 5 per cent. World temperatures could rise by between 1.1 and 6.4°C during the twenty-first century leading to increased sea levels, more frequent warm spells, heat waves and heavy rainfall and an increase in droughts, tropical cyclones and extreme high tides. The growing concern with impacts of climate change throws up both new challenges for local and regional development and returns attention to old problems of the physical geography of development. Shalizi and Lecocq have argued that,

Until recently, policymakers and development experts could at least assume that where there was water today, there would be water in the future. Or that where there was coastline suitable for a port, that coastline would still be there in the future. In other words, the geographical and physical foundations for development, and for the determination of competitive advantage, were treated as stable and reliable. This presumption is no longer true, as climate change threatens to bring about important shifts in precipitation and weather patterns, sea levels, and water flows, ratcheting up pressure on the land and on ecosystems, thereby making stable parameters less stable (Shalizi and Lecocq, 2010).

Basic questions of the management of natural resources and habitats and access to food, water and energy are likely to loom large in policies for local and regional development, which in turn will be affected by international policies frameworks in these fields. These ecological challenges will affect both developed and developing countries and will require local planning to cope with their diversity, although cities and regions will have uneven capacities to adapt and mitigate depending on differential access to knowledge, finance and technology.

Notwithstanding the uncertainties, the scientific consensus, together with the precautionary principle, form the broad case for policies aimed at mitigation and adaptation to climate change. The Stern Review for the UK government concluded that the benefits of strong, early action on climate change outweigh the costs. Among other things it suggested that the transition to a low-carbon economy will bring challenges for competitiveness but also opportunities for growth, while policies to support the development of a range of low-carbon and high-efficiency technologies are required urgently. Stern (2007) made the case for establishing a carbon price, through tax, trading or regulation, as an essential foundation for climate change policy. This is not merely a technocratic exercise, but a deeply political one in which social and spatial costs and benefits of different forms of change need to be carefully weighed (Christopherson, this volume).

But the costs of climate change – as well as those of addressing it – will be unevenly distributed. As the Garnaut Report (Garnaut 2008) showed for Australia the introduction of carbon pricing will have highly uneven regional consequences. For instance, Garnaut identified the specific threat to the Latrobe Valley brown coal-mining region in Victoria – which produces 80 per cent of the state's electricity – arising from his proposed carbon emission trading scheme, suggesting it might need structural adjustment measures to assists its adaptation, although in general it saw market mechanisms as the means of regional adjustment. Such restructuring is likely to become commonplace and produce new patterns of local and regional change and shifts attention to what solutions to these problems might be found at the regional scale (Jonas et al., this volume)

Climate change impacts such as rising sea levels are likely to affect some of the poorest regions in the world. Thus climate change and broader development objectives, such as tackling poverty and inequality are likely to be interlinked in both developed and developing countries. Thus, according to Stern,

> Strategies for managing the risks of climate change for meeting the other great challenge of this century – overcoming poverty – must be intertwined and built together: if we fail on one we will fail on the other.
>
> (Stern, 2009: no page; see also UNDP, 2007)

Adaptation and mitigation in the face of climate change occur in the context of – and are linked to – population growth and rising living standards for some, which are leading to increased demand for energy, water and food. The UK government's Chief Scientific Adviser posits a possible "perfect storm" of global food, water and energy shortages by 2030 (Beddington, 2009). Stable and reliable supplies of food, water and energy cannot be assumed in any part of the world according to this analysis and addressing these issues will be a task for policy-makers' regions in both the developed and developing world.

Demographic change forms an important component of the context for local and regional development (Vaiou and Wills et al., this volume). Global population growth is a key factor in the development resource pressures. Poverty is a factor compelling migration from, for instance, Central America to the United States, or from Africa to Europe and Asia to Australia comprising refugees and legal and illegal migrants. In Europe, major migrations occurred between Central/Eastern and Western Europe in the 2000s. Regions in developed countries, moreover, now compete internationally for global talent via skilled regional migration programmes of the types pioneered in Scotland, the Australian state of Victoria and the Canadian province of Manitoba.

The impact of these migratory movements on local and regional donor and host economies are profound (Coombes and Champion, this volume). Incorporating migrants, whether lower or higher skilled, into local labour markets and social structures is likely to be a central challenge for local and regional development policy. At the higher end of the labour market migration of skilled workers between developed countries – or from developing to developed countries – is a significant component of regional change in Canada, Australia the Gulf States and some Western European economies. In developed countries the ageing of populations is a regionally uneven process leading to the creation of retirement regions such as the coastal areas of Queensland in Australia, the coast of Florida or South West England, throwing up new challenges for the development of these regions. The issue of whether ageing populations are a welfare burden or an economic opportunity is an open and context-specific question (Glasgow and Brown, 2007).

A final factor shaping the conditions for local and regional development is the trend toward decentralisation of governance across both the developed and developing world. There is a long-standing debate about the potential contribution of decentralisation to economic efficiency (through better matching of the heterogeneous preferences of citizens in different localities to public spending thus enhancing allocative efficiency) and its impact on geographical inequality (because differences in economic endowments among regions mean poorer regions may lose out to richer ones in the struggle for resources). The economic impact of decentralisation is, however, far from settled. There is limited evidence of a positive impact of fiscal and political decentralisation on overall economic growth and "the relationship between decentralization and the evolution of disparities at subnational level seems strongly affected by the level of wealth of a country, the dimension of its existing disparities, and the presence of solid fiscal redistribution systems" (Rodríguez-Pose and Ezcurra, 2009: 34). Thus, although the trend toward decentralised systems of governance is important, local and national contexts will continue to shape its character.

In short, coping with population change, climate change adaptation and mitigation, securing supplies of energy, water and food – including localising production of these – are likely to figure strongly in local and regional development strategies, which are increasingly likely to be enacted by decentralised institutions. Tackling these problems with an eye to impacts on inequality will also be a challenge for policy-makers. Moreover, the ability of the nations to respond to these challenges is likely to depend on local and regional action.

Values and principles

The terms and prospects for local and regional development will be determined not merely by global trends, but also by social and political action which, in turn, will be determined by the values and principles which attend such action. In defining such values and principles it is necessary to consider the different (and competing) concepts that have arisen to explain contemporary patterns of local and regional development. One highly influential body of theory in national finance ministries and international organisations such as the World Bank (2009) is the "new economic geography" (NEG), which focuses on how increasing returns affect the spatial agglomeration economic activity producing both growth and inequality (Krugman, 1991; Venables, 2006, 2008). For instance, an analysis by the UK Treasury in 2006 argued that:

> Theory and empirical evidence suggests that allowing regional concentration of economic activity will increase national growth. As long as economies of scale, knowledge spillovers and a local pool of skilled labour result in productivity gains that outweigh congestion costs, the economy will benefit from agglomeration, in efficiency and growth terms at least … policies that aim to spread growth amongst regions are running counter to the natural growth process and are difficult to justify on efficiency grounds, unless significant congestion costs exist.
>
> (quoted in Martin, 2009: 21)

The view embodied here is of a trade-off between national efficiency and regional equity. However, despite the formal complexity of the models developed by the new economic geography its analysis represents a highly simplified view of the regional development process, which emphasises how market forces under conditions of monopolistic competition facilitate the *adjustment* of productive capacity. Its policy implications, when taken to its conclusions disavow the effectiveness of regional policy or at least see

it having a mainly ameliorative effect. For instance, in the UK, it has been suggested that there is no hope of regenerating northern cities and that policy should focus on boosting agglomerations by investments in infrastructures, thus accelerating the growth of financial services in London and the South East (Leunig and Swaffield, 2008).

The NEG can be criticised for its simplified theoretical assumptions which fail to capture the wide range of economic and political factors that shape development and on empirical grounds for overlooking the evidence of growth potential outside major urban areas. Agglomerations do not always lead to sustained high annual average growth, while there are opportunities for growth in peripheral regions which cannot be explained by the axioms of NEG (OECD, 2009a). Moreover, agglomerations are the product of the decisions of public as well as private actors (Barca, 2009). This suggests that there is potential for growth in a wide range of regions, including regions which do not exhibit strong agglomerations (OECD, 2009a). Such analysis leads to a different set of policy conclusions to those that are associated with NEG. Accordingly, over recent years it has become possible to identify a new or emergent model of regional policy, which has been adopted, in adapted fashion, in developed and developing countries and which at its heart focuses on the identification and mobilisation of endogenous assets:

> In response to poor outcomes, regional policy has evolved, and continues to evolve, from a top-down, subsidy-based group of interventions designed to reduce regional disparities, into a much broader family of policies designed to improve regional competitiveness. These policies are characterised by: a strategic concept or development strategy that covers a wide range of direct and indirect factors that affect the performance of local firms; a focus on endogenous assets, rather than

exogenous investments and transfers; an emphasis on opportunity rather than on disadvantage; and a collective/negotiated governance approach, involving national, regional and local government plus other stakeholders, with the central government playing a less dominant role. The new regional approach is based on the principle that opportunities for growth exist in the entire territory, across all types of regions. The aim is to maximise national output by encouraging each individual region to reach its growth potential from within. Before, policy makers regarded regional polices as a zero sum game. Recent reforms of regional policy in a number of OECD countries provide evidence that this thinking has undergone a paradigm shift.

(OECD, 2009: 5)

Such approaches can form a component of a "place-based policy" aimed at tackling underutilised economic potential and reducing social exclusion, through supply of integrated goods and services tailored to local contexts and triggering institutional changes (Barca, 2009). There is evidence that this broad approach has been adopted in Europe (Tödtling, this volume) and North America (Green Leigh and Clark, this volume) and Latin America (Vázquez-Barquero, this volume). This approach to local and regional policy gains support from alternative theorisations, such as those which emphasise notions of "constructed advantage" (DG Research, 2006), drawing on developments in evolutionary economics which provide a stronger foundation for public policy interventions to shape patterns of local and regional development. The focus here is on how public policy can aid the process of industrial *adaptation* through interventions in the development of indigenous innovation assets. Structural change in the economy, including the emergence of "disruptive technologies" may create "locational windows of opportunity", which

can alter economic geographies (Boschma and van der Knaap, 1999; Bower and Christiansen, 1995; Scott, 1998). Such approaches can contribute to territorial competition which can make a limited contribution to development (Bristow, Gordon, this volume), leading to strategies of "pure waste" as incentive wars develop (Rodríguez-Pose and Arbix, 2001). A key question then concerns how strategies make a positive sum contribution to development through the development of local assets (Cheshire and Gordon, 1998; Camagni, 2002) and the role of national and international regulation in limiting wasteful forms of territorial competition.

It is also important, however, to consider approaches which go beyond a narrow focus on improvements in the rates of GDP growth as the main measure of development. While growth is desperately needed to improve the conditions of the "bottom billion", in richer countries the relationship between economic growth and human development is more uncertain. Indeed, recent research has drawn attention to the decreasing returns to society and personal well-being of more economic growth in rich countries. Levels of health and well-being vary significantly between and within richer countries and there is convincing evidence that this reflects not levels of growth, but levels of inequality at both national and regional scales. Notwithstanding the general growth in inequality, Japan and Scandinavian societies with comparatively low levels of inequality exhibit fewer of the social problems that characterise more unequal societies such as the United States, while the same is true of more of individual US states. Moreover, evidence suggests that inequality is not just a problem for the poor in such societies, but for all social groups — for instance, levels of ill-health are higher among all social groups in more unequal societies (Wilkinson and Pickett, 2009; Sustainable Development Commission, 2009). This suggests that local and regional development should not just be about promoting greater growth, but also about reducing levels of inequality, and that mobilising resources in lagging and/or peripheral areas may constitute a valid recipe for both greater overall growth and lower territorial polarisation. More importantly, it suggests that tackling local and regional inequalities may be necessary for the achievement of national well-being. In this context, Sen's (1999a) notion that the focus of development should be informed by the formation of "capabilities" rather than the pursuit of utility would seem to be especially pertinent at the local and regional scale (Morgan, Perrons, this volume).

The focus on the relationship between inequality and well-being raises profound questions about how we theorise the economy and understand the nature of growth (Sen, 1999a; Stiglitz *et al.*, 2009; Sustainable Development Commission, 2009; Perrons, Turok, this volume) and is the background to renewed interest in "Steady State Economics" drawn from classical economics, but recast in the context of growing ecological pressures, which posits an economy based on a constant stock of physical capital, capable of being maintained by a low rate of material throughput that lies within the regenerative and assimilative capacities of the ecosystem (Daley and Farley, 2003). These ideas are in their intellectual infancy but, along with ideas about the relationship between inequality and well-being, point to the importance of a more rounded consideration of the question of "what kind of regional development and for whom?", which emphasises the social and the ecological as well the narrowly defined economic (Pike *et al.*, 2007).

Democratic decision-making is central to the task of finding answers to the question of "what kind of development and for whom?" Sen is clear about the advantages of democratic practices in the formulation of development priorities, regardless of the level of development of given countries or regions:

The value of democracy includes its *intrinsic importance* in human life, its *instrumental role* in generating political incentives, and its *constructive function* in the formation of values (and in understanding the force and feasibility of claims of needs, rights, and duties). These merits are not regional in character. Nor is the advocacy of discipline or order. Heterogeneity of values seems to characterize most, perhaps all, major cultures. The cultural argument does not foreclose, nor indeed deeply constrain, the choices we can make today.

(Sen, 1999b: 16)

These arguments apply at all scales of multi-level governance systems in developed and developing countries: democracy is a universal value. Designing effective and accountable local and regional institutions is by no means straightforward and is marked by social conflicts but is essential to long-run success of strategies (Crouch, this volume). Questions of state and social power will continue to determine the space(s) for action (Cochrane, and Cumbers and Mackinnon, Jessop, and Jones and MacLeod, Lovering, this volume).

Strategies and politics

The design of local and regional development strategies embodies values and principles. The definition of local and regional development is a starting point for strategy-making. Defining the purposes and objects of development is a matter of debate. Democratic debate is intrinsically, instrumentally and constructively important in the process of strategy development. Partnerships between local actors are an essential complement to formal democratic structures and a means of mobilising constructive engagement. We tried to show above some of the general challenges which affect localities and regions in all parts of the globe, but we have emphasised the value of decentralised responses to these and place-based solutions. We have asserted the central objectives of tackling climate change and inequality simultaneously. We have raised the question of whether and to what extent a simple and undifferentiated focus on growth is sufficient to meet these objectives.

As we outlined in the introduction to this Handbook, context sensitivity is at the heart of the kinds of place-based approaches to local and regional and development that require a detailed grasp of local social and economic conditions. This requires an approach which emphasises research and evidence in the identification and mobilisation of endogenous assets and the planning of investment priorities in relation to them. Decentralised and accountable institutions are necessary conditions for the success of this approach, but so too is a supportive system of fiscal redistribution and macro-economic management in the context of multi-level governance. Without such a supportive context, there are limits to local to regional and development.

The dominant forms of economic policy and modes of growth over the last thirty years have produced and tolerated large social and territorial inequalities. But the costs of the inequalities – even under conditions of rapid growth, let alone periods of austerity – are becoming more evident (Wilkinson and Pickett, 2009). A focus on measures to alleviate poverty as a response to inequality – adopted in both rich and poor countries – neglects the degree to which poverty cannot be considered independently of its social context and the evidence which suggests inequality is bad for society as a whole. Poverty and its implications vary according to context, but unequal societies are more prone to produce socially excluded groups, a process which has a clear spatial dimension: "place effects" play a part in producing inequality and exclusion. For all of these reasons there is compelling case for putting the tackling of inequality alongside economic growth at the centre of policies to promote local and regional development. At the core of this approach is the creation of employment opportunities in places where they are needed because of the benefits this will produce for society as a whole. In this context, there is likely to be a growing a concern with the character and quality of growth, especially in the context of a shift to a low carbon economy – already evidenced in the green stimulus packages adopted in places such as South Korea, Japan and the United States. Such an outcome would require action at the national (and international) as well as the local and regional scale, including interventions to support development outside metropolitan regions.

References

Australia Parliament House of Representatives (2009) Standing Committee on Infrastructure, Transport, Regional Development and Local Government, *The Global Financial Crisis and Regional Australia*. Canberra: Commonwealth of Australia.

Barca, F. (2009) *An Agenda for a Reformed Cohesion Policy. A Place-based approach to meeting European Union Challenges and Expectations*. Brussels: DG Region, European Commission.

Bennington, J. (2009) *Food, Energy, Water and The Climate: A Perfect Storm Of Global Events?* London: Government Office for Science.

Birdsall, N. (2001) "Why inequality matters: some economic issues", *Ethics & International Affairs*, 15 (2): 3–29.

Birdsall, N. (2006) "Rising inequality in the new global economy", *International Journal of Development Issues*, 5 (1): 1–9.

Birrell, B. and O'Connor, K. (2000) "Regional Australia and the 'new' economy", *People and Place*, 8 (4): 52–62.

Boschma, R. and van der Knaap, G.A. (1999) "New high tech industries and locational windows of opportunity", *Geografiska Annaler*, 81 B: 73–89.

Bower, J.L. and Christiansen, C.M. (1995) "Disruptive technologies: catching the wave", *Harvard Business Review*, 73 (1): 43–54.

Bradley, J. (2006) "Committing to growth in a small European country", in D. Coyle, W. Alexander, and B. Ashcroft *New Wealth for Old Nations. Scotland's Economic Prospects*. Princeton, NJ: Princeton University Press.

Camagni, R. (2002) "On the concept of territorial competitiveness: sound or misleading?", *Urban Studies*, 39 (13): 2396–2411.

Carnoy, M. and Castells, M. (2001) "Globalization, the knowledge society, and the Network State", *Global Networks*, 1 (1): 1–18.

Cheshire, P. and Gordon, I. (1998) "Territorial competition: some lessons for policy", *Annals of Regional Science*, 32 (1): 321–346.

Collier, P. (2007) *The Bottom Billion. Why the Poorest Countries are Failing and What Can be Done About it*. Oxford: Oxford University Press.

Daley, H. and Farley, J. (2003) *Ecological Economics: Principles and Applications*. Washington, DC: Island Press.

DG Research (2006) *Constructing Regional Advantage*. Brussels: DG Research, European Commission.

European Union (2007) *Growing Regions, Growing Europe. Fourth Report on Economic and Social Cohesion*. Brussels: European Commission.

Florida, R. (1995) "Toward the learning region", *Futures*, 27 (5): 527–536.

Galbraith, K. (2009) "Obama signs stimulus package with clean energy provisions", *New York Times*, 17 February.

Garnaut, R. (2008) *The Garnaut Climate Change Review*. Melbourne: Cambridge University Press.

Glasgow, N. and Brown, D. (2007) *Retirement Migration and the Road to Rural American*. Dordrecht: Springer.

Harvey, D. (2005) *A Brief History of Neoliberalism*. Oxford: Oxford University Press.

Hirst, P. Q. and Thompson, G. F. (1999) *Globalization in Question: The International Economy and the Possibilities of Governance*, 2nd edn. Cambridge: Polity Press.

Hosking, P. and Jagger, S. (2009) "'Wake up, gentlemen', world's top bankers warned by former Fed chairman Volcker", *The Times*, 9 December 2009 (http://business.timesonline.co.uk/tol/business/industry_sectors/banking_and_finance/article6949387.ece) accessed: 9 December 2009.

Hudson, R. (1999) "The learning economy, the learning firm and the learning region", *European Urban and Regional Studies*, 6 (1): 59–72.

Industry Canada (1999) *Micro-economic Monitor Special Report – Canada's Regions and the Knowledge-based Economy: A Compelling Journey to a Promising Future*, March. Ottawa: Industry Canada.

Inman, P. (2009) "Financial Services Authority Chairman backs tax on 'socially useless' banks", *Guardian*, 27 August.

IPCC (2007) *Climate Change 2007: Synthesis Report. Summary for Policymakers*. Geneva: Intergovernmental Panel on Climate Change.

Knight, R. (1995) "Knowledge-based development: policy and planning implications for cities", *Urban Studies*, 32 (2): 225–260.

Krugman, P. (1997) "Good news from Ireland. A geographical perspective", in A. W. Gray (ed.) *International Perspectives on the Irish Economy*. Dublin: Indecon.

Krugman, P. (1991) "Increasing returns and economic geography", *Journal of Political Economy*, 49: 137–150.

Leunig, T. and Swaffield, J. (2008) *Cities Unlimited. Making Urban Regeneration Work*. London: Policy Exchange.

Martin, R. (2009) "The recent evolution of regional disparities – a tale of boom and bust", in J. Tomaney (ed.) *The Future of Regional Policy*. London: Smith Institute.

Milanovic, B. (2005) *Worlds Apart: Measuring International and Global Inequality*. Princeton: Princeton University Press.

Morgan, K. (1997) "The learning region: institutions, innovation and regional renewal", *Regional Studies*, 31 (5): 491–503.

NEF (2009) *The Ecology of Finance*. London: New Economics Foundation.

ODI (2008) *Achieving the Millennium Development Goals: The Fundamentals*. Briefing Paper 43. London: Overseas Development Institute.

OECD (2007) *Higher Education and Regions. Globally Competitive, Locally Engaged*. Paris: OECD.

OECD (2009) *How Regons Grow. Trend and Analysis*. Paris: OECD.

Peck, J. and Theodore, N. (2007) "Variegated capitalism", *Progress in Human Geography*, 31 (6): 731–772.

Pike, A., Rodríguez-Pose, A. and Tomaney, J. (2007) 'What kind of local and regional development and for whom', *Regional Studies*, 41 (9): 1253–1269.

Rodríguez-Pose, A. and Crescenzi, R. (2008) 'Mountains in a flat world: why proximity still matters for the location of economic activity', *Cambridge Journal of Regions, Economy and Society*, 1 (3): 371–388.

Rodríguez-Pose, A. and Ezcurra, R. (2009) "Does decentralization matter for regional disparities? A cross country analysis", IMDEA Working Papers Series in Economics and Social Sciences, 2009/4. Madrid: IMDEA.

Scott, A. (1998) "The geographical foundations of industrial performance", in A.D. Chandler, P. Hagström and Ö. Solvell, (eds) *The Dynamic Firm: The Role of Technology, Strategy, Organization, and Regions*. Oxford: Oxford University Press.

Sen, A. (1999a) *Development as Freedom*. Oxford: Oxford University Press.

Sen, A. (1999b) "Democracy as a universal value", *Journal of Democracy*, 10 (3): 3–17.

Shalizi, Z. and Lecocq, F. (2010) "To mitigate or to adapt: is that the question? Observations on an appropriate response to the climate change challenge to development strategies", *World Bank Research Observer*. 25 (2): 295–321.

Stern, N. (2007) *The Economics of Climate Change: The Stern Review*. Cambridge: Cambridge University Press.

Stiglitz, J. (2006) *Making Globalisation Work*. London: Penguin.

Stiglitz, J., Sen, A. and Fitoussi, J-P. (2009) *Report by the Commission on the Measurement of Economic Performance and Social Progress. – www. stiglitz-sen-fitoussi.fr* published online only.

Sustainable Development Commission (2009) *Prosperity Without Growth? The Transition to a Sustainable Economy*. London: Sustainable Development Commission.

UNCTAD (2009) *Trade and Development Report 2009*. Geneva: United Nations Conference on Trade and Development.

UNDP (2007) *Human Development Report 2007/8*. Basingstoke: Palgrave MacMillan.

UNEP (2009) *A Global Green New Deal*. Geneva: United Nations Environment Programme.

UN HABITAT (2008) *State of the World's Cities 2008/9*. London: Earthscan/Nairobi: UN HABITAT.

Venables, A. J. (2006) "Shifts in economic geography and their causes", *Federal Reserve Bank of Kansas City Economic Review*, 91 (4) Q IV: 61–85.

Venables, A. J. (2008) "New economic geography", in Steven N. Durlauf and Lawrence E. Blume (eds) *The New Palgrave Dictionary of Economics. Second Edition*. Basingstoke: Palgrave Macmillan.

Wang, X-F. (2009) Knowledge-based Urban Development in China. PhD Thesis, Centre for Urban and Regional Development Studies, University of Newcastle upon Tyne.

Wilkinson, R. and Pickett, K. (2009) *The Spirit Level. Why More Equal Societies Almost Always Do Better*. London: Allen Lane.

Wolf, M. (2009) "The post post-Thatcher era begins", *Financial Times*, 3 December.

World Bank (2009) *World Development Report 2009: Reshaping Economic Geography*. Washington, DC: The World Bank.

Yigitcanlar, T., O'Connor, K. and Westerman, C. (2008) "The making of knowledge cities: Melbourne's knowledge-based urban development experience", *Cities*, 25 (2): 63–72.

Index

Printed and bound by CPI Group (UK) Ltd, Croydon, CR0 4YY

08/05/2025

01864327-0016